ORGANIZATIONAL BEHAVIOR

▼ SEVENTH EDITION

ORGANIZATIONAL BEHAVIOR

 **SEVENTH EDITION**

Don Hellriegel
Texas A&M University

John W. Slocum, Jr.
Southern Methodist University

Richard W. Woodman
Texas A&M University

WEST PUBLISHING COMPANY
Minneapolis/St. Paul   New York   Los Angeles   San Francisco

West's Commitment to the Environment

In 1906, West Publishing Company began recycling materials left over from the production of books. This began a tradition of efficient and responsible use of resources. Today, up to 95 percent of our legal books and 70 percent of our college and school texts are printed on recycled, acid-free stock. West also recycles nearly 22 million pounds of scrap paper annually—the equivalent of 181,717 trees. Since the 1960s, West has devised ways to capture and recycle waste inks, solvents, oils, and vapors created in the printing process. We also recycle plastics of all kinds, wood, glass, corrugated cardboard, and batteries, and have eliminated the use of Styrofoam book packaging. We at West are proud of the longevity and the scope of our commitment to the environment.

 TEXT IS PRINTED ON 10% POST CONSUMER RECYCLED PAPER

British Library Cataloguing-in-Publication Data. A catalogue record for this book is available from the British Library.

Production Credits

Copyediting: Jerrold Moore

Text Design: Roslyn Stendahl/Dapper Design

Composition: Parkwood Composition

Artwork: Alexander Teshin and Associates and Wiest International

Cover Image and Design: Roslyn Stendahl/Dapper Design
Production, Printing, PrePress, and Binding by West Publishing Company.

Library of Congress Cataloging-in-Publication Data

Hellriegel, Don.
    Organizational behavior / Don Hellriegel, John W. Slocum, Jr.,
Richard W. Woodman. — 7th ed.
        p. cm.
    Includes index.
    ISBN 0-314-04472-8 (hard)
    1. Organizational behavior.   I. Slocum, John W.   II. Woodman,
Richard W.   III. Title.
HD58.7.H44   1995
158.7—dc20   94-32601
                                                    CIP

To Jill, Kim, and Lori (DH)
Christopher, Bradley, and Jonathan (JWS)
David and Anna (RWW)

BRIEF CONTENTS

Contents   *ix*
Preface   *xxi*

CHAPTER 1   Managers and Organizational Behavior   2

▼ **PART I: INDIVIDUAL PROCESSES**   37

CHAPTER 2   Personality and Attitudes   38

CHAPTER 3   Perception and Attribution   68

CHAPTER 4   Individual Problem-Solving Skills   104

CHAPTER 5   Learning and Reinforcement   136

CHAPTER 6   Work Motivation   168

CHAPTER 7   Motivating Performance: Goal Setting and Reward Systems   206

CHAPTER 8   Work Stress   234

▼ **PART II: INTERPERSONAL AND GROUP PROCESSES**   265

CHAPTER 9   Dynamics Within Groups and Teams   266

CHAPTER 10   Dynamics Between Groups and Teams   308

CHAPTER 11   Leadership   340

CHAPTER **12** Interpersonal Communication 386

CHAPTER **13** Conflict and Negotiation 426

▼ **PART III: ORGANIZATIONAL PROCESSES** **461**

CHAPTER **14** Organizational Culture 462

CHAPTER **15** Power and Political Behavior 494

CHAPTER **16** Job Design 526

CHAPTER **17** Organization Design 562

CHAPTER **18** Organizational Decision Making 610

▼ **PART IV: CHANGE PROCESSES** **647**

CHAPTER **19** Nature of Planned Organizational Change 648

CHAPTER **20** Approaches to Planned Organizational Change 684

CHAPTER **21** Career Planning and Development 718

Appendix: Tools and Techniques for Studying Organizational Behavior 757

Integrating Cases C–1

Name Index I–1

Subject and Organization Index I–11

CONTENTS

Preface xxi

CHAPTER 1   Managers and Organizational Behavior   2

Preview Case: Cunningham Communications, Inc.   4

Diversity at Work   7

Managing Diversity: Hoechst Celanese Diversity Programs   9

Organizational Issues for the 1990s   11

Managing Quality: USAA   13

Managing Ethics: What to Do   15

Managing in Practice: How Managers Learn Global Skills at Colgate-Palmolive   16

Developing Skills   17

Managerial Roles   19

Managing Across Cultures: Getting the Best from Managers in Different Cultures   23

Fundamental Concepts of Organizational Behavior   24

Managing in Practice: Cultural Influences on Behavior   25

Organizational Behavior: A Framework   28

▼ **Developing Skills**

Self-Diagnosis: How Much Do You Value Diversity?   34

A Case in Point: Wanda Hill at Trust Consultants   35

▼ PART I: INDIVIDUAL PROCESSES   37

CHAPTER 2   Personality and Attitudes   38

Preview Case: Individual Differences in Reactions to Downsizing   40

Personality: An Introduction   41

Sources of Personality Differences   41

Managing Diversity: Generational Tension in the Office   43

Personality Structure   45

Managing in Practice: America's Toughest Bosses   46

Personality and Behavior   48

The Person and the Situation   51

Attitudes: An Introduction   52

Attitudes and Behavior   52

Managing Quality: Reengineering Attitudes   54

Work Attitudes: Job Satisfaction   55

Managing Across Cultures: A Comparison of Japanese and U.S. Work
Attitudes   56

Work Attitudes: Organizational Commitment   58

Individual Differences and Ethical Behavior   59

Managing Ethics: Three Types of Management Ethics   60

▼ **Developing Skills**

  Self-Diagnosis: Measuring Locus of Control   63

  A Case in Point: Chuck Holeman—Retail Sales Representative   64

CHAPTER 3   Perception and Attribution   68

Preview Case: Whom Should I Hire   70

The Perceptual Process   71

Managing in Practice: The Icon Crisis   71

Perceptual Selection   74

Managing Diversity: Selective Perception of Managers   75

Managing Across Cultures: Time Perception   78

Perceptual Organization   79

Managing in Practice: Office Design, Layout, and Decor—What Do They Tell
You?   81

Person Perception   82

Managing Across Cultures: Perceptions of Japanese and American Business
Associates   84

Perceptual Errors   86

Managing Ethics: Perceptions of Ethics in Organizations   86

Managing Diversity: Sex Stereotypes in the Workplace   88

Attributions: Perceiving the Causes of Behavior   90

Managing in Practice: Searching for Causes of Job Applicant Behavior   90

▼ **Developing Skills**

  Self-Diagnosis: Measuring Perceptions of Women as Managers   97

  A Case in Point: The Internship   99

CHAPTER 4   Individual Problem-Solving Styles   104

Preview Case: Ben & Jerry's Homemade Ice Cream, Inc.   106

Individual Problem-Solving Processes   106

Psychological Functions in Problem Solving   108

Managing Across Cultures: Problem-Solving Styles of Canadian and Japanese Students   113

Individual Problem-Solving Styles   114

Managing in Practice: Against the Grain   116

Managing in Practice: The CEO as Organizational Architect   119

Managing in Practice: Body Shop International   121

Managing in Practice: Herb Kelleher of Southwest Airlines   124

Organizational Implications   125

Managing Ethics: What's Your Decision?   126

Managing Diversity: Reengineering at GTE   128

▼ **Developing Skills**

    Self-Diagnosis: Problem-Solving Style   131

    A Case in Point: Whole Foods Market   133

CHAPTER 5   Learning and Reinforcement   136

Preview Case: Driver Behaviors at UPS   138

Types of Learning   139

Managing Diversity: Diversity at Coopers & Lybrand   143

Contingencies of Reinforcement   144

Managing Across Cultures: Attracting Japan's Brightest   146

Organizational Rewards   147

Managing in Practice: Generating Ideas at Peak Electronics   148

Managing Ethics: Are You Sick or Well?   149

Managing in Practice: Positive Discipline at Tampa Electric   154

Schedules of Reinforcement   155

Managing Quality: Diamond International's 100 Club   157

Behavioral Modification   158

Managing in Practice: Thin Promises   161

▼ **Developing Skills**

    A Case in Point: Stonebriar Country Club   165

    A Case in Point: Synerdyne   165

CHAPTER 6   Work Motivation   168

Preview Case: Bill Gates and Microsoft   170

Essentials of Motivation   172

Content Theories of Motivation   174

ERG Theory   176

Managing Diversity: When English Isn't So Plain   178

Managing in Practice: Instant Rewards for Big Deals   182

Managing Across Cultures: Motorola's Guadalajara Employees   184

Process Theories of Motivation   187

Managing Across Cultures: Defining Productivity in Japan   191

Managing Quality: Working at Home Depot   193

Managing Ethics: To Steal or Not: That's the Question   196

▼ **Developing Skills**

Self-Diagnosis: What Do You Want From Your Job?   201

A Case in Point: Robert Princeton   202

CHAPTER 7   Motivating Performance: Goal Setting and Reward Systems   206

Preview Case: One-Page Company Game Plan   208

Essentials of Goal Setting   208

Managing Quality: ISO 9000: Making the Grade   211

Goal Setting and Performance   212

Managing in Practice: Cheryl Womack   214

Managing Across Cultures: Mexican Workers Get Raises   217

Managing Ethics: Churning Accounts   219

Managing Diversity: Beyond Good Faith   221

Enhancing Performance Through Reward Systems   223

Managing in Practice: Long John Silver's Seafood   224

Managing in Practice: Playcare Development Center   226

▼ **Developing Skills**

Self-Diagnosis: Goal-Setting Questionnaire   229

A Case in Point: Survival at Westinghouse Electronic Plant   230

CHAPTER 8   Work Stress   234

Preview Case: Stress on the Job   236

Nature of Stress   236

Managing in Practice: The Navy Pilot   239

Sources of Stress   239

Managing Across Cultures: Siesta Sunset   239

Managing Ethics: Welcome to the Age of Overwork   241

Managing Diversity: Work and Family—Business as Usual?   244

Effects of Stress   246

Managing Across Cultures: Karoushi or Stress Death   247

Managing in Practice: "Just Enough But Not Too Much"   248

Managing Diversity: The "New-Collar" Workers   252

Personality and Stress   252

Stress Management   255

Managing Quality: AT&T's Wellness Program   258

▼ **Developing Skills**

   Self-Diagnosis: Identifying Your Strategies for Coping with Stress   261

   A Case in Point: The Stress of Shift Work   261

▼ PART II: INTERPERSONAL AND GROUP PROCESSES   265

CHAPTER 9   **Dynamics Within Groups and Teams   266**

Preview Case: Teams at MPI   268

Individual–Group Relations   269

Group Types and Development   270

Managing Quality: Teams at Mary T.   273

Influences on Groups and Teams   276

Managing in Practice: Groupware at Westinghouse   278

Managing Across Cultures: Apple's Global Videoconferencing   279

Managing Ethics: "Dateline" Crashes   280

Managing Diversity: United Nations at Tabra, Inc.   284

Managing in Practice: It's Only Fair   286

Managing Ethics: Beech-Nut's Groupthink   290

Improving Team Decision Making   291

Managing Across Cultures: Group Meetings in China   295

Fostering Team Creativity   296

Managing in Practice: Brainstorming to Action   299

▼ **Developing Skills**

   Self-Diagnosis: People are Electric   302

   A Case in Point: Great Majestic Company   302

CHAPTER 10   **Dynamics Between Groups and Teams   308**

Preview Case: Developing Aurora   310

Key Influences on Outcomes   311

Managing Ethics: Dow Brazil   313

Managing Across Cultures: Medtronic's Global Soul   318

Managing in Practice: Fluor Reengineers   323

Fostering Effective Outcomes   325

Managing Diversity: CIGNA's Dialogue   326

Managing Quality: Alcoa's Quality-Driven Vision and Values   329

Managing in Practice: Hope Creek   332

▼ **Developing Skills**

   Self-Diagnosis: Interteam Dynamics Questionnaire   335

   A Case in Point: Madison Electronics Company   336

CHAPTER 11

Leadership   340

Preview Case: Monte Peterson at Thermos   342

Foundations of Leadership   344

Managing Diversity: Janet McLaughlin at Corning Glass   346

Traditional Leadership Models   348

Managing Across Cultures: The Europeans are Coming   351

Contingency Models of Leadership   352

Managing in Practice: Stern's Record at Northern Telecom   359

Managing Quality: Making Contact Lenses at Johnson & Johnson   363

Managing Quality: Rachel Blaylock at Primacare   367

Emerging Leadership Models   371

Managing Ethics: You Make the Decision   373

Managing in Practice: Tom's of Maine   377

▼ **Developing Skills**

   Self-Diagnosis: What's Your Leadership Style?   380

   A Case in Point: Southwestern Manufacturing Company   382

CHAPTER 12

Interpersonal Communication   386

Preview Case: Communicating Assertively   388

Elements of Interpersonal Communication   389

Managing in Practice: Bypassing   395

Managing Diversity: Communication Biases   397

Managing Across Cultures: Nonverbal Cues and Tips   400

Interpersonal Networks   401

Managing Diversity: African-American Network at Xerox   405

Fostering Dialogue   407

Managing in Practice: A Merger with Communication Openness   410

Managing Quality: How Honda Listens   414

Nonverbal Communication   414

Managing Across Cultures: Nonverbal Expectations in Mexico   415

▼ **Developing Skills**

   Self-Diagnosis: Personal Communication Practices   419

   A Case in Point: Xographics   422

CHAPTER 13   **Conflict and Negotiation   426**

Preview Case: Charlie Olcott   428

Conflict Management   429

Managing Quality: Motorola's Balanced Use of Conflict   431

Levels of Conflict   432

Managing in Practice: The Silent Saboteurs   434

Managing in Practice: USA Truck Cuts Role Conflicts   436

Managing in Practice: U-Haul's Family Feud   437

Managing Diversity: Bridging Differences at General Computer Inc.   440

Conflict-Handling Styles   440

Managing Ethics: Wal-Mart's Failed Compromise   445

Negotiation in Conflict Management   446

Managing Across Cultures: Business Negotiations in Mexico   450

▼ **Developing Skills**

   Self-Diagnosis: Conflict-Handling Styles   455

   A Case in Point: Sue's Dilemma   457

▼ **PART III: ORGANIZATIONAL PROCESSES   461**

CHAPTER 14   **Organizational Culture   462**

Preview Case: Bank of America   464

Types of Organizational Culture   465

Dynamics of Organizational Culture   466

Managing Across Cultures: Effects of National Cultural Values on Organizations   469

Managing in Practice: McKinsey & Co.—"The Firm"   474

Managing in Practice: The Failed Courtship of Bell Atlantic and TCI   476

Performance and Organizational Culture   477

Managing Quality: Gillette's Total Quality Culture   479

Ethical Behavior and Organizational Culture   479

Managing Ethics: Selling Auto Repair Service at Sears   480

Managing Cultural Diversity   482

Managing Diversity: Corporate Culture Versus Ethnic Culture   482

Organizational Socialization   485

Managing in Practice: Herb Kelleher and Southwest Airlines   487

▼ **Developing Skills**

Self-Diagnosis: Assessing Ethical Culture   490

A Case in Point: Procter & Gamble   490

CHAPTER 15   **Power and Political Behavior   494**

Preview Case: The Politics of Innovation   496

Power   497

Managing in Practice: The King is Dead   497

Interpersonal Sources of Power   498

Managing Across Cultures: Power and the Japanese CEO   501

Structural Sources of Power   503

Managing Quality: Computer Links Empower Employees   504

Managing Across Cultures: Power in Chinese and British Organizations   506

Managing Diversity: African-American Business Networking   508

The Effective Use of Power   510

Political Behavior   512

Managing in Practice: Picking a Successor at Booz, Allen, & Hamilton, Inc.   513

Managing Ethics: The Politics of Employee Appraisal   516

Personality and Political Behavior   517

▼ **Developing Skills**

Self-Diagnosis: How Much Power Do You Have in Your Group?   520

A Case in Point: The NASA Moonlander Monitor   522

CHAPTER 16   **Job Design   526**

Preview Case: Maids International   528

Introduction to Job Design   529

Managing Quality: Job Redesign at Vortex   530

Common Job Design Approaches   532

Managing in Practice: Job Engineering by Teams at NUMMI   534

Managing Diversity: The Disabled and Job Design   536

Technology and Job Design   537

Managing Quality: Metz Baking Company   539

Job Characteristics Enrichment Model   541

Managing Ethics: Electronic Monitoring of Work   545

Managing in Practice: Technology and Redesign of Tellers' Jobs   550

Sociotechnical Systems Model   552

Managing Across Cultures: Volvo's Uddevalla Versus NUMMI   555

▼ **Developing Skills**

   Self-Diagnosis: Redesign of the Data Entry Operator Job   558

   A Case in Point: McGuire Industry   559

CHAPTER 17   Organization Design   562

Preview Case: Xerox's New Design   564

Key Factors in Design   565

Managing in Practice: Fannie Mae   572

Managing Quality: Ford Reengineers Accounts Payable   575

Mechanistic Versus Organic Systems   576

Managing in Practice: Gore's Organic System   578

Managing Diversity: Sexual Harassment Complaint Procedures   580

Functional Design   581

Managing Ethics: Ethics Positions and Offices   584

Place Design   585

Product Design   586

Managing in Practice: Johnson & Johnson's Multidivisional Design   588

Integration of Units   589

Managing Quality: NCR's US Group Quality Improvement Design   591

Multinational Design   594

Managing Across Cultures: Ford's New Global Design   596

Network Design   596

Managing in Practice: Eastman Chemical's Network Design   597

Managing Across Cultures: Procter & Gamble's New Network Design   601

▼ **Developing Skills**

   Self-Diagnosis: Inventory of Effective Design   604

   A Case in Point: Aquarius Advertising Agency   604

CHAPTER 18   Organizational Decision Making   610

Preview Case: Rules to Decide By   612

Ethical Decision Making   613

Managing Diversity: Denny's Errors and Recovery   616

Managing Ethics: Designing an Effective Code   618

Decision-Making Models   620

Managing Quality: Providing Reliable Service   622

Phases of Managerial Decision Making   625

Managing in Practice: The Challenger Disaster   627

Managing in Practice: Challenger Flashback   631

Managing Across Cultures: Royal Dutch/Shell's Decision Making   634

Stimulating Creativity   635

▼ **Developing Skills**

   Self-Diagnosis: Individual Ethics Profile   640

   A Case in Point: Olson Medical Systems   642

▼ PART IV: CHANGE PROCESSES   647

CHAPTER 19   Nature of Planned Organizational Change   648

Preview Case: Managing in the Midst of Chaos   650

Goals of Planned Change   651

Pressures for Change   653

Managing Across Cultures: Arvin Industries   654

Managing Quality: The Non-manager Managers   658

Managing Across Cultures: 12,000 World Managers View Change   660

Resistance to Change   661

Managing Diversity: Ineffective Training Increases Resistance   662

Managing Ethics: Overcoming Resistance to Integrity   666

Organizational Diagnosis   669

Managing in Practice: The Chairman's Rice Pudding   669

Changing Organizations   672

Managing in Practice: The Nuts and Bolts of Innovation   674

▼ **Developing Skills**

   Self-Diagnosis: Rate Your Readiness for Change   678

   A Case in Point: Planned Change at the Piedmont Corporation   679

CHAPTER 20   Approaches to Planned Organizational Change   684

Preview Case: A Grim Fairy Tale   686

The Challenge of Change   686

People- and Culture-Focused Approaches   689

Managing Diversity: Workplace Flexibility at Corning   696

Managing in Practice: Changing Big Blue's Culture   698

Task- and Technology-Focused Approaches   700

Managing Across Cultures: Quality Circles in Japan   703

Managing Quality: Quality at AT&T Universal Card Services   706

Design- and Strategy-Focused Approaches   706

Managing in Practice: The Adaptive Organization   707

Ethical Issues in Organizational Change   711

Managing Ethics: The Tyranny of Change   711

▼ **Developing Skills**

   Self-Diagnosis: Attitudes Toward Change   714

   A Case in Point: Understanding Quality Systems—The Westinghouse Corporation   714

CHAPTER 21

Career Planning and Development   718

Preview Case: Winning the Career Game   720

Organizational Socialization: The Process of Joining Up   721

Managing Quality: Realistic Job Previews at Nissan   723

Managing Diversity: Pepsi-Cola's Designate Program   725

Career Changes   726

Managing Across Cultures: Speed Bumps on a Career Path   727

Managing in Practice: Cross Colours   729

Career Stages   733

Career Planning Issues   743

Managing Across Cultures: 3M   745

Managing in Practice: Coping with Job Loss   749

▼ **Developing Skills**

   Self-Diagnosis: Life Success Scale   752

   A Case in Point: Trade-offs   754

Appendix: Tools and Techniques for Studying Organizational Behavior   757

Integrating Cases   C–1

Name Index   I–1

Subject and Organization Index   I–11

PREFACE

We approached this seventh edition as though we were engaged in writing the first edition of the book. We asked ourselves what competencies, knowledge, and skills in organizational behavior will be needed by the users of this book both today and in the future. We recognize that many readers of this book may never become managers in the traditional sense of the word but *are* likely to be members and leaders of teams. Thus, even if you do not aspire to become a manager, this edition is filled with insights, needed skills, and concepts that will assist you in becoming an effective employee, whatever your role in the organization may be.

Organizational Behavior is the study of human behavior, individual differences, and performance in organizational settings. It is an interdisciplinary field, drawing on concepts from a variety of areas. Time and again, we see employees and managers who work hard and have all the necessary technical skills. But because of the lack of organizational behavior competencies, knowledge and skills, they never reach their full potential to contribute most effectively to the organization. A theme introduced in Chapter 1 and repeated throughout the book is that effective employees and managers need to understand and use organizational behavior concepts and skills. We use models and research to help you enhance your understanding and skills. We designed this book to be used flexibly, so chapters need not necessarily be studied in the same sequence as presented.

▼ GOALS OF THIS EDITION

Each chapter opens with a statement of the learning objectives unique to that chapter. These learning objectives are presented in terms of the competencies, knowledge, and skills that you should have acquired after carefully studying the chapter. In addition to these chapter-by-chapter learning objectives, a variety of goals are woven throughout the book.

▲ *The further development of your interpersonal skills*. These skills include the abilities to lead, motivate, manage conflict, manage stress, participate effectively as a team member, work constructively with others, and the like. Increased self-awareness may be the most important outcome from the development of your interpersonal skills. Self-awareness is fundamental to setting personal and professional goals and taking the constructive actions needed to achieve those goals.

▲ *The further development of your communication skills*. These skills include the abilities to send and receive thoughts, facts, beliefs, attitudes, and feelings to produce a response. Two of the most important of these skills are active listening and constructive feedback. Studying this book will enhance your abilities to engage in *assertive communication*, which means confidently expressing what you think, feel, and believe—and standing up for your beliefs while respecting the beliefs of others. In contrast, there appears to be a crisis of too much *aggressive communication*. It occurs when individuals express themselves in ways that intimidate, demean, or degrade others and simply pursue what they want in ways that violate the beliefs of others.

▲ *The further development of your conceptual skills.* These skills include the abilities to (1) reason deeply and clearly, (2) apply models and theories to problems and issues facing employees in organizations, (3) differentiate between symptoms and causes in situations, (4) identify assumptions underlying current and proposed practices, (5) apply concepts and techniques to enhance individual, team, and organizational creativity, (6) learn as a lifelong endeavor, and (7) analyze organizations as complex and interdependent systems and processes. We have increased the emphasis on recognizing and analyzing organizations in relation to customers, suppliers, shareholders, government agencies, and other stakeholders. We explicitly recognize that the pressures and demands from them are key influences on employee behavior in organizations.

▲ *The further development of your technical skills.* These skills involve the abilities to apply specific methods, procedures, and techniques in a specialized field. We focus on methods, procedures, and techniques in organizational behavior. We have substantially increased our discussion of the development and use of various information technologies as they relate to team and group processes, interteam decision making, job design, and interpersonal communication.

▲ *The further development of your understanding of the close links between organizational behavior concepts and skills with problems and issues actually faced by individuals, teams, and organizations.* We have drawn on the experiences of service, manufacturing, and not-for-profit organizations from around the world. We have maintained a balance between large and small organizations and between managerial and nonmanagerial employees.

▲ *The further development of your abilities and skills to diagnose and deal with ethical dilemmas and issues.* Rather than attempting to achieve this goal through a discussion of ethical issues in a single chapter, we have integrated the discussion of ethical issues and dilemmas in virtually every chapter of the book.

▲ *The further development of your knowledge and skills for positively dealing with culturally diverse individuals and groups in work settings.* We have integrated our presentation of diversity issues and challenges throughout the book. Organizational diversity involves a mixture of people who vary by age, gender, race, religion, life style, and other distinctive characteristic. The importance of managing diversity at work is increasing rapidly for both domestic and multinational organizations.

▲ *The further development of your knowledge and skills for working in organizations that have adopted the total quality management philosophy and its related practices.* Total quality management is an organizational philosophy and strategy for the long term that makes customer satisfaction and continuous improvement a responsibility of all employees. It represents dedication to meet customers' needs and exceed their expectations. Throughout the book, we discuss how employees, managers, and teams can use various methods to improve quality.

▲ *The further development of your understanding and appreciation of organiza-tional behavior issues and problems across cultures.* With the development of a global economy, organizations clearly need employees who appreciate and are sensitive to the diversity of values, communication styles, deci-sion practices, negotiation approaches, and leadership styles of other cultures.

▼ SPECIAL FEATURES

We addressed the goals just mentioned by revising completely all chapters, retaining features that our *customers* indicated should be kept, and adding several new features. The following special features aid in the achievement of the goals for this edition.

▲ *Preview Case.* In this edition we continue to open each chapter with a Preview Case. Twenty of the 21 Preview Cases are new to this edition. Each immediately links chapter content to real-world issues and prob-lems faced by organizations, teams, or individuals. They also integrate key concepts in each chapter.

▲ *Managing Across Cultures.* Each chapter contains one or more Managing Across Cultures feature. Twenty-two of the 30 Managing Across Cultures features are new to this edition. Additional issues and concepts related to them are presented as part of the regular content in a number of chapters. For example, new to this edition in the Interpersonal Com-munication chapter is a section on potential cultural barriers in interper-sonal communication. The Conflict and Negotiations chapter has a new section on negotiating across cultures. The Organization Design chapter has an expanded discussion of multinational design. Hence cultural is-sues have been woven into the text in addition to the special Managing Across Cultures features in each chapter.

▲ *Managing Diversity.* Each chapter contains a new feature entitled Man-aging Diversity. Twenty-three of 24 Managing Diversity features in the text are new to this edition. The one carryover feature appeared in the previous edition as a Managing in Practice item. Several chapters have additional textual discussions of diversity at work issues. Chapter 1 be-gins with a major presentation on diversity at work. It poses issues that will face all employees whether they work for U.S. or foreign orga-nizations.

▲ *Managing Quality.* All but two of the 21 chapters include new Managing Quality features. Twenty of the 22 Managing Quality features are new to this edition. The two carryover features appeared in the previous edi-tion as Managing in Practice items. Several of the chapters, beginning with Chapter 1, contain additional discussions of total quality manage-ment concepts and issues. The total quality management movement draws on many of the concepts, techniques, and models of organiza-tional behavior.

▲ *Managing Ethics.* Nineteen of the chapters contain a new Managing Ethics feature. Eighteen of the 20 Managing Ethics features are new to this edition. The one carryover feature appeared in the previous edition as a Managing in Practice item. We emphasize the importance of managing ethics in virtually all areas of organizational behavior. We introduce the importance of managing ethics in Chapter 1, noting that employees and managers must make decisions that have multiple values and ethical dilemmas associated with them. The Organizational Decision Making chapter has an extended discussion of ethical decision making. In other chapters we introduce special ethical concepts and issues in addition to the Managing Ethics feature in those chapters.

▲ *Managing in Practice.* This edition continues the well-received Managing in Practice feature that appeared in the previous edition. This edition, contains 50 Managing in Practice features, 35 of which are new to it. The Managing in Practice feature illustrates and applies the concepts, models, and skills relevant to the portion of the chapter in which it appears.

▲ *Developing Skills.* At the end of each chapter is a Developing Skills section. In 20 of the chapters it begins with a feature entitled *Self-Diagnosis*. This feature may include a self assessment questionnaire, a series of incidents that you are to respond to, or an exercise that you need to work on with others. Ten of the Self-Diagnosis features are new to this edition. The second feature in this section is entitled *A Case in Point*. Short cases are presented to sharpen your interpersonal, communication, conceptual, or technical skills. For the most part, these cases focus on the development of your conceptual skills. But they also present an opportunity to develop other skills related to problem solving with team members (requiring interpersonal skills), developing and applying procedures or techniques to the case (requiring technical skills), and writing or orally presenting a diagnosis and proposed solutions (requiring communication skills). These cases primarily focus on the content of the chapter. However, in some instances, the instructor can easily draw concepts and issues from other chapters in diagnosing a case. Of the 22 Case in Point features in this book, 15 are new to this edition.

▲ *Integrating Cases.* Six integrating cases appear at the end of this book, continuing a popular feature from the previous edition. Three of the six cases are new to this edition. These cases are more comprehensive and complex than the short cases that appear at the end of each chapter. They require the reader to draw on concepts, models, and skills from several areas of the book. The Integrating Cases may be assigned as individual projects for written and oral analysis and presentation, or they may be used as team projects.

▼ FRAMEWORK

As developed in Chapter 1 (and outlined in Figure 1.4), the framework for understanding the behavior of employees in organizations consists of five basic components: (1) the environment, (2) individual processes, (3) interpersonal and team processes, (4) organizational processes, and (5) change processes. Chapter 2 in the previous edition, Learning About Organizational Behavior, is now provided as an Appendix. This Appendix is entitled Tools and Techniques for Studying Organizational Behavior.

This edition contains four major parts, each of which is discussed briefly in Chapter 1.

▲ Part I, Individual Processes, includes seven chapters that focus on factors that influence an individual's behavior. Chapters are included on Personality and Attitudes (Chapter 2), Perception and Attribution (Chapter 3), Individual Problem-Solving Styles (Chapter 4), Learning and Reinforcement (Chapter 5), Work Motivation (Chapter 6), Motivating Performance: Goal Setting and Reward Systems (Chapter 7), and Work Stress (Chapter 8).

▲ Part II, Interpersonal and Group Processes, focus on groups and teams, leadership, interpersonal communications, and conflict and negotiations. It contains five chapters: Dynamics within Groups and Teams (Chapter 9), Dynamics between Groups and Teams (Chapter 10), Leadership (Chapter 11), Interpersonal Communication (Chapter 12), and Conflict and Negotiation (Chapter 13).

▲ Part III, Organizational Processes, [both sets the context for individual and interpersonal processes as well as emerge out of those processes]. The notion of organizations as systems and interdependent processes is emphasized in this part and Part IV. The five chapters included in this part are Organizational Culture (Chapter 14), Power and Political Behavior (Chapter 15), Job Design (Chapter 16), Organization Design (Chapter 17), and Organizational Decision Making (Chapter 18).

▲ Part IV, Change Processes, considers the issues and topics in the preceding chapters from a change perspective. This part contains three chapters: Nature of Planned Organizational Change (Chapter 19), Approaches to Planned Organizational Change (Chapter 20), and Career Planning and Development (Chapter 21).

▼ SUPPLEMENTS

Ten supplements are available for use with this book.

▲ A new edition of *Organizational Behavior: Experiences and Cases*, written by Dorothy Marcic, contains experiential exercises and cases that closely parallel material presented in this edition.

▲ A new *Student Study Guide*, prepared by Roger Roderick, contains learning objectives, chapter outlines, practice questions, and a programmed study supplement to *Organizational Behavior*.

▲ A new *Instructor's Resource Guide*, authored by Michael McCuddy, contains (1) lecture resource materials including Enrichment Modules, (2) answers to all discussion questions, (3) answers to *A Case in Point* questions, (4) instructor's notes for using *Self-Diagnosis instruments*, (5) answers to end-of-book *Integrating Cases* questions, and (6) instructor's notes for videos that accompany this text. This *Instructor's Resource Guide* is also available on disk in ASCII.

▲ A new *Test Manual*, prepared by David M. Leuser, contains more than 2,600 true–false and multiple-choice questions, as well as essay questions with possible responses.

▲ *Westest*, a computer-based test bank.

▲ A set of over 200 Transparency Masters.

▲ A set of four-color transparency acetates of the key Transparency Masters.

▲ A new video library is available to qualified adopters.

All of these supplements are available from West Publishing Company.

ACKNOWLEDGMENTS

We express our deep appreciation to those whose suggestions led to improvements in the seventh edition of *Organizational Behavior*. In alphabetical order, they are as follows:

David J. Abramis	California State University, Long Beach
Peggy Anderson	University of Wisconsin-Whitewater
Judith A. Babcock	Rhode Island College
Richard D. Babcock	University of San Francisco
Robert A. Cooke	University of Illinois at Chicago
Arthur L. Darrow	Bowling Green State University
Gene Deszca	Wilfrid Laurier University
Brian Graham-Moore	University of Texas at Austin
Samuel Gray	University of Richmond
James L. Hall	Santa Clara University
Jack L. Howard	Lamar University
Dev Jennings	University of British Columbia
Halsey Jones	University of Central Florida
Bruce Kemelgor	University of Louisville
Bonnie Kerr	Northern Alberta Institute of Technology
David M. Leuser	Plymouth State College
Sara J. McQuaid	University of Texas at Dallas
Barbara M. Pitts	McMaster University
Allen N. Shub	Northeastern Illinois University
Roger Volkema	American University
Sarah Williams Jacobson	North Dakota State University

Our working relationship with the people at West Publishing spans almost 25 years. We have worked with numerous individuals there over these many years and have always found them to be totally professional, ethical, and committed to the common goal of creating material that will well serve its users, both instructors and students. We want to single out several people at West for special recognition. Dick Fenton, acquisitions editor, worked with us through the first six editions of this book and a portion of this edition. We will always be grateful for his support. It was a pleasure to work with John Szilagyi, our new acquisitions editor. As with several of the previous editions, we worked closely with Esther Craig, our developmental editor. We feel blessed to have the opportunity to continue to work with Esther. Jayne Lindesmith, the assistant production editor on this edition, did a fine job in orchestrating the many paths and processes associated with turning a manuscript into a finished product. From the very beginning of this process, we had the good fortune once again to work with Jerrold Moore as our copy editor.

For their help with the many tasks of manuscript preparation, we express our special thanks and gratitude to Kimberly Bravenec and Argie Butler of Texas A&M University and Billie Boyd of Southern Methodist University. We are grateful to Dean Benton Cocanougher and former Interim Dean Gary Trennephol of Texas A&M University and the late President A. Kenneth Pye of Southern Methodist University for creating and supporting an environment that made this significant revision possible.

Finally, our colleagues and friends at Southern Methodist University and Texas A&M University play a critical role in creating a work environment that encourages and sustains our own learning and professional development.

Don Hellriegel
Texas A&M University

John W. Slocum, Jr.
Southern Methodist University

Richard W. Woodman
Texas A&M University

ORGANIZATIONAL BEHAVIOR

▼ SEVENTH EDITION

Chapter

1 Managers and Organizational Behavior

LEARNING OBJECTIVES

When you have finished studying this chapter, you should be able to:

▲ Discuss diversity in today's organizations.

▲ Describe seven critical challenges facing organizations.

▲ State the skills that employees need to develop to work effectively in a diverse organization.

▲ Describe the roles that managers play.

▲ Explain the fundamental concepts of organizational behavior.

OUTLINE

Preview Case: Cunningham Communications, Inc.

Diversity at Work

The Work Force

Managing Diversity: Hoechst-Celanese Diversity Programs

Gender

Race and Ethnicity

Age

Organizational Issues for the 1990s

Downsizing

Promotion

Expanding Service Organizations

Total Quality Management

Managing Quality: USAA

Ethics

Managing Ethics: What To Do

Global Challenge

Managing in Practice: How Managers Learn Global Skills at Colgate-Palmolive Company

Use of Technology

Organizational Challenges

Developing Skills

Technical Skills

Interpersonal Skills

Conceptual Skills

Communication Skills

Managerial Roles

Interpersonal Roles

Informational Roles

Decision Roles

Summary of Roles

Managing Across Cultures: Getting the Best from Managers in Different Countries

Fundamental Concepts of Organizational Behavior

Basics of Human Behavior

Managing in Practice: Cultural Influences on Behaviors

Organization Design

Organizations as Social Systems

Interaction Between Organization Design and Process

Organizational Behavior: A Framework

Environmental Forces

Individual Processes

Interpersonal and Team Processes

Organizational Processes

Change Processes

DEVELOPING SKILLS

Self-Diagnosis: *How Much Do You Value Diversity?*

A Case in Point: *Wanda Hill at Trust Consultants*

PREVIEW CASE

Cunningham Communications, Inc.

Andrea Cunningham had just returned to work from her first vacation since starting her public relations agency three years ago. She was preparing to meet with the vice-president she had left in charge. During her European vacation, she had phoned and faxed work to the office between bike rides and excursions with her husband to keep in touch with the business. She also had taken along business books to read, hoping that they would give her some new insights into management.

Located in Silicon Valley, her business was making a profit but had some unresolved internal problems. She had left her previous employer to make more money, take on more responsibility, and be an entrepreneur. Her clients included Hewlett-Packard, Borland International, Aldus Corporation, and NeXT, among others. Current billings were more than $3 million, and she employed twenty people. But Cunningham was dissatisfied. Clients still relied on her personally for most of the advice they had hired her company to provide. She felt that she had failed to delegate and hadn't created the caring and growing organization she had been determined to build. The two top people she had hired to help lead the company had no use for each other, fighting openly despite her efforts to keep the peace. In fact, a year ago she had considered selling the business.

Now she was reviewing the to-do list left with the vice-president. She discovered that many of the items on the list had not been done. Moreover, her secretary told her that the vice-president had led a mini-insurrection against her while she was gone. He had even crumpled up her mission statement and thrown it on the floor, telling the employees that he would be running the show. As she reviewed the disregarded to-do list with the vice-president, something snapped. She said, "I want you to leave. Now. You're fired."

After he left, she tried to figure out what had happened. She had believed that, by dividing people who worked on accounts into teams with each team accountable for its own profit-and-loss record, managing them would be relatively easy. People in each team would earn bonuses based on the team's profits, taking a lot of responsibility themselves and leaving her time to attract new clients. However, team rivalries destroyed companywide cooperation. People on different teams didn't share ideas because they wanted to protect their own profits. Individuals also balked at taking on responsibility. Andrea had thought that, if she presented them with some goals and gave them a chance to succeed, people would be productive and satisfied. In fact, just the opposite happened. During one six-month period, almost her entire staff had left.[1]

As Cunningham discovered, being a manager isn't easy. She faced ethical and quality control problems along with leadership and motivational challenges. She'd tried many different management practices with only marginal results. Supervisors didn't follow directives, subordinates didn't accept goals, and employees at all levels quit when they became dissatisfied.

There are no easy or complete answers as to why people and organizations fail to function smoothly. However, your study of organizational behavior should give you a systematic way of looking at and understanding the behavior of people in organizations. **Organizational behavior** is the study of human behavior, attitudes, and performance in organizations. It is interdisciplinary, drawing concepts from social and clinical psychology, sociology, cultural anthropology, industrial engineering, and organizational psychology.

Why should you study organizational behavior? Most people who do so are or will be employees in organizations and many will eventually become managers. Studying organizational behavior should help you be an effective employee and manager. The knowledge you gain should help you diagnose, understand, and explain what is happening around you in your job.

Andrea Cunningham had made organizational changes to remain competitive, but she still had some unanswered questions.

▲ Is my organization structured properly?

▲ Should I consult with my employees about a decision before I make it, or should I just make it?

▲ If I pay people more, will they stay longer?

▲ Should I continue to set goals for all employees? Or should I involve them in the process? If so, how?

▲ How can employees benefit from feedback they receive?

Effective managers try to find answers to these and many similar questions. They also try to understand how their behavior affects others in their organization. In this book we present information that will help you answer such questions and be aware of the importance of behavior (both overt and covert)—including your own—in an organization.

As Figure 1.1 suggests, one way to recognize why people behave as they do at work is to view an organization as an iceberg. What sinks ships isn't what sailors can see, but what they can't see. Using this analogy, let's analyze Cunningham's company. Its formal (overt) aspects include:

▲ *goals,* which are to make a profit, be a good community citizen, and let employees make their own decisions;

▲ *technology,* comprising the latest computers, fax machines, and electronic equipment to serve clients;

▲ *structure,* by which the organization is organized around account teams, with each team responsible for its own profit-and-loss record;

▲ *financial resources,* or the firm's current assets and liabilities, owner's equity, and the like; and

▲ *skills and abilities,* which are the technical, interpersonal, communication, and leadership skills of the owner and all employees.

To serve the public relations needs of her clients, Cunningham hired employees with good research skills, broad-based knowledge of the high-tech industry in which her firm specializes, and an in-depth understanding of how a client's business works. She had tried to discover what hindered employee performance and remove obstacles. However, by looking only at the goals, technology, structure, financial resources, and skills and abilities of her employees, she had focused only on the tip of the iceberg.

When Cunningham finally looked below the tip of the iceberg, she found that employee attitudes, communication patterns, and team processes—and her leadership style—needed to be changed. To begin making these changes, Cunningham took several actions. First, she sent all employees to an off-site meeting and asked her director of human resources to find out what her employees wanted. The answer was that they wanted a voice in running the company. They didn't complain about money or bonuses; they wanted to help run the company. Second, after receiving this information, she let them create an organizational structure that would allow the firm to satisfy customer goals, reach its financial targets, and maintain employee morale. The employees decided to organize into six teams: marketing, professional development, finance, quality, fun, and community relations. Except for finance, every task

FIGURE 1.1

Organizational Iceberg

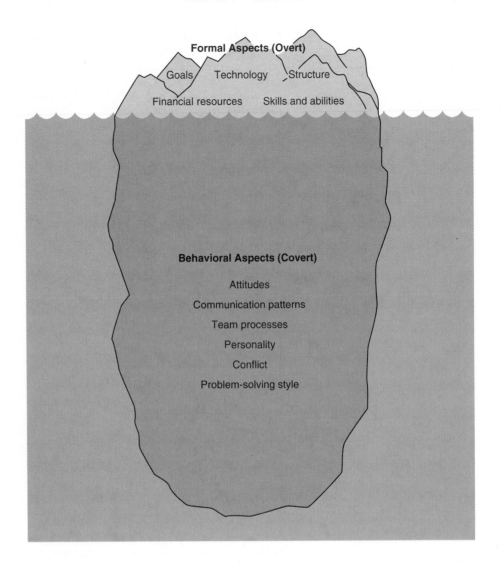

would be performed by teams of seven to eleven employees. Cunningham now gives each team its mission for the year. Each team then comes up with plans, budgets, and strategies for the year. Third, employees learned that it's hard to make decisions, accept trade-offs, and live with their own decisions. Now they are responsible for setting goals and taking the responsibility of meeting them. Teams meet to go over the past month's work and set goals for the next month. Employees adopted the motto, "Don't bitch. Fix it." Cunningham also learned that running the company wasn't her only leadership role. Coaching the teams, helping them stay on track, and removing obstacles became an integral part of her leadership role.

What were the results of these efforts? The firm's revenues increased by almost 20% during the past year, surpassing its goal by nearly 5%. Employee turnover now is minimal. Cunningham Communications has become the largest public relations firm in Santa Clara County, California.

An examination of an organization's structure, systems, technologies, goals, and employee skills and abilities is only a part of understanding why people behave as they do on the job. These factors set conditions that affect their behavior. Only after Cunningham changed her behavior did the organization's performance improve. As Cunningham discovered, what people want from their jobs can be much different from what leaders think people want. We next focus on what people want from their jobs and the changing nature of the work force.

▼ DIVERSITY AT WORK

Many people use the word *diversity* to refer to anyone who is not a white male. We define **diversity** as a mixture of people who vary by age, gender, race, religion, and/or life-style.[2] Think of diversity as a forest with various species of trees. Most U.S. managers have focused primarily on the species of race and gender, devoting little attention to the scope and breadth of the forest. One management challenge is to help people understand diversity so that they can establish productive relationships with people at work. Managing diversity doesn't mean addressing only one or two aspects of diversity and ignoring all others. Rather, effectively managing a diverse work force means adopting practices that recognize all aspects of diversity. Throughout this book, we suggest ways of understanding and appreciating individual differences. The Managing Diversity features that appear in most chapters are intended to help you promote a work environment that is comfortable for everyone.

Perhaps nothing has greater implications for managing diversity than the changing characteristics of the work force. Increasingly, managers realize that they can no longer assume work force homogeneity and high skill levels. Currently, there are just over five billion people on the earth, and by the year 2000 the world's population will be about six billion.[3] Most of the existing population and the projected population growth is in Asia. The U.S. population is growing more slowly than at any time in this nation's history, and there will be fewer young workers by the year 2000 than now. Let's examine how these changes will affect you and others entering the work force between now and the end of this decade.

▼ The Work Force

The makeup of the U.S. work force will change during the next five years. An estimated 25 million people will join the work force for the first time. About 85% of these new workers will be women, members of minority groups, and people with disabilities. Organizations such as Arthur Andersen, Boeing, DuPont, Hewlett-Packard, Hoechst Celanese, and Xerox recognize the value of a diverse work force comprising men and women of different races, national origins, and ethnic backgrounds, and they promote diversity in their organizations. For example, Hewlett-Packard conducts workshops for all employees in which the emphasis is on educating and encouraging managers to understand culturally different employees and to create an environment that will foster productivity.[4] Some organizations observe Hispanic Awareness Days, featuring food and cultural displays that reflect the Hispanic heritage.

By the end of this decade, immigrants from Asia and Mexico will represent a much larger share of the U.S. work force than they did in the 1980s. Two-thirds or more of all immigrants are expected to settle in the Southern and Western states. Immigration into Europe by people from less developed countries also is expected to continue, with the newcomers filling many jobs that Europeans don't want. This situation already has created workplace and other societal tensions in Germany, the United Kingdom, and other European countries.

Diversity in the work force affects managers in many ways. Let's consider two of them. First, people value work, but the type of work that interests them has changed. People want challenging jobs that allow them to make decisions. They also want the opportunity to learn, believe that work should be fun and unstructured, and desire small unexpected rewards for jobs well done.[5] For example, Patagonia, a manufacturer of products for outdoor enthusiasts, has nontraditional open workspaces (no offices with walls between), flexible work schedules, and flexible personal leave times.

The new buzz word in employee values is **empowerment,** which is the employees' right to make decisions within their areas of responsibility. Alfred West, founder of SEI Corporation, a $123 million financial services company in Wayne, Pennsylvania, organized his company into entrepreneurial divisions. Employees own as much as a 20% interest in their divisions. After some period of time, West asks an investment bank to assess each division's worth. He then pays the employees of the division that price. If the division has failed to make a profit, the members get only their salaries. Similarly, Tom Zidek, an employee at L-S Electro-Galvanizing Company in Cleveland, believes that most workers want to determine how to do their work and to participate in setting gain-sharing goals. Gain-sharing (discussed in Chapter 7) essentially is a form of bonus payment awarded to employees for achieving their production goals.[6]

Second, managers who are 40 or older generally believe that experience is the necessary road to promotion and have been willing to wait their turn. That is, they have typically moved their families geographically for the "good" of the organization. They have endured long working hours, postponed vacations, or taken overseas assignments in less developed countries in order to gain promotions. By contrast, younger employees believe that they should advance as rapidly as their competencies permit. Even in Asia (where the average employee works as much as 40% more hours than the average employee in North America) and Western Europe, there is some evidence that younger workers want to benefit from the hard work of their parents. Many such workers aren't willing to endure the personal sacrifices (such as long commutes to work, living in crowded apartments, etc.) that their parents did to get ahead.[7]

Work forces in Asia, Western Europe, Latin America, and North America are growing more complex and diverse. Thus managers need to recognize differences resulting from this diversity, particularly in terms of what employees want from the job. What are some of the challenges that organizations face with a diverse work force?[8]

First, there are language differences. Unless employees can understand each other, communication is difficult or even impossible. Employees cannot train each other or work together if they can't communicate. Translators may be used for hiring, but for the day-to-day communication that fosters a friendly, informal, and productive work setting, language barriers pose real and often serious problems. Such problems may lead to misunderstandings regarding performance standards, work methods, safety measures, and other essential working conditions.

Second, natural ethnic groupings within an organization may develop. Employees, especially if they do not speak English, may seek out others of the same ethnic group. Although such grouping develops a strong sense of teamwork within a group, it doesn't promote working with others who don't share the same language and cultural heritage.

Third, attitudes and cultural differences are another possible challenge. Most people have developed attitudes and beliefs about others by the time they seek a job. However, some attitudes and beliefs create frustration, anger, and bitterness in those at whom they're aimed. Managers who want to foster employee tolerance are opting for major change. Employees usually accept change only if the potential benefits are clear and worthwhile. In many organizations women and minorities are bypassed when important, formal decisions are made. Informally, these people often are left out when others go to lunch or a sporting event. These informal get togethers give older employees a chance to counsel junior employees about coping with problems. For managers to effectively create an environment where everyone can contribute to the organization's goals, attitudes usually must change. What are your attitudes toward diversity? Before reading any further, complete the "Diversity Self Assessment Questionnaire" in the Developing Skills section of this chapter on page 34.

How do organizations address these and other problems in promoting diversity in the workplace? Let's look at how Hoechst Celanese, a New Jersey–based maker of chemicals, fibers, and film, encourages diversity in its work force.

MANAGING DIVERSITY

Hoechst Celanese Diversity Programs

When Ernie Drew became CEO of Hoechst Celanese in 1988, he set out to study the human resource practices of the organization. When he began to examine the diversity of its work force, he found it unacceptable. To change hiring and promotion practices, his team drew up a 20-point plan, a major portion of which focused on respect for individuals and the need for diversity. Today half of the firm's skilled and professional entry-level jobs go to women and minorities. Celanese has found that it is easier to recruit a diverse work force if role models already exist within the organization. To reinforce the management of these talented employees, employees give blind evaluations of their manager's diversity practices, as well as their goal-setting and decision-making abilities. Retention and promotion opportunities require that women and minority members be given opportunities for operations and production jobs, as opposed to human resources, legal affairs, and other staff jobs. Often, operations and production jobs are more likely to lead into top man-

MANAGING DIVERSITY —*Continued*

agement jobs than are human resources jobs. Since most production work is done in teams, Celanese forms teams that include people from different departments, levels, races, and cultures. At Celanese, employees are reminded to observe religious holidays of all employees, translate instructions and other materials if needed, and to invite speakers to raise awareness of cultural variety.[9]

▼ Gender

Women accounted for about 60% of total U.S. work-force growth between 1970 and 1985. They are expected to be a large percentage of new entry-level employees between 1995 and 2000. Many women entering the job market are better educated than those who entered the work force during the 1970s. Although women represent 35% of all managers, less than one-half of 1% hold *top* management jobs.[10] Of the women in top managerial positions, 35% hold accounting and/or finance department jobs in their organizations.

Let's consider two of the main gender diversity challenges for organizations. First, women's talents and abilities should be fully utilized on the job. There is considerable evidence that women face a glass ceiling in management. The **glass ceiling** refers to a barrier so subtle that it is transparent, yet so strong that it prevents women and minorities from moving up in management.[11] Because women represent such a large portion of the work force, maximizing their productivity is essential to competitiveness. A recent poll of 241 *Fortune* 1,000 CEOs showed that nearly 80% said that stereotypes and preconceptions kept women from reaching top managerial jobs.[12] Many of these stereotypes and preconceptions are rooted in traditions, such as President's Golf Day, annual hunting trips, and the like, that preclude women's participation. Organizations such as Corning Glass Works, Avon, American Express, and Pacific Bell, among many others, have started to change their male-dominated practices to attract and retain highly qualified and productive women.[13]

Second, many women with children hold full-time jobs and still bear primary responsibility for family care. Approximately 75% of working women by the year 2000 will be in their child-bearing years. J.C. Penney, American Airlines, Dayton Hudson, and New England Telephone, among many other organizations, are setting up full-time child care centers and are offering workshops to teach parents about effective day care. These organizations recognize that developing programs to ease parents' concern for their children's welfare makes economic sense.[14] Not only are organizations providing subsidized day care centers on site, they also are arranging daily work schedules and vacation time to accommodate the demands of parenting. Still, a survey by the Society for Human Resource Management reports that only 10% of U.S. organizations provide child care assistance. However, nearly 50% of those surveyed are considering some form of assistance for employees responsible for child and/or elder care.

▼ Race and Ethnicity

One-third of the newcomers to the U.S. work force between now and the year 2000 will be minority group members. By then the work force will contain

16.5 million African-Americans, up almost 20% from 1988. Hispanics, Asians, and other minorities will comprise 14% of the work force, up 4% from 1988.[15] There is evidence that minority group members also face the glass ceiling. For example, only one African-American heads a *Fortune* 1,000 company, and less than 4% of top management positions are held by African-Americans, Asians, and Hispanics. As organizations strive to create a diverse work force, the recruitment, retention, and advancement of minority workers is essential. US West, Avon, C & P Telephone, and Whirlpool, among other corporations, actively seek to attract and retain minority group members. Katherine Davalos Ortega—who serves on the Board of Directors of Diamond-Shamrock Corporation, Ralston-Purina, and Kroger Company—believes that Hispanic managers can be effective if given a chance. To break through the glass ceiling, she advises minority group members to find mentors who can help them enter the power bases of the organization.[16]

▼ Age

The U.S. and Canadian work forces are aging along with the baby boomers. Between 1990 and 2000, the number of people aged 35 to 47 will increase by 38%, whereas the number between 48 and 53 will increase by 67%.[17] In the past, older workers have been less likely to relocate or train for new occupations than younger workers.

This increase in the number of middle-aged workers may collide with organizational efforts to reduce middle management in order to remain competitive. Because many of their skills and their productivity are valuable only to the firms they work for, older employees who lose jobs will have great difficulty matching previous salaries even when they are able to find new jobs. However, many experts believe that, to maintain adequate staffing, older men and women need to be kept on the job longer.[18]

▼ ORGANIZATIONAL ISSUES FOR THE 1990s

Just as diversity is requiring managers and employees to change their behaviors, organizations are under pressure to change. Let's briefly review several primary organizational issues.

▼ Downsizing

One of the results of the merger mania that swept through U.S. and Canadian organizations in the latter part of the 1980s is downsizing. **Downsizing** involves letting people go in an attempt to improve efficiency and competitive position. A survey by the American Management Association showed that almost 40% of the 1,000 organizations surveyed planned to reduce their work force by downsizing.[19] Organizations that have done so include IBM, which now employs 225,000 people, down from 344,400 in 1992; and Digital Equipment, now employing 98,000, down from 126,000 in 1989. The central question in downsizing is how best to do it. Options typically include attrition, layoffs, early retirement, and shortened workweeks, each of which affects organizations' costs differently. Organizations also must be aware that the survivors, along with those forced to leave, have concerns about the future. Managers of those remaining often encounter employees who report loss of identity or purpose, high levels of anxiety about their personal lives, emotional problems at home, and an obsession with self-survival. As one manager stated, "People were spending a lot of time worrying about their stock and personal futures rather than doing their work."

▼ Promotion

The tremendous expansion in the number of middle-aged workers will increase competition for fewer high-level management jobs. In 1987, one person in twenty was promoted into a top management position; in 2001, the ratio is expected to be one in fifty. The traditional incentive of promotion—to keep people working hard—appears to be threatened. The lower odds of promotion within an organization also may lead talented people to become entrepreneurial and form their own businesses rather than continue working for others. Sandra Kurtzig of ASK Computers, Debbi Fields of Mrs. Fields' Cookies, Michael Mackey of Whole Foods Market, and Michael Dell of Dell Computer Company, among others, are talented people who chose to start their own businesses rather than work their way up the corporate ladder.

▼ Expanding Service Organizations

The focus of many of tomorrow's organizations will continue to be on services, not manufacturing. In 1993, the service sector accounted for more than 68% of the U.S. gross national product and 71% of its employment.[20] In fact, the service sector accounts for nearly 90% of all nonfarm jobs created in the past thirty years. Nurturant service workers—those who tend the sick or people who are recuperating in their own homes—now hold more than three million jobs.

　　Many experts believe that the most successful service firms in the year 2000 will not be traditional service firms, but those that deliver an "experience." For example, half the U.S. population east of the Mississippi River has visited Disney World in Orlando, Florida, at least once. Today entertainment represents the second biggest U.S. export, after aerospace.

▼ Total Quality Management

Total quality management (TQM) is an organizational philosophy and long-term strategy that makes continuous improvement a responsibility of all employees. Total quality management requires dedication to meeting customers' needs and expectations, which includes (1) designing quality into products and services; (2) preventing defects but correcting those that do appear; and (3) continuously improving the quality of goods and services to the extent economically and competitively feasible.[21]

　　In 1951, W. Edwards Deming conducted a quality control seminar for Japanese executives.[22] Deming believed that to be more competitive, organizations had to begin with quality. He also believed that poor quality is 85% a management problem and 15% a worker problem. Among his recommendations for improving quality were the following.

▲ Establish and maintain zero tolerance for defective materials, workmanship, products and services.

▲ Gather statistical facts of quality during the process, not at its end. The earlier an error is caught, the less the cost will be to correct it.

▲ Rely on a few suppliers that historically have provided quality.

▲ Depend not on slogans but on training and retraining of employees to use statistical methods in their jobs to improve quality.

▲ Encourage employees to report any conditions that detract from quality.

Today most organizations are committed to productivity and quality improvement. Ford, Chrysler, and General Motors are changing management philosophies and past practices to foster new and creative ways of doing things. Numerous other organizations, such as Motorola, Corning, Hewlett-Packard, 3M, Federal Express, Xerox, and USAA, have used Deming's concepts or some variation of them to improve quality. The following Managing Quality piece illustrates how USAA has begun to use TQM concepts to improve customer services.

MANAGING QUALITY

USAA

Located in San Antonio, USAA is a life insurance and investment firm for military officers, former officers, and their dependents. Robert McDermott, USAA's CEO, believes that technology can improve quality and increase customer satisfaction, but only if programmers understand the need to do so.

Working with IBM, USAA computer programmers developed a program that sorts documents, arranges them in order of importance, and assigns them to an employee qualified to process them. Employees access documents electronically rather than removing papers from a file manually. The document is displayed on the employee's computer screen. The employee files completed work or routes documents that need further work to someone else for completion.

Another program aids policy service representatives who deal with customers by phone. Each rep can call up customers' complete records and display them on the computer screen as soon as customers identify themselves. Equipped in this manner, reps often settle matters during customers' first calls.

The results of McDermott's drive for TQM have been spectacular. More than 99% of USAA policyholders renew their policies annually. A *Consumer Reports* opinion survey of fifty-one car insurers rated USAA second for quick and fair claims settlements. The firm's reputation for being a good place to work also has spread. It receives more than 20,000 job applications a year—far more than it has positions to fill.[23]

In 1987, Congress established the Malcolm Baldrige Award to recognize organizations that excel in quality achievement and management.[24] Organizations are evaluated in terms of leadership, information and analysis, human resource utilization, customer satisfaction, and other factors that cover all the major components of an integrated TQM system. Motorola, 3M, Federal Express, Xerox, and Cadillac are among the firms that have won this prestigious award.

The constant provision of quality services and goods is an ideal that can't always be attained. Therefore how managers and employees respond to quality problems is crucial. There are three specific prescriptions for managing quality.

▲ Encourage customers to complain and make it easy for them to do so. Customer service cards and toll-free telephone numbers are only two of the possible alternatives.

▲ Make timely, personal communication a key part of the organization's strategy. For example, North Carolina's Wachovia Bank & Trust has a "sundown rule": Employees must contact a complaining customer before sunset the day the complaint was received.

▲ Encourage employees to respond directly to customer problems and give them the means to solve the problems themselves. When American Express cardholders telephone the 800 number shown on their monthly statements, they talk to highly trained customer service representatives. These representatives are able to solve 85% of customer problems on the spot.

▼ Ethics

The ethical issues facing managers and other employees have grown in significance in recent years, fueled by public concern about how business is conducted. Ethical behavior sometimes is difficult to define, especially in a global economy with its myriad beliefs and practices. We can define **ethics** as the values and rules that distinguish right from wrong.[25] Although there is clearly a legal component to ethical behavior in business, there may be few absolutes. Such behavior usually is interpreted relative to some guiding frame of reference. At Body Shop International, Anita Roddick runs her retail outlets with a strong commitment to the environment and human rights.[26] When the firm needed to build a new soap factory, it could have easily expanded the headquarters plant in Sussex, England. But Roddick decided to build a plant in Scotland, creating 100 jobs in an area that had about 70% unemployment. Honesty, integrity, and caring form the foundation of the organization. Says Roddick, "The stroke you get is not in the shares going up another bloody pence, but rather in an enthusiastic work force that's proud of what you do and is motivated by it."

Managers and other employees face many situations in which there are no right or wrong answers: The burden is on individuals to make ethical decisions. Such a situation is called an **ethical dilemma** when the individual must make a decision that has multiple values. An ethical dilemma doesn't simply involve choosing right over wrong because the opposite of one value may be several other competing values. Some ethical dilemmas arise from competitive and time pressures.

The following ethical dilemmas were presented in a survey of *Harvard Business Review* readers. Decide what you would do in each case before looking at the *HBR* readers' answers.

MANAGING ETHICS

What To Do

▼ Case 1: Foreign Payment

The minister of a foreign government asks you to pay a special consulting fee of $200,000. In return for the money, the official promises special assistance in obtaining a $100 million contract for your firm that would produce at least a $5 million profit. The contract will be awarded to a foreign competitor if not won by you.

Your Choice: Pay the fee   Do not pay the fee

▼ Case 2: Competition's Employee

You learn that a competitor has made an important scientific breakthrough. If this is true, it will substantially reduce your profits for about a year. There is the possibility of hiring one of the competitor's employees who worked on the project and knows its details.

Your Choice: Hire the person   Do not hire the person

▼ Case 3: Expense Account

You learn that a manager in your organization who earns $50,000 a year has been padding his expense account by $1,500 a year.

Your Choice: Report the person   Do not report the person

Now compare your answers with those of *HBR* readers. In Case 1, 42% would refuse to pay; 22% would pay but consider it unethical; 36% would pay and consider it ethical in the foreign context. In Case 2, 50% would hire the person, and 50% wouldn't. In Case 3, 89% believe that padding is okay if superiors know about it; only 9% believe that padding is unacceptable regardless of the circumstances.[27]

Managerial ethics are affected by personal experiences and the background of the person. Family influences, religious values, and personal standards and needs all influence a person's ethical conduct in any given situation. Throughout the book, we present Managing Ethics situations to illustrate ethical problems that managers and employees face.

▼ Global Challenge

Hewlett-Packard assembles computers in Guadalajara, Mexico, and 3M makes tapes and chemical and electrical parts in Bangalore, India. The reasons for these and other U.S. organizations' choosing international locations for some of their new facilities are complex.[28] These organizations want to establish sophisticated manufacturing and service operations that promise growth, not just exploit cheap labor. New technology and the continuing drive for greater profits push organizations to build plants and offices in other countries—plants that require only a fraction of the employees used in plants back home. Moreover, firms are outsourcing tasks previously performed by the organization. In **outsourcing,** firms hire independent suppliers rather than doing all the work themselves. Although not permanent, such workers often are highly skilled. In Fermony, Ireland, Metropolitan Life employs 150 medical claims insurance people to determine whether claims from Canada and the United States are reimbursable. A considerable knowledge of medicine and the insurance business is required. In addition, each worker is required to spend eighteen weeks in training before being allowed to start processing claims.

North American organizations are part of a global economy. Some experts believe that more than one-third of these organizations' profits are derived from international business, along with one-sixth of the jobs. Today's managers must understand the complexities of diverse work forces in order to compete globally. How do new managers acquire the skills and knowledge needed to become effective global managers? That question is the focus of the following Managing in Practice piece.

MANAGING IN PRACTICE

How Managers Learn Global Skills at Colgate-Palmolive

Colgate-Palmolive Company calls them "globalites." But it will take a lot of training before a trainee like Sebastian de Kleer becomes a global manager. The Dutch-born manager visited a grocery store in the U.S. for the first time last year and felt overwhelmed by the large assortment of "things people do not need" on the shelves. American born Catherine Sheldon had a similar rude shock during her business trip to Romania. She got puzzled looks when she asked a salesperson about her favorite soap brand. They said, "What do you mean? You just go in and buy the available soap."

Colgate tries to reduce the risk of failure in its global marketing-management training program by carefully screening applicants. Colgate looks for people who have the ability to work with people of other cultures as equals, who can adapt to living in many foreign countries, who are willing to learn about different cultures, who can understand the business from a global perspective, and who want to continuously learn from people in other cultures. Those trainees who pass this screening, 25% of whom are foreign, spend up to 24 months in a training program. After intensive language training, trainees perform three-month stints of duty in several foreign countries learning the marketing techniques for developing new products for those countries. Usually this means working with a local manufacturer, arranging distribution channels, developing an advertising campaign with a local advertising agency, working with shopkeepers to secure shelf space for their products, and the like.

It is important for Colgate, PepsiCo, Raychem, American Express, Honda Manufacturing of America, G.E. and other organizations to develop globally competent managers. This means that global organizations must recruit from around the world, use selection criteria that are not biased to favor one culture, and promote the most competent people without regard to national passport.[29]

▼ Use of Technology

Managers have begun to design their organizations to take advantage of advances in computer-based information systems.[30] About 16 million employees now work out of their homes instead of going to offices. The use of "electronic offices" will continue to expand as computers link more and more people without their having to meet face-to-face. The challenge is how to motivate and lead people effectively when the manager has little or no personal contact with them.

▼ Organizational Challenges

The workplace challenge for all employees is how to simultaneously deal with a diverse work force (characterized by changing attitudes and values) and a changing organization (required to maintain competitiveness). As the work force continues to diversify, organizations will need to be especially attuned to different expectations. The organization in the year 2000 will reflect society's melting pot of backgrounds, cultures, and expectations.

How can we help you meet these challenges? One way is to provide frameworks and concepts that give you insights into these challenges. A good starting point is to focus on the skills needed to become an effective professional.

▼ DEVELOPING SKILLS

Successful professionals must be able to work with people. Although strong analytical and quantitative skills are important, organizations are emphasizing skills that enable employees to become effective members of a team, division, or corporation. **Skills** are abilities related to performance that can be learned. For our purpose, we separate professional skills into four groups: technical, interpersonal, conceptual, and communication. Sometimes, however, telling where one skill begins and another ends may be difficult.[31] Throughout this book, both within the text and in the Developing Skills section at the end of each chapter, we focus on the basic skills you should develop to be a more effective professional.

▼ Technical Skills

Technical skills involve the ability to apply specific methods, procedures, and techniques in a specialized field. Imagine the technical skills needed by design engineers, market researchers, tax accountants, and computer operators. Their skills are concrete and usually are learned in college courses and on the job. Managers use these skills to varying degrees, depending on the problems they face. Technical skills change as a manager's responsibility increases. Generally, people are promoted into management because of their technical skills. First-line managers need to be technically skilled enough to train new employees and supervise the technical aspects of their work. As managers' responsibilities increase, they may have less need for hands-on detailed knowledge. But they still have to keep up with changes while learning new skills, such as problem-solving and negotiating, that are essential to their jobs.

▼ Interpersonal Skills

Interpersonal skills include the abilities to lead, motivate, manage conflict, conduct group meetings, and work with others. Whereas technical skills involve working with things, interpersonal skills involve working with people. Because every organization's most valuable asset is its people, interpersonal skills are a key part of every manager's job.

Managers with excellent interpersonal skills encourage participation in decision making and let others express themselves without fear of embarrassment. People with good interpersonal skills respect other people and are respected by them. Such managers are able to implement decisions, defend the interests of their work groups, and obtain special rewards for deserving subordinates. They understand the balance between personal and work life, help others reach their goals, and develop ways to reduce stress in the workplace. Managers who lack effective interpersonal skills may be rude, abrupt, and unsympathetic, and make employees feel resentful.

▼ Conceptual Skills

Conceptual skills involve viewing the organization as a whole and applying planning and thinking abilities. Managers with good conceptual skills are able to see how an organization's departments and functions relate to one another. Poor conceptual skills often lead managers into conceptual ruts, where they rely on habitual ways of thinking rather than look for new ways to solve problems.

▼ Communication Skills

Communication skills involve the abilities to send and receive information and to convey and understand thoughts, feelings, and attitudes. Few work activities are more criticized than group meetings. Managers and employees alike complain that they have to go to meetings whose purposes are ill defined, sit through boring presentations, and waste time discussing a decision a higher level manager should have made. Garbled communications and committee meetings often are the butts of office jokes.

Gender, cultural, and ethnic diversity demands new and better communication skills. To overcome language barriers, Pepsi-Cola International developed a system for use by people from many different cultures and countries. The company had found, for example, that ''handle business complexity'' might be translated differently in China and France. In China it might mean to produce a product and get it to the loading dock. In France it might mean being concerned with producing, marketing, distributing, and merchandising the product. Because ''handling business complexity'' translates differently,

Pepsi-Cola International needed a way to get individuals to behave consistently regardless of country and language. Therefore the company created its own multinational vocabulary to state performance criteria in a consistent, globally acceptable, and understood way.

The need to communicate effectively is basic to managing people, as shown in Figure 1.2. Communication skills serve as the building blocks for the development of all other skills. Note the breakdown of technical skills into detailed and broader knowledge. Detailed knowledge permits someone to perform a job because of "hands-on" ability, whereas broader knowledge refers to a person's understanding of how a combination of various technical skills is required to produce a good and/or service. For example, the admitting clerk at a local hospital needs detailed knowledge of the admissions procedure; the hospital administrator needs to know how this process interfaces with billing department activities.

To use either technical or conceptual skills effectively, managers must be able to communicate well with others. Especially in companies that operate in various countries, managers will have to spend more and more time building a consensus with a highly diverse work force to meet the organizations' objectives. As Colgate-Palmolive discovered, newly hired managers need to be able to learn about other cultures, learn other languages, and learn how to work effectively with local manufacturers, advertisers, and merchants.

▼ MANAGERIAL ROLES

Related to the skills that managers need is what managers actually do on their job. According to Henry Mintzberg, there are ten different managerial roles.[32] We define a **role** as a set of behaviors associated with a particular job in an

FIGURE 1.2

Skills for Employees

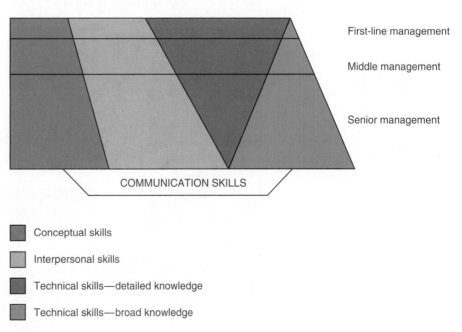

Source: Ripley, D. A. Trends in management development. *Personnel Administrator*, May 1989, 94.

organization. Figure 1.3 shows that these ten roles fall into three major categories: interpersonal, informational, and decisional.

Before discussing each role, we need to point out that (1) every manager's job consists of some combination of roles; (2) the roles played by managers often influence the type(s) of skills needed; (3) although described separately to aid understanding, roles actually are highly integrated; and (4) the importance of these roles may vary considerably by managerial level (first-line, middle, or top) and organization.

▼ Interpersonal Roles

Interpersonal roles refer to relationships with others and flow directly from a manager's formal authority. Interpersonal roles differ from the other types of roles in that their prime purpose is the development of relationships between the manager and other people. The key is interpersonal contact, not analyzing data or making decisions.

Figurehead Role   The **figurehead role** includes handling of symbolic and ceremonial tasks for a department or organization. The president who greets a touring dignitary, the mayor who gives a key to the city to a local hero, the first-line manager who attends the wedding of a machine operator, the sales manager who takes an important customer to dinner—all are performing ceremonial duties that are important to the organization's success. Although such duties may not seem important, managers are expected to perform them. They show that managers care about employees, customers, and others who deserve recognition.

Leadership Role   The **leadership role** involves directing and coordinating the tasks of subordinates in order to accomplish organizational goals. Some

FIGURE 1.3
───────────

Managerial Roles

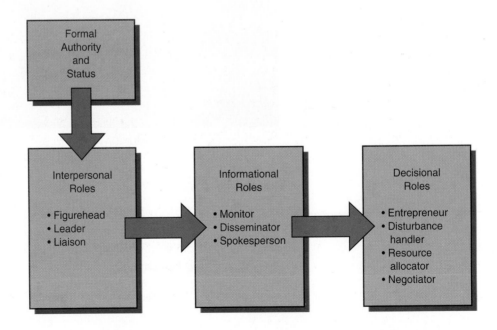

aspects of the leadership role have to do with staffing, such as hiring, evaluating, and rewarding employees. The essence of the leadership role is integrating the needs of individual employees with the goals and purposes of the organization.

Subordinates are sensitive to a leader's behavior. Everything a leader does may be screened by others who are looking for messages. Formal authority gives a person a great deal of potential power, but how that person behaves in the leadership role determines how much of that power will be realized.

Liaison Role   The **liaison role** is concerned with the development of information sources, both inside and outside the organization. The manager's prime motive is to establish, maintain, and extend a network of personal contacts that can feed information to the manager. Presidents of organizations spend time with other presidents and government officials to build a network of contacts through which they learn of trends or impending legislation that can affect their organizations. Within the organization, an ability to generate unsolicited information and ideas keeps managers informed about operations. The liaison role helps the manager build an information system and is closely related to the informational role of monitor.

▼ Informational Roles

Through their **informational roles,** managers build a network of contacts. These contacts enable managers to receive and send large amounts of information.

Monitor Role   In the **monitor role,** the managers seek and receive information. Managers are like radar systems, scanning the environment for information that may affect their department or organization's performance. Managers need current information because they must react quickly to events taking place around them. Therefore much of the information they receive is verbal.

Disseminator Role   What do managers do with the information received? In the **disseminator role,** managers share and distribute information to others in the organization. Sometimes it is passed along as privileged information, meaning that, unless a manager passed it along, other managers and employees wouldn't have access to it. Information sharing goes on all the time, but adequately informing subordinates may be difficult and time-consuming. Managers must sort through the information they have received—most of it verbally—and decide whom to share it with and how best to do so. Managers must then convey the information to others verbally or in writing, both of which take time to do.

Spokesperson Role   Managers' role in the information system doesn't end with being a disseminator. They also must pass along information to those outside the organization. In the **spokesperson role,** managers make official statements to outsiders through speeches, reports, television commercials (such as David Thomas, CEO and founder of Wendy's Old Fashioned Hamburgers), and other media. In this case, if the manager says it, the company says it.

▼ Decision Roles

Authority, interpersonal contacts, and information all are necessary for any organization to function but don't accomplish anything by themselves. Only when the organization produces something—a product or a service—does it perform its primary function. And a prerequisite to action is a decision. In their **decisional roles,** managers commit the organization to courses of action.

Entrepreneurial Role   In the **entrepreneurial role,** managers initiate projects or identify needed changes. Jack Welch, CEO of General Electric, introduced the concept of "workout" to generate ideas and make decisions about how to streamline operations and cut waste. Employees get the opportunity to tell management what they don't like and what they want to change. Issues range from food served in the cafeterias to reserved parking spaces for senior managers to managing in a "boundaryless" organization. In a boundaryless organization employees can get information from anyone who has it, and employees are evaluated both by their subordinates and managers.

The entrepreneurial role isn't confined to those working within an organization. Often, a successful entrepreneur is someone who starts a new organization. Anita Roddick, founder and managing director of Body Shop International, started the cosmetics company in 1976 because she wanted products that were based on all-natural ingredients that could be sold in refillable, recyclable containers. Detailed labeling information appealed to a new generation of environmentally conscious customers. Starting from a single store in West Sussex, England, the company has grown to more than 600 shops operating in forty countries around the world.

Disturbance Handler Role   In the **disturbance handler role,** managers resolve conflicts between subordinates or departments. In some cases, such as a strike, work stoppage, or the bankruptcy of a supplier, managers need to resolve conflicts between organizations. Even the best of managers cannot always anticipate or prevent such disturbances. However, effective managers learn how best to handle them as and when they do occur. Poor managers not only have to deal with such problems, they also typically fail to anticipate and resolve those that are preventable.

Resource Allocator Role   In the **resource allocator role,** managers are responsible for deciding who will get which resources and how much they will get. These resources may include budgeted or extra funds, equipment, personnel, and access to managers' time. Managers must continually make choices as to how resources will be distributed. Should money be spent for improving the quality of a product, or should a new product be developed? What proportions of the budget should be earmarked for advertising and for improving existing services? Should a second shift be added, or should the company pay overtime to handle new orders?

Negotiator Role   Closely linked to the resource allocator role is the negotiator role. In the **negotiator role,** managers represent a department or the company in negotiating with suppliers, customers, unions, and governments. For example, a purchasing manager negotiates with suppliers for lower costs and faster delivery times, and a sales manager negotiates a price reduction to keep a major customer happy. These negotiations are an integral part of the job because managers often have the information needed for a decision and the authority necessary to commit the organization to a course of action.

▼ Summary of Roles

Ten managerial roles add up to one manager. A manager who does not perform all ten roles probably is not performing as effectively as possible. Nevertheless, an individual may perform some roles more ably and vigorously than others, depending on personal background and style, managerial level, type of organization, and career path.

Every nation has a heritage that has created certain cultural expectations about the roles of manager and subordinate. What one culture encourages as participatory management, another may see as managerial incompetence. What one culture values as employee initiative and leadership, another may consider selfish and destructive to group harmony. Thus nothing is carved in stone about the way managers and subordinates are supposed to act. Managers must understand why people behave as they do and respond in an appropriate manner in terms of the situation.

In the following Managing Across Cultures feature, we look at how managers from several countries fulfill the three major categories of roles—interpersonal, informational, and decisional. We did not single out any one country, trying to give you an idea of how managers in several countries act.

MANAGING ACROSS CULTURES

Getting the Best from Managers in Different Cultures

▼ Interpersonal Roles

In some countries, authority is inherited; that is, key positions are filled from certain families. In other countries, a manager commands respect by virtue of position, age, or expertise.

In Mexico machismo is important. In Germany polish, decisiveness, and breadth of knowledge give a manager power. In Asia, the Arab world, and Latin America, a manager needs to be warm and personal. Managers often demonstrate this quality by appearing at birthday parties, soccer matches, and other social events and by walking through work areas, recognizing employees by name, talking to them, and listening to their concerns. In China managers periodically visit workers socially, inquiring about their health and morale without discussing specific work problems. Without singling out any person, managers thus compliment the entire work group.

In the United States and Canada, subordinates might have give-and-take discussions and present recommendations to their managers. Subordinates in the previously mentioned countries expect their managers to give them instructions. A U.S. manager who tries to get German workers to make a group decision may be told: "No, let the forepersons decide."

MANAGING ACROSS CULTURES —*Continued*

▼ Decisional Roles

Canadian and U.S. managers are being told to involve employees in making decisions that affect them; that is, participation strengthens commitment to the firm's goals and values and improves performance. Conversely, French, Italian, Indian, and German managers believe that rigid controls and strict obedience to authority are needed to obtain high job performance; that is, subordinates are not expected to try to influence their managers. These managers believe that subordinates want strong managers and that subordinates do not question the actions of their superiors.

▼ Informational Roles

In Japan, many workers identify completely with the organization for which they work. They focus their attention and energies on the organization—their personal life is their company life, and their company's future is their future. Compared to U.S. and Canadian employees, who tend to be job-oriented rather than company-oriented, the Japanese worker tends to be better informed about the organization's business and more ready to help other workers.

Latin Americans tend to work for an individual, not the job or organization, striving for personal power. Relationships and loyalties are much more personalized than in North America. Managers can obtain high performance only by effectively gathering information and working through individual members of a group.

In the United States and Canada, competition often is the name of the game: Everyone wants a winner. In other countries, competition in the workplace means that everyone loses. In Greece, managers say: "Two Greeks will do badly what one will do well." Greek teams work well only when a strong leader is available to set goals and settle conflicts. The leader often acts as a spokesperson and transmits information to others.

In the United States and Canada, a subordinate is supposed to accept criticism of performance as valuable feedback. In other countries, such criticism might be a mistake. To Arabs, Africans, Asians, and Latin Americans, preservation of dignity or "face" is an all-important value. Those who lose self-respect dishonor both themselves and their families. Public criticism is intolerable.[33]

▼ FUNDAMENTAL CONCEPTS OF ORGANIZATIONAL BEHAVIOR

One purpose of this book is to present as clearly as possible the basic knowledge we have about the behavior of people in organizations. Students of physics or accounting learn certain fundamental principles. The law of gravity is the same in Dallas, Paris, and Singapore; a hydrogen atom in New York is the same as a hydrogen atom in Brussels. An account receivable is carried on the books of a company in Calgary the same way it is carried on the books of a company in Atlanta. A cash transaction credit and debit are the same in London as they are in Tokyo. Although such rigid rules do not exist for behavior in the workplace, four fundamental concepts help explain the behavior of employees and managers in most situations.

▼ Basics of Human Behavior

One of the primary concepts of psychology is that people are different from each other. From birth, each person is unique, and experiences in life increase the differences among people. Hence managers can get the best performance from employees by treating them as individuals.

Both internal and external factors shape a person's behavior on the job. Internal factors include learning ability, motivation, perception, attitudes, personality, and values. We examine these individual differences closely in Part I of this book. What the people of one country value may not be valued by people of another country. Even though managers now operate in a global economy, they tend to fall back on their own cultural values when making decisions. Thus they must not only understand the cultural values of the people they are working with, at times they must hold their own values in check to build effective global working relationships. The following Managing in Practice example highlights how cultural values influence behavior at work.

MANAGING IN PRACTICE

Cultural Influences on Behavior

Let's compare the behaviors of workers in Japan, France, and the Netherlands to those in the United States. These differences can be partially explained by the cultural values of their respective countries.

▼ Japan

In the United States, managers are the core of the organization. Employees in the United States are expected to look after themselves. In Japan, the organization is a permanent work group; for all practical purposes, workers stay with the same firm throughout their careers. The group looks out for its own members. University graduates join a firm and are paid according to seniority rather than position. Rules and regulations govern relationships between workers with different levels of seniority. The behaviors of Japanese workers are controlled by peer groups, not by managers, as is the case in the United States. A worker who violates his peer group's norms is isolated until the group takes the worker back. Japanese workers believe that peer groups will protect them, and they give these groups their loyalty, even during punishment.

▼ France

In the United States, the worker exchanges services for a salary. Salaries can be used to buy goods and services, serve as status symbols, and generally indicate a person's worth to the organization. In France, which remains highly class-oriented, the governing principle is the honor of each class. Different

MANAGING IN PRACTICE —*Continued*

social classes accept rules that have been passed down for centuries. Supervisors behave in superior ways (such as giving orders and having large offices and other perks), which subordinates accept because they belong to a lower social class. The French do not think in terms of managers versus nonmanagers but in terms of cadres versus noncadres; a person becomes a cadre member by attending the proper schools and remains one forever regardless of managerial position. Cadre membership brings with it the privileges of a higher social class.

▼ The Netherlands

Americans place more importance on salary, advancement, benefits, a good working relationship and security in their employment than do the Dutch. In the Netherlands, employees attach a great deal of importance to their freedom to adopt their own approaches to a job, being consulted by their managers with regard to making decisions, training opportunities, fully utilizing their skills, and helping others. In terms of leadership, Dutch managers demonstrate modesty—as opposed to assertiveness in the United States—and are supposed to consult with their subordinates in an effort to reach a consensus.[34]

Among the external factors that affect a person's behavior are the organization's reward system, organizational politics, group behavior, managerial leadership styles, and the organization's design. We examine these factors in Parts II, III, and IV of this book.

▼ Organization Design

For years, behavioral scientists have stressed that individual behavior is a function of the interaction between the personal characteristics of the individual and the situation. To understand a person's behavior at work, we must analyze the pressures that the organization's design places on the individual. **Organization design** involves a set of decisions about the shape (tall versus flat) and features (number of departments, rules and regulations) of the organization's formal structure. Bureaucratic organizations, such as the Internal Revenue Service, the U.S. Postal Service, and United Parcel Service (UPS), are efficient because employees perform routine tasks. Rules and regulations increase an organization's effectiveness when its environment—customers, suppliers, and regulatory bodies—remains rather stable.

For years, Procter & Gamble dominated the soap and packaged food industry. Its large bureaucratic structure had worked effectively, but recently its environment changed. Crest was losing market share to Colgate, and Tide was losing market share to liquid detergents introduced by major competitors. Procter & Gamble responded by changing its organization design. The company introduced teams to increase coordination among brands. Production employees were brought into the decision-making process and made responsible for day-to-day operating results. With its new organization design, Procter & Gamble is introducing more products now than in the past and marketing those products faster than before.[35]

▼ Organizations as Social Systems

People in organizations have both psychological and social needs (for approval, status, and power), and they play various roles (interpersonal, informational, and decision making). Because individuals' behavior is influenced by their groups, managers may be able to use groups to improve performance and also to satisfy employees' needs for belonging. Celestial Seasonings, the $50 million herbal-tea company in Boulder, Colorado, has a strong employee orientation. It was founded in 1969 on a specific set of "Corporate Beliefs," including one outlining a long-term commitment to the development of people. That means empowering people to make decisions, having managers share full financial and market data with employees, and helping employees learn new skills. Empowerment requires managers not just to ask for suggestions, but to let employees make decisions and then act to generate change. At Celestial, members of teams are encouraged to work on specific problems, such as reducing milling waste by 20%, while at the same time learning how to analyze processes and develop appropriate solutions.[36]

▼ Interaction Between Organization Design and Process

Accomplishing something in organizations often involves knowing who to see and how to present an idea to that person. An organization design often indicates how people are grouped in the organization. For example, the basic UPS organization design feature is the service center. Drivers deliver packages to customers from each service center, which is responsible for making its own deliveries on time. **Process** refers to how the tasks of the organization are carried out. Decision-making, leadership, communication, motivation, and conflict-resolution practices are examples of processes.

Let's return to the opening case involving Andrea Cunningham and diagnose the interaction between her organization's design and process. She had organized her firm by client account (e.g., Apple, NeXT, etc.) and assigned teams of employees to each account. Each team had its own profit goals, on which bonuses were based. Her staff consisted of a vice-president and a secretary. Problems arose when teams didn't share information; they became minicompanies within the firm. Thus Cunningham's organization design fostered self-serving entrepreneurship, not interteam cooperation. Helping other teams solve their clients' problems brought no rewards, just more work. Her leadership style was to hire competent people and let them become entrepreneurs. She also thought that team members would get feedback from profit-and-loss statements, which would be sufficient motivation. She initially set goals herself without input from others. Her employees felt left out because the decision-making process didn't let them help determine their own goals. They wanted a voice in the decision-making process. Cunningham discovered that she needed to make changes both in design and process for her public relations firm to survive and prosper.

▼ ORGANIZATIONAL BEHAVIOR: A FRAMEWORK

The framework for understanding the behavior of employees in organizations consists of five basic components: (1) the environment; (2) individual processes; (3) interpersonal and group processes; (4) organizational processes; and (5) change processes. Figure 1.4 shows the relationships among these components, as well as the principal aspects of each. These relationships are much too dynamic—in terms of variety and change—to define them as laws or rules. As we analyze each component, the dynamics and complexities of organizational behavior will become clear.

▼ Environmental Forces

What happens when a company suddenly finds that the environment in which it has been competing suddenly shifts? Until the middle of 1991, the athletic footwear industry had been steadily growing at 20% a year. Sales accounted for more than 40% of all shoes sold in the United States. Since then, the industry has been in a severe slump for three reasons: market saturation, recession, and a shift in consumer tastes. Whether an organization has been able to survive this downturn is contingent on three factors: the environment, its behavior, and the consequences.

The slump in demand has caused the failure of small manufacturers that competed directly with Nike and Reebok. Nike and Reebok, with more than 50% of the market and combined sales of $3.3 billion, dominate the market. Jim Davis, CEO of New Balance, is attempting to create a market niche by catering to people who want high quality and need special sizes. Width sizing, for example, requires manufacturers to customize their manufacturing processes. Customizing means shorter production runs and the use of multiple lasts, the molds on which shoes are built. New Balance owns its manufacturing plants, but Nike and Reebok don't. They outsource their manufacturing to companies in China, Taiwan, Korea, and other Pan-Pacific countries. Outsourcing keeps Nike and Reebok's costs down, but they cannot fill custom orders quickly because they don't control production schedules.

Davis also knew that he had to get workers to focus on quality instead of volume. To reinforce New Balance's commitment to quality, 70% of workers' pay is based on quality and 30% on volume. Currently, 99.9% of New Balance shoes can be shipped as produced, in contrast to the industry average of 92%.

The consequences of Davis's decisions must be understood in terms of this environment. Nike and Reebok spend more money on advertising than New Balance generates in sales. Therefore the decision to manufacture high-quality shoes for people with sizing problems is a feasible solution for survival in a changing market environment.[37]

▼ Individual Processes

People make assumptions about those with whom they work, supervise, or spend time in leisure activities. To some extent, these assumptions influence a person's behavior toward others. Effective employees understand what affects their own behavior before attempting to influence the behavior of others. (In Chapters 2–8, we focus on the behavior of individuals.)

FIGURE 1.4

Framework for Understanding Organizational Behavior

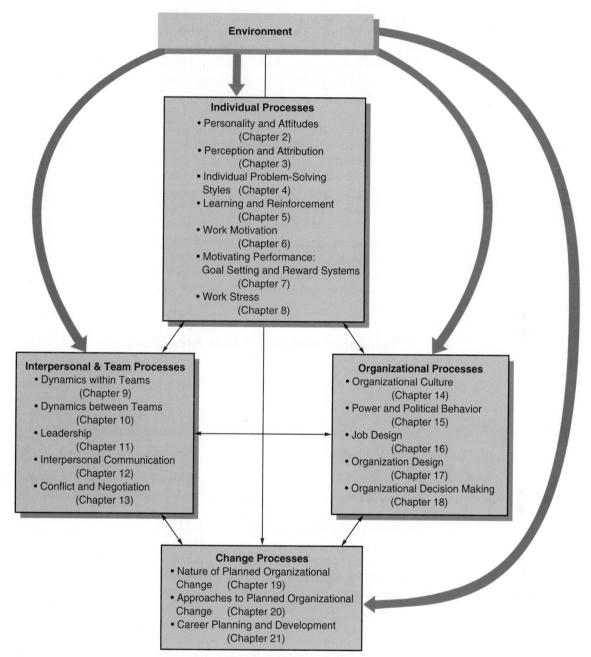

Individual behavior is the foundation of organizational performance. Understanding individual behavior, therefore, is crucial for effective management, as illustrated by the Cunningham Communications, Inc., case. Each person is a physiological system composed of a number of subsystems—digestive, nervous, circulatory, and reproductive—and a psychological system composed of a number of subsystems—attitudes, perceptions, learning capabilities, personality, needs, feelings, and values. In this book, we concentrate on the individual's psychological system.

Chapter 2 examines how personality and attitudes can affect an individual's capacity to learn, which depends on perception. Chapter 3 discusses behavior on the job. Different individuals give their own meaning to situations and so may view the same situation differently. To verify this assertion, compare your score on the Diversity Self Assessment Questionnaire (page 34) with those of others. How similar or dissimilar are they? Think about the reasons for these differences and discuss them with your classmates.

How various individuals use data to make decisions is the subject of Chapter 4. We present a framework for studying the effects of decisions on employee motivation and commitment to the organization. Chapter 5 identifies ways that managers can use rewards to communicate decisions and encourage or inhibit employee behaviors. Chapter 6 explains how to stimulate, sustain, and stop behavior in organizations. We explore various motivators and the importance of motivation in terms of performance. Chapter 7 examines how goal-setting and performance enhancement techniques have been used successfully. Chapter 8 focuses on work-related stress and how employees at all levels are attempting to cope with it, including the use of organizationally sponsored fitness and wellness activities, such as exercise programs and alcohol and substance abuse counseling.

▼ Interpersonal and Team Processes

Being inherently social, people generally do not choose to live or work alone. Almost all our time is spent interacting with others: We are born into a family group; we worship in groups; we work in groups; we play in groups. Much of our personal identity is based on the ways that other group members perceive and treat us. For these reasons—and because many managers spend more than two-thirds of their working days in meetings—skills in group dynamics are vital to all managers and employees.

Many organizational goals can be achieved only with the cooperation of others. The history of such organizations as Home Depot, Wal-Mart, Kentucky Fried Chicken, Kodak, and Boeing clearly illustrates the creative use of teams to improve the quality of life and to satisfy the needs of their employees and customers. The productivity generated by effective team action makes the development of team skills one of the most essential aspects of managerial training. Furthermore, membership in productive and cohesive groups is essential to maintaining psychological health throughout a person's life.

Being an effective team member requires an understanding of the dynamics within and between groups. Team members must be skillful in eliminating barriers to achieving their goals, solving problems, maintaining productive interaction among team members, and overcoming obstacles to team effectiveness. Chapters 9 and 10 present methods of increasing team effectiveness.

Organizations need leaders who can integrate employee and organizational goals. The ability of organizations to achieve their goals depends on the degree to which leadership abilities and styles enable managers to control, influence, and act effectively. Chapter 11 examines how leaders influence others and choose their own leadership styles.

How employees communicate with superiors, peers, and others can help make them effective team members or lead to low morale and lack of commitment. For that reason—and because most managers spend considerable amounts of time dealing with others—Chapter 12 stresses interpersonal communication. Conflict often arises among teams and/or team members over a variety of issues. Chapter 13 explains why conflict arises and how managers and employees can effectively resolve conflict, including the process of negotiation.

▼ Organizational Processes

Individuals enter organizations to work, earn money, and pursue career goals. Chapter 14 describes how they learn what is expected of them. They do so through the organization's culture, which is the set of shared assumptions and understandings about how things really work—that is, which policies, practices, and norms are important—in the organization. Newcomers have to understand the organization's culture in order to be accepted and become productive. Some organizations use formal programs, others simply rely on co-workers, and still others use a combination of these methods to teach the newcomer what to do and what not to do on the job.

Not all behaviors are aimed at improving performance. As Andrea Cunningham discovered when she returned from her vacation, power and political behavior, the subjects of Chapter 15, are realities of organizational life. Employees and managers use power to accomplish goals and, in many cases, to strengthen their own positions. A person's success or failure in using or reacting to power is largely determined by understanding power, knowing how and when to use it, and being able to predict its probable effects on others.

To work effectively, all employees must clearly understand their jobs and the organization's design. Chapter 16 describes the process of designing jobs, work methods, and relationships among employees at various levels. The technology utilized by the organization has a tremendous impact on job design and employee behavior.

As presented in Chapter 17, organization design refers to the features and shape of the organization. An organization chart presents a simplified view of organizational authority, responsibility, and functions. However, organization design is far more complex than can be depicted on such a chart. We identify factors that influence organization design and present some typical organization designs.

The world of managerial decision making is not particularly orderly or totally within the control of managers. Chapter 18 focuses on the factors, both internal and external, that influence managers' decisions. We identify and explore the phases of decision making and some ethical dilemmas encountered in decision making.

▼ Change Processes

The management of change involves adapting an organization to the demands of the environment and modifying the actual behaviors of employees. If employees do not change their behaviors, the organization cannot change. Many things must be considered when undertaking organizational change, including the types of pressures being exerted on the organization to change, the kinds of resistance to change that are likely to be encountered, and who should implement change. Chapter 19 presents a general model of organizational change. Chapter 20 discusses six basic strategies for achieving change:

▲ *people approaches*—using behavioral science techniques to involve employees in diagnosing organizational problems and planning actions to correct them;

▲ *cultural approaches*—changing the shared beliefs, values, expectations, and norms that comprise the organization's culture;

▲ *technological approaches*—changing the methods by which work is accomplished;

▲ *design approaches*—rearranging organizational authority, responsibility, and decision making;

▲ *task approaches*—redesigning individuals' jobs; and

▲ *strategy approaches*—changing the organization's intended courses of action to attain its goals or selecting new goals.

Most individuals look to organizations to provide satisfying work throughout their careers. Chapter 21 emphasizes that a career consists of both attitudes and behaviors over a long period of time. How people react to organizational events, such as relocation, promotion, demotion, or firing, reflects their personality, career stage, and career alternatives.

Summary

Several themes developed in this chapter have broad implications for everyone. Workplace diversity is increasing. As the work-force characteristics change and globalization of the marketplace accelerates, more and more people from diverse backgrounds will have to work together. Although few organizations and individuals are likely to be exposed to all forms of diversity, we highlighted how four types—changes in the work force, gender, race and ethnicity, and age—will affect most employees, managers, and organizations. These types of diversity are important because they reflect differences in perspectives, life-styles, attitudes, values, and behaviors. How employees respond to diversity will greatly influence organizational performance.

Next, we identified seven issues facing organizations: downsizing, lack of traditional promotional opportunities, the expanding service sector, total quality management, ethics, global competition, and the use of technology. These issues, coupled with diversity, will require organizations to change their traditional ways of operating. To help them adjust to the challenges of work force diversity and organizational change, individuals can develop and utilize four basic skills: technical, interpersonal, conceptual, and communication skills.

To accomplish their work and use their skills, managers perform ten different roles, which can be grouped into three broad categories: interpersonal, informational, and decisional. Through the interpersonal roles of figurehead, leader, and liaison, managers exercise their formal authority within the system. The informational roles of monitor, disseminator, and spokesperson enable managers to establish and maintain a network of personal contacts, which they use to give and receive a wide range of information. Information, of course, is the basic input to managers' decisional roles. As decision makers, managers are entrepreneurs, disturbance handlers, resource allocators, and negotiators.

The final topic developed in this chapter focused on the development of the five major components of organizational behavior: the environment, individual processes, interpersonal and group processes, organizational processes, and change processes.

Key Words and Concepts

Communication skills	Ethics	Organization design
Conceptual skills	Figurehead role	Organizational behavior
Decisional roles	Glass ceiling	Outsourcing
Disseminator role	Informational roles	Process
Disturbance handler role	Interpersonal roles	Resource allocator role
Diversity	Interpersonal skills	Role
Downsizing	Leadership role	Skills
Empowerment	Liaison role	Spokesperson role
Entrepreneurial role	Monitor role	Technical skills
Ethical dilemma	Negotiator role	Total Quality Management

Discussion Questions

1. What types of diversity does your organization face today? How is your university or organization responding?

2. What roles did Andrea Cunningham play in her public relations firm? How effectively did she perform these roles?

3. The most successful organizations will be those that recognize the challenge and opportunity of maintaining a diverse work force. In light of the recent emphasis on downsizing, what obstacles stand in the way of maintaining a diverse workforce?

4. If more people are entering the work force and organizations are promoting people more slowly, what motivational challenges does this situation present for managers?

5. What are some ethical dilemmas you have faced? How did you resolve them?

6. How might organizations shape the behavior, attitudes, and values of their employees?

7. How can you develop each of the four types of skills on your first job?

8. What are some of the difficulties you might face in taking a managerial position in a foreign country?

9. What are some of the challenges that women and minority group members face in organizations?

▲ Developing Skills

Self-Diagnosis:
How Much Do You Value Diversity?

Rate yourself on how you respond to the statements listed below. Use a scale of 5 to 1 to indicate how strongly you agree with the statements (5 is strongly agree and 1 is strongly disagree).

SA = Strongly Agree (5)
A = Agree (4)
N = Neutral (3)
D = Disagree (2)
SD = Strongly Disagree (1)

	SA	A	N	D	SD
1. I make a conscious effort to not think stereotypically.	5	4	3	2	1
2. I listen with interest to the ideas of people who don't think like me.	5	4	3	2	1
3. I respect other people's opinions, even though I may disagree.	5	4	3	2	1
4. If I were at a social event with people who differed ethnically from me, I would make every effort to talk to them.	5	4	3	2	1
5. I have a number of friends who are not my age, race, or gender, or of the same economic status and education.	5	4	3	2	1
6. I recognize the influence that my upbringing has had on my values and beliefs and that my way is not the only way.	5	4	3	2	1
7. I like to hear both sides of an issue before making a decision.	5	4	3	2	1
8. I don't care how the job gets done, as long as I see results.	5	4	3	2	1
9. I don't get uptight when I don't understand everything going on around me.	5	4	3	2	1
10. I adapt well to change and new situations.	5	4	3	2	1
11. I enjoy traveling, seeing new places, eating different foods, and experiencing different cultures.	5	4	3	2	1
12. I enjoy people-watching and trying to understand the dynamics of human interactions.	5	4	3	2	1
13. I have learned from my mistakes.	5	4	3	2	1
14. When I am in unfamiliar surroundings, I watch and listen before acting.	5	4	3	2	1
15. When I get lost, I don't try to figure it out for myself but ask directions.	5	4	3	2	1
16. When I don't understand what someone is telling me, I ask questions.	5	4	3	2	1
17. I really try not to offend or hurt others.	5	4	3	2	1
18. People are generally good, and I accept them as they are.	5	4	3	2	1
19. I watch for people's reactions whenever I'm speaking to them.	5	4	3	2	1
20. I try not to assume anything.	5	4	3	2	1

Scoring

Total your answers. If your score is 80 or above, you probably value diversity and can adapt easily to a multicultural work environment. Continue to look for areas of improvement. If you scored below 50, you probably need to work on understanding the need to value diversity.[38]

A Case in Point: Wanda Hill at Trust Consultants

It didn't surprise Wanda Hill that her lunch with José Rodriguez had turned into an uncomfortable experience. Rodriguez had been hired almost a year ago to develop the Hispanic market in the Los Angeles area for Trust Consultants. The company had used a similar strategy to develop the Taiwanese, Korean, and Japanese markets. It believed that, to attract these investors, it needed people in the office who understood their culture and could easily relate to them. During Rodriguez's first year, he had obtained numerous Hispanic accounts for Trust Consultants and was the top performer in the L.A. office.

Over lunch, Hill and Rodriguez reviewed his past year's performance. Hill told him that she was pleased but reminded him about the company's policy regarding investment advice. The policy of Trust Consultants was not to encourage clients to invest in high-risk ventures, but rather to suggest that they invest in mainstream stocks and bonds.

Rodriguez ignored the reminder and stated that he had been actively developing relationships with members of the Hispanic business community and expected to bring in more accounts soon. He asserted that, as the top performing financial consultant in the office, he deserved and needed a private office. He felt that the way to develop the Hispanic market further was to increase his visibility and prestige within the firm.

Hill was stunned by Rodriguez's request. There were only six private offices for the thirty-three financial consultants in the L.A. office, and they went to the most senior and experienced brokers. She had just moved into a private office herself after being with the firm for fourteen years. Rodriguez went on to say that, if he didn't get a private office, he might leave Trust Consultants and join Merlin Lawrence.

As the lunch ended, Hill started thinking about Rodriguez's request. When she became a vice-president at Trust Consultants and moved from Toronto to California, she wanted to build a winning team in L.A.—one that would be recognized for quality and professionalism, that would excel at matching clients with products, and that would utilize all the services of Trust Consultants.

Hill then thought about Rodriguez's day-to-day behaviors. He related well to his co-workers. He remembered what people took in their coffee and would bring it to them. He bought Danish or bagels and surprised people in the office with them. He carefully noted others' national and religious holidays.

Hill also had observed that, when he had clients in the office, they spoke only Spanish. He didn't allow others to work with his clients or even use his desk. If someone needed to use a desk for an informal meeting, they simply asked another person's permission, but few asked Rodriguez because the answer was always *no*.

Hill made it a point to circulate and talk with the brokers as often as she could. She usually spent several hours a day helping them on the phone or monitoring stock market indicators. She liked to do informal coaching and frequently would sit down at a person's desk and say, "Hi. How's it going?" From these discussions she kept the pulse of the office.

Hill also persuaded the more experienced brokers to take on younger brokers as junior partners. These mentors gave the younger brokers tips on how to make cold calls, handle rejection, and manage a client's assets effectively. She hoped that this effort also would revitalize the careers of some of the older brokers while giving the younger ones much needed advice and supervision. Many of the younger brokers sought such advice, but Rodriguez didn't. Hill couldn't understand why.

Hill had to make a decision on Rodriguez's office request by the following Monday.

Questions

1. What are some diversity issues in this case?
2. What roles did Hill play? How effective was she?
3. Should Hill give Rodriguez a private office? What factors influenced your decision?

References

1. Adapted from Brokaw, L. Playing for keeps. *INC.*, May 1992, 30–41.
2. Thomas, R. R., Jr. Managing diversity: A conceptual framework. In S. E. Jackson and Associates (eds.), *Diversity in the Workplace.* New York: Guilford Press, 1992, 307.
3. Jamieson, D., and O'Mara, J. *Managing the Workforce 2000.* San Francisco: Jossey-Bass, 1991; Jackson, S. E., and Alvarez, E. B. Working through diversity as a strategic imperative. In S. E. Jackson and Associates (eds.), *Diversity in the Workplace.* New York: Guilford Press, 1992, 13–36.

4. Schuler, R. S. World class HR departments: Six critical issues. Unpublished working paper, New York University, 1993.

5. Drucker, P. F. The new society of organizations. *Harvard Business Review*, September–October 1992, 95–105.

6. Macy, H. Personal interview, July 1994; Uchitelle, H. Empowering labor held key to more jobs. *New York Times*, July 27, 1993, D1 & D9.

7. Kiechel, W., III. How we will work in the year 2000. *Fortune*, May 17, 1993, 38–52; Hall, D. T., and Parker, V. A. The role of workplace flexibility in managing diversity. *Organizational Dynamics*, Summer 1993, 5–19.

8. DeLuca, J. M., and McDowell, R. N. Managing diversity: A strategic "Grass Roots" approach. In S. E. Jackson and Associates (eds.), *Diversity in the Workplace*. New York: Guilford Press, 1992, 227–247; Watson, W. E., Kumar, K., and Michaelsen, L. K. Cultural diversity's impact on interaction process and performance: Comparing homogeneous and diverse task groups. *Academy of Management Journal*, 1993, 36, 590–602.

9. Hall, C. Hoechst Celanese diversifying its ranks. *Dallas Morning News*, September 27, 1992, 1H, 5H.

10. Fisher, A. B. When will women get to the top? *Fortune*, September 21, 1992, 44–48, 52, 56; Ibarra, H. Personal networks of women and minorities in management: A conceptual framework. *Academy of Management Journal*, 1993, 18, 56–87.

11. Morrison, A. M., White, R. P., Van Velsor, E., and the Center for Creative Leadership. *Breaking the Glass Ceiling*. Reading, Mass.: Addison-Wesley, 1987; Morrison, A. M. *The New Leaders: Guidelines on Leadership Diversity in America*. San Francisco: Jossey-Bass, 1992.

12. Fisher, A. B. When will women get to the top? *Fortune*, September 21, 1992, 44–48, 52, 56.

13. Ragins, B. R., and Cotton, J. Gender and willingness to mentor. *Journal of Management*, 1993, 19, 97–112.

14. Kossek, E. E., and Nichol, V. The effects of on-site child care on employee attitudes and performance. *Personnel Psychology*, 1992, 45, 485–510.

15. Kunde, D. Workers cite hesitancy to discuss racial issues. *Dallas Morning News*, November 11, 1992, 1A, 13A. Also see Cooper, J. N., and Parrott, C. S. 25 years: An update on a new and changing workforce. *Equal Opportunity*, Winter 1993, 28–36; Thomas, D. A. Racial dynamics in cross-race developmental relationships. *Administrative Science Quarterly*, 1993, 38, 169–194.

16. Gomez, M. A place at the table. *Hispanic*, October 1992, 16–20. Also see Chao, G. T., Walz, P. M., and Gardner, P. D. Formal and informal mentorships: A comparison on mentoring functions and contrast with nonmentored counterparts. *Personnel Psychology*, 1992, 45, 619–636.

17. Green, G. M., and Baker, F. *Work, Health, and Productivity*. New York: Oxford University Press 1991; Varca, P. E., and Pattison, P. Evidentiary standards in employment discrimination: A view toward the future. *Personnel Psychology*, 1993, 46, 239–258.

18. Cascio, W. F. Downsizing: What do we know? What have we learned? *Academy of Management Executive*, 1993, 7, 95–104; Denton, D. K. Delayered, downsized, and demotivated. *Business Forum*, Summer 1992, 5–8.

19. Johnston, W. B. *Workforce 2000*. Indianapolis: Hudson Institute, 1987; Hall, D. T., and Richter, J. Career gridlock: Baby boomers hit the wall. *Academy of Management Executive*, 1990, 4, 7–22; Coates, J. F., Jarratt, J., and Mahaffie, J. B. *Future work: Seven critical forces reshaping work and the work force in North America*. San Francisco: Jossey-Bass, 1990; Hage, D., Grant, L., and Impoco, J. White Collar Wasteland. *U.S. News & World Report*, June 28, 1993, 42–53.

20. Schneider, B., and Bowen, D. E. The service organization: Human resources management is crucial. *Organizational Dynamics*, Spring 1993, 39–52.

21. Belohlav, J. A. Quality, strategy, and competitiveness. *California Management Review*, 1993, 35(3), 55–67.

22. Deming, W. E. *Out of the Crises*. Cambridge, Mass.: MIT Center for Advanced Engineering Study, 1986.

23. Adapted from Henkoff, R. Make your office more productive. *Fortune*, February 25, 1991, 72–84.

24. Easton, G. S. A Baldrige examiner's view of U.S. total quality management. *California Management Review*, 1993, 35(3), 32–54; Blackburn, R., and Rosen, B. Total quality and human resources management: Lessons learned from Baldrige Award-Winning Companies. *Academy of Management Executive*, 1993, 7, 49–66; Hill, R. C. When the going gets rough: A Baldrige Award winner on the line. *Academy of Management Executive*, 1993, 7, 75–79.

25. Hellriegel, D., and Slocum, J. W., Jr. *Management*, 6th ed. Reading, Mass.: Addison-Wesley 1992, 146.

26. Bartlett, C. A., Elderkin, K., and McQuade, K. The Body Shop International. *Harvard Business School*, Case number 9-392-032, 1992; Brock, P. Anita Roddick. *People*, May 10, 1993, 101–106.

27. Brenner, S. N., and Mollander, E. A. Is the ethics of business changing? *Harvard Business Review*, January–February 1977, 57. Also see Vogel, D. The globalization of business ethics: Why America remains distinctive. *California Management Review*, 1992, 35(1), 30–49.

28. Lei, D., and Slocum, J. W., Jr. Global strategy, competence-building and strategic alliances. *California Management Review*, 1992, 35(1), 81–97.

29. Lublin, J. S. Younger managers learn global skills. *Wall Street Journal*, March 31, 1992, 33.

30. Boynton, A. C. Achieving dynamic stability through information technology. *California Management Review*, 1993, 35(2), 58–77; Lei, D., and Goldhar, J. D. Implementation of CIM technology: The key role of organizational learning. *International Journal of Human Factors in Manufacturing*, 1993, 3(3), 217–230.

31. Ripley, D. E. Trends in management development. *Personnel Administrator*, May 1989, 93–96; Adler, N. J., and Bartholomew, S. Managing globally competent people. *Academy of Management Executive*, 1992, 6, 52–65.

32. Mintzberg, H. *The Nature of Managerial Work*. New York: Harper & Row, 1973; Stewart, R. Studies of managerial jobs and behavior: The way forward. *Journal of Management Studies*, 1989, 26, 1–10.

33. Adapted from Copeland, L., and Griggs, L. Getting the best from foreign employees. *Management Review*, June 1986, 19–26; Jackofsky, E. F., McGuaid, S. J., and Slocum, J. W., Jr. Cultural values and the CEO: Alluring companions? *Academy of Management Executive*, 1988, 2, 39–49.

34. Hofstede, G. Cultural constraints in management theories. *Academy of Management Executive*, 1993, 7, 81–94.

35. Hagerty, L. Personal interview. July 1993.

36. Rothman, H. The power of empowerment. *Nation's Business*, June 1993, 49–52.

37. Finegan, J. Surviving in the Nike/Reebok jungle. *INC.*, May 1993, 98–108.

38. Adapted from Hill-Storks, H. Diversity Self-Assessment Questionnaire. Used with permission, 1994.

Part I

Individual Processes

Chapter 2
Personality and Attitudes

Chapter 3
Perception and Attribution

Chapter 4
Individual Problem-Solving Styles

Chapter 5
Learning and Reinforcement

Chapter 6
Work Motivation

Chapter 7
Motivating Performance: Goal Setting and Reward Systems

Chapter 8
Work Stress

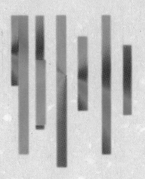

Chapter

2 Personality and Attitudes

LEARNING OBJECTIVES

When you have finished studying this chapter, you should be able to:

▲ Define personality and describe the basic sources of personality differences.

▲ Identify the "Big Five" personality factors and explain why these concepts are useful.

▲ Provide some examples of specific personality traits that have important relationships to work behavior.

▲ Explain the concept of attitudes and describe their components.

▲ Describe the general relationship between attitudes and behavior.

▲ Define job satisfaction and explain why it is important.

▲ Explain the concept of organizational commitment and identify important work outcomes of commitment.

OUTLINE

Preview Case: Individual Differences in Reactions to Downsizing

Personality: An Introduction

Sources of Personality Differences

Heredity

Environment

Managing Diversity: Generational Tension in the Office

Personality Structure

Managing in Practice: America's Toughest Bosses

Personality and Behavior

Self-Esteem

Locus of Control

Introversion and Extraversion

Dogmatism and Authoritarianism

Organizational Implications

The Person and the Situation

Attitudes: An Introduction

Attitudes and Behavior

Managing Quality: Reengineering Attitudes

Work Attitudes: Job Satisfaction

Managing Across Cultures: A Comparison of Japanese and U.S. Work Attitudes

Sources of Job Satisfaction

Job Satisfaction and Job Behavior

Work Attitudes: Organizational Commitment

Individual Differences and Ethical Behavior

Managing Ethics: Three Types of Management Ethics

DEVELOPING SKILLS

Self-Diagnosis: *Measuring Locus of Control*

A Case in Point: *Chuck Holeman— Retail Sales Representative*

PREVIEW CASE

Individual Differences in Reactions to Downsizing

Allied Products recently underwent a major downsizing after several quarters of disappointing sales and an anticipated further drop in product demand. Let's listen in as Anna and David, two middle managers at Allied Products, puzzle over some observed employee behaviors. As we join them, Anna is speaking.

"It happened again today. Amy lost her temper and threatened to quit for probably the sixth time this week. Ever since we had that layoff, she has been almost impossible to work with. I realize that two of her best friends were let go, but still. . . ." "I know what you mean," responded David. "Terry has been the same way. The slightest little thing sets him off. It puzzles me. He no longer gets along well with the rest of the department. You'd think that people would be worried about their own jobs since the downsizing and try harder."

"Well, some do," observed Anna. "For example, Kate's productivity has skyrocketed lately. She has become a real

team player—she clearly sees that we all have to do more with less resources. She's become a real star." "Hmmm," said David noncommittally, "I don't have too many people who have responded that positively, although I guess a few have. I've also had some really odd responses to the downsizing. You remember Reilly—I think you met her at the company picnic?" "Yes," said Anna, "I did." "Anyway," David continued, "Reilly has been extremely withdrawn and sad since the downsizing. I talked to her about it and she said that she feels guilty that she survived the cuts when so many others were let go. It seems to have taken away some of the enjoyment that she used to get from her job. Amazing!"

"Well, one thing about it," said Anna. "The wide range of reactions to this challenge makes me wonder if I know anything at all about people. After all, we're all in the same boat. Why such differences in behavior? Sometimes human behavior is such a mystery."

D ownsizing is one of the major challenges facing organizations and their employees in the 1990s, as we discussed in Chapter 1. As the Preview Case indicates, people often react very differently to downsizing and other organizational changes. Some 2,000 years ago, the Greek philosopher Theophrastus asked, "Why is it that while all Greece lies under the same sky and all Greeks are educated alike, it has befallen us to have characters variously constituted?"[1] This question—Why are people different?—is as important for understanding human behavior today as it was in ancient Greece. Managers and employees must comprehend and appreciate individual differences in order to understand the behavior of people in complex social settings, such as organizations.[2]

The behavior of an employee always involves a complex interaction of the person and the situation. Events in the surrounding environment (including the presence and behavior of others) strongly influence the way people behave at any particular time; yet people always bring something of themselves to the situation. This "something," which represents the unique qualities of the individual, is *personality*.

Part I of the book covers "individual processes" within organizations. We focus first on the individual in order to develop an understanding of organizational behavior. The term **individual differences** refers to the fact that people differ in a variety of ways. In this chapter, we discuss some of these individual differences, specifically personality and attitudes.

▼ PERSONALITY: AN INTRODUCTION

No single definition of personality is accepted universally. However, one key idea is that personality represents personal characteristics that lead to consistent patterns of behavior.[3] People naturally seek to understand these behavioral patterns in interactions with others. Certainly in organizations, managers and employees need to understand others' behaviors in various situations.

A well-known personality theorist, Salvatore Maddi, proposed the following definition of **personality:**

> Personality is a stable set of characteristics and tendencies that determine those commonalities and differences in the psychological behavior (thoughts, feelings, and actions) of people that have continuity in time and that may not be easily understood as the sole result of the social and biological pressures of the moment.[4]

This definition contains some important ideas. First, the definition does not limit the influence of personality only to certain behaviors, certain situations, or certain people. Rather, personality theory is a **general theory of behavior**—an attempt to understand or describe all behavior all the time.[5] In fact, some people argue that attempting to define the concept of personality means trying to explain the very essence of being human.

Second, the phrase "commonalities and differences" suggests an important aspect of human behavior. An often quoted adage states that, in certain respects, every person is like

- ▲ all other people;
- ▲ some other people; and
- ▲ no other person.

Theories of personality often describe what people have in common and what sets people apart. To understand the personality of an individual, then, is to understand both what that individual has in common with others and what makes that particular individual unique. Thus each employee in an organization is unique and may or may not respond as others do in a particular situation, as indicated in the Preview Case. This complexity makes managing and working with people extremely challenging.

Finally, Maddi's definition refers to personality as being "stable" and having "continuity in time." Most people intuitively recognize this stability. If your entire personality could change suddenly and dramatically, your family and friends would confront a stranger. Although significant changes normally do not occur suddenly, an individual's personality may change over time. Personality development occurs to a certain extent throughout life, but the greatest changes occur in early childhood.[6]

▼ SOURCES OF PERSONALITY DIFFERENCES

What determines an individual's personality? This question has no single answer because too many variables contribute to the development of each individual's personality. As Figure 2.1 shows, two primary sources shape personality differences: heredity and environment—or nature and nurture. Examining these categories helps us to understand why individuals are different.

FIGURE 2.1

Sources of Personality Differences

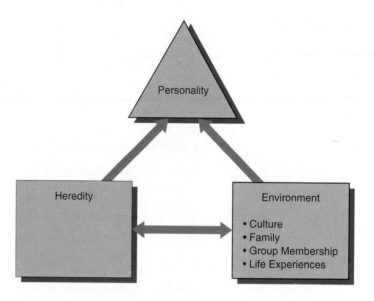

▼ Heredity

Historically, the **nature–nurture controversy** in personality theory was a sharp disagreement about the extent to which genetic factors influence personality. Those holding the extreme *nature* position argued that personality is inherited. Those adhering to the extreme *nurture* position argued that a person's experiences determine personality. Current thinking is more balanced—both heredity (biology) and environment (experiences) are important, although some personality characteristics may be influenced more by one factor than the other. That is, some personality traits seem to have a strong genetic component whereas other traits seem to be largely learned (based on experiences). Deeply ingrained in many people's notions of personality is a belief in its genetic basis. Expressions such as "She is just like her father" and "He gets those irritating qualities from your side of the family, dear," reflect such beliefs. In fact, some personality theorists argue that heredity sets limits on the range of development of characteristics and that only within this range do environmental forces determine personality characteristics.[7]

Moreover, recent research on the personalities of twins who have been raised apart indicates that genetic determinants may play a larger role than many experts had believed. Some studies of twins suggest that as much as 50%–55% of personality traits may be inherited,[8] which has some interesting implications. For example, it explains about 50% of the variance in occupational choice.[9] In other words, you probably inherited some interests that will influence your career choices. (We discuss careers and occupational choices in Chapters 4 and 21.)

▼ Environment

Many behavioral experts still believe that the environment plays a larger role in shaping personality than do inherited characteristics. Environmental components include culture, family, group membership and life experiences.

Culture   **Culture** refers to the distinctive ways that different human populations or societies organize their lives. Anthropologists working in different cultures have clearly demonstrated the important role that culture plays in personality formation.[10] Individuals born into a particular culture are exposed to family and societal values and to their norms of acceptable behavior. Culture also defines how the different roles in that society are to be performed. For example, U.S. culture generally rewards people for being independent and competitive, whereas Japanese culture generally rewards individuals for being cooperative and group oriented.

Culture helps determine broad patterns of behavioral similarity among people, but differences—at times extreme—in behavior usually exist among individuals within a culture; that is, most cultures are not homogeneous. For example, the work ethic (hard work is valued; an unwillingness to work is sinful) usually is associated with Western cultures. But this value doesn't influence everyone within those cultures to the same degree. Thus, although culture has an impact on the development of employees' personalities, not all individuals respond to cultural influences equally. Indeed, one of the most serious errors that managers can make is to assume that their subordinates are just like themselves. As indicated in the following Managing Diversity feature, individuals possess and exhibit many important differences even though they may be raised in the same culture and socialized into the same organization.

MANAGING DIVERSITY

Generational Tension in the Office

As if managers didn't have enough diversity concerns with gender and race issues, they must also sometimes contend with tensions between different generations of workers. The 78 million Americans born between 1946 and 1964 are popularly known as the *Baby Boom* generation. The *Baby Busters* generation comprises the 38 million born from 1965 to 1975. In some respects, we might regard these terms as convenient labels for workers employed, say, 15–20 years, and those in their first few years with an organization. Table 2.1 captures, in a somewhat tongue-in-cheek fashion, some of the dynamics that exist between these generations in the workplace.

The generation that entered the work force in the 1960s rebelled strongly against authority and a culture it viewed as repressive. Today's twentysomethings (the X generation, as some like to call themselves) face economic and career prospects that seem increasingly bleak. Their concerns bring the workplace to center stage.

Members of the X generation express their concerns about baby boomers in the workplace in terms such as "boomers spend too much time politicking and not enough time working. Boomer managers claim to be seeking younger employees' input when in reality they couldn't care less what Xers think. Worst of all, boomers seem threatened by young, cheap-to-employ hotshots who come in brimming with energy and superior technological savvy." For their part, fortysomethings see Xers as cocky, unwilling to pay their dues,

MANAGING DIVERSITY —*Continued*

TABLE 2.1   Tension Between the "Baby Boom" and the "Baby Bust" Generations

What "Baby Busters" Hate About "Baby Boomers"	The "Boomers" Response
You're blocking our way.	Wait your turn.
Too much political behavior—not enough work.	Can you spell naive?
Too much emphasis on hierarchy and structure.	You have no respect for authority.
You're not current on information technology. You don't know a PC from your left elbow.	You're right. Stop rubbing it in.

Source: Adapted from Ratan, S. Generational tension in the office: Why busters hate boomers. *Fortune*, October 4, 1993, 57–70.

disloyal, and uncommitted to the organization. Paradoxically, the boomers, who came of age challenging all authority, seem upset when a younger generation doesn't defer to *their* authority.

Although the sentiments presented in Table 2.1 have an amusing side, the tensions between these generations of employees are all too real. A difficult economic scene for young job seekers and the clash of workplace values creates a significant managerial challenge. Because organizations always need younger employees' energy and ideas, this challenge in managing diversity involves balancing the attitudes and values of the different generations of workers while at the same time capturing the younger workers' loyalty and enthusiasm.[11]

Family   The primary vehicle for socializing an individual into a particular culture is the person's immediate family. Both parents and siblings play important roles in personality development for most individuals. Members of an extended family—grandparents, aunts, uncles, and cousins—also can influence personality formation. In particular, parents—or a single parent—influence their children's development in three important ways.

▲ Through their own behaviors, they present situations that bring out certain behaviors in children.

▲ They serve as role models with which children often strongly identify.

▲ They selectively reward and punish certain behaviors.[12]

The family's situation also is an important source of personality differences. Situational influences include the family's socioeconomic level, size, race, religion, and geographic location; birth order within the family; parents' educational level; and so on. For example, a person raised in a poor family simply has different experiences and opportunities than does a person raised in a wealthy family. Being an only child is different in some important respects from being raised with several brothers and sisters.

Group Membership   The first group to which most individuals belong is the family. People also participate in various groups during their lives, beginning with their childhood playmates and continuing through teenaged school-mates, sports teams, and social groups, and on into adult work and social groups. The numerous roles and experiences people have as members of groups represent another important source of personality differences. Although playmates and school groups early in life may have the strongest influences on personality formation, social and group experiences in later life continue to influence and shape personality. Understanding someone's personality requires understanding the groups—past and present—to which that person belongs.

Life Experiences   Each person's life also is unique in terms of specific events and experiences, which serve as important determinants of personality. For example, the development of self-esteem (a personality dimension to be discussed shortly) depends on a series of experiences that include the opportunity to achieve goals and meet expectations, evidence of the ability to influence others, and a clear sense of being valued by others. Thus a complex series of events and interactions with other people helps shape the adult's level of self-esteem.

PERSONALITY STRUCTURE

The number and variety of specific personality traits or dimensions are bewildering. **Personality trait** typically refers to the basic "units" or components of the personality. Investigators have identified, named, and examined literally *thousands* of traits over the years. Trait names simply represent the terms that people use to describe each other. However, a list containing hundreds or thousands of terms isn't very useful either in understanding the structure of personality in a scientific sense or in describing individual differences in a practical sense. Thus these terms need to be organized into a small set of concepts or descriptions. Interestingly, recent research on personality has done just that—identified several factors that provide a useful way to talk about the "structure" of a person's personality.

Five main factors—often referred to as the "Big Five."—summarize the structure of an individual's personality.[13] The **"Big Five" personality factors** describe the individual's adjustment, sociability, conscientiousness, agreeableness, and intellectual openness (see Figure 2.2). Each factor includes a potentially large number of specific traits or dimensions. That is, each is not, by itself, a single trait, but rather a collection of related traits. Further, each factor is a continuum. For example, an individual at one extreme in terms of her degree of "agreeableness" might be described as warm and considerate. But with a personality at this factor's other extreme, she would be considered cold or rude.

Our society often places great importance on personality. Individuals with certain personality traits are admired, whereas those with other traits are intensely disliked or even feared. Note the emphasis on the personalities of the Chief Executive Officers described in the following Managing In Practice feature.

FIGURE 2.2

The "Big Five" Personality Factors

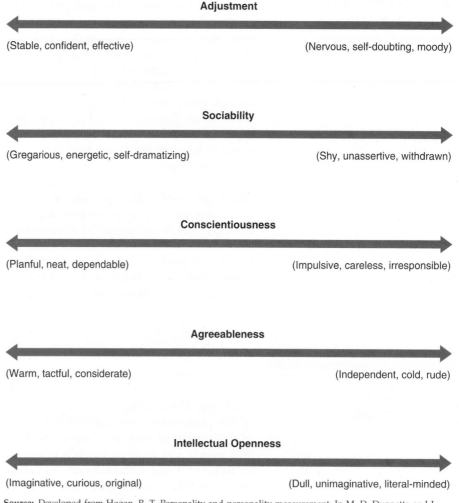

Adjustment

(Stable, confident, effective)   (Nervous, self-doubting, moody)

Sociability

(Gregarious, energetic, self-dramatizing)   (Shy, unassertive, withdrawn)

Conscientiousness

(Planful, neat, dependable)   (Impulsive, careless, irresponsible)

Agreeableness

(Warm, tactful, considerate)   (Independent, cold, rude)

Intellectual Openness

(Imaginative, curious, original)   (Dull, unimaginative, literal-minded)

Source: Developed from Hogan, R. T. Personality and personality measurement. In M. D. Dunnette and L. M. Hough (eds.), *Handbook of Industrial and Organizational Psychology*, 2nd ed., vol. 2. Palo Alto, Calif.: Consulting Psychologists Press, 1991, 878–879.

MANAGING IN PRACTICE

America's Toughest Bosses

Fortune magazine has created a dubious honor by selecting the "toughest" Chief Executive Officers in the United States. What does it take to make the list? According to Brian Dumaine of *Fortune*, merely being an iron-fisted cost cutter who has laid off hundreds or thousands of employees isn't enough. To make the *Fortune* list of tough bosses requires a certain type of personality— one that engages in "psychological oppression." Psychological oppression is defined as "an especially sadistic way of making a point, say, or a bullying quality that can transform underlings into quivering masses of Jell-O." Peller Marion, a San Francisco psychologist, says that overly abusive or demanding bosses often "do what works without looking at the consequences of their

MANAGING IN PRACTICE —*Continued*

behavior on other people." Dr. Gerald Kraines, head of the Levinson Institute in Waltham, Massachusetts, believes that such bosses have extremely rigid personalities: "They have such high expectations and are so unyielding that they are impossible to please. The abusive boss is constantly angry at himself and others for falling short of his ideal." Stanley Foster Reed labels mentally abusive bosses as "toxic executives" and suggests that their most troubling behaviors (to their subordinates and others around them in the workplace) are that they frequently

- ▲ invade the privacy of others,
- ▲ have secrets to protect,
- ▲ are changeable and unpredictable,
- ▲ have bad manners,
- ▲ are late for appointments and meetings,
- ▲ are control freaks,
- ▲ are highly competitive,
- ▲ hate others' ideas,
- ▲ are credit snatchers, and
- ▲ blame others when things go wrong.

Table 2.2 lists the "winners" of *Fortune's* search for America's toughest bosses, developed by soliciting nominations from business professors, top managers, financial analysts, and executive search firms. *Fortune* conducted more than 500 follow-up interviews to check out those leads. Dumaine describes the seven CEOs in Table 2.2 as "the most ego-squashing, tongue-lashing, tail-kicking bosses in U. S. business."[14]

TABLE 2.2   *Fortune* **Magazine's Toughest Bosses**

Chief Executive Officer	*Fortune's* "Label"	Descriptions by Co-workers and Others
T. J. Rodgers CEO, Cypress Semiconductor	*The Turret Gunner*	Punishing . . . expects you to know all the answers . . . uses intimidation to get what he thinks is right . . . a master of mind games.
Steven Jobs CEO, Next Computer	*The Rabid Perfectionist*	Brilliant and charming but explosive and abusive . . . inhuman drive for perfection can burn out even the most motivated employee.
Linda Wachner CEO, Warnaco	*The Queen of Impatience*	Smart, impatient . . . rewards employees but demands absolute loyalty . . . a screamer who is not above swearing like a trooper.
Harvey and Robert Weinstein Co-Chairmen, Miramax Films	*The Good Cop/Bad Cop Duo*	They play good and bad cop to keep people off balance . . . drive their employees excessively . . . Japanese management on acid.
Herbert Haft CEO, Dart Group	*The Pompadoured Bully*	An extremely hard negotiator . . . no long-standing relationship he has not broken . . . an intimidating military style . . . I say so, do it.
John Connors CEO, Hill Holliday	*Dr. Jekyll and Mr. Hyde*	A control freak with a split personality . . . generous and engaging, but also cold, calculating, and mean . . . hot-tempered.

Source: Adapted from Dumaine, B. America's toughest bosses. *Fortune*, October 18, 1993, 39–48.

▼ PERSONALITY AND BEHAVIOR

The main reason that we are interested in individual personality in the study of organizational behavior is because of the linkage between personality and behavior. For example, researchers have extensively investigated the relationships between the Big Five personality factors and job performance.[15] These investigations indicate that employees who are responsible, dependable, persistent, and achievement oriented (the *conscientiousness* factor in Figure 2.2), perform better than those who do not have these traits.

Recall that each personality factor represents a collection or grouping of related traits. However, the link between personality and specific behaviors often is most clear when we focus on a single trait rather than one of the five factors. The following material describes several *specific* personality traits that are particularly important for understanding aspects of organizational behavior.[16] Throughout the book we explain additional personality traits as they relate to topics under discussion—for example, in relation to perception (Chapter 3), individual problem-solving styles (Chapter 4), work stress (Chapter 8), and political behavior (Chapter 15).

▼ Self-Esteem

Self-esteem is the evaluation that an individual makes of himself or herself. People have opinions of their own behaviors, abilities, appearance, and worth. These general assessments, or judgments, of worthiness are affected somewhat by situations, success or failure, and the opinions of others. Nevertheless, they are stable enough to be widely regarded as a basic personality trait or dimension. In terms of the Big Five personality factors, self-esteem most likely would be part of the *adjustment* factor (see Figure 2.2).

Self-esteem affects behavior in organizations and other social settings in several important ways. For example, self-esteem is related to initial vocational choice. Individuals with high self-esteem take risks in job selection, are attracted to high-status occupations, and are more likely to choose unconventional or nontraditional jobs than individuals with low self-esteem. A study of college students looking for a job reported that those with high self-esteem (1) received more favorable evaluations from organizational recruiters, (2) were more satisfied with the job search, (3) received more job offers, and (4) were more likely to accept jobs before graduation than were students with low self-esteem.[17]

Self-esteem is related to numerous social and work behaviors. For example, individuals with low self-esteem are more easily influenced and individuals with high self-esteem are less easily influenced by the opinions of other workers. Individuals with low self-esteem set lower goals for themselves than do employees with high self-esteem. Further, individuals with high self-esteem place more value on actually attaining those goals than do employees with low self-esteem.[18] Individuals with low self-esteem are more susceptible than are high self-esteem employees to adverse job conditions—stress, conflict, ambiguity, poor supervision, poor working conditions, and the like.[19] In a general sense, self-esteem is positively related to attempts to achieve or a willingness to expend effort to accomplish tasks. Clearly, self-esteem is an important individual difference in terms of effective work behavior.

▼ Locus of Control

Locus of control refers to the extent to which individuals believe that they can control events affecting them. On the one hand, individuals who have a high **internal locus of control** (internals) believe that their own behavior and actions primarily (but not necessarily totally) affect the events in their lives. On the other hand, individuals who have a high **external locus of control** (externals) believe that chance, fate, or other people primarily determine the events in their lives. Locus of control typically is considered to be a part of the *conscientiousness* factor (see Figure 2.2).

Many differences between internals and externals are significant in explaining some aspects of behavior in organizations and other social settings.[20] Evidence indicates that internals control their own behavior better, are more active politically and socially, and seek information about their situations more actively than do externals. Compared to externals, internals are more likely to try to influence or persuade others and are less likely to be influenced by others. Internals often are more achievement oriented than externals. Compared to internals, externals appear to prefer a more structured, directive style of supervision. A recent study showed that managers with a high internal locus of control adjusted more readily to international transfers than did managers with a high external locus of control.[21]

Recall that we are particularly interested in the relationship between these personality dimensions and specific behaviors. Figure 2.3 on p. 50 shows some of the important relationships between locus of control and job performance. The Developing Skills section of this chapter contains a questionnaire on pages 63–64 that you can use to measure your own locus of control beliefs.

▼ Introversion and Extraversion

In everyday speech, the labels *introvert* and *extravert* describe a person's congeniality: An introvert is shy and retiring, whereas an extravert is socially gregarious and outgoing. The terms have similar meanings when used to refer to a personality dimension. **Introversion** is a tendency to be directed inward and have a greater sensitivity to abstract ideas and personal feelings. Introverts are quiet, introspective, and emotionally unexpressive. **Extraversion** is an orientation toward other people, events, and objects. Extraverts are sociable, lively, impulsive, and emotionally expressive. Introversion and extraversion are part of the collection of traits that comprise the *sociability* factor (see Figure 2.2).

Although some people exhibit the extremes of introversion and extraversion, most are only moderately introverted or extraverted or relatively balanced between the extremes. Introverts and extraverts are widely distributed across educational levels, genders, and occupations. As might be expected, extraverts are well represented in managerial occupations because the manager's decisional role often involves identifying and solving problems with and through other people (see Chapter 1). Research even suggests that some extraversion may be essential to managerial success. However, either extreme extraversion or extreme introversion can interfere with an individual's effectiveness in an organization.

FIGURE 2.3

The Effects of Locus of Control on Performance

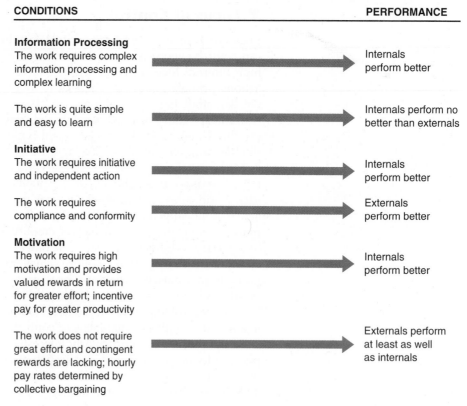

Source: Miner, J. B. *Industrial-Organizational Psychology.* New York: McGraw-Hill, 1992, 151. Reprinted with permission of McGraw-Hill.

One of the most striking implications of the introversion–extraversion personality dimension involves task performance in different environments. The evidence suggests that introverts perform better alone and in an environment that is quiet, whereas extraverts perform better in an environment with greater sensory stimulation, such as a noisy office with many people and a high level of activity.

Recall our discussion of the sources of personality differences among people. Interestingly, many experts consider introversion and extraversion to be a personality dimension with a relatively high genetically determined component.[22]

▼ Dogmatism and Authoritarianism

Dogmatism refers to the rigidity of a person's beliefs. The highly dogmatic individual perceives the world as a threatening place, often regards legitimate authority as absolute, and accepts or rejects other people on the basis of their agreement or disagreement with accepted authority or doctrine. In short, the high dogmatic (HD) individual is close-minded, and the low dogmatic (LD) person is open-minded.

As a result, HDs appear to depend more on authority figures in the organization for guidance and direction and are more easily influenced by them than are LDs. Some relationship between the degree of dogmatism and interpersonal and group behavior also seems to exist. For example, HDs typically need more group structure than LDs to work effectively with others. Hence the performance of HDs on task force and committee assignments may vary somewhat depending on how the group goes about its task. A high degree of dogmatism is related to a limited search for information in decision-making situations, which sometimes leads to poor managerial performance.

Authoritarianism is closely related to dogmatism but is narrower in scope. The events of World War II spurred the original research on authoritarianism. It was designed to identify personalities susceptible to fascist or otherwise antidemocratic appeals. Over time, however, the concept broadened. The **authoritarian personality** now describes someone who adheres to conventional values, obeys recognized authority, exhibits a negative view of society, respects power and toughness, and opposes the expression of subjective feelings. In organizations, the authoritarian personality probably is subservient to authority figures and may even prefer superiors who have a highly directive, structured leadership style. Both dogmatism and authoritarianism are related to the *intellectual openness* factor (see Figure 2.2).

▼ Organizational Implications

The personality dimensions identified and discussed have important implications for organizational behavior. Note that we identified *specific* relationships for each personality dimension. However, you must not conclude that managers or work groups should try to change or otherwise directly control employee personality, which, of course, is impossible anyway. Even if such control were possible, it would be highly unethical. Rather, the challenge for managers and employees is to understand the crucial role played by personality in explaining some aspects of human behavior in the workplace. Knowledge of important individual differences provides managers, other employees, and students of organizational behavior with valuable insights and a framework that they can use to diagnose events and situations.

▼ THE PERSON AND THE SITUATION

At this point in examining individual differences, again recognizing that behavior always occurs within a particular situation or context is essential. Although understanding differences in personality is important, remember that behavior always involves an interaction of the person and the situation. Sometimes the demands of the situation may be so overwhelming that individual differences are relatively unimportant. For example, if a room is burning, everyone in it will try to flee. However, the fact that everyone behaved the same way says nothing about the differences among those individuals. In other cases, individual differences may explain more about behavior. In the Preview Case, employees facing the same downsizing situation reacted very differently because of their individual differences.

The relative importance of situational versus personal determinants of behavior continues to be debated, but considerable evidence exists for roles by both.[23] Taking an **interactionist perspective** helps in understanding behavior in organizations. That is, you must consider both the person and the situation in order to understand and explain the individual's behavior.[24] Consequently, we present an interactionist perspective consistently throughout this book. You will discover that many of the topics covered—such as leadership, political behavior, power differences, stress, and resistance to change—examine both personal and situational causes for the organizational behavior discussed. Both *interact* to determine behavior.

▼ ATTITUDES: AN INTRODUCTION

Attitudes represent another type of *individual difference* that affects behavior. **Attitudes** are relatively lasting feelings, beliefs, and behavior tendencies directed toward specific persons, groups, ideas, issues, or objects.[25] An individual's attitudes reflect the person's background and various life experiences. As with personality development, significant people in a person's life—parents, friends, and members of social and work groups—strongly influence attitude formation. Also, some evidence points to genetic influences on the attitudes that people develop.[26]

People often think of attitudes as a simple concept, but in reality attitudes and their effects on behavior can be extremely complex.[27] An attitude consists of three core components:

▲ an *affective* component, or the feelings, sentiments, moods, and emotions about some person, idea, event, or object;

▲ a *cognitive* component, or the beliefs, opinions, knowledge, or information held by the individual; and

▲ a *behavioral* component, or the predisposition to act on a favorable or unfavorable evaluation of something.[28]

These components do not exist or function separately. An attitude represents the *interplay* of a person's feelings, cognitions, and behavioral tendencies with regard to something—another person or group, an event, an idea, and so on. For example, suppose that an individual holds a strong, negative attitude about the use of nuclear power. During a job interview with the representative of a large corporation, he discovers that the company is a major supplier of nuclear power generation equipment. He might feel a sudden intense dislike for the company's interviewer (the affective component). He might form a negative opinion of the interviewer based on beliefs and opinions about the kinds of people who would work for such a company (the cognitive component). He might be tempted to make an unkind remark to the interviewer or suddenly terminate the interview (the behavioral component). However, the person's actual behavior will depend on several factors, including the strength of the attitude toward nuclear power.

▼ ATTITUDES AND BEHAVIOR

To what extent do attitudes predict or cause behavior? For a long time, behavioral scientists believed that individuals' behaviors were consistent with their attitudes. However, they now widely accept the premise that a simple, direct link between attitudes and behavior frequently does not exist. In the preceding interviewing example, the person being interviewed might have the negative feelings, opinions, and intentions described and yet choose not to behave negatively toward the interviewer because (1) the individual desperately needs a job; (2) the norms of courteous behavior outweigh the person's desire to express a negative attitude; (3) the individual decides that the interviewer is an inappropriate target for the negative behavior; or (4) the individual acknowledges the possibility of having incomplete information.

Pollsters, among others, often measure attitudes in order to predict subsequent behavior. Yet, finding the relationship between attitudes and behavior may be difficult. Predicting behavior from attitudes can be improved by observing three principles.

▲ General attitudes best predict general behaviors.

▲ Specific attitudes best predict specific behaviors.

▲ The less the time that elapses between attitude measurement and behavior, the more consistent will be the relationship between attitude and behavior.[29]

For example, attitudes toward conservation in general are not as good a predictor of whether someone will join the Sierra Club as are specific attitudes toward the Sierra Club. General attitudes toward religion are not good predictors of specific behavior, such as giving to a certain church-related charity or observing a specific religious holiday. However, these general attitudes may accurately predict general religious behavior, such as the overall level of involvement in church activities. Finally, attitudes may change over time. Generally, the longer the elapsed time between the measurement of an attitude and some behavior, the less likely a strong relationship between them will be observed. This third principle is well-known to political pollsters (after some earlier embarrassments), and they typically are careful not to predict voting behavior too far ahead of an actual election. (Or they may be careful to add certain qualifiers to published polls, such as "If the election were held today. . . .")

In their model of the attitude–behavior relationship, the **behavioral intentions model,** Ajzen and Fishbein suggested that focusing on a person's specific *intentions* to behave in a certain way makes behavior more predictable (and understandable).[30] Figure 2.4 illustrates the model and shows that intentions depend on both attitudes and norms regarding the behavior. **Norms** are rules of behavior, or proper ways of acting, that members of a group or a society have accepted as appropriate. Norms thus impose "social pressures" to perform or not to perform the behavior in question. (We explore more fully the concept of norms in Chapter 9.) If both attitudes and norms are positive with regard to a behavior, an individual's intention to behave in a certain way will be strong. If attitudes and norms conflict, their relative strengths may determine the individual's intentions and subsequent behavior.

According to the behavioral intentions model, the individual's beliefs regarding specific behaviors affect both attitudes and norms (see Figure 2.4.). In the case of attitudes, beliefs concern the relationship between the behavior and its consequences (outcomes). Beliefs regarding norms reflect an individual's perceptions of how others expect that person to act. The behavioral intentions model helps explain why the relationship between attitudes and behavior sometimes is strong and at other times is weak.

FIGURE 2.4

Behavioral Intentions Model

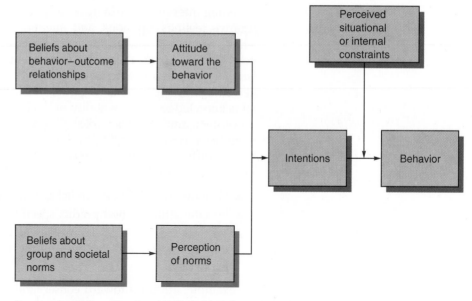

Source: Adapted from Ajzen, I. and Fishbein, M. *Understanding Attitudes and Predicting Social Behavior.* Englewood Cliffs, N.J.: Prentice-Hall, 1980, 8.

The behavioral intentions model was revised to include another possible explanation of social behavior: Real or perceived situational or internal obstacles or constraints may prevent a person from performing an intended behavior.[31] For example, someone might fully intend to perform a task quickly and efficiently but lack the skill to do so. Moreover, merely the perception or belief that she lacks the necessary skills might prevent her from performing the task (having the same effect as the actual lack of skill).

Over the years, behavioral scientists have proposed various models to explain attitude–behavior relationships. However, the simple model shown in Figure 2.4 predicts behavior about as well as more complex explanations do.[32] This model seems particularly useful for predicting certain specific behaviors in organizations, such as turnover.[33] In sum, attitude–behavior relationships are important for understanding some aspects of organizational behavior. For example, in some circumstances attitudes may be so important that managers can change an organization successfully only when supportive attitudes exist. The following Managing Quality feature provides an example of this.

MANAGING QUALITY

Reengineering Attitudes

The term *reengineering* is currently the rage among top executives, business school professors, and consultants concerned with improving quality in organizations. **Reengineering** refers to a radical redesign of processes to achieve real gains in service or product quality, reduce performance time, or cut costs. Reengineering isn't about "fixing" things that are broken in the organization; rather it means starting over, from scratch. Reengineering starts from the future—what do we want the business to look like?—and works backward. True

MANAGING QUALITY —*Continued*

TABLE 2.3 Traditional Versus Reengineered Work Attitudes

Traditional Work Attitudes	Reengineered Work Attitudes
My boss pays my salary. My objective is to keep my boss happy.	Customers pay all our salaries. My objective is to keep our customers happy.
I'm just a small cog in a big machine. My best strategy is to keep my head down and not make waves.	Every job in this company is essential and important. I get paid to create value.
If something goes wrong, I dump the problem onto someone else. Only suckers take the blame.	I must accept responsibility for problems and solve them.
The person with the biggest empire wins. The more people that I have reporting to me, the more important I am.	I belong to a team. We win or lose as a team. When we lose, nobody's empire wins.
Tomorrow will be just like today. Studying the past is the key to success.	Nobody knows what tomorrow will bring. Constant learning is part of my job.

Source: Adapted from The promise of reengineering. *Fortune*, May 3, 1993, 96; Hammer, M., and Champy, J. *Reengineering the Corporation: A Manifesto for Business Revolution*. New York: HarperCollins, 1993.

organizational reengineering is unconstrained by existing work methods, departmental structure, or work-force availability. Everything is subject to examination and change.

However, merely starting over is no guarantee of success. Reengineering is always difficult—by some estimates about 50%–70% of reengineering programs fail. Slowly and painfully, organizations are learning important lessons about what works and what doesn't in reengineering. One of them is that employee attitudes play a crucial role in the reengineering process. Employees and managers may have attitudes about how to do their jobs, their roles in the organization, and their responsibilities that are ineffective or even incorrect. Such work attitudes can derail a reengineering effort if not addressed. Table 2.3 lists some traditional work attitudes along with corresponding reengineered attitudes that are likely to be consistent with the reengineered organization and that are necessary for success. An organization cannot possibly do "more with less" unless the attitudes of individual employees support this initiative.[34]

▼ WORK ATTITUDES: JOB SATISFACTION

In organizational behavior, perhaps the attitude of greatest interest is the general attitude toward work or toward a job—often called **job satisfaction**.[35] Managers are particularly interested in understanding the sources of job satisfaction because these sources often suggest actions for improving employee job satisfaction. Further, managers are interested in the sometimes complex relationship between job satisfaction and job performance. In fact, job satisfaction is of interest to managers of organizations throughout the world. The Managing Across Cultures piece explores some interesting comparisons between the work attitudes of Japanese and U.S. workers.

MANAGING ACROSS CULTURES

A Comparison of Japanese and U.S. Work Attitudes

Investigators gathered data from 8,300 employees of 106 factories in the United States and Japan in an effort to identify possible productivity differences in the two countries. Among other things, the investigators suspected that Japanese and U.S. factory workers might have some different work attitudes.

Commitment to the company (one of the attitudes measured) seemed to be essentially the same for employees in the two countries. However, responses to survey questionnaires did reveal important differences in average job satisfaction scores between the two groups of factory workers. Contrary to some people's expectations, U.S. employees reported higher satisfaction than did their Japanese counterparts. Table 2.4 shows the average satisfaction scores obtained, along with some of the questions asked in order to measure job satisfaction.

Study results also indicated that certain organizational practices had the same positive effects on employee job satisfaction and commitment in both Japanese and U.S. factories. For example, participation in quality circles, company-sponsored recreation opportunities, and training opportunities outside the firm had similar positive effects on work attitudes in both countries.[36]

TABLE 2.4   A Comparison of Job Satisfaction Between U.S. and Japanese Employees

Job Satisfaction Question	Japanese Mean	U.S. Mean
All in all, how satisfied would you say you are with your job? (0 = not at all, 4 = very)	2.12*	2.95
If a good friend of yours told you that he or she was interested in working at a job like yours at this company, what would you say? (0 = would advise against it, 1 = would have second thoughts, 2 = would recommend it)	.91	1.52
Knowing what you know now, if you had to decide all over again whether to take the job you now have, what would you decide? (0 = would not take job again, 1 = would have some second thoughts, 2 = would take job again)	.84	1.61
How much does your job measure up to the kind of job you wanted when you first took it? (0 = not what I wanted, 1 = somewhat, 2 = what I wanted)	.43	1.20

*The differences in average response to each question are statistically significant, which means that the differences between U.S. and Japanese responses are large enough that they do not appear to be chance results.

Source: Adapted from Lincoln, J. R. Employee work attitudes and management practice in the U.S. and Japan: Evidence from a large comparative survey. *California Management Review*, Fall 1989, 91.

▼ Sources of Job Satisfaction

People sometimes regard job satisfaction as a single concept; that is, a person is satisfied with the job or not. However, it actually is a collection of related job attitudes that can be divided into a variety of job aspects. For example, a popular measure of job satisfaction—the Job Descriptive Index (JDI)—measures satisfaction in terms of five specific aspects of a person's job: pay, promotion, supervision, the work itself, and co-workers.[37] Obviously, an employee may be satisfied with some aspects of the job and, at the same time, dissatisfied with others.

The sources of job satisfaction and dissatisfaction vary from person to person. Sources thought to be important for many employees include the challenge of the job, the degree of interest that the work holds for the person, the extent of required physical activity, the characteristics of working conditions, the types of rewards available from the organization (such as the level of pay), the nature of co-workers, and the like. Table 2.5 lists work factors that often are related to levels of employee job satisfaction. An important implication of the relationships suggested is that job satisfaction perhaps should be considered primarily as an *outcome* of the individual's work experience. Thus high levels of dissatisfaction might indicate to managers that problems exist, say,

TABLE 2.5   **Effects of Various Work Factors on Job Satisfaction**

Work Factors	Effects
Work itself	
Challenge	Mentally challenging work that the individual can successfully accomplish is satisfying.
Physical demands	Tiring work is dissatisfying.
Personal interest	Personally interesting work is satisfying.
Reward structure	Rewards that are equitable and that provide accurate feedback for performance are satisfying.
Working conditions	
Physical	Satisfaction depends on the match between working conditions and physical needs.
Goal attainment	Working conditions that promote goal attainment are satisfying.
Self	High self-esteem is conducive to job satisfaction.
Others in the organization	Individuals will be satisfied with supervisors, co-workers, or subordinates who help them attain rewards. Also, individuals will be more satisfied with colleagues who see things the same way they do.
Organization and management	Individuals will be satisfied with organizations that have policies and procedures designed to help them attain rewards. Individuals will be dissatisfied with conflicting roles and/or ambiguous roles imposed by the organization.
Fringe benefits	Benefits do not have a strong influence on job satisfaction for most workers.

Source: Adapted from Landy, F. J. *Psychology of Work Behavior*, 4th ed. Pacific Grove, Calif.: Brooks/Cole, 1989, 470.

with the plant's working conditions, the organization's reward system, or the employee's role in the organization.

▼ Job Satisfaction and Job Behavior

Of particular interest to managers are the possible relationships between job satisfaction and various job behaviors and other outcomes in the workplace. A commonsense notion suggests that job satisfaction leads directly to effective task performance. ("A happy worker is a good worker.") Yet, numerous studies have shown that a simple, direct linkage between job attitudes and job performance often does not exist.[38] The difficulty of relating attitudes to behavior is pertinent here. Earlier, we noted that general attitudes best predict general behaviors and that specific attitudes relate most strongly to specific behaviors. These principles explain, at least in part, why the expected relationships often do not exist. Overall job satisfaction, as a collection of numerous attitudes toward various aspects of the job, represents a general attitude. Performance of a specific task, such as preparing a particular monthly report, cannot necessarily be predicted on the basis of a general attitude. However, a recent study showed that job satisfaction and the organization's overall performance are linked. That is, organizations with satisfied employees tend to be more effective than organizations with unsatisfied employees.[39]

Although job satisfaction does not necessarily lead an individual to perform a specific task well, it is important for several reasons. Satisfaction represents an outcome of work experience, so high levels of dissatisfaction help managers identify organizational problems that need attention. In addition, job dissatisfaction is strongly linked to absenteeism, turnover, and physical and mental health problems.[40] For example, highly dissatisfied employees are likely to be absent from work and are likely to leave a job for other employment. High levels of absenteeism and turnover are costly for organizations. Thus the strong relationship between dissatisfaction and absence and turnover is a compelling reason for concern about employee job satisfaction.

▼ WORK ATTITUDES: ORGANIZATIONAL COMMITMENT

Another work attitude of value for understanding organizational behavior is commitment to the organization. **Organizational commitment** refers to the strength of an employee's involvement in and identification with the organization. Strong organizational commitment, for example, is characterized by

- ▲ a strong belief in and acceptance of the organization's goals and values;
- ▲ a willingness to exert considerable effort on behalf of the organization; and
- ▲ a strong desire to maintain membership in the organization.[41]

Organizational commitment goes beyond loyalty to an active contribution in accomplishing organizational goals. Organizational commitment is a broader work attitude than job satisfaction because it applies to the entire organization rather than just to the job. Further, commitment typically is somewhat more stable than satisfaction because day-to-day events are less likely to change it.

As with job satisfaction, the sources of organizational commitment may vary from person to person. Employees' initial commitment to an organization is determined largely by their individual characteristics (such as personality and values) and how well their expectations about the job actually match their initial job experiences. Later, organizational commitment continues to be influenced by job experiences, with many of the same factors that lead to job satisfaction also contributing to organizational commitment or lack of commitment: pay, relationships with supervisors and co-workers, working conditions, opportunities for advancement, and so on. Over time, organizational commitment tends to become stronger for several reasons: (1) Individuals develop stronger ties to the organization and their co-workers as they spend more time with them; (2) seniority often brings advantages that tend to develop more positive work attitudes; and (3) opportunities in the job market may decrease with age, causing workers to become more strongly attached to their current job.[42]

As with job satisfaction, managers are interested in the relationships between organizational commitment and job behavior. One of the most important to organizations is the relationship between organizational commitment and turnover.[43] Simply stated, the stronger an employee's commitment is to the organization, the less likely the person is to quit. Strong commitment also is often correlated with low absenteeism and relatively high productivity. Attendance at work (being on time, taking little time off) is usually higher for employees with strong organizational commitment. Further, committed individuals tend to be more goal-directed and waste less time while at work, with a positive impact on typical productivity measures. Thus, as with job satisfaction, organizational commitment is an attitude of great interest to managers.

INDIVIDUAL DIFFERENCES AND ETHICAL BEHAVIOR

Ethical behavior in businesses and other organizations is receiving increased attention during the 1990s. Part of this attention focuses on the influence that individual differences might have on ethical behavior. For example, a recent study suggested that locus of control and cognitive moral development are important in helping explain whether people will behave ethically or unethically.[44] **Cognitive moral development** refers to an individual's level of moral judgment. People seem to pass through stages of moral reasoning and judgment as they mature. Judgment with regard to right and wrong becomes less dependent on outside influences (such as parents) and also less self-centered ("It's right because it's right for me."). At higher levels of cognitive moral development, individuals develop a deeper understanding of the principles of justice, ethical behavior, and balancing individual and social rights.

Research has demonstrated that individuals with high internal locus of control exhibit more ethical behavior when making organizational decisions than do individuals with high external locus of control. Further, individuals with higher levels of cognitive moral development are more likely to behave ethically than are others. The following Managing Ethics feature describes different types of management ethics, perhaps reflecting differences in cognitive moral development.

MANAGING ETHICS

Three Types of Management Ethics

Archie Carroll, a management professor, has suggested that the terms *immoral*, *amoral*, and *moral management* identify important ethical differences among managers.

▼ Immoral Management

Managerial behaviors devoid of any ethical principles represent **immoral management.** Its operating strategy is maximum exploitation of opportunities for corporate or personal gain to the exclusion of other considerations. Any "corner will be cut" if doing so appears useful. Even legal standards are barriers to be overcome rather than guides for appropriate behavior.

The Frigitemp Corporation provides an example of immoral management at the highest levels of the firm. According to testimony provided during federal investigations and criminal trials, corporate officials (including the chairman of the board of directors and the president) admitted making illegal payoffs of millions of dollars. In addition, corporate officers embezzled funds, exaggerated earnings in reports to shareholders, took kickbacks from suppliers, and even provided prostitutes for customers. Frigitemp eventually went bankrupt because of management's misconduct.

▼ Moral Management

The opposite extreme from immoral management is **moral management.** That is, managerial behaviors focus on and follow ethical norms, professional standards of conduct, and compliance with applicable regulations and laws. Moral management does *not* mean lack of interest in profits. However, the moral manager will not pursue profits outside the boundaries of the law and sound ethical principles.

McCulloch Corporation, a manufacturer of chain saws, provides a good example of moral management. Chain saws can be dangerous to use, and studies have consistently shown large numbers of injuries from saws not equipped with chain brakes and other safety features. The Chain Saw Manufacturers Association fought hard against mandatory federal safety standards, preferring to rely on voluntary standards even in the face of evidence that voluntary standards were neither high enough nor working. However, McCulloch consistently supported and practiced higher safety standards; in fact, chain brakes have been standard on McCulloch saws since 1975. McCulloch made numerous attempts to persuade the Chain Saw Manufacturers Association to adopt higher standards when research results indicated that they could greatly reduce injuries. When McCulloch failed to persuade the association to support these higher standards, it withdrew from the association.

▼ Amoral Management

Managerial behaviors that are indifferent to ethical considerations—as though different standards of conduct apply to business than to other aspects of life— characterize **amoral management.** Amoral managers seem to lack awareness

MANAGING ETHICS —*Continued*

of ethical or moral issues and act with no thought for the impact that their actions might have on others.

An example of amoral management was Nestlé's decision to market infant formula in Third World countries. Nestlé received massive amounts of negative publicity for this marketing strategy, and governments in several countries launched investigations. These investigations indicated that Nestlé apparently gave no thought to the possible disastrous health consequences of selling the formula to illiterate and impoverished people in areas where the likelihood was high that it would be mixed with impure, disease-ridden water.[45]

A story is often told about President Calvin Coolidge, who was famous for being a "man of few words." One Sunday, President Coolidge had attended church without his wife. Later in the day, Mrs. Coolidge inquired as to the subject of the minister's sermon. "Sin," replied Coolidge. "What did he say about it?" his wife persisted. "He was against it," answered Coolidge. This story illustrates part of the problem of dealing with a topic such as ethics or ethical behavior in organizations. To be against unethical behavior isn't enough. Managers and employees need a framework of ethical beliefs and behavior in order to diagnose and address ethical problems in the workplace. In this book, we explore ethical issues involved in various aspects of organizational behavior.

As we discussed earlier, an organization cannot directly manage personality dimensions (such as locus of control) or cognitive individual differences (such as cognitive moral development). Still, managers can take steps such as the following to instill moral management by fostering ethical attitudes in the work force.

▲ Identify ethical attitudes crucial for the firm's operation. For example, a security firm might stress honesty, whereas a drug manufacturer may identify responsibility as most important to ensure product quality. After identifying important ethical attitudes, training programs can focus on developing these ethical attitudes among employees.

▲ Select employees with desired attitudes. The firm might develop and use standard interview questions that assess an applicant's ethical values.

▲ Incorporate ethics in the performance evaluation process. Criteria that individuals are evaluated on will have an important influence on work-related attitudes that they develop. Organizations should make ethical concerns part of the job description and evaluation.

▲ Establish a work culture that reinforces ethical attitudes. Managers and organizations can take many actions to influence organizational culture. This culture, in turn, has a major influence on ethical behavior in the organization.[46] (We explore organizational culture, including its relationship to ethical behavior, in detail in Chapter 14.)

Citicorp is one organization that stresses development of ethical attitudes among its employees. Citicorp is a huge, multinational financial services corporation with some 88,000 employees in 91 countries. Its concerns about ethical behavior resulted in the development and use of an ethics game, or exercise, entitled "The Work Ethic—An Exercise in Integrity." Managers use the game in training programs, staff meetings, and department retreats—and to orient new employees. The goals of the game are to help employees recognize ethical dilemmas in decision making, to teach employees how Citicorp responds to misconduct, and to increase understanding of its rules and policies regarding ethical behavior. Citicorp does not require use of the game, but it has proved so popular that the firm estimates that almost 40,000 of its employees around the world have played it.[47] The ethics game is not the only ethics training that Citicorp uses, but it is an excellent example of how an organization can foster ethical attitudes among managers and employees.

Summary

Personality represents a person's characteristics and traits that in turn account for consistent patterns of behavior in various situations. Each individual in some ways is like other people and in some ways is unique. An individual's personality is the product both of inherited traits or tendencies and experiences. These experiences occur within the framework of the individual's biological, physical, and social environment—all of which are modified by the culture, family, and other groups to which the person belongs. An individual's personality may be described by a set of factors known as the "Big Five." In addition, specific personality dimensions, such as self-esteem, locus of control, and introversion and extraversion, affect behavior. The study of personality and an understanding of interactions between the person and the situation are important for comprehending organizational behavior.

Attitudes are patterns of feelings, beliefs, and behavior tendencies directed toward specific persons, groups, ideas, issues, or objects. Attitudes have affective, cognitive, and behavioral components. The relationship between attitudes and behavior isn't always clear, although important relationships exist. The attitude–behavior relationship becomes clear when an individual's intentions to behave in a certain way are known and the specific attitudes and norms that might be related to the behavior are understood. Job satisfaction— the general collection of attitudes that a worker holds toward the job—is of great interest for organizational behavior. Another attitude of interest is organizational commitment. Both satisfaction and commitment are related to important organizational behaviors.

Some individual differences, such as locus of control and cognitive moral development, are related to ethical behavior. Organizations can take constructive steps to foster ethical attitudes among managers and employees.

Key Words and Concepts

Amoral management	Culture	Individual differences
Attitudes	Dogmatism	Interactionist perspective
Authoritarian personality	External locus of control	Internal locus of control
Behavioral intentions model	Extraversion	Introversion
"Big Five" personality factors	General theory of behavior	Job satisfaction
Cognitive moral development	Immoral management	Locus of control

Moral management
Nature–nurture controversy
Norms

Organizational commitment
Personality
Personality trait

Reengineering
Self-esteem

Discussion Questions

1. Describe the concept of personality and give some examples of how personality might affect employee behaviors in the workplace.

2. Discuss the basic categories of factors that influence personality development.

3. State the opposing positions in the nature–nurture controversy over personality formation. What influences on personality formation seem most important to you? Why?

4. Explain the "Big Five" personality factors. Use these factors to describe your perceptions of the President of the United States.

5. Compare and contrast self-esteem and locus of control.

6. Which of the personality dimensions discussed in this chapter seems most important for managerial behavior? Why?

7. Discuss the relationships among personality, situations, and behavior in terms of their interactions.

8. What are attitudes? Describe the basic components of attitudes.

9. How does the behavioral intentions model help explain that attitude–behavior relationships sometimes may appear to be weak and at other times may appear to be strong?

10. What is the meaning of job satisfaction? Why is it important?

11. Describe the concept of organizational commitment and explain why organizations seek strong employee commitment.

12. Compare and contrast moral management, immoral management, and amoral management. Give an example of each.

13. Suggest some specific actions that organizations may take to encourage ethical behavior by managers and employees.

▲ Developing Skills

Self-Diagnosis: Measuring Locus of Control

Instructions:

The following thirty statements represent employees' opinions toward their work in an organization. Think about your own work experience—a job you have held or currently hold. Read each statement carefully; then indicate the extent to which you agree with it by writing a number in the blank provided. There are no right or wrong choices; the one that is right for you is the correct answer. If the responses do not adequately indicate your own opinion, use the number closest to the way you feel. Use the following key for your responses:

$$4 = \text{strongly agree}$$
$$3 = \text{generally agree}$$
$$2 = \text{agree somewhat}$$
$$1 = \text{agree only slightly}$$
$$0 = \text{seldom or never agree}$$

_____ 1. I determine what matters to me in the organization.

_____ 2. The course of my career depends on me.

_____ 3. My success or failure depends on the amount of effort I exert.

_____ 4. The people who are important control matters in this organization.

_____ 5. My career depends on my seniors.

_____ 6. My effectiveness in this organization is determined by senior people.

_____ 7. The organization a person joins or the job he or she takes is an accidental occurrence.

_____ 8. A person's career is a matter of chance.

_____ 9. A person's success depends on the breaks or chances he or she receives.

_____ 10. Successful completion of my assignments is due to my detailed planning and hard work.

_____ 11. Being liked by seniors or making good impressions on them influences promotion decisions.

_____ 12. Receiving rewards in the organization is a matter of luck.

_____ 13. The success of my plans is a matter of luck.

_____ 14. Receiving a promotion depends on being in the right place at the right time.

_____ 15. Preferences of seniors determine who will be rewarded in this organization.

_____ 16. My success depends on my competence and hard work.

_____ 17. How much I am liked in the organization depends on my seniors.

_____ 18. Getting people in this organization to listen to me is a matter of luck.

_____ 19. If my seniors do not like me, I will not succeed in this organization.

_____ 20. The way I work determines whether or not I receive rewards.

_____ 21. My success or failure in this organization is a matter of luck.

_____ 22. My success or failure depends on those who work with me.

_____ 23. Any promotion I receive in this organization will be due to my ability.

_____ 24. Most things in this organization are beyond the control of the people who work here.

_____ 25. The quality of my work influences decisions on my suggestions in this organization.

_____ 26. The reason I am acceptable to others in my organization is a matter of luck.

_____ 27. I determine what happens to me in the organization.

_____ 28. The degree to which I am acceptable to others in this organization depends on my behavior with them.

_____ 29. My ideas are accepted if I make them fit with the desires of my seniors.

_____ 30. Pressure groups in this organization are more powerful than individual employees are, and they control more things than individuals.

Scoring Instructions

The numbers below correspond to the numbers of the items in the Locus of Control Inventory. Please transfer the numbers you assigned by writing them in the appropriate blanks below. Then total the numbers you transferred to each column.

Item number	Number you assigned	Item number	Number you assigned	Item number	Number you assigned
1.	_____	4.	_____	7.	_____
2.	_____	5.	_____	8.	_____
3.	_____	6.	_____	9.	_____
10.	_____	11.	_____	12.	_____
16.	_____	15.	_____	13.	_____
20.	_____	17.	_____	14.	_____
23.	_____	19.	_____	18.	_____
25.	_____	22.	_____	21.	_____
27.	_____	29.	_____	24.	_____
28.	_____	30.	_____	26.	_____
Column total	_____ I	Column total	_____ EO	Column total	_____ EC

Interpretation

On each scale, your scores could range from zero to 40. The "I" scale measures internal locus of control. The higher your "I" score, the more you tend to believe that you are generally responsible for what happens to you. The "EO" scale measures external locus of control (others). The higher your "EO" score, the more you tend to believe that powerful other people determine much of what happens to you. The "EC" scale measures external locus of control (chance). The higher your "EC" score, the more you tend to believe that chance or fate plays a large role in what happens to you.

The data below were collected from over 300 managers who responded to the Locus of Control Inventory. These data show the average score of these managers for each scale as well as numbers indicating comparatively high or low internal and external locus of control beliefs.[48] Your scores do not necessarily reflect your locus of control beliefs in general because you responded to these items with regard to a particular set of work experiences.

Scale	Mean	Standard Deviation	Very High	High	Low	Very Low
I	25	8	33	29	21	17
EO	25	9	34	29.5	20.5	16
EC	19	9	28	23.5	14.5	10

A Case in Point: Chuck Holeman—Retail Sales Representative

When he joined the company, Chuck Holeman gave every indication of becoming an outstanding employee. As a sales trainee, he was consistently at the top of his group on the written examinations covering such matters as the characteristics of the company's products, policies of the company, and various sales techniques. In his field training he also demonstrated a high level of proficiency. The people he traveled with and worked with reported that he was a rapid learner who was, in contrast to many of the trainees, a real help. He did what he was told and did it right. The owners of the various retail outlets through which the company sold its products seemed to like him. Everyone commented on the time and effort he devoted to his job. The company had not had a young trainee who worked as hard in years. He wanted to learn everything about sales work that there was to be learned. Probably this constant search for new knowledge and the rapidity with which he absorbed it was a major factor in his popularity; another was his complete openness and honesty. When he was promoted and given his own territory, most of the company's sales managers who knew him considered this promotion as merely the first step in a succession of moves that would take him to a high-level position in a few years.

However, the first figures that came in from the new sales representative's territory were very disappointing. There were losses on nearly all products—in some cases, very sizable losses. The supervisor was disturbed. This was not what she had expected. Nevertheless, the territory was known to be in bad shape, and any new person would inevitably have trouble there at first. The man who had been in it previously drank rather heavily, and partly because of this and partly because of a flippant attitude, he had lost a number of customers. In large part the choice of Chuck Holeman for this territory had been dictated by this state of affairs. He appeared to be the kind of young man who could convey a more favorable image of the company and thus gain back the lost business.

When the figures for the second period came in, however, they were no better. In fact, they were slightly worse. The supervisor was sure she would be called on the carpet herself very shortly if this poor showing continued. She began to check into Chuck's background to see if there was anything that would explain his difficulties. Several facts were unearthed as a result of conversations with people in the company. Although Chuck had done extremely well as a trainee, there was some question as to whether he had really mastered the work on financial management, bookkeeping, and pricing. One of the people with whom Chuck had worked in the field had noted some difficulty in the bookkeeping area and also felt that the young man was lacking in aggressiveness and vitality. Chuck worked hard, but he never got very enthusiastic about anything. He rarely seemed to get any enjoyment out of doing something well.

The supervisor decided that it was time to talk with the people who worked in various retail establishments in Chuck's territory. The picture she got was not entirely what she had expected, but it did fit a pattern she had seen several times before. Chuck was generally liked or, rather, had no enemies. People considered him to be honest and reliable. He was, as management had hoped, a welcome relief after his predecessor. Many commented that he seemed worn out and solemn; at the same time, he clearly seemed to work hard. He would come in and get right down to business, often without even saying hello. He would run down the order sheet in a mechanical manner, ask if he could help with anything, and then hurry out. No one really felt he knew Chuck well. Chuck never did anything more than take

orders. He always seemed in a hurry to leave, and he was so unenthusiastic about everything, including his job and the products on his list, that it was somewhat depressing to have him around. He was a nice young man, though. No, he had never offered to help out with any bookkeeping and pricing problems related to his products. He acted as if he knew very little about such things. A check on several outlets that had dropped the company's products while the former sales representative was still in the territory revealed that, as far as anyone could remember, the new man had never called on them.

There were a number of other problems that were less evident at the retail level. Chuck was clearly not making use of the promotional material he received, and he was not pushing the high-profit items, as he had been instructed to do. In fact, he was deviating from company policy in so many ways that the supervisor clearly had to have a talk with him. In most such instances, such a talk did very little good, but at least it protected the supervisor against criticism for not having issued a warning should more drastic action be required later.

As expected, the supervisor's talk with Chuck did not go very well. When faced with the facts, Chuck did not deny them. He wanted to do well and to follow company policy. He understood what he was supposed to do, but he could not help seeing things from the point of view of the customers too. They were human beings and it was not fair to take advantage of them. He pointed out that the high-priced items were almost identical with the less expensive ones and that some of the promotional material was, to say the least, questionable. It was hard to sell when you did not believe the prescribed sales pitch. He felt the company was not being entirely socially responsible in what it was doing. Chuck admitted that sometimes the territory seemed to be more than he could handle, but said that he would lick it somehow. He was upset now, but things would get better. The supervisor did not think so, but decided to wait a little longer and see.

Not unexpectedly, the losses continued. Obviously, putting pressure on Chuck had done no good. The young man got more upset as a result, but otherwise there was little change in his behavior. Evidently things were not getting better and Chuck was not finding a way to solve his problems with the territory. Some other solution was required before sales disappeared entirely.[49]

Questions

1. What attitudes contributed to Chuck Holeman's problems on the job? How did they manifest themselves?
2. How would you describe Holeman's level of organizational commitment?
3. Would you find it difficult to follow the prescribed policies in this situation? What would you do if you were a salesperson in this company?
4. What would you do if you were Holeman's supervisor?

References

1. Quoted in Eysenck, H. J. *Personality, Genetics, and Behavior*. New York: Prager, 1982, 1.
2. George, J. M. The role of personality in organizational life: Issues and evidence. *Journal of Management*, 1992, 18, 185–213; Weiss, H. M., and Adler, S. Personality and organizational behavior. In B. M. Staw and L. L. Cummings (eds.), *Research in Organizational Behavior*, vol. 6. Greenwich, Conn.: JAI Press, 1984, 1–50.
3. Engler, B. *Personality Theories*, 3rd ed. Boston: Houghton Mifflin, 1991; Liebert, R. M., and Spiegler, M. D. *Personality: Strategies and Issues*, 6th ed. Pacific Grove, Calif.: Brooks/Cole, 1990; Schultz, D. *Theories of Personality*, 4th ed. Pacific Grove, Calif.: Brooks/Cole, 1990.
4. Maddi, S. R. *Personality Theories: A Comparative Analysis*, 5th ed. Homewood, Ill.: Dorsey, 1989, 10.
5. Hall, C. S., and Lindzey, G. *Theories of Personality*, 3rd ed. New York: Wiley, 1978, 17–19.
6. Collins, W. A., and Gunnar, M. R. Social and personality development. *Annual Review of Psychology*, 1990, 41, 387–416.
7. Pervin, L. A. *Current Controversies and Issues in Personality*, 2d ed. New York: Wiley, 1984, 36–38.
8. Brody, N. *Personality: In Search of Individuality*. San Diego, Calif.: Academic Press, 1988, 68–101; Holden, C. The genetics of personality. *Science*, August 7, 1987, 598–601.
9. Lykken, D. T., Bouchard, T. J., McGue, M., and Tellegen, A. Heritability of interests. *Journal of Applied Psychology*, 1993, 78, 649–661.
10. Buss, D. M. Evolutionary personality psychology. *Annual Review of Psychology*, 1991, 42, 459–491; Hettma, P. J. (ed.). *Personality and Environment: Assessment of Human Adaptation*. New York: Wiley, 1989; Low, B. S. Cross-cultural patterns in the training of children: An evolutionary perspective. *Journal of Comparative Psychology*, 1989, 103, 311–319.
11. Adapted from Ratan, S. Generational tension in the office: Why busters hate boomers. *Fortune*, October 4, 1993, 57–70.
12. Pervin, L. A. *Personality: Theory and Research*, 4th ed. New York: Wiley, 1984, 10.
13. Digman, J. M. Personality structure: Emergence of the five-factor model. *Annual Review of Psychology*, 1990, 41, 417–440; Hogan, R. T. Personality and personality measurement. In M. D. Dunnette and L. M. Hough (eds.), *Handbook of Industrial & Organizational Psychology*, 2nd ed., vol. 2. Palo Alto, Calif.: Consulting Psychologist Press, 1991, 873–919; Wiggins, J. S., and Pincus, A. L. Personality: Structure and assessment. *Annual Review of Psychology*, 1992, 43, 473–504.
14. Drawn from Dumaine, B. America's toughest bosses. *Fortune*, October 18, 1993, 39–50; Toxic executives. *Psychology Today*, September/October 1993, 22.
15. Barrick, M. R., and Mount, M. K. Autonomy as a moderator of the relationships between the big five personality dimensions and job performance. *Journal of Applied Psychology*, 1993, 78, 111–118; Barrick, M. R., and Mount, M. K. The big five personality dimensions and job performance: A meta-analysis. *Personnel Psychology*, 1991, 44, 1–26.
16. Descriptions of the following personality dimensions are based on Blass, T. (ed.). *Personality Variables in Social Behavior*. Hillsdale, N.J.: Lawrence Erlbaum Associates, 1977; Engler, *Personality Theories*; Jackson, D. N., and Paunonen, S. V. Personality structure and assessment. *Annual Review of Psychology*, 1980, 31, 503–551;

Lefcourt, H. M. *Locus of Control: Current Trends in Theory and Research*, 2nd ed. Hillsdale, N.J.: Lawrence Erlbaum Associates, 1982; Liebert and Spiegler, *Personality: Strategies and Issues*; Schultz, *Theories of Personality*.
17. Ellis, R. A., and Taylor, M. S. Role of self-esteem within the job search process. *Journal of Applied Psychology*, 1983, 68, 632–640.
18. Hollenbeck, J. R., and Brief, A. P. The effects of individual differences and goal origins on goal setting and performance. *Organizational Behavior and Human Decision Processes*, 1987, 40, 392–414.
19. Pierce, J. L., Gardner, D. G., Dunham, R. B., and Cummings, L. L. Moderation by organization-based self-esteem of role condition-employee response relationships. *Academy of Management Journal*, 1993, 36, 271–288; Rosse, J. G., Boss, R. W., Johnson, A. E., and Crown, D. F. Conceptualizing the role of self-esteem in the burnout process. *Group & Organization Studies*, 1991, 16, 428–451.
20. Lefcourt, H. M. Durability and impact of the locus of control construct. *Psychological Bulletin*, 1992, 112, 411–414.
21. Black, J. S. Locus of control, social support, stress, and adjustment in international transfer. *Asia Pacific Journal of Management*, April 1990, 1–30.
22. Engler, *Personality Theories*, 329–334; Eysenck, *Personality, Genetics, and Behavior*, 161–197.
23. Carson, R. C. Personality. *Annual Review of Psychology*, 1989, 40, 227–248; Pervin, L. A. Personality: Current controversies, issues, and directions. *Annual Review of Psychology*, 1985, 36, 83–114.
24. See, for example, Greenberger, D. B., and Strasser, S. The role of situational and dispositional factors in the enhancement of personal control in organizations. In L. L. Cummings and B. M. Staw (eds.), *Research in Organizational Behavior*, vol. 13. Greenwich, Conn.: JAI Press, 1991, 111–145; Mitchell, T. R., and James, L. R., Theory development forum—Situational versus dispositional factors: Competing explanations of behavior. *Academy of Management Review*, 1989, 14, 330–407; Woodman, R. W., and Schoenfeldt, L. F. Individual differences in creativity: An interactionist perspective. In J. A. Glover, R. R. Ronning, and C. R. Reynolds (eds.), *Handbook of Creativity*. New York: Plenum, 1989, 77–91.
25. Myers, D. G. *Social Psychology*, 4th ed. New York: McGraw-Hill, 1993, 112; Olson, J. M., and Zanna, M. P. Attitudes and beliefs. In R. M. Baron, W. G. Graziano, and C. Stangor (eds.), *Social Psychology*. Fort Worth, Texas: Holt, Rinehart, and Winston, 1991, 196.
26. Tesser, A. The importance of heritability in psychological research: The case of attitudes. *Psychological Review*, 1993, 100, 129–142.
27. Eagly, A. H., and Chaiken, S. *The Psychology of Attitudes*. San Diego, Calif.: Harcourt, Brace, Jovanovich, 1992; Tesser, A., and Shaffer, D. R. Attitudes and attitude change. *Annual Review of Psychology*, 1990, 41, 479–523.
28. Breckler, S. J. Empirical validation of affect, behavior, and cognition as distinct components of attitude. *Journal of Personality and Social Psychology*, 1984, 47, 1191–1205; Olson, J. M., and Zanna, M. P. Attitudes and attitude change. *Annual Review of Psychology*, 1993, 44, 120–122.
29. Penrod, S. *Social Psychology*. Englewood Cliffs, N.J.: Prentice-Hall, 1983, 345–347.

30. Ajzen, I., and Fishbein, M. *Understanding Attitudes and Predicting Social Behavior*. Englewood Cliffs, N.J.: Prentice-Hall, 1980.

31. Ajzen, I. From intentions to actions: A theory of planned behavior. In J. Kuhl and J. Beckmann (eds.), *Action-Control: From Cognition to Behavior*. Heidelberg: Springer, 1985, 11–39.

32. Ajzen, I. The theory of planned behavior. *Organizational Behavior and Human Decision Processes*, 1991, 50, 1–33; Olson and Zanna, Attitudes and attitude change, 131–135.

33. Hulin, C. Adaptation, persistence, and commitment in organizations. In M. D. Dunnette and L. M. Hough (eds.), *Handbook of Industrial & Organizational Psychology*, 2nd ed., vol. 2. Palo Alto, Calif.: Consulting Psychologists Press, 1991, 469–471.

34. Hammer, M., and Champy, J. *Reengineering the Corporation: A Manifesto for Business Revolution*. New York: HarperCollins, 1993; Stewart, T. A. Reengineering: The hot new managing tool. *Fortune*, August 23, 1993, 41–48; The promise of reengineering. *Fortune*, May 3, 1993, 94–97.

35. O'Reilly, C. R. Organizational behavior. *Annual Review of Psychology*, 1991, 42, 427–458.

36. Based on Lincoln, J. R. Employee work attitudes and management practice in the U.S. and Japan: Evidence from a large comparative survey. *California Management Review*, Fall 1989, 89–106.

37. Hanisch, K. A. The job description index revisited. *Journal of Applied Psychology*, 1992, 77, 377–382; Smith, P. C., Kendall, L. M., and Hulin, C. L. *The Measurement of Satisfaction in Work and Retirement*. Chicago: Rand McNally, 1969.

38. Iaffaldano, M. T., and Muchinsky, P. M. Job satisfaction and job performance: A meta-analysis. *Psychological Bulletin*, 1985, 97, 251–273.

39. Ostroff, C. The relationship between satisfaction, attitudes, and performance: An organizational level analysis. *Journal of Applied Psychology*, 1992, 77, 963–974.

40. Miner, J. B. *Industrial-Organizational Psychology*. New York: McGraw-Hill, 1992, 119-124; Muchinsky, P. M. *Psychology Applied to Work*, 3rd ed. Pacific Grove, Calif.: Brooks/Cole, 1990, 327–337; Saal, F. E., and Knight, P. A. *Industrial/Organizational Psychology: Science and Practice*. Pacific Grove, Calif.: Brooks/Cole, 1988, 312–322.

41. Mowday, R. T., Porter, L. W., and Steers, R. M. *Employee–Organization Linkages: The Psychology of Commitment, Absenteeism, and Turnover*. New York: Academic Press, 1982, 27. See also, Mathieu, J. E., and Zajac, D. M. A review and meta-analysis of the antecedents, correlates, and consequences of organizational commitment. *Psychological Bulletin*, 1990, 108, 171–194.

42. This section is drawn largely from Miner, *Industrial-Organizational Psychology*, 124–128.

43. Cohen, A. Organizational commitment and turnover: A meta-analysis. *Academy of Management Journal*, 1993, 36, 1140–1157; Hulin, Adaptation, persistence, and commitment, 488–491.

44. Trevino, L. K., and Youngblood, S. A. Bad apples in bad barrels: A causal analysis of ethical decision making behavior. *Journal of Applied Psychology*, 1990, 75, 378–385.

45. Based on Carroll, A. B. In search of the moral manager. *Business Horizons*, March/April 1987, 2–6.

46. Goddard, R. W. Are you an ethical manager? *Personnel Journal*, March 1988, 38–47.

47. Trevino, L. K. A cultural perspective on changing and developing organizational ethics. In W. A. Pasmore and R. W. Woodman (eds.), *Research in Organizational Change and Development*, vol. 4. Greenwich, Conn.: JAI Press, 1990, 195–230.

48. The author of Internal, Powerful Others, and Chance Scales is Hanna Levenson Ph.D. Reprinted with permission from Hanna Levenson, *Locus of control inventory, Journal of Consulting and Clinical Psychology*, 1973, 41, 397–404. U. Pereek adapted Hanna Levenson's work for his article. Pereek, U. Locus of control inventory. In J. W. Pfeiffer (ed.), *The 1992 Annual: Developing Human Resources*. San Diego: Pfeiffer & Company, 1992, 135–148. Reprinted with permission.

49. Miner, J. B. *Industrial-Organizational Psychology*. New York: McGraw-Hill, 1992, p. 140–142. Reprinted with permission of McGraw-Hill.

3 Perception and Attribution

LEARNING OBJECTIVES

When you have finished studying this chapter, you should be able to:

▲ Describe the major elements in the perceptual process and explain why this process is important.

▲ Define perceptual selection and perceptual organization.

▲ Describe the factors that determine how one person perceives another.

▲ Discuss the issue of accuracy in person perception.

▲ Identify five kinds of perceptual errors.

▲ Explain the process of attribution and how attributions influence behavior.

▲ Describe important attributions that people make in the work setting.

OUTLINE

Preview Case: Whom Should I Hire?

The Perceptual Process

Managing in Practice: The Icon Crisis

Perceptual Selection

External Factors

Internal Factors

Managing Diversity: Selective Perception of Managers

Managing Across Cultures: Time Perception

Perceptual Organization

Managing in Practice: Office Design, Layout, and Decor—What Do They Tell You?

Person Perception

Characteristics of the Person Perceived

Characteristics of the Perceiver

Managing Across Cultures: Perceptions of Japanese and American Business Associates

The Situation

Impression Management

Perceptual Errors

Managing Ethics: Perceptions of Ethics in Organizations

Accuracy of Judgment in Person Perception

Perceptual Defense

Stereotyping

Managing Diversity: Sex Stereotypes in the Workplace

Halo Effect

Projection

Expectancy Effects

Attributions: Perceiving the Causes of Behavior

Managing in Practice: Searching for Causes of Job Applicant Behavior

The Attribution Process

Internal Versus External Causes of Behavior

Attributions of Success and Failure

DEVELOPING SKILLS

Self-Diagnosis: *Measuring Perceptions of Women as Managers*

A Case in Point: *The Internship*

PREVIEW CASE

Whom Should I Hire?

Todd Costanza intently examined the two personnel folders on his desk. As the credit manager of the company, he was faced with replacing two employees who had just left the company from his department. One was for a verifier position, the other was an account executive. A verifier was someone who would verify the accuracy of information presented on a credit application form. Prospective customers seeking an approved line of credit would fill out an application, and the verifier's job was to ensure that the information was accurate. Since it was an entry clerical position, most verifiers didn't stay in their jobs for much over two years. Most were either promoted or they quit (often citing boredom as their reason for leaving). The account executive position was a much higher level position. An account executive authorized large amounts of credit, some as high as $50,000 per month. The position entailed staying on top of all accounts, being sure each account paid invoices on time, and regulating the amount of credit each account could handle financially. These positions made or cost the company a great deal of money because the account executive's judgment in appraising accounts was critical to the success of the Credit Department. Accounts that were delinquent or that forfeited their payments were a direct loss to the company. Accounts that weren't extended enough credit to run their business would go to a competitor for a larger line of credit. Either way represented a loss of income for the company. Thus, the account executive walked a fine line between extending the accounts too much or not giving enough credit.

The two folders contained the results of assessments by the Human Resources Department of the recommended candidates for the two positions. Neither candidate looked very inspiring. Carl Worrell was the best applicant for the verifier's position. However, his test score was only aver-

age, and his performance in the interview had been adequate, but nothing more. Cheryl Catrell emerged as the best possible account executive, but she too appeared as a marginal case. While her test scores were acceptable, her previous experience was limited and her interview was weak. Yet she received a favorable evaluation from her previous employer. Costanza wished there had been better applicants to select from, but these two people represented the best of their respective applicant pools.

After examining the candidates' credentials one last time, Costanza decided to hire Worrell as the verifier. He reasoned the job was not that critical to the success of his department, and it was a high turnover job. While Worrell didn't appear to be a surefire hit, Costanza figured Worrell wouldn't hurt the company too badly if he bombed. However, Catrell seemed to be a different story. Although her respective qualifications were no worse that Worrell's, the consequences of Catrell's failing in the account executive job were far greater than Worrell's potential failure as a verifier. Costanza believed he really had to feel confident about hiring a new account executive, and Catrell didn't inspire that confidence. Therefore, Costanza would elect not to fill the account executive position at this time but would reopen the recruiting process to find a better-qualified applicant.

Costanza knew what awaited him. The Human Resources Department would want to know why he decided to hire the male but not the female. It would be particularly concerned because Catrell's respective qualifications were no worse that Worrell's. Costanza was worried about how people would react to his decision. He appeared to be giving the benefit of the doubt to the male but not the female. Costanza saw it as a question of two different jobs, not a male and a female. However, Costanza had been around long enough to know that not everyone saw things the way he did.[1]

T he Preview Case illustrates the importance of perceptions in organizational behavior. Todd Costanza is justified in worrying about how others will perceive his decisions and behaviors and what attributions they might make concerning the reasons for his decisions. Todd knows that no two people will necessarily perceive a situation in exactly the same way. Further, people base their behaviors on what they perceive reality to be, not necessarily what it *is*. In a very real sense, people live in their own perceptual worlds. Hence recognizing the difference between the perceptual worlds of employees and managers and the reality of the organization is important in understanding organizational behavior. In this chapter, we continue to explore *individual differences*. Here, we focus on the important processes of *perception* and *attribution*.

▼ THE PERCEPTUAL PROCESS

Perception is the selection and organization of environmental stimuli to provide meaningful experiences for the perceiver. Perception involves searching for, obtaining, and processing information. It represents the psychological process whereby people take information from the environment and make sense of their worlds.[2]

The key words in the definition of perception are *selection* and *organization*. Different people often perceive a situation differently, both in terms of what they selectively perceive and how they organize and interpret the things perceived. Figure 3.1 summarizes the basic elements in the perceptual process from initial observation to final response.

People receive stimuli from the environment through the five senses: taste, smell, hearing, sight, and touch. Everyone selectively pays attention to some aspects of the environment and selectively ignores other aspects at any particular time. For example, an apartment dweller may listen expectantly for a friend's footsteps in the hall but ignore sounds of the people upstairs. In an office, a secretary ignores the bell announcing the arrival of the elevator but jumps at the sound of the coffee cart's bell. There are examples of a selection process involving both external and internal factors that filters sensory perceptions and determines which will receive the most attention. The individual then organizes the stimuli selected into meaningful patterns.

How people interpret what they perceive also varies considerably. A wave of the hand may be interpreted as a friendly gesture or as a threat, depending on the circumstances and the state of mind of those involved. As indicated in the Preview Case, the interpretation of things perceived is very important. In organizations, managers and employees therefore must confront the possibility of inaccurately interpreting their perceptions of events and others' behavior. The following Managing In Practice account provides an interesting example of the importance of accurate interpretations.

MANAGING IN PRACTICE

The Icon Crisis

Icons are those little figures on a computer screen that help users issue commands to their PCs through a hand control known as a mouse. Easily interpreted icons make computer use quick and instinctive. Xerox introduced icons in 1981, and Apple popularized their use with introduction of its Macintosh personal computer in 1984. Microsoft dramatically increased icon usage with its "Windows" software for IBM machines and their clones. In the 1990s, however, a proliferation of icons has brought on a crisis: Creating a good icon is getting harder.

Amazingly enough, designers are running out of images that clearly communicate their functions to users. In the past, interpreting the meaning of

(continued on page 71)

FIGURE 3.1

Basic Elements in the Perceptual Process

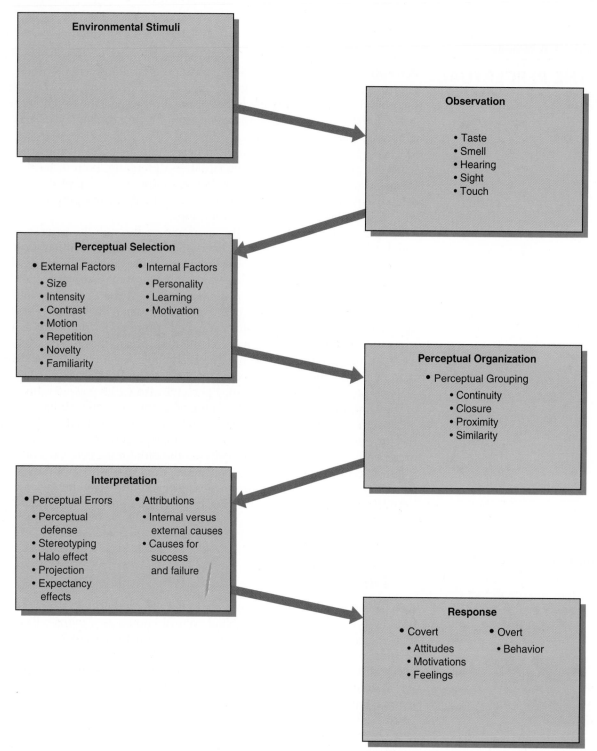

MANAGING IN PRACTICE —*Continued*

FIGURE 3.2

Identify the Icon

Match the icon with its function

1.   2.   3.   4.   5.

6.   7.   8.   9.   10.

a. Rotate image
b. Enlarge or reduce object
c. Delete file
d. Merge document
e. Undo

f. Move through document
g. Enlarge or reduce view
h. Draw chart
i. Fill with color
j. Erase image

Source: Adapted from Kansas, D. The icon crisis: Tiny pictures cause confusion. *Wall Street Journal,* November 17, 1993, B1.

icons—little pencils, manila folders, a mailbox, tiny trash cans, and the like—was simple. But, the more complex the functions that your PC can perform and the more icons that are used, the more difficult creating new ones with clear meanings becomes. When an icon is so abstract that its meaning isn't clear, it is no better than the words it replaces.

An icon cannot be copyrighted unless the design is distinctive and clever. For example, the Apple trash-can icon, representing the ''delete'' function, is copyrighted. But most icons that represent everyday objects cannot be copyrighted; thus the same icon often means different things in different software programs. Try to match each icon in Figure 3.2 with its function. (The correct answers are in the Developing Skills section of this chapter on p. 97.

Another difficult problem that icon designers face stems from cultural differences. Internationally, the most offensive icon potentially is the human hand. Early icons often showed hands doing all kinds of things. However, various hand positions mean different things in different cultures, and their use often caused problems. For example, Apple Computer discovered that an open hand with palm forward, intended to mean ''stop,'' conveyed something entirely different (and obnoxious) in Greece. So icon developers have learned to be very careful not to assume that a hand gesture that is acceptable in the United States will be equally inoffensive around the world.[3]

A person's interpretation of sensory stimuli will lead to a response, either overt (actions) or covert (motivation, attitudes, and feelings), or both. Each person selects and organizes sensory stimuli differently and thus has different interpretations and responses. Perceptual differences help to explain why people behave differently in the same situation. People often perceive the same things in different ways, and their behavioral responses depend, in part, on these perceptions. We next explore the external and internal factors that influence perception, the ways that people organize perceptions, the process of *person perception*, and various errors in the perceptual process.

▼ PERCEPTUAL SELECTION

The phone is ringing, your television is blaring, a dog is barking outside, your PC is making a strange noise, and you smell coffee brewing. Which of these stimuli will you ignore? Which will you pay attention to?

Perceptual selection is the process by which people filter out most stimuli so that they can deal with the most important ones. Perceptual selection depends on several factors, some of which are in the external environment and some of which are internal to the perceiver.[4]

▼ External Factors

External perception factors are characteristics that influence whether the stimuli will be noticed. The following external factors may be stated as *principles* of perception. In each case we present an example to illustrate the principle.

▲ *Size.* The larger the size of an external factor, the more likely it is to be perceived. A hiker is far more likely to notice a fully grown fir tree than a seedling.

▲ *Intensity.* The more intense an external factor, the more likely it is to be perceived (bright lights, loud noises, and the like). Even the language in a memo from a boss to an employee can reflect the intensity principle. A memo that reads ''Please stop by my office at your convenience'' would not fill you with the same sense of urgency as a memo that reads ''Report to my office *immediately*!''

▲ *Contrast.* External factors that stand out against the background or that are not what people expect are the most likely to be perceived. In addition, the contrast of objects with others or with their background may influence *how* they are perceived. Figure 3.3 illustrates this aspect of the contrast principle. Which of the solid center circles is larger? The one on the right appears to be larger, but it isn't: the two circles are the same size. The solid circle on the right appears to be larger because its background—its frame of reference—is composed of much smaller circles. The solid circle on the left appears to be smaller because its background consists of larger surrounding circles.

FIGURE 3.3

Contrast Principle of Perception

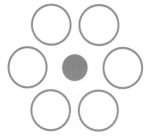

▲ *Motion.* A moving factor is more likely to be perceived than a stationary factor. Soldiers in combat learn this principle very quickly. Video games also illustrate the principle that motion is quickly detected.

▲ *Repetition.* A repeated factor is more likely to be perceived than a single factor. Marketing managers use this principle in trying to get the attention of prospective customers. An advertisement may repeat key ideas, and the advertisement itself may be presented many times for greater effectiveness.

▲ *Novelty* and *familiarity.* Either a familiar or a novel factor in the environment can attract attention, depending on circumstances. People quickly notice an elephant walking along a city street. (Both novelty and size increase the probability of perception.) You are likely to first perceive the face of a close friend among a group of people walking toward you.[5]

A combination of these or similar factors may be operating at any time to affect perception. In combination with certain internal factors of the person doing the perceiving, they determine whether any particular stimulus is more or less likely to be noticed.

▼ Internal Factors

Internal perception factors are aspects of the perceiver that influence perceptual selection. Some of the more important internal factors include personality (Chapter 2), learning (Chapter 5), and motivation (Chapter 6). The powerful role that internal factors play in perception manifests itself in many ways, as the following Managing Diversity feature demonstrates.

MANAGING DIVERSITY

Selective Perception of Managers

Twenty-three executives enrolled in a company-sponsored training program participated in an experiment concerning the impact of internal factors on perception. Six of these executives were in sales, five in production, four in accounting, and eight in other functional areas of the company. Researchers gave the participants in the training program a 10,000-word case history dealing with another company's organization and activities. The assignment was to examine the case history and to determine the most important problem facing the firm. Five of the six sales executives felt that the problem was in sales. Four of the five production people said that the problem related to production. Three of the four accounting people (who worked closely with sales) believed that the problem was in sales. The researchers concluded that, although the case history called for looking at the problem from a company-wide rather than a departmental perspective, most of the executives perceived the problem in terms of their own backgrounds.[6] This research is a classic example of selective perception by managers. These results are not the end of the story, however.

Recently, 121 managers attending a graduate program at a large university participated in a similar but more rigorous study. As in the earlier study, the

MANAGING DIVERSITY —*Continued*

participants read a case history and were asked to (1) identify problems facing the firm and (2) indicate additional information that they might need. Results both partially supported and partially refuted the earlier study. On the one hand, the managers tended to frame the issues in terms of their own backgrounds. (For example, accounting and finance managers sought more accounting and financial information than did managers with other backgrounds.) On the other hand, these managers demonstrated an ability to recognize problems in areas other than their own and sought information about those other areas also.[7]

These studies have some important implications for organizational behavior. First, managers should avoid overly simplistic assumptions about the abilities of people to process information and make decisions. Internal factors clearly influence and even bias which information managers and employees might be most attentive to. At the same time, through education and experience, people can overcome perceptual biases. Second, the existence of these biases presents yet another diversity management challenge. That is, employees from different areas of the organization may have trouble working together on task forces and teams because each will tend to see problems and issues from the perspective of their own departments or functions. Thus, in order to be effective, managers and employees must learn how to deal with this type of diversity.

Personality   Personality has an interesting relationship to perception. In part, perceptions shape personality; in turn, personality affects what and how people perceive. In Chapter 2, we discussed several personality dimensions. Any of them, along with numerous other traits, may influence the perceptual process. Under many circumstances, personality appears to affect strongly how an individual perceives other people—the process of "person perception," which we discuss shortly.[8]

An aspect of the personality called **field dependence/independence** provides a specific example of the relationship between personality and perception. A field-dependent person tends to pay more attention to external environmental cues, whereas a field-independent person relies mostly on bodily sensations. For example, in a test where a subject has to decide whether an object is vertically upright, a field-dependent individual will rely on cues from the environment, such as the corners of rooms, windows, and doors. A field-independent individual will rely mostly on bodily cues, such as the pull of gravity, to make the same judgment. A field-dependent person needs more time to find hidden figures embedded in complex geometrical designs than does a field-independent person. A field-dependent person is influenced more by the background or surrounding design than is a field-independent person.

Field dependence/independence has some implications for organizational behavior. For example, in comparison to a field-dependent employee, a field-independent employee interacts more independently with others in the organization. That is, a field-independent employee relies less on cues from others (such as a team leader or supervisor) to identify appropriate interpersonal behavior. In addition, a field-independent employee seems to be more aware of important differences in others' roles, status, and needs.[9]

Learning   Another internal factor affecting perceptual selection is learning, which can lead to the development of perceptual sets. A **perceptual set** is an expectation of a perception based on past experience with the same or similar stimuli. What do you see in Figure 3.4? If you see an attractive, elegantly dressed woman, your perception concurs with the majority of first-time viewers. However, you may agree with a sizable minority and see an ugly, old woman. The woman you see depends on your perceptual set.

In organizations, managers' and employees' past experiences and learning strongly influence their perceptions. For example, imagine an architect, a lawyer, and a real estate appraiser—all employed by the international design and engineering firm CRSS—approaching a tall office building in Toronto. These three individuals may notice distinctly different things about the building. The architect may first notice the architectural style and the construction materials used in the building. The lawyer may quickly perceive that the size and placement of advertising on the building violates a zoning regulation. The appraiser may focus on the general condition of the building and of the surrounding area, factors that would influence the building's price and salability. Each person pays attention to a different aspect of the same general stimulus because of the individual's training and work experiences.

The culture into which a person is born determines many life experiences, and learned cultural differences influence the perceptual process. For example, a recent study demonstrated differences in perceptions of punctuality among managers in Japan, Mexico, Taiwan, and the United States.[10] On average, U.S. managers would consider a colleague late for an important business meeting after about seven minutes. Managers in the other three countries are somewhat more tolerant of tardiness and would perceive a colleague as late only after about 10 or 11 minutes. The following Managing Across Cultures examines some other interesting differences in the perception of time in different cultures.

FIGURE 3.4

Test of Perceptual Set

MANAGING ACROSS CULTURES

Time Perception

Understanding and appreciating the sense of time in other cultures has value. However, for the traveler or the person attempting to live in another culture, adjusting to a different perception of time may be quite difficult. For example, an investigation of "culture shock" among U.S. Peace Corps volunteers revealed that two of the three greatest sources of adjustment difficulties related to perceptions of time: the "general pace of life" and the "punctuality of the people."

Researchers have attempted to measure the general pace at which people live their lives in various cultures. One study has compared the pace of life in six countries: England, Japan, Indonesia, Italy, Taiwan, and the United States. In each country, researchers collected data from the largest city and one medium-sized city on three measures of the pace or tempo of life.

▲ *The accuracy of bank clocks.* The researchers checked 15 clocks in each downtown area and compared the times they showed to a verifiable correct time.

▲ *The speed at which pedestrians walk.* The researchers timed 100 pedestrians, walking alone, for 100 feet.

▲ *The length of time needed to purchase a stamp.* The researchers measured the response time to a written request to purchase a commonly used denomination of postage stamp.

Figure 3.5 shows the results of this study. Japanese cities rated the highest on all three measures: They had the most accurate bank clocks, the fastest pedestrians, and the quickest postal clerks. U.S. cities were second in two of

FIGURE 3.5

The Pace of Life in Six Countries

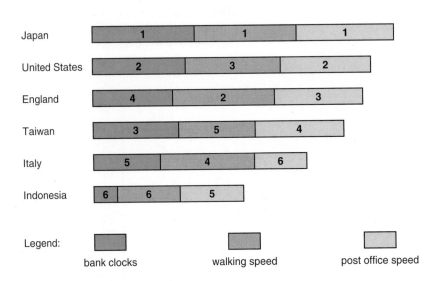

Numbers on the chart (1 is the top value) indicate the comparative rankings of cities in each country for each indicator of time sense.

Source: Adapted from Levine, R. V. The pace of life. *American Scientist*, September/October, 1990, 453.

MANAGING ACROSS CULTURES —*Continued*

the three categories. Indonesian cities had the least accurate clocks and the slowest pedestrians. Italian cities had the slowest postal clerks.

From this and related studies, researchers have concluded that a city and a culture have a "pace of life" that influences people's behaviors. This pace of life varies in different cultures and can be important in understanding the perceptions of time in these cultures. Adjusting to a new pace of life is one of the challenges facing employees and managers of multinational corporations when they are transferred from their home country to a foreign assignment.[11]

Motivation   Motivation also plays an important role in determining what a person perceives. A person's most urgent needs and desires at any particular time can influence perception.

> Everyone has had the following maddening experience. While taking a shower, you faintly hear what sounds like the telephone ringing. Do you get out of the shower, dripping wet, to answer it? Or do you conclude that it is only your imagination?
>
> Your behavior in this situation may depend on factors other than the loudness of the ringing. If you are expecting an important call, you are likely to scurry out of the shower. If you are not expecting a call, you are more likely to attribute the ringing sound to shower noises. Your decision, then, has been influenced by your expectations and motivations.[12]

This example illustrates a significant aspect of perception: Internal factors such as motivation influence the interpretation of sensory information. Similarly, an employee whose firm has just announced the pending layoff of 5,000 workers is more sensitive to help-wanted advertisements than is an employee at another firm whose job is not threatened.

In general, people perceive things that promise to help satisfy their needs and that they have found rewarding in the past. They tend to ignore mildly disturbing events (a barking dog) but will perceive dangerous ones (the house being on fire). Summarizing an important aspect of the relationship between motivation and perception is the **Pollyanna principle,** which states that people process pleasant stimuli more efficiently and accurately than unpleasant stimuli. For example, an employee who receives both positive and negative feedback during a performance appraisal session with her boss may more easily, clearly, and pleasantly remember the positive statements rather than the negative statements.

▼ PERCEPTUAL ORGANIZATION

Perceptual organization is the process by which people group environmental stimuli into recognizable patterns. In the perceptual process, following selection, organization takes over. The stimuli selected for attention now appear as a whole. For example, most people have a mental picture of an object with the following properties: wood, four legs, a seat, a back, and armrests. This is our image of a chair. When people see an object that has all these properties, they recognize it as a chair. They have organized the incoming information into a meaningful whole.

A great deal remains to be learned about how the human mind assembles, organizes, and categorizes information.[13] However, certain factors in perceptual organization, such as perceptual grouping, are helpful in understanding perceptual organization. **Perceptual grouping** is the tendency to form individual stimuli into a meaningful pattern by means such as continuity, closure, proximity, and similarity.

Continuity is the tendency to perceive objects as continuous patterns. Continuity is a useful organizing principle, but it may also have negative aspects. For example, the tendency to perceive continuous patterns may result in an inability to perceive uniqueness and detect change. In economic or business forecasting, a common continuity error is to assume that the future will be a simple continuation of current events and trends.

Closure is the tendency to complete an object and perceive it as a constant, overall form. In other words, it is the ability to perceive a whole object, even though only part of the object is evident. Most people somehow perceive the odd-shaped inkblots in Figure 3.6 as a dalmatian dog walking toward a tree. Someone who had never seen a dalmatian wouldn't be able to make the closure. People can also organize their perceptions in terms of the closure principle when dealing with ideas and information. For example, a manager facing a complex decision may be able to develop a fairly accurate understanding of the issues even though her information isn't complete. Based on her experience and imagination, she "fills in the missing pieces" needed in order to make a decision.

The **proximity** principle states that a group of objects may be perceived as related because of their nearness to each other. Employees often perceive other employees working together in a department as a team or unit because of their physical proximity. Suppose that four people on the third floor of a large office building quit their jobs. Even if they did so for completely unrelated reasons, the human resources department may perceive the resignations as a problem on the third floor and examine morale, pay, and working conditions there in an attempt to determine what is wrong.

The **similarity** principle states that the more alike objects (or ideas) are, the greater is the tendency to perceive them as a common group. Similarity is very important in most team sports—thus the use of different colors of uni-

FIGURE 3.6

An Example of Closure

Source: Reproduced by permission from Sekuler, R., and Blake, R. *Perception*, 2nd ed. New York: McGraw-Hill, 1990, 129.

forms by the opposing teams. In football, for example, the quarterback must be able to spot an open receiver without a moment's hesitation, which would be extremely difficult (if not impossible) if both teams wore uniforms of the same color. Many organizations, especially those in buildings with open floor plans, color code the partitions and other accessories of each department to define separate functions and responsibilities visually. A company might require visitors to its plant to wear yellow hard hats and employees to wear white hard hats. Employees can then easily identify people who are unfamiliar with everyday safety precautions and routines when they are in the work area.

These principles and, in general, the ways that individuals organize their perceptions to make sense of their worlds are not something that managers and organizations can safely ignore. The following Managing in Practice account explores the impact that office design, layout, and decor can have on perceptions.

MANAGING IN PRACTICE

Office Design, Layout, and Decor—What Do They Tell You?

Office design—lighting, colors, and arrangement of furnishings, and other physical objects—influences the perceptions of customers, suppliers, prospective employees, and other visitors. Moreover, the design of their offices may affect employees in various ways. Many managers, though, seem unaware of the relationships between office design and employee perceptions, attitudes, and behaviors.

Office layout—who is located next to whom—influences perceptions of which individuals and functions the organization values most. For example, offices arranged by rank, where the highest level managers occupy the top floors, the most desirable office space, and so on, convey the message that the organization highly values status. By contrast, when Union Carbide moved into new corporate headquarters, all its managers received offices of identical size to emphasize for managers, employees, and visitors alike the importance of equality to the company.

Even the arrangement of furniture influences perceptions of the firm. For example, one study showed that visitors had very different impressions of an organization depending on whether the chairs in the reception area faced one another or were at right angles to one another. Organizations that placed chairs facing one another were perceived as more "rigid," "tense," and "deliberate" than organizations using the right-angle layout for visitor seating. Further, executives visiting the firms where seating was arranged at right angles perceived these organizations as "warmer," "friendlier," and more "comfortable." Significantly, the executive visitors strongly preferred to do business with the "warmer and friendlier" firms.

Finally, office decor influences perceptions. Students perceived that professors who had posters on the wall and plants in their offices were more friendly than professors who didn't display these objects. In organizations, people perceive that items such as flags, corporate logos, and pictures of company officers indicate a highly structured organization where employees have limited

MANAGING IN PRACTICE —*Continued*

autonomy. People are likely to perceive an organization that displays certificates of achievement, plaques, and trophies as one that values and rewards good performance. Workplace studies consistently show that flowers and plants increase perceptions of warmth and friendliness. Artwork, though, is likely to be tricky. Having art on the walls is generally perceived positively, but the content of some pictures might have the opposite effect. For example, one firm that was having trouble recruiting women discovered that pictures of men on horseback displayed prominently throughout the building gave prospective women employees the impression that the firm was cold, hostile, and generally unfriendly.[14]

▼ PERSON PERCEPTION

Of particular interest in organizational behavior is the process of *person* or *social* perception. **Person perception** is the process by which individuals attribute characteristics or traits to other people. It is closely related to the *attribution* process, which we discuss later in this chapter.[15]

The person perception process is the same as the general process of perception shown in Figure 3.1. That is, the process follows the same sequence of observation, selection, organization, interpretation, and response. However, the object being perceived in the environment is another person. Although perceptions of situations, events, and objects are important, individual differences in perceptions of other people are crucial to understanding behavior in complex social settings. For example, suppose that you meet a new employee. In order to get acquainted and to make him feel at ease, you invite him to lunch. During lunch, he begins to tell you his life history and spends a great deal of time describing his accomplishments. Because he talks only about himself (he asks you no questions about yourself), you may form the impression that he is very self-centered. Later, you may come to see other aspects of his personality, but your perceptions may always be strongly affected by this first impression, which is called a **primacy effect.**

In general, the factors influencing person perception are the same as those that influence perceptual selection. That is, both external and internal factors affect person perception. However, we may usefully categorize factors that influence how a person perceives another as:

▲ characteristics of the person being perceived;

▲ characteristics of the perceiver; and

▲ the situation or context within which the perception takes place.

▼ Characteristics of the Person Perceived

In perceiving someone else, an individual processes a variety of cues about that person: facial expressions, general appearance, skin color, posture, age, gender, voice quality, personality traits, behaviors, and so on. Some cues may contain important information about the person, but many do not. People seem to have **implicit personality theories** about which physical characteristics, personality traits, and specific behaviors relate to others.[16] Table 3.1 illustrates implicit personality theory "in action." People often seem to believe that some voice quality characteristics indicate that the speaker has certain personality traits. However, you should realize that there is no real basis for the relationships contained in Table 3.1. Think about your first contact with someone over the telephone. Later, upon meeting, did that person look and act as you expected?

Implicit personality theories may affect how individuals view, treat, and remember others. At best, the way that people group individual characteristics and personality traits helps them organize their perceptions to understand their worlds better. At worst, implicit personality theories lead to perceptual errors, such as stereotyping (to be discussed shortly).

▼ Characteristics of the Perceiver

Listening to an employee describe the personality of a co-worker may tell you as much about the employee's personality as it does about the personality of the person being described. Does this surprise you? It shouldn't if you recall that factors internal to the perceiver, including personality, learning, and motivation influence perception and that internal factors are particularly important in person perception. A person's own personality traits, values, attitudes, current mood, past experiences, and so on determine, in part, how that person perceives someone else. For example, accurately perceiving the personality of an individual raised in another culture often is difficult.[17] One reason is that the perceiver interprets the perceptions of the other person's traits and behavior in light of his or her own cultural experiences, attitudes, and values. Often these factors are inadequate for making accurate judgments about the personality and behavior of people from a different culture as the following Managing Across Cultures feature shows.

TABLE 3.1   **Personality Judgments on the Basis of Voice Quality**

Voice Quality: High in	Male Voice	Female Voice
Breathiness	Younger, artistic	Feminine, pretty, petite, shallow
Flatness	Similar results for both sexes: masculine, cold, withdrawn	
Nasality	Similar results for both sexes: having many socially undesirable characteristics	
Tenseness	Cantankerous (old, unyielding)	Young, emotional, high-strung, not highly intelligent

Source: Adapted from Hinton, P. R. *The Psychology of Interpersonal Perception.* London: Routledge, 1993, 16.

MANAGING ACROSS CULTURES

Perceptions of Japanese and American Business Associates

In a large U.S. office tower, three American executives sat around a conference table with their boss, Akiro Kusumoto, the newly appointed head of a Japanese firm's American subsidiary, and two of his Japanese lieutenants. The meeting was called to discuss ideas for reducing operating costs. Kusumoto began by outlining his company's aspirations for its long-term U.S. presence. He then turned to the current budgetary matter. One Japanese manager politely offered one suggestion, and an American then proposed another. After gingerly discussing the alternatives for quite some time, the then exasperated American blurted out: "Look, that idea is just not going to have much impact. Look at the numbers! We should cut this program, and I think we should do it as soon as possible!" In the face of such bluntness, uncommon and unacceptable in Japan, Kusumoto fell silent. He leaned back, drew air between his teeth, and felt a deep longing to "return East." He realized his life in this country would be filled with many such jarring encounters, and lamented his posting to a land of such rudeness.[18]

As this brief description indicates, Japanese managers in the United States (and American managers in Japan) may face disorienting experiences as they try to learn how to deal with business associates from another culture. Table 3.2 contains some common negative Japanese and American perceptions of their business associates. Many of these differences in perception stem from cultural differences in accepted patterns of behavior. That is, individuals may misperceive what their associates from the other country are really like because they do not fully understand the cultural differences involved.

TABLE 3.2   American and Japanese Business Associates' Perceptions of Each Other

Context	Japanese Perceptions of Americans	American Perceptions of Japanese
Interpersonal contacts	Assertive	Disturbing
	Frank	Arrogant
	Egotistical	Withdrawn
	Glib	Cautious
	Impulsive	Excessively sensitive
Business practices	Shortsightedness	Vagueness, delay
	Lackluster service	Overworked employees
	Hasty dealmaking	Ethical violations
	Legal minefields	Influence peddling

Source: Adapted from Linowes, R. G. The Japanese manager's traumatic entry into the United States: Understanding the American–Japanese cultural divide. *Academy of Management Executive*, 1993, 7, 26.

▼ The Situation

The situation or setting also influences how one person perceives another. The situation may be particularly important in understanding first impressions or primacy effects. For example, if you meet someone for the first time and he is with another person that you respect and admire, that may positively influence your assessment of the new acquaintance. But, if he is with someone you dislike intensely, you may form a negative first impression. Of course, these initial perceptions (whether positive or negative) may change over time if you continue to interact with him and get to know him better. Nevertheless, the first impression may continue to color your later perception of the individual.

Thus, in understanding the perceptual process, you have yet another use for the interactionist perspective introduced in Chapter 2. Both person and situation *interact* to determine how you perceive others.

▼ Impression Management

People often engage in **impression management,** which is an attempt to manipulate or control the impressions that others form about them:[19]

> We all ''put on a show'' at times, by using our nonverbal communication to create a deliberate impression. The clothes we choose to wear for an interview or a date, wearing sunglasses even when it's cloudy as it looks ''cool,'' having our hair cut in a certain style, putting on a ''telephone voice,'' feigning interest in a boring lecture given by our instructor, behaving ''nicely'' when grandparents come to visit; these are all ways of managing impressions.[20]

Impression management has two distinct facets, as Figure 3.7 shows.[21] The first facet, **Impression motivation,** concerns the degree to which individuals actively manage the impressions they make. Sometimes a person might be strongly motivated to manage the impression he makes on others; at other times there is little or no motivation. For example, in dressing for a job interview he might be acutely conscious of trying to make a favorable impression. But, when meeting old friends, he might be far less concerned about how he dresses.

The second facet in impression management is impression construction. **Impression construction** refers to individuals consciously choosing (1) the image they want to convey, and (2) how they go about it. For example, a woman applying for a job as a bank manager might choose to convey stability and conservatism. When interviewing for this position, she probably would wear a conservative business suit. Further, she may rewrite her resume to emphasize job tenure (to appear stable and dependable) and to omit her skydiving hobby (to not appear reckless).

Impression management provides another example of an individual difference. Some people are preoccupied with impression management; others are less concerned about how they might be perceived. In sum, however, impression management is an important part of understanding person perception. Almost everyone cares about the impression he or she makes on others, at least part of the time.

FIGURE 3.7

The Facets of Impression Management

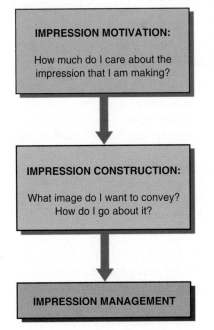

▼ PERCEPTUAL ERRORS

The perceptual process may result in errors in judgment or understanding in various ways. We first explore accuracy of judgment in person perception. We then discuss five of the most common types of perceptual errors: perceptual defense, stereotyping, the halo effect, projection, and expectancy effects. The following Managing Ethics account demonstrates the possibility of perceptual errors and the importance of accuracy of judgment.

MANAGING ETHICS

Perceptions of Ethics in Organizations

Perceptions of ethics have important implications for ethical behavior in organizations. In particular, perceptions of ethical behavior by managers will have a strong impact on the ethical behavior of employees throughout an organization.

Researchers collected data from 385 managers about perceptions of their own ethical behavior and leadership. In addition, for each of these 385 managers, the researchers collected data from four to six subordinates, peers, or superiors familiar with the manager's work behavior.

Managers in this study rated their own ethical behaviors better than their co-workers rated them. One conclusion drawn by the researchers was that these managers would benefit from knowing that their self-judgments differed from the judgments of others. Such knowledge might prompt them to re-examine their approaches to the ethical aspects of decisions and actions.

A second interesting finding was the direct relationship between perceptions of ethics and judgments of leadership. Ethical behavior appeared to enhance a manager's stature as a leader. That is, managers who were perceived as more ethical also tended to be perceived as being better leaders.[22]

▼ Accuracy of Judgment in Person Perception

How accurate are people in their perceptions of others? This question is important in organizational behavior.[23] For example, misjudging the characteristics, abilities, or behaviors of an employee during a performance appraisal review could result in an inaccurate assessment of the employee's current and future contributions to the firm. Another example of the importance of accurate person perception comes from the employment interview. Many people have long been concerned about the judgmental and perceptual errors that interviewers could make when basing employment decisions on information gathered in face-to-face interviews. The following types of interview errors are the most common:

▲ *Similarity error.* Interviewers are positively predisposed toward job candidates who are similar to them (in terms of background, interests, or hobbies, and the like) and negatively biased against job candidates who are unlike them.

▲ *Contrast error.* Interviewers have a tendency to compare job candidates to other candidates interviewed at the same time, rather than to some absolute standard. For example, an average candidate might be rated too highly if she were preceded by several mediocre candidates; a candidate might be scored too low if she were preceded by an outstanding applicant.

▲ *Overweighting of negative information.* Interviewers tend to overreact to negative information as though looking for an excuse to disqualify a job candidate.

▲ *First-impression error.* The primacy effect previously discussed may play a role in the job interview as some interviewers tend to form impressions quickly that are resistant to change.[24]

There are no easy answers to the general problems of accuracy in person perception. We do know that accuracy in person perception represents another important *individual difference.* That is, some people are quite accurate in judging and assessing others, and some people are extremely inept in doing so. We also know that people can learn to make more accurate judgments in person perception. For example, perceptions of others will be more accurate if the perceiver can avoid (1) generalizing from a single trait to many traits; (2) assuming that a single behavior will show itself in all situations; and (3) placing too much reliance on physical appearance. In addition, as person perception is influenced by characteristics of both the perceiver and the situation, accuracy in person perception can be improved when the perceiver understands these potential biases. Unfortunately, the errors that individuals make in person perception (and in other aspects of the perceptual process) are so common that names have been given to some of them. We now turn to these perceptual errors.

▼ Perceptual Defense

Perceptual defense is the tendency for people to protect themselves against ideas, objects, or situations that are threatening. A well-known folk song suggests that people hear what they want to hear and disregard the rest. Once established, an individual's way of viewing the world may become highly resistant to change. In the discussion of perceptual selection we mentioned that people tend to perceive things that are supportive and satisfying and ignore disturbing things. Avoiding unpleasant stimuli often is more than escapism; it may be a sensible defensive device. People can become psychologically deaf or blind to disturbing parts of the environment. For example, an employee who really enjoys his work, likes most of his colleagues, and is satisfied with his pay, might simply ignore some aspect of his work experience that is negative (such as an irritating co-worker).

▼ Stereotyping

Stereotyping is the tendency to assign attributes to someone solely on the basis of a category in which that person has been placed. People generally expect someone identified as a doctor, president of a company, or minister to have certain positive attributes, even if they have met some who didn't. A person categorized as a dropout, ex-convict, or alcoholic is automatically perceived negatively. Even identifying an employee by such broad categories as

African-American, older worker, or female, which should not bring to mind any attributes beyond the obvious physical characteristics, can lead to misperceptions. The perceiver may dwell on certain characteristics expected of all persons in that category and fail to recognize the characteristics that distinguish the person as an individual. The following Managing Diversity feature suggests some of the problems that gender stereotyping can create for individuals and organizations.

MANAGING DIVERSITY

Sex Stereotyping in the Workplace

Nine years of attorney fees and court costs, portrayal in national media coverage as an employer that discriminates, a $371,000 judgment for back pay, and a court order to reinstate and partner a former employee would be a nightmare for any firm. But this nightmarish scenario was precisely the cost to one employer for engaging in sex stereotyping.

Ann Hopkins billed more that $34 million in consulting contracts for her employer, Price Waterhouse—more than anyone else among the firm's 88 partner candidates. She was the sole female candidate. Nevertheless, she was denied partnership on the basis that she needed to "walk more femininely, talk more femininely, and wear makeup."

Unfortunately, Hopkins' experience is too common for women in business who face the pernicious effects of sex stereotyping. Ruined careers, glass ceilings, lost job opportunities, and hostile working environments are causing some women to leave corporate America to start their own businesses. Employers, on the other hand, lose valuable employees, face discrimination suits, and generate negative public images. Managers need to be aware of the risks associated with gender bias in the workplace, and take appropriate measures to remove it. Given the recent Price Waterhouse decision, managers that fail to minimize or eliminate sex stereotyping face substantial potential liability.[25]

▼ Halo Effect

Evaluation of another person solely on the basis of one attribute, either favorable or unfavorable, is called the **halo effect.** In other words, a *halo* blinds the perceiver to other attributes that also should be evaluated to obtain a complete, accurate impression of the other person. Managers have to guard against the halo effect in rating employee performance. A manager may single out one trait and use it as the basis for judging all other performance measures. For example, an excellent attendance record may produce judgments of high productivity, quality work, and industriousness—whether they are accurate or not.

▼ Projection

Projection is the tendency for people to see their own traits in other people. That is, they project their own feelings, personality characteristics, attitudes, or motives onto others. This tendency may be especially strong for undesirable traits that perceivers possess but fail to recognize in themselves. For example, an employee frightened by rumors of impending organizational changes may not only judge others to be more frightened than they are but may also assess various policy decisions as more threatening than they really are. People whose personality traits include stinginess, obstinacy, and disorderliness tend to rate others higher on these traits than do people who do not have these personality traits.

▼ Expectancy Effects

Expectancy effects in the perceptual process are the extent to which prior expectations bias perceptions of events, objects, and people. Sometimes the extent to which people perceive what they expect to perceive is amazing, as in the following dialogue from Shakespeare's *Hamlet*.

> **Polonius:** My lord, the Queen would speak with you, and presently.
>
> **Hamlet:** Do you see yonder cloud that's almost in the shape of a camel?
>
> **Polonius:** By th' mass, and 'tis like a camel indeed.
>
> **Hamlet:** Methinks it is like a weasel.
>
> **Polonius:** It is back'd like a weasel.
>
> **Hamlet:** Or like a whale?
>
> **Polonius:** Very like a whale.
>
> (Act III, scene ii)

Of course, Shakespeare was making a joke about an individual (Polonius) who seemingly would agree with anything to curry favor with the Prince of Denmark (Hamlet). Faced with an ambiguous stimulus, however (in this case, a cloud), many individuals could be led to expect to see a particular object, and this expectation would color their perceptions.

Expectancy effects may also bias perceptions even in less ambiguous situations. For example, your perceptions of a committee to which you have been assigned recently may be positive if your boss told you that the committee's work is important and that it will be staffed by talented people from several departments. However, your perceptions may be negative if she told you that the committee exists solely for "political reasons" and contains some real "deadwood" from other departments. You might also perceive identical behavior by other members of the committee quite differently under each set of expectations. Earlier, we noted that past experiences and learning are important to the perceptual process. As a result, people often approach situations expecting certain things to happen or other people to have certain attributes. These expectations may strongly influence their perceptions of reality.

Another aspect of expectancy effects is the **self-fulfilling prophecy.** Expecting certain things to happen shapes the behavior of the perceiver in such a way that the expected is more likely to happen.[26] For example, a team leader who has been led to believe that a new employee has great potential might do two things: (1) she might assess the employee's performance as being better than it really is (an expectancy effect); and (2) she might behave toward the new employee in such a way (for example, by providing encouragement or additional training) that the new employee's performance is, in fact, very good (a self-fulfilling prophecy).

▼ ATTRIBUTIONS: PERCEIVING THE CAUSES OF BEHAVIOR

The **attribution process** refers to the ways in which people come to understand the causes of others' (and their own) behaviors.[27] Attributions play an important role in the process of person perception. Attributions made about the reasons for someone's behavior may affect judgments about that individual's fundamental characteristics or traits (what he or she is "really like"). Note the attributions made in the following Managing In Practice piece.

MANAGING IN PRACTICE

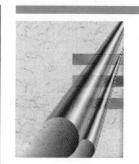

Searching for Causes of Job Applicant Behavior

Christie Johnson decided that she wanted to discuss the job candidates further and attempt to pin down the reasons for their applications. She called the interviewers together to review the files one final time.

"I don't think Richard Thomas would be suitable," said Linda Herrera. "Many of his answers sounded very pat. Our clients would be put off if he's too slick." "It could have been because he was nervous," suggested Kent Robinson. "He might be very different on the job." "Well," said Johnson, who had Thomas's résumé in front of her, "Don't forget that he's worked for Albanese & Hitt for several years. He must be pretty good with the clients." "So, why is he leaving now?" asked Herrera, unconvinced. "Maybe they are trying to get rid of him." "He said he wanted a new challenge," answered Johnson. "And we would be paying him more than Albanese & Hitt." "It could be, I suppose," said Herrera slowly.

"What about the others?" asked Johnson. "I was quite impressed with Mary Pat Slavic," said Robinson. Now it was Johnson's turn to be unconvinced. "I didn't find her very dynamic. Also she's earning the same money as we're offering already. And she would be working longer hours with us." "It could mean that she's really interested," suggested Robinson. "Or that she has some other reason. Isn't her company having a rough time? She could be trying to get out while the getting is good," observed Herrera. "Possibly," answered Robinson, "I've heard the rumors. Still, I don't think that should enter into our decision." "But," Herrera persisted, "It could mean that she's willing to settle for anything to get out and might not stay with us very long. She's not really committed to our position."

"What about David Cohen?" asked Johnson. "It is a natural progression from his current job," answered Robinson. "And he's been there a few years. It's the right time for him to move on." "But, he didn't seem to have a natural friendliness," interrupted Herrera. "He hardly looked at me and sounded rather abrupt."

The others nodded in agreement. . . . And so the discussion went on long past quitting time, as Johnson and her staff explored the characteristics and motivations of the applicants.[28]

The attributions that employees and managers make concerning the causes of behavior are important in understanding behavior in organizations. For example, managers who attribute poor performance directly to their subordinates tend to behave more punitively than managers who attribute poor performance to circumstances beyond their subordinates' control. A manager who believes that an employee failed to perform a task correctly because she lacked proper training might be understanding and give the employee better instructions or training. The same manager might be quite angry if he believes that a subordinate made mistakes simply because the subordinate did not try very hard. The relationship between attributions and behavior will become clearer as we examine the attribution process.

▼ The Attribution Process

Basically, people make attributions in an attempt to understand the behavior of other people and to make better sense of the environment. Individuals do not *consciously* make attributions in all circumstances (although they may do so *unconsciously* much of the time). However, under certain circumstances, people are likely to make causal attributions consciously. For example, causal attributions are common in the following situations:

▲ The perceiver has been asked an explicit question about another's behavior. (Why did Anna do that?)

▲ An unexpected event occurs. (I've never seen him behave that way. I wonder what's going on?)

▲ The perceiver depends on another person for a desired outcome. (I wonder why my boss made that comment about my expense account?)

▲ The perceiver experiences feelings of failure or loss of control. (I can't believe I failed my midterm exam!)

Figure 3.8 presents a basic model of the attribution process. People infer "causes" to behaviors they observe in others, and these interpretations often largely determine their reactions to those behaviors. The perceived causes of

FIGURE 3.8

The Attribution Process

Antecedents — Factors internal to the perceiver
- Information
- Beliefs
- Motivation

Attributions made by the perceiver
- Perceived causes of behavior (such as internal versus external causes)

Consequences for the perceiver
- Behavior
- Feelings
- Expectations

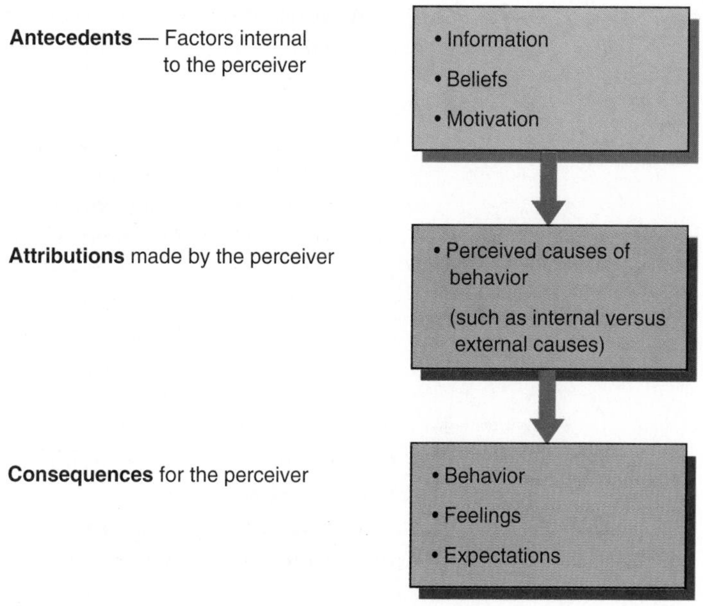

behavior reflect several *antecedents*: (1) the amount of information the perceiver has about the people and the situation and how that information is organized by the perceiver; (2) the perceiver's beliefs (implicit personality theories, what other people might do in a similar situation, and so on); and (3) the motivation of the perceiver (for example, the importance to the perceiver of making an accurate assessment). Recall our discussion of the internal factors influencing perception—learning, personality, and motivation. In the attribution process, you can see another example of the influence of these internal factors. The perceiver's information and beliefs depend on previous experience and are influenced by the perceiver's personality.

Based on information, beliefs, and motives, the perceiver often distinguishes between internal and external causes of behavior; that is, whether people did something because of a real desire or because of the pressure of circumstances. The assigned cause of the behavior—whether internal or external—helps the perceiver attach meaning to the event and is important for understanding the subsequent *consequences* for the perceiver. Among the consequences of this attribution process are the subsequent behavior of the perceiver in response to the behavior of others, the impact on feelings or emotions (how the perceiver now feels about events, people, and circumstances), and the effects on the perceiver's expectations of future events or behavior.

▼ Internal Versus External Causes of Behavior

Imagine the following scene in a busy department. Hector Gallegos, the office manager, and Jan DiAngelo, a section head for accounts receivable, are arguing loudly in Gallegos's private office. Even though they had closed the door before starting their discussion, their voices have gotten louder until everyone else in the office has stopped working and is staring in discomfort and embarrassment at the closed door. After several minutes, DiAngelo jerks open the door, yells a final, unflattering remark at Gallegos, slams the door, and stomps out of the department.

Anyone observing this scene is likely to wonder about what is going on and make certain attributions about why DiAngelo behaved the way she did. On the one hand, attributions regarding her behavior could focus on internal causes: She gets mad easily because she has a bad temper; she behaves this way because she is immature and doesn't handle pressure well; or she isn't getting her work done, and Gallegos called her on the carpet for it. On the other hand, attributions could focus on external causes: She behaves this way because Gallegos provoked her; or both their behaviors are the result of unreasonable workloads imposed on the department by top management. Some of the individuals who witnessed the events may perceive more than a single cause in such an interaction. Also, as should be clear by now, different individuals in the department are likely to interpret the events they witnessed differently.

A central question in the attribution process concerns how perceivers determine whether the behavior of another person stems from internal causes (such as personality traits, emotions, motives, or ability) or external causes (other people, the situation, or chance). A widely accepted model proposed by Harold Kelley attempts to explain how people determine why others behave as they do.[29] This explanation states that in making attributions, people focus on three major factors:

▲ *consistency*—the extent to which the person perceived behaves in the same manner on other occasions when faced with the same situation;

▲ *distinctiveness*—the extent to which the person perceived acts in the same manner in different situations; and

▲ *consensus*—the extent to which others, faced with the same situation, behave in a manner similar to the person perceived.[30]

As Figure 3.9 suggests, under conditions of high consistency, high distinctiveness, and high consensus, the perceiver will tend to attribute the behavior of the person perceived to external causes. When distinctiveness and consensus are low, the perceiver will tend to attribute the behavior of the person to internal causes. Of course, other combinations of high and low consistency, distinctiveness, and consensus are possible. Some combinations, however, may not provide the perceiver with a clear choice between internal and external causes.

Note that consistency is high under both attribution outcomes in Figure 3.9. When consistency is low, the perceiver may attribute the behavior to either or both internal and external causes. For example, imagine that a candidate running for President of the United States gives a speech in favor of gun control while campaigning in Washington, D.C., and then speaks in opposition to gun control when addressing the National Rifle Association. In this case, an observer might make either or both internal and external attributions—the audience "causes" the politician to change his speech or a character flaw "causes" the politician to tell these people what he thinks they want to hear.

In the example of the argument between Gallegos and DiAngelo, an observer would likely attribute causation to DiAngelo if others typically do not

FIGURE 3.9

Kelley's Theory of Causal Attributions

Consistency:
Does person usually
behave this way
in this situation?

External attribution
(to the person's situation)

Distinctiveness:
Does person behave
differently in different
situations?

Internal attribution
(to the person's disposition)

Consensus:
Do others behave
similarly in this situation?

Source: Myers, D. G. *Social Psychology*, 4th edition. New York: McGraw-Hill, 1993, 77. Reprinted with permission from McGraw-Hill.

have similar arguments with Gallegos (low consensus) and DiAngelo often has similar arguments with others in various work situations (low distinctiveness). But, if other individuals frequently have run-ins with Gallegos (high consensus) and DiAngelo seldom has arguments in other situations with her fellow employees (high distinctiveness), observers may attribute her behavior to external causes (in this case, Gallegos). You may want to reread this paragraph while examining Figure 3.9 to make sure that you understand the differences that lead to either external or internal attributions of behavior.

With regard to internal versus external causes of behavior, observers often make what is known as the **fundamental attribution error.** This error is the tendency to *underestimate* the impact of situational or external causes of behavior and to *overestimate* the impact of personal or internal causes of behavior when seeking to understand why people behave the way they do.[31] In organizations, employees often tend to assign blame for conflict (Chapter 13), political behavior (Chapter 15), or resistance to change (Chapter 19) to the individuals involved and fail to recognize the effects of the dynamics of the situation. For example, a CEO might attribute a high level of political behavior on the part of his vice-presidents to aspects of their personalities, not recognizing that competition for scarce resources is causing much of the political behavior.

Interestingly, there may be some cultural differences in the fundamental attribution error. For example, in North America, this error would be as just described (underestimating external causes and overestimating internal causes). In India, however, evidence indicates that the more common attribution error is to *overestimate* situational or external causes for the observed behavior.[32] This difference may be the result of cultural differences in the way people view personal responsibility and in "average" locus of control beliefs in the respective societies.

The fundamental attribution error isn't the only bias that can influence judgments concerning internal versus external causes of behavior. For example, a study of 188 supervisors showed that these individuals were more likely to attribute effective performance to internal causes for high-status employees and less likely to attribute success to internal causes for low-status employees. Similarly, supervisors were more likely to attribute ineffective performance to internal causes for low-status employees and less likely to attribute failure to internal causes for high-status employees.[33]

▼ Attributions of Success and Failure

In terms of task performance, the attributions that employees and managers make regarding success or failure are very important. Managers may base decisions about rewards and punishments on their perceptions of *why* subordinates have succeeded or failed in performing some task. In general, individuals often attribute their own (and others') success or failure to four causal factors: *ability, effort, task difficulty,* and *luck.*

▲ I succeeded (or failed) because I had the skills to do the job (or because I did not have the skills to do the job). Such statements are *ability* attributions.

▲ I succeeded (or failed) because I worked hard (or because I did not work hard). Such statements are *effort* attributions.

▲ I succeeded (or failed) because it was easy (or because it was too hard). Such statements are attributions about *task difficulty*.

▲ I succeeded (or failed) because I was lucky (or unlucky). Such statements are attributions about *luck* or the circumstances surrounding the task.[34]

Causal attributions of ability and effort are internal, and causal attributions of task difficulty and luck are external. These attributions about success or failure reflect differences in self-esteem and locus of control—personality dimensions discussed in Chapter 2.[35] For example, individuals with high self-esteem and high internal locus of control are likely to assess their own performance positively and to attribute their good performance to internal causes.

The organizational importance of these success and failure attributions is demonstrated by research in hospitals that examined the feedback provided to nurses by their managers.[36] When the managers perceived that poor performance was the result of lack of effort, their feedback messages to nurses tended to be punitive or negative in tone. Their attributions also affected the specific content of the feedback. For example, when the managers inferred that poor performance reflected lack of ability, their messages to nurses focused on *instructions* for doing the job better; when they thought that poor performance meant lack of effort, their messages to nurses tended to stress *orders* to be followed. Thus the managers' attributions about the reasons for performance failures by staff nurses influenced their communications behavior, as suggested by the model of the attribution process shown in Figure 3.8.

Not surprisingly, people have a strong tendency to attribute their success with a task to internal factors (ability or effort) and to attribute their failures to external factors (task difficulty or luck). This tendency is known as a **self-serving bias.** The tendency of employees to accept responsibility for good performance but to deny responsibility for poor performance often presents a serious challenge for managers and supervisors during performance appraisals. A self-serving bias may also create other types of problems. For example, it prevents an individual from accurately assessing his or her own performance and abilities and makes more difficult determining why a manager's course of action has failed. The general tendency to blame others for a person's own failures often is associated with poor performance and inability to establish satisfying interpersonal relationships at work and in other social settings.[37]

A slightly different version of the self-serving bias seems to arise when people compare themselves to others in the workplace. For example, research indicates that managers and workers compare themselves to others in the following ways.

▲ Most businesspeople see themselves as more ethical than the average businessperson.

▲ Managers tend to see their leadership as more encouraging of openness and innovation than do their subordinates.

▲ Ninety percent of business managers rate their performance as superior to "average" managerial performance.

▲ In Australia, 86 percent of people rated their job performance as above average. Only 1 percent saw their performance as below average.[38]

Recall that the Managing Ethics feature in this chapter on p. 86 reported that the managers interviewed believed that they behaved more ethically than their co-workers believed they did.

Summary

Perception is the psychological process whereby people select information from the environment and organize it to make sense of their worlds. Two major components of the perceptual process are selection and organization. People use perceptual selection to filter out less important information in order to focus on more important environmental cues. Both external factors in the environment and factors internal to the perceiver influence perceptual selection. Perceptual organization represents the process by which people assemble, organize, and categorize information from the environment. This organization process groups environmental stimuli into recognizable patterns (wholes) that allow people to interpret what they perceive.

How people perceive each other is particularly important for understanding organizational behavior. Person perception is a function of the characteristics of the person perceived, the characteristics of the perceiver, and the situation within which the perception takes place. People may go to great lengths to manage the impressions that others form about them. Unfortunately, the perceptual process may result in errors of judgment or understanding in various ways, such as denying the reality of disturbing information or assigning attributes to someone solely on the basis of some category or group they belong to. Fortunately, through training and experience, individuals can learn to judge or perceive others more accurately.

Attribution deals with the perceived causes of behavior. People infer causes for the behavior of others, and their perceptions of why behavior is occurring influences their own subsequent behavioral responses and feelings. Whether behavior is internally caused by the nature of the person or is externally caused by circumstances is an important attribution that people make about the behavior of others. Individuals also make attributions concerning task success and failure, which have important implications for behavior in organizations.

Key Words and Concepts

Attribution process
Closure
Continuity
Expectancy effects
Field dependence/independence
Fundamental attribution error
Halo effect
Implicit personality theories
Impression construction

Impression management
Impression motivation
Perception
Perceptual defense
Perceptual grouping
Perceptual organization
Perceptual selection
Perceptual set
Person perception

Pollyanna principle
Primacy effect
Projection
Proximity
Self-fulfilling prophecy
Self-serving bias
Similarity
Stereotyping

Discussion Questions

1. Explain the various "steps" in the process of perception.

2. Identify the factors that determine the probability that some stimulus will be perceived.

3. Give an example from your own experience of when people seemed to interpret the same situation differently. Why did they do this?

4. Describe the key factors in person perception.

5. Provide two examples of impression management from your own experiences.

6. Identify and explain the most common perceptual errors.

7. From your own experience, which of the perceptual errors discussed seems most likely to occur? Give an example of a situation in which this type of error was made.

8. What perceptual errors by managers could create special problems in their evaluation of subordinates' job performance? In their evaluation of a job applicant?

9. Describe how a person determines whether someone else's behavior represents what he or she is truly like or simply reflects the circumstances of the situation.

10. Explain the fundamental attribution error. Provide an example—either from your own experience or something you have read—of when an observer apparently made the fundamental attribution error.

11. From your own experience, give an example of attributions made following either success or failure on some task.

12. Provide two real examples of the occurrence of a self-serving bias.

 ## Developing Skills

Answers to Identify the Icon (Figure 3.2):

1-b, 2-f, 3-i, 4-j, 5-g, 6-c, 7-d, 8-a, 9-h, 10-e

Self-Diagnosis: Measuring Perceptions of Women as Managers

Gender-role stereotypes limit the opportunity for women to advance to managerial positions in many firms. Although these stereotypes are slowly changing, the attitudes toward women as managers held by many individuals present a barrier to career opportunities for many women.

Because specific attitudes and stereotypes can be pervasive and powerful influences on behavior, considering their role in the treatment—by both men and other women—of women in managerial positions is important. Attitudes about the managerial abilities of women may affect how a manager or executive judges a woman's performance in a managerial role. In addition, such attitudes may influence the granting or withholding of developmental opportunities.

The following questionnaire is designed to help you explore your attitudes toward women as managers. Note that each set of three statements asks you to select the one with which you *most* agree or which is most characteristic of your beliefs. From the two remaining statements, you then are to select the one with which you *least* agree.

Instructions:

From each *set* (of three) statements below, select the one statement with which you *most agree* and place a M (for "most agree") in the blank to the right of that statement. For each *set*, also select the one statement with which you *least agree* and place an L (for "least agree") in the blank to the right of that statement. Note that one statement in each set will not be chosen at all.

1. A. Men are more concerned with the cars they drive than with the clothes their wives wear. _____

   B. Any man worth his salt should not be blamed for putting his career above his family. _____

   C. A person's job is the best single indicator of the sort of person he is. _____

2. A. Parental authority and responsibility for discipline of the children should be divided equally between the husband and the wife. _____

   B. It is less desirable for women to have jobs that require responsibility than for men. _____

C. Men should not continue to show courtesies to women, such as holding doors open for them and helping them with their coats. _____

3. A. It is acceptable for women to assume leadership roles as often as men. _____
   B. In a demanding situation, a female manager would be no more likely to break down than would a male manager. _____
   C. There are some professions and types of businesses that are more suitable for men than for women. _____

4. A. Recognition for a job well done is less important to women than it is to men. _____
   B. A woman should demand money for household and personal expenses as a right rather than a gift. _____
   C. Women are temperamentally fit for leadership positions. _____

5. A. Women tend to allow their emotions to influence their managerial behavior more than men. _____
   B. The husband and the wife should be equal partners in planning the family budget. _____
   C. If both husband and wife agree that sexual fidelity is not important, there is no reason why both should not have extramarital affairs. _____

6. A. A man's first responsibility is to his wife, not to his mother. _____
   B. A man who is able and willing to work hard has a good chance of succeeding in whatever he wants to do. _____
   C. Only after a man has achieved what he wants from life should he concern himself with the injustices in the world. _____

7. A. A wife should make every effort to minimize irritations and inconveniences for the male head of the household. _____
   B. Women can cope with stressful situations as effectively as men can. _____
   C. Women should be encouraged not to become sexually intimate with anyone, even their fiancés, before marriage. _____

8. A. The "obey" clause in the marriage service is insulting to women. _____
   B. Divorced men should help to support their children but should not be required to pay alimony if their former wives are capable of working. _____
   C. Women have the capacity to acquire the necessary skills to be successful managers. _____

9. A. Women can be aggressive in business situations that demand it. _____
   B. Women have an obligation to be faithful to their husbands. _____
   C. It is childish for a woman to assert herself by retaining her maiden name after marriage. _____

10. A. Men should continue to show courtesies to women, such as holding doors open for them or helping them with their coats. _____
    B. In job appointments and promotions, females should be given equal consideration with males. _____
    C. It is all right for a wife to have an occasional, casual, extramarital affair. _____

11. A. The satisfaction of her husband's sexual desires is a fundamental obligation of every wife. _____
    B. Most women should not want the kind of support that men traditionally have given them. _____
    C. Women possess the dominance to be successful leaders. _____

12. A. Most women need and want the kind of protection and support that men traditionally have given them. _____
    B. Women are capable of separating their emotions from their ideas. _____
    C. A husband has no obligation to inform his wife of his financial plans. _____

Score your responses by using the form and following the instructions on the next page. Your total score indicates your feelings about women managers. The higher your score, the more prone you are to hold negative gender-role stereotypes about women in management. Possible total scores range from 10 to 70; a "neutral" score (one that indicates neither positive nor negative attitudes about women as managers) is in the range of 30 to 40.[39]

Instructions:

1. Record your response for the indicated items in the spaces provided.
2. On the basis of the information provided below, determine the points for each item and enter these points in the space provided to the right. For example, if in item 3, you chose alternative A as the one with which you *most* agree and alternative B as the one with which you *least* agree, you should receive three points for item 3. Note that items 1 and 6 are "buffer items" and are *not* scored.
3. When you have scored all ten scorable items, add the points and record the total at the bottom of this page in the space provided. This is your total score.

Your Response	Item No.	Points per Item Response*				Points
		1	3	5	7	
	1	Not Scored				
M ____	2	C(M)	A(M) C(M)	A(M) B(M)	B(M)	
L ____		B(L)	B(L) A(L)	C(L) A(L)	C(L)	
M ____	3	A(M)	A(M) B(M)	C(M) B(M)	C(M)	
L ____		C(L)	B(L) C(L)	B(L) A(L)	A(L)	
M ____	4	C(M)	C(M) A(M)	B(M) A(M)	B(M)	
L ____		B(L)	A(L) B(L)	A(L) C(L)	C(L)	
M ____	5	C(M)	C(M) B(M)	A(M) B(M)	A(M)	
L ____		A(L)	B(L) A(L)	B(L) C(L)	C(L)	
	6	Not Scored				
M ____	7	B(M)	B(M) C(M)	A(M) C(M)	A(M)	
L ____		A(L)	C(L) A(L)	C(L) B(L)	B(L)	
M ____	8	C(M)	C(M) A(M)	B(M) A(M)	B(M)	
L ____		B(L)	A(L) B(L)	A(L) C(L)	C(L)	
M ____	9	A(M)	A(M) C(M)	B(M) C(M)	B(M)	
L ____		B(L)	C(L) B(L)	C(L) A(L)	A(L)	
M ____	10	B(M)	B(M) C(M)	A(M) C(M)	A(M)	
L ____		A(L)	C(L) A(L)	C(L) B(L)	B(L)	
M ____	11	C(M)	C(M) B(M)	A(M) B(M)	A(M)	
L ____		A(L)	B(L) A(L)	B(L) C(L)	C(L)	
M ____	12	B(M)	B(M) C(M)	A(M) C(M)	A(M)	
L ____		A(L)	C(L) A(L)	C(L) B(L)	B(L)	

Total____

*M indicates item chosen as "most"; L indicates item chosen as "least."

A Case in Point: The Internship

"Well, Ken, it's been a pleasure, and if I can ever do anything for you, feel free to give me a call." These words were spoken by Don Ahearn, industrial relations manager at ARC Corporation, to Ken Barrett, student intern, as they shook hands on the final day of Ken's internship project. As he drove away from ARC's plant in Boston, Ken could not help thinking about Mr. Ahearn's parting remark. Although the internship may have been a pleasure for Mr. Ahearn, Ken thought the most enjoyable part about it was getting it over with.

It all began in September. As a junior at Babson College in Wellesley, Massachusetts, Ken had enrolled in "Problems in Organizational Behavior," a course coordinated by Dr. Ned Berry. It was a field placement course, in which Dr. Berry placed students in a management internship position for the semester, and they would report back to him weekly with progress reports. For a final grade in the course, the students had to submit (1) a report of their particular project, counting 30 percent, (2) an organizational setting analysis of the impact of physical facilities on employee attitudes and behavior in each student's host organization, counting 40 percent, (3) an oral presentation to class members at the end of the semester, counting 15 percent, and (4) a grade submitted by the host organization, counting 15 percent. Dr. Berry produced a list of participating organizations and a brief description of the projects required at each. ARC Corporation listed its project as "research concerning the implementation of an advanced information technology system." Since Ken was majoring in management and taking a minor in computer science, he requested placement at ARC. He received the placement, wrote a letter of introduction to Mr.

Don Ahearn, and scheduled an appointment to meet with Mr. Ahearn one week later.

In that following week, Dr. Berry kept his students busy. Since each student was now placed in a host organization and was scheduled to meet with his or her contact person at the organization within two weeks, Dr. Berry used class periods to prepare the students for the internship experience. Through discussion and role-playing, Dr. Berry stressed the importance of setting project parameters at the initial interview. He felt it would benefit both the host company and the student to know exactly what to expect from each other in terms of time spent with the company, work space provided, expense reimbursement, support systems such as use of copy machines and secretarial service, and, most important, what specific project outcomes were expected from the student by the end of the semester. He also stressed the fact that each student was on his or her own in setting the project parameters. Dr. Berry was available as an advisor, but each student was responsible for seeing his or her own project through.

The next Monday morning, Ken found ARC located in an old manufacturing facility in an industrial section of Boston. He met Mr. Ahearn in his basement office and began the interview by asking for a more detailed description of the project. Mr. Ahearn looked puzzled and replied, "Oh Ken, there is no project." He went on to explain that he had an idea of using more sophisticated information technology (IT) to cut down on time he spent meeting the heavy reporting demands of the Office of Federal Contract Compliance and similar government agencies. He wanted Ken to do some research on IT. Ken thought this was fine but pressed Mr. Ahearn for more details on what he wanted the computing system to do, whether or not he would integrate payroll functions into the system, whether individual employee workstations would be linked to it, and how much he wanted to pay for the system.

Throughout the next hour, Mr. Ahearn remained vague and did not really address Ken's questions. Consequently, the entire time was spent attempting to define the project. Ken had little time to discuss other parameters. He did mention that a requirement of the internship was to conduct an organizational setting analysis which would require him to distribute a questionnaire to thirty or so ARC employees. Mr. Ahearn said that was fine but asked to see the questionnaire before it was distributed. At the end of the hour, Ken left disappointed. He had had no time to discuss parameters and still had only a vague idea of what he was to do. Since Mr. Ahearn would be out of town, Ken's next appointment with him was set for three weeks later.

During this first meeting, however, Ken did learn some things about ARC. It processed sheet aluminum for construction and was a division of a large Fortune 500 diversified communications firm. ARC employed roughly 700 people, 450 of which were hourly production workers. Although Mr. Ahearn made passing mention of a computer already used by ARC in payroll, Ken did not see it, and Ahearn did not seem interested in talking much about it.

Not sure where to begin, Ken decided to begin in the college library. He found a great deal of information on IT—indeed he was overwhelmed by how much information was available. After this research, he called four computer firms to gather information and to try to arrange interviews. At this point, two problems developed. First, when the sales representatives asked Ken for details on the applications of the system, he was unable to give them, as he did not know them himself. Second, the computer firms were generally not very enthusiastic about spending much time speaking with a college student "doing research," because this would probably not lead to a sale. To complicate matters, Mr. Ahearn had asked Ken not to use the name ARC Corporation in any of his inquiries, for reasons Mr. Ahearn did not disclose. Only one computer firm, Sonex Equipment, offered to speak with Ken in person but only if he would bring a letter of introduction from "whatever firm you're doing work for." Although disheartened, Ken called Mr. Ahearn and obtained the letter. He then spent two hours with the sales representative at Sonex and left with a great deal of information on a system priced at twenty-four thousand dollars.

At his next appointment with Mr. Ahearn, Ken planned to present the information he had received at Sonex and get Mr. Ahearn's reaction to it. However, when he appeared for his appointment, Mr. Ahearn led Ken into a vacant office, brought in a large box, and placed it on the desk. He then told him, "There's a computer in the box. Why don't you set it up and play around with it for a while, so you'll know what we already have available." He explained that not much had been done with the computer since ARC purchased it. Before opening the box, Ken explained about his interview with Sonex and handed Mr. Ahearn the sales material he had received. Mr. Ahearn said, "Oh," placed the sales material on the desk, and went back to his office. Ken was disappointed that Mr. Ahearn did not take the time to look at the material, but he proceeded to open the box on the desk. It contained a small personal computer—a somewhat out-of-date 386 machine—a standard keyboard, and a LaserJet Hewlett Packard printer. At least the printer is "state of the art," Ken thought to himself. Since Mr. Ahearn did not seem interested in discussing his research at Sonex, Ken set the computer up and "played around with it" for about two hours. When he went to find Mr. Ahearn around noon, which was his scheduled time to leave, Mr. Ahearn had already left the building for lunch. Ken left a note with Mr. Ahearn's secretary that read:

Mr. Ahearn: I will be back next week at this same time. If that's not a good time for you, give me a call at home at 555-1234. Also, I will bring a copy of my organizational setting analysis questionnaire for you to look at. If you like it, maybe you could give me that plant tour you promised, and we could distribute the questionnaire to twenty or so people. Sincerely, Ken.

In the following week, Ken wrote his questionnaire and first presented it to Dr. Berry, who remarked, "It is one of the better surveys I've seen." With that, Ken brought his questionnaire to ARC the following week. Since Mr. Ahearn had meetings scheduled all day, he only had a moment to speak to Ken and put the questionnaire in his "in" basket. They had a short conversation about ARC's personal computer, and Mr. Ahearn asked Ken, "Do you think we can use it?" Ken explained briefly some of the limitations of such a small, relatively slow machine, but since Mr. Ahearn was on his way to a meeting, there was not much time to talk. Ken's next appointment with Mr. Ahearn was two weeks later.

During those next two weeks, Ken did some thinking about the project. He felt he had accomplished nothing, and the semester was half over. Since he sensed that ARC was really not interested in a large computer system but more interested in the personal computer, he thought he should change the direction of the project to center on the personal computer. He was beginning to feel that the outside research work was only "busy work," so he decided to present Mr. Ahearn with an alternative project. He would suggest that he discontinue the outside research and concentrate on attempting to identify exactly what could and could not be done with the PC they already had. Although he did not think the PC was appropriate for sophisticated statistical analyses and the high-speed data sorting required, Mr. Ahearn did. Ken thought the best way to illustrate the computer's limitations might be to outline its strengths and weaknesses. He would offer this alternative to Mr. Ahearn at their next meeting. He also resolved to get Mr. Ahearn's approval on the organizational setting analysis questionnaire so he could get started on that project.

When Ken visited ARC for his next appointment, Mr. Ahearn's secretary informed him that Mr. Ahearn had left on a business trip two days ago and had left no message. She suggested that he give Mr. Ahearn a call the following Friday to schedule another appointment.

When he called on Friday, neither he nor Mr. Ahearn mentioned the business trip, but they did set up another appointment. Ken also took the opportunity to ask Mr. Ahearn if he had looked over the questionnaire. Mr. Ahearn said yes, so Ken asked him what he thought of it. Mr. Ahearn replied, "I find it unacceptable." Ken pressed for elaboration, but Mr. Ahearn was vague, replying, "You know we have three unions here, and the situation is volatile. I can't have you asking my people some of these questions." This surprised Ken, because although he did know that Mr. Ahearn dealt with three unions, he also remembered Mr. Ahearn bragging about how great relations were with all three unions. He told Mr. Ahearn that they would need to discuss it at their next meeting, and Mr. Ahearn agreed. In the interim, he reviewed his questionnaire to try and determine which questions might be objectionable to ARC. He could pinpoint none. He hoped that Ahearn did not object to more than five or six of

the thirty-one questions, as the questionnaire worked best when taken as a whole. Dropping or modifying more than a few questions would render the questionnaire far less useful.

At the next meeting, Ken was shocked to find that Mr. Ahearn objected to sixteen of the thirty-one questions and did not like any of the remaining questions either. In a mocking tone of voice, Mr. Ahearn read some of the questions back to Ken and asked what they were supposed to measure. Although Ken attempted to explain, he could see he was getting nowhere. He then told Mr. Ahearn that the organizational setting analysis was required of all interns and that if he could not distribute a questionnaire, he would have to conduct interviews. They both agreed that interviews were too time-consuming, but Mr. Ahearn still did not want to distribute a questionnaire, and Ken still could not get a clear reason why. Mr. Ahearn remarked that ARC had conducted an extensive attitude survey two years ago and offered to get the results for Ken, saying, "Maybe you can look at those results and do something with them." At a loss for what to do next, Ken agreed to look at the results. Mr. Ahearn said he would leave the results with his secretary so Ken could pick them up on the following Friday.

When Ken went to ARC the following Friday to pick up the results, Ahearn's secretary said that Mr. Ahearn had left nothing with her and had left several days ago on business. Not knowing what to do next, Ken turned to Dr. Berry. During their weekly meetings, he had kept Dr. Berry informed of the problems he had been having at ARC, and the professor had suggested possible solutions. However, at this point, Dr. Berry offered him the option of doing some outside research work in lieu of the organizational setting analysis. Dr. Berry said, "This is bound to prove more valuable than continued fighting over the questionnaire." Since his classmates were still required to do the analysis, this again felt a little like defeat, but Ken gladly agreed.

When Ken finally did obtain the results of the ARC study, they turned out to be the text of a speech the company president had made to the workers, summarizing some of the firm's problems. Ken was glad he had taken Dr. Berry's option, as the speech provided no information for analyzing the organizational setting.

Over the next several weeks, Ken worked on developing corporate applications for ARC's personal computer. He then scheduled an appointment with Mr. Ahearn to present his final report. Since Mr. Ahearn had been busy at meetings during Ken's last few appointments, he had not seen much of what the student had been doing. Mr. Ahearn informed Ken that he had invited his boss, Nancy Baker, the human resources manager, to hear the presentation with him. In addition to his analysis of PC applications, Ken prepared a six-page report on what qualities he felt ARC should look for in a larger system. Since he knew that Mr. Ahearn and his department did not know much about computers, he thought an informational report of this type would be most helpful.

Based on the criteria set forth in the report, he concluded with a recommendation that the small personal computer not be used. Since he felt that Mr. Ahearn really did want to use the existing computer, he hesitated before making this recommendation, but based on the criteria set up in his report, his only choice was to recommend that the existing PC not be used.

The presentation to Mr. Ahearn and Nancy Baker was well received. At the end of Ken's presentation, Ms. Baker remarked, "That's an excellent report, Ken. It looks like you put a lot of work into it." Mr. Ahearn agreed, then shook hands with Ken and made the remark appearing at the beginning of the case. Ken handed him the report and his internship was over.

One week later, Dr. Berry received the grade determined for Ken by ARC: a B minus. Ken was disappointed and wondered what he had done wrong and what exactly he had learned from the whole experience.[40]

Questions

1. Make a list of the possible differences in the way Ken and Mr. Ahearn perceived the internship.
2. To what might Ken attribute Mr. Ahearn's behavior?
3. To what would you expect Ken to attribute his "failure"?
4. What were the main problems Ken faced during his internship? Why did these problems arise?
5. If you had been given this internship, what would you have done to improve the situation?

References

1. From *Psychology Applied to Work*, by P. M. Muchinsky, Copyright © 1990, 1993 by Wadsworth Inc. Reprinted by permission of Brooks/Cole Publishing Company, Pacific Grove, Calif. 93950.
2. Banks, W. P., and Krajicek, D. Perception. *Annual Review of Psychology*, 1991, 42, 305–331; Sekuler, R., and Blake, R. *Perception*, 2nd ed. New York: McGraw-Hill, 1990.
3. Adapted from Kansas, D. The icon crisis: Tiny pictures cause confusion. *Wall Street Journal*, November 17, 1993, B1, B10.
4. Kinchla, R. A. Attention. *Annual Review of Psychology*, 1992, 43, 711–742.
5. Barber, P. *Applied Cognitive Psychology*. London: Methuen, 1988, 35–66.
6. Dearborn, D., and Simon, H. A. Selective perception: A note on the departmental identifications of executives. *Sociometry*, 1958, 21, 140–144.
7. Walsh, J. P. Selectivity and selective perception: An investigation of managers' belief structure and information processing. *Academy of Management Journal*, 1988, 31, 873–896.
8. Hogan, R. T. Personality and personality measurement. In M. D. Dunnette and L. M. Hough (eds.), *Handbook of Industrial and Organizational Psychology*, 2nd. ed., vol. 2. Palo Alto, Calif.: Consulting Psychologist Press, 1991, 886–891.
9. McBurney, D. H., and Collings, V. B. *Introduction to Sensation/Perception*, 2nd ed. Englewood Cliffs, N.J.: Prentice-Hall, 1984, 327–345.
10. Dorfman, P. W., Howell, J. P., Bautista, J., Hibino, S., Snyman, J. H., and Mayes, B. T. Perceptions of punctuality: Cultural differences and the impact of time perceptions on job satisfaction and organizational commitment. Paper presented at the Pan Pacific Conference, Beijing, China, June 8–10, 1993.
11. Based on Levine, R. V. The pace of life. *American Scientist*, September/October, 1990, 450–459; Levine, R. V., and Wolff, E. Social Time: The heartbeat of culture. *Psychology Today*, March 1985, 28–35.
12. Adapted from Sekuler and Blake, *Perception*, 16.
13. Roitblat, H. L., and von Fersen, L. Comparative cognition: Representations and processes in learning and memory. *Annual Review of Psychology*, 1992, 43, 671–710; Squire, L. R., Knowlton, B., and Musen, G. The structure and organization of memory. *Annual Review of Psychology*, 1993, 44, 453–495.
14. Based on Ornstein, S. The hidden influences of office design. *Academy of Management Executive*, 1989, 3, 144–147; Ornstein, S. Impression management through office design. In R. A. Giacalone and T. Rosenfeld (eds.), *Impression Management in the Organization*. Hillsdale, N.J.: Lawrence Erlbaum, 1989, 411–426.
15. Fiske, S. T. Social cognition and social perception. *Annual Review of Psychology*, 1993, 44, 155–194.
16. Baron, R. M., Graziano, W. G., and Stangor, C. *Social Psychology*. Fort Worth: Holt, Rinehart, and Winston, 1991, 122–123.
17. See, for example, Zebrowitz-McArthur, L. Person perception in cross-cultural perspective. In M. H. Bond (ed.), *The Cross-Cultural Challenge to Social Psychology*. Newbury Park, Calif.: Sage, 1988, 245–265.
18. Linowes, R. G. The Japanese manager's traumatic entry into the United States: Understanding the American–Japanese cultural divide. *Academy of Management Executive*, 1993, 7, 21. Reprinted with permission of Academy of Management Publications.
19. Schlenker, B. R., and Weigold, M. F. Interpersonal processes involving impression regulation and management. *Annual Review of Psychology*, 1992, 43, 133–168.
20. Hinton, P. R. *The Psychology of Interpersonal Perception*. London: Routledge, 1993, 23.
21. Leary, M. R., and Kowalski, R. M. Impression management: A literature review and two-component model. *Psychological Bulletin*, 1990, 107, 34–47.
22. Based on Morgan, R. B. Self- and co-worker perceptions of ethics and their relationships to leadership and salary. *Academy of Management Journal*, 1993, 36, 200–214.
23. Cook, M. (ed.), *Issues in Person Perception*. London: Methuen, 1984; DePaulo, B. M., Kenny, D. A., Hoover, C. W., Webb, W., and Oliver, P. V. Accuracy of person perception: Do people know what kinds of impressions they convey? *Journal of Personality and Social Psychology*, 1987, 52, 303–315; Kenny, D. A., and DePaulo, B. M. Do people know how others view them? An

empirical and theoretical account. *Psychological Bulletin*, 1993, 114, 145–161; Kruglanski, A. W. The psychology of being right: The problem of accuracy in social perception and cognition. *Psychological Bulletin*, 1989, 106, 395–409.

24. Fisher, C. D., Schoenfeldt, L. F., and Shaw, J. B. *Human Resource Management*, 2nd ed. Boston: Houghton Mifflin, 1993, 323–325.

25. Kelly, E. P., Young, A. O., and Clark, L. W. Sex stereotyping in the workplace: A manager's guide. *Business Horizons*, March–April, 1993, 23. Reprinted with permission from JAI Press.

26. Baron, Graziano, and Stangor, *Social Psychology*, 129.

27. Baron, R. A., and Byrne, D. *Social Psychology: Understanding Human Interaction*, 6th ed. Boston: Allyn & Bacon, 1991, 55–83; Harvey, J. H., and Wells, G. (eds.). *Attribution: Basic Issues and Applications*. New York: Academic Press, 1988, 282–311; Myers, D. G. *Social Psychology*, 4th ed. New York: McGraw-Hill, 1993, 74–108.

28. Adapted from Hinton, *The Psychology of Interpersonal Perception*, 138.

29. Kelley, H. H. The process of causal attribution. *American Psychologist*, 1973, 28, 107–128.

30. For explanations of Kelley's model see Baron and Byrne, *Social Psychology*, 57–64; Hinton, *The Psychology of Interpersonal Perception*, 143–146.

31. Myers, *Social Psychology*, 78–80.

32. Miller, J. G. Culture and the development of everyday causal explanation. *Journal of Personality and Social Psychology*, 1984, 46, 961–978.

33. Heneman, R. L., Greenberger, D. B., and Anonyus, C. Attributions and exchanges: The effects of interpersonal factors on the diagnosis of employee performance. *Academy of Management Journal*, 1989, 32, 466–476.

34. Babladelis, G. *The Study of Personality*. New York: Holt, Rinehart and Winston, 1984, 76.

35. Levy, P. E. Self-appraisal and attributions: A test of a model. *Journal of Management*, 1993, 19, 51–62.

36. Kim, Y. Y., and Miller, K. I. The effects of attributions and feedback goals on the generation of supervisory feedback message strategies. *Management Communication Quarterly*, 1990, 4, 6–29.

37. Tennen, H., and Affleck, G. Blaming others for threatening events. *Psychological Bulletin*, 1990, 108, 209–232.

38. Myers, *Social Psychology*, 90.

39. Adapted from Yost, E. B., and Herbert, T. T. Attitudes toward women as managers. In L. D. Goodstein and J. W. Pfeiffer (eds.), *The 1985 Annual: Developing Human Resources*. San Diego, Calif.: University Associates, 1985, 117–127. Reprinted with permission.

40. Case prepared by Professors Neal Thornberry and Joseph Weintraub of Babson College with the help of student Carl Brooks based on his experiences as a student intern and reprinted with permission. Copyright 1981. Revised 1993.

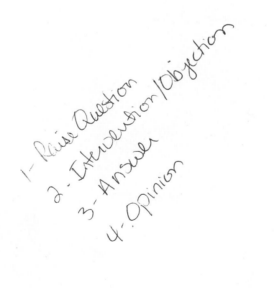

4 Individual Problem-Solving Styles

LEARNING OBJECTIVES

When you have finished studying this chapter, you should be able to:

▲ Describe the four stages of problem solving.

▲ Explain two methods that individuals use to gather data.

▲ Describe two methods that individuals use to evaluate information.

▲ Identify your own problem-solving style.

▲ List the strengths and weaknesses of four individual problem-solving styles.

OUTLINE

Preview Case: Ben & Jerry's Home-made Ice Cream, Inc.

Individual Problem-Solving Processes

Psychological Functions in Problem Solving

Sensation Versus Intuition in Gathering Information

Feeling Versus Thinking in Evaluating Information

Managing Across Cultures: Problem-Solving Styles of Canadian and Japanese Students

Individual Problem-Solving Styles

Sensation-Thinkers

Managing in Practice: Against the Grain

Intuitive-Thinkers

Managing in Practice: The CEO as Organizational Architect

Sensation-Feelers

Managing in Practice: Body Shop International

Intuitive-Feelers

Managing in Practice: Herb Kelleher of Southwest Airlines

Summary of Problem-Solving Styles

Organizational Implications

Managing Ethics: What's Your Decision?

Managing Diversity: Reengineering at GTE

DEVELOPING SKILLS

Self-Diagnosis: *Problem-Solving Style Questionnaire*

A Case in Point: *Whole Foods Market*

PREVIEW CASE

Ben & Jerry's Homemade Ice Cream, Inc.

From the very beginning, Ben & Jerry's was determined to be a company with a strong set of unique values. The owners wanted to be a force for social change and operate innovatively to improve people's quality of life. In 1963 founders Ben Cohen and Jerry Greenfield opened their first homemade ice cream shop in Burlington, Vermont, with an investment of $12,000. The shop was an immediate success.

Cohen and Greenfield's philosophy has been referred to as caring capitalism. Not interested in managing the details of building the company, they were concerned about the company's social mission. The company does no marketing research, media advertising, or test marketing of new flavors. Cohen decided that marketing and promotions should be educational events, rather than gimmicks, that focus on social issues and be fun. He developed a variety of creative promotional activities, such as the company's pint containers, to increase social awareness of such issues as supporting the family farm and banning bovine growth hormone. The company also sponsored summer music festivals throughout the country. Half the money earned from guided tours of their ice cream plant is donated to local charities. Their annual board meetings became highly publicized events that promoted world peace, environmental issues, and social causes.

The company is dedicated to its employees. It provides free employee assistance programs, on-site day care facilities, and comprehensive employee benefits. The work setting is informal, dress is casual, and there is no organization chart. Managers and employees agree on the important aspects of each job. The salary range between the newest, lowest paid employee hired and the owners is 7-to-1. This policy was designed to recognize the contribution of lower level employees, link top-management rewards to companywide compensation, and reflect the owners' respect for the dignity of each employee. Greenfield left the company in 1982 because, with its 20 employees, it was becoming too large and impersonal for his liking. However, after several years, Cohen convinced his friend to rejoin the company as head of the Joy Gang, whose purpose is to "spread joy" in the company.[1]

H ow would you like to work for Ben & Jerry's Homemade Ice Cream, Inc.? What contributes to the organization's success? You might answer by saying that the company employs talented people who believe in its social mission. Although these factors obviously contribute to the organization's success, hidden factors also often underlie such success. These factors have to do with perceptions, attributions, personality, and attitudes. Yet because they are hidden or covert, they are hard for others to see. All these factors contribute to a **problem-solving style** that reflects the way a person perceives and thinks about situations.

▼ INDIVIDUAL PROBLEM-SOLVING PROCESSES

People have various problem-solving abilities, which they use in playing chess, analyzing stocks, making business deals, learning languages, and myriad other ways. Problem-solving skills are not easily learned, sometimes requiring years of experience and countless hours of practice. And yet, amazingly, people compress years of experience and learning into split-second decision making.

The same problem-solving processes that underlie the greatest mental accomplishments also create some problems. For instance, people sometimes believe that important events occur more frequently than they do and that each event is a crisis. People also tend to be overconfident and make complex decisions based on little information. Finally, people often are not very good at assessing the interrelationships of factors affecting a decision. That is, people may look at factors one at a time without seeing how they merge into a coherent whole. Unless complex relationships are very clear, many people tend to rely on prior experiences and perceive things that are not there.[2]

In making day-to-day decisions, individuals rely on a general problem-solving process. Figure 4.1 illustrates how people process information and make decisions. Starting at the left, note that the decision maker responds to two major sources of environmental stimuli: (1) internal, such as job requirements and communications with employees; and (2) external, such as customers, governmental units, suppliers, and competitors. The decision maker's frame of reference includes such factors as needs, personality, past experiences, and attitudes.[3] Perceptual selection, or information bias, relates to the person's personality, learning, and motivation (see Chapter 3). Based on past experiences and personality, a person's selection of information to attend to may be too narrow and rigid. Recall that in Chapter 2 we described a person having a rigid belief system as a highly dogmatic person. Such a person holds fast to attitudes and beliefs, even in the face of facts to the contrary. A less dogmatic person isn't as likely to ignore new information or ways of doing things.

The amount of external information to be processed also affects that person's ability to make a decision. Let's return to the Ben & Jerry's Homemade

FIGURE 4.1

Individual Problem-Solving Process

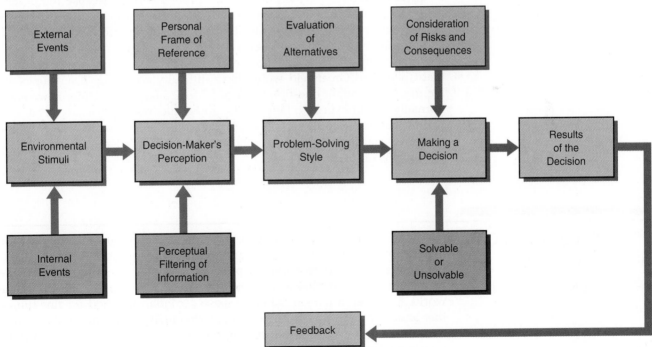

Source: Adapted from Rowe, A. J., and Mason, R. O. *Managing with Style: A Guide to Understanding, Assessing, and Improving Decision Making.* San Francisco: Jossey-Bass, 1987, 61.

Ice Cream, Inc., case and determine the amount of environmental information the owners have to process before deciding how much ice cream to produce. This decision affects the number of employees and amounts of ingredients needed and the number of outlets that can be supplied. Let's look at some of the external environmental factors that affect Cohen and Greenfield's decision making.

Americans ate more than 925.7 million gallons of ice cream last year, or about 18.5 quarts per person, which was up slightly from the previous year. The per capita consumption of ice cream varies between 21.2 quarts in the Pacific Northwest to a low of 9.7 quarts in the Mountain States. Ninety-four percent of all households bought ice cream, and families with young children and persons over 55 ate the most. Ice cream consumption is not as seasonal as you might suspect, with the summer months accounting for about 30% of annual consumption. Supermarket sales of ice cream generate five times more profit than other products per square foot of shelf space. The highest quality products cost the most to produce because of the ingredients. Ben & Jerry's products are famous for the large chunks of added ingredients, such as cherries, nuts, and peaches and for the use of quality cream, all of which increase costs. Competition for Ben & Jerry's products include those made by Kraft (Frusen Gladje) and Pillsbury (Häagen-Dazs), among others. The company's share of the U.S. ice cream market is 27%, ranging from a high of 53% in the Boston area to a low of 20% in the Los Angeles area. Its market share in metropolitan areas along the East Coast is its largest.

How do these data and the owners' personal frame of reference affect the evaluation of alternatives, such as expansion into additional markets? What risks are they willing to consider? One risk is that, as more people are hired to increase production, the potential for problems rises because the organization lacks structure and formal control processes (rules and regulations). Not everyone hired subscribes to its caring social philosophy. Departments and procedures might have to be created to maintain the organization's profitability, making the company a more traditional organization—a consequence that Cohen and Greenfield would have difficulty accepting. If managers are recruited, they might question the firm's 7-to-1 salary ratio. Other newcomers normally would expect to be paid the going rate, not some salary arbitrarily tied to that of the company's lowest-paid employee. Maintaining the organization's social mission greatly influences the owners' decisions, as do their perceptions of the market.

▼ PSYCHOLOGICAL FUNCTIONS IN PROBLEM SOLVING

Psychologist Carl Gustav Jung defined four psychological functions that are involved in information gathering and evaluation: sensation, intuition, thinking, and feeling.[4] A person usually prefers one way of gathering data and one way of evaluating it, that is, of perceiving and making judgments about the world. However, a person may also use a secondary method for fine-tuning that basic approach. According to Jung, individuals gather information either by sensation or intuition—but not by both simultaneously. These two functions represent the orientation extremes in gathering information. **Sensing** means that a person prefers to work with known possibilities and facts rather than look for new possibilities. **Intuition** means that a person prefers to look for possibilities rather than work with facts. Similarly, the thinking and feeling functions represent the orientation extremes in evaluating information. **Thinking** means that a person bases judgments more on impersonal analysis and logic than on personal values. **Feeling** means that a person bases judgments more on personal values than on impersonal analysis.

Before reading further, complete the questionnaire in the Developing Skills section at the end of this chapter on pages 131–132. Because this questionnaire has been validated with many students, your scores should be reasonably accurate and remain relatively constant for some time. With knowledge of your problem-solving style and how it affects others, you can change your problem-solving preferences over time if you so desire.

According to Jung, only one of the four functions is dominant in an individual. The dominant function normally is related to one of the functions from the other set of paired opposites. For example, the sensation function may support the thinking function, or vice versa. The sensation-thinking combination characterizes many people in today's Western industrialized societies. As a result, intuition and feeling are the functions most likely to be disregarded, undeveloped, or repressed. However, as they mature, individuals tend to move toward a balance, or integration, of the four psychological functions.

Let's first consider each of the four psychological functions as a dominant type. Then let's consider the two information-gathering orientations (sensation and intuition) in combination with the two information-evaluating orientations (thinking and feeling) as they relate to managerial styles.

▼ Sensation Versus Intuition in Gathering Information

Individuals perceive or gather information differently, according to whether they prefer sensation or intuition. Table 4.1 describes behavioral patterns and general characteristics of people with sensation- and intuitive-type information-gathering styles. More than 56% of U.S. managers report a preference for gathering information through sensation, whereas 44% indicate a preference for intuition. People usually belong to one group or the other.[5]

Sensation-Type Person   The **sensation-type person** wants, trusts, and remembers facts and would rather work with facts than look for possibilities and relationships. Such a person believes in experience and relies on the past in approaching current problems. When interviewing someone for a job, a sensation-type manager wants to know the details of the applicant's past experience to help form an opinion of the person and make a decision. The sensation-type person uses words such as *actual, down-to-earth, realistic,* and *practical* when making a presentation to others. In terms of a problem-solving style, the sensation-type person tends to:

▲ dislike new problems, unless there are standard ways to solve them;

▲ enjoy using skills already acquired more than learning new ones;

▲ work steadily with a realistic idea of how long a task will take;

▲ work through a task or problem to a conclusion;

TABLE 4.1   Comparisons of Sensation and Intuitive Types of People

Characteristic	Sensation Type	Intuitive Type
Focus	Details, practical, action, getting things done quickly	Patterns, innovation, ideas, long-range planning
Time Orientation	Present, live life as it is	Future achievement, change, rearrange
Work Environment	Pay attention to detail, patient with details and don't make factual errors, not risk takers	Look at the "big picture," patient with complexity, risk takers
Strengths	Pragmatic, results-oriented, objective, competitive	Original, imaginative, creative, idealistic
Possible Weaknesses	Impatient when projects get delayed, decide issues too quickly, lack long-range perspective, can oversimplify a complex task	Lack follow-through, impractical, make errors of facts, take people's contributions for granted.

Source: Adapted from Quenk, N. L. *Beside Ourselves: Our Hidden Personality in Everyday Life*. Palo Alto, Calif.: CCP Books, 1993; Nutt, P. C. Flexible decision styles and choices of top executives. *Journal of Management Studies*, 1993, 30, 695–721.

▲ be impatient when details get complicated; and

▲ distrust creative inspirations.

The sensation-type person dislikes dealing with unstructured problems because of the uncertainty involved. Such problems usually require the individual to exercise judgment in deciding what to do and how to do it. The person may experience great anxiety in making this type of decision because the consequences are not clear-cut. The sensation-type person is mentally oriented to physical reality, external facts, and concrete experiences. This person is not inclined to be reflective or introspective.

The sensation-type person emphasizes action, urgency, and results. Through an assertive, quick-paced, and "let's do it now" approach to life and work, the individual learns by doing, not by imagining or thinking.

Intuitive-Type Person   An **intuitive-type person** looks first at ideas and possibilities rather than facts. Such an individual likes to solve new problems, dislikes repetitive work, may jump to conclusions, becomes impatient with routine details, and dislikes taking time to be precise.[6]

An intuitive-type person probably would dislike and may perform poorly the routine and structured job that the sensation-type individual enjoys and often performs well. The intuitive-type person is better at coming up with ideas than implementing them. The intuitive-type person tends to perceive the organization as a whole—as it is and as it might change—and lives in anticipation. When conducting a job interview, the intuitive-type manager is not likely to examine in detail the applicant's experience. This type of manager is much more interested in the applicant's imagination, ability to understand the organization's growth possibilities, and creativity in solving a messy problem.

The intuitive-type person's speaking and writing are filled with metaphors and imagery. Such a person often uses the words *possible, fascinating, ingenious,* and *imaginative,* among others, to describe people and events—and often day-dreams and fantasizes. The sensation-type person may believe that the intuitive-type person's head is in the clouds. If so, the intuitive-type person may make more errors of fact than the sensation-type person. A person once described an intuitive manager as someone "who can see around corners." In terms of a problem-solving style, the intuitive-type person tends to:

▲ keep the total picture or overall problem continually in mind as problem solving proceeds;

▲ show a tendency, willingness, and openness to continually explore possibilities;

▲ rely on hunches and nonverbal cues;

▲ almost simultaneously consider a variety of alternatives and options and quickly discard those judged unworkable; and

▲ jump around or back and forth among the usual sequence of steps in the problem-solving process and may even suddenly want to reassess whether the "real" problem has even been identified.

Unlike the sensation-type person, the intuitive-type person feels suffocated by stable conditions and seeks to create new possibilities. Such a person is often a venture capitalist, politician, or entrepreneur. Often starting and promoting new enterprises, services, concepts, and other innovations in both the public and private sectors, this type of person skips from one activity to the next, perhaps completing none. Jung described the intuitive-type person as one who plants a field and then is off to something new before the crop is even beginning to break ground. Instead of staying around to see the crop mature, the individual is off looking for new fields to plow.

Intuitive-type people are imaginative, creative, and futuristic. They enjoy playing mind-testing games, such as chess, checkers, and bridge. Technical details often elude them. They become impatient with people who do not see the immediate value of their ideas. Although they may appear to be day-dreaming, they are probably forming ideas and reflecting on experiences in relation to these ideas.

▼ Feeling Versus Thinking in Evaluating Information

Information evaluation involves making a judgment based on the information gathered. Jung believed that people rely on two basic psychological functions when making a judgment: thinking and feeling. Some people are more comfortable with making impersonal, objective judgments and are uncomfortable with making personal, subjective judgments. Other people are just the opposite. However, both ways of making judgments are necessary and useful. Table 4.2 summarizes the characteristics typically associated with these functions. About 64% of the U.S. population uses thinking when evaluating information, whereas the other 36% emphasizes feeling.[7]

Feeling-Type Person A **feeling-type person** is aware of other people and their feelings, likes harmony, needs occasional praise, dislikes telling people

TABLE 4.2　Comparisons of Thinking and Feeling Types of People

Characteristic	Thinking Type	Feeling Type
Focus	Logic of situation, truth, organization principles	Human values and needs, harmony, feelings, emotions
Time Orientation	Past, present, future	Past
Work Environment	Businesslike, impersonal, treat others fairly, well organized	Naturally friendly, personal, harmony, care and concern for others
Strengths	Good at putting things in logical order, tend to be firm and tough-minded, rational, objective, predict logical results of decisions	Enjoy pleasing people, sympathetic, loyal, draw out feelings in others, take interest in person behind the job or idea
Possible Weaknesses	Overly analytical, unemotional, too serious, rigid, verbose	Sentimental, postpone unpleasant tasks, avoid conflict

Source: Adapted from Quenk, N. L. *Beside Ourselves: Our Hidden Personality in Everyday Life.* Palo Alto, Calif.: CCP Books, 1993; Nutt, P. C. Flexible decision styles and choices of top executives. *Journal of Management Studies*, 1993, 30, 695–721.

unpleasant news, is sympathetic, and relates well to most people. Such an individual bases decisions on how they will affect the well-being of others, looking to moral values for guidance. The feeling-type individual probably would conform highly to norms and make accommodations for other people. This type of person strives to make decisions that win approval from others (peers, subordinates, and superiors). In terms of a problem-solving style, the feeling-type person tends to:

▲ enjoy pleasing people, even in ways that others consider unimportant;
▲ dislike dealing with problems that require telling other people something unpleasant;
▲ be responsive and sympathetic to other people's problems; and
▲ emphasize the human aspects in dealing with organizational problems and view the causes of inefficiency and ineffectiveness as interpersonal and other human problems.

Feeling-type people emphasize emotional and personal factors in decision making. They usually avoid problems that are likely to result in disagreements. When avoidance or smoothing over of differences isn't possible, they often change their positions to those that are more acceptable to others. Establishing and maintaining friendly relations may be more important to them than achievement, effectiveness, and decision making. Feeling-type managers may have difficulty suspending or discharging subordinates for poor performance, even when the need to do so is widely recognized by others, including the employees' peers.

In other words, feeling-type people are emotional and spontaneous, and known for their love of people. Whether buying a car or choosing a friend, they base their decisions on feelings, and they often are self-indulgent. They choose words that reflect a personal tone, such as *subjective, values, intimacy, extenuating circumstances,* among others. The ready use of such words makes the feeling-type person good at persuasion or negotiating.

Thinking-Type Person   At the other extreme, a **thinking-type person** prefers impersonal principles and isn't comfortable unless there is a logical or analytical basis for a decision. Such a person generally is unemotional and uninterested in other people's feelings. The individual's activities and decisions usually are controlled by intellectual processes based on external data and generally accepted ideas and values. This type of person fits problems and their solutions into standardized formulas and, when making decisions, may lose sight of all personal considerations.

Thinking-type people are organized and structured. They doggedly pursue facts, seldom leaping to conclusions and preferring to consider options carefully before deciding. They are not risk takers, being painstaking in their research and stressing its accuracy and timeliness. Thinking-type people may get bogged down in analyzing situations over and over. At worst, they are perceived by others to be rigid, blunt, aloof, and too impersonal. In terms of a problem-solving style, a thinking-type person is likely to:

▲ make a plan and look for a method to solve a problem;

▲ be extremely conscious of and concerned with the approach to a problem;

▲ define carefully the specific constraints in a problem;

▲ proceed by increasingly refining an analysis; and

▲ search for and obtain additional information in an orderly manner.

In the following Managing Across Cultures piece, we illustrate the problem-solving preferences of Canadian and Japanese students. As more and more organizations seek to form joint ventures in other countries, people must learn how to deal with others who do not share the same problem-definition and problem-solving style. Frustration often occurs and negotiations may even fail because people have different perspectives and ways of doing things.

MANAGING ACROSS CULTURES

Problem-Solving Styles of Canadian and Japanese Students

How do students from Canada and Japan process information? Differences between nationalities not only reflect cultural values, but differing attitudes and personalities. Figure 4.2 indicates that Canadian students strongly prefer thinking, a problem-solving style that tends to be logical, impersonal, and objective. It results in quick, impersonal, and analytically based decisions, with rapid closure on fact-finding as soon as enough information is available for the decision. Canadian students tend to underplay the human element by discounting "personal" types of data in favor of abstract/theoretical data.

The Japanese students display a strong preference for a more feeling-based problem-solving style that emphasizes the human element in decision making. This style has a concern for group harmony, and a tendency to be sympathetic and friendly in human relations. These students do not make decisions quickly and appear to be particularly adaptable to new situations.[8]

FIGURE 4.2

Comparison of Student Problem-Solving Styles

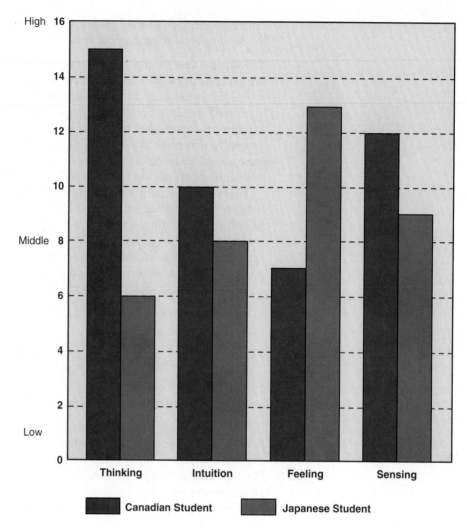

Source: Adapted from Abramson, N., Lane, H. W., Nagai, H., and Takagi, H. A comparison of Canadian and Japanese cognitive styles: Implications for management interaction. *Journal of International Business Studies*, 1993, 575–587.

So far, we've focused on each of the four dominant psychological functions used by people to gather and evaluate information. Think back to the Preview Case for a moment. What is the dominant combination of psychological functions that the owners exhibit? If you answered that they exhibit many of the characteristics of intuitive-feeling managers, you would agree with our assessment.

▼ INDIVIDUAL PROBLEM-SOLVING STYLES

The combination of information gathering and information evaluation results in a problem-solving style. Figure 4.3 illustrates individual problem-solving styles based on the four psychological functions. The vertical axis represents the thinking–feeling continuum, and the horizontal axis represents the sensation–intuition continuum. Although most people gather and evaluate information both ways in their daily lives, they usually prefer one way of gathering information and one way of evaluating information. Go back to the questionnaire we asked you to complete in the Developing Skills section of this chapter on pages 131–132. Look at your results and then locate yourself on the grid in Figure 4.3. According to your scores, are you primarily an ST, NT, NF, or SF person? Or do your scores suggest a balance among the four psychological functions? Compare your scores with those of students from Canada and Japan.

Much can be learned about someone's problem-solving style from a person's brief written description of an ideal organization. Take ten minutes and write such a description. Then compare it with the ideas culled from those of numerous managers (presented in the following sections) to identify your own problem-solving style.[9]

▼ Sensation-Thinkers

Sensation-thinkers (STs) want to establish order, control, and certainty. They want to know the details of a situation before making a decision. They may oversimplify and quantify messy or novel decisions to obtain order and meaning, and they seldom make errors of fact. They can absorb, remember, manipulate, and manage many details, objects, or facts. They tend to downplay qualitative (subjective) information because it disrupts the order and structure of factual data. They like to clarify, settle, and conclude problems and situations. They may reject novel or innovative solutions when little ''hard'' data supports such solutions. They are not risk takers, and their preference for analytic precision means that they don't follow hunches. They persevere, work steadily, and have realistic ideas of how long tasks will take to complete. As managers, they are tough-minded individuals who can get others to do their jobs.

An organization that does not have some ST managers may not be as efficient and effective as one that has such managers. Plant use may be inefficient, and control over materials and organizational procedures may be lax. An organization without any ST managers may find itself in a constant state of change without a foundation of sound, accepted policy and regulations on which to operate.

Relating to Others Sensation-thinkers want others to get to the point fast and stick to it. They enjoy dealing with others who can present data in a highly

FIGURE 4.3

Individual Problem-Solving Styles

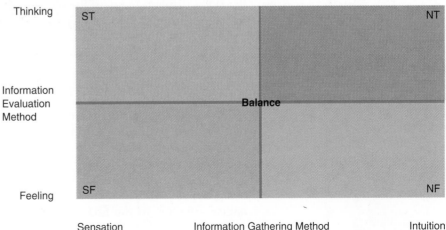

organized way. When relating to other people, however, they may become frustrated by not always being able to get facts. They may express this frustration, for example, by insisting that others follow formal procedures and policies.

These people withhold rewards unless they believe the rewards to be fully deserved. They may have difficulty giving symbolic rewards, such as certificates and trophies, but are more comfortable giving verbal or monetary rewards based on measurable performance objectives.

Possible Limitations   Sensation-thinkers get impatient with project delays. At times, they may decide too quickly on a course of action and not notice complications or new developments that need attention. Because they excel in preserving the organization's procedures and rules, they may hold on to some that no longer are valuable in an attempt to maintain stability. Doing so may not be desirable when rapid change is necessary.

Such people often overlook the personal touch, such as complimenting people, in favor of getting the job done. Their relationships with others often are tense, and they may blame others when things don't go their way. They are concerned about the possibility of negative consequences. They may repeatedly analyze situations and thus expend a great deal of energy worrying about dealing with situations that never occur. They believe that everyone can contribute to the organization if only they work hard and long enough.

Professions   Thirty-seven percent of U.S. managers are sensation-thinkers. They are interested in occupations that deal with the physical and impersonal side of the organization. These individuals may be attracted to jobs in fields such as accounting, production, quality control, computer programming, scheduling, copy editing, drafting, engineering, statistics, stock-brokerage, and finance. Their idea of organizational effectiveness tends to focus on objective indicators, such as sales per full-time salesperson, inventory cost per dollar of sales, scrap loss per unit produced, rate of return on invested capital, profits, value of production per labor hour, and cost of goods sold. Most organizations, as well as the advanced industrialized societies and their educational systems, emphasize developing and using the problem-solving style characteristics of sensation-thinkers.

The following Managing in Practice feature illustrates how one sensation-thinking manager makes decisions. Enita Nordeck, president of Unity Forest Products, displays many of the effective characteristics that sensation-thinking managers bring to their jobs.

MANAGING IN PRACTICE

Against the Grain

Enita Nordeck had no dream of running an organization. Being a single mother of four children didn't leave her too much time to think about managing a business. However, when three business associates approached her about running an old lumber mill where she had been controller, she took advantage of the opportunity. Although she had been concerned about lumber being a male-dominated field, her associates convinced her that her near fanatical attention to the financial side of the business was crucial for the organization's success.

MANAGING IN PRACTICE —*Continued*

Unity Forest Products sells exterior siding, paneling, fencing, and specialty items to builders, remodelers, and handy homeowners in the Pacific Northwest. Before Nordeck took over, the organization had been losing money. Now, it is a money maker. She achieved the turnaround by paying attention to the smallest details. She tracks cash flow daily and makes all deals. When she and another manager were traveling to Idaho to look at some computer hardware, she found a failing lumber mill that had installed a computerized milling system but that was going out of business. New equipment would have cost $800,000. She bought the used equipment for $180,000 and, under the terms of the sales agreement, didn't have to pay for it until it was needed.

When work began on Unity's new office building, Nordeck drove an hour every morning to make sure that the contractors were at the site. If they weren't, she called them and got them going. She then laid out all the work she expected them to accomplish that day. After working all day, she drove back to the work site to make sure that everything had been done as promised.

Some of her employees say that she runs Unity as tightly as a submarine. She insists that her customers pay her within ten days, for which she offers a 1% discount. By collecting bills in ten days versus the industry average of twenty-seven days, she gains the use of their cash. Unity itself has never missed a discount period. All employees are paid a flat guaranteed rate per month and a bonus. There are no separate commissions for salespersons. Monthly bonuses can range from 0 to 15% or more if the organization meets its profit goal. If a customer doesn't pay on time, all the employees lose some of their monthly bonus, encouraging employees to get on the phone with customers who might run late on their payments. Nordeck's strategy is to make sure that customers pay Unity before they pay someone else.

She walks the yard every Monday with the sales crew, inspecting every stack of lumber to be milled. If the lumber has been there for more than four days, she notes that there is an inventory problem. At Unity, sales are made first and then the mill produces whatever is required to fill the order. This approach requires unusual teamwork between sales and manufacturing. Nordeck and her key people hold at least three meetings a day to coordinate the mill's activities. Although the mill sometimes has to scramble to get product out on time, Unity turns its inventory at least once a week; the industry average is fifty-eight days. This turnover saves Unity money but places stress on employees. Nordeck compensates for the high energy levels required from her employees by paying them well above the industry average.[10]

▼ Intuitive-Thinkers

Effective managers who are **intuitive-thinkers** (NTs) are architects of progress and ideas. Such people are interested in the principles on which the organization was built and seek answers to why events occur. An ability to see and analyze across departmental lines enables NT managers to make sense of those events. They focus on possibilities but analyze them impersonally. For example, when they move into an organization, they are likely to analyze immediately the power base and determine how things actually get done. The intuitive-thinker is intellectually demanding and excels as a technical and administrative innovator. Such individuals favor long-term, open-ended projects.

An organization that does not have some NT managers will undergo minimal change, and sooner or later profits will decline. If NT managers perceive that the organization's goal is stability, they drift off to other jobs or form quiet pockets of passive resistance, ignoring rules out of sheer boredom.

They may prefer to work with other NTs, but they also need to work with those who can persuade, conciliate, and negotiate cooperation. As managers, they should be supported by a staff that can carry out the details of projects and ideas. They value administrative assistants who can digest contracts, keep track of details, check records, proofread, call attention to needed actions, and patiently perform these tasks over and over.

Relating to Others   Intuitive-thinkers typically follow the thought processes and ideas of others quite easily—and enjoy doing so. They respond well to others' new ideas, and they also champion their own causes. They enjoy solving new problems and feel stimulated rather than put upon by having to solve a colleague's problem. They have the courage of their convictions, even if others believe that they are wrong.

Employees know where these managers stand, but only if the employees ask. Such managers believe that their positions are obvious and to state them therefore would be redundant. They answer questions about their opinions frankly. They admire reason, logic, and intelligence in others and don't feel a need to minimize the contributions of others.

In an organization, NT managers are labeled the "architects of ideas," easily focusing on desired results and goals. They are most comfortable in organizations that emphasize long-term results rather than procedures and rules.

They must consciously try to remember social rituals that are important to others. Although they may be most grateful for others' ideas and contributions, they may fail to express their appreciation. They are most likely to respond to praise that recognizes accomplishments and, in particular, the influence of their work on others.

Possible Limitations   When involved in the creative process, intuitive-thinkers have enormous drive. After a program has been developed, however, they are more than willing to let someone else implement it. Because they focus on principles and abstract thinking, they tend to discount arguments based on data. They tend to operate with little specific data and rely on their intuitive abilities to identify patterns. At times, they may not be aware of others' feelings and may not consider employees (subordinates or superiors) to be valuable unless they believe them to be intellectually competent.

They may have trouble with interpersonal relations because they believe that everyone should be competent, adequate, and professional. Thus NTs expect a great deal of themselves and others—often more than they or anyone else can deliver. They need to remind themselves that people have both strengths and weaknesses. They often feel restless and unfulfilled, tending to raise standards for themselves and others and often being intolerant of mistakes and reflection after a decision has been made.

Professions   Positions that deal with new possibilities and nonroutine tasks attract NTs. Twenty-six percent of U.S. managers have this problem-solving style. They are entrepreneurs and teachers in such fields as economics, business, philosophy, and the physical sciences. They also are in systems design and analysis, architectural design, law, mathematics, and engineering design. They probably measure organizational effectiveness by the rate of new product development, market share, cost of capital, growth in earnings and long-run profits, new market development, and degree of action on and response to environmental changes.

Today many managers are trying to redesign their organizations to make them more responsive to changes in technology, markets, and global competition. Paul Allaire, CEO of Xerox, has rebuilt that company by using many of the problem-solving techniques common to intuitive-thinkers. His innovative creation of self-managed divisions is described in the following Managing in Practice piece.

MANAGING IN PRACTICE

The CEO as Organizational Architect

As CEO of the Xerox Corporation, Paul Allaire moved quickly to turn the company around. When Xerox introduced its first copier in 1959, it had invented a new industry and entered two decades of spectacular growth and profits. By the early 1980s, however, Xerox had lost its focus and market share. Low-cost Japanese competitors had entered the market, cutting Xerox's profits sharply.

In the mid 1980s, Xerox embarked on a long-term effort to generate new growth and regain its dominant position in the world copier market. The appointment of Allaire as CEO in 1990 was an integral part of the company's strategy. He has positioned Xerox at the intersection of two worlds: paper and electronics. To do so, he helped create a new organization design that balances independent business divisions with integrated research and development and technological customer operations. With his team of managers, he championed new managerial values and skills, redefined managerial roles and responsibilities, and changed the way managers are selected and compensated.

Prior to Allaire's appointment, Xerox had a "functional" organization structure, with manufacturing, marketing, finance, accounting, and other departments. Managers had a tendency to shift problems and departmental conflicts to others and wait for a decision to be made for them. Allaire redesigned the company as nine autonomous business divisions—such as the Advanced Office Documents Division—that rely on a common technology. These stand-alone businesses are organized around specific products and markets, with each having its own profit accountability. He organized sales and service into geographical customer-operation divisions so that the customer deals with only one Xerox representative. He also created a new department of strategic services that provides support for specialized manufacturing and purchasing.

Allaire believes that this new design is remarkably easy to change. When new markets or new technologies emerge that don't fit into Xerox's current structure, it can easily add another business division. Allaire gives the division presidents the freedom to run their businesses and communicate with anyone they need to—so long as they meet the objectives (e.g., sales, costs) they presented to him and his staff.

MANAGING IN PRACTICE —*Continued*

Allaire's vision for Xerox is that the firm will consist of many small groups of people who have the technical expertise, business knowledge, and information to design their own work processes to get the job done. These groups will be tied directly to customers and will be working more or less independently. For example, product designers now have to be more knowledgeable about computer systems and electronics and be able to work with customers to redesign their businesses. Allaire's goal is to organize and reorganize Xerox into "productive work communities."[11]

▼ Sensation-Feelers

Effective managers who are **sensation-feelers** (SFs) stress interpersonal relations and dealing with concrete problems methodically. They negotiate with ease and are natural troubleshooters or diplomats. They are good at putting out fires and unsnarling interpersonal problems that arise among employees—and doing so quickly. They have a talent for getting people to cooperate with them and with each other. They possess a certainty that causes others to have total confidence in their decisions and direction. If sensation-feelers experience self-doubt, they do not share it with those around them. They are adept at analyzing day-to-day work systems, spotting breakdowns and errors, and determining the types of corrections needed.

As managers, SFs understand the organization better than any other type of manager because they astutely observe operational details. They excel at getting others to cooperate in planning and decision making and in verbal and written communication. They can spot trouble in an organization while it is still minor, thus preventing small problems from becoming larger ones, allowing operations to run smoothly. Subordinates working for such managers say that things seem to happen effortlessly, without wasted time and motion. These managers do not fight the current system; they use the means available to solve problems rather than to try to change the system.

They spur action in a management team and promote group activities. Productivity is apt to be high, in part because SF managers are aware of employee comfort and working conditions. They are not likely to allow poor working conditions to exist without attempting to do something about them.

Sensation-feelers typically do not judge their co-workers, accepting their behaviors at face value rather than seeking underlying motives and meanings. To motivate subordinates, SF managers reward them only when they have completed a task. They prefer symbolic rewards, such as plaques, lapel pins, and company newspaper stories to tangible rewards.

Relating to Others   Sensation-feelers usually respond better to others' ideas if those ideas are concrete. They are predictable in working with colleagues, who find them easy to get along with. They consult with others before making decisions and try to reach consensus and acceptance of the decision. The possibility of their own failure or that of others doesn't threaten SFs, who take calculated risks and encourage others to do the same. They can change their position easily, as facts change and new situations arise. They don't worry about what might have been; they deal with what is.

Possible Limitations   Sensation-feelers may be reluctant to accept radical new theories and may become impatient with abstract ideas. Such managers often seem more interested in promoting group discussion than actually solving a problem, especially if it is an abstract problem. Their need for acceptance by others may prompt them to promote others' ideas instead of their own. They are adaptable up to the point of breaking rules and procedures. They live primarily for the moment and may have difficulty honoring commitments and decisions made in the past when they do not expect group support.

Professions   Sensation-feelers usually are interested in jobs that require personal contact with others in the organization or with customers; they enjoy working with people. Seventeen percent of U.S. managers are sensation-feelers. Such managers excel at selling, counseling, negotiating, teaching, human resource management, and many types of customer service work. For them, organizational effectiveness is influenced by employee loyalty, attitudes, turnover, and absenteeism.

In Chapter 1, we briefly introduced you to Anita Roddick, CEO of Body Shop International. In the following Managing in Practice piece, we examine how her problem-solving style influences the decisions she makes.

MANAGING IN PRACTICE

Body Shop International

Founder of the Body Shop International, an almost-all-natural cosmetics company, Roddick is one of the five richest women in England. She owns more than 950 shops in 42 countries, including more than 130 shops in the United States. In the beginning she and her husband were the only employees, selling cosmetics from their home. They decided on a name that would catch people's attention and beat back an attempt by two funeral-parlor directors on her street to block the name of the store.

Roddick crisscrosses the globe several times a year to gather leaves and other ingredients to make cosmetics. She routinely visits tribal communities, such as Brazil's Kayapo Indians and the Bedouin women of Oman, to find ingredients. She also is a social activist. Her stores hand out pamphlets promoting everything from human rights to saving the rain forest. She has funded projects for orphanages in India and Romania.

Roddick strives to create a unique environment in her stores, stressing honesty, excitement, and fun. Rather than focusing on overly sophisticated marketing gimmicks, she emphasizes consumer education, giving customers the feeling that they are buying from people they know and can trust. To make sure that her store managers believe in her philosophy, she maintains tight control over hiring. The process involves a personality test, a home visit, and an assessment of the candidate's business sense and attitude toward people—and can take three years to complete. Roddick herself always completes the final interview and has been known to ask the candidate, "How would you like to die?" The objective of the entire interview process is to select people who believe in the organization's products and its environmental and social causes. The success of the Body Shop depends largely on its ability to recruit and retain people who share Roddick's values.

MANAGING IN PRACTICE —*Continued*

She also believes that the cosmetics industry had become dishonest and exploitive of women. She believes that companies should operate on the principles of care and love. To instill these principles into her organization, she encourages upward communication through a suggestion system known as DODGI (the Department of Dammed Good Ideas). A "Red Letter" system allows any employee to bypass management and communicate directly with a managing director. She encourages employees to "think frivolously" and ties bonuses to innovative suggestions. All her staff are assessed by an immediate superior and their subordinates. She detests bureaucracy and keeps meetings short by requiring all participants to stand during them.

Extending the family feeling, the company built a modern day care facility for employees' younger children. Employees pay a nominal amount for this service. Free day care slots are offered to social service organizations for emergency placements. She encourages employees to take courses that will broaden their perspectives on life, such as sociology and urban survival.[12]

▼ Intuitive-Feelers

Effective managers who are **intuitive-feelers** (NFs) rely on charisma and commitment to the people they lead. Such managers are organizational "cheerleaders." They usually use language well and, through it, express their caring and enthusiasm for customers, suppliers, employees, and others. They easily see abstract possibilities for their organizations and particularly for the people in democratically run organizations. They excel at considering loosely structured problems that enable others to participate in the decision-making process with them. They enjoy creative problem solving and often reject traditional methods and standard operating procedures in favor of novel solutions. They are patient in complicated situations and wait for the right time to move on an idea; they are like chemical catalysts. Reasoning by analogy helps NFs explain new ideas to others. Intuitive-feelers make excellent top managers, especially if they must represent and promote the organization to customers, employees, and government agencies.

The employees of an organization that doesn't have NF managers may find the environment cold, sterile, joyless, and dull. Such managers focus on developing individuals within the organization. They are committed to the career progress of subordinates and encourage subordinates' personal growth. When NFs are in leadership roles, their focus may be primarily on developing the potential of employees, with the development of the organization being secondary. They look for and react to the best in others and give them feedback and coaching.

They head an organization well if they are given free rein to manage, but they may rebel if they believe that the system places too many constraints on them. To motivate others, NF managers give many psychological rewards. If they receive sufficient praise, they are excellent managers; if not sufficiently praised, they can become ineffective, discouraged, and uninvolved—and will look outside the organization for rewards.

Relating to Others   Intuitive-feelers relate well to others, who often view them as the most popular people in the organization. They hunger for personal contact and go out of their way to find it. They are sociable, adventurous, risk taking, and enjoy being where people are gathered. They frequently consult and maintain close personal contact with their bosses. They find the organization a source of social satisfaction as well as a place to work.

Possible Limitations   Intuitive-feelers may find themselves making decisions on the basis of their personal likes and dislikes rather than on the basis of performance measures. Powered by enthusiasm, they work in great bursts of energy, but they need to recharge their energy levels frequently. They seek the approval of both subordinates and superiors and at times may find themselves to be the champion of two opposing groups. They understand the emotions of others so well that they are vulnerable to them and want to "please all the people all the time," which inevitably gets them into difficult managerial situations.

They are likely to feel pressured because their belief systems make it necessary for every person, especially significant others, to love and admire them. This belief may cause NFs to spend too much time seeking approval and to constantly check with others until they show approval. Under these conditions, such individuals may become so responsive to the demands of others that they lose sight of their own values, beliefs, and goals.

Professions   Intuitive-feelers, like SFs, usually prefer professions that deal with the human side of the organization. They deal comfortably with all types of people—individuals and groups alike—either directly or indirectly. They excel at public relations work and shine as spokespersons because they can sell their organizations to others and help employees feel good about themselves and the organization. These individuals often do well in such occupations as public relations, politics, advertising, human resource management, some types of sales, art, and teaching. They believe that organizational effectiveness is reflected in consumer satisfaction, social responsibility, ability to identify problems or new opportunities, quality of life, and community satisfaction with the organization.

The problem-solving style of Herb Kelleher, CEO of Southwest Airlines, reflects that of the intuitive-feeler manager: a genuine respect for customers, employees, and suppliers. His problem-solving philosophy deeply influences the decisions made at Southwest Airlines. Anyone who has ever flown Southwest can sense his impact on the company he founded. His zany behaviors are well known in the airline industry. For example, when Bob Crandall, CEO of American Airlines and a native of Rhode Island, asked Kelleher what he was going to do with all the whale droppings from Southwest's newly painted plane "Shamu One," Herb said, "I'm going to turn them into chocolate mousse and feed them to the Yankees." The next day he had a tub of chocolate mousse delivered to Crandall's office with a king-sized Shamu spoon.

MANAGING IN PRACTICE

Herb Kelleher of Southwest Airlines

Herb Kelleher, Southwest's CEO, has three pillars that guide his decision-making: (1) work should be fun, so enjoy it; (2) work is important, so don't spoil it with being too serious; and (3) people are important, so remember that each one makes a difference. With these guiding principles, he has built Southwest Airlines into one of the largest and most profitable carriers in the United States. It has posted a yearly profit since 1973, a record no other airline can match. On-time arrivals and departures, a major quality measure, rank it among the best commercial carriers in the United States.

A sense of humor has always been one of the hiring principles at Southwest. Kelleher looks for employees that are broad-gauged thinkers, flexible team players, and love to fly. Tolerance for individual differences and peculiarities is important. Ann Rhoades, Southwest's vice-president—people, has turned down technically good pilots because they were rude to the reservations agent who booked them on a flight to Dallas's Love Field for an interview. Reservation agents are the backbone of this airline because it doesn't belong to a computerized reservations system like United, Delta, and American. Therefore Kelleher believes that how a person treats a reservations agent is probably a good indication of how that person will treat passengers. The ratio of applicants to hires is 10 to 1 because of the company's desire to hire only those people who will fit into Southwest's culture.

Kelleher has dressed up as Elvis Presley, a woman, the Easter bunny, and as a flight attendant to promote the airline and its values. His behavior serves as a role model for others. For example, when Southwest finished its new headquarters building at Love Field, all the staff except the dispatchers were moved into the new building. To retaliate, the dispatchers arrived early at the new building's "open house" party and set up their own valet parking just for dispatchers. They even used flags and parking cones to block off part of the parking lot for their own use. Everyone in the headquarters building then got together and decorated the dispatchers' offices like a funeral parlor, including old flowers with wilted heads. Such shenanigans are a regular element in Southwest's culture that stresses "fun."

The importance of caring for people is key for Herb Kelleher. When he read about a two-year old child who was dying of leukemia, he told the employees. The employees sent the child more than 3,000 get-well cards. Kelleher and about 25% of Southwest's people volunteer some of their time and talent to help at Ronald McDonald Houses all over the United States.[13]

▼ Summary of Problem-Solving Styles

Table 4.3 summarizes the major characteristics associated with each of the four problem-solving styles. If you are comfortable with the words used for your problem-solving style, they probably describe accurately how you gather and process information. If you aren't comfortable with the words, there may be a good reason for why you're not: You may not be sure what you prefer; you may be trying to be something different from what you are in an attempt to

TABLE 4.3   Summary of Problem-Solving Styles

ST (Sensation-Thinker)	*NT (Intuitive-Thinker)*
Concerned with technical detail	Speculative
Logical analysis of hard data	Emphasize understanding
Orderly, precise	Synthesize and interpret
Careful about rules and procedures	Ideas oriented with logic
Responsible and dependable	Objective, impersonal, idealistic
Good at:	Good at:
Observing and ordering	Discovery and inquiry
Filing and recalling	Problem solving
Goal: To do it right	Goal: To think things through
SF (Sensation-Feeler)	*NF (Intuitive-Feeler)*
Interpersonal	Insightful, mystical
Specific human detail	Personal, idealistic
Sympathetic and friendly	Creator/originator
Open communication	Global ideas oriented to people
Respond to people now	Human potential
Good at:	Good at:
Empathizing	Imagining
Cooperating	Making new combinations
Goal: To be helpful	Goal: To make things beautiful

(Axis labels: T at top, S at left, N at right, F at bottom)

Source: Adapted from McIntyre, R. P., and Capen, M. M. A cognitive style perspective on ethical questions. *Journal of Business Ethics*, 1993, 12, 631.

please others; or some other equally important reason. If the words describing your problem-solving style don't seem right for you, have a friend answer the questionnaire on pages 131–132 as they see you. This feedback might give you valuable information and help you define your natural problem-solving style.

▼ ORGANIZATIONAL IMPLICATIONS

Being able to identify a preferred problem-solving style may help clarify a person's approach to gathering and processing information. For example, perceptions of ethical situations are likely to be influenced by a person's problem-solving style. Of course, ethics do not exist in isolation, being constantly shaped by family values and income, occupation and organizational position, level of education, and various other factors.

In the following Managing Ethics feature, we give you an opportunity to compare your reasons for making a decision with those of other students. When choosing what to do, write a brief note of the reason(s) for your decision.

MANAGING ETHICS

What's Your Decision?

Assume that you are a salesperson for an organization. Please indicate what you would do in the following situations by writing your response in the space provided.

▼ Situation

1. Seeking information from purchasers on competitor's quote for the purpose of submitting another quote.

Your Response.

_____
_____
_____

2. Allowing personal feelings to affect price, and delivery regarding the sale.

Your Response.

_____
_____
_____

3. Giving gifts as sales promotions to a purchaser.

Your Response.

_____
_____
_____

4. Having less competitive prices for buyers who use your firm as their sole supplier.

Your Response.

_____
_____
_____

5. Attempting to contact other employees rather than going through purchasing to increase the likelihood of a sale.

Your Response.

_____
_____
_____

Let's compare your reasons with those of other students. Intuitive-feelers based their decisions on the morality of the situation and the organization's past practices. They follow their consciences and rely on personal integrity to determine proper behavior. Sensation-thinkers based their decisions on the

MANAGING ETHICS —*Continued*

firm's rules and regulations. They do not do anything illegal. Intuitive-thinkers, who dislike specific facts, based their decisions on overall economic impact on the organization. They make decisions through impersonal analysis. Sensation-feelers based their decisions on specific, realistic information and the interpersonal relationships of the situation.[14]

A person's problem-solving style also affects that individual's behavior in teams. Effective teamwork calls for the recognition and use of certain valuable differences of team members. Effective teams often do not have members who agree all the time, nor do ineffective teams have members who disagree constantly. A good team needs a division of labor, mutual respect, communication, openness, appreciation of differences, and a desire to act. In fact, a team often comprises individuals who have different problem-solving styles. Hence the effective team leader needs to understand how each person's problem-solving style affects other team members and, ultimately, the team's effectiveness.[15]

Many organizations (IBM, Citicorp, Exxon, General Electric, Apple, and Allstate Insurance Company, among others) use an understanding of various problem-solving styles to improve team effectiveness. For example, at Loral Vought Systems an intuitive-thinking manager headed one team. Team meetings frequently became far-ranging and undisciplined discussions of ideas, theories, and possibilities. The team leader glossed over facts and instead fostered the generation of "far out" ideas. The sensation-thinker team members felt lost and constantly tried to bring the group back to "reality." They frequently complained about the lack of focus and tended to skip meetings. The manager thought of these people as stick-in-the-muds. When a consultant pointed out these differences, the manager agreed to spend more time on agenda issues. The manager also agreed that more down-to-earth discussions would generate more productive ideas. Once the sensation-thinking team members were satisfied with the problem's definition and resulting goals, the team's effectiveness and morale increased.

If individual differences are respected and appreciated, teamwork often is actually most effective when team members have different problem-solving styles. Allstate Insurance Company put NTs with SFs on the same team. On the surface, this combination seems to be a poor one. The NT is an architect of ideas, whereas the SF is a persuader. But, as it worked out, the SF often sold NTs' ideas to the others. Generally, an NT might be consumed with an idea, but the SF can anchor the NT by skillfully getting others to accept the ideas. Similarly, combining NF and ST problem solvers might create an effective team. The NF often is a crusader, championing environmental causes, having a drug-free workplace, and the like. The NF questions the meaning of life and what the organization is doing to improve the human condition. The ST is likely to think of specific ways that these idealistic notions can be integrated into the organization. The NF thinks about long-range problems and solutions, whereas the ST thinks about short-range problems and the implementation of solutions.

One of the newest trends in management problem solving is reengineering. **Reengineering** is the search for, and implementation of, needed changes in an organization's processes.[16] Understanding the organization's environment and competitive stance helps pinpoint the processes (e.g., logistics, communications, and marketing) that really matter. Designed by management consultants whose problem-solving style reflects that of an intuitive thinker, reengineering begins with a blank sheet of paper on which employees are asked to answer the question, "If we were to start a new organization, how should this place be run?"

Reengineering experts believe that improvements in an organization's performance do not come from recycling old procedures and/or downsizing, but starting with a blank slate that is not constrained by existing methods, departments, or people—in other words, starting with an organization that has no boundaries. According to one AT&T manager, reengineering works when employees step into their customers' shoes and then participate in the effort. This approach helps challenge employees' thinking and problem-solving biases.

Facing new competitive threats from AT&T, MCI, and Sprint, GTE assembled a group of employees with different problem-solving styles to discuss ways to offer dramatically better customer service in order to attract and retain customers. This highly diverse team decided to try a reengineering project in its Garland, Texas, plant. The following Managing Diversity feature shows how employees with different problem-solving styles can be organized into a highly effective team. We inserted in parentheses the different problem-solving styles where they most likely had their greatest impact on the project's success.

MANAGING DIVERSITY

Reengineering at GTE

The reengineering team decided to focus its attention on the telephone operations of GTE because it accounts for more than 80% of the company's revenues, or about $16 billion. After examining the organization from its customers' perspective and studying the external environment, the team decided that, rather than eke out slow gains in GTE's repair, billing, and marketing departments, a radical program of change was needed. The team concluded that its customers wanted one-stop shopping—one number to call to get a dial tone fixed, question a bill, sign up for call waiting—at any time of the day (NT).

GTE's top management agreed to set up a pilot customer care center in Garland, Texas, to test the practicality of this vision. The team started with repair clerks, whose main job had been to take information from a customer, fill out a trouble ticket, and then send it to others who tested switches and lines until they solved the problem. The team wanted these tasks done while the customer was on the phone. To do so, it had to move the testing and switching equipment to the repair clerks (now called front-end technicians) and train them in using this new equipment (SF). Job descriptions had to be

MANAGING DIVERSITY —*Continued*

rewritten, computer systems revamped, and pay systems changed. For example, GTE had to stop measuring how fast people handled customer calls and start tracking how often customer problems were solved without passing them on to other employees (ST). Presently, seven of ten problems are passed on for someone else to handle. GTE's goal is to have only three of ten problems passed on to others.

The next step was to link sales and billing with repair. The team's engineers devised a system whereby customers with push-button phones could use the phone to identify any service needed (ST). The engineers had to design and install new software so that any front-end technician could handle almost any customer request. Finally, the reengineering team wanted everyone at the plant to see the results of their work and to be recognized for their efforts. The solution was a program that shows employee contributions in terms of dollars saved (SF). The company estimates that, so far, it has increased productivity at the Garland center by more than 30%.[17]

As GTE management discovered, employees with different problem-solving styles can all contribute to solving a problem, but at different times and performing different tasks. The nature and scope of the tasks often indicate which type of person may be best suited to carry them out. If the task is structured and has numerous facts and details, sensation-thinkers might be better suited for it than intuitive-feelers. Sensation-thinkers like to organize facts and set rules to guide their decision making. They are more interested in the present than in future possibilities. They are happy performing tasks that demand factual accuracy. The intuitive-feeler may question such a straightforward analysis just to challenge the group to look at various alternatives. However, if solving the problem requires a close-knit group, the intuitive-feeler may be better suited to lead the group. Because NF managers value people highly, they tend to focus on ways to improve communication and gain members' loyalty to the group. They try to help people see others' viewpoints in a nonthreatening manner.

Summary

The discussion of individual problem-solving styles focused on why and how individuals differ in terms of gathering and evaluating information. This chapter—along with the preceding two chapters on personality, attitudes, perception, and attribution—suggests ways of understanding how people affect others, view themselves and others, and learn to appreciate and build on differences between themselves and others. Individuals gather data from the environment by using their senses or intuition. Sensing people gather specific, factual data, whereas intuitive people gather global, abstract data. After gathering data, people make decisions on the basis of thinking or feeling. Thinking people solve a problem by breaking it into logical parts, whereas feeling people use their instincts when solving a problem.

The discussion of problem-solving styles concentrated on four distinct styles. Sensation-thinkers (STs) gather facts and numbers from their environment and then apply logic to solve problems. Intuitive-thinkers (NTs) use abstract principles and logic to solve problems. Intuitive-feelers (NFs) use intuition to gather data and then apply personal values when making a decision. Sensation-feelers (SFs) gather specific facts and figures from their environment and then rely on personal values when making a decision. However, many people exhibit characteristics of each style at various times and in different situations. People also tend to move toward a balance and integration of the four styles. Although one problem-solving style isn't necessarily better than another, the requirements of certain positions or roles in an organization may favor one style over the others.

Key Words and Concepts

Feeling	Intuitive-type person	Sensation-thinkers
Feeling-type person	Problem-solving style	Sensation-type person
Intuition	Reengineering	Thinking
Intuitive-feelers	Sensing	Thinking-type person
Intuitive-thinkers	Sensation-feelers	

Discussion Questions

1. Use the problem-solving chart shown in Figure 4.1 to describe how you chose the academic course(s) you are taking.

2. What is the likely influence of your problem-solving style on your selection of a job? Why do some people want to match the demands of the job with their preferred problem-solving style?

3. If an organization has managers with all four problem-solving styles, what diversity issues does this pose for employees?

4. Given the external environmental factors affecting Ben & Jerry's Homemade Ice Cream, why has it been so successful?

5. After fourteen years of legal battles, on October 2, 1990, a federal judge told Eastman Kodak to pay Polaroid $909.5 million for violating its instant-photography patents. After federal and state taxes, there is still some $600 million left. What kinds of arguments would I. McAllister Booth, CEO of Polaroid, present for spending the $600 million to the shareholders of Polaroid if he were either an NF or ST?

6. The following stories were written by senior managers while attending an executive development program. Identify the problem-solving style of each and state the reasons for your choice.

Story 1

The organization I would like to work for would need to be highly attentive to the personal needs of the employees. Also, I would need to produce a good product—one that society thinks is important. The organization should have a fine service department to service the product it sells. To keep moving forward, the company would need to be innovative and able to stay in front of the competition. These factors all lead to a more profitable organization.

Story 2

Organizations that have the greatest success in reaching established goals and objectives are those that have a staff of people who know what they are doing. Ideally, the organization would have a unique product, be a medium size (less than a thousand employees), have formal lines of communication, and produce a return on investment of at least 12 percent on operating assets. The organization would be located in a single facility in the Sun Belt. The unique product line would have limited competition, and the competition would have relatively similar quality standards.

   The organization would consist of a chief executive officer with a staff of officers of marketing, finance, operations, human resources, and accounting. The structure below these officers would allow a hands-on management style that would capitalize on the ideas of all personnel.

Story 3

Characteristics: (1) one product, (2) a highly centralized location, and (3) a small staff of professionals.

My organization operates through the efforts of several groups. Each group is loosely organized to achieve its goals and objectives and has professional personnel with the various skills required to produce our product. Each group has an adviser or consultant who functions to help the group in its task. He or she does not function as the group leader but knows all aspects of the job.

The groups set their own goals, choose their own leaders, and discipline and reward their members. Their production rates and quality are closely monitored and reported to the leaders. To some extent, the group is rewarded for high profitability. Leaders are elected by the group and change from time to time.

Story 4

My ideal organization would consist of people who are all dedicated to achieving the goals of the organization and who are willing to do so in a friendly, cooperative way. To be effective, all the people must have a servant attitude toward one another (that is, they must think not of their own interests first, but of the interests of others). An attitude of humility would prevail, and the needs of others would be met before our own.

I think of the New Testament church in its beginnings as an ideal organization. There was a structure, but it permitted everyone to share everything so no one was in need. As the organization grew and prospered, so did the people. People's needs come before the organization.

7. Should organizations attempt to select people for positions on the basis of their problem-solving styles? What would be the benefits? The dangers?

▲ Developing Skills

Self-Diagnosis: Problem-Solving Style

Please indicate the response that usually describes *your* concerns and behaviors. There are no *right* or *wrong* answers to the questions. For each question, indicate which of the two alternative statements is most characteristic of you. Some statements may seem to be equally characteristic or uncharacteristic of you. While we anticipated this, try to choose the statement that is *relatively more* characteristic of what you do or feel in your everyday life. You will be working with pairs of statements and will have 5 points to distribute among the statements. Points may be divided between each A and B statement in any of the following combination pairs:

▲ If A is completely characteristic of you and B is
completely uncharacteristic, write a "5" on your
answer sheet under A and "0" under B, thus:

A	B
5	0

▲ If A is considerably more characteristic of you
and B is somewhat characteristic, write a "4" on
your answer sheet under A and a "1" under B,
thus:

A	B
4	1

▲ If A is only slightly more characteristic of you
than B, write a "3" on your answer sheet under
A, and a "2" under B, thus:

A	B
3	2

▲ Each of the above three combinations may be
used in reverse order. For example, should you
feel that B is slightly more characteristic of you
than A, write a "2" on your answer sheet under
A and a "3" under B, thus: (And so on, for
A = 1, B = 4, or A = 0, B = 5).

A	B
2	3

Be sure that the numbers you assign to each pair sum to 5 points. Relate each question in the index to your own behavior. *Remember, there is no right or wrong answer.* Attempts to give a "correct" response merely distort the meaning of your answers and render the inventory's results valueless.

Questions		Score
1. Are you more	(a) pragmatic (b) idealistic	A B
2. Are you more impressed by	(a) standards (b) sentiments	A B
3. Are you more interested in that which	(a) convinces you by facts (b) emotionally moves you	A B
4. It is worse to be	(a) impractical (b) having a boring routine	A B

5. Are you more attracted to
   - (a) a person with good common sense
   - (b) a creative person

   A   B

6. In judging others, are you more swayed by
   - (a) the rules
   - (b) the situation

   A   B

7. Are you more interested in
   - (a) what has happened
   - (b) what can happen

   A   B

8. Do you more often have
   - (a) presence of mind
   - (b) warm emotions

   A   B

9. Are you more frequently
   - (a) a realistic sort of person
   - (b) an imaginative sort of person

   A   B

10. Are you more
    - (a) faithful
    - (b) logical

    A   B

11. Are you more
    - (a) action-oriented
    - (b) creation-oriented

    A   B

12. Which guides you more
    - (a) your brain
    - (b) your heart

    A   B

13. Do you take pride in your
    - (a) realistic outlook
    - (b) imaginative ability

    A   B

14. Which is more of a personal compliment
    - (a) you are consistent in your reasoning
    - (b) you are considerate of others

    A   B

15. Are you more drawn to
    - (a) basics
    - (b) implications

    A   B

16. Is it better to be
    - (a) fair
    - (b) sentimental

    A   B

17. Would you rather spend time with
    - (a) realistic people
    - (b) imaginative people

    A   B

18. Would you describe yourself as
    - (a) hard
    - (b) soft

    A   B

19. Would your friends say that you are
    - (a) someone who is filled with new ideas
    - (b) someone who is a realist

    A   B

20. It is better to be called a person who shows
    - (a) feelings
    - (b) reasonable consistency

    A   B

Answer Form

Please enter the numbers for your response to each question in the appropriate columns.

Questions	Column I A	Column II B	Questions	Column III A	Column IV B
1	——	——	2	——	——
3	——	——	4	——	——
5	——	——	6	——	——
7	——	——	8	——	——
9	——	——	10	——	——
11	——	——	12	——	——
13	——	——	14	——	——
15	——	——	16	——	——
17	——	——	18	——	——
19	——	——	20	——	——
Total Score	☐	☐		☐	☐
	S	N		T	F

Scoring

1. Add down each column to obtain a total for score "A" and write it in the total box. Do the same for "B."
2. Compare the totals for columns I and II. If your highest point total is for "A," circle the letter **S**. "S" refers to sensation. If your highest point total is for "B," circle the letter **N**. "N" refers to intuitive. If your total scores for A and B are equal, circle the letter **S**.
3. Compare the totals for columns III and IV. If your highest point total is for "A," circle the letter **T**. "T" refers to thinking. If your highest point total is for "B," circle the letter **F**. "F" refers to feeling. If your total scores for A and B are equal, circle the letter **T**.

Source: This questionnaire is based on the earlier works by Kiersay, D., and Bates, M. *Please Understand Me*. Del Mar, Calif.: Prometheus Nemesis Book Company, 1987; Agor, W. H. *Intuitive Management: Integrating Left and Right Brain Management Skills*. Englewood Cliffs, N.J.: Prentice-Hall, 1984; and Hirsh, S., and Kummerow, J. M. *Lifetypes*. New York: Warner Books, 1989.

A Case in Point: Whole Foods Market

Whole Foods Market was born when Safer Way Natural Foods, in Austin, Texas, decided that a supermarket format for natural foods was an idea whose time had come. It features foods made from natural ingredients and free from unnecessary additives. When it opened on September 20, 1980, there were only a handful of natural food supermarkets in the entire country. Under the leadership of John Mackey, president, it grew from one store with nineteen employees to twenty stores throughout Texas, Louisiana, California, Massachusetts, and Rhode Island.

Mackey believes that people have powerful needs and desires for affiliation and community. Whole Foods Market stores typically employ between 60 and 140 people, and each store is organized into various teams to develop a sense of community. Each team is responsible for doing its own work and selecting new team members. A new team member must be voted on by the team, requiring a two-thirds majority at the end of a trial period to become a team member. At least every four weeks, each team meets to discuss problems and make team decisions. These meetings are followed by storewide meetings to discuss news and update information and to recognize and reward outstanding work. These meetings also encourage employees to express their positive feelings toward one another. This sharing builds by turning attention away from judgment and critical fault-finding and toward respect and admiration.

Whole Foods Market practices the principle of shared fate. That is, everyone shares the organization's successes, as well as its hard times. An organizationwide bonus plan rewards employees for team profitability. All company financial information is available to employees, which Mackey believes builds trust and promotes partnership because it lessens uncertainty and fear.

Another basic principle practiced is self-responsibility. Mackey believes that too many people feel that they are victims of events beyond their control. That is, when things don't go well, someone or something else is to blame. At Whole Foods Market, he has established this principle of self-responsibility by placing authority and responsibility at the store and team member level rather than at corporate headquarters. He encourages team member participation at every opportunity and in every area that affects their daily work. He knows that team members will make mistakes because of their inexperience, but the company is dedicated to learning and growing and team members learn and grow from their mistakes. Mackey recognizes that there are many different approaches to getting things done and encourages creativity and experimentation at each store and by each team. Such experimentation may lead to new information that can help other stores and team members improve.

Whole Foods Market has made participative management possible by recognizing that there are three types of decisions: command, consultative, and consensus. Command decisions tend to be short-term operating or crisis decisions. Deciding what price to put on an item or when to reorder it are examples of command decisions. Consultative decisions usually require consideration of their impact on the entire organization. These decisions often are made by two or three people in an informal setting. Consensus decisions have strategic implications and are dealt with by the entire team. Examples of these types of decisions are whether to provide a new service, to vote a new employee onto a team; and to make any change in the organization's direction that will affect shareholders. Consensus decisions usually are taken up at the monthly meetings because they need to be discussed by the entire organization.[18]

Questions

1. What is John Mackey's problem-solving style? How is it demonstrated in the management of Whole Foods Market?
2. What are some of the challenges that Mackey and his organization face as it expands into new regions?

References

1. Adapted from Theroux, J. *Ben & Jerry's Homemade Ice Cream Inc: Keeping the Mission(s) Alive.* Harvard Business School, Case Number 9-392-025, 1992; Bellafante, G. Just Desserts. *Time,* May 17, 1993, 73; Calta, M. The ice-cream sorcerer: Will Ben & Jerry's flavor expert discover the newest taste in the eye of Knute Drawer? *New York Times,* March 21, 1993, 9; and Bittman, M. Ben & Jerry's Caring Capitalism. *Restaurant Business Magazine,* 1990, 89(17), 132–134.

2. Ruble, T. L., and Cosier, R. A. Effects of cognitive style and decision making on performance. *Organizational Behavior and Human Decision Processes,* 1990, 46, 283–295; Stumpf, S. A., and Dunbar, R. L. M. The effects of personality type on choices made in strategic decision situations. *Decision Sciences,* 1991, 22, 1047–1072. Gardner, W. L., and Martinko, M. J. Using the Myers-Briggs type indicator to study managers: A conceptual model and research agenda. *Journal of Management,* 1994, in press.

3. Taylor, R. N. Strategic decision making. In M. D. Dunnette and L. M. Hough (eds.), *Handbook of Industrial and Organizational Psychology, Vol. 3.* Palo Alto, Calif.: Consulting Psychologist Press, 1992, 961–1008; Haley, U., and Stumpf, S. A. Cognitive trails in strategic decision-making: Linking theories of personality and cognition. *Journal of Management Studies,* 1989, 26, 447–467.

4. Jung, C. G. *Psychological Types.* London: Routledge and Kegan Paul, 1923. For an expansion of Jung's ideas, see Kiersay, D., and Bates, M. *Please Understand Me.* Del Mar, Calif.: Prometheus Nemesis Book Company, 1984; Quenk, N. L. *Beside Ourselves: Our Hidden Personality in Everyday Life.* Palo Alto, Calif.: CPP Books, 1993.

5. Roach, B. Organizational decision-makers: Different types at different levels. *Journal of Psychological Type,* 1986, 12, 16–24.

6. Hoy, F., and Vaught, B. C. The relationship between problem-solving styles and problem-solving skills among entrepreneurs. *Research in Psychological Type,* 1981, 4, 38–45; Tett, R., Jackson, D., and Rothstein, M. Personality measures as predictors of job performance: A meta-analytic review. *Personnel Psychology,* 1991, 44, 703–734.

7. McCaulley, M. H. The selection ratio type table: A research strategy for comparing type distributions. *Journal of Psychological Type,* 1985, 10, 46–56; Davey, A. J., Shell, B. H., and Morrison, K. The Myers Briggs personality indicator and its usefulness for problem solving in mining industry personnel. *Group and Organization Studies,* 1993, 18(1), 50–66.

8. Abramson, N. R., Lane, H. W., Nagai, H., and Takagi, H. A. Comparison of Canadian and Japanese cognitive styles: Implications for management interaction. *Journal of International Business Studies,* 1993, 575–587.

9. Hirsch, S. H. *Using the Myers-Briggs Type Indicator in Organizations.* Palo Alto, Calif.: Consulting Psychologists Press, 1985; Hellriegel, D., and Slocum, J. W., Jr. Managerial problem-solving styles. *Business Horizons,* December 1975, 29–37; Kroeger, O., and Thusen, J. M. *Type Talk at Work.* New York: Tilden Press, 1992.

10. Adapted from Finegan, J. Against the grain. *INC.,* November 1992, 116–125; Gabriel, G. Partners in profit. *Success,* September 1992, 30–34.

11. Adapted from Howard, R. The CEO as organizational architect: an interview with Xerox's Paul Allaire. *Harvard Business Review,* September–October 1992, 106–123; Hooper, L. Xerox plans to withdraw completely from the financial-services industry. *Wall Street Journal,* January 19, 1993, A3; Dumaine, B. The bureaucracy busters. *Fortune,* June 17, 1991, 36–42; Norman, J. R. Xerox on the move. *Forbes,* June 10, 1991, 70–72.

12. Adapted from Brock, P. Anita Roddick. *People,* May 10, 1993, 101–106; Bartlett, C. A., Elderkin, K., and McQuade, K. *The Body*

Shop International. Harvard Business School, Case Number 9-392-032, 1992; Elmer-DeWitt, P. Anita the agitator. *Time,* January 25, 1993, 52–55; Butcher, L. Body Shop founder gives retail success stylish new rules. *Kansas City Business Journal,* April 24, 1992, 1–3.

13. Adapted from Quick, J. C. Crafting an organizational culture: Herb's hand at Southwest Airlines. *Organizational Dynamics,* Autumn 1992, 45–56; Maxon, T. Jet set. *Dallas Morning News Life Magazine,* January 12, 1992, 8–13, 18; Woodbury, R. Prince of midair. *Time,* January 25, 1993, 55–56; Donlan, T. G. The state bird of Texas. *Barron's,* October 19, 1992, 10–11; Welles, E. O. Captain Marvel, *INC.,* January 1992, 44–48.

14. McIntyre, R. P., and Capen, M. M. A cognitive style perspective on ethical questions. *Journal of Business Ethics,* 1993, 12, 629–634; Fleming, J. E. A suggested approach to linking decision styles with business ethics. *Journal of Business Ethics,* 1985, 4, 137–144; Dubinsky, A. J., and Ingram, T. N. Correlates of salespeople's ethical conflict: An exploratory investigation. *Journal of Business Ethics,* 1984, 3, 343–353.

15. Hirsch, S. K. *MBTI Team Building Program.* Palo Alto, Calif.: Consulting Psychological Press, 1992; For some examples of using problem-solving styles in team building, see Coe, C. K. The MBTI: potential uses and misuses. *Personnel Administration,* 1992, 21, 511–552; Bushe, G. R., and Gibbs, B. W. Predicting organizational development consulting competence from the Myers-Briggs type indicator and ego development. *Journal of Applied Behavioral Science,* 1990, 26, 357–378; McClure, L., and Werther, W. B., Jr. Personality variables in management development interventions. *Journal of Management Development,* 1993, 12(3), 39–47.

16. Davenport, T. H. *Process Innovation: Reengineering Work Through Information Technology.* Boston: Harvard Business School Press, 1993.

17. Adapted from Stewart, T. Reengineering: The hot new managing tool. *Fortune,* August 23, 1993, 41–43, 46, 48. Also see King, J. Reengineering repercussions. *Computerworld,* June 28, 1993, 149–152; Angrist, S. W. Reengineering the corporation: A manifesto for business revolution. *Wall Street Journal,* June 1, 1993, A10.

18. Adapted from Reed, J., and Cunningham, R. *Team Member General Information Guidebook.* Austin, Tex.: Whole Foods Market, 1993; *1992 Annual Stakeholders Report.* Austin, Tex.: Whole Foods Market, 1993; Personal interview with John Mackey, CEO, Whole Foods Market, June, 1993, Dallas.

5 Learning and Reinforcement

LEARNING OBJECTIVES

When you have finished studying this chapter, you should be able to:

▲ Discuss the differences among classical, operant, and social learning.

▲ Describe the contingencies of reinforcement.

▲ List the methods used to increase desired behaviors and reduce undesired behaviors.

▲ Describe the principles and procedures of behavioral modification.

▲ State two limitations of behavioral modification.

OUTLINE

Preview Case: Driver Behaviors at UPS

Types of Learning

Classical Conditioning

Operant Conditioning

Social Learning

Managing Diversity: Diversity at Coopers & Lybrand

Contingencies of Reinforcement

Positive Reinforcement

Managing Across Cultures: Attracting Japan's Brightest

Organizational Rewards

Managing In Practice: Generating Ideas

Negative Reinforcement

Managing Ethics: Are You Sick or Well?

Omission

Punishment

Managing In Practice: Positive Discipline at Tampa Electric

Using Contingencies of Reinforcement

Schedules of Reinforcement

Continuous and Intermittent Reinforcement

Fixed Interval Schedule

Variable Interval Schedule

Fixed Ratio Schedule

Variable Ratio Schedule

Comparison of Intermittent Reinforcement Schedules

Managing Quality: Diamond International's 100 Club

Behavioral Modification

Identifying Relevant Behaviors

Charting Behavior

Choosing a Contingency of Reinforcement

Problem Solved?

Limitations of Behavioral Modification

Managing in Practice: Thin Promises

Ethics of Behavioral Modification

DEVELOPING SKILLS

A Case in Point: *Stonebriar Country Club*

A Case in Point: *Synerdyne*

PREVIEW CASE

Driver Behaviors at UPS

For United Parcel Service (UPS), the slogan "the tightest ship in the shipping business" is gospel. With revenues of more than $16.5 billion dollars and 165,000 drivers and sorters, UPS is among the largest and most profitable shippers in the world. It serves customers in Canada, Europe, and Asia. In competition with Federal Express Company and Roadway Package System, UPS is now stressing customer satisfaction. Flexible pickup and delivery times and customized shipment plans are available to corporate clients. It operates the tenth largest airline in the United States. How does UPS deliver?

At 8:45 each morning, all UPS drivers begin their routes in freshly washed trucks. Packages are arranged by sorters from midnight to 7:00 A.M. Sorters are expected to sort 1,124 packages per hour and make no more than one mistake per 2,500 packages. Employees then load each truck according to strict guidelines. Drivers must be able to see the packaging labels quickly and easily. Drivers start at $16 per hour and can earn more with overtime. Every route

has been timed, and some drivers have to make 15 deliveries or pickups an hour. Drivers are trained to perform their tasks over and over again without wasted effort. They are told to keep the clipboard under the right arm and the package under the left. Keys, teeth up, are on the middle finger of the driver's right hand. They are told to look at the package only once to fix the address in their mind. They walk to the customer's place of business or home at three feet a second. The driver takes the customer's money or charge number and starts back toward the truck. Along the way, the paperwork for that stop is completed. The driver's left foot should hit the truck's first step. During an average day, a driver will make about 145 stops to deliver 246 packages and pick up 70 others.

United Parcel Service relies on extensive written records and has installed computer systems to keep accurate records. Operating costs are constantly compared to those of its largest competitors. Daily worksheets specifying performance objectives and production quotas. These production records are accumulated weekly and monthly.[1]

United Parcel Service's efficiency is based on specific principles drawn from an area of psychology called learning theory. The **learning theory** approach stresses the assessment of behavior in objective, measurable (countable) terms. Behavior must be publicly observable, which de-emphasizes the unobservable, inner, or cognitive aspects of behavior. In this chapter, we use learning theory to explore the development, maintenance, and change of employee work behaviors.

Desirable work behaviors contribute to achieving organizational goals. Conversely, undesirable work behaviors hinder achieving these goals. Labeling behavior as "desirable" or "undesirable" is entirely subjective and depends on the value system of the person making the assessment. For example, a secretary who returns late from a coffee break exhibits (1) undesirable behavior from the manager's viewpoint; (2) desirable behavior from the viewpoint of friends with whom the worker chatted during the break; and (3) desirable behavior from the worker's viewpoint because social needs were satisfied.

From management's perspective the work setting and organizational standards are the bases for determining whether a behavior is desirable or undesirable. The more a behavior deviates from organizational standards, the more undesirable it is. At UPS, undesirable behavior includes anything that results in poor quality and causes packages not to be delivered to customers on time. Standards and expectations vary considerably from one organization to another. For example, a research and development laboratory may encourage scientists to question top management's directives because professional judgment is crucial to the organization's product. A military organization, however, would consider such questioning to be insubordination and justification for severely reprimanding the questioner.

Effective managers don't try to change employees' personalities or basic beliefs. Rather, they identify observable employee behaviors and the environmental conditions that affect these behaviors. Then they attempt to control external events in order to influence employee behavior. As discussed in Chapters 2–4, an individual's personality, attitudes, and problem-solving style influence behavior. Because they often have trouble uncovering these characteristics in employees, managers usually have to focus on those behaviors that they can observe.

▼ TYPES OF LEARNING

Learning is a relatively permanent change in the frequency of occurrence of a specific individual behavior.[2] In an organization, a manager wants employees to learn productive work behaviors, which to a great extent depends on environmental factors. The manager's goal, then, is to provide learning experiences in an environment that will promote employee behaviors desired by the organization. In the work setting, learning can take place in one of three ways: classical conditioning, operant conditioning, and social learning. Of these three types of learning, operant conditioning and social learning are most important in helping the manager understand the behaviors of others in the organization.

▼ Classical Conditioning

Classical conditioning is the process by which individuals learn reflex behavior. A **reflex** is an involuntary or automatic response that is not under an individual's conscious control. Table 5.1 lists examples of reflexive behavior. In classical conditioning, an unconditioned stimulus (environmental event) causes a reflexive response. Sometimes a neutral environmental event, called a conditioned stimulus, is initially paired with the unconditioned stimulus. Eventually, the conditioned stimulus alone yields the reflexive behavior. Environmental events that precede a reflexive response control it.

The person most frequently associated with classical conditioning is Ivan Pavlov, the Russian physiologist whose experiments with dogs pioneered classical conditioning theory.[3] In Pavlov's famous experiment, he paired the

TABLE 5.1   **Examples of Reflexive Behavior**

Stimulus (S)	Response (R)
The Individual	
▲ is stuck by a pin and	flinches.
▲ is shocked by an electric current and	jumps or screams.
▲ has something in an eye and	blinks.
▲ hits an elbow on the corner of a desk and	flexes arm.

sound of a metronome (the conditioning stimulus) with food (the unconditioned stimulus). The dogs eventually salivated (the reflex response) to the sound of the metronome alone. Figure 5.1 describes the classical conditioning process.

Classical conditioning helps explain a variety of behaviors that occur in everyday organizational life. At Baylor Hospital's emergency room, special colored lights in the hallway indicate that a patient needing treatment has just been admitted. Nurses and other hospital staff state that they feel nervous when the lights go on. Similarly, Gary McPherson, Manager of Human Resources for Loral Vought Systems, was praised by Tom Cunningham, his boss, for introducing a new work system at a recent luncheon in the organization's dining room. Now whenever McPherson sees that room, he experiences a good feeling.

The distinction between reflexive and nonreflexive behaviors has become somewhat blurred. The individual can control some behaviors formerly thought to be exclusively reflex responses. For example, the use of biofeedback techniques can effectively change heart rate, blood pressure, muscle tension, and galvanic skin response—responses once considered to be exclusively reflexive.

From the managerial viewpoint, classical conditioning usually is not considered applicable to the work setting. Desired employee behaviors typically do not include reflexive responses that can be changed by using classical conditioning techniques. Instead, managers are interested in the voluntary behaviors of employees and how those behaviors can be influenced.

▼ Operant Conditioning

The person most closely linked with operant conditioning learning is B. F. Skinner.[4] He coined the term **operant conditioning** to refer to a process by which individuals learn voluntary behavior. Voluntary behaviors are operants because they operate, or have some influence, on the environment. Learning occurs because of the consequences that follow the behavior. Many employee work behaviors are operant behaviors. In fact, most behaviors in everyday life (such as talking, walking, reading, or working) are forms of operant behavior. Table 5.2 shows some examples of operant behaviors and consequences.

Operant behaviors are of interest to managers because they can influence, or manage, such behaviors by changing the results of those behaviors. The

FIGURE 5.1
───────
Classical Conditioning

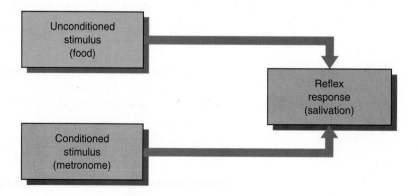

TABLE 5.2   Examples of Operant Behaviors and Their Consequences

Behaviors	Consequences
The Individual	
▲ works and	is paid.
▲ is late to work and	is docked pay.
▲ enters a restaurant and	eats.
▲ enters a football stadium and	watches a football game.
▲ enters a grocery store and	buys food.

crucial aspect of operant conditioning is what happens as a consequence of the behavior. That is, consequences largely determine the strength and frequency of operantly conditioned behaviors. Thus managers must understand the effects of different consequences on the task behaviors of employees. For example, at UPS one consequence of a driver wasting thirty seconds on each stop is to work an hour longer that day to deliver every package.

▼ Social Learning

Albert Bandura and others have extended and expanded Skinner's work by demonstrating that people can learn new behavior by watching others in a social situation and then imitating or modeling their behavior after that of the other person.[5] This type of learning is called social learning. **Social learning** refers to the behaviors we learn from observing and imitating others. People first watch others, then develop a mental picture of the behavior and its results, and finally try the behavior themselves. If the results are positive, they repeat the behavior; if the results are negative, they don't repeat the behavior. Bandura has suggested that observers often learn faster than others because they don't have to unlearn behaviors, thereby avoiding needless and costly errors.

Social learning integrates modeling, symbolism, and self-control, as Figure 5.2 shows. People imitate parents, friends, teachers, heroes, and others because they can identify with them. The symbolic process yields guidelines for behavior. If a weekend golfer observes Nancy Lopez or Jack Nicklaus swinging a golf club with good results, the observation creates an image in that person's mind. Such images, or mental road maps, help the person swing a golf club properly the next time he or she plays golf. In social situations, when those at the head table at a formal dinner begin to eat, their actions let the other diners know (serve as a model) that starting to eat now is an appropriate behavior. People also invoke self-control to not engage in observed behaviors that harm the people engaging in them. Many people, for example, have stopped smoking because of its link to cancer. They have seen or read how smoking has adversely affected the health of others.

Central to social learning theory is the concept of self-efficacy. **Self-efficacy** refers to a person's belief that he or she can handle a situation adequately. It is the individual's personal estimate of his or her ability to perform a specific task.[6] The greater an employee's ability to perform a task, the higher self-

FIGURE 5.2

A Model of Social Learning

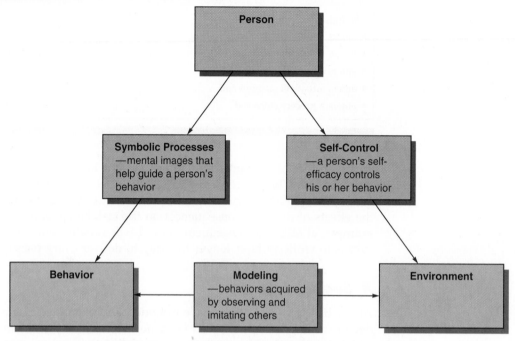

Source: Adapted from Kreitner, R., and Luthans, F. A Social learning approach to behavioral management: radical behaviorists "mellowing out." *Organizational Dynamics,* Autumn 1984, 55.

efficacy will be. Employees with high self-efficacy believe that (1) they have the ability needed, (2) they are capable of the effort required, and (3) no outside events will prevent them from performing well. If workers have low self-efficacy, they believe that no matter how hard they try, something will happen to prevent them from performing well. Self-efficacy influences choices of tasks and how long someone will strive to reach a goal.[7] For example, a novice golfer who has taken only a few lessons might shoot a good round. Under such circumstances, the golfer probably would attribute the score to "beginner's luck" and not to ability (recall the discussion of attribution theory in Chapter 3). After many lessons and hours of practice, though, if a golfer with low self-efficacy still can't break 100 (the goal), the person may conclude that the goal isn't worth the effort. However, an individual with high self-efficacy will try even harder to reach the goal. This might include taking more lessons, watching videotapes, and practicing even harder.

Generally, past experience exerts the greatest influence on self-efficacy. At work, the manager's challenge is to create situations in which employees can respond successfully to their task(s). The expectations that a manager or team members have about someone's behavior can affect that person's self-efficacy. If a manager has high expectations and gives a person the proper training to succeed, that person's self-efficacy is likely to increase.[8] If a manager has low expectations, doesn't train a subordinate properly, and the subordinate performs poorly, that behavior might persist. The reason is that the subordinate is likely to feel inadequate to the task.

People with high self-efficacy generally focus and concentrate their attention on a task better than people with low self-efficacy. People with low self-efficacy often view potential obstacles as greater than they really are and don't focus their attention on solving the problems. At Honeywell, low-performing managers were more likely than high-performing managers to dwell on obstacles hindering their ability to perform a task. When people believe that they aren't capable of doing the required work, their motivation to perform the task will be low.[9]

Applications of social learning theory for improving behavior in organizations are just starting to emerge.[10] Researchers have suggested the managers

▲ identify the behaviors that will lead to improved performance;

▲ select the appropriate model for employees to observe;

▲ make sure that employees are capable of meeting the technical skills required;

▲ create a positive learning situation to increase the likelihood that employees will learn the new behaviors and act properly;

▲ provide positive feedback (praise or bonuses) for employees who have learned behaviors and those who have served as models; and

▲ develop organizational practices that maintain these newly learned behaviors.

Coopers & Lybrand, a worldwide, 15,000-person accounting and consulting firm, applies the principles of social learning theory. In the following Managing Diversity example, we highlight several of Coopers & Lybrand's human resources practices that reward diversity.

MANAGING DIVERSITY

Diversity at Coopers & Lybrand

In an organization as large and old as Coopers & Lybrand, managing diversity effectively means managing change. Approximately 50% of the company's entry-level professionals are women. Flexible work arrangements, mentoring for female professionals, transfers of dual-career couples, and alternative career paths were issues that these professionals wanted Coopers & Lybrand to address.

With offices scattered around the world, the company urged its human resources managers to design diversity programs at local offices. If they worked, managers in other offices were encouraged to try them. For example, if a telecommuting pilot program for single parents was successful in the Newark, N.J. office, its human resource manager let others know about its success so that they could try it.

To help managers learn, the company rewarded successful diversity programs in several ways. First, it highlighted "best practices," showing managers at other offices productivity and cost reduction data. Second, it made available resources (including training aids) to help other offices implement these successful programs. Third, managers who successfully implemented diversity programs were rewarded, either by promotion or salary increase. Finally, Coopers & Lybrand established a clearinghouse that collected, summarized, and distributed information on a wide variety of diversity issues, both inside and outside the firm.[11]

In the next section, we return to the operant conditioning theory that behavior is influenced by its consequences. It is the most widely used theory of learning and has implications for designing effective organizational reward systems. We begin by reviewing its basic elements.

▼ CONTINGENCIES OF REINFORCEMENT

A **contingency of reinforcement** is the relationship between a behavior and the preceding and following events that influence that behavior. A contingency of reinforcement consists of an antecedent, a behavior, and a consequence.[12]

An **antecedent** precedes and is a stimulus to a behavior. The probability that a particular behavior will occur can be increased by presenting or withdrawing a particular antecedent. At UPS each driver prepares a "to do" list, routing the driver's deliveries for the day. The drivers are simply organizing their tasks and focusing their attention on specific behaviors. The "to do" list is an antecedent that the drivers use to influence their behavior.

A **consequence** is the result of a behavior. A consequence of a behavior can be either positive or negative in terms of goal or task accomplishment. A manager's response to an employee is contingent on the consequence of the behavior (and sometimes on the behavior itself, regardless of consequence). The consequence for the UPS driver is completion of tasks on time and getting to go home.

Figure 5.3 shows an example of a contingency of reinforcement. First, the employee and manager jointly set a goal (say, selling $100,000 worth of equipment next month). Next, the employee performs tasks to achieve this goal (such as calling on four new customers a week, having regular lunches with current buyers, and attending a two-day management training program on

FIGURE 5.3

Example of Contingent Reinforcement

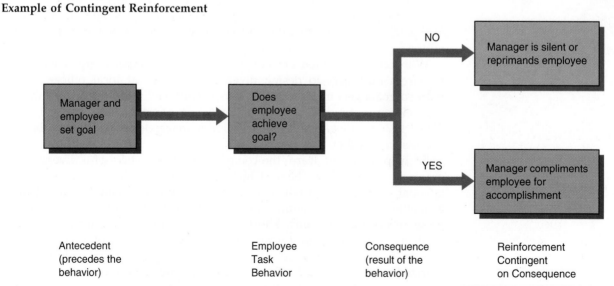

Antecedent (precedes the behavior)	Employee Task Behavior	Consequence (result of the behavior)	Reinforcement Contingent on Consequence

new methods of selling). If the employee reaches the sales goal, the manager praises the employee—an action contingent on achievement of the goal. If the employee doesn't reach the goal, the manager says nothing or reprimands the employee.

To explore the contingency of reinforcement concept further, we have to identify the principal types of contingency. First, an event can be presented (applied) or withdrawn (removed), contingent on employee behavior. The event also may be positive or aversive. **Positive events** are desired, or pleasing, to the employee. **Aversive events** are undesired, or displeasing, to the employee. Figure 5.4 shows how these events can be combined to produce four primary types of contingencies of reinforcement. It also shows whether a particular type of contingency leads to more or less frequent use of the employee behavior. **Reinforcement** is a behavioral contingency that follows and increases the frequency of a particular behavior. Reinforcement, whether positive or negative, always increases the frequency of the employee behavior. Omission and punishment always decrease the frequency of the employee behavior.

▼ Positive Reinforcement

Positive reinforcement presents a pleasant consequence for performance of a desired behavior. That is, a manager recognizes in some way an employee's desirable behavior in completing a task or leading toward achievement of organizational goals.

Reinforcement Versus Reward   The terms reinforcement and reward often are confused in everyday usage. A **reward** is an event that a person finds desirable or pleasing. Thus whether a reward acts as a reinforcer is subjective to the individual. A team leader who singles out and praises a member in front of other team members for finding an error in the group's report believed

FIGURE 5.4

Types of Contingencies of Reinforcement

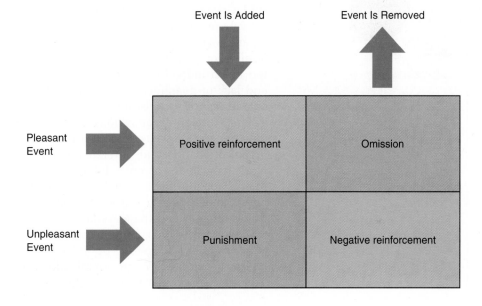

that the desired behavior was being reinforced. Later, however, the team leader learned that co-workers gave the person the silent treatment and that the employee stopped looking for errors. To qualify as a reinforcer, a reward must increase the frequency of the behavior it follows. At UPS drivers can earn more money by working overtime scheduled by management. The extra money can be regarded as a positive reinforcer for a particular individual only if the frequency of desired behavior (in this case, high performance) increases. A reward doesn't act as a reinforcer if the frequency of the behavior decreases or remains unchanged.

Primary and Secondary Reinforcers   A **primary reinforcer** is an event that has a value already known to the individual. Food, shelter, and water are primary reinforcers for most people. However, primary reinforcers do not always reinforce. For example, food may not be a reinforcer to someone who has just completed a five-course meal.

Most behavior in organizations is influenced by secondary reinforcers. A **secondary reinforcer** is an event that once had neutral value but has taken on some value (positive or negative) for an individual because of past experience. Money is an obvious example of a secondary reinforcer. Although it cannot directly satisfy a basic human need, money has value because an individual can use it to purchase both necessities and nonessentials.

Organizations often give employees information about benefits when they are hired. These benefits are secondary reinforcers. The following Across Cultures feature describes how some foreign organizations in Japan are attempting to recruit top Japanese students. Note the emphasis that these organizations place on secondary reinforcers when recruiting employees.

MANAGING ACROSS CULTURES

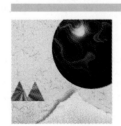

Attracting Japan's Brightest

To expand their businesses in Japan, many foreign organizations (including IBM, Coca-Cola, Pfizer Pharmaceutical, Citibank, and Johnson & Johnson) are actively recruiting more Japanese students who understand Japanese markets. Japanese organizations warn students of the potential dangers of working for foreign companies, such as being transferred out of Japan, cultural differences, too much individualism that often causes isolation from their peer groups, and lack of guaranteed employment. Nevertheless, foreign organizations are able to recruit successfully in Japan. Why?

First, foreign organizations in Japan typically require employees to work only five days a week, in contrast to a five and a half day week for Japanese organizations. Second, foreign organizations rarely ask their employees to work long hours or on holidays, observing the traditional 9-to-5 workday. Many Japanese firms "ask" their employees to work overtime entertaining guests and engage in corporate bonding activities in bars after work. These duties often extend the workday to midnight without extra pay. Most people who work in Tokyo commute by train, so late hours may mean arriving home after 1:00 A.M. and getting up at 5:00 A.M. to begin another day.

Third, because foreign organizations don't cover housing or educational expenses, employees are free to think about such matters and make their own

MANAGING ACROSS CULTURES —*Continued*

decisions instead of being pressured by the organization. Fourth, employees working for foreign organizations often feel freer to express their opinions to co-workers and their bosses than do employees working for Japanese organizations. In Japanese organizations, "fitting in" often requires employees to withhold their opinions if they want to be accepted by their co-workers.

Finally, Japanese organizations usually recruit all the employees they need for the next year and assign them to jobs. Foreign organizations typically recruit employees to fill specific jobs, such as systems engineer, investor, or brand manager. Career paths are easier to follow in these organizations than in many traditional Japanese firms.[13]

Principles of Positive Reinforcement   Several factors can influence the intensity of positive reinforcement. These factors may be thought of loosely as principles because they help to explain optimum reinforcement conditions.[14]

The **principle of contingent reinforcement** states that the reinforcer must be administered only if the desired behavior is performed. According to this principle, a reinforcer loses effectiveness if it is administered when the desired behavior hasn't been performed.

The **principle of immediate reinforcement** states that the reinforcer will have more effect if it is administered immediately after the desired behavior has occurred than sometime later. The more time that passes, the less effective the reinforcer will be. Thus the reinforcer should be delivered as soon as practical following completion of the desired behavior.

The **principle of reinforcement size** states that the larger the reinforcer is, the more effect it will have on the rate of the desired behavior. The size of the reinforcer is relative. A reinforcer that may be large to one person may be small to someone else. Thus the size of the reinforcer should relate both to the behavior and the individual.

The **principle of reinforcement deprivation** states that the more a person is deprived of the reinforcer, the more it affects the future occurrence of the desired behavior. However, if an employee recently has had enough of a reinforcer and is satisfied, the reinforcer will have less effect.

▼ **ORGANIZATIONAL REWARDS**

What types of rewards do organizations commonly use? Material rewards—salary, bonuses, fringe benefits, and so on—are obvious. In addition, most organizations offer a wide range of other rewards, many of which aren't immediately apparent. They include verbal approval, assignment to desired tasks, improved working conditions, and extra time off. At Sharp, a Japanese electronics manufacturer, top performers are rewarded by being assigned to a "gold badge" project team that reports directly to the company president. The privilege instills pride and encourages other employees to generate new ideas and products in the hope that they, too, will make the team. In addition, self-administered rewards are important. Self-congratulation for accomplishing a particularly difficult assignment can be an important personal reinforcer.

TABLE 5.3   Rewards Used by Organizations

Material Rewards	Supplemental Benefits	Status Symbols
▲ Pay	▲ Company automobiles	▲ Corner offices
▲ Pay raises	▲ Health insurance plans	▲ Offices with windows
▲ Stock options	▲ Pension contributions	▲ Carpeting
▲ Profit sharing	▲ Vacation and sick leave	▲ Drapes
▲ Deferred compensation	▲ Recreation facilities	▲ Paintings
▲ Bonuses/bonus plans	▲ Child care support	▲ Watches
▲ Incentive plans	▲ Club privileges	▲ Rings
▲ Expense accounts	▲ Parental leave	▲ Private restrooms

Social/Interpersonal Rewards	Rewards from the Task	Self-Administered Rewards
▲ Praise	▲ Sense of achievement	▲ Self-congratulation
▲ Developmental feedback	▲ Jobs with more responsibility	▲ Self-recognition
▲ Smiles, pats on the back, and other nonverbal signals	▲ Job autonomy/self-direction	▲ Self-praise
▲ Requests for suggestions	▲ Performing important tasks	▲ Self-development through expanded knowledge/skills
▲ Invitations to coffee or lunch		▲ Greater sense of self-worth
▲ Wall plaques		

Table 5.3 contains an extensive list of potential organizational rewards. Remember, however, such rewards will act as reinforcers only if the individual receiving one believes that it is desirable or pleasing.

The following Managing In Practice piece illustrates how E. J. Yancy, president of Peak Electronics, an electronics-fabricating organization in Orange, Connecticut, uses rewards and principles of reinforcement to motivate employees.

MANAGING IN PRACTICE

Generating Ideas at Peak Electronics

President E. J. Yancy wants each of Peak Electronics' 125 employees to contribute one idea a month. One such idea allowed the company to more than double its capacity to scrub circuit boards, and another allowed it to code and track its circuit boards after they have left the plant. To encourage ideas, Yancy asks all employees—assembly and office employees alike—to think about how they could improve their jobs by changing something within two arms' length of their workstations. Employees submit suggestions to their managers, who have the authority to approve a change on the spot or pass the suggestion on

MANAGING IN PRACTICE —*Continued*

to the plant manager or Yancy. Yancy promises an answer within twenty-four hours. He doesn't give people cash, but he does reward with recognition. Each month two employees are named "Thinker of the Month" and given reserved parking spaces closest to where they work, with their names on them. Yancy further emphasizes his desire to hear suggestions by holding a daily fifteen-minute morning meeting between managers and employees. Both managers and employees must be able to review the previous day's operations and preparations for the current day.[15]

▼ Negative Reinforcement

In **negative reinforcement** (see Figure 5.4), an unpleasant event is presented before the employee behavior occurs and is then removed when the behavior does occur. This procedure increases the likelihood of the desired behavior. Negative reinforcement sometimes is confused with punishment because both use unpleasant events to influence behavior. Negative reinforcement is used to increase the frequency of a desired behavior. Punishment is used to decrease the frequency of an undesired behavior.

Managers frequently use negative reinforcement when an employee hasn't done something that is desired. For example, air-traffic controllers want to be able to activate a blinking light and a loud buzzer in cockpits when airplanes come too close together. The air-traffic controllers wouldn't shut off the devices until the planes moved farther apart. This type of procedure is called escape learning because the pilots begin to move their planes away from each other in order to escape the light and buzzer. In **escape learning,** an unpleasant event occurs until an employee performs a behavior, or escape response, to terminate it.

Avoidance is closely related to escape. In **avoidance learning,** a person prevents an unpleasant event from occurring by completing the proper behavior before the unpleasant event is presented. For example, after several unpleasant encounters with a computer software package, you will learn the program's commands in order to avoid error messages. Escape and avoidance both are types of negative reinforcement that increase desired behavior and remove unpleasant events.

What happens if an organization rewards the wrong behavior? The following Managing Ethics feature illustrates how health care practices sometimes reward behaviors that many people, including President Clinton, find expensive and unnecessary.

MANAGING ETHICS

Are You Sick or Well?

Is it better for a doctor to incorrectly diagnose a healthy person as sick or a sick person as well? It may depend on the reward system. During the past few years, the number of lawsuits filed against doctors has risen dramatically. Juries have awarded millions of dollars to patients whose conditions have been incorrectly diagnosed and treated by their doctors. Consequently, malpractice insurance premiums paid by doctors have increased tremendously. To reduce their liability exposure and thereby lower insurance premiums, physicians have engaged in defensive medicine. Such practices include order-

MANAGING ETHICS —*Continued*

ing unnecessary diagnostic tests or prolonged hospitalization of mental patients. The annual costs of defensive medicine have been estimated to be more than $12 billion. If a doctor pronounces a well person sick, the doctor is paid for testing, office visits, and the like. The doctor also is less likely to be sued by the patient than if the doctor pronounced a sick person well.

If you were a doctor, what decision would you make?[16]

▼ Omission

Omission means that all reinforcing events are stopped. Whereas reinforcement increases the frequency of a desirable behavior, omission decreases the frequency of an undesirable behavior and eventually extinguishes it (see Figure 5.4). Omission reduces the occurrence of employee behaviors that do not lead to achievement of organizational goals. The omission procedure consists of

1. identifying the behavior to be reduced or eliminated;
2. identifying the reinforcer that maintains the behavior; and
3. stopping the reinforcer.

Omission is a useful technique for reducing undesirable behaviors that disrupt normal work flow. For example, a group reinforces the disruptive behavior of a member by laughing at the behavior. When the group stops laughing (the reinforcer), the disruptive behavior will diminish and eventually stop.

Omission can also be regarded as a failure to reinforce a behavior positively. In this regard, the omission of behaviors can be quite accidental. If individuals fail to reinforce desirable behaviors, they may be using omission without recognizing it. As a result, the frequency of desirable behaviors may inadvertently decrease.

Although omission may effectively decrease undesirable employee behavior, it doesn't automatically replace the undesirable behavior with desirable behavior. An undesirable behavior is likely to return if desirable behaviors haven't replaced it. Therefore, when omission is used, it should be combined with other methods of reinforcement to develop the desired behaviors.

▼ Punishment

Punishment (see Figure 5.4) is an unpleasant event that follows a behavior and decreases its frequency. As in positive reinforcement, a punishment may include a specific antecedent that lets the employee know that a consequence (punisher) will follow a specific behavior. A positive reinforcement contingency increases the frequency of a desired behavior. A punishment contingency decreases the frequency of an undesired behavior.

To qualify as a punishment, an event must actually reduce or stop the undesirable behavior. Just because an event may be unpleasant, it isn't necessarily a punishment. Organizations typically use several types of unpleasant events to punish individuals. Material consequences for failure to perform adequately include a pay cut, a disciplinary layoff without pay, a demotion, or a transfer to a dead-end job. The ultimate punishment is the firing of an employee for failure to perform. In general, organizations use unpleasant material events only in cases of serious behavior problems.

Interpersonal punishment is used extensively on a day-to-day basis. Examples include a manager's oral reprimand of an employee or nonverbal expressions, such as frowns, grunts, and aggressive body language, for unacceptable behavior. Certain tasks themselves can be unpleasant. The fatigue that follows hard physical labor can be considered a punishment, as can harsh or dirty working conditions. However, care must be exercised in labeling an event a punishment. In coal-mining or farming, for example, harsh or dirty working conditions may be considered to be part of the job.

The principles of positive reinforcement discussed earlier have equivalents in punishment. For maximum effectiveness, a punishment should be linked directly to the undesirable behavior (principle of contingent punishment); the punishment should be administered immediately (principle of immediate punishment); and in general, the more serious the punishment, the stronger its effect will be on the undesirable behavior (principle of punishment size).

Negative Effects   An argument against the use of punishment is the chance of its negative effects, especially over long or sustained periods of time. Even though punishment may stop an undesirable employee behavior, the potential negative consequences may be greater than the original undesirable behavior. Figure 5.5 on p. 152 illustrates some potential negative effects of punishment.

Punishment may cause undesirable emotional reactions. For example, a worker who has been reprimanded for staying on break too long may react angrily. This reaction may lead to behavior detrimental to the organization. Sabotage, for example, often is a result of a punishment-oriented behavioral management system.[17]

Punishment frequently leads only to short-term suppression of the undesirable behavior, rather than to its elimination. Continuous suppression of an undesirable behavior over a long period of time usually requires continued punishment. Another problem is that control of the undesirable behavior becomes contingent on the manager's presence. When the manager is not present, the undesirable behavior is likely to recur.

In addition, the punished individual may try to avoid or escape the situation. From an organizational viewpoint, this reaction may be undesirable if an employee avoids an essential task. High absenteeism is a form of avoidance and is likely to occur in situations where punishment is used frequently. Quitting the job is the employee's final form of escape. Organizations that depend on punishment are likely to have high rates of employee turnover. Some turnover is desirable, but excessive rates aren't because of increased recruitment and training costs and because skilled, productive employees are the ones most likely to leave.

Punishment suppresses employee initiative and flexibility. Reacting to punishment, many an employee has said, "I'm going to do just what I'm told and nothing more." Such an attitude is undesirable because organizations depend on the initiative and creativity that employees bring to their jobs. Overusing punishment produces apathetic employees, who are not an asset to an organization. Sustained punishment can also lead to negative employee self-esteem. Low self-esteem, in turn, undermines the employee's self-confidence, which is necessary for performing most jobs (see Chapter 2).

Punishment produces a conditioned fear; that is, employees develop a general fear of a punishment-oriented manager. The manager becomes an environmental cue that indicates to the employee the probability of an aversive event. This type of problem is especially serious when tasks require normal, positive interaction between employees and the manager. Responses to fear, such as "hiding" or reluctance to communicate with the manager, may well hinder employee performance.

Some managers rely on punishment because it often produces fast results in the short run. In essence, using punishment reinforces the manager because the approach produces an immediate change in an employee's behavior. However, the manager may overlook punishment's long-term detrimental negative effects, which can be cumulative. A few incidents of punishment may not produce negative effects. Its long-term, sustained use, however, most often results in negative outcomes for the organization, such as shoddy work.

FIGURE 5.5

Potential Negative Effects of Punishment

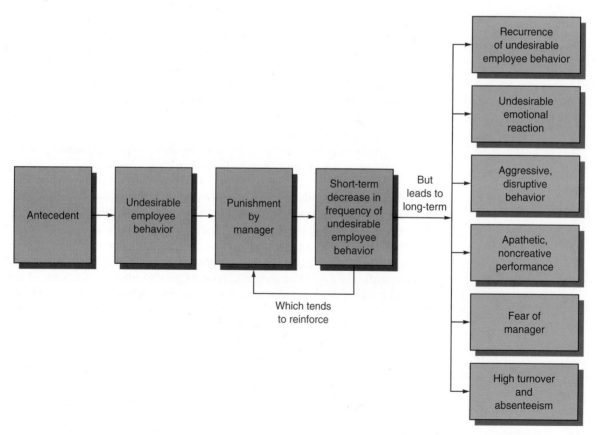

Effective Use of Punishment   Positive reinforcement is more effective than punishment over the long run. Effectively used, however, punishment does have a place in organizations.

The most common form of punishment in organizations is the oral reprimand. It is intended to diminish or stop an undesirable employee behavior. An old rule of thumb is, "Praise in public; punish in private." Private punishment establishes a different type of contingency of reinforcement than public punishment does. In general, a private reprimand can be constructive and instructive in nature. A public reprimand is likely to have negative effects.

Punishment should be connected to the undesirable behavior as immediately, directly, and obviously as possible. An unnecessarily long interval between the behavior and the punishment makes the punishment less effective. Oral reprimands should never be given about behavior in general and especially never about a so-called bad attitude. An effective reprimand pinpoints and specifically describes the undesirable behavior to be avoided in the future. It focuses on the target behavior and avoids threatening the employee's self-image. The effective reprimand punishes specific undesirable behavior, not the person. Behavior changes more easily than personal characteristics and attitudes.

Punishment (by definition) trains a person in what not to do, not in what to do. Therefore a manager must specify an alternative, desired behavior for the employee. When the employee performs the desired alternative behavior, the manager should reinforce that behavior positively and quickly.

Finally, a manager should balance the use of pleasant and unpleasant events. What is important is the ratio of positive to unpleasant events, not the absolute number of unpleasant events. The frequent use of positive reinforcement makes an occasional deserved punishment quite effective. However, never using positive reinforcement and relying entirely on punishment is likely to produce long-run negative effects that counteract any short-term benefits. Positive management procedures should dominate in any well-run organization.

John Huberman, a Canadian psychologist, began promoting the idea of positive discipline in the mid 1960s. But not until the 1970s when Richard Grote started positive discipline at Frito-Lay did the idea become widespread. Grote began searching for a better management technique after a disgruntled worker wrote a vulgar message on a corn chip and it was discovered by a consumer. Grote gave the employee a day off with pay and called it "positive discipline." **Positive discipline** emphasizes changing employee behaviors by reasoning rather than by imposing increasingly severe punishments.[18] One of management's primary duties is to help employees understand that the needs of the organization require that they meet certain standards of behavior and performance. One managerial task is to coach employees, issuing oral and then written reminders, when they fail to maintain stated behavioral and performance standards. The employee's responsibility is to exercise self-discipline to achieve those standards. More than 200 companies, including AT&T, General Electric, and Union Carbide, use positive discipline to change undesirable employee behaviors. The following Managing in Practice account shows how Tampa Electric Company uses this form of punishment to achieve positive results.

MANAGING IN PRACTICE

Positive Discipline at Tampa Electric

On the face of it, positive discipline sounds like a contradiction in terms. How can discipline be positive? According to Donna Minton, Administrator of Supervisory Training at Tampa Electric, the process works like this: "The positive discipline process is one that places responsibility for behavior change with the one person who can best change the behavior—the *employee*." An employee who comes to work late, does a sloppy job, or mistreats another employee gets an oral reminder about the behavior rather than a written reprimand. If the undesirable behavior persists, next comes a written reminder, then the paid day off—called a "decision-making leave day." The purpose of this day is for the employee to decide whether to conform to expected standards. After a paid day off to think things over, the employee must agree in writing to stop the undesirable behavior for the next year.

Tampa Electric's program has been highly successful. Ninety percent or more of the employees going through the positive discipline program have stayed with the company. Minton says that the paid day off is a one-shot chance at reform. Any employee who doesn't "shape up" faces the prospect of being terminated. The company lets the employee know what is expected, and the employee then decides whether he or she wants to meet those expectations. Sometimes the best decision is for the employee to leave Tampa Electric and go to work for a company that has different expectations. *But* the power to decide rests with the employee.[19]

▼ Using Contingencies of Reinforcement

For positive reinforcement to cause a desired behavior to be repeated, it must have value for the employee. If the employee is consistently on time, the manager may positively reinforce this behavior by complimenting the employee. But, if the employee has been reprimanded in the past for coming to work late and then reports to work on time, the manager uses negative reinforcement and refrains from saying anything to embarrass the employee. The manager hopes that the employee will learn to avoid unpleasant comments by coming to work on time.

If the employee continues to come to work late, the manager may use either omission or punishment to try to stop this undesirable behavior. The manager who chooses omission doesn't praise the tardy employee but simply ignores the employee. The manager who chooses punishment may reprimand, fine, suspend, and ultimately fire the employee if the behavior persists.

The following guidelines are recommended for using contingencies of reinforcement in the work setting.

▲ Do not reward all employees the same.

▲ The failure to respond to behavior has reinforcing consequences; superiors are bound to shape the behavior of subordinates by their use or nonuse of rewards. Carefully examine the consequences of nonactions as well as actions.

▲ Let employees know which behaviors get reinforced.

▲ Let employees know what they are doing wrong.

▲ Do not punish employees in front of others.

▲ Make the response equal to the behavior by not cheating workers of their just rewards.[20]

▼ SCHEDULES OF REINFORCEMENT

Schedules of reinforcement determine when reinforcement is applied. Deliberately or not, reinforcement is always delivered according to some schedule.[21]

▼ Continuous and Intermittent Reinforcement

In **continuous reinforcement** the behavior is reinforced each time it occurs, which is the simplest schedule of reinforcement. An example of continuous reinforcement is when you drop coins in a soft-drink vending machine. Your coin behavior is reinforced (on a continuous schedule) by the consequence of the machine delivering a can of soda. Verbal recognition and material rewards generally are not delivered on a continuous schedule in organizations. In organizations such as Mary Kay Cosmetics, Tupperware, and Amway, salespeople are paid a commission for each sale, usually earning commissions of 25 to 50% of their sales. Merrill Lynch and Company changed the commission rates for its more than 11,000 stockbrokers to help increase the firm's profits. In the past, stockbrokers were paid 30 to 46% of the commission income they generated from buying and selling stocks. Under the new plan, the minimum commission rate was reduced to 25%, and payouts for small trades that generate from $50 to $100 were reduced because small trades increase administrative costs and are not as profitable as larger trades.[22] Most managers who supervise people who aren't in sales, however, seldom have the opportunity to deliver reinforcement every time their employees demonstrate a desired behavior. Therefore behavior is typically reinforced intermittently.

In **intermittent reinforcement** a reinforcer is delivered after some, but not every, occurrence of the desired behavior. Intermittent reinforcement can be subdivided into interval and ratio and fixed and variable schedules. An **interval schedule** means that reinforcement is delivered after a certain amount of time has passed. A **ratio schedule** means that reinforcement is delivered after a certain number of behaviors have been performed. These two main schedules can be further subdivided into fixed (not changing) or variable (constantly changing) schedules. Thus there are four major types of intermittent schedules: fixed interval, variable interval, fixed ratio, and variable ratio.

▼ Fixed Interval Schedule

In a **fixed interval schedule** a constant amount of time must pass before reinforcement is provided. The first desired behavior to occur after the interval has elapsed is reinforced. For example, in a fixed interval, one-hour schedule, the first desired behavior that occurs after an hour has elapsed is reinforced.

Such reinforcement tends to foster uneven behavior. Before the reinforcement, the behavior is frequent and energetic. Immediately following the reinforcement, the behavior is less frequent and energetic. The reason is that the individual rather quickly figures out that another reward will not immediately follow the last one. A common example of administering rewards on a fixed interval schedule is the payment of employees weekly, biweekly, or monthly. That is, monetary reinforcement comes regularly at the end of a specific period of time. Such time intervals, unfortunately, are generally too long to be an effective form of reinforcement for newly learned work-related behavior.

▼ Variable Interval Schedule

In a **variable interval schedule** the amount of time between reinforcement varies. For example, Art Homma, Group Director of Technology at Rayovac Corporation, makes a point of walking through the laboratory, on average, once a day. However, he varies the times, going perhaps twice on Monday, once on Tuesday, not on Wednesday, not on Thursday, and twice on Friday. During these walks, he reinforces any desirable behavior he observes.

▼ Fixed Ratio Schedule

In a **fixed ratio schedule** the desired behavior must occur a certain number of times before it is reinforced. The exact number of times is specified. Administering rewards under a fixed ratio schedule tends to produce a high response rate and steady behavior. The employee soon determines that reinforcement is based on the number of responses and performs them as quickly as possible to receive the reinforcement. The individual piece-rate system used in many manufacturing plants is an example of such a schedule. Production worker pay is based on the number of acceptable pieces produced (number of responses). Other things being equal, employee performance should be steady. In reality, other things are never equal, and a piece-rate system may not lead to the desired behavior. For example, peer pressure can influence employee behavior regardless of the reinforcement system offered by the organization.

▼ Variable Ratio Schedule

In a **variable ratio schedule** a certain number of desired behaviors must occur before reinforcement is delivered, but the number of behaviors varies around some average. Managers frequently use a variable ratio schedule with praise and recognition. Team leaders at Lone Star Steel, for example, use this schedule of reinforcement when they give employees verbal approval from time to time. The interval of time varies. Gambling casinos, such as Bally's and Harrah's, and state lotteries use this schedule of reinforcement to lure people to play craps and slot machines and buy lottery tickets. Patrons win, but not on a regular basis.

▼ Comparison of Intermittent Reinforcement Schedules

Table 5.4 summarizes the four types of intermittent reinforcement schedules. Which is superior? The ratio schedules—fixed and variable—appear to improve performance more than interval schedules do. The reason is that ratio schedules are more closely related to the occurrence of desired behaviors than are interval schedules, which are based on the passage of time.

TABLE 5.4   Comparison of Schedules of Reinforcement

Schedule	Form of Reward and Example	Influence on Performance	Effects on Behavior
Fixed interval	Reward on fixed time basis: weekly or monthly paycheck	Leads to average and irregular performance	Fast extinction of behavior
Fixed ratio	Reward tied to specific number of responses: piece-rate pay system	Leads quickly to very high and stable performance	Moderately fast extinction of behavior
Variable interval	Reward given after varying periods of time: unannounced inspections or appraisals and rewards given randomly each month	Leads to moderately high and stable performance	Slow extinction of behavior
Variable ratio	Reward given for some behaviors: sales bonus tied to selling X accounts but X constantly changing around some mean	Leads to very high performance	Very slow extinction of behavior

Let's see how one organization used a combination of reinforcement schedules to increase productivity and morale. Daniel Boyle, vice-president of Diamond International, started The 100 Club only after everything else had failed to improve productivity and increase morale at the company's Palmer factory. The plant employs 240 hourly workers who daily turn out 1.6 million egg cartons—enough to pack 19 million eggs. After reading this Managing In Practice piece, you should be able to identify the various schedules of reinforcement the company uses.

MANAGING QUALITY

Diamond International's 100 Club

The 100 Club at Diamond International Corporation focuses on teamwork and improving the quality of production. The number in the club's name stands for 100 points. An employee earns 25 points a year for perfect attendance, 20 points for going through a year without formal disciplinary action, and 15 points for working a year without a lost-time injury accident. For each full or partial day's absence, the company deducts 5 points. Workers earn points for coming up with cost-saving ideas and participation in community service,

MANAGING QUALITY —*Continued*

such as blood drives, United Way, or Little League. Employees in the various departments also earn points by working together effectively as a team. Maintenance department employees earn 4 points for keeping machine downtime under a specified level and improving safety. Shipping department employees earn points for reaching their hourly shipment goals. Production employees earn points if they reach their production targets.

What does the employee receive for 100 points? A nylon and cotton jacket with the Diamond logo and the words "The 100 Club." The average employee reaches the 100 club in eight to eleven months. At each 50-point level between 150 and 600, an employee may choose from among twenty-five to forty gifts. An employee choosing a gift starts over from a 100-points base. An employee reaching 600 points—usually in three or more years—may select gifts such as luggage, cameras, and cordless phones.

What happened to quality? Quality rose 14.7% the first year and has steadily improved at 2.7% a year. The plant has saved more than $5.2 million since 1981 and increased productivity by 14.5%. Quality-related mistakes have declined by 40%. The cost of machine downtime has decreased from $19.50 to $16.00 per hour.[23]

BEHAVIORAL MODIFICATION

Behavioral modification refers to procedures and principles that are based on operant conditioning. Figure 5.6 illustrates the procedures used in behavioral modification.[24]

▼ Identifying Relevant Behaviors

Not all employee behaviors are desirable or undesirable from a managerial viewpoint. Many behaviors are neutral; they neither add to nor detract from the achievement of organizational goals. Thus the first and most important step in applying behavioral modification principles is to identify the behaviors that have a major impact on an employee's overall performance. The manager should concentrate on them, trying to increase desirable behaviors and decrease undesirable behaviors. Identifying relevant behaviors consists of

1. observing the behaviors;
2. measuring the behaviors; and
3. describing the situation in which the behaviors occur.

Training often is necessary to enable managers to identify behaviors. Frequently, the untrained manager confuses employee attitudes, feelings, and values with behaviors.

▼ Charting Behavior

One way to keep track of employee behaviors is by **charting,** or measuring, them over time. Figure 5.7 shows an example of an employee behavior chart. The horizontal axis represents time in months. The vertical axis represents

FIGURE 5.6

Behavioral Modification Procedures and Principles

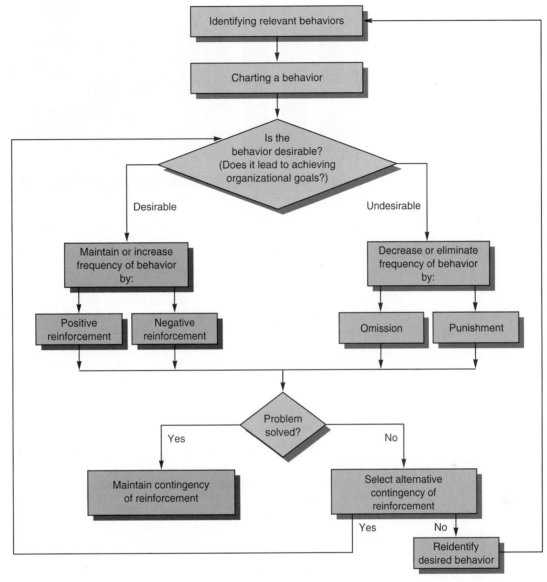

employee behavior for past-due projects. Each bar on the chart represents measurement of the employee's behavior during a one-month period.

Typically, an employee behavior chart is divided into at least two periods. The first is the baseline period, during which behavior is measured before any attempt is made to change it. In Figure 5.7, the baseline period covers June–September. Usually, the manager makes observations during the baseline period without the employee's knowledge in order to get an accurate measurement.

The second is the intervention period. During this time, the manager measures the employee's behavior after applying one or more contingencies of

FIGURE 5.7

Employee Behavior Chart

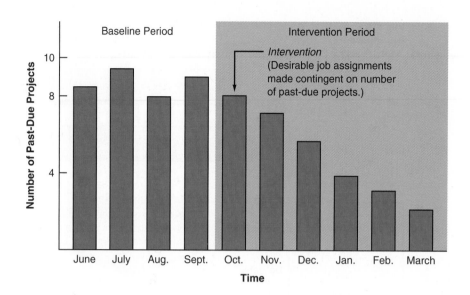

reinforcement—positive reinforcement, negative reinforcement, omission, or punishment. During the intervention period (October–March in Figure 5.7), the employee might be shown the chart—a type of feedback—which may be enough to cause a change in behavior. However, a reward or penalty frequently accompanies feedback and may affect the behavior.

Charting has two overall objectives. First, observations during the baseline period show the frequency of certain behaviors. Sometimes charting a behavior reveals that the behavior isn't as much of a problem as the manager originally thought. Second, by charting through the intervention period, the manager can determine whether the intervention strategy is working. Charting then becomes an evaluation method. Sometimes a chart reveals no change in behavior, which means that the intervention was not successful.

▼ Choosing a Contingency of Reinforcement

After a behavior has been identified and charted for a baseline period, the manager needs to select a contingency of reinforcement and apply it to change the behavior (see Figure 5.7). For desirable behaviors, techniques to increase or maintain them should be used. Obviously, positive reinforcement is the first alternative to consider. In doing so, the manager must decide which type of reward is likely to have the desired effect on the employee's behavior. The other alternative, of course, is to apply negative reinforcement.

However, if the behavior is undesirable, the manager's objective will be to decrease or stop it. Either punishment or omission would be appropriate. The manager might also decide to use a combination of reinforcement contingencies to extinguish undesirable behaviors while reinforcing desirable behaviors.

▼ Problem Solved?

Experience gives the effective manager a valuable tool in choosing contingencies of reinforcement for modifying employee behaviors. The ability to generalize from similar past situations or from similar incidents with the same employee is essential. If the manager has indeed successfully affected the target behavior, the contingency of reinforcement must be maintained for lasting results.

There is no guarantee that a chosen contingency of reinforcement will be effective. Every manager encounters situations in which the first intervention fails. The manager should then either try a different contingency of reinforcement or re-identify the desired behavior (see Figure 5.7). In either case, the manager must again consider the various steps of the procedure. In addition, the manager can simplify the procedure by evaluating the previous effort.

Changing behavior may be as difficult as reshaping concrete because people often resist changing. Over the past decade, millions of people have tried various weight-loss programs, making the diet industry a $33 billion dollar a year industry. Weight-loss clinics have sprouted in shopping centers around the country and use principles of behavioral modification to entice customers to lose weight. The following Managing In Practice feature illustrates how many diet centers use the principles of behavioral modification. Consultants and governmental agencies estimate that 95% of the people who go to a commercial diet center fail to maintain their lower weights five years after participating in a program.

MANAGING IN PRACTICE

Thin Promises

Disc jockeys, celebrities, and others endorse weight-loss programs they swear work on them. Liquid diets, such as Optifast, and other diet plans—Weight Watchers and Jenny Craig, among others—advertise weight-loss accomplishments by those who use their diet programs. But do they really work?

Typically, the weight-loss center weighs and measures the dieter to start the program's baseline period. The dieter and the counselor then establish weight-loss goals. Usually, two or more pounds drop off the first week because early losses are water, not fat. This early loss give the dieter positive reinforcement that the diet program is working. The dieter normally has to buy food from the diet center and, in some programs, forgoes food altogether. Food substitutes account for 85% of the center's revenues because they are sold solely through its diet centers. At Jenny Craig, for example, the average dieter wants to lose 30 pounds. At a rate of $1^{1}/_{2}$ to 2 pounds per week (the usual goal), the food bill would be $920. For liquid diets, the dieter substitutes from two to six packets of liquid formula a day for food, depending on their calorie allotment. As the person loses additional weight, he or she receives counseling on types of food and how to eat, exercise sessions, and motivational programs. The positive reinforcement received each week further encourages the dieter to buy additional foods, attend more exercise classes, and participate in other activities sponsored by the diet center. The diet center's counselor charts progress and each weight-loss achievement.

What are the results? About 50% of the people drop out of programs before reaching their ultimate weight-loss goals. Of those who remain in programs, about two out of three keep off half or more of their lost weight up to two years. These results are not surprising considering that some liquid diet manufacturers lure doctors with promises that they can make good money by moonlighting in a diet center. Counselors also are rewarded by being given as many dieters as they can handle. This approach prompted the president of the American Society of Bariatric Physicians to state that many counselors' philosophy is simply "Here you are, here's your packet. Wham, bam, get out the door."[25]

▼ Limitations of Behavioral Modification

There are two general limitations to the use of behavioral modification procedures and principles: individual differences and group norms. We describe each limitation and then briefly describe ways in which the effective manager can overcome them.

Individual Differences   Behavioral modification often ignores individual differences in needs, values, abilities, and desires.[26] When Diamond International Corporation set up its positive reinforcement system, it assumed that all employees valued prizes and that all employees could perform their assigned tasks. However, the company found that what is reinforcing to one person may not be to another.

These individual differences can be recognized in two ways. First, organizations can try to select and hire employees who value the rewards offered. Proper selection can lead to hiring employees whose needs most closely match the reinforcers provided by the organization. Although not easy to do, it can be an effective way for organizations to minimize individual differences.

Second, employees can be allowed to participate in determining their rewards. Thus, if the present contingencies of reinforcement are ineffective, managers can ask employees what they would do to correct the situation. This method allows employees to have a greater voice in designing their work environment and should lead to greater employee involvement. However, if this method is used simply to exploit employees, they will look for ways to get around it.

Group Norms   When workers feel that management is trying to exploit them, group norms emerge that aim to control the degree of cooperation with management. This control typically takes the form of restricting output. When this situation exists, the implementation of a program (particularly one that relies on praise and other nonmaterial rewards) is likely to meet with stiff resistance. Workers feel that they have little reason to cooperate with management because cooperation may lead to pressure to increase productivity, without a corresponding increase in pay.

The power of group norms can reduce the effectiveness of most organizational reward systems. When employees and managers have a history of distrust, the principles covered in this chapter probably will not help. In that case, building an atmosphere of trust between employees and managers is a necessary first step. Once that has been done, these principles have a better chance of working.

▼ Ethics of Behavioral Modification

Behavioral modification continues to stir controversy in organizations, centering on a person's freedom and dignity. According to proponents of behavioral modification, the way to manage people effectively is to establish control systems that shape their behaviors. Recognizing that behaviors are shaped by their consequences, managers should administer rewards in ways that promote desirable behaviors from the organization's point of view. They shouldn't worry too much about the individuals' freedom to choose which behaviors to engage in to satisfy their own needs and desires.

Opponents of behavioral modification argue that there is an ethical question involved in deciding what is good or beneficial for other people and in having the power to force or manipulate them into doing what has been decided. These individuals object to what coercion and manipulation do to a person's sense of self-worth. Promising employees a reward for doing a task they already enjoy doing can lead them to view the reward as an incentive for performing the task, thus undermining their enjoyment of the task. A person may think, "If I have to be bribed or forced into doing this, I must not enjoy doing the task for its own sake." In essence, shouldn't employees enjoy doing a task rather than have managers manipulate them into doing it? Furthermore, in contrast to the widespread use of punishment, wouldn't the use of positive reinforcement be more humanitarian?[27]

There are other problems to consider as well. Employees may engage only in those behaviors that can be measured and ignore those that can't be. For example, managers may reward the quantity of work produced and overlook its quality. Or they may rely on measuring tardiness or absenteeism of employees, both of which can easily be measured, rather than evaluate the quality of their employees' work, which often is more difficult to measure. Under such conditions, the quality of the employees' work may suffer, but they show up on time for work. Second, many managers feel societal pressure to reinforce behaviors that they really don't want to reinforce. Employees may engage in behaviors such as recycling campaigns or carpooling, even though such behaviors may interfere with employees' effectiveness. For example, carpooling might limit an employee's ability to work overtime to finish a priority project.

Summary

Classical conditioning began with the work of Pavlov, who studied reflex behaviors. A metronome (conditioning stimulus) was started when food was placed in the dog's mouth (unconditioned stimulus). Soon, the sound of the metronome alone evoked salivation.

Operant conditioning focuses on the effects of reinforcement on desirable and undesirable behaviors. Changes in behavior result from the consequences of previous behavior. People tend to repeat a behavior that leads to a pleasant result and not repeat a behavior that leads to an unpleasant result. In short, when a behavior is reinforced, it is repeated; when it is punished or not reinforced, it isn't repeated.

Social learning theory focuses on people learning new behaviors by observing others and then modeling their own behavior on that person's. A central part of the theory is the concept of self-efficacy. A person's self-efficacy influences how the person performs in a situation, how long the person persists in doing a task, and how much effort the person will expend on a task.

There are two types of reinforcement: (1) positive reinforcement, which increases a desirable behavior because the person is provided with a pleasurable outcome after the behavior has occurred; and (2) negative reinforcement, which also maintains the desirable behavior by presenting an unpleasant event before the behavior occurs and stopping the event when the behavior occurs. Both positive and negative reinforcement increase the frequency of a desirable behavior. Conversely, omission and punishment reduce the frequency of an undesirable behavior. Omission involves stopping everything that reinforces the behavior. Punishment is an unpleasant event that follows a behavior and reduces the probability that the behavior will be repeated.

There are four schedules of reinforcement. The fixed interval schedule gives rewards at regular intervals (for example, a weekly or monthly paycheck). In the variable interval schedule the reward is given around some average time during a specific period of time (for example, the plant manager walking through the plant on the average of five times a week). The fixed ratio schedule ties rewards to certain outputs (for example, a piece-rate system). In the variable ratio schedule the reward is given around some mean, but the number of behaviors varies (as does a slot machine).

The procedures that can be used in applying the principles of behavior modification include identifying behaviors, charting these behaviors, and choosing a contingency of reinforcement to obtain desirable behaviors and stop undesirable behaviors.

Key Words and Concepts

Antecedent
Aversive events
Avoidance learning
Behavioral modification
Charting
Classical conditioning
Consequence
Contingency of reinforcement
Continuous reinforcement
Escape learning
Fixed interval schedule
Fixed ratio schedule
Intermittent reinforcement
Interval schedule

Learning
Learning theory
Negative reinforcement
Omission
Operant conditioning
Positive discipline
Positive events
Positive reinforcement
Primary reinforcer
Principle of contingent
 reinforcement
Principle of immediate
 reinforcement

Principle of reinforcement
 deprivation
Principle of reinforcement size
Punishment
Ratio schedule
Reflex
Reinforcement
Reward
Secondary reinforcer
Self-efficacy
Social learning
Variable interval schedule
Variable ratio schedule

Discussion Questions

1. How can managers apply the principles of learning to improve the employees' performance?

2. What ethical considerations should an organization consider before using a behavioral modification program?

3. How can team leaders use punishment effectively?

4. Why do some people find gambling addictive? What types of reinforcement schedules do gambling casinos use?

5. Which are the most effective reinforcement schedules for maintaining desirable behaviors over the long run?

6. Identify the types of reinforcement used by managers at Diamond International Corporation. Why are they effective?

7. Describe the basic differences among classical conditioning, social learning, and operant conditioning. Which theory is most important for managers? Why?

8. What are some of the pitfalls in the rewards used in the U.S. health care system? How can they be overcome?

9. Visit either a local health club or diet center and interview the manager. What types of rewards does it give members who achieve their targets? Does it use punishment?

10. Can managers use positive discipline principles effectively in managing diversity in the workplace? What are some limitations to their use?

11. How can you use social learning theory to improve your own performance?

▲ Developing Skills

A Case in Point: Stonebriar Country Club

Stonebriar Country Club has an exercise and physical fitness program for its 400 members. A person who joins this program first meets with one of two fitness directors for a general health and fitness assessment. This assessment includes a comprehensive physical examination by the person's own doctor and the person's statement of goals. After the evaluation, the director determines fitness-related activities for the participant.

The fitness director also presents the program's overall goal. It is based on a point system that relates directly to cardiovascular fitness. For example, jogging two miles in twenty minutes is worth six points. Walking on a treadmill at 3.7 miles per hour on an incline of eight degrees for twenty minutes is worth five points. For general fitness, a person should achieve 30 points per week.

With the overall goal of 30 points, the directors set specific week-by-week goals for members during the first ninety days. These short-term goals are always measurable and objective. For example, a member's goal might be to get 10 points the first week, walk two miles a day for two weeks,

and attend two fitness classes. As members reach goals, they receive rewards, such as a tote bag, sweatshirt, T-shirt, or jogging suit. Numerous other rewards are given for specific behaviors, such as earning a place on the pounds-lost list.

Members log points on the computer after completing aerobic activities. The computer keeps track of the number of points earned and provides each member with immediate feedback on the total number of points earned to date. Each month, members receive printouts showing their total points. The two directors also receive copies of each report. Members who haven't been logging points receive a cartoon card from a director saying that they were missed. If a member still doesn't log any points during the next month, the director calls the person to find out if there are any physical reasons why the member isn't doing so. If there are no physical reasons, the director tries to get the member to return to the program.

Questions

1. What types of reinforcement does the Stonebriar Country Club use?
2. What schedule of reinforcement does it use with its members?

A Case in Point: Synerdyne

Jan Perkins has just retired after thirty years with your firm. She was well liked by everyone and earned $73,125 in commissions on printing sales per year. As her replacement you

are having dinner with one of her best customers, Mary Stevens. She works for Beta Corporation and bought $150,000 in printing services from your company last year. Perkins's commissions on these sales were $9,000. You have been emphasizing to Stevens how you plan to continue the same high-quality service that Perkins was providing.

Stevens responds that she has recently talked to several other printers who also provide good service. She wonders if you intend to continue Perkins's special support activities. You say that you aren't sure what these activities entail. Stevens indicates that Perkins paid $2,000 for Stevens's trip to Hawaii each winter to help relieve her arthritis and get some sun. She also indicates that she had received other "deals," such as theater tickets, because of her large orders. She indicates that, because everybody in the industry does it, she sees no problem with it.

You face a difficult choice. The president of Synerdyne has recently drafted a corporate policy on ethics and the importance of high moral standards in dealing with customers and employees. There have been no well-defined guidelines for moral conduct for situations like this in the past. You guess that the president probably doesn't know about the deals that Perkins gave Stevens. Without that account, you probably can't reach your sales quota for the year. If you don't, you won't get a bonus and may be given a cheaper company car to drive.[28]

Question

1. Be prepared to play the role of a salesperson in front of the class or some other small group. What would you say? How does the Synerdyne's reward system affect your answer?

References

1. Adapted from Vogel, T., and Hawkins, C. Can UPS deliver goods in the new world? *Business Week,* June 4, 1990, 80–82; Labich, K. Big changes at big brown. *Fortune,* January 18, 1988, 56–64; Hawkins, C. After a U-turn, UPS really delivers: The giant shipper has radically changed its corporate culture. *Business Week,* May 31, 1993, 92–94.

2. Akin, G. Varieties of managerial learning. *Organizational Dynamics,* Autumn 1987, 36–48.

3. Rescorla, R. A. Pavlovian analysis of goal-directed behavior. *American Psychologist,* 1987, 42, 119–129.

4. Skinner, B. F. *About Behaviorism.* New York: Knopf, 1974.

5. For excellent overviews, see Wood, R., and Bandura, A. Social cognitive theory of organizational management. *Academy of Management Review,* 1989, 13, 361–384; Bandura, A. *Social Learning Theory.* Englewood Cliffs, N.J.: Prentice-Hall, 1977; Ostroff, C., and Kozlowski, S. W. J. Organizational socialization as a learning process: The role of information acquisition. *Personnel Psychology,* 1992, 45, 849–874.

6. Gist, M. E., and Mitchell, T. R. Self-efficacy: A theoretical analysis of its determinants and malleability. *Academy of Management Review,* 1992, 17, 183–211.

7. Mathieu, J. E., Martineau, J. W., and Tannenbaum, S. I. Individual and situational influences on the development of self-efficacy: Implications for training effectiveness. *Personnel Psychology,* 1993, 46, 125–148.

8. Bandura, A. Social cognition theory of self-regulation. *Organizational Behavior and Human Decision Processes,* 1991, 50, 248–287.

9. For excellent examples of social learning theory in organizations, see Sims, H. P., Jr., and Lorenzi, P. *The New Leadership Paradigm: Social Learning and Cognition in Organizations.* Newbury Park, Calif.: Sage, 1992.

10. For an insightful review, see Manz, C. C., and Sims, H. P., Jr. *SuperLeadership: Leading Others to Lead Themselves.* New York: Prentice-Hall, 1989.

11. Adapted from DeLuca, J. M., and McDowell, R. N. Managing Diversity: A Strategic "Grass Roots" Approach. In S. E. Jackson and Associates (eds.), *Diversity in the Workplace: Human Resources Initiatives.* New York: Guilford Press, 1992, 227–247.

12. These principles are based on Thorndike's law of effect and can be found in Thorndike, E. L. *Educational Psychology: The Psychology of Learning,* vol. 2. New York: Columbia Teachers College, 1913.

13. Adapted from Kim, J. A. Japanese firms competing for workers. *Japan Times,* May 21, 1992, 3.

14. For an excellent overview, see Luthans, F., and Kreitner, R. *Organizational Behavior Modification and Beyond.* Glenview, Ill.: Scott, Foresman, 1985.

15. Adapted from Yancy, E. J. Modernizing the suggestion box. *Inc.,* October 1992, 36.

16. Adapted from Boettger, R. D., and Greer, C. R. On the wisdom of rewarding A while hoping for B. *Organization Science,* 1994, in press.

17. Trevino, L. K., and Ball, G. A. The social implications of punishing unethical behavior: observers' cognitive and affective reactions. *Journal of Management,* 1992, 18, 717–768; Dalton, D. R., and Todor, Wm. D. Turnover, transfer, absenteeism: An interdependent perspective. *Journal of Management,* 1993, 19, 193–220.

18. Sherman, M., and Lucia, A. Positive discipline and labor arbitration. *Arbitration Journal,* June 1992, 56–58.

19. Based on telephone conversations with Ms. Donna Minton, Administrator of Supervisory Training, Tampa Electric, September, 1993.

20. Hamner, W. C., and Hamner, E. Behavior modification on the bottom line. *Organizational Dynamics,* Winter 1976, 2–21.

21. Bandura, A. *Principles of Behavior Modification.* New York: Holt, Rinehart and Winston, 1969.

22. Dalrymple, D. J., and Cron, Wm. L. *Sales Management,* 5th ed. New York: John Wiley & Sons, 1995.

23. Adapted from Boyle, D. C. The 100 club. *Harvard Business Review,* March–April 1987, 26–27.

24. Luthans, F., and Schweizer, J. How behavior modification techniques can improve total organizational performance. *Management Review,* September 1979, 43–50.

25. Adapted from Barrett, A. How can Jenny Craig keep on gaining? *Business Week,* April 12, 1993, 52–53; Cake eaters dream. *Time,* July 26, 1993; Long, P. Thin promises. *Vogue,* October 1990, 400–401, 440.

26. Komaki, J. L., Desselles, M. L., and Bowman, E. D. Definitely not a breeze: Extending an operant model of effective supervision to teams. *Journal of Applied Psychology,* 1989, 74, 522–529; Locke, E. A. The myths of behavior mod in organizations. *Academy of Management Review,* 1977, 2, 543–553.

27. Organ, D. W. *Organizational Citizenship Behavior: The Good Soldier Syndrome.* Lexington, Mass.: Lexington, 1988; Trevino, L. K. The social effects of punishment in organizations: A justice perspective. *Academy of Management Review,* 1992, 17, 647–676; Taylor, S. M., and Giannantonio, C. A. Forming, adapting and terminating the employment relationship: A review of the literature from individual, organizational, and interactionist perspective. *Journal of Management,* 1993, 19, 461–515.

28. Adapted from Dalrymple, D. J., and Cron, Wm. L. *Sales Management,* 4th ed. New York: John Wiley & Sons, 1992, 241.

6 Work Motivation

When you have finished studying this chapter, you should be able to:

▲ Define motivation and the challenges of motivating others.

▲ Explain and apply the needs hierarchy, ERG, achievement motivation, and motivator-hygiene content theories of motivation.

▲ Describe and apply the expectancy and equity process theories of motivation.

▲ State the organizational implications for each of the motivation theories.

OUTLINE

Preview Case: Bill Gates and Microsoft

Essentials of Motivation

Core Processes

Challenges in Motivating Others

Content Theories of Motivation

Needs Hierarchy Theory

ERG Theory

Managing Diversity: When English Isn't So Plain

Achievement Motivation Theory

Managing in Practice: Instant Rewards for Big Deals

Motivator-Hygiene Theory

Managing Across Cultures: Motorola's Guadalajara Employees

Matching Content Theories

Process Theories of Motivation

Expectancy Theory

Managing Across Cultures: Defining Productivity in Japan

Managing Quality: Working at Home Depot

Equity Theory

Managing Ethics: To Steal or Not: That's the Question

Matching Process Theories

DEVELOPING SKILLS

Self-Diagnosis: *What Do You Want from Your Job?*

A Case in Point: *Robert Princeton*

PREVIEW CASE

Bill Gates and Microsoft

In 1975, Microsoft Corporation had three employees, and its first year's sales were only $16,000. By 1993, Microsoft employed more than 14,430 people and had sales of more than $3.75 billion. Headquartered at the Microsoft campus in Redlands, Washington, ten miles east of Seattle, it has manufacturing plants throughout the world. Despite its rapid growth, Microsoft tries to retain the feeling of a small firm. For example, once a year, all Microsoft employees attend a presentation by top management at each location throughout the world. During the Holiday Season, employees at each location gather for an annual party and each summer hold a picnic.

During the early 1980s, Bill Gates, Microsoft's CEO, and key employees developed the motivational and teamwork programs that have been an integral part of the company's unparalleled success. The motivational program was simple: reverence for the individual. Gates pays attention to employees' needs and gives people the feeling that their work is important in achieving the company's mission.

Gates lets people do their own thing in an informal atmosphere. Employees work long, hard hours to develop products that they hope will make them wealthy someday. Employees receive profit and loss statements that clearly identify which products are making and losing money. Microsoft pays employees working on products making money more than those working on products that customers aren't buying. The company also encourages employees to buy Microsoft stock. The use of electronic, or "E," mail to communicate directly, even with Gates himself, maintains openness from top to bottom in the organization.

Gates and his managers also try hard to build successful teams to tackle tough problems. They divide employees into work groups and establish goals that small teams of employees can handle. These teams are small enough for Gates and his managers to sit around a table and chat with them. Although Gates delegates freely, his grasp of details enables him to help employees do their jobs better. He is as likely to check the math in meeting handouts as he is to clarify fuzzy marketing programs.[1]

I n the summer of 1994, Bill Gates looked back on Microsoft's remarkable technical and financial achievements. Its growth and consistently high profits demonstrate its past success. Microsoft now needs to identify new opportunities for growth and develop new ways to continue to generate innovative computer software applications. As the business becomes more complex, Gates realizes that, more than ever, employees must have fun and feel empowered to make decisions. He knows that these will be difficult challenges.

Motivation represents the forces acting on or within a person that cause the person to behave in a specific, goal-directed manner. Employee motivation affects productivity, so one of management's jobs is to channel employee motivation effectively to achieve organizational goals. Alain Gomez, Chairman and CEO of Thomson, a high-technology French industrial corporation, says that his greatest challenge is to attract, manage, and develop a worldwide work force. With Thomson's RCA and GE brands competing for the high end of the U.S. television market, Gomez must come up with and use cost-effective motivational systems that will maintain timely, high-quality workmanship. Permitting employees to participate in incentive programs in its Marion, Indiana, plant has improved productivity. The company achieved the same result by providing employee housing and safe working conditions in Thomson's new Bangkok, Thailand, plant.[2] Table 6.1 highlights some of the factors that managers must address when dealing with multicultural work force motivation. Note the diversity in what employees say they want. An effective manager, however, must be able to identify and understand these differences and help people satisfy their wants and needs in the organization.[3]

TABLE 6.1   Diversity in the Work Force: What Do People Want?

Younger and Older Employees Want

To have more respect for their life experiences
To be taken seriously
To be challenged by their organizations, not patronized

Women Want

To be recognized as equal contributors
To have active support of male colleagues
To have work and family issues actively addressed by organizations

Men Want

To have the same freedom to grow/feel that women have
To be perceived as allies, not the enemy
To bridge the gap with women at home and at work

People of Color Want

To be valued as unique individuals, as members of ethnically diverse groups, as people of
    different races, and as equal contributors
To establish more open, honest, working relationships with people of other races and ethnic
    groups
To have the active support of white people in fighting racism

White People Want

To have their ethnicity acknowledged
To reduce discomfort, confusion, and dishonesty in dealing with people of color
To build relationships with people of color based on common goals, concerns, and mutual
    respect for differences

Disabled People Want

To have greater acknowledgment of and focus on abilities, rather than on disabilities
To be challenged by colleagues and organizations to be the best
To be included, not isolated

Able-Bodied People Want

To develop more ease in dealing with physically disabled people
To give honest feedback and appropriate support without being patronizing or
    overprotective

Gay Men and Lesbians Want

To be recognized as whole human beings, not just sexual beings
To have equal employment protection
To have increased awareness among people regarding the impact of heterosexism in the
    workplace

Heterosexuals Want

To become more aware of lesbian and gay issues
To have a better understanding of the legal consequences of being gay in America
To increase dialogue about heterosexist issues with lesbians and gay men

Source: Adapted from Loden, M., and Rosener, J. *Workforce America!*, Homewood, Ill.: Business One
Irwin, 1991, 76–78.

Motivational experts might not agree about everything that motivates individuals and the effects of working conditions over their careers, but they do
agree that the following organizational and work-setting factors are crucial.

▲ Individuals must be attracted not only to join the organization but also
    to remain in it.

▲ Individuals must be allowed to perform the task for which they were hired.

▲ Individuals must go beyond routine performance and become creative and innovative in their work.

Thus for an organization to be effective management must tackle the motivational problems involved in stimulating people's desires to be members of the organization and productive workers.

▼ ESSENTIALS OF MOTIVATION

A key motivational principle states that an individual's performance is a function of both ability and motivation. Mathematically, we may state this principle as

Performance = f(ability × motivation).

According to this principle, no task can be performed successfully unless the person who is to carry it out has the ability to do so. **Ability** is the person's talent for performing specific tasks. This talent might include intellectual competencies (such as verbal, abstract, and spatial skills) and manual competencies (such as physical strength and dexterity).

However, regardless of how intelligent, skilled, or dexterous a person may be, ability alone isn't enough to ensure a high level of performance. The person must also want to achieve that level. Discussions of motivation generally center on (1) what drives behavior, (2) which direction behavior takes, and (3) how to maintain this behavior.

▼ Core Processes

The motivational process begins with identifying a person's needs (step 1 in Figure 6.1). **Needs** are deficiencies that a person experiences at any particular time. These deficiencies may be psychological (such as the need for recognition), physiological (such as the need for water, air, or food), or social (such as the need for friendship). Needs create tensions within the individual, who finds them uncomfortable and wants to reduce or eliminate them. Hence

FIGURE 6.1

Core Motivational Process

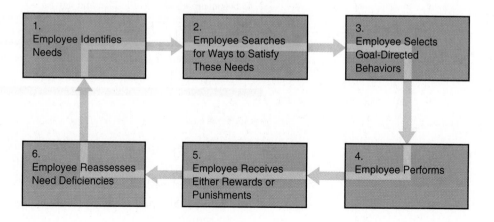

needs may act as energizers, their presence spurring the individual to act (step 2) to meet them.

Motivation is goal directed (step 3). A **goal** is a specific result an individual wants to achieve.[4] Accomplishing goals may significantly reduce the individual's needs. Some employees have a strong desire for advancement and an expectation that working long hours will lead to a promotion. However, such needs, desires, and expectations may create tension, making employees feel uncomfortable. In such cases employees can overcome this feeling by acting to reduce the tension. For example, employees who want to advance may seek work on major problems facing the organization in order to influence attainment of its goals and gain senior managers' attention (step 4). By giving promotions and raises, the company sends signals (feedback) to these employees that their need for advancement and their behaviors are appropriate (step 5). When the employees receive these rewards (or punishments in the event of failure), they reassess their needs (step 6).

▼ Challenges in Motivating Others

The general model of the motivational process just described is simple and straightforward. In the real world, of course, the process isn't so clear-cut. The first challenge is that motives can only be inferred; they cannot be seen. Return to Table 6.1 and note what different groups of employees want. Can managers observe any of these factors, or must they infer all of them? Melissa Driscoll, manager at Consolidated Edison's Reactor and Fuel Engineering Indian Point Station in New York City, observes two engineers in the quality control department inspecting engineering diagrams. She knows that both employees are responsible for the same type of work, have similar abilities, and have been with the organization for about five years. One employee is able to spot design problems more easily and faster than the other. Driscoll knows that both employees have similar abilities and training, so the difference in their output strongly suggests different levels of motivation. She makes a note to investigate further to determine what specifically motivates each engineer.

A second challenge centers on the dynamic nature of needs, desires, and expectations. Not only do these factors change, but they may also conflict with each other. Employees who put in many extra hours at work to fulfill their needs for accomplishment may find that these extra work hours conflict directly with needs for affiliation and their desires to be with their families.

A third challenge is the considerable differences in the way people select certain motives over others and in the energy with which they express these motives. Just as various organizations manufacture different products or offer different services, people have different motivations. Ken Rosenthal knew that he wanted to open a bakery/cafe after visiting his brother one weekend in San Francisco. Working 70 hours a week didn't bother him. Once he developed and perfected his idea, he created his own product line and opened his first store in St. Louis. By mid 1993, his Saint Louis Bread Company employed more than 565 people at its corporate office and 17 locations throughout the city. Rosenthal was motivated to be his own boss and operator of a chain of bakeries in the St. Louis area.[5] In contrast, Frank McGrew, a broker with Salomon Brothers, took a one-year job assignment with his firm's Tokyo office. McGrew joined a group of U.S. managers living in Tokyo to satisfy his needs for belonging and to learn Japanese business customs. Through these associations, he discovered that Japanese managers learn to be indirect in conversation and carefully edit their remarks to reflect both good manners and the status of their listeners. He also learned that many Japanese managers believe that Americans are impatient, noisy, disruptive, and confrontational—often saying things that are better left unsaid. Through his understanding of Japanese customs, he was able to more effectively conduct business for Salomon Brothers.

There is no shortage of motivation theories and tactics that managers use to motivate employees.[6] However, we can group the theories into two general categories: content and process theories.

▼ CONTENT THEORIES OF MOTIVATION

Content theories of motivation try to explain the factors within a person that energize, direct, and stop behavior, that is, the specific factors that motivate people. For example, an attractive salary, good working conditions, and friendly co-workers are important to most people. Hunger (the need for food) or a desire for a steady job (the need for job security) also are factors that cause people to set specific goals (earning money to buy food or working in a financially stable industry). Four widely recognized content theories of motivation are Maslow's needs hierarchy, Alderfer's ERG theory, McClelland's achievement motivation theory, and Herzberg's two-factor theory.

▼ Needs Hierarchy Theory

The most widely recognized theory of motivation is the **needs hierarchy theory.** Abraham Maslow suggested that people have a complex set of exceptionally strong needs, which can be arranged in a hierarchy.[7] Underlying this hierarchy are the following basic assumptions.

▲ A satisfied need does not motivate. However, when one need is satisfied, another need emerges to take its place, so people are always striving to satisfy some need.

▲ The needs network for most people is complex, with several needs affecting the behavior of each person at any one time.

▲ In general, lower level needs must be satisfied before higher level needs are activated sufficiently to drive behavior.

▲ There are more ways to satisfy higher level needs than lower level needs.

This theory states that a person has five primary types of needs: physiological, security, affiliation, esteem, and self-actualization. Figure 6.2 shows these five needs categories, arranged in Maslow's hierarchy.

Physiological Needs   The needs for food, water, air, and shelter are all **physiological needs** and are the lowest level in Maslow's hierarchy. People concentrate on satisfying these needs before turning to higher order needs. Managers and others should understand that, to the extent that employees are motivated by physiological needs, their concerns do not center on the work they are doing. They will accept any job that serves to meet their needs. Man-

FIGURE 6.2

Maslow's Needs Hierarchy

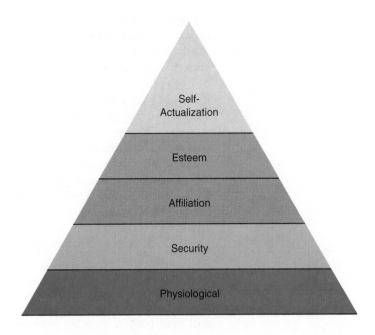

agers who focus on physiological needs in trying to motivate subordinates assume that people work primarily for money and are primarily concerned with comfort, avoidance of fatigue, and the like.

Security Needs   The needs for safety, stability, and absence of pain, threat, or illness are all **security needs.** Like physiological needs, unsatisfied security needs cause people to be preoccupied with satisfying them. People who are motivated primarily by security needs value their jobs mainly as a defense against the loss of basic need satisfactions. Managers who believe that security needs are most important focus on them by emphasizing rules, job security, and fringe benefits. Such managers may not encourage innovation by employees and will not reward risk taking. Employees who are most concerned about security will follow rules strictly.

Affiliation Needs   The needs for friendship, love, and a feeling of belonging are all **affiliation needs.** When physiological and security needs have been satisfied, affiliation needs emerge and motivate people. Managers must realize that when affiliation needs are the primary source of motivation, people value the workplace as an opportunity for finding and establishing warm and friendly interpersonal relationships. Greg Woodson of Colgate-Palmolive Company wanted to satisfy his affiliation needs while stationed in Hong Kong. He and his wife joined a group of U.S. managers and their spouses to help satisfy this need. Managers and team leaders who believe that employees are striving primarily to satisfy these needs are likely to act in supportive and permissive ways. They emphasize employee acceptance by co-workers, extra-curricular activities (such as organized sports programs and company picnics), and team-based norms.

Esteem Needs   Personal feelings of achievement and self-worth and recognition or respect from others meet **esteem needs.** People with esteem needs want others to accept them for what they are and to perceive them as competent and able. Managers who focus on esteem needs try to motivate employees with public rewards and recognition for services. These managers may use lapel pins, articles in the company paper, achievement lists on the bulletin board, and the like to promote employee pride in their work.

Self-Actualization Needs   Self-fulfillment comes from meeting **self-actualization needs.** People who meet self-actualization needs readily accept themselves and others and gain confidence in their problem-solving abilities. Managers who emphasize self-actualization may involve employees in designing jobs, make special assignments that capitalize on employees' unique skills, or give employee teams leeway in planning and implementing work procedures. When Ken Rosenthal opened his first St. Louis Bakery/Cafe, he achieved a measure of self-fulfillment.

Significance for the Workplace   Maslow's needs hierarchy theory implicitly states the goals that people value. It also suggests the types of behavior that will help people meet various needs. The three lowest needs, physiological, safety, and social, are also known as **deficiency needs.** According to Maslow, unless these needs are satisfied, an individual will fail to develop into a healthy person, both physically and psychologically. In contrast, esteem and self-actualization needs are known as **growth needs.** Satisfaction of these needs will help a person grow and develop to his or her potential.

This theory provides incomplete information about the origin of needs. However, it implies that, potentially, higher level needs are present in most people. Moreover, higher level needs will emerge and motivate most people if conditions do not block them.

Managers, as well as psychologists, pay attention to Maslow's work.[8] Research indicates that top managers satisfy their esteem and self-actualization needs more easily than lower level managers; top managers have more challenging jobs and opportunities for self-actualization. Employees who work on a team often satisfy their higher level needs by participating in decisions that affect their team and company positively. For example, at Loral Vought's Camden, Arkansas, plant, employees are trained to perform multiple tasks, including hiring, training, and firing team members who fail to meet performance standards. As team members learn new tasks, they start satisfying their higher level needs. Employees who have little or no control over their work (such as assembly-line workers) may not even experience higher level needs in relation to their jobs. Studies also show that the fulfillment of needs differs according to the job a person performs, a person's age or race, and the size of the company.

▼ ERG THEORY

Clay Alderfer agrees with Maslow that individuals have a hierarchy of needs. Instead of the five categories of needs suggested by Maslow, however, Alderfer's **ERG theory** holds that the individual has three sets of basic needs: existence, relatedness, and growth.[9] Alderfer describes them in the following manner.

▲ **Existence needs,** or material needs, are satisfied by food, air, water, pay, fringe benefits, and working conditions.

▲ **Relatedness needs** are met by establishing and maintaining interpersonal relationships with co-workers, superiors, subordinates, friends, and family.

▲ **Growth needs** are expressed by an individual's attempt to find opportunities for unique personal development by making creative or productive contributions at work.

The arrangement of these categories of needs is similar to Maslow's. Existence needs are similar to Maslow's physiological and safety needs; relatedness needs are similar to Maslow's affiliation needs; and growth needs are similar to Maslow's esteem and self-actualization needs.

The two theories differ, however, in their views of how people may satisfy the different sets of needs. Maslow states that unfilled needs are motivators and that the next higher level need is not activated until the preceding lower level need is satisfied. Thus a person progresses up the needs hierarchy by satisfying each set of lower level needs. In contrast, ERG theory suggests that, in addition to this fulfillment-progression process, a frustration-regression process is at work. That is, if a person is continually frustrated in attempts to satisfy growth needs, relatedness needs will reemerge as a significant motivating force. The individual will return to satisfying this lower level need instead of attempting to satisfy growth needs, and frustration will lead to regression. Figure 6.3 illustrates these relationships. The solid lines indicate direct relationships between sets of needs, desires, and needs satisfaction. The dashed lines represent what happens when a set of needs is frustrated. For example, if a person's growth needs are frustrated, the importance of relatedness needs increases. The same behavior that had led to the frustration of

FIGURE 6.3

ERG Needs Model

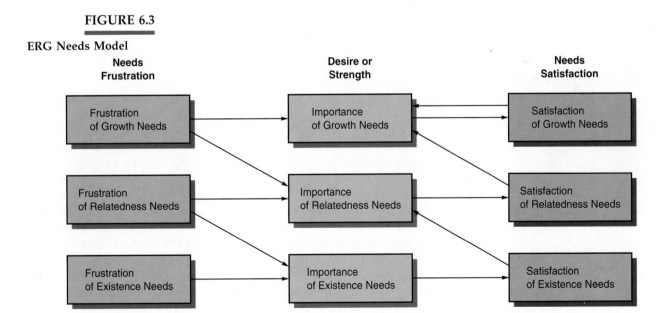

Source: From *Psychology of Work Behavior,* 4th edition by F. J. Landy, Copyright ©1989 by Wadsworth, Inc. Reprinted by permission of Brooks/Cole Publishing Company, Pacific Grove, CA 93950.

growth needs now becomes the means for satisfying relatedness needs. The frustration–regression process assumes that existence, relatedness, and growth needs vary along a continuum of concreteness, with existence being the most concrete and growth being the least concrete. Alderfer further assumes that, when the less concrete needs are not met, more concrete need fulfillment is sought. (Note that the direction of the dotted lines in Figure 6.3 is downward from needs frustration to needs importance.)

Significance for the Workplace   The ERG theory states that individuals are motivated to engage in behavior to satisfy one of the three sets of needs. Thus Alderfer's ERG theory provides an important insight for managers and team leaders. If a team leader observes that a subordinate's growth needs are blocked (perhaps because the job doesn't permit satisfaction of these needs or there are no resources to satisfy them), the team leader should try to redirect the employee's behavior toward satisfying relatedness or existence needs.[10]

Few research studies have tested the ERG theory of motivation. However, several studies do support the three sets of needs in the ERG theory, rather than the five categories in Maslow's hierarchy. At the same time, some managers question the theory's universality, finding that it does not help them understand what motivates employees.[10]

We believe that Maslow's need and Alderfer's ERG theories both offer a useful way of thinking about employee motivation. Note but don't dwell on the disagreement over the exact number of categories of needs because both theories hold that satisfying needs is an important part of motivating employees.

Managers in global organizations find that needs models help them understand the motivations of their employees. The following Managing Diversity account indicates how one company used these theories to help it motivate its workers. Note what occurs when growth needs are frustrated and employees' relatedness needs become the driving motivational force.

MANAGING DIVERSITY

When English Isn't So Plain

Growing diversity in the work force is forcing many small-company managers to give their workers training in English. When Datatec, a $40 million computer installer, decided to do its own manufacturing, it faced a problem. Prior to that time, its workers only assembled the equipment. Now they needed to be trained to manufacture the parts. More than 70% of its work force was foreign born; most were Hispanic, who didn't speak or understand English. They struggled to understand their new and more technical job descriptions. They became frustrated because they couldn't do the work. As a result, they stayed home, avoiding coming to work and becoming frustrated.

Datatec's manager, Larry Tourjee, decided that providing English classes would help them become better workers and citizens. The company hired a bilingual instructor and paid employees to take English two hours a week. To foster a sense of affiliation and commitment to the company, Tourjee asked employees to sign a contract spelling out when they'd practice their new language skills. Employees came up with creative ideas, such as speaking English all day every Friday, eating lunch with managers and speaking only English, and agreeing to teach English to others. After several months, absenteeism no longer was a problem, and errors from misinterpretation of instructions declined dramatically. Hispanic team leaders now write instruction notes to each other in English.[11]

▼ Achievement Motivation Theory

David McClelland proposed a theory of motivation that he believes is rooted in culture.[12] He stated that we all have three particularly important needs: for achievement, affiliation, and power. When a need is strong in a person, its effect will be to motivate that person to act to satisfy the need. Individuals who possess a strong **power motive** take action that affects the actions of others and has a strong emotional impact on them. That is, these individuals are concerned with providing status rewards to their followers. Individuals who have a strong **affiliation motive** tend to establish, maintain, and restore close personal relationships with others. McClelland's research focused mainly on ways that managers can develop subordinates' desire to achieve. Individuals who have a strong **achievement motive** exhibit long-term involvement, competition against some standard of excellence, and unique accomplishment.

McClelland studied achievement motivation extensively, especially with regard to entrepreneurship. **Achievement motivation theory** states that people are motivated according to the strength of their desire either to perform in terms of a standard of excellence or to succeed in competitive situations. McClelland indicates that most people believe that they have an "achievement motive" but that probably only 10% of the U.S. population is strongly motivated to achieve. The amount of achievement motivation that people have depends on their personal childhood and adult (including occupational) experiences and the type of organization for which they work. Table 6.2 shows an application of McClelland's theory to presidents of the United States.

According to McClelland's theory, motives are "stored" in the preconscious mind just below the level of full awareness. They lie between the conscious and the unconscious—in the area of daydreams—where people talk to themselves without quite being aware of doing so. A basic premise of the theory is that the pattern of these daydreams can be tested and that people can be taught to change their motivation by changing these daydreams.

Measuring Achievement Motivation   McClelland measures the strength of a person's achievement motivation by using the **Thematic Apperception Test (TAT).** The TAT uses unstructured pictures that may arouse many kinds of reactions in the person being tested. Examples include an ink blot that a person may perceive as many different objects or a picture that may generate a variety of stories. There are no right or wrong answers, and the person is not given a limited set of alternatives from which to choose. A major objective of the TAT is to obtain the individual's own perception of the world. It is called a *projective method* because it emphasizes individual perceptions of stimuli, the

TABLE 6.2   Presidents' Needs for Power, Achievement, Affiliation

	Needs		
President	*Power*	*Achievement*	*Affiliation*
Clinton, B.	Moderate	High	High
Bush, G.	Moderate	Moderate	Low
Reagan, R.	High	Moderate	Low
Kennedy, J. F.	High	Low	High
Roosevelt, F. D.	High	Moderate	Low
Lincoln, A.	Moderate	Low	Moderate
Washington, G.	Low	Low	Moderate

Source: Adapted from House, R. J., Spangler, Wm. D., and Woycke, J. Personality and charisma in the U.S. President: A psychological theory of leader effectiveness. *Administrative Science Quarterly*, 1992, 36, 395.

meaning each individual gives to them, and how each individual organizes them. (Recall the process of perception discussed in Chapter 3.)

One projective test involves looking at the picture in Figure 6.4 for 10–15 seconds and then writing a short story about it that answers the following questions.

▲ What is going on in this picture?
▲ What is the woman thinking?
▲ What has led up to this situation?

Write your own story about the picture. Then compare it with the following story written by a manager who exhibits strong achievement motivation.

> The individual is an executive officer of a large corporation who wants to get a contract for her company. She knows that the competition will be tough, because all the big firms are bidding on this contract. She is taking a moment to think how happy she will be if her company is awarded the large contract. It will mean stability for the company and probably a large raise for her. She is satisfied because she has just thought of a way to manufacture a critical part that will enable her company to bring in a low bid and complete the job with time to spare.

Characteristics of High Achievers   Self-motivated high achievers have three major characteristics.[13] First, they like to set their own goals. Seldom content to drift aimlessly and let life happen to them, they nearly always try to accomplish something. High achievers seek power and influence and do not back down from making tough decisions. They are selective about the goals to which they commit themselves. For this reason, they are unlikely to accept automatically the goals that other people, including their superiors, select for them. They tend to seek advice or help only from experts who can provide needed knowledge or skills. High achievers prefer to be as fully responsible for attaining their goals as possible. If they win, they want the credit; if they lose, they accept the blame. For example, assume that you are given a choice between rolling dice with one chance in three of winning or working on a problem with one chance in three of solving the problem in the time allotted.

FIGURE 6.4

Sample Picture Used
in a Projective Test

Which would you choose? A high achiever would choose to work on the problem, even though rolling the dice obviously is less work and the odds of winning are the same. High achievers prefer to work at a problem rather than leave the outcome to chance or to other people.

Second, high achievers avoid selecting extremely difficult goals. They prefer moderate goals that are neither so easy that attaining them provides no satisfaction nor so difficult that attaining them is more a matter of luck than ability. They gauge what is possible and then select as difficult a goal as they think they can attain—the hardest practical challenge. The game of ringtoss illustrates this point. Most carnivals have ringtoss games that require participants to throw rings over a peg from some minimum distance but specify no maximum distance. Imagine the same game but with people allowed to stand at any distance from the peg. Some will throw more or less randomly, standing close and then far away. Those with high achievement motivation will calculate carefully where they should stand to have the greatest chance of winning a prize and still feel challenged. Thus they will not stand so close that the task is ridiculously easy and not so far away that it is impossible. They set a distance moderately far away but from which they can potentially ring a peg. Thus they set challenges for themselves and enjoy tasks that stretch themselves.

Third, high achievers prefer tasks that provide immediate feedback. Because of the goal's importance to them, they want to know how well they're doing. This desire is one reason that the high achiever often enters a profession, sales, or entrepreneurial activities. Golf appeals to most high achievers: Golfers can immediately compare their scores to par, to those of playing partners, and to previous rounds; they can easily relate performance to both feedback (score) and goal (par).

Monetary Incentives   Money has a complex effect on high achievers. They usually value highly their services and place a high price on them. High achievers are self-confident because they are aware of their abilities and limitations and thus are confident when they choose to do a particular job. They are unlikely to remain with an organization that does not pay them well for high performance. Whether an incentive plan actually increases their performance is questionable because they normally work at peak efficiency anyway. They value money as a strong symbol of their achievement and adequacy, but money may create dissatisfaction if they believe that it inadequately reflects their contributions.

When achievement motivation is operating, the opportunity to demonstrate good job performance may be very attractive to high achievers. Achievement motivation, however, does not operate when they have to perform routine or boring tasks or when they have no competition. Steve Braccini, President of Pro Fastener, has tackled a challenging job for the past ten years. He used his knowledge of achievement motivation to solve the thorny problem of how to motivate high achievers, as described in the following Managing in Practice account.

MANAGING IN PRACTICE

Instant Rewards for Big Deals

Pro Fasteners, Inc. sold industrial hardware in Canada and the United States until 1990. Spurred by its biggest customers, it began making deals not only for nuts and bolts, but also to manage customers' inventories of hundreds of parts. Converting a customer from a parts contract to a long-term inventory management contract took time and was stressful for the company's ten-person sales force. The salespeople's excitement about handling a new contract quickly faded when they realized that they had to wait months for commissions to kick in.

Steve Braccini, President of Pro Fasteners, Inc., decided to change the system. Instead of making his salespeople wait until customer payments are received, he pays them a commission when customers enter into contracts. The checks are like signing bonuses because they give instant feedback and recognition. The system works well for salespeople because the instant feedback motivates them to move on to the next potential long-term deal, which is what he wants. However, Braccini's plan doesn't work for everyone. Employees who handle service and support, for example, need incentives for maintaining close contact with clients. He is working on an incentive system for his support people. If the employees are high achievers, what do you recommend?[14]

Significance for the Workplace   McClelland and his associates conducted most of the research supporting the achievement motivation theory at McBer and Company. This research led to the following conclusions.

▲ Arrange tasks so that employees receive periodic feedback about their performance. Feedback enables employees to modify their performance, if necessary.

▲ Managers should provide good role models of achievement. Employees should be encouraged to have heroes to emulate.

▲ Managers should help employees modify self-images when necessary. High-achievement individuals accept themselves, seek job challenges and responsibilities, and are productive.

▲ Managers should help employees control their imaginations. Employees should learn how to set realistic goals and how to attain them.

▲ Successful managers rank higher in power motivation than in affiliation.

One of the primary problems with the achievement motivation theory is also its greatest strength.[15] The TAT method is valuable because it allows the researcher to tap individuals' preconscious motives. This method has some advantages over questionnaires, but the interpretation of a story is more of an art than a science. As a result, the method's reliability and permanency of its three needs are questionable. Further research is needed to determine the theory's validity.

▼ Motivator-Hygiene Theory

The **motivator-hygiene theory** is one of the most controversial theories of motivation because of two unique features. First, the theory stresses that some job factors lead to satisfaction, whereas others may prevent dissatisfaction but not be sources of satisfaction. Second, it states that job satisfaction and dissatisfaction do not exist on a single continuum.

Frederick Herzberg and his associates examined the relationship between job satisfaction and productivity in a group of accountants and engineers. Through the use of semistructured interviews, they accumulated data on various factors that these employees said had an effect on their feelings about their jobs. Two different sets of factors emerged: motivators and hygienes.[16]

Motivator Factors   The first set of factors, **motivator factors,** includes the work itself, recognition, advancement, and responsibility. These factors are associated with an individual's positive feelings about the job and are related to the content of the job itself. These positive feelings, in turn, reflect the individual's experiences of achievement, recognition, and responsibility. The factors are predicated on lasting rather than temporary achievement in the work setting.

Motivators are **intrinsic factors,** or internal factors directly related to the job. Intrinsic factors (for example, a feeling of accomplishment after successful task performance) are largely internal to the individual. The organization's policies have only an indirect impact on them. Thus, by defining exceptional performance, an organization may enable individuals to feel that they have performed their tasks exceptionally well.

Hygiene Factors   The second set of factors, **hygiene factors,** includes company policy and administration, technical supervision, salary, working conditions, and interpersonal relations. These factors are associated with an individual's negative feelings about the job and are related to the context or environment in which the job is performed. Hygienes are **extrinsic factors,** or factors external to the job. In other words, the organization largely determines extrinsic factors (for example, salary, policies and rules, and fringe benefits).

They serve as rewards for high performance only if the organization recognizes high performance.

Effects of Diversity   One of the important themes of this book is managing diversity in the work force. As U.S. organizations continue to expand overseas and foreign organizations establish manufacturing sites in Canada, Mexico, and the United States, managers must be aware of cultural differences and how they affect employee motivation. Herzberg believes that, despite cultural differences, hygiene and motivator factors affect workers similarly around the world.[17] The data in Table 6.3 support his viewpoint. They show that, for U.S. workers, about 80% of the factors that lead to job satisfaction can be traced to motivators. For workers in other countries, motivators account for 60%–90% of job satisfaction. Hygiene factors account for most of the reasons that workers are dissatisfied with their jobs. In Finland, 80% of the workers indicated that hygiene factors contribute mainly to job dissatisfaction, whereas only 10% said that hygiene factors contribute to job satisfaction.

With passage of the North American Free Trade Agreement (NAFTA), employees in North America will be working closer with others who don't necessarily share the same work motivations. The following Managing Across Cultures piece highlights some of the main differences that Motorola managers observed between employees in its Guadalajara, Mexico, plant and in its U.S. plants. Note the importance that Mexican employees seem to place on hygiene factors.

MANAGING ACROSS CULTURES

Motorola's Guadalajara Employees

It didn't take Motorola's U.S. managers long to realize that its employees in Mexico have different work motives than their U.S. counterparts. The latter often take the initiative, exercising individual responsibility and taking failure personally. The former are comfortable operating in groups, and the group shares both success and failure. Motorola's U.S. employees are competitive, have high goals, and live for the future. The company's Mexican employees tend to be cooperative, flexible, and enjoy life as it is now.

In Mexico, employees' priorities are family, religion, and work. During the year, the Guadalajara plant's manager hosts family dinners to celebrate the anniversaries of employees who have worked there 5, 10, 15, and 20 years. Employees may borrow the company clubhouse for weddings, baptisms, anniversary parties, and other family celebrations. Motorola also hosts a family day during which all family members can tour the plant, enjoy entertainment and food, and participate in sports.

The typical workday in Mexico is 8 A.M. to 5:30 P.M. The company bus picks up employees at central locations throughout the city. Employees like to eat their main meal in the middle of the day. Motorola subsidizes meal costs (70%) In the spirit of cooperation, managers serve employees.

These practices have helped to increase output steadily and spur on-time deliveries to approach 100%. Employees are confident that their plant can become a world-class operation.[18]

TABLE 6.3   Motivators and Hygienes Across Cultures

Motivators	Satisfying Job Events	Dissatisfying Job Events
United States	80%	20%
Japan	82%	40%
Finland	90%	18%
Hungary	78%	30%
Italy	60%	35%
Hygienes		
United States	20%	75%
Japan	10%	65%
Finland	10%	80%
Hungary	22%	78%
Italy	30%	70%

Source: Adapted from Alder, N. J., and Graham, J. L. Cross-cultural interaction: The international comparison fallacy. *Journal of International Business Studies*, Fall 1989, 515–537; Herzberg, F. Workers needs: The same around the world. *Industry Week*, September 21, 1987, 29–32.

The hygiene-motivator theory also states that satisfaction and dissatisfaction do not form a single continuum but are on a separate and distinct continuum, as Figure 6.5 indicates. It illustrates the continua—from ideal to poor—of both hygiene and motivator factors. Note that, according to this theory, hygiene factors cannot increase or decrease job satisfaction; they can only affect the amount of job dissatisfaction.

Significance for the Workplace   The research designed to test the motivator-hygiene theory does not provide clear-cut evidence that either supports or rejects it. One aspect of the theory that appeals to managers is the use of common terms to explain how to motivate people. There is no need to translate psychological terms into everyday language.

Hygiene factors also are easy to identify and have become targets of complaints by shareholders when share prices fall. For example, when IBM management announced that it was eliminating more jobs and that its 1993 sales were down $8.73 billion, shareholders began questioning the purposes of IBM's perks (hygienes). Shareholders wanted to know why the company still maintained its three country clubs, with golf courses, bowling alleys, and skeet-shooting. They wanted to know why it still sends employees to its own management school that is housed on a 26-acre campus and has a 160-room hotel. They wanted to know why IBM still has nine private jets, spent $75,000 on a 12-minute video to teach people how to use its phone system, and has five staff people who oversee the naming of new IBM products. Finally, they wanted to know why IBM spent more than $33 million on entertainment for recognition events, hosted by Liza Minnelli, the Dixie Chicks, and other big-name acts, for its top-producing salespeople.[19]

Herzberg recommends that managers focus on motivators and not hygiene factors to motivate employees. That is, managers should rely on job chal-

FIGURE 6.5

Motivator-Hygiene Situations

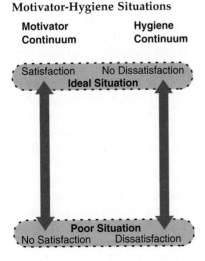

lenge, responsibility, and achievement to increase employees' motivations to perform.

Despite its attractive features, several criticisms have been leveled at motivator-hygiene theory.[20] One telling criticism is that Herzberg used a method-bound procedure; that is, the method he used to measure the factors determined the results. He asked two key questions: "Can you describe, in detail, when you felt exceptionally good about your job?" and "Can you describe, in detail, when you felt exceptionally bad about your job?" In response to such questions, people tend to give socially desirable answers, that is, answers that they think the researcher wants to hear or that sound "reasonable." Also, people tend to attribute good results to their own efforts and to attribute poor results to the actions of others (recall the discussion of the self-serving bias attribution in Chapter 3).

Another principal criticism of the motivator-hygiene theory questions whether satisfaction and dissatisfaction are two separate dimensions, as Figure 6.5 indicates. Research results are mixed. Some researchers identified factors that can contribute to both satisfaction and dissatisfaction, whereas others observed that motivator factors can contribute to dissatisfaction and hygiene factors can contribute to satisfaction. For example, in Hungary, employees reported that, although hygiene factors were related to many dissatisfying features of their jobs, some hygiene factors also were related to satisfying events (see Table 6.3). These findings raise serious questions about Herzberg's theory but have not disproved that satisfaction and dissatisfaction operate on two different continua.

Some evidence, although not strong, links experiences such as increasing job responsibility, challenge, and advancement opportunities to high performance. Unfortunately, researchers have paid little attention to constructing a theory that explains why certain job factors affect performance positively or negatively. Similarly, few researchers have attempted to use content theories to explain why certain outcomes are attractive to employees or why people choose one type of behavior over another to obtain a desired outcome.

▼ Matching Content Theories

The four content theories emphasize the basic motivational concepts of needs, achievement, and hygiene-motivator factors. Figure 6.6 highlights the relationships among these four theories. The needs hierarchy theory served as the basis for the ERG theory, hence the similarities between the two: Self-actualization and esteem needs comprise growth needs; affiliation needs are similar to relatedness needs; and security and physiological needs are the building blocks of existence needs in ERG theory. A significant difference between these two theories is that the needs hierarchy theory offers a static five-needs system based on fulfillment–progression, whereas the ERG theory presents a flexible three-needs classification system based on frustration–regression.

The motivator-hygiene theory draws on both of the needs theories. Thus, if hygiene factors are present, security and physiological needs (needs hierarchy) are likely to be met. Similarly, if hygiene factors are present, relatedness and existence needs (ERG theory) are not likely to be frustrated. Motivator factors focus on the job itself and the opportunity for the individual to satisfy personal higher order needs, or growth needs (ERG theory).

Achievement motivation theory does not recognize lower order needs. A person can satisfy the need for affiliation by realizing hygiene factors on the job. If the job itself is challenging and provides an opportunity for the individual to make meaningful decisions, it is motivating. These conditions go far toward satisfying the need for achievement.

The content theories give managers an understanding of the particular work-related factors that start the motivational process. These theories, however, provide little understanding of why people choose a particular behavior to accomplish task-related goals. This aspect of choice is the focus of process theories of motivation.

▼ PROCESS THEORIES OF MOTIVATION

Process theories try to describe and analyze how personal factors (internal to the person) interact to produce certain kinds of behavior. The four best known process theories of motivation are expectancy, reinforcement, equity, and goal setting. In this section, we cover the expectancy and equity theories of motivation. In Chapter 5, we discussed reinforcement theory, and in Chapter 7, we present goal-setting theory.

▼ Expectancy Theory

Expectancy theory differs widely from the content theories just described. Instead of focusing on factors in the work environment that contribute to job dissatisfaction or satisfaction, expectancy theory looks at the entire work environment.[21] **Expectancy theory** states that people are motivated to work when they believe that they can get what they want from their jobs. Such

FIGURE 6.6

Matching Content Theories

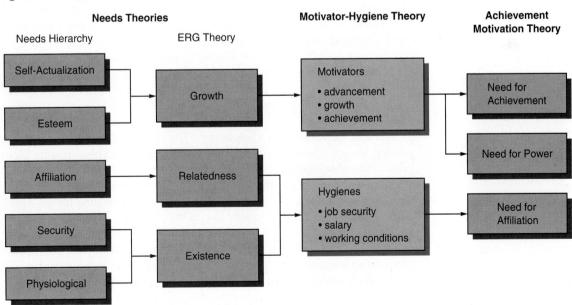

results might include satisfaction of safety needs, the excitement of doing a challenging task, or the ability to set and achieve challenging goals. A basic premise of expectancy theory is that employees are rational people who think about what they have to do to earn rewards—and how much the rewards mean to them—before they perform their jobs. Four assumptions about the causes of behavior in organizations provide the basis for this theory.

First, a combination of forces in the individual and the environment determines behavior (recall the discussion of the interactionist perspective in Chapter 2). Neither the individual nor the environment alone determines behavior. People join organizations with expectations about their jobs that are based on their needs, motivations, and past experiences. These factors all influence how people respond to an organization. But these factors can and do change over time.

Second, individuals decide their own behaviors in organizations, although rules, technology, and work-group norms place many constraints on individual behavior. Most individuals make at least two kinds of conscious decisions: (1) decisions about coming to work, staying with the same organization, and joining another organization (membership decisions); and (2) decisions about how much to produce, how hard to work, and the quality of workmanship (job-performance decisions).

Third, different individuals have different needs and goals, as Table 6.1 illustrates. Moreover, different employees want different rewards from their work (for example, job security, promotion, good pay, or challenge). Recall that, as Frank McGrew discovered, Japanese employees have far different expectations about their work than most U.S. workers have about theirs.

Fourth, individuals decide among alternatives based on their perceptions of whether a certain behavior will lead to a desired outcome. Individuals do the things that they perceive will lead to desirable rewards and avoid doing the things that they perceive will lead to undesirable outcomes.[22]

In general, expectancy theory holds that individuals have their own needs and ideas about what they desire from their work (rewards). They act on these needs and ideas when making decisions about what organization to join and how hard to work. The theory also holds that individuals are not inherently motivated or unmotivated, that motivation depends on the situations individuals face and how it fits their needs.

To understand expectancy theory requires defining the important variables of the theory and explaining how they operate. The five most important variables of the theory are: first-level and second-level outcomes, expectancy, instrumentality, and valence.

First- and Second-Level Outcomes   The results of behaviors associated with doing the job itself are called **first-level outcomes.** These results include productivity, absenteeism, turnover, and quality of work. **Second-level outcomes** are rewards (either positive or negative) that first-level outcomes are likely to produce, such as a pay increase, promotion, acceptance by co-workers, and job security.

Expectancy.   The belief that a specific level of effort will be followed by a particular level of performance is called **expectancy.** It can vary from the belief that effort and performance are completely unrelated to the certainty that some level of effort will result in a corresponding level of performance. Expectancy values range from 0 to +1. Zero indicates that there is no chance that a first-level outcome will occur after the behavior. A +1 indicates certainty that a particular first-level outcome will follow a behavior. For example, if you believe that you have no chance of getting a good grade on the next exam by studying this chapter, your expectancy value would be 0. With this expectancy, you may choose not to study this chapter.

Instrumentality   The relationship between first-level outcomes and second-level outcomes is called **instrumentality.** Its values range from −1 to +1. A −1 indicates that attainment of a second-level outcome is inversely related to the achievement of a first-level outcome. For example, if one of your desired second-level outcomes is to pass this course but you consistently receive failing grades on exams, you couldn't achieve your second-level outcome. A +1 indicates that the first-level outcome is positively related to the second-level outcome. For example, if you received an A on some of your exams, the probability that you would achieve your desired second-level outcome (passing this course) approaches +1. If your performance on a test and either passing or failing this course were unrelated, your instrumentality would be 0.

Valence   An individual's preference for a particular second-level outcome is called **valence.** The NAFTA negotiations among the United States, Canada, and Mexico caused political controversy in all three countries. In the United States, many union and political leaders argued that a free-trade agreement with Mexico would cost many U.S. workers their jobs. Conversely, President Clinton and corporate leaders argued that such an agreement would provide an economic stimulus for all workers.

An outcome is positive when it is preferred and negative when it is not preferred or is to be avoided. An outcome has a valence of zero when the individual is indifferent about receiving it.

Putting It Together   In brief, expectancy theory holds that individual beliefs regarding effort–performance–outcome relationships and the desirability of various work outcomes associated with different performance levels determine work motivation. Simply put, you can remember its important features by the proposition that:

> **People exert work effort to achieve performance and receive work-related outcomes.**

Expectancy Theory in Action   Using these five variables, we can demonstrate the expectancy theory of motivation, as shown in Figure 6.7. Motivation is the force that causes individuals to expend effort. Effort alone isn't enough, however. Unless an individual believes that effort will lead to some desired performance level (first-level outcome), that person won't make much of an effort. The effort–performance relationship is based on a perception of the difficulty of achieving a particular outcome (say, getting an A in this course) and the probability of achieving that outcome. For example, if you expect that, by attending class, studying the book, taking good notes, and preparing for exams, you could receive an A in this class, you probably will make the effort

FIGURE 6.7

Expectancy Theory in Action

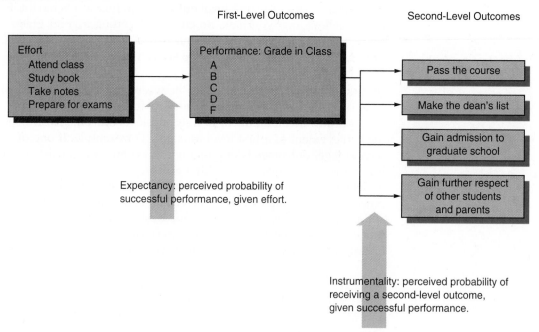

to do so. But, if you believe that the same behaviors give you only a 20% chance of receiving an A, you may decide not to make the effort.

Performance level is important in obtaining desired second-level outcomes. Figure 6.7 shows four desirable outcomes: passing the course, making the dean's list, gaining admission to graduate school, and gaining the respect of other students and your parents. In general, if you believe that a particular level of performance (A, B, C, D, or F) will lead to these desired outcomes, you are likely to try to perform at that level. If you strongly desire these four second-level outcomes and you can achieve them only if you get an A in this course, the instrumentality between receiving an A and these four outcomes will be +1. However, if you believe that getting an A in this course means that you will lose some friends and that these friends are most important to you, the instrumentality between an A and this outcome will be negative. That is, the higher the grade, the more your friends will ignore you, and for that reason you might decide not to get an A in this course.

Research Findings   Researchers are still working on ways to test the expectancy theory, which presents some problems.[23] The theory tries to predict choice or the amount of effort an individual will expend on one or more tasks. However, because there is little agreement about what represents choice or effort for different individuals, accurate measurement of this variable is difficult. In addition, the theory does not specify which second-level outcomes are important to a particular individual in a specific situation. Although researchers are expected to address this issue, comparison of the limited results to date often is difficult because many studies are unique. Take another look at the second-level outcomes in Figure 6.7. Would you choose them? What others might you choose? Finally, the theory contains an implicit assumption that motivation is a conscious choice process. That is, the individual consciously calculates the pain or pleasure that he or she expects to attain or avoid when making a choice. Expectancy theory says nothing about unconscious motivation or personality characteristics. But people often do not make conscious choices about which outcomes to seek. Can you recall going through this process concerning your grade while taking this course?

Significance for the Workplace   Although some research problems with expectancy theory remain, it has some direct implications for motivating employees. These implications can be grouped into several suggestions for action.[24]

Managers should try to determine the outcomes that each employee values. They can do so by (1) using a questionnaire; (2) observing employee reactions to different rewards; and (3) asking employees about the kinds of rewards they want from their jobs. However, managers must understand that employees can and do change their minds about desired outcomes.

Managers should determine and state clearly the performance desired because employees need to understand what is expected of them. Moreover, managers should define good, adequate, and poor performance in terms that are observable and measurable. Historically, most Japanese organizations have not measured the performance of their white-collar employees. However, global competitors have begun closing the performance gap between their workers and Japanese workers. As a result, Fujitsu, Japan Airlines, Nippon Trust Bank, and Sanyo Electric, among other Japanese companies, can no longer support the huge costs associated with poor performance of their white-collar employees. They have begun to emphasize improving the performance and innovativeness of their white-collar work force, as the following Managing Across Cultures feature points out.

MANAGING ACROSS CULTURES

Defining Productivity in Japan

One of Sanyo management's greatest challenges is to measure productivity of employees who are not engaged in the actual manufacturing process or delivery of a service. In the past, every April employees would receive a computer printout of their new monthly salary. No attempt was made to link salary to performance, and the difference between all employees doing the same job might be only 2%–3%. The mutual commitment of the employee and employer was, in a sense, unconditional. Poor performers were "put by the window" (*madogiwazoku*). They would have no subordinates and be left alone. Good performers eventually would be promoted, in keeping with the seniority system of the firm. Incentive compensation made little sense in a culture where the work ethic so closely equated hard work with success in life.

In an effort to control costs, Honda, Fujitsu, and other companies instituted performance reviews. Rather than measuring hours at the office (which are

MANAGING ACROSS CULTURES —*Continued*

long), Japanese managers began to measure the value created during those hours. Managers at Honda are now required to sit down with their employees and set performance objectives for the future and review past results against targets. Goals, such as "to reduce by 40% the time spent on producing the monthly forecast" or "eliminate by 50% the amount of paperwork in the department" are set and monitored by managers.[25]

Managers should make sure that desired levels of performance set for employees can be attained. If employees believe that the level of performance necessary to get a reward is higher than they can reasonably achieve, their motivation to perform will be low. For example, Nordstrom's tells its employees to "respond to unreasonable customer requests." Employees are urged to keep scrapbooks with "heroic" acts, such as hand delivering items purchased by phone to the airport for a customer with a last-minute business trip, changing a customer's flat tire, or paying a customer's parking ticket when in-store gift wrapping has taken longer than expected. Not surprisingly, Nordstrom's pays its employees about twice what they would earn at a rival's store, but for those who love to sell and can meet such demanding standards, Nordstrom's is nirvana.[26]

Managers should directly link the specific performance they desire to the outcomes employees desire (recall the discussion in Chapter 5 of how operant conditioning principles can be applied to improve performance). If an employee has achieved the desired level of performance required for a promotion, the employee should be promoted as soon as possible. If a high level of motivation is to be created and maintained, employees must clearly see the reward process at work in a timely manner. Concrete acts must accompany statements of intent in linking performance to rewards.

Never forget that perceptions, not reality, determine motivation. For example, a manager's conviction that employee pay and raises are related to performance means little if the employees don't perceive the relationship. Too often, managers misunderstand employee behavior because they tend to rely on their own perceptions of the situation and forget that employee perceptions may be different.

Managers should analyze a situation for conflicts. Having set up positive expectancies for employees, managers need to look at the entire situation to see whether other factors (such as the informal work group or the organization's formal reward system) conflict with the desired behaviors. Motivation will be high only when employees recognize that many rewards and few negative outcomes are associated with good performance.

Managers should make sure that changes in outcomes or rewards are large enough to motivate significant behavior. Trivial rewards may result in minimal efforts, if any, to improve performance. Rewards must be large enough to motivate individuals to make the effort required to significantly change performance. Home Depot managers have relied on these practices to create a retail chain of stores that excels at satisfying the customer. Home Depot has been able to build customer loyalty by doing little extra things for customers and making sure that they get exactly what they want. The following Managing Quality example illustrates some of Home Depot's practices that convert a shopper into a lifetime customer.

MANAGING QUALITY

Working at Home Depot

Once inside the doors of a Home Depot store, you know that you are dealing with a different kind of company. A few feet from the entrance is a makeshift classroom, with bleacher seating, a chalkboard, a bulletin board, and a work-table. You see an orange-aproned Home Depot employee teaching customers how to install a pedestal sink, rewire an electrical outlet, build a fence, or do any number of home improvements. Salespeople are hired not only for their product knowledge, but, as President Art Blank notes, also for "their ability to raise a customer's enthusiasm about a project. We hire cheerleaders as well as coaches." Contractors asked for special checkout areas near the lumber racks; Home Depot obliged and also found out that these lumber racks speeded up customer checkout.

Teaching isn't focused just on the customer. Before a new Home Depot store opens, employees receive nearly four weeks of training. Home Depot also holds quarterly Sunday morning meetings during which all 23,000 employees learn, via satellite TV hookup in each store. Known as "Breakfast with Bernie and Arthur" these meetings inform employees of the company's past financial performance, instill the Home Depot "quality service spirit," and outline growth plans. Employees are rewarded publicly for introducing new products, such as a bridal registry for the newly married homeowner, and recommendations for improving customer quality.[27]

▼ Equity Theory

Feelings of unfairness were among the sources of job dissatisfaction reported most frequently to Herzberg and his associates. Some researchers have made this desire for fairness, justice, or equity a central focus of their theories. Assume that you just received a 5% raise. Are you satisfied with it? Would your satisfaction with it vary with the consumer price index, with what you expected to get, or with what others performing the same job at the same performance level received? Answers to such questions reflect a person's feelings about **distributive justice,** or the extent to which someone perceives that rewards are related to performance. Although the distribution of raises and other benefits often are beyond an individual manager's control, treating subordinates fairly and equitably is important to maintaining their performance and job satisfaction.

Equity theory focuses on an individual's feelings of how fairly he or she is treated in comparison with others.[28] The theory is based on two major assumptions. The first is that individuals evaluate their interpersonal relationships just as they would evaluate the buying or selling of a home, shares of stock, or a car. The theory views interpersonal relationships as exchanges in which individuals make contributions and expect certain results.

They compare their situations with those of others to determine equity in a situation. How people view an exchange is influenced by what happens to them in comparison to what happens to the others involved (such as co-workers, relatives, and neighbors).

General Equity Model   Equity theory is based on the comparison of two variables: inputs and outcomes. **Inputs** represent what an individual contributes to an exchange; **outcomes** are what an individual receives from the exchange. Table 6.4 shows some typical inputs and outcomes. The items in the two lists are not paired and do not represent specific exchanges.

According to equity theory, individuals assign weights to various inputs and outcomes according to their perceptions of the situation. Most situations involve multiple inputs and outcomes, so the weighting process isn't precise. However, people generally can distinguish between important and less important inputs and outcomes. After they balance inputs and outcomes for themselves, they compare that with their perceived balance of inputs and outcomes of others in the same or a similar situation.

Equity exists whenever the ratio of a person's outcomes to inputs equals the ratio of outcomes to inputs for similar others. For example, an individual may feel properly paid in terms of what she puts into a job compared to what other workers are getting for their inputs. **Inequity** exists when the ratios of outcomes to inputs are not equal. For example, let's say that a person who works harder than her co-workers, completes all her tasks on time while others do not, and puts in longer hours than others receives the same pay raise as the others. What happens? She believes that her inputs are greater than those of co-workers and therefore should merit a larger raise. Inequity can also occur when someone is overpaid. In this case, the overpaid employee might be motivated by guilt or social pressure to work harder to reduce the imbalance between his inputs and outcomes in comparison to his co-workers.

TABLE 6.4   Examples of Inputs and Outcomes in Organizations

Inputs	Outcomes
Age	Challenging job assignments
Attendance	Fringe benefits
Communication skills	Job perquisites (parking space or
Interpersonal skills	office location)
Job effort (long hours)	Job security
Level of education	Monotony
Past experience	Promotion
Performance	Recognition
Personal appearance	Responsibility
Seniority	Salary
Social status	Seniority benefits
Technical skills	Status symbols
Training	Working conditions

Consequences of Inequity Inequity causes tension in an individual and among individuals. Tension is not pleasurable, so a person is motivated to reduce it to a tolerable level. To reduce a perceived inequity and the corresponding level of tension, the person can choose among the following types of action. Figure 6.8 depicts this tension-reduction process.

▲ People may increase or decrease their inputs to what they perceive to be an equitable level. For example, underpaid people may reduce the quantity of their production, work shorter hours, be absent more frequently, and so on. Figure 6.9 shows these relationships graphically.

▲ People may change their outcomes to restore equity. Many union organizers try to attract nonmembers by pledging to improve working conditions, hours, and pay without an increase in employee effort (input).

▲ People may distort their own inputs and outcomes. As opposed to actually changing inputs or outcomes, people may mentally distort them to achieve the same result. For example, people who feel inequitably treated may distort how hard they work ("This job is a piece of cake.") or attempt to increase the importance of the job to the organization

FIGURE 6.8

Inequity as a Motivational Process

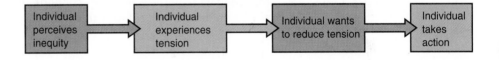

FIGURE 6.9

Performance Levels for Underpaid and Overpaid Employees

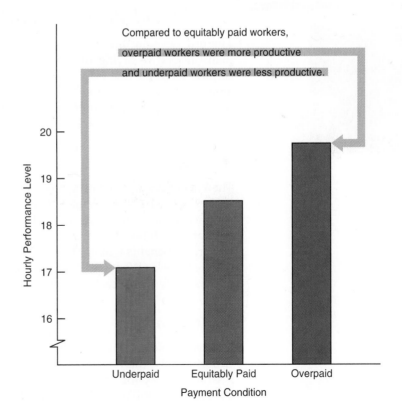

("This is really an important job!"). By mentally distorting the input–outcome ratio, people achieve a more favorable balance in their own minds.

▲ People may leave the organization or request a transfer to another department. In doing so, they hope to find a more favorable balance between inputs and outcomes.

▲ People may shift to a new reference group to reduce the source of an inequity. The star high school athlete who does not get a scholarship to a Big Ten university might decide that a smaller school has more advantages, thereby justifying a need to look at smaller schools when making a selection.

▲ People may distort the inputs or outcomes of others. People may come to believe that those in the comparison group actually work harder than they do and therefore deserve greater rewards.

Keeping these six actions in mind, let's consider employee theft as a reaction to underpayment. Employee theft is one of the most serious problems facing organizations. The American Management Association estimates that employee theft costs U.S. organizations more than $10 billion a year. The following Managing Ethics feature contains two accounts of reasons for an across-the-board pay cut and their effect on employee theft.

MANAGING ETHICS

To Steal or Not: That's the Question

The organization reduced everyone's payroll by 15% for ten weeks in each plant instead of laying off people. Management drafted two accounts concerning the reduction in pay and read only one account at each plant. Before announcing the reduction in pay, theft was running at about 3% annually. Read each account and predict which group increased its level of theft: group A, group B, or both groups.

▼ Account A

The reason why I'm sharing this information with you is that I want you to understand what's happening here. As you probably know, we've lost a key contract, which will make things fairly lean around there. Starting Monday, each of us will take a 15% cut in pay. This applies to you, to me, to everyone. Our fringe benefits will not be touched. I expect that this cut will not last more than ten weeks. We hope to be stronger than ever after this trying time. I want to personally thank each of you for gutting it out with us.

▼ Account B

It is inevitable in a business like ours that cost-cutting measures are needed. Unfortunately, the time has come for us to take such measures. I know that it won't be easy for anyone, but the President has decided that a 15% across-the-board cut will be instituted starting Monday. All employees, including the

MANAGING ETHICS —*Continued*

President, will share in this effort to save our company. We're reasonably sure that the cuts will last only ten weeks. I'll answer a few questions, but then I have to catch a plane for another meeting.

Theft by those employees who heard account B increased by more than 250%. Why? They believed that they were not hearing the entire story. They reduced their inequities by acts of theft. To be effective, equity explanations must be perceived to be honest, genuine, and not manipulative.[29] Employees who heard about Account A maintained their level of productivity.

Equity Theory Findings   Most of the research on equity theory focuses on pay or other compensation issues.[30] A review of these studies indicates some shortcomings, including the fact that the comparison group is always known. What happens if the comparison group or situation changes? Do people change comparison groups frequently throughout their careers?

Also, the research focuses mainly on short-term comparisons. Do factors such as pay cuts, temporary assignments, longer working hours, and the like remain the same over time? Do perceptions of inequity or equity increase, decrease, or stabilize over time? In the preceding Managing Ethics feature, what is likely to happen to the amount of theft after the ten-week period if salaries are not restored? Would theft increase in group A? Answers to these types of questions help managers understand better the dynamic character of equity and inequity.

Finally, equity theory does not specify the type of action (from among the actions listed) that a person would choose to reduce inequity in a particular situation. In other words, is one strategy used primarily when pay is involved, another when theft or absenteeism is involved, and yet another when productivity is involved?

Significance for the Workplace   Managers use equity theory implicitly in making decisions about granting pay raises, assigning a person to an office (size, location, windows, decor, and the like), assigning parking places, and parceling out other perks. Equity theory makes two primary points. First, employees should be treated fairly. When individuals believe that they are not being treated fairly, they will try to correct the situation and reduce tension by taking one or more of the types of actions just discussed. A sizable inequity increases the probability that individuals will choose more than one type of action to reduce it. For example, an employee may partially withdraw from the organization by being absent more often, arriving at work late, not completing assignments on time or by stealing from the organization. Management may retaliate by reducing the employee's inputs—assigning him to monotonous jobs, taking away some of his perquisites, and giving him small raises, if any.

Second, people make decisions concerning equity only after they compare their inputs and outcomes with those of comparable employees.[31] These other employees may be members of the same organization or of other organizations. The latter presents a sticky problem for managers, who cannot control what other organizations pay their employees. For example, the vice-president for human resources at a large corporation hired a recent business school graduate for $28,500, the maximum the company could pay for the job. The new employee thought that this salary was very good until she compared it to the $31,000 that fellow graduates were getting at other firms. She then felt underpaid in comparison to her former classmates, causing an inequity problem for her (and the company). However, when comparing her salary of $28,500 against that of Stephen Wynn, CEO of Mirage Resorts, who earned more than $34 million in 1992, she may not perceive inequity because of Wynn's far greater inputs than her own. However, Jack Welch, CEO of General Electric, and Charles Lazarus, CEO of Toys 'R' Us, might perceive an inequity after comparing their salaries of $14 million and $7 million, respectively, against Wynn's because they are CEOs of comparable organizations.

Managers have given a great deal of attention to the idea that fairness in organizations is determined by more than just money. Organizational fairness also is influenced by how rules and procedures are applied and how much employees are consulted in decisions that affect them. The perceived fairness of rules and procedures is referred to as **procedural justice**.[32] Employees now seek fairness in how decisions are made, as well as what those decisions are. Research shows that if they believe that pay raises are administered fairly, employees are more satisfied with their raises than if they judge the procedures used to make these increases to be unfair. That is, the perceived fairness of the procedures used to allocate pay raises is a better predicator of pay satisfaction than the absolute amount of pay received.

Employee assessments of procedural justice also are related to their trust in management, intention to leave the organization, evaluation of their supervisor, employee theft, and job satisfaction. Consider a few of the many relatively small day-to-day issues in an organization that involve procedural justice: decisions about who will cover the phones during lunch while others are away from their desks, the choice of the site of the company picnic, or who gets the latest software for her personal computer.

Procedural justice affects the attitudes of those workers who survive a layoff. When workers are laid off, survivors (those who remain on the job) often are in a good position to judge the fairness of how the layoffs were made. When the layoffs are handled fairly, survivors feel more committed to the organization than when they believe that the laid-off workers were not fairly treated.[33]

Think about your behavior in this class. If you receive a high grade, you may think that it is fair because it benefits you. You may think of yourself as a good student, and good students deserve high grades. But what if you receive a low grade? Thinking of yourself as a good student, you might not like the grade. But you will accept the grade if you believe that the instructor graded everyone fairly. You might think that your grade was unfair if you perceive that the instructor had class favorites who received all the high grades.

▼ Matching Process Theories

The expectancy and equity theories emphasize different aspects of motivation. Expectancy theory is based on the assumption that employees are rational and evaluate how much a reward means to them before they perform their jobs.

How well employees perform their jobs depends, in part, on what they believe is expected of them. Once their managers or team leaders communicate these expectations, employees decide which efforts will lead to desired first-level outcomes (performance, quality, absenteeism, and so on). These outcomes are linked to valued rewards (high pay, job security, and the like) they desire from their jobs. The manager's job is to make the desired rewards attainable to employees by clearly linking rewards and performance. Allowing employees to choose among rewards (such as improved insurance, child-care and elder-care facilities for family members, and additional vacation days) is important because all employees do not value the same rewards. **Cafeteria-style benefit plans** are reward systems that permit employees to select their fringe benefits from a menu of alternatives and are becoming popular in organizations. In many organizations, fringe benefits represent 35% of payroll costs. So, letting employees choose those that they find rewarding and linking these to their performance is important for organizations.[34]

In contrast to expectancy theory, equity theory assumes that employees determine what is equitable by comparing themselves to similar others. According to equity theory, people are motivated to escape inequitable situations and are induced to remain on the job and perform at high levels in equitable situations. Because equity theory deals with perceptions of fairness among employees, expecting that they react to inequitable situations in different ways is reasonable.

Both theories emphasize the future role of rewards and an individual's decision-making processes. These theories suggest that managers concerned about improving employee performance should actively create proper work environments, match employees to jobs, and establish clear performance–reward systems. Motivation for high performance will not exist unless managers recognize such performance when it occurs and reward it quickly.

Summary

Individuals behave in certain ways to satisfy their needs. Their reasons for doing so were the focus of this chapter. To understand these reasons, we examined two major classes of theories of motivation: content and process. Content theories focus on the factors within a person that drive, sustain, or stop behavior. Among the most widely recognized content theories of motivation are those of Maslow, Alderfer, McClelland, and Herzberg, which attempt to determine the specific needs that motivate people. Process theories provide a description and analysis of how behavior is driven, sustained, or stopped. Expectancy and equity theories of motivation are two of the most important process theories.

Maslow assumed that people have five types of needs: physiological, security, affiliation, esteem, and self-actualization. Once a need is satisfied, it no longer serves to motivate a person. Alderfer agreed with Maslow that needs motivate people but claims that people have only three types of needs: existence, relatedness, and growth. If a person's growth needs cannot be satisfied, the person then focuses on relatedness needs to find satisfaction. McClelland believes that people have three types of needs (achievement, affiliation, and power), which are rooted in the culture. We focused on achievement needs and indicated the characteristics associated with high achievers. Herzberg claimed that two types of factors affect a person's motivation: hygienes and motivators. Hygiene factors, such as working conditions, can only prevent job dissatisfaction; they cannot lead to job satisfaction. Motivators, such as job challenge, can only lead to job satisfaction; they cannot lead to job dissatisfaction.

Expectancy theory holds that individuals have their own ideas about what they desire from work. They decide to undertake activities only when they believe that these activities will satisfy their needs. The essential components of this theory are first- and second-level outcomes, expectancy, instrumentality, and valence. Unless the individual believes that effort leads (expectancy) to some desired level of performance (first-level outcome) and that this level of performance will lead (instrumentality) to desired rewards (second-level outcomes and valences), that person will not be motivated to expend any effort.

Equity theory focuses on personal feelings of how fairly an individual is treated in comparison to others. To make this judgment, an individual compares his or her inputs (experience, age) and outcomes (salary) to those of others. If equity exists, the person is not motivated to change the situation. If inequity exists, the person can engage in any one of six behaviors to reduce this inequity.

Key Words and Concepts

Ability
Achievement motivation theory
Achievement motive
Affiliation motive
Affiliation needs
Cafeteria-style benefit plans
Content theories
Deficiency needs
Distributive justice
Equity
Equity theory
ERG theory
Esteem needs
Existence needs

Expectancy
Expectancy theory
Extrinsic factors
First-level outcomes
Goal
Growth needs
Hygiene factors
Inequity
Inputs
Instrumentality
Intrinsic factors
Motivation
Motivator-Hygiene theory
Motivator factors

Needs
Needs hierarchy theory
Outcomes
Physiological needs
Power motive
Procedural justice
Process theories
Relatedness needs
Second-level outcomes
Security needs
Self-actualization needs
Thematic Apperception Test (TAT)
Valence

Discussion Questions

1. Think about the worst job you have ever had. What approach to motivation did that organization use? Now think about the best job you have ever had. What approach to motivation did that organization use?

2. How does expectancy theory explain the behaviors of the employees who stole from their company after it announced that all employees would take a 15% pay cut for the next ten weeks?

3. Compare and contrast the role of financial incentives in the needs, ERG, and hygiene-motivator theories.

4. What lessons are to be learned from Motorola's motivational approach with its employees in its Guadalajara plant? Which of Maslow's categories of needs is Motorola trying to satisfy for its employees?

5. How could a manager apply ERG theory to motivate employees?

6. How can cafeteria-style benefits plans motivate employees?

7. What is the value of the motivator-hygiene theory?

8. If high achievers are better performers, why don't organizations simply hire high achievers?

9. Discuss the organizational implications for overpayment and underpayment.

10. Evaluate the statement: "A satisfied worker is a productive worker." Under what conditions is the statement false? True?

▲ Developing Skills:

Self-Diagnosis:
What You Want from Your Job?

We have listed the 16 most mentioned characteristics that employees want from their jobs in random order.[35] Please rank these in order of their *importance* to you and then in terms of *satisfaction* for you. Assign number 1 to the most important, 2 to the next most important, 3 to the next most important, and so on. Use the same procedure to identify the characteristics that satisfy you. Compare your answers to those of employees working in a wide variety of jobs and industries, which are provided at the end of this Self-Diagnosis.

Job Characteristics	Importance	Satisfaction
1. Working independently	15	13
2. Chances for promotion	6	12
3. Contact with people	7	9
4. Flexible Hours	4	11
5. Health insurance and other benefits	1	10
6. Interesting work	2	1
7. Work important to society	16	16
8. Job security	9	6
9. Opportunity to learn new skills	10	7
10. High income	3	4
11. Recognition from team members	12	14
12. Vacation time	9	3
13. Regular hours	11	4
14. Working close to home	8	2
15. Little job stress	13	15
16. A job in which I can help others	14	8

Responses

For *job importance*, the rank order of employee responses by question number was 1-6; 2-14; 3-15; 4-16; 5-1; 6-2; 7-13; 8-3; 9-4; 10-11; 11-7; 12-5; 13-8; 14-12; 15-10; and 16-9.

For *job satisfaction*, the rank order of employee responses by question number was 1-3; 2-14; 3-2; 4-6; 5-13; 6-4; 7-9; 8-7; 9-11; 10-12; 11-15; 12-8; 13-5; 14-1; 15-16; 16-10.

Questions

1. Choose any theory of motivation and think about your answers. What situational factors (such as being in school, looking for a new job, wanting more responsibility, or desiring to work for a foreign organization) influenced your rankings of *importance*?

2. How do most of the managers who responded gain their job satisfaction? What theory of motivation helps you understand those rankings?

A Case in Point:
Robert Princeton

In May 1994, Robert Princeton, 24, graduated from Middlebury College with a Bachelor's degree in Theatre. In October 1994, he accepted a job as the Assistant Manager of Falls Video, a rapidly growing chain of video rental outlets in northeastern New York State.

"Momma and Poppa" Valenchia had founded Falls Video in 1990. The operation began as a video rental business in a corner of their Glens Falls grocery store. They were immediately successful and expanded the operation to include four new video rental outlets by 1992. At the same time, they also expanded their grocery business, opening three new stores in surrounding towns. Momma Valenchia was the mastermind behind this growth; Poppa Valenchia was content to remain in the Glens Falls office and keep the books for the growing business. One of the decisions that Momma Valenchia had made was to separate the grocery and video stores. As they expanded the number of grocery and video outlets, she recognized the need for managerial assistance. In June 1992, she split the management duties of the organization. She continued to manage the grocery stores, but she brought in her son, Mario, to run the video business. Mario Valenchia had just earned an Associate Degree in Business from a nearby community college and was eager to take charge of the rapidly growing video business. He was in charge of hiring, firing, and supervision of personnel, loss prevention, video buying, and the day to day management of all video stores.

By the summer of 1994, Falls Video had eight rental outlets within a 25-mile radius of Glens Falls. However, problems had begun to arise. Losses from stolen or misplaced videotapes were up, supplies of newly released films were inadequate to satisfy customer demand, and turnover, absenteeism, and tardiness were way up among the 35 full- and part-time employees of the chain. Momma Valenchia was particularly puzzled by the personnel problems because she had no such difficulties with her grocery store employees. When she asked her son about it, he replied that she had only four stores to manage and that he had eight! Besides, he insisted, attracting competent workers was hard at the low wages they had to pay to remain profitable.

In the early fall of 1994, Momma Valenchia decided to hire Robert Princeton as Assistant Manager of Falls Video to help her son. Momma Valenchia believed that he had a lot of potential and hired him at an annual salary of $29,500.

Princeton began work with enthusiasm. He made it a point to visit each store at least twice a week and, over time, got to know every staff member personally. He found that by taking a staff member to lunch or dinner he could get them to open up about their jobs and the organization. Princeton found this contact with the staff very gratifying. However, he quickly ran into problems with his boss. On one occasion, he allowed a part-time employee to take the weekend off in order to attend an out-of-state funeral. When Mario Valenchia found out, he was furious that the store had been understaffed during the busy weekend period. He informed Princeton that all future schedule changes would have to have his personal approval. Feeling somewhat embarrassed, Princeton sheepishly agreed. On another occasion, Princeton offered to train the staff in the basics of film appreciation because he felt that such training would help them to better assess and satisfy customer needs. The younger Valenchia said that it was a foolish idea, and told Princeton not to waste any company time on it. Although Princeton felt that it was indeed a good idea, he didn't pursue it. At one point Princeton mentioned that many of the full-time employees wanted the company to institute an employee health insurance program. Mario Valenchia's casual response was that the company could not afford the expense and that Princeton should be channeling his efforts into saving money rather than spending it. Even though Princeton was convinced that such a program would boost morale and reduce turnover, he let the matter drop.

Despite all these frustrations, Princeton kept working hard. Although he was troubled by the lack of guidance that he received, he felt that he could demonstrate his value to the organization. After all, when he had approached Momma Valenchia with his concerns about his working relationship with her son, she had said: "Mario is a good and capable boy, and so are you. Work hard and you will be successful." This discussion motivated Princeton to take a strategic view of his efforts.

He initiated a survey of customer preferences in movies to help determine which new titles to purchase. He initiated exit interviews with employees who quit and, as a result, did an informal survey of staff members' perceptions of Falls Video management. Finally, he developed a proposal to track video rentals and customer creditworthiness on a microcomputer system.

In early January of 1995, Princeton scheduled a meeting with Mario Valenchia to discuss his accomplishments during the preceding three months. Valenchia was silent and looked sullen as Princeton presented the results of his work. Princeton provided detailed recommendations for the purchase and resale of new titles and suggested various changes in personnel policies and management practices to boost morale and reduce absenteeism and turnover. He explained how the computer tracking system could reduce losses of videos and improve customer service. Princeton was taken aback by Valenchia's sudden response.

Valenchia: "Who the hell do you think you are?" (followed by a long pause). "Strategic management is *my* job!

Your job is to supervise the workers. I tell *you* what to do, and *you* tell *them* what to do! It's as simple as that. Any questions?''

Princeton: ''Well, yes . . . but . . . I thought. . . .''

Valenchia: ''You're not paid to think—you're paid to do what you're told.'' Poppa showed me your expense account yesterday. The poor old guy almost had a coronary when he tallied it. It's off the wall! Your travel and entertainment expenses in one week are more than mine in a whole month! We give you an office and a telephone here in Glens Falls. I expect you to use them! We're not rich like your family and that snobby private school they sent you to. We have to run this operation on a shoestring. As I've told you before, that's where I need your help. Now get to work on making a real contribution to this organization's bottom line.''

Princeton was flabbergasted! He was proud of his accomplishments and thought that he had proved himself. But, rather than get into a heated argument on the spot, Princeton felt that he had better sleep on it.

The next morning when Princeton arrived for work he found a sealed envelope on his desk with his name on it, marked ''Personal and Confidential.'' At first he assumed that it must be an apology from Mario. He was surprised to find that it was a letter of reprimand for abuse of his expense account and insubordination, signed by both Poppa and Mario Valenchia. It concluded with the statement: ''If you wish to continue your employment with Falls Video, you must learn to become more cost conscious!''

Princeton spent the rest of the morning in his office with the door closed, thinking. At 11:30, he asked Momma Valenchia to have lunch with him. After some hesitation, she agreed. During lunch, Princeton complained that he was not being allowed to have a strategic impact on the organization.

Momma responded: ''Roberto, I hired you as Assistant Manager. Your job is to work for Mario. His job is strategic planning. I still believe that you have a lot of potential. But you must understand the ways of the family. Poppa and Mario run the business. You must cooperate with them. Without cooperation, we cannot run a successful family business.''

At 1:30 Robert Princeton submitted his resignation. He had no job prospects and wasn't sure what his next move would be.[36]

Memorandum

To: Students
From: Faculty Member
Re: Robert Princeton Memo Assignment

Assignment

Write a memo, directed to me, explaining why Robert Princeton quit his job. Also explain how the situation could have been avoided, or at least handled more effectively. Be specific about who should have done what differently at which point in time.

Use the concepts and theories presented in this chapter in order to support your explanations and recommendations. Note that the appropriate use of the concepts and theories is sufficient; you don't need to define them. You may assume that I have a sufficient understanding of all textbook concepts and terminology.

If necessary, you may make appropriate assumptions to compensate for missing or unclear data. However, you must identify your assumptions and justify their appropriateness.

Format

Report your conclusions in memo format. Your response does not have to be limited to one page. However, I urge you to keep your recommendations short and to the point.

References

1. Adapted from Rosenzweig, P. M. *Bill Gates and the Management of Microsoft.* Soldiers Field, Mass.: Harvard Business School, Case Number 9-392-019, 1992; Moore, S. F. The tough interface between execs and techs. *Wall Street Journal,* August 16, 1993, A12; Baker, M. S. Microsoft says growth will slow: Analysts agree. *Puget Sound Business Journal,* August 6, 1993, 31–32.
2. Adapted from Thomson Corporation's *Annual Report.* Paris: 1993; Toor, M. Thomson bids for Sony status. *Marketing,* September 5, 1991, 2–3.
3. Church, G. J. Jobs in an age of insecurity. *Time,* November 22, 1993, 37–38; Harari, O. Back to the future of work. *Management Review,* 1993, 82, 33–36; Poindexter, J. T. Labor and economic trends: Effect on U. S. workforce. *Review of Business,* Summer/Fall, 1993, 34–37; Pearce, J. L. Toward an organizational behavior of contract laborers: Their psychological involvement and effects

on co-workers. *Academy of Management Journal,* 1993, 36, 1082–1096.
4. Locke, E. A., and Latham, G. P. *A Theory of Goal Setting and Task Performance.* Princeton, N.J.: Prentice-Hall, 1990, 6–8.
5. Adapted from Brokaw, L. Minding the store. *Inc.,* November, 1993, 66–78.
6. For an excellent overview of motivation theory, see Kanfer, R. Motivation theory and industrial and organizational psychology. In M. D. Dunnette and L. M. Hough (eds.), *Handbook of Industrial and Organizational Psychology,* Vol. 1. Palo Alto, Calif.: Consulting Psychologist Press, 1990, 75–170.
7. Maslow, A. H. *Motivation and Personality.* New York: Harper & Row, 1970.
8. Elizur, D. Facets of work values: A structural analysis of work outcomes. *Journal of Applied Psychology,* 1984, 69, 379–389; Betz,

E. L. Two tests of Maslow's theory of need fulfillment. *Journal of Vocational Behavior*, 1984, 24, 204–220.

9. Alderfer, C. P. *Existence, Relatedness and Growth: Human Needs in Organizational Settings.* New York: Free Press, 1972.

10. Winer, B. *Human Motivation.* New York: Holt, Rinehard and Winston, 1980; Landy, F. L. and Becker, W. S. Motivation theory reconsidered. In L. L. Cummings and B. M. Staw (eds.), *Research in Organizational Behavior*, Vol. 9. Greenwich, Conn.: JAI Press, 1987, 1–38.

11. Adapted from Cronin, M. P. Teaching workers English. *Inc.*, November, 1993, 127.

12. McClelland, D. C. *Motivational Trends in Society.* Morristown, N.J.: General Learning Press, 1971.

13. McClelland, D. C. and Burnham, D. Power is the great motivator. *Harvard Business Review*, March–April 1976, 100–111; McClelland, D. C., and Boyatzis, R. E. Leadership motive pattern and long-term success in management. *Journal of Applied Psychology*, 1982, 67, 744–751.

14. Adapted from Greco, S. Instant rewards for big deals. *Inc.*, August 1993, 23. Also see Lambert, R. A., Larcker, D. F., and Weigelt, K. The structure of organizational incentives. *Administrative Science Quarterly*, 1993, 38, 438–461.

15. Winter, D. G. The power motive in women and men. *Journal of Personality and Social Psychology*, 1988, 54, 510–519.

16. Herzberg, F. I., Mausner, B., and Snyderman, B. B. *The Motivation to Work.* New York: John Wiley & Sons, 1959.

17. Herzberg, F. I. Worker's needs: The same around the world. *Industry Week*, September 21, 1987, 29–32.

18. Banning, K., and Wintermantel, D. Motorola turns vision to profits. *Personnel Journal*, February 1991, 55; Swort, E. B., Virgile, L., Tucker, T., and Hiser, T. Semiconductor industry. *Value Line*, 1993, 48, 1058–1076. Mariah, E. F. Thinking of a plant in Mexico? *Academy of Management Executive*, 1994, 8, 33–40.

19. Adapted from Miller, M. W. Vestiges of success: As IBM losses mount, so do the complaints about company perks. *Wall Street Journal*, October 27, 1993, A1, A14.

20. Boettger, R. D. and Greer, C. R. On the wisdom of rewarding A while hoping for B. *Organization Science*, 1994, [in press].

21. Vroom, V. H. *Work and Motivation.* New York: John Wiley & Sons, 1964.

22. Ilgen, D. R., Nebeker, D. M., and Pritchard, R. D. Expectancy theory measures: An empirical comparison in an experimental simulation. *Organizational Behavior and Human Performance*, 1981, 28, 189–223.

23. Harrell, A., and Stahl, M. J. Additive information processing and the relationship between expectancy of success and motivational force. *Academy of Management Journal*, 1986, 29, 424–433.

24. Larson, U. R. Supervisor's performance feedback to subordinates: The effect of performance valence and outcome dependence. *Organizational Behavior and Human Decision Processes*, 1986, 37, 391–409.

25. Adapted from Linowes, R. G. The Japanese manager's traumatic entry into the United States: Understanding the American-Japanese cultural divide. *Academy of Management Executive*, November, 1993, 21–40; Hori, S. Fixing Japan's white-collar economy: A personal view. *Harvard Business Review*, November–December 1993, 157–172.

26. Goss, T., Pascale, R., and Athos, A. Risking the present for a powerful future. *Harvard Business Review*, November–December 1993, 97–108.

27. McGill, M. E., and Slocum, J. W., Jr. Unlearning the organization. *Organizational Dynamics*, Fall 1993, 67–79; Kane, S., and Keeton, R. Dream merchants. *Business Atlanta*, June 1993, 34–39; Thompson, R. There's no place like Home Depot. *Nation's Business*, February 1992, 30–33.

28. Adams, J. S. Toward an understanding of inequity. *Journal of Abnormal and Social Psychology*, 1963, 67, 422–436. Also see Harder, J. W. Play for pay: Effects on inequity in a pay-for-performance context. *Administrative Science Quarterly*, 1992, 37, 321–325; Cowherd, D. M. and Levine, D. I. Product quality and pay equity between lower-level employees and top management: An investigation of distributive justice theory. *Administrative Science Quarterly*, 1992, 37, 302–320.

29. Adapted from Greenberg, J. Employee theft as a reaction to underpayment inequity: The hidden costs of pay cuts. *Journal of Applied Psychology*, 1990, 75, 561–568; Wahn, J. Organizational dependence and the likelihood of complying with organizational pressures to behave unethically. *Journal of Business Ethics*, 1993, 12, 245–251; Niehoff, B. P. and Moorman, R. H. Justice as a mediator of the relationship between methods of monitoring and organizational citizenship behavior. *Academy of Management Journal*, 1993, 36, 527–556.

30. Wilhelm, P. Application of distributive justice theory to the CEO pay problem: Recommendations for reform. *Journal of Business Ethics*, 1993, 12, 469–482; Jackson, L. A., Gardner, P. D., and Sullivan, L. A. Explaining gender differences in self-pay expectations: Social comparison standards and perceptions of fair pay. *Journal of Applied Psychology*, 1992, 77, 651–663.

31. Glenn, J. R., Jr., and Van Loo, M. F. Business students' and practitioners' ethical decisions over time. *Journal of Business Ethics*, 1993, 12, 835–847; Serwer, A. E. PayDay! PayDay! *Fortune*, June 14, 1993, 102–111; Howard, L. W., and Miller, J. L. Fair pay for fair play: Estimating pay equity in professional baseball with data envelopment analysis. *Academy of Management Journal*, 1993, 36, 882–894.

32. Greenberg, J. Looking fair vs. being fair: Managing impressions of organizational justice. In L. L. Cummings and B. M. Staw (eds.), *Research in Organizational Behavior*, Vol. 12. Greenwich, Conn.: JAI Press, 1990, 111–158; Ferris, G. R. and Kacmar, K. M. Perceptions of Organizational Politics. *Journal of Management*, 1992, 18, 93–116; Kim, W. C., and Mauborgne, R. A. Procedural justice, attitudes, and subsidiary top management compliance with multinationals' corporate strategic decisions. *Academy of Management Journal*, 1993, 36, 502–526.

33. Gutknecht, J. E., and Keys, B. Mergers, acquisitions and takeovers: Maintaining morale of survivors and protecting employees. *Academy of Management Executive*, August 1993, 26–36; LaFarge, V., and Nurick, A. J. Issues of separation and loss in the organizational exit. *Journal of Management Inquiry*, 1993, 2, 356–365.

34. Personal conversation with Finley, D. Vice-President, Human Resources, Southland Corporation, Dallas, June 15, 1994. Also see Barber, A. E., Dunham, R. B., and Formisano, R. A. The impact of flexible benefits on employee satisfaction: A field study. *Personnel Psychology*, 1992, 45, 55–76.

35. Adapted from a survey of employees conducted by Caggiano, C. What do workers want? *Inc.*, November 1992, 101.

36. Adapted from Leuser, David M., Ph.D. Plymouth State College of the University System of New Hampshire, 1992. Reprinted with permission.

7 Motivating Performance: Goal Setting and Reward Systems

LEARNING OBJECTIVES

After you have finished studying this chapter, you should be able to:

▲ Explain the role of customers, suppliers, and others in the goal-setting process.

▲ List the key factors in goal setting and performance and describe their relationships.

▲ State how management by objectives (MBO) can be applied as a management philosophy and system.

▲ Describe four reward systems for encouraging high performance.

OUTLINE

Preview Case: One-Page Company Game Plan

Essentials of Goal Setting

Purposes of Goal Setting

Impact of Stakeholders

Customer Service Quality Goals

Managing Quality: ISO 9000: Making the Grade

Goal Setting and Performance

Goal Setting Model

Managing In Practice: Cheryl Womack

Managing Across Cultures: Mexican Workers Get Raises

Management by Objectives

Managing Ethics: Churning Accounts

Managing Diversity: Beyond Good Faith

Enhancing Performance Through Reward Systems

Gain-Sharing Plans

Managing in Practice: Long John Silver's Seafood

Flexible Benefit Plans

Managing in Practice: Playcare Development Center

Banking Time Off

Skill-Based Pay

DEVELOPING SKILLS

Self-Diagnosis: *Goal-Setting Questionnaire*

A Case in Point: *Survival at Westinghouse Electric Plant*

PREVIEW CASE

One-Page Company Game Plan

A producer of large-scale metal casting, Elyria Foundry of Elyria, Ohio, was losing $3 million a year on sales of $4 million when Greg Foster took over ten years ago. He recalls that the company was begging for work and took anything that it could find. If a mistake was made, employees blamed management for not asking for their input. Today, Elyria is a $29 million per year, profitable firm. Foster solicited ideas from employees and posted lists of goals to guide and motivate them.

During the past five years, goal setting has emerged as a key management tool at the foundry. All employees are encouraged to submit five to ten goals in November and December for the following year. These goals—such as 100% on-time delivery, answer all telephone calls on the second ring, 50% reduction in personal injuries, 50 employees to visit customers during the year—are discussed at companywide meetings. At these meetings, Foster grades the previous year's performance, goal by goal, and explains what the company will be aiming for next year. Each year's goals cover a broad range of issues from employee retirement programs to applying for a quality certification program (ISO 9000) required for certain European customers. What makes a goal good enough to appear on Elyria's single-page summary?

First, a goal should be attainable by a wide variety of employees and must be meaningful and measurable. Although hundreds of things in the office and shop are important, employees must agree on the key goals for the coming year. Second, a specific and measurable goal gives people something to dig their teeth into because it creates not only a picture of where the company wants to be but also gives employees something to talk about. Third, because employees write each goal, they are committed to those that appear on the single page.[1]

To survive in today's competitive global market, setting challenging goals that take into account both time and quality is no longer an option. Designing a new telephone at AT&T used to take two years. But, says John Hanley, an AT&T vice-president of product development, "We came to the realization that if you get to market sooner with new technology, you can charge a premium until the others follow." For example, AT&T began developing a new cordless phone for the home called the 4200 in early 1988. Rather than trying to save 10% in time here and 5% there, Hanley's goal was to reduce the development cycle by 50%. He says, "It made us change the way we did everything."[2]

The common elements of the achievements cited in the Preview Case are setting goals and developing feedback and reward systems that guide individuals and teams toward those goals. In this chapter, we first outline the role played by customers, suppliers, and other stakeholders and how they affect goal setting. We then present a model of goal setting and performance. We describe how this model provides the foundation for the discussion of management by objectives as a management philosophy and system that attempts to integrate goal setting into organizational life. To close the chapter, we return to the topic of reward systems (also considered in Chapters 5 and 6). Here, we review reward systems being used by organizations to reinforce desired employee behaviors.

ESSENTIALS OF GOAL SETTING

Goal setting is a process intended to increase efficiency and effectiveness by specifying desired outcomes toward which individuals, departments, teams, and organizations should work. **Goals** are the future outcomes (results) that individuals, teams, and organizations desire and strive to achieve.[3] An example of an individual goal is: "I am planning to graduate with a 2.5 grade-point average by the end of the spring semester, 1998."

▼ Purposes of Goal Setting

Even though goal setting is no easy task, the purposes served by establishing goals generally make the effort worthwhile. The following are among the more important purposes of goals.

▲ Goals guide and direct behavior. They increase role clarity by focusing effort and attention in specific directions, thereby reducing uncertainty in day-to-day decision making.

▲ Goals provide challenges and standards against which individual, departmental, team, or organizational performance can be assessed.

▲ Goals serve as a source of legitimacy. They justify various activities and the use of resources to pursue them.

▲ Goals define the basis for the organization's structure. They determine, in part, communication patterns, authority relationships, power relationships, and division of labor.

▲ Goals serve an organizing function.

▲ Goals reflect what the goal setters consider important and thus provide a framework for planning and control activities.[4]

▼ Impact of Stakeholders

Goals and goal setting often are the object of disagreement and conflict, as we demonstrate in Chapter 13. Because diverse groups have a stake in organizational decisions, managers are faced with the continuing need to develop, modify, and discard goals. **Stakeholders** are groups having potential or real power to influence the organization's decisions, such as choice of goals and actions. Stakeholders commonly include customers or clients, employees, suppliers, shareholders, government agencies, unions, public interest groups, and lenders.

Table 7.1 contains several categories of organizational goals of particular interest to five stakeholder groups. Some of these categories may be incompatible with others. Creating a unified and logical system of goal setting for an organization is difficult when

▲ each stakeholder group has substantial power in relation to the organization;

▲ each stakeholder group pushes to maximize its own interests and perceives the interests of some or all other groups as incompatible with its own.

▲ the stakeholders keep changing what they expect (want) from the organization; and/or

▲ the management team itself is divided into competing groups within the organization.[5]

Taken together, these situations represent a worst-case scenario. Thus some of the goals in Table 7.1, if pushed to extremes, will be incompatible and require

TABLE 7.1   Typical Stakeholder Goals

Bankers
▲ Financial strength of the organization
▲ Maintenance of assets that serve as collateral on loans
▲ Improvements in productivity to keep costs competitive
▲ Repayment schedule

Customers
▲ Good service
▲ Competitive prices
▲ Product quality
▲ Product variety
▲ Product satisfaction guaranteed

Employees
▲ Good compensation and job security
▲ Opportunity to learn
▲ Opportunities for fun on the job
▲ Sense of meaning or purpose in the job
▲ Opportunities for advancement
▲ Opportunities for personal development
▲ Good management of diversity issues

Stockholders
▲ Growth in dividend payments
▲ Increase in stock price
▲ Growth in market share
▲ Ethical behavior of employees

Suppliers
▲ Timely debt payment
▲ Repeat customers
▲ Prompt service
▲ Business growth

managers to use keen negotiating skills to balance or resolve the resulting conflicts. Fortunately, managers and other employees don't usually confront such diversity and incompatibility of demands in setting goals.

The most important stakeholders for any organization are its customers or clients. Their goals should be reflected in the goals of the organization as a whole, as well as in the goals of individual employees and groups within the organization. The goal-setting process at Elyria Foundry certainly reflects this perspective, as did the goal of reducing the development cycle time by 50% for the 4200 model telephone at AT&T.

▼ Customer Service Quality Goals

What's involved in setting customer service quality goals? Two core concerns need to be recognized in answering this question. First, customers or clients are the sole judge of service quality. They assess it by comparing the service they receive to the service they desire. An organization can build a strong reputation for quality service only by consistently meeting or exceeding customer service expectations. Second, managers and other employees easily forget the first concern when competitors start vying for business.[6]

Customer service goals may be grouped into five overall categories. In the following list, each category includes a definition and a sample comment from a dissatisfied customer.

▲ *Reliability:* the ability to perform the promised service dependably and accurately. Car leasing customer: "Too often they take care of your problems too fast. They fix your car and two days later you have to take it back for the same problem. They could be a little more attentive and fix the problem permanently."

▲ *Tangibles:* the appearance of physical facilities, equipment, personnel, and communication materials. Hotel customer: "They get you real pumped up with the beautiful ad. When you go in, you expect bells and whistles to go off. Usually, they don't."

▲ *Responsiveness:* the willingness to help customers and to provide prompt service. Business equipment repair customer: "You put in a service call and wait. No one calls back; there is no communication."

▲ *Assurance:* the knowledge and courtesy of employees and their ability to convey trust and confidence. Life insurance customer: "I quote pages out of my policy and my agent cannot interpret what it means to me in language that I can understand."

▲ *Empathy:* the provision of caring, individualized attention to customers or clients. Airline customer: "They'll out-and-out lie to you about how delayed a flight will be so that you won't try to get a flight on another airline."

As demonstrated in the following Managing Quality account, setting and achieving service goals is an evolving process. The service output of an organization is intangible. Moreover, it cannot be stored: A customer evaluates the quality of a service when it is delivered. The system described contains standards that manufacturing organizations are using to evaluate the quality of their services.

MANAGING QUALITY

ISO 9000: Making the Grade

What is ISO 9000—a new fortune teller card or a dial-a-horoscope? No, **ISO 9000** is a set of standards for quality, which is popular in Europe and is taking hold throughout the world. Europeans use it for products traded across international boundaries. DuPont, GE, Eastman Kodak, British Telecom, and Philips Electronics are some of the big-name companies that require their suppliers to meet service standards in order to continue to do business with them. To become certified as an ISO 9000 member, the organization must prove that

MANAGING QUALITY —*Continued*

it is following its own procedures for inspecting production processes, updating engineering drawings, maintaining machinery, calibrating equipment, training employees, and dealing with customer complaints. Unified standards are intended to reduce the number of on-site visits to suppliers. The ISO 9000 standards do not tell GE how to design a more efficient washing machine. However, they do show customers how GE tests products, trains employees, keeps records, and fixes defects. The program is designed to demonstrate that the organization uses quality methods in developing and testing their products.

In its drive to be certified as an ISO 9000 company, Caterpillar has undergone a massive customer service program. In the past when customers complained that an engine wasn't performing well, engineers might order a design change. But Caterpillar had no systematic way of verifying that employees were using these new designs. Today, Caterpillar regularly audits all employees to make sure they are using only the latest documents. This procedure helps identify mistakes that used to be caught only during final product testing or, worse, when the engine reached the customer. Caterpillar doesn't believe that ISO 9000 is going to solve all its manufacturing and customer service problems. But when customers visit any Caterpillar plant, they know that all employees are working from the same standards.[7]

▼ GOAL SETTING AND PERFORMANCE

The key elements of goal setting and performance are the focus of this section. Just as organizations strive to achieve certain goals, individuals are motivated to strive for and attain goals. In fact, the goal setting process is one of the most important motivational tools affecting employees in organizations. We review one of the most accepted theories of goal setting and then indicate how goal setting techniques can be applied to motivate individuals and teams to improve their performance.

▼ Goal-Setting Model

Ed Locke and Gary Latham developed a sophisticated model of individual goal setting and performance. Figure 7.1 shows a simplified version of their model.[8] It identifies the key variables and the general relationships that can lead to high individual performance, some of which we've discussed in previous chapters. The basic idea of the model is that a goal serves as a motivator because it causes people to compare their present performance with that required to achieve the goal. If people believe that they will fall short of a goal, they will feel dissatisfied; they will then work harder to attain the goal so long as they believe that they can do so. Having a goal may improve performance because the goal makes clear the type and level of performance expected. Greg Foster's goal at Elyria Foundry was clear: receive ISO 9000 certification by June 1994. It clearly communicated performance expectations to all employees. By reviewing individual goals each year, Foster also provided information to all employees on how well they were performing in terms of the agreed upon

FIGURE 7.1

Goal-Setting Model

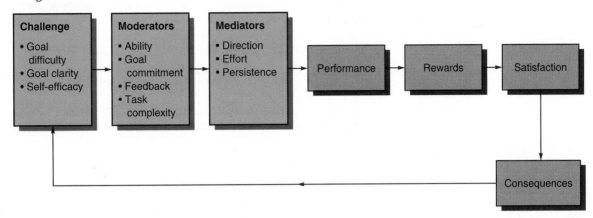

Source: Adapted from Locke, E. A., and Latham, G. P. *A Theory of Goal Setting and Task Performance.* Englewood Cliffs, N.J.: Prentice-Hall, 1990, 253.

targets. With these general ideas in mind, let's consider the basics of the Locke–Latham goal-setting model.

Challenge   Goal setting is the process of developing, negotiating, and establishing targets that challenge the individual. Employees with unclear goals or no goals are likely to work slowly, perform poorly, lack interest, and accomplish less than employees whose goals are clear. In addition, employees with clearly defined goals appear to be energetic and productive. They get things done on time and then move on to other activities (and goals).

Goals may be implicit or explicit, vague or clearly defined, and self-imposed or externally imposed. Whatever their form, goals serve to structure the individual's time and effort. Two key attributes of goals are particularly important.

  ▲ **Goal difficulty.** A goal should be challenging. If it is too easy, the individual may delay or approach the goal lackadaisically. If a goal is too difficult, the individual may not accept it and thus not try to meet it.

  ▲ **Goal clarity.** A goal must be clear and specific if it is to be useful in directing effort. The individual thus will know what is expected and not have to guess.

Clear and challenging goals lead to higher performance than do vague or general goals. Bloomingdale's store in Manhattan has set an annual goal of half a million dollars for each salesperson in its shoe department. Management found it better to set a salesperson's goal at a specific amount than to set a vague goal of "trying to increase sales" or "doing your best." Goals that are difficult but not impossible will lead to higher performance than will easy goals. Unrealistically high goals that cannot be reached may not be accepted or may lead to high performance only in the short run. Individuals eventually get discouraged and stop trying, as predicted by expectancy theory (see Chap-

TABLE 7.2   Impact of Goals on Performance

When Goals Are	Performance Will Tend To Be
Specific and clear	Higher
Vague	Lower
Difficult and challenging	Higher
Set participatively	Higher
Accepted by employees	Higher
Rejected by employees	Lower
Accompanied by positive incentives	Higher

ter 6). Goal setting may be used to enhance creativity. In order to be creative, many individuals need to focus their attention and effort on either a do-your-best or a difficult goal.[9]

With clear and challenging goals, employees are likely to focus on job-related tasks, high levels of performance, and goal achievement. Table 7.2 provides a summary of the key links between goal setting and individual performance.

A third key factor that influences the establishment of challenging goals is self-efficacy. In Chapter 6, we defined *self-efficacy* as the individual's belief that he or she can perform at a certain level in a given situation. It may be assessed by having individuals rate their confidence in attaining different performance levels. Predictably, individuals who set high goals have higher self-efficacy than those who set lower goals.[10]

The following Managing In Practice piece demonstrates how goal difficulty, goal clarity, and high self-efficacy techniques enabled Cheryl Womack to achieve outstanding results at VCW. This organization sells insurance, drug-testing services, and audiotapes to 8,600 independent truckers. In ten years, VCW has grown from a one-woman operation to a company with more than 70 employees and annual revenues of $25 million.

MANAGING IN PRACTICE

Cheryl Womack

People who work for Womack and don't give their jobs 110% don't last long. If they aren't willing to come in early and leave late during a crunch or can't cooperate with each other, they are "written-up" by their department heads and are given firm deadlines for improving. Those who can't take responsibility and work hard are urged to leave.

Tough, yes. Womack hires people not so much for their credentials as for their attitudes—passion for work, personal flexibility, and excitement. Once hired, the individual writes a personal goal statement. Goals are specific and measurable, such as the number of insurance policies per month a person is to write or the number of workers' compensation claims a person is to settle per month. Employees review the goals monthly to verify progress. Teamwork is important. If an employee isn't a team player, someone usually says something. Most people who can't handle the challenge of working with others leave within the first month.[11]

Moderators Figure 7.1 also shows four of the factors that moderate the strength of the relationship between goals and performance. *Ability* limits the individual's capacity to respond to a challenge. The relation of goal difficulty to performance is curvilinear. That is, performance levels off when a person reaches the limits of his or her ability.

The second factor, **goal commitment,** refers to the individual's determination to reach a goal, regardless of whether the goal was set by the person or a manager. How committed are you to achieving a top grade in this class? Take a minute and complete the questionnaire in Table 7.3. Your commitment to a goal is likely to be stronger if you make a public commitment to achieve it, if you have a high need for achievement, and if you believe that you can control those activities that will help you reach that goal.[12] The effect of participation on goal commitment is a complex one. Positive goal commitment is more likely if employees participate in goal setting, which often leads to a sense of ownership. Not expecting or wanting to be involved in goal setting reduces the importance of employee participation in terms of goal commitment. Even when a manager has to assign goals without employee participation, doing so leads to more focused efforts and better performance than if no goals were set.

The expected rewards for achieving goals play an important role in the degree of goal commitment.[13] The greater the extent to which employees believe that positive rewards (merit pay raises, bonuses, promotions, opportunities to perform interesting tasks, and the like) are contingent on achieving goals, the greater will be their commitment to the goals. These ideas are similar to those of the expectancy theory of motivation. Similarly, if employees expect to be punished for not achieving goals, the probability of goal commitment also is higher.[14] However, recall that punishment and the fear of

TABLE 7.3   Goal Commitment Questionnaire

Items	Strongly Agree	Agree	Undecided	Disagree	Strongly Disagree
1. I am strongly committed to pursuing a top grade.	——	——	——	——	——
2. I am willing to expend a great deal of effort beyond what I'd normally do to achieve this top grade.	——	——	——	——	——
3. I really care if I achieve a top grade.	——	——	——	——	——
4. Much is to be gained by trying to achieve this grade.	——	——	——	——	——
5. Revising this goal, depending on how things go this term, isn't likely.	——	——	——	——	——
6. A lot would have to happen for me to abandon this goal.	——	——	——	——	——
7. Expecting to reach my goal is realistic for me.	——	——	——	——	——

Scoring: Give yourself 5 points for each Strongly Agree response; 4 points for each Agree response; 3 points for each Undecided response; 2 points for each Disagree response; and 1 point for each Strongly Disagree response. The higher your score, the greater your goal commitment to achieve a top grade in this class.

Source: Adapted from Hollenback, J. R., Williams, C. R., and Klein, H. J. An empirical examination of the antecedents of commitment to goals. *Journal of Applied Psychology,* 1989, 74, 18–23.

punishment as primary means of guiding behavior may create problems (see Chapter 5).

Employees compare expected rewards to rewards actually received. If the expected and received rewards are the same, the reward system is likely to continue to support goal commitment. For example, at VCW salaries are average, but benefits include full health insurance, profit sharing, generous spot bonuses for reaching difficult goals, and on-site day care. If employees perceive that the rewards they receive are much less than the rewards they expected, they may sense inequity. If inequity actually exists, employees eventually lessen their goal commitment. Teamwork and peer pressure are other factors that affect a person's commitment to a goal.[15]

Feedback makes goal setting and individual responses to goal achievement (performance) a dynamic process. It provides information to an employee and others about outcomes and the employee's degree of goal achievement.[16] Feedback gives the individual an external way to assess performance and compare expected rewards to those received. Such stock taking, in turn, can influence an employee's degree of goal commitment.

Task complexity is the last moderator of the relationship between goals and performance that we consider. For simple tasks (for example, stuffing envelopes), the effort encouraged by challenging goals leads directly to task performance. For more complex tasks (for example, studying to achieve a high grade), effort doesn't lead directly to effective performance. The individual also must decide where and how to allocate effort. We consider a variety of issues associated with simple and complex jobs in Chapter 16 when we discuss job design.

Mediators   Let's assume that the individual has challenging goals and that the moderating factors support the achievement of these goals. How do the three mediators—direction, effort, and persistence—shown in Figure 7.1 affect performance? *Direction* of attention focuses behaviors on activities expected to result in goal achievement and at the same time steers people away from activities irrelevant to achieving the goals. The amount of *effort* a person exerts depends on the difficulty of the goal. Generally, the greater the challenge, the greater will be the effort expended to achieve the goal, assuming that the person is trying to reach and is committed to the goal. Finally, *persistence* refers to a person's willingness to work at the task over an extended period of time and overcome obstacles in order to achieve the goals. Most sports require individuals to practice long and hard to raise their skills to a high level and maintain them at that level.

Performance   Performance is likely to be high when (1) challenging goals are set, (2) moderators are present, and (3) mediators are operating. Three basic types of quantitative measures of outcome may be used to assess performance: units of production or quality (amount produced, number of errors); dollars (profits, costs, income, sales); and time (job attendance, ability to meet deadlines).

When such measures are unavailable or inappropriate, qualitative goals and indicators may be used. Accordingly, many organizations have developed a **code of ethics** to guide employee behavior and to help management assess employees qualitatively. Creating ethical guidelines has several advantages that Boeing, GTE, and Johnson & Johnson, among others, consider important:

▲ to help employees identify what their organization recognizes as acceptable business practices;

▲ to legitimize the consideration of ethics as part of decision making.

▲ to avoid discussions among employees about what is right and wrong; and

▲ to avoid ambivalence in decision making caused by an organizational reward system that appears to reward unethical behavior.[17]

Rewards   We discussed rewards at length in Chapters 5 and 6, so we merely summarize them here. When an employee attains a high level of performance, rewards can be important inducements to maintain that level. Recall that rewards can be external (bonuses, promotions, public recognition, and so on) or internal (a sense of achievement, pride in accomplishment, feelings of success and efficacy, and the like).

The following Managing Across Cultures feature indicates some of the challenges facing Canadian, Mexican, and U.S. companies under the North American Free Trade Agreement (NAFTA). One of the main problems is that of Mexican industrial wages, averaging $1.99 an hour, which need to be raised and tied to productivity.

MANAGING ACROSS CULTURES

Mexican Workers Get Raises

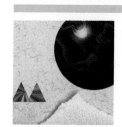

Mexican manufacturers have been suffering through hard economic times and are in no mood to pay workers more. There is pressure from the government to boost wages, but slowly so as not to fuel inflation. Canadian and U.S. exporting firms are worried that, unless wages increase, Mexican workers will lack the buying power to purchase their goods.

For the more than 8 million Mexicans who work for large companies, the government has proposed that gains in productivity be tied to bonuses based on individual performance rather than overall wages. Telmex (Mexican telephone company) has established a $150 million incentive pool and started awarding bonuses to workers based on their performance. It used to be that repairpersons would complete half of their rounds during regular working hours, and save the rest to do at costly overtime. Then, complaining of low salaries, they would demand a "tip" from customers to do the job right. Under the new bonus plan, if workers meet monthly performance goals, they can earn bonuses equal to as much as 30% of their salary.[18]

Satisfaction   Many factors—including challenging work, interesting co-workers, salary, the opportunity to learn, and good working conditions—influence a person's satisfaction with the job. However, in the Locke–Latham model, the primary focus is on the employee's degree of satisfaction with having achieved goals. Employees who set unrealistically high and difficult goals may be less satisfied than employees who set lower, achievable goals. Difficult goals are less frequently achieved, and satisfaction with performance is positively associated with the number of successes experienced. Thus some compromise regarding goal difficulty may be necessary to maximize both satisfaction and performance. However, sources of satisfaction are associated simply with striving for difficult goals, such as responding to a challenge, making some progress toward the goals, and the belief that benefits may be derived from the experience regardless of the outcome.

Consequences   Individuals who are both satisfied with and committed to the organization are more likely to stay with the organization and to accept the challenges that it presents than are individuals who are less satisfied and committed. Turnover and absenteeism rates for satisfied and committed individuals are low. This link brings us full circle to the beginning of the Locke–Latham goal-setting model.

What might happen if things go badly and the individual experiences dissatisfaction rather than satisfaction? Individual responses fall into at least six possible categories: (1) job avoidance (quitting); (2) work avoidance (absenteeism, arriving late, and leaving early); (3) psychological defenses (alcohol and drug abuse); (4) constructive protest (complaining); (5) defiance (refusing to do what is asked); and (6) aggression (theft, assault). Quitting is the most common outcome of severe dissatisfaction.[19]

Managerial Significance   The goal-setting model has important implications for both employees and managers. First, it provides an excellent framework to assist the manager or team in diagnosing the potential problems with low- or average-performing employees. Several diagnostic questions might be: (1) How were the goals set? (2) Are the goals challenging? (3) What is affecting goal commitment? and (4) Does the employee know when he or she has done a good job? Second, the goal-setting model provides concrete advice to the manager on how to create a high-performance work environment. Third, it portrays the system of relationships and interplay among key factors such as goal difficulty, goal commitment, feedback, and rewards to achieve high performance.

▼ Management by Objectives

Management by objectives (MBO) is a philosophy and system of management that serves as both a planning aid and a method of working. A widely used management approach, it reflects a positive philosophy about people and a participative management style. Hewlett-Packard and Procter & Gamble are among the organizations that use MBO successfully.

Management by objectives involves managers and their subordinates in jointly setting goals for work performance and personal development, evaluating progress toward these goals, and integrating individual, team, departmental, and organizational goals. The manager and employee periodically evaluate the employee's success in attaining the goals.

Although many people have contributed to the development of MBO, Peter Drucker coined the term *management by objectives* in about 1950.[20] The process

FIGURE 7.2

Management by Objectives
Process

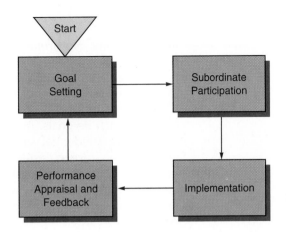

contains four basic components, each of which has several dimensions. As Figure 7.2 shows, these components are goal setting, subordinate participation, implementation, and performance appraisal and feedback. The arrows indicate that a strong interrelationship exists among the components and that all should operate simultaneously to make the MBO process effective.

Goal setting Subordinates and superiors define and focus on job goals rather than rules, activities, and procedures. Here, we consider goals, objectives, outputs, quotas, results, ends, and performance standards as equal concepts. The goal-setting process includes identifying specific areas of job responsibility, developing performance standards in each area, and, possibly, formulating a work plan for achieving the goals. At Innovative Office Systems, Inc., a sales representative for the cellular phone company has a goal of selling $1,000 worth of equipment a month and five new cellular phone systems every two weeks. To achieve these goals, Innovative Office Systems management believes that each sales representative should complete 20 sales call per week.

What happens when employees don't reach their goals? Many employees under extreme pressure to meet their organization's goals resort to overcharging customers for auto repairs, falsifying medical tests, and countless other stratagems. Reliance on a numerically based reward system often produces such unintended behaviors, which harm customers. The following Managing Ethics story highlights an incident that occurred at the Prudential Bache Securities branch in Dallas.

MANAGING ETHICS

Churning Accounts

Charles Grose, a manager in the Prudential Bache Securities Branch in Dallas, noticed that a broker was rapidly buying and selling securities that brought clients less than $200 in profits but generated more than $1,000 in sales commissions for the broker. The broker was preying on old women who didn't understand the mechanics of buying and selling stocks. Grose wrote a confidential memo to the regional director. The regional director, rather than discipline the stockbroker, had another idea: destroy the memo. Prudential had

MANAGING ETHICS —*Continued*

an honor code: No broker should just trade for commissions. But why did these abuses occur?

At the core of the regional director's decision to destroy the memo was the fact that he didn't want to discipline a broker who brought the firm more than $700,000 in commissions during the year. If the broker left the firm, the branch couldn't reach its goals. In an effort to meet the required sales and commissions levels, Prudential stockbrokers also traded customers' shares without authorization, forged customers' signatures, made trades for dead customers, and put customers in questionable investments. With money pouring into both the firm and brokers, everyone benefited except the customer. Managers gained because their bonuses were based on branch income. Brokers gained because they earned higher commissions on firm-sponsored products, such as mutual funds or limited partnerships.

Prudential has been trying to clean up such practices in the Dallas office. New managers have been put in place and Prudential is cooperating with numerous federal regulatory agencies. Customer lawsuits against the firm cost it $371 million.[21]

Particular job responsibilities usually change less dramatically and less frequently over time than does the specific goal associated with each area of responsibility. At Innovative Office Systems, the salesperson is responsible for sales volume. However, specific sales volumes can vary sharply because of general economic conditions, changes in market demand, more or fewer opportunities in a sales territory, and so on. Highland Super Stores, Inc., an electronics and appliance chain, recently eliminated daily quotas because it discovered that salespeople were becoming too aggressive with customers. Management replaced the quotas with monthly goals for entire departments.

Various guidelines have been offered to managers and team leaders on how to set goals. Here is one example.

▲ State what must be done. If you are setting goals with a subordinate, you may find a job description helpful. It should list the tasks to be performed, the outcomes expected, the other jobs with which this one coordinates, necessary equipment, supervisory duties, and so on. Critical job requirements, on which job success depends, can further clarify the job description.

▲ Specify how performance will be measured. Often you can use time, money, or physical units. Sometimes, though, success is more subjective and hard to measure objectively. We can still define performance by specifying behaviors or actions that we know will lead to success.

▲ Specify the performance standard. A readily accepted approach is to start goal setting by letting previous performance set the standard. Most employees consider their average previous performance, or that of their team, to be a fair goal. Performance in some jobs, though, cannot be measured so precisely. The job may be unique or so new that no previous performance measures are available. If so, goal setting becomes a matter of judgment.

▲ Set deadlines to reach goals. Some goals lend themselves to daily or weekly accomplishment. Others can be accomplished only monthly, quarterly, or annually.

▲ Rank goals in order of importance. Clear understanding of priorities helps employees achieve their purpose. People work best when they have compelling goals.

▲ Rate goals as to difficulty and importance. We may need to be precise when we deal with multiple goals, as in the case of an employee's job description or a departmental goal.[22]

Many managers at Pacific Bell, Coopers & Lybrand, Pepsi-Cola, American Express, and Digital Equipment, among others, also have used these guidelines to manage diversity in their organizations. As we pointed out in previous chapters, managing diversity is now a simple fact of life that influences employee recruitment, retention, motivation, and performance. A wide variety of tools for changing the behaviors of employees exist, but setting goals is a key component. The following Managing Diversity feature indicates how Pacific Bell used the preceding guidelines to modify its recruiting practices.

MANAGING DIVERSITY

Beyond Good Faith

Affirmative action programs are supposed to involve a good-faith effort on the part of the organization to seek out, recruit, and encourage minority applicants for jobs. Yet in many organizations, this means placing the words "We are an equal opportunity employer" at the bottom of advertisements, and running those ads in selected "minority publications." Such efforts certainly do not discourage minority applicants, but they do very little to encourage them also. Pacific Bell decided to take some actions that went beyond the minimum good-faith program.

It established goals for departments in terms of minority representation. To achieve these goals, recruiters from the human resources and engineering departments were sent to colleges that tended to enroll higher proportions of minority students. Students' scores on standardized tests were examined to determine racial or gender bias. Recruiters were asked to contact minority faculty and staff to identify deserving students. Once the students were identified, recruiters helped them with such basic tools as résumé writing, interviewing techniques, and job hunting.

To further help identify talent, Pacific Bell's managers developed two programs. First, they designed a summer management program to prepare minority students in their junior year for entry-level management jobs upon graduation. To reach this goal, a Bell manager was assigned to coach each student. Before the coaching started, both the coach and student were required to attend a half-day seminar on diversity issues. During the summer, senior managers were introduced to all summer students through workshops, recreational events, and the like. As a result of the program, Pacific Bell offered jobs to 64 percent of these students upon graduation from college. Second, 17 California colleges developed scholarship programs to lessen the financial burdens facing these students.

What did these programs accomplish? In 1980, minority managers were 17.5% of the total. Today, they represent more than 28% of the total.[23]

Participation In the MBO process, a moderate to high level of participation by subordinates in goal setting seems to be effective. However, before subordinates can effectively participate in MBO, they must have some autonomy in their jobs or an increase in autonomy must be planned as part of the process. Autonomy enables employees to plan and control what they do and how they do it, rather than merely doing what they are told. Thus highly routine and programmed jobs should be redesigned before applying the MBO approach to them.

Implementation Implementation of the MBO process requires translating the outcomes from goal setting into actions that ultimately will lead to the attainment of the desired goals. Action planning, which indicates how goals are to be achieved, often accompanies the implementation phase. During implementation, superiors must give greater latitude and choice to subordinates, perhaps by discontinuing day-to-day oversight of their activities. But superiors must be available to coach and counsel subordinates to help them reach their goals. They must play a helping or facilitating role rather than a judgmental role. Superiors should hold periodic meetings during the year with subordinates to review progress, discuss any assistance needed, and modify goals as needed. This approach prevents employees from perceiving MBO as a rigid system and encourages them to address significant new problems or changes as they occur.

Performance Appraisal and Feedback Performance appraisal under MBO involves (1) identifying goals and measurement factors, (2) measuring performance against those goals, (3) reviewing performance with the employee, and (4) developing ways to improve future performance. Subordinates develop a clear understanding of their progress through performance appraisal and feedback. Feedback is a key element of MBO because it identifies the extent to which employees have attained their goals. The knowledge of results is essential to improving job performance and fastening personal development in the form of new skills, attitudes, and motivation. There are many ways to recognize and reward performance beyond pay. Ultimately, however, the satisfaction of achieving goals is one of the most cherished rewards.[24]

Management by objectives encourages self-evaluation of performance. Honest self-evaluation by employees can provide insight into their own performance and the possible need to modify their behaviors to achieve their goals. When people are motivated, managers can turn their attention to other issues, recognizing that their subordinates are taking charge of attaining the agreed upon goals.

At Electronic Systems Personnel, a $2 million a year executive search firm in Minneapolis, about 20% of the compensation package of a new salesperson is activity based. The firm tracks three activities weekly: daily calls to potential job candidates, company visits by candidates, and "balls in the air," or leads that could convert into sales. A salesperson who meets these goals can—in addition to salary—make up to $400 a month in bonuses. Salespeople also can evaluate their own performance. They know that placing 30 calls per day reaps a $100 bonus that month and that making three visits a week also nets a $100 bonus. One to four balls in the air weekly is good for an additional $100. Doing all three things brings in another $100.[25]

Managerial Significance   Critics have attacked MBO, particularly with respect to ways that organizations apply it. These criticisms relate mainly to how managers actually use the process, rather than to how it is supposed to be used. These criticisms include the following.

▲ Too much emphasis is placed on reward–punishment psychology (that is, people are rewarded for accomplishing goals and punished for not doing so).

▲ An excessive amount of paperwork and red tape develops, the very things that MBO is supposed to reduce.

▲ The process is really controlled and imposed from the top, allowing little opportunity for real employee participation.

▲ The process turns into a zero-sum (win–lose) game between superior and subordinate.

▲ Aspects of jobs that can be objectively rather than subjectively measured receive the most emphasis.

▲ Too much emphasis on individual goals and performance drives out recognition of the need for collaborative teamwork and group goals. Individuals may satisfy their own goals to the detriment of overall goals.[26]

ENHANCING PERFORMANCE THROUGH REWARD SYSTEMS

In Chapters 5 and 6, we discussed the typical rewards that organizations give to employees. They include fringe benefits and opportunities to engage in challenging assignments and achieve difficult goals. In this section, we discuss reward systems that organizations use to motivate employees. These reward systems include gain-sharing, flexible benefit plans, banking time off, and skill-based pay.[27] Table 7.4 summarizes the strengths and limitations of each system.

TABLE 7.4   Reward Systems That Improve Productivity

Reward System	Strengths	Limitations
Gain-sharing/Scanlon plan	Plans reward employees who reach specified production levels and control labor costs.	Formula can be complex; trust on part of employees and management is needed.
Flexible benefit plans	Plans are tailored to fit employee needs.	Administrative costs are high for management.
Banking time off	Additional time off is contingent on employee performance.	Managers must give high performers more time off than poor performers.
Skill-based pay	Employee acquires new skills before being paid more.	Training costs to improve employee skills may be high. Employees can "top out." Labor costs increase as employees master more skills.

▼ Gain-Sharing Plans

Through **gain-sharing plans,** organizations provide regular cash bonuses to employees for higher productivity, cost reductions, or improved quality.[28] Many organizations (such as TRW, Mead, GE, and Goodyear) are discovering that, when designed correctly, gain-sharing plans can increase employee motivation and involvement. Specific formulas tailored to each organization measure performance and determine gain-sharing awards. Many gain-sharing plans encourage employees to become involved in making decisions that will affect their rewards.

Gain-sharing plans differ from **profit-sharing plans,** which give employees a portion of the company's profits.[29] In contrast, gain-sharing plans are tied to improvements at a plant, division or department. Profit sharing may have a limited effect on the individual because an employee may have little ability to influence the organization's overall profitability. Many factors—such as competitors' products, state of the economy, or inflation—that are well beyond the control of employees influence company profits. Profit-sharing plans are popular in Japan. For example, at Seiko Instruments, many workers and managers receive a bonus twice a year that equals four or five months' salary. The actual amount of the bonus is based on overall company performance.[30]

A popular version of gain-sharing is the Scanlon plan, named after Joe Scanlon, a union leader in the 1930s.[31] The **Scanlon plan** is a system of rewards by which management shares with employees the benefits from improved productivity. Working together, employees and managers set a formula for distributing rewards based on a ratio of total labor costs to total sales volume. If actual labor costs are less than expected, the difference goes into a bonus pool. The bonus pool often is split equally between the company and employees, with all employees receiving bonuses that are percentages of their salaries.[32] Both employees and managers need to share in developing the plan and receiving the gain for the plan to work. Long John Silver's Seafood Shoppes, Inc., developed a Scanlon plan that targets hourly workers and each restaurant's profitability. The following Managing in Practice account illustrates how that plan works.

MANAGING IN PRACTICE

Long John Silver's Seafood

Long John Silver's has more than 16,000 employees who work in its 1,451 restaurants. The program gives hourly employees quarterly bonuses according to improvements in their restaurant's sales and profits. The "improvements" are based on quarterly performance compared to the same quarter in the preceding year. For managers, annual bonuses are tied to the company's overall performance and its stock price. According to William Flock, senior vice-president of human resources, managers are expected to have a longer time horizon and can affect the entire company's performance to a much greater extent than can hourly employees.

Expectations and opportunity are different for hourly employees. The reason that the Scanlon plan works for these employees is that they are rewarded

MANAGING IN PRACTICE —*Continued*

for things they can control. What can hourly workers do to be more sales-oriented? Every piece of pie they sell earns them more money. Serving customers faster enables the restaurant to serve more customers each day. Giving customers "TLC" (tender loving care) brings in more repeat business and fewer complaints. At one restaurant, hourly employees suggested to management that it open up the store's limited menu. Management agreed, and the number of luncheon customers increased by more than 400 per week.[33]

▼ Flexible Benefit Plans

Flexible benefit plans allow employees to choose the benefits they want, rather than having management choose for them. According to Towers Perrin, a global compensation consulting firm, a corporation's benefit plan costs about 37% of its employee cash compensation package.[34] This amount represents a huge cost to organizations, considering that most organizations set aside only 5% or less for merit pay increases. Under flexible benefit plans, employees decide how they want to receive the benefit amounts, tailoring the benefit package to their needs. The plans are based on the assumption that employees can make important and intelligent decisions about their benefits. Some employees take all their benefits in cash; others choose additional life insurance, child or elder care, dental insurance, or retirement plans. Extensive benefit options may be very attractive to an employee with a family, whereas fewer benefits might be attractive to a young, single employee. Older employees value retirement plans more than younger employees do, and generally put more money into retirement funds. Employees with elderly parents may desire financial assistance in providing care for them. At Traveler's Insurance Company, for example, employees may choose benefits of up to $5,000 a year for the care of dependent elderly parents.

Thousands of organizations now offer flexible benefits plans.[35] Why have they become so popular? Flexible benefit plans offer three distinct advantages. First, they allow employees themselves to make important decisions about their personal finances. Second, the organization doesn't have to assume a paternalistic role of knowing what is best for each employee. Employees may choose what gives them the greatest personal benefit. Many traditional benefit plans were targeted for employees who have families and are in the middle of their working careers. Although there still are many such individuals, their number is dwindling. More and more families have two wage earners, the number of single-parent families has increased, medical costs have skyrocketed, and inflation has increased retirement living expenses. Third, such plans highlight the economic value of many benefits to employees. Most employees have little idea of the cost of such benefits because their organizations have been willing to pay for all or part of the benefits even though many employees might not want all of them.

The following Managing in Practice feature illustrates how Dow Chemical and River West Medical Center worked together to establish a child development center to help employees balance work and family demands. Dow and River West recognized that the life-styles and needs of Dow's employees were changing. The increase in dual wage earner families and working single parents presented Dow with an opportunity to use its benefits plan creatively. The program was designed to meet both traditional child development needs and employees' child care needs.

MANAGING IN PRACTICE

Playcare Development Center

The River West Playcare Child Development Center is an innovative program designed to satisfy the needs of employees at Dow Chemical. Dow wanted to provide a child care center for its employees but didn't want to manage it. River West Medical Center had extra space and rented it to Dow.

The 4,800 square foot center is open from 6:00 A.M. until 6:00 P.M., Monday through Friday. The children are predominantly preschool aged and infants. However, after-school activities are planned for school aged children; places to watch movies and do homework also are provided. The center features a sick bay that enables parents to have sick children treated while the parents are at work. Nurses from the hospital staff the sick bay. The center has space for 75 children and one staff person for every 4 children. Dow subsidizes the cost of this care, which parents who use the facility basically pay for. Dow also provides summer program transportation, on-site inspections by Dow's safety and security personnel, and other services.

Dow employees are happy with the center. The company also is pleased because working parents are absent and late less often owing to child care problems. The center has received a lot of in-house publicity and has helped Dow's recruiting efforts. Michael Geissler, a manager at the center, believes that, in tight labor markets and difficult economic times, "benefits are the key to holding employees, not salaries."[36]

Flexible benefit plans have some limitations. First, because of the different choices among employees, record keeping becomes more complicated. Sophisticated computer systems are essential to keep straight the details of employees' records. Second, organizations can't accurately predict the number of employees who might choose each benefit. This inability may affect the firm's group rates for life and medical insurance because they are based on the number of employees covered by the plans.

▼ Banking Time Off

Time off from work with pay is attractive to some people. Typically, vacation schedules and their lengths are based on the number of years an employee has worked for the organization. An extension of such a system is to base the amount of time off on performance. That is, employees can bank time-off credit if they perform well. At Tandem Computers, high-performing employees earn extra vacation time and can bank this time for one year. If the employees do not use their vacation time, they can roll the credit over to a savings plan. In setting up such programs, organizations should be aware of some potential issues. For example, what if an employee wants to use banked time during a rush period for the organization? What if an employee's extended absence could negatively affect productivity? How long should an employee be able to retain banked time?

A version of banking time off is SelectTime, which NationsBank and other organizations offer. SelectTime gives employees the option of reducing their work hours for family reasons. They can use this time to care for any dependent family member, whether child, spouse, or parent. This time off is not vacation time. As soon as the need is satisfied, the employee returns to work full time. If the employee's manager agrees, the person's salary and benefits are reduced in proportion to the reduction in hours. NationsBank President Hugh McColl believes that this program permits the bank to utilize its human resources more fully. "The beauty of this concept is that it accommodates people." The program has reduced NationsBank training costs because there is less need to recruit new employees.

▼ Skill-Based Pay

Paying people according to their value in the labor market makes a great deal of sense. After all, employees who develop multiple skills become even more valuable to the organization. **Skill-based pay** depends on the number and level of job-related skills the employee has learned.[37] About 40 percent of the largest U.S. organizations, such as TRW, Honeywell, and Westinghouse, use skill-based pay for at least some of their blue-collar employees.

Skill-based pay is easiest to describe for a production team in a manufacturing plant. Typically, management can rather easily identify all the skills needed to perform the team's tasks and pinpoint the skills that employees need. Each skill receives a financial value, say $0.50 per hour. Initially, the size of a raise is the same regardless of the content of the job learned. But as an employee learns a new skill, the amount of pay increases. This approach fits particularly well those employees who set high but attainable goals and who want to manage themselves and participate in decisions that affect their performance. The Shell Canada chemical plant in Sarnia, Ontario, permits individuals to learn all the jobs in the plant. Employees reach top pay only when they have attained this level of competency, which typically can take eight or more years. At Loral Vought Systems, some employees are rewarded for economic skills and knowledge of the business and corporation.[38]

The most obvious advantage of skill-based pay in a production situation is flexibility. When employees can perform multiple tasks, managers gain tremendous flexibility in utilizing the work force. Largely as a result of the Tylenol poisoning tragedy, Johnson & Johnson decided to redo completely its packaging of Tylenol to increase safety. Because of the firm's skill-based pay system, employees understood the technology involved and were able to introduce the new packaging changes quickly. Johnson & Johnson also found that skill-based pay can increase productivity while decreasing supervisory costs. Employees are motivated to gain and use new skills because the organization equitably rewards them for learning.

Skill-based pay has some disadvantages. The most obvious one has to do with the high pay rates that it tends to produce. The very nature of the plan encourages individuals to become more valuable to the organization and, as a result, to be paid more. Learning multiple skills requires a large investment in training and lost production time as employees gain new skills. Thus the organization sometimes may have inexperienced and overpaid employees doing the work. A worst case scenario for the organization is that many employees know how to do every job, but at any particular time, all the jobs are being done by employees who aren't highly proficient at them. Finally, employees may become frustrated when no job openings are available in areas for which they have learned these new skills. Most skill-based programs require employees to perform skills regularly and competently in order to be paid for them.

Summary

Goal setting is intended to increase efficiency and effectiveness by specifying the desired outcomes toward which individuals, teams, departments, and organizations should work. Goal setting doesn't take place in a vacuum. Stakeholders such as customers, shareholders, and employees influence the selection of organizational and individual employee goals. On a day-to-day basis, customers or clients probably are the main driving force in the selection of key goals.

The goal-setting model presented begins with the challenges provided for the individual. Challenges are explained in terms of goal difficulty, goal clarity, and self-efficacy. Four moderating factors—ability, goal commitment, feedback, and task complexity—influence the strength of the relationship between challenging goals and performance. Then, three mediators—direction, effort, and persistence—act as facilitators of goal attainment. Performance, rewards, satisfaction, and consequences complete the model.

Management by objectives (MBO) is both a philosophy and a management process. Managers and subordinates jointly set goals, evaluate performance, and modify the goals and behavior as required.

The chapter concludes with a discussion of four reward systems designed to enhance performance. We explored the features, advantages, and limitations of gain-sharing plans, flexible benefit plans, banking time-off plans, and skill-based pay plans.

Key Words and Concepts

Code of ethics	Goal difficulty	Profit-sharing plans
Flexible benefit plans	Goal setting	Scanlon plan
Gain-sharing plans	Goals	Skill-based pay
Goal clarity	ISO 9000	Stakeholders
Goal commitment	Management by Objectives (MBO)	

Discussion Questions

1. Imagine that you are establishing goal setting in an organization that you're familiar with. How might various stakeholders influence the goal-setting process?

2. Think of an organization for which you currently work or have worked. How would you evaluate the organization and its employees in terms of the five service quality goals stated in the chapter?

3. List your five most important personal goals. Evaluate each for difficulty and clarity. What are the implications, if any, of this assessment?

4. Think of a current or previous job. Evaluate your level of goal commitment. What factors influenced your level of goal commitment? Did your level of commitment affect your performance?

5. In 1994, investigators revealed that researchers at St. Luc's Hospital in Montreal falsified data on breast cancer patients. Although the fabricated data didn't affect the results of the entire study, why do people engage in such behaviors?

6. What are the similarities and differences between gain-sharing and profit-sharing plans? Explain how each relates to goal-setting techniques.

7. What are some problems for employees working for an organization that has adopted skill-based pay systems?

8. Can management equitably tie flexible benefit plans to employee performance? If so, what are the advantages of doing so? The disadvantages?

▲ Developing Skills

Self-Diagnosis: Goal-Setting Questionnaire

Instructions

The following statements refer to a job you currently hold or have held. Read each statement and then select a response from the scale that best describes your view. You may want to use a separate sheet of paper to record your responses and compare them with others in class or at work.

Scale

Almost Never   1   2   3   4   5   Almost Always

_____ 1. I understand exactly what I am supposed to do on my job.

_____ 2. I have specific, clear goals to aim for on my job.

_____ 3. The goals I have on this job are challenging.

_____ 4. I understand how my performance is measured on this job.

_____ 5. I have deadlines for accomplishing my goals on this job.

_____ 6. If I have more than one goal to accomplish, I know which ones are most important and which are least important.

_____ 7. My goals require my full effort.

_____ 8. My manager tells me the reasons for giving me the goals I have.

_____ 9. My manager is supportive with respect to encouraging me to reach my goals.

_____ 10. My manager lets me participate in the setting of my goals.

_____ 11. My manager lets me have some say in deciding how I will go about implementing my goals.

_____ 12. If I reach my goals, I know that my manager will be pleased.

_____ 13. I get credit and recognition when I attain my goals.

_____ 14. Trying for goals makes my job more fun than it would be without goals.

_____ 15. I feel proud when I get feedback indicating that I have reached my goals.

_____ 16. The other people I work with encourage me to attain my goals.

_____ 17. I sometimes compete with my co-workers to see who can do the best job in reaching their goals.

_____ 18. If I reach my goals, my job security will be improved.

_____ 19. If I reach my goals, my chances for a pay raise are increased.

_____ 20. If I reach my goals, my chances for a promotion are increased.

_____ 21. I usually feel that I have a suitable action plan(s) for reaching my goals.

_____ 22. I get regular feedback indicating how I am performing in relation to my goals.

_____ 23. I feel that my training was good enough so that I am capable of reaching my goals.

_____ 24. Organization policies help rather than hurt goal attainment.

_____ 25. Teams work together in this company to attain goals.

_____ 26. This organization provides sufficient resources (e.g., time, money, equipment) to make goal setting effective.

_____ 27. In performance appraisal sessions, my supervisor stresses problem solving rather than criticism.

_____ 28. Goals in this organization are used more to help you do your job well rather than punish you.

_____ 29. The pressure to achieve goals here fosters honesty as opposed to cheating and dishonesty.

_____ 30. If my manager makes a mistake that affects my ability to attain my goals, he or she admits it.

Scoring and Interpretation

Add the points shown for items 1–30. Scores of 120–150 may indicate a high-performing, highly satisfying work situation.

Your goals are challenging and you are committed to reaching them. When you achieve your goals, you are rewarded for your accomplishments. Scores of 80–119 may suggest a highly varied work situation with motivating and satisfying attributes on some dimensions and just the opposite on others. Scores of 30–79 may suggest a low-performing, dissatisfying work situation.[39]

A Case in Point:
Survival at Westinghouse Electronic Plant

The Westinghouse Electronic Assembly Plant in College Station, Texas has been recognized by manufacturing experts as one of the most advanced manufacturing assembly plants in the United States. Various events have significantly affected employee productivity and plant efficiency during the past 11 years.

When the doors opened in 1983, Westinghouse's management strongly emphasized human and technical training of its newly hired work force. As an assembly contractor for a highly sophisticated radar defense system for the U.S. military, Westinghouse needed a highly trained work force to ensure total quality at each step of the operation.

In an effort to promote employee development through advanced training, the company implemented a "pay for knowledge" reward system during the first year of operation. Under this system, employees received wages for each level of advanced training they completed successfully. The motivation to earn salary increases challenged employees to broaden and deepen the understanding of their jobs at each level of training. Westinghouse believed that this type of reward system would create a more flexible and knowledgeable work force.

Westinghouse management also was aware of some of the drawbacks to this type of compensation–training system. Some employees' salaries would eventually "top out." That is, at that point an employee could not further increase his or her salary for additional knowledge or skills learned. Most reward systems are built on merit programs that are generally in line with area and industry wage growth factors or organizational programs, such as incentive compensation systems, bonus opportunities, and the like.

In 1986, Westinghouse management knew that the company faced the "top out" situation in its reward system. Approximately 64 percent of all employees would have achieved all possible levels of training by the end of the year. The area wage growth factors were showing no signs of increasing, and merit increases therefore could not be justified to Westinghouse's corporate human resources management in Pittsburgh. Employees were vocal about the situation, as they had become accustomed to having a goal to strive for that, when attained, would result in a financial reward. Management at this non-union plant was well aware of the fact that most other Westinghouse plants were unionized.

Management established a task force during 1986 to investigate the current reward problems. As with any reward system, the task proved to be difficult. During the task force's meetings, bonus, gain-sharing, profit-sharing, and flexible benefits plans all were discussed at one time or another. As a result of these discussions, the Westinghouse corporate human resource department allowed the plant to give lump-sum payments to employees based on certain labor indicators. The formula was complex, and neither employees nor management at the College Station plant understood it very well. Little attempt was made to inform them about the formula. What everyone knew was that lump-sum payments were to be made for three years. Although these payments seemed to ease the frustrations created by "topping out," employees quickly learned to expect this year-end payment. The lump-sum payments were available to technicians but not to managers. Although the payments were not large, managers at the plant felt excluded and resented the payment.

In 1988, the College Station plant faced a new and more crucial problem. Competition in the electronic assembly industry was becoming increasingly intense as companies built numerous manufacturing plants in Third-World countries and paid workers extremely low wages for assembly operations similar to those performed at the College Station plant. In this labor-intensive assembly business, the survival of the College Station plant was severely threatened. Rumors began circulating that, unless something could be done to increase the plant's productivity and drive down its labor costs, the plant might close.

Although the College Station plant was competitive domestically, international pressures created a new challenge. In an effort to solve the wage and productivity problems, plant managers decided to implement an MBO system.[40]

Questions

1. What were some of the problems with the lump-sum payment plan?
2. If Westinghouse hired you as a consultant to advise them on developing an MBO process, what would you recommend?
3. Using the goal-setting model, diagnose the "pay for knowledge" system. What features of the goal-setting model are present in this system?

References

1. Adapted from Brokaw, L. One-page company game plan. *Inc.,* June 1993, 111–113.

2. Adapted from Tully, S. Your paycheck gets exciting. *Fortune,* November 1, 1993, 83–84, 88–89, 95, 98.

3. Locke, E. A., Latham, G. P. *A Theory of Goal Setting & Task Performance.* Englewood Cliffs, N.J.: Prentice-Hall, 1990, 7.

4. Earley, P. C., and Shalley, C. E. New perspectives on goals and performance: Merging motivation and cognition. In G. R. Ferris and K. M. Rowland (eds.), *Research in Personnel Human Management,* vol. 9. Greenwich, Conn.: JAI Press, 1991, 121–157.

5. Hill, C. W., and Jones, G. R. *Strategic Management: An Integrated Approach,* 2nd ed. Boston: Houghton Mifflin, 1992.

6. Berry, L. L., Zeithaml, V. A., and Parasuraman, A. Five imperatives for improving service quality. *Sloan Management Review,* Summer 1990, 29–38.

7. Adapted from Brokaw, L. ISO 9000: Making the grade. *Inc.,* June 1993, 98–99; Henkoff, R. The hot new seal of quality. *Fortune,* June 28, 1993, 116–118.

8. Locke, E. A., and Latham, G. P. *A Theory of Goal Setting and Task Performance.* Englewood Cliffs, N.J.: Prentice-Hall, 1990, 252–267.

9. Saavedra, R., Earley, C. P., and Van Dyne, L. Complex interdependence in task-performing groups. *Journal of Applied Psychology,* 1993, 78, 61–72.

10. Lindsley, D. H., Brass, D. J., and Thomas, J. B. Efficacy-performance spirals: A multilevel perspective. Paper presented at the MESO Conference, Atlanta, February 1994; Mathieu, J. E., Martineau, J. W., and Tannenbaum, S. I. Individual and situational influences on the development of self-efficacy: Implications for training effectiveness. *Personnel Psychology,* 1993, 46, 125–148.

11. Adapted from Burack, C. Succeeding with tough love. *Fortune,* November 29, 1993, 188.

12. Hollenback, J. R., Williams, C. R., and Klein, H. J. An examination of the antecedents of commitment to difficult goals. *Journal of Applied Psychology,* 1989, 74, 18–23.

13. Brett, J. F., Cron, W. L., and Slocum, J. W., Jr. Economic dependency on work: A moderator of the relationship between organizational commitment and performance. *Academy of Management Journal,* 1995, in press.

14. Matsui, T., Kakuyama, T., and Onglatco, L. U. Effects of goals and feedback on performance in groups. *Journal of Applied Psychology,* 1987, 72, 407–415.

15. Lee, C., Earley, P. C., Lituchy, T. R., and Wagner, M. Relations of goal setting and goal sharing to performance and conflict for independent tasks. *British Journal of Management,* 1991, 2, 33–39.

16. Chowdhury, J. The motivational impact of sales quotas on effort. *Journal of Marketing Research,* 1993, 30, 28–41; Wright, P. M., George, J. M., Farnsworth, S. R., and McMahan, G. C. Productivity and extra-role behavior: The effects of goals and incentives on spontaneous helping. *Journal of Applied Psychology,* 1993, 78, 374–382; Earley, P. C., Northcraft, G. B., Lee, C., and Lituchy, T. R. Impact of process and outcome feedback on the relation of goal setting to task performance. *Academy of Management Journal,* 1990, 33, 87–105.

17. Lamb, C. W., Jr., Hair, J. F., Jr., and McDaniel, C. *Principles of Marketing.* Cincinnati: South-Western, 1994, 672–674; Harrington, S. J. What corporate America is teaching about ethics. *Academy of Management Executive,* February 1991, 21–30.

18. Smith, G. Congratulations, Mexico, you're in for a raise. *Business Week,* September 27, 1993, 58. Also see, Harpaz, I. The importance of work goals: An international perspective. *Journal of International Business Studies,* First Quarter 1990, 75–93.

19. Wright, T. A., and Bonnett, D. G. The role of employee coping and performance in voluntary employee withdrawal: A research refinement and elaboration. *Journal of Management,* 1993, 19, 147–160; Tett, R. P. and Meyer, J. P. Job satisfaction, organizational commitment, turnover intentions and turnover: Path analyses based on meta-analytic findings. *Personnel Psychology,* 1993, 46, 259–294.

20. Greenwood, R. G. Management by Objectives: As Developed by Peter Drucker, Assisted by Harold Smidy. *Academy of Management Review,* 1981, 6, 225–230.

21. Adapted from Eichenwald, K. Prudential execs ignored churning by Dallas brokers. *Dallas Morning News,* May 24, 1993, D1–2; Steinmetz, G., and Siconolfi, M. Chip off the rock: Partnership problems at Prudential embroil insurance business. *Wall Street Journal,* December 1, 1993, A1; Zimmerman, M. Prudential, investors in a tactical tug of war. *Dallas Morning News,* March 20, 1994, H1–2.

22. Weihrich, H. *Management Excellence: Productivity Through MBO.* New York: McGraw-Hill, 1985.

23. Adapted from Roberson, L., and Gutierrez, N. C. Beyond good faith: Commitment to recruiting management diversity at Pacific Bell. In S. E. Jackson and Associates (eds.), *Diversity in the Workplace.* New York: Guilford Press, 1992, 65–88. Also see Ellis, C., and Sonnenfeld, J. Diverse approaches to managing diversity. *Human Resource Management,* 1994, 33, 79–110.

24. Locke, E. A., and Latham, G. P. *Goal Setting: A Motivational Technique That Works!* Englewood Cliffs, N.J.: Prentice-Hall, 1984, 27–40.

25. Adapted from Greco, S. Bonuses for the right moves. *Inc.,* October 1993, 29.

26. Latham, G. P. *Increasing Productivity Through Performance Appraisal.* Reading, Mass.: Addison-Wesley, 1992.

27. Lawler, E. E. III. *Strategic Pay: Aligning Organizational Strategies and Pay Systems.* San Francisco: Jossey-Bass, 1990.

28. Adapted from Ehrenfeld, T. Gain-Sharing. *Inc.,* August 1993, 87–89. Also see Bowie-McCoy, S. W., Wendt, A. C., and Chope, R. Gainsharing in public accounting: Working smarter and harder. *Industrial Relations,* 1993, 32, 432–445.

29. Schuler, R. S., and Huber, V. L. *Personnel and Human Resource Management.* St. Paul, Minn.: West, 1990, 316–317.

30. Rehfeld, J. E. *Alchemy of a Leader.* New York: John Wiley & Sons, 1994.

31. Schuler and Huber, *Personnel and Human Resources Management,* 315–316.

32. Tyler, L. S., and Fisher, B. The Scanlon concept: A philosophy as much as a system. *Personnel Administrator,* July 1983, 33–37.

33. Adapted from Allen, R. L. Long John's sails on in wake of Clark's exit. *Nation's Restaurant News,* July 26, 1993, 27, 3–5; Deutsch, C. H. The trickle-down effects in perks. *New York Times,* November 4, 1990, F25.

34. Personal conversation with Jeffrey Joyce, Towers Perrin, March 16, 1994.

35. Gomez-Majia, L. R., and Balkin, D. B. *Compensation, Organizational Strategy, and Firm Performance.* Cincinnati: South-Western, 1992.

36. Adapted from Neale, M. B., Chapman, N. J., Ingersol, D., and Arthur, E. *Balancing Work and Caregiving for Children, Adults and Elders.* Newbury Park, Calif.: Sage, 1993; personal conversation with L. B. Donges, Manager, Public Affairs, Dow Chemical Corporation, April 1994.

37. French, W. *Human Resources Management,* 3rd. ed. Boston: Houghton Mifflin Company, 1994.

38. Personal conversation with Gary McPherson, Loral Vought Systems, March 9, 1994. For a description of how Xerox used skill-based pay systems to develop its work force, see Jones, F. R. Transition to skill-based pay. *Journal of Career Planning & Employment,* 1993, 54, 6–8.

39. Adapted from Locke, E. A., and Lathum, G. P. *A Theory of Goal Setting & Task Performance,* Englewood Cliffs, N.J.: Prentice-Hall, 1990, 355–358.

40. McMahan, G. C. Gaining Systems Revisited: A Survival Strategy Inside Westinghouse Electric Corporation. Unpublished case study. Center for Effective Organizations, School of Business, University of Southern California, Los Angeles: 1994. Reprinted by permission of the author.

8 Work Stress

LEARNING OBJECTIVES

When you have finished studying this chapter, you should be able to:

▲ Define the concepts of stress and stressors.

▲ Explain the general nature of the body's response to stressors.

▲ Diagnose the sources of stress in organizations.

▲ State the effects of stress on health.

▲ Explain the relationship between stress and job performance.

▲ Understand the nature and causes of job burnout.

▲ Describe several methods for coping with stress.

OUTLINE

Preview Case: Stress on the Job

Nature of Stress

Fight-or-Flight Response

The Stress Experience

Managing in Practice: The Navy Pilot

Sources of Stress

Managing Across Cultures: Siesta Sunset

Work Stressors

Managing Ethics: Welcome to the Age of Overwork

Managing Diversity: Work and Family—Business as Usual?

Life Stressors

Effects of Stress

Health and Stress

Managing Across Cultures: Karoushi, or Stress Death

Performance and Stress

Managing In Practice: "Just Enough but Not Too Much"

Job Burnout

Managing Diversity: The "New-Collar" Workers

Personality and Stress

Type A and B Personalities

The Hardy Personality

Stress Management

Individual Stress Coping Methods

Organizational Stress Coping Methods

Managing Quality: AT&T's Wellness Program

DEVELOPING SKILLS

Self-Diagnosis: *Identifying Your Strategies for Coping with Stress*

A Case in Point: *The Stress of Shift Work*

PREVIEW CASE

Stress on the Job

An important deadline is drawing near and you realize that you are not prepared. Although you have been trying to avoid him all day, the boss's steely gaze finally catches your attention. Your body reacts: Your muscles tense, your breathing speeds up and deepens, and your heart rate quickens.

Suddenly the phone rings. An angry voice informs you that serious problems have arisen with the project that you thought had been successfully completed last week. It seems that work has ground to a halt downstairs until you resolve the crisis. Your physical reactions worsen. Your blood vessels constrict, which raises your blood pressure. Adrenal glands pump more hormones into your system. You start sweating profusely. Your stomach and intestines halt the digestion of the lunch you hurriedly ate. The pupils of your eyes dilate involuntarily.

A cup of coffee and a moment to relax do little to get you off the stress cycle. Last night's insomnia is catching up with you. That argument with your spouse didn't help either. You can feel the beginnings of a headache.

The boss beckons angrily. You shudder. Not only is last week's project down the drain, but today's project is late. The boss's choice of words—"You're a disappointment to me"—makes you feel like you did when your parents scolded you for a bad report card.

After the unpleasant exchanges with the people downstairs, the run-in with your boss, and several hours of overtime to catch up, it's time to head home. No time for the kids, though. There's only time for a few bites of dinner and another quick but ugly argument with your spouse. Exhaustion sets in and your only thought is of bed. . . .

"Ring!" The alarm clock sounds. It seems like your head just hit the pillow. Already you are tensing up for the day ahead.[1]

From time to time, everyone experiences a "bad day" and the resulting stress. Moreover, small amounts of stress can sometimes have positive effects. However, the Preview Case illustrates an unfortunate situation when bad days seem to go on and on without letup. If you keep up that sort of routine long enough, the resulting stress may seriously affect your health and personal life as well as harm your job performance.

Both managers and employees need to understand the effects of work stress, the relationship between stress and performance, and the sources of stress within an organization. In particular, everyone should understand the relationships between stress and health. In this chapter, we examine the nature of stress, the sources of stress at work, and the effects of stress. People can handle varying amounts of stress effectively, and we explore some of these individual differences. Finally, we examine ways that employees and organizations can cope with stress.

▼ NATURE OF STRESS

Stress is a consequence of or a general response to an action or situation that places special physical or psychological demands, or both, on a person. Stress involves the interaction of a person and that person's environment. The physical or psychological demands from the environment that cause stress are called **stressors**.[2] Stressors can take a variety of forms, but all stressors have one thing in common: They create stress or the potential for stress when an individual perceives them as representing a demand that may exceed his or her ability to respond.

▼ Fight-or-Flight Response

The Preview Case described some of the possible changes in a person's body during a stress reaction, which everyone has experienced at one time or another. These biochemical and bodily changes represent a natural reaction to an environmental stressor: the **fight-or-flight response**.[3] An animal attacked by a predator in the wild basically has two choices: to fight or to flee. The animal's bodily responses to the stressor (the predator) increase its chances of survival. Similarly, our cave-dwelling ancestors benefited from this biological response mechanism. People gathering food away from their cave would have experienced a great deal of stress upon meeting a saber-toothed tiger. In dealing with the tiger, they could have run away or stayed and fought. The biochemical changes in their bodies prepared them for either alternative and contributed to the probability of their survival.[4]

The human nervous system still responds the same way to environmental stressors that it did for our ancestors. This response continues to have survival value in a true emergency. However, for most people most of the time, the "tigers" are imaginary rather than real. In work situations, a fight-or-flight response usually isn't appropriate. If an employee receives an unpleasant work assignment from a manager, physically assaulting the manager or storming angrily out of the office obviously is inappropriate. Instead, the employee is expected to accept the assignment calmly and do the best job possible. Remaining calm and performing effectively may be especially difficult when the employee perceives an assignment as threatening and the body is prepared to act accordingly.

Medical science has discovered that the human body has a standard response to demands placed on it—whether psychological or physical. Medical researcher Hans Selye first used the term *stress* to describe the body's biological response mechanisms. Selye considered stress to be the nonspecific response of the human body to any demand made on it.[5] However, the body has only a limited capacity to respond to stressors. The workplace makes a variety of demands on people, and too much stress over too long a period of time will exhaust their ability to cope with those stressors.

▼ The Stress Experience

Several factors determine whether an individual experiences stress at work or in other situations. Figure 8.1 identifies four of the primary factors: (1) the person's perception of the situation; (2) the person's past experiences; (3) the presence or absence of social support; and (4) individual differences with regard to stress reactions.

Perception   In Chapter 3 we defined *perception* as a key psychological process whereby a person selects and organizes environmental information into a concept of reality. Employee perceptions of a situation can influence how (or whether) they experience stress. For example, two employees had their job duties substantially changed—a situation likely to be stressful for many people. The first employee viewed the new duties as an opportunity to learn new skills and thought that the change was a vote of confidence from management

FIGURE 8.1

The Relationship Between
Stressors and Stress

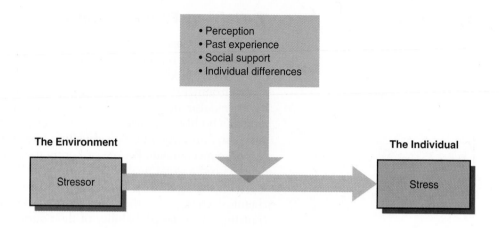

in her ability to be flexible and take on new challenges. The second employee perceived the same situation to be extremely threatening and concluded that management was unhappy with his performance in his original job.

Past Experience   A person may experience a situation as more or less stressful, depending on how familiar that person is with the situation and prior experience with the particular stressors involved. Past practice or training may allow some employees in an organization to deal calmly and competently with stressors that would greatly intimidate less experienced employees. The relationship between experience and stress is based on reinforcement (see Chapter 5). Positive reinforcement or previous success in a similar situation can reduce the level of stress that a person experiences in the present situation; punishment or past failure under similar conditions can increase stress in the present situation.

Social Support   The presence or absence of other people influences how individuals in the workplace experience stress and respond to stressors.[6] The presence of co-workers may increase an individual's confidence, allowing that person to cope more effectively with stress. For example, working alongside a person who performs confidently and competently in a stressful situation may help an employee behave similarly. Conversely, the presence of fellow workers may irritate people or make them anxious, reducing their ability to cope with stress.

Individual Differences   Personality characteristics may explain some of the differences in the ways that employees experience and respond to stress. For example, the Big Five personality factor that we labeled *adjustment* in Chapter 2, seems to be particularly important in individual responses to various stressors.[7] Individual differences in motivations, attitudes, and abilities also influence how employees experience work stress.[8] Simply stated, people are different. What one person considers a major source of stress, another may hardly notice as the following Managing in Practice story shows.

MANAGING IN PRACTICE

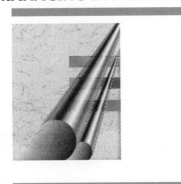

The Navy Pilot

The story is told of a Harvard University undergraduate who had to drop out of college due to serious psychological problems brought on by stress from the demands of school. Eventually, this individual enlisted in the U.S. Navy and became a pilot. He was based on an aircraft carrier much of the time. Military pilots usually consider taking off and landing on carriers to be particularly dangerous. Despite this danger, the Navy pilot served with distinction for a number of years and felt psychologically well during this time. When he finally retired from the Navy, he again enrolled in Harvard. As before, the individual experienced psychological difficulties, which became so severe this time that he required hospitalization.[9]

This story dramatically illustrates individual differences in stress reactions. Situations that cause stress in one individual may not in another. Most people would find flying a plane from an aircraft carrier to be extremely stressful, whereas being a student would be relatively less so. Yet, for this Navy pilot, exactly the opposite was the case. We further discuss relationships between personality and stress later in this chapter.

▼ SOURCES OF STRESS

Individuals commonly experience stress both in their personal and work lives. Understanding these sources of stress and their possible interaction is important. For a manager to consider either source in isolation gives an incomplete picture of the stress that an employee may be experiencing. Note the combined effects of work stress and stress from other aspects of life on the residents of Mexico City as described in the following Managing Across Cultures feature.

MANAGING ACROSS CULTURES

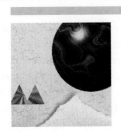

Siesta Sunset

Mexicans, particularly residents of Mexico City, are gulping stress medication in record numbers. Mañana-land isn't supposed to be like this—what is going on?

There are signs that Mexico's breakneck pace to urbanize and modernize has brought both opportunities and stress to Mexican workers. In the past few years, Mexican doctors have reported increases in cigarette smoking, drinking, and drug abuse. (However, drug abuse is at relatively low levels compared to the United States.) Claudio Garcia Barriga, chief of the outpatient department of a large psychiatric hospital in Mexico City, observed, "In the past five years, there's been a very important increase in the problem of stress, and we continue to see a steady increase in stress crises." Garcia reports that some 15% of the hospital's patients show stress symptoms.

MANAGING ACROSS CULTURES —*Continued*

Mexico City has 20 million residents, and, traditionally, problems associated with overcrowding were blamed for most stress. Recently however, Mexico's changing economy seemingly is the source of much stress. The North American Free Trade Agreement among Canada, Mexico, and the United States is feeding job insecurity fears among Mexican workers just as it has north of the border. The fears are well founded. As Mexico has opened up to private investment, hundreds of thousands of workers have lost jobs to cost-cutting, downsizing, and closing of businesses in the face of new competition. Time-honored work rules are changing as well. For example, many firms no longer tolerate traditional on-the-job siestas. In addition, wage controls and inflation have squeezed average workers' buying power. These economic uncertainties, coupled with the pollution and traffic that are overwhelming Mexico City, have sent stress levels soaring.[10]

▼ Work Stressors

Several nationwide surveys have indicated that, in many firms, an average of about 25% of all employees suffer from stress-induced problems. A 1992 Northwestern National Life Insurance survey reported that

▲ one in three workers said that they have thought about quitting because of stress;

▲ one in two workers said that job stress reduces their productivity; and

▲ one in five workers said they took sick leave in the past month because of stress.[11]

Work stressors take various forms, and numerous studies have identified specific stressors and their effects. For example, in a worldwide comparative study of work stress, researchers gathered information from 1,065 managers in ten countries on five continents: Brazil, the United Kingdom, Egypt, Germany, Japan, Nigeria, Singapore, South Africa, Sweden, and the United States. Fifty-five percent of all respondents mentioned time pressures and deadlines as a stressor, followed closely by work overload, mentioned by almost 52%. Other frequently identified stressors included inadequately trained subordinates, long working hours, attending meetings, and conflicts between work and family and other social relationships.[12]

Similar studies have identified many stressors that seem common to both managers and employees in different types of organizations. In addition, some jobs seem to generate more stress than others. For example, a recent survey indicated that telecommunications, financial services, and nonprofit organizations had the most stressful working environments. A study of suicide found an elevated suicide risk in 18 occupations, including psychologists, pharmacists, physicians, securities and financial-service salespeople, lawyers, police, and farmers.[13]

Managers and employees need a framework for thinking about and diagnosing sources of work stress. Figure 8.2 presents such a framework by identifying six principal sources of work stress. It also shows, as previously discussed, that internal factors influence the ways in which individuals experience these stressors.

FIGURE 8.2

Sources of Work Stress

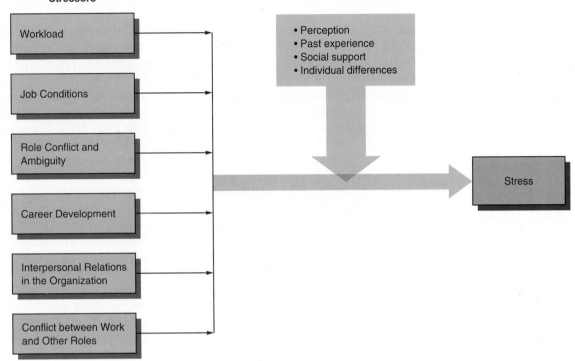

Workload   For many people, having too much work to do and not enough time or resources to do it can be stressful. **Role overload** exists when demands exceed the capacity of a manager or employee to meet all of them adequately. Many stressful jobs may be described as perpetually being in a condition of role overload. Surveys commonly identify work overload or "working too hard" as a major source of stress. The following Managing Ethics piece explores this overload situation.

MANAGING ETHICS

Welcome to the Age of Overwork

The U.S. Bank of Washington was closed on Columbus Day. However, Robert Kakiuchi, Vice-President of Human Resources, went to his Seattle office anyway to catch up on paperwork. He signed in at the front desk and counted the names of other managers who had arrived before him. There were 99.

Kakiuchi wasn't surprised. He had observed that his colleagues often work late into the evening and on weekends and holidays. The workload at the bank became heavier following a merger and subsequent layoffs. In Kakiuchi's

MANAGING ETHICS —*Continued*

department, six people now are responsible for work formerly done by a staff of 70.

This situation isn't unusual. For many workers, the years just ahead seem to be shaping up as the "Age of Overwork." Contributing to overwork is the wave of restructuring and downsizing sweeping corporate America. Amoco, AT&T, Citicorp, Digital Equipment, Eastman Kodak, Exxon, General Motors, Goodyear, IBM, TRW, and Xerox are among the giant firms that have recently announced major staff reductions. An estimated 85% of the 1,000 largest industrial corporations in the United States have downsized their work forces, in many cases dramatically. The survivors of leveraged buyouts, mergers, cost-cutting, and downsizing may be hard pressed to even get a day off during the 1990s. Unfortunately, most companies seem to downsize without figuring out how to reduce the workload. This shortsightedness leads directly to extra work and high stress for the people who remain.

In addition to stress, organizations are taking another serious risk when they push people too hard for too long. Michael Josephson, president of an ethics institute in Marina del Rey, California, describes this risk as *overtasking*—expecting managers and employees to meet unrealistically high goals. Overtasking has ethical implications as employees may cheat or succumb to various other forms of dishonesty to make their numbers look acceptable. For example, Josephson argues that the recent scandal at Sears auto repair shops (where customers were charged for services not received) was the result of demands on service managers and other employees to meet unreasonable sales goals. The scandal and subsequent investigation cost Sears more than $10 million in fines and refunds.

In addition to the obvious costs of such wrongdoing, the greatest cost to organizations from stressing their employees may be more subtle. How much better might the company be doing if its employees weren't quite so busy or so tired? How many bad decisions might be avoided?[14]

Interestingly, having too little work to do also may create stress. Have you ever had a job with so little to do that the work day seemed never to end? If so, you can understand why many people find an "underload" situation stressful. Managers sometimes are guilty of trying to do their subordinates' work, or "micromanage," when their jobs aren't challenging enough. Although "micromanaging" might reduce the manager's stress from boredom, it is likely to increase subordinates' stress.

Job conditions   Poor working conditions represent another important set of job stressors. Temperature extremes, loud noise, too much or too little lighting, radiation, and air pollution are just a few examples of the working conditions that can cause stress for employees. Job performance deteriorates, sometimes markedly, when environmental stressors (such as bad lighting, noise, or unpleasant temperatures) are present. Further, the effects of these environmental stressors are cumulative over time, and they interact with other sources of stress. Heavy travel demands or commuting to work over long distances are other aspects of jobs that employees may find stressful. Poor working conditions, excessive travel, and long hours all add up to increased stress and decreased performance.[15]

Role Conflict and Ambiguity   Differing expectations of or demands on a person's role at work produce **role conflict.** (We discuss role conflict in detail in Chapter 13.) **Role ambiguity** describes the situation in which the employee is uncertain about assigned job duties and responsibilities. Role conflict and role ambiguity are particularly significant sources of job-related stress.[16]

Many employees suffer from role conflict and ambiguity, but conflicting expectations and uncertainty particularly affect managers. For example, managers often must make decisions in the face of financial uncertainty. When Campgrounds of America (KOA) decided to expand into another business, it purchased Sir Speedy, a chain of stores in the copier business. This purchase was successful because it capitalized on KOA's ability to run franchises. However, KOA failed when it purchased Gardner Motor Homes. In this case, KOA management was unable to learn how to manufacture and market recreational vehicles effectively in a highly competitive industry.

Having responsibility for the behavior of others and a lack of opportunity to participate in important decisions affecting the job are other aspects of employees' roles that may be stressful.

Career Development   Major stressors related to career planning and development involve job security, promotions, transfers, and developmental opportunities. (We explore career planning and development in Chapter 21). As with too much or too little work, an employee can feel stress by underpromotion (failure to advance as rapidly as desired) or overpromotion (promotion to a job that exceeds the individual's capabilities).

The current wave of reorganization and downsizing may seriously threaten careers. When jobs, departments, work teams, or entire organizations are restructured, employees often have numerous career-related concerns: Can I perform competently in the new situation? Can I advance? Is my new job secure? Typically, employees find these concerns stressful.[17]

Interpersonal Relations in the Organization   Groups have a tremendous impact on the behavior of people in organizations. (We explore these dynamics in Chapters 9 and 10.) Good working relationships and interactions with peers, subordinates, and superiors are a crucial part of organizational life, helping people achieve personal and organizational goals; when poor or missing, they are sources of stress. For example, a study of clerical employees indicated that intrusions by others—interruptions from noisy co-workers, ringing telephones, and other people walking into and around their work stations—were principal sources of stress.[18] A high level of political behavior, or "office politics," also may create stress for managers and employees (see Chapter 15). Thus the nature of relationships with co-workers may influence how employees react to other stressors. In other words, interpersonal relationships can be either a source of stress or the social support that affects how employees react to stressors.

Conflict between Work and Other Roles   A person plays many roles in life, only one of which is typically associated with work (although some individuals may hold more than one job at a time). These roles may present conflicting demands that become sources of stress. Furthermore, work typically meets only some of employees' goals and needs. Other personal goals and needs may conflict with career goals, presenting an additional source of stress. For example, employees' personal needs to spend time with their families may conflict with the extra hours they must work to advance their careers. Current demographic trends, such as the increasingly higher number of dual-career couples, have brought work and family role conflicts into sharp focus.[19] Such conflicts are obvious in the following Managing Diversity feature.

MANAGING DIVERSITY

Work and Family—Business as Usual?

Many organizations claim to be attuned to the needs of their employees' families. In 1993, *Working Mother* magazine received more than 300 entries from organizations vying for their "Best Companies for Working Mothers" award— a 30% increase in entries over the previous year. Corporate support for families is the "in" thing to do. Despite this response, for many workers life seemingly hasn't changed much, as the following examples show.

Raylynn McIntire, a lab operator at a Chevron refinery in California, told her supervisor that she needed time off to be with a sick child. She received a disciplinary pay cut and counseling. McIntire says, "It was kind of degrading. The message was, 'You don't get sick, and your kids don't get sick. You come to work.'"

At the same refinery, Ruth Bennett combed the Yellow Pages to find a licensed child-care professional when her son got the flu and the regular sitter was unavailable. When Bennett couldn't find anyone, she had to miss two days of work. Her supervisor docked her pay.

Dawn Dodge, an honors graduate of Michigan Technological University, was pleased when she landed a job at Wisconsin Energy Corporation. She believed that she could "have it all," based on articles in the company's publications about flexible benefits and part-time and work-at-home options. When Dodge asked permission to extend her three-month maternity leave because her new baby needed surgery, she was told it would be better if she just quit. When her husband, a chemical engineer for Wisconsin Energy offered to quit instead, the company granted her request. Later, her son needed further surgery and she requested a part-time schedule, but the company turned her down. Wisconsin Energy states that, even though alternative work schedules and arrangements are touted in company publications, they are still "experimental" and are "not something every employee can count on."[20]

▼ Life Stressors

The distinction between work and nonwork stressors isn't always clear. For example, as the previous Managing Diversity feature indicates, one source of stress lies in potential conflicts between work and family. As Figure 8.3 illustrates, both work and family stressors may contribute to work–family conflict because stress in one area can reduce a person's ability to cope with stress in

FIGURE 8.3

Stressors and Work–Family Conflict

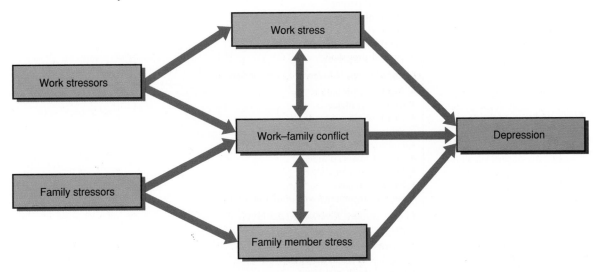

Source: Adapted from Frone, M. R., Russell, M., and Cooper, M. L. Antecedents and outcomes of work–family conflict: Testing a model of the work–family interface. *Journal of Applied Psychology*, 1992, 77, 66.

the other. This conflict represents a further source of stress which, in turn, leads to problems such as depression.

Much of the stress felt by managers and employees may stem from stressors in their personal lives, or **life stressors.** As in the work setting, people must cope with a great variety of life stressors. In addition, different individuals deal with life stressors differently. Events that cause stress for one person may not do so for another person. However, life stressors that affect almost everyone are those caused by major changes: divorce, marriage, death of a family member, and the like. As mentioned previously, the human body has a limited capacity to respond to stressors. Too much change too quickly can exhaust the body's ability to respond, with negative consequences for physical and mental health (to be discussed shortly).

Table 8.1 contains some stressful events that college students typically face. These events are rated on a 100-point scale, with 1 indicating the least stressful event and 100 the most stressful. For example, events labeled "high levels of stress" might be assigned 71 to 100 points, depending on the specific circumstances of the student being evaluated. "Moderate levels of stress" might be scored from 31 to 70 points, and "low levels of stress" assigned scores from 1 to 30. During the course of a year, if a student faces events that total 150 points or more, the student has a 50–50 chance of getting sick as a result of excessive stress.[21]

Recall that Selye's medical science definition emphasized that stress is the body's general response to any demand made on it. Note that the list of stressful events in Table 8.1 contains both unpleasant events, such as failing a course, and pleasant events, such as finding a new love interest. Note particularly that life stressors are not limited to negative occurrences in a person's life but also may include positive experiences. For example, vacations and

TABLE 8.1   Stressful Events for College Students

Events Having High Levels of Stress
▲ Death of parent
▲ Death of spouse
▲ Divorce
▲ Flunking out
▲ Unwed preganancy

Events Having Moderate Levels of Stress
▲ Academic probation
▲ Change of major
▲ Death of close friend
▲ Failing important course
▲ Finding a new love interest
▲ Loss of financial aid
▲ Major injury or illness
▲ Parents' divorce
▲ Serious arguments with romantic partner

Events Having Relatively Low Levels of Stress
▲ Change in eating habits
▲ Change in sleeping habits
▲ Change in social activities
▲ Conflict with instructor
▲ Lower grades than expected
▲ Outstanding achievement

Source: Adapted from Baron, R. A., and Byrne, D. *Social Psychology: Understanding Human Interaction*, 6th ed. Boston: Allyn and Bacon, 1991, 573.

holidays actually may be quite stressful for some people. In addition, viewing life events as having only negative effects is incorrect. People often can both cope with unpleasant events and enjoy the stimulation of pleasurable events, such as significant accomplishments, vacations, gaining a new family member, and so on.

▼ EFFECTS OF STRESS

Work stress may have both positive and negative effects. However, research on work stress tends to focus on its negative effects, which seems well targeted. The Research Triangle Institute estimated the cost to the U.S. economy from stress-related disorders at $187 billion per year. Other estimates are more conservative, but they invariably run into the billions of dollars.[22] These costs include lost productivity, job errors, and medical treatment.

The effects of work stress occur in three main areas: physiological, emotional, and behavioral. Examples of the effects of excessive stress in these three areas are as follows.

▲ **Physiological effects of stress** include increased blood pressure, increased heart rate, sweating, hot and cold spells, breathing difficulties, muscular tension, and increased gastrointestinal disorders.
▲ **Emotional effects of stress** include anger, anxiety, depression, lowered self-esteem, poorer intellectual functioning (including an inability to con-

centrate and make decisions), nervousness, irritability, resentment of supervision, and job dissatisfaction.

▲ **Behavioral effects of stress** include decreased performance, absenteeism, higher accident rates, higher turnover rates, higher alcohol and other drug abuses, impulsive behavior, and difficulties in communication.

These effects have important implications for organizational behavior. We examine some of the implications of work stress for the health and performance of managers and employees, including the phenomenon of *job burnout*.

▼ Health and Stress

There is a strong link between stress and coronary heart disease. Other major health problems commonly associated with stress include back pain, headaches, stomach and intestinal problems, and various mental problems. Medical researchers recently have discovered possible links between stress and cancer. Although determining the precise role that stress plays in health in all individual cases is difficult, many illnesses appear to be stress-related.[23] In Japan, a phenomenon known as *karoushi*—death by overwork—is well known. Sometimes called stress-death, *karoushi* is examined in the following Managing Across Cultures piece.

MANAGING ACROSS CULTURES

Karoushi, *or Stress Death*

Karoushi is a Japanese word usually translated as "sudden death from overwork." The Japanese people worked long and hard to rebuild their country from the devastation of World War II. They have been admired by the whole world for the economic achievements they have attained as a result. In Japan, however, people recently have become alarmed by some of the risks associated with the problems of overwork. The Japanese press has reported many examples of *karoushi*.

A 60-year old man, Noboru Sato, died of a heart attack and his widow became eligible for survivor benefits under workmen's compensation insurance because the labor standards inspection office in Kobe determined that his death was caused by overwork. He had been working a 24-hour shift every other day as an attendant at a ferry terminal in Kobe. One day, after finishing his shift, his replacement called in sick and he was forced to put in eight more hours. He died of a heart attack a week later. It was assumed that the extra eight hours was the "last straw" or the "final cause" of his death.

Some *karoushi* victims were working fifty days straight and working more than 100 hours of overtime per month. Nakamura, an employee of a construction company, had recorded 135 hours of overtime a month around the time of his collapse. He was barely able to squeeze in five hours of sleep a night. Assigned to a job in Tokyo, he had to commute daily from Osaka for more than two months. Some days, he worked so late that he spent the night at his office, rather than trying to go home.

The Nara Labor Standards Inspection Office ruled that the death of Taro Kimura, a worker in a ball-bearing factory, was caused by overwork. On his job, workers were not allowed to take any days off in order to keep the company's machines in operation for 24 hours a day.

MANAGING ACROSS CULTURES —*Continued*

The interest in *karoushi* suggests a possible shift in Japanese attitudes toward work and a recognition that work stress is contributing to health problems among Japanese workers. Current thinking is that *karoushi* is not just "death from overwork" (which the Japanese recognize is an overly simplistic explanation). Perhaps it is more accurately described as death from strong feelings of depression and helplessness combined with overwork. This description is similar to the U.S. phenomenon of "job burnout."[24]

Stress-related illnesses place a considerable burden on people and organizations. The costs to individuals often are more obvious than the costs to organizations. However, identifying at least some of the organizational costs associated with stress-related disease is possible.[25] First, costs to employers include not only increased premiums for health insurance but also lost work days from serious illnesses, such as heart disease, and less-serious illnesses, such as stress-related headaches. Estimates are that each employee who suffers from a stress-related illness loses an average of 16 days of work a year. Second, over three-fourths of all industrial accidents are caused by a worker's inability to cope with emotional problems worsened by stress. Third, legal problems for employers are growing. For example, the number of stress-related workers' compensation claims is growing at a tremendous rate.

▼ Performance and Stress

The positive and negative aspects of stress are most apparent in the relationship between stress and performance. Figure 8.4 depicts the general performance–stress relationship. At low levels of stress, employees may not be sufficiently alert, challenged, or involved to perform at their best. As the curve indicates, increasing a low amount of stress may improve performance—up to a point. An optimal level of stress probably exists for most tasks. Beyond this point, performance begins to deteriorate. At excessive levels of stress, employees are too agitated, aroused, or threatened to perform at their best. The following Managing in Practice account provides an example of the relationship between performance and stress.

MANAGING IN PRACTICE

"Just Enough But Not Too Much"

Laura Taylor was puzzled. During the past several months, she had presented three major reports to the executive committee of the board of directors. The first had been a catastrophe. She had been so nervous that she could actually remember little that had gone on. Taylor did know, however, that she had somehow gotten through her formal presentation—which seemed to go okay—before disaster struck. It came in the form of a series of questions, each more confusing than the last. The board members eventually took pity on her and suddenly stopped the questioning. They thanked her for her efforts on

MANAGING IN PRACTICE —*Continued*

the report, and turned their attention to other matters. Later, Elizabeth Rainey—her boss and the firm's president—helped Taylor analyze her performance. They determined that, with one or two exceptions, Taylor actually knew the answers to the questions asked. What seemed to happen, they decided, was that she had been far too agitated to think clearly. Indeed, Taylor had been so upset that she even had trouble focusing on what was being asked. Several times she had had to ask that questions be repeated. Rainey's advice was preparation and practice. "You have to make stress work for you—but you can't be so stressed out that you can't think straight."

Taylor didn't fully understand the implications of Rainey's last comment, but she carefully prepared for her next presentation to the board. Like a highly trained athlete before the big game, she was actually looking forward to the presentation. Although "keyed up" when the time came, Taylor made a superb presentation full of energy and enthusiasm and fielded the board members' questions with confidence. Board members were effusive in their praise (and probably a little relieved because the first experience had gone so badly).

Now Taylor had just come from her third presentation to the board. Even though well prepared, today she had been "flat." She hadn't been nervous. In fact, she had been working on another project right up until the time she went into the boardroom for her presentation. Although her presentation certainly went better than the first one, she knew without being told that it hadn't measured up to the peak performance of last time. "What's going on?" she wondered. With Rainey's help, she again attempted to diagnose her performance. After some discussion, they finally decided that, whereas Taylor had felt too much stress during her first presentation, this time she had, ironically, probably not felt enough.

Managers often want to know the optimum stress points for both themselves and their subordinates. This information, however, is difficult to obtain. For example, an employee may be absent from work frequently because of boredom (too little stress) or because of overwork (excessive stress). Also, the curve in Figure 8.4 on p. 250 changes with the situation; that is, the curve varies for different people and different tasks. Too little stress for one employee may be just right for another on a particular task. The optimum amount of stress for a specific individual for one task may be too much or too little for that person's effective performance of other tasks.

As a practical matter, managers should be more concerned about the excessive stress side of the curve than with how to add to employee stress. Motivating individuals to perform better is always important, but attempting to do so by increasing their stress is shortsighted.

The downsizing that many organizations are going through yields many examples of the effects on performance from excessive stress. A survey of 531 large companies indicated that 85% expected their restructuring to raise profits. However, only 46% saw increased earnings after restructuring. Further research into firms such as Jostens Learning Corporation, the biggest U.S. maker of educational software, revealed some reasons for these disappointing results. Although layoffs may lower direct labor costs, these lower costs are

FIGURE 8.4

**Typical Relationship Between
Performance and Stress**

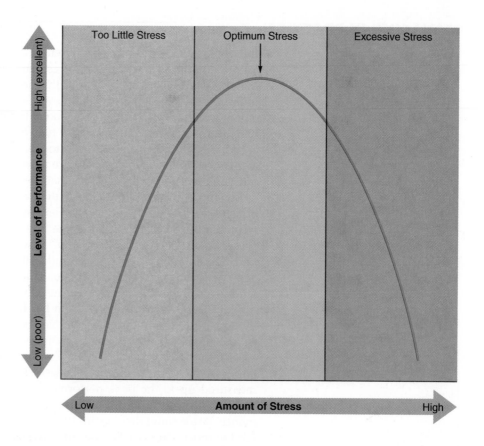

often more than offset by declines in productivity because of increased stress and lowered morale among the survivors.[26]

Studies of the performance–stress relationship in organizations often show a strong negative correlation between the amount of stress in a work team or department and its overall performance.[27] That is, the greater the stress that employees are experiencing, the lower will be their productivity. This negative relationship indicates that these work settings are operating on the right-hand side (excessive stress) of the curve in Figure 8.4. Managers and employees in these situations need to find ways to reduce the number and magnitude of stressors.

▼ Job Burnout

Job burnout refers to the adverse effects of working conditions where stressors seem unavoidable and sources of job satisfaction and relief from stress seem unavailable. The burnout phenomenon typically contains three components:

▲ a state of *emotional exhaustion*;

▲ *depersonalization* of individuals; and

▲ *feelings of low personal accomplishment*.[28]

Depersonalization refers to the treatment of people as objects. For example, a nurse might refer to the "broken knee" in room 107, rather than use the patient's name.

Most job-burnout research has focused on the human services sector of the economy—sometimes called the "helping professions." Burnout is thought to be most prevalent in occupations characterized by continuous direct contact with people in need of aid. The professionals who may be most vulnerable to job burnout include social workers, nurses, physicians, police officers, air traffic controllers, teachers, and lawyers. However, burnout also may affect managers, shopowners, professionals and others, who constantly face stressors with little relief or who must deal extensively with other people as part of their jobs. Figure 8.5 suggests that the highest probability of burnout occurs among those professionals who have both high frequency and high intensity of interpersonal contact. This level of interpersonal contact is believed to lead to emotional exhaustion, a key component of job burnout.

Individuals who experience job burnout seem to have some common characteristics. Three characteristics in particular are associated with a high probability of burnout.

▲ Burnout candidates experience a great deal of stress as a result of job-related stressors.

▲ Burnout candidates tend to be idealistic and self-motivating achievers.

▲ Burnout candidates often seek unattainable goals.[29]

Job burnout thus represents a combination of certain individual characteristics and job situations. Individuals who suffer from burnout often have unrealistic expectations concerning their work and their ability to accomplish desired goals, given the nature of the situation in which they find themselves. Unrelieved stressful working conditions, coupled with an individual's unrealistic expectations or ambitions, may lead to physical, mental, and emotional exhaustion. In burnout, the individual can no longer cope with job demands, and the willingness to even try drops dramatically.

Evidence suggests that women, on average, face somewhat higher probabilities of burnout than men, as described in the following Managing Diversity feature. Note also that the "high burnout" cell in Figure 8.5 contains occupations that have traditionally attracted more women than men.

FIGURE 8.5

Predicted Level of Job Burnout Based on Frequency and Intensity of Interpersonal Contact

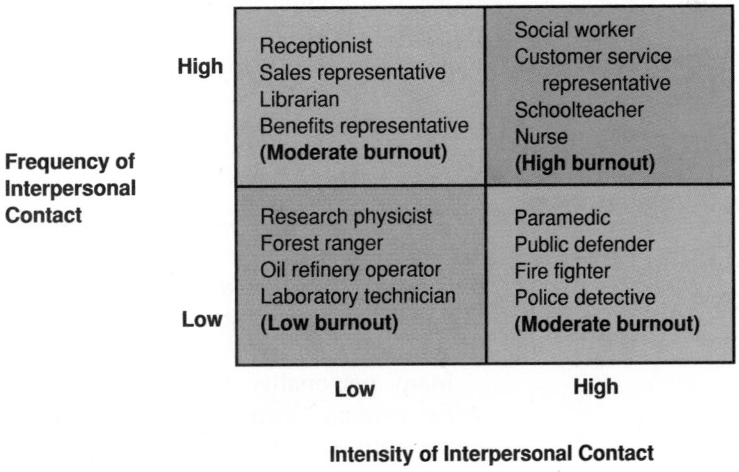

Source: Cordes, C. L., and Dougherty, T. W. A review and integration of research on job burnout. *Academy of Management Review*, 1993, 18, 643. Reprinted with permission.

MANAGING DIVERSITY

The "New-Collar" Workers

Bev Demille is having a bad night. The 51-year-old telemarketer is on her fourteenth phone call of the shift, but so far she has sold just one magazine renewal. "Come on computer, move it," she says, waiting for the next beep in her headset and the next name to flash on her screen. Around her, co-workers tethered to their desks by telephone cords gesture as they speak and signal supervisors to listen to the confirmation of a sale. A young supervisor half DeMille's age reprimands her: "You're low, girl—one in 14."

DeMille glares at her video screen. "I don't know where he gets off saying that," she says. But she knows that pressure goes with the job. Working for nine other employers in her 10 years in telemarketing, she has seen co-workers take tranquilizers to relieve stress. She has seen people fired for missing sales targets. When confronted once on a previous job for leaving her desk to go to the ladies' room without permission, she retorted: "My bladder couldn't see you."

Many of the estimated 3–4 million telephone sales representatives in the United States feel this type of stress. A telemarketer often talks to hundreds of indifferent or hostile customers during a shift. Supervisors constantly monitor them, expecting them to stick closely to a prepared script and remain cheerful no matter how rudely they are treated. Little wonder that telemarketers feel unappreciated and tend to burn out quickly. About 70% of telemarketers are women.

Sometimes called *new-collar* workers, telemarketers, other similar sales people, and data processors comprise about 40% of the work force born after 1945. These new-collar workers, working primarily with computers and telephones, in a sense perform blue-collar work in a white-collar world. In terms of stress, lack of variety in their work, limited opportunity for advancement, and heavy performance pressure, the new-collar worker has been described as similar to "turn-of-the-century factory workers except that they are educated and use high technology."

Perhaps not surprisingly, because women comprise so much of the new-collar employment, surveys have indicated that 11% more women than men report that high stress has affected their health. Further, a Northwestern National Life Insurance study found that the job burnout rate was 36% for women versus 28% for men.[30]

▼ PERSONALITY AND STRESS

To a very real extent, the problems caused by stress depend on the type of person involved. Personality influences (1) how individuals are likely to perceive situations and stressors, and (2) how they will react to these environmental stressors.

Many personality dimensions or traits can be related to stress, including self-esteem and locus of control (personality traits discussed in Chapter 2). A personality trait may affect the probability that someone will perceive a situation or an event as a stressor.[31] For example, an individual with low self-esteem may be more likely to experience stress in demanding work situations than will a person with high self-esteem. The reason may be that individuals high in self-esteem typically have more confidence in their ability to meet job demands. Employees with high internal locus of control may take more effective action, more quickly, in coping with a sudden emergency (a stressor) than will employees with high external locus of control. Individuals high in internal locus of control are likely to believe that they can moderate the stressful situation.

Before reading further, please respond to the statements in Table 8.2. This self-assessment exercise is related to the discussion that follows.

▼ Type A and B Personalities

People with a **Type A personality** are involved in a never-ending struggle to achieve more and more in less and less time. Characteristics of this personality type include

▲ a chronic sense of urgency about time;[32]

▲ an extremely competitive, almost hostile orientation;

▲ an aversion to idleness; and

▲ an impatience with barriers to task accomplishment.

Two medical researchers first identified the Type A personality when they noticed a recurrent personality pattern in their patients who suffered from premature heart disease.[33] In addition to the characteristics mentioned, extreme Type A individuals often speak rapidly, are preoccupied with themselves, and are dissatisfied with life.

The questionnaire in Table 8.2 measures four sets of behaviors and tendencies associated with the Type A personality: (1) time urgency, (2) competitiveness and hostility, (3) polyphasic behavior (trying to do too many things at once), and (4) a lack of advance planning. Medical researchers have discovered that these behaviors and tendencies often relate to life and work stress. They tend to cause stress or to make stressful situations worse than they otherwise might be.

Evidence links Type A behavior with a vulnerability to heart attacks. For years, the conventional wisdom among medical researchers was that Type A individuals were two to three times more likely to develop heart disease than were Type B individuals. The **Type B personality** is considered to be the opposite of the Type A personality. Type B individuals tend to be more easygoing and relaxed, less concerned about time pressures, and less likely to overreact to situations in hostile or aggressive ways. Recent research, however, suggests that the Type A personality description is too broad to predict coronary heart disease accurately. Rather, research indicates that only certain aspects of the Type A personality—particularly anger, hostility, and aggression—are strongly related to stress reactions and heart disease.[34]

▼ The Hardy Personality

A great deal of interest has emerged in identifying aspects of the personality that might buffer or protect individuals from, in particular, the negative health

TABLE 8.2   A Self-Assessment of Type A Personality

Choose from the following responses to answer the questions below:

A. Almost always true   C. Seldom true
B. Usually true   D. Never true

Answer each question according to what is generally true for you:

_____ 1. I do not like to wait for other people to complete their work before I can proceed with my own.

_____ 2. I hate to wait in most lines.

_____ 3. People tell me that I tend to get irritated too easily.

_____ 4. Whenever possible, I try to make activities competitive.

_____ 5. I have a tendency to rush into work that needs to be done before knowing the procedure I will use to complete the job.

_____ 6. Even when I go on vacation, I usually take some work along.

_____ 7. When I make a mistake, it is usually due to the fact that I have rushed into the job before completely planning it through.

_____ 8. I feel guilty for taking time off from work.

_____ 9. People tell me I have a bad temper when it comes to competitive situations.

_____10. I tend to lose my temper when I am under a lot of pressure at work.

_____11. Whenever possible, I will attempt to complete two or more tasks at once.

_____12. I tend to race against the clock.

_____13. I have no patience for lateness.

_____14. I catch myself rushing when there is no need.

Score your responses according to the following key:

▲ *An intense sense of time urgency* is a tendency to race against the clock, even when there is little reason to. The person feels a need to hurry for hurry's sake alone, and this tendency has appropriately been called "hurry sickness." Time urgency is measured by items 1, 2, 8, 12, 13, and 14. Every A or B answer to these six questions scores one point.

Your Score = [ ]

▲ *Inappropriate aggression and hostility* reveals itself in a person who is excessively competitive and who cannot do anything for fun. This inappropriately aggressive behavior easily evolves into frequent displays of hostility, usually at the slightest provocation or frustration. Competitiveness and hostility is measured by items 3, 4, 9, and 10. Every A or B answer scores one point.

Your Score = [ ]

▲ *Polyphasic behavior* refers to the tendency to undertake two or more tasks simultaneously at inappropriate times. It usually results in wasted time due to an inability to complete the tasks. This behavior is measured by items 6 and 11. Every A or B answer scores one point.

Your Score = [ ]

▲ *Goal directedness without proper planning* refers to the tendency of an individual to rush into work without really knowing how to accomplish the desired result. This usually results in incomplete work or work with many errors, which in turn leads to wasted time, energy, and money. Lack of planning is measured by items 5 and 7. Every A or B response scores one point.

Your Score = [ ]

TOTAL SCORE = _____

If your score is 5 or greater, you may possess some basic components of the Type A personality.

Source: Reproduced with permission of the Robert J. Brady Co., Bowie, Maryland, 20715, from its copyrighted work *The Stress Mess Solution: The Causes and Cures of Stress on the Job,* by G. S. Everly, and D. A. Girdano, 1980, 55.

consequences of stress. A collection of personality traits that seem to counter the effects of stress is known as the *hardy personality*. As a personality type, **hardiness** is defined as "a cluster of characteristics that includes feeling a sense of commitment, responding to each difficulty as representing a challenge and an opportunity, and perceiving that one has control over one's own life."[35] Hardiness thus includes

▲ a sense of positive involvement with others in social situations;

▲ a tendency to attribute one's own behavior to internal causes (recall the discussion of attribution in Chapter 3); and

▲ a tendency to perceive or welcome major changes in life with interest, curiosity, and optimism[36] (recall the earlier discussion in this chapter of change as a major life stressor).

A high degree of hardiness reduces the negative effects of stressful events.[37] Hardiness seems to reduce stress by altering the way that people perceive stressors. The concept of the hardy personality provides a useful insight into the role of individual differences in reactions to environmental stressors. An individual having a high level of hardiness perceives few events as stressful; an individual having a low level of hardiness perceives many events as stressful. A person with high levels of hardiness is not overwhelmed by challenging or difficult situations. Rather, faced with a stressor, the high-hardiness individual copes or responds constructively by trying to find a solution—to control or influence events. This behavioral response typically reduces stress reactions, lowers blood pressure, and reduces the probability of illness.

▼ STRESS MANAGEMENT

Articles in newspapers and popular magazines often suggest various ways of coping with stress. The frequency with which these articles appear demonstrates the prevalence of stress in our society. In addition, organizational programs to help employees cope with stress have become increasingly popular as the tremendous toll taken by stress has become more widely known. We next explore some methods that individuals and organizations can use to manage stress and reduce its harmful effects. **Stress management** refers to any program that reduces stress by understanding the stress response, recognizing stressors, and using coping techniques to minimize the negative consequences of stress.[38]

▼ Individual Stress Coping Methods

Stress management by individuals includes activities and behaviors designed to (1) eliminate or control the sources of stress and (2) make the individual more resistant to stress or better able to cope with stress. The first step in individual stress management involves recognizing the stressors that are affecting a person's life. Next, the individual needs to decide what to do about them. The following are some of the many practical suggestions for individual stress management.

▲ Plan ahead and practice good time management.

▲ Get plenty of exercise, eat a balanced diet, get adequate rest, and generally take care of yourself.

▲ Develop a sound philosophy of life and maintain a positive attitude.

▲ Concentrate on balancing your work and personal life. Always take the time to have fun.

▲ Learn a relaxation technique.

Among the advantages of relaxation techniques are that individuals can use them during the workday to cope with job demands. For example, a common approach to learning a "relaxation response" when stressed is to

▲ choose a comfortable position;

▲ close your eyes;

▲ relax your muscles;

▲ become aware of your breathing;

▲ maintain a passive attitude when thoughts surface;

▲ continue for a set period of time (20 minutes is recommended); and

▲ practice the technique twice daily.[39]

An in-depth study of six successful top executives revealed that they use similar stress coping methods.[40] First, they worked hard at balancing work and family concerns. Work was central to their lives, but it wasn't their sole focus. These executives also made effective use of leisure time to reduce stress. In addition, they were skilled time managers and goal setters. Important components of their effective use of time were identifying crucial goals and constructively planning their attainment. Finally, these executives cited the essential role of social support in coping with stress. They did not operate as loners; rather, they received emotional support and important information from a diverse network of family, friends, co-workers, and industry colleagues. Additionally, these executives worked hard at maintaining fair exchanges in these relationships. That is, they both received support from others and gave support to others in their networks.

▼ Organizational Stress Coping Methods

After a major layoff last year, Phillips Petroleum Company formed a team to respond to problems created by stress among its current and former employees. Further, Phillips paid for outside help to supplement the counseling available within the organization. Ford Motor Company currently offers stress management classes and free counseling services for workers who feel overloaded. Chevron Corporation conducts workshops to help employees deal with stress.[41] In the 1990s, a large percentage of organizations have in place or are developing various stress management programs.

As Figure 8.6 on p. 257 shows, stress management by organizations is designed to reduce the harmful effects of stress in three ways: (1) identify and then modify or eliminate work stressors, (2) help employees modify their perceptions and understandings of work stress, and (3) help employees to cope more effectively with the consequences of stress.[42]

Stress management programs aimed at eliminating or modifying work stressors often include

▲ improvements in the physical work environment;

▲ job redesign to eliminate stressors;

FIGURE 8.6

Targets of Organizational Stress Management Programs

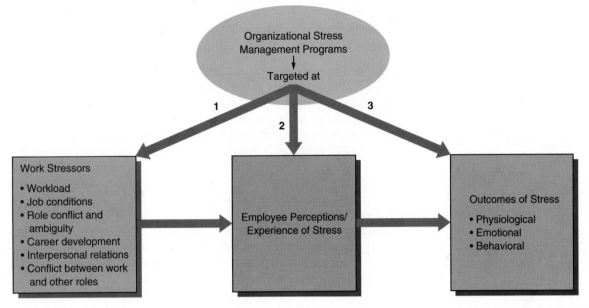

Source: Adapted from Ivancevich, J. M., Matteson, M. T., Freedman, S. M., and Phillips, J. S. Worksite stress management interventions. *American Psychologist*, 1990, 45, 253.

- ▲ changes in workloads and deadlines;
- ▲ structural reorganization;
- ▲ changes in work schedules, more flexible hours, and sabbaticals;
- ▲ management by objectives or other goal-setting programs;
- ▲ greater levels of employee participation, particularly in planning changes that affect them; and/or
- ▲ workshops dealing with role clarity and role analysis.

Programs that promote role clarity and role analysis can be particularly useful in removing or reducing role ambiguity and role conflict—two major sources of stress. When diagnosing stressors in the workplace, managers should be particularly aware of the large amount of research showing that uncertainty and perceived lack of control heighten stress. For example, Figure 8.7 on p. 259 shows the relationships commonly observed between work stressors and an individual's control over his or her work. As shown, the greatest stress occurs when jobs are high in stressors and low in controllability.[43] Thus involvement of employees in organizational change efforts, work redesign that reduces uncertainty and increases control over the pace of work, and improved clarity and understanding of roles all should help reduce employee stress.

Programs of stress management targeted at perceptions and experiences of stress and outcomes of stress include

- ▲ team building;
- ▲ behavior modification;

▲ career counseling and other employee assistance programs;

▲ workshops on time management;

▲ workshops on job burnout to help employees understand its nature and symptoms;

▲ training in relaxation techniques; and/or

▲ physical fitness or "wellness" programs.

Dividing stress management programs into these categories doesn't mean that they are necessarily separate in practice. In addition, programs that appear in the preceding lists might overlap in terms of their impact on the three target areas shown in Figure 8.6. For example, a workshop dealing with role problems might clarify roles and thus reduce the magnitude of this potential stressor. At the same time, through greater knowledge and insight into roles and role problems, employees might be able to cope more effectively with this source of stress. Similarly, career counseling might reduce career concerns as a source of stress while improving the ability of employees to cope with career problems.

Wellness programs currently are extremely popular. In general, **wellness programs** are activities that organizations sponsor to promote good health habits or to identify and correct health problems.[44] Estimates are that more than 50,000 U.S. firms provide some type of company-sponsored health promotion program. The following Managing Quality account describes the wellness program at AT&T.

MANAGING QUALITY

AT&T's Wellness Program

AT&T's Total Life Concept (TLC) program began in 1983 at several test sites. Some 2,400 employees took part in the first wellness program, which began with ambitious goals and an agenda designed to improve stress coping skills, fitness, and health among AT&T's employees. One year after the start of this program, AT&T observed substantial improvements in health and morale. Program participants reduced their cholesterol levels by 10% on average, and 78% of the employees who wanted to lower their blood pressure had managed at least a 10% decrease. Over 80% of the employees who joined smoking-cessation courses quit smoking; after one year, 50% remained nonsmokers. The director of TLC says, "People's attitudes changed. We sent a message to employees that said, 'We care about your health and well-being.' They got the message."

Eighty thousand AT&T employees are enrolled in TLC. The first step in joining the program is free blood-pressure and cholesterol tests. Employees can then choose among various courses designed to address concerns about blood pressure, cholesterol, nutrition, stress, cancer, and the like. Some courses are free; others might cost small amounts, depending on the facilities and resources required. People typically need encouragement after they have started an exercise program or have quit smoking, so "graduates" of the courses get together in support groups to help each other make the life-style changes last.

The TLC motto is "A healthy workplace makes good business sense," and AT&T managers seem to take this slogan seriously. AT&T is spending about $50 for each employee in the program. With 80,000 employees participating, this contribution amounts to about $4 million annually.[45]

FIGURE 8.7

Impacts of Employee Control and
Amount of Work Stressors

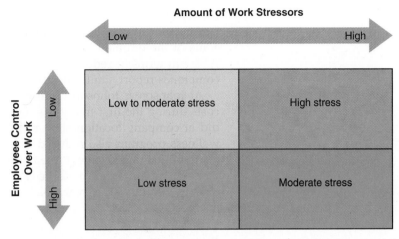

FIGURE 8.7

Impacts of Employee Control and
Amount of Work Stressors

Source: Adapted from Fox, M. L., Dwyer, D. J., and Ganster, D. C. Effects of stressful job demands and control on physiological and attitudinal outcomes in a hospital setting. *Academy of Management Journal,* 1993, 36, 291.

There are three major types of wellness programs.[46] The first are programs aimed at raising awareness and providing information. These programs may or may not directly improve health; rather, they are designed to inform employees about the consequences of unhealthy behavior. For example, Sara Lee provides female employees with a series of workshops on prenatal care, nutrition, and strategies for preventing disease. Johnson & Johnson has lunch-hour seminars on stress-coping techniques. Companies often use these programs to generate interest in more active exercise and life-style change programs.

A second type of wellness program involves employees in ongoing efforts to modify their life-styles. Such efforts might involve physical fitness programs (such as jogging or walking), smoking-cessation programs, weight control programs, and the like. For example, L. L. Bean has a running club for employees and programs that offer lessons in ballroom dancing and cross-country skiing. Bonne Bell encourages employees to ride bicycles to work and has arranged for its employees to purchase bikes at cost. Bonne Bell also provides an extensive series of exercise programs for employees and has built tennis and volleyball courts, a running track, and shower and locker facilities. Employees may use all of these facilities at no cost and even get an extra 30 minutes for lunch if they want to exercise. The firm sells running suits and shoes at discount prices and currently offers a $250 bonus for employees who exercise at least four days a week.

A third variety of wellness program has as its goal the creation of an environment that will help employees maintain the healthy life-style developed in the other programs. An example is the AT&T employees who formed support groups to help each other maintain their healthy life-style changes. The exercise facilities provided free of charge to employees by Bonne Bell are another example. At Safeway, employees built their own fitness center on company grounds. The firm now provides a full-time fitness director to oversee the exercise programs and activities.

Wellness programs can provide substantial benefits to both individuals and organizations. Safeway estimates that its wellness program has almost completely eliminated workplace accidents and reduced tardiness and absenteeism by more than 60%. The preceding Managing Quality feature described some of the dramatic health benefits obtained by participating employees at AT&T in terms of reduced blood pressure and cholesterol levels. Many other companies report similar positive health consequences.

At Johnson & Johnson locations that used the wellness program, hospital costs during the first five years increased by only one-third as much as they did at company locations that didn't use the program. Johnson & Johnson's wellness program also reduced absenteeism by 18%. In addition to showing a substantial improvement in employee morale, an evaluation of Honeywell's wellness program indicated the cost of its health-care services is increasing an average of only 4% a year. (Nationwide, health-care costs are increasing an average 14% a year.)[47]

Summary

Stress is a consequence of or a response to a situation that places either physical or psychological demands, or stressors, on a person. The body's general biological response to stressors prepares the individual to fight or flee—behaviors generally inappropriate in the workplace. Many factors determine how employees experience work stress, including their perception of the situation, past experiences, the presence or absence of other employees, and a variety of individual differences.

Stressors at work stem from many sources, including (1) workload, (2) job conditions, (3) role conflict and ambiguity, (4) career development, (5) interpersonal relations, and (6) conflict between work and other roles. In addition, significant changes or other events in an individual's personal life may also be sources of stress.

Stress affects people physiologically, emotionally, and behaviorally. Researchers have linked stress to several serious health problems, particularly coronary heart disease. An inverted U-shaped relationship exists between stress and performance. An optimal level of stress probably exists for any particular task, and less or more stress than that level leads to reduced performance. Job burnout is a major result of unrelieved job-related stress.

Several personality dimensions are related to stress. Individuals having a Type A personality are prone to stress and have an increased chance of heart disease. Some specific dimensions of the Type A personality, such as hostility, are particularly important in terms of stress-related illness. In contrast, the collection of personality traits known as hardiness seems to reduce the effects of stress.

Stress is a crucial issue for both individuals and organizations. Fortunately, various techniques and programs can help people manage stress in the workplace. These programs may focus on identifying and removing workplace stressors and helping employees cope with stress. Wellness programs are particularly promising in this latter regard.

Key Words and Concepts

Behavioral effects of stress	Emotional effects of stress	Hardiness
Depersonalization	Fight-or-flight response	Job burnout

Life stressors
Physiological effects of stress
Role ambiguity
Role conflict

Role overload
Stress
Stress management
Stressors

Type A personality
Type B personality
Wellness programs

Discussion Questions

1. Write a paragraph that summarizes the most important influences on how individuals experience stress.

2. Explain the role of individual differences in experiencing stress.

3. Describe some of the stressors in a job that you have held. Which were the most difficult ones to deal with? Why?

4. Give an example of a time when the fight-or-flight response seemed particularly inappropriate for your own behavior.

5. Identify the possible health consequences of excessive stress.

6. Describe the general relationship between performance and stress.

7. Discuss the conditions and circumstances leading to job burnout.

8. Compare and contrast the hardy personality with the Type A personality.

9. Design a stress management program for an organization. Justify the various components of your suggested program.

 ## Developing Skills

Self-Diagnosis:
Identifying Your Strategies for Coping with Stress

On a separate sheet of paper, develop responses to the following questions. Be prepared to share your responses with other members of your group or class.[48]

Successful Experience

1. Describe a situation in which you coped well with stress. (How did you perceive and/or assess the situation? What did you think was happening?)

2. What perceptions, thoughts, feelings, behaviors, and resources helped you to succeed in this situation?

3. How have you integrated these perceptions, thoughts, feelings, behaviors, and resources into your typical style of dealing with stress?

4. What other perceptions, thoughts, feelings, behaviors, and resources could you use in order to cope even better with stress?

Unsuccessful Experience

1. Describe a situation in which you did not cope well with stress. (How did you perceive and/or assess the situation? What did you think was happening?)

2. What perceptions, thoughts, feelings, and behaviors prevented you from dealing with this situation effectively?

3. As a result of this experience, what did you learn about coping with stress? What would (or did) you do differently the next time?

Comparison

Review your responses to the "successful experience" and the "unsuccessful experience." Describe the differences in how you perceived and handled the two situations.

A Case in Point:
The Stress of Shift Work

Marilyn Baker sat at her kitchen table and leafed through the entertainment section of the local paper, slowly sipping her second cup of coffee. An Academy Award-winning movie was playing in town, and she hoped that it would stay for several weeks so that she and her husband, Carl, could fit it into their hectic schedules. Carl Baker had changed jobs re-cently and was now working for St. Regis Aluminum, a manufacturer of lightweight metal products. St. Regis worked shifts, and he was about to start a two-week stint on the night shift (midnight to 8 A.M.). Neither of the Bakers had had previous experience with shift work, and the switch from normal working hours was proving to be difficult.

Carl worked cycles that included two weeks of day shift (8 A.M. to 4 P.M.), two weeks of swing shift (4 P.M. to mid-night), and two weeks of night shift. Then, the whole cycle began again. The couple had to plan their family life around this changing schedule, but Marilyn couldn't seem to get the hang of it. Little things that would have been minor irritants before now seemed to become major problems. For example, the boy next door was taking trumpet lessons and practiced after school. When Carl needed to sleep in the afternoon, the noise of the trumpet often woke him. The couple had already had two arguments about whether to call the boy's mother to request that he practice at another time.

Marilyn was an excellent cook and particularly enjoyed preparing foods that her family liked. Yesterday, beef roasts, one of Carl's favorite foods, had been on sale. However, with Carl starting the night shift, Marilyn decided to freeze the roast and wait for a time when the entire family could enjoy it. Even though Carl could sit down to a "full" meal after coming off the night shift, that early morning time was not very appealing to the rest of the family. So, Marilyn was learning that "special" meals were pretty much restricted to the times when Carl worked the day shift.

Shift work was also proving awkward for their social life. The Bakers were members of a poker club that met twice a month on Friday nights. Couples in the club usually met at 8 P.M. and played for four or five hours. When Carl was on the swing shift, there was no way they could play. When he worked the night shift, they could stay for only part of the evening, as Carl would have to leave in time to get ready for work. Only when he was on the day shift could they participate fully. So, now they were playing with their club only once or twice every two months. Their friends had gotten another couple to substitute for them, but the Bakers were afraid they might have to drop out of the club because the substitute couple was playing more frequently than they were.

Marilyn had started to feel a bit sorry for herself. Still, she admitted to herself that this shift work must be more stressful to Carl than it was to her. She remembered that he was working the swing shift on the weekend when the Custom Boat and Trailer Show came to town. He had been looking forward to seeing the new bass boats for weeks but got to visit the show for only about an hour before leaving for work. Weekends seemed particularly hard on Carl Baker. On Saturdays and Sundays, just when he found something he liked to do, it often was time to go to work.

Their ten-year-old son, Tom, wandered into the kitchen holding a Little League schedule in his hand. "Mom," Tom said, "the regional tournament is in three weeks. Will you and Dad be able to see my games?" Marilyn got up to look at Carl's work schedule, which was taped to the refrigerator door. "Dad will be working the swing shift that week, but I can come. I'll work some extra hours and can trade days off with someone on my work team. So, I'll be able to take off enough time to see all your games," Marilyn said. Tom loved to have his mother at his baseball games, but still his face fell. "Dad sure doesn't see many of my games any more," he said, as he slowly walked from the kitchen.[49]

Questions

1. Identify the stressors that exist in this situation. Which do you think are the most important sources of stress?

2. Can you predict other possible disruptions in the Bakers' family life that might stem from shift work?

3. Suggest some things that St. Regis Aluminum might do to reduce stress for shift workers.

4. Suggest some stress coping strategies that Marilyn and Carl Baker could use.

References

1. Adapted from Riecher, A. Job stress: What it can do to you. *Bryan-College Station Eagle*, August 15, 1993, D1.

2. Jax, S. M., Beehr, T. A., and Roberts, C. K. The meaning of occupational stress items to survey respondents. *Journal of Applied Psychology*, 1992, 77, 623–628; Kahn, R. L., and Byosiere, P. Stress in organizations. In M. D. Dunnette and L. M. Hough (eds.), *Handbook of Industrial and Organizational Psychology*, Vol. 3, 2nd ed. Palo Alto, Calif.: Consulting Psychologists Press, 1992, 571–650.

3. Contrada, R., Baum, A. S., Glass, D., and Friend, R. The social psychology of health. In R. M. Baron, W. G. Graziano, and C. Stangor (eds.), *Social Psychology*. Fort Worth: Holt, Rinehart and Winston, 1991, 620–624.

4. This example is based on Matteson, M. T., and Ivancevich, J. M. *Controlling Work Stress: Effective Human Resource and Management Strategies.* San Francisco: Jossey-Bass, 1987, 12–14.

5. Selye, H. History and present status of the stress concept. In L. Goldberger and S. Breznitz (eds.), *Handbook of Stress.* New York: Free Press, 1982, 7–17; Selye, H. *The Stress of Life,* rev. ed. New York: McGraw-Hill, 1976, 1.

6. See, for example, Cummins, R. C. Job stress and the buffering effect of supervisory support. *Group & Organization Studies,* 1990, 15, 92–104; Ganster, D. C., Fusilier, M. R., and Mayes, B. T. Role of social support in the experience of stress at work. *Journal of Applied Psychology,* 1986, 71, 102–110.

7. Burke, M. J., Brief, A. P., and George, J. M. The role of negative affectivity in understanding relations between self-reports of stressors and strains: A comment on the applied psychology literature. *Journal of Applied Psychology,* 1993, 78, 402–412; Schaubroeck, J., Ganster, D. C., and Fox, M. L. Dispositional affect and work-related stress. *Journal of Applied Psychology,* 1992, 77, 322–335.

8. Lazarus, R. S. From psychological stress to the emotions: A history of changing outlooks. *Annual Review of Psychology*, 1993, 44, 1–21.

9. This story is attributed to Henry Murray, as described by Pervin, L. A. Persons, situations, interactions: The history of a controversy and a discussion of theoretical models. *Academy of Management Review*, 1989, 14, 350–360.

10. Adapted from Ellison, K. Siesta sunset: Stress invades mañana-land. *Houston Chronicle*, July 28, 1992, 7A.

11. O'Boyle, T. F. Fear and stress in the office take toll. *Wall Street Journal*, November 6, 1990, B1, B3; Riecher, Job stress, D1, D5; Stewart, T. A. Do you push your people too hard? *Fortune*, October 22, 1990, 121–128.

12. Cooper, C. L., and Arbose, J. Executive stress goes global. *International Management*, May 1984, 42–48.

13. Trost, C. Workplace Stress. *Wall Street Journal*, December 1, 1992, A1.

14. Adapted from Fisher, A. B. Welcome to the age of overwork. *Fortune*, November 30, 1992, 64–71. The downsizing information in this feature is based on Cascio, W. F. Downsizing: What do we know? What have we learned? *Academy of Management Executive*, 1993, 7, 95–104.

15. Nykodym, N., and George, K. Stress busting on the job. *Personnel*, July 1989, 56–59; Shostak, A. B. *Blue-Collar Stress.* Reading, Mass.: Addison-Wesley, 1980, 19–28.

16. See, for example, Leigh, J. H., Lucas, G. H., and Woodman, R. W. Effects of perceived organizational factors on role stress–job attitude relationships. *Journal of Management*, 1988, 14, 41–58; Miner, J. B. *Industrial-Organizational Psychology.* New York: McGraw-Hill, 1992, 158–159.

17. Isabella, L. A. Downsizing: Survivors' assessments. *Business Horizons*, May/June 1989, 35–41.

18. Sutton, R. I., and Rafaeli, A. Characteristics of work stations as potential occupational stressors. *Academy of Management Journal*, 1987, 30, 260–276.

19. Frone, M. R., Russell, M., and Cooper, M. L. Antecedents and outcomes of work-family conflict: Testing a model of the work–family interface. *Journal of Applied Psychology*, 1992, 77, 65–78.

20. Adapted from Shellenbarger, S. So much talk, so little action. *Wall Street Journal Reports*, June 21, 1993, R1, R4.

21. Baron, R. A., and Byrne, D. *Social Psychology: Understanding Human Interaction*, 6th ed. Boston: Allyn and Bacon, 1991, 571–573. The type of rating scale shown in Table 8.1 is based on the work of Holmes, T. H. and Rahe, R. H. The social readjustment rating scale. *Journal of Psychomatic Medicine*, 1967, 11, 213–218.

22. Ganster, D. C., and Schaubroeck, J. Work stress and employee health. *Journal of Management*, 1991, 17, 235–271; Stewart, Do you push your people too hard?, 121.

23. Ader, R., and Cohen, N. Psychoneuroimmunology: Conditioning and stress. *Annual Review of Psychology*, 1993, 44, 53–85; Cohen, S., and Williamson, G. M. Stress and infectious disease in humans. *Psychological Bulletin*, 1991, 109, 5–24; Maes, S., Spielberger, C. D., Defares, P. B., and Sarason, I. G., (eds.). *Topics in Health Psychology.* Chichester, England: John Wiley & Sons, 1988; Quick, J. C., and Quick, J. D. *Organizational Stress and Preventive Management.* New York: McGraw-Hill, 1984.

24. Adapted from Tubbs, W. *Karoushi*: Stress-death and the meaning of work. *Journal of Business Ethics*, 1993, 12, 869–877.

25. Allen, D. S. Less stress, less litigation. *Personnel*, January 1990,

26. Lublin, J. A. Walking wounded: Survivors of layoffs battle angst, anger, hurting productivity. *Wall Street Journal*, December 6, 1993, A1.

27. See, for example, Greer, C. R., and Castro, M. A. D. The Relationship between perceived unit effectiveness and occupational stress: The case of purchasing agents. *Journal of Applied Behavioral Science*, 1986, 22, 159–175; Motowidlo, S. J., Packard, J. S., and Manning, M. R. Occupational stress: Its causes and consequences for job performance. *Journal of Applied Psychology*, 1986, 71, 618–629; Sullivan, S. E., and Bhagat, R. S. Organizational stress, job satisfaction, and job performance: Where do we go from here? *Journal of Management*, 1992, 18, 353–374.

28. Cordes, C. L., and Dougherty, T. W. A review and integration of research on job burnout. *Academy of Management Review*, 1993, 18, 621–656; Lee, R. T., and Ashforth, B. E. On the meaning of Maslach's three dimensions of burnout. *Journal of Applied Psychology*, 1990, 75, 743–747.

29. Niehouse, O. I. Controlling burnout: A leadership guide for managers. *Business Horizons*, July–August 1984, 81–82.

30. Milbank, D. "New-collar" work: Telephone sales reps do unrewarding jobs that few can abide. *Wall Street Journal*, September 9, 1993; Offerman, L. R., and Armitage, M. A. Stress and the woman manager: Sources, health outcomes, and interventions. In E. A. Fagenson (ed.), *Women in Management*, Vol. 4. Newbury Park, Calif.: Sage, 1993, 131–161. Reicher, A. Burnout, cancer rates plot women's stress. *Bryan-College Station Eagle*, August 15, 1993, A1, A8.

31. Kahn and Byosiere, Stress in organizations, 611–622; Miner, *Industrial-Organizational Psychology*, 160–162.

32. Landy, F. J., Rastegary, H., Thayer, J., and Colvin, C. Time urgency. *Journal of Applied Psychology*, 1991, 76, 644–657.

33. Friedman, M., and Rosenman, R. *Type A Behavior and Your Heart.* New York: Knopf, 1974.

34. Friedman, H. S., and Booth-Kewley, S. Personality, Type A behavior and coronary heart disease: The role of emotional expression. *Journal of Personality and Social Psychology*, 1987, 53, 783–792; Ganster, D. C., Schaubroeck, J., Sime, W. E., and Mayes, B. T. The nomological validity of the Type A personality among employed adults. *Journal of Applied Psychology*, 1991, 76, 143–168; Lyness, S. A. Predictors of differences between Type A and B individuals in heart rate and blood pressure reactivity. *Psychological Bulletin*, 1993, 114, 266–295.

35. Baron and Byrne, *Social Psychology*, 606.

36. Contrada, Baum, Glass, and Friend, The social psychology of health, 626–627.

37. Baron and Byrne, *Social Psychology*, 574–575; Contrada, R. J. Type A behavior, personality hardiness, and cardiovascular responses to stress. *Journal of Personality and Social Psychology*, 1989, 57, 895–903; Roth, D. L., Wiebe, D. J. Fillingham, R. B., and Shay, K. A. Life events, fitness, hardiness, and health: A simultaneous analysis of proposed stress-resistance effects. *Journal of Personality and Social Psychology*, 1989, 57, 136–142.

38. Byrum-Robinson, B. Stress-management training for the nineties. In J. W. Pfeiffer (ed.), *The 1993 Annual: Developing Human Resources.* San Diego: Pfeiffer & Company, 1993, 264.

32–35; Hollis, D., and Goodson, J. Stress: The legal and organizational implications. *Employee Responsibilities and Rights Journal*, 1989, 2, 255–262.

39. Byrum-Robinson, Stress-management training for the nineties, 277.

40. Nelson, D. L., Quick, J. C., and Quick, J. D. Corporate warfare: Preventing combat stress and battle fatigue. *Organizational Dynamics*, Summer 1989, 65–79.

41. Trost, Workplace stress, A1.

42. Ivancevich, J. M., Matteson, M. T., Freedman, S. M., and Phillips, J. S. Worksite stress management interventions. *American Psychologist*, 1990, 45, 252–261.

43. Fox, M. L., Dwyer, D. J., and Ganster, D. G. Effects of stressful job demands and control on physiological and attitudinal outcomes in a hospital setting. *Academy of Management Journal*, 1993, 36, 289–318; Lee, C., Ashford, S. J., and Bobko, P. Interactive effects of Type A behavior and perceived control on worker performance, job satisfaction, and somatic complaints. *Academy of Management Journal*, 1990, 33, 870–881.

44. Gebhardt, D. L., and Crump, C. E. Employee fitness and wellness programs in the workplace. *American Psychologist*, 1990, 45, 262–272.

45. Adapted from Roberts, M., and Harris, T. J. Wellness at work. *Psychology Today*, May 1989, 55.

46. Gebhardt and Crump, Employee fitness and wellness programs in the workplace.

47. Company examples in this section are drawn from Roberts and Harris, Wellness at work, 54–58.

48. Gregory, A. M. Coping strategies: Managing stress successfully. Reproduced from *The 1992 Annual: Developing Human Resources* by J. W. Pfeiffer (ed.). Copyright © 1992 by Pfeiffer & Company, San Diego, Calif. Used with permission.

49. Adapted from Muchinsky, P. M. *Psychology Applied to Work*, 3rd ed. Pacific Grove, Calif.: Brooks/Cole, 1990, 556–557.

Part
II
Interpersonal and Group Processes

Chapter
9

Dynamics Within Groups and Teams

Chapter
10

Dynamics Between Groups and Teams

Chapter
11

Leadership

Chapter
12

Interpersonal Communication

Chapter
13

Conflict and Negotiation

9 Dynamics Within Groups and Teams

When you have finished studying this chapter, you should be able to:

▲ State the potential tensions between group and individual goals.

▲ Define the most common types of groups and teams in organizations.

▲ Express the evolving impact of groupware tools on groups and teams.

▲ Describe the five-stages model of group development.

▲ Discuss the key factors that influence group and team outcomes.

▲ Explain the six-phase model of team decision making.

▲ Apply the nominal group technique and electronic brainstorming to foster team creativity.

OUTLINE

Preview Case: Teams at MPI

Individual–Group Relations

Individualism and Collectivism

Individual and Team Goals

Group Types and Development

Types of Task Groups

Types of Teams

Managing Quality: Teams at Mary T.

Coalitions

Stages of Group Development

Influences on Groups and Teams

Context

Managing in Practice: Groupware at Westinghouse

Managing Across Cultures: Apple's Global Videoconferencing

Goals

Managing Ethics: ''Dateline'' Crashes

Size

Member Composition and Roles

Managing Diversity: United Nations at Tabra, Inc.

Managing in Practice: It's Only Fair

Cohesiveness

Managing Ethics: Beech-Nut's Groupthink

Leadership

Improving Team Decision Making

Six-Phase Model

Assessment of Model

Managing Across Cultures: Group Meetings in China

Fostering Team Creativity

Nominal Group Technique

Brainstorming

Managing in Practice: Brainstorming to Action

DEVELOPING SKILLS

Self-Diagnosis: *People Are Electric*

A Case in Point: *Great Majestic Company*

PREVIEW CASE

Teams at MPI

Maryland Plastics, Inc. (MPI) is a Federalsburg, Maryland, firm with about 300 employees. It produces injection molded plastic cutlery, and scientific and custom molded products. The company has developed a comprehensive quality system to carry out its quality goals and support its overall mission. The system includes a quality steering committee, quality improvement teams, department quality improvement teams and corrective action teams. These teams are both departmental and cross-functional and are guided by a common mission and vision.

Although company leaders provide the vision for quality, all MPI employees are involved in making quality a way of life. "We use the Quality Improvement Team concept as our key mechanism to apply the total quality process," explains Raymond Appler, MPI's total quality manager. "We presently have twelve quality improvement teams representing every department at MPI. They are self-directed, have their own facilitators and develop improvements relating to their specific areas." Employees are empowered to make improvements and to take corrective action. Teams are recognized for their quality improvements through a variety of programs which keep the commitment to quality strong. Management fosters open communication among all MPI associates (employees) through employee surveys, company newsletters, infor-mational bulletin boards, team meetings, and plantwide meetings and celebrations. "All employees feel they are part of the company and participate in the continuous improvement process," Appler says.

The teams at MPI continually improve working partnerships with customers and suppliers. "Facility visits and efforts to foster open communication at all employee levels have improved these partnerships," says Appler. A customer bulletin board in the cafeteria informs everyone about customers' products, issues, and concerns, demonstrating the customer's importance. Teams hold monthly production planning meetings with customers to avoid scheduling and quality pitfalls. An annual customer appreciation day allows customers and employees to meet informally and develop closer customer–supplier relationships. The company conducts customer surveys and participates in many customer audits, taking action (by teams) in any areas of concern that are revealed.

Has MPI's commitment to human resource excellence and to the quality process through teams yielded positive results? Indeed! Reject rates at the company have been continually improving. Innovative devices and techniques have increased operator safety, improved product consistency, reduced required production floor space, enhanced the "value-added" to products, increased productivity, and improved the quality of working life.[1]

Maryland Plastics, Inc. (MPI), is just one of many organizations that are using teams and other types of groups to make decisions, perform tasks, and accomplish their goals. This chapter focuses on the factors and processes that determine whether formal groups and teams are efficient and effective—like the quality steering committee and quality improvement teams at MPI—or inefficient and ineffective. There are no simple prescriptions for creating and maintaining effective *formal* groups and teams (those specifically created by management) or *informal* groups (those that form from the day-to-day interactions of individuals).[2]

In this chapter, we focus on ways to *diagnose* formal and informal groups and—based on the diagnosis—ways to increase their performance and effectiveness. We emphasize (1) the relations between individuals and groups, (2) the principal factors that affect group and team effectiveness, (3) effective team decision-making processes, and (4) ways to stimulate team creativity. As might be expected, many of the other topics discussed in this book—such as leadership, interpersonal communication, and conflict management—contribute to the skills needed for effective management of and participation in groups and teams.

A **group** comprises people with shared goals who often communicate with one another over a period of time and are few enough so that each individual may communicate with all the others person-to-person.[3] For our purposes, a group is a small number of individuals who communicate person-to-person to achieve one or more common goals. Accordingly, we do not focus on large groups such as a political party, ethnic group, or occupational group.

▼ INDIVIDUAL–GROUP RELATIONS

In many countries, people strongly believe in the importance and centrality of the individual. In the United States and Canada, educational, governmental, and business institutions frequently state that they exist to serve individual goals. The two cultural values that affect the use of groups and teams in organizations are individualism and collectivism.

▼ Individualism and Collectivism

The cultural belief in individualism creates uneasiness over the influence that groups or teams have in organizations. **Individualism** means being distinct and separate from the group, emphasizing personal goals, and showing less concern and emotional attachment to groups, especially in work organizations. Employees in individualistic cultures are expected to act on the basis of their personal goals and self-interests.

The cultural belief in collectivism in such countries as China and Japan seems to have the opposite effect in organizations. The use of teams is a natural extension of their cultural values. Their uneasiness revolves around the relative influence and assertiveness of the individual in teams. **Collectivism** means being an integral part of the group, subordinating personal goals to group goals, showing deep concern for the welfare of the group, and feeling intense emotional ties to the group.[4] Thus we might characterize the basic difference between individualism and collectivism in certain cultures as the uneasiness between "fitting into the group" versus "standing out from the group."[5] Even in societies that value individualism, the actual use of groups and teams is substantial, as demonstrated at MPI. The company encourages all employees, including those with individualistic orientations, to be contributing team members through (1) intensive training on team participation and decision making, (2) empowerment of small teams to implement improvements and take corrective action (which serves to increase individual participation), and (3) assessment, recognition, and reward of each individual for his or her contributions to team decision making and goals. Even so, MPI employees spend most of their time performing work tasks individually.

▼ Individual and Team Goals

The potential for the group and individuals to have incompatible goals clearly exists. But these goals need not always conflict and in fact often are compatible.[6] The potential for conflicting and common goals in teams and groups relative to individuals is suggested in the following observations.

▲ They do exist, and all employees need to take them into account.

▲ They mobilize powerful forces that create important effects for individuals.

▲ They may create both good and bad results.

▲ They can be managed to increase the benefits from them.[7]

The free rider concept is one example of conflicting team and individual goals. A **free rider** refers to a team member who obtains benefits from membership but doesn't bear a proportional share of the responsibility for generating the benefit.[8] Students sometimes experience the free-rider problem when a faculty member assigns a team project for which all the members receive the same (team) grade. Let's assume that seven students are in a team and that two members make little or no contribution. The noncontributing members obtain the benefit of the team grade but didn't bear a proportional share of the work in earning the team grade. Free riders are likely to be highly individualistic people who believe that they can minimize their contributions to a team effort so long as they are not held accountable individually.

Free riding is repulsive to most group and team members for three reasons. First, free riding violates an equity standard: Team members don't want others to receive the same rewards for less effort. Second, it violates a standard of social responsibility: Everyone should do their fair share. Third, it violates a standard of reciprocity or exchange.[9] A team may do poorly if too many of its members are free riders who contribute little or nothing to the task.

▼ GROUP TYPES AND DEVELOPMENT

Individuals usually belong to many types of groups, and there are numerous ways of classifying them. For example, a person concerned with the degree of difficulty in gaining membership or becoming accepted as a group member might develop a classification scheme that separates it according to whether the group is *open* or *closed* to new members. A person evaluating groups in an organization according to the primary goal they serve might find useful the classification of friendship group and task group. A **friendship group** evolves informally to meet its members' personal needs of security, esteem, and belonging. Management formally creates a **task group** to accomplish organizational goals. However, a single group or team in an organization may serve both friendship and task goals. The 12 quality improvement teams at MPI are examples of task groups, which we focus on in this chapter.

▼ Types of Task Groups

Task groups may be classified on the basis of the relationships between group members. The three basic types of task groups are counteracting, coacting, and interacting.[10]

A **counteracting group** exists when members interact to resolve some type of conflict, usually through negotiation and compromise. A labor-management negotiating group is one example of a counteracting group. Management and union representatives usually believe that at least some of their goals conflict.

When group members perform their jobs relatively independently in the short run, a **coacting group** exists. *Relatively* and *in the short run* indicate that, without interdependence over time, there would be no task group. For example, college students enrolled in the same course may participate relatively independently of each other in class discussions but act interdependently with others in undertaking a team project. Another example of a coacting group is a bowling team where the team score is the sum of the team members' scores. Coacting groups are likely to be the effective when individual efforts do not require much coordination. For example, a regional sales manager may need to bring her sales representatives together quarterly to review common problems and issues. However, the day-to-day activities of each sales representative doesn't involve communication and coordination with the other sales representatives. In addition, the total regional sales and profits are primarily the sum of each sales representative's performance.

An **interacting group** exists when a group or team cannot accomplish its goal(s) until all members have completed their shares of the task. For example, the assembly team of a large luggage manufacturer consists of about ten people who perform the separate jobs required to assemble a complete piece of luggage. If one job isn't done, the goal—the finished suitcase—cannot be completed. Common forms of interacting groups include committees, task forces, teams, boards, advisory councils, work crews, review panels, and the like. An increasing portion of the work force is being called upon to work in a team environment, such at Maryland Plastics Inc.[11]

The types of issues and decisions that a group or team addresses may vary widely. Table 9.1 provides a brief questionnaire for assessing the degree of autonomy and responsibility that resides with a group or team and higher management. As you review Table 9.1, please relate it to your own experi-

TABLE 9.1   Questionnaire for Assessing Group or Team Autonomy

Instructions: Check the appropriate column for each of the 12 types of issues or decisions.

For the most part in my group/team, the autonomy and responsibility for handling the following issues or decisions resides with:

Issues or Decisions	Group/Team	Higher Management
1. Primary influence on its qualitative goals	——	——
2. Primary influence on its quantitative goals	——	——
3. Propose and/or formulate budget	——	——
4. Monitor activities against budget	——	——
5. Rotate tasks and assignments among members	——	——
6. Decide on team leadership	——	——
7. Assess performance and progress toward goals	——	——
8. Call and conduct meetings	——	——
9. Implement solutions within scope of team responsibilities	——	——
10. Inspect quality of team's outputs	——	——
11. Evaluate and dismiss team members	——	——
12. Other (add other types of issues or decisions relevant to the team)	——	——

ence—such as the autonomy and responsibilities of a class project team relative to your instructor (higher management). In general, the greater the number of marks in the team/group column in Table 9.1, the greater is the autonomy of the group/team.

▼ Types of Teams

A **team** is a small number of people with complementary skills who are committed to a common purpose, set of performance goals, and approach for which they hold themselves mutually accountable.[12] The heart of any team is a shared commitment by the members to their collective performance. Team goals could be as basic as responding to all customers within 24 hours to reducing defects by 20 percent over the next six months. The key is that these goals cannot be achieved without the cooperation of team members. A team must be formed with or develop the right mix of complementary skills among the members to achieve its goals. Team members need to decide how they will work together to accomplish the team's purpose.[13] Recall the quality improvement teams at MPI in the Preview Case. They are self-directed, have their own coordinators, are expected to develop improvements in their specific areas of responsibility, and are empowered to implement improvements. There are various types of teams. Let's consider three of the most common types.

Problem-solving teams identify specific concerns in their areas of responsibility, develop potential solutions, and often are empowered to take action within defined limits.[14] Such teams frequently address quality or cost problems. The members usually are employees of a specific department and meet at least once or twice a week for an hour or two. The teams may be empowered to implement their own solutions if those solutions don't require major changes in procedures that might adversely affect other departments, teams, or external stakeholders (customers, suppliers, regulatory agencies, etc.) or require substantial new resources. Problem-solving teams do not fundamentally reorganize work or change the role of managers. In essence, managers delegate certain problems and decision-making responsibilities to a team as a whole. This approach contrasts to delegating specific tasks and authority on a person-by-person basis.[15] For example, management at U.S. Steel's plant in Gary, Indiana, formed a team of hourly workers to help solve numerous quality problems. The team helped reduce the amount of steel rejected by automotive customers by 80%.[16]

Cross-functional teams bring together the knowledge and skills of people from various work areas to solve mutual problems. Unlike problem-solving teams, cross-functional teams (1) draw members from several departments or functions, (2) deal with problems that cut across departments and functions, and (3) typically disband after the problem is solved.[17] Cross-functional teams may design and introduce quality improvement programs and new technology, meet with customers and suppliers to improve inputs or outputs, and link separate functions (e.g., marketing, finance, manufacturing, and human resources) to increase product or service innovations. For example, Precision Industries, a distributor of industrial parts in Omaha, Nebraska, put together a team of people from three departments to improve its computer invoicing.

Employees from the collections, data entry, and customer service departments met with the firm's software developers to address practical problems with the writing of the software. "We would chart out how to solve those problems in fairly short meetings and come up with three or four solutions," says Mike Keim, chief financial officer for Precision Industries, adding that "all of it is not only working but we have state-of-the-art technology."[18]

Self-managed teams normally consist of employees who must work together and cooperate on a daily basis to produce an entire good (or major identifiable component) or service. These teams perform a variety of managerial tasks, such as (1) scheduling work and vacations, (2) rotating tasks and assignments among members, (3) ordering materials, (4) deciding on team leadership, which can rotate among team members, (5) setting key team goals, (6) budgeting, (7) hiring replacements for departing team members, and (8) sometimes even evaluating one another's performance.[19] Each member often learns all the jobs that have to be performed by the team. The impacts of self-managed teams may be enormous. They have raised productivity 30% or more and have substantially raised quality in organizations that have used them. They fundamentally change how work is organized and empower the team to make many decisions. The introduction of such teams typically eliminates one or more managerial levels, thereby creating a flatter organization.

The following Managing Quality feature reveals how Mary T., Inc., uses self-managed teams to achieve a variety of goals with particular emphasis on quality and customer satisfaction.

MANAGING QUALITY

Teams at Mary T.

Mary Tjosvold is the chief executive officer of Mary T., Inc. This 600-employee company in Minneapolis provides residential social services for people with disabilities. Tjosvold says, "I've never had a hierarchy. I've always managed with a team [approach]." Employees have a good deal of sway within the company, Tjosvold says, but the greatest influence over a business should come from its customers. Mary T.'s organizational chart "puts the clients in the center," Tjosvold explains, and the company's teams revolve around them. Mary T. regularly uses teams to guarantee product and service quality.

Mary T.'s quality team consist of several staff members who visit the firm's clients and "make sure that the programs we run are up to the standards we set," says Tjosvold. The quality assurance team at Mary T. also directs its own activities, and another team is moving toward self-management. The self-governing team draws up its own budgets and schedules, and, whenever possible, it even makes its own disciplinary decisions. "When they can't do that, they call me in," says Tjosvold. The self-directed team also appoints, by rotation, a person to be the "single point of contact" to whom Tjosvold could go immediately for answers to questions about the team's work.

Mary T. also uses problem-solving teams and cross-functional teams. For example, the company formed a team to implement a smoke-free policy and environment within 18 months.[20]

▼ Coalitions

A **coalition** is a set of individuals (or organizations) who band together to pursue a specific goal. An informal group that operates to control and reduce the influence of higher management is one type of coalition. A coalition has four key features: (1) it is deliberately created by the members; (2) it operates independently of the formal organization; (3) it is formed to achieve a specific and mutual goal(s); and (4) it requires united action by its members.[21] A co-alition could be as simple as ten students banding together to try to reverse a decision to deny tenure to their favorite faculty member. A more complex coalition is the Organization of Petroleum Exporting Countries (OPEC). It at-tempts to persuade member countries to limit the supply of oil as a means of keeping prices, and thus total revenues for member countries, high.

▼ Stages of Group Development

Groups and teams often go through a five-stage developmental sequence: forming, storming, norming, performing, and adjourning.[22] The types of task-oriented behaviors and relations-oriented (social) behaviors that may be ob-served in groups and teams differ from stage to stage. Figure 9.1 shows the five stages on the horizontal axis, and the level of group maturity on the vertical axis. Figure 9.1 also indicates that a group can fail and disband during a stage or when moving from one stage to another. Pinpointing the devel-opmental stage of a group at any specific time is difficult. Nevertheless, man-agers and team members need to understand these developmental stages because each can influence performance. Let's consider the behaviors that might occur in each stage. As we do so, you need to realize that groups may not evolve in the straightforward manner shown. For example, time pressures owing to a competitor's actions or a customer's demands could speed up or otherwise change the evolution of a team.[23]

Forming   Members focus their efforts on defining goals and developing pro-cedures for performing their task in the forming stage. Relations-oriented be-haviors deal with members' feelings and the tendency of most members to depend too much on one or two other members. Group development in this stage involves getting acquainted and understanding leadership and other member roles. Individual members might (1) keep feelings to themselves until they know the situation, (2) act more secure than they actually feel, (3) ex-perience confusion and uncertainty about what is expected of them, (4) be nice and polite, or at least certainly not hostile, and (5) try to size up the personal benefits relative to the personal costs of being involved with the group or team.[24]

Storming   Things get serious in the storming stage. Conflicts emerge over task behaviors, relative priorities of goals, who is to be responsible for what, and the task-related guidance and direction of the leader. Relations-oriented behaviors are a mixture of expressions of hostility and strong feelings. Com-petition over the leadership role and conflict over goals dominate this stage. Some members may withdraw or try to isolate themselves from the emotional tension generated. The key is to manage conflict during this stage, not to

FIGURE 9.1

Stages of Group Development

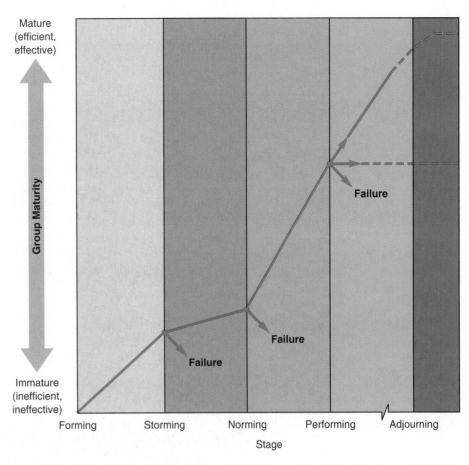

Source: Adapted from Tuckman, B. W., and Jensen, M. A. C. Stages of Small-Group Development Revisited. *Groups and Organization Studies*, 1977, 2, 419–442.

suppress it or withdraw from it. The group cannot effectively evolve into the third stage if the leader and members go to either extreme. Suppressing conflict will likely create bitterness and resentment, which will last long after group members attempt to express their differences and emotions. Withdrawal may cause the group to fail.

This stage may be shortened or mostly avoided if the group's members use a *team-building* process from the beginning. This process involves the development of decision-making, interpersonal, and technical skills where they are lacking. (We discuss team building in detail in Chapter 20.) Team-building facilitators can help members work through the inevitable conflicts that will surface during this and the other stages.[25] For example, PPG Industries—a manufacturer of glass, paint, and chemicals and headquartered in Pittsburgh—utilizes self-managed teams in three of its plants. The firm provides extensive classroom training and consulting services for team members. Teams are not charged for these services, which the corporate training development and education department provide.[26]

Norming Task-oriented behaviors in the norming stage evolve into a sharing of information, acceptance of different opinions, and positive attempts to make decisions which may require compromise. During this stage the group sets the rules by which it will operate. Relations-oriented behaviors focus on empathy, concern, and positive expressions of feelings that lead to a sense of cohesion. Cooperation and a sense of shared responsibility develop among team members.

Performing   During the performing stage, the group or team shows how effectively and efficiently it can achieve results. The roles of individual members are accepted and understood. The members usually understand when they should work independently and when they should help each other. The two dashed lines in Figure 9.1 suggest that teams may differ after the performing stage. Some groups continue to learn and develop from their experiences, becoming more efficient and effective. Other groups—especially those that developed norms not fully supportive of efficiency and effectiveness—may perform only at the level needed for their survival. Excessive self-oriented behaviors, development of norms that inhibit task effectiveness and efficiency, poor leadership, or other factors may hurt performance.[27]

Adjourning.   The termination of task behaviors and disengagement from relations-oriented behaviors occurs in the adjourning stage. Some teams, such as a cross-functional team created to investigate and report on a specific problem within six months, have well-defined points of adjournment. Other teams, such as the quality-assurance teams at Mary T., Inc., may go on indefinitely. Adjourning for this type of team is more subtle and takes place when one or more key members leave the organization or if Mary Tjosvold, the CEO, decides to revise the system for dealing with quality issues.

The developmental stages of groups—regardless of the framework used to describe and explain them—are not easy to traverse.[28] Failure can occur at any point in the sequence, as noted in Figure 9.1. In the next section, we review the primary factors that affect team or group behaviors and effectiveness. These factors also further explain why there can be so much diversity between teams and within a specific team over time.

▼ INFLUENCES ON GROUPS AND TEAMS

Figure 9.2 identifies seven influences on group and team outcomes, and, as you might expect, they are interrelated. All of them need to be diagnosed separately and in relation to each other to gain an understanding of team dynamics and outcomes.

▼ Context

The context (external environment) can directly affect each of the six other influences shown in Figure 9.2 and group or team behaviors and outcomes. The **context** includes the conditions and factors that are *givens* for a team. The team's context might include technology, physical working conditions, management practices, formal organizational rules, influences of higher management, and organizational rewards and punishments.[29] We focus here on one

FIGURE 9.2

Key Influences on Group and
Team Outcomes

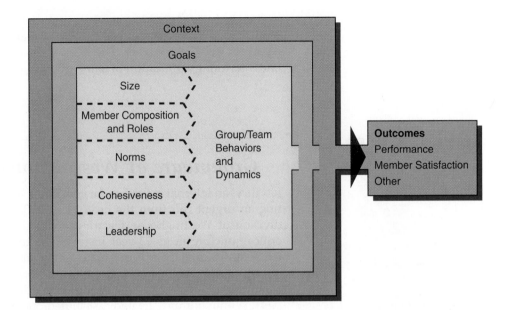

of the contextual influences that fundamentally shapes the ways individuals and teams work and interact, namely, the growing array of information technologies.

Information Technology   The term **information technology** refers to the means of assembling and electronically storing, transmitting, processing, and retrieving words, numbers, images, and sounds, as well as to the electronic means for controlling machines of all kinds—from everyday appliances to automated factories.[30] Information technology isn't just computers and computer software. It also includes communications aids (including telephone, video, and radio) and office equipment (e.g., word processors, copiers, and fax machines). Let's assume that management wants to introduce a technological change, such as automatically controlled machines, and turns the problem over to a problem-solving team. The team's investigation and findings influence how this technology is introduced into the organization.

Groupware   Computer-based information technologies are beginning to have a significant impact on how team and group members network with each other. These technologies are part of a concept known as **groupware,** an approach to using specialized computer aids, communication tools, and designated physical facilities. Groupware helps teams work faster, share information, make decisions, and achieve their goals.[31] The basic groupware tools are the telephone, the computer (with software), and the conference room. As is typical of emerging technologies and approaches, they may initially be known by a variety of names. A few of the other names for groupware include computer-mediated communications, computer-supported cooperative work (CSCW), computer-supported groups, group decision support systems (GDSS), and group support systems (GSS). Groupware tools revolve around *time* and *place* and reflect their four basic combinations.[32]

Face-to-face networking involves the *same time/same place* combination. Obviously, it is the most common mix of time and place when we think of team members working together. The following Managing in Practice piece reveals one interesting application of same time/same place groupware.

MANAGING IN PRACTICE

Groupware at Westinghouse

Jeff Jury, an internal management consultant at Westinghouse, remembers getting an urgent call from the head of a $150 million per year manufacturing division of Westinghouse Electric Corporation. The division had reached a critical juncture in its 12-year history. The top management team was deadlocked in its attempts to formulate a new strategic business plan.

Jury called a meeting of the division's top managers. He took his laptop computer out of his briefcase, along with a dozen small electronic voting keypads. Within minutes, he had distributed one of the devices to every executive in the room. The keypads were linked via thin wires to the laptop, which was running a voting software application called Option-Finder.

Jury began probing the team's attitudes by asking questions about the division's fundamental strategy. Participants answered the questions by pressing the keypads in front of them. Questions included: "Are you trying to be a low-priced competitor? Do you differentiate on value? Serve the entire market or just a niche?" Jury showed the executives the results, displayed in full-color graphs on an overhead projector. The team was stunned to find that "answers were scattered across the board, with absolutely no agreement or consensus," says Jury. "Yet if I'd asked them this question vocally, we probably wouldn't have gotten any challenge."

Through *Option-Finder*, team members can see not only which issues "won" but by how much—and whether the team is splintered. They can even calculate subgroups of agreement and disagreement according to preset characteristics of attendees. Because the process is totally anonymous, people feel freer to express (vote) their own minds.[33]

The *same time/different place* combination comes into play when team members can't get together face-to-face because they work in different locations and travel time and costs are substantial. The conference call is the simplest form of groupware for meetings held at the same time in different locations. Also, participants can exchange personal computer (PC), fax, and graphic images and messages simultaneously with a conference call. Videoconferencing, a new groupware tool, is a dramatic application; its cost has fallen by a factor of 10 in recent years. With digital technology, the quality of images is improving rapidly. Videoconferencing is helping to make the cliché that we now live in a global village a reality. The following Managing Across Cultures account clearly illustrates this development.

MANAGING ACROSS CULTURES

Apple's Global Videoconferencing

Apple Computer began installing videoconferencing systems in 1988, partly because it does so much business abroad. Apple's videoconference manager, Peter Kavanagh, says, "When you ask someone, 'How'd you like to go to Paris on Friday for a meeting?' they say, 'Yeah, great!' But when you say, 'How'd you like to go every other week for the next six months?' it gets old very fast."

One of Apple's first important uses of the technology was after Iraq's invasion of Kuwait, when many feared terrorist attacks on airlines. The company had just begun working with Sony to develop the lowest priced model of Apple's PowerBook computer. To minimize air travel, the two companies' engineers did a lot of their joint work via video. Apple now has video meeting rooms at ten sites in the U.S., three in Europe, and two in Japan (both are in Tokyo and also save engineers agonizing journeys across town).

Apple has spent about $6 million on developing groupware capabilities over the past four years. But Kavanagh estimates that video meetings cut travel costs by $28 million in that period. "The technology is not very cheap," he says, "but it's very, very cost-effective."

Kavanagh maintains that videoconferencing also means better meetings because all who should attend can do so without incurring extra costs. That eliminates the need for time-consuming debriefings when participants return home. Also, more travel is eliminated when they find answers to questions they could only shrug their shoulders at the first time around. Decision making is faster, Apple has found, and the company can bring products to market more swiftly.[34]

On the surface, the *different time/same place* combination may be difficult to imagine. However, consider these examples. A team in a manufacturing plant could include members from different work shifts. A bedside workstation in a hospital may be served by a team of health care providers around-the-clock. The groupware tools most often used in this situation include voice mail and computers (including electronic mail, or E-mail). Shift workers may then come together for face-to-face meetings infrequently, such as once a month.

The *different time/different place* combination is the most extreme and difficult configuration for team members. Groupware tools focus on storing and forwarding information, problems, suggestions, and the like. Once again, E-mail and voice mail are common day-to-day groupware tools. The members check into the system, see what has been entered since the last check, record comments, and leave the system. The main advantage of groupware tools in this situation is flexibility—gathering team members at the same time and place regularly may be difficult. Limitations of this method include stretching "meetings" out over time, not getting immediate feedback, and not receiving visual (including nonverbal) communication cues.

Because of the revolution in groupware tools, the work of groups and teams clearly is no longer limited to being in the same place at the same time.

▼ Goals

We addressed many aspects of goals in Chapter 7. Here, as throughout the book, we return repeatedly to the concept that goals influence individual, team, and organizational outcomes. Obviously, individual and organizational goals are likely to influence the types of group or team goals and actual group behaviors in pursuit of these goals. **Team goals** are the results desired for the group or team as a whole, not just those desired by the individual members.[35]

Both compatible and conflicting goals may exist within a team. For example, teams typically have both relations-oriented and task-oriented goals. Effective teams spend two-thirds or more of their time on task-oriented issues and roughly one-third or less on relations-oriented issues. The pursuit of only one or the other goal over the long run can reduce performance, increase conflicts, and cause the group or team to disband. The influence of goals on group dynamics and outcomes becomes even more complex when the possible compatibilities and conflicts among member goals, broader team goals, and even broader organizational goals are considered. The following Managing Ethics account describes how such tensions and problems can lead to indefensible actions.

MANAGING ETHICS

"Dateline" Crashes

But for a puff of smoke, it all might have turned out differently. General Motors Corporation might still be reeling from a $105.2 million jury verdict awarded to an Atlanta couple whose son died when his GM truck exploded in a collision. NBC News might be touting itself for having exposed the danger of GM's controversial "sidesaddle" gas tanks in a riveting "Dateline NBC" segment. Instead, the network singed its reputation, and the car company won in the court of public opinion the safety battle it had lost in the court.

"Dateline"'s report featured 14 minutes of balanced debate, capped by 57 seconds of crash footage that explosively showed how the gas tanks of certain old GM trucks could ignite in a sideways collision. Following a tip, GM hired detectives, searched 22 junkyards for 18 hours, and found evidence to debunk almost every aspect of the crash sequence. In a press conference devastating to "Dateline," GM showed that the crash was rigged, its causes misattributed, its severity overstated, and other facts distorted. Two crucial errors: NBC said the truck's gas tank had ruptured, yet an X ray showed that it hadn't; NBC consultants set off explosive miniature rockets beneath the truck split seconds before the crash—yet no one told the viewers.

How could the "Dateline" producers and staff go so far wrong? One veteran correspondent wasn't surprised: "The whole atmosphere" has been so competitive and overeager, he said, that this was "an accident waiting to happen."

Video newsmagazines are proliferating because they are cheaper, and thus more profitable, than comedy or drama. But to beat the tabloid "news" and talk shows, network magazines increasingly concentrate on crime, celebrities and scandals—and on graphic visual imagery. "Dateline" would have had a perfectly sound, valid and sensible 14-minute story about the controversy without a crash. But the producers felt the story would be stronger with one. They were wrong![36]

▼ Size

The effective size of a team can range from 2 members to a normal upper limit of 16 members. However, groupware tools are enabling larger teams to work on some issues. Twelve members probably is the largest size that enables each member to interact easily with every other member.[37] Table 9.2 shows six dimensions of teams in terms of leader behaviors, member behaviors, and team process and the likely effects of team size on each dimension. Note that members of teams of 7 or less interact differently than do members of teams or groups of 13–16. A 16-member board of directors will operate differently from a board of 7 members. Large boards of directors often form committees of 5–7 members to consider specific matters in greater depth than the entire board can.

As with all of the influences on teams, the effects identified in Table 9.2 need to be qualified.[38] For example, adequate time and sufficient member commitment to the team's task and goals might lead to better results from a team of eight or more members than from a hurried and less committed team of the same size. If a team's primary task were to tap the expertise of the members and arrive at decisions based primarily on expertise rather than judgment, a larger team would not necessarily reflect the effects identified in Table 9.2.

▼ Member Composition and Roles

Similarities and differences among members and their roles influence team behavior, dynamics, and outcomes.

Problem-Solving Styles   In Chapter 4, we described how different individual problem-solving styles influence decision making and behaviors. Recall that we classified individuals by their preferences in obtaining information from the outside world (either by sensation or intuition) and by the two basic ways

TABLE 9.2   Some Possible Effects of Size on Teams

	Team Size		
Dimension	*2–7 Members*	*8–12 Members*	*13–16 Members*
1. Demands on leader	Low	Moderate	High
2. Direction by leader	Low	Low to moderate	Moderate to high
3. Member tolerance of direction by leader	Low to moderate	Moderate	High
4. Member inhibition	Low	Low to moderate	High
5. Formalization of rules and procedures	Low	Low to moderate	Moderate to high
6. Time required for reaching judgment decisions	Low to moderate	Moderate	Moderate to high

of making a decision (either by thinking or feeling). Combining the two information-gathering approaches and the two decision-making approaches resulted in a model containing four basic types of problem-solving styles: sensation-thinker, sensation-feeler, intuitive-thinker, and intuitive-feeler.

The particular combination of member styles in a problem-solving group or team can affect its process and decisions.[39] For example, a team with three strong sensation-thinkers and three intuitive-feelers, all of whom are extroverts, is likely to generate more conflict and divergence of opinion than a team consisting of members who all use the same problem-solving style. Although divergence of viewpoint may be highly desirable, it can also lead to conflict, which, if not managed, may render the team ineffective.

Managers can rarely alter the problem-solving styles of team members. Thus they may find trying to influence the behavioral roles in the group or team more useful. These roles may be classified as task-oriented, relations-oriented, and self-oriented.[40] Each member has the potential for performing all of these roles over time.

Task-Oriented Role   The **task-oriented** role of members facilitates and coordinates decision-making tasks. This role may be divided into the following subroles.

▲ *Initiators* offer new ideas or different ways of considering team problems or goals and suggest solutions to group difficulties, including modified team procedures.

▲ *Information seekers* try to clarify suggestions and obtain authoritative information and pertinent facts.

▲ *Information givers* offer facts or generalizations that are authoritative or relate experiences that are pertinent to the team problem.

▲ *Coordinators* clarify relationships among ideas and suggestions, pull ideas and suggestions together, and coordinate members' activities.

▲ *Evaluators* assess the team's functioning; they may evaluate or question the logic, facts, or practicality of other members' suggestions.

Relations-Oriented Role   The **relations-oriented role** of members build team-centered tasks, sentiments, and viewpoints. This role may be divided into the following subroles.

▲ *Encouragers* praise, agree with, and accept the ideas of others; they indicate warmth and solidarity toward other members.

▲ *Harmonizers* mediate intrateam conflicts and relieve tension.

▲ *Gatekeepers* encourage participation of others by saying things such as "Let's hear from Sue," "Why not limit the length of contributions so all can react to the problem?" and "Bill, do you agree?"

▲ *Standard setters* express standards for the team to achieve or apply in evaluating the quality of team processes, raise questions about team goals, and assess team movement in light of these goals.

▲ *Followers* go along passively and serve as friendly members.

Team observers tend to stay out of the group process and give feedback to the team as detached evaluators.

Self-Oriented Role The **self-oriented role** focuses only on members' individual needs, possibly at the expense of the team or group. This role may be divided into the following subroles.

▲ *Blockers* are negative, stubborn, and unreasoningly resistant; for example, they may repeatedly try to bring back an issue that the team considered carefully and rejected.

▲ *Recognition seekers* try to call attention to themselves; they may boast, report on personal achievements, and, in unusual ways, struggle to avoid being placed in an inferior position.

▲ *Dominators* try to assert authority by manipulating the group or certain individuals in the group; they may use flattery or proclaim their superior status to gain attention; and they may interrupt contributions of others.

▲ *Avoiders* maintain distance from others; these passive resisters try to remain insulated from interaction.

Effective problem-solving groups and teams often are composed of members who play both task-oriented and relations-oriented roles. Again, each individual member may perform various subroles over time. A particularly adept individual who can perform certain subroles valued by the team probably has relatively high *status*—the relative rank of an individual in the group or team. A group dominated by individuals who are performing mainly self-oriented subroles is likely to be ineffective.

Table 9.3 provides a questionnaire for evaluating some of your task-oriented, relations-oriented, and self-oriented behaviors as a team member. The scale enables you to assess how often you perform each role. Member

TABLE 9.3 Assessing Your Behaviors as a Team Member

	Strongly Disagree	Disagree	Undecided	Agree	Strongly Agree
Task-oriented behaviors: In this team, I . . .					
1. initiate ideas or actions.	1	2	3	4	5
2. facilitate the introduction of facts and information.	1	2	3	4	5
3. summarize and pull together various ideas.	1	2	3	4	5
4. keep the team working on the task.	1	2	3	4	5
5. ask whether the team is near a decision (determine consensus).	1	2	3	4	5
Relation-oriented behaviors: In this team, I . . .					
6. support and encourage others.	1	2	3	4	5
7. harmonize (keep the peace).	1	2	3	4	5
8. try to find common ground.	1	2	3	4	5
9. encourage participation.	1	2	3	4	5
Self-oriented behaviors: In this team, I . . .					
10. express hostility.	1	2	3	4	5
11. avoid involvement.	1	2	3	4	5
12. dominate the team.	1	2	3	4	5

composition and roles greatly influence group or team behavior. Either too much or too little of certain member behaviors or roles can adversely affect team performance and member satisfaction.[41] Scores of 20–25 on task-oriented behaviors, 16–20 on relations-oriented behaviors, and 3–6 on self-oriented behaviors by each member indicate an effectively functioning team.

Team Diversity   The growing diversity of the work force adds complexity—beyond differences in problem-solving styles and behavioral roles of individuals in teams—to understanding team behavior and processes. As we discussed in Chapter 1, the composition of the work force is undergoing continued change in terms of age, gender, race, physical well-being, life-style preferences, ethnicity, educational background, religious preferences, and the like. Team effectiveness will be hampered if members hold false stereotypes about each other in terms of such differences.[42] As suggested in the following Managing Diversity feature, member differences can be both rewarding and challenging to organizations.

MANAGING DIVERSITY

United Nations at Tabra, Inc.

Tabra Tunoa is the founder and chief executive of Tabra, Inc., a jewelry-making company in Novato (near San Francisco), California. Flags from 11 countries hang from the ceiling at Tabra, Inc., as jewelry workers string beads, position stones, and polish silver pieces. The banners offer more than decoration. They represent the many homelands of the employees. The company has shown that a diverse array of employees can create both an interesting and successful workplace. Eighty-five percent of the more than 100 employees are foreign born. They come from such places as Laos, Cambodia, Thailand, Samoa, India, Singapore, and Vietnam.

Tunoa regularly travels abroad to find the unique stones and beads—and the inspiration for the designs—that make her line so distinctive. Yet, as her creations express her own artistic and worldly style, Tunoa realizes her work force is as much a reflection of her business as the jewelry itself.

Joyce Shearer, the human resource manager, notes that such a patchwork of cultures offers plenty of rewards. Employees share their backgrounds and heritage with potluck lunches, where they talk about the food from their native lands and bring family photos and maps. The company also adopts customs from the various homelands. A 3:00 P.M. "stretch" period, common in many Asian countries, is a welcome break every afternoon. Tabra celebrates the holidays of the countries represented by its employees. "We had a fabulous Laotian New Year celebration with twenty-five women dancing in their native dress," Shearer recalls. "We were all sprayed with warm water, because that is part of their new year well-wishing."

Cultural prejudices do surface and must be addressed. Vietnamese men, for instance, believed they were superior to their co-workers from other countries. At one time, they held all the coveted soldering jobs in the company. They refused to teach anyone—especially Laotians and women—how to master the skill. Women shied away from soldering jobs because they considered

MANAGING DIVERSITY —*Continued*

it "men's work." Tunoa had to take the men aside and make it clear that their attitudes and behavior were not acceptable. Then she demonstrated to the women that because she could do the job, other women could as well. Today, men and women from various countries are filling these positions.

Communicating other key company values can also be challenging. Tabra regularly holds seminars on topics including human rights sensitivity, sexual harassment, conservation, and other timely topics. Yet, in Asian societies, Shearer explains, talking directly about a difficult issue is considered rude. "We are the only society that confronts issues so openly, and sometimes that's difficult for our workers," she says. "They're accustomed to speaking around a problem."

Despite the difficulties, Tunoa is committed to maintaining a mix of cultures in her company—not just because it helps a segment of society that often has trouble finding decent employment, but because it makes her company superior.[43]

▼ Norms

Norms are the rules and patterns of behavior that are accepted and expected by members of a group or team.[44] In general, norms define the kind of behaviors that members believe are necessary to help them reach their goals. Individuals may join groups and teams in which many of the norms have already been established.

Norms Versus Organizational Rules   Norms differ from organizational rules. Managers may write and distribute organizational rules to employees in the form of manuals and memorandums. At times, employees refuse to accept such rules and widely ignore them. Norms usually are unwritten and are enforced by group members. If a group member consistently and excessively violates the norms, the other members sanction the individual in some way. Sanctions may range from physical abuse to threats to ostracism to positive inducements (rewards) for compliance. Those who consistently adhere to the group's norms typically receive praise, recognition, and acceptance from the other members.

Members may be only vaguely aware of some of the norms that operate in their group or team. Members should be made aware of these norms for at least two reasons. First, awareness increases the potential for individual and group freedom and maturity. Second, norms can positively or negatively influence the effectiveness of individuals, teams, and organizations.[45] For example, team norms of minimizing and correcting defects are likely to reinforce an organization's formal quality standards.

Relation to Goals   Teams often adopt norms to help them attain their goals.[46] Moreover, some organizational development efforts are aimed at helping members evaluate whether their norms are consistent, neutral, or conflicting in relation to team and organizational goals. (See Chapter 19 for a discussion of organization development efforts.) For example, a team may claim that one of its goals is to improve its efficiency to meet organizational goals. The members' behaviors might actually reveal norms inconsistent with this stated goal, that is, norms that inhibit production and making changes.

Even if team members are aware of such norms, they may rationalize them as being necessary in order to achieve their goals. Members may claim that producing more than the norm will "burn them out" or reduce product or service quality and result in lower long-term effectiveness. If group goals include minimizing managerial influence and increasing the opportunity for members to interact socially, members could perceive norms restricting employee output as desirable. Take the case of Ginny in the following Managing in Practice account. She is socializing a new packer by telling him that packing 80 pieces is the production goal for ensuring a "fair day's work for a fair day's pay."

MANAGING IN PRACTICE

It's Only Fair

For 18 years, Ginny has been doing about the same thing: packing expandrium fittings for shipment. She is so well practiced that she can do the job perfectly without paying the slightest attention. This, of course, leaves her free to socialize and observe the life of the company around her. Today, Ginny is breaking in a new packer.

"No, not that way, Look, Jim, if you hold it that way, well, then you have to twist your arm when you pack this corner, see. This way it's easier."

"But that's the way Mr. Wolf [the methods engineer] said we had to do it." "Sure he did, Jim. But he's never had to do it eight hours a day like me. You just pay attention to what I say."

"But what if he comes around and says I should pack the other way?"

"Oh, that's easy. When he's here, you do it his way. Anyway, after a couple of weeks, you won't see him again. Slow down. You'll wear yourself out. No one's going to expect you to do even eighty pieces for another couple of weeks."

"But Mr. Wolf said ninety."

"Sure he did. Let him do it. Look, here's how to pace yourself. It's the way I was taught, and it works. You know the 'Battle Hymn of the Republic'?" Ginny hums a few bars. "Well, you just work to that, hum it to yourself, use the way I showed you, and you'll be doing eighty next week."

"But what if they make me do ninety?"

"They can't. You know, you start making mistakes when you go that fast. No, eighty is right. I always say, a fair day's work for a fair day's pay."[47]

This account illustrates several things about groups and teams in organizations. First, norms and goals may differ from the standards or goals management sets for employees. Second, co-workers may have as much, if not more, influence than management in pressuring employees to accept certain norms and goals. Third, employees are concerned with both task-oriented and relations-oriented behaviors. In their efforts to change task-oriented behaviors, managers must consider their possible impact on relations-oriented behaviors. The failure to do so is likely to lead to group or team resistance.

Enforcing Norms   Groups and teams do not establish norms for every conceivable situation. They generally form and enforce norms with respect to behaviors that they believe to be particularly important. Members are most likely to enforce norms under one or more of the following conditions:[48]

▲ The norms aid in group survival and provide benefits. For instance, a team might develop a norm not to discuss individual salaries with other members in the organization to avoid calling attention to pay inequities in the team.

▲ The norms simplify or make predictable the behaviors expected of members. When colleagues go out for lunch together, there can be some awkwardness about how to split the bill at the end of the meal. A group may develop a norm that results in some highly predictable way of behaving: split the bill evenly, take turns picking up the tab, or individually pay for what each ordered.

▲ The norms help avoid embarrassing interpersonal problems. There might be norms about not discussing romantic involvements (so that differences in moral values do not become too obvious) or about not getting together socially in members' homes (so that differences in taste or income do not become too obvious).

The norms express the central values or goals of the group or team and clarify what is distinctive about its identity. When employees of an advertising agency label the wearing of unstylish clothes as deviant behavior, they say: "We think of ourselves, personally and professionally, as trendsetters, and being fashionably dressed conveys that to our clients and the public."

Conforming to Norms   Some writers criticize large organizations for maintaining and encouraging conformity to norms such as "It is best to keep opinions to yourself and play it safe" and "The most important thing is to appear to work hard, regardless of the results." Unfortunately, there isn't much data on the extent to which conformity to these types of norms actually exists in organizations.

The pressures to adhere to norms may result in conformity.[49] The two basic types of conformity are compliance and personal acceptance. **Compliance conformity** occurs when a person's behavior reflects the group's desired behavior because of real or imagined pressure. In fact, some individuals may conform, even though they don't personally agree with the norms.

People may comply without personal acceptance for a variety of reasons. They may believe that the appearance of a united front is necessary for success in accomplishing group goals. On a more personal level, a person may comply in order to be liked and accepted by others. Meeting this need may apply especially to members of lower status in relation to those of higher status, such as a subordinate and a superior. Finally, someone may comply because the costs of conformity are much less than the costs of nonconformity, which could threaten the personal relationships in the group or team.

The second type of conformity is based on positive personal support of the norms. In **personal acceptance conformity,** the individual's behavior and attitudes are consistent with the group's norms and goals. By definition, this type of conformity is much stronger than compliance conformity because the person is a true believer in the goals and norms.

All of this helps explain why some members of highly conforming groups and teams may easily change their behavior (compliance type of conformity), whereas others may oppose changes and find them highly stressful (personal acceptance type of conformity). Without norms and reasonable conformity to them, teams would be chaotic, and few tasks could be accomplished. Conversely, excessive and blind conformity may threaten expressions of individualism and a group's ability to change and learn.

▼ Cohesiveness

Cohesiveness is the strength of the members' desire to remain in the group or team and their commitment to it. It is influenced by the degree of compatibility between group goals and individual members' goals. Members who have a strong desire to remain in the group and personally accept its goals form highly cohesive groups.

The relationship between cohesiveness and conformity is complex. Low cohesiveness usually is associated with low conformity. However, high cohesiveness does *not* exist only in the presence of high conformity. High performing teams may have high member commitment and a desire to stick together while simultaneously respecting and encouraging individual differences in behavior and thought. This situation is more likely when cohesion is based on a common commitment to performance goals. In confronting complex problems, members of such a cohesive team are likely to encourage and support nonconformity.[50]

Relation to Groupthink   When decision-making teams are both conforming and cohesive, a phenomenon called groupthink might emerge. **Groupthink** is an agreement-at-any-cost mentality that results in ineffective team decision making and poor decisions. Irving L. Janis, who coined the term, focused his research on high-level government policy teams faced with difficult problems in a complex and dynamic environment. Team decision making is quite common in all types of organizations, so the possibility of groupthink exists in private-sector organizations as well as those in the public sector.

Figure 9.3 outlines the initial conditions that are likely to lead to groupthink, its characteristics, and the types of defective decision making that will result from it. The characteristics of groupthink include the following.

▲ An *illusion of invulnerability* is shared by most or all team members, which creates excessive optimism and encourages taking extreme risks. "No one can stop up now" or "The other group has a bunch of jerks" are statements made by members suffering from an illusion of invulnerability.

▲ *Collective rationalization* discounts warnings that might lead the members to reconsider their assumptions before committing themselves to major policy decisions. For example, "We are confident that only a small segment of auto buyers are willing to buy Japanese-made autos." This type of statement was made by North American auto executives in the early 1970s.

▲ An unquestioned belief in the *team's inherent morality* leads members to ignore the ethical or moral consequences of their decisions.

FIGURE 9.3

The Groupthink Phenomenon

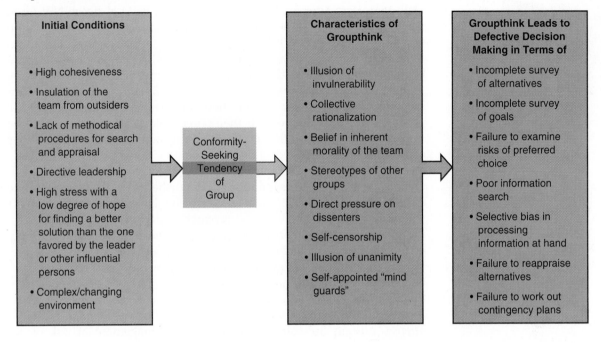

▲ *Stereotyped views* of rivals and enemies (other groups) picture them as too evil to warrant genuine attempts to negotiate or too weak or stupid to counter whatever attempts are made to defeat their purposes.

▲ *Direct pressure* is exerted on any member who expresses strong arguments against any of the team's illusions, stereotypes, or commitments, making clear that such dissent is contrary to what is expected of all loyal members. The leader might say: "What's the matter? Aren't you a member of the team anymore?"

▲ *Self-censorship* of deviations from any apparent team consensus reflects the inclination of members to minimize the importance of their doubts and not present counterarguments. A member might think: "If everyone feels that way, my feelings must be wrong."

▲ A shared *illusion of unanimity* results, in part, from self-censorship and is reinforced by the false assumption that silence implies consent.

▲ The emergence of *self-appointed "mind-guard"* members serves to protect the team from adverse information that might shatter the shared complacency about the effectiveness and morality of their decisions.[51]

The following Managing Ethics feature about the Beech-Nut Nutrition Corporation portrays some of the features of groupthink. The result was unethical and illegal decisions and behaviors several years ago, which have since been corrected.

MANAGING ETHICS

Beech-Nut's Groupthink

Only two years after joining the company, the CEO of Beech-Nut found evidence suggesting that the apple juice concentrate supplied by the company's vendors for use in Beech-Nut's "100% pure" apple juice contained nothing more than sugar water and chemicals. The CEO could have destroyed the bogus inventory and withdrawn the juice from grocers' shelves. But, he was under extraordinary pressure to turn the company around. Eliminating the inventory would have killed any hope of turning even the meager $700,000 profit promised to Beech-Nut's then parent, Nestle.

Numerous people in the corporation, it turned out, had doubted the purity of the juice for several years before the new CEO arrived. But the 25% price advantage offered by the supplier of the bogus concentrate allowed the operations head to meet cost-control goals. Furthermore, the company lacked an effective quality control system. A conclusive lab test for juice purity did not yet exist. When a member of the research department voiced concerns about the juice to operating management, he was accused of not being a team player and of acting like "Chicken Little." His judgment, his supervisor wrote in an annual performance review, was "colored by naiveté and impractical ideals." No one else seemed to have considered the company's obligations to its customers or to have thought about the potential harm of disclosure. No one considered the fact that the sale of adulterated or misbranded juice is a legal offense, putting the company and its top management at risk of criminal liability.

A Food and Drug Administration investigation taught Beech-Nut the hard way. The company pleaded guilty to selling adulterated and misbranded juice. Two years and two criminal trials later, the CEO pleaded guilty to ten counts of mislabeling. The total cost to the company—including fines, legal expenses, and lost sales—was an estimated $25 million.[52]

Groupthink isn't inevitable, and several steps can be taken to avoid it. For example, a leader should try to remain neutral and encourage dialogue and new ideas. Small subgroups or outside consultants can be used to introduce new viewpoints. People holding diverse views can be encouraged to present them.

Impact on Outcomes   The degree of cohesion is important because it can affect both team performance and productivity. **Productivity** is the relationship between the inputs consumed (labor hours and costs, raw materials, money, machines, and the like) and the outputs created (quantity and quality of goods and services). Cohesion and productivity can be interrelated, particularly for teams having high performance goals. If the team is successful in reaching its performance goals, the positive feedback of its successes may heighten member commitment and satisfaction. For example, a winning basketball team is more likely to be cohesive than one with a poor record, everything else being equal. Also, a cohesive basketball team may be more likely to win games.

Conversely, low cohesiveness may interfere with a team's ability to obtain its goals. The reason is that members are not as likely to communicate and cooperate to the extent necessary to reach the team's goals. High cohesiveness in teams actually may be associated with low efficiency if team goals are contrary to organizational goals. They might think that "the boss holds us accountable" rather than "we hold ourselves accountable" to achieve these results. Therefore the relationships among cohesion, productivity, and performance cannot be anticipated or understood unless the team's goals and norms are also known.

▼ Leadership

Studies of small groups in organizations have emphasized the importance of emergent, or informal, leadership in accomplishing goals. An **informal leader** is an individual whose influence in the group grows over time. It usually is based on a unique ability to help the group reach its goals.

Multiple Leaders   We often think of group or team leadership in terms of one person. However, a group often has both relations-oriented and task-oriented goals, so it may easily have two or more leaders. For example, one person may provide leadership with respect to relations-oriented goals, while another may provide leadership with respect to task-oriented goals. Achieving these two types of goals may require different personal characteristics and skills, creating a total set of demands that one person may have difficulty satisfying.[53] Informal leaders of work teams are not likely to emerge unless the formal leader ignores task-related responsibilities or lacks the necessary skills to carry them out.[54] In contrast, relations-oriented leaders of task groups are likely to emerge informally.

Effective Team Leaders   Leaders greatly influence virtually all aspects of group or team behaviors (such as size, member composition and roles, norms, goals, and context). A leader often assumes a key role in the relations between the team and external groups or higher management. Also, the leader often influences the selection of new members. Even when the team participates in the selection process, the team leader may screen potential members, thereby limiting the number and range of candidates. We have only touched on the behaviors and qualities of effective group and team leaders, which we discuss in detail in Chapter 11. Based on the seven key influences on group and team behaviors and dynamics reviewed thus far (see Figure 9.2), the establishment of effective groups and teams clearly is no easy task.

▼ IMPROVING TEAM DECISION MAKING

Organizations face different types of tasks and rely on varying degrees of interdependency to solve different problems over time. They require both individual and team decision making. Organizations incur excessive costs with the inappropriate use of either individual or team decision-making approaches. The inappropriate use of team decision making is wasteful because the participants' time could have been used more effectively on other tasks, it creates boredom, and it results in a feeling that time is being squandered. Thus it reduces motivation. Conversely, the inappropriate use of individual decision making can result in poor coordination, less creativity, and more errors.[55] In brief, team decision making is likely to be superior to individual decision making when (1) the greater diversity of information, experience, and approaches to be found in a team are important to the tasks at hand; (2) the acceptance of the decisions arrived at is crucial for effective implementation by team members; (3) participation is important for reinforcing the democratic values of representation versus authoritarianism and demonstrating respect for individual members through team processes; and (4) the team members rely on each other in performing their jobs.

▼ Six-Phase Model

After management has decided that a high degree of team involvement is appropriate, how should it go about obtaining effective team decision making? Figure 9.4 shows a six-phase model for effective team decision making.[56] Its use may improve decision making in all types of teams—from a class project team to the quality improvement teams at Maryland Plastics, Inc. (see the Preview Case). The model is based on the assumption the team or group has achieved the performing stage of development (see Figure 9.1).

Phase I: Problem Definition   Team members may assume that they know what the problem is in a situation, but they may be wrong. They could be looking at only a symptom or a part of the problem. In Phase I, the team should fully explore, clarify, and define the problem. Even when it has correctly identified the problem, the team may need to collect more detailed information and define it more sharply. Thus a key part of problem definition is generation and collection of information. Problem definition also requires that the team identify or recognize the goals that it is trying to achieve by solving the problem. When group or team members are clear about goals— which in itself may be a major problem area—they can determine better

FIGURE 9.4

Team Decision-Making Model

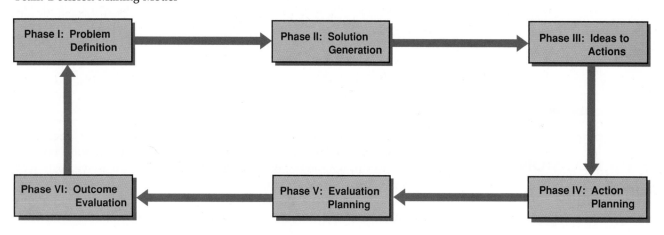

whether the problem really exists and, if it does, the relative priority that should be assigned to solving it.

If team members can respond *yes* to questions such as the following, the dynamics in Phase I probably have been effective.

▲ Was everyone who might have relevant data present or represented at the team meeting?

▲ Were those most directly involved in defining the problem encouraged by the leader and other team members to give information?

▲ Did the team take the information relating to the problem and consider how it all "fits together"?

▲ Was everyone asked whether they agree with the final problem statement as written?

Phase II: Solution Generation   Groups and teams often tend to be more solution-oriented than problem-oriented. They may choose the first or one of the first solutions suggested. Phase II prolongs the idea-generating process and discourages premature conclusions. An eventual solution can be much better if the team considers many ideas and several alternative solutions. The more ideas generated and creativity encouraged, the more likely the team is to come up with *good* potential solutions.

The dynamics in Phase II are likely to have been effective if team members can respond *yes* to questions such as the following.

▲ Have all the resources of the team been used to generate ideas?

▲ Did the leader and other team members take time to encourage those who might be slower at expressing ideas, pausing and asking for more ideas when necessary?

▲ Did the team take time to examine all the ideas and combine them into sets of alternatives?

▲ Was criticism tactfully discouraged and evaluative comments postponed (e.g., asking for another alternative instead of criticism)?

Phase III: Ideas to Actions   In Phase III, the team evaluates ideas and alternative solutions to come up with a likely solution. Even though one alternative may not work alone, it could provide a useful part of the solution. Thus the team should take time to combine the best parts of alternative solutions. It then can carefully evaluate each possibility. Rather than weeding out poor alternatives (and making those who suggested them feel defensive), the team should select the best ones and concentrate on them until everyone can agree on a solution or recognize the need to move on.

A *yes* to questions such as the following suggests that team dynamics are on target in Phase III.

▲ Did the team examine the alternatives in terms of human, financial, and other costs associated with each and in terms of new problems that might arise?

▲ Was the team able to evaluate ideas critically without attacking individuals who proposed or supported those ideas?

▲ Is the chosen solution related to the problem statement and goals discussed earlier?

▲ Was final consensus reached on a trial solution? If not, was the extent of agreement among team members clearly established?

Phase IV: Action Planning   Now that there is a solution to implement, careful planning of actions to put it into operation is needed to make it work smoothly. In Phase IV, the team anticipates implementation problems, makes plans to involve those whose support will be needed, and assigns and accepts action responsibilities. Only if the team determines who is to do what and when can the agreed-on solution get a fair test.

Key questions requiring a *yes* response in Phase IV dynamics include the following.

▲ Did the team identify the various forces that might help or hinder the action steps being planned?

▲ Were all team members involved in the discussion, particularly in giving information needed to define action steps and ensure that essential steps weren't left out?

▲ Were all the needed resources (material as well as human, including persons not present) for accomplishing each of the action steps clearly identified?

▲ Did each person who accepted a task responsibility make a clear commitment to carry out that responsibility?

Phase V: Evaluation Planning   Sometimes teams stop at Phase IV, losing the chance to learn from experience. Even if a solution is a tremendous success, a team benefits from knowing exactly what made the solution work so that it can be repeated when appropriate. If a solution is a total disaster, team members may feel like hiding the fact that they had anything to do with it. However, a team that knows what went wrong can avoid making the same mistakes in the future. In real life, solutions generally work moderately well; most are neither great successes nor great failures. By keeping track of what is happening, a team can make minor improvements or adjustments that will help significantly in other team problem-solving efforts. Diagnosis should not be based on guesswork but on hard, accurate information about the effect of actions. Phase V offers the greatest potential for team learning in decision making. In order to take advantage of this opportunity, a team must determine what type of evaluation information is needed, who will obtain it, and when it must be collected.

Questions requiring a *yes* response for effective dynamics in Phase V include the following.

▲ Has the team reviewed the desired outcomes and developed measures to indicate the degree of success in attaining the outcomes?

▲ Were any differences among team members regarding definitions and measures of success openly discussed, explored, and resolved?

▲ Were contingency plans outlined for critical steps (such that the overall plan could continue with modification but without major interruption)?

▲ Was a timetable developed for step-by-step interim evaluation (monitoring of effects as action plans are implemented)?

Phase VI: Outcome Evaluation   When enough information has been collected to evaluate how well the solution worked, the team should make a comprehensive evaluation of the outcome. The outcome demonstrates whether the problem was solved. If the problem or some part of it remains, the team can recycle it by looking at the information, perhaps even redefining the problem, and coming up with new ideas or trying a previously rejected alternative. Phase VI also involves a review and evaluation of how well the team members worked together. As we suggested in the discussion of group development stages, mature groups and teams can openly and constructively evaluate outcomes.

A response of *yes* to each of the following questions indicates effective dynamics during Phase VI.

▲ Was the team able to compare, in detail, the outcomes with the goals set earlier?

▲ Were all team members involved in influencing both what the team did and how the team operated?

▲ Did the team determine whether any new problems were created and, if so, then make plans to deal with them?

▲ Did the team learn to solve problems in accordance with this model (Figure 9.4)?

▼ Assessment of Model

Team decision making *rarely* proceeds so neatly or systematically as suggested in the descriptions of these six phases.[57] Problem-solving groups and teams often jump around or skip phases. However, this team decision-making model, if followed as closely as possible, should improve the decision making of most teams. This model stresses that *members have expertise* and that a norm of *full participation* among members emerges during the team process.

Teams and other types of groups—even if operating properly—probably are more effective in Phase III (ideas to actions) through Phase V (evaluation planning) than in Phases I, II, and VI. Phase I (problem definition) and Phase II (solution generation) benefit from processes different from the usual face-to-face interactions.

Various other processes and procedures have been developed for improving the effectiveness of decision-making groups in addition to those suggested here. For example, in the last section of this chapter, we consider two aids especially designed to improve team effectiveness in Phases I and II. First, we present a Managing Across Cultures feature to demonstrate the potential impact of the broader *context*, such as cultural values and norms, on understanding the actual process of some small groups and teams in different societies.

MANAGING ACROSS CULTURES

Group Meetings in China

In working at the Institute of International Economic Management in Beijing China, we had the opportunity to teach Chinese businesspeople American management techniques. This experience has given us some insights into Chinese responses to Western management theory and application, as well as some knowledge of Chinese organizational behavior.

MANAGING ACROSS CULTURES *—Continued*

During the year, 200 students attended the institute. The majority of the students worked as interpreters and employees in various import/export corporations in diverse regions of China. The remaining students were employed as engineers, scientists, commune workers, or in various other occupations. A number of decision-making groups of four to six members each were used in the training program. We and the students developed a list of behaviors and related cultural norms and beliefs that characterize the Chinese group-process style, which we can summarize as follows: high dependence on authority figures; participation by followers in "discussion," but not in decision making; strictly patterned "discussion" flows; and avoidance of public conflict. We traced each of these aspects to its root in either traditional Chinese culture or modern socialist development.

Students identified their high dependence on the leader as resulting from a traditional Chinese norm of deference to authority; one student said, "It is not right to disagree with the leader." They had a more difficult time explaining "discussion" without participation in decision making, for the general consensus of the students was that they had participated in arriving at the decision. Some students reported that they felt required to participate but were afraid of being too outspoken. Although modern Communist ideals support participative decision making, ancient Chinese norms prohibit such boldness in the face of authority figures. Apparently, these two contradictory norms for appropriate behavior had merged to produce this style.

Students insisted that strict patterning of discussion was "correct" polite behavior, an example of "right participation." In discussions of this point, students sometimes referred to the Confucian tradition of "five relationships," which defines social rules of communication among the following five different pairs of related individuals: ruler and minister, father and son, husband and wife, brothers and/or sisters, and friends. This belief in the propriety of such defined behavior may stem from early experiences with traditional Chinese culture. This structured communication is reinforced by the childhood experience of being criticized by elders for offering opinions.

Avoidance of conflict stems from the face-saving rituals of traditional Chinese culture, which perceive conflict as "confusion" and detrimental to social well-being. All of these aspects of the Chinese meeting style presented themselves repeatedly in subsequent interactions.[58]

FOSTERING TEAM CREATIVITY

Let's now turn to two approaches for fostering team and group creativity. These approaches can assist members with Phase I (problem definition), Phase II (solution generation) and the initial part of Phase III (ideas to action) in the team decision making model (see Figure 9.4).

▼ Nominal Group Technique

The **nominal group technique** (NGT) is a structured process designed to foster creative team decision making where agreement is lacking or the members have incomplete knowledge of the nature of the problem. This technique has a special purpose: to make individual judgments the essential inputs in arriving at a team decision. That is, members must pool their judgments in order to solve the problem and determine a satisfactory course of action.

The NGT is most useful for (1) identifying the crucial variable in a specific situation; (2) identifying key elements of a plan designed to implement a particular solution to some problem; or (3) establishing priorities with regard to the problem to be addressed and goals to be attained. In all such circumstances, aggregating individual judgments into team decisions often seems beneficial. The NGT isn't particularly well suited for routine team meetings that focus primarily on task coordination or information exchange. Nor is it usually appropriate for the negotiating that takes place in counteracting groups (such as a union and management bargaining committee, if each has conflicting goals). The NGT consists of four distinct stages.[59] Various useful ideas for modifying or tailoring these stages to specific situations have been advanced.[60]

Generating Ideas   The first stage in the process is to have the members generate ideas. Each participant separately writes down ideas in response to a statement of the problem, a *stimulus question*, or some other central focus of the team. A question could be something as simple as: "What problems do you think we should consider over the next year?" followed by "Take five minutes to write some of your own ideas on the piece of paper in front of you." The generation of ideas or solutions privately by individuals while in a team setting avoids direct pressures resulting from status differences or competition among members to be heard. Yet it retains some of the peer and creative tension in the individual generated by the presence of others. This stage and the subsequent stages provide time for thinking and reflection to avoid premature choosing among ideas.[61]

Recording Ideas   The second stage is to record one idea (generated in the first stage) from each group member in turn on a flip chart or other device visible to all members of the team. A variation is to have members submit their ideas anonymously on index cards. The process continues until the team members are satisfied that the list reflects all the ideas individually generated. This round-robin approach emphasizes equal participation by all members and avoids losing ideas that individuals consider significant. Listing the ideas for everyone to see depersonalizes the ideas and reduces the potential for conflict. Team members often are impressed and pleased with the list of ideas presented, which provides momentum and enthusiasm for continuing the process.

Clarifying Ideas   The team then discusses in turn each idea on the list during the third stage. The purpose of this discussion is to clarify the meaning of each idea and to allow team members to agree or disagree with any item. The intent is to present the logic and thinking behind the ideas and to reduce misunderstanding. It is *not* to win arguments concerning the relative merits of the ideas. Differences of opinion are not resolved at this stage, but rather by the voting procedure in the fourth stage.

Voting on Ideas   A list of at least 12 and perhaps as many as 30 ideas often is developed. There are several ways to proceed at this point. Perhaps the most common voting procedure is to have the team members individually select a specific number (say, 5) of the ideas that they believe are most important. Each person writes these five ideas on individual index cards. The team leader then asks the members to rank their 5 items from most to least important. The index cards are collected and the votes tabulated to produce a priority list. An alternative to this single vote is to feed back the results of a first vote, allow time for discussion of the results, and then to vote again. Feedback and discussion is likely to result in a final decision that most closely reflects members' true preferences.

Regardless of format, the voting procedure determines the outcome of the meeting: a team decision that incorporates the individual judgments of the participants. The procedure is designed to document the collective decision and to provide a sense of accomplishment and closure.

Assessment   The advantages of the NGT over traditional team discussion may include greater emphasis and attention to idea generation, increased attention to each idea, and greater likelihood of balanced participation and presentation by each member. Nominal groups may not be superior when the task of problem identification is performed by people who are both (1) aware of the existing problems and (2) willing to communicate them. The approach may be most effective when there are certain blockages or problems in a team, such as a few dominating members.

▼ Brainstorming

Traditional Brainstorming   Usually done with 5–12 people, **brainstorming** is a process in which individuals state as many ideas as possible during a 20–60-minute period. Guidelines for brainstorming include: (1) the wilder the ideas the better; (2) don't be critical of any ideas; and (3) hitchhike on or combine previously stated ideas. The group setting for brainstorming was supposed to generate many more and better ideas than if the same number of individuals worked alone.[62] However, research indicates that brainstorming isn't very effective. In fact, the nominal group technique (NGT) has proven to be much more effective than traditional brainstorming as an aid for generating ideas.[63] Why?

To brainstorm effectively is to think of an idea, express it, and get on with thinking of and expressing more new ideas. In face-to-face brainstorming, however, people may be prevented from producing an idea and immediately producing another idea because someone else is talking. As a result, team members may get bogged down waiting for other people to finish talking. Team members also may be anxious about how others will view them if they express their ideas. This problem may be particularly acute when ideas can be interpreted as critical of current practice or when superiors or others who may affect team members' futures are present. Withholding ideas for these reasons defeats the purpose of brainstorming.[64] Electronic brainstorming is a type of groupware that can reduce such problems.

Electronic Brainstorming   **Electronic brainstorming** makes use of computer technology to enter and automatically disseminate ideas in real time to all group members, each of whom may be stimulated to generate other ideas. For example, GroupSystems has a software tool called *Electronic Brainstorming*. With this system, each member has a computer terminal that is connected to all other members' terminals. The software allows individuals to enter their ideas as they occur. Every time an individual enters an idea, a random set of the teams' ideas is presented on each person's screen. The individual can continue to see new random sets of ideas at will by pressing the appropriate key.[65]

Preliminary research on electronic brainstorming is encouraging. It tends to produce significantly more fresh ideas than traditional brainstorming.[66] Electronic brainstorming has considerable potential because it removes a major barrier of traditional brainstorming: members seeing and hearing which ideas are whose. Electronic brainstorming permits anonymity and thus lets team members contribute more freely to idea generation. They need not fear "sounding like a fool" to other employees and managers when spontaneously generating ideas. These advantages appear to be greater for teams of seven or more people.[67] The following Managing in Practice account reveals how the elements of brainstorming, the nominal group technique, and the ideas to action phase of team decision making may be integrated by means of several groupware tools.

MANAGING IN PRACTICE

Brainstorming to Action

Jim Westland, regional vice-president of North American Life and Casualty (NALC), decided that fresh ideas were needed about ways to cut costs and improve efficiency at the northeast head office. Pressures were mounting to reduce costs, attract new business, and maintain service. He decided to bring his senior management team and selected lower level employees to a one-day, electronic brainstorming session at a local university's computer-supported decision center. The team consisted of seven senior managers, two clerical staff, and one sales representative. The day began with an electronic brainstorming session. The question was: How can we cut costs at NALC? The process started tentatively, with people typing in an idea and hitting a function key to enter that idea. Someone mentioned that she saw an idea on her screen that she didn't enter. The facilitator explained that this is the essence of the electronic brainstorming process: People will see a random selection of their own and other people's ideas on their screens that will help them think of other ideas. Suddenly everyone was typing in ideas. In 20 minutes, the team produced more than 85 cost-cutting ideas.

"Now comes the hard part," Jim thought. "How are we going to sort and evaluate all these ideas?" The team decided to use the "idea organizer" software tool to put the ideas into categories for easier evaluation. Each person scanned the ideas and created categories, which appeared on a large screen at the front of the room. There were some common, well-defined categories, and most participants agreed about how the ideas fit into them. The process took quite a while (about an hour-and-a-half), but all felt that it helped them

MANAGING IN PRACTICE —*Continued*

better understand the categories and the remaining ideas. The outcome of the "idea organizer" process was a list of 49 ideas divided into seven categories. Each person rated each idea in the first category on feasibility and benefits (using a ten-point scale). Then the software collected the ratings and displayed them for the team on the large screen. The team thought that some ideas were less feasible and had fewer benefits than others. The participants decided that two ideas were very good ones and should be implemented immediately. They went on to rate ideas in the rest of the categories (with a break for lunch) and selected six more good ideas.

Now the team had to flesh out the eight ideas and assign responsibilities for implementing them. The "topic commenter" tool was used. Each idea became the title of one of the eight windows created in the topic commenter tool. For each idea window, team members entered their comments on how the idea should be implemented and any problems or concerns that might arise during implementation. The system gathered and displayed this information, and the team considered the ideas one at a time. To indicate responsibility, team members entered their names beside one or two of the ideas or beside certain implementation steps, along with completion dates.

The meeting ended at about 4:30 P.M.. The team had eight ideas that could be implemented. Jim knew that follow-up would be crucial, but felt that the team was committed and motivated to make the changes happen.[68]

Summary

Groups and teams have far-reaching effects on organizations and life in general. With the cultural belief in individualism, there can be an uneasiness over their impacts on our lives. One potential source of tension between group and individual interests is that of the free rider.

Groups are classified in numerous ways. In organizations, a basic classification is according to the group's primary purpose, including friendship groups and task groups. Task groups may be classified further as counteracting, coacting, or interacting. The three types of interacting teams discussed were problem-solving teams, cross-functional teams, and self-managed teams.

There are a variety of ways of understanding the developmental sequence of groups and teams. One is the five-stage developmental stages of forming, storming, norming, performing, and adjourning. The issues and challenges a team faces change with each stage.

Primary factors that affect team dynamics or behaviors and outcomes include context, goals, size, member composition and roles, norms, cohesiveness, and leadership. One type of changing contextual influence on how teams work, interact, and network with other teams is that of information technology, especially the rapid developments in groupware tools. Teams no longer are limited to face-to-face meetings (same time/same place) in carrying out their tasks and goals. Group member behavioral roles may be task-oriented, relations-oriented or self-oriented. Norms differ from rules in important ways and can positively or negatively affect organizational goals and performance. The pressures to adhere to norms may result in either compliance conformity or personal acceptance conformity. Another factor affecting groups is cohesiveness, which is related to conformity, groupthink, and productivity. Team leaders may be selected formally or emerge informally.

We presented three approaches for improving team decision making and creativity: a team decision-making model, the nominal group technique, and brainstorming. They can help both team members and leaders become more effective. The core themes addressed in the presentation of team decision making include when to use team decision making versus individual decision making; the relationship between team processes and their relative autonomy; and suggestions for improving team processes and creativity to enhance performance outcomes and member satisfaction.

Key Words and Concepts

Brainstorming	Friendship group	Problem-solving teams
Coacting group	Group	Productivity
Coalition	Groupthink	Relations-oriented role
Cohesiveness	Groupware	Self-managed teams
Collectivism	Individualism	Self-oriented role
Compliance conformity	Informal leader	Task group
Context	Information technology	Task-oriented role
Counteracting group	Interacting group	Team
Cross-functional teams	Nominal group technique	Team goals
Electronic brainstorming	Norms	
Free rider	Personal acceptance conformity	

Discussion Questions

1. Think about a team of which you have been a member. Was there any evidence of free riders on the team? Why were behaviors associated with free riding present or not present?

2. For the same team, was there any evidence that the team evolved according to the five-stage developmental sequence (see Figure 9.1)?

3. What were the effects of the size of that team in terms of the dimensions shown in Table 9.2? Were these effects consistent with those predicted in Table 9.2?

4. Was this a self-managed team? Use Table 9.1 to explain your answer.

5. Describe the context of another group or team of which you have been a member in terms of technology, organizational rules, influence of higher level management, and organizational rewards and punishments. In what ways did the context appear to affect the group's or team's dynamics and outcomes?

6. What were the formal and informal goals of this team or group? Were the informal goals consistent and supportive of the formal goals? Explain.

7. How would you describe this group or team as a whole in terms of task-oriented behaviors, relations-oriented behaviors, and self-oriented behaviors? Which of the behaviors seemed to contribute the most to its performance? The least?

8. State three norms of a task group of which you have been a member. Did you or other members conform to these norms on the basis of compliance or personal acceptance? How did this conformity affect behavior? Explain.

9. The team decision-making model (see Figure 9.4) presents a phased sequence by which teams should proceed. How may the factors identified in Figure 9.2 help to work for or against the implementation of this model?

10. What are the similarities and differences between the nominal group technique (NGT) and electronic brainstorming?

▲ Developing Skills

Self-Diagnosis: People Are Electric[69]

Introduction

Team effectiveness is sometimes limited by the judgmental thinking of team members. Especially in ambiguous or uncertain circumstances, people tend to use heuristics (rules of thumb) to make judgments or decisions. Examples of heuristics might be certain opening moves in chess or arriving at this year's budget by adding 10% to last year's budget. Essentially heuristics are ways that people simplify thinking and decision making. Problems occur when these heuristics lead to wrong conclusions. Selective perception, or just viewing problems from a personal perspective, is an example of a heuristic that can lead to problems.

Goals

This activity has the following primary goals: (1) to encourage the team participants to think creatively; (2) to help the participants to discover heuristics in their thinking patterns; and (3) to improve team effectiveness by uncovering judgmental thinking and biases.

Process

The participants are to form into teams of approximately five members each. After the stated time has elapsed, the facili-
tator (instructor) reconvenes the teams. Each team is to note how it reached consensus and presented its answers to the scenario questions. Also, each team should review its process by modifying and applying Table 9.3 to assess the team as a whole, rather than each individual member.

Scenario Questions

Begin by answering the following questions yourself. Then discuss your answers with the other members of the team. When you reach a consensus, write the answers on a large sheet of paper, such as newsprint. Take particular note of how your team's thinking process affects consensus. You will have about 20–30 minutes for this activity.

What if human beings were electrically powered rather than having their energy supplied through food, water, and rest?

1. How would your personal life be affected?
2. How would your professional life be affected?
3. How would the following areas be changed?
   Employment
   Education
   Family
   Leisure activities
   Government programs
   Global affairs
   Other

A Case In Point: Great Majestic Company

Susan Hoffman, manager of the Great Majestic Lodge, was sitting at her desk and debating what she would say and what action she would take at a meeting with her bellmen, which was scheduled to begin in two hours. She has just weathered a stormy encounter with Bob Tomblin, the general manager of the Great Majestic Company's recreational and lodging facilities in the area.

Tomblin was visibly upset by an action taken by the bellman at Great Majestic Lodge three weeks ago. At the end of the explosive meeting, Tomblin roared, "Sue, I don't care if you fire the whole bunch! I want you to do something about this right now!"

Background

The Great Majestic Lodge was located in a popular park in the western United States. It was rather remote, yet offered
all the modern conveniences featured at any fine metropolitan hotel. Because of its size and accommodations, the lodge was a favorite spot for large, organized tours. Most of the tours stayed one night and none stayed over two days. They were good moneymakers for the lodge because they always met their schedules, paid their bills promptly, and usually were gone very early on checkout day.

Most of the employees hired by the Great Majestic Company were college students. This situation was ideal because the opening and closing dates of the lodge corresponded to most universities' summer vacations. The employees lived and ate at the company facilities and were paid about $300 a month.

The Lodge Bellmen

The bellmen at the Great Majestic Lodge were directly responsible to Hoffman. They were college students who, before being chosen for a bellman position, had worked for the company at least three summers. A total of seven were chosen on the basis of their past performance, loyalty, efficiency, and ability to work with the public. However, Tomblin chose the bellmen.

Employees considered the position of bellman to be prestigious and important. In the eyes of the public, the bellmen represented every aspect of the Great Majestic Lodge. They were the first ones to greet the guests upon arrival, the people the guests called when anything was needed or went wrong, and the last ones to see the guests off upon their departure. Clad in their special cowboy apparel complete with personalized name tags and company insignia, the bellmen functioned as an effective public relations team for the lodge, as well as providing prompt and professional service for each guest.

The bellmen all lived together in the back area of the most secluded employees' dorm at the lodge. They shared this facility with other lodge employees who had been with the company for two years or more. The older student employees were especially close-knit, and all were looking forward to the time they would have the opportunity to be chosen as bellmen. The first-year employees usually occupied a dorm to themselves, adjacent to the senior dorm. For the most part, a warm team spirit existed among all the staff at the lodge.

Traditionally, the bellmen had a comfortable relationship with Tomblin, so this latest incident was of great concern to Hoffman. She realized that Tomblin was dead serious about firing them. It was midsummer, and finding qualified replacements would be difficult. The bellmen this year had been especially productive. They received $2.00 per hour plus tips, which they pooled and divided equally at the end of each week; daily tips averaged $25 per person. Hoffman was particularly concerned about the situation because it involved employees for whom she was directly responsible.

Organized Tours

The bellmen had the responsibility of placing the tour luggage in the guests' rooms as soon as the bus arrived. The front desk provided them with a list of guests' names and the assigned cottage numbers. Speed was particularly important because the guests wanted to freshen up and demanded that their bags be delivered promptly. On the morning of departure, the guests left their packed bags in their rooms while they went to breakfast. The bellmen picked up the bags, counted them, and then loaded them on the bus.

As payment for the service rendered by the bellmen, tour directors paid the standard gratuity of $0.75 per bag. It was considered a tip, but it was included in the tour expenses by each company. For large tours, the tip could be as high as $100, although the average was $50.

Jones Transportation Agency

The Jones Transportation Agency had a reputation throughout the area of being fair and equitable with its tips. How-

ever, one of their tour directors, Don Sirkin, didn't live up to the company's reputation. On a visit to the Great Majestic Lodge, Sirkin had not given a tip. The bellmen knew that their service to Sirkin's group had been very good. They were upset about the situation but assumed that Sirkin had forgotten the tip in the rush before his tour departed. The tour was large and the tip would have amounted to $90.

Sirkin's tour also stayed at several other nearby resorts. Several of the Great Majestic Lodge bellmen knew the bellmen at the other lodges and, in discussing the situation, discovered that Sirkin had neglected the tip at each of the other lodges. Sirkin apparently had pocketed more than $1,000 on his group's four-day tour through the region.

The Letter

Upon hearing of Sirkin's actions, the Majestic Lodge bellmen decided that some action had to be taken. They immediately ruled out telling Hoffman. On previous occasions when there had been a problem, Hoffman had done very little to alleviate the situation.

Roger Sikes, a first-year bellman and a business undergraduate, suggested that they write a letter directly to the president of Jones Transportation Agency. He felt that the agency would appreciate knowing that one of its tour directors had misused company funds. After some discussion, the other bellmen present agreed. Sikes prepared a detailed letter, which told the Jones president the details of the Sirkin incident. The bellmen didn't expect to recover the money from the tour, but they felt that this was the appropriate action to take.

Five of the bellmen signed the letter as soon as it was completed. Two more opposed but, after more discussion and considerable peer pressure, agreed to sign the letter. They mailed it with the expectation of a speedy reply and justice for the offending Don Sirkin.

Reaction to the Letter

Three weeks after the bellmen's letter had been mailed to the Jones Transportation Agency, Tomblin was thumbing through his morning mail. He noticed a letter from his good friend Grant Cole, the president of the Jones Transportation Agency. Tomblin opened this letter first. Cole had written that there was a problem at the Great Majestic Lodge and he thought that Tomblin should be made aware of it. He enclosed the letter from the bellmen and suggested that, if the bellmen had any problems with any Jones directors in the future, it might be wise for them to speak to Tomblin before taking any action. Cole informed Tomblin that Jones was investigating the Sirkin incident.

Tomblin was enraged. The bellmen had totally ignored their supervisor and had written a letter without first consulting the lodge manager or any of the other managers of the Great Majestic Company. This action not only was a breach of company policy, but also a personal humiliation for Tomblin.

Tomblin, yelling with outrage, leaped to his feet and charged through the lobby to Hoffman's office. He spotted bellman George Fletcher and ordered him to get out of his sight. The bewildered Fletcher quickly obeyed.

Hoffman's meeting with Tomblin was unpleasant. She had never seen Tomblin so upset at the actions of employees. Tomblin was a proud person, and, because his pride has been hurt, he wanted revenge. He showed Hoffman the bellmen's letter and the reply from Cole. Tomblin made it clear that he expected some quick action. Hoffman knew that the action had to meet Tomblin's approval. Her position as lodge manager suddenly was precarious.

Several employees had been in the lobby when Tomblin roared through. Hoffman knew that gossip would spread quickly throughout the lodge. The bellmen were well liked by the other employees, and she knew that they would be concerned about the bellmen's fate.

Hoffman called the still shaken George Fletcher into her office and told him to summon the off-duty bellmen for a meeting. After Fletcher left, she attempted to think of alternatives that would satisfy Tomblin and also maintain the quality of service expected by guests.[70]

Questions

1. What social influences and norms appear to have played a part in the behaviors of the bellmen?
2. What contextual influences and goals are relevant in this situation to (1) the bellmen, (2) Hoffman, and (3) Tomblin?
3. What should Hoffman do? Why?

References

1. Adapted from Bizup, A. Maryland Plastics, Inc. *Maryland Workplace*. College Park, Md.: Newsletter of the Maryland Center for Quality and Productivity. Fall 1992, 9, 11.
2. Worchel, S., Wood, W., and Simpson, J.A. (eds.). *Group Process and Productivity*. Newbury Park, Calif.: Sage, 1991; Krackhardt, D., and Hanson, J. R. Informal networks: The company behind the chart. *Harvard Business Review*, July–August, 1993, 104–111.
3. Homans, G. C. *The Human Group*. New York: Harcourt, Brace and World, 1959, 2. Also see Miller, J. Living systems: The group. *Behavioral Science*, 1971, 16, 302–398.
4. Erez, M. Toward a model of cross-cultural industrial and organizational psychology. In H. C. Triandis, M. D. Dunnette, and L. M. Hough (eds.), *Handbook of Industrial and Organizational Psychology*, Vol. 4, 2nd ed. Palo Alto: Calif.: Consulting Psychologists Press, 1994, 559–607.
5. Hofstede, G., Neuijen, B., Ohayv, D. D., and Sanders, G. Measuring organizational cultures: A qualitative and quantitative study across twenty cases. *Administrative Science Quarterly*, 1990, 35, 286–316.
6. Mitchell, T. R., and Scott, W. G. America's problems and needed reforms: Confronting the ethic of personal advantage. *Academy of Management Executive*, August 1990, 23–35.
7. Zander, A. *The Purpose of Groups and Organizations*. San Francisco: Jossey-Bass, 1985.
8. Albanese, R., and Van Fleet, D. D. Rational behavior in groups: The free-riding tendency. *Academy of Management Review*, 1985, 10, 244–255.
9. Schnake, M. E. Equity in effort: The "sucker effect" in co-acting groups. *Journal of Management*, 1991, 17, 41–55.
10. Fiedler, F. E. and Garcia, J. E. *New Approaches to Effective Leadership*. New York: John Wiley & Sons, 1987, 3–4.
11. Harsman, C. L. and Phillips, S. L. *Teaming Up: Achieving Organizational Transformation*. San Diego: Pfeiffer, 1993.
12. Katzenbach, J. R., and Smith, D. K. The discipline of teams. *Harvard Business Review*, March–April 1993, 111–120.
13. Katzenbach, J. R., and Smith, D. K. *The Wisdom of Teams: Creating the High Performance Organization*. Boston: Harvard Business School Press, 1993.
14. Stoner, C. R., and Hartman, R. I. Team building: Answering the tough questions. *Business Horizons*, September–October 1993, 70–78.
15. Nelson, R. B. *Empowering Employees Through Delegation*. Burr Ridge, Ill.: Richard D. Irwin, 1994.
16. Healey, J. R. U.S. Steel learns from experience. *USA Today*, April 10, 1992, 1, 3.
17. Dean, J. W., Jr., and Evans, J. R. *Total Quality: Management Organization and Strategy*. St. Paul, Minn.: West, 1994, 176–179.
18. McKee, B. Turn your workers into a team. *Nation's Business*, July 1992, 36–38.
19. Cotton, J. L. *Employee Involvement: Methods for Improving Performance and Work Attitudes*. Newbury Park, Calif.: Sage, 1993.
20. Adapted from Tjosvold, D. W. and Tjosvold, M. M. *Leading the Team Organization*. New York: Lexington Books, 1992; McKee, B. Turning your workers into a team, *Nation's Business*, July 1992, 36–38.
21. Stevenson, W. B., Pearce, J. L., and Porter, L. W. The concept of "coalition" in organization theory and research. *Academy of Management Review*, 1985, 10, 256–268.
22. Tuckman, B. W. Development sequence in small groups. *Psychological Bulletin*, 1965, 62, 384–399; Tuckman, B. W., and Jensen, M. A. C. Stages of small group development revisited. *Group & Organization Studies*, 1977, 2, 419–427; Obert, S. L. Developmental patterns of organizational task groups: A preliminary study. *Human Relations*, 1983, 36, 37–52.
23. Kormanski, C. A situational leadership approach to groups using the Tuckman model of group development. In L. D. Goodstein and J. W Pfeiffer (eds.), *The 1985 Annual: Developing Human Resources*. San Diego: University Associates, 1985, 217–226; Gersick, C. J. Time and transition in work teams: Toward a new model of group development. *Academy of Management Journal*, 1988, 31, 9–41.
24. Napier, R. W., and Gershenfeld, M. K. *Groups: Theory and Expe-*

rience, 3rd ed. Boston: Houghton Mifflin, 1985, 459–460.

25. Schein, E. H. On dialogue, culture, and organizational learning. *Organizational Dynamics*, Autumn 1993, 40–51.

26. Liebowitz, J. Self-managing work teams at PPG. *Self-managed Work Teams Newsletter*. Denton, Tex.: Center for the Study of Work Teams (University of North Texas), Winter 1993, 1–4.

27. Bolman, L. G., and Deal, T. E. What makes a team work? *Organizational Dynamics*, Autumn, 1992, 34–44.

28. Gersick, C. J. G. Time and transition in work teams: Toward a new model of group development. *Academy of Management Journal*, 1988, 31, 9–41; Gersick, C. J. G. Revolutionary change theories: A multilevel exploration of the punctuated equilibrium paradigm. *Academy of Management Review*, 1991, 16, 10–36.

29. Trist, E. and Murray, H. (eds.). *The Social Engagement of Social Science: A Tavistock Anthology*, Vol. II. Philadelphia: University of Pennsylvania Press, 1993.

30. Gerstein, M. S. *The Technology Connection*. Reading, Mass.: Addison-Wesley, 1987, 5.

31. Johansen, R. *Groupware: Computer Support for Business Teams*. New York: Free Press, 1988.

32. Johansen, R., Martin, A., Mittman, R., Saffo, P., Sibbet, D., and Benson, S. *Leading Business Teams: How Teams Can Use Technology and Group Process Tools to Enhance Performance*. Reading, Mass.: Addison-Wesley, 1991, 13–30.

33. Adapted from La Plante, A. Brainstorming. *Forbes ASAP*, October 25, 1993, 45–61; Nolle, T. Groupware: The next generation. *Business Communication Review*, August 1993, 54–58.

34. Adapted from Kupfer, A. Prime time for videoconferences. *Fortune*, December 28, 1992, 90–95; Halhed, B. R., and Scott, D. L. There really are practical uses for videoconferencing. *Business Communications Review*, June 1992, 41–44.

35. Herman, S. M. *A Force of Ones*. San Francisco: Jossey-Bass, 1994.

36. Adapted from Henry, W. A. III. Where NBC went wrong. *Time*, February 22, 1993, 59; Frame, P. How GM trumped Dateline. *Automotive News*, February 15, 1993, 1, 3.

37. Berelson, B., and Steiner, G. A. *Human Behavior: An Inventory of Scientific Findings*. New York: Harcourt, Brace and World, 1964, 356–360.

38. Stoneman, K. G., and Dickinson, A. M. Individual performances as a function of group contingencies and group size. *Journal of Organizational Behavior Management*, 1989, 10, 131–150; Hare, A. P. Group size. *American Behavioral Scientist*, 1981, 24, 695–708.

39. Driskill, J. E., Hogan, R., and Salas, E. Personality and group performance. In C. Hendrick (ed.), *Group Processes and Intergroup Relations*. Newbury Park, Calif.: Sage, 1987, 91–112.

40. Hoffman, L. R. Applying experimental research on group problem solving to organizations. *Journal of Applied Behavioral Science*, 1979, 15, 375–391.

41. Bales, R. F. *Personality and Interpersonal Behavior*. New York: Holt, Rinehart, and Winston, 1970; Lustig, M. W. Bales' interpersonal rating forms: Reliability and dimensionality. *Small Group Behavior*, 1987, 18, 99–107.

42. Triandi, H. C., Kurowski, L. L., and Gelfand, M. J. Workplace diversity. In H. C. Triandis, M. D. Dunnette, and L. M. Hough (eds.), *Handbook of Industrial and Organizational Psychology*. Vol. 4, 2nd Ed. Palo Alto: Calif.: Consulting Psychologists Press, 1994, 769–827.

43. Adapted from Scott, J. United Nations. Reprinted with permission from *Business Ethics Magazine*, 52 S. 10th Street, Suite 110, Minneapolis, MN 55403.

44. Bettenhausen, K. L., and Murnighan, J. K. The development of an intragroup norm and the effects of interpersonal and structural changes. *Administrative Science Quarterly*, 1991, 36, 20–35.

45. Diamond, M. A. *The Unconscious Life of Organizations*. Westport, Conn.: Quorum Books, 1993.

46. Roethlisberger, F. J., and Dickson, W. J. *Management and the Worker: Technical versus Social Organization in an Industrial Plant*. Cambridge, Mass.: Harvard University Press, 1939.

47. Adapted and reprinted with permission from Ritti, R. Richard, and Funhouser, G. Ray. *The Ropes to Skip and the Ropes to Know*. Columbus, Ohio: Grid, 1977, 188–189.

48. Feldman, D. C. The development and enforcement of group norms. *Academy of Management Review*, 1984, 9, 47–53. Also see Spich, R. S., and Keleman, R. S. Explicit norm structuring process: A strategy for increasing task-group effectiveness. *Group and Organization Studies*, 1985, 10, 37–59.

49. Hackman, J. R. Group influences on individuals. In M. D. Dunnette and L. M. Hough (eds.), *Handbook of Industrial and Organizational Psychology*. Vol. 3, 2nd ed. Palo Alto: Calif.: Consulting Psychologists Press, 1992, 199–267.

50. Galem, S., and Moscovici, S. Toward a theory of collective phenomena: Consensus and attitude changes in groups. *European Journal of Social Psychology*, 1991, 21, 49–74; Cosier, R. A., and Schwenk, C. R. Agreement and thinking alike: Ingredients for poor decisions. *Academy of Management Executive*, February 1990, 69–74.

51. Janis, I. L. Groupthink, 2nd ed. Boston: Houghton Mifflin, 1982; Whyte, G. Groupthink reconsidered. *Academy of Management Review*, 1989, 14, 40–56; Sims, R. R. Linking groupthink to unethical behavior in organizations. *Journal of Business Ethics*, September 1992, 651–652.

52. Adapted from Paine, L. S. Managing for organizational integrity. *Harvard Business Review*, March–April 1994, 106–117; Kindel, S. Bad apple for baby: Exchanged its future reputation for profit. *Financial World*, June 27, 1989, 1–3.

53. Shipper, F., and Manz, C. C. Employee self-management without formally designated teams: An alternative road to empowerment. *Organizational Dynamics*, May 1992, 48–60.

54. Larson, C. E., and Lafasto, F. M. J. *Teamwork: What Must Go Wrong/What Can Go Wrong*. Newbury Park, Calif.: Sage, 1989.

55. Kinlaw, D. C. *Developing Superior Work Teams: Building Quality and the Competitive Edge*. Lexington, Mass.: Lexington Books, 1991.

56. Morris, W. C., and Sashkin, M. *Organization Behavior in Action: Skill Building Experiences*. St. Paul: West, 1976; Campion, A., Medsker, G. J., and Higgs, A. C. Relations between work group characteristics and effectiveness: Implications for designing effective work groups. *Personnel Psychology*, 1993, 46, 823–850.

57. Trist, E., and Murray, H. (eds.). *The Social Engagement of Social Science: A Tavistock Anthology*, Vol. I. Philadelphia, PA: University of Pennsylvania Press, 1990.

58. Adapted from Lindsay, C. P., and Dempsey, B. L. Experiences in training Chinese business people to use U.S. management techniques. *Journal of Applied Behavioral Science*, 1985, 21, #1, pp. 65–78, copyright © 1985. Reprinted by permission of Sage Publications, Inc.

59. Major portions of this discussion for the nominal group technique were excerpted from Woodman, R. W. Use of the nominal group technique for idea generation and decision making. *Texas Business Executive*, Spring 1981, 50–53; Delbecq, A. L., Van de Ven, A. H., and Gustafon, D. H. *Group Techniques for Program*

Planning: A Guide to Nominal and Delphi Processes. Glenview, Ill.: Scott, Foresman, 1975, 60.

60. Bartunek, J. M., and Murninhan, J. K. The nominal group technique: Expanding the basic procedure and underlying assumptions. *Group and Organization Studies*, 1984, 9, 417–432; Burton, G. E. The "clustering effect": An idea-generation phenomenon during nominal grouping. *Small Group Behavior* 1987, 18, 224–238.

61. Hirokawa, R. Y. and Rost, K. M. Effective group decision making in organizations: Field test of the vigilant interaction theory. *Management Communication Quarterly*, 1992, 5, 267–288.

62. Osborn, A. F. *Applied Imagination*, rev. ed. New York: Scribner, 1957.

63. Diehl, M., and Strobe, W. Productivity loss in brainstorming groups: Toward the solution of the riddle. *Journal of Personality and Social Psychology*, 1987, 53, 497–509.

64. Mullen, B., Johnson, C., and Salas, E. Productivity loss in brainstorming groups: A meta-analytical integration. *Basic and Applied Social Psychology*, 12, 1991, 3–23.

65. Gallupe, R. B., Cooper, W. H., Grise, M. L., Bastianutti, L. M.

Blocking electronic brainstorms. *Journal of Applied Psychology*, 1994, 79, 77–86.

66. Olaniran, B. A. Group performance in computer-mediated and Face-to-Face communication media. *Management Communication Quarterly*, 1994, 7, 256–281.

67. Gallupe, R. B., Dennis, A. R., Cooper, W. H., Valacich, J. S., Bastianutti, L. M., and Nunamaker, J. F., Jr. Electronic brainstorming and group size. *Academy of Management Journal*, 1992, 35, 350–359.

68. Adapted from Gallupe, R. B. and Cooper, W. H. Brainstorming electronically. *Sloan Management Review*, Fall 1993, 27–36.

69. Adapted from Smith, T. People are electric: Understanding heuristics in the creative process. Adapted from *The 1993 Annual: Developing Human Resources* by J. W. Pfeiffer (Ed.) Copyright © 1993 by Pfeiffer & Company, San Diego, CA. Used with permission.

70. Prepared by and adapted with permission from Barnes, F. C., professor, University of North Carolina at Charlotte (presented at Southern Case Research Association).

10 Dynamics Between Groups and Teams

When you have finished studying this chapter, you should be able to:

▲ State how the interactions between groups and teams impact their performance.

▲ Explain how certain key influences affect the dynamics and outcomes between groups and teams.

▲ Diagnose the causes of cooperative versus competitive relations between groups and teams.

▲ Describe several approaches that can be used to foster effective outcomes between groups and teams.

OUTLINE

Preview Case: Developing Aurora

Key Influences on Outcomes

Uncertainty and Uncertainty Absorption

Managing Ethics: Dow Brazil

Goals

Attitudinal Sets

Managing Across Cultures: Medtronic's Global Soul

Diversity

Task Relations

Resource Sharing

Managing in Practice: Fluor Reengineers

Substitutability

Fostering Effective Outcomes

Dialogue

Managing Diversity: CIGNA's Dialogue

Superordinate Group Goals and Rewards

Managing Quality: Alcoa's Quality-Driven Vision and Values

Plans and Hierarchy

Linking Roles

Cross-Functional Teams

Integrating Roles and Teams

Managing in Practice: Hope Creek

Groupware

DEVELOPING SKILLS

Self-Diagnosis: *Interteam Dynamics Questionnaire*

A Case in Point: *Madison Electronics Company*

PREVIEW CASE

Developing Aurora

In mid 1994, the first Auroras began to appear in Oldsmobile dealer showrooms. The Aurora, also known as the G-car within General Motors, is the first of Oldsmobile's new products. Aurora's *architecture*—the body, mechanical and electrical components, and power train and suspension systems—will be the basis for a future generation of Oldsmobiles, Cadillacs, Pontiacs, and Buicks, starting with the 1997 Buick Park Avenue.

Aurora illustrates GM's progress toward fixing its product development efforts, which have long been fragmented by bickering fiefdoms. Aurora is the first product from GM's new vehicle development process. The process has five phases: determining what customers want, using that knowledge to develop the vehicle's concept, two phases of converting the concept into vehicles and processes, and manufacturing.

Using this process, all departments from engineering to marketing worked simultaneously on Aurora, cooperating in the early stages to reduce costly glitches later. GM is convinced that nurturing cooperation between established departments will result in the best new products. Responsibility for each project is spread among an overlapping network of smaller teams, each with its own goals and managers. Still, the current system is far more unified than in the past. "What's important now is that everyone is tied together," says CEO Smith.

For Aurora, GM design engineers in Flint joined efforts with Oldsmobile's marketing team in Lansing and GM factory managers at the Lake Orion (Michigan) plant. In cases where the various teams have a sense of common purpose, the results can be impressive. But GM hasn't yet demonstrated that it can consistently and repeatedly inspire such teamwork. "I'm waiting for them to convince me," says one GM supplier. "There's still too much bickering and infighting going on."

There are encouraging signs of interteam cooperation and problem solving in the development of Aurora. Resolving a dispute about how to attach the Aurora's roof to the rear quarter panel required flexibility and cooperation that have been rare at GM. The designers wanted a smooth, flowing line where the two parts met. The engineers didn't want to use conventional welding to join the two pieces. This would require putting a big hole in the frame for the welder to reach through, weakening the rigid structure. In-stead, the engineers suggested a new manufacturing process they had been tinkering with. They devised a way for robots to spray molten silicon bronze smoothly into the roof seam. To make sure the technique was perfected before Aurora's launch, the Orion plant pioneered it in 1992 on other Olds and Buick cars.

The plant manager, Tim Sprecher, started to work the bugs out of several new processes. Because Aurora's engine is too big and complex to be lowered into the body, Sprecher and his team created *stop stations*, where the chassis comes up to meet the sheet-metal bodies. Teams of five operators work at their own pace to bolt the assemblies together. Helping Sprecher iron out the details of assembling the new car was a rotating group of 50 hourly workers and Aurora's engineers. In a three-year collaboration, they made 80% of the major changes in how Aurora is put together before it left the engineering center, avoiding costly changes in the plant. "In the past, the engineers would drop off the designs at the front door and say, 'O.K., now you build it,'" Sprecher says. "And sometimes, we couldn't." To shepherd Aurora through its final stages, Olds formed its first *launch team*, headed by Bob Romero, then the unit's head of strategic marketing. This team coordinated the efforts of marketing, public relations, engineering, manufacturing, and dealers.[1]

There is no guarantee that GM's process, including its revamped system of interteam cooperation and problem solving, will lead to Aurora's market success. However, based on learning from failures in the past and the greater effectiveness of the new development process, GM's leadership wants it to be a model for future vehicle development projects. To ensure this, GM has established the vehicle launch center in Warren, Michigan. When a car project is begun, everyone involved, from designers to accountants, spends nearly a year at the center under the guidance of a staff of engineers and purchasing agents. The teams working on the 1997 Chevrolet Corvette and the 1997 Park Avenue were among the first through the center. The center coordinates the flow of new products and coaches each program through its critical early stages. It urges teams to use common GM parts and share engineering expertise. "We stay on the learning curve," says Roger Masch, chief engineer of GM's luxury car engineering and manufacturing division. "We take all the knowledge we gain and apply it on the next vehicle, so we never make the same mistakes twice."[2]

A s General Motors was so slow to learn, the ability to diagnose and manage interteam relations is vital to most organizations because (1) teams often must work with and through other teams to accomplish their goals; (2) teams within the organization often create problems for and demands on other teams; and (3) the quality of the dynamics between teams can affect an organization's effectiveness. Recall the comment by one of GM's suppliers in the Preview Case: "There's still too much bickering and infighting going on." If this comment is valid, GM is still in the process of learning how to diagnose and manage its interteam dynamics better.

The meaning of *group* in this chapter goes beyond the definition presented in Chapter 9, which focused on person-to-person relations. In this chapter, a group or team may refer to (1) the many types of groups and teams previously discussed, (2) a department (such as the engineering department at GM), (3) a formal classification of employees (such as the hourly workers at the Orion, Michigan, plant), and (4) many other classifications based on common attributes or goals (race, gender, ethnic background, religion, occupation, physical characteristics, educational background, language skills, and so on).[3] Groups need not always be a part of the formal organizational structure, such as the coalition launch team for the Aurora. This concept (discussed in Chapter 9) is especially useful in understanding and coping with intergroup dynamics that are not revealed through the formal organization, such as GM's vehicle launch center in Warren, Michigan. We defined a *coalition* as a set of individuals or groups that band together to pursue a specific goal. Coalitions may form for many reasons, including race, gender, or a specific issue (such as a no-smoking policy). In this chapter we first present seven basic influences on interteam outcomes. Then we present seven approaches that can lead to more effective team outcomes. Although we consider some aspects of intergroup conflict, we discuss conflict more extensively in Chapter 13.

▼ KEY INFLUENCES ON OUTCOMES

The seven key influences on outcomes from interactions between groups and teams are uncertainty, goals, attitudinal sets, diversity, task relations, resource sharing, and substitutability. The potential impact of these influences and group interactions must be diagnosed to obtain a complete understanding of intergroup dynamics and outcomes. As Figure 10.1 suggests, the degree of uncertainty and the nature of group goals are fundamental to a diagnosis of any set of relationships between groups. These two influences must be assessed first to interpret properly the impact of the other five influences.

▼ Uncertainty and Uncertainty Absorption

Uncertainty is the inability to predict something accurately.[4] Individuals and teams in organizations often are concerned with three types of uncertainty: state, effect, and response.

State uncertainty means that an individual, team, or organization does not understand how factors in its environment might change. Uncertainty about whether a labor union will call a strike, whether top management will sell the division for which you work, and whether competitors will react in a certain

FIGURE 10.1

Key Influences on Outcomes
Between Groups and Teams

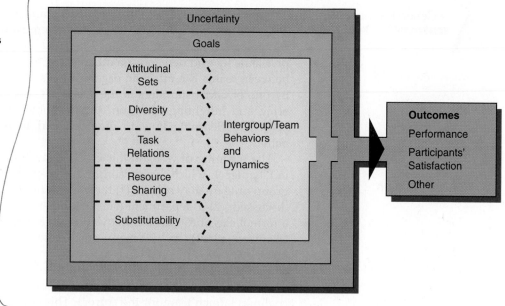

way if deregulation takes place are examples of state uncertainty. In the Preview Case, GM faced state uncertainty in not knowing how other manufacturers of directly competitive cars (e.g., Mercedes-Benz, BMW, or Lexus) might respond to the introduction of the Aurora.

Effect uncertainty is the inability to predict the impact of a future state of the environment on the individual, team, or organization. Effect uncertainty is a lack of understanding of cause–effect relationships. For example, let's assume that there is little uncertainty that the union will strike or that top management will sell the division for which you work. However, uncertainty could still exist about the possible effect (impact) of such a strike or sale of the division on your work team. In the Preview Case, GM faced effect uncertainty in not knowing the impact on sales forecasts for the Aurora if direct competitors cut their car prices by 10–15%.

Response uncertainty is a lack of knowledge of alternatives and/or the inability to predict the likely consequences of alternatives.[5] Top management may experience response uncertainty over how to deal with a strike. Or, when the Southland Corporation (which operates 7-Eleven stores) cut its management and staff employees, many employees experienced response uncertainty about their career alternatives. In the Preview Case, GM faced response uncertainty in not being sure of the best course of action to take as a result of a possible price reduction for cars competing in the same market segment as the Aurora.

One way of managing these types of uncertainty involves assigning specific teams or individuals to deal with them. Thus management may use individuals or teams to absorb particular types of uncertainty for others in the organization. **Uncertainty absorption** occurs when one team makes particular decisions for another team or sets the decision-making guidelines for another team.[6] GM's vehicle launch center in Warren, Michigan, is intended to absorb some of the uncertainties that would otherwise have been experienced by the teams working on the 1997 Chevrolet Corvette and the 1997 Buick Park Avenue.

Effects on Relative Power   Uncertainty and uncertainty absorption often have an important impact on the relative power of groups. Power has three major dimensions: weight, domain, and scope.[7] The *weight* of a group's power is the degree to which it can affect the behavior of another group. The *domain* of a group's power is the number of other groups it can affect. The *scope* of a group's power is the range of behaviors or decisions that the group can determine for another group. An accounting department has a great weight with respect to expense account procedures. Its domain in expense account matters is broad, affecting virtually everyone in an organization. But its scope in a department such as marketing probably is small; marketing has much more important behaviors and goals to be concerned about than accounting procedures. We further diagnose the sources of power in organizations—as well as the relationships of individual and group power to decision making, information, and resources—in Chapter 15.

Effects of Expert Power   The technical expertise of one group or team relative to others strongly influences the process of uncertainty absorption.[8] The amount of power it gives one group relative to others normally is limited to specific areas of knowledge and skills. Recall the dispute between the designers and engineers on how to attach the roof to the rear quarter panel of the Aurora. The designers had the power to insist on a smooth flowing line where the two parts met. The engineers had the technical expertise and related power to refuse to use conventional welding because it would weaken the car's rigid structure. Rather than engage in endless bickering, the engineering unit came up with an alternative satisfactory to both groups. They refined and tested a new process whereby robots sprayed molten silicon bronze into the roof seam to make a smooth joint.

The following Managing Ethics feature illustrates the concepts of uncertainty, uncertainty absorption, and power in the development and implementation of an ethics program at Dow Brazil.

MANAGING ETHICS

Dow Brazil

Dow Brazil was facing challenges common to many international businesses. Global economic pressures were forcing downsizing, cost-containment measures, government regulatory changes, tightened control to eliminate white-collar crime, and ongoing quality improvement initiatives (illustrates new uncertainties and the important power of external groups—customers, regulatory agencies, and competitors).

Top-level executives at Dow headquarters charged the executives of each division with tightening legal compliance, improving audit control procedures, and enhancing ethical expectations and practices (illustrates high relative power of corporate headquarters to issue mandates on giving attention to ethics by divisions).

MANAGING ETHICS —*Continued*

Dow's top-level executives hired Organizational Ethics Associates (OEA) of Cincinnati, Ohio, to serve as a consultant to Dow headquarters and the divisions regarding ethics (illustrates expert power and uncertainty absorption by OEA in addressing ethics needs). OEA conducted and reported on a company-wide *Ethical Climate/Needs Assessment Survey*. This survey provided ethical climate profiles of the company's workers as well as discrepancies between senior management and employee perceptions regarding high-priority ethical issues at the company. Dow Brazil's management team, in consultation with OEA, responded in a variety of ways to reduce the uncertainties created when employees respond to ethical issues in their own personal ways, which may not reflect the intent of Dow Brazil or corporate headquarters (illustrates greater relative power of top management over lower level managerial and employee groups in defining and implementing desired ethical decisions and climate).

To absorb uncertainty surrounding ethical issues, Dow Brazil's top-level management team

▲ endorsed the role of an ethics committee to bridge the gap between legal compliance and quality commitment;

▲ created the position of organizational ethics officer;

▲ communicated the survey results to employees and developed action plans to transform a paternalistic work culture into one that emphasizes participatory justice processes; and

▲ set up an ongoing ethics development system for addressing priority ethical issues in each location and at each level of the organization in Brazil.[9]

Significance   Uncertainty absorption by groups is significant for three reasons. First, uncertainty absorption requires that managers decide which teams will have the authority to make decisions that affect others. Second, uncertainty absorption influences the relative power of various groups—and individuals within those groups—in organizations. These power differences can be important in diagnosing conflicts and other intergroup problems. Third, uncertainty absorption requires that managers make sure that the uncertainties being absorbed by teams are consistent with their knowledge and expertise.

▼ Goals

Goals can have a powerful effect on the dynamics and outcomes between groups (see Chapter 7). Like individuals, groups reveal their preferences through stated and unstated goals.[10] An ideal state exists in an organization when each group views its goals, the goals of the entire organization, and the goals of other groups as compatible and mutually reinforcing. This is a win–win situation. Each group can attain its goals if the other groups achieve theirs. The Preview Case clearly demonstrates a potential win–win situation for the teams involved in developing and introducing the Aurora as a successful new entry in 1994 with the marketing goal of selling 40,000 units per year.[11] A win–win situation is likely to stimulate free-flowing communication, cooperation, mutual concern, respect for each other's problems, and rapid problem solving between groups and teams. But employees and teams don't always perceive goals to be compatible and mutually reinforcing. This situation may exist even when a diagnosis of the situation reveals that they should be perceived as such.

Goal Conflict   Goal conflict occurs when one group's goals are viewed by other groups as preventing them from attaining most or all of their goals. Widespread goal incompatibility, that is, a win–lose situation, is unlikely in an organization. However, a win–lose situation does exist when one group attains its goals at the expense of another group. On occasion, confrontation between a union and management takes on the characteristics of an extreme win–lose situation, particularly during bitter strikes or negotiations. Such situations deteriorate into hostility, physical violence and property damage, unwillingness of the parties to listen to one another or to compromise, and the like. Goal conflict pitted the management of American Airlines against members of the Association of Professional Flight Attendants. The flight attendants' union went on strike for five days against American during November 1993, just prior to the peak Thanksgiving travel period. There were conflicting goals (preferences) involving pay, health insurance, staffing, and scheduling. The strike ended after both sides agreed to binding arbitration at President Clinton's request.[12] This outcome was widely perceived as a *win* for the flight attendants and a *loss* for the management of American Airlines.

Mixed Goal Conflict   Goal conflict between groups more often is *mixed* than a total win–lose situation. Mixed goal conflict may serve as a basis for creating coalitions in organizations.[13] Let's consider briefly an example of a coalition's potential power. Some years ago, an executive of one of the divisions of Dresser Industries, a supplier of tools and equipment for oil and gas drilling, issued a memo to the 8,000 employees in the division forbidding women to wear slacks at work. At that time, the division had centralized computer operations. In response to that memo, 28 women who operated the centralized computer system walked off the job. The entire division needed daily information and reports from the computer center. Only those women knew how to operate it. The executive reversed the order within 48 hours. This small coalition of women discovered that they had real power.

Significance   Goal conflict or mixed goal conflict often is revealed through various forms of intergroup competition. It is most obvious when the groups are highly interdependent. Recall the Preview Case in which one of GM's suppliers commented, "There's still too much bickering and infighting going on," even though GM had taken action to reduce intergroup competition. Outcomes are predictable when groups or teams are both interdependent and competing. The following questions and answers highlight those potential outcomes.[14]

> *What happens within each competing team?* Each team becomes more cohesive and demands greater loyalty from its members; members close ranks and bury many of their personal differences. Each team increases its task-

oriented behaviors. Leadership becomes more structured and directive, and the team members become more willing to accept this type of leadership to win. Finally, each team demands more loyalty and conformity so that it can present a united front to the other team(s).

What happens between the competing teams? Each team may begin to see the other as the enemy. Distortion of perceptions takes place. Members view their own team in positive terms and the other team in negative terms. Each team soon forms stereotypes and makes negative attributions of the other(s); for example, "They're just ——— engineers. What do they know about the marketplace?" Each feels and expresses increasing hostility toward the other. Communication between the teams declines. When the teams *do* communicate, they tend to emphasize and listen only to their own concerns and to discount the statements of the other team(s).

What happens to the winner? The winning team often becomes more cohesive and tends to release the tension created by the competition in a victory celebration. Over time, the winner may become complacent ("fat and happy") and feel little need to change. This outcome doesn't appear to be the case for the Association of Professional Flight Attendants. A day after the strike's end, Denise Hedge, the union's president said that she felt the team had "won a major victory that not only will bring the union closer to its contract goals but also will build the self-esteem of the flight attendants who waged the walkout."[15]

What happens to the loser? The loser(s) may deny or distort the reality of losing. In sports, statements such as the following are common: "The referees were biased." "It was an unlucky day." or "They had a home court advantage." When the losing team fails to accept the defeat, conflicts within the team may surface, fights may break out, and members may blame others for the loss. The result is more tension and less cooperation than in the winning team. Over time, the losing team may reevaluate its behaviors and stereotypes about others. Doing so could lead to reorganization, new leadership, and other changes.

▼ Attitudinal Sets

Attitudinal sets are the thoughts and feelings—either positive or negative—that members of two or more groups have toward each other.[16] These sets of attitudes may be both a cause and a result of the dynamics and outcomes between groups. The dynamics might begin with the groups trusting and cooperating with each other. If two teams trust each other, each tends to consider the other's point of view, avoid blaming the other when problems occur, and check with each other before making decisions that jointly affect them. If the dynamics begin with attitudes of distrust, competitiveness, secrecy, and closed communication, the opposite tendencies can be expected, as suggested in the preceding discussion of the results of interteam competition.

Consider what is likely to happen if top management evaluates the performance of its internal auditing department solely on the basis of its ability to find errors in other departments and report them to higher management. These other departments probably will develop attitudes of distrust, competitiveness, and closed communication toward the auditing department. These attitudes are likely to intensify if top management uses the reports from auditing primarily to punish the audited departments, rather than to help them improve operations. In this situation, the audited departments may appear to be cooperative and open in their communications with the auditing department when in fact they are not.[17]

Cooperation Versus Competition   The attitudinal sets that groups and teams hold about each other often become *stereotypes*, that is, standardized shortcut evaluations that reflect present or past perceptions of relations between groups or specific individuals within the groups (see Chapter 2).[18] Various attitudinal and behavioral consequences have been identified for groups that stereotype their relationships as basically cooperative or competitive.[19]

Table 10.1 provides a brief questionnaire for diagnosing the attitudinal sets and behavioral relations between two groups or teams. Take a few minutes and complete this questionnaire for a work group or class project team of which you've been a member. The relationships may range from extremely cooperative to competitive. In extremely competitive relationships, teams tend to be distrustful, emphasize self-interests, communicate only when required to do so, and resist influence or control from each other. Conversely, a highly cooperative relationship tends to be characterized by trust, emphasis on mutual interests, open and frequent communication, and acceptance of mutual influence or control. However, the dynamics between teams in organizations rarely focus at one extreme or the other.

The following Managing Across Cultures account presents several of the core attitudinal sets of Medtronic in relation to conducting business abroad

TABLE 10.1   Questionnaire for Diagnosing Relations Between Teams and Groups

Instructions: For each of the characteristics shown, place a check mark in the response category that best represents your view of the relationships between the two teams or groups. The middle response category, which shows a "3," should be used only if the relationships are "neutral" or you are undecided.

Cooperative		Competitive
1. Trust	1 2 3 4 5	Distrust
2. Flexibility	1 2 3 4 5	Rigidity
3. Openness and authenticity	1 2 3 4 5	Secrecy and deceptiveness
4. Mutual interests and goals	1 2 3 4 5	Self-interest and goals
5. Friendliness or neutrality	1 2 3 4 5	Aggressiveness or enemy status
6. Listening to each other	1 2 3 4 5	Listening to selves
7. Accepting mutual control	1 2 3 4 5	Resisting control of each other
8. Collaboration and compromise	1 2 3 4 5	Force and avoidance

Scoring: For items 1–8, sum the point values shown in each category checked. Total scores of 8–16 suggest a high level of cooperation between the two teams. Total scores of 32–40 suggest a high level of competition and conflict.

through portions of an interview with Bill George, the firm's president and chief executive officer. Medtronics is a Minneapolis-based manufacturer of heart pacemakers and related products. The firm has 9,000 employees around the world.

MANAGING ACROSS CULTURES

Medtronic's Global Soul

Bill George, the president and CEO of Medtronics, comments: "We've spent forty years building our soul at Medtronic. We've been constantly restoring and renewing the soul of this company. And it gets harder. Earl Bakken built the company. Now, at age sixty-nine, he still meets with every new employee at Medtronic—all over the world. He tells the history and mission of the company. He gives everyone a medallion with a representation of our mission statement on the front: 'Towards Man's Full Life.' He says, 'Put it on your desk, and when you look at it when you are working, it will remind you that you are not here just to make money. But you're here to help people lead full lives.' George's response to the interviewer's comments and questions, which appear in italics, follow.

The company still has to earn a profit, though. The business world is still too much of a mind that our role is to maximize shareholder wealth. That cannot be a basis for a company's existence.

That's a radical statement. I don't think it's so radical.

But Milton Friedman says that the only social responsibility of a corporation is to increase profits for the shareholders. You do have to have profits. We reward our shareholders very well. If you had invested $1,000 in Medtronic in 1960, that would be worth $2 million today. If in 1985 you put in $1,000, it would be worth about $10,000 today. That's a pretty good return.

If you read our mission, you can see we serve our customers first. We enable the doctors to help patients lead full lives. We do that job well and enable our employees to be empowered and motivated. If they feel they really have a worthwhile mission themselves and are a part of carrying out this corporate mission, then the result is that we make a lot of money. But if you do it the other way around by saying, "We're here to make a lot of money. We'll figure everything else out later," it doesn't work. You can't sustain it."

You've had to deal with various sorts of ethical dilemmas? We had to terminate the head of our Italian company. Three years before we acquired an Italian distributor, they had loaned a car to a doctor in Sicily. Last November the police showed up and arrested the doctor. They were also talking about arresting one of our own employees because it appeared we had bribed the doctor with the car. The Italian manager's mistake was that he didn't tell us about it. Our president of International was there, and he asked him how things were going, check to see if he wanted talk about any ethical issues, and he covered it up. It turned out there were some other things he was covering up as well. To me the major fault was not that the problem existed, but that he wasn't open and straightforward with us. He put the corporation at risk. We didn't violate the Foreign Corrupt Practices Act, but that wasn't the point. It sets a climate in which you don't know what's going on, decisions are being made behind closed doors. You have to get the ethical issues out on the table.

MANAGING ACROSS CULTURES —*Continued*

That must be a big challenge in a global corporation like yours, where the tendency would be to say that such compromises are necessary to market successfully in some countries. When I first came here, we reorganized the international business. In Europe we had a split organization reporting to about five or six people back here. We promoted a Dutchman who came from a subsidiary to become the president of Europe. We found out three or four months later that he had engaged in a scheme with a subsidiary company before he came to Medtronic, setting up a private fund for an Italian distributor in a Swiss bank account. We checked the log books and found out that he had been involved with this Italian distributor, so we had to fire him and go public with it. He said, "We do things differently here. What I did was legal under Dutch law. Bribes are deductible." We have a worldwide standard of ethics. Particularly in the medical field, it's hard to convey because practices are so different around the world. We had to pull out of Korea because we couldn't tolerate some of the practices there.

So you have had to walk away from some markets? We decided to back away from the market and look for another way of doing business there.[20]

Significance   Attitudinal sets—whether cooperative or competitive—can significantly affect the ability and willingness of teams to work together to achieve organizational goals. If teams are interdependent, competitive attitudinal sets will hurt the chances for goal accomplishment. The reason is that these teams must expend considerable time and energy trying to "get one up" on the other. We further develop the importance of attitudinal sets and differences in the following discussion of diversity as an influence on the dynamics and outcomes between groups and teams.

▼ Diversity

Many interactions between individuals have an intergroup component. The way individuals act toward one another reflects to some degree (1) the attitudes and behaviors of their respective groups, (2) the stereotypes that the groups hold about each other, and (3) the types of relationships between the groups. These dynamics are especially pronounced when the interacting individuals hold a strong group identification.

   Group identification refers to the idea that a person's identity, and thus the perception of others' identity, is defined (at least in part) by reference to who is *in* and who is *out* of various groups or teams. The in or out concept creates enormous challenges for managing diversity in organizations, which often is the basis of intergroup dynamics and behaviors.[21] The Preview Case suggested many types of diversity that could lead to group identification, including engineering, marketing, purchasing, factory managers, designers, suppliers, hourly workers, public relations, dealers, launch team, and vehicle launch center. The individuals at GM who may partly define their group identification according to such categories also may be likely to hold other forms of group identification, which they use to define who is in or out, such as race, gender, religion, and ethnicity. *Diversity* reflects any characteristic that individuals or groups are likely to use to tell themselves: *That person (group) is different from me (us).*[22]

Although changing in some organizations, diversity too often is viewed more negatively than positively. This negative reaction may be due, in large part, to six underlying attitudinal sets involving stereotypical false assumptions in group and organizational cultures.

▲ *Otherness* is a deficiency.

▲ Diversity poses a threat to the organization's effective functioning.

▲ Expressed discomfort with the dominant group's values is perceived as oversensitivity by the *minority* groups.

▲ Members of all diverse groups want to become and should be more like the dominant group.

▲ Equal treatment means the same treatment.

▲ Managing diversity simply requires changing the people, not the organizational culture.[23]

An in-depth survey of U.S. workers shows continued deep divisions by race and gender. The study involved hour-long telephone interviews with a nationally representative sample of about 3,000 wage and salaried employees. Employees under 25 showed no greater preference than older employees for working with individuals of other races, ages, or ethnic groups. Slightly over half of those surveyed indicated that they prefer to work with individuals of the same race, gender, and educational level. Minority men and women and white women rated white men's chances of advancement higher than did white men themselves. Surveyed women managers were more than twice as likely as men to rate their career advancement opportunities as poor or fair, with 39% choosing those labels, compared to 16% of the men.[24]

Female and Male Managers   One interesting example of attitudinal sets based on diversity is demonstrated by gender differences among managers. Three distinct attitudinal sets have emerged in response to the question: Do female and male managers differ? A summary of the attitudinal sets and research evidence on this question follows.[25]

No differences. Women who pursue the nontraditional career of manager reject the feminine stereotype and have needs, values, and leadership styles similar to those of men who pursue managerial careers.

Stereotypical differences. Female and male managers differ in ways predicted by stereotypes. This is a result of early socialization experiences in schools, sports, and home that reinforce masculinity in males and femininity in females.

Nonstereotypical differences. Female and male managers differ in ways opposite to the stereotypes. The reason is that female managers have to be exceptional to compensate for early socialization experiences that are different from those of men.

Before reading further, select the attitudinal set that best represents your personal attitudes.

Research shows *no consistent gender differences* in task-oriented behavior, people-oriented behavior, performance ratings, and subordinates' responses to women or men as managers. Stereotypical differences in some types of managerial behavior and in some ratings of managers in laboratory studies favor male managers, who typically were viewed as more decisive and better planners. However, when differences in motivational profiles for managerial roles are considered, the slight stereotypical differences are eliminated. The results regarding gender differences in commitment are inconclusive. Moreover, when gender differences are found, they are not as extensive as other types of differences. On balance, the research evidence supports the *no differences* view of gender differences in management. Gary Powell, author of *Women and Men in Management*, comments: "Managers are a self-selecting population. Those who choose managerial careers, like firefighters, have a lot in common. The best embody stereotypes of both genders."

Top management shouldn't assume that male and female managers differ in personal qualities. It also should make sure that policies, practices, and programs minimize the creation of gender differences in managers' experiences on the job. There is little reason to believe that either women or men make superior managers or that women and men are different types of managers. Instead, there are likely to be excellent, average, and poor male and female managers. Success in today's highly competitive marketplace calls for organizations to make the best use of the talent available to them. To do so, they need to identify, develop, encourage, and promote the most effective managers, regardless of gender, race, or other nonjob attributes.

Significance   The abundance of diversity creates unique challenges in making it work for rather than against the long-term interests of individuals, teams, and organizations. Once a we–they distinction is perceived, people tend to discriminate against out–group members and in favor of in–group members. Moreover, they tend to further perceive out–group members as inferior, adversaries, and competitive.[26]

Jim Engel, senior vice-president of claims and lost contracts for CIGNA's property and casualty division expressed the business significance of creating a work environment that embraces diversity in these words:

> We ask our employees to work hard at understanding the goals and values of the company, such as the focus on the customer and adequate returns. In turn, we need to take care of the needs of our employees. When I see employee anger at not being included, I see that we're not thinking about employees the way we should. Stupid things people do that may be racially or gender-motivated are preventing us from developing the kind of environment that values all people. If we were the kind of company that valued all people, wouldn't senior management look different? We want to change the environment so that employees can feel as good as possible about the settings they work in; so that we don't unnecessarily keep them from focusing on what's important to our company.[27]

The attitude expressed by Jim Engel of CIGNA—and presented throughout this book about diversity—is that of **positive multiculturalism.** It is the condition that allows an individual to acquire new skills, perspectives, and attitudes that improve that person's chances of relating effectively to members of other groups. Positive multiculturalism is *additive*; that is, individuals maintain their self-defining attributes and add skills and positive attitudes that facilitate relationships with members of other groups. For example, a person can become bilingual by learning English but retaining a native language.[28]

▼ Task Relations

The three principal types of task relations between teams, departments, and other groups in organizations are independent, interdependent, and dependent, as shown in Figure 10.2. Although our discussion focuses on the relations between teams, the concepts apply to relations between all kinds of groups (departments, committees, coalitions, informal groups, divisions, etc.).

Independent   **Independent task relations** means that none or few interactions are needed between two groups or that those that do occur take place at the discretion of the two groups. This type of task relations between groups is based on a view of organizations as loosely coupled systems. **Loose coupling** occurs when groups affect each other occasionally (rather than constantly), negligibly (rather than significantly), and indirectly (rather than directly).[29] Self-managed teams reflect loose coupling.

Some large organizations maintain internal consulting teams that contract, on mutually agreeable terms, to work with various departments. For example, Corning Glass's organizational development team operates principally in this way. Say that a department at Corning wants to improve its problem-solving effectiveness in team meetings. The managers call in a representative from the organizational development department to diagnose the problems and help the department change its processes.

Once groups start working together, their relations are interdependent, at least to some extent, for the duration of the project. However, if both groups have the freedom to withdraw from the relationship at any time, they probably perceive it to be a relatively independent task relation. In this case neither group has much power relative to the other.

Interdependent   **Interdependent task relations** means that collaboration, integration, and mutual decision making are necessary and desirable between groups for them to achieve their own goals. For effective interdependent task relations to exist, no single group or individual within a group should dictate or unilaterally determine the outcome of interactions.[30] Cross-functional teams

FIGURE 10.2

Task Relations Between Teams

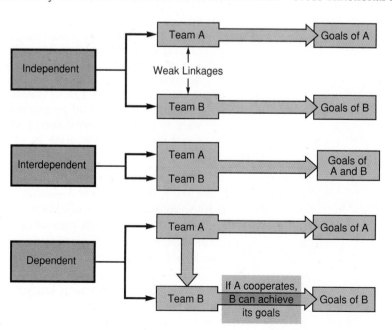

usually are formed to facilitate interdependent task relations. Recall the Preview Case on development of the new Aurora automobile. The groups and teams that had interdependent task relations during the development process included engineering, marketing, purchasing, designers, plant managers, hourly workers, public relations, dealers, and potential customers.

Dependent   **Dependent task relations** means that one group has the ability and power to determine the behaviors and outputs of other groups.[31] Dependent task relations often occur when (1) one group absorbs uncertainty for another group, (2) the services that one group provides for another group are not readily substitutable, or (3) groups depend on another group for needed resources. A dramatic example is that of the dependent task relations between an organization's top-management planning and budget committee and its operating departments. Resource allocations and possibly even the survival of departments depend on the budget committee's decisions.

When individuals are dependent on the actions of another individual or group, they may unite by forming a coalition or respond by joining an organization that represents their interests. One goal of such a coalition is to reduce the dependency of the individuals or group on the unilateral actions of those who are perceived as having more power.[32] Some employees form or join unions to reduce their dependency on the actions of management. They believe that, in unity there is strength, that is, less dependency.

Significance   The diagnosis of task relations between groups or teams is essential to long-term effectiveness. First, the achievement of important organizational goals—such as productivity, innovation, and customer satisfaction—often is influenced by the nature and degree of task relations between groups and individuals. Second, some degree of interdependent task relations between groups—such as quality control and production—usually is needed and must be managed. Third, a wide range of task relations exists between groups in organizations.[33]

▼ Resource Sharing

Resource sharing refers to the degree to which two or more groups must obtain needed goods or services from a common group and the degree to which these goods or services are adequate to meet the needs of all the groups.[34] The following Managing in Practice item presents the changes made in one of the divisions of Fluor Corporation to share and use valuable resources more efficiently.

MANAGING IN PRACTICE

Fluor Reengineers

Since 1990, the engineering projects of Fluor's mining and metal unit have grown 230%—from $300 million to more than $1 billion—with only a 25% increase in the work force. How could this be? Before reengineering its operations, each local office operated autonomously, with its own team of engineering, procurement, marketing, and operations managers responsible for the bottom line at its site. Besides adding overhead, this setup kept the offices from cooperating and sharing talent. Today one team of mobile managers, who communicate constantly via fax, phone, and E-mail, presides over all the

MANAGING IN PRACTICE —*Continued*

offices, moving work and technical talent among sites as needed. Victor Medina, the general manager of the mining and metals division, says: "We are conscious of the fact that we're in the business to run projects. We're not in the business to run offices."

Through electronic work-sharing (and related groupware tools), engineers in New Orleans are preparing drawings for a copper mine expansion on the Indonesian island of Irian Jaya. Similarly, the Vancouver office has done structural engineering work for Fluor's challenging Quebrada Blanca project—a copper mine being built 14,000 feet up in the Andes. The Vancouver engineers used to be fully utilized about 40% of the time; now it's 90%.[35]

Significance The need for two or more groups or teams to share a common pool of resources can generate either competition or cooperation between them.[36] Collaborative problem solving among groups that share a pool of scarce resources may be encouraged through the use of cross-functional teams and other approaches discussed later in this chapter. These approaches, including interventions by higher management, can help set priorities to minimize unnecessary competition and destructive conflicts. Of course, higher level managers also are in a unique position to influence the attitudinal sets that groups have toward each other. Improved attitudes can avoid difficulties when teams share resources or work together. This type of change is clearly reflected in the previous comment by Victor Medina, a general manager at Fluor: "We are conscious of the fact that we're in the business to run projects. We're not in the business to run offices."

▼ Substitutability

Substitutability is the degree to which one group can obtain the services or goods provided by another group from alternative sources. If alternative services or goods are readily available, the power of the provider group is weaker than if no alternatives existed.[37] For example, in the California State University System, the academic departments have neither the authority nor the ability to select alternative means for obtaining travel expense reimbursements. The fiscal departments at the state universities handle all travel reimbursements.

In order to utilize resources fully, organizations frequently have rules requiring that departments use the services provided by other departments within the organization. For example, if the department of management at Texas A&M University wants a new brochure printed, it is required to go through the university's printing department unless it receives an exception. The university might enforce this rule even if the department of management could get an outside firm to do the job faster and cheaper. From an organizational standpoint, the decreased costs to the department of management might be less significant than the low utilization of labor and equipment in the university's printing department. However, an increasing number of organizations are eliminating entire departments or work teams by contracting for the services they perform—called *outsourcing*. Subcontracting has hit many groups, such as custodial, food, printing, maintenance, information processing, and even production departments that manufacture component parts.

Significance   Everything else being equal, the lower the substitutability of a group's or team's goods or services, the greater is its power within the organization.[38] Groups that provide vital, nonsubstitutable services sometimes find that groups to which they furnish these services try to (1) win them over by providing extra rewards or (2) eliminate the service group or its management by complaining to top management. For example, some information processing department managers have been dismissed because the amount of their control over critical information threatened higher management. Thus even a perceived attempt to exercise too much power and control by a computer processing manager can create a backlash from others.

▼ FOSTERING EFFECTIVE OUTCOMES

In this section we present seven approaches for fostering effective dynamics and outcomes between interdependent groups or teams. These approaches may be used singly or in various combinations. Two of the approaches—dialogue and superordinate team goals and rewards—provide a foundation for the use of the other approaches. Figure 10.3 identifies the seven approaches and suggests the crucial importance of dialogue and superordinate team goals and rewards.

▼ Dialogue

Dialogue is a process whereby people suspend defensive exchanges to allow a free flow of inquiry into their own and others' assumptions and beliefs. Dialogue can build mutual trust and common ground and helps people learn how to think together. They do so by stating assumptions and beliefs that they hold about each other and gaining insights into what they do. Dialogue also

FIGURE 10.3

Fostering Effective Outcomes Between Groups and Teams

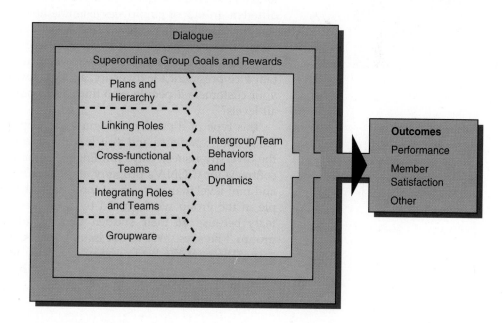

is concerned with discovering how our thought processes work and how our past experiences influence current perceptions.[39]

A union representative who had gone through a dialogue process with the management of a troubled steel company told a group of managers from many companies that "we have learned to question fundamental categories and labels that we have applied to each other." A manager in the audience asked: "Can you give us an example?" "Yes. Labels like *management* and *union*."[40]

The following are some basic guidelines for fostering dialogue between individuals and groups.

▲ Suspend your own assumptions and sense of certainty about others and the issues at hand.

▲ Listen to see if you are truly understanding or simply engaging in negative evaluations of the comments by others.

▲ Slow down the inquiry because dialogue requires time to develop.

▲ Reject polarization of views as acceptable.[41]

Through dialogue, false stereotypes and competitive relations between individuals and groups are likely to be resolved or reduced. (Chapter 12 focuses on the development of dialogue skills.) Diversity issues often get in the way of dialogue. As portrayed in the following Managing Diversity feature, CIGNA, the large insurance company, is making efforts to create dialogue and resolve diversity issues.

MANAGING DIVERSITY

CIGNA's Dialogue

Diversity dialogue has been implemented companywide at CIGNA as part of its effort to create a more inclusive corporate culture. In awareness sessions different groups of employees examine how they feel and develop an understanding of why change is necessary. The goals of this effort are to heighten personal awareness and understanding and to link resolving diversity issues with improving organizational performance. Bobby Espinosa, CIGNA's assistant vice president for diversity, asks: "'How can you pitch your products to your customers if people who think like your customers aren't represented at all levels?"

This type of diversity dialogue hits people at the gut level. "It's a pretty emotional experience and you leave with a better understanding of some of the diversity issues," says Jim Engel, senior vice-president of claims and loss contracts for CIGNA's property and casualty division. His group of 26 senior and mid-level managers spent three days at a diversity seminar. "All the people in the group were moved by the experience, and some were moved to tears because of their sudden understanding of the differences between groups," he says. "We're not issuing edicts and creating hiring goals," Engel says. "We're at the beginning of a journey toward a more inclusive culture; we have set out on a path. Exactly where that will take us isn't yet clear, but we're looking for better ways of operating, and we're creating better systems to support all our employees."

MANAGING DIVERSITY —*Continued*

Susan Wood, an assistant vice-president at CIGNA Worldwide, says she thinks CIGNA sees a compelling need to change the composition of senior management. But the company has had a hard time making the changes because senior management has been insulated from what those on the front lines have had to face. "White males by and large haven't had the experiences and opportunities to understand what not being included means," she says. "Women and minorities have moved up by sheer grit; they've had to restrain their anger and behave well. And sometimes they've had to give up their alliances to succeed. They sometimes have become isolated; they have feared talking to each other at cocktail parties. For a long time, white males wouldn't tolerate women talking to each other; now it's become acceptable. There is more of a willingness to see the other side, the other group's point of view. In the past couple of years, there has been a genuine interest in exploring the issue and being more inclusive. All systems—not just pay and selection—are being openly discussed. It's still too early to see how effective all this will be, but it is definitely changing. We're making a conscious effort to be more inclusive. We're pushing back on behavior and really questioning things at this point."[42]

▼ Superordinate Group Goals and Rewards

Superordinate group goals are ends that two or more groups might pursue but can't be achieved without their cooperation.[43] Such goals do not replace or eliminate individual group goals. Superordinate group goals may be qualitative or quantitative. An example of a qualitative goal is: "Marketing and production need to pull together for the good of the company." An example of a quantitative goal is: "Marketing and production need to work together if we are to reach the company goals of launching the new X line within 9 months and achieving sales of 5,000 units per month within 15 months. The company's survival is at stake." Many industry analysts believe that development of the Aurora automobile is one key to the survival (one superordinate goal) of GM's Oldsmobile division. John Rock, head of the Oldsmobile division, commented on the many rumors of Olds's demise: "There's nothing like the fear of death to give you a little focus. Without the scare maybe we would still be studying and struggling."[44]

Superordinate group goals are likely to have a more powerful effect on the willingness of groups to cooperate if they are accompanied by superordinate group rewards.[45] **Superordinate group rewards** are the benefits received by members of the cooperating groups that are partially determined by the results of their joint efforts. With the introduction of Aurora, the superordinate group rewards were the increased likelihood of job security for many employees and the financial incentives for key people in the Oldsmobile division if Aurora is a success in the marketplace.

Range of Use   Superordinate group goals and rewards vary widely in complexity and in the resources required to meet them. A company president might state: "During this past year, we needed extensive cooperation among all our departments and divisions in order to achieve our company goal of a twelve percent increase in profits. I would like to express my appreciation to all of you for pulling together—even when we had to deal with several sticky issues involving some teams and departments. Through everyone's efforts, we did it—and more! I am pleased to report that profits are up sixteen percent, well over our goal." This statement is fairly simple in terms of the degree of complexity and inexpensive in terms of the resources required.

Let's assume that she adds the following: "Under our profit sharing program, I am pleased to report that ninety percent of our employees will receive bonuses ranging from ten to fifteen percent of their salaries. As all of you should know, these bonuses are based on a weighted system of (1) individual merit rating, (2) achievement of departmental goals, and (3) overall company profitability." These additional comments suggest that the superordinate group rewards are more complex and expensive in terms of the additional resources required. Of course, these expenses actually may represent an investment with a high rate of return.

Total Quality Management   Total quality management (TQM) provides a good example of a program based on superordinate group goals and rewards. The organizationwide foundation for TQM is the superordinate group goal of total dedication to meet or exceed customers' needs and expectations.[46] It means thinking about quality in terms of all of the functions, teams, and levels in the organization. It involves systems thinking—from start (inputs) to transformation (process) to finish (final goods and services to customers) to follow-up with customers. Total quality management considers every interaction among the individuals, teams, groups, and levels of the organization.[47] It is vitally concerned with the dynamics between groups or teams and their behaviors to achieve desired outcomes, especially as they may affect meeting or exceeding customer expectations.

A task force created at Alcoa, the largest aluminum company in the world, investigated the possible use of total quality management. Consistent with the creation of superordinate group goals and rewards, the task force concluded that quality is a focal point around which the entire company could be energized. Total quality management appealed to most Alcoa employees, building on their desire to excel and control their destiny and was more inspiring than purely financial goals. The task force recognized that TQM can be a win–win proposition vis-à-vis the union because it holds that 80% of the problems are with the "system." On the cautionary side, the task force realized that TQM is not a quick fix and that those companies that view it as such fail in their TQM initiatives. It recognized that TQM does not become "real" until it permeates the values, norms, and culture of the organization.[48]

The Alcoa task force went on to develop a statement of vision and values based on the TQM approach, which also expressed the superordinate group goals and rewards for all of Alcoa's employees. The following Managing Quality account presents Alcoa's quality-driven vision and values.

MANAGING QUALITY

Alcoa's Quality-Driven Vision and Values

▼ Alcoa's Vision

Alcoa is a growing worldwide company dedicated to excellence through quality—creating value for customers, employees, and shareholders through innovation, technology, and operational expertise. Alcoa will be the best aluminum company in the world, and a leader in other businesses in which we choose to compete.

▼ Alcoa's Values

Integrity: Alcoa's foundation is the integrity of its people. We will be honest and responsible in dealing with customers, suppliers, co-workers, shareholders, and the communities where we have an impact.

Safety and Health: We will work safely in an environment that promotes the health and well-being of the individual.

Quality and Excellence: We will provide products and services that meet or exceed the needs of our customers. We will relentlessly pursue continuous improvement and innovation in everything we do to create significant competitive advantage compared to world standards.

People: People are the key to Alcoa's success. Every *Alocan* will have equal opportunity in an environment that fosters communication and involvement while providing reward and recognition for teams and individual achievement.

Profitability: We are dedicated to earning a return on assets that will enable growth and enhance shareholder value.

Accountability: We are accountable—individually and in teams—for our actions and results.[49]

▼ Plans and Hierarchy

Planning can help groups and teams achieve effective outcomes. **Planning** develops an organization's, team's, or individual's (1) destination (vision and goals), (2) strategies for getting there, (3) targets for achievement by specific dates, (4) anticipated obstacles, and (5) alternatives for dealing with those obstacles.[50]

By following accepted or agreed on plans, teams and even interrelated organizations can act and make day-to-day decisions without constantly communicating with each other. Plans foster integrated and interdependent team actions in achieving goals. For example, construction crews in England and France started working on different sections of the tunnel under the English Channel. Because engineers and managers had prepared precise plans, construction crews made accurate decisions based on the plans and met exactly where they were supposed to meet.

Plans that involve coordination between teams often require the participation of a common manager. **Hierarchy** allows a common manager to coordinate teams or individuals. Its use is based on the fact that people at upper levels in an organization have more power (and possibly more knowledge) than those at lower levels. Its exclusive use to resolve integration problems may be especially appropriate when coordination requirements are few and differences between the teams are only minor. Hierarchy doesn't prevent team members from sitting down with their common manager and working through issues together. Recall that, in the development of the Aurora, Olds formed its first launch team headed by Bob Romero, then the unit's head of strategic marketing. Because of his higher level position in the company's hierarchy, Romero had the clout to facilitate, coordinate, and make tough decisions when the interrelated departments couldn't reach a consensus.

▼ Linking Roles

Linking roles are performed by individuals in specialized positions who facilitate communication and problem solving between interdependent teams. The creation of such a role is important when the use of hierarchy, plans, or both is too slow or time-consuming. If minor issues were continually referred up the hierarchy, the project manager might become overloaded, increasing the response time. Someone in a linking role could solve these minor problems and reduce that workload. A linking role may involve nothing more than handling and tracking the flow of paperwork between teams and following up on requests.

Boundary-Spanning Roles   People performing specialized linking roles also can tie teams to other teams or organizations. These **boundary-spanning roles** often are essential in facilitating information flow and decision making.[51] For example, safety managers at Rubbermaid fill boundary-spanning roles between Rubbermaid and the U.S. Occupational Safety and Health Administration (OSHA) with respect to work-related safety issues. Boundary-spanning roles also may involve representing the team or organization to outside groups. For example, boundary spanners in the collective bargaining process with unionized trucking companies include negotiators representing the firms on one side and those representing the Teamsters on the other. An organization spokesperson often deals with the media, responding to questions related to a crisis or disaster.[52] Research on groups and teams revealed four basic types of boundary-spanning roles.

- ▲ The *ambassador* obtains personnel, funding, equipment, and legitimacy from higher management or other teams. This role appears to be somewhat political: identifying opposition at the top levels of the organization and other teams and working to win their support.
- ▲ The *task coordinator* facilitates integration and synchronization with other teams, typically those involved with a specific product or project.
- ▲ The *scout* engages in general scanning aimed at obtaining competitive, market, and technical ideas.
- ▲ The *guard* reduces dependence by controlling the information flow from the team.[53]

All of these forms of boundary-spanning activity may occur in linking and in representing a team or group with external groups. These roles may be performed by more than one person, not just the team leader.

▼ Cross-Functional Teams

Cross-functional teams bring together the knowledge and skills of people from various parts of the organization to produce solutions to joint problems. These teams usually are formed to work on temporary issues or problems and are disbanded when those items are resolved. Some members of a cross-functional team may be engaged in its work full-time and others part-time. Team members often link the team with their own groups. Members usually can provide information and ideas regarding common problems, serve as transmitters of ideas and information between the cross-functional team and their groups, and help assess the impact of the team's decisions on their own groups or teams.[54]

Thermos Corporation recently adopted the use of cross-functional teams to help it break out of its bureaucratic, top-down culture. Thermos is headquartered in Schaumburg, Illinois, and primarily makes Thermos bottles, lunch boxes, and gas and electric cookout grills. A cross-functional product development team created and developed the new Thermal Electric Grill. The grill uses an entirely new technology to give food a barbecued taste, it burns cleaner than gas or charcoal, it has won four design awards, and it has been a major market success. After the grill was introduced, the cross-functional development team was disbanded.[55]

▼ Integrating Roles and Teams

Integrating roles are performed by employees who are permanently assigned to help teams work together. One person performs an integrating role, whereas several people comprise an integrating team. Positions and teams that often have integrating responsibilities include product managers, program coordinators, project managers, group vice-presidents, plant productivity teams, corporate and division general managers, boards of directors, union leaders, union–management committees, chief information officers, chief technology officers, and human resource managers. Such positions and teams clearly provide boundary-spanning functions but typically have much more formal authority than the boundary-spanning roles described previously.

One typical role of the integrating person or team is to help resolve conflicts that develop between groups or teams. Such conflicts often surface between production and marketing departments and between union and management. Intergroup issues include disagreements over major capital investment priorities, production schedules, cost estimates, quality standards, human resource problems, and the like. The decision to use one person or a specialized team to achieve integration usually depends on the situation. Using an integrating team obviously costs more than using an integrating person. Organizations tend to use integrating teams when (1) intergroup differences are large, (2) the need for integration increases because of interdependent task relations, and (3) the need to deal with nonroutine problems between the teams increases.

The following Managing in Practice piece reveals how one organization successfully used a variety of approaches to create effective dynamics and outcomes both within and between teams.

MANAGING IN PRACTICE

Hope Creek

The organizations involved in the construction of Hope Creek Generating Station, a nuclear power plant located in southern New Jersey, faced tight budget and schedule constraints. The only way they could complete the project was to increase productivity. The question was: "How?" The primary owner, Public Service Electric & Gas Company (PSE&G), decided to implement a program designed to boost productivity by tapping the creativity of a vast and diverse work force. It required an atmosphere in which ideas and feelings could move up, down, and across the participating organizations. They had to work as cooperating teams.

The Hope Creek project was an enormous undertaking. Its total cost was more than $3.5 billion, and almost 8,000 people were employed in the effort. Some 3,500 were members of 14 craft unions, another 2,000 were salaried contractor employees, 1,500 were from 20 subcontractors (e.g., General Electric), and 500 were from PSE&G.

Employee participation was the cornerstone of the Hope Creek program. A steering team, which included representatives from all major groups, held executive powers for the overall project. The program was named PRIDE (People Respecting Integrity, Dedication, Excellence). A logo was designed that eventually found its way onto all stationery, hard hats, flagpoles, and posters. The PRIDE program included the following interrelated teams.

▲ *Steering team*—included representatives of management, salaried employees, and unions; the steering team authorized or approved PRIDE activities and provided ongoing evaluation of the program.

▲ *Suggestion team*—included representative members who reviewed all suggestions and made awards.

▲ *Quality teams*—created from a large pool of volunteers; were formed and dissolved on an ad hoc basis.

▲ *Recognition team*—included representative members who considered nominations of employees for recognition of excellent service.

▲ *Survey team*—included representative managers who undertook comprehensive annual and spot surveys of employee opinions.

▲ *Events and recreation team*—included representative volunteers who provided project celebrations at key points of completion, as well as fishing, golf, softball, football, and tennis tournaments.

Other teams were formed to improve parking facilities and litter disposal. Still others addressed issues relating directly to the work at hand, such as cable pulling, heating, ventilation, air conditioning installation, and so on. The most important factor in maintaining the program and team viability was prompt response by higher management. Team facilitators had to have constant access to senior management and management had to respond quickly and openly to ideas developed in the program.[56]

▼ Groupware

In Chapter 9, we discussed the use of groupware—computer aids, communication tools, and designated facilities—to enable groups and teams to work faster, share more information, communicate more accurately, and achieve their goals better. Here we highlight the four main categories of groupware aids that aid team-to-team communications.[57]

▲ *Basic groupware* combines a messaging system with a database containing work records and memos and changes the way information flows in an organization. Unlike plain E-mail, it doesn't require figuring out who needs to know a fact or hear an idea. Instead, you simply forward your memo to the appropriate bulletin board. Anyone who needs to know about a subject will check the bulletin board and find it.

▲ *Workflow software* is designed to remake and streamline business processes, especially in paper-clogged bureaucracies. Workers understand better the steps that comprise a particular process, and workflow software also allows them to redesign those steps. It also routes work automatically from employee to employee and team to team.

▲ *Meeting software* allows participants in face-to-face or videoconference gatherings to "talk" simultaneously by typing on PC keyboards. Because people read faster than they speak and don't have to wait for others to finish talking, the software can dramatically speed progress toward consensus. It also helps ensure that everyone gets a chance to take part. A Boeing study found that this software shortened the time it took some teams to complete projects by as much as 90%.

▲ *Scheduling software* uses a network to coordinate employee's electronic datebooks and figure out when they can all get together.

The organizational effects of groupware can be profound. With groupware, people use computers and related software, in effect, to manage networks of relationships, whereas the traditional use of computers is to manage data. To be effective, groupware typically requires a change in both vertical and lateral power relationships (i.e., manager to subordinate and department to department). In some organizations, knowledge (information) is power, and sharing it doesn't come easily. In intensely competitive organizational cultures, some employees and groups still don't openly share all relevant information through the groupware networks[58] (see Chapter 15). Thus prevailing attitudinal sets are likely to have a great impact on whether the use of groupware is successful in an organization.

Summary

In this chapter we demonstrated the importance of the relationships between groups or teams. Seven principal influences may independently or in combination affect the dynamics and outcomes between groups or teams: uncertainty, goals, attitudinal sets, diversity, task relations, resource sharing, and substitutability.

When the goals of two or more groups are perceived as being incompatible, conflict and poor coordination are likely. When one group absorbs uncertainty for other groups, its power usually increases. When the attitudinal sets that groups hold toward each other are characterized by trust, flexibility, openness, mutuality of interests, and friendliness, high levels of cooperation often result. Competition and conflict go hand in hand with opposing attitudinal sets. Diversity reflects any factor that is used to define *in* or *out* individuals or groups. Leadership in managing diversity is now a central concern in organizations. If diversity leads to hostility because of false stereotypical assumptions between in and out members, the organization isn't likely to achieve its goals. When task relations between teams are highly interdependent, extensive collaboration, coordination, and mutual decision making are required. When groups have to share resources, the likelihood of conflict is greater than when sharing isn't needed. Groups and teams need to establish priorities and ground rules for sharing common resources. When substitutability of the services or goods of a group is not permitted, the group's power often is greater than it otherwise would be.

Seven primary approaches for fostering effective outcomes between teams and groups are dialogue, superordinate group goals and rewards, plans and hierarchy, linking roles, cross-functional teams, integrating roles and teams, and groupware. Each approach may be used independently or in combination with one or more of the others. Only after careful diagnosis can someone draw conclusions about the best approach or combination of approaches for creating effective dynamics and outcomes. Management may pay too little or too much attention to intergroup relations. Too little attention can result in poor integration, duplication of effort, and destructive conflict. Too much attention can result in unnecessary paperwork and meetings, excessive expenditure of resources on achieving integration, and a lack of accomplishment by groups and teams.

Key Words and Concepts

Attitudinal sets	Independent task relations	Response uncertainty
Boundary-spanning roles	Integrating roles	State uncertainty
Dependent task relations	Interdependent task relations	Substitutability
Dialogue	Linking roles	Superordinate group goals
Effect uncertainty	Loose coupling	Superordinate group rewards
Goal conflict	Planning	Uncertainty
Group identification	Positive multiculturalism	Uncertainty absorption
Hierarchy	Resource sharing	

Discussion Questions

1. Identify a group of which you are a member and another group which is important to your group. How may this other group create state uncertainty, effect uncertainty, and response uncertainty for your group?

2. With respect to the other group identified, how does it affect the weight, domain, and scope of your group's power?

3. Consider the relationships between the student government and the administration of your college or university. Give an example of mutual goals, goal conflict, and mixed goal conflict for the two groups.

4. How does the concept of substitutability apply to dormitories, food services, the copy center, and the bookstore on your campus? What policies or practices does

your college or university pursue to limit the substitutability of these services? Are they effective? If so, how?

5. In what ways can a human resources department absorb uncertainty for other departments in an organization?

6. What are the types of task relations that probably exist between a purchasing department and a production department? Between purchasing and the human resources department? Between purchasing and the top management team? What factors probably influence the differences in these profiles of task relations?

7. Is resource sharing becoming a smaller or larger problem in organizations? Why?

8. Give examples of how attitudinal sets affect the relationships between any two groups or teams that are highly interdependent. Use the diagnostic questionnaire shown in Table 10.1 to develop the profile of the attitudinal sets between these two groups or teams.

9. What aspects of intergroup relationships are likely to be aided by groupware technologies? Why?

10. Based on your experiences in organizations, have the methods they used for integrating groups worked well or poorly? Illustrate and explain your conclusion.

 Developing Skills

Self-Diagnosis:
Interteam Dynamics Questionnaire[59]

Instructions

The following items focus on the dynamics between two teams or groups. It is assumed that the person answering this questionnaire is a member of one of the teams or groups. Identify the teams in the spaces provided:

Team #1_____ Team #2_____

Indicate the extent to which you agree or disagree with each of the statements. Record one of the following responses next to each statement.

SA = Strongly Agree
A = Agree
? = Neither Agree Nor Disagree
D = Disagree
SD = Strongly Disagree

____ 1. When we have to arrive at an agreement with the other team, the outcome depends most on which team can get more powerful support for its position.

____ 2. Members of each team feel free to get together with persons in the other team.

____ 3. Members of the other team generally have positive feelings toward members of my team.

____ 4. We can generally work out a fair bargain with the other team.

____ 5. Members of the two teams generally avoid one another.

____ 6. There is no personal animosity between members of the two teams.

____ 7. When we have a problem it is usually resolved by a solution that satisfies members of both teams.

____ 8. Members of the other team generally dislike us.

____ 9. There is quite a bit of interaction between members of the two teams.

____10. The relationship between the two teams would best be described as collaborative, open, and friendly.

Scoring

Use the following grid to determine the point scores for each statement, by circling the numbers that correspond to your responses (i.e., SA, A, ?, D, SD). Then place the number in the box at the bottom of each column. Finally, add the appropriate column scores to obtain the three subscores and all ten column scores to obtain the total score.

Response	Question Number									
	1	2	3	4	5	6	7	8	9	10
SA	1	5	5	5	1	5	5	1	5	5
A	2	4	4	4	2	4	4	2	4	4
?	3	3	3	3	3	3	3	3	3	3
D	4	2	2	2	4	2	2	4	2	2
SD	5	1	1	1	5	1	1	5	1	1
	A	B	C	D	E	F	G	H	I	J

Joint Decision Process: $A + D + G =$ _____

Openness of Contact: $B + E + I =$ _____

Feelings about Others: $C + F + H =$ _____

Total Score: $A + B + C + D + E + F + G + H + I + J =$ _____

Interpretation

The higher the total score, the more interteam dynamics can be characterized as *cooperative*; the lower the score, the more *competitive* these dynamics. Scores can range from 10 to 50. High scores are above 40, moderate from 25 through 40, and low from 10 through 24. Any score below 30 should be a cause for concern. The three subscale scores may range from 3 through 15. Lower scores suggest *competitive* dynamics. Any score below 10 should be cause for concern.

Discussion Questions

1. Is one of the three factors that comprise the interteam dynamics more important than the others? Which one? Why?
2. What would you conclude if one of the three subscale scores is much higher than the other two? Much lower?
3. Can high scores on one subscale *make up for* low scores on another?

A Case in Point:
Madison Electronics Company

The Madison Electronics Company (MEC) is a nonunionized manufacturer of electrical components for a number of major U.S. firms. The standards for the components vary with the customer but usually must conform to rather close tolerances. Historically, MEC competed successfully with its larger competitors. However, a couple of years ago, MEC started being underbid by many of its competitors. A consulting team was hired to evaluate the production and pricing policies of MEC.

The consultants interviewed managers, researched the practices of competing firms, and reached the conclusion that MEC was not as efficient as its competitors. The consultants mostly made what all managers and most employees agree were minor changes in jobs and work flow to lower unit costs and to increase efficiency. One major change was the introduction of a piece-rate incentive system. Time and motion studies were used to establish rates for the various jobs throughout the company. While there was initial resistance to using such a system, most employees discovered that they can exceed the base rate and thus earn more than their base pay. Management's goal of lowering per unit costs has been achieved, and worker output increased faster than increases in wages. Most employees were happy because their earning ability increased with the new incentive system.

One department that has been unable to meet the established piece rate is the trimming department. The department trims the various parts prior to their being assembled and sold to the customers. The parts are sent directly to trimming from the casting department. The trimmers insert the part into a shearing machine, which trims away burrs and other irregular formations on the parts. After trimming, the parts are sent to milling, where they are smoothed and prepared for assembly and shipped to the intended customer. The work flow is shown in Figure 10.4. If the part does not fit into the shearing equipment, it is rejected and returned to the casting department for possible reworking.

The standard rate set for the trimmer is five hundred units per hour, or four thousand units per day. When the casting machines are properly adjusted, this rate can be attained by a trained employee. However, if the trimmer rejects a part because it does not fit the shearing machine, it is not counted as a unit completed and does not count toward the rate set for the operator. As the dies in the casting department become worn, it becomes increasingly difficult for trimming employees to achieve their established rates of production. This creates special problems since, once the parts are trimmed, employees in the assembly and shipping operations are able to achieve their rates and earn their bonus. Trimmers are quire dissatisfied with the existing system, and turnover for the department is excessive. The manager of the trimming department has asked the casting manager numerous times to replace the dies before they become so worn. The casting manager is reluctant to replace the dies sooner than is absolutely necessary because this increases the downtime for casting employees and keeps them from achieving their established rates. Doing "extra" maintenance on the dies increases overhead costs, which the casting manager wants to avoid.

Management has been very reluctant to change the established piece-rate system. The standard reply has been that the system was developed by specially trained time-and-motion experts and that they knew what they were doing.[60]

Questions

1. What are the major problems facing the managers and groups at MEC? Explain.
2. How would you advise the managers in this case to resolve the problems identified?
3. What do you think of the individual piece-rate compensation system? Why?
4. Evaluate the boundary-spanning roles of the managers of the casting and trimming departments in solving the problems identified.

FIGURE 10.4

Work Flow for Cast Components

Casting → Trimming → Milling → Assembly → Shipping

References

1. Adapted from Kerwin, K. GM's Aurora. *Business Week*, March 21, 1994, 88–95; Plumb, S. E. Aurora team: New day dawning at Oldsmobile. *Ward's Auto World*, September 1993, 77–80; Keebler, J. The new Oldsmobile: Aurora the shining hope of GM division's future. *Automotive News*, July 19, 1993, 1i–12i.

2. Kerwin, K. GM's Aurora. *Business Week*, March 21, 1994, 95.

3. Fisher, R. J. *The Social Psychology of Intergroup and International Conflict Resolution*. New York: Springer-Verlag, 1990.

4. Milliken, F. J. Three types of perceived uncertainty about the environment: State, effect, and response uncertainty. *Academy of Management Review*, 1987, 12, 133–143.

5. Boynton, A. C., Gales, L. M., and Blackburn, R. S. Managerial search activity: The impact of perceived role uncertainty. *Journal of Management*, 1993, 19, 725–747.

6. Thompson, J. D. *Organizations in Action*. New York: McGraw-Hill, 1967.

7. Kaplan, D. Power in perspective. In R. L. Kahn and K. E. Boulding (eds.), *Power and Conflict in Organizations*. London: Tavistock, 1964, 11–32.

8. Rotemberg, J. J. Power in profit-maximizing organizations. *Journal of Economics & Management Strategy*, 1993, 2, 165–198.

9. Adapted from Petrick, J. A. and Quinn, J. F. Developing ethical work cultures at home and abroad. *Business Ethics*, September–October 1993, 30–31.

10. Locke, E. A., and Latham, G. P. *A Theory of Goal Setting and Task Performance*. Englewood Cliffs, N.J.: Prentice-Hall, 1990.

11. Kerwin, K. GM's Aurora. *Business Week*, March 21, 1994, 88–95.

12. Greenwald, J. A growing itch to fight. *Time*, December 6, 1993, 34–35.

13. Boeker, W. The development and institutionalization of subunit power in organizations. *Administrative Science Quarterly*, 1989, 34, 388–410.

14. Schein, E. H. *Organizational Psychology*. Englewood Cliffs, N.J.: Prentice-Hall, 1980, 172–176; Tjosvold, D. *The Conflict-Positive Organization: Stimulate Diversity and Create Unity*. Reading, Mass.: Addison-Wesley, 1991.

15. Hightower, S. Toughing it out. *Bryan–College Station Eagle*, November 28, 1993, C1.

16. Simon, B., and Pettigrew, T. F. Social identity and perceived group homogeneity: Evidence for the ingroup homogeneity effect. *European Journal of Social Psychology*, 1990, 20, 269–286.

17. Cobb, A. T. Political diagnosis: Applications in organization development. *Academy of Management Review*, 1986, 11, 482–496.

18. Sherif, M., and Sherif, C. *Groups in Harmony and Tension: An Integration of Studies on Intergroup Relations*. New York: Octagon, 1966, 231; Smith K. K. Social comparison processes and dynamic conservatism in intergroup relations. In L. L. Cummings and B. M. Staw (eds.), *Research in Organizational Behavior*. Greenwich, Conn.: JAI Press, 1983, 199–233.

19. Blake, R. R., and Morton, J. S. *Solving Costly Organizational Conflicts*. San Francisco: Jossey-Bass, 1984; Likert, R., and Likert, J. G. *New Ways of Managing Conflict*. New York: McGraw-Hill, 1976.

20. Adapted from interview of Bill George—In care of the company soul. *Business Ethics*, November/December 1993, 17–19.

21. Guzzo, R. A. and Shea, G. P. Group performance and intergroup relations in organizations. In M. D. Dunnette and L. M. Hough (eds.), *Handbook of Industrial and Organizational Psychology*, Vol. 3, 2nd Ed. Palo Alto, Calif.: Consulting Psychologists Press, 1992, 269–313.

22. Triandis, H. C., Kurowski, L. L., Gelfand, M. J. Workplace diversity. In H. C. Triandis, M. D. Dunnette, and L. M. Hough (eds.), *Handbook of Industrial and Organizational Psychology*, Vol. 4, 2nd ed. Palo Alto, Calif.: Consulting Psychologists Press, 1994, 769–827.

23. Laden, M., and Rosener, J. B. *Workforce America: Managing Employee Diversity as a Vital Resource*. Homewood, Ill.: Business One-Irwin, 1991, 27–30.

24. Shellenbarger, S. Work-force study finds loyalty is weak: Divisions of race and gender are deep. *Wall Street Journal*, September 3, 1993, B1, B2. Also see Powell, G. N., and Butterfield, D. A. Investigating the "glass ceiling phenomenon: An empirical study of actual promotions to top management. *Academy of Management Journal*, 1994, 37, 68–86.

25. Adapted from Powell, G. N. One more time: Do female and male managers differ? *Academy of Management Executive*, August 1990, 68–75; Powell, G. N. *Women and Men in Management*, 2nd ed. Newbury Park, Calif.: Sage, 1993.

26. Jackson, S. E., and Associates. *Diversity in the Workplace: Human Resource Initiatives*. New York: Gulford Press, 1993.

27. Thornburg, L. Journey toward a more inclusive culture. *HR Magazine*, February 1994, 79. Also see: Keck, S. L., and Tushman, M. L. Environmental and organizational context and executive team structure. *Academy of Management Journal*, 1993, 36, 1314–1344.

28. Triandis, H. C., Kurowski, L. L., and Gelfand, M. J. *Workplace Diversity*, 769–825.

29. Orton, J. D., and Weick, K. E. Loosely coupled systems: A reconceptualization. *Academy of Management Review*, 1990, 15, 203–223.

30. Victor, B., and Blackburn, R. S. Interdependence: An alternative conceptualization. *Academy of Management Review*, 1987, 12, 486–498.

31. Salancik, G. R. An index of influence in dependency networks. *Administrative Science Quarterly*, 1986, 31, 194–211.

32. Pfeffer, J. *Managing with Power: Politics and Influence in Organizations*. Boston: Harvard Business School Press, 1993.

33. Kahn, W. A. and Kram, K. E. Authority at work: Internal models and their organizational consequences. *Academy of Management Review*, 1994, 19, 17–50.

34. Walker, G., and Poppo, L. Profit centers, single-source suppliers, and transaction costs. *Administrative Science Quarterly*, 1991, 36, 66–87.

35. Adapted from Perry, N. J. How to mine human resources. *Fortune*, February 21, 1994, 94.

36. Limerick, D., and Cunnington, B. *Managing the New Organization: A Blueprint for Networks and Strategic Alliances*. San Francisco: Jossey-Bass, 1994.

37. Lackman, R. Power from what? A reexamination of its relationships with structural conditions. *Administrative Science Quarterly*, 1989, 34, 231–251.

38. Hickson, D. J., Hinnings, C. R., Lee, C. A., Schneck, R. E., and Pennings, J. M. Strategic contingencies theory of organizational power. *Administrative Science Quarterly*, 1971, 16, 216–229.

39. Schein, E. H. On dialogue, culture, and organizational learning. *Organizational Dynamics*, Autumn 1993, 40–51; Gudykunst, W. B. *Bridging Differences: Effective Intergroup Communication*. Newbury Park, Calif.: Sage, 1991.

40. Isaacs, W. N. Dialogue, collective thinking, and organizational learning. *Organizational Dynamics*, Autumn 1993, 27.

41. Ibid., 24–39.

42. Adapted from Thornburg, L. Journey toward a more inclusive culture. *HR Magazine*, February 1994, 79–86. Reprinted with the permission of *HR Magazine* published by the Society for Human Resource Management, Alexandria, VA.

43. Sherif, M. Superordinate goals in the reduction of intergroup conflict. *American Journal of Sociology*, 1958, 68, 349–358.

44. Kerwin, K. A chunk of true grit named John Rock. *Business Week*, March 21, 1994, 95.

45. Kramer, R. M. Intergroup relations and organizational dilemmas: The role of categorization processes. In B. M. Staw and L. G. Cummings (eds.), *Research in Organizational Behavior*, Vol. 13. Greenwich, Conn.: JAI Press, 1991, 191–288.

46. Ciampa, D. *Total Quality*. Reading, Mass.: Addison-Wesley, 1992, 10.

47. Omachonu, U. K., and Ross, J. E. *Principles of Total Quality*. Debray Beach, Fla.: St. Lucie Press, 1994.

48. Kolesar, P. J. Visions, values, milestones: Paul O'Neill starts total quality at Alcoa. *California Management Review*, Spring 1993, 146.

49. Ibid., 133–165 (adapted from) .

50. Mintzberg, H. *The Rise and Fall of Strategic Planning: Reconceiving Roles for Planning, Plans, and Planners*. New York: Free Press, 1994.

51. Schwab, R. C., Ungson, G. R., and Brown, W. B. Redefining the boundary spanning–environment relationship. *Journal of Management*, 1985, 11, 75–86.

52. Theus, K. T. Organizations and the media: Structures of miscommunication. *Management Communication Quarterly*, 1993, 7, 67–94.

53. Ancona, D. G., and Caldwell, D. Beyond boundary-spanning: Managing external dependence in product development teams. *Journal of High Technology Management Research*, 1990, 1, 121–135.

54. Mink, O. G., Esterhuysen, P. W., Mink, B. P., and Owen, K. Q. *Change at Work: A Comprehensive Management Process for Transforming Organizations*. San Francisco: Jossey-Bass, 1994.

55. Dumaine, B. Payoff from the new management. *Fortune*, December 13, 1993, 103–110.

56. Adapted from McCume, W. B. Internal communications and participatory management: An experiment in team building. *Public Relations Quarterly*, Fall 1989, 14–18. Reprinted with permission from *Public Relations Quarterly*, Rhinebeck, NY.

57. Kirkpatrick, D. Groupware goes boom. *Fortune*, December 27, 1993, 99–106.

58. Wilke, J. R. Computer links erode hierarchical nature of workplace culture. *Wall Street Journal*, December 9, 1993, A1, A7.

59. Adapted from Sashkin, M., and Morris, W. C. *Organizational Behavior: Concepts and Experiences*. Englewood Cliffs, N.J.: Prentice-Hall, 1984, 239–240. Used with permission.

60. Thomas, J. G. Madison Electronics Company. In S. L. Willey (ed.), *Annual Advances in Business Cases: 1988*. Ames, Iowa: Midwest Society for Case Research, 1988, 289–290. This case was prepared by Professor Joe G. Thomas, Middle Tennessee State University, as a basis for class discussion, rather than to illustrate either effective or ineffective handling of an administrative situation. Presented to the Midwest Society for Case Research Workshop, 1988. All rights reserved to the author. Copyright © 1988 by Joe Thomas. Used with permission.

11 Leadership

LEARNING OBJECTIVES

When you have finished studying this chapter, you should be able to:

▲ Identify the differences between leaders and managers.

▲ List the skills and sources of power that leaders can use to influence subordinates.

▲ Describe the traits model of leadership.

▲ Define two key behavioral leadership dimensions.

▲ Describe Fiedler's contingency model.

▲ Explain the leadership and contingency variables in both Hersey and Blanchard's situational model and House's path–goal model.

▲ Discuss the situational variables in the Vroom–Jago model.

▲ Describe the attributional and charismatic models of leadership.

OUTLINE

Preview Case: Monte Peterson at *Thermos*

Foundations of Leadership

Leader–Subordinate Relationships

Leadership Skills

Managing Diversity: Janet *McLaughlin at Corning Glass*

Sources of Power

Uses of Power

Traditional Leadership Models

Traits Model

Behavioral Models

Managing Across Cultures: The Euro-*peans Are Coming*

Contingency Models of Leadership

Fiedler's Contingency Model

Hersey and Blanchard's Situational Model

Managing In Practice: Stern's Record *at Northern Telecom*

House's Path–Goal Model

Managing Quality: Making Contact *Lenses at Johnson & Johnson*

Vroom–Jago Leadership Model

Managing Quality: Rachel Blaylock at *Primacare*

Comparing the Four Contingency Models

Emerging Leadership Models

Attribution Model

Managing Ethics: You Make the *Decision*

Transformational Model

Managing in Practice: Tom's of *Maine*

DEVELOPING SKILLS

Self-Diagnosis: What's Your *Leadership Style?*

A Case in Point: Southwestern *Manufacturing Company*

PREVIEW CASE

Monte Peterson at Thermos

When Monte Peterson took over as CEO of Thermos Corporation in 1990, he faced his toughest leadership challenge. He needed to reinvent totally the company that was famous for its Thermos bottles and lunch boxes. Sales were lukewarm and the competition (including Sunbeam, Char-Broil, and Weber) was constantly innovating and creating goods that gave their customers high quality at the right price. He believed that, unless employees understood their customers and top management provided them with backing to make changes to satisfy their customers, Thermos was headed for financial trouble.

He created a team of managers and employees from various departments, such as engineering, marketing, and manufacturing, to create new products that used Thermos's vacuum technology. At first, some employees resisted working on the team, but Peterson patiently reminded them that they had a great opportunity to make the market grow. He emphasized how important the project could be to all aspects of the company's business. The team, named lifestyle, went out into the field to learn about people's needs and invent a product to satisfy these. Peterson made sure that no single team member rode roughshod over the others by suggesting that leadership be rotated according to the most pressing task. When the team needed to do field research, for example, the marketing person would take the lead.

Peterson and the team also agreed on a firm deadline and made sure that the project was the primary responsibility of its members. The team discovered that the image of dad with apron and chef's hat, slaving over a smoky charcoal grill, was changing. Women were barbecuing and wanted a grill that would use electricity but get hot enough to sear food and give it that cookout taste. Research and development designed an electric grill with electric heat rods built directly into the surface of the grill and a domed vacuum top that kept the heat inside the grill. The team invited customers to use some sample grills, took notes on their ideas, and based changes to the grill on their suggestions.

Was it worth it? Peterson thinks so. Thermos revenues from its electric grills have grown from 2% to 20% in two years. Thermos has won four design awards for the grill's aesthetics and ease of use. Peterson also found out that he didn't need to offer a special bonus to motivate people. Their reward is being a part of a team that gives them a sense of accomplishment when the product takes off and flies.[1]

Peterson is an effective leader. If we examine how he steered the rebirth of Thermos, two important behaviors stand out. First, he developed an agenda for himself and the company that included a new vision of what the company could and should be. It was a vision of a competitive and profitable firm that produced high-quality, innovative products using the Thermos vacuum technology to keep liquids cold or hot. Second, he gained cooperation from employees by motivating them to buy into this vision. He worked hard to delegate decision making to a team of employees who could make decisions. Employees now had a sense of belonging, recognition, and self-esteem, along with a feeling of control over their work and the ability to live up to their own ideals. These feelings elicited a powerful motivational response from all team members. Peterson maintained these feelings by regularly providing support (financial and marketing) for members of the lifecycle team. Because he did those things, employees' work became intrinsically motivating.

Leadership is the process whereby one person influences others to work toward a goal[2] and helps them pursue a vision. Monte Peterson exercised leadership by guiding and influencing employees in developing a new product line for Thermos.

Not all employees or managers exercise leadership. A good manager isn't necessarily a good leader. A **manager** is a person who directs the work of employees and is responsible for results. An effective manager brings a degree of order and consistency to tasks. A **leader,** by contrast, inspires employees with a vision and helps them cope with change. Let's explore these differences more closely.[3]

Managers handle complexity through *planning* and *budgeting*: setting goals, determining how to achieve those goals, and then allocating resources to achieve those goals. By contrast, leaders start by articulating a *direction* or *vision* of what the future might look like and then developing strategies for producing changes needed to move in that direction. According to William McCowan, chairman and CEO of MCI Communications, vision is the art of seeing beyond the present to seeing the possible. In uncertain times, employees look to leaders for vision. Like yeast, it is a leavening agent, and it stimulates the organization to grow and change. In its earliest days, MCI's vision of leadership in the global communications industry kept the company on course. This vision helped MCI beat the competition and enabled employees to take risks and be innovative entrepreneurs.

Managers achieve their goals by *organizing* and *staffing*: creating an organizational structure and sets of jobs for accomplishing the plan's requirements, staffing the jobs with qualified employees, communicating the goals to those employees, and devising systems to monitor the employees' progress toward achieving those goals. Leaders *recruit* and *keep* employees who understand and share their visions.

Finally, managers ensure that employees reach goals by *controlling* their behaviors: monitoring results in great detail by means of reports and meetings and noting deviations from plans. Leaders *motivate* and *inspire* teams of employees, as Monte Peterson did at Thermos. Leaders tap employees' needs, values, and emotions.[4] Peterson successfully motivated employees to overcome obstacles, such as the lack of product development, that the company faced when he took over by empowering them to make decisions. In doing so, he changed his job from one of monitoring others to one of motivating them.

Hence some managers are leaders, but others are not, as Figure 11.1 shows. Each role—manager and leader—requires different behaviors. Return to the

FIGURE 11.1

Behaviors of Leaders and Managers

Managers Who Also Are Leaders

Leaders' Behaviors

• Vision and direction

• Align employees

• Inspire and motivate

Managers' Behaviors

• Plan and budget

• Organize and staff

• Control

Preview Case and evaluate Monte Peterson's behaviors. What role(s) did he play at Thermos to help the lifecycle team achieve its goal?

▼ FOUNDATIONS OF LEADERSHIP

Leadership always has been, and probably always will be, important to organizations. Recently, the need for leadership and the difficulty of providing it have grown dramatically because of ever-increasing complexity of business. Hundreds of firms and dozens of industries have been restructured to remain competitive. The banking industry provides a good example. Since federal deregulation, the local bank's competition is not just the bank down the street. It also is Sears, Merrill Lynch, American Express, foreign banks, and General Electric. Similarly, the airline, insurance, automobile, health care, and other industries face new competitive pressures every day.

▼ Leader–Subordinate Relationships

Subordinates consider leadership to be valuable, but leaders become an integral part of an organization, group, or team only after proving their competence and value. People in leadership positions receive economic and psychological rewards. Many top executives are paid up to 150 times as much as their lowest paid employees. (However, opposition to the great—and growing—disparity between executive and workers' pay is beginning to emerge.) But some people seek positions of leadership even when there are no economic rewards. The captain of a collegiate basketball team, a union steward, and the chairperson of a civic or church committee do not hold paid positions, but they usually exercise leadership. Leadership grants people power over others; with this power, people believe that they can influence to some extent the well-being of others and can affect their own destinies.

Leaders receive their authority from subordinates because the subordinates have accepted them as leaders. To maintain a leadership position, a person must enable others to gain satisfactions that are otherwise beyond their reach. In return, they satisfy the leader's need for power and prominence and give the leader the support necessary to reach organizational goals.

▼ Leadership Skills

Both Monte Peterson and William McCowan are successful leaders, but the processes they use to reach their goals are quite different. Both share several common skills (shown in Figure 11.2) with many other successful leaders.[5]

Creating a Vision Leaders attract employees by creating a vision. People want to be part of an organization that has a vision larger than reality. When a leader can share a vision with others and get them committed to it, this vision "grabs" them. Both Peterson of Thermos and McCowan of MCI are such leaders. Their employees become so caught up in what they are doing that they absorb and commit themselves to their leaders' goals and values. The visions that leaders convey instill confidence in others, a confidence that leads them to believe that they can succeed.

FIGURE 11.2

Effective Leadership Skills

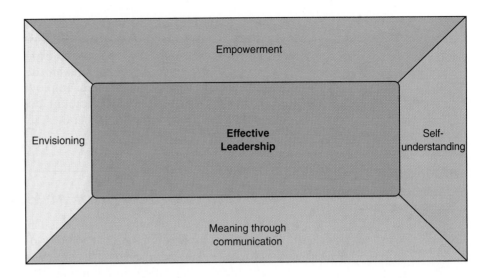

Meaning Through Communication   Successful leaders communicate effectively with their employees. Such leaders can articulate a compelling vision of what can be accomplished—the kind of vision that induces enthusiasm and commitment in others. The old method of telling people what to do just doesn't work in many cases any more. In Peterson's case, he used the National Hardware Show held in Chicago to focus the team's enthusiasm and commitment; he and the team agreed to have the new product ready for the show. The team also responded positively to what consumers told them about their prototype grill (e.g., such as the legs needed to be straight and the shelves needed to be stronger).

Empowerment   The sharing of influence and control with employees is **empowerment.** It gives employees a stake in developing goals and strategies, being productive, and deriving satisfaction from reaching those goals. At Thermos the team talked directly to customers and involved them in the decision-making process, such as suggesting a price range for the grill, stronger shelves, and the like. Effective leaders usually are not dictators but rather are sensitive to the needs of employees. They tap the motivations and capabilities in others to pursue shared goals. The behaviors associated with empowerment include taking delight in an employee's development, realizing that visions are achieved by teams and not by individual employees, and helping employees reach their personal goals.[6] Responsible employees don't often make decisions that are inconsistent with their goals, especially goals that they helped shape.

Self-Understanding   Effective leaders recognize their strengths and weaknesses and tend to hire employees who can offset their weaknesses. They are eager to receive feedback on their performance and continually take an inventory of themselves: "What am I really good at?" "What are my strengths?" "What do I lack?" and "What do I need to work on?"

These leadership skills can be learned. In many organizations (e.g., Texas Instruments, General Foods, and Johnson & Johnson), potential leaders early in their careers get the types of job experience that help them develop these skills. Many global organizations are developing leaders to deal with great diversity in terms of customers, employees, and other stakeholders. The following Managing Diversity account describes how Corning, a $3.7 billion glass-products manufacturer, handles diversity in its leadership program.

MANAGING DIVERSITY

Janet McLaughlin at Corning Glass

When James Houghton took over as Chairman of Corning Glass, his vision for the company emphasized valuing diversity and the integrity of all employees. He also believed that employees should spend 5% of their time in meaningful education and training. Based on this vision and belief, Janet McLaughlin, head of Corning's strategic corporate education, launched programs designed to enhance how women, African-Americans, and others could grow, be challenged, and contribute fully. Using her leadership skills, she and her staff created programs that changed the way employees do business at Corning.

McLaughlin and her staff created a course entitled "Valuing Diversity" that all employees are required to attend. The 18-month program begins with an awareness-raising course that outlines Corning's beliefs. McLaughlin encourages participants to talk about gender issues, sexual harassment, and the expanding opportunities for women and minority employees. Seeing a group of employees talking about a child care issue or that the language just used in a meeting was offensive because it belittled women or a minority group isn't unusual.

To put some teeth into the program, managers are evaluated on how well they support women and minorities in their departments. Managers who aren't actively involved in the careers of such employees usually are not promoted. McLaughlin and her staff also actively lobbied a local cable television service to add the Black Entertainment Television network to its schedule and helped the local school district recruit more minority teachers. The company also built a day care center near its main plant in Corning, New York, added flexible work schedules, and a 20-week parental-leave policy (compared to 12 weeks offered by most employers). Promotions depend partly on how successfully employees implement what they learn in these courses.[7]

▼ Sources of Power

To influence others, a person must appeal to one or more of their needs. If a robber is pointing a gun at a bank teller and is ready to fire it, chances are that the teller will do what the robber asks. However, history proves that, in many situations, people refuse to obey an order even when faced with death. Similarly, effective leadership depends as much on acceptance by the follower as what the leader does. Power and influence are central to a leader's job. In Chapter 15, we discuss the sources of a manager's power; so here we consider only briefly the sources of a leader's power.[8]

Legitimate Power   Employees may do something because the leader has the right to request them to do it and they have an obligation to comply. This **legitimate power** comes from the leader's position in the organization. Employees in the cosmetics division of Liz Claiborne, Inc., follow the directions of Susan Doelz in making marketing decisions because she is the head of marketing in that division. Speeders usually pull over when they see blue and/or red lights flashing on a police car because they believe that police have a legitimate right to ticket speeders.

Reward Power   Employees may do something to get rewards that the leader controls (such as promotions, pay raises, and better assignments). Thus **reward power** comes from the leader's ability to provide something desired by team members in return for their desired behaviors. Janet McLaughlin's vision for Corning's diversity programs enabled the company to become more competitive in its industry and to reward employees with pay raises.

Coercive Power   Employees may do something to avoid punishments that the leader controls, such as demotions, reprimands, no pay raises, and termination. **Coercive power** is the potential to influence others through the use of sanctions or punishment. Unfortunately, coercive power doesn't necessarily encourage desired behavior. In Chapter 5, we described how team members whom managers reprimand for poor workmanship may suddenly slow production, stop working altogether, be absent more often, and take other negative actions.

Referent Power   Employees may do something because they admire the leader, want to be like the leader, and want to receive the leader's approval. **Referent power** usually is associated with individuals who possess admired personal characteristics, such as charisma, integrity, and courage. Anita Roddick, CEO of the Body Shop, possesses referent power because of her environmental, political, and human rights stands.

Expert Power   Employees may do something because they believe that the leader has special knowledge and expertise and knows what is needed to accomplish the task. **Expert power** has a narrow scope: Employees are influenced by a leader only within that leader's area of expertise. The expert power of Janet Reno, U.S. Attorney General and a member of President Clinton's cabinet, are confined to the Justice Department, whereas Janet McLaughlin's expert powers are confined to human resource issues.

▼ Uses of Power

Figure 11.3 divides these sources of power into the personal and the organizational. Legitimate, reward, and coercive powers are organizational, and company rules prescribe them. Part of the leader's job is to use them wisely to motivate group or team members. A team probably will not achieve exceptional levels of performance if its leader relies solely on organizational power. Thus reliance on referent and expert power—personal power—can lead to greater job satisfaction and less absenteeism and turnover. However, a leader normally uses all five sources of power at various times, depending on the situation, to obtain both follower satisfaction and productivity.[9]

FIGURE 11.3

Sources of a Leader's Power and Effectiveness

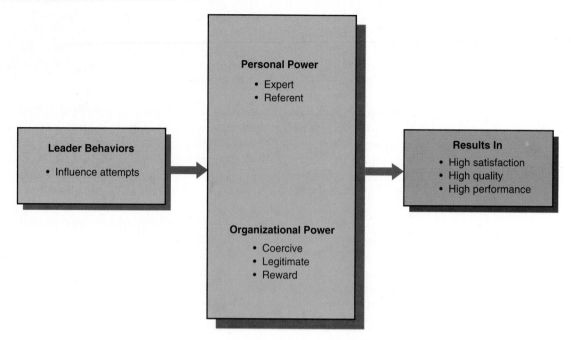

The bases of power in organizations are changing because of changing technology, the increasing ability of employees to obtain and use information to make decisions, and the flattening of the management hierarchy. For example, as employees at Thermos became experts in making decisions pertaining to the electric grill, the need for the CEO to display his expertise in this area lessened. Leaders must empower employees to get results. Another leader who has done so is Ralph Stayer, CEO of Johnsonville Foods, a specialty foods and sausage maker in Sheboygan, Wisconsin. Said Stayer, "Flattening pyramids doesn't work if you don't transfer the power, too. Before, I didn't have power because I had people wandering around not giving a damn. Real power is getting people committed. It comes from giving it to others who are in a better position to do things than you are. The only control a leader can possibly have comes when people are controlling themselves."[10]

▼ TRADITIONAL LEADERSHIP MODELS

Many people believe that they have the intuitive ability to identify outstanding leaders. Often they believe that people with pleasing personalities will be highly successful leaders and select those who have personal charm as leaders. Although some people have that intuitive ability, most do not. However, there are better ways to assess leadership potential and effectiveness. In the remainder of this chapter, we present and examine five general approaches to assessing leadership: traits, behavioral, contingency, and two of the latest approaches—attributional and charismatic.

▼ Traits Model

The **traits model** is based on observed characteristics of many leaders—both successful and unsuccessful. The resulting lists of traits—drive, originality, high energy, extraversion, introversion, and so on—are then compared to those of potential leaders to predict their success or failure. There is support for the notion that effective leaders have interests and abilities and, perhaps, even personality traits that are different from those of less effective leaders. Most researchers, however, believe that the traits approach is inadequate for successfully predicting leadership performance for at least three reasons.[11]

First, although more than 100 personality traits of successful leaders have been identified, no consistent patterns have been found. The trait stereotypes of successful leaders in charge of salespeople include optimism, enthusiasm, and dominance. Successful production leaders are usually progressive, introverted, cooperative, and genuinely respectful of employees. However, many successful leaders of salespeople and production employees do not have all, or even some, of these characteristics. In fact, the list of personality traits never ends, and researchers often disagree over which traits are the most important for an effective leader. Furthermore, two leaders with significantly different traits have been successful in the same situation.[12]

Despite these difficulties, the evidence suggests that most (but not all) successful leaders share four traits. These traits are more likely to be found in middle-level and top managers than in team leaders or first-line supervisors.

- ▲ *Intelligence.* Leaders tend to have somewhat higher intelligence than their subordinates.
- ▲ *Maturity and breadth.* Leaders tend to be emotionally mature and have a broad range of interests.
- ▲ *Inner motivation and achievement drive.* Leaders want to accomplish things; when they achieve one goal, they seek another. They don't depend primarily on employees for their motivation to achieve goals.
- ▲ *Employee-centered.* Leaders are able to work effectively with employees in a variety of situations. They respect others and realize that, to accomplish tasks, they must be considerate of others' needs and values.

The second criticism of the traits model relates physical characteristics such as height, weight, appearance, physique, energy, and health to effective leadership. Most of these factors are related to situational factors that can significantly affect a leader's effectiveness. For example, military or law enforcement people must be a particular minimum height, weight, and strength in order to perform certain tasks effectively. Such characteristics may help an individual rise to a leadership position in an organization, but height, weight, and strength don't correlate highly with leadership performance. Moreover, in educational or business organizations, height, weight, and strength play no role in task performance and thus are not requirements for a leadership position.

The final criticism of the traits model is that leadership itself is complex. A relationship between personality and a person's interest in particular types of jobs could well exist but a study relating personality and effectiveness does not reflect it. For example, one study found that high earners (a measure of success) in small firms were more ambitious, were more open-minded, and described themselves as more considerate than low earners. But in small firms, a leader usually performs numerous jobs. People who like performing multiple jobs may seek out small firms that permit them to do so.

▼ Behavioral Models

Because of the failure of the traits model to predict successful leadership accurately, researchers shifted their emphasis from trying to identify leaders' traits to studying leaders' behaviors. That is, what leaders actually *do* and how they do it instead of studying *who* they are. Behavioral models suggest that effective leaders help individuals and teams achieve their goals in two ways: (1) by having task-centered relations with members that focus attention on the quality and quantity of work accomplished; and (2) by being considerate and supportive of members' attempts to achieve personal goals (e.g., work satisfaction, promotions, and recognition), settling disputes, keeping people happy, providing encouragement, and giving positive reinforcement.

Ohio State University Leadership Studies   The largest number of studies of leader behavior have come from the Ohio State University leadership studies program, which began in the late 1940s under the direction of Ralph Stogdill.[13] That research was aimed at identifying leader behaviors that foster the attainment of team and organizational goals. These efforts resulted in the identification of two essential dimensions of leader behavior: consideration and initiating structure.

Consideration is the extent to which leaders are likely to have job relationships that are characterized by mutual trust, two-way communication, respect for employees' ideas, and consideration for their feelings. Leaders with this style emphasize the needs of the employee. They typically find time to listen to employees, are willing to make changes, look out for the personal welfare of employees, and are friendly and approachable. A high degree of consideration indicates psychological closeness between leader and employee; a low degree shows greater psychological distance and a more impersonal leader.

Initiating structure is the extent to which managers are likely to define and structure their roles and those of employees. Managers with this style emphasize direction of group activities through planning, communicating information, scheduling, assigning tasks, emphasizing deadlines, and giving directions. They maintain definite standards of performance and ask subordinates to follow standard rules. In short, leaders with a high degree of initiating structure concern themselves with accomplishing tasks by giving directions and expecting them to be followed.

The research also indicates that a leader who emphasizes consideration generally fosters employee satisfaction, group harmony, and cohesion. A leader who emphasizes initiating structure generally improves productivity, at least in the short run. However, leaders that rank high on initiating structure and low on consideration generally have large numbers of grievances, absenteeism, and high turnover rates among employees. We might rank Monte Peterson of Thermos high on consideration and low on initiating structure. We might rank Janet McLaughlin of Corning as moderate on initiating structure and high on consideration.

The Ohio State University researchers made the assumption that leader behavior is related not only to indirect measures of performance, such as absenteeism, grievances, and turnover, but also to direct measures of performance, such as the number of units produced. Later studies by others have failed to show a significant relationship between leadership behavior and group performance.[14] This failure indicates that individual productivity is influenced by other factors, including (1) the employee's social status within the group, (2) the technology used, (3) the employee's expectations of a certain style of leadership, and (4) the employee's psychological rewards from working with a particular type of leader.

When Is Consideration Effective?   The most positive effects of leader consideration on group members' productivity and job satisfaction occur when (1) the task is routine and denies employees any job satisfaction, (2) employees are predisposed toward participative leadership, (3) team members must learn something new, (4) employees feel that their involvement in the decision-making process is legitimate and affects their job performance, and (5) few status differences exist between leader and subordinate.

When Is Initiating Structure Effective?   The most positive effects of leader initiating structure on members' productivity and job satisfaction occur when (1) a high degree of pressure for output is imposed by someone other than the leader, (2) the task satisfies employees, (3) employees depend on the leader for information and direction on how to complete the task, (4) employees are psychologically predisposed toward being told what to do and how to do it, and (5) no more than 12 employees report to the leader.[15]

The following Managing Across Cultures item illustrates some of the leadership problems facing European leaders. Many European companies, such as Daimler-Benz, BMW, and Thomson Consumer Electronics, realize that they are having to fight for business. Driven by stiffer competition, a steady erosion of both market share and profits as costs rise out of control, a new type of leader is taking charge. These new leaders are unlike their predecessors who often relied on an easygoing, collegial style to get things done. In the past, employees rarely challenged their leaders. Now that performance counts, employees are challenging their leaders to make decisions that will improve productivity and save their jobs.

MANAGING ACROSS CULTURES

The Europeans Are Coming

Noel Goutard, CEO of the French auto parts company Valeo, has changed most things about this business. Budgets now are prepared once every six months so that Valeo can shift or readjust its marketing strategy to the demands of Europe's auto industry. He grouped workers into teams that are responsible for organizing their own activities. Each team meets for five minutes or so every morning and for an hour once a week to talk about production problems and ways to improve. Every worker is expected to make

MANAGING ACROSS CULTURES —*Continued*

ten suggestions for improvement per year. The rallying cry heard throughout the plant is "quality, service, and price." Goutard reinforces these buzzwords daily by posting reminders on bulletin boards throughout the plant.

Another new leader is Percy Barnevik, CEO of ABB, a Swedish engineering company. Barnevik turned a sleepy company into a highly effective global competitor by creating profit centers, each with its own balance sheet, and reducing staff at headquarters in Zurich from 4,000 to 200. Instead of using staff, he now relies on getting some administrative work, such as training and development, done for less money outside ABB. He insists that managers work with suppliers to lower costs and that suppliers show ABB's managers how that can be done. Instead of giving suppliers a new design, ABB asks the supplier to create its own design within certain guidelines.[16]

What style of leadership do these leaders use? What are their bases of power? Would their style be effective in the United States?

Limitations of the Behavioral Model   The Ohio State University research paid attention primarily to relationships between leader and employee. Its principal limitation was that it paid little attention to the situation in which the relationships occurred and its effects on leadership style. For example, compare the situations facing the two European leaders to those facing Thermos's Peterson and Corning's McLaughlin. Do these different situations account for the success of the different leadership styles? The importance of the situation is the basis of the contingency, or situational, models of leadership.

▼ CONTINGENCY LEADERSHIP MODELS

Research into the leadership process before the mid 1960s showed no consistent relationship between leadership style and measures of performance, group processes, and job satisfaction. Although many researchers concluded that the situation in which a leader functions plays a significant role in determining the leader's effectiveness, they did little to identify the key situational variables.

Contingency leadership theorists, in contrast, direct their research toward discovering the variables that make certain leadership characteristics and behaviors effective in a specific situation. For example, contingency theorists would say that a team leader at Chaparral Steel in charge of buying a new $2.3 million steel mill and the director of marketing at Baxter International creating an advertising strategy for a new drug face substantially different situations. Hence they may choose different leadership styles to reach their objectives. According to contingency models, both leaders can be effective if they do so.

The contingency variables most often suggested as influences on a leader's behavior are (1) a leader's personal characteristics, (2) employees' personal characteristics, (3) the group's characteristics, and (4) the structure of the group, department, or organization. As suggested in Figure 11.4, these four variables interact to influence a leader's style of behavior. The leadership pro-

FIGURE 11.4

Contingency Variables That Affect Leader Behavior

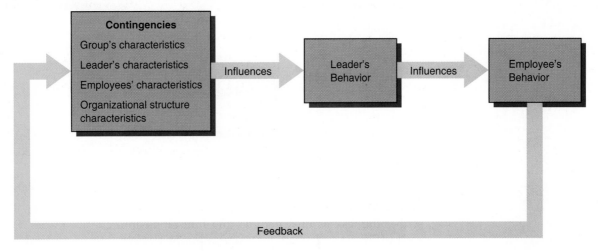

cess is complex, and simple prescriptions (such as "democratic leaders have more satisfied employees than autocratic leaders") just do not work.

In this section, we present and discuss four specific contingency models of leadership: Fiedler's contingency model, Hersey and Blanchard's situational leadership model, House's path–goal model, and the Vroom–Jago model. Each at least partially explains how some of the contingency variables affect leadership.

▼ Fiedler's Contingency Model

Fred Fiedler and his associates developed the first contingency model of leadership.[17] **Fiedler's contingency model** specifies that performance is contingent upon both the leader's motivational system and the degree to which the leader controls and influences the situation. Figure 11.5 shows the model's three contingency variables: group atmosphere, task structure, and the leader's position power.

Group Atmosphere   Group atmosphere refers to a leader's acceptance by the team. The leader who is accepted by and inspires loyalty in employees needs few displays of rank to get them to commit themselves to a task. When a leader and employees get along well together, there is less friction. In groups that reject a leader, the leader's basic problem is to keep employees from bypassing him or her or sabotaging the task.

Task Structure   The extent to which a task performed by employees is routine or nonroutine is the degree of **task structure.** A routine task is likely to have clearly defined goals, to comprise only a few steps or procedures, to be verifiable, and to have a correct solution. At the other extreme is the nonroutine task, which the leader may no more know how to perform than the employees do. Such a task is likely to have unclear goals and multiple paths to accomplishment; the task cannot be done by the "numbers."

FIGURE 11.5

Variables in Fiedler's Contingency Model

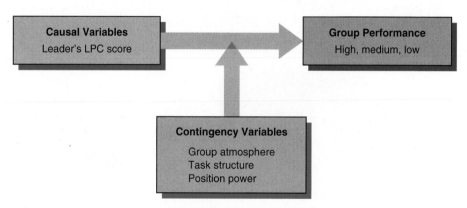

Source: Yukl, G. A. *Leadership in Organizations*, 196. Copyright © 1989 by Prentice-Hall, Inc., Englewood Cliffs, N.J. Adapted with permission.

Jean-Marie Descarpentries runs Franco-British CMB Packaging. He describes the task as unstructured and himself as an orchestra leader. He runs each of his 94 organizations as separate businesses, but in the end they all must work together to achieve the organization's goals. Instead of tight budgets, he and his staff set financial targets that are designed to stretch all employees, including themselves. He uses these targets primarily to get employees to dream the impossible. Because each business has its own set of problems and opportunities, he evaluates them mainly on how well they do this year versus last year and how they stack up against industry leaders. Descarpentries calls it "management by pride." As a leader, his job is offering consulting advice, not orders.[18]

Position Power   Position power is the extent to which a leader has reward, coercive, and legitimate power. In most business organizations, leaders have high position power, including the authority to hire, discipline, and fire employees. In most voluntary organizations, committees, and social organizations, leaders tend to have low position power.

Leadership Style   Fiedler developed the **least preferred co-worker** (LPC) scale to measure leadership style. Scores are obtained by asking employees first to think about all the people with whom they have worked and then to identify the individual with whom they have worked least well. The person then rates this least preferred co-worker on a set of 18 scales, 5 of which are as follows:

Pleasant									Unpleasant
	8	7	6	5	4	3	2	1	
Friendly									Unfriendly
	8	7	6	5	4	3	2	1	
Accepting									Rejecting
	8	7	6	5	4	3	2	1	
Relaxed									Tense
	8	7	6	5	4	3	2	1	
Close									Distant
	8	7	6	5	4	3	2	1	

Low-LPC leaders describe their least preferred co-worker in negative terms. Low LPC leaders are primarily motivated by the task and gain satisfaction from accomplishing the task. If tasks are being accomplished satisfactorily, low-LPC leaders will try to form and maintain relationships with their subordinates. Thus low-LPC leaders focus on improving relationships with their subordinates *after* they are assured that the assigned tasks are being completed. *High-LPC* leaders give a more positive description of their least preferred co-worker and are sensitive to others. They are motivated primarily by establishing and maintaining close interpersonal relationships. High-LPC leaders focus on establishing good relationships with their subordinates and *then* concentrate on task accomplishment.

How Well Does It Work?   Fiedler's answer to how well it works is: It all depends. What it all depends on are the situational factors—leader–member relations, task structure, and leader power. Fiedler suggests that whether low-LPC or high-LPC leaders are more effective depends on the degree to which the situation is favorable to the leader. In other words, effectiveness depends on the degree to which the situation provides the leader with influence over others.

The three contingency variables create eight situations, as shown in Figure 11.6, which graphically represents Fiedler's contingency model. It shows the average results of the studies that Fiedler and his associates conducted. Task-motivated (low-LPC) leaders performed more effectively than high-LPC leaders in the most favorable situations (1, 2, and 3) and in the least favorable

FIGURE 11.6

Continuum of the Three Basic Leadership Variables

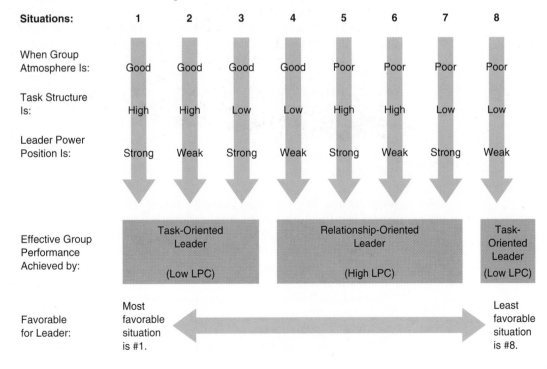

situation (8). Low-LPC leaders are motivated basically by task accomplishments. In the most favorable situation, (1), they will strive to develop pleasant work relations while directing group members. They realize that conditions are good and that successful task performance is likely. As a result, they can turn their attention to improving their relations with team members and often adopt a "hands off" style. Employees value such treatment, and satisfaction and performance remain high. In many respects, this situation was the one that Monte Peterson faced at Thermos. Recall that he essentially let the life-cycle team work on the new electric grill without much direction after the team agreed on the deadline and the type of product to be introduced. In the least favorable situation (8), leaders will strive to achieve organizational goals by telling employees what to do. In many respects, this situation was the one that both Percy Barneik at ABB and Noel Goutard at Valeo faced.

Figure 11.6 also shows situations in which high-LPC leaders probably will perform more effectively than low-LPC leaders. High-LPC leaders get the best performance under conditions that are moderately favorable (situations 4–7). Situations 4 and 5 describe cases in which (1) the group has a structured task but dislikes the leader, who must demonstrate concern for the emotions of employees; or (2) the group likes the leader but has an unstructured task, and the leader must depend on the willingness and creativity of group members to accomplish its goals. As a result, high-LPC leaders may shift their attention to task performance. Ygnacio Dominquez, a business development manager at IBM, is a high-LPC leader who provides guidance to his team members when they start a new task. When they have learned how to proceed and their task becomes more structured, he delegates decision-making authority to them and supports their decisions.

Fiedler's contingency model has several problems.[19] In particular, critics have questioned the use of LPC, arguing that better measures of leader behaviors are needed. They call LPC a one-dimensional concept; that is, it implies that, if individuals are highly motivated toward task accomplishment, they are unconcerned with relations among employees and vice versa. Fiedler also assumes that a person's LPC score is constant over time and unlikely to change. In addition, critics say that Fiedler's model doesn't consider that leaders can influence both the task structure and group atmosphere because of their knowledge of the situation. That is, the task can be changed by the leader and therefore isn't a contingency variable. The nature of the employee's task can be determined, at least in part, by the leader's style. In other words, a leader can take a messy, poorly defined problem and structure it before presenting it to others.

Implications for Leaders.   Despite these criticisms, Fiedler's contingency model has three important implications for leaders. First, both relationship-motivated and task-motivated leaders perform well in certain situations but not in others. Outstanding people at one level who are promoted may fail at the higher level because their leadership style doesn't match the demands of the situation.[20]

Second, leaders' performance depends both on their motivational bases and the situation. Therefore an organization can affect leadership by changing the reward system for the leader or by modifying the situation.

Third, leaders can do something about their situations. Table 11.1 presents some of Fiedler's suggestions for changing particular contingency variables.

TABLE 11.1   Leadership Actions to Change Contingency Variables

Modifying Group Atmosphere

1. Spend more—or less—informal time with your employees (lunch, leisure activities, etc.).

2. Request particular people to work in your team.

3. Volunteer to direct difficult or troublesome employees.

4. Suggest or effect transfers of particular employees into or out of your department.

5. Raise morale by obtaining positive outcomes for team members (e.g., special bonuses, time off, attractive jobs).

Modifying Task Structure

If you want to work with less structured tasks, you can

1. ask your leader, whenever possible, to give you the new or unusual problems and let you figure out how to get them done; and

2. bring the problems and tasks to your team members and invite them to work with you on the planning and decision-making phases of the tasks.

If you want to work with more highly structured tasks, you can

1. ask your leader to give you, whenever possible, the tasks that are more structured or to give you more detailed instructions; and

2. break the job down into smaller subtasks that can be more highly structured.

Modifying Position Power

To raise your position power, you can

1. show others "who's boss" by exercising fully the powers that the organization provides; and

2. make sure that information to others gets channeled through you.

To lower your position power, you can

1. call on team members to participate in planning and decision-making functions; and

2. delegate decision making to others.

Source: Developed from Fiedler, F. E., and Garcia, J. E. *New Approaches to Effective Leadership.* New York: John Wiley & Sons, 1987, 49–93.

He suggests that leaders can be taught how to become better leaders. **Leader match** is a self-teaching process utilizing a programmed learning text that instructs the individual on matching his or her LPC level with the situation. A leader could achieve this match either by changing the situation to fit the leader's LPC style or by moving to a new position in the organization.

▼ Hersey and Blanchard's Situational Model

Hersey and Blanchard's model is based on the amount of relationship (supportive) and task (directive) behavior that a leader provides in a situation. The amount of either relationship or task behavior is based on the readiness of the follower.[21]

Task behavior is the extent to which a leader spells out to followers what to do, where to do it, and how to do it. Leaders who use task behavior structure, control, and closely supervise the behaviors of their followers. **Relationship behavior** is the extent to which a leader listens, provides support and encouragement, and involves followers in the decision-making process. **Follower readiness** is subordinates' ability and willingness to perform the task. Followers have various levels of readiness (R), as Figure 11.7 shows. At R1

FIGURE 11.7

Hersey and Blanchard's
Situational Leadership Model

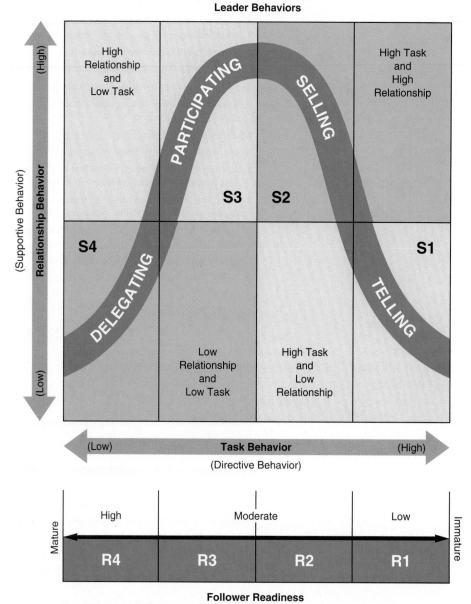

Source: Hersey, P., and Blanchard, K. H. *Management of Organizational Behavior: Utilizing Human Resources*, 5th ed., Englewood Cliffs, N.J.: Prentice-Hall, 1988. Used by permission from Ronald Campbell, President, Leadership Studies, Escondido, California, June 1994.

the followers are either unable or unwilling to perform the task, whereas at R4 they are able, willing, and confident that they can achieve the task. At R2 followers are unable but willing or confident to perform a task. At R3 subordinates are able to do the task but are either unwilling or not totally confident about their abilities to do so. According to situational leadership, as the readiness level of individuals increases from R1 to R4, a leader should change his or her style to increase subordinates' commitment, competence, and performance.

Leader's Style and Followers' Readiness Figure 11.7 also shows how the model links task and relationship leader behaviors and follower readiness. The curve running through the four leadership quadrants identifies the appropriate style of leadership.

A **telling style** provides clear and specific instruction. If subordinates are either unable or unwilling to perform the task, specific direction and close supervision are needed. The leader tells subordinates what to do and where to perform various tasks.

A **selling style** is effective when the subordinates are willing but somewhat unable to carry out their task. The selling style provides both task and relationship leader behaviors. With subordinates who still are unable to perform the task but are eager to do it, a selling style is most effective. This style encourages two-way communication between the leader and subordinates and helps them build confidence in their ability to perform the task.

A **participating style** works best when the subordinates are able but not fully confident of their ability to perform the task. This moderate level of follower readiness requires the leader to maintain two-way communication and to encourage and support the skills the followers have developed.

When followers are able, willing, and confident to perform their tasks, a delegating style of leader behavior is most appropriate. A **delegating style** involves few leader task or relationship behaviors because subordinates are empowered to make decisions. They decide how and when to do things.

The following Managing in Practice account focuses on Paul Stern's leadership practices at Northern Telecom Ltd. In 1990, it had recruited Paul Stern to become its CEO, but in January 1993 he announced his intention to leave. During his tenure, he had driven the company to record profits but also huge financial losses, created furious customers, and watched morale drop to new low levels. What happened? Using Hersey and Blanchard's model, we can gain some insight into his failure as a leader. The numbers and letters in parentheses indicate the parts of Hersey and Blanchard's model that apply to his leadership style and his subordinates' readiness levels.

MANAGING IN PRACTICE

Stern's Record at Northern Telecom

Paul Stern's leadership style has been described as "relentless, and imperial" **(S1).** He told employees what to do instead of asking for their input **(R1).** He decided, for example, that all employees who dealt with customers should start wearing uniforms. A vice-president who made the mistake of questioning this order was dismissed. He reorganized the company to create separate global product divisions so that he could monitor business results more closely. His concern with making profits caused him to put off launching much-needed, but expensive, research programs to revamp Northern's products.

He knew nothing about marketing and didn't trust employees in that department to design new products that would satisfy Northern's customers **(R1).** Many of these employees had built long-standing relationships with customers and wanted to continue satisfying their needs **(R4).** He even issued an order threatening to dismiss any employee involved with a holiday party on

MANAGING IN PRACTICE —*Continued*

company time. Employees who disagreed with his strategy lived in fear of losing their jobs. Many sales employees viewed his strategy, called Vision 2000, as unattainable. They had no input into the sales numbers and knew that they couldn't deliver the products **(R3).** This heightened the morale problem in the company and caused several senior marketing managers to resign.[22]

Implications for Leaders   Hersey and Blanchard's situational model has generated a lot of interest. The idea that people should be flexible in choosing a leadership style is appealing to many leaders and organizations. The model is relatively simple to understand and its recommendations are straightforward. The leader must constantly check the readiness level of employees in order to determine which combination of task and relationship behaviors would be most appropriate at any particular time. An inexperienced employee (low readiness) may perform as well as an experienced employee if directed and closely supervised. An appropriate style also should help employees increase their level of readiness. Thus, as a leader develops a team and helps them learn to manage themselves, leadership style needs to change to fit the situation.

This model has some drawbacks.[23] First, if each team member has a different readiness level, how does a leader decide which style is most appropriate? Does the leader assume an average readiness and choose a leadership style accordingly? Second, the model relies only on one contingency factor—follower readiness. In most situations, time, work, and other pressures also influence a leader's choice of behavior and must be taken into account. Third, the model holds that leaders can adapt their leadership style to fit the situation. How adaptable might Paul Stern's leader behaviors be? Fourth, although thousands of organizations use the model to train people to improve their diagnostic abilities, research doesn't strongly support its results. Some studies verify positive outcomes, but others haven't been able to do so.

▼ House's Path–Goal Model

Puzzled by the contradictory research findings on leadership, Robert J. House developed a model based on the expectancy theory of motivation (see Chapter 6). **House's path–goal model** suggests that, to be effective, a leader must select a style that enhances employees' satisfaction with their jobs and increases their performance levels. A leader can do so by clarifying the nature of the task, reducing roadblocks to successful task completion, and increasing opportunities for employees to feel worthwhile. The model further states that employees will be motivated when the leader performs these functions. Employees are satisfied with their jobs to the extent that performance leads to rewards they value highly.[24] Figure 11.8 shows House's general model.

Leader Behaviors   The model identifies four distinct types of leader behavior.

▲ **Supportive leadership** includes considering the needs of employees, displaying concern for their welfare, and creating a friendly climate in the

FIGURE 11.8

House's Path–Goal Model

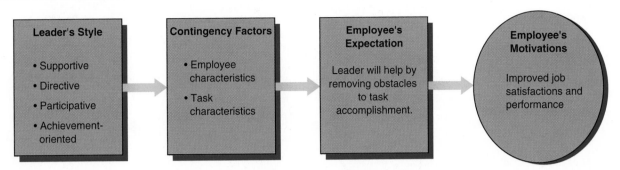

work group. This behavior is similar to the Ohio State University consideration style.

▲ **Directive leadership** involves letting members know what they are expected to do, giving them specific guidance, asking them to follow rules and regulations, scheduling and coordinating their work, and setting standards of performance for them. This behavior is similar to the initiating structure style previously discussed.

▲ **Participative leadership** includes consulting with others and evaluating their opinions and suggestions when making decisions.

▲ **Achievement-oriented leadership** entails setting challenging goals, seeking improvements in performance, emphasizing excellence in performance, and showing confidence that members will perform well.

Contingency Variables   House's model has two contingency variables: *employee needs* and *task characteristics*. Employee needs (e.g., safety, esteem, belongingness, etc.) determine how they will react to a leader's behavior. Employees with strong acceptance and affiliation needs may find that a supportive leader satisfies their needs. However, employees with strong autonomy, responsibility, and self-actualization needs probably will be motivated more by participative and achievement-oriented leaders than by supportive leaders.

Recall that tasks generally may be classified as routine and nonroutine. A routine task (1) requires the use of only a few skills, (2) represents bits and pieces of a job rather than the whole job, (3) involves few decisions regarding scheduling and methods to be used, and (4) provides little information about how well it has been performed. A nonroutine task has the opposite characteristics. Figure 11.9 illustrates the application of supportive and directive leadership styles to routine and nonroutine tasks.

Effects of Different Leadership Styles   A leader can make performing a task that is tedious, boring, or routine more pleasant by considering and supporting the employees' needs. For example, employees taking parking tolls at airports all day derive little self-esteem or self-actualization from this highly structured and routine task. They probably would feel that a directive leadership style is excessive and unnecessary. A leader with a supportive style,

FIGURE 11.9

Applying House's Path–Goal Model

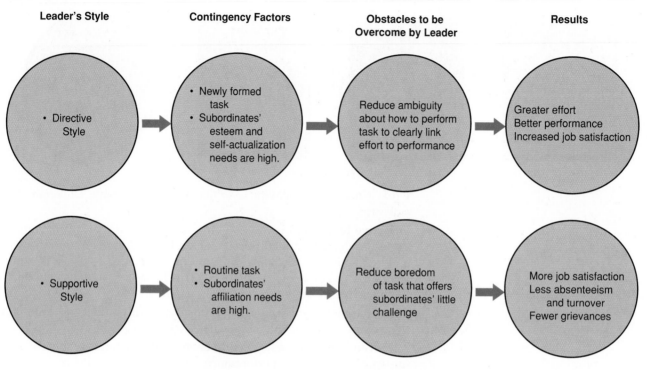

Leader's Style	Contingency Factors	Obstacles to be Overcome by Leader	Results
• Directive Style	• Newly formed task • Subordinates' esteem and self-actualization needs are high.	Reduce ambiguity about how to perform task to clearly link effort to performance	Greater effort Better performance Increased job satisfaction
• Supportive Style	• Routine task • Subordinates' affiliation needs are high.	Reduce boredom of task that offers subordinates' little challenge	More job satisfaction Less absenteeism and turnover Fewer grievances

however, could increase employee satisfaction with the work by asking employees about their outside interests and preferred working hours.

A more directive leadership style is appropriate for highly unstructured, complex, and nonroutine tasks. Directive leaders can help employees cope with task uncertainty and clarify the paths to high job satisfaction and performance. For example, this style was appropriate for Percey Barnevik when he became CEO at ABB because employees didn't know what to do. They wouldn't have felt that this style was excessive when given guidance and direction about how to improve the manufacturing process. Directive leadership helps employees achieve job satisfaction by completing their tasks properly and being rewarded for doing so.

Participative leadership involves sharing information, power, and influence between the leader and employees. When the task is clear and employees' egos are not involved in the work, participative leadership will likely contribute to satisfaction and performance only for highly independent employees. For ambiguous, ego-involving tasks, participative leadership will have positive effects on performance and job satisfaction regardless of an employee's needs for self-esteem or achievement.

Achievement-oriented leaders set challenging goals, expect employees to perform at their highest level, and show a high degree of confidence that employees will assume responsibility for accomplishing difficult tasks. This type of leadership can motivate employees to strive for high standards and build confidence in meeting challenging goals, especially among employees who are working on unstructured tasks. The Preview Case illustrates how an achievement-oriented team leader can get great results from employees.

Implications for Leaders   Research reveals that employees who perform highly routine or tedious tasks report higher job satisfaction when their leader uses a supportive (as opposed to directive) leadership style.[25] However, employees who perform unstructured tasks are more productive and satisfied when their leader uses a more directive style.

Achievement-oriented leadership has little effect on members' performance and job satisfaction when they are performing routine and repetitive tasks. Unless employees have some discretion over the what, when, and how of performing a task, the achievement-oriented leader can have little impact on employees' performance and job satisfaction. Participative leadership increases employees' efforts if they are performing an unstructured task. When they participate in decision making about tasks, goals, plans, and procedures, employees learn more about the tasks and feel that they have a better chance of successfully completing them. If employees have a highly structured task and a clear understanding of the job, however, participative leadership has little effect on performance.

We can gain some insight into how this model works by looking at how Bernard Walsh, president of Johnson and Johnson's (J&J's) Vistakon company, changed it into one of J&J's most aggressive and successful companies. The challenge of turning a company with barely $20 million in sales and low profits into a profitable company was a gamble that attracted Walsh. Headquarters managers promised to leave him alone as he attempted to develop the company. In the following Managing Quality feature, we identify (in parentheses) Walsh's leadership styles, which he varied to fit the situation.

MANAGING QUALITY

Making Contact Lenses at Johnson & Johnson

In 1983, a Johnson & Johnson (J&J) employee got word of a new Danish technology to produce disposable contact lenses cheaply. The company bought the rights and, under Walsh's leadership, began developing packaging and manufacturing processes. Within a few years, Vistakon had assembled a management team and built a high-volume plant in Jacksonville, Florida, to manufacture "Acuvue," J&J's disposable lens. Walsh hired employees because of their ability to make decisions without close supervision and their attention to quality (achievement-oriented leadership). Choosing the right employees was crucial because Acuvue lenses cost the consumer about $150 a year more to wear than conventional extended-wear lenses. Today, sales of these contact lenses bring in more than $250 million annually.

One reason for Acuvue's success is Walsh's leadership. His company is small enough that he and his employees can make rapid-fire decisions (participative leadership) on issues ranging from work-force diversity to manufacturing processes to marketing. The customers' initial reactions to the new lenses weren't what Walsh expected because competitors challenged the lenses' safety. Vistakon immediately shipped some 17,000 lenses to eye-care professionals. The speedy reaction to this complaint indicated to eye-care professionals how much service they could expect from J&J (achievement-oriented leadership). When Walsh urged Vistakon employees to think about other new products, they responded with Surevue lenses. Unlike Acuevue lenses, Surevue lens users cannot sleep with them in place, but they get twice the wear out of the lenses.[26]

▼ Vroom–Jago Leadership Model

Victor Vroom and Arthur Jago developed a leadership model that focuses on the role played by leaders in making decisions.[27] The **Vroom–Jago leadership model** indicates that various degrees of participative decision making are appropriate in different situations. These researchers assume that the leader can choose a leadership style along a continuum from highly autocratic to highly participative, as Table 11.2 shows. Vroom and Jago's shorthand notation AI refers to instances in which the leader makes the decision alone without seeking further information; AII is similar, but the leader obtains certain information from others. The "A" represents *autocratic*, and the roman numerals refer to degrees of autocracy. The notation CI means *one-to-one consultation*, and CII means *group consultation*. The notation GII represents *group decision making* with consensus as the goal.

Decision Effectiveness   **Decision effectiveness** depends on decision quality, acceptance, and timeliness. *Decision quality* refers to the extent to which a method of handling a situation produces a desired decision. The degree to which employee commitment is generated is termed *decision acceptance*. Employees are more likely to implement a decision that is consistent with their values and preferences than one that they view as harmful to them (such as a layoff, demotion, or cut in pay). *Decision time penalty* means that decisions must be made in a timely manner, that is, when needed and not at someone's leisure. For example, air traffic controllers, emergency rescue squads, and nuclear energy plant operators may have limited time to get inputs from others before making a decision. Decision effectiveness is represented by the following relationship:

$$\text{Decision effectiveness} = \text{Decision Quality} + \text{Decision Acceptance} - \text{Decision time penalty.}$$

The time penalty term has a value of zero when the leader is under no severe time pressures to make a decision.

Decision effectiveness criteria should be used only if the leader has ample time to make a decision and team members' development isn't important. If time isn't available or development is important, another criterion is needed.

TABLE 11.2   Decision Styles for Leading a Group

Leading a Group

AI   You solve the problem or make the decision yourself, using information available to you at that time.

AII   You obtain any necessary information from employees, then decide on the solution to the problem yourself. The role played by your employees in making the decision is clearly one of providing specific information that you request, rather than generating or evaluating solutions.

CI   You share the problem with relevant team members individually, getting their ideas and suggestions without bringing them together as a group. Then you make the decision. This decision may or may not reflect their influence.

CII   You share the problem with your employees in a group meeting. In this meeting, you obtain their ideas and suggestions. Then you make the decision, which may or may not reflect their influence.

GII   You share the problem with your subordinates as a group. Together, you generate and evaluate alternatives and attempt to reach a consensus on a solution. Your role is much like that of chairperson, coordinating the discussion, keeping it focused on the problem, and making sure that the critical issues are discussed. You do not try to influence the group to adopt "your" solution, and you are willing to accept and implement any solution that has the support of the entire group.

Source: Vroom, V. H., and Yetton, P. W. *Leadership and Decision Making.* Pittsburgh: University of Pittsburgh Press, 1973, 13.

Overall Effectiveness   Overall effectiveness is influenced not only by decision effectiveness but also by the cost of time and the benefits of employee development, or

$$\text{Overall effectiveness} = \text{Decision effectiveness} - \text{Cost} + \text{Development}$$

Negative effects on what Vroom and Jago call *human capital* occur because participative and consultative leadership processes use time and energy, which can be translated into costs if there are no severe time constraints. Many managers spend almost 70% of their time in meetings. Time always has a value, although its precise cost varies with how it is utilized. For example, while Marsha Huffer, a marketing manager for GTE, is in a meeting, what other marketing decisions are being delayed while waiting for her input? Do these delays represent a cost to GTE? Some of the benefits of employee participation in a meeting might include strengthening team membership, increasing commitment to organizational goals, and gaining leadership skills (mainly self-understanding and communication). Thus the costs of holding a meeting and not holding a meeting must be compared. Costs therefore represent the value of time lost through the use of participative decision making.

If participation has costs, it also can have some positive effects, as at Vistakon. Participative leader behaviors help develop the technical and managerial talents of employees, build teamwork, and strengthen loyalty and commitment to organizational goals and objectives. Walsh used these positive factors to build Vistakon into one of J&J's most profitable companies.

Decision Tree   The Vroom–Jago model considers the trade-offs among four criteria by which a leader's decision-making behavior may be evaluated: decision quality, employee commitment, time, and employee development. Figure 11.10 shows a decision tree representing the Vroom–Jago model. Note the eight problem attributes or situational variables that can be used to describe differences among decision-making situations.

FIGURE 11.10

Vroom–Jago Decision Tree

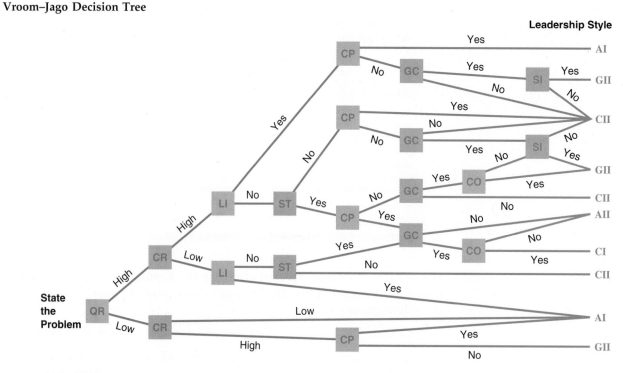

Problem Attributes

QR	Quality requirement:	How important is the technical quality of this decision?
CR	Commitment requirement:	How important is subordinate commitment to the decision?
LI	Leader's information:	Do you have sufficient information to make a high-quality decision?
ST	Problem structure:	Is the problem well structured?
CP	Commitment probability:	If you were to make the decision by yourself, is it reasonably certain that your subordinate(s) would be committed to the decision?
GC	Goal congruence:	Do subordinates share the organizational goals to be attained in solving this problem?
CO	Subordinate conflict:	Is conflict among subordinates over preferred solutions likely?
SI	Subordinate information:	Do subordinates have sufficient information to make a high-quality decision?

Source: Reprinted from Vroom, V. H., and Jago, A. G. *The New Leadership*. Englewood Cliffs, N.J.: Prentice-Hall, 1988, 184.

At the end of each branch of the decision tree, the letters and roman numerals correspond to those used to identify leadership styles in Table 11.2. That is, AI represents a leadership style in which you solve the problem yourself, using the information available to you at that time, and so on for the various leadership styles. Leader styles and problem attributes are combined through a series of complex equations that are beyond the scope of our presentation. The decision tree, however, represents the solution of those equations.

The following Managing Quality feature helps explain how the Vroom–Jago model works. It focuses on Rachel Blaylock, a manager at Primacare, a manager who wants to save organizational time and money by improving Primacare's medical chart. Following this account, we "walk you through" the decision tree solution.

MANAGING QUALITY

Rachel Blaylock at Primacare

Primacare medical clinics were begun to serve a transient patient population. In each clinic, two physicians, two nurses, and support staff usually treat patients on an emergency basis or treat those who for various reasons are unable to see their own family physicians. They also treat a large number of patients for job-related injuries and provide preemployment assessments. Because the clinics treat so many transient patients, doctors need to record as much medical information on the patient's chart as possible.

When a patient checks into a Primacare facility, a staff support person generates the patient's chart manually at the registration desk. The chart needs to reflect demographic data, a brief clinical history, physician records and diagnostic information, nursing notes and treatments, and patient treatment instructions. In addition, written patient or parental consent needs to be obtained and noted on the front of the chart before any treatment can begin. The patient chart is Primacare's single most important medical/legal document. Its design should reflect efficient and competent patient management and the latest insurance and government reporting requirements.

Primacare has computerized its patient registration and billing systems but not the patient's chart, which is still maintained manually. Moreover, the patient population that Primacare serves is changing. Many patients are now using Primacare for routine family medical needs because of its extended office hours and convenient locations. In order to provide continuity of care for returning patients, the chart needs to reflect more detailed treatment and follow-up information. Medical chart information needs to be recorded and stored in a computerized patient database where physicians and nurses can retrieve, review, and add to the patient's history quickly.

Thus a new medical chart could benefit doctors, nurses, and administrative staff by eliminating the need for redundant paperwork, documenting patient progress and follow-up contacts and treatment, and integrating the medical records, insurance, and other parts of the information system. Rachel Blaylock faces the challenge of designing a new medical chart to meet all these requirements and gain the acceptance of those who will have to use it.

MANAGING QUALITY —*Continued*

Some 62% of health care total quality management (TQM) plans fail because they are not implemented properly, so making changes that everyone understands and accepts and that will have a positive impact on the system is essential. Furthermore, most patient care activities require teamwork between doctors, nurses, and other staff members. What style of leadership should Blaylock use when deciding to change the format of patients' medical charts?[28]

If you were Rachel Blaylock and using the decision tree in Figure 11.10, what leadership style would you choose? Start with State the Problem on the left-hand side of Figure 11.10. The first box to the right is QR (quality requirement). You must make a decision about whether the importance of quality requirements is high or low. After you make that decision, go to the next box, CR (commitment required). Once again you must make a decision about the importance of having doctors, nurses, and other staff members committed to the final design of the new medical chart. After you have made that decision, you face another decision and then another. As you make each decision, follow the proper line to the next box. Eventually, at the far right-hand side of Figure 11.10, you will arrive at the best style of leadership for use, based on your previous eight decisions. We used this method as follows to determine the style of leadership that we would use.

Analysis		**Answers**
QR	Quality requirement: How important is the technical quality of the decision?	Highly Important
CR	Commitment requirement: How important is employee commitment to the decision?	Highly Important
LI	Leader's information: Do you have sufficient information to make a high-quality decision?	Probably Not
ST	Problem Structure: Is the problem well structured?	No
CP	Commitment probability: If you were to make the decision by yourself, is it reasonably certain that your team members would be committed to the decision?	Probably Not
GC	Goal congruence: Do employees share the organizational goals to be attained in solving this problem?	Yes
CO	Subordinate conflict: Is conflict among employees over preferred solutions likely?	Yes
SI	Subordinate information: Do employees have sufficient information to make a high-quality decision?	Yes

Factors Not Considered

TC	Time constraints: Are time constraints important?
MD	Motivation development: Do you want to develop your employees' skills?

Answer

We choose GII style of leadership. What did you choose?

The GII style of leadership seems to be most appropriate in this case. In other words, Rachel Blaylock probably would recognize that, unless doctors, nurses, and other staff members provide input to help redesign the chart, they won't accept and willingly use the new chart.

Implications for Leaders   The Vroom–Jago model represents a significant breakthrough in thinking about leadership.[29] Moreover, it is consistent with earlier work on leadership and the effective use of teams (see Chapter 9). If leaders can diagnose situations correctly, choosing the best leadership style for those situations becomes easier. These choices, in turn, will enable them to make high-quality, timely decisions. If the situation requires delegation, the leader must learn how to establish the desired goals and limitations—and then let employees determine how best to achieve the goals within those limitations. If the situation calls for the leader alone to make the decision, the leader should be aware of potential positive and negative consequences of not asking others for their input.

However, the model does have some drawbacks. First, most subordinates have a strong desire to participate in decisions affecting their jobs even though use of the model might suggest an autocratic decision-making approach. If subordinates are kept in the dark, they become frustrated and not committed to the decision. Second, certain characteristics of the leader play a key role in determining the relative effectiveness of the model. For example, in situations involving conflict, only leaders skilled in conflict resolution should use the type of participative decision-making strategy suggested by the model. A leader who hasn't developed these skills probably would obtain better results with a more autocratic style, even though use of the model might suggest the opposite. Third, the model is based on the premise that decisions involve a single process. However, decision making often goes through several cycles and is part of broader considerations. In Blaylock's case, not involving key employees in redesigning the medical chart probably would come back to haunt her as she makes various decisions about Primacare's patient registration and records policies.

▼ Comparing the Four Contingency Models

Choosing the most appropriate leadership style can be difficult. A strongly stated preference for democratic, participative decision making in organizations prevails in the business community today. Evidence from Thermos, J&J, and other organizations shows that this leadership style can result in productive, healthy organizations. Participative management, however, is not appropriate for all situations, as contingency theorists note. Table 11.3 shows the differences in leader behaviors, situational variables, and outcomes for the four contingency models that we have discussed.

Leadership Differences   Fiedler's model is based on the LPC style of a leader (high or low LPC) and the degree to which the situation is favorable for the leader. Fiedler considers the leadership style of a leader to be relatively rigid and recommends that a leader choose a situation that matches his or her leadership style. Hersey and Blanchard use the same two leadership dimensions that Fiedler identified: task and relationship behaviors. They went one step further by considering each as either high or low and then combining them into four specific leadership styles: directive, supportive, participating, and

TABLE 11.3   Comparing the Four Contingency Leadership Models

Model	Leader Behaviors	Contingency Variables	Leader Effectiveness Criteria
Fiedler's	Task-oriented: Low LPC Relationship-oriented: High LPC	Group atmosphere Task structure Leader position power	Performance
Hersey and Blanchard's	Task and Relationship	Readiness level of team members	Performance and job satisfaction
House's Path–Goal	Supportive Directive Participative Achievement-oriented	Employee characteristics Task characteristics	Employee job satisfaction Job performance
Vroom–Jago	Continuum of autocratic to participative	Eight problem attributes	Employee development Time Decision effectiveness Overall effectiveness

delegating. House's path–goal model states that leaders should try to improve the job satisfaction and performance of employees by removing roadblocks that stand in their way. The leader can choose a supportive, participative, directive, or achievement-oriented leadership style. Vroom and Jago believe that leaders can choose from among a variety of leadership styles, ranging from highly autocratic to highly consultative. The leader's role in choosing a style is to (1) improve the quality and acceptance of the decision, (2) increase the probability that employees will accept and implement the decision on a timely basis, and (3) develop effective leadership skills in employees. Thus each of the four contingency models identifies different styles of leadership and views the leader's ability to choose among styles differently.

Contingency Variables   All four models emphasize somewhat different contingency variables. Fiedler's model suggests that the way the variables (group atmosphere, task structure, and leader position power) are arranged in a situation determines whether and to what extent the situation is favorable or unfavorable to the leader. As the combination of the three contingency variables changes, so do the leadership requirements. A leader who is effective in one situation may not be effective in another.

Hersey and Blanchard's contingency variable is the readiness of the employee. If the employee has a low level of readiness, he or she is unable or unwilling to take on responsibility or to do something independently. If an employee's readiness level is high, he or she is both willing and knows what to do, can work independently, and always meets deadlines. As the readiness level of the subordinate changes, the leader's style should change also to match the readiness level of subordinates.

House's model uses the contingency variables of task structure and the employees' characteristics. Employees who believe that rewards are based on their own efforts generally feel more satisfied with a participative style of leadership. If the task is unstructured, a directive style of leadership will lead to higher job satisfaction and performance than a participative style because it eases the "unknown" for the employee.

The Vroom–Jago model identifies eight different contingencies for the leader to consider in deciding whether a more autocratic or a more participative style would be more effective in a particular situation. Subordinate participation in the decisions that a leader encounters increases quality, generates commitment, and develops employee leadership skills—but increases the length of time required for the leader to make a decision.

Leadership Effectiveness   All four models use somewhat different criteria for evaluating leadership effectiveness. Fiedler emphasizes performance; Hersey and Blanchard and House use both employee job satisfaction and performance; and Vroom and Jago emphasize decision effectivenes and overall effectiveness. If a decision must be made with a group, the Vroom–Jago model may best assist leaders in choosing the most appropriate leadership style. But, if improving individual performance is most important, perhaps Fiedler's, Hersey and Blanchard's, or House's model may be more useful.

▼ EMERGING LEADERSHIP MODELS

The four contingency theories of leadership don't answer every question about leadership. For example, what impact do leaders' perceptions of their employees have on their choice of leadership style? What about a leader's charisma? In the final section of this chapter, we focus on two emerging models—attribution and transformational leadership models—that attempt to answer these questions.

▼ Attribution Model

In Chapter 3, we discussed attribution theory in relation to perception. Recall that attribution theory attempts to explain the causes of behavior. When something happens, people want to attribute it to something. The **attribution model** suggests that a leader's judgment about employees is influenced by the leader's attributions regarding employee performance.[30] A leader's attributions, as much as employees' behaviors, determine how the leader responds to their performance. A leader obtains information about employees and their behaviors by observing their work frequently (sometimes daily). Based on this information, the leader makes an attribution of each employee's behaviors and selects actions to deal with these behaviors.

Leaders' Attributions   As part of diagnosing a situation, leaders must determine whether personal or situational factors cause an employee's behavior. As explained in Chapter 3, attributions are based on the leader's ability to process information concerning three dimensions of behavior: *distinctiveness* (Did the behavior occur on this task only?), *consensus* (Is this level of performance usual for other employees?), and *consistency* (Is this level of performance usual for this employee?). The answers to these three questions identify for the leader either external (situational) or internal (personal) causes for the employee's performance.

The attribution process is crucial to leader–employee relations. An employee whose successes or failures are attributed to personal skills will have different interpersonal relations with the leader than a subordinate whose successes or failures are attributed to environmental factors over which the employee has little control. Leaders attempt to change an employee's behavior only when they make an internal attribution. For example, if Ellen Larson, a sales manager at the Loew's Hotel, believes that her subordinate's poor performance is caused by the situation, she is more likely to provide resources, redesign the job, or change the situation in some way. If she believes that his poor performance is attributable to personal reasons, she probably will try to get him to improve his behavior, offer him training to improve his skills, or reprimand him. Figure 11.11 illustrates the attribution model of leadership.

Employees' Attributions   Employees, too, attribute certain causes to their leader's behavior. Employees tend to believe that their leader has an effect on their performance—whether the leader does or not—and develop either positive or negative attitudes about their leader. Past performance of employees sometimes influences their rating of the leader's effectiveness. When employ-

FIGURE 11.11

Attributional Leadership Model

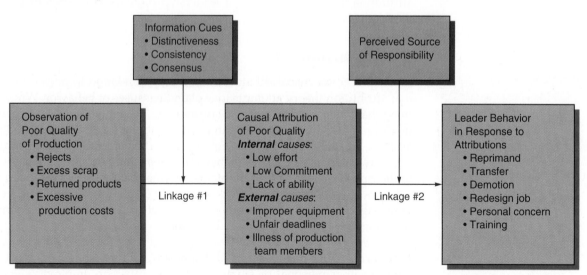

Source: Adapted from Mitchell, R., and Wood, R. E. An Empirical Test of an Attribution Model of Leader's Responses to Poor Performance. In *Academy of Management Proceedings*, Richard C. Huseman, ed. Starksville, Miss.: Academy of Management, 1979, p. 94.

ees are successful, they tend to rate their leader as successful. When they are unsuccessful, employees will try to distance themselves from their leader. Employees perceive their leader as ineffective and attribute their team's or their personal performance problems to the leader's actions, rather than their own. (Recall the discussion of self-serving bias in Chapter 3.) In professional sports, the team owner usually fires the manager, not the players, when the team does poorly. In organizations, the CEO gets fired. The firing of the top executive symbolizes the board's or the shareholders' conviction that steps must be taken to improve effectiveness.

Implications for Leaders   Leaders tend to be biased toward making internal attributions about poor employee performance, often leading to punitive actions. Employees who do not feel responsible for a problem usually resent punitive actions (see Chapters 6 and 7). After attributing a problem to employees, a leader is apt to give less support, coaching, and resources. Therefore leaders need to learn to be careful, fair, and systematic about evaluating employee performance and making attributions about poor performance. They need to become more aware of the various options available for dealing with different causes of poor performance and the importance of selecting an appropriate one.

The following Managing Ethics account describes an ethical problem facing a manager. After reading the account, please select one of the courses of action suggested for each item. Following the items, we provide responses from a sample of managers working for 260 different companies.

MANAGING ETHICS

You Make the Decision

Assured Self Storage Company has an employee assistance program (EAP) that offers counseling for alcohol and substance abuse and mental and psychiatric problems. In 1989, Bob Gordon, a 20-year sales staff veteran and frequent winner of annual performance awards, told his boss Paula Hill, "I have been drinking a lot because I am depressed about my personal problems." Hill referred him to the EAP. Hill doesn't have access to Gordon's medical records and doesn't know whether he ever obtained or is currently receiving counseling for depression. His performance has remained high since he told her about his drinking problem. In 1994, Hill was promoted to president of Assured Self Storage. She received an application from Gordon to fill a vacancy for the high-stress position of vice-president for sales and marketing for the Midwest region. The position requires supervising 35 salespeople, lots of travel, and making decisions on the spot to fix customer service problems. Judging by Gordon's past sales performance, his application merits serious consideration.

MANAGING ETHICS —*Continued*

1. Hill should (pick one):
   a. Ask Gordon if he is still "depressed"; his response is relevant to whether he qualifies for the job.
   b. Not discuss the issue with Gordon, but consider his statement about being depressed.
   c. Ignore Gordon's depression because his performance remains high.
   d. Exclude the depression incident because it occurred more than five years ago.

2. In making her decision Hill (pick one):
   a. Is confronting ethical as well as business issues.
   b. Can resolve the issues by conforming to the human resource practices stated in the company's manual.

3. Hill's policy with respect to known employee health complaints should be to (pick one):
   a. Exclude health issues in making promotions.
   b. Consider them when performance is related.
   c. Consider them if performance is related but exclude them if they occurred more than three years ago.[31]

What answers did you pick? Generally, managers choose
1(a) = 37%; 1(b) = 1%; 1(c) = 33%; 1(d) = 29%; 2(a) = 72%; 2(b) = 28%; 3(a) = 5%; 3(b) = 75%; 3(c) = 20%.

According to the attribution model of leadership, managers determine whether subordinate performance is caused by either internal or external factors. Then, on the basis of such attributions, they take specific actions to change the present situation and perhaps the subordinate's performance. The attribution model suggests that leaders base such actions, at least in part, on explanations of the subordinate's behavior. The managers' response reported in the Managing Ethics account indicate that most of them perceived that Gordon's problems stemmed from external, rather than internal, sources and would promote him. How did you respond? Why did you choose those actions? What attributions did you make about Gordon's problems?

▼ Transformational Model

World history and the history of organizations are filled with examples of individuals who have had extraordinary success in changing the beliefs, values, and actions of their followers. Joan of Arc, Abraham Lincoln, Franklin D. Roosevelt, Hitler, John F. Kennedy, Martin Luther King, and others have transformed entire societies through their words and by their actions. Individuals who accomplish such changes often are described as charismatic or transformational leaders. **Charismatic leaders** concern themselves with developing a common vision of what could be, discovering or creating opportunities, and increasing people's desire to control their own behaviors.[32] Charismatic leaders use dominance, self-confidence, a need for control, and a conviction of moral righteousness to increase their hold over their followers. When Lee Iacocca took over as president of Chrysler, he refused to believe that it was a dead company as most financial analysts predicted. Instead, he launched a political campaign to unite the company's managers and union members behind his vision and lobbied Congress to approve loans necessary for Chrysler's continued operation. Cutting his salary to $1, he urged all employees to sacrifice for the good of the company. Chrysler survived and again is a profitable U.S. automobile company.

Leaders who use their charismatic ability to inspire others often are called transformational leaders. **Transformational leaders** rely on their referent and personal sources of power to arouse intense feelings and heighten employee motivation.[33] Lee Iacocca used his transformational leadership abilities and his charismatic skills to turn Chrysler around. What methods do transformational leaders use to profoundly affect their followers and generate this type of response? Transformational leaders exhibit three behaviors: vision, framing, and impression management. Figure 11.12 shows these behaviors and followers' reactions.

Vision   Perhaps the most important behavior that transformational leaders have developed is their ability to create a **vision** that binds people to each other. A dramatic example of a vision was Martin Luther King's "I Have a Dream" speech, in which he said:

> It is a dream rooted in the American dream that one day this nation will rise up and live out the true meaning of its creed—we hold these truths to be self-evident, that all men are created equal.

In this speech, King provided an emotional message that inspired and motivated many people to change their attitudes and behaviors toward civil rights issues in the United States. Iacocca used the same emotional language in his appeal to Congress to lend Chrysler millions of dollars to bail out the financially failing company when he said, "Would you rather have people on welfare or working at Chrysler? The choice is yours." Both leaders had more than just a vision: They also had a road map for attaining it. What is important is that followers "buy into" the vision and that the leader has a plan to energize people to reach that goal.

Framing   Mary Kay Ash, founder and president of Mary Kay Cosmetics, began her company in 1963 with an objective to help women earn as much money as men do. She paid her salespeople on the basis of their contributions, not because they were women or men. She *framed* her vision by giving women a purpose for working for her new organization.

Transformational leaders are willing to take risks and nontraditional career paths to reach their goals. Joan Lappin vividly remembers her introduction into the men's world of Wall Street. As an analyst with Equity Research Corporation, she had been invited to lunch at the New York Stock Exchange's lunch club. The security guard wouldn't let her in because club rules denied women admission. Spurred on by this rule, and after several years of training, she founded her own firm, which specializes in investing in stocks that she believes are grossly underpriced. Since forming Gramacy in 1986, she has built the firm into one of the best investment houses on Wall Street. Now she gets a kick out of declining invitations to the NYSE lunch club (now open to women).[34]

Impression management   Transformational leaders use methods that enhance their attractiveness and appeal to others, referred to as **impression management**.[35] When Mary Kay Ash arrives at her company's annual meeting to give out awards to her beauty consultants (salespeople) her entrance befits a

FIGURE 11.12

Transformational Leadership
Model

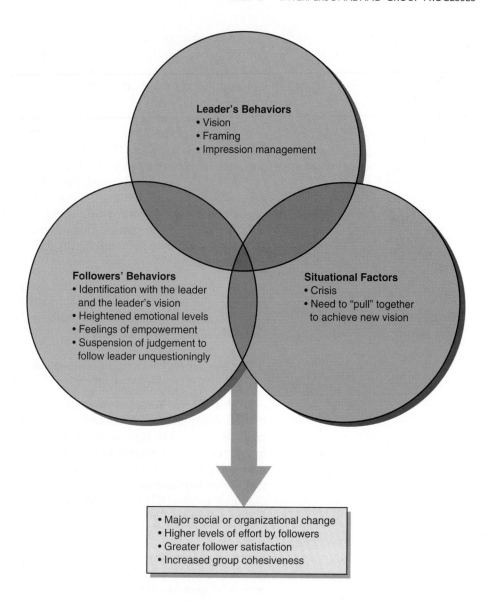

Leader's Behaviors
• Vision
• Framing
• Impression management

Followers' Behaviors
• Identification with the leader
  and the leader's vision
• Heightened emotional levels
• Feelings of empowerment
• Suspension of judgement to
  follow leader unquestioningly

Situational Factors
• Crisis
• Need to "pull" together
  to achieve new vision

• Major social or organizational change
• Higher levels of effort by followers
• Greater follower satisfaction
• Increased group cohesiveness

queen and sets the mood for the event. She is lowered on a throne from above into billowing clouds below. She descends from her throne in a long flowing pink ball gown, adorned with jewels. The more than 8,000 beauty consultants are captivated by her presence. She leads them in songs, crowns top performers, and personally asks each winner to repeat the "Mary Kay oath." She has the ability to inspire others by her words, vision, and actions.

In addition to Lee Iacocca and Mary Kay Ash, who are some other transformational business leaders? Steve Jobs of Apple and NEXT Computer, Wayne Huizenga of Blockbuster Video, Anita Roddick of the Body Shop, Ben Cohen of Ben and Jerry's Ice Cream, and the late Walt Disney are among some of the leaders you might have read about. Their charisma has transformed their organizations.

In the following Managing in Practice piece, Tom Chappell, president and co-founder with his wife Kate, describes his company. The $17 million company they operate is Tom's of Maine and sells personal care products.

MANAGING IN PRACTICE

Tom's of Maine

Tom's of Maine sells environmentally correct, all-natural toothpastes and deodorants. At its recent annual meeting, Tom Chappell reported that profits have climbed more than 40%, sales by more than 31%, and personal growth 50%.

What's personal growth? Tom believes that his company is responsible for both the environment and its employees' physical and spiritual growth. The company donates at least 10% of its pretax profits to charities in the Kennebunk area, pledged more than $100,000 for a rain-forest alliance, and gave the city more than $25,000 to start a curbside recycling program. He and his wife are as much concerned about their mission as they are about their market share.

The company remains faithful to its environmentalist roots by doing no animal testing, printing cartons with soy-based ink, and using recycled milk jugs to bottle its shampoo. His book, *The Soul of a Business*, outlines his management principles, such as informal dress and no reserved parking spaces. It is required reading for all prospective employees. He wants employees to work for him only if they share his vision and desire to make products that will not harm the environment.[36]

Tom Chappell exemplifies transformational leaders who consider themselves to be change agents, are courageous risk takers, believe in teamwork and try to empower others, and can dream and share this dream with others. Transformational leaders build confidence among their employees by helping them become more competent and giving them the freedom to demonstrate initiative.

Implications for Leaders   Using their charismatic leadership skills, transformational leaders may be most effective when an organization is new or when its survival is threatened. The poorly-structured problems that such organizations face call for leaders with vision, confidence, and determination. These leaders must influence others to assert themselves, to join enthusiastically in team efforts, and arouse their feelings about what they are attempting to do.

Transformational leadership is not a cure-all for organizations.[37] Because transformational leaders' effects may be more emotional than rational, such leadership has definite limitations. First, followers can be so zealous that they are blind to conditions surrounding the leader, a bit like the children who followed the Pied Piper of Hamelin. For example, Steve Jobs achieved unwavering loyalty and commitment from his employees during the late 1970s and early 1980s. He created a vision for them that personal computers would dramatically change the way people lived. However, once the need for this vision was fulfilled, Jobs became a liability to Apple. He was unable to listen to what experts in the PC industry were saying about Apple, became uncomfortable when employees challenged his views, and began to hold an unjustifiable belief in his "rightness" about issues. Because of these problems, the board of directors replaced him with a less charismatic leader, John Sculley.

At worst, transformational leaders emotionally manipulate followers and create visions for their own self-aggrandizement. They can even wreak havoc on the rest of the world (e.g., Attila the Hun or Adolph Hitler). A tragic example of the negative aspects of transformational leadership was David Koresh, the Branch Davidian cult leader who died along with his followers in a fiery farmhouse outside Waco, Texas, in 1993. A similar tragedy occurred in the 1970s when 912 followers of the Jim Jones cult drank a flavored drink containing a fatal dose of cyanide in Jonestown, Guyana. Jones said that they all must commit mass suicide for the glory of his vision.

Second, such leaders may lack communications and impression management skills. Because people and organizations become dependent on transformational leaders, the danger is that these leaders will surround themselves with "yes people" and thus fail to receive important information that might challenge their vision.

Finally, some transformational leaders are known for their autocratic management style. Ross Perot, for example, was used to running his own organization, Electronic Data Systems (EDS). When EDS merged with General Motors and Perot was made a GM board member, he became one of GM management's most outspoken critics. He insisted that any changes made in EDS procedures be cleared through him. His style and outspokenness were revealed again during his TV campaign against NAFTA and his TV face-off with Vice President Al Gore in 1993.

Although some organizations have prospered under transformational leadership, organizations in the 1990s generally must support and have an understanding and appreciation for managers and employees who are willing to make unpopular decisions, who know when to reject traditional ways of doing something, and who can accept reasonable risks. A "right to fail" must be nurtured and embedded in the organization's culture.

Summary

Leadership is a process of creating a vision for others and having the power to translate the vision into reality. The ways in which leaders attempt to influence others depend in part on the power available to them and in part on their skills. Leaders draw on five sources of power to influence others: legitimate, reward, coercive, referent, and expert. Visioning, empowerment, meaning through communication, and self-understanding are skills that help leaders become more effective.

The traditional leadership models include traits and behavioral. The traits model emphasizes the personal qualities of leaders and attributes success to certain abilities, skills, and personality characteristics. However, this model fails to determine why certain people succeed and others fail as leaders. The behavioral model emphasizes leaders' actions instead of their personal traits. We focused on two leader behaviors—initiating structure and consideration—and how they affect employee performance. However, most research indicates a need to analyze also the situation in which the leader operates.

The contingency approach emphasizes the importance of various situations, or contingencies. The four principal contingency models are those of Fiedler, Hersey and Blanchard, House, and Vroom and Jago. Fiedler focuses on the effective diagnosis of the situation in which the leader will operate. He emphasizes understanding the nature of the situation and then matching the correct leadership style to that situation. According to Fiedler's model, three contingency variables need to be diagnosed: group atmosphere, task structure, and the leader's position power. It also holds that all leaders have a motivational system (LPC) that indicates the combinations of situations in which their styles probably will be effective.

Hersey and Blanchard state that leaders should choose a style that matches the readiness level of their employees. If employees are not ready to perform the task, then a directive leadership style will be more effective than a relationship style. As the readiness level of the employees increases, the leadership style should become more participative and less directive.

House suggests that leadership behavior is contingent on the characteristics of subordinates and the nature of the task. The leader's goal is to reduce the obstacles that keep employees from reaching their goals. For a routine task, a leader who is considerate of employees is more likely to have satisfied and productive employees than a leader who isn't considerate of them.

Vroom and Jago base their model on an analysis of how a leader's style affects decision effectiveness and overall effectiveness. The Vroom–Jago model proposes five leadership styles that managers can use. Its set of rules can help a manager determine the leadership style to avoid in a given situation because decision effectiveness and overall effectiveness might be low.

Two emerging leadership models were reviewed. The attribution leadership model suggests that a leader's judgment about subordinates is influenced by the leader's attribution of the causes of employee behaviors. These causes may either be external or internal. Effective leaders identify the correct cause and then act accordingly.

The transformational leadership model focuses on the abilities of the leader to create a new vision and—through charismatic skills—to excite, arouse, and inspire employees to greater efforts to achieve goals. Such leaders have a clear vision, can communicate this vision to others, and pay attention to the developmental needs of their subordinates.

Key Words and Concepts

Achievement-oriented leadership
Attribution model
Charismatic leaders
Coercive power
Consideration
Decision effectiveness
Delegating style
Directive leadership
Empowerment
Expert power
Fiedler's contingency model
Follower readiness
Group atmosphere
Hersey and Blanchard's situational model

House's path–goal model
Impression management
Initiating structure
Leader
Leader match
Leadership
Least-preferred co-worker
Legitimate power
Manager
Overall effectiveness
Participating style
Participative leadership
Position power
Referent power

Relationship behavior
Reward power
Selling style
Supportive leadership
Task behavior
Task structure
Telling style
Traits model
Transformational leaders
Vision
Vroom–Jago leadership model

Discussion Questions

1. What skills must a person learn in order to lead?

2. When someone once asked Bill Miller, president of EmCare, a leading emergency medical care management group, what it took to be an effective leader, his response was: "Great team members!" What does this response mean?

3. Under what conditions have you been a successful leader? Under what conditions have you failed? Were both situations similar? Explain the similarities or differences.

4. Suppose that a leader's style doesn't seem to match the situation. Can a leader's style change to produce a better match? What does Fiedler's theory say about that possibility?

5. Are transformational leaders really different from other types of leaders? If so, in what ways? Under what situations are transformational leaders likely to be effective? Ineffective?

6. Kathleen Manella, the director of housekeeping at a St. Paul hospital, discovered that she could get better performance from her staff by making the decisions autocratically rather than consultatively. Following the Vroom–Jago model, under what conditions would her leadership style be effective?

7. According to William Howell, president of J.C. Penney, "At Penney's, our philosophy is that the best ideas come from associates—employees—on the firing line rather than managers sitting in their offices." What style of leadership works most effectively in promoting this philosophy? Explain.

8. Ralph Stayer, CEO of Johnsonville Foods, says that a leader must develop a vision or employee job performance declines. Why is creating a vision so important?

9. What are some major differences between the four contingency models? Why do they exist?

10. Assume that you are a student in a class and have been assigned to do a team project with five other classmates. How might Hersey and Blanchard's leadership model help you choose a leadership style? How might House's path–goal model help you choose a leadership style?

11. What are some conditions under which leaders don't seem to make a difference?

12. Some managers believe that female leaders adopt a different style than male leaders: a style that shows more concern with interpersonal relations and encourages subordinates to participate in decisions. Do you agree? Why or why not?

13. Consider all the men who have been president of the United States since you were born. How many of them would you classify as charismatic? How would you rate them as president?

▲ Developing Skills

Self-Diagnosis: What's Your Leadership Style?

Instructions

The following questions analyze your leadership style according to the Ohio State model. Read each item carefully. Think about how you usually behave when you are the leader. Then, using the following key, circle the letter that most closely describes your style. Circle only one choice per question.

> A = Always
> O = Often
> ? = Sometimes
> S = Seldom
> N = Never

1. I take time to explain how a job should be carried out.   A   O   ?   S   N

2. I explain the part that co-workers are to play in the group.   A   O   ?   S   N

3. I make clear the rules and procedures for others to follow in detail.   A   O   ?   S   N

4. I organize my own work activities.   A   O   ?   S   N

5. I let people know how well they are doing.   A   O   ?   S   N

6. I let people know what is expected of them.   A   O   ?   S   N

7. I encourage the use of uniform procedures for others to follow in detail.   A   O   ?   S   N

8. I make my attitude clear to others.   A   O   ?   S   N

9. I assign others to particular tasks.   A   O   ?   S   N

10. I make sure that others understand their part in the group.   A   O   ?   S   N

11. I schedule the work that I want others to do.   A   O   ?   S   N

12. I ask that others follow standard rules and regulations.   A   O   ?   S   N

13. I make working on the job more pleasant.   A   O   ?   S   N

14. I go out of my way to be helpful to others.   A   O   ?   S   N

15. I respect others' feelings and opinions.   A   O   ?   S   N

16. I am thoughtful and considerate of others.   A   O   ?   S   N

17. I maintain a friendly atmosphere in the group.   A   O   ?   S   N

18. I do little things to make it more pleasant for others to be a member of my group.   A   O   ?   S   N

19. I treat others as equals.   A   O   ?   S   N

20. I give others advance notice of change and explain how it will affect them.   A   O   ?   S   N

21. I look out for others' personal welfare.   A   O   ?   S   N

22. I am approachable and friendly toward others.   A   O   ?   S   N

Column 1

1	2
A = 5 O = 4 ? = 3 S = 2 N = 1	A = 5 O = 4 ? = 3 S = 2 N = 1

3	4
A = 5 O = 4 ? = 3 S = 2 N = 1	A = 5 O = 4 ? = 3 S = 2 N = 1

5	6
A = 5 O = 4 ? = 3 S = 2 N = 1	A = 5 O = 4 ? = 3 S = 2 N = 1

7	8
A = 5 O = 4 ? = 3 S = 2 N = 1	A = 5 O = 4 ? = 3 S = 2 N = 1

9	10
A = 5 O = 4 ? = 3 S = 2 N = 1	A = 5 O = 4 ? = 3 S = 2 N = 1

11	12
A = 5 O = 4 ? = 3 S = 2 N = 1	A = 5 O = 4 ? = 3 S = 2 N = 1

Column 2

13	14
A = 5 O = 4 ? = 3 S = 2 N = 1	A = 5 O = 4 ? = 3 S = 2 N = 1

15	16
A = 5 O = 4 ? = 3 S = 2 N = 1	A = 5 O = 4 ? = 3 S = 2 N = 1

17	18
A = 5 O = 4 ? = 3 S = 2 N = 1	A = 5 O = 4 ? = 3 S = 2 N = 1

19	20
A = 5 O = 4 ? = 3 S = 2 N = 1	A = 5 O = 4 ? = 3 S = 2 N = 1

21	22
A = 5 O = 4 ? = 3 S = 2 N = 1	A = 5 O = 4 ? = 3 S = 2 N = 1

Scoring

The following boxes are numbered to correspond to the questionnaire items. In each box, circle the number next to the letter of the response alternative you picked. Add up the numbers you circled in each of the columns

Total Column 1 = _____   Total Column 2 = _____

Interpretation

The questions scored in Column 1 reflect an initiating-structure leadership style. A score of greater than 47 would indicate that you describe your leadership style as high on initiating structure. You plan, organize, direct, and control the work of others.

The questions scored in Column 2 reflect a considerate style. A total score of greater than 40 indicates that you are a considerate leader. A considerate leader is one who is concerned with the comfort, well-being, and contributions of others.

In general, managers rated high on initiating structure and moderate on consideration tended to be in charge of higher-producing groups than those whose leadership styles are the reverse.[38]

A Case in Point:
Southwestern Manufacturing Company

Ramona Ortega pulled the trailer into the parking lot of the Loew's Anatole Hotel in Dallas and sighed with relief that her long trip from Santa Fe, New Mexico, was over. The trailer was packed with samples of handmade Native American dolls from her factory. She hoped that she would get many orders for them during the next three days at the Southwestern art and furniture shows at the World Trade Center. As she checked into her room, she recalled many of the difficult times she and her husband Hector Ortega had overcome during the last three years.

First, productivity at the factory had been lower than they thought it should be. They had hired local workers to help them and her husband had devised a piecework system to pay workers. He had carefully explained the system to the workers and offered them the opportunity to ask questions about how the system worked. Because many of the workers had never made dolls, they didn't ask any questions. Their only request was to be paid a straight hourly wage. Although the Ortegas had thought that an incentive system would encourage workers to be more productive, they finally agreed to pay them on an hourly basis. The manual skills required for assembling the dolls were similar, so all employees were paid at the same rate.

The Ortegas soon found that the work habits of their employees were erratic. They were surprised one day when none of the workers showed up for work. They soon learned that it was the first day of deer hunting season and that many employees in Santa Fe treated it like a holiday. As the workers explained later, it was a tradition to take this day off.

Hector Ortega knew of potential markets for other products handcrafted by Native American artifacts, so he had held a meeting the previous month with several of the employees to discuss making new products. Because the buying for dolls was seasonal—especially before Christmas and Mother's Day—he thought that employees could work on other products, such as small drums, at other times. This approach would increase the firm's productivity and overall profitability. The workers listened to his suggestions, but explained that they only knew how to make the dolls. He decided not to pursue the idea until he and his wife could figure out why the workers were unwilling to cooperate. However, the Ortegas knew that competition from other companies eventually would require their workers to learn new skills to produce other products.

Several squabbles among employees had erupted in the plant. Usually they involved some of the Hispanic and Native American women. None of the squabbles were serious or prolonged, but they contributed to an underlying tension among the workers. The previous week, Ramona Ortega had been in the factory when Rosa Gonzalez complained that Carla Lightfoot and Paula Jimenez were making fun of her. When Hector Ortega asked Gonzalez what they had said, she didn't know because they were speaking in Tewa, a language that she didn't understand. He had been in the middle of negotiating a large contract with Toys "R" Us and was unable to drop everything to sort out the situation. Ramona Ortega was uncertain about what to do because she didn't understand Tewa either.

These minor squabbles between workers may have been one of the reasons why the Ortegas' efforts to develop a team leader had failed. Ramona Ortega had attended a week-long seminar in Albuquerque for small business owners that focused on building good working relationships among employees. When she came back to the plant, she and her husband began applying some of these techniques. For example, they began forming workers into teams that consisted of one person from each of the three stages in making dolls. After introducing the concepts to the workers, Hector Ortega asked the teams to discuss ways that they could cooperate with each other to increase their productivity and report back to him or Judith Ramirez within a week. When the teams came back the following week, each team said that they hadn't come up with any ideas on how to cooperate with each other. When he asked more specifically about what they had discussed, he found out that the teams hadn't even met, much less discussed anything.

The Ortegas then decided to appoint a leader for each group. This time they gave the workers a month to meet informally and report back on the group's progress. At the end of the month, the employees gathered in the office and the results were the same: No one had discussed teamwork and cooperation. The Ortegas decided to drop the team concept temporarily until they could think of a way to gain employee support and help them work together to make the company more successful.[39]

Questions

1. What are some of the leadership problems facing the Ortegas?

2. If they decided to select a contingency model to help them choose a leadership style, which one might help the most?

3. What specific transformational leadership behaviors might the Ortegas try in dealing with the workers?

4. If the Ortegas hired you as a leadership consultant to advise them, which leadership style would you suggest to them? Why?

References

1. Adapted from Dumaine, B. Payoff from the new management. *Fortune*, December 13, 1993, 103–114.

2. Yulk, G., and VanFleet, D. D. Theory and research on leadership in organizations. In M. D. Dunnette and L. M. Hough (eds.), *Handbook of Industrial and Organizational Psychology*, Vol. 3. Palo Alto, Calif.: Consulting Psychologists Press, 1992, 147–198.

3. Kotter, J. P. *The Leadership Factor*. New York: Free Press, 1988; Sayles, R. L. *The Working Leader*. New York: Free Press, 1993.

4. Conger, J. A. Inspiring others: The language of leadership. *Academy of Management Executive*, 1991, 5, 31–45.

5. Bennis, W., and Nanus, B. *Leaders: The Strategies for Taking Charge*. New York: Harper & Row, 1985.

6. Lawler, E. E. III, Mohrman, S. A., and Ledford, G. E., Jr. *Employee Involvement and Total Quality Management: Practices and Results in Fortune 1000 Companies*. San Francisco: Jossey-Bass, 1992.

7. Adapted from Solomon, C. M. Careers under glass. *Personnel Journal*, April 1990, 97–105; Lang, S. Corning's blueprint for training in the '90's. *Training*, July 1991, 33–36.

8. French, J. R. P. and Raven, B. H. The bases of social power. In D. Cartwright and A. Zander (eds.), *Group Dynamics: Research and Theory*, 2nd ed. New York: Harper & Row, 1960, 607–623; Schriesheim, C. A., Hinkin, T. R., and Podsakoff, P. M. Can ipsative and single-item measures produce erroneous results in field studies of French and Raven's (1959) five bases of power? *Journal of Applied Psychology*, 1991, 76, 106–114.

9. Lachman, R. Power from what? A reexamination of its relationships with structural conditions. *Administrative Science Quarterly*, 1989, 34, 131–151; Hinkin, T. R., and Schriesheim, C. A. Relationship between subordinate perceptions of supervisory influence tactics and attributed bases of power. *Human Relations*, 1990, 43, 221–238; Yukl, G. A., and Falbe, C. M. Influence tactics and objectives in upward, downward, and lateral influence attempts. *Journal of Applied Psychology*, 1990, 75, 132–140.

10. Belasco, J. A., and Stayer, R. C. *Flight of the Buffalo*. New York: Warner Books, 1993, 16–23.

11. Bass, B. M. *Bass and Stogdill's Handbook of Leadership*. New York: Free Press, 1990.

12. Hughes, R. L., Ginnett, R. C., and Curphy, G. J. *Leadership: Enhancing the Lessons of Experience*. Homewood, Ill.: Irwin, 1993.

13. Stogdill, R. M. *Handbook of Leadership: A Survey of the Literature*. New York: Free Press, 1974.

14. Schriesheim, C. A., and Kerr, S. Theories and measures of leadership: A critical appraisal. In J. G. Hunt and L. L Larson (eds.), *Leadership: The Cutting Edge*. Carbondale: Southern Illinois University Press, 1977, 9–45.

15. Kerr, S., Schriesheim, C. A., Murphy, C., and Stogdill, R. M. Toward a contingency theory of leadership based on consideration and initiating structure. *Organizational Behavior and Human Performance*, 1974, 12, 68–82.

16. Adapted from Hofheinz, P. Europe's tough new managers. *Fortune*, September 6, 1993, 111–116.

17. Fiedler, F. E. *A Theory of Leadership*. New York: McGraw-Hill, 1967.

18. Adapted from Chang, G. Let the manager do his thing or replace him. *Fortune*, March 26, 1990, 42; Tully, S. The CEO who sees beyond budgets. *Fortune*, June 4, 1990, 186.

19. Peters, L. H., Hartke, D. D., and Pohlmann, J. T. Fiedler's contingency theory of leadership: An application of the meta-

analysis procedures of Schmidt and Hunter. *Psychological Bulletin*, 1985, 97, 224–285; Ayman, R., and Chemers, M. M. The effect of leadership match on subordinate satisfaction in Mexican operations: Some moderating influences of self-monitoring. *Applied Psychology: An International Review*, 1991, 40, 299–314.

20. Fiedler, F. E., and Chemers, M. M. *Improving Leadership Effectiveness: The Leader Match Concept*, 2nd ed. New York: John Wiley & Sons, 1982.

21. Hersey, P., and Blanchard, K. H. *Management of Organizational Behavior*, 5th ed. Englewood Cliffs, N.J.: Prentice-Hall, 1988.

22. Adapted from Paige, R. Was Dr. Paul Stern a Great Leader at Northern Telecom? Unpublished manuscript, Cox School of Business, Southern Methodist University, Dallas, used with permission, 1994; Surtees, L. Northern Telecom: The morning after. *The Globe and Mail*, Toronto, July 5, 1993, B1ff

23. Yulk, G. A., and VanFleet, D. D., Theory and research in organizations. In M. D. Dunnette and L. M. Hough (eds.), *Handbook of Industrial and Organizational Psychology*, Vol. 3. Palo Alto, Calif.: Consulting Psychologist Press, 1992, 147–198; Blanchard, K. H., Zigarmi, D., and Nelson, R. B. Situational leadership after 25 years: A retrospective. *Journal of Leadership Studies*, 1993, 1, 21–36.

24. House, R. J., and Mitchell, T. R. Path–goal theory of leadership. *Journal of Contemporary Business*, 1974, 3, 81–97.

25. Wofford, J. C., and Liska, L. Z. Path–goal theories of leadership: A meta-analysis. *Journal of Management*, 1993, 19, 857–876.

26. Adapted from Weber, J. How J&J's foresight made contact lenses pay. *Business Week*, May 4, 1992, 132; Weber, J. A big company that works. *Business Week*, May 4, 1992, 124–132.

27. Vroom, V. H., and Jago, A. G. *The New Leadership*. Englewood Cliffs, N.J.: Prentice-Hall, 1988.

28. Adapted from Blaylock, R. Decision Making at Primacare. Unpublished manuscript, Cox School of Business, Southern Methodist University, Dallas, 1994, used with permission.

29. Field, R. H. G., and House, R. J. A test of the Vroom–Yetton model using manager and subordinate reports. *Journal of Applied Psychology*, 1990, 75, 362–366; Pasewark, W. E. and Strawser, J. R. Subordinate participation in audit budgeting decisions: A comparison of decisions influenced by organizational factors to decision conforming with the Vroom–Jago model. *Decision Sciences*, 1994, 25, 281–300.

30. Meindl, J. R., and Ehrlich, S. B. The romance of leadership and the evaluation of organizational performance. *Academy of Management Journal*, 1987, 30, 91–109; Cropanzano, R., James, K., and Citera, M. A goal hierarchy model of personality, motivation, and leadership. In L. L. Cummings and B. M. Staw (eds.), *Research in Organizational Behavior*, Vol. 15. Greenwich, Conn.: JAI Press, 1993, 267–322.

31. Adapted from Berenbeim, R. E. The corporate ethics test. *Business and Society Review*, Spring 1992, 77–89.

32. Shamir, B., House, R. J., and Arthur, M. B. The motivational effects of charismatic leadership: A self-based theory. *Organization Science*, 1993, 4, 577–594; House, R. J., and Howell, J. M. Personality and charismatic leadership. *Leadership Quarterly*, 1992, 3, 81–108; House, R. J., Spangler, W. D., Woycke, J. Personality and charisma in the US presidency: A psychological theory of leader effectiveness. *Administrative Science Quarterly*, 1991, 36, 364–395.

33. Howell, J. M., and Avolio, B. J. Transformational leadership,

transactional leadership, locus of control and support for innovations: Key predictors of consolidated-business-unit performance. *Journal of American Psychology*, 1993, 78, 545–568; Keller, R. T. Transformational leadership and performance of research and development project groups. *Journal of Management*, 1994, in press.

34. Adapted from Marcial, G. G. Very fancy returns. *Business Week*, June 8, 1992, 83.

35. Sims, H. P., Jr., and Lorenzi, P. *The New Leadership Paradigm*. Newbury Park, Calif.: Sage, 1992; Trice, H. M., and Beyer, J. M. *The Cultures of Work Organizations*. Englewood Cliffs, N.J.: Prentice-Hall, 1993.

36. Adapted from Bamford, J. Changing business as usual. *Working Woman*, November 1993, 99–100.

37. Conger, J. A. The dark side of leadership. *Organizational Dynamics*, Autumn 1990, 44–55; Conger, J. A. Inspiring others: The language of leadership. *Academy of Management Executive*, 1991, 5,

31–45; Meindl, J. R. On leadership: An alternative to the conventional wisdom. In B. M. Staw and L. L. Cummings (eds.), *Research in Organizational Behavior*, Vol. 12. Greenwich, Conn.: JAI Press, 1990, 159–204; Bass, B. M., and Avolio, B. J. The implications of transactional and transformational leadership for individual, team, and organizational development. In W. A. Pasmore and R. W. Woodman (eds.), *Research in Organizational Change and Development*, Vol. 4. Greenwich, Conn.: JAI Press, 1990, 231–272.

38. Schriesheim, C. *Leadership Instrument*. Miami: University of Miami, 1994. Used by permission.

39. Reproduced with permission from Caitlin, L., and White, T. "Case Study: Southwestern Manufacturing Company," *International Business: Cultural Sourcebook and Case Studies* with the permission of South-Western College Publishing. © 1993 by South-Western College Publishing. All rights reserved.

12 Interpersonal Communication

LEARNING OBJECTIVES

When you have finished studying this chapter, you should be able to:

▲ Describe the elements of interpersonal communication and their relationships to one another.

▲ State the potential interpersonal and cultural barriers to dialogue.

▲ Evaluate the effects of different types of communication networks.

▲ Describe how groupware aids support networking.

▲ Explain the skills and behaviors that are needed to foster dialogue.

▲ Give feedback, engage in self-disclosure, and actively listen.

▲ State how nonverbal cues may support dialogue between individuals.

OUTLINE

Preview Case: Communicating Assertively

Elements of Interpersonal Communication

Sender and Receiver

Transmitters and Receptors

Messages and Channels

Meaning, Encoding, Decoding, and Feedback

Potential Interpersonal Barriers

Managing in Practice: Bypassing

Managing Diversity: Communicating Biases

Potential Cultural Barriers

Managing Across Cultures: Nonverbal Cues and Tips

Interpersonal Networks

Variety of Networks

Impacts of Networks

Implications of Networks

Managing Diversity: African-American Network at Xerox

Groupware-Based Networking

Fostering Dialogue

Communication Openness

Managing in Practice: A Merger With Communication Openness

Constructive Feedback

Appropriate Self-Disclosure

Active Listening

Managing Quality: How Honda Listens

Nonverbal Communication

Types of Nonverbal Cues

Managing Across Cultures: Nonverbal Expectations in Mexico

Status and Nonverbal Cues

Gender Differences and Nonverbal Cues

DEVELOPING SKILLS

Self-Diagnosis: *Personal Communications Practices*

A Case in Point: *Xographics*

PREVIEW CASE

Communicating Assertively

Kim: "Sam, I'd like to talk to you about your work. Will you join me in my office?" (Kim is Sam's manager.)

Sam: "Oh, okay, I'll be right with you."

Kim: "As a follow-up to our previous conversation, I'll come right to the point. Your work has been deteriorating recently. Your productivity has fallen off and you've failed to meet three more deadlines."

Sam: "My work is as good as ever."

Kim: "I'm not talking about how well you do things. I'm referring to how *much* you do and how *quickly* you do them."

Sam: "Well, ever since we had to start using the new setup procedure, nobody has been doing as much as before."

Kim: "Sam, everyone in the section was consulted for their opinions before we installed it—including you. Nobody expressed any objections. If you want to talk about the production of the others, take a look at this production chart first."

Sam: "Well, okay—so *they're* doing fine, but this new setup throws *me* off."

Kim: "Sam, your production started dropping before we began the new procedure."

Sam: "Well, believe me, the new setup procedure didn't help. Anyway, as they say, you can't teach an old dog new tricks."

Kim: "Didn't your team leader explain it all to you?"

Sam: "Yes, he did—but I guess I just didn't get it."

Kim: "He told me he spent several hours with you."

Sam: "I suppose he did—maybe I'm just thick."

Kim: "We'll give you whatever assistance you need to understand it. If necessary, I'll arrange to streamline the production procedure on your line. Now, what about the deadlines, Sam—that's another matter."

Sam: "Yes, but I can't possibly meet them with all these changes taking place."

Kim: "Sam, you can take measures to make yourself more effective. I will do what I can to remove barriers to your performance. I'm setting up another meeting with you to go over positive measures that you can take to meet production standards. Let's start our next meeting with a discussion of your ideas."[1]

Kim's meeting with Sam suggests that she has handled this meeting professionally. She has not been manipulated or confused by Sam's self-serving statements. Kim made a commitment to removing possible barriers to performance and made clear her expectations for improved performance. Her messages to Sam were open, candid (honest), and supportive. At the same time, she refrained from demeaning Sam and kept her cool. Kim avoided communicating aggressively with Sam. To give Sam a chance to start responding effectively, Kim empowered Sam to propose at their next meeting the positive measures that he might take to meet production standards.

Three basic interpersonal communication approaches were available to Kim during her meeting with Sam: assertive, nonassertive, and aggressive.[2] Fortunately, she followed the assertive approach. **Assertive communication** means confidently expressing what you think, feel, and believe (values)—and standing up for your rights while respecting the rights of others. By actions and words, you convey meaning and expectations without humiliating or degrading the other person. Assertive communication is based on respect for yourself and respect for other people's needs and rights.

Nonassertive communication is a reluctance or inability to express consistently what you think, feel, and believe (values) and allows others to violate your rights without challenge. It reflects a lack of respect for your own preferences. With this approach, others can easily disregard your thoughts, feelings, and beliefs. A variation of this approach is *passive–aggressive communication,* which involves some degree of resentment and subtle hostility—pouting, stewing, and fretting. It may involve a sense of being a *victim,* even if such a feeling isn't valid. In the Preview Case, Sam appeared to exhibit the passive–aggressive communication approach in a number of his comments, such as: "Well, ever since we had to start using the new setup procedure, nobody has been doing as much as before." **Aggressive communication** means expressing yourself in ways that intimidate, demean, or degrade another person and pursuing what you want in ways that violate the rights of another person. This approach carries such messages as: "This is what I think. You're dumb for thinking differently" and "Do as I say or you're out of here."

We described the central role of communications in the daily work of all employees in Chapter 1. In this chapter, we develop the process, types, and patterns of verbal, nonverbal, and other forms of interpersonal communication used by employees on the job. We emphasize the ways to foster effective dialogue in organizations. Most often, people think of the active part of interpersonal communication as only the words, emotions, gestures, and other cues provided by the sender to the receiver. However, even the most eloquent speaker is doomed to failure if the receiver doesn't actively listen. **Interpersonal communication** is the transmission and reception of thoughts, facts, beliefs, attitudes, and feelings—through one or more information media—that produce a response. Through active listening, the messages intended by the sender are likely to be accurately understood and interpreted by the receiver.[3] In the Preview Case, apparently Sam wasn't listening actively. Kim's responses to Sam's feedback suggested that she understood his apparent inability to engage in active listening. At the follow-up meeting, Kim will learn how well Sam understood, interpreted, and responded to the theme of her repeated key message.

▼ ELEMENTS OF INTERPERSONAL COMMUNICATION

Accurate interpersonal communication takes place only if the thoughts, facts, beliefs, attitudes, or feelings that the sender intended to transmit are the same as those understood and interpreted by the receiver. Management and labor representatives may well disagree with each other while negotiating a new contract. But so long as opposing viewpoints are being transmitted, received, and understood with the intended meaning, accurate interpersonal communication is taking place. Interpersonal communication obviously requires two or more people. Figure 12.1 presents the core elements of interpersonal communication involving only two people.

▼ Sender and Receiver

Interpersonal communication usually includes exchanges between people. Thus labeling one person as the *sender* and the other as the *receiver* is arbitrary.

FIGURE 12.1

Elements of Interpersonal Communication

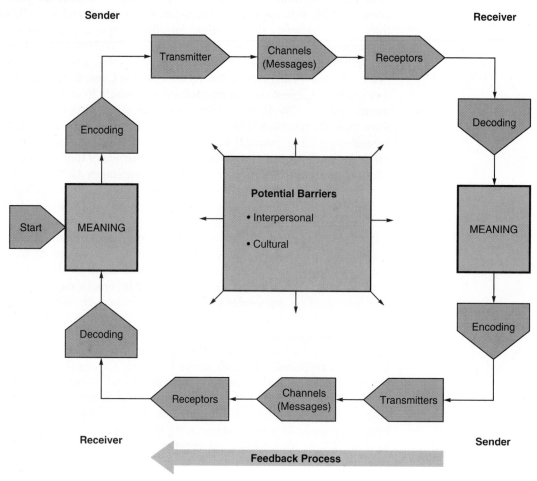

These roles shift back and forth, depending on where the individuals are in the process. When the receiver responds to the sender, the original receiver becomes the sender and the initiating sender becomes the receiver.

Consider the comment of a supervisor of security services about dealing with a vice-president of operations:

> I wanted an assistant so that I could have some help in managing my department and would not have to handle the petty problems of my employees. I (sender) tried to convince my general manager (receiver) that I was overworked since my staff had almost doubled and I was having a lot of people problems. I failed because I was just trying to make it easier on myself and wanted an assistant to do the job that I was supposed to be doing. I was also asking to increase the payroll of the company with no plans to increase revenue or profits. After my general manager (sender) turned me (receiver) down, I pouted for a few weeks and later learned that

he thought I was immature. I then decided to forget about past disappointments and only worry about the future.[4]

The supervisor's statement suggests that the goals of the sender and receiver substantially influence the communication process. For example, the sender may have certain goals for communicating, such as adding to or changing the thoughts, beliefs, attitudes, and/or behaviors of the receiver or changing the relationship with the receiver. These intentions may be presented openly (the supervisor wanted a new assistant) or developed in a deceptive manner.[5] If the receiver doesn't agree with them, the probability of distortion and misunderstanding can be quite high (general manager concluded that the supervisor was immature). The fewer the differences in goals, attitudes, and beliefs, the greater is the probability that accurate communication will occur. This quote also suggests that the sender used a passive–aggressive communication approach with his general manager.

▼ Transmitters and Receptors

Transmitters (used by the sender) and **receptors** (used by the receiver) are the means (media) available for sending and receiving messages. In interpersonal communication, they usually involve one or more of the senses: seeing, hearing, touching, smelling, and tasting. Transmission can take place both verbally and nonverbally. Once transmission begins, the communication process moves beyond the direct control of the sender. A message that has been transmitted cannot be brought back. How many times have you thought to yourself, "I wish I hadn't said that?"

Several types of communication media are available for transmitting and receiving messages. They vary in terms of **media richness,** which is a medium's capacity for carrying multiple cues and providing rapid feedback. The richness of each medium is based on a blend of four factors: (1) the rapidity and use of feedback to correct and/or confirm intended meanings; (2) the tailoring of messages to the personal circumstances of the receiver; (3) the ability to convey multiple cues simultaneously; and (4) language variety (for example, verbal and nonverbal versus just numbers).[6] Figure 12.2 relates nine different media to these four factors, each of which is presented as a continuum. The factors are labeled *feedback* (slow to rapid), *personalization* (low to high), *cues* (single to multiple), and *language* (standard to varied). The media may vary somewhat along these continua, depending on their use by the sender and receiver.[7] For example, electronic mail (E-mail) may be associated with slower or quicker feedback than shown in Figure 12.2. The speed depends on the accessibility of E-mail messages and the receiver's tendency to reply immediately or later. Communications that require a long time to digest or that cannot overcome biases are low in richness.

Data simply are the output of communication. Words spoken face-to-face, telephone calls, letters and memos, and computer printouts represent various forms of data. They become information when they reinforce or change the understanding of receivers with respect to their thoughts, feelings, attitudes, or beliefs. The use of groupware (various information technologies) may help such information exchange but cannot always substitute for face-to-face dialogue.[8] Why? As suggested in Figure 12.2, face-to-face dialogue is considered

FIGURE 12.2

Examples of Media Richness for Sending and Receiving Messages

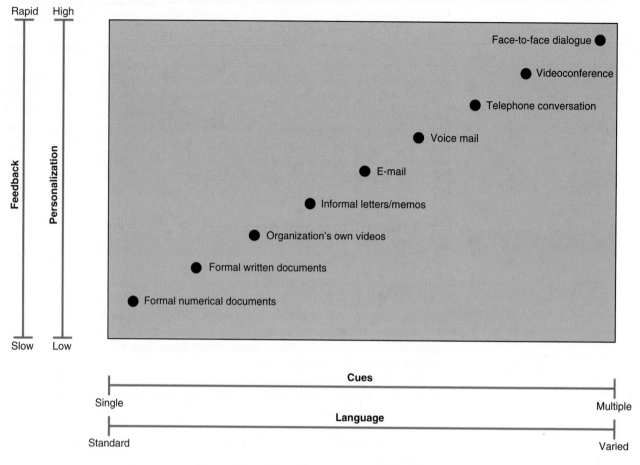

Source: Adapted from Soft, R.L., and Lengel, R. H. Organizational information requirements, media richness, and structural design. *Management Science*, 1986, 32, 554–571.

to be the richest medium. It provides immediate feedback so that receivers can check the accuracy of their understanding and make corrections if needed. It also allows the sender and receiver simultaneously to observe body language, tone of voice, and facial expression. These observations communicate more than just the spoken words. Finally, it enables the sender and receiver more quickly to identify and use language that is natural and personal. Because of these characteristics, solving important and tough problems—especially those involving uncertainty and ambiguity—almost always requires face-to-face dialogue.[9]

▼ Messages and Channels

Messages include the transmitted data and the coded (verbal and nonverbal) symbols that give particular meanings to the data. The sender hopes that messages are interpreted as meant. To understand the difference between the original meaning and the received message, think about an occasion when you tried to convey inner thoughts and feelings of happiness, rage, or fear to another person. Did you find it difficult or impossible to transmit your true "inner meaning?" The greater the difference between the interpreted meaning and the original message, the poorer will be the interpersonal communication. Words and nonverbal symbols have no meaning by themselves. Their meaning is created by the sender *and* the receiver and the situation or context.[10] In our discussion of potential interpersonal and cultural barriers, we explain why messages aren't always interpreted as they were meant to be. **Channels** are the means by which messages travel from sender to receiver. For example, a conversation may be carried by the air in a face-to-face conversation or by a telephone line.

▼ Meaning, Encoding, Decoding, and Feedback

As Figure 12.1 indicates, the sender's message is transmitted through channels to the receiver's receptors, or senses. The received messages are changed from their symbolic form (such as spoken words) to a form that has meaning. **Meanings** represent a person's thoughts, feelings, beliefs (values), and attitudes.

Encoding is the personal translation of meanings into messages that can be sent. Vocabulary and knowledge play an important role in the sender's ability to encode. For example, some professionals have difficulty communicating with the general public. They often encode meanings in a form that only other professionals in the same field can understand. Lawyers often encode (write) contracts that directly affect consumers on the assumption that only other lawyers will decode them. Consumer groups have pressed to have such contracts written in language that most everyone can understand—a reaction to legal terminology that only lawyers can understand. As a result, many banks, credit card firms, and other organizations have simplified the language in their contracts.

Decoding is the personal translation of received messages into interpreted meanings. Using a shared language, people can decode many messages so that the meanings received are reasonably close to the meanings transmitted. Decoding messages accurately often is a major challenge in communicating across cultures. The following comments made by Japanese and Japanese-Americans who have worked closely with North Americans illustrate the gaps that may occur between sent messages and interpreted meanings.

▲ Sometimes Americans don't understand that we are smiling and laughing not because we like what they are doing but because they are making us nervous.

▲ Americans ought to watch us more carefully as we are not as verbal as they are. We don't like to say no for instance, but when we suck air in through our teeth and grab the back of our necks, we mean no.

▲ Americans just don't understand the process of establishing relationships with the Japanese; the investment of time and expense seems like too much for them. They just aren't comfortable with the expectations, and they are not used to creating lasting, permanent business relationships. They think once the deal is done, it's over. They need to learn how to nurture relations: pay attention, follow up, make return visits—not only when something goes wrong.[11]

The accuracy of interpersonal communication is evaluated in relation to the *ideal state*. In this state, the sender's intended meanings and the receiver's interpretation of them are the same. The transmission of factual information of a nonthreatening nature most easily approximates the ideal state. For example, the sharing of the time, place, and procedures for high school or college commencement generally resulted in easy and accurate interpersonal communication. The communication between a manager and a subordinate during a performance feedback session is another matter.

Feedback is the receiver's response to the message. Feedback lets the sender know whether the message was received as intended. Through feedback, interpersonal communication becomes a dynamic, two-way process, rather than just an event. Reread the Preview Case. It illustrates the dramatic differences in Kim's constructive feedback and efforts to engage Sam in dialogue and Sam's use evasive and defensive responses.

▼ Potential Interpersonal Barriers

There are numerous perspectives for considering potential interpersonal communication barriers. We have discussed many of the potential underlying interpersonal barriers in previous chapters. We briefly review the more central ones here.

▲ Individual personality traits that serve as potential barriers include low adjustment (nervous, self-doubting, moody), low sociability (shy, unassertive, withdrawn), low conscientiousness (impulsive, careless, irresponsible), low agreeableness (independent, cold, rude), and low intellectual openness (dull, unimaginative, literal-minded). Introverts are more likely to be quiet and emotionally unexpressive. Dogmatics are rigid and closed-minded and accept or reject other people on the basis of their agreement or disagreement with accepted authority or their own beliefs. (See Chapter 2.)

▲ Individuals with a low level of cognitive moral development, which is associated with extreme self-centeredness ("It's right because it's right for me."), are likely to present barriers to interpersonal communication. (See Chapter 2.)

▲ Individual perceptual errors that serve as potential barriers include perceptual defense (protecting oneself against ideas, objects, or situations that are threatening), stereotyping (assigning attributes to someone solely on the basis of a category in which the person has been placed), halo effect (evaluating another person based solely on one impression, either favorable or unfavorable), projection (tendency for people to see their own traits in others) and high expectancy effect (prior expectations serving to bias how events, objects, and people are actually perceived). Individuals who make the fundamental attribution error (underestimating the impact of situational or external causes of behavior and overestimating the impact of personal causes of behavior when seeking to understand why people behave the way they do) are less likely to communicate effectively. This error too readily results in communicating blame or credit to individuals for outcomes. A related attribution error is the self-serving bias (that is, communicating personal responsibility

for good performance but denying responsibility for poor performance).
(See Chapter 3.)

▲ Individual differences in problem-solving styles (based on differences in
gathering information—sensation versus intuition and differences in
evaluating information—feeling versus thinking) create potential barriers. (See Chapter 4.)

In addition to these potential underlying interpersonal communication barriers, we provide an overview of several potential direct barriers. Of course,
most of these more direct interpersonal communication barriers are caused,
at least in part, by one or more of the underlying barriers.

Communication Approach   Early in this chapter, we identified several basic
interpersonal communication approaches—assertive, nonassertive, passive–
aggressive and aggressive. With the exception of the assertive approach, they
are characterized by transmission and reception processes that create potential
barriers to effective dialogue between two or more individuals. The aggressive
approach creates communication barriers by criticizing, belittling, reprimanding, threatening, failing to be open to options, stressing conformity, focusing
on weaknesses, and the like.[12]

Noise   **Noise** is any interference with the intended message in the channel.
A radio playing loud music while someone is trying to talk to someone else
is an example of noise. Noise can be overcome by repeating the message or
increasing the intensity (for example, the volume) of the message.

Bypassing and Semantics   **Bypassing** refers to an *apparent* agreement and
understanding between two or more individuals and ultimately leads to expectations by each person about the near-term behavior of the other person.[13]
Bypassing occurs because (1) individuals assume that meanings are simply in
the words spoken, rather than in the intended thoughts and feelings of people,
(2) individuals think they can communicate the same way and with the same
degree of success in both high-pressure (stress) and low-pressure situations,
and (3) individuals treat communication as easier to accomplish than it is.
Consider the encounter in the following Managing in Practice story.

MANAGING IN PRACTICE

Bypassing

Phil is walking past the vending machines, a place where social and work-
related communications often take place. Suddenly, Sue, the vice-president of
operations, appears. She is obviously late for an important Monday morning
meeting. As Sue breezes by Phil, she says, "How about the report for production planning? Don't they want it soon!" Before Phil can respond, other
than to say "okay," Sue enters an office off of the corridor and shuts the door.
Phil heard the words Sue muttered. She was informing him that production
planning needed the report soon.

Phil decides to get in touch with production planning to find out when
they want it. Phil has a leisurely conversation over coffee with the manager

MANAGING IN PRACTICE —*Continued*

and two other members of the production planning department. It is agreed that the report will be submitted by the end of the week. On Wednesday, Phil receives an early morning call from Sue.

Sue: "Phil, where the heck is my copy of that report for production planning? I needed it yesterday."

Phil: "But I spoke with production planning, and they said it would be okay to have it to them on Friday. I was going to be working on it tomorrow morning."

Sue: "That's not good enough, Phil. I told you to get it done on Tuesday."

Phil (biting his tongue): "I'll get on it immediately and should have it to you later this afternoon."[14]

When the Monday morning short conversation between Phil and Sue ended, both thought they had agreed with each other. They also seem to have experienced a semantics barrier. **Semantics** refers to the special meanings assigned to words. The same words may mean different things to different people.[15] Recall Sue's comment to Phil: "How about the report for production planning? Don't they want it soon!" She could have intended one of several meanings in the message sent to Phil.

Directing: "You should get the report to me now. That's an order."

Suggesting: "I suggest that we consider getting the report out now."

Requesting: "Can you do the report for me now? Let me know if you can't."

Informing: "A report is needed soon by production planning."

Questioning: "Does production planning want the report soon?"

Phil said "okay," which implied to Sue that they were on the same wavelength.

Consider the semantics for basic words such as *sale*, *airport*, and *train* in the following organizations. At Digital Equipment Corporation, a sale to the indirect marketing organization happens when a distributor or reseller orders a computer. To direct marketing (sells to ultimate customers), a sale occurs only when the end customer takes delivery. Even within direct marketing, there are differences of opinion: Salespeople record a sale when the order is placed, manufacturing and logistics when the product is delivered, and finance when it is paid for. At American Airlines, some managers argue that an airport is any location to which American has scheduled service; others count an airport as any facility granted that status by the international standards body. At Union Pacific Railroad, there's little consensus on what a train is. Is it a locomotive, all cars actually pulled from an origin to a destination, or a scheduling sheet?[16]

Language Routines **Language routines** are patterned responses to situations, often reflecting the person's unique communication approach, or language choices that have become habits.[17] For example, language routines might be observed for the ways employees greet one another each morning. In many instances they are quite useful because they reduce the amount of thinking time needed to produce common messages. They provide predictability in terms of being able to anticipate what was going to be said and how it was going to be said. The unique culture of Ford Motor Company and its identity is reinforced through language routines, including slogans such as "Quality is Job 1.

"Conversely, language routines sometimes cause discomfort, offend, and alienate when they serve to discriminate against individuals or groups. Many demeaning stereotypes of individuals and groups are perpetuated through language routines. The following Managing Diversity feature provides examples of the stereotypic biases and several language routines used to communicate some of those stereotypes, as perceived by diverse groups. This feature is based on specific incidents reported by Dr. Alan Weis, an organizational consultant.

MANAGING DIVERSITY

Communicating Biases

The anecdotes and accounts presented are from some of the best run and most successful organizations in the U.S. *In a group of all white men*, one participant responsible for interviewing candidates in research and technical areas reported that "if I see ten candidates, only one is likely to be a minority, and that person will never be the best of the group." I asked, "Do you mean because he or she is a minority, that person will not be the best?" He replied, "Absolutely." To my greater astonishment, not one of the other 14 people in the room saw fit to contradict or qualify that statement.

In a group of women, a woman silenced the room during her revelation that she was four months pregnant and afraid to tell anyone in her work unit. "I wake up every morning praying that I don't 'show' for a little while longer," she explained. Although the company has a competitive family leave program, all the women acknowledged that there was intense pressure from superiors to return to work as soon as possible, despite the provisions in the leave policy. (And it was a "career-ender" for a man to use the family leave policy.) *A group of minorities and women* stated flatly that "we have to be twice as good as the white males to obtain equivalent positions." When I asked if they felt that this was an arrogant attitude and whether it was difficult to arise every morning feeling you have to be twice as good just to be treated equally, a woman responded—to applause from the group—"That's the way it is, so why be bitter about it? Let's just get on with work, whatever the rules may be."

African-American men repeatedly cited instances during interviews of white males approaching them when talking in an all-black group and asking, "Hey, what are you guys up to?" Although stated jokingly, the respondents pointed out that there was never an analogous situation when a group of white males were clustered in discussion. "It's as if we were engaged in some drug deal going down right in the hallway," stated one interviewee. *Asian-Americans* frequently cited "labeling" which included two career-stopping elements: "Asians are excellent in technical areas, but are unable to serve as leaders because they cannot muster the assertiveness necessary to confront tough situations." Consequently, Asian-Americans were relegated to technical areas with career paths that excluded management positions.[18]

Lying and Distortion   **Lying** is an extreme form of deception in which the sender states what is believed to be false in order to seriously mislead one or more receivers. The intention to deceive implies a belief that the receiver will hopefully accept the lie as a fact. In contrast, **honesty** means that the sender abides by consistent and rational ethical principles to respect the truth. Everyday social flattery in conversations usually isn't completely honest, but it is normally considered acceptable and rarely regarded as dishonest (lying).[19] **Distortion** represents a wide range of messages that a sender may use between the extremes of lying and complete honesty. Of course, the use of vague, ambiguous, or indirect language doesn't necessarily indicate the sender's intent to mislead.[20] This form of language may be viewed as acceptable political behavior (see Chapter 15). Not wanting to look incompetent, a subordinate may remain quiet instead of expressing an opinion or asking a question of a manager.

Personal distortion in interpersonal communications may occur through **impression management,** or the process by which a sender consciously attempts to influence the perceptions that the receivers form (see Chapter 3). Three impression management strategies are commonly used.

▲ *Ingratiation*—using flattery, supporting the opinions of the other person, doing favors, smiling excessively in support of the person, and so on.

▲ *Self-promotion*—communicating one's personal attributes in a highly positive and exaggerated way;

▲ *Face-saving*—communicating *apologies* in a way to convince the receiver that the bad outcome is not a fair indication of what he or she is really like as a person; making *excuses* by admitting that one's behavior in some way caused a negative outcome, but strongly suggesting that he or she is not really as responsible as it seems (because the outcome was not intentional or there were extenuating circumstances); or presenting *justifications* by appearing to accept responsibility for an outcome, [but denying the outcome really led to any major problems.][21]

Impression management strategies can range from relatively harmless and minor forms of distortion (being courteous to another even if you don't like the individual) to messages that use extreme ingratiation and self-promotion to obtain a more favorable raise or promotion relative to others. The personal ethics and self-awareness of the sender and the political nature of the individual's organization (see Chapter 15) combine to influence the degree to which distortion tactics are used.[22] In brief, the greater the frequency of distortion tactics and the more they approach the lying end of the distortion continuum, the more they will serve as a barrier to interpersonal communication.

▼ Potential Cultural Barriers

As discussed in Chapter 2, *culture* refers to the distinctive ways that different populations, societies or smaller groups organize their lives or activities. **Intercultural communication** occurs whenever a message that must be understood by a member of one culture is received by a member of another culture.[23] The effects of cultural differences on barriers to interpersonal communications can be wide ranging. They depend on the degree of difference (or similarity) between people in terms of languages, religious beliefs, economic beliefs, social values, physical characteristics, use of nonverbal cues, and the like. The greater the differences, the greater are the barriers—and challenges—to achieving effective intercultural communication.

Cultural Context   One framework for considering potential barriers to intercultural communication is **cultural context** or the conditions that surround and influence the life of an individual, group, or organization. Cultures may vary on a continuum from low context to high context.[24] Figure 12.3 places various cultures approximately on this continuum. In a **high context culture,** interpersonal communication is characterized by (1) the establishment of social trust before engaging in task-based discussions, (2) the value placed on personal relationships and goodwill, and (3) the importance of the surrounding circumstances during an interaction. In this context, people rely on paraphrasing, tone of voice, gesture, posture, social status, history, and social setting to interpret the spoken words. High-context communication requires time. Factors such as trust, relationships between friends and family members, personal needs and difficulties, weather, and holidays must be considered. An example of this kind of communication in organizations is the Japanese practice of socializing after work.

In contrast, a **low-context culture** is characterized by (1) directly and immediately addressing the tasks, issues, or problems at hand; (2) the high value placed on personal expertise and performance; and (3) the importance of clear, precise, and speedy interactions. *The One-Minute Manager*, a management best seller in North America, promotes a managerial approach based on low-context communication. The book describes how a manager can motivate employees with one-minute statements focusing on positive or corrective feedback and goal setting.[25] Within the diverse cultural context of countries such as the United States, a subcultural context continuum exists, reflecting the various characteristics of its subcultures. In contrast, the cultural context of a homogeneous country, such as South Korea, reflects the more uniform characteristics of its people.

FIGURE 12.3

Examples of Cultures on the Cultural Context Continuum

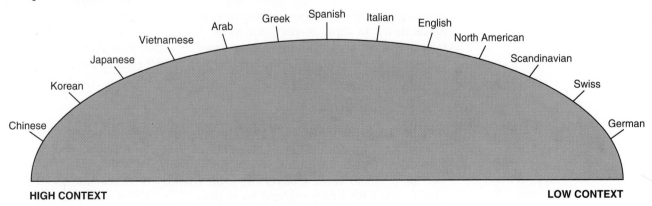

Source: Based on Hall, E. *Understanding Cultural Differences.* Yarmouth, Me.: Intercultural Press, 1989; Munter, M. Cross-culture communication for managers, *Business Horizons*, May–June 1993, 67–78.

The following Managing Across Cultures feature focuses on the vital role of nonverbal cues across cultures and how they can become communication barriers if not understood.

MANAGING ACROSS CULTURES

Nonverbal Cues and Tips

Two of the many sets of challenges in cross-cultural nonverbal communication include body language and the personal space around an individual. We present a few tips for helping you to understand and use nonverbal cues across cultures.

▼ Body Language

Ideas of appropriate posture, gestures, eye contact, facial expression, touching, pitch, volume, and speaking rate differ across cultures. As a simple but potentially disastrous example, nodding the head up and down in Bulgaria means "no," not "yes." You must avoid using any gestures considered rude or insulting. For instance, in Buddhist cultures, the head is considered sacred, so you must never touch anyone's head. In Muslim cultures, the left hand is considered unclean, so never touch, pass, or receive with the left hand. Pointing with the index finger is rude in cultures ranging from the Sudan to Venezuela to Sri Lanka. The American circular "A-OK" gesture carries a vulgar meaning in Brazil, Paraguay, Singapore, and Russia. Crossing your ankle over your knee is rude in such places as Indonesia, Thailand, and Syria. Pointing your index finger toward yourself insults the other person in Germany, the Netherlands, and Switzerland. Avoid placing an open hand over a closed fist in France, saying "tsk tsk" in Kenya, and whistling in India.

Prepare yourself to recognize gestures that have meaning only in the other culture. Chinese stick out their tongues to show surprise and scratch their ears and cheeks to show happiness. Japanese suck in air, hissing through their teeth to indicate embarrassment or "no." Greeks puff air after they receive a compliment. Hondurans touch a finger to the face below the eyes to indicate caution or disbelief. Finally, resist applying your own culture's nonverbal meanings to other cultures. Vietnamese may look at the ground with their heads down to show respect, not to be "shifty." Russians may exhibit less facial expression and Scandinavians fewer gestures than Americans are accustomed to, but that doesn't mean that they aren't enthusiastic.

▼ Personal Space

A second aspect of nonverbal communication has to do with norms regarding space. North Americans generally feel comfortable in the following zones of space: 0–18 inches for intimacy only (comforting or greeting); 18 inches to 4 feet for personal space (conversing with friends); 4–12 feet for social space (conversing with strangers); and more than 12 feet for public space (standing in lobbies or reception areas). Different cultures define the acceptable extents of these zones differently. Venezuelans tend to prefer much closer personal

MANAGING ACROSS CULTURES —*Continued*

and social space and might consider it rude if you back away. The British may prefer more distant personal and social space and might consider it rude if you move too close. Closely related to this is the concept of touch. Anglos usually avoid touching each other very much. In studies of touching behaviors, researchers observed people seated in outdoor cafes in each of four countries and counted the number of touches during one hour of conversation. The results were: San Juan, 180 touches per hour; Paris, 110 per hour; Gainesville, Florida, 1 per hour; and London, 0 per hour.[26]

Ethnocentrism   The greatest barrier to intercultural communication occurs when a person believes that "only my culture makes sense, espouses the 'right' values, and represents the 'right' and logical way to behave." This mode of thinking is called **ethnocentrism.** When two ethnocentric people from different cultures interact, there is little chance that they will achieve understanding. Common ethnocentric reactions to strongly differing views are anger, shock, or even amusement.[27]

▼ INTERPERSONAL NETWORKS

An **interpersonal communication network** refers to a pattern over time of communication flows between individuals.[28] It emphasizes communication *relationships* among individuals over time, rather than on the individuals themselves. Networks involve the ongoing flow of oral, written, and nonverbal signals (data) between two people or between one person and all other network members simultaneously. The concept doesn't focus on whether a specific signal sent was received as intended by the sender. However, communication networks can increase the likelihood of a match between messages as sent and as actually received and interpreted.

▼ Variety of Networks

The elements of interpersonal communication shown in Figure 12.1 are based on the involvement of only two people. Obviously, communication often takes place among many individuals and larger groups. For example, a manager normally has ongoing links with many people both inside and outside an organization. A manager's communication network extends laterally, vertically, and externally. *Vertical networks* typically include the manager's immediate superior and subordinates and the superior's superiors and the subordinates' subordinates. *Lateral networks* include people in the same department at the same level (peers) and people in different departments at the same level. *External networks* for managers may include customers, suppliers, regulatory agencies, pressure groups, professional peers, and friends. As you can readily see, an employee's communication network can become quite involved. This networking is based on a combination of formally prescribed and informally developed relationships.[29] Group size limits the possible communication networks within a group. In principle, as the size of a group increases arithmetically, the number of possible communication interrelationships increases exponentially. Accordingly, communication networks are much more varied and complex in a 12-person team than in a 5-person team. Although every member (theoretically) may be able to communicate with all other group members, the direction and number of communication channels in an organization often are somewhat limited. In committee meetings, for example, varying levels of formality influence who may speak, what may be discussed, and in what order. The relative status or ranking of group members also may differ. Members having higher status probably will dominate a communication network more than those with lower status. Even when an open network is encouraged, group members may actually use a limited network arrangement.

To provide a sense of the potential and powerful effects of communication networks, let's consider a single group—which could be a work team or informal social group—of five members. This approach reduces the complicating effects of different numbers of members in groups. A five-person group has about 60 possible communication networks. We consider only the five basic communication networks for a group of this size: the *star* (sometimes called the *wheel*), the *Y*, the *chain*, the *circle*, and the *all-channel network*. These five networks—presented in Figure 12.4—illustrate the communication possibilities in a five-person group. Each line between each pair of names rep-

FIGURE 12.4

Five Alternative Communication Networks for a Five-Person Group

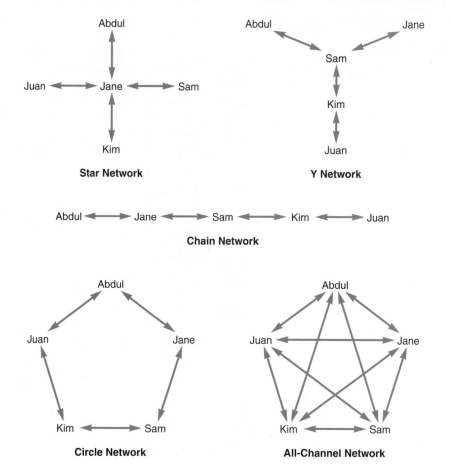

resents two-way communication. The degree of restriction on members in communicating with each other differentiates the networks. At one extreme, the star network is the most restricted: All communication between members must flow through Jane. At the other extreme, the all-channel network is the least restricted and most open: Each member communicates with all other members directly.

▼ Impacts of Networks

The importance of communication networks lies in their potential impacts on selecting group leaders, predicting effectiveness and efficiency, and ensuring member satisfaction.[30] Table 12.1 provides a brief comparison of the communication networks in terms of four assessment criteria. The first criterion, *degree of centralization,* is the extent to which some group members have access to more communication possibilities than other members. The star network is the most centralized, because all communication flows from and to only one member. The all-channel network is the least centralized, because any member can communicate with all other members. The criterion of *leadership predictability* is the ability to anticipate which group member is likely to emerge as the leader. In Figure 12.4, the following individuals are likely to emerge as leaders: Jane in the star network; Sam in the Y network; and possibly Sam in the chain network. In each of these three networks, the anticipated leaders should have more information and greater control over its dissemination than the other members.

The third and fourth assessment criteria in Table 12.1 address the average satisfaction of the group members as a whole within each network and the range in satisfaction between group members. Several interesting relationships exist between these two criteria. In the star network, the average member satisfaction in the group is likely to be the lowest compared to the other networks. However, the range in individual member satisfaction is likely to be the highest relative to the other networks. Jane might find the star network highly satisfying, because she is the center of attention and has considerable influence over the group. In contrast, the other members are highly dependent on Jane and may well play a small role in the decision process. Accordingly,

TABLE 12.1   Effects of Five Communication Networks

	Types of Communications Networks				
	Star	*Y*	*Chain*	*Circle*	*All-Channel*
Degree of centralization	Very high	High	Moderate	Low	Very low
Leadership predictability	Very high	High	Moderate	Low	Very low
Average group satisfaction	Low	Low	Moderate	Moderate	High
Range in individual member satisfaction	High	High	Moderate	Low	Very low

the average satisfaction of the group as a whole is likely to be relatively low. The all-channel network creates the potential for greater participation by all members in terms of their interests and abilities to contribute to the group. Average group satisfaction may be relatively high, and the range of satisfaction scores for individuals probably will be smaller than for the other networks.

▼ Implications of Networks

Knowing the types of communication networks used is especially important in understanding power and control relationships among employees in organizations.[31] Powerful individuals may limit access to information by others as one way of maintaining or increasing their power. (We discuss information as a source of power in Chapter 15.)

Problems may be thought of as simple or complex. Simple problems, such as scheduling overtime work, make few demands on group members in terms of (1) collecting, categorizing, and evaluating information, (2) generating goals to be achieved, (3) developing and evaluating alternatives, and (4) coping with interpersonal problems associated with the tasks at hand. Simple networks (e.g., superior to subordinate) often are effective for solving simple problems. However, complex problems (e.g., deciding whether to build a new plant) are characterized by a high degree of the types of demands just identified. All-channel or open networks (as in a self-managed team) often are more effective for solving complex problems.

Another factor is the degree to which members must work together to accomplish the team's tasks. With problems requiring little member interdependence, communication may be handled effectively through one of the more centralized networks. Think about various sports and the types of communication networks needed in them. In swimming, track, and golf, the coach usually is the central person in task coordination and communication. Team members can perform most of their tasks with minimal interactions with other team members. With a high degree of member interdependence—as in basketball, ice hockey, and soccer—the all-channel network is much more effective than a simple, centralized network. A complex communication network is required—both between coach and players and among players—as they perform their tasks.

Networks also have several implications for day-to-day communications in organizations. First, no single network is likely to prove effective in all situations for a team with a variety of tasks and goals. The apparently efficient, low-cost, and simple method of a superior instructing subordinates is likely to be ineffective if used exclusively. Dissatisfaction may become so great that members will leave the team or lose their motivation to contribute. Second, teams that face complex problems requiring high member interdependence may deal with them ineffectively because of inadequate sharing of information, consideration of alternatives, and so on. Third, a team must consider trade-offs or opportunity costs. A team committed to the exclusive use of the all-channel network may deal inefficiently with simple problems and tasks that require little member interdependence. In such cases, members also may become bored and dissatisfied with the meetings. They often simply come to feel that their time is being wasted. Another trade-off with the all-channel network is its implied labor costs. That is, team members must spend more time on processing a problem in meetings with the all-channel network. Hence, a team should use the type of network that is most appropriate to its tasks and problems.[32]

Informal networks in many organizations often create barriers for minorities and women as they seek opportunities and representation in white-male–dominated roles and departments, especially in upper level managerial networks. These informal managerial networks may value similarities among members in terms of gender, race, educational level, and the like.[33] Xerox is unique in its support of the establishment of *caucus groups* as a way to manage, value and nurture diversity. The caucus groups encourage networking to (1) link caucus members and upper management, (2) assist with personal and professional development; (3) provide support within the caucus, and (4) serve as role models to majority employees for managing diversity.[34] The following Managing Diversity account gives a sense of how African-Americans at Xerox developed their network—now a caucus group—to diversify the firm's established networks.

MANAGING DIVERSITY

African-American Network at Xerox

It all started in 1971 with the disappearance of Algy Guy. The ten other recently hired black sales representatives in Xerox Corporation's Washington (D.C.) office had no idea why their friend had abruptly left the company. The mystery ate at everyone. "We didn't know what happened, but if it happened to Algy, it could happen to us," recalls Gilbert H. Scott, who joined Xerox earlier that year. Fearing Guy's failure had something to do with race, Scott and his fellow African-Americans banded together to form a survival network. They named themselves the "Corporate Few," and met in each other's apartments to coach one another on presentation skills, sales techniques, and pricing strategies. The three more senior sales reps tutored the others on the nuances of Xerox culture: what to wear, whom to cultivate, and whom to avoid. They concluded that the subtle stuff helps shape careers.

"We couldn't risk having low performers," recalls Barry Rand. "We did not have the luxury to be mediocre." If one group member's performance was slipping, the others would lend a hand. "We'd take a day out of our territories and go help," Scott says. "There were 13 people selling in your territory in one day. You would get the recognition for the sales." Soon, the performance of some of the "Corporate Few" distinguished them on a national level. By 1973, the Washington network contacted two similar groups in California to schedule a national meeting in Philadelphia. About 100 of Xerox's 4,053 black employees showed up. Fellow workers noticed, the top executives in Stamford, Connecticut, noticed, but many Xerox managers were unhappy. "People thought we could be a unionizing effort," says Scott. "They asked, 'How come all these black people are meeting, and what are they trying to do?'" Although some grumbled, then-president David T. Kearns backed the idea, which squelched most of the complaints.

Xerox is now widely acclaimed for its acceptance of minorities. The internal African-American network is thriving, and 27 of Xerox's 264 vice-presidents

MANAGING DIVERSITY —*Continued*

are African-Americans. One of those is Scott, 46, who is vice-president in charge of U.S. field operations for Xerox Business Services. As for Rand, 48, he's Xerox's executive vice-president for operations and, as one of three top executives, in the running to succeed Chairman Paul A. Allaire. He stands a chance of becoming the first African-American chief executive of a major public company. Rand is proud of that, but he sees Xerox's success at promoting minorities in the context of corporate America's failure generally. "Xerox stands out," Rand laments. "And it's unfortunate that it does."[35]

▼ Groupware-Based Networking

An increasing range of groupware aids (information technologies) is available to support and extend interpersonal communication networks. Groupware aids (see Chapters 9 and 10) may substitute for direct face-to-face communication. In this section, we highlight a few of the groupware aids that make it easier for people at work to communicate with one another.

Electronic mail (E-mail) is a computer-based system that enables participating individuals to exchange and store messages with their computers. In sophisticated E-mail systems, the user gets a digest of all the incoming mail, with headings noting the name of the sender, the time and date an item was sent, and what it is about. The user can then choose which full messages to call up. In addition to transmitting messages between employees down the hall or overseas, E-mail technology even permits computer-to-computer exchanges of purchase orders, invoices, electronic payment of bills, and so on.[36] E-mail reduces barriers of time and distance in the creation of communication networks. It also minimizes "phone tag," in which individuals trade numerous phone calls before catching up with each other. Kimber Edwards, a senior sales representative for Banyon Systems in San Francisco, comments: "I am completely addicted to E-mail. I log in the first thing when I wake up and the last thing before I go to bed. I was even up at 11 P.M. on Christmas eve 'talking' with customers and work mates." Edwards sends and receives about 30 E-mail messages each day.[37]

Voice mail is a computer-based messaging system that people access by telephone. They may use it as they would an answering machine to receive recorded messages or as they would memoranda to send recorded messages to others. Although more expensive to operate than an E-mail system, voice mail is a richer information medium than E-mail. Voice mail is an excellent medium for sending short, simple, and noncontroversial messages.[38]

Telecommuting refers to the practice of working at home while linked to the office or plant with groupware. It also includes those who work out of a customer's office or communicate with the office or plant via a laptop computer or mobile phone. Telecommuting often incorporates computer-based software, E-mail, voice mail, fax machines, and related technologies. Telecommuting jobs usually involve some combination of

   ▲ tasks that can be performed and transmitted with the use of groupware aids;

   ▲ regular telephone use;

▲ routine information handling;

▲ tasks that can be performed independently of others and, if necessary, be coordinated with others via groupware aids; and/or

▲ project-oriented jobs with well-defined targets and schedules.

Telecommuting jobs include salesperson, real estate agent, computer systems analyst, data entry clerk, consultant, author, security broker, and copy editor. An estimated 8 million U.S. and Canadian employees have already formed telecommuting arrangements with their employers, and the number is growing. Among the more well-known companies with successful telecommuting programs for some employees are IBM, Xerox, American Express, Du Pont, Pacific Bell, J.C. Penney, and Apple Computer.[39] However, telecommuting isn't for everyone. Some telecommuters experience a sense of isolation, stagnation, or compulsive overwork. Julie Rohrer, who works full time from her home as a transcriber for a hospital in Madison, Wisconsin, says: "Every day is the same. You put in your eight hours and there isn't anybody to talk to, and you miss what's going on in the outside world. You feel you're in your house constantly."[40] Rohrer clearly misses face-to-face interactions on the job.

The potential advantages of groupware aids are fairly obvious. They allow people to communicate with one another more easily, quickly, and less expensively. However, some problems need to be guarded against. First, as suggested by Julie Rohrer's comment, these aids haven't been effective for relationship building or complex group problem solving where face-to-face dialogue (the richest medium) continues to be crucial. Second, groupware aids can break down the boundaries between work time and nonwork time. These boundaries are especially useful for many employees in managing work stress (see Chapter 8). If not managed carefully, these technologies can evolve into a continuous invasion of privacy by enabling managers and other workers to contact the employee easily at any time. Third, groupware aids may erode the delegation of authority by creating too much and too frequent communications between superiors and subordinates. That is, superiors may start to oversupervise the work of subordinates because giving and getting constant feedback is too easy. Fourth, groupware aids open the possibility of wasting time on increased volumes of meaningless data (junk) with the consequence of unnecessary work overload. These problems are not inevitable, and awareness is the first step in avoiding them.[41]

▼ FOSTERING DIALOGUE

In the remainder of this chapter, we focus on the skills and behaviors that directly foster dialogue between individuals. The absence or lack of these skills and behaviors will hinder or prevent dialogue. In Chapter 10, we introduced *dialogue* as a process where people have learned to suspend their defensive exchanges to enable a free flow of inquiry into their own and others assumptions and beliefs. Dialogue can build mutual trust and common ground.[42] A necessary, but not sufficient condition for dialogue, is the assertive communication approach. Recall that, in the Preview Case, Kim employed the assertive communication approach, but Sam didn't. True dialogue requires that interacting individuals demonstrate multiple skills and behaviors. Figure 12.5 presents the idea that the *ultimate* in dialogue is characterized by a network

FIGURE 12.5

Network of Skills and Behaviors
That Foster Dialogue

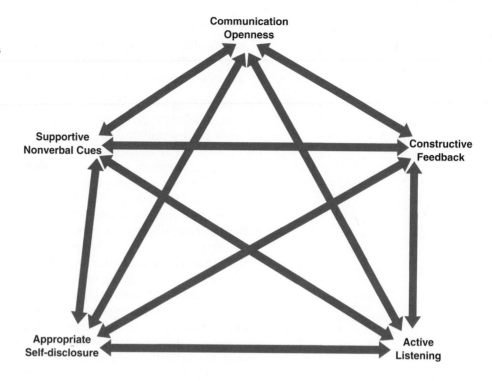

of skills and behaviors, including communication openness, constructive feedback, appropriate self-disclosure, active listening, and supportive nonverbal cues.

▼ Communication Openness

Communication openness may be viewed as a continuum ranging from closed, guarded, and defensive to open, candid, and nondefensive.[43] Figure 12.6 shows that, at the extreme left side of the continuum, every message (regardless of the medium of transmission) is weighed, analyzed, and scrutinized. Communication occurs on the direct level and the meta-communication level. **Meta-communication** refers to the (hidden) assumptions, inferences, and interpretations of the parties that form the basis of overt messages. In closed communications, senders and receivers *consciously* and *purposely* hide their real agendas and "messages." Thus game playing is rampant. Meta-communications focus on inferences such as: (1) "what I think you think about what I said"; (2) "what I think you really mean"; (3) "what I really mean but hope you don't realize what I mean"; (4) "what you're saying but what I think you really mean"; and (5) "what I think you're trying to tell me but aren't directly telling me because...(you're afraid of hurting my feelings, you think being totally open could hurt your chances of promotion, etc.)."

At the extreme right side of the continuum, the communications are totally open, candid, and supportive. The words and nonverbal cues sent convey an authentic message that the sender chose without a hidden agenda. The purpose of communication is to reveal intent, not conceal it. The individuals express what they mean and mean what they convey. Breakdowns in

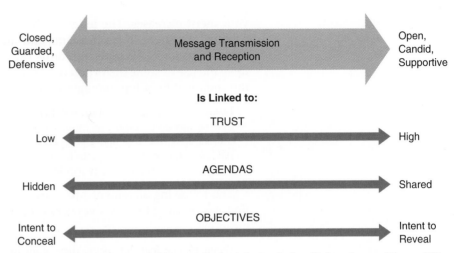

FIGURE 12.6

The Communication Openness Continuum

Source: Adapted from Sussman, L. Managers: On the defensive. *Business Horizons*, January–February 1991, 83, Copyright © 1991 by the Foundation for the School of Business at Indiana University. Used with permission.

communication at this end of the continuum are due primarily to honest errors (e.g., as the different meanings that people assign to words such as soon or immediately).

Communication openness usually is a matter of degree rather than an absolute. The nature of language, linguistics, and different interpersonal relationships (co-worker to co-worker, subordinate to superior, friend to friend, spouse to spouse, etc.) create the situational forces that allow for degrees of shading, coloring, amplification, and deflection in the use of words and nonverbal cues as symbols of meaning.

Key Implications   The degree of openness must be considered in relation to the situational risk factors associated with such openness. (We address these factors at length in Chapter 13 on conflict and negotiation, Chapter 14 on organizational cultures, and Chapter 15 on power and political behavior.) We note just three of them here briefly. First, the history of the relationship is perhaps the most significant factor affecting trust and risk taking in interpersonal communication. Has the other person violated your or others' trust in the past? Has the other person provided cues (verbal and/or nonverbal) soliciting or reinforcing your attempts to be open and candid? Or has the other person provided cues to the contrary? Has the history of the relationship created a level of such comfort that both you and the other person can focus on direct communication, rather than meta-communication?[44] Second, if the encounter is likely to be partly adversarial (such as union and management in wage negotiations) or the other person is committed to damaging or weakening your position or gaining at your expense, engaging in guarded communication is rational. Conversely, if the encounter is likely to be friendly and the other person is trying to please you, strengthen your position, or enhance your esteem, guarded communication may be viewed as irrational. Third, when you communicate with someone of higher status and power, you are communicating with someone who has some control over your fate. This person may appraise your performance, judge your promotability, and determine your merit increases. The tendency is to project a favorable image, to encode negative messages in euphemisms and qualifiers, which may be understandable and rational. This perception is especially valid if past encounters reinforce the use of some distortion over completely honest disclosures.[45] Consider the comment by a top manager of a Fortune 500 company:

> Listen, I've attended enough seminars and read enough self-help books to know that relationships ought to be based on honesty, mutual support, and open communications. But I've also managed long enough in this company and other companies to know that complete honesty can hurt both parties and the organization. The principle isn't always worth the cost of hurt feelings and ruined relationships.[46]

The following statement provides an interesting summary of the research findings on closed (defensive) versus open (supportive) interpersonal communications:

> When people feel defensive, they want to strike out; when they feel understood, they want to reach out. When people feel defensive, they want to do something to the other person; when they feel understood, they want to do something for the other person and for people in general.[47]

The following Managing in Practice account illustrates the communication openness, constructive feedback, and active listening involved in the merger of Federal Express and Flying Tiger Airline.

MANAGING IN PRACTICE

A Merger with Communication Openness

Several years ago Federal Express (FedEx) acquired Flying Tiger Line, Inc., its rival in the international air freight business. FedEx senior managers realized that the organization's "strategic fit" would mean little if the people in the organizations could not be convinced that the merger made sense. The FedEx credo of "People-Service-Profit" was about to be put to a highly visible test. As Jim Perkins, senior vice president for personnel at FedEx said: "We wanted a merger our people would be proud of, to reflect who we are as a company, our people philosophy. We wanted a merger that would bring the merged company on to the FedEx team." Employees throughout the organizations were concerned, however. Careers, loyalty, and years of trust were at stake.

FedEx management didn't waste much time in beginning to address these concerns. In fact, some believe that its communication measures were extraordinary. Less than two hours after the Dow Jones wire service announced the merger, FedEx Chairman Fred Smith and Chief Operating Officer Jim Barksdale gave a spontaneous address over the company's satellite television network—FXTV—to 35,000 employees in 800 locations. From the start, Smith and Barksdale described the move as a "merger," not an "acquisition." The phrasing had symbolic importance to people in both organizations. The choice of terminology "didn't require a lot of debate or discussion," said Carol Presley, senior vice president for marketing and corporate communications. "We wanted Flying Tiger people to feel we really did want them."

Still, FedEx employees had serious concerns. Most Flying Tiger employees, for instance, were unionized. Moreover, some had been employed by their company longer than FedEx had been in existence. To FedEx employees, there-

MANAGING IN PRACTICE —*Continued*

fore, joining forces with these outsiders could threaten their seniority. Altogether, the hopes and dreams of 70,000 people were involved. And the FedEx management team would spend what some might view as an extravagant amount of time and money to communicate—talk *and* listen—with employees. For months following the merger announcement, questions and answers traveled back and forth, up and down the organization. The means of communication included face-to-face meetings, company publications, videos, and television programs, including the daily company news broadcast, "FX Overnight."

FedEx managers considered the effort well worth the expense. In fact, openly addressing the concerns proved vital to the achievement of all of the goals that both sides wanted. Barksdale described the payoff: "Placing such an emphasis on internal communication has made us the company we are. We couldn't be anywhere near the size we are, and have the profitability or the relationship with our employees we have, if we weren't deeply into the business of communicating with people."[48]

▼ Constructive Feedback

In giving feedback, we share our thoughts and feelings about others with them. Feedback may involve personal feelings or abstract thoughts, as when we react to others' ideas or proposals. The emotional impact of feedback varies according to how personally it is focused. When we attempt to achieve dialogue, feedback should be *supportive* (reinforcing ongoing behavior) or *corrective* (indicating that a change in behavior is appropriate). The following are principles of constructive feedback that can foster dialogue.

- ▲ Constructive feedback is based on a foundation of trust between sender and receiver. If the organization is characterized by extreme personal competitiveness, emphasis on the use of power to punish and control, and rigid superior–subordinate relationships, it will lack the level of trust necessary for constructive feedback, thereby contributing to closed communications and limited dialogue.

- ▲ Constructive feedback is specific rather than general. It uses clear and recent examples. Saying "You are a dominating person" is not as useful as saying "Just now when we were deciding the issue, you did not listen to what others said. I felt I had to accept your argument or face attack from you."

- ▲ Constructive feedback is given at a time when the receiver appears to be ready to accept it. When a person is angry, upset, or defensive, it probably isn't the time to bring up other, new issues.

- ▲ Constructive feedback is checked with the receiver to determine whether it seems valid. The sender can ask the receiver to rephrase and restate the feedback to see whether it matches what the sender intended.

- ▲ Constructive feedback includes behaviors the receiver may be capable of doing something about.

▲ Constructive feedback doesn't include more than the receiver can handle at any particular time. For example, the receiver may become threatened and defensive if the feedback includes everything the receiver does that annoys the sender.[49]

Giving people personal feedback helps them look at their behaviors by sharing how you feel. People who are given and accept accurate feedback don't necessarily change their behaviors. Individual change usually isn't that easy.[50] Constructive feedback is vital to an organization's effectiveness. Consider one customer feedback practice: the apology. "I get a lot of people saying, 'If that doctor had just said he was sorry, I wouldn't be here suing him,'" says Robert Sullivan, a New York City attorney specializing in personal injury lawsuits. Although Sullivan acknowledges that an apology could come back to haunt someone in a legal action—as in "he felt so guilty he even said he was sorry"—he believes that it is worth the risk. "I think 'I'm sorry' goes a long way, and I recommend it," he says.[51]

"Often when you're mistreated as a consumer, it's not just your pocketbook that hurts, it's your pride," says Cleo Manuel of the National Consumers League. "A lot of people call us for sympathy, so we do a lot of apologizing for companies we have no control over. Half the time when we say 'I'm sorry this happened,' there's this weight lifted off our shoulders." Manuel's telephone service was recently cut off by mistake. Apologies? The telephone company "not only didn't say they were sorry for the inconvenience, they said I was lucky they didn't make me pay an extra deposit," Manuel says.[52]

▼ Appropriate Self-Disclosure

Self-disclosure is any information that individuals communicate (verbally or nonverbally) about themselves to others. People often unconsciously disclose much about themselves by what they say and how they present themselves to others.[53] The ability to express yourself to other individuals usually is basic to personal growth and development. The relationship between self-disclosure and effectiveness in an organization appears to be curvilinear. Nondisclosing individuals may repress their real feelings because to reveal them is threatening. Conversely, total-disclosure individuals, who expose a great deal about themselves to anyone they meet, actually may be unable to communicate with others because they are too preoccupied with themselves. The presence of appropriate self-disclosure between superior and subordinate, co-workers, or employees and customers can facilitate dialogue and sharing of work-related problems.[54] The ties among personality and self-disclosure have been expressed as follows:

> Healthy personality is manifested by a model of what we call authenticity, or more simply, honesty. Less healthy personalities, people who function less than fully, who suffer recurrent breakdowns or chronic impasses, may usually be found to be liars. They say things they do not mean. Their disclosures have been chosen more for cosmetic value than for truth. The consequences of a lifetime of lying about oneself to others, of saying and doing things for their sound and appearance, is that ultimately the person loses contact with his or her real self. The authentic being manifested by healthier personalities takes the form of unself-conscious disclosure of self in words, decisions, and actions.[55]

A person's level in the organization often complicates self-disclosure. Individuals are likely to dampen self-disclosure to those with higher formal power because of their ability to give raises and promotions or demotions and dismissals. Even when a subordinate is able and willing to engage in "appropriate" forms of self-disclosure at work, a perception of the superior's trustworthiness in not using the revealed information to punish, intimidate, or ridicule is likely to influence the amount and form of self-disclosure.[56]

▼ Active Listening

Active listening is necessary to encourage maximum levels of feedback and openness. **Listening** is a process that integrates physical, emotional, and intellectual inputs in a search for meaning and understanding.[57] Listening is effective when the receiver understands the sender's message as intended.

As much as 40% of an eight-hour work day of many employees is devoted to listening. However, tests of listening comprehension suggest that people often listen at only 25% efficiency.[58] Listening skills influence the quality of peer, superior–subordinate, and employee–customer relationships. Employees who dislike their superior may find it extremely difficult to listen attentively to the superior's comments during performance review sessions. The following guidelines are suggested for increasing listening skills to foster dialogue.

- ▲ Active listening involves having a reason or purpose for listening. Good listeners tend to search for value and meaning in what is being said, even if they are not predisposed to be interested in the particular issue or topic. Poor listeners tend to rationalize any or all inattention on the basis of a lack of initial interest.
- ▲ Active listening involves suspending judgment, at least initially. Good listening requires concentrating on the sender's whole message, rather than forming evaluations on the basis of the first few ideas presented.
- ▲ Active listening involves resisting distractions, such as noises, sights, and other people, and focusing on the sender.
- ▲ Active listening involves pausing before responding to the sender.
- ▲ Active listening involves rephrasing in your own words the content and feeling of what the sender seems to be saying, especially when the message is emotional or unclear.
- ▲ Active listening seeks out the sender's important themes in terms of the overall content and feeling of the message.
- ▲ Active listening involves using the time differential between the rate of thought (400 or 500 words per minute) and the rate of speech (100 to 150 words per minute) to reflect on content and search for meaning.[59]

Most of these active listening skills are interrelated. That is, you cannot practice one without improving the others. Unfortunately, like the guidelines for improving feedback, the listening-skills guidelines are much easier to understand than to develop and practice. The more that you practice active listening skills, the greater will be the likelihood that you can enter into effective dialogue. Active listening is not just important within an organization; it is vital to TQM, which strives to meet or exceed customer expectations. The following

Managing Quality feature describes Honda's approach to listening actively to current and prospective customers.

How Honda Listens

Honda uses all the standard research tools, including focus groups and surveys, to listen to current and prospective customers. The company even videotapes drivers as they test new cars. In response to all this customer input, Honda has made thousands of changes in the Accord since introducing it in 1976. The improvements range from installing a new suspension handling system to changing the shape of the rear window so that a large soft drink can be passed into the car without spilling. In the process, Honda just happened to produce the best-selling car in the United States from 1989 until 1992, when the Ford Taurus edged it out. Says Ben Knight, vice-president for R&D of Honda North America: "We believe that the market and the customer will always find the truth."

Honda's manufacturing unit kicked off its most extensive customer listening effort yet, the E.T. Phone Home Project, in November 1992. (The name and notion were lifted from the film *E.T.*) Over the following three months, factory workers who actually assembled the Accord in Ohio called more than 47,000 recent U.S. and Canadian Accord buyers. They represented about half the owners who registered their cars with the company the previous spring. Honda's goal: to find out if customers were happy with their autos and to get more ideas for improvements. Because of the long lead times in the auto industry, the impact of the E.T. Phone Home project showed up on the 1995 Accords.[60]

▼ NONVERBAL COMMUNICATION

Nonverbal communication includes nonlanguage human responses (such as body motions and personal physical attributes) and environmental characteristics (such as a large or small office). Nonverbal cues may contain many hidden messages and can influence the process and outcome of face-to-face communication. Even a person who is silent or inactive in the presence of others may be sending a message, which may or may not be the intended message (e.g., boredom, fear, anger, or depression).[61]

▼ Types of Nonverbal Cues

Table 12.2 identifies the basic types of nonverbal cues. It also illustrates the numerous ways people can and do communicate without saying or writing a word. Nonverbal communication is important to verbal communication in that neither is adequate by itself for effective dialogue. Verbal and nonverbal cues can be related in the following ways:

▲ by repeating, as when verbal directions to some location are accompanied by pointing;

TABLE 12.2 Types of Nonverbal Cues

Basic Type	Explanation and Examples
Body motion	Gestures, facial expressions, eye behavior, touching, and any other movement of the limbs and body
Personal physical characteristics	Body shape, physique, posture, body or breath odors, height, weight, hair color, and skin color
Paralanguage	Voice qualities, volume, speech rate, pitch, nonfluencies (saying "ah," "um," or "uh"), laughing, yawning, and so on
Use of space	Ways people use and perceive space, including seating arrangements, conversational distance, and the "territorial" tendency of humans to stake out a personal space
Physical environment	Building and room design, furniture and other objects, interior decorating, cleanliness, lighting, and noise
Time	Being late or early, keeping others waiting, cultural differences in time perception, and the relationship between time and status

▲ by contradicting, as in the case of the person who says, "What, me nervous?" while fidgeting and perspiring anxiously before taking a test—a good example of how the nonverbal message might be more believable when verbal and nonverbal signals disagree;

▲ by substituting nonverbal for verbal cues, as when an employee returns to the office with a stressful expression that says, "I've had a horrible meeting with my manager," without a word being spoken; and

▲ by complementing the verbal cue through nonverbal "underlining," as when a person pounds the table, places a hand on the shoulder of a co-worker, or uses a tone of voice indicating the great importance attached to the message.[62]

Earlier in the chapter, we presented nonverbal cues and tips for a variety of cultures. In the following Managing Across Cultures account, we present some of the common nonverbal expectations, the *silent language*, in Mexico.

MANAGING ACROSS CULTURES

Nonverbal Expectations in Mexico

A somewhat soft handshake is the customary greeting among both men and women. Men normally let the woman make the first move toward handshaking. After the second or third meeting, Mexican men may begin with or add the *abrazo*, the embrace, along with a few pats on the back. Women friends will embrace lightly and pretend to kiss a cheek. In some areas of Mexico, you may encounter an unusual addition to the handshake. After gripping the palm, the two people slide their hands upward to grasp each other's thumbs.

Many Mexicans are "touch oriented." This means they may linger over a handshake, they may touch the forearm or elbow, or they may even casually finger the lapel of the other person's suit. All these touches merely signify a willingness to be friendly, nothing more.

MANAGING ACROSS CULTURES —*Continued*

While eating, both hands should be kept above the table, not in the lap. When passing an object to another person, hand it—don't toss it. The same is true when handing over change—don't put it on the counter, place it in the hand. In public, men should not stand with their hands in their pockets. A man standing with his hands on his hips suggests hostility or a challenge. To beckon others, extend the arm, palm down, with the fingers making a scratching motion inward. Deference is shown to the elderly, so give way to them in public places and don't object if they are waited on first. Patience is important; avoid showing anger if and when you encounter delays or interruptions.[63]

Nonverbal cues have been linked to a wide variety of concepts and issues. We briefly consider two: (1) status, in terms of the relative ranking of individuals and groups; and (2) gender differences.

▼ Status and Nonverbal Cues

Here we present only three of the many relationships between organizational status and nonverbal cues.

▲ Employees of higher status typically have better offices than employees of lower status. Executive offices tend to be more spacious, located on the top floors of the building, and have finer carpets and furniture than those of first-line managers. Most senior offices will be at the corners so they have windows on two sides.

▲ The offices of higher status employees are better "protected" than those of lower status employees. By protected, we mean how much more difficult it would be for you to arrange to visit the governor of your state than for the governor to arrange to visit you. Top executive areas are typically least accessible and are often sealed off from others by several doors and assistants. Even lower level managers and many staff personnel are "protected" by having an office with a door and a secretary who answers the telephone.

▲ The higher the employee's status, the easier that employee finds it to invade the territory of lower status employees. A superior typically feels free to walk right in on subordinates, whereas subordinates are more careful to ask permission or make an appointment before visiting a superior.[64]

Carried to excess, these and other nonverbal status cues are likely to create barriers to dialogue, especially from the perspective of the employees with lower formal status. However, effective managers often use supportive nonverbal cues when meeting with subordinates, such as (1) lightly touching subordinates on the arm when they arrive and shaking hands, (2) smiling appropriately, (3) nodding to affirm what was said, (4) slightly pulling their chairs closer to subordinates and maintaining an open posture, and (5) engaging in eye contact to further demonstrate listening and interest.[65]

▼ Gender Differences and Nonverbal Cues

Physical differences between men and women contribute to differences in their nonverbal behavior. They are minor compared to the differences based on cultural influences. In addition to communicating gender, body language may communicate status and power. Many signs of dominance and submission are exchanged through nonverbal communication. Some nonverbal behaviors are associated with the subordinate position for either gender. But many of these same behaviors have been associated with women, regardless of status. In this section, we describe three nonverbal patterns, and note how they may differ by gender.[66] These patterns reflect generalities and certainly do not apply to all men and women. Moreover, we know that in some segments of U.S. and Canadian societies, these patterns have changed or are changing.[67]

Use of Space   Women's bodily behavior more often is restrained and restricted than men's. In fact, their femininity is gauged by how little space they take up. Masculinity is judged by men's expansiveness and the strength of their gestures. Men control greater territory and personal space, a property associated with dominance and status. Studies have found that people tend to approach women more closely than men, seat themselves closer to women, and cut across women's paths in hallways, and so on.

Eye Contact   Gender may influence eye contact. In personal interactions, women tend to look more at the other person than men do—and they maintain more woman-to-woman eye contact. Some research suggests that women are more skilled than men in accurately decoding nonverbal cues.[68] People tend to maintain more eye contact with those from whom they want approval. Women are stared at and reciprocate by not looking back more than men. Men routinely stare at women in public. Our language even has specific words, *ogling* and *leering*, for this practice.

Touching   Touching may be another gesture of dominance. Cuddling in response to touch may be a corresponding gesture of submission. Just as a manager can put a hand on a worker, a master on a servant, and a teacher on a student, so men frequently put their hands on women, despite folklore to the contrary.

Another side to touching is much better understood: Touching symbolizes friendship and intimacy. The power aspect of touching doesn't rule out its intimacy aspect. A particular touch may have both components and more, but it is the *pattern* of touching between individuals that tells us the most about their relationship. When touching is reciprocal—that is, when both people have equal touching privileges—we have information about the intimacy of the relationship. Much touching indicates closeness, and little touching indicates distance. When one person is free to touch the other but not vice versa, we have information about status and power. The person with greater touching privileges probably has higher status or more power.

Breaking the Mold   Many women have been reversing these nonverbal interaction patterns. Women now feel freer to stop smiling when they are unhappy, stop lowering their eyes, stop getting out of men's way on the street, and stop letting themselves be interrupted. They can stare people in the eye, address someone by first name if that person addresses them by their first name, and touch when they feel it is appropriate. Men need to become more aware of what they are signifying nonverbally. Men can restrain their invasions of personal space by avoiding staring, touching (if not by mutual consent), and interrupting.[69]

Summary

When individuals engage in effective interpersonal communication, they increase their own sense of well-being and become more productive. The essential elements in the communication process include: senders, receivers, transmitters, receptors, messages, channels, noise, meaning, encoding, decoding, and feedback. All are interrelated. Individuals may approach communication differently: They may be assertive, nonassertive, or aggressive.

Face-to-face interpersonal communication has the highest degree of information richness. An information-rich medium is especially important for performing complex tasks and resolving social and emotional issues that involve considerable uncertainty and ambiguity. Important issues usually contain significant amounts of uncertainty, ambiguity, and people-related (especially social and emotional) problems.

There are numerous potential barriers to interpersonal communication. We briefly reviewed the underlying interpersonal barriers discussed in previous chapters. Direct potential barriers include the nonassertive and aggressive communication approaches, noise, bypassing and semantics, demeaning language routines, and lying and distortion. The potential for barriers owing to cultural differences always is present but may be especially high when the interaction takes place between individuals from high context and low context cultures.

Through their many communication networks, individuals may repeat the interpersonal communication process dozens of times each day. Individuals' communication networks operate both vertically and laterally. These networks can range from closed and centralized to open and decentralized and may hinder or support organizational diversity. Groupware-based networking by means of E-mail, voice mail, and telecommuting is growing rapidly.

People need to use certain skills and behaviors to foster dialogue. They include communication openness, constructive feedback, active listening, appropriate self-disclosure, and supportive nonverbal cues. Nonverbal cues play a powerful role in fostering dialogue, either supporting or contradicting what is being said. For example, formal organizational status often is tied to nonverbal cues, and status and gender differences in the use of nonverbal cues exist. If not used appropriately, nonverbal cues may hinder dialogue.

Key Words and Concepts

Aggressive communication	Data	Ethnocentrism
Assertive communication	Decoding	Feedback
Bypassing	Distortion	High context culture
Channels	Electronic mail (E-mail)	Honesty
Cultural context	Encoding	Impression management

Intercultural communication
Interpersonal communication
Interpersonal communication
   network
Language routines
Listening
Low-context culture

Lying
Meanings
Media richness
Messages
Meta-communication
Noise
Nonassertive communication

Nonverbal communication
Receptors
Self-disclosure
Semantics
Telecommuting
Transmitters
Voice mail

Discussion Questions

1. What difficulties might most people have in trying to use the assertive communication approach consistently?

2. Give two examples of how interpersonal classroom communication is likely to vary in a high-context culture and in a low-context culture.

3. Describe your communication network. Would you like to make any changes in it? Why or why not?

4. What types of problems are less likely to be communicated effectively by E-mail than in face-to-face discussion? Explain.

5. Think of an organization or team of which you are a member. How would you assess it in terms of the continuum of communication openness? (See Figure 12.6.)

6. What types of problems and limitations prevent meaningful self-disclosure between superiors and subordinates?

7. How are constructive feedback skills and active listening similar and different?

8. Describe the common nonverbal cues used by someone you have worked for or by someone you know well. Are they usually consistent or inconsistent with this person's verbal expressions? Explain.

9. If you take a job in a foreign culture, what communication practices must you be sensitive to?

10. If you are supervised by a person of a different gender, what nonverbal problems might you encounter?

▲ Developing Skills

Self-Diagnosis: Personal Communication Practices[70]

Instructions

This survey is designed to assess your interpersonal communication practices. For each item on the survey, you are requested to indicate which of the alternative reactions would be more characteristic of the way *you* would handle the situation described. Some alternatives may by equally characteristic of you or equally uncharacteristic. Although this is a possibility, please choose the alternative that is *relatively* more characteristic of you. For each item, you will have five points that you may *distribute* in any of the following combinations, where 5 = most characteristic and 0 = least characteristic. The following are example responses.

	A	B
1.	5	0
2.	4	1
3.	3	2
4.	2	3
5.	1	4
6.	0	5

Thus, there are six possible combinations for responding to the pair of alternatives presented to you with each survey item. *Be sure the numbers you assign to each pair sum to 5.*

To the extent possible, please relate each situation in the survey to your own personal experience. In this survey, we alternate the words *he/she* and *him/her* to include both the feminine and masculine genders with balanced frequency.

1. If a friend of mine had a personality conflict with a mutual acquaintance of ours with whom it was important for her to get along, I would:
   ____A. Tell my friend that I felt she was partially responsible for any problems with this other person and try to let her know how the person was being affected by her.
   ____B. Not get involved because I would not be able to continue to get along with both of them once I had entered into the conflict.

2. If one of my friends and I had a heated argument in the past and I realized that he was ill at ease around me from that time on, I would:
   ____A. Avoid making things worse by discussing his behavior and just let the whole thing drop.
   ____B. Bring up his behavior and ask him how he felt the argument had affected our relationship.

3. If a friend began to avoid me and act in an aloof and withdrawn manner, I would:
   _____A. Tell her about her behavior and suggest she tell me what was on her mind.
   _____B. Follow her lead and keep our contacts brief and aloof since that seems to be what she wants.

4. If two of my friends and I were talking and one of my friends slipped and brought up a personal problem of mine that involved the other friend, and of which he was not yet aware, I would:
   _____A. Change the subject and signal my friend to do the same.
   _____B. Fill in my uninformed friend on what the other friend was talking about and suggest that we go into it later.

5. If a friend were to tell me that, in her opinion, I was doing things that made me less effective than I might be in social situations, I would:
   _____A. Ask her to spell out or describe what she has observed and suggest changes I might make.
   _____B. Resent the criticism and let her know why I behave the way I do.

6. If one of my friends aspired to an office in our student organization for which I felt he was unqualified and if he had been tentatively assigned to that position by the president of the student society, I would:
   _____A. Not mention my misgivings to either my friend or the president and let them handle it in their own way.
   _____B. Tell my friend and the president of my misgivings and then leave the final decision up to them.

7. If I felt that one of my friends was being unfair to me and her other friends, but none of them had mentioned anything about it, I would:
   _____A. Ask several of those people how they perceived the situation to see if they felt she was being unfair.
   _____B. Not ask the others how they perceived our friend but wait for them to bring it up to me.

8. If I were preoccupied with some personal matters and a friend told me that I had become irritated with him and others and that I was jumping on him for unimportant things, I would:
   _____A. Tell him I was preoccupied and would probably be on edge a while and would prefer not to be bothered.
   _____B. Listen to his complaints but not try to explain my actions to him.

9. If I had heard some friends discussing an ugly rumor about a friend of mine that I knew could hurt her and she asked me what I knew about it, if anything, I would:
   _____A. Say I didn't know anything about it and tell her no one would believe a rumor like that anyway.
   _____B. Tell her exactly what I had heard, when I had heard it, and from whom I had heard it.

10. If a friend pointed out the fact that I had a personality conflict with another friend with whom it was important for me to get along, I would:
    _____A. Consider his comments out of line and tell him I didn't want to discuss the matter any further.
    _____B. Talk about it openly with him to find out how my behavior was being affected by this.

11. If my relationship with a friend has been damaged by repeated arguments on an issue of importance to us both, I would:
    _____A. Be cautious in my conversations with her so the issue would not come up again to worsen our relationship.
    _____B. Point to the problems the controversy was causing in our relationship and suggest that we discuss it until we get it resolved.

12. If in a personal discussion with a friend about his problems and behavior, he suddenly suggested we discuss my problems and behavior as well as his own, I would:
    _____A. Try to keep the discussion away from me by suggesting that other, closer friends often talked to me about such matters.
    _____B. Welcome the opportunity to hear what he felt about me and encourage his comments.

13. If a friend of mine began to tell me about her hostile feelings about another friend who she felt was being unkind to others (and I wholeheartedly agreed), I would:
    _____A. Listen and also express my own feelings to her so she would know where I stood.
    _____B. Listen but not express my own negative views and opinions because she might repeat what I said to her in confidence.

14. If I thought an ugly rumor was being spread about me and suspected that one of my friends had quite likely heard it, I would:
    _____A. Avoid mentioning the issue and leave it to him to tell me about it if he wanted to.
    _____B. Risk putting him on the spot by asking him directly what he knew about the whole thing.

15. If I had observed a friend in social situations and thought that she was doing a number of things that hurt her relationships, I would:
    _____A. Risk being seen as a busybody and tell her what I had observed and my reactions to it.
    _____B. Keep my opinions to myself, rather than be seen as interfering in things that are none of my business.

16. If two friends and I were talking and one of them inadvertently mentioned a personal problem that involved me but of which I knew nothing, I would:
    _____A. Press them for information about the problem and their opinions about it.
    _____B. Leave it up to my friends to tell me or not tell me, letting them change the subject if they wished.

17. If a friend seemed to be preoccupied and began to jump on me for seemingly unimportant things and to become irritated with me and others without real cause, I would:
    ____A. Treat him with kid gloves for a while on the assumption that he was having some temporary personal problems that were none of my business.
    ____B. Try to talk to him about it and point out to him how his behavior was affecting people.

18. If I had begun to dislike certain habits of a friend to the point that it was interfering with my enjoying her company, I would:
    ____A. Say nothing to her directly but let her know my feelings by ignoring her whenever her annoying habits were obvious.
    ____B. Get my feelings out in the open and clear the air so that we could continue our friendship comfortably and enjoyably.

19. In discussing social behavior with one of my more sensitive friends, I would:
    ____A. Avoid mentioning his flaws and weaknesses so as not to hurt his feelings.
    ____B. Focus on his flaws and weaknesses so he could improve his interpersonal skills.

20. If I knew I might be assigned to an important position in our group and my friends' attitudes toward me had become rather negative, I would:

____A. Discuss my shortcomings with my friends so I could see where to improve.
____B. Try to figure out my own shortcomings by myself so I could improve.

Scoring Key

In the Personal Communication Practices Survey, there are ten items that deal with your receptivity to feedback and ten that are concerned with your willingness to self-disclose. Transfer your scores from each item to this scoring key. Add the scores in each column. Now, transfer these scores to Figure 12.7 by drawing a vertical line through the feedback score and a horizontal line through the self-disclosure line.

Receptivity to Feedback		Willingness to Self-Disclose	
2. B	____	1. A	____
3. A	____	4. B	____
5. A	____	6. B	____
7. A	____	9. B	____
8. B	____	11. B	____
10. B	____	13. A	____
12. B	____	15. A	____
14. B	____	17. B	____
16. A	____	18. B	____
20. A	____	19. B	____
Total: ____		Total: ____	

FIGURE 12.7

Personal Openness in Interpersonal Communications

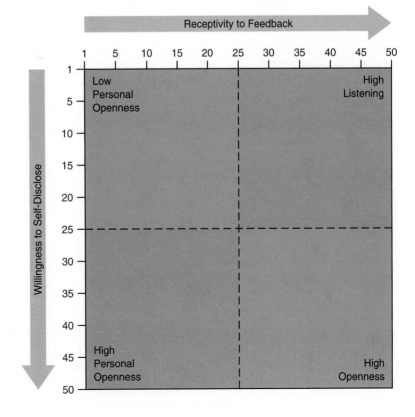

As Figure 12.7 suggests, higher scores in *receptivity to feedback* and *willingness to self-disclose* indicate a greater willingness to engage in personal openness in interpersonal communications. Of course, you need to be mindful of the situational factors that may influence your natural personal preference to be relatively more open or closed in interpersonal communication.

A Case in Point: Xographics[71]

Part A

Xographics was a division of a large telecommunications company, Ellen Bohn, the new production superintendent, had recently moved to Xographics from Rolm Communications where she had been a manager of a large office staff. The three line managers reporting to Bohn all had 20 or more years' experience with Xographics. They had seen it go from a productive company to one that was badly troubled with problem workers and poor performance.

In talking with one of the supervisors, Bohn learned that many of them were upset because they had to report any machine breakdown to the production manager or one of his assistants within 15 minutes of the breakdown. They felt that this did not give the workers the opportunity to repair the machine themselves. The breakdown report was forwarded to the production superintendent's office. The assistant told Bohn that the word was that once a worker got five reports, he or she was taken off the machine and given a lower paying job.

Questions

1. What should Bohn do?
2. What other problems (unidentified by Bohn) might be present?
3. What additional steps might the supervisors take?

Part B

One of the major problems that Bohn faced was that only about 40% of the jobs listed for scheduled maintenance shutdowns were ever performed. During an informal conversation with Ken Viet, Xographics personnel director, Bohn learned that the maintenance department was operating at about 30% efficiency. Viet said that the maintenance workers had recently staged a slowdown in order to force the company to increase their wages. Viet also told Bohn that maintenance workers usually quit about an hour early in order to wash up.

The head of the maintenance department had worked his way up through the ranks. He started with Xographics immediately after graduation from high school and had been with the company 25 years. His reason for the "inefficiency" was the lack of qualified maintenance people in the area, with the personnel department sending him individuals not qualified to maintain the mill's machines. He didn't have time to train each newly hired worker, assigning this responsibility to other workers who had been around for a while.

Questions (continued)

4. How might Bohn approach the maintenance head?
5. Who else should Bohn talk to?

Part C

Two months after Bohn joined Xographics, the company held its annual picnic at a local park. Most of the employees and their families were there. Bohn saw Viet at the picnic and handed him a beer. The following conversation then took place.

Ken: Hey, Ellen, got a minute?

Ellen: Sure. What's up?

Ken: Well, I was talking with one of your supervisors that I know pretty well. You know, an off-the-record chat about the company.

Ellen: Yeah?

Ken: He told me that the company's management style is the mushroom style: Keep them in the dark and feed 'em a lot of manure. He said that nobody knew you were hired until you showed up at the plant. We heard that the guard didn't even know who you were.

Ellen: Yeah, I guess that's so.

Ken: This supervisor said that he has been doing his job for ten years and has never received any performance appraisal. His raises are just added into his check. No one has pointed out his strong and weak points.

Ellen: Yeah, I guess that's so. But, I'm not totally sure. You know that I've been here only a few months myself.

Ken: Yeah, I know that, but listen to this. Tom Kerr, the new head of industrial engineering, hasn't talked to or even been introduced to anybody in the paper-machine area, and Tom has been on the job for three months.

Ellen: Ken, how widespread do you think this feeling is about the mushroom style of management?

Ken: I don't know, Ellen, but I think you ought to find out if you want this place to produce.

Questions (continued)

6. What steps can Bohn take?
7. What does this conversation tell you about the company?

What barriers to communication may exist?
8. What role has the company's informal communication network played in this situation?

References

1. Adapted from Albano, C. *Transactional Analysis on the Job.* New York: AMACOM, 1974, 53–54.
2. Based on Carr-Ruffino, N. *The Promotable Woman: Advancing Through Leadership Shells,* 2nd ed. Belmont, Calif.: Wadsworth, 1993, 164–208; Lange, A., and Jakubowski, P. *Responsible Assertive Behavior.* Champaign, Ill.: Research Press, 1983.
3. Putnam, L. L., and Pacanowsky, M. E. (eds.). *Communication and Organizations: An Interpretive Approach.* Thousands Oaks, Calif.: Sage, 1993.
4. Adapted from Keys, J. B., and Case, T. L. How to become an influential manager. *Academy of Management Executive,* November 1990, 38–51.
5. Stiles, W. B. *Describing Talk: A Taxonomy of Verbal Response Modes.* Thousand Oaks, Calif.: Sage, 1992.
6. Russ, G. S., Daft, R. L., and Lengel, R. H. Media selection and managerial characteristics in organizational communications. *Management Communication Quarterly,* 1990, 4, 151–175.
7. Yates, J., and Orlikowski, W. J. Genres of organizational communication: An approach to studying communication and media. *Academy of Management Review,* 1992, 17, 299–326.
8. Fulk, J. Social construction of communication technology. *Academy of Management Journal,* 1993, 36, 921–950.
9. Daly, J. A., and Wieman, J. M. (eds.), *Strategic Interpersonal Communication.* Hillsdale, N.J.: Lawrence Erlbaum Associates, 1994.
10. Dibble, J. A., and Langford, B. Y. *Communication Skills and Strategies: Guidelines for Managers at Work.* Cincinnati, OH: South-Western, 1994.
11. Barnum, C. F. Mirror on the wall: Who's the wisest one of all? *International Executive,* July–August 1989, 39–41.
12. Garko, M. G. Persuading subordinates who communicate in attractive and unattractive styles. *Management Communication Quarterly,* 1992, 289–315.
13. Sullivan, J., Kameda, N., and Nobu, T. Bypassing in managerial communications. *Business Horizons,* January—February 1991, 73.
14. Ibid., 71–80.
15. Munter, M. Cross-cultural communication for managers. *Business Horizons,* May–June 1993, 69–78.
16. Davenport, T. H. Saving IT's soul: Human-centered information management. *Harvard Business Review,* March–April 1994, 119–131.
17. Daily, B., and Finch, M. Benefiting from nonsexist language in the workplace. *Business Horizons,* March–April 1993, 30–34.
18. Adapted from Weiss, A. A hidden bias. Reprinted with permission from *Managing Diversity Newsletter,* JALMC, P.O. Box 819, Jamestown, NY 14702-0819; (716) 665-3654.
19. Murphy, K. R. *Honesty in the Workplace.* Pacific Grove, Calif.: Brooks/Cole, 1993.
20. Huk Ng, S. and Bradac, J. J. *Power in Language: Verbal Communication and Social Influence.* Newbury Park, Calif.: Sage, 1993.
21. Gardner, W. L. III. Lessons in organizational dramaturgy: The art of impression management. *Organizational Dynamics,* Summer 1992, 33–46.
22. Kenny, D. A., and De Paulo, B. M. Do people know how others view them? An empirical and theoretical account. *Psychological Bulletin,* 1993, 114, 145–161; Rusk, T., and Miller, D. P. *The Power of Ethical Persuasion: Winning Through Understanding in Difficult Communications.* New York: Penguin Books, 1993.
23. Porter, R. E., and Samovar, L. A. An introduction to intercultural communication. In L. A. Samovar and R. E. Porter (eds.), *Intercultural Communication: A Reader,* 7th ed. Belmont, Calif.: Wadsworth, 1994, 4–26; La Fromboise, T., Coleman, H. L. K., Gerton, J. Psychological impact of biculturalism: Evidence and theory. *Psychological Bulletin,* 1993, 114, 395–412.
24. Hall, E. *Understanding Cultural Differences.* Yarmouth, Me.: Intercultural Press, 1989.
25. Halverson, C. B. Cultural-context inventory: The effects of culture on behavior and work style. In J. W. Pfeiffer (ed.), *The 1993 Annual: Developing Human Resources.* San Diego: Pfeiffer & Company, 1993, 131–145; Blanchard, K., and Johnson, S. *The One-Minute Manager,* New York: Berkely, 1987.
26. Adapted from Munter, M. Cross-cultural communication for management. *Business Horizons,* May–June 1993, 76–77.
27. Kogod, S. K. Managing diversity in the workplace. In J. W. Pfeiffer (ed.), *The 1992 Annual: Developing Human Resources.* San Diego: Pfeiffer & Company, 1992, 241–249; Gudykunst, W. B. *Bridging Differences: Effective Intergroup Communication,* 2nd ed. Thousand Oaks, Calif.: Sage, 1994.
28. Monge, P. R., and Eisenberg, E. M. Emergent communication networks. In F. M. Jablin, L. L. Putnam, K. H. Roberts, and L. W. Porter (eds.), *Handbook of Organizational Communication.* Newbury Park, Calif.: Sage, 1987, 304–342.
29. Krackhardt, D., and Hanson, J. R. Informal networks: The company behind the chart. *Harvard Business Review,* July–August 1993, 104–111.
30. Toshio, Y., Gilmore, M. R. and Cook, K. S. Network connections and the distribution of power in exchange networks. *American Journal of Sociology,* 1988, 93, 833–851.
31. Gargiulo, M. Two-step leverage: Managing constraint in organization politics. *Administrative Science Quarterly,* 1993, 38, 1–19.
32. Eisenberg, E. M., and Witten, M. G. Reconsidering openness in organization communication. *Academy of Management Review,* 1987, 12, 418–426; Beck, C. E., and Beck, E. A. The manager's open door and the communication climate. *Business Horizons,* January–February 1986, 15–19.
33. Ibarra, H. Personal networks of women and minorities in management: A conceptual framework. *Academy of Management Review,* 1993, 18, 56–87; Blum, T. C., Fields, D. L., Goodman, J. S. Organization-level determinants of women in management. *Academy of Management Journal,* 1994, 37, 237–268.
34. Sessa, V. I. Managing diversity at the Xerox Corporation: Bal-

anced workforce goals and caucus groups. In S. E. Jackson and Associates (eds.), *Diversity in the Workplace: Human Resource Initiatives.* New York: Gulford Press, 1992, 37–64.

35. Ibid, 37–64; Lesly, E. Sticking it out at Xerox by sticking together. *Business Week*, November 29, 1993, 77.

36. Tetzeli, R. The internet and your business. *Fortune,* March 7, 1994, 86–96.

37. Malone, M. S. Perpetual motion executives—Call them PMXs. *Forbes ASAP*, February 11, 1994, 93–97.

38. Reinsch, N. L., Jr., and Beswick, R. W. Voice mail versus conventional channels: A cost minimization analysis of individuals' preferences. *Academy of Management Journal*, 1990, 33, 801–816.

39. Berner, J. *The Joy of Working from Home: Making a Life While Making a Living*, San Francisco: Berrett-Kolhler, 1994.

40. Shellenbarger, J. Some thrive, but many wilt working at home. *Wall Street Journal*, December 14, 1993, B1, B10; Shellenbarger, S. I'm still here! Home workers worry they're invisible. *Wall Street Journal*, December 16, 1993, B1, B2.

41. Marlow, E. The electrovisual manager: Media and American corporate management. *Business Horizons*, March–April 1994, 61–67; La Plante, A. Data liberation. *Forbes ASAP*, February 28, 1994, 59–68.

42. Isaacs, U. N. Taking flight: Dialogue, collective thinking, and organizational learning. *Organizational Dynamics*, Autumn 1993, 24–39; Schein, E. H. On dialogue, culture, and organizational cues. *Organizational Dynamics*, Autumn 1993, 40–51.

43. This section draws heavily from Sussman, L. Managers: On the defensive. *Business Horizons*, January–February 1991, 81–87. Also see Thompson, M. P. The skills of inquiry and advocacy: Why managers need both. *Management Communication Quarterly*, 1993, 7, 95–106.

44. Ibid., 84.

45. Ibid., 85. Also see Denton, D. K. Open communication. *Business Horizons*, September–October 1993, 64–69.

46. Sussman, L., Managers: On the defensive. *Business Horizons*, January–February 1991, 82.

47. Gordon, R. D. The difference between feeling defensive and feeling understood. *Journal of Business Communication*, Winter 1988, 53–64.

48. Adapted from Yound, M., and Post, J. E. Managing to communicate, communicating to manage: How leading companies communicate with employees. Reprinted by permission of publisher, from *Organizational Dynamics*, Summer / 1993, American Management Association, New York, NY. All rights reserved.

49. Karp, K. The lost art of feedback. In J. W. Pfeiffer (ed.), *The 1987 Annual: Developing Human Resources*. San Diego: University Associates, 1987, 237–245; Albrecht, T. L., and Adelman, M. B. *Communicating Social Support*. Newbury Park, Calif.: Sage, 1987.

50. Brett, J. M., Feldman, D. C., and Weingart, L. R. Feedback-seeking behavior of new hires and job changers. *Journal of Management*, 1990, 16, 737–749; Downs, T. M. Predictors of communication satisfaction during performance appraisal interviews. *Management Communication Quarterly*, 1990, 3, 334–354.

51. Crossen, C. Simple apology for poor service is in sorry state. *Wall Street Journal*, November 29, 1990, B1, B6.

52. Ibid., Kiechkel, W. III. How to escape the echo chamber. *Fortune*, June 18, 1990, 129–130.

53. Derlega, V. J., Metts, S., Petronio, S., and Margulis, S. T. *Self-Disclosure*. Newbury Park, Calif.: Sage, 1993.

54. Dindra, K., and Allen, M. Sex differences in self-disclosure: A meta-analysis. *Psychological Bulletin*, 1992, 112, 3–23.

55. Jourard, S. M. *Disclosing Man to Himself.* New York: Van Nostrand Reinhold, 1968, 46–47. Also see Markus, H., and Nurius, P. Possible selves. *American Psychologist*, 1986, 41, 954–969.

56. Gioia, D. A., and Longenecker, C. O. Delving into the dark side: The politics of executive appraisal. *Organizational Dynamics*, Winter 1994, 47–58.

57. Chartier, M. R. Five components contributing to effective interpersonal communications. In J. W. Pfeiffer, and J. E. Jones (eds.), *1974 Annual Handbook for Group Facilitators*. La Jolla, Calif.: University Associates, 1974, 125–128.

58. Hamlin, S. *How to Talk So People Listen.* New York: Harper & Row, 1988.

59. Brownell, J. *Building Active Listening Skills*. Englewood Cliffs, N.J.: Prentice-Hall, 1986; Kurtz, T. Dynamic listening: Unlocking your communication potential. *Supervisory Management*, September 1990, 7.

60. Adapted from Pare, T. P. How to find out what they want. *Fortune*, Autumn/Winter 1993, 39–41.

61. Wieman, J. M. and Harrison, R. P. (eds.), *Nonverbal Interaction*. Newbury Park, Calif.: Sage, 1983.

62. Harper, R. G., Wiens, A. N., and Matarzzo, J. D. *Nonverbal Communication: The State of the Art.* New York: John Wiley & Sons, 1978.

63. Adapted from Axtell, R. E. *Gestures: The Do's and Taboos of Body Language Around the World.* New York: John Wiley & Sons, 1991; de Forest, M. E. Thinking of a plant in Mexico? *Academy of Management Executive*, February 1994, 33–40.

64. Strati, A. Aesthetic understanding of organizational life. *Academy of Management Review*, 1992, 17, 568–581; Rafaeli, A., and Pratt, M. G. Tailored meanings: On the meaning and impact of organizational dress. *Academy of Management Review*, 1993, 18, 32–55.

65. Heintzman, M., Leathers, D. G., Parrott, R. L., Cairns, A. B. III. Nonverbal rapport-building behaviors/effects on perceptions of a supervisor. *Management Communication Quarterly*, 1993, 7, 181–208.

66. Henley, N., and Thorne, B. Womanspeak and manspeak: Sex differences and sexism in communication, verbal and nonverbal. In A. G. Sargent (ed.), *Beyond Sex Roles*. St. Paul, Minn.: West, 1977, 201–218; De Paulo, B. M. Nonverbal behavior and self-presentation. *Psychological Bulletin*, 1992, 111, 203–243.

67. Carr-Ruffins, N. *The Promotable Woman: Advancing Through Leadership*, 2nd ed. Belmont, Calif.: Wadsworth, 1993.

68. Graham, G. H., Unruh, J., and Jennings, P. The impact of nonverbal communication in organizations: A survey of perceptions. *Journal of Business Communication*, 1991, 28, 45–60.

69. Arliss, L. P. *Gender Communication.* Englewood Cliffs, N.J.: Prentice-Hall, 1991.

70. Source: Douglas Roberts, formerly Manager of Training, LTV Missiles and Electronics Group, Grand Prairie, Texas. Used with permission.

71. Adapted from Hellriegel, D., and Slocum, J. W., Jr. *Management*, 4th ed. Reading, Mass.: Addison-Wesley, 1986, 511–512. Used with permission. Copyright © by Don Hellriegel and John W. Slocum, Jr.

13 Conflict and Negotiation

LEARNING OBJECTIVES

When you have finished studying this chapter, you should be able to:

▲ Define four basic forms of conflict.

▲ Explain the negative, positive, and balanced views of conflict.

▲ Identify the principal levels of conflict within organizations.

▲ Describe and apply five interpersonal conflict-handling styles.

▲ Explain the basic types of negotiations.

▲ Describe various negotiation strategies.

OUTLINE

Preview Case: Charlie Olcott

Conflict Management

Forms of Conflict

Views of Conflict

Managing Quality: Motorola's Balanced Use of Conflict

Levels of Conflict

Intrapersonal Conflict

Managing in Practice: The Silent Saboteurs

Interpersonal Conflict

Managing in Practice: USA Truck Cuts Role Conflicts

Intragroup Conflict

Managing in Practice: U-Haul's Family Feud

Intergroup Conflict

Managing Diversity: Bridging Differences at General Computer Inc.

Conflict-Handling Styles

Avoiding Style

Forcing Style

Accommodating Style

Collaborating Style

Compromising Style

Managing Ethics: Wal-Mart's Failed Compromise

Key Implications

Negotiation in Conflict Management

Basic Types of Negotiations

Integrative Process

Distributive Process

Matrix of Outcomes

Negotiating Across Cultures

Managing Across Cultures: Business Negotiations in Mexico

Third-Party Facilitation

DEVELOPING SKILLS

Self-Diagnosis: *Conflict-Handling Styles*

A Case in Point: *Sue's Dilemma*

PREVIEW CASE

Charlie Olcott

Charlie Olcott had the career most of us only dream of. By the time he was thirty-nine years old, he'd worked his way up the corporate ladder to become president of Burger King USA, a division of Minneapolis-based Pillsbury Corporation. "I thought I had it all figured out," he says. "I ran a $5 billion company with 250,000 employees and five thousand stores. But I hope I'm never again as smart as I was in my thirties."

"I was taught growing up that each rung of the ladder would give me more satisfaction, but I found the view from the top held no more real satisfaction than the other rungs. I was supposed to feel better about having a big bank account, but I was still searching for fulfillment. The needs in my life just weren't being met by having a corporate jet, a seven-figure salary, or controlling a boardroom. Still, you don't suddenly leave something you've worked your whole life to achieve. Sometimes, you need a little push."

In October 1988, Pillsbury management began what Olcott calls a desperate attempt to defend the company from a hostile takeover by Grand Metropolitan PLC. "A professional difference of opinion on the accuracy of the numbers used in the defensive strategy forced a showdown with Pillsbury's new chairman," Olcott says. "The chairman told me, 'Defend my numbers or you're off the team.'" Olcott refused, walked out, and called his wife to tell her he had been fired. "This was a career vaporizing

move, and I knew it. You don't get to that position at thirty-nine by being a rabble rouser—the most radical thing I'd done in corporate life was not shave on vacation."

His wife was supportive, though, and the family of five had enough savings to live on while Olcott began searching for something more satisfying. After nearly a year of searching, Olcott became a partner in a four-person small business consulting practice in Miami, where he'd continued to live after he left Burger King. Still, after two years, the business wasn't making much money and the family's savings were depleted. "If I'd focused on the loss of title and money, I could have been extremely unhappy," he says. "Instead, we found that this was the happiest time we'd ever had as a family. I was largely never home when I was with Burger King, but now I had time with my three sons."

It wasn't long before he was introduced to Tim Joukowsky and his Boston-based social venture capital firm, HFG Expansion Fund. Olcott liked what he saw, and became a general partner as well as chairman and CEO of two of the fund's four portfolio companies. He's making a lot less money than before, and he doesn't control the resources he used to, but Olcott couldn't be happier. "The particulars of your circumstance are less important than your attitude," he says. "I've been rich and poor, and I would like to be rich again. But it doesn't matter because I realize that you win in the end."[1]

Managing conflict is a common process in organizations. **Conflict** is the process that begins when one person perceives that another person has negatively affected, or is about to negatively affect, something that the first person, a group, or an organization cares about. This definition implies some interdependence and interaction, along with the perception of incompatible concerns, among the people involved. It is sufficiently broad to cover a variety of conflict issues and events.[2] As Charlie Olcott demonstrated, a person's attitudes, values, and style play an important role in determining whether conflict leads to beneficial or destructive outcomes.

We examine conflict and negotiations from several viewpoints. First, we consider the basic forms of conflict and examine three views of conflict. Second, we review four levels of conflict often present in organizations. Third, we discuss five interpersonal styles in conflict management and the conditions under which each style may be appropriate. Fourth, we address the core elements of negotiation, basic negotiation strategies, and some of the complexities involved in negotiating across cultures. We conclude with some highlights of third-party facilitation in the negotiation process.

▼ CONFLICT MANAGEMENT

Effective conflict management requires much more than the use of specific techniques. The ability to understand and correctly diagnose conflict is essential to managing it. This chapter emphasizes the proper diagnosis of conflict and then how to best manage it in organizations. **Conflict management** consists of diagnostic processes, interpersonal styles, negotiating strategies, and other interventions that are designed to avoid unnecessary conflict and reduce or resolve excessive conflict.[3] Charlie Olcott resolved his work—family conflicts by deciding that time with his family was more important than the relentless pursuit of bigger titles and more money.

▼ Forms of Conflict

Conflict comes in four basic forms. Regardless of form, the essence of conflict is incompatability.

Goal conflict occurs when two or more desired or expected outcomes are incompatible. Goal conflict may involve inconsistencies between the individual's or group's values and norms (e.g., standards of behavior) and the demands or goals assigned by higher levels in the organization.[4] Recall Charlie Olcott's comment in the Preview Case: "A professional difference of opinion on the accuracy of the numbers used in the defensive strategy forced a showdown with Pillsbury's new chairman. The chairman told me, 'Defend my numbers or you're off the team.'" Olcott's personal goal was honesty in reporting as he saw it, whereas Olcott's perception of the demands from the chairman was extreme distortion in reporting to ward off the hostile takeover effort by Grand Metropolitan PLC.

More frequently, goal conflict occurs when an individual or group is assigned or selects incompatible goals. A student may set goals of earning $200 a week and achieving a 3.50 grade point average (4 point system) while being enrolled full-time during the coming semester. After a month into the semester, the student may realize that there aren't enough hours in the week to achieve both goals. This situation also is related to the concept of *goal difficulty* (see Chapter 7). It refers to the extent to which an individual's or group's goal is at odds with the capacity to achieve the goal.[5] Thus, even without the goal of earning $200 per week, the student could face inner conflicts because of the extreme difficulty in achieving a 3.5 grade point average.

Cognitive conflict occurs when the ideas and thoughts within an individual or between individuals are incompatible. In the Preview Case, Charlie Olcott appeared to be reflecting on one of his cognitive conflicts when he stated: "I thought I had it all figured out. I ran a $5 billion company with 250,000 employees and five thousand stores. But I hope I'm never again as smart as I was in my thirties."

Affective conflict occurs when the feelings and emotions within an individual or between individuals are incompatible. Charlie Olcott's reflection on inner affective conflict is implied when he comments: "I was supposed to feel better about having a big bank account, but I was still searching for fulfillment. The needs in my life weren't being met by having a corporate jet, a seven-figure salary, or controlling a boardroom." The more obvious forms of affective conflict occur between individuals, such as the anger by the chairman of Pillsbury when he told Olcott: "Defend my numbers or you're off the team."

Procedural conflict occurs when people differ over the process to use for resolving a matter. Union—management negotiations often involve procedural conflicts before negotiations actually begin. The parties may have procedural conflicts over *who* will be involved in the negotiations, *where* they will take place, and *when* sessions will be held (and how long they will be). Different interpretations about how a grievance system is to operate provides another example of procedural conflict.

▼ Views of Conflict

The four basic forms of conflict need not necessarily lead to ineffectiveness. In fact, there are three views of conflict: positive, negative, and balanced.

Positive View   Conflict in organizations can be a positive force. The creation and/or resolution of conflict often leads to constructive problem solving. The need to resolve conflict can lead people to search for ways of changing how they do things. The conflict-resolution process often is a stimulus for positive change within an organization. The search for ways to resolve conflict may not only lead to innovation and change, but it may make change more acceptable.[6] A recent study of managers demonstrated this view. The positive effects they noted generally fell into three main categories: beneficial effects on productivity ('Our work productivity went up" and "We produced quality products on time"), relationship outcomes ("Sensitivity to others was increased" and "Better communication methods were developed"), and constructive organizational change ("We adopted more effective controls" and "Better job descriptions and expectations were drawn up").[7]

The intentional introduction of conflict into the decision-making process may even be beneficial. In group decision making, a problem may arise when a cohesive group's desire for agreement interferes with its ability to consider alternative solutions. A group may encounter *groupthink* (see Chapter 9), which it can reduce if the introduction of conflict takes the form of one or more dissenting opinions. Finally, people may come to quite different conclusions about what is fair and ethical in specific situations. A positive view of conflict encourages people to work out their differences, participate in developing an ethical and fair organization, and deal directly with injustices.[8]

Negative View   Conflict also may have serious negative effects and divert efforts from goal attainment. Instead of directing organizational resources primarily toward reaching desired goals, the conflict may deplete resources, especially time and money. Conflict also may negatively affect the psychological well-being of employees. If severe, conflicting thoughts, ideas, and beliefs may result in resentment, tension, and anxiety. These feelings appear to result from the threat that conflict poses to important personal goals and beliefs. Over an extended period of time, conflict may make the establishment of supportive and trusting relationships difficult.[9] In one study, the vast majority of women participants revealed personal images of conflict that were negative. They viewed conflict as a battle that proceeds at great personal cost, creates negative results, and may even be hopeless. Words that they associated with conflict were pain, loss, danger and even death. Their other principal image of conflict was as a process in which they had little or no input. Many of the women saw themselves, at worst, as victims in conflict and, at best, as bystanders (e.g., "I'm in the middle" and "A losing proposition—the good old boys support each other strongly").[10]

Deep conflicts and competition when cooperation between employees is required typically bring performance down.[11] Pressure for results tends to emphasize immediate and measurable goals—such as sales costs—at the expense of longer range and more important goals—such as product quality. When high product quality is a primary organizational goal, conflict based on competition between co-workers is often ill-advised.

Balanced View   Many individuals have a balanced view of conflict. They recognize that conflict may sometimes be highly desirable and at other times destructive. These individuals know that, although they can reduce conflict, they will have to resolve and properly manage that which remains. The balanced view is sensitive to the consequences of conflict, ranging from negative outcomes (loss of skilled employees, sabotage, low quality of work, and personal stress) to positive outcomes (creative alternatives, increased motivation and commitment, high quality of work, and personal satisfaction).[12]

The balanced view acknowledges that conflict arises in organizations whenever interests collide. Sometimes, employees will think differently, want to act differently, and pursue different goals. When these differences divide interdependent people, conflicts are inevitable and must be constructively managed.[13] The following Managing Quality feature suggests how Motorola uses balanced conflict to increase quality and maintain its competitive edge. Headquartered in Schaumburg, Illinois, Motorola is a worldwide leader in wireless communications. The firm manufactures cellular telephones, pagers, two-way radios, semiconductors, and other electronic items. Motorola also is widely viewed as one of the leaders in total quality management.

MANAGING QUALITY

Motorola's Balanced Use of Conflict

Gary Tooker, the engineer who recently became vice-chairman and CEO of Motorola comments, "Fame is a fleeting thing. When the alarm clock rings tomorrow morning, you'd better get up and understand that your customers expect more from you than they did the day before. You'd better find ways to be better." To do this, Motorola uses a process of candid internal debate that remains rare in organizations. Tooker is a master of the company's debates and challenging discussions that pit manager against manager and business unit against business unit, often in pursuit of conflicting technologies.

Christopher Galvin, president and chief operating officer, explains: "Since its inception, Motorola has been managing on the concept of renewal, a willingness to renew our technologies and to renew the processes by which we run the institution." Jack Scanlon, general manager of the cellular business says, "The fact that I may conflict with another business's turf is tough beans. Things will sort themselves out in the marketplace." Motorola continues to push quality, cycle time reduction, and teamwork to levels that many companies can scarcely imagine. Motorola is a model of how to use TQM to re-

MANAGING QUALITY —*Continued*

invigorate a corporation. Harvard Business School professor Rosabeth Moss Kanter states, "A lot of companies have used TQM as a device to discipline the work force. Motorola has taken it as a way to examine what everyone does, including managers."

Motorola's intellectual property rights department was drowning in paperwork. It was backlogged in filing applications for patents on products and processes invented by company scientists. Engineers were spending hours, even days, filling out disclosure forms. Patent attorneys spent even more time rewriting those disclosures into legalese. Working together for 18 months, a team of lawyers and engineers, not the most natural of bedfellows, trimmed the standard invention disclosure form from 15 pages to 2. They cut the backlog without adding staff. The streamlined disclosure process saved the company the equivalent of 44 years of engineering time in 1993. This quality team won a gold medal at Motorola's annual Total Customer Service team competition in 1994. The team won from a field of 4,300 teams from 11 countries.[14]

▼ LEVELS OF CONFLICT

There are five major levels of conflict within organizations: intrapersonal (within an individual), interpersonal (between individuals), intragroup (within a group), intergroup (between groups), and interorganizational (between organizations). However, we discuss interorganizational conflict only briefly in this chapter. These levels of conflicts are often interrelated, as Figure 13.1 suggests. For example, an employee struggling with whether to stay on a certain career path may act aggressively toward fellow workers, thus triggering interpersonal conflicts.

▼ Intrapersonal Conflict

Intrapersonal conflict occurs within an individual and often involves some form of goal, cognitive, or affective conflict. It is triggered when a person's

FIGURE 13.1

Levels of Conflict in Organizations

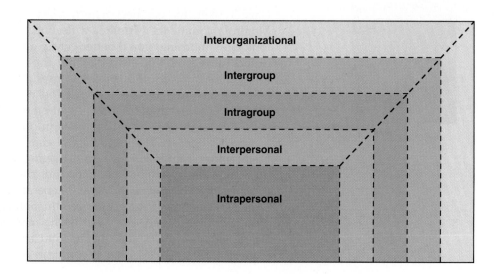

behavior will result in outcomes that are mutually exclusive.[15] Inner tensions and frustrations commonly result. A graduating senior may have to decide between jobs that offer different challenges, pay, security, and locations. Trying to make such a decision may create one (or more) of three basic types of intrapersonal goal conflict.

▲ **Approach–approach conflict** means that an individual must choose among two or more alternatives, each of which is expected to have a positive outcome (such as a choice between two jobs that appear to be equally attractive).

▲ **Avoidance–avoidance conflict** means that an individual must choose among two or more alternatives, each of which is expected to have a negative outcome (such as relatively low pay or much out-of-town traveling).

▲ **Approach–avoidance conflict** means that an individual must decide whether to do something that is expected to have both positive and negative outcomes (such as accepting an offer of a good job in a bad location).

Day-to-day decisions frequently involve the resolution of intrapersonal goal conflict. However, the intensity of intrapersonal goal conflict generally increases under one or more of the following conditions: (1) several realistic alternative courses of action are available for coping with the conflict; (2) the positive and negative consequences of the alternative courses of action are roughly equal; or (3) the source of conflict is important to the individual.

Cognitive Dissonance   Intrapersonal conflict may also be a consequence of **cognitive dissonance,** which occurs when individuals recognize inconsistencies in their own thoughts and/or behaviors.[16] The existence of substantial and recognized inconsistencies is usually stressful and uncomfortable. Sufficient discomfort usually motivates a person to reduce the dissonance and achieve balance. Balance can be achieved by (1) changing thoughts and/or behaviors or (2) obtaining more information about the issue that is causing the dissonance. Both goal conflict and cognitive conflict accompany many important personal decisions. The greater the goal conflict before the decision, the greater the cognitive dissonance is likely to be after the decision. Individuals experience dissonance because they know that the alternative accepted has negative (avoidance) outcomes and the alternative rejected has positive (approach) outcomes. The more difficulty individuals have in arriving at the original decision, the greater is their need to justify the decision afterward. Some cognitive dissonance is inevitable. Otherwise, the inner world and the external world as an individual who interprets it would be in perfect harmony.

Neurotic Tendencies   **Neurotic tendencies** are irrational personality mechanisms that an individual uses—often unconsciously—which create inner conflict. In turn, inner conflict often results in behaviors that lead to conflict with others.[17] The psychological sources of neurotic tendencies are beyond the scope of this discussion, but we briefly describe some ways that managers and others with strong neurotic tendencies may think and act in the workplace.[18] Neurotic managers might make excessive use of tight organizational controls (e.g., budgets, rules and regulations, and monitoring systems) because they distrust people. Some neurotic individuals may be fearful of uncertainty and risk, not just distrustful of others. Thus they are driven to plan and standardize every detail of their unit's operation, again emphasizing formal controls. Still other neurotic individuals may be excessively bold and impulsive in their actions. They may be predisposed to rely on hunches and impressions rather than to seek out available facts. Such managers may not use participation and consultation in their decision making unless required to do so.

Individuals with strong neurotic tendencies usually struggle unsuccessfully with intrapersonal conflict. Because they cannot resolve their own problems, they often trigger conflict with others. The excessive distrust and need to control exhibited by neurotic managers is likely to trigger conflict with others, especially subordinates who come to feel overcontrolled and distrusted. A common reaction to leaders with neurotic tendencies is open or covert (hidden) aggression and hostility. Subordinates often try to even the score and protect themselves from further abuse. These actions give the manager an even stronger sense of employee worthlessness. The manager's hostility and attempts to control and punish become ever more vigorous.[19] The following Managing in Practice account demonstrates this vicious cycle.

MANAGING IN PRACTICE

The Silent Saboteurs

A consultant was called to a lumber company for advice. Profits were slipping and management couldn't figure out what was causing it, but all other performance measures were stable or increasing. The consultant talked with many employees and won their trust. He observed many things about this company, including bad working conditions and an autocratic, almost abusive, dominant leadership style.

One day, the consultant asked an employee why—in light of the difficult working conditions and harsh leadership style—there wasn't more absenteeism, poor production, or other symptoms of an organization that was "hard" on its workers. The employee answered, "Oh that's easy. When we get frustrated or angry we just feed the hog." Seeing the puzzled look in the consultant's face, the employee explained: "The hog is the big mechanical wood chipper at the back of the plant." All unusable scrap is fed to the hog to make the wood chips that go into particle board, one of the least profitable products the company manufactured. "When we get upset we take finished lumber and feed the hog."

The consultant was still puzzled. That explained the slipping profits but not the absence of the typical symptoms of an organization in distress. "I still don't see why people don't just call in sick and avoid coming to work." The employee explained: "We don't really want to miss work. We all have hog quotas. If we aren't here to feed the hog, we are fined $20. That money goes into the party kitty and pays for our quarterly family picnic."[20]

With increasing frequency, unresolved intrapersonal conflicts of employees or customers trigger violent interpersonal conflict. Violence in the workplace has its source in severe intrapersonal conflicts. The gunman in the 1991 massacre at the U.S. Postal Service office in Royal Oak, Michigan, had warned co-workers that if he didn't win his job back, he would make the workplace look like Edmond, Oklahoma, where a postal carrier killed 14 people in 1986. Dr. E. Wolf, a consultant to the Postal Service, noted that the gunman had been dismissed from the military for disciplinary problems, which included using a tank to run over the car of a person with whom he'd had a dispute.[21]

▼ Interpersonal Conflict

Interpersonal conflict involves two or more individuals who believe that their attitudes, behaviors, or preferred goals are in opposition. Many interpersonal (and intrapersonal) conflicts are based on some type of role conflict or role ambiguity.

Role Conflict   A **role** is the cluster of tasks that others expect a person to perform in doing a job. Figure 13.2 presents a role episode model, which involves role senders and a focal person. A role episode begins before a message is sent because role senders have expectations, perceptions, and evaluations of the focal person's behaviors. These attributions, in turn, influence the actual role messages that the senders transmit. The focal person's perceptions of these messages and pressures may then lead to role conflict. **Role conflict** occurs when a focal person perceives incompatible messages and pressures from the role senders. The focal person responds with coping behaviors that serve as inputs to the role senders' attribution process.

A **role set** is the group of role senders that directly affect the focal person. A role set might include the employee's manager, other team members, close friends, immediate family members, and important clients or customers served. Four types of role conflict may occur as a result of incompatible messages and pressures from the role set.

▲ **Intrasender role conflict** may occur when different messages and pressures from a single member of the role set are incompatible.

▲ **Intersender role conflict** may occur when the messages and pressures from one role sender oppose messages and pressures from one or more other senders.

FIGURE 13.2

Role Episode Model

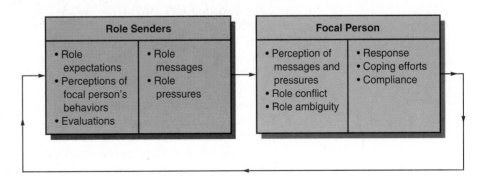

Source: Based on Kahn, R. L., et al. *Organizational Stress: Studies in Role Conflict and Ambiguity.* New York: John Wiley & Sons, 1964, 26.

▲ **Interrole conflict** may occur when role pressures associated with membership in one group are incompatible with pressures stemming from membership in other groups.

▲ **Person–role conflict** may occur when the role requirements are incompatible with the focal person's own attitudes, values, or views of acceptable behavior.[22] *Intrapersonal conflict* typically accompanies this type of conflict.

The following Managing in Practice piece describes the actions taken by USA Truck to reduce role conflicts experienced by its truck drivers. The company hauls truckload quantities of tire fabric, auto parts, and other products for firms such as Goodyear and General Motors. It is one of the most efficient carriers in the industry, and the way it now treats its drivers has a lot to do with its strong performance.

MANAGING IN PRACTICE

USA Truck Cuts Role Conflicts

A breakdown room is the place truckers call when something goes wrong on the road: a blown tire, a broken fan belt, or a slipping clutch. In most trucking firms, the drivers who call the breakdown room rarely expect to be greeted like long-lost family members. A sign in the breakdown room of USA Truck, Inc.'s Van Buren, Arkansas, headquarters reads: "Please communicate with our drivers as if one of your family members were sitting in the passenger seat." On getting a call from a stranded driver, a USA Truck supervisor checks the computer for the nearest shop that can fix the problem. Then, the supervisor develops a solution with the driver that will get the goods delivered on time. "Some outfits talk to you like you're a dog," says USA Truck driver Carlton Curry. "But it's first class here, man."

USA Truck's other actions to reduce the role conflicts experienced by truck drivers began in 1989. At that time, USA Truck's managers paid $30 million to buy the company from another firm. Brock Speed became chairman and Robert Powell became president. Speed and Powell decided to go directly to the source to ask for advice about reducing driver turnover. They began attending quarterly meetings with 18 senior drivers at the nonunion shop. They got an earful. The drivers wanted antilock brakes and air-ride suspensions. They got them. When USA Truck built a drivers' dormitory at its West Memphis, Arkansas, terminal, the drivers suggested installing private shower stalls instead of a communal shower. This was done. Drivers wanted to get home more often. USA Truck added the time a driver had been on the road to the information provided to dispatchers assigning loads. This cut average tours on the road from six to two weeks.

Some have accused Speed and Powell of coddling the truck drivers. Speed responds: "Treating people fairly isn't coddling. Drivers who are late just twice in a year are out of a job." Speed figures he's simply treating the truckers with respect, and he expects them to show respect for the company's health.[23]

Despite USA Truck's efforts, long-haul truck driver turnover continues to be a problem—at 85% per year. However, USA's rate is much less than the industry's—typically well over 100% a year. The continuing problem appears to relate to severe work–family role conflicts. However, many groups of employees experience work–family role conflicts, especially those in professional and managerial jobs and women, regardless of their occupation.[24] Working women generally bear a disproportionate share of family role expectations and pressures in addition to intense self-defined responsibilities for their families.[25]

Role ambiguity   Uncertainty or lack or clarity surrounding expectations about a single role often creates **role ambiguity**.[26] Like role conflict, severe role ambiguity may cause stress and subsequent coping behaviors. These coping behaviors may include (1) aggressive action and hostile communication, (2) withdrawal, and (3) approaching the role sender or senders to attempt joint problem solving. Research findings are not clear-cut on the relationships among role conflict, role ambiguity, and outcomes. These outcomes include stress reactions, aggression, hostility, and withdrawal behaviors (turnover and absenteeism).[27] However, stress is a common reaction to severe role conflict and role ambiguity. Effective individuals possess the ability to cope with the many ambiguities inherent in their roles.[28]

▼ Intragroup Conflict

Intragroup conflict involves clashes among some or all of the group's members, which often affect the group's processes and effectiveness. Family-run businesses can be especially prone to severe intragroup and other types of conflicts.[29] These conflicts are most evident when an owner–founder approaches retirement, retires, or dies. The following Managing in Practice account dramatizes some of the many types of conflict that exist in family-run businesses.

MANAGING IN PRACTICE

U-Haul's Family Feud

A man or woman who builds a business for a living doesn't often think about dying. Usually, a near-fatal illness or the death of a close friend is needed to shake the founder into admitting that everything has a season. Even so, getting down to particulars is tough. Peter Davis, who runs the family business program at the Wharton School, comments, "The founder feels that anything given up to the children is another nail in the coffin."

You couldn't blame Leonard S. Shoen for seeing it that way. Shoen, who started U-Haul International, the Phoenix-based car and truck rental business, began transferring stock to his children while they were still young. The trouble was, the Shoen kids kept coming—eight sons (one of them adopted) and five daughters from three different mothers. Shoen parceled out the shares as the kids arrived and ultimately gave away 95% of the company.

U-Haul grew into Amerco, with annual revenues of about $1 billion. Two of Shoen's sons, Edward and Mark, seized control. The senior Shoen found

MANAGING IN PRACTICE —*Continued*

himself voted out of the business. Soon after, his eldest son, Sam, who had been running the company, quit. The family has since split into two camps. Edward and Mark continue to run the business, and Leonard and Sam are suing to regain control of it. Both sides have filed numerous law suits. They accuse each other of mismanagement, incompetence, violence, and mental instability, among other things.

The battle has even been violent, with shareholders' meetings turning into slugfests. In the most outlandish incident, Michael Shoen was reportedly beaten up by Edward and Mark. A photograph of Michael, complete with bruises, was splashed across the business section of the Arizona Republic newspaper. Says dad, "I created a monster."[30]

Only three in ten family-run businesses make it to the second generation, and one in ten survives into the third generation. The most formidable obstacles to succession are the relationships among the family members who own the business and bear responsibility for keeping it alive for another generation. What determines whether a family business soars or nose-dives? It depends, in large part, on the respect family members give each other in the workplace, their willingness to take on work roles different from those they have at home, and their ability to manage conflict. Randall Carlock, a consultant on family business and founder of the Audio King electronic stores chain, comments, "Families don't express their needs and wants clearly and don't deal with conflict very well. When that moves into their place of business, that spells real trouble. Take the way most parents negotiate with their kids in the business. They basically tell them what they're going to do, or they threaten them, or they tell them, 'You're lucky to have this job.' That's not how you handle an employee, and that's not how you develop a future leader."[31]

▼ Intergroup Conflict

Intergroup conflict involves opposition and clashes between groups. It often occurs in union–management relations.[32] Such conflicts may be highly intense, drawn out, and costly to the groups involved. Under extreme conditions of competition and conflict (see Chapter 10), the groups develop attitudes toward each other that are characterized by distrust, rigidity, a focus only on self-interests, failure to listen, and the like. We briefly consider four categories of intergroup conflicts within organizations.

Vertical Conflict Clashes between employees at different levels in an organization are called **vertical conflict.** It often occurs when superiors attempt to control subordinates too tightly and the subordinates resist.[33] This type of conflict was illustrated in The Managing in Practice piece "The Silent Saboteurs." Subordinates may resist because they believe that the controls infringe too much on their freedom to do their jobs. Vertical conflicts also may arise because of inadequate communication, goal conflict, or a lack of agreement concerning information and values (cognitive conflict). Consider the situation of airline flight attendants. In 1994, US Air abandoned the weight chart, one of the last vestiges of female flight attendants as sex objects. The company settled the dispute with the flight attendants and the Equal Employment Opportunity Commission after the airline was sued for sex and age discrimination. The new agreement simply requires flight attendants to: ". . . fit comfortably down the aisle of US Air's smallest aircraft, facing forward and single file, and fit quickly through the cabin exits."[34]

Horizontal Conflict   Clashes between groups of employees at the same hierarchical level in an organization are called **horizontal conflict.** It occurs when each department or team strives only for its own goals, disregarding the goals of other departments and teams, especially if those goals are incompatible. Contrasting attitudes of employees in different departments and teams may also lead to conflict (see Chapter 10). Smoking in the workplace is an issue that causes both horizontal and vertical conflicts. Matt Shade, from Atlanta, Georgia, must go outside at work to smoke. He says, "It's unfair. It's an assault on people who smoke."[35] Nonsmokers usually disagree, and, for the most part, smokers have lost to nonsmokers.

Line-Staff Conflict   Clashes over authority relationships often involve **line-staff conflict.** Most organizations have staff departments to assist the line departments. Line managers normally are responsible for some process that creates part or all of the firm's goods or services. Staff managers often serve an advisory or control function that requires specialized technical knowledge.[36] Line managers may feel that staff managers are imposing on their areas of legitimate authority (which we discuss in Chapter 15). Staff personnel may specify the methods and partially control the resources used by line managers. In many manufacturing organizations, staff engineers specify how each product is to be made and what materials are to be used. At the same time, line managers are held responsible for the outcomes. Line managers may experience conflict when they perceive that the engineers are directing production tasks. Line managers often believe that staff managers reduce their authority over workers while their responsibility for the outcomes remains unchanged; that is, their perceived authority is less than their perceived responsibility because of staff involvement.

Diversity-based conflict   As discussed in several previous chapters, serious intergroup conflicts may be based on diversity. The toughest diversity-based conflicts in organizations appear to be related to issues of race, gender, ethnicity, and religion.[37] They may encompass all five levels of conflict—intrapersonal, interpersonal, intragroup, intergroup, and interorganizational. Interorganizational conflicts come into play, for example, in disputes between an organization and the U.S. Equal Employment Opportunity Commission, which pursues discrimination charges by individuals or groups.

The following Managing Diversity feature presents some of the initiatives at General Computer, Inc., to avoid, reduce, and resolve diversity-based conflicts. The firm recognizes that it hasn't yet fully addressed or resolved all its diversity-based conflicts.

MANAGING DIVERSITY

Bridging Differences at General Computer, Inc.

Diversity initiatives at General Computer, Inc. (GCI) span more than one program. They involve a philosophical orientation and a range of opportunities to discuss and learn about cultural differences. Martha Webster, who helped design and manage GCI's diversity program, explains that GCI has developed a series of programs that enable employees to explore cultural differences and a corporation-wide ideology that values those differences.

Employees have the opportunity to begin exploring race- and gender-related topics in an introductory diversity workshop. Then they may move on to participate in continual, in-depth training and personal cross-cultural interaction. Designed to introduce employees to GCI's diversity philosophy, the initial workshop is led by an internal management education group. If participants are inspired by the program, they may join or form a discussion group. Typically, ten male and female employees from varied cultural backgrounds comprise a discussion group. They meet approximately once a month to explore their own differences and stereotypes. Webster explains, "The groups were established to ask all the dirty questions about race and gender." She says the personal cross-cultural interaction and exploration that takes place in these groups is a potentially powerful form of self-exploration and enhances the participants' ability to communicate effectively with a diverse range of employees. Webster points out that the program groups typically realize that what they have in common as human beings and as members of a firm supersede differences associated with their genetic and cultural heritages. She explains that the commonalty among the participants naturally becomes evident as they learn more about one another.

To become a member of a discussion group, employees must attend a two-day training program. It is designed to increase participants' knowledge of and sensitivity to race and gender issues and to teach them about basic group dynamics. The company implemented this program in response to conflicts that erupted in early discussion groups, which hurt individual members and were destructive to the group. Webster estimates that 200 discussion groups currently are in place at GCI and speculates that about 50% of GCI's employees have participated in one at some time. The groups tend to last from 12 to 18 months. They dissolve as members either work through issues or transfer to other positions in the company.[38]

▼ CONFLICT-HANDLING STYLES

Individuals attempt to manage interpersonal conflict in various ways.[39] Figure 13.3 provides a basic model for understanding and comparing five interpersonal conflict-handling styles. They are identified by their locations on two dimensions: *concern for self* and *concern for others*. The desire to satisfy your own concerns depends on the extent to which you are *assertive* or *unassertive* in pursuing personal goals. Your desire to satisfy the concerns of others depends on the extent to which you are *cooperative* or *uncooperative*. The five

FIGURE 13.3

Interpersonal Conflict-Handling Styles

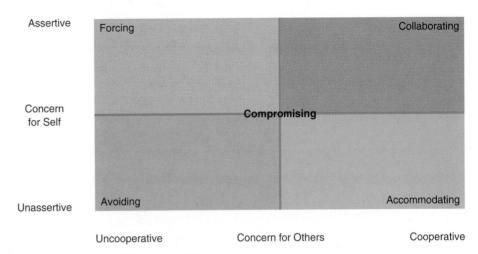

Source: Adapted with permission from Thomas, K. W. Conflict and conflict management. In M. D. Dunnette (ed.), *Handbook of Industrial and Organizational Psychology*. Chicago: Rand McNally, 1976, 900.

interpersonal conflict-handling styles thus represent different combinations of assertiveness and cooperativeness. Although you may have a natural tendency toward one or two of the styles, nothing precludes your using all the styles as the context and people change.[40] For example, the style you use in working through a conflict with a good friend may be quite different than that you utilize with a stranger after a minor auto accident.

▼ Avoiding Style

The **avoiding style** involves unassertive and uncooperative behaviors. People use this style to stay away from conflict, ignore disagreements, or remain neutral. This approach might reflect a decision to let the conflict work itself out, or it might reflect an aversion to tension and frustration. Because ignoring important issues often frustrates others, consistent use of this interpersonal conflict-handling style usually results in unfavorable evaluations by others.[41] An avoiding style is reflected in statements such as the following.

- ▲ "If there are rules that apply, I cite those. If there aren't, I leave the other person free to make his or her own decision."
- ▲ "I usually don't take positions that will create controversy."
- ▲ "I shy away from topics that are sources of disputes with my friends."
- ▲ "That's okay. It wasn't important anyway. Let's leave well enough alone."

When unresolved conflicts affect goal accomplishment, the avoiding style will lead to negative results for the organization. This style may be desirable under some situations, as when (1) the issue is minor or only of passing importance and thus not worth the individual's time or energy to confront the conflict; (2) there isn't enough information available to the individual to effectively deal with the conflict at that time; (3) the individual's power is so low relative to the other person's that there's little chance of causing change (such as disagreement with a new strategy approved by top management); and (4) other individuals can more effectively resolve the conflict.

▼ Forcing Style

The **forcing style** involves assertive and uncooperative behaviors and reflects a win–lose approach to interpersonal conflict. Those who use this style try to achieve their own goals without concern for others. The forcing style includes aspects of coercive power and dominance.[42] The forcing person feels that one side must win and that one side must lose. This style sometimes helps a person achieve individual goals, but like avoidance, forcing tends to result in unfavorable evaluations by others. Recall the Preview Case and the chairman's comment to Charlie Olcott: "Defend my numbers or you're off the team." The forcing style is reflected in the following statements.

- ▲ "I like to put it plainly: Like it or not, what I say goes, and maybe when others have had the experience I have, they will remember this and think better of it."
- ▲ "I convince the other person of the logic and benefits of my position."
- ▲ "I insist that my position be accepted during a disagreement."
- ▲ "I usually hold on to my solution to a problem after the controversy starts."

Forcing-prone individuals assume that conflict involves win–lose situations. When dealing with conflict between subordinates or departments, forcing-style managers may threaten or actually use demotion, dismissal, negative performance evaluations, or other punishments to gain compliance. When conflict occurs between peers, an employee using the forcing style might try to get his or her own way by appealing to the manager. This approach represents an attempt to use the manager to force the decision on the opposing individual. Recall the earlier account about the silent sabateurs and how the employees got back at managers because of their heavy reliance on the forcing style.

Overreliance on forcing by a manager lessens employees' work motivation because their interests have not been considered. Relevant information and other possible alternatives usually are ignored. In some situations the forcing style may be necessary, such as when (1) emergencies require quick action, (2) unpopular courses of action must be taken for long-term organizational effectiveness and survival (such as cost-cutting and dismissal of employees for unsatisfactory performance), and (3) the person needs to take action for self-protection and to stop others from taking advantage of him or her.

▼ Accommodating Style

The **accommodating style** represents cooperative and unassertive behaviors. Accommodations may represent an unselfish act, a long-term strategy to encourage cooperation by others, or a submission to the wishes of others. Accommodators usually are favorably evaluated by others, but they also are perceived as weak and submissive. Statements that reflect an accommodating style include the following.

- ▲ "Conflict is best managed through the suspension of my personal goals to maintain good relationships with those whom I value."
- ▲ "If it makes other people happy, I am all for it."

▲ "I like to smooth over disagreements by making them appear less important."

▲ "I ease conflict by suggesting that our differences are trivial and then show good will by blending my ideas into those of the other person."

When using the accommodating style, individuals may act as though the conflict will go away in time and appeal for cooperation. These individuals try to reduce tensions and stress by reassurance and support. This style shows concern about the emotional aspects of conflict but little interest in working on its substantive issues. The accommodating style simply encourages individuals to cover up or gloss over their feelings. It is generally ineffective if used as a dominant style.[43] The accommodating style may be effective on a short-term basis when (1) the individuals are in a potentially explosive emotional conflict situation, and smoothing is used to defuse it; (2) keeping harmony and avoiding disruption are especially important in the short run; and (3) the conflicts are based primarily on the personalities of the individuals and cannot be easily resolved.

▼ Collaborating Style

The **collaborating style** involves strongly cooperative and assertive behaviors and is the win–win approach to interpersonal conflict. The collaborating style represents a desire to maximize joint outcomes. People who use this style tend to have the following characteristics: (1) they see conflict as natural, helpful, and even leading to a more creative solution if handled properly; (2) they exhibit trust in and candor with others; and (3) they recognize that when conflict is resolved to the satisfaction of all, commitment to the solution is likely. Individuals who use the collaborating style often are dynamic and evaluated favorably by others. Charlie Olcott's comments in the Preview Case, when taken as a whole, suggest that he primarily uses the collaborating style. Statements consistent with this style include the following.

▲ "I first try to overcome any distrust that might exist between us. Then I try to get at the feelings that we both have about the topics. I stress that nothing we decide is cast in stone and suggest that we find a position we can both give a trial run."

▲ "I tell the other person my ideas, actively seek out the other person's ideas, and search for a mutually beneficial solution."

▲ "I like to suggest new solutions and build on a variety of viewpoints that may have been expressed."

▲ "I try to dig into an issue to find a solution good for all of us."

With this style, conflict is recognized openly and evaluated by all concerned. Sharing, examining, and assessing the reasons for the conflict should lead to the development of an alternative that effectively resolves it and is fully acceptable to everyone involved.[44] **Collaboration** is most practical when there is (1) sufficient *required interdependence* so that expending the extra time and energy needed with collaboration to work through individual differences makes sense; (2) sufficient *parity in power* among individuals so that they feel free to interact candidly, regardless of their formal superior/subordinate status; (3) the potential for *mutual benefits*, especially over the long run, for resolving the dispute through a win–win process; and (4) sufficient *organizational support* for taking the time and energy to resolve disputes through collaboration. The norms, rewards, and punishments of the organization—especially those set by top management—provide the framework for encouraging or discouraging collaboration.[45]

▼ Compromising Style

The **compromising style** represents behaviors at an intermediate level in terms of cooperation and assertiveness. This style is based on give and take, typically involves a series of concessions, and is commonly used and widely accepted as a means of resolving conflict. The compromising style is reflected in statements such as the following.

- ▲ "I want to know how and what others feel. When the timing is right, I explain how I feel and try to show them where they are wrong. Of course, it's often necessary to settle on some middle ground."
- ▲ "After failing in getting my way, I usually find it necessary to seek a fair combination of gains and losses for both of us."
- ▲ "I give in to others if they are willing to meet me halfway."
- ▲ "As the old saying goes, a half a loaf is better than nothing. Let's split the difference."

Those who compromise with others tend to be evaluated favorably. Various explanations are suggested for the favorable evaluation of the compromising style, including: (1) it may be seen primarily as a cooperative "holding back;" (2) it may reflect a pragmatic way for dealing with conflicts; and (3) it may help maintain good relations in the future.

In one study, individuals with a preference for the compromising style felt that it did provide a solution ("not coming up with a solution is weak") but that it required strength to accept the other person's ideas as important. Implicit in these two ideas seems to be the notion that insisting on your own viewpoint can be self-indulgent, as it fails to recognize the ideas of others. Individuals with a strong preference for the forcing style simply viewed it as a quick way to deal with conflict. Most thought that the initially positive reactions to a compromise are soon replaced by doubts about the fairness of the outcome, the equality of each person's concessions, and the other person's motives and honesty.[46] The compromising style usually is most effective as a backup to the collaborating style.

The compromising style may create several problems if used too early in trying to resolve conflict. First, the people involved may be encouraging compromise on the stated issues rather than on the real issues. The first issues raised in a conflict often are not the real ones, so premature compromise may prevent full diagnosis or exploration of the real issues. For example, students telling professors that their courses are tough and challenging may be trying to negotiate an easier grading system. Second, accepting an initial position presented is easier than searching for alternatives that are more acceptable to everyone involved. Third, compromise may be inappropriate to all or part of the situation because it may not be the best decision available. Further debate may reveal a better way of resolving the conflict.

Compared to the collaborating style, the compromising style tends not to maximize joint satisfaction. Compromise achieves moderate, but only partial, satisfaction for each person. This style is likely to be appropriate when (1) agreement enables each person to be better off or at least not worse off than if no agreement were reached; (2) achieving a total win–win agreement simply isn't possible; and (3) conflicting goals or opposing interests block agreement on one person's proposal.

When faced with apparent ethical dilemmas, individuals or groups often seek some kind of compromise. As suggested in the following Managing Ethics feature, the attempt to negotiate or impose a compromise solution doesn't always work.

MANAGING ETHICS

Wal-Mart's Failed Compromise

Mary Marquardt and Wal-Mart have waged a three-year battle over her religious principles. Marquardt believes that the giant discount chain discriminated against her when it offered her a job, then withdrew the offer after she cited her biblical convictions in refusing to work on Sundays. So far, Wal-Mart has lost every legal decision.

The case centers on just how far employers must go to accommodate workers' religious beliefs and how much religious believers may have to compromise their beliefs for a job. Marquardt's story starts in 1990, when Wal-Mart began hiring for a store it was opening in Manitowoc, Wisconsin. On her application, she noted that, for religious reasons, she could not work Sundays. Marquardt says she has been a born-again Christian since 1978. A Wal-Mart assistant manager offered her a job in June 1990. He told her that the clerical position, which paid $4.50 an hour, would require her to work two Sundays a month. When Marquardt reiterated her beliefs about Sundays, the assistant manager told her that at least one Sunday a month would be required. Marquardt reluctantly accepted. At the time, she said, she was living at home with her parents. They were urging her to move out on her own. "I felt under pressure to have to take the job," Marquardt said. Ten days after accepting the offer but before beginning work, she visited the store and told the assistant manager that as much as she wanted to work for Wal-Mart, her conscience wouldn't allow her to work on Sunday.

The store's manager, Jeffrey Hindes, told her he would have to withdraw the job offer. If he made an exception in her case, "it would ultimately snowball," he later testified. "We would have to give the same privilege to each and every person that would request it." Marquardt filed a complaint against Wal-Mart with the Equal Rights Division of the Wisconsin Department of Industry, Labor and Human Relations. In 1992, an administrative law judge sided with her. The judge ruled that Wal-Mart could have modified its policy on Sunday work without suffering an undue burden. Wal-Mart appealed to the Labor and Industry Review Commission. In June 1993, the commission largely criticized the judge but also criticized Wal-Mart for failing to tell Marquardt about its policy that allowed employees to swap shifts with management approval. The commission claimed that this policy might have allowed Marquardt to take the job without compromising her beliefs.

MANAGING ETHICS —*Continued*

In fighting the claim, Wal-Mart presented various defenses, all to no avail. For example, the company argued that its offer to have Marquardt work just one Sunday a month when it usually required two Sundays and that her initial acceptance of the offer signified that the store was making a "reasonable accommodation," as expected under the state's fair employment law. Wal-Mart further argued that a decision in Marquardt's favor could cause the store "to discriminate against non-Sabbath observers by forcing others in the work force to sacrifice their Sunday in order to allow Marquardt her requested time off." The commission rejected these and other arguments. In December 1993, a county circuit judge upheld the commission's ruling. Wal-Mart has appealed to a higher court.[47]

▼ Key Implications

Studies conducted on the use of different interpersonal conflict-handling styles indicate that collaboration tends to be characteristic of (1) more successful rather than less successful individuals and (2) high-performing rather than medium- and low-performing organizations. People tend to perceive collaboration in terms of the constructive use of conflict. The use of collaboration seems to result in positive feelings in others, as well as favorable self-evaluations of performance and abilities.

The same studies reveal that, in contrast to collaboration, forcing and avoiding often have negative effects. Forcing and avoiding tend to be associated with a less constructive use of conflict, negative feelings from others, and unfavorable evaluations of performance and abilities. The effects of accommodation and compromise appear to be mixed. The use of accommodation sometimes results in positive feelings from others. But these individuals do not form favorable evaluations of the performance and abilities of those using the accommodating style. The use of the compromising style generally is followed by positive feelings from others.[48]

▼ NEGOTIATION IN CONFLICT MANAGEMENT

Negotiation is a process in which two or more people or groups, having both common and conflicting goals, state and discuss proposals for specific terms of a possible agreement. Negotiation normally includes a combination of compromise, collaboration, and possibly some forcing on particular vital issues.[49]

▼ Basic Types of Negotiations

The four basic types of negotiations are distributive, integrative, attitudinal structuring, and intraorganizational.[50]

Distributive Negotiations Traditional win–lose, fixed-amount situations— where one party's gain is another party's loss—characterize **distributive negotiations.** They often occur over economic issues. The interaction patterns may include guarded communications, limited expressions of trust, use of threats, and distorted statements and demands. In short, the parties are engaged in intense emotion laden conflict. The forcing and compromise conflict-handling styles are dominant in distributive negotiations.

During 1993 and 1994, Frank Lorenzo, previously chairman of Continental Airlines and now defunct Eastern Airlines, negotiated with the U.S. Department of Transportation to start a small airline. Because of bitter past relations between Lorenzo and airline unions and other groups, they pressured the department to reject Lorenzo's efforts to start this airline. These groups also lobbied numerous key members of Congress to stop Lorenzo. In a press release, the pilots' union declared: "He is the very embodiment of evil." Joseph Corr, a former Continental chief executive testified at a public hearing on Lorenzo's application. He described Lorenzo's management style as "dishonest, inattentive to matters of safety, [and] generally unqualified." The Department of Transportation rejected Lorenzo's application in 1994. Lorenzo is expected to fight the ruling in the courts.[51] Clearly, the unions and Lorenzo were engaged in distributive (I win, you lose) negotiations through a third-party, namely the Department of Transportation.

Integrative Negotiations Joint problem solving to achieve solutions by which both parties can gain is called **integrative negotiations.** The parties identify mutual problems, identify and assess alternatives, openly express preferences, and jointly reach a mutually acceptable solution. Rarely perceived as equally acceptable, the choice is simply advantageous to both sides. Those involved are strongly motivated to solve problems, exhibit flexibility and trust, and explore new ideas. The collaborative and compromise conflict-handling styles are dominant in integrative negotiations.

Motorola fosters mostly integrative negotiations with its suppliers by looking for suppliers that share its values. Then it sharpens their skills by teaching them its own TQM techniques. While nurturing long-term partnerships, Motorola sparks some competition among partners by grading them. Motorola teams tour suppliers' plants every two years, grading them on how well they stack up against their competitors in terms of meeting quality and scheduling agreements. Motorola's purchasing managers also rate suppliers monthly on an index that combines cost and quality. Again, they compare suppliers to their competitors (listed anonymously) and show them how much of Motorola's business each competitor gets. Motorola procurement chief Tom Slaninka states, "The better performers should earn a greater share of our business. We're teaching and coaching and pushing them in a direction that's been successful for us, toward a culture and a mindset that show that quality and cycle times have a direct relation to the cost of the product."[52]

Attitudinal Structuring Throughout any negotiations, the parties exhibit an interpersonal relationship pattern (such as hostility or friendliness and competitiveness or cooperativeness) that influences their interactions. **Attitudinal structuring** is the process by which the parties seek to establish desired attitudes and relationships. Hostile and competitive attitudes prevailed between airline union leaders and Frank Lorenzo, which reflected their direct negotiations with the Department of Transportation. In contrast, Motorola works hard to create friendly and cooperative attitudes with suppliers while engaging in tough-minded negotiations with them. Motorola demonstrates to its suppliers that they are valued and are part of the team. Motorola even established a 15-member council of suppliers to rate Motorola's own practices and offer suggestions for improvement.[53]

Intraorganizational Negotiations   Groups often negotiate through representatives. However, the representatives first may have to obtain the agreement of their respective groups before they can agree with each other. In **intraorganizational negotiations,** each set of negotiators tries to build consensus for agreement and resolve intragroup conflict before dealing with the other group's negotiators. For example, the president of the flight attendants union recently spent a considerable amount of time building agreement among the union's members that a strike of American Airlines was necessary and would be effective.

▼ Integrative Process[54]

In the highly publicized best-seller *Getting to Yes,* R. Fisher and W. Ury outline four key concepts for integrative (win–win) negotiations. These concepts comprise the foundation of an integrative negotiation strategy, which they call "principled negotiation," or "negotiation on the merits."[55]

▲ *Separate the people from the problem.* The first concept in reaching a mutually agreeable solution is to disentangle the substantive issues of the negotiation from the interpersonal relationship issues between the parties and deal with each set of issues separately. Negotiators should perceive themselves as working side-by-side, attacking the substantive issues or problems instead of attacking each other.

▲ *Focus on interests, not positions.* People's egos tend to become identified with their negotiating positions. Furthermore, focusing only on stated positions often obscures what the participants really need or want. Rather than focusing only on the positions taken by each negotiator, a much more effective strategy is to focus on the underlying human needs and interests that had caused them to adopt those positions.

▲ *Invent options for mutual gain.* Designing optimal solutions under pressure in the presence of an adversary tends to narrow people's thinking. Searching for the one right solution inhibits creativity, particularly when the stakes are high. These blinders can be offset by establishing a forum in which a variety of possibilities are generated before deciding which action to take.

▲ *Insist on using objective criteria.* The parties should discuss the conditions of the negotiation in terms of some fair standard such as market value, expert opinion, custom, or law. This steers focus away from what the parties are willing or unwilling to do. By using objective criteria, neither party has to give in to the other, and both parties may defer to a fair solution.

▼ Distributive Process

Some individuals and groups still believe in extreme distributive (win–lose) negotiations, and you have to be prepared to counter them. Awareness and understanding probably are the most important means for dealing with win–lose negotiation ploys by the other party. Four of these more common win–lose strategies are as follows.[56]

▲ *I want it all.* By making an extreme offer and then granting concessions grudgingly, if at all, the other party hopes to wear down your resolve. You will know that you have met such a negotiator when you encounter the following tactics: (1) the other party's first offer is extreme; (2) minor concessions are made grudgingly; (3) you are pressured to make significant concessions, and (4) the other party refuses to reciprocate.

▲ *Time warp.* Time can be used as a very powerful weapon by the win–lose negotiator. When any of the following techniques are used, you should refuse to be forced into an unfavorable position: (1) the offer is valid only for a limited time; (2) you are pressured to accept arbitrary deadlines; (3) the other party stalls or delays the progress of the negotiation; and (4) the other party increases pressure on you to settle quickly.

▲ *Good cop, bad cop.* Negotiators using this strategy hope to sway you to their side by alternating sympathetic with threatening behavior. You should be on your guard when you are confronted with the following tactics: (1) the other party becomes irrational or abusive; (2) the other party walks out of a negotiation; and (3) irrational behavior is followed by reasonable, sympathetic behavior.

▲ *Ultimatums.* This strategy is designed to try to force you to submit to the will of the other party. You should be wary when the other party tries any of the following: (1) you are presented with a take-it-or-leave-it offer; (2) the other party overtly tries to force you to accept his/her demands; (3) the other party is unwilling to make concessions; and (4) you are expected to make all the concessions.

▼ Matrix of Outcomes

Although negotiators may realize the importance of cooperatively creating value by means of the integrative negotiation process, they must also acknowledge the fact that both sides may eventually seek gain through the distributive process. The negotiator's dilemma lies in the fact that the tactics of self gain may tend to repel moves to create self-gain. An optimal solution normally results when both parties openly discuss the problem, respect each other's substantive and relationship needs, and creatively seek to satisfy each other's interests. However, such behavior cannot always be expected to occur.

In negotiations between a win–lose negotiator and a win–win negotiator, the latter is highly vulnerable to the former's tactics. Negotiators may develop an inherent uneasiness about the use of integrative strategies to the extent that they may come to expect the other party to use distributive strategies. Such mutual suspicion may cause negotiators to leave joint gains on the table. Moreover, after being stung in several encounters with experienced win–lose strategists, the pull toward self-gain tactics becomes insidious and win–win strategists may "learn" to become win–lose strategists. Finally, if both negotiators choose to employ distributive strategies, the probability of high value being created through the negotiating process is virtually eliminated. The negotiations will likely result in both parties receiving only mediocre benefits.

FIGURE 13.4

Matrix of Negotiated Outcomes

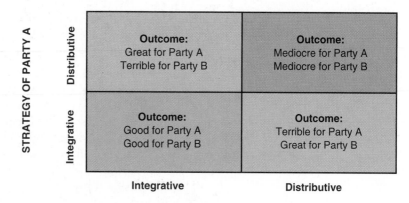

STRATEGY OF PARTY B

Source: Adapted from Anderson, T. Step into my parlor: A survey of strategies and techniques for effective negotiation. *Business Horizons*, May–June 1992, p. 75.

Graphically, the integrative and distributive negotiating strategies may be placed on vertical and horizontal axes, representing the two negotiating parties. Then, a matrix of possible outcomes emerging from the negotiation process can be developed to illustrate the negotiator's dilemma, as shown in Figure 13.4, for parties A and B.

▼ Negotiating Across Cultures

The numerous issues and complexities relevent to domestic negotiations are compounded in negotiating across cultures.[57] The following Managing Across Cultures feature highlights some of the unique aspects of negotiations and union–management relations in Mexico.

MANAGING ACROSS CULTURES

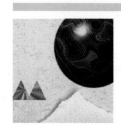

Business Negotiations in Mexico

Personal relationships are an important part of business negotiations in Mexico. Hospitality is a first priority in doing business, and negotiations are initiated with social graces. Trust and respect must be secured for successful negotiations. Executives in Mexico frequently express strong objections to U.S. negotiators' tendency to "get to the point." They find this urgency to produce results distasteful and ill-mannered.

Mexican negotiators initially tend to be cautious, perhaps even suspicious. Their wanting not to appear ill-informed and not to be taken advantage of may slow the opening phases of negotiations. Therefore the opening conversation should be indirect, cautious, and exploratory. Direct questions or statements should be postponed until later. Consequently, although talk will be plentiful, there will be little engagement in substantive negotiations.

Mexican negotiators prefer to start with a general proposal and then define the issues. The ultimate conclusions will be arrived at with minimal consid-

MANAGING ACROSS CULTURES —*Continued*

eration of details. Mexican negotiators prefer agreements that are bound by a strong oral understanding. They believe that the written agreement is secondary and only represents the strong bond of the oral obligation. At times, however, the seemingly positive oral statements during negotiations are simply used to save face. A negative decision may come later by mail.

Equality in union–management relations in Mexico is valued by employees, management, and the union. This norm is sometimes difficult for Americans to understand because they are accustomed to union and management being adversaries. Under Mexican labor law, union and management roles often are complementary and equal. They both strive to maintain a "foundation of employment," one accountable for workers and the other for managing the business. Day-to-day relations often fall short of this ideal. Direct management communications to the work force are welcomed by unions as a way to cement relations, and management solicitation of grievances is encouraged. The union cooperates in disciplining workers, and management's role is to discipline supervisors. Few significant problems arise so long as wages do not fall below the legal minimum, supervisors act reasonably, and recreational or other social activities are available. Mexican employees view peaceful relations between the union and management as normal and desirable.

The recognition of an individual's place through symbolic formalities or a bit of flattery is the bedrock of human relations and negotiations in Mexico. For example, a union president was deeply insulted when a U.S. plant manager failed to introduce him to visitors from the home office. The plant manager regarded him as just another employee. However, the union leader's place was that of commander of the entire labor force and, under labor law, he possessed equal status with the employer.[58]

Table 13.1 provides additional insights into the complexities and sensitivities in negotiating across cultures. It presents the *traditional* cultural assumptions that underlie the Japanese, U.S. and Canadian, and Latin American approaches toward negotiations. However, as demonstrated in this and other chapters, many of the leading organizations in the United States and other countries have moved somewhat away from these traditional assumptions. Table 13.1 provides a thumbnail sketch of these traditional negotiating assumptions in terms of five dimensions: emotions, power, decision making, social interaction, and persuasion.

The traditional assumptions and generalizations shown may not always apply to negotiations and conflict resolution between the parties when long-term and insider relationships have been established. This situation applies particularly to negotiations by the Japanese with those whom they view as *insiders*. Almost by definition Westerners are considered to be *outsiders*. Thus Westerners often incorrectly assume that the Japanese never use direct or confrontational approaches to conflict resolution and negotiations. In fact, they often are very direct in resolving differences of opinion with insiders. They explicitly state the principal differences among group members and state demands, rejections, and counteroffers directly.

A consultant from the United States recently had this experience while working in Japan. The consultant, who speaks Japanese fluently, was involved

TABLE 13.1 Traditional Negotiating Assumptions Across Three Cultural Groupings

| Dimensions | Traditional Negotiating Assumptions | | |
	Japanese	U.S. and Canadian	Latin American
Emotions	Emotions valued but must be hidden.	Emotions not highly valued. Transactions with others mostly unemotional.	Emotional sensitivity valued. Highly emotional and even passionate interactions.
Power	Subtle power plays. Conciliation sought.	Power games played all the time. Litigation, not so much conciliation, pursued. Strength highly valued.	Great power plays. To be stronger than the others particularly valued.
Decision making	Team decision making.	Team inputs for decision makers.	Decisions made by individuals in charge.
Social interaction	Face-saving crucial. Decisions often made on the basis of saving someone from embarrassment.	Decisions made on a cost/benefit basis. Face-saving not openly important.	Face-saving for oneself critical to preserve honor and dignity.
Persuasion	Not argumentative. Quiet when right. Respectful and patient. Modesty and self-restraint highly valued.	Argumentative when right or wrong. Impersonal when arguing. Practical when presenting arguments.	Passionate and emotional when arguing. Enjoys a warm interaction and a lively debate.

Source: Adapted from Casse, P., and Doel, S. *Managing Intercultural Negotiations: Guidelines for Trainers and Negotiators.* Washington, D.C.: SEITAR International, 1985, p. 10.

in the renewal and renegotiation of a consulting contract. He met one-on-one with the lead person of a longtime client firm. The negotiation was conducted in Japanese, in a private room. The main issues were the price for new services and the criteria for assessing performance. Instead of using the wording more typical of public meetings, the Japanese client stated directly that the proposed price was too high and the criteria were too vague. The consultant replied in equal directness that the price requested was below industry norms and the criteria demanded could not be met. The discussion continued at this level of openness until a compromise was reached. The Japanese can "say no" directly and state whatever else is on their minds without any traditional indirectness. The key is negotiating in private with someone defined as an insider.[59]

▼ Third-Party Facilitation

Most negotiations occur directly between the involved parties. But, when the parties are likely to get locked into win–lose conflict, a third-party facilitator, acting as a *neutral* party, may be able to help them resolve their differences.[60]

Skills and Functions The role of a third-party facilitator is difficult, and effective third-party facilitators need special skills: (1) they must be able to diagnose the conflict, (2) they must be skilled at breaking deadlocks and facilitating discussions at the right time, and (3) they must show mutual acceptance and have the ability to provide emotional support and reassurance. In brief, the third-party facilitator's style must instill confidence in and acceptance by the parties in conflict. Key functions of this role include the following:

▲ *Ensure mutual motivation.* Each party should have incentives for resolving the conflict.

▲ *Achieve a balance in situational power.* If the situational power of the parties is not equal, it may be difficult to establish trust and maintain open lines of communication.

▲ *Coordinate confrontation efforts.* One party's positive moves must be coordinated with the other party's readiness to do likewise. A failure to coordinate positive initiatives and readiness to respond can undermine future efforts to work out differences.

▲ *Promote openness in dialogue.* The third party can help to establish norms of openness, provide reassurance and support, and decrease the risks associated with openness.

▲ *Maintain an optimum level of tension.* If the threat and tension are too low, the incentive for change or finding a solution is minimal. However, if the threat and tension are too high, the parties may be unable to process information and see creative alternatives. They may begin to polarize and take rigid positions.[61]

Intergroup Dialogue Technique A third-party facilitator usually tries to assist negotiations without setting down a specific set of procedures for everyone to follow. Occasionally, however, a structured approach is useful to ensure that everyone concentrate on the appropriate issues and direct their efforts toward resolving them. One example of such an approach is the intergroup dialogue technique.[62]

▲ Each group meets in a separate room and develops two lists. On one list, the members indicate how they perceive themselves as a group, particularly in their relationship with the other group. On the second list, they indicate how they view the other group.

▲ The two groups come together and share perceptions. The third-party facilitator helps them clarify their views and come to a better understanding of themselves and the other group.

▲ The groups return to their separate rooms to look deeper into the issues, diagnose the current problem, and determine what each group contributes to the conflict.

▲ The groups meet again to share their new insights. The third-party facilitator urges them to identify common issues and plan the next stages for seeking solutions.

Like most methods of negotiation and conflict management, the intergroup dialogue technique doesn't guarantee successful conflict resolution. Instead, it provides a process for the parties in conflict to explore and work through their differences. A skillful third-party facilitator uses the technique to move the parties toward a resolution.

Summary

Conflict is inevitable in organizational life. Four basic forms of conflict are goal conflict, cognitive conflict, affective conflict, and procedural conflict. Conflict need not have destructive outcomes for individuals or an organization. Through effective conflict management, its negative effects may be minimized and its positive effects maximized, yielding a balanced view of conflict. Effective conflict management is based, in part, on a solid understanding of the different ways in which conflict emerges and can be resolved.

Conflict occurs at five different levels within organizations: intrapersonal, interpersonal, intragroup, intergroup, and interorganizational. We discussed the key aspects of each level, with the exception of interorganizational conflict. The model presented for understanding and comparing interpersonal conflict-handling styles identified them as avoiding, forcing, accommodating, collaborating, and compromising. An individual may have a natural preference for one or two of these styles but may use all of them over time when dealing with various interpersonal conflict situations.

Negotiation is an important part of conflict management. The four basic types of negotiations are distributive, integrative, attitudinal structuring, and intraorganizational. The two basic approaches to negotiating tactics and behaviors are the win–win and win–lose processes. Negotiating across cultures is even more complex than domestic negotiating. Third-party facilitation can be helpful when the negotiating parties anticipate or experience difficulties in reaching agreement.

Key Words and Concepts

Accommodating style
Affective conflict
Approach–approach conflict
Approach–avoidance conflict
Attitudinal structuring
Avoidance–avoidance conflict
Avoiding style
Cognitive conflict
Cognitive dissonance
Collaborating style
Collaboration
Compromising style
Conflict

Conflict management
Distributive negotiations
Forcing style
Goal conflict
Horizontal conflict
Integrative negotiations
Intergroup conflict
Interpersonal conflict
Interrole conflict
Intersender role conflict
Intragroup conflict
Intraorganizational negotiations
Intrapersonal conflict

Intrasender role conflict
Line–staff conflict
Negotiation
Neurotic tendencies
Person–role conflict
Procedural conflict
Role
Role ambiguity
Role conflict
Role set
Vertical conflict

Discussion Questions

1. Would you have any difficulties in negotiating in Mexico or Latin America? Explain why or why not and identify the skills you possess or may need to develop to overcome any difficulties.

2. Have you been involved in negotiations where the other party used or tried to use win–lose tactics? If yes, describe the situation. What did you do in response to these tactics? How did you feel? What was the outcome?

3. Give four recommendations for reducing diversity-based conflicts in organizations. Explain the rationale for these recommendations.

4. What is your personal view of conflict—positive, negative, or balanced? Cite two incidents from your personal experience to illustrate your view.

5. How might goal conflict, cognitive conflict, and affective conflict all come into play in a conflict situation? Illustrate your answer by referring to a personal conflict situation.

6. Give personal examples of your experience with approach–approach conflict, avoidance–avoidance conflict, and approach–avoidance conflict.

7. What are the similarities and differences among intra-sender role conflict, intersender role conflict, and person–role conflict?

8. In which of your roles do you experience the most role ambiguity? Explain.

9. Why isn't the collaborative conflict-handling style used in all conflict situations?

10. What difficulties might an individual encounter in trying to apply win–win tactics in negotiations?

 ## Developing Skills

Self-Diagnosis: Conflict-Handling Styles[63]

Instructions

Each numbered item contains two statements that describe how people deal with conflict. Distribute five points between each pair of statements. The statement that more accurately reflects your likely response should receive the higher number of points.

For example, if response (a) strongly describes your behavior, then record

<u>5</u> a.

<u>0</u> b.

However, if (a) and (b) are both characteristic, but (b) is slightly more characteristic of your behavior than (a), then record

<u>2</u> a.

<u>3</u> b.

1. ____ a. I am most comfortable letting others take responsibility for solving a problem.
____ b. Rather than negotiate differences, I stress those points upon which agreement is obvious.

2. ____ a. I pride myself in finding compromise solutions.
____ b. I examine all the issues involved in any disagreement.

3. ____ a. I usually persist in pursuing my side of an issue.
____ b. I prefer to soothe others' feelings and preserve relationships.

4. ____ a. I pride myself in finding compromise solutions.
____ b. I usually sacrifice my wishes for the wishes of a peer.

5. ____ a. I consistently seek a peer's help in finding solutions.
____ b. I do whatever is necessary to avoid tension.

6. ____ a. As a rule, I avoid dealing with conflict.
____ b. I defend my position and push my view.

7. ____ a. I postpone dealing with conflict until I have had some time to think it over.
____ b. I am willing to give up some points if others give up some too.

8. ____ a. I use my influence to have my views accepted.
____ b. I attempt to get all concerns and issues immediately out in the open.

9. ____ a. I feel that most differences are not worth worrying about.
____ b. I make a strong effort to get my way on issues I care about.

10. ____ a. Occasionally I use my authority or technical knowledge to get my way.
____ b. I prefer compromise solutions to problems.

11. ____ a. I believe that a team can reach a better solution than any one person can working independently.
____ b. I often defer to the wishes of others.

12. ____ a. I usually avoid taking positions that would create controversy.
____ b. I'm willing to give a little if a peer will give a little, too.

13. ____ a. I generally propose the middle ground as a solution.
    ____ b. I consistently press to "sell" my viewpoint.

14. ____ a. I prefer to hear everyone's side of an issue before making judgments.
    ____ b. I demonstrate the logic and benefits of my position.

15. ____ a. I would rather give in than argue about trivialities.
    ____ b. I avoid being "put on the spot."

16. ____ a. I refuse to hurt a peer's feelings.
    ____ b. I will defend my rights as a team member.

17. ____ a. I am usually firm in pursuing my point of view.
    ____ b. I'll walk away from disagreements before someone gets hurt.

18. ____ a. If it makes peers happy, I will agree with them.
    ____ b. I believe that give-and-take is the best way to resolve any disagreement.

19. ____ a. I prefer to have everyone involved in a conflict generate alternatives together.
    ____ b. When the team is discussing a serious problem, I usually keep quiet.

20. ____ a. I would rather openly resolve conflict than conceal differences.
    ____ b. I seek ways to balance gains and losses for equitable solutions.

21. ____ a. In problem solving, I am usually considerate of peers' viewpoints.
    ____ b. I prefer a direct and objective discussion of any disagreement.

22. ____ a. I seek solutions that meet some of everyone's needs.
    ____ b. I will argue as long as necessary to get my position heard.

23. ____ a. I like to assess the problem and identify a mutually agreeable solution.
    ____ b. When people challenge my position, I simply ignore them.

24. ____ a. If peers feel strongly about a position, I defer to it even if I don't agree.
    ____ b. I am willing to settle for a compromise solution.

25. ____ a. I am very persuasive when I have to be to win in a conflict situation.
    ____ b. I believe in the saying, "Kill your enemies with kindness."

26. ____ a. I will bargain with peers in an effort to manage disagreement.
    ____ b. I listen attentively before expressing my views.

27. ____ a. I avoid taking controversial positions.
    ____ b. I'm willing to give up my position for the benefit of the group.

28. ____ a. I enjoy competitive situations and "play" hard to win.
    ____ b. Whenever possible, I seek out knowledgeable peers to help resolve disagreements.

29. ____ a. I will surrender some of my demands, but I have to get something in return.
    ____ b. I don't like to air differences and usually keep my concerns to myself.

30. ____ a. I generally avoid hurting a peer's feelings.
    ____ b. When a peer and I disagree, I prefer to bring the issue out into the open so we can discuss it.

Scoring

Record your responses (number of points) in the space next to each statement number below and then sum the points in each column.

Column 1	Column 2	Column 3	Column 4	Column 5
3(a) ___	2(a) ___	1(a) ___	1(b) ___	2(b) ___
6(b) ___	4(a) ___	5(b) ___	3(b) ___	5(a) ___
8(a) ___	7(b) ___	6(a) ___	4(b) ___	8(b) ___
9(b) ___	10(b) ___	7(a) ___	11(b) ___	11(a) ___
10(a) ___	12(b) ___	9(a) ___	15(a) ___	14(a) ___
13(b) ___	13(a) ___	12(a) ___	16(a) ___	19(a) ___
14(b) ___	18(b) ___	15(b) ___	18(a) ___	20(a) ___
16(b) ___	20(b) ___	17(b) ___	21(a) ___	21(b) ___
17(a) ___	22(a) ___	19(b) ___	24(a) ___	23(a) ___
22(b) ___	24(b) ___	23(b) ___	25(b) ___	26(b) ___
25(a) ___	26(a) ___	27(a) ___	27(b) ___	28(b) ___
28(a) ___	29(a) ___	29(b) ___	30(a) ___	30(b) ___
Total ___	Total ___	Total ___	Total ___	Total ___

Next, carry-over the totals from the column totals and then plot your total scores on the following chart to show the profile of your conflict-handling styles. A total score of 36 to 45 for each style, such as the forcing style in column one, may indicate a strong preference and use of that style. A total score of 0 to 18 for each style, such as the compromising style in column two, may indicate little preference and use of that style. A total score of 19 to 35 for each style may indicate a moderate preference and use of that style.

	Total	0	10	20	30	40	50	60
Column 1 (Forcing)	___			•	•	•	•	•
Column 2 (Compromising)	___		•	•	•	•	•	

Column 3
(Avoiding)

Column 4
(Accommodating)

Column 5
(Collaborating)

0   10   20   30   40   50   60

Interpretation

As discussed in the chapter, when used appropriately, each of these styles can be an effective approach to conflict resolution. Any one style or a mixture of the five can be used during the course of a dispute. Are you satisfied with this profile? Why or why not? Is this profile truly representative of your natural and primary conflict-handling styles?

A Case in Point: Sue's Dilemma

Sue was faced with a dilemma as to what course of action to take. She had recently started her job with a national accounting firm and she was already confronted with a problem that could affect her future with the firm. On an audit, she encountered a client who had been treating payments to a large number, but by no means a majority, of its workers as payments to independent contractors. This practice saves the client the payroll taxes (such as social security and unemployment compensation taxes) that would otherwise be due on the payments if the workers were classified as employees. In Sue's judgment, this was improper as well as illegal and should have been noted in the audit. She raised the issue with John, the senior accountant to whom she reported. He thought it was a possible problem, but did not seem willing to do anything about it. He encouraged her to talk to the partner in charge if she did not feel satisfied.

She thought about the problem for a considerable time before approaching the partner in charge. The ongoing professional education classes she had received from her employer emphasized: (1) ethical responsibilities that she has as a certified public accountant, and (2) the fact that her firm endorsed adherence to high ethical standards. This finally swayed her to pursue the issue with the partner in charge of the audit. The visit was not unsatisfactory. Paul, the partner, virtually confirmed her initial reaction that the practice was wrong. But, he said that many other companies in the industry follow such a practice. He went on to say that if an issue was made of it, they would lose the account. He was not about to take such action. Sue came away from the meetings with the distinct feeling that should she choose to pursue the issue, she would create an enemy.

Sue still felt disturbed and decided to discuss the problem with some of her co-workers. She approached Bill and Mike, both of whom had been working for the firm a couple of years. They were familiar with the problem since they had encountered it when doing the audit the previous year. They expressed considerable concern about her going over the head of the partner in charge of the audit. Bill and Mike noted that they could be in big trouble since they had failed to question the practice during the previous audit. They said that they realized it was probably wrong, but they went ahead because it had been ignored in previous years. They knew their supervisor wanted them to ignore it again as well. They did not want to cause problems. Bill and Mike encouraged her to be a "team player" and drop the issue.

Sue considered her dilemma. She could go over the head of the partner in charge of the audit and take her chances. She realized that even if she was vindicated, she would probably have to change jobs. Certainly, her co-workers would not appreciate her actions. Another course of action was to do nothing. She thought the people in her firm would be the happiest with that alternative and it would probably help her career in the company. The only problem was she would still have to deal with her conscience. She knew she had to decide soon.[64]

Questions

1. Is there evidence of goal conflict, cognitive conflict, and affective conflict in this case? Explain.
2. What types of role conflict is Sue probably experiencing?
3. How would you use the concepts of approach–approach conflict, avoidance–avoidance conflict, and approach–avoidance conflict to diagnose this situation?
4. State the role ambiguities that Sue is experiencing.
5. What should Sue do? Why?

References

1. Adapted from Kaeter, M. From hell to happiness. *Business Ethics*, July/August 1993, 22–26. This article reprinted with permission from *Business Ethics Magazine*, 52 S. 10th St., Suite 110, Minneapolis, MN 55403-2001.

2. Thomas, K. W. Conflict and negotiation processes in organizations. In M. D. Dunnette and L. M. Hough (eds.), *Handbook of Industrial and Organizational Psychology*, vol. 3, 2nd ed. Palo Alto, Calif.: Consulting Psychologists Press, 1992, 651–717.

3. Kottler, J. *Beyond Blame: A New Way of Resolving Conflicts in Relationships*. San Francisco: Jossey-Bass, 1994.

4. Kolb, D. M., and Bartunek, J. M. (eds.), *Hidden Conflict in Organizations: Uncovering Behind-the-Scenes Disputes*. Thousand Oaks, Calif.: Sage, 1992.

5. Wright, P. M. A theoretical examination of the construct validity of operationalizations of goal difficulty. *Human Resource Management Review*, 1992, 2, 275–298.

6. Cosier, R. A. and Dalton, D. R. Positive effects of conflict: A field experiment. *International Journal of Conflict Management*, 1990, 1, 81–92.

7. Baron, R. A. Positive effects of conflict: A cognitive perspective. *Employee Responsibilities and Rights Journal*, 1991, 4, 25–35.

8. Tjosvold, D. *Learning to Manage Conflict: Getting People to Work Together Productively*. New York: Lexington Books, 1993.

9. Baron, R. A., and Richardson, D. R. *Human Aggression*, 2nd ed. New York: Plenum Press, 1991.

10. Burrell, N. A., Buzzanell, P. M., and McMillan, J. J. Feminine tensions in conflict situations as revealed by metaphoric analyses. *Management Communication Quarterly*, 1992, 6, 115–149.

11. Kohn, A. *No Contest: The Case Against Competition*. Boston: Houghton Mifflin, 1986.

12. Kolb, D. M., and Silbey, S. S. Enhancing the capacity of organizations to deal with disputes. *Negotiation Journal*, October 1990, 297–304.

13. Morgan, G. *Imaginization: The Art of Creative Management*. Thousand Oaks, Calif.: Sage, 1993.

14. Adapted from Henkoff, R. Keeping Motorola on a roll. *Fortune*, April 18, 1994, 67–77; Slutsker, G. The company that likes to obsolete itself. *Forbes*, September 13, 1993, 139–144; Galvin, R. W. Linking research to applications: Looking to the future of technology at Motorola. *Across the Board*, October 1993, 47–48.

15. Locke, E. A., Smith, K. G., Erez, M., Chah, D., Schaeffer, A. The effects of intra-individual goal conflict on performance. *Journal of Management*, 1994, 20, 67–91.

16. Festinger, L. *A Theory of Cognitive Dissonance*. Evanston, Ill.: Row, Peterson, 1967; Kofodimas, J. *Balancing Act: How Managers Can Integrate Successful Careers and Fulfilling Personal Lives*. San Francisco: Jossey-Bass, 1993.

17. Czander, W. H. *The Psychodynamics of Work and Organizations: Theory and Applications*. New York: Gulford Press, 1993.

18. Kets de Vries, M. F. R., and Miller D. *The Neurotic Organization*. San Francisco: Jossey-Bass, 1984; Rothstein, L. R. The case of the temperamental talent. *Harvard Business Review*, November–December 1992, 16–19.

19. Ibid., 73–94; Zaleznik, A. *Learning Leadership: Cases and Commentaries on Abuse of Power in Organizations*. Chicago: Bonus Books, 1993.

20. Adapted from Navran, F. J. Silent saboteurs. *Executive Excellence*, April 1991, 11–13.

21. Rigdon, J. E. Companies see more workplace violence. *Wall Street Journal*, April 12, 1994, B1, B6.

22. Kahn, R. L., Wolfe, D. M., Quinn, R. P., Snoek, J. D., and Rosenthal, R. A. *Occupational Stress: Studies in Role Conflict and Ambiguity*. New York: John Wiley & Sons, 1964.

23. Adapted from Sullivan, R. E. It's first class here, man. *Forbes*,

March 14, 1994, 102–103; Schulz, J. D. USA Truck turned spinoff into success by staying focused on customer service. *Traffic World*, March 22, 1993, 18–20.

24. Galen, M. Work and family: Companies, are starting to respond to workers' needs—And gain from it. *Business Week*, June 28, 1993, 80–88.

25. Wharton, A. S., and Erickson, R. J. Managing emotions on the job and at home: Understanding the consequences of multiple emotional roles. *Academy of Management Review*, 1993, 18, 457–486; Duxbury, L. E., and Higgins, C. A. Gender differences in work-family conflict. *Journal of Applied Psychology*, 1991, 76, 60–74.

26. Ilgen, D. R., and Hollenbeck, J. R. The structure of work: Job design and roles. In M. D. Dunnette and L. M. Hough (eds.), *Handbook of Industrial and Organizational Psychology*, vol. 2, 2nd ed. Palo Alto, Calif.: Consulting Psychologists Press, 1991, 165–207.

27. Jackson, S. E., and Schuler, R. S. A meta-analysis and conceptual critique of research on role ambiguity and role conflict in work settings. *Organizational Behavior and Human Decision Processes*, 1985, 36, 16–78.

28. Oneal, M. Just what is an entrepreneur? *Business Week/Enterprise*, 1993, 104–112; Boynton, A. C., Gales, L. M., and Blackburn, R. S. Managerial search activity: The impact of perceived role uncertainty and role threat. *Journal of Management*, 1993, 19, 725–747.

29. Kabanoff, B. Equity, equality, power, and conflict. *Academy of Management Review*, 1991, 16, 416–441.

30. Adapted from Pare, T. P. Passing on the family business. *Fortune*, May 7, 1990, 81–85; Gupta, U., and Robichaux, M. At family firms, reins tangle easily. *Wall Street Journal*, August 9, 1989, 81; Sims, C. Shurgard sues, citing U-Haul's family feuds. *New York Times*, December 21, 1993, D5.

31. Kahn, A. Taking on a family business can call for greater expertise. *Bryan–College Station Eagle*, March 20, 1994, C6; Schifrin, M., and Moshavi, S. When heirs fall out. *Forbes*, December 6, 1993, 140–143.

32. Nulty, P. Look what the unions want now. *Fortune*, February 8, 1993, 128–133.

33. Pondy, L. R. Organizational conflict: Concept and models. *Administrative Science Quarterly*, 1967, 12, 296–320.

34. Weintraub, R. USAir lifts attendant weight rule. *Houston Chronicle*, February 11, 1994, B1.

35. Mallory, M. Is the smoking lamp going out for good? *Business Week*, April 11, 1994, 30–31.

36. March, S., and Simon, H. *Organizations*, 2nd ed. Cambridge, Mass.: Blackwell, 1993.

37. Triandis, H. C., Kurowski, L. S., and Gelfand, M. J. Workplace diversity. In H. C. Triandis, M. D. Dunnette, and L. M. Hough (eds.), *Handbook of Industrial and Organizational Psychology*, vol. 4, 2nd. ed. Palo Alto, Calif.: Consulting Psychologists Press, 1994, 769–827; Fagenson, E. A. (ed.), *Women in Management: Trends, Issues and Challenges in Managing Diversity*. Newbury Park, Calif.: Sage, 1993.

38. Adapted from Ellis, C., and Sonnenfeld, J. A. Diversity approaches to managing diversity. *Human Resource Management*, 1994, 33, 79–109.

39. Thomas, K. W. The conflict handling modes: Toward more precise theory. *Management Communication Quarterly*, 1988, 1, 430–436. For a more complex model of conflict-handling styles,

see Nicotera, A. M. Beyond two dimensions: A grounded theory model of conflict-handling behavior. *Management Communication Quarterly*, 1993, 6, 282–306.

40. King, W. C. and Miles, E. W. What we know—and don't know—about measuring conflict: An examination of the ROCI-OO and the OCCI conflict instruments. *Management Communication Quarterly*, 1990, 4, 222–243.

41. Baron, R. A., Fortin, S. P., Frei, R. L. Hauver, L. A., and Shack, M. L. Reducing organizational conflict: The role of socially induced positive affect. *International Journal of Conflict Management*, 1990, 1, 133–152.

42. DeWine, S., Nicotera, A. M., and Parry, D. Argumentativeness and aggressiveness: The flip side of gentle persuasion. *Management Communication Quarterly*, 1991, 4, 386–411.

43. Lee, Chang-Won. Relative status of employees and styles of handling interpersonal conflict: An experimental study with Korean managers. *International Journal of Conflict Management*, 1990, 1, 327–340.

44. Weeks, D. *The Eight Essential Steps to Conflict Resolution*. Los Angeles: Jeremy P. Tarcher, 1992.

45. Blake, R. R., and Mouton, J. S. *Solving Costly Organizational Conflicts*. San Francisco: Jossey-Bass, 1984.

46. Kabanoff, B. Why is compromise so favorably viewed? In F. Hoy (ed.), *Academy of Management Best Paper Proceedings*. Mississippi State, Miss.: Academy of Management, 1987, 280–284.

47. Adapted from Gunn, E. Religious employee challenges Wal-Mart over working Sunday. *Houston Chronicle*, January 2, 1994, 3F; Johnson, J. L. We're all associates. *Discount Merchandiser*, August 1993, 50–80.

48. Rahim, M. A. *Managing Conflict in Organizations*, 2nd ed., New York: Praeger, 1992.

49. Lewicki, R. J., Litterer, J. A., Minton, J. W., and Saunders, D. *Negotiation*, 2nd. ed., Burr Ridge, Ill.: Irwin, 1994.

50. Walton, R. E., and McKersie, R. B. *A Behavioral Theory of Labor Negotiations*. New York: McGraw-Hill, 1965.

51. O'Brian, B. For Lorenzo, getting a new airline aloft is proving treacherous. *Wall Street Journal*, January 25, 1994, A1, A9; Mintiz, B. Lorenzo airline at risk of losing investors. *Houston Chronicle*, April 15, 1994, 2D.

52. Magnet, M. The new golden rule of business. *Fortune*, February 21, 1994, 60–64.

53. *Ibid.*

54. This section was adapted from Anderson, T. Step into my parlor: A survey of strategies and techniques for effective negotiations. *Business Horizons*, May–June 1992, 71–76.

55. Fisher, R., and Ury, W. *Getting to Yes: Negotiating Agreement Without Giving In*. New York: Penguin Books, 1981. Also see Hall, L. (ed.), *Negotiating: Strategies for Mutual Gain*. Thousand Oaks, Calif.: Sage, 1992.

56. Economy, P. *Business Negotiating Basics*. Burr Ridge, Ill.: Irwin, 1994.

57. Lewicki, R. J., Sheppard, B. H., and Bazerman, M. H. (eds.), *Handbook of Negotiation Research*, vol. 4. Greenwich, Conn.: JAI Press, 1994; Zartman, I. W. (ed.), *International Multilateral Negotiation: Approaches to the Management of Complexity*. San Francisco: Jossey-Bass, 1994.

58. Adapted from de Forest, M. E. Thinking of a plant in Mexico. *Academy of Management Executive*, February 1994, 33–40; Hellweg, S. A., Samovar, L. A., and Skow, L. Cultural variations in negotiation styles. In L. A. Samovar and R. E. Proter (eds.), *Intercultural Communications: A Reader*, 2nd. ed. Belmont, Calif.: Wadsworth, 1994, 286–292; Schmidt, K. D. *Doing Business in Mexico*. Menlo Park, Calif: SRI International, 1980.

59. Black, J. S., and Mendenhall, M. Resolving conflicts with the Japanese: Mission Impossible. *Sloan Management Review*, Spring 1993, 49–59; Weiss, S. E. Negotiating with the "Romans"—Part I. *Sloan Management Review*, Winter 1994, 51–61.

60. Schwarz, R. M. *The Skilled Facilitator: Practical Wisdom for Developing Effective Groups*. San Francisco: Jossey-Bass, 1994.

61. Peterson, R. B. Organizational goverance and the grievance process: In need of a new model for resolving workplace issues. *Employee Responsibilities and Rights Journal*, 1994, 7, 9–21; Klaas, B. S., and Feldman, D. C. The evaluation of disciplinary appeals in non-union organizations. *Human Resource Management Review*, 1993, 3, 49–81.

62. Blake, R. R., Shepard, H. A., and Mouton, J. S. *Managing Intergroup Conflict in Industry*. Houston: Gulf, 1964. Also see Conlon, D. E., and Ross, U. H. The effects of partisan third parties on negotiators behavior and outcome perceptions. *Journal of Applied Psychology*, 1993, 78, 280–290.

63. Adapted from Baskerville, D. M. How do you manage conflict. *Black Enterprise*, May 1993, 63–66; Holton, B., and Holton, C. *The Manager's Short Course: A Complete Course in Leadership Skills for the First-Time Manager*. New York: John Wiley & Sons, 1992; Thomas, K. W., and Kilmann, R. H. *The Thomas-Kilmann Conflict Mode Instrument*. Tuxedo, N.Y.: Xicom, 1974; Rahim, M. A. A measure of styles of handling interpersonal conflict. *Academy of Management Journal*, 1983, 26, 368–376.

64. Kilpatrick, J., Gantt, G., and Johnson, G. The audit. In R. A. Cook (ed.), *Annual Advances in Business Cases 1990*. South Bend, Ind.: Midwest Society for Case Research, 1990, 67–68. This case was prepared by John Kilpatrick, Gamewell Gantt, and George Johnson of Idaho State University as a basis for class discussion, rather than to illustrate either effective or ineffective handling of an administrative situation. Presented to the Midwest Society for Case Research Workshop, 1990. All rights reserved to the authors. Copyright © 1990 by John Kilpatrick, Gamewell Gantt, and George Johnson. Used with permission.

Part III Organizational Processes

Chapter
14

Organizational Culture

Chapter
15

Power and Political Behavior

Chapter
16

Job Design

Chapter
17

Organization Design

Chapter
18

Organizational Decision Making

461

14 Organizational Culture

LEARNING OBJECTIVES

When you have finished studying this chapter, you should be able to:

▲ Explain the concept of organizational culture.

▲ Describe how organizational cultures are developed, maintained, and changed.

▲ Understand the relationships between organizational culture and performance.

▲ Discuss the implications of organizational culture for ethical behavior in organizations.

▲ Explain the importance of effectively managing cultural diversity.

▲ Describe the process of organizational socialization and explain its relationship to organizational culture.

OUTLINE

Preview Case: Bank of America

Types of Organizational Culture

Dynamics of Organizational Culture

Developing Organizational Culture

Managing Across Cultures: Effects of National Cultural Values on Organizations

Maintaining Organizational Culture

Managing in Practice: McKinsey & Co.—"The Firm"

Changing Organizational Culture

Managing in Practice: The Failed Courtship of Bell Atlantic and TCI

Performance and Organizational Culture

Managing Quality: Gillette's Total Quality Culture

Ethical Behavior and Organizational Culture

Managing Ethics: Selling Auto Repair Service at Sears

Managing Cultural Diversity

Managing Diversity: Corporate Culture Versus Ethnic Culture

Organizational Socialization

Socialization Process

Managing in Practice: Herb Kelleher and Southwest Airlines

Socialization Outcomes

DEVELOPING SKILLS

Self-Diagnosis: *Assessing Ethical Culture*

A Case in Point: *Procter & Gamble*

PREVIEW CASE

Bank of America

Bank of America has rediscovered its original culture. A. P. Giannini founded the bank to provide banking services for the Italian immigrants of San Francisco. In its early years, the bank pioneered many services to make banking more customer friendly. It attracted thousands of small personal accounts by offering convenient branch banking, clever advertising, and well-designed, "inviting" offices. At the same time, Giannini took large risks, including backing projects as diverse as the Golden Gate Bridge and Walt Disney's movie *Snow White and the Seven Dwarfs*.

The Bank of America discovered a great many things that worked well and institutionalized them, becoming both efficient and predictable. This success gave rise to a new set of assumptions that characterized its organizational culture for some years: Don't risk failure; take a short-term view; don't be frank when evaluating products or programs; seniority is more important than perfor-

mance; study every new idea to death; protect your own turf. In the 1980s, a loss of market share and the resources used in fending off a hostile takeover attempt left Bank of America in a weakened position. In addition, just when it needed to respond to increased competition in a deregulated market, its culture resisted needed changes. The bank's ways of doing business no longer worked.

Rather than responding with new rules and regulations, Bank of America chose to reemphasize its core values and to promote change by refocusing on its original company culture. Core values included putting the customer first and respecting and rewarding both customers and bank employees. The bank communicated the new (original) culture throughout the organization by means of meetings, publications, and training programs. The new culture, coupled with a changed business strategy, including an aggressive acquisition program, returned the Bank of America to profitability and preeminence.[1]

The effectiveness and success of an organization are not determined solely by the abilities and motivations of employees and managers. Nor is effectiveness measured solely by how well groups and teams work together, although both individual and group processes are crucial for organizational success. In other words:

> The organization itself has an invisible quality—a certain style, a character, a way of doing things—that may be more powerful than the dictates of any one person or any formal system. To understand the soul of the organization requires that we travel below the charts, rule books, machines, and buildings into the underground world of corporate cultures.[2]

In this chapter, we introduce a part of the book devoted to organizational processes. So far, we have focused first on individual behavior and then on interpersonal and group behavior. We now shift our attention to the organization as a whole. We examine the concept of organizational culture and how cultures are formed, maintained, and changed. We also explore some possible relationships between organizational culture and performance; the relationship between organizational culture and ethical behavior; the challenge of managing a culturally diverse work force; and, finally, how organizations socialize individuals to their particular cultures. We begin with a brief overview of some types of organizational cultures.

TYPES OF ORGANIZATIONAL CULTURE

The labels of baseball team, club, academy, and fortress have been used to describe some common types of organizational cultures in the business world.[3] Each has distinctive characteristics.

Organizations with a **baseball team culture** attract entrepreneurs, innovators, and risk takers and pay employees for what they produce. Top performers often receive large salaries or other financial rewards and considerable autonomy. However, risks are high, and long-term security is virtually nonexistent. High performers tend to see themselves as free agents, much like professional athletes. Job hopping is common, with employees readily leaving one firm for greater rewards or freedom at another. Baseball team cultures are common in advertising agencies, biotechnology firms, consulting firms, investment banks, law firms, and computer software developers, such as Microsoft and Lotus.

Age and experience are valued in the **club culture.** Organizations with a club culture reward seniority and provide stable, secure employment. The club culture also rewards loyalty, commitment, and "fitting in." Managers typically work at various jobs in different functions during a slow, steady progression up the corporate hierarchy; quick upward mobility is unusual. Employees often start young and may spend 35–40 years with the same firm. For example, at United Parcel Service (UPS), the CEO and his entire top management team began their UPS careers as clerks, delivery drivers, or management trainees. Other club cultures include Delta Airlines, most commercial banks, many utilities (such as the Bell companies), government agencies, and the U.S. military.

Organizations with an **academy culture** also tend to hire recruits early—often directly from college—as do those with club cultures. However, academy cultures emphasize training employees to become expert in a particular function. For example, someone hired as a marketing representative would be unlikely to serve a stint in manufacturing. The academy culture stresses continuity of service, functional expertise, and institutional wisdom. Although there is some opportunity for "fast trackers," the academy culture is more likely to appeal to the steady climber who enjoys mastering the job. Academy cultures exist at Coca-Cola, IBM, Procter & Gamble and many other consumer product firms, the big three U.S. automakers, pharmaceutical companies, and many electronic and office products companies.

The **fortress culture** is preoccupied with survival. Organizations with a fortress culture promise little in the way of job security and have difficulty in rewarding employees for good performance. Typically, they may be in the process of downsizing or restructuring, causing the dismissal of many employees. A fortress culture might appeal to individuals who relish the challenge of turning a company around, but wouldn't appeal to those who desire a sense of belonging, opportunities for professional growth, or secure future income. Some fortress culture organizations that have fallen on hard times previously had baseball team, club, or academy cultures. Others are firms in businesses that are characterized by periodic boom and bust cycles. Currently, the ranks of fortress companies include some forest products firms, hotels, oil and gas companies, publishers, large retailers, and textile firms.

Most organizations probably cannot be categorized neatly as having a baseball team, club, academy, or fortress culture. Some may be a blend of these types; others may be in transition between types or even be different types at different times. For example, Bank of America, described in the Preview Case, began as a baseball team culture, matured into a club culture, and then returned to its original culture. Another example is Apple Computer, which also started with a baseball team culture but has matured into an academy culture.

These cultural types are offered as a way of introducing the concept of culture and understanding some important distinctions among organizations. However, other labels or categories of cultural types are commonly used. Not oversimplifying the concept of culture with the use of labels is important. Two organizations might be in essentially the same business, be located in the same geographic area, have similar forms of organizational structure, and yet, somehow, be very different places to work. What makes organizations different? How do they get that way? The concept of organizational culture provides a useful way to answer such questions.

▼ DYNAMICS OF ORGANIZATIONAL CULTURE

Organizational culture represents a complex pattern of beliefs, expectations, ideas, values, attitudes, and behaviors shared by the members of an organization.[4] More specifically, organizational culture includes the following components:

▲ *routine behaviors* when people interact, such as organizational rituals and ceremonies and the language commonly used;

▲ the *norms* that are shared by working groups throughout the organization, such as "a fair day's work for a fair day's pay";

▲ the *dominant values* held by an organization, such as "product quality" or "price leadership";

▲ the *philosophy* that guides an organization's policy toward employees and customers;

▲ the *rules* of the game for getting along in the organization or the "ropes" that a newcomer must learn in order to become an accepted member; and

▲ the *feeling* or *climate* that is conveyed in an organization by the physical layout and the way in which members of the organization interact with customers or other outsiders.[5]

None of these components individually represents the culture of the organization. Taken together, however, they reflect and give meaning to the concept of organizational culture.

Organizational culture exists on several levels, as indicated by Figure 14.1, which differ in terms of visibility and resistance to change. The least visible or deepest level is shared assumptions. These represent beliefs about reality and human nature that are taken for granted. For example, a basic assumption that guides some organizations in the development of reward systems, rules, and procedures is that employees are naturally lazy and must be tightly controlled in order to enhance their performance.

FIGURE 14.1

Levels of Organizational Culture

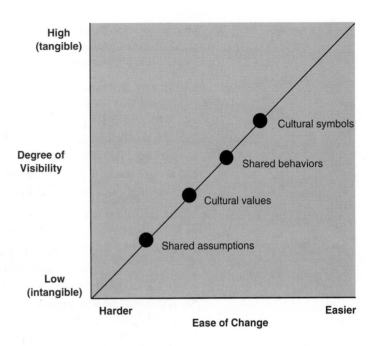

The next level of culture is **cultural values.** These shared values represent collective beliefs, assumptions, and feelings about what things are good, normal, rational, valuable, and so on.[6] Cultural values might be very different in different companies; in some, employees may care deeply about money but, in others, about technological innovation or employee well-being. These values tend to persist over time even when organizational membership changes. Shared behaviors, including norms (see Chapter 9), are more visible and somewhat easier to change than values, in part because people may be unaware of the values that bind them together.[7]

The most superficial level of culture consists of symbols. **Cultural symbols** are words (jargon or slang), gestures, and pictures or other physical objects that carry a particular meaning within a culture. Some expressions used at McDonald's Corporation provide an example of corporate jargon. McDonald's employees take training classes at Hamburger University; loyal employees are said to have "ketchup in their veins." Important cultural symbols sometimes take the form of **cultural heroes,** or people (alive or dead, real or imaginary) who possess characteristics highly valued by the culture and thus serve as role models.[8] For example, at the University of Virginia, which was founded by Thomas Jefferson, administrators reportedly still ask, "What would Mr. Jefferson do?" when faced with a challenging decision.

▼ Developing Organizational Culture

How does an organizational culture develop? Edgar Schein suggests that organizational culture forms in response to two major challenges that confront every organization: (1) external adaptation and survival; and (2) internal integration.[9]

External adaptation and survival has to do with how the organization will find a niche in and cope with its constantly changing external environment. External adaptation and survival involve addressing the following issues.

▲ *Mission and strategy*: Identifying the primary mission of the organization; selecting strategies to pursue this mission.

▲ *Goals*: Setting specific goals.

▲ *Means*: Determining how to pursue the goals; means include selecting an organizational structure and reward system.

▲ *Measurement*: Establishing criteria to measure how well individuals and teams are accomplishing their goals.

Internal integration concerns the establishment and maintenance of effective working relationships among the members of the organization. Internal integration involves addressing the following issues.

▲ *Language and concepts*: Identifying methods of communication; developing a shared meaning for important concepts.

▲ *Group and team boundaries*: Establishing criteria for membership in groups and teams.

▲ *Power and status*: Determining rules for acquiring, maintaining, and losing power and status.

▲ *Rewards and punishments*: Developing systems for encouraging desirable behaviors and discouraging undesirable behaviors.

An organizational culture emerges when members share knowledge and assumptions as they discover or develop ways of coping with external adaptation and internal integration issues.

Figure 14.2 shows a common pattern in the emergence of organizational cultures. In new companies, a founder, top manager, or a few key individuals may largely determine the organization's culture. Later in the life of the organization, its culture will reflect a complex mixture of the assumptions, values, and ideas of the founder or other early top managers and the subsequent learning and experiences of organizational members.

The national culture, customs, and societal norms of the country within which the firm operates also shape organizational culture. In other words, the culture of the larger society influences the culture of organizations operating within it.[10]

The dominant values of a national culture can be reflected in the constraints imposed on organizations by their environments. For example, the form of government may have a dramatic impact on how an organization does business in a country. In addition, the members of the organization have been raised in a particular society and thus bring the dominant values of the society into the firm. For example, individuals learn values, such as freedom of speech or respect for individual privacy, from their societies. The presence or absence of these and other values within the larger society has implications for organizational behavior. Finally, increased global operations have forced an awareness that differences in national culture may seriously affect organizational effectiveness. Multinational corporations such as IBM, Ford, and GE are discovering that organizational structures and cultures that might be effective in one part of the world may be ineffective in another.[11] The following Managing

FIGURE 14.2

One Common Pattern in the
Emergence of Corporate Cultures

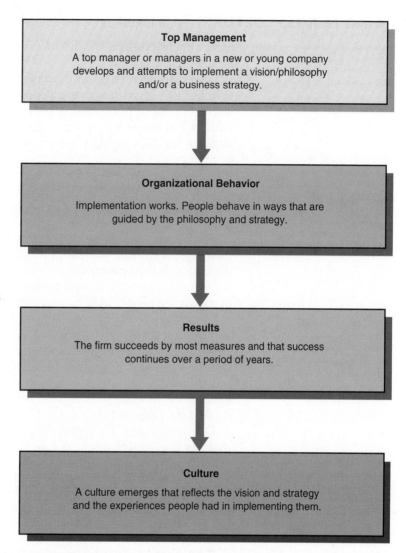

Top Management

A top manager or managers in a new or young company develops and attempts to implement a vision/philosophy and/or a business strategy.

Organizational Behavior

Implementation works. People behave in ways that are guided by the philosophy and strategy.

Results

The firm succeeds by most measures and that success continues over a period of years.

Culture

A culture emerges that reflects the vision and strategy and the experiences people had in implementing them.

Source: Reprinted with the permission of The Free Press, an imprint of Simon and Schuster from *Corporate Culture and Performance* by John P. Kotter and James L. Heskett. Copyright © 1992 by Kotter Associates, Inc. and James L. Heskett.

Across Cultures account illustrates the impact of a society's culture on the organizational culture of firms operating in that society.

MANAGING ACROSS CULTURES

Effects of National Cultural Values on Organizations

Geert Hofstede, a Dutch social scientist, has developed a framework consisting of several cultural dimensions that can be used to compare national cultural values. Recently, Hofstede's cultural dimensions have been used to examine the potential impacts of national culture on organizations. Two of these cul-

MANAGING ACROSS CULTURES —*Continued*

tural dimensions—power distance and uncertainty avoidance—are examined here.

Power distance refers to the extent to which a society encourages unequal distributions of power among people. In low power distance societies, more interaction takes place among people from different social classes, and individuals can move up in social status more easily. Examples of low power distance societies include Austria, Sweden, and the United States. Examples of high power distance countries are India, Mexico, and the Philippines. In these societies the distance between individuals of high and low status typically is considerable, and advancement into the upper classes often is difficult. Table 14.1 shows some differences between organizations in low and high power distance cultures.

These organizational characteristics can lead to important differences in organizational culture. For example, managers and employees are highly interdependent in low power distance societies and may prefer a more democratic style of management. In high power distance societies, a more autocratic style of managing people may be expected and even preferred by employees.

Uncertainty avoidance refers to the extent to which individuals in a society feel threatened by ambiguous and unstable situations and try to avoid them. In a high uncertainty avoidance culture, organizations tend to have many written rules and procedures, impose structure on employee activities, and reward managers for risk avoidance. The opposite tendencies characterize organizations in a national culture where uncertainty avoidance is low, as indicated by Table 14.2.

One implication for global corporations is that an organizational culture that fits one society might not be readily transferable to other societies. For example, one study examined the Hong Kong subsidiary of Hewlett-Packard in relation to its fit with Hong Kong's cultural values. The subsidiary's organizational culture was low power distance and low uncertainty avoidance—identical to the parent firm's culture in the United States. However, Hong

TABLE 14.1   Some Effects of the Power Distance Dimension on Organizations

Power Distance Dimension	
Low (Austria, Denmark, Israel, Sweden, United States)	*High* (Brazil, Hong Kong, India, Mexico, Philippines)
▲ Less centralization	▲ Greater centralization
▲ Fewer levels in organizational hierarchy	▲ More levels in organizational hierarchy
▲ Fewer supervisory personnel	▲ More supervisory personnel
▲ Smaller wage differentials	▲ Large wage differentials
▲ White-collar jobs and blue-collar jobs are valued equally	▲ White-collar jobs are valued more than blue-collar jobs

Source: Adapted from Jackofsky, E. F., Slocum, J. W., Jr., and McQuaid, S. J. Cultural values and the CEO: Alluring companions? *Academy of Management Executive*, 1988, 2, 40.

MANAGING ACROSS CULTURES —*Continued*

TABLE 14.2 Some Effects of the Uncertainty Avoidance Dimension on Organizations

Uncertainty Avoidance Dimension	
Low (Denmark, Great Britain, Hong Kong, Sweden, United States)	*High* (France, Greece, Japan Peru, Portugal)
▲ Less task structure	▲ Greater task structure
▲ Fewer written rules	▲ More written rules
▲ More generalists	▲ More specialists
▲ Greater willingness to take risks	▲ Less willingness to take risks
▲ Less ritualistic behavior	▲ More ritualistic behavior

Source: Adapted from Jackofsky, E. F., Slocum, J. W., Jr., and McQuaid, S. J. Cultural values and the CEO: Alluring companions? *Academy of Management Executive*, 1988, 2, 41.

Kong's culture was high power distance and low uncertainty avoidance. The study's authors predicted that the subsidiary's Hong Kong employees might not fully accept Hewlett-Packard's corporate culture. Some effects of this cultural mismatch might include low job satisfaction and high absenteeism and turnover.[12]

▼ Maintaining Organizational Culture

The ways in which an organization functions and is managed may have both intended and unintended effects on maintaining or changing organizational culture. Figure 14.3 shows a basic method of maintaining an organization's culture: The organization attempts to hire individuals who, in some sense, *fit* the organizational culture. (Later in the chapter, we discuss the socialization of new employees.) In addition, organizations maintain cultures by removing employees who consistently or markedly deviate from accepted behaviors and activities.

Specific methods for maintaining organizational culture, however, are a great deal more complicated than just hiring and firing the right people. The most powerful reinforcers of the organization's culture are (1) what managers and teams pay attention to, measure, and control; (2) the ways managers (particularly top managers) react to critical incidents and organizational crises; (3) managerial and team role modeling, teaching, and coaching; (4) criteria for allocating rewards and status; (5) criteria for recruitment, selection, promotion, and removal from the organization; and (6) organizational rites, ceremonies, and stories.[13]

What Managers and Teams Pay Attention to One of the more powerful methods of maintaining organizational culture involves the processes and behaviors that managers and teams pay attention to, that is, the things that get noticed and commented on. Dealing with things systematically sends strong

FIGURE 14.3

Methods of Maintaining
Organizational Culture

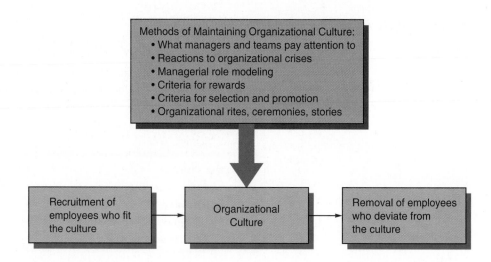

signals to employees about what is important and expected of them. For example, a large toy manufacturer installed a management-by-objectives (MBO) performance appraisal system (see Chapter 7). After a few years, top management discovered that the MBO process was working well in one part of the corporation but not in another. An investigation revealed that MBO was working well where senior management was enthusiastic and committed. These managers perceived real benefits from the program and conveyed these beliefs to others. Where MBO was failing, senior management viewed MBO as just another bureaucratic exercise. Subordinates quickly learned to complete the paperwork but ignore the purpose of the MBO system. The firm's top management concluded that MBO would work only when employees believe that managers care about the results and pay attention to them.[14]

Reactions to Incidents and Crises   When an organization faces a crisis, the handling of that crisis by managers and employees reveals a great deal about the culture. The manner in which the crisis is dealt with can either reinforce the existing culture or bring out new values and norms that change the culture in some way. For example, an organization facing a dramatic reduction in demand for its product might react by laying off or firing employees. Or it might reduce employee hours or rates of pay with no work-force reduction. The alternative chosen indicates the value placed on human resources and may reinforce and maintain the current culture or indicate a major change in the culture. Such a situation occurred at Hewlett-Packard early in its history. The company responded to declining demand for its products by reducing hours. It went to a schedule of working nine days every two weeks—a 10% reduction in time with a corresponding cut in pay—rather than fire or lay off employees. Hewlett-Packard thus sent a clear message to its employees about their value to the company. This response became deeply ingrained in the company's folklore and now serves to reinforce this aspect of its culture.

Role Modeling, Teaching, and Coaching   Aspects of the organization's culture are communicated to employees by the way managers fulfill their roles. In addition, managers and teams may specifically incorporate important cultural messages into training programs and day-to-day coaching on the job. For example, training films shown to new employees might emphasize customer service. Also, managers might demonstrate good customer or client service practices in their interactions with customers. The repeated emphasis on good customer relations in both training and day-to-day behavior would help create and maintain a customer-oriented culture throughout the organization. Arthur Anderson, the large public accounting firm, sends all newly hired accountants to a 15-week training program not only to learn accounting procedures used by the firm, but also to become steeped in the organization's culture.

Allocation of Rewards and Status   Employees also learn about their organization's culture through its reward system. The rewards and punishments attached to various behaviors convey to employees the priorities and values of both individual managers and the organization. Similarly, the organization's status system maintains certain aspects of its culture. The distribution of *perks* (e.g., a corner office on an upper floor, carpeting, a private secretary, or a private parking space) demonstrates which roles and behaviors are most valued by the organization. However, an organization may use rewards and status symbols ineffectively and inconsistently. If it does, it misses a great opportunity to influence its culture because an organization's reward practices and its culture appear to be strongly linked.[15] In fact, some authorities believe that the most effective method for influencing organizational culture may be through the reward system.

Recruitment, Selection, Promotion, and Removal   As Figure 14.3 suggests, one of the fundamental ways that organizations maintain a culture is through the recruitment process. In addition, the criteria used to determine who is assigned to specific jobs or positions, who gets raises and promotions and why, who is removed from the organization by firing or early retirement, and so on reinforce and demonstrate basic aspects of a culture. These criteria become known throughout the organization and can maintain or change an existing culture.

Organizational Rites, Ceremonies, and Stories   **Organizational rites and ceremonies** are organized, planned activities or rituals that have important cultural meaning.[16] Certain managerial or employee activities can become organizational rituals that are interpreted as part of the organizational culture. Rites and ceremonies that sustain organizational culture include rites of passage, degradation, enhancement, and integration. Table 14.3 contains examples of each of these four types of rites and identifies some of their desirable consequences.

A ceremony used at Mary Kay Cosmetics Company provides a good example of rites of enhancement. During elaborate awards ceremonies, gold and diamond pins, fur stoles, and the use of pink Cadillacs are presented to saleswomen who achieve their sales quotas. The ceremonies are held in a setting reminiscent of a Miss America pageant with all the participants dressed in glamorous evening clothes. The setting is typically an auditorium with a stage in front of a large, cheering audience.[17] The ceremonies clearly are intended

TABLE 14.3   Organizational Rites and Ceremonies

Type	Example	Possible Consequences
Rites of passage	Basic training, U.S. Army	Facilitate transition into new roles; minimize differences in way roles are carried out
Rites of degradation	Firing a manager	Reduce power and identity; reaffirm proper behavior
Rites of enhancement	Mary Kay Cosmetics Company ceremonies	Enhance power and identity; emphasize value of proper behavior
Rites of integration	Office party	Encourage common feelings that bind members together

Source: Adapted from Trice, H. M., and Beyer, J. M. *The Cultures of Work Organizations.* Englewood Cliffs, N.J.: Prentice-Hall, 1993, 111.

to increase the identity and status of high-performing employees and emphasize the rewards for performance.

Many of the underlying beliefs and values of an organization's culture are expressed as legends and stories that become part of its folklore.[18] These stories and legends transmit the existing culture from older to new employees and emphasize important aspects of that culture. Some stories may persist for a long time. For example, a Fortune 500 manufacturer had a factory with a history of hostile labor–management relations, low productivity, and poor quality. The company hired a consultant who started out by talking with the employees in the plant. They eagerly told him about the plant manager, a 300-pound gorilla named Sam with a disposition that made King Kong look like Bonzo the chimp. Employees told a number of outrageous stories about Sam's behavior. The stunned consultant made an appointment to see the plant manager. When the consultant walked into the manager's office, he saw a slim, pleasant-looking man behind the desk who introduced himself as Paul. "Where's Sam?" asked the consultant. Paul, looking puzzled, replied, "Sam has been dead for nine years."[19]

The following Managing in Practice item about the culture of McKinsey and Company reveals several of the methods that organizations use to maintain their cultures.

MANAGING IN PRACTICE

McKinsey & Co.—"The Firm"

Members of McKinsey & Co. have long called their organization "The Firm"—doing so before release of the popular book and movie of the same title. McKinsey & Co. has been called the "most well-known, most secretive, most high-priced, most prestigious, most consistently successful, most envied, most trusted, and the most disliked management consulting firm on earth." The culture of McKinsey—unique and eccentric—seems to set it apart from other consulting firms. This organizational culture often mystifies outsiders including McKinsey's clients.

MANAGING IN PRACTICE —*Continued*

Marvin Bower, 90, is McKinsey's founding father. (Mac McKinsey, Bower's partner in starting the firm, and whose name the firm still bears, died in 1937 at a relatively young age.) Bower has been likened to Sam Walton of Wal-Mart and Tom Watson of IBM in terms of his impact on the organization's culture. Bower laid down principles that have been emphasized so consistently over the years that they now define the culture.

First, McKinsey consultants are supposed to put the client's interests ahead of consulting revenues. They should keep their mouths shut about the client's activities. They should always tell the truth and not be afraid to disagree with a client's opinion. They should only agree to perform work that is truly needed and that McKinsey has the expertise to do. Bower prefers "professional" to "business" language as part of the culture. Thus, McKinsey is "The Firm," never the "company;" jobs are "engagements;" and The Firm doesn't have a business—it has a "practice."

A defining moment in the McKinsey culture came in 1960 when Bower sold his shares back to the firm for book value, rather than selling to outsiders at a huge multiple of earnings. This incident set an example for partners that they still follow 35 years later.

One view of why the McKinsey culture seems to function so well is that the firm only recruits consultants that fit with the prevailing culture (see Figure 14.3). A former employee says, "Basically they hire the same people over and over. At other consulting firms there is a lot more diversity." Of the 465 partners, 21 are women and only 2 are African-American. Only 3 of 151 firm directors (a higher rank than partner) are women. The vast majority of people who run McKinsey were educated at one of only seven universities.[20]

▼ Changing Organizational Culture

The same basic methods used to maintain an organization's culture may be used to change it. Culture might be changed by (1) changing what managers and teams pay attention to, (2) changing how crisis situations are handled, (3) changing criteria for recruiting new members, (4) changing criteria for promotion within the organization, (5) changing criteria for allocating rewards, and (6) changing organizational rites and ceremonies. For example, an organizational culture that tends to punish risk taking and innovation and reward risk avoidance might be deliberately altered through changes in the reward system. Employees could be encouraged to set riskier and more innovative goals for themselves in coaching and goal-setting sessions. In performance appraisal sessions and through merit raises, individuals could be rewarded for attempting more challenging tasks, even if they failed sometimes, than for attaining safe goals that required no innovative behavior.

Changing organizational culture can be a tricky business, and at least two perspectives suggest caution. One concern is articulated by well-known management expert Peter Drucker who has questioned whether the deep, core values of organizational culture are amenable to change.[21] In his view, focusing managerial efforts on changing ineffective behaviors and procedures is more meaningful than attempting to change organizational culture. Drucker further argues that changing behavior will work only if it can be based on the existing culture.

A second perspective that suggests caution in cultural change considers the difficulties in accurately assessing organizational culture. Most large, complex organizations actually have more than one culture. General Electric, for example, has distinctly different cultures in different corporate units. Sometimes these multiple cultures are called **subcultures**.[22] Faced with a variety of subcultures, management may have difficulty, first, in accurately assessing them and, second, in effecting needed changes.

Despite these concerns, we believe that changing organizational cultures is both feasible and, in the case of failing organizations, sometimes essential. Successfully changing organizational culture requires

▲ understanding the old culture first because a new culture can't be developed unless managers and employees understand where they are starting from;

▲ providing support for employees and teams who have ideas for a better culture and are willing to act on their visions;

▲ finding the most effective subculture in the organization and using it as an example from which employees can learn;

▲ not attacking culture head on but finding ways to help employees and teams do their jobs more effectively;

▲ treating the vision of a new culture as a guiding principle for change, *not* as a miracle worker;

▲ recognizing that significant organizationwide cultural change takes five to ten years; and

▲ living the new culture because actions speak louder than words.[23]

We cover planned organizational change extensively in Chapters 19 and 20. Many of the specific techniques and methods for changing organizational behaviors presented in those chapters also may be used to change organizational culture. Indeed, any comprehensive program of organizational change, in some sense, is an attempt to change the culture of the organization.

We can't overemphasize how difficult changing organizational cultures may be. In fact, the incompatibility of organizational cultures and their resistance to change has been one of the most significant barriers to successful corporate mergers.[24] For a merger to be effective, at least one (and sometimes both) of the merging organizations may need to change its culture. The following Managing in Practice account describes just such a situation.

MANAGING IN PRACTICE

The Failed Courtship of Bell Atlantic and TCI

From the beginning, the proposed merger of Bell Atlantic Corporation, the giant regional phone company, and Tele-Communications, Inc. (TCI), the biggest cable operator in the U. S., had management experts shaking their heads. Conventional wisdom held that these two corporate giants had cultures that were just too different to allow successful integration. The critics of the merger seemed to have been correct when, after many weeks of breathless headlines

MANAGING IN PRACTICE —*Continued*

in the business press, the two firms announced in February 1994 that the merger was off.

Despite intense efforts to shed its bureaucratic culture, Bell Atlantic retains many characteristics from its regulated monopoly past. In contrast, TCI is an aggressive, cost-conscious entrepreneur. The concern was that these firms would lock horns over the speed of decision making, methods of conflict resolution, the importance of cost cutting, and even attitudes toward customer service.

Conceivably, the two firms had much to learn from each other. Cable companies such as TCI often excel at cutting costs, but have a poor reputation for customer service. Bell Atlantic possesses a customer-oriented culture but is hampered by a bureaucracy that does little to promote independent thinking. Bell Atlantic, in particular, seemed eager to change its culture and gave every indication that it expected to do so in order to merge successfully with TCI.

Despite the most serious of intentions throughout the courtship, the companies suddenly called off their merger plans. The merger that seemed destined to shape the interactive video world of the twenty-first century failed because the culture gap between the two organizations proved just too difficult to bridge. Publicly, the firms were quick to blame the Federal Communications Commission and other federal authorities in Washington for proposed regulatory changes that made merger less attractive. However, most knowledgeable observers blame what has been described as "the largest flameout in the history of corporate mergers" on differences in corporate culture.[25]

▼ PERFORMANCE AND ORGANIZATIONAL CULTURE

An underlying assumption of cultural change is that an organization's culture and its performance or effectiveness are directly related. Thus the rationale for attempting cultural change is to create a more effective organization.

The common theme of a number of popular books is that strong, well-developed cultures are an important characteristic of organizations that have outstanding performance records.[26] The term **strong culture** implies that most managers and employees share a set of consistent values and methods of doing business.[27]

Strong cultures may be associated with strong performance for three reasons. First, a strong culture often provides for a good fit between strategy and culture. This fit is considered essential for successfully implementing corporate strategy. Second, a strong culture may lead to the alignment of goals among employees. That is, the majority of organizational participants share the same goals and have some basic agreement as to how to pursue them. Finally, a strong culture leads to employee commitment and motivation. In this view, culture is crucial for developing the dedication to excellent performance that characterizes successful organizations.

Organizational culture and performance clearly are related, although the evidence regarding the exact nature of this relationship is mixed.[28] For example, strong cultures may not always be superior to weak cultures. Some studies indicate that the *type* of culture may, in fact, be somewhat more important than its strength. A comparison of the cultures of 334 institutions of

higher education revealed no differences in organizational effectiveness between those with strong cultures and those with weak cultures.[29] However,
the type of culture possessed by these institutions was related to their effectiveness. Colleges and universities that possessed a type of culture whose features matched their market niche and mission were more effective than
institutions whose cultures lacked such a match.

Another cautionary note comes from studies showing that the relationship
between many cultural attributes (featured in the popular press as being important for performance) and high performance hasn't been consistent over
time.[30] Based on what we know about culture-performance relationships, a
contingency approach seems to be a good one for managers and organizations
to take. Further investigations of this issue are unlikely to discover one "best"
organizational culture (either in terms of strength or type).

A four-year study conducted of a large number of organizations resulted
in the following conclusions about the relationships between culture and
performance.

▲ Organizational culture can have a significant impact on a firm's long-
   term economic performance.

▲ Organizational culture will probably be an even more important factor
   in determining the success or failure of firms in the next decade.

▲ Organizational cultures that inhibit strong long-term financial performance are not rare; they develop easily, even in firms that are full of reasonable and intelligent people.

▲ Although tough to change, organizational cultures can be made more
   performance enhancing.[31]

High degrees of participative management and an emphasis on teamwork
often are cited as characteristics of successful organizational cultures. In **participative management,** managers share decision-making, goal-setting, and
problem-solving activities with employees. Of course, high levels of
participation do not fit all settings and tasks. Further, changing an organization from a more traditional management approach to greater collaboration
with employees may be extremely difficult. A type of organizational culture
designed to foster high performance with high levels of employee involvement
is called a **high performance–high commitment work culture.** As with participative management, cultures that foster high involvement and commitment
on the part of employees often exist in organizations that have a record of
high performance. We examine high performance–high commitment work cultures or systems in greater detail in Chapter 20.

Another type of organizational culture often associated with organizational
effectiveness is a **total quality culture,** which values customers, continuous
improvement, and teamwork. Employees in such a culture believe that customers are the key to the organization's future. Employees expect their jobs
to change as they constantly strive to improve and seek better ways of doing
things. Moreover, employees in such a culture almost instinctively act as a
team. Gillette provides an example of an organization with a focus on customers, continuous improvement, and teamwork, as the following Managing
Quality item demonstrates.

MANAGING QUALITY

Gillette's Total Quality Culture

Gillette dominates the "wet shaving" market and has for several generations. For example, in 1923 Gillette was the market share leader and remained so in 1994. In today's rapidly changing economy this observation, by itself, indicates something rather remarkable about the Gillette organization.

Gillette has about two-thirds of the U.S. market and its share of the world market is even higher. In Latin America, for example, Gillette's market share is over 80%. In some parts of the world, the word Gillette *means* razor blade. Global sales continue to expand with joint ventures in China, Russia, and India. Over the years, Gillette has been faced with numerous competitive challenges, yet has always responded with improved products.

This type of success doesn't just happen. It is the result of a relentless quest for improvements in shaving technology and high levels of commitment and teamwork from employees. The CEO of Gillette shaves half of his face with his product and half with a competitor's to compare the closeness of the shaves. Each day, about 200 employees come to work unshaven (including women with unshaven legs) in order to test their own and competitor's shaving products.

This continuous improvement and ongoing desire to satisfy the customer is expressed by Donald Chaulk, vice-president in charge of Gillette's shaving technology lab: "We test the blade edge, the blade guard, the angle of the blades, the balance of the razor. . . . What happens to the chemistry of the skin? What happens to the hair when you pull it? What happens to the follicle? We own the face. We know more about shaving than anybody. I don't think obsession is too strong a word."[32]

We can summarize the effects of organizational culture on employee behavior and performance with four key ideas. First, knowing the culture of an organization allows employees to understand the firm's history and current approach. This knowledge provides guidance about expected behaviors for the future. Second, organizational culture can foster commitment to corporate philosophy and values. This commitment gives organizational members shared feelings of working toward common goals. Third, organizational culture, through its norms, serves as a control mechanism to channel employee behaviors toward desired and away from undesired behaviors. Finally, certain types of organizational cultures may be related directly to greater effectiveness and productivity than others.

▼ ETHICAL BEHAVIOR AND ORGANIZATIONAL CULTURE

Ethical problems in organizations continue to concern managers and employees greatly. However, researchers are only now beginning to explore the potential impact that organizational culture can have on ethical behavior. Early findings indicate that organizational culture appears to affect ethical behavior in several ways.[33]

The ethics component of organizational culture is a complex interplay of formal and informal systems that may support either ethical or unethical organizational behavior. The formal systems include leadership, structure, policies, reward systems, orientation and training programs, and decision-making processes. Informal systems include norms, heroes, rituals, language, myths, sagas, and stories.[34]

Ethical business practices stem from ethical organizational cultures. For example, a culture emphasizing ethical norms provides support for ethical behavior. In addition, top management plays a key role in fostering ethical behavior. Moreover, all authority figures—managers and other professionals—in the organization can encourage or discourage ethical behavior. The presence or absence of ethical behavior in managerial actions both influences and reflects the prevailing culture. The organizational culture may promote taking responsibility for the consequences of actions, thereby increasing the probability that individuals will behave ethically. Alternatively, the culture may diffuse responsibility for the consequences of unethical behavior, thereby making such behavior more likely. The following Managing Ethics account demonstrates the impact of organizational culture on ethical practices, including management's behaviors and policies.

MANAGING ETHICS

Selling Auto Repair Service at Sears

In 1992, consumers inundated Sears with complaints about its automobile repair and service business. They accused the company of selling unnecessary parts and services in more than 40 states. Sears management didn't set out to defraud customers, so what went wrong?

Faced with declining revenues and reduced market share, Sears attempted to improve the profitability of its auto repair centers. Management adopted new performance goals and incentive programs. Service representatives received higher sales quotas and mechanics received higher minimum work quotas. For example, goals called for larger numbers of parts and services—such as springs, shock absorbers, alignments, and brake jobs—to be sold each shift. Failure to meet quotas could result in transfers or a reduction in work hours. Employees felt pressured to bring in sales.

An internal analysis of what went wrong conducted by Sears concluded that management failed to clarify the line between legitimate preventive maintenance and unnecessary service. Tremendous pressures were brought to bear on employees who seemed to have few legitimate options for meeting sales and service goals. The culture and management practices neither supported ethical practices nor provided mechanisms to detect questionable sales practices and poor work. Under these pressures and work rules, some employees resorted to unethical behaviors and careless repairs.

Sears has discontinued the sales commissions and quotas for selling specific parts and services that led to the fraudulent practices. For example, mechanics who no longer earn commissions now solely determine whether repairs are needed. Further, Sears instituted a plan to monitor auto repair service and sales continuously. The lapse in ethical culture was quite harmful to Sears. In addition to the potential loss of future business, which will take some time to measure, Sears spent $60 million in settling lawsuits and giving customer refunds.[35]

An important concept linking organizational culture to ethical behavior is **principled organizational dissent,** by which individuals in an organization protest, on ethical grounds, some practice or policy.[36] Some cultures permit and even encourage principled organizational dissent; other cultures punish such behavior.

An employee might use various strategies in attempting to change unethical behavior, including

▲ secretly or publicly blowing the whistle within the organization;

▲ secretly or publicly blowing the whistle outside the organization;

▲ secretly or publicly threatening an offender or a responsible manager with blowing the whistle; or

▲ quietly or publicly refusing to implement an unethical order or policy.[37]

As a form of principled organizational dissent, **whistle-blowing** means challenging the authority structure of an organization by exposing a practice that the organization's leaders or some of its members support. The whistle-blower lacks the power to change the undesirable practice directly and so appeals to a higher authority either inside or outside the organization.[38]

An example of publicly blowing the whistle inside an organization occurred when John Young, the chief of the National Aeronautic and Space Administration's (NASA) astronaut office, wrote a 12-page internal memorandum following the Challenger explosion that killed seven astronauts. He sent the memo, which detailed a large number of safety problems that endangered space shuttle crews to 97 key individuals in NASA. This communication was instrumental in broadening NASA's safety investigations and getting safety improvements.

An example of secretly blowing the whistle outside an organization occurred when an employee of Commonwealth Electric Company anonymously sent a letter to the Justice Department that identified instances of bid rigging among the largest U.S. electrical contractors. These contractors paid more than $20 million in fines as a result of investigations into illegal bidding practices.

These types of whistle-blowing activities are not without their risks. The risks to the individuals engaging in principled organizational dissent are obvious—dismissal, demotion, isolation, and ostracism, among others. There is also the possibility that the whistle-blower could be wrong about individual or organizational actions. Thus misguided attempts to stop unethical behavior might unnecessarily harm employees or organizations.

Much remains to be learned about creating organizational cultures that encourage ethical behavior.[39] The following suggestions are a beginning.

▲ Be realistic in setting values and goals regarding employment relationships. Do not promise what the organization cannot deliver.

▲ Encourage input from throughout the organization regarding appropriate values and practices for implementing the culture. Choose values that represent the views of employees as well as managers.

▲ Do not automatically opt for a "strong" culture. Explore methods to provide for diversity and dissent, such as grievance or complaint mechanisms or other internal review procedures.

▲ Provide training programs for managers and teams on adopting and implementing the organization's values. These programs should explain the underlying ethical and legal principles and present the practical aspects of carrying out procedural guidelines.[40]

An effective organizational culture should encourage ethical behavior and discourage unethical behavior. Admittedly, ethical behavior may "cost" the organization. A global firm that refuses to pay a bribe to secure business in a particular country may lose sales. Individuals may gain financially by behaving unethically (particularly if they don't get caught). Similarly, an organization might seem to gain from unethical actions. For example, a purchasing agent for a large corporation might take bribes to purchase all needed office supplies from a particular supplier. However, such gains are often short-term. The Sears experience provides a clear example of short-term gain but long-term loss for the organization. In the long run, an organization cannot successfully operate if its prevailing culture and values are not congruent with those of society. That is just as true as the observation that, in the long run, an organization cannot survive unless it provides goods and services that society wants and needs. An organizational culture that promotes ethical behavior is not only more compatible with prevailing cultural values but also makes good business sense.

▼ MANAGING CULTURAL DIVERSITY

In Chapter 1, we emphasized that organizations are becoming increasingly diverse in terms of gender, race, ethnicity, and nationality. More than half the U.S. work force consists of women, minorities, and recent immigrants. Only about 15% of the expected increase in the U.S. work force during the remainder of this decade will be white males.[41] The growing diversity of employees in many organizations can bring substantial benefits, such as more successful marketing strategies for different types of customers, improved decision making, and perhaps greater creativity and innovation.[42] But there are costs and concerns as well, including communication difficulties, intraorganizational conflict, and turnover. Effectively managing cultural diversity promises to be a significant challenge for organizations during the 1990s and beyond.

There are no easy answers to the challenges of managing a culturally diverse work force. Hence successful organizations have to work hard at acculturation. **Acculturation** refers to methods by which cultural differences between a dominant culture and minority or subcultures are resolved and managed.[43] Consider the following Managing Diversity example.

MANAGING DIVERSITY

Corporate Culture Versus Ethnic Culture

Lakeview Enterprises has 20,000 employees worldwide. Keisha Gibson started as a word processor for Lakeview and has performed well, receiving two promotions. Currently, she is the secretary for Alan Hirsh, who is director of benefit programs in the human resources department.

Gibson and Hirsh have a good working relationship. Hirsh describes Gibson as conscientious and highly skilled. Gibson describes Hirsh as a good boss who provides the right amount of responsibility, feedback, and recognition.

MANAGING DIVERSITY —*Continued*

Gibson is an African-American. She frequently wears attractive African-style prints, jewelry, and headwraps. Gibson is proud of her heritage and expresses it through her style of clothing. Hirsh, who is white, considers himself a proponent of equal employment opportunity and affirmative action.

A problem arose when Gibson requested Hirsh's recommendation to participate in a vacation substitute program for secretaries of the firm's top executives. Understandably, Gibson wants this visibility to senior management and knows this could put her in line for promotion to the highest paying secretarial positions. Hirsh's dilemma arises because he knows the executive floor is a bastion of conservatism, particularly with regard to dress. With *no* exceptions, secretaries and executives observe unwritten rules or norms with regard to their attire—dark suits and white shirts for the men, business suits or dresses for the women.

If Gibson, despite her skills and potential for advancement, fails to find acceptance on the executive floor, will it be because she is an African-American or because she expresses this ethnic identity through her manner of dress? But if everyone else is required to conform to this dress code, why should Gibson be an exception? How should Hirsh manage this potential clash between corporate and ethnic cultures?[44]

The Prudential Insurance Company provides an example of managing cultural diversity.[45] Prudential became alarmed when many African-American employees were leaving the company. Surveys showed that the complaints of African-Americans actually were shared by female, Asian, and other minority employees as well. Among other problems uncovered, Prudential management was viewed as insensitive to diversity issues. Prudential embarked on a massive diversity training effort that by now has included 12,000 managers. During their diversity training, managers must develop personal goals and plans that identify actions and behaviors to improve organizational diversity. Top management then holds them financially accountable for accomplishing the goals. Even the most senior-level executives in the organization are required to submit plans for addressing diversity concerns. Prudential also established diversity councils throughout the firm to monitor the effectiveness of the effort. Prudential believes that its diversity effort has gone beyond a mere program and has become institutionalized. The company believes that the core values of the culture now promote respect for diversity.

Many companies rely on teams, task forces, and committees to address work-force diversity issues. For example, Digital Equipment Company initiated core groups of employees from different backgrounds who try to work through diversity and stereotype issues. Corning, Inc., established two teams led by members of top management to focus on women's and African-American's concerns. These teams have broad charters to identify gender and race issues, find remedial actions, design and fund diversity programs, and measure the results of these efforts. Each team is a cross section of the organization to ensure representation by race, gender, and organizational levels, departments, and functions.[46]

Managers such as Alan Hirsh cannot necessarily wait for the organization to come to their rescue with a corporate program every time they face conflict between cultures. The following guidelines can help in managing cultural diversity.

▲ Don't avoid the issue of diversity. Bring it out in the open and talk about it.

▲ Explore how all employees come to the workplace with a unique combination of background influences. Start with yourself and your own background.

▲ Be an intercultural ambassador by making tact and respect the rule for discussions of ethnic, cultural, racial, or gender differences.

▲ Don't tolerate racist or sexist behaviors. Stay within equal employment opportunity (EEO) guidelines.

▲ Help employees balance personal and professional needs.

▲ Explain the unwritten rules of the organization to employees.

▲ Encourage employees to talk with co-workers about their concerns so they are exposed to a variety of viewpoints.[47]

Table 14.4 contains a questionnaire that you can use to examine your awareness of diversity issues.

TABLE 14.4   Diversity Questionnaire

Respond to the following questions using either true (T) or false (F).

1. I know about the rules and customs of several different cultures. _____

2. I know that I hold stereotypes about other groups. _____

3. I feel comfortable with people of different backgrounds from my own. _____

4. I associate with those who are different from me. _____

5. I find working on a multicultural team satisfying. _____

6. I find change stimulating and exciting. _____

7. I enjoy learning about other cultures. _____

8. When dealing with someone whose English is limited, I show patience and understanding. _____

9. I find that spending time building relationships with others is useful because more gets done. _____

The more true responses you have, the more adaptable and open you are to diversity. If you have five or more true responses, you are probably someone who finds value in cross-cultural experiences.

If you have less than five true responses, you may be resistant to interacting with people who are different from you. If that is the case, you may find that your interactions with others are sometimes blocked.

Source: Adapted from Gardenswartz, L., and Rowe, A. What's your diversity quotient? *Managing Diversity Newsletter*, Jamestown, New York (undated).

ORGANIZATIONAL SOCIALIZATION

Organizational socialization is the systematic process by which an organization brings new employees into its culture. The general meaning of the term *socialization* is the process by which older members of a society transmit to younger members the social skills and knowledge needed to function effectively in that society. Organizational socialization has a similar meaning: the transmission of culture from senior to new employees, providing the social knowledge and skills needed to perform organizational roles and tasks successfully.[48]

Socialization provides the means by which individuals learn the ropes upon joining an organization. It includes learning work group, departmental, and organizational values, rules, procedures, and norms; developing social and working relationships; and developing skills and knowledge needed to perform the new job. Interestingly, the stages that an employee goes through during socialization resemble, in many respects, the stages in group development discussed in Chapter 9. We discuss further the socialization of new employees in Chapter 21.

▼ Socialization Process

Figure 14.4 presents an example of an organizational socialization process. It isn't intended to depict the socialization process of all organizations. However, many firms with strong cultures—such as IBM, P&G, AT&T, and Delta Airlines—frequently follow these seven steps for socializing new employees.

Step One. Entry-level candidates are selected carefully. Trained recruiters use standardized procedures and seek specific traits that tie to success in the business.

Step Two. Humility-inducing experiences in the first months on the job cause employees to question their prior behaviors, beliefs, and values. Such experiences might include giving a new employee more work to do than can reasonably be done. The self-questioning promotes openness toward accepting the organization's norms and values.

Step Three. In-the-trenches training leads to mastery of one of the core disciplines of the business. Promotion is tied to a proven track record.

Step Four. Careful attention is given to measuring operational results and rewarding individual performance. Reward systems are comprehensive and consistent and focus on those aspects of the organization that are tied to success and corporate culture.

Step Five. Adherence to the organization's values is emphasized. Identification with common values allows employees to justify personal sacrifices caused by their membership in the organization.

Step Six. Reinforcing folklore provides legends and interpretations of important events in the organization's history that validate its culture and goals. Folklore reinforces a code of conduct for "how we do things around here."

FIGURE 14.4

An Example of an Organizational Socialization Process

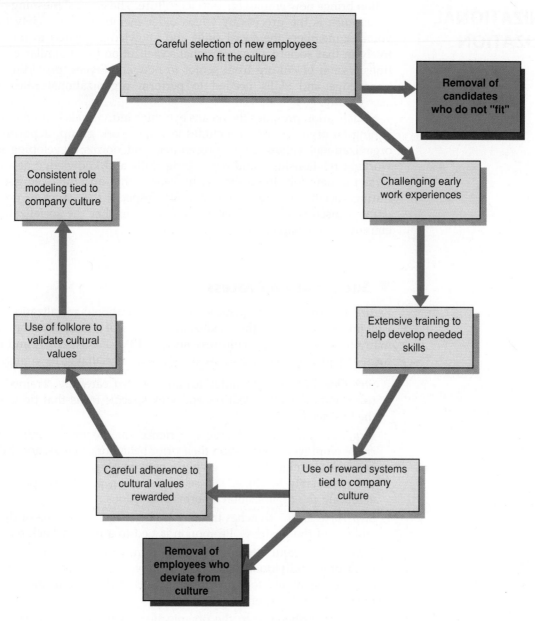

Step Seven. Consistent role models and consistent traits are associated with those recognized as being on the fast track to promotion and success.[49]

Southwest Airlines has developed a strong culture based on customer service. The following Managing in Practice account describes the main characteristics of its strong culture and socialization process.

MANAGING IN PRACTICE

Herb Kelleher and Southwest Airlines

Herb Kelleher of Southwest Airlines attributes the firm's success to a simple corporate philosophy: "We dignify the customer." This sounds strange coming from the CEO of an airline that has no first-class seating, no assigned seats, and no transfers of bags to other airlines—and serves no food on flights other than peanuts, potato chips, and cookies. However, Southwest must be doing something right. In an era when airlines as a group are consistently losing money, Southwest's revenues are increasing 15% annually and the company is adding 200 new employees a month.

For starters, Southwest charges about one-third as much as competitors for its tickets. But cheap fares are not all that is going on here. Southwest takes its customer-oriented culture seriously. For example, the job of one executive vice-president is to oversee every aspect of the business that touches the public and to make that contact as pleasant as possible. The word *customer* is always capitalized in company ads and publications. Frequent fliers receive birthday cards from the company. The 1,000 customers that write the company during a typical week receive a personal response—not a form letter—within one month. When five medical students who commuted weekly to their out-of-state medical school complained that their regularly scheduled flight got them to class 15 minutes late, Southwest moved the departure time forward by 15 minutes.

For Kelleher, treating the customer right begins with treating employees right. "If you don't treat your own people well, they won't treat other people well," he has said. Kelleher believes that work should be fun, and this belief permeates the organizational culture. For example, every Friday at noon, employees in the Dallas office gather in the parking lot for a cookout. Employees throughout the organization typically wear costumes on Halloween, Valentine's Day, and other special occasions and "fun uniforms" on Fridays. Upper level managers reinforce an egalitarian culture by working as baggage handlers, ticket agents, and flight attendants once each quarter.

As do many firms with a strong culture and socialization process, Southwest places a great deal of emphasis on its hiring practices. Kelleher believes so strongly that work should be fun and that too much seriousness is ineffective, that a sense of humor is actually one of the criteria for hiring new employees. Kelleher looks for people with a certain attitude and approach to life that is humorous, broad-minded, and tolerant of individual differences. In keeping with its customer orientation, Southwest uses frequent fliers to help select new flight attendants.[50]

▼ Socialization Outcomes

All organizations and groups socialize new members in some way, but the process can vary greatly in terms of how explicit, comprehensive, and lengthy it is. Generally, rapid socialization is advantageous. For the individual, it quickly reduces the uncertainty and anxiety surrounding a new job. For the organization, it helps the new employee become productive quickly. Organizations with strong cultures may be particularly skillful at socializing individ-

TABLE 14.5   Possible Outcomes of Socialization Process

Successful Socialization Is Reflected In	Unsuccessful Socialization Is Reflected In
▲ Job satisfaction	▲ Job dissatisfaction
▲ Role clarity	▲ Role ambiguity and conflict
▲ High work motivation	▲ Low work motivation
▲ Understanding of culture, perceived control	▲ Misunderstanding, tension, perceived lack of control
▲ High job involvement	▲ Low job involvement
▲ Commitment to organization	▲ Lack of commitment to organization
▲ Tenure	▲ Absenteeism, turnover
▲ High performance	▲ Low performance
▲ Internalized values	▲ Rejection of values

uals. If the culture is effective, the socialization process will contribute to organizational success. However, if the culture needs changing, a strong socialization process reduces the prospects for making the needed changes.

Some additional dilemmas are created by strong socialization processes. For example, business schools are concerned with issues surrounding the socialization of their students. How strong should their socialization be? Does the business school want students to think alike, at least in terms of a certain level of logic and intelligent analysis? To have the same appropriate values and sense of professionalism? In some sense, the answer to these questions has to be *yes*. Yet, oversocialization runs the risk of creating rigid, narrow-minded corporate men and women. The ideal goal of business school socialization, then, may be to develop independent thinkers committed to what they believe to be right, while at the same time educating students to be collaborative team players who have good interpersonal skills and are able to relate well to others. These goals pose a challenge for the socialization process, which, in order to be effective, must balance these demands. Although this example is of the business school, to a certain extent the same need for balance exists for all organizations.

The socialization process may affect employee and organizational success in a variety of ways.[51] Table 14.5 lists some possible socialization outcomes. We don't claim that these outcomes are determined solely by an organization's socialization process. For example, job satisfaction is a function of many things, including the nature of the task, the individual's personality and needs, the nature of supervision, opportunities to succeed and be rewarded, and so on (see Chapter 2). Rather, the point here is that successful socialization may contribute to job satisfaction, whereas unsuccessful socialization may contribute to job dissatisfaction.

Summary

Organizational culture is the pattern of beliefs and expectations shared by organizational members. Culture includes norms, common values, company philosophy, the "rules of the game" for getting along and getting things done, and ways of interacting with outsiders, such as customers. Some aspects of organizational culture are indicated by cultural symbols, heroes, rites, and ceremonies.

Organizational culture develops as a response to the challenges of external adaptation and survival and of internal integration. The formation of an organization's culture also is influenced by the culture of the larger society within which the firm must function.

The primary methods for both maintaining and changing organizational culture include (1) what managers and teams pay attention to, measure, and control; (2) the ways managers and employees react to crises; (3) role modeling, teaching, and coaching; (4) criteria for allocating rewards; (5) criteria for recruitment to, selection and promotion within, and removal from the organization; and (6) organizational rites, ceremonies, and stories.

Organizational culture can affect employee behaviors and commitment to the organization. There is some evidence that culture may be related to effective organizational performance, although there is no evidence that a "best" organizational culture exists. In addition, organizational culture can affect ethical behavior by managers and employees of the firm. Managing cultural diversity is expected to be one of the principal managerial challenges for many years to come.

Socialization is the process by which new members are brought into the organization's culture. At firms having a strong culture, the socialization process is well developed and the focus of careful attention. All organizations socialize new members, but depending on how this is done, the outcomes could be either positive or negative in terms of job performance, satisfaction, and commitment to the organization.

Key Words and Concepts

Academy culture
Acculturation
Baseball team culture
Club culture
Cultural heroes
Cultural symbols
Cultural values
External adaptation and survival

Fortress Culture
High performance–high
   commitment work culture
Internal integration
Organizational culture
Organizational rites and
   ceremonies
Organizational socialization

Participative management
Principled organizational dissent
Strong culture
Subcultures
Total quality culture
Whistle-blowing

Discussion Questions

1. Provide three examples of how culture is manifested or revealed in an organization with which you are familiar.

2. What factors significantly influence the formation of organizational culture?

3. Describe an organizational culture with which you are familiar. How did the organization develop its culture?

4. What are the primary methods used to maintain the organizational culture you identified in Question 3?

5. Identify and discuss some constraints or limitations on changing the culture you selected in Question 3.

6. How are organizational culture and performance related?

7. How might an organization use culture to increase the probability of ethical behavior and/or decrease the probability of unethical behavior by its members?

8. Discuss the issue of managing cultural diversity. How can organizations and managers deal with this challenge?

9. Describe the process of organizational socialization. Identify some key issues in organizational socialization.

10. Describe the socialization process used by an organization with which you are familiar. What were the results of this socialization process?

 Developing Skills

Self-Diagnosis:
Assessing Ethical Culture

Instructions

Think of a job you currently hold or used to have. Indicate whether you agree or disagree with the following statements about that organization. Use the following scale and write the number of your response in the space next to each question.

Completely False	Mostly False	Somewhat False	Somewhat True	Mostly True	Completely True
1	2	3	4	5	6

_____1. In this organization, employees are expected to follow their own personal and moral beliefs.

_____2. Employees are expected to do anything to further the organization's interests.

_____3. In this organization, employees look out for each other's welfare.

_____4. It is very important to strictly follow the rules and procedures of this organization.

_____5. In this organization, the major consideration is whether a decision violates any law or ethical codes.

_____6. In this organization, employees protect their own interests above other considerations.

_____7. An important consideration is what is best for everyone in the organization.

_____8. The most efficient way is always the right way in this organization.

_____9. In this organization, employees are always expected to do what is right for the customer and the public.

Scoring

Add the responses to questions 1, 3, 5, 7, and 9: _____ Reverse the scores on questions 2, 4, 6 and 8 (1 = 6, 2 = 5, 3 = 4, 4 = 3, 5 = 2, 6 = 1) and add these responses: __

Total: _____

Scores could range from 9 to 54 on this questionnaire. Scores of 36 and above indicate an organizational culture that tends to support or encourage ethical behavior. Scores of 28–35 indicate a culture that may be somewhat ambivalent with regard to ethical issues. Scores of 27 or below indicate a culture that tends to increase the probability that individuals will behave in an unethical manner.[52]

A Case in Point:
Procter & Gamble

This 150-year-old consumer products giant is well-known as an innovator in such areas as brand management, profit sharing, advertising and promotion, and innovative work design. Concentrating first on soap and then for decades on a range of "high quality consumer products found within every home," the corporation is now a $20 billion company with 73,000 employees worldwide. The strong, methodical culture is seen by many current and past employees as a key factor in the company's steady doubling in size every decade. While P&G has been quite profitable, performance is remarkable not so much for its level, but for its predictability.

At the core of the P&G culture is a highly rational, objective view of the world. Research, on both markets and products, is central to all decisions. When making or discussing a proposal, one must always "know the numbers." A central goal has always been to develop a technically superior product that will win in a blind taste test. A classic example of this logic is Olestra, a new synthetic cooking oil and food ingredient free of fats, calories, and cholesterol. It grew out of years of basic research, and the product will not only be sold directly to consumers, but also will serve as a technically superior base for other P&G food products.

Heavy attention is paid to socialization by P&G. New employees in the brand management organization, for example, are socialized as a cohort, and many see this peer competition and cooperation as the real source of learning and motivation for new members. New assignments, which usually included a period of structured training, are alternated on a regular basis in short cycles of 6–24 months. P&G careers, in general, are like a tournament in which the members continually move up or out. Requirements for performance and conformity to the P&G way lead many new recruits to leave the organization after a few years. Ironically, P&G often trains the key employees of many of their competitors, although some in the organization will claim that they "never lost an employee that they wanted to keep."

Strong emphasis is also placed on written communication. Lessons on writing a memo in the proper P&G form are of central importance in a new recruit's socialization. This system results in efficient communication in a common "language," and the creation of a written corporate record of all significant events. The system is intended to be independent of any one person, and everything important can always be quickly reconstructed from the records. This is one of many systems used to reinforce the idea that work at P&G is the product of the organization, and not of any one individual.

In manufacturing plants P&G is highly innovative, if largely secretive, in their design of organizations. Principles of sociotechnical design are used to build progressive, high commitment systems that place a high level of autonomy and responsibility on workers. They were among the first American corporations to see these innovations as a source of competitive advantage, and to see them as an outgrowth of their organization's traditional assumption that the interests of the individual and the organization overlap. This assumption led to the use of innovative practices such as profit sharing as early as 1887.

A qualitative examination of P&G's culture supports the idea that it is a high involvement organization, but the context in which involvement occurs is highly structured. Involvement seems to reflect the high overlap of interest between the individual and the organization more than voluntarism and autonomy. Furthermore, this involvement takes place within a structured competition created by the organization, in a context with a high degree of normative integration, commitment, and a common language and symbolic system.

P&G is a classic example of a "strong culture" system. As many past and current members of the organization have noted, this characteristic of the culture has both positive and negative impacts on effectiveness; P&G is an organization that seldom makes big mistakes, but is often beaten to the punch by smaller, faster companies. Their historical limitation has been a difficulty in moving quickly primarily because of their commitment to research, objectivity, and methodical reviews. Their key capabilities are often described as "science, not art." The P&G system is also generally seen as being very well suited to the consumer goods mass market where objectivity and a methodical approach pay off, but slow and ponderous in fast-moving markets that are driven primarily by taste and fashion. Recent acquisitions and expansions into food, health, and beauty products may test the adaptability of P&G culture. As one past employee put it, "the question is, does the 'corporate gene pool' have the variety necessary for future adaptation?"[53]

Questions

1. List the major issues and ideas from this chapter that appear, in one form or another, in this case.
2. Would you describe the P&G culture as most like a baseball team, club, academy, or fortress culture? Explain and defend your choice.
3. Using the culture of Procter and Gamble as an example, identify and discuss some of the positive and negative aspects of strong cultures.

References

1. Adapted from McGill, M. E., and Slocum, J. W. Unlearning the organization. *Organizational Dynamics*, Autumn 1993, 70.
2. Kilmann, R. H. Corporate culture. *Psychology Today*, April 1985, 63.
3. The description of these cultural types is based on Thompson, G. Fitting the company culture. In T. Lee (ed.), *Managing Your Career*. New York: Dow Jones & Company, 1990, 16.
4. Hatch, M. J. The dynamics of organizational culture. *Academy of Management Review*, 1993, 18, 657–693; Sackman, S. A. Culture and subcultures: An analysis of organizational knowledge. *Administrative Science Quarterly*, 1992, 37, 140–161; Trice, H. M., and Beyer, J. M. *The Cultures of Work Organizations*. Englewood Cliffs, N.J.: Prentice-Hall, 1992.
5. Schein, E. H. *Organizational Culture and Leadership*. San Francisco: Jossey-Bass, 1985, 6.
6. Hofstede, G., Neuijen, B., Ohayv, D. D., and Sanders, G. Measuring organizational cultures: A qualitative and quantitative study across twenty cases. *Administrative Science Quarterly*, 1990, 35, 286–316.
7. Reprinted with the permission of The Free Press, an imprint of Simon & Schuster from *Corporate Culture and Performance* by John P. Kotter and James L. Heskett. Copyright © 1992 by Kotter Associates, Inc. and James L. Heskett.
8. Hofstede, G., Neuijen, B., Ohayv, D. D., and Sanders, G. Mea-

suring organizational cultures: A qualitative and quantitative study across twenty cases. *Administrative Science Quarterly*, 1990, 35, 286–316.

9. Schein, E. H. How culture forms, develops, and changes. In Kilmann, R. H., Saxton, M. I., and Serpa, R. (eds.), *Gaining Control of the Corporate Culture*. San Francisco: Jossey-Bass, 1985, 17–43; Schein, E. H. *Organizational Culture and Leadership*. San Francisco: Jossey-Bass, 1985, 49–84; Schein, E. H. Organizational culture. *American Psychologist*, 1990, 45, 109–119.

10. Doktor, R. H. Asian and American CEOs: A comparative study. *Organizational Dynamics*, Winter 1990, 46–56; Linowes, R. G. The Japanese manager's traumatic entry into the United States: Understanding the American–Japanese cultural divide. *Academy of Management Executive*, 1993, 7(4), 21–37; Triandis, H. C. Cross-cultural industrial and organizational psychology. In H. C. Triandis, M. D. Dunnette, and L. M. Hough (eds.), *Handbook of Industrial and Organizational Psychology*, vol. 4, 2nd ed. Palo Alto, Calif.: Consulting Psychologists Press, 1994, 103–172.

11. Evans, P. A. L. Organizational development in the transnational enterprize. In R. W. Woodman and W. A. Pasmore (eds.), *Research in Organizational Change and Development*, vol. 3. Greenwich, Conn.: JAI Press, 1989, 1–38; Hofstede, G. Cultural constraints in management theory, *Academy of Management Executive*, 1993, 7(1), 81–94; Solomon, C. M. Transplanting corporate cultures globally. *Personnel Journal*, October 1993, 78–88.

12. Based on Kirkbride, P. S., and Chaw, S. W. The cross-cultural transfer of organizational cultures: Two case studies of corporate mission statements. *Asia Pacific Journal of Management*, 1987, 5, 55–66; Jackofsky, E. F., Slocum, J. W., Jr., and McQuaid, S. J. Cultural values and the CEO: Alluring companions? *Academy of Management Executive*, 1988, 2, 39–49. Also see Hodgetts, R. A. Conversation with Geert Hofstede. *Organizational Dynamics*, Spring 1993, 53–61.

13. The description of these methods is based on Schein, E. H. *Organizational Culture and Leadership*, San Francisco: Jossey-Bass, 1985, 223–243; Schein, E. H. Organizational culture. *American Psychologist*, 1990, 45, 109–119.

14. O'Reilly, C. R. Corporations, culture, and commitment: Motivation and social control in organizations. *California Management Review*, Summer 1989, 9–25.

15. See, for example, Kerr, J., and Slocum, J. W., Jr. Managing corporate culture through reward systems. *Academy of Management Executive*, 1987, 1, 99–108; Sethia, N. K., and Von Glinow, M. A. Arriving at four cultures by managing the reward system. In Kilmann R. H., Saxton, M. I., and Serpa, R. (eds.), *Gaining Control of the Corporate Culture*. San Francisco: Jossey-Bass, 1985, 400–420.

16. Trice, H. M., and Beyer, J. M. Using six organizational rites to change culture. In Kilmann, R. H., Saxton, M. I., and Serpa, R. (eds.), *Gaining Control of the Corporate Culture*. San Francisco: Jossey-Bass, 1985, 372.

17. Farnham, A. Mary Kay's lessons in leadership. *Fortune*, September 20, 1993, 68–77.

18. Boje, D. M. The storytelling organization: A study of story performance in an office-supply firm. *Administrative Science Quarterly*, 1991, 36, 106–126; Trice, H. M., and Beyer, J. M. *The Cultures of Work Organizations*. Englewood Cliffs, N.J.: Prentice-Hall, 1992, 101–107.

19. Dumaine, B. Creating a new company culture. *Fortune*, January 15, 1990, 127–131.

20. Adapted from Huey, J. How McKinsey does it. *Fortune*, November 1, 1993, 56–81.

21. Drucker, P. F. Don't change corporate culture—Use it! *Wall Street Journal*, March 28, 1991, A14. Also see Fitzgerald, T. H. Can change in organizational culture really be managed? *Organizational Dynamics*, Autumn 1988, 5–15.

22. Sackmann, S. A. Culture and subcultures: An analysis of organizational knowledge. *Administrative Science Quarterly*, 1992, 37, 140–161.

23. Dumaine, B. Creating a new company culture. *Fortune*, January 15, 1990, 128.

24. Cartwright, S., and Cooper, C. L. The role of culture capability in successful organizational marriage. *Academy of Management Executive*, 1993, 7(2), 57–70.

25. Adapted from Kneale, D., Roberts, J. L., and Cauley, L. Why the mega-merger collapsed: Strong wills and a big culture gap. *Wall Street Journal*, February 25, 1994, A1, A16; Lublin, J. S., and Lopez, J. A. Aggressive frugal TCI, meet the bureaucrats at Bell Atlantic. *Wall Street Journal*, October 14, 1993, B1, B6.

26. See, for example, Deal, T. E., and Kennedy, A. A. *Corporate Cultures: The Rites and Rituals of Corporate Life*, Reading, Mass.: Addison-Wesley, 1982; Peters, T. J., and Austin, N. *A Passion for Excellence*. New York: Random House, 1985; Peters, T. J., and Waterman, R. H. *In Search of Excellence*. New York: Harper & Row, 1982.

27. Kotter, J. P., and Heskett, J. L. *Corporate Culture and Performance*. New York: Free Press, 1992, 15.

28. Hofstede, G., Neuijen, B., Ohayv, D. D., and Sanders, G. Measuring organizational cultures: A qualitative and quantitative study across twenty cases. *Administrative Science Quarterly*, 1990, 35, 286–316; Marcoulides, G. A., and Heck, R. H. Organizational culture and performance: Proposing and testing a model. *Organization Science*, 1993, 4, 209–225.

29. Cameron, K. S., and Freeman, S. J. Cultural congruence, strength, and type: Relationships to effectiveness. In R. W. Woodman and W. A. Pasmore (eds.), *Research in Organizational Change and Development*, vol. 5. Greenwich, Conn.: JAI Press, 1991, 23–58.

30. Hitt, M. A., and Ireland, R. D. Peters and Waterman revisited: The unended quest for excellence. *Academy of Management Executive*, 1987, 1, 91–98.

31. Kotter, J. P., and Heskett, J. L. *Corporate Culture and Performance*. New York: Free Press, 1992, 11–12.

32. Adapted from Dean, J. W., and Evans, J. R. *Total Quality: Management, Organization, and Strategy*. St. Paul, Minn.: West, 1994, 150–152.

33. Gatewood, R. D., and Carroll, A. B. Assessment of ethical performance of organization members: A conceptual framework. *Academy of Management Review*, 1991, 16, 667–690; Sinclair, A. Approaches to organizational culture and ethics. *Journal of Business Ethics*, 1993, 12, 63–73.

34. Trevino, L. K. A cultural perspective on changing and developing organizational ethics. In W. A. Pasmore and R. W. Woodman (eds.), *Research in Organizational Change and Development*, vol. 4. Greenwich, Conn.: JAI Press, 1990, 195.

35. Adapted from Fuchsberg, G. Sears reinstates sales incentives in some centers. *Wall Street Journal*, March 7, 1994, B1, B6; Paine, L. S. Managing for organizational integrity. *Harvard Business Review*, March–April, 1994, 106–117.

36. Graham, J. W. Principled organizational dissent: A theoretical essay. In B. M. Staw and L. L. Cummings (eds.), *Research in Organizational Behavior*, vol. 8. Greenwich, Conn.: JAI Press, 1986, 2.

37. Intervention strategies and the following examples are based on Nielsen, R. P. Changing unethical organizational behavior. *Academy of Management Executive*, 1989, 3, 123–130.

38. Near, J. P., and Miceli, M. P. Whistle-blowers in organizations. In L. L. Cummings and B. M. Staw (eds.), *Research in Organizational Behavior*, vol. 9. Greenwich, Conn.: JAI Press, 1987, 321–368.

39. See, for example, Byrne, J. A. The best laid ethics programs. *Business Week*, March 9, 1992; Morgan, R. B. Self- and co-worker perceptions of ethics and their relationships to leadership and salary. *Academy of Management Review*, 1993, 36, 200–214; Stark, A. What's the matter with business ethics? *Harvard Business Review*, May–June 1993, 38–48.

40. Drake, B. H., and Drake, E. Ethical and legal aspects of managing corporate cultures. *California Management Review*, Winter 1988, 120–121.

41. Cox, T. H., Lobel, S. A., and McLeod, P. A. Effects of ethnic group cultural differences on cooperative and competitive behavior on a group task. *Academy of Management Journal*, 1991, 34, 827–847; Thomas, R. R. From affirmative action to affirming dignity. *Harvard Business Review*, March–April 1990, 107–117.

42. Cox, T. H., and Blake, S. Managing cultural diversity: Implications for organizational competitiveness. *Academy of Management Executive*, 1991, 5(3), 45–56; Watson, W. E., Kumar, K., and Michaelsen, L. K. Cultural diversity's impact on interaction process and performance: Comparing homogeneous and diverse task groups. *Academy of Management Journal*, 1993, 36, 590–602.

43. Cox, T. The multicultural organization. *Academy of Management Executive*, 1991, 5(2), 35.

44. Adapted from Goldstein, J., and Leopold, M. Corporate culture versus ethnic culture. *Personnel Journal*, November 1990, 83.

45. Caudron, S. Training can damage diversity efforts. *Personnel Journal*, April 1993, 54.

46. Overman, S. Managing the diverse workforce. *HR Magazine*, April 1991, 32–36.

47. Goldstein, J., and Leopold, M. Corporate culture versus ethnic culture. *Personnel Journal*, November 1990, 83–92.

48. Harrison, J. R., and Carroll, G. R. Keeping the faith: A model of cultural transmission in formal organizations. *Administrative Science Quarterly*, 1991, 36, 552–582; Morrison, E. W. Longitudinal study of the effects of information seeking on newcomer socialization. *Journal of Applied Psychology*, 1993, 78, 173–183.

49. Pascale, R. The paradox of "corporate culture": Reconciling ourselves to socialization. *California Management Review*, Winter 1985, 29–33.

50. Adapted from Quick, J. C. Crafting an organizational culture: Herb's hand at Southwest Airlines. *Organizational Dynamics*, Autumn 1992, 45–56; Teitelbaum, R. S. Southwest Airlines: Where service flies right. *Fortune*, August 24, 1992, 115–116; Trice, H. M., and Beyer, J. M. *The Cultures of Work Organizations*. Englewood Cliffs, N.J.: Prentice-Hall, 1992, 3.

51. Abelson, M. A. Turnover cultures. In G. Ferris (ed.), *Research in Personnel and Human Resources Management*, vol. 11. Greenwich, Conn.: JAI Press, 1993, 339–376; Allen, N. J., and Meyer, J. P. Organizational socialization tactics: A longitudinal analysis of links to newcomer's commitment and role orientation. *Academy of Management Journal*, 1990, 33, 847–858; Jones, G. R. Socialization tactics, self-efficacy, and newcomers' adjustments to organizations. *Academy of Management Journal*, 1986, 29, 262–279; O'Reilly, C. R., Chatman, J., and Caldwell, D. F. People and organizational culture: A profile comparison approach to assessing person-organization fit. *Academy of Management Journal*, 1991, 34, 487–516.

52. Adapted from Cullen, J. B., Victor, B., and Stephens, C. An ethical weather report: Assessing the organization's ethical climate. *Organizational Dynamics*, Autumn 1989, 56.

53. Reprinted by permission of Denison, D. R., and Mishra, A. K. Toward a theory of organizational culture and effectiveness. *Organization Science*, in press. Copyright The Institute of Management Sciences, 290 Westminster Street, Providence, Rhode Island 02903–USA. Reprinted with permission.

15 Power and Political Behavior

When you have finished studying this chapter, you should be able to:

▲ Define the concepts of organizational power and organizational politics.

▲ Describe the main interpersonal sources of power.

▲ Identify and explain the primary categories of structural sources of power.

▲ Discuss effective and ineffective uses of power.

▲ Identify the personal and situational factors that contribute to the occurrence of political behavior.

▲ Describe some personality dimensions that are related to political behavior.

OUTLINE

Preview Case: The Politics of Innovation

Power

Managing in Practice: The King is Dead

Interpersonal Sources of Power

Reward Power

Coercive Power

Legitimate Power

Expert Power

Managing Across Cultures: Power and the Japanese CEO

Referent Power

Key Relationships

Structural Sources of Power

Knowledge as Power

Managing Quality: Computer Links Empower Employees

Resources as Power

Decision Making as Power

Managing Across Cultures: Power in Chinese and British Organizations

Networks as Power

Managing Diversity: African-American Business Networking

Lower-Level Employee Power

The Effective Use of Power

Political Behavior

Organizational Politics

Managing in Practice: Picking a Successor at Booz, Allen, & Hamilton, Inc.

Forces Creating Political Behavior

Managing Ethics: The Politics of Employee Appraisal

Personality and Political Behavior

Need for Power

Machiavellianism

Locus of Control

Risk-Seeking Propensity

DEVELOPING SKILLS

Self-Diagnosis: *How Much Power Do You Have in Your Group?*

A Case in Point: *The NASA Moonlander Monitor*

PREVIEW CASE

The Politics of Innovation

In 1873, Christopher Sholes invented the typewriter. Some 122 years later, this same typewriter keyboard is still the principle tool that most of us use to communicate with our computers. What is unknown to most people, however, is that the particular configuration of keys (referred to as the QWERTY keyboard) was purposely engineered to *slow down* typists in order to accommodate the limitations of the typewriter introduced in 1873. The original typewriters, which relied on gravity to return struck keys to their resting positions, could jam if keys were struck in quick succession. Thus the keyboard was designed to prevent typists from striking keys too rapidly, particularly keys located next to each other. This mechanical problem with modern typewriters no longer exists, nor is this a problem with PC keyboards.

Surprisingly, a keyboard with a significantly improved configuration of keys has been in existence since 1932. The Dvorak Simplified Keyboard (DSK) has repeatedly been shown to be faster and more accurate than the standard keyboard in use, yet this innovation has never been adopted. Why?

The story of the DSK keyboard pits a solitary inventor against large organizations with a stake in maintaining the status quo. For some 30 years, Dr. August Dvorak fought to have his keyboard adopted as the standard. Dvorak and his associates conducted time and motion studies, participated in international typing contests, and even arranged for trial tests to be conducted by the federal government. Studies and tests showed the DSK keyboard to result in productivity improvements in the range of 35–100% with approximately 50% fewer mistakes. From 1934 to 1941, DSK-trained typists won the World Typewriting Championships. Dvorak failed to gain a government contract for his typewriters despite government tests that showed an average of 74% productivity gains. Both the U.S. Navy and the General Services Administration rejected converting to the DSK keyboard based on the costs of replacing obsolete equipment and retraining typists. The U.S. Navy assigned a security classification to test results of the DSK, thereby assuring that few people would be aware of them.

Dvorak also faced active resistance from typewriter manufacturers. Manufacturers sponsored most of the typing contests and routinely attempted to prevent DSK typists from competing. Results of typing contests typically failed to list the machines that typists used in instances when DSK typists won. There were even documented instances of sabotage of Dvorak's machines.

Adoption of the DSK was defeated by political resistance on the part of typewriter manufacturers who had little incentive to use the improved keyboard. The increased productivity from the new keyboard could reduce sales of typewriters as an office would need less machines if each typist could produce more. Further, manufacturers would have been required to pay royalties on the DSK, which was a patented invention.[1]

I n this chapter, we focus on power and political behavior in organizations. People often are uncomfortable discussing the concepts of power and organizational politics. Both terms carry emotional, often negative, implications. We argue that this should not be the case; these labels are simply descriptive terms that apply to certain aspects of the behavior of people in organizations. Managers and employees need to understand power and political behavior in order to understand organizational behavior fully.

Certainly, political behavior can be unproductive for an organization, and people can use power in unfair or harmful ways as demonstrated in the Preview Case. Managers and employees must try to avoid such outcomes, but they cannot change reality by refusing to accept the existence of power differences or political behavior. In this chapter, we discuss the nature of power, the sources of power in organizations, and the effective and ineffective uses of power. We also explore political behavior in organizations and some relationships between personality and political behavior.

▼ POWER

Power is the capacity to influence the behavior of others.[2] The term power may be applied to individuals, groups, teams, organizations, and countries. For example, a certain group or team within an organization might be labeled as powerful, which suggests that it has the ability to influence the behavior of individuals in other groups or departments. This influence may affect resource allocations, space assignments, goals, hiring decisions, or many other outcomes and behaviors in an organization.

People continually attempt to influence the behavior of others in the normal course of everyday living. For example, people quite naturally attempt to *reinforce* the pleasing or satisfying behaviors of family members and friends. Likewise—and often without conscious awareness—people fail to reinforce or even attempt to *punish* undesirable behaviors. The behavior of people at work is no different.

Power is a *social* term; that is, an individual has power in relation to other people, a group or team has power in relation to other groups, and so on.[3] The concept of power characterizes interactions among people—more than one person must be involved for the concept to apply. Further, power is never absolute or unchanging. It is a dynamic relationship that changes as situations and individuals change. For example, a manager may strongly influence the behavior of one subordinate but, at the same time, only marginally influence another. Managers may be powerful with respect to their own subordinates, yet be unable to influence the behavior of employees in other departments. In addition, relationships change with time. Last month's successful influence attempt may fail tomorrow, even though the same people are involved in both situations. The following Managing in Practice account illustrates the dynamic, changing nature of CEO power in corporate America.

MANAGING IN PRACTICE

The King is Dead

American industry is going through a reversal of a decades-old trend that saw corporate power accrue to top managers and executives. If the Chief Executive Officer (CEO) ever was King, those days are gone. The King is dead. Gigantic institutions that hold large amounts of stock (such as retirement funds), activist shareholders, boards of directors, and even lower level managers increasingly are wielding power formerly controlled almost exclusively by CEOs.

Chief executive officers report major changes in who has power in their organizations and how that power is used. According to a survey of 216 top executives of the largest U.S. corporations, formerly powerful headquarters staffs have been reduced in size, and their power has shrunk. Louis Pepper, CEO of Washington Mutual Savings Bank in Seattle, states: "The headquarters staff, at one point, were running the entire show. That power has been diminished to allow more of management to become involved." Moreover, the corporate hierarchy has been flattened and layers of management reduced. One result has been to push decision making lower in the organization. Consequently, the majority of CEOs surveyed report that middle management's power has increased.

MANAGING IN PRACTICE —*Continued*

In comparing the balance of power between organizations and their customers, these CEOs say that customer power is growing. In response, Square D, an electrical equipment manufacturer, reorganized to give employees who deal with customers greater autonomy and power, says Jerry Stead, CEO. In addition, CEOs must listen more to their boards of directors, which increasingly contain more outside representatives. The majority of these CEOs report that their boards are more powerful than they were five years ago.

The CEOs agree that consensus building characterizes their management style. Compared to the traditional, more autocratic or "imperial" CEO, 74% of these CEOs describe themselves as more participatory, more consensus-oriented, and more reliant on communication skills than on "command and control" skills. Harry Todd, CEO of Rohr Industries, says, "No more one-man band. We're all group-oriented." This theme was echoed by Vincent Sarni of PPG Industries, who describes the new style of successful CEOs as team-oriented and participatory. In this view, CEOs should set a strategic direction, get employees to agree, give them resources and authority, and leave them alone.

Indeed, these powerful corporate heads agree that personality and leadership skills are the most important sources of power in today's organization. The exercise of control has become less important than the exercise of leadership. Reuben Mark, CEO of Colgate-Palmolive, sums up the new power-sharing philosophy: "The more [power] you have, the less you should use. You consolidate and build power by empowering others."[4]

The terms *power* and *authority*, although closely related, do not mean exactly the same thing. **Authority** is power legitimated by (1) being formally granted by the organization and (2) being accepted by employees as being right and proper.[5] The most obvious organizational example is the superior–subordinate relationship. An organization has a formal authority structure with individuals, groups, teams, departments, and divisions being charged with responsibility for certain activities and functions. When individuals join an organization, they generally recognize the authority structure as legitimate; that is, employees accept the manager's right to set policy and give direction. So long as directives are reasonable and related to the job, employees generally obey them. Authority is narrower in scope than power and applies to fewer behaviors in an organization.

In addition to exercising authority, an individual or group may be able to influence the behavior of other people in an organization for many other reasons. In general, power sources in an organization may be categorized as (1) interpersonal and (2) structural, as shown in Figure 15.1.

▼ INTERPERSONAL SOURCES OF POWER

Many studies of power in organizations have focused on interpersonal relationships between manager and subordinates or leader and followers. French and Raven identified five interpersonal sources of power: reward power, co-

FIGURE 15.1

Sources of Power in Organizations

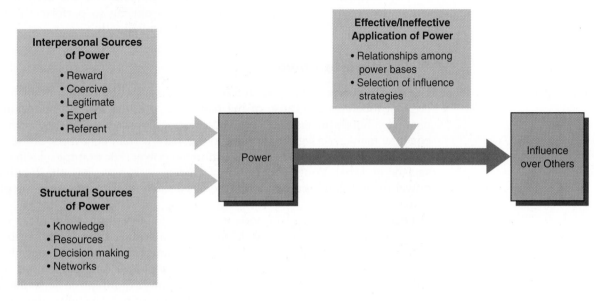

ercive power, legitimate power, expert power, and referent power.[6] We introduced you to these concepts in Chapter 11, discussing them in the context of a leader's ability to influence the behavior of followers. Here, we explore these sources of power in a broader organizational context.

▼ Reward Power

Reward power is an individual's ability to influence others' behavior by rewarding their desirable behavior. For example, to the extent that subordinates value rewards that the manager can give—praise, promotions, money, time off, and so on—they may comply with requests and directives. A manager who controls the allocation of merit pay raises in a department has reward power over the employees in that department. In sum, employees may comply with some influence attempts by managers because they expect to be rewarded for their compliance.

▼ Coercive Power

Coercive power is an individual's ability to influence others' behavior by means of punishment for undesirable behavior. For example, subordinates may comply because they expect to be punished for failure to respond favorably to managerial directives. Punishment may take the form of reprimands, undesirable work assignments, closer supervision, tighter enforcement of work rules, suspension without pay, and the like. The ultimate punishment, from the organization's perspective, is firing the employee.

Recall, however, that punishment can have undesirable side effects (see Chapter 5). For example, the employee who receives an official reprimand for shoddy work may find ways (other than the obvious one the organization wants) to avoid the punishment, such as by refusing to perform the task, falsifying performance reports, or being absent frequently.

▼ Legitimate Power

Legitimate power most often refers to a manager's ability to influence subordinates' behavior because of the manager's position in the organizational hierarchy. Subordinates may respond to such influence because they acknowledge the manager's legitimate right to prescribe certain behaviors. Sometimes nonmanagerial employees possess legitimate power. For example, a safety inspector at Loral Vought's plant in Camden, Arkansas, has the legitimate power to shut down production if there is a safety violation, even if the plant manager objects.

Legitimate power is an important organizational concept. Typically, a manager is empowered to make decisions within a specific area of responsibility, such as quality control, marketing, or accounting. This area of responsibility, in effect, defines the activities for which the manager (and sometimes other employees) can expect to exercise legitimate power to influence behavior. The farther that managers get from their specific area of responsibility, the weaker their legitimate power becomes. Employees have a **zone of indifference** with respect to the exercise of managerial power.[7] Within the zone of indifference, employees will accept certain directives without questioning the manager's power, and the manager may have considerable legitimate power to influence subordinates' behavior. Outside that zone, however, legitimate power disappears rapidly. For example, a secretary will type letters, answer the phone, open the mail, and do similar tasks for a manager without question. However, if the manager asks the secretary to go out for a drink after work, the secretary may refuse. The manager's request clearly falls outside the secretary's zone of indifference. The manager has no legitimate right to expect the secretary to comply.

▼ Expert Power

Expert power is an individual's ability to influence others' behavior because of recognized skills, talents, or specialized knowledge. To the extent that managers can demonstrate competence in implementing, analyzing, evaluating, and controlling the tasks of subordinates, they will acquire expert power. Expert power often is relatively narrow in scope. For example, a team member might carefully follow the advice of her team leader about how to program a numerically controlled lathe yet ignore advice from the team leader regarding which of three company health plans she should choose. In this instance, the team member is recognizing expertise in one area while resisting influence in another. A lack of expert power often plagues new managers and employees. Even though a young accountant might possess a great deal of knowledge about accounting theory and procedures, that expertise must be demonstrated and applied over time to become known and accepted. The following Managing Across Cultures feature describes the role of expert power, as well as other sources of power.

MANAGING ACROSS CULTURES

Power and the Japanese CEO

Japanese CEOs sometimes have been portrayed as powerless. This observation is based on a misunderstanding of the bottom-up decision-making processes common in large Japanese organizations. The assumption is that the complex process of decision making by consensus (*ringi*) relegates the Japanese CEO to a role of rubber stamping decisions collectively agreed to at lower levels of the organization.

Contrary to this view, many observers believe that Japanese CEOs wield strong influence over their organizations. This influence is derived both from the personal power of the CEO and his position in the firm, as indicated by Figure 15.2.

A Japanese CEO presides over the company's top management team (whose members are called *torishimariyaku*). This group's members are the organization's environmental scanners, strategy formulators, and policy implementers. Thus CEOs are at the center of the most powerful group in the organization. They often personally control both the frequency and agenda of top-management team meetings, and the selection of new *torishimariyaku*. In addition, most large Japanese firms are members of industrial groups characterized by complex overlapping ownership and a strong sense of community. These industrial groups have "president's clubs" that serve as a decision-making body for each group. Many of the most important contacts in the industrial group thus occur at the CEO level. The Japanese CEO serves as the primary link between the individual firm and the industrial group and is in a powerful position in terms of access to external resources and influence. The position power of the Japanese CEO is solidified by organizational and

FIGURE 15.2

Sources of Japanese CEO Power

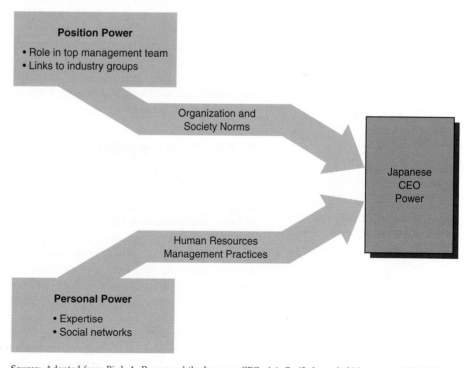

Source: Adapted from Bird, A. Power and the Japanese CEO. *Asia Pacific Journal of Management*, 1990, 7(2), 3.

MANAGING ACROSS CULTURES —*Continued*

societal norms that emphasize and reinforce hierarchical relationships, respect for authority, and the like.

The personal power of Japanese CEOs resides in the expert and charismatic influence developed through the human resources management practices of Japanese organizations. Through slow promotion practices, extensive job rotation (which broadens knowledge), and intensive on-the-job training, Japanese managers acquire considerable expertise as they advance through the company. Those receiving promotions are widely viewed as legitimate recipients of greater authority. A second source of personal power is the CEO's social network (*jimmyaku*). This far-reaching network, too, is a product of Japanese human resources practices. For example, the policy of job rotation gives interpersonally skillful managers an opportunity to establish broad networks of acquaintances both inside and outside the organization.[8]

▼ Referent Power

Referent power is an individual's ability to influence others' behavior as a result of being liked or admired. For example, subordinates' identification with a manager often forms the basis for referent power. This identification may include the desire of the subordinates to emulate the manager. A young manager may copy the leadership style of an older, admired, and more experienced manager. The older manager thus has some ability—some referent power—to influence the behavior of the younger manager. Referent power usually is associated with individuals who possess admired personality characteristics, charisma, or a good reputation. Thus it often is associated with political leaders, movie stars, sports figures, or other well-known individuals (hence their use in advertising to influence buying behavior). However, managers and employees also may have considerable referent power because of the strength of their personalities. Anita Roddick, CEO of the Body Shop, and Herb Kelleher, CEO of Southwest Airlines, use their referent power to motivate employees to achieve their organization's goals.

▼ Key Relationships

Managers and other employees possess varying amounts of interpersonal sources of power. As implied by Figure 15.1, these sources do not operate independently. A study conducted in two paper mills provides an example of how power sources are related.[9] One of the mills dropped an incentive pay plan based on performance in favor of a pay plan based strictly on seniority. Compared to the second plant, which retained the incentive system, subordinates' perceptions of the use of various sources of power by supervisors in the first plant changed noticeably. Discontinuing the incentive plan lowered the perceived reward power of supervisors, as might be expected, but other results were more complex. Perceptions of supervisors' use of punishment increased (attributable perhaps to less control over rewards). The perceived use of referent and legitimate power decreased, but expert power appeared to be unaffected. These findings suggest that the interpersonal sources of power that influence behavior are complex and interrelated.

The ways in which managers and other employees use one type of power can either enhance or limit the effectiveness of power from another source. For example, managers who administer rewards to subordinates also tend to be well liked and seem to have greater referent power than managers who do not give out rewards. However, the use of coercive power can reduce referent power. The threatened or actual use of punishment appears to reduce liking or admiration, leading to a reduction in referent power. Further, employees often view managers who possess knowledge valuable to them as having greater legitimate power in addition to having expert power.

These five sources of interpersonal power may be divided into two broad categories: organizational and personal. Reward power, coercive power, and legitimate power have organizational bases; that is, top managers can give to or take away from lower level managers or others the right to administer rewards and punishments. The organization can change employees' legitimate power by changing their positions in the authority hierarchy or by changing job descriptions, rules, and procedures. Referent power and expert power, however, depend much more on personal characteristics—personalities, leadership styles, and knowledge brought to the job. In the long run, the organization may influence expert power by, for example, making additional training available. But the individuals determine how they use that training, that is, the extent to which they apply the new knowledge. Recall that in the Managing in Practice description of CEO power, CEOs reported that personal sources of power (expert and referent power) were more important than organizational sources (legitimate, reward, and coercive power).

▼ STRUCTURAL SOURCES OF POWER

Much of the attention directed at power in organizations tends to focus on the power of managers over subordinates. An additional perspective is that many aspects of a situation, in part, determine power. They include the design of the organization, the type of departmental structure, the opportunity to influence, access to powerful individuals and critical resources, the nature of the position an individual holds, and so on.[10] For example, the power associated with a particular position or job is affected by its visibility to upper management and its importance or relevance with respect to the organization's goals or priorities. Table 15.1 contains some examples of position characteristics that determine relative power within an organization. Note that, whereas the legitimate power previously discussed applies primarily to managerial positions, the characteristics described in Table 15.1 are relevant for both managerial and nonmanagerial positions.

Structural and situational sources of power reflect the division of labor and membership in different departments, teams, and groups. These work assignments, locations, and roles naturally result in unequal access to information, resources, decision making, and other people. Any of an almost infinite variety of specific situational factors could become a source of power in an organization. We next discuss several important categories of these factors, including knowledge as power, resources as power, decision making as power, and networks as power.

▼ Knowledge as Power

Organizations are information processors that must use knowledge to produce goods and services. The concept of **knowledge as power** means that individ-

TABLE 15.1   Position Characteristics Associated with Power

Characteristic	Definition	Example
Centrality	Relationship among positions in a communication network	More-central positions will have greater power
Criticality	Relationship among tasks performed in a work-flow process	Positions responsible for the most critical tasks will have more power.
Flexibility	Amount of discretion in decision making, work assignments, and so on	More-autonomous positions will have more power.
Visibility	Degree to which task performance is seen by higher management in the organization	More-visible positions will have more power.
Relevance	Relationship between tasks and high-priority organizational goals	Positions most closely related to important goals will have more power.

Source: Adapted from Whetten, D. A., and Cameron, K. S. *Developing Managerial Skills.* Glenview, Ill.: Scott Foresman, 1984, 259.

uals, teams, groups, or departments that possess knowledge crucial to attaining the organization's goals have power. People and groups in a position to control information about current operations, develop information about alternatives, or acquire knowledge about future events and plans have enormous power to influence the behavior of others. Thus certain staff and support activities—a data processing center, for example—sometimes seem to have influence disproportionate to their relationship to the organization's major goals and activities.

The increased use of personal computers and computerized work stations is having a dramatic impact on access to and use of information—and thus on power relationships—in many organizations. Information is rapidly becoming more widely available to many employees. Greater access to information tends to flatten the hierarchy and make hoarding information by employees or departments more difficult. Information sharing has important implications for the quality of decision making and other aspects of performance, as indicated in the following Managing Quality feature.

MANAGING QUALITY

Computer Links Empower Employees

The extensive use of computer networks is spreading and presenting management with both opportunities and challenges. These networks enable many employees to share information simultaneously. Further, computer networks provide workers with information that previously was available only to management. Networks also provide another access: the ability to join discussions of senior executives or other top managers.

When on-line, people are judged more by what they say than by their rank in the organizational hierarchy. For example, the computer networks at

MANAGING QUALITY —*Continued*

Wright-Patterson Air Force Base in Ohio don't follow the lines of command. "Rank doesn't really matter when you're on-line," says Lt. Col. Donald Potter. "An enlisted man could send a message to a colonel." Formerly, he says, there wouldn't have been an easy way for a sergeant to share an idea with a colonel without making a formal appointment to see him in his office.

An on-line computer network also altered the chain of command at the insurance firm of Johnson & Higgins. When Mary Jo Dirkes, a young employee in Chicago, posted a particularly well-crafted statement about the firm's efforts in workers' compensation, the memo immediately came to the attention of top management in New York. They were impressed and rewarded Dirkes with praise and broadened her responsibilities. Her boss said, "In the past I wouldn't have thought of going to her for help because she is relatively new."

Perhaps because knowledge is power, at some firms sharing of information doesn't come easily. A study at Price Waterhouse found that some junior employees wouldn't share information on the computer network because of the firm's intensely competitive culture. Esther Dyson, an industry consultant, observes that computer networks can "create a flatter, more democratic organization. But that really only happens if the organization is ready for it."[11]

It is now claimed that *intellectual capital* is corporate America's most valuable asset. **Intellectual capital** represents the knowledge, know-how, and skill that exists in the organization. This intellectual capital can provide an organization with a competitive edge in the marketplace. For example, Dr. P. Roy Vagelos, CEO of Merck & Company, states, "A low-value product can be made by anyone anywhere. When you have knowledge no one else has access to—that's dynamite." In the annual *Fortune* magazine poll, Merck was voted the most admired U.S. company seven years in a row (1986–1992) and has invented more new medicines than any other U.S. pharmaceutical company.[12]

▼ Resources as Power

Organizations need a variety of resources, including human resources, money, equipment, materials, supplies, and customers to survive. The importance of specific resources to a firm's success and the difficulty of obtaining them vary. The concept of **resources as power** suggests that departments, groups, or individuals who can provide essential or difficult-to-obtain resources acquire power in the organization. Which resources are the most important depends on the situation, the organization's goals, the economic climate, and the goods or services being produced. The old saying that "he who has the gold makes the rules" sums up the idea that resources are power.

At Weirton Steel, employees now own 77% of the voting stock in the company. Employees and management are locked in a bitter battle for control of the board of directors stemming from disagreements over strategies (such as issuing new stock) the firm is pursuing. Although some employees are angry that they don't wield as much power as they think they should, the employees undoubtedly have more power over corporate strategy as a result of their ownership interests than they would otherwise.[13]

▼ Decision Making as Power

Decisions in organizations often are made sequentially, with many individuals or groups participating (discussed in Chapter 18). The decision-making process creates additional power differences among individuals or groups. The concept of **decision making as power** means that individuals or groups acquire power to the extent that they can affect some part of the decision-making process. They might influence the goals being developed, premises being used in making a decision, alternatives being considered, outcomes being projected, and so on. For example, a task force at the Fort Worth Museum of Science and History was charged with studying attendance problems and making recommendations for ways to increase attendance. Even though the task force did not make the final decision, it had a great deal of power because it controlled the consideration of possible solutions. A powerful machine politician in New York City once reportedly said, "I don't care who does the electing, as long as I have the power to do the nominating."

The ability to influence the decision-making process is a subtle and often overlooked source of power. Decision-making power doesn't necessarily reside with the final decision-maker in an organization. For example, Southern California Edison uses a technique known as *scenario planning* to develop strategic plans for the future of the electric utility.[14] Scenario planners might look ahead ten years and develop a dozen possible versions of the future—another Middle East oil crisis, heightened environmental concerns, an economic boom in southern California, a major recession, and so on. Each scenario has implications for needed capacity, investment funds, human resources, and the like. The individuals and departments involved in scenario planning at Edison wield considerable influence, regardless of whether they make the final decisions regarding resource allocations.

Although decision making is an important aspect of power in every organization, cultural differences make for some interesting differences in the relationship, as the following Managing Across Cultures piece indicates.

MANAGING ACROSS CULTURES

Power in Chinese and British Organizations

Relationships between power and decision making were examined in 11 Chinese and 10 British companies. Data were collected about making decisions in 18 areas, such as assigning employees to training, selecting supervisors, and assigning specific tasks to be performed. Organizations studied represented both manufacturing and service industries. Patterns of decision making revealed both organizational and cultural differences.

In the Chinese organizations, decision-making power was more decentralized in manufacturing firms than in service organizations. The reverse was true in British firms, with power being more decentralized in the service organizations than in the manufacturing firms. Organizational and cultural differences were more pronounced for medium- and long-range decisions than for short-term decisions. In China the service sector of the economy is relatively new, which may account for its greater centralization of power compared to manufacturing firms. However, the central government has

MANAGING ACROSS CULTURES —*Continued*

attempted to decentralize power in manufacturing firms as part of its economic reforms. In the United Kingdom, by contrast, the service sector of the economy is well developed and prosperous and is characterized by decentralized decision-making procedures.

In the British firms, managers and trade union representatives had larger differences in perceptions of which individuals had decision-making power than did their counterparts in the Chinese firms. Chinese management and trade unions seemed to have more common objectives, and they more readily agreed about who held power and who didn't. In part because of the strong influence of the Communist party, management and unions cooperate more in Chinese organizations than is typical of British organizations.

Decision-making power was more centralized at the middle and top levels of Chinese firms than it was in British organizations. This condition, too, may reflect important cultural differences between China and the United Kingdom as, in general, Chinese society relies more on strong central authority than does British society. Thus the study demonstrated that decision-making power is affected by various factors, including the type of decision task, the type of industry, and the prevailing culture.[15]

▼ Networks as Power

The existence of structural and situational power depends not only on access to information, resources, and decision making, but also on the ability to get cooperation in carrying out tasks. Managers and departments that have connecting links with other individuals and departments in the organization will be more powerful than those who don't. As suggested by Figure 15.3, traditional superior–subordinate vertical relationships are important aspects of power. In addition, the horizontal linkages provided by both internal and external networks help explain power differences. The concept of **networks as power** implies that various affiliations, networks, and coalitions, both inside and outside the organization, represent sources of power.

For example, power is provided by the following connecting links, each of which relates to the factors already discussed.

▲ *Information links.* To be effective, managers and employees must be "in the know" in both the formal and informal sense. (Knowledge is power.)

▲ *Supply links.* Outside links provide managers with the opportunity to bring materials, money, or other resources into their departments or teams. (Resources are power.)

▲ *Support links.* A manager's job must allow for decision-making discretion—the exercise of judgment. Managers must know that they can make decisions and assume innovative, risk-taking activities without each decision or action having to go through a stifling, multilayered approval process. Managers and other professionals need the backing of other important figures in the organization, whose support becomes another resource they bring to their own work unit. (Participation in decision making is power and an important indicator of support links.)[16]

FIGURE 15.3

Work Relationships and Power

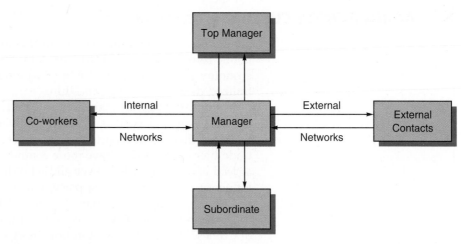

Source: Adapted from Ragins, B. R., and Sundstrom, E. Gender and power in organizations: A longitudinal perspective. *Psychological Bulletin*, 1989, 105, 65.

Internal networks are key to understanding how the organization gets work done. To identify and determine how they operate, managers and employees can undertake a **network analysis,** whereby they attempt to diagram important relationship networks within the organization. For example, the *advice network* reveals employees that others depend on to solve problems and provide technical information. The *trust network* shows which employees share delicate political information with each other. The *communication network* (see chapter 12) indicates who talks to whom on a regular basis.[17] By understanding these and other networks, managers can diagnose the informal organization and understand more about how work actually gets done (or fails to get done) in the organization, as well as identify power differences among individuals and groups.

The following Managing Diversity feature illustrates the notion of networks as power. Motown Records was in serious difficulty until its CEO was able to utilize external networks to solve problems and bring needed resources into the firm.

MANAGING DIVERSITY

African-American Business Networking

Jheryl Busby, the CEO of Motown Record Co. was in big trouble during the summer of 1991. He was desperately trying to save Motown Records, an enterprise rich in tradition but not cash. Motown still had a tremendous record library, but big names such as Michael Jackson and Smokey Robinson had defected to other labels for more money. Busby was in the midst of a major lawsuit filed against its distributor and part-owner, MCA, Inc., for failing to promote Motown's label and acts adequately.

So what did Busby do? He turned to the black business community for help with these problems. For example, he asked Clarence Avant, an influential music impresario, to introduce him to Earl Graves, publisher of *Black Enterprise*

MANAGING DIVERSITY —*Continued*

magazine. Busby's face soon appeared on the cover of the national publication. The magazine gave extensive coverage to Busby's plans for "the new Motown." About the same time, Busby spent hours in conversation with Graves, Avant, and Robert L. Johnson, CEO of Black Entertainment Television.

Busby's brain trust helped him develop a strategy to create Motown TV specials and theme restaurants. Johnson made an offer to buy out MCA, giving Busby time to find a new distributor and develop new acts. Busby says, "I had never before asked for a favor or advice. But when you're driven by fear, you reach for help from those who understand you best."[18]

▼ Lower Level Employee Power

Although we commonly think of power as something that managers have, lower level employees also may wield considerable power.[19] Some sources of interpersonal power—expert power, in particular—may allow subordinates to influence their managers. For example, the secretary who can use a *Windows* spreadsheet has the power to influence her manager's decisions if the manager cannot personally use the spreadsheet and must rely on the secretary's expertise.

Although lower level employees may have some interpersonal power, their ability to influence others' behavior more likely stems from structural or situational sources. Figure 15.4 suggests that their power is a result of their positions in the organization. Refer back to Table 15.1 for a description of important position characteristics related to power. In addition to these characteristics, lower level employees may be able to control access to information or resources and important aspects of the decision-making process. Networks

FIGURE 15.4

Model of Lower Level Employee Power

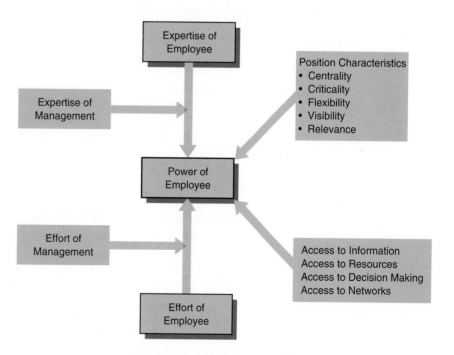

or affiliations with powerful individuals or groups may be yet another source of their power. Further, the expertise of employees and the amount of effort expended also influence the extent of their power. As Figure 15.4 illustrates, whether expertise and effort increase employees' power depends, in part, on their superior's expertise and effort. For example, if an employee's manager has little knowledge about a certain task and the employee has considerable knowledge, the relative power of the employee increases. Employees also can acquire power by expending effort in areas where management puts little effort.

▼ THE EFFECTIVE USE OF POWER

When managers, employees, or teams face a situation in which they want to influence the behavior of others, they must choose a strategy. **Influence strategies** are the methods by which individuals or groups attempt to exert power or influence others' behavior. Table 15.2 lists various influence strategies that managers and employees use in the workplace.

Researchers and others are interested in identifying effective influence strategies and understanding the situations in which each might be used. For example, studies have indicated that the influence strategies of rational persuasion, inspirational appeal, and consultation shown in Table 15.2 often are the most effective in a variety of circumstances. Overall, the least effective strategies seem to be pressure, coalition, and legitimating.[20] However, it is a mistake to assume that certain strategies always will work and that others won't. Differences in effectiveness occur when attempts to influence are downward rather than upward or lateral in the hierarchy and when they are used in combination rather than independently. In general, a manager or employee must take into account the power sources available, the direction of attempts to influence, and the goals being sought when selecting an influence strategy.

TABLE 15.2   Influence Strategies

Influence Strategy	Definition
Rational persuasion	Use logical arguments and factual evidence
Inspirational appeal	Appeal to values, ideals, or aspirations to arouse enthusiasm
Consultation	Seek participation in planning a strategy, activity, or change
Ingratiation	Attempt to create a favorable mood before making request
Exchange	Offer an exchange of favors, share of benefits, or promise to reciprocate at later time
Personal appeal	Appeal to feelings of loyalty or friendship
Coalition	Seek aid or support of others for some initiative or activity
Legitimating	Seek to establish legitimacy of a request by claiming authority or by verifying consistency with policies, practices, or traditions
Pressure	Use demands, threats, or persistent reminders

Source: Adapted from Yukl, G., Falbe, C. M., and Youn, J. Y. Patterns of influence behavior for managers. *Group & Organization Management*, 1993, 18, 7; Yukl, G., and Tracey, J. B. Consequences of influence tactics used with subordinates, peers, and the boss. *Journal of Applied Psychology*, 1992, 77, 526.

Having the *capacity* to influence (power) the behavior of others and effectively using this capacity aren't the same thing. Managers who believe that they can effectively influence the behavior of others by acquiring enough power to simply order other people around generally are unsuccessful. In addition, the evidence indicates that the ineffective use of power has many negative implications, both for the individual and the organization. For example, one study examined the consequences of overreliance on assertiveness and persistence as an influence strategy (the "pressure" strategy in Table 15.2). Managers who were very assertive and persistent with others—characterized by a refusal to take no for an answer, reliance on repeated reminders, frequent use of face-to-face confrontations, and the like—suffered negative consequences. Compared to other managers studied, these aggressive managers (1) received the lowest performance evaluations, (2) earned less money, and (3) experienced the highest levels of job tension and stress.[21]

In addition to selecting the correct influence strategy, effective influence in organizations often depends on an exchange process somewhat related to the "exchange" influence strategy shown in Table 15.2. The **exchange process** in power relationships is based on the "law of reciprocity"—the almost universal belief that people should be paid back for what they do.[22] Imagine a situation in which an employee is asked by her manager to work through the weekend on an important project. The employee does so but receives no recognition, no extra time off, no extra pay—not even a "thank you." The employee later discovers that her manager took sole credit for the project, which was quite successful. This employee, and most observers, would agree that the manager has violated an important aspect of a good working relationship.

The expectation of reciprocal actions, or exchange, occurs repeatedly in organizations. In part, because people expect to be "paid back," influence becomes possible in many situations. The exchange process is particularly important in relationships, such as networks of peers or colleagues, where formal authority to compel compliance is absent. Power in the exchange process stems from the ability to offer something that others need. The metaphor of *currencies* provides a useful way to understand how the exchange process influences behavior. Table 15.3 provides some interesting examples of the

TABLE 15.3   Organizational Currencies Traded in the Exchange Process

Currency	Example
Resources	Lending or giving money, budget increases, personnel, space
Assistance	Helping with existing projects or undertaking unwanted tasks
Cooperation	Giving task support, providing quicker response time, approving a project, or aiding implementation
Information	Providing organizational or technical knowledge
Advancement	Giving a task or assignment that can aid in promotion
Recognition	Acknowledging effort, accomplishment, or abilities
Network/contacts	Providing opportunities for linking with others
Personal support	Giving personal and emotional backing

Source: Adapted from Cohen, A. R., and Bradford, D. L. Influence without authority: The use of alliances, reciprocity, and exchanges to accomplish work. *Organizational Dynamics*, Winter 1989, 11.

many types of currencies traded in organizations. Note the similarities between these currencies and the sources of power previously discussed.

The effective use of power is a difficult challenge for managers, employees, and organizations. The goal is to influence the behavior of others in ways that are consistent with both the needs of the organization and its employees. If the use of power isn't carefully managed, powerful individuals may exploit those with less power in the organization and substitute their self-interests for the legitimate interests of the organization. Effective managers and employees often have the following five characteristics.[23]

First, they understand both the interpersonal and the structural sources of power and the most effective methods of using them to influence people. For example, professionals (e.g., research and development scientists, engineers, lawyers, or professors) tend to be more readily influenced by expertise than by other interpersonal sources of power. Effective managers and employees often recognize the structural and situational problems that exist in a power relationship and modify their own behavior to fit the actual situation. As a result, they tend to develop and use a wide variety of power sources and influence strategies. Some ineffective managers rely too much on one or a few power bases or influence strategies.

Second, they understand the nature of the exchange process underlying many successful attempts to influence others. They recognize that, over time, unless reciprocal exchanges are roughly equivalent and fair, hard feelings will result and their ability to influence others will decline.

Third, they understand what is and what is not legitimate behavior in acquiring and using power. The misuse or lack of understanding of a source of power can destroy its effectiveness. For example, individuals erode expert power if they attempt to demonstrate expertise in areas in which they do not have the required knowledge. Individuals may lose referent power by behaving in ways that are inconsistent with characteristics or traits that are attractive to others.

Fourth, they tend to seek positions that allow the development and use of power. In other words, they choose jobs that immerse them in the crucial issues and concerns of an organization. These jobs provide opportunities for and, indeed, demand influencing the behavior of others. Successful performance in these positions, in turn, allows the individual to acquire power.

Finally, they temper their use of power with maturity and self-control. They recognize that their actions influence the behaviors and lives of others. Although they are not necessarily reluctant or afraid to use their power—recognizing that influencing the behavior of employees is a legitimate and necessary part of the manager's role—they nevertheless apply power carefully. They do so in principled and fair ways that are consistent with organizational needs and goals.

▼ POLITICAL BEHAVIOR

Political behavior of individuals and groups consists of their attempts to influence the behavior of others and the course of events in the organization in order to protect their self-interests, meet their own needs, and advance their own goals. Described in this way, almost all behavior may be regarded as political. Labeling behavior as political, however, usually implies a judgment that individuals or groups are gaining something at the expense of other employees, groups, or the organization. People often are self-centered and biased when labeling actions as political behavior. For example, employees may justify their own behavior as defending legitimate rights or interests yet call similar behavior by others "playing politics."

▼ Organizational Politics

Organizational politics involves actions by individuals or groups to acquire, develop, and use power and other resources in order to obtain preferred outcomes when there is uncertainty or disagreement about choices.[24] When people share power and differ about what must be done, many decisions and actions quite naturally will be the result of a political process. The following Managing in Practice account, which describes the selection of a new CEO at Booz, Allen & Hamilton, Inc. describes the political process at work.

MANAGING IN PRACTICE

Picking a Successor at Booz, Allen, & Hamilton, Inc.

Booz, Allen, & Hamilton, Inc., a large New York–based management consulting firm, had a policy that top managers should step aside when they reached 55 years of age. Managers didn't necessarily need to leave the firm or retire at 55, but they were expected to return to consulting work and pass executive responsibility to younger, supposedly more energetic people. Consequently, when he turned 54, James Farley, head of Booz, Allen, proposed a plan for selecting his successor. Rather than simply handpicking a qualified successor, which, as chief executive, he might have done, Farley proposed a "winner-take-all" race among the top partners of the firm. Farley established a selection committee of 15 partners, which he would chair. His intention was to stay out of the process and allow the committee to select his successor democratically. The selection committee would develop a list of desirable criteria for the top job, interview prospective candidates, and gather other information about them. Farley announced that anyone interested should step forward; seven of the firm's best and brightest declared their candidacy, and the race was on.

By all accounts, it was a disaster. Farley's intent may have been to reduce organizational politics and to increase the probability that his successor would be the best person for the job. However, his approach apparently had the opposite effect. The selection process went on for ten months and disrupted many normal operations. Gossip flourished, and work slowed. The openly political contest pitted candidates against each other in attempting to influence the selection process in ways that some members of the firm resented. One former partner was quoted as saying, "To say the process created bad feelings does not capture the essence."

The selection process at Booz, Allen is widely regarded as one that produced the candidate who was least offensive to the largest number of people. The new CEO hasn't received high marks for subsequent performance. He immediately reorganized the company in a manner that generated enormous ill-will and a large number of resignations. Booz, Allen, & Hamilton, Inc., has continued to lose market share to rival consulting firms, such as McKinsey & Company.[25]

Employees often are concerned about office politics.[26] Typically, they also believe that an ideal work setting would be free from political behavior. Negative attitudes about political behavior and organizational politics can block understanding of this crucial aspect of organizational behavior. People tend to assume that political behavior does not yield the best organizational decisions or outcomes—that somehow, by advocating their own positions, individuals or groups produce inferior actions or decisions. Although this result seems to have been the case at Booz, Allen, political behavior isn't always detrimental to an organization. For example, a study involving 90 managers in 30 organizations indicated that these managers were able to identify beneficial, as well as harmful, effects of political behavior. Beneficial effects included career advancement, recognition and status for individuals looking after their legitimate interests, and achievement of organizational goals—getting the job done—as a result of the normal political process in the organization. Harmful effects included demotions and loss of jobs for "losers" in the political process, a misuse of resources, and creation of an ineffective organizational culture.[27] The effect on culture may be among the most undesirable consequences of continual political behavior. Organizational politics may arouse anxieties that cause employees to withdraw emotionally from the organization.[28] This withdrawal, in turn, makes creating an organizational culture characterized by high performance and high commitment very difficult (see Chapter 14).

Political behavior, then, can meet appropriate and legitimate individual and organizational needs, or it can result in negative outcomes. In any event, managers and employees must understand political behavior because it will occur. Eliminating all political behavior isn't possible—it can only be managed.

▼ Forces Creating Political Behavior

The probability of political behavior increases in proportion to disagreements over goals, unclear goals, different ideas about the organization and its problems, different information about the situation, the need to allocate scarce resources, and so on. If these forces didn't exist, perhaps political behavior would not occur. Unfortunately, outcomes are never certain, resources are never infinite, and people must make difficult choices among competing goals and methods to attain them. Thus political behavior will occur as employees and groups attempt to obtain their preferred outcomes. Managers should not try to prevent the inevitable, but rather should try to ensure that these activities do not have negative consequences for the organization and its employees.

One perspective on political behavior suggests that managers and employees are likely to act politically when (1) decision-making procedures and performance measures are highly uncertain and complex and (2) competition among individuals and groups for scarce resources is strong. Conversely, in more stable and less complex environments where decision processes are clear and competitive behavior is less, excessive political behavior is unlikely.[29] Figure 15.5 illustrates these ideas. Using it, we could have predicted that the search for James Farley's successor at Booz, Allen would result in intensive political behavior.

FIGURE 15.5

Probability of Political Behavior
in Organizations

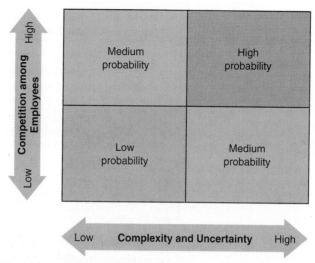

Source: Adapted from Beeman, D. R., and Sharkey, T. W. The use and abuse of corporate politics. *Business Horizons*, March–April 1987, 27.

Whereas certain individual differences may contribute to political behavior (to be discussed shortly), political behavior probably is more strongly influenced by aspects of the situation. Organizations make engaging in political behavior easier when they provide few rules or policies. Ambiguous circumstances allow individuals to define situations in ways that satisfy their own needs. Such redefinition of the situation may be considered political behavior.[30] Further, when employees want more of a resource (such as computer time or office space) than is available, political behavior is likely to occur.

In addition to the dimensions shown in Figure 15.5, political behavior will be higher in organizations that reward such behavior. A reward system may focus solely on individual accomplishment and minimize group and team contributions. When that is the case, individuals may be tempted to behave politically to ensure that they receive some of the rewards. If their political actions result in rewards, employees may be even more likely to engage in such actions in the future. Similarly, individuals who had avoided political behavior, may start behaving politically when they observe such behavior being rewarded. In sum, the organizational reward system can be a major factor in the occurrence of political behavior.[31]

Decisions in some areas can be made less political by increasing the resources available (thus reducing conflict over scarce resources) or by making the decisions seem less important than they really are. However, strategies to reduce the political behavior associated with organizational decisions may have some unintended consequences that translate into real costs for the firm. Table 15.4 shows several examples of strategies used to avoid organizational politics and the potential costs associated with each strategy.

The performance appraisal process provides a good example of forces in the workplace that may create political behavior. Performance for many employees isn't easily measured, and the process results in the allocation of scarce resources based on complex criteria. The following Managing Ethics account describes political behavior in the performance appraisal process.

TABLE 15.4   Strategies for Avoiding the Use of Political Behavior in Decision Making and Their Possible Costs

Strategy	Costs
Slack or excess resources, including additional administrative positions	Inventory, excess capacity, extra personnel and salary
Strong culture—similarity in beliefs, values, and goals produced through recruitment, socialization, use of rewards and punishments	Fewer points of view, less diverse information represented in decision making, potentially lower quality decisions
Make decisions appear less important	Decision avoided; critical analysis not done; important information not uncovered
Reduce system complexity and uncertainty	Creation of rigid rules and procedures; reduction of capacity for change

Source: Adapted from Pfeffer, J. *Power in Organizations.* Marshfield, Mass.: Pitman, 1981, 93; and Pfeffer, J. *Managing with Power: Politics and Influence in Organizations.* Boston: Harvard Business School Press, 1993.

MANAGING ETHICS

The Politics of Employee Appraisal

There is really no getting around the fact that whenever I evaluate one of my people, I stop and think about the impact—the ramifications of my decisions on my relationship with the guy and his future here. I'd be stupid not to. Call it being politically minded, or using managerial discretion, or fine-tuning the guy's ratings, but in the end, I've got to live with him, and I'm not going to rate a guy without thinking about the fallout. There are a lot of games played in the rating process, and whether we (managers) admit it or not, we are all guilty of playing them at our discretion.

That statement comes from one of 60 executives that participated in in-depth interviews concerning their performance appraisal processes. These 60 executives—from 7 large corporations—had performance appraisal experience in a total of 197 different companies. An analysis of over 100 hours of tape-recorded interviews resulted in the following conclusions.

▲ Political considerations were nearly always part of the performance evaluation process.

▲ Politics played a role in the performance appraisal process because (1) executives took into consideration the daily interpersonal dynamics between them and their subordinates; (2) the formal appraisal process results in a permanent written document; and (3) the formal appraisal can have considerable impact on the subordinate's career and advancement.

In addition, these executives believed there was usually a justifiable reason for generating appraisal ratings that were less than accurate. Overall, they felt it was within their managerial discretion to do so. Thus, the findings suggest that the formal appraisal process is indeed a political process and that few ratings are determined without some political consideration.

MANAGING ETHICS *—Continued*

Perhaps the most interesting finding from the study (because it debunks a popular belief) is that accuracy is *not* the primary concern of these practicing executives when appraising subordinates. Their main concern is how best to use the appraisal process to motivate and reward subordinates. Hence, managerial discretion and effectiveness, not accuracy, are the real goals. Managers made it clear that they would not allow excessively accurate ratings to cause problems for themselves and that they attempted to use the appraisal process to their own advantage.[32]

Many organizations ignore the existence of politics in the appraisal process or may assume that use of the proper performance appraisal instruments will minimize it. However, research indicates that, as indicated in the preceeding Managing Ethics feature, political behavior may be a fact of life in many appraisal processes. In particular, because of the ambiguous nature of managerial work, appraisals of managers are susceptible to political manipulation. What is the risk, ethical or otherwise, of using performance appraisal as a political tool? Among other things, overly political performance appraisals can:

▲ Undermine organizational goals and performance;

▲ compromise the link between performance and rewards (see Chapter 6);

▲ encourage politics in the rest of the organization; and

▲ expose an organization to litigation if managers are terminated.[33]

Some experts who have studied politics in the appraisal process suggest that organizations adopt the following guidelines to help cope with the problem.

▲ Articulate goals and standards as clearly and specifically as possible.

▲ Link specific actions and performance results to rewards.

▲ Conduct structured, professional reviews, providing specific examples of observed performance and explanations for ratings given.

▲ Offer performance feedback on an ongoing basis, rather than once a year.

▲ Acknowledge that appraisal politics exists and make this topic a focus of ongoing discussions throughout the organization.[34]

▼ PERSONALITY AND POLITICAL BEHAVIOR

So far, we have stressed the situational and structural determinants of political behavior. Just as power has both personal and situational sources, some individuals appear more likely to engage in political behavior than others. Several personality traits are related to a willingness to do so (and in some cases, a willingness to use power). We discuss four of them: the need for power, Machiavellianism, locus of control, and risk-seeking propensity.[35]

▼ Need for Power

The **need for power** is a motive, or basic desire, to influence and lead others and to control the current environment. As a result, individuals with a high need for power are likely to engage in political behavior in organizations. Successful managers often have high needs for power.[36] The desire to have an impact, to control events, and to influence others often is associated with effective managerial behaviors, equitable treatment of subordinates, and, hence, higher morale.

However, some aspects of strong power needs may not be particularly useful for effective management. The need for power may take two different forms: personal power and institutional power. On the one hand, managers who emphasize personal power strive to dominate others; they want loyalty to themselves, rather than to the organization. When this type of manager leaves the organization, the work group may fall apart. On the other hand, managers who emphasize institutional power demonstrate a more socially acceptable need for power. They create a good climate or culture for effective work, and their subordinates develop an understanding of and loyalty to the organization. Interestingly, some research indicates that female managers often demonstrate greater needs for institutional power and lesser needs for personal power than their male counterparts.[37]

▼ Machiavellianism

Niccolo Machiavelli was a sixteenth-century Italian philosopher and statesman whose best-known writings include a set of suggestions for obtaining and holding governmental power. Over the centuries, Machiavelli has come to be associated with the use of deceit and opportunism in interpersonal relations. Thus **Machiavellians** are people who view and manipulate others for their own purposes.

As a personal style of behavior toward others, **Machiavellianism** is characterized by (1) the use of guile and deceit in interpersonal relationships, (2) a cynical view of the nature of other people, and (3) a lack of concern with conventional morality.[38] A person who scores high on a test to measure Machiavellianism probably agrees with the following statements.

▲ The best way to handle people is to tell them what they want to hear.

▲ Anyone who completely trusts anyone else is asking for trouble.

▲ Never tell anyone the real reason you did something unless it is useful to do so.

▲ It is wise to flatter important people.

Machiavellians are likely to be effective manipulators of other people. They often effectively influence others, particularly in face-to-face contacts, and tend to initiate and control social interactions. As a result, Machiavellianism can be associated with a tendency to engage in political behavior. For example, a study that examined the relationship between a propensity to engage in political behavior in organizations and a variety of individual differences reported that Machiavellianism was the strongest correlate of political behavior among the variables investigated.[39] The study concluded that Machiavellianism may be a good predictor of political behavior in many organizational situations.

▼ Locus of Control

Recall that **locus of control** refers to the extent to which individuals believe that they can control events that affect them (see Chapter 2). Individuals with a high internal locus of control believe that events result primarily from their own behavior. Those with a high external locus of control believe that powerful others, fate, or chance primarily determine events. Internals tend to exhibit more political behaviors than externals and are more likely to attempt to influence other people. Further, they are more likely to assume that their efforts will be successful. The study of relationships among political behavior and individual differences referred to in the preceding section also supported the notion that the propensity to engage in political behavior is stronger for individuals who have a high internal locus of control than for those who have a high external locus of control.

▼ Risk-Seeking Propensity

Individuals differ (sometimes markedly) in their willingness to take risks, or in their **risk-seeking propensity.** Some people are risk avoiders, and others can be described as risk seekers.[40] Negative outcomes (such as demotions, low performance ratings, and loss of influence) are possible for individuals and groups who engage in political behavior in organizations. Engaging in political activity isn't risk free; to advocate a position and to seek support for it is to risk being perceived as opposing some other position. In many situations, risk seekers are more willing to engage in political behavior, whereas risk avoiders tend to avoid such behavior because of its possible consequences.

Summary

Power is the capacity to influence the behavior of others. Sources of power stem from interpersonal and structural factors in an organization. Interpersonal power sources can be categorized as reward power, coercive power, legitimate power, expert power, and referent power. Structural power differences stem from unequal access to information, resources, decision making, and networks with others. Lower level employees, despite their location in the organizational hierarchy, may have considerable power to influence events and behavior. Individuals who can effectively influence others' behavior usually understand clearly the sources of power—and the appropriate and fair uses of power. Such individuals also usually understand the important role that the exchange process plays in the ability to influence the behavior of others.

Organizational politics involves the use of power and other resources by individuals or groups to obtain their own preferred outcomes. Political behavior is inevitable, owing to naturally occurring disagreements and uncertainty about choices and actions. Political behavior can have both positive and negative consequences; it may or may not result in optimal decisions, and some real costs are associated with avoiding political behavior. Political behavior is more likely to occur when resources are scarce and/or rules and procedures are unclear. The performance appraisal process often invites political behavior, sometimes with negative consequences.

Certain personality traits predispose some people to political behavior. Specifically, the probability that individuals will engage in political influence attempts increases if they have (1) a high need for power, (2) a Machiavellian interpersonal style, (3) a high internal locus of control, and (4) a preference for risk taking.

Key Words and Concepts

Authority
Coercive power
Decision making as power
Exchange process
Expert power
Influence strategies
Intellectual capital
Knowledge as power

Legitimate power
Locus of control
Machiavellianism
Machiavellians
Need for power
Network analysis
Networks as power
Organizational politics

Political behavior
Power
Referent power
Resources as power
Reward power
Risk-seeking propensity
Zone of indifference

Discussion Questions

1. Compare and contrast interpersonal and structural sources of power in organizations.

2. Were you ever in a situation in which you had the power to influence the behavior of others? If so, explain the source or sources of your power.

3. Were you ever in a situation in which someone else had the power to influence your behavior? If so, explain the source or sources of their power.

4. Provide some suggestions for the effective use of power.

5. What is the nature of the exchange process in power relationships? Provide some examples of currencies that were commonly exchanged in an organization with which you are familiar.

6. Based on your own experiences, give examples of both the effective and ineffective use of power. Explain why each outcome occurred.

7. Define political behavior. What are some of the factors that can contribute to organizational politics?

8. Based on your own experience, describe a situation in which political behavior seemed to be excessive. Why did it occur?

9. Why is the performance appraisal process prone to political abuse? How can the probability of political behavior be minimized in this process?

▲ Developing Skills

Self-Diagnosis:
How Much Power Do You Have in Your Group?

Instructions

Think of a group of which you are a member. It could be a work group or team, a committee, a group project at your school, or the like. Respond to the statements below using the following scale.

Strongly Disagree	Disagree	Slightly Disagree	Neither Agree nor Disagree	Slightly Agree	Agree	Strongly Agree
1	2	3	4	5	6	7

_____ 1. I am one of the more vocal members of the group.

_____ 2. People in the group listen to what I have to say.

_____ 3. I often volunteer to lead the group.

_____ 4. I am able to influence group decisions.

_____ 5. I often find myself on "center stage" in group activities or discussions.

_____ 6. Members of the group seek me out for advice.

_____ 7. I take the initiative in the group and often am one of the first to speak out on important issues.

_____ 8. I receive recognition in the group for my ideas and contributions.

_____ 9. I would rather lead the group than be a participant.

_____10. My opinion is held in high regard by group members.

_____11. I volunteer my thoughts and ideas without hesitation

_____12. My ideas often are implemented.

_____13. I ask questions in meetings just to have something to say.

_____14. Group members often ask for my opinions and input.

____15. I often play the role of scribe, secretary, or note taker during meetings.

____16. Group members usually consult me about important matters before they make a decision.

____17. I clown around with other group members.

____18. I have noticed that group members often look at me, even when not talking directly to me.

____19. I jump right into whatever conflict the group members are dealing with.

____20. I am very influential in the group.

Scoring

Visibility	
Item	Your Score
1.	_____
3.	_____
5.	_____
7.	_____
9.	_____
11.	_____
13.	_____
15.	_____
17.	_____
19.	_____
Total	_____

Influence	
Item	Your Score
2.	_____
4.	_____
6.	_____
8.	_____
10.	_____
12.	_____
14.	_____
16.	_____
18.	_____
20.	_____
Total	_____

Use the scores calculated and mark your position on the Visibility/Influence matrix in Figure 15.6. The combinations of visibility and influence shown are described as follows.

1. *High visibility/high influence.* Group members in quadrant I exhibit behaviors that bring high visibility and allow them to exert influence on others. In organizations, these people may be the upwardly mobile or "fast trackers."

2. *High visibility/low influence.* Group members in quadrant II are highly visible but have little real influence. This condition could reflect their personal characteristics but also could indicate that formal power resides elsewhere in the organization. Often these people may hold staff, rather than line, positions that give them visibility but that lack "clout" to get things done.

3. *Low visibility/low influence.* Group members in quadrant III, for whatever reason, are neither seen nor heard. Individuals in this category may have difficulty advancing in the organization.

4. *Low visibility/high influence.* Group members in quadrant IV are "behind the scenes" influencers. These individuals often are opinion leaders and "sages" who wield influence but are content to stay out of the limelight.[41]

FIGURE 15.6

Visibility/Influence Matrix

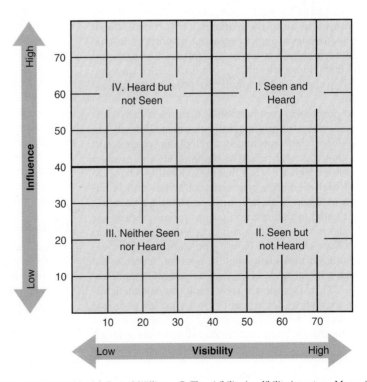

Source: Adapted from Reddy, W. B., and Williams, G. The visibility/credibility inventory: Measuring power and influence. In J. W. Pfeiffer (ed.), *The 1988 Annual: Developing Human Resources.* San Diego: University Associates, 124.

A Case In Point:
The NASA Moonlander Monitor

As a young engineer, Chuck House played a key role at Hewlett-Packard (H-P) in developing new applications for oscilloscope technology. The company's technology eventually was used in NASA's moon missions, although this happy ending was not without its political battles.

The story began when the Federal Aviation Administration (FAA) advertised for an improved airport control tower monitor. Hewlett-Packard developed such a monitor but lost out when the FAA selected another firm's design. However, House was convinced that the H-P design represented a significant technological breakthrough. The model that his team developed was smaller, faster, more energy efficient, and brighter than conventional monitors. Unfortunately, the model didn't seem to have a niche in the marketplace.

House set out to convince H-P of the merits of his team's monitor, even though the firm had lost the FAA contract. He proved to be a master political gamesman who violated a number of organizational rules and procedures. First, he collected his own market research data in direct violation of organizational boundaries, circumventing the marketing department. During an unauthorized trip, he visited 40 computer manufacturers to demonstrate the prototype. Not only did this arouse the ire of the marketing department, but it violated a security rule against showing prototypes to customers. However, based on marketing information gathered during the trip, House was able to convince senior management at H-P to continue development of the monitor, at least temporarily.

The next obstacle to continuation of the project came during an annual review of progress by senior management. The marketing department conducted a telephone survey and concluded that the total projected demand for the product was 32 monitors. House argued that the marketing data were flawed and that marketing was resistant to the project because of his invasion of their "turf." Further, the marketing department failed to understand the appropriate strategy for marketing the new monitor and had called only upon current oscilloscope customers. House's position was that new products required new customers. In addition, because the product was difficult to describe, only in-person demonstrations could sell it. Despite this reasoning, management accepted the marketing department's projection of potential demand rather than House's projection. (House again had obtained data through organizationally illegitimate means.)

As if the political resistance from marketing weren't enough, the project also lacked the support of the chief corporate engineer, who favored an alternative technology.

Not surprisingly, the senior management annual review concluded that there was insufficient market demand and a lack of technological support from others in the organization for this product. The project was to be canceled. David Packard, one of the two founders of H-P, even said: "When I come back next year, I don't want to see that project in the lab!"

At this point, House's political skills were put to their greatest test. House chose to interpret Packard's statement to mean that the project should be out of the lab in one year and in production, rather than that the project should be scrapped. With covert support from his boss, House and his group hid the development cost of the new monitor under other items in the budget. They then raced to complete the project within a year's time (easily only one-half of the normal time such development might be expected to take). The marketing department mounted continual opposition to the project, but House countered by convincing interested potential customers to intervene personally with senior management and express interest in the monitor.

Fortunately for House and the project, he and his team made the deadline. When Packard returned for the next annual review, the monitor was in the marketplace. Packard was said to be both angered and amused by this obvious reinterpretation of his order. However, perhaps because he himself was something of a maverick, Packard now chose to support the monitor. Rather than being punished, House and his development team were given the green light to continue to seek additional applications. The eventual uses for this oscilloscope monitor included the NASA moon mission, the medical monitor used in the first artificial heart transplant, and a large-screen oscilloscope that was part of a television special effects system that won an Emmy award. These important innovations could easily have fallen victim to opposing political forces in Hewlett-Packard.[42]

Questions

1. List and explain the sources of power that House used.
2. Identify and explain the factors that increased political behavior in Hewlett-Packard during this time.
3. Did House use power effectively or ineffectively? Defend your answer.
4. Suggest some strategies that House might have utilized to reduce the political resistance to this innovation.

References

1. Adapted from Frost, P. J., and Ergi, C. P. The political process of innovation. In L. L. Cummings and B. M. Staw (eds.), *Research in Organizational Behavior*, vol. 13. Greenwich, Conn.: JAI Press, 1991, 230, 251–252.

2. Finkelstein, S. Power in top management teams: Dimensions, measurement, and validation. *Academy of Management Journal*, 1992, 35, 505–538; Hollander, E. P., and Offerman, L. R. Power and leadership in organizations. *American Psychologist*, 1990, 45, 179–189; Keys, B., and Case, T. How to become an influential manager. *Academy of Management Executive*, 1990, 4(4), 38–51; Pfeffer, J. *Managing with Power: Politics and Influence in Organizations*. Boston: Harvard Business School Press, 1993.

3. Townley, B. Foucault, power/knowledge, and its relevance for human resource management. *Academy of Management Review*, 1993, 18, 518–545.

4. Adapted from Stewart, T. A. CEOs see clout shifting. *Fortune*, November 6, 1989, 66; Stewart, T. A. New ways to exercise power. *Fortune*, November 6, 1989, 52–64; Stewart, T. A. The king is dead. *Fortune*, January 11, 1993, 34–40.

5. Biggart, N. W., and Hamilton, G. G. The power of obedience. *Administrative Science Quarterly*, 1984, 29, 540–549; Hamilton, G. G., and Biggart, N. W. Why people obey: Theoretical observations on power and obedience in complex organizations. *Sociological Perspectives*, 1985, 28, 3–28; Pfeffer, J. *Power in Organizations*. Marshfield, Mass.: Pitman, 1981, 4–6.

6. French, J. R. P., and Raven, B. The bases of social power. In D. Cartwright (ed.), *Studies in Social Power*. Ann Arbor: University of Michigan Institute for Social Research, 1959, 150–167. Also see Hinkin, T. R., and Schriesheim, C. A. Development and application of new scales to measure the French and Raven (1959) bases of social power. *Journal of Applied Psychology*, 1989, 74, 561–567; Podsakoff, P. M., and Schrieshiem, C. A. Field studies of French and Raven's bases of power: Critique, reanalysis, and suggestions for future research. *Psychological Bulletin*, 1985, 97, 387–411; Yukl, G., and Falbe, C. M. Importance of different power sources in downward and lateral relations. *Journal of Applied Psychology*, 1991, 76, 416–423.

7. Barnard, C. I. *The Functions of the Executive*. Cambridge, Mass.: Harvard University Press, 1938. For additional perspectives on this issue, see Zelditch, M., and Walker, H. A. Legitimacy and the stability of authority. In S. B. Bacharach and E. J. Lawler (eds.), *Advances in Group Processes*, vol. 1. Greenwich, Conn.: JAI Press, 1984, 1–25.

8. Adapted from Bird, A. Power and the Japanese CEO. *Asia Pacific Journal of Management*, 1990, 7(2), 1–20.

9. Greene, C. N., and Podsakoff, P. M. Effects of withdrawal of a performance-contingent reward on supervisory influence and power. *Academy of Management Journal*, 1981, 24, 527–542.

10. Brass, D. J., and Burkhardt, M. E. Potential power and power use: An investigation of structure and behavior. *Academy of Management Journal*, 1993, 36, 441–470; Krackhardt, D. Assessing the political landscape: Structure, cognition, and power in organizations. *Administrative Science Quarterly*, 1990, 35, 342–369; Lackman, R. Power from what? A reexamination of its relationships with structural conditions. *Administrative Science Quarterly*, 1989, 34, 231–251. Pfeffer, J. *Power in Organizations*. Marshfield, Mass.: Pitman, 1981, 101–122.

11. Adapted from Wilke, J. R. Computer links erode hierarchical nature of workplace culture. *Wall Street Journal*, December 9, 1993, A1, A7.

12. Stewart, T. A. Brainpower. *Fortune*, June 3, 1991, 44–60; Welsh, T. Best and worst corporate reputations. *Fortune*, February 7, 1994, 58–66.

13. Baker, S., and Alexander, K. L. The owners vs. the boss at Weirton Steel. *Business Week*, November 15, 1993, 38.

14. Henkoff, R. How to plan for 1995. *Fortune*, December 31, 1990, 70–81.

15. Adapted from Wang, Z., and Heller, F. A. Patterns of power distribution in managerial decision making in Chinese and British industrial organizations. *International Journal of Human Resource Management*, 1993, 4(1), 113–128.

16. Kanter, R. M. Power failure in management circuits. *Harvard Business Review*, July–August 1979, 66. Also see Ibarra, H., and Andrews, S. B. Power, social influence, and sense making: Effects of network centrality and proximity on employee perceptions. *Administrative Science Quarterly*, 1993, 38, 277–303.

17. Krackhardt, D., and Hanson, J. R. Informal networks: The company behind the chart. *Harvard Business Review*, July–August 1993, 104–111.

18. Adapted from Lesly, E., and Mallory, M. Inside the black business network. *Business Week*, November 29, 1993, 70–71.

19. See, for example, Blackburn, R. S. Lower participant power: Toward a conceptual integration. *Academy of Management Review*, 1981, 6, 127–131; Mechanic, D. Sources of power of lower participants in complex organizations. *Administrative Science Quarterly*, 1962, 7, 349–364; Porter, L. W., Allen, R. W., and Angle, L. L. The politics of upward influence in organizations. In L. L. Cummings and B. M. Staw (eds.), *Research in Organizational Behavior*, vol. 3. Greenwich, Conn.: JAI Press, 1981, 109–149.

20. Falbe, C. M., and Yukl, G. Consequences of managers using single influence tactics and combinations of tactics. *Academy of Management Journal*, 1992, 35, 638–652; Kipnis, D., Schmidt, S. M., Swaffin-Smith, C., and Wilkinson, I. Patterns of managerial influence: Shotgun managers, tacticians, and bystanders. *Organizational Dynamics*, Winter 1984, 60–61; Yukl, G., Falbe, C. M., and Youn, J. Y. Patterns of influence behavior for managers. *Group & Organization Management*, 1993, 18, 5–28; Yukl, G., and Tracey, J. B. Consequences of influence tactics used with subordinates, peers, and the boss. *Journal of Applied Psychology*, 1992, 77, 525–535.

21. Schmidt, S. M., and Kipnis, D. The perils of persistence. *Psychology Today*, November 1987, 32–34. Also see Judge, T. A., and Bretz, R. D. Political influence behavior and career success. *Journal of Management*, 1994, 20, 43–65.

22. Cohen, A. R., and Bradford, D. L. Influence without authority: The use of alliances, reciprocity, and exchange to accomplish work. *Organizational Dynamics*, Winter 1989, 5–17.

23. These characteristics of managerial effectiveness are based, in part, on Kotter, J. P. Power, dependence, and effective management. *Harvard Business Review*, April 1977, 125–136; Kotter, J. P. *Power and Influence*. New York: Free Press, 1985.

24. Ferris, G. R., and Judge, T. A. Personnel/human resources management: A political influence perspective. *Journal of Manage-*

ment, 1991, 17, 447–488; Pfeffer, J. *Power in Organizations*. Marshfield, Mass.: Pitman, 1981, 7.

25. Adapted from Machan, D. Gladiators' ball. *Forbes*, December 26, 1988, 130–134.

26. Ferris, G. R., and Kacmar, K. M. Perceptions of organizational politics. *Journal of Management*, 1992, 18, 93–116.

27. Madison, D. L., Allen, R. W., Porter, L. W., Renwick, P. A., and Mayes, B. T. Organizational politics: An exploration of managers' perceptions. *Human Relations*, 1980, 33, 79–100.

28. Baum, H. S. Organizational politics against organizational culture: A psychoanalytic perspective. *Human Resource Management*, Summer 1989, 191–206.

29. Beemon, D. R., and Sharkey, T. W. The use and abuse of corporate politics. *Business Horizons*, March–April 1987, 26–30.

30. Kacmar, K. M., and Ferris, G. R. Politics at work: Sharpening the focus of political behavior in organizations. *Business Horizons*, July–August, 1993, 70–74.

31. Ibid.

32. Excerpted with permission from Longenecker, C. O., Sims, H. P., and Gioia, D. A. Behind the mask: The politics of employee appraisal. *Academy of Management Executive*, 1987, 1, 183–193.

33. Gioia, D. A., and Longenecker, C. O. Delving into the dark side: The politics of executive appraisal. *Organizational Dynamics*, Winter 1994, 54.

34. Ibid., 56.

35. The sections on these personality differences are based, in part, on House, R. J. Power and personality in complex organizations. In B. M. Staw and L. L. Cummings (eds.), *Research in Organizational Behavior*, vol. 10. Greenwich, Conn.: JAI Press, 1988, 305–357; Porter, L. W., Allen, R. W., and Angle, L. L. The politics of upward influence in organizations. In L. L. Cummings and

B. M. Staw (eds.), *Research in Organizational Behavior*, vol. 3. Greenwich, Conn.: JAI Press, 1981, 120–122; Ragins, B. R., and Sundstrom, E. Gender and power in organizations: A longitudinal perspective. *Psychological Bulletin*, 1989, 105, 70–72.

36. House, R. J., and Singh, J. V. Organizational behavior: Some new directions for I/O psychology. *Annual Review of Psychology*, 1987, 38, 672–678; McClelland, D. C. *Human Motivation*. Glenview, Ill.: Scott, Foresman, 1985; McClelland, D. C., and Boyatzis, R. E. Leadership motive pattern and long-term success in management. *Journal of Applied Psychology*, 1982, 67, 737–743.

37. Ragins, B. R., and Sundstrom, E. Gender and power in organizations: A longitudinal perspective. *Psychological Bulletin*, 1989, 105, 70.

38. Christie, R., and Geis, F. L. *Studies in Machiavellianism*. New York: Academic Press, 1970.

39. Woodman, R. W., Wayne, S. J., and Rubinstein, D. Personality correlates of a propensity to engage in political behavior in organizations. *Proceedings of the Southwest Academy of Management*, 1985, 131–135. Also see Nelson, G., and Gilbertson, D. Organizational Machiavellianism: The ruthlessness of opportunism. *Proceedings of the Southwest Academy of Management*, 1991, 119–122.

40. Sitkin, S. B., and Pablo, A. L. Reconceptualizing the determinants of risk behavior. *Academy of Management Review*, 1992, 17, 9–38.

41. Adapted from Reddy, W. B., and Williams, G. The visibility/credibility inventory: Measuring power and influence. In J. W. Pfeiffer (ed.), *The 1988 Annual: Developing Human Resources*. San Diego: University Associates, 1988, 115–124.

42. Adapted from Frost, P. J., and Egri, C. P. The political process of innovation. In L. L. Cummings and B. M. Staw (eds.), *Research in Organizational Behavior*, vol. 13. Greenwich, Conn.: JAI Press, 1991, 246–248.

16 Job Design

After you have finished this chapter, you should be able to:

▲ Describe five approaches to job design and indicate the differences between them.

▲ Discuss the relationship between reengineering and job design.

▲ Indicate the problems caused by poorly designed jobs.

▲ Discuss the linkages between technology and job design.

▲ Describe the job characteristics enrichment model and explain how it may affect performance, work motivation, and satisfaction.

▲ Explain the primary components of the sociotechnical systems approach to job design.

OUTLINE

Preview Case: Maids International

Introduction to Job Design

Relation to Reengineering

Managing Quality: Job Redesign at Vortex

Comparative Framework

Common Job Design Approaches

Job Rotation

Job Engineering

Managing in Practice: Job Engineering by Teams at NUMMI

Job Enlargement

Job Enrichment

Sociotechnical Systems

Managing Diversity: The Disabled and Job Design

Technology and Job Design

Work-Flow and Task Uncertainty

Task Interdependence

Managing Quality: Metz Baking Company

Job Characteristics Enrichment Model

Basic Framework

Job Characteristics

Individual Differences

Managing Ethics: Electronic Monitoring of Work

Job Diagnosis

Implementation Approaches

Technology and Job Characteristics

Managing in Practice: Technology and Redesign of Tellers' Jobs

Social Information Processing

Sociotechnical Systems Model

Social System

Technological System

Moderators

Key Principles

Managing Across Cultures: Volvo's Uddevalla Versus NUMMI

Organizational Significance

DEVELOPING SKILLS

Self-Diagnosis: Redesign of the Data Entry Operator Job

A Case in Point: McGuire Industry

PREVIEW CASE

Maids International

Maids International is a highly successful housecleaning service franchise. It hires mostly women, including part-timers with young children, and pays them between $4.25 and $7.50 an hour. This wage rate means that the company draws from the same labor pool as fast-food and other such businesses. To be successful, management believed that the company couldn't afford the high turnover normally associated with those types of businesses. So, says CEO Dan Bishop, "We focused the whole concept of the company on the labor. Fatigue and boredom are what burns people out. We tried to eliminate them."

Maids International management studied employees to determine how they worked, minute by minute. Examination of every task performed revealed that a lot of unnecessary work was being done. Changes were made. Now the maids wind a vacuum cord in three seconds rather than the eight seconds it used to take. They bend over 30 times rather than the 72 times it used to take to clean the average house. By working in foursomes, they are able to rotate jobs better. A maid who cleans a kitchen in one house may do a bedroom in another. The job design approach of Maids International concentrated on eliminating work and forming small work teams. The teams created opportunities for social interaction to reduce boredom. Also, they enabled job rotation to increase variety in the specific tasks performed.

Has all this concentration on how the job is designed paid off? If turnover is one measure of success, the answer is yes. Maids International's employees stay with the job about nine months, compared to five months at such places as fast-food businesses.[1]

To enhance jobs while eliminating work, you must remain focused on what you are trying to accomplish. In discussing white-collar jobs, Carl Paonessa, a partner at Anderson Consulting in Chicago, says, "Conditions cannot be improved by blindly computerizing office work. Rather than just automating something, it is better to eliminate bottlenecks, reduce mistakes, focus on the customer, and then introduce (labor-saving) new technology."[2] As discussed in previous chapters, new information technologies are affecting how employees perform their jobs, as well as the tasks that make up their jobs. In addition, social forces and attitudes must be taken into account in how jobs are designed.[3] (In Chapter 19, we discuss the broader implications of information technologies for organizational change.)

This chapter contains five sections. First, we introduce job design by (1) defining it, (2) explaining its relationship to reengineering, and (3) proposing a method for comparing job design approaches. Second, we present an overview of five common job design approaches, two of which we discuss in greater detail in the last two sections of the chapter. Third, we present a framework for determining how job design is likely to vary in different technological situations. Fourth, we provide a fairly detailed discussion of the job characteristics enrichment model; it is one of the best known job design approaches for addressing the motivational needs of individuals. Finally, we describe the sociotechnical systems model, the most complex and significant job design approach discussed in this chapter.

▼ INTRODUCTION TO JOB DESIGN

We have emphasized the importance of appropriately designed jobs in our discussion of work motivation, commented on the importance of designing jobs to give individuals challenging goals, and discussed many ideas relevant to job design in terms of the dynamics within groups and teams (see Chapters 6, 7, and 10, respectively). For example, the introduction of problem-solving teams, special-purpose teams, and self-managed teams into organizations changes and enlarges the tasks performed by employees. In this chapter, we further develop and extend the job design concepts and issues introduced in those earlier chapters.

Job design is the specification of tasks that are to be performed by employees, including expected interpersonal and task relationships. Job design occurs every time individuals are assigned work, given instructions, or empowered to perform tasks and pursue goals. Consciously or unconsciously, their managers, team members, or others may change the job-related tasks of employees. Because both the tasks and the best means for performing them change, managers and teams need to know how to design and redesign jobs formally to make them as motivating and meaningful as possible. We share the view that the needs and goals of employees and the organization both should be considered in the design or redesign of jobs.[4] The job design changes for house-cleaning personnel at Maids International benefited both the employees and the firm.

The ideal situation is the effective use of employees' competencies and skills to create and deliver quality products and services most efficiently.[5] Although this ideal state isn't always attainable, substantial improvements in job design usually are possible and can also benefit the consumer. For example, improving the design of production workers' jobs in automobile plants has improved the quality of cars. These efforts directly benefited the workers and enhanced car owners and the firms' positions in the market.

▼ Relation to Reengineering

Job design is one of the cornerstones of organizational reengineering efforts. **Reengineering** refers to radically new ways of thinking about organizations, including breaking away from the outdated rules and assumptions that underlie how tasks have been performed in the past. The purpose of reengineering is to eliminate—or prevent—the erection of barriers that create a distance between employees and consumers. The design of an organization should be based on collections of tasks that create value. The term used to describe such collections is *processes*. Processes are value-adding and value-creating collections of activities and tasks. Some examples are product development, customer acquisition, customer service, and order fulfillment.[6] Michael Hammer, an MIT professor, first coined the term *reengineering* in a 1990 article entitled *Reengineering Work: Don't Automate, Obliterate.*[7] More recently, he stated the cornerstone role of job design in reengineering as follows:

> Reengineering means radically changing how we do our work. That's a very important word—work. People often ask me questions about managing, but for me the issue is work. Work is the way in which we create value for customers, how

we design, invent and make products, how we sell them, how we serve customers. Reengineering means radically rethinking and redesigning those processes by which we create value and do work.[8]

The reengineering process is more comprehensive than four of the five job design approaches discussed in this chapter. The three "R's" of reengineering—rethink, redesign, and retool—represent separate but related phases.

▲ *Rethink*: This phase requires examining the organization's current goals and underlying assumptions to determine how well they incorporate a renewed commitment to customer satisfaction. Another element in this phase is to examine crucial success factors—those areas that set the organization apart from its competition. Do they contribute to the goal of customer satisfaction?

▲ *Redesign*: This phase requires an analysis of the way an organization produces the products or services it sells—how jobs are structured, who accomplishes what tasks, and the results of each procedure. Then, a determination must be made as to which elements should be redesigned to increase job satisfaction and customer focus.

▲ *Retool*: This phase requires a thorough evaluation of the current use of advanced technologies, especially groupware aids, to identify opportunities for change to improve the quality of services, products, and customer satisfaction.[9]

The application of reengineering isn't limited to large organizations, as the following Managing Quality feature on Vortex Industries of Costa Mesta, California, demonstrates. Vortex is a $10 million, 130-employee, family-owned company that repairs and replaces warehouse doors. The grandfather of the current president, Frank Fulkerson, founded it in 1937.

MANAGING QUALITY

Job Redesign at Vortex

Frank Fulkerson, the current president of Vortex, had been away from the company for most of the preceding three years, helping his wife establish an insurance agency. During that time his partner, a man 20 years his senior, ran Vortex. Fulkerson had sold him a one-third interest in the business in 1978. "It was a great partnership," Fulkerson says, "and probably still would be today if it hadn't been for just one area of disagreement." The partner wanted Vortex to be a highly centralized, top-down organization, and Fulkerson didn't. As a result, Fulkerson bought out his partner. The company had three locations, but most of its people and equipment were at one location near downtown Los Angeles—even though Vortex's customers were spread across six counties. Fulkerson says, "We were trying to handle so much business at headquarters that we lost control of it. Vortex had 'stratified' itself. Each person was stuck in his or her little cut-out job. The receptionist only answered the phone. The material people only ordered and received. The billing clerk only billed. They each felt like what they did was such a small part of the equation that they didn't make a difference."

MANAGING QUALITY —*Continued*

As an experiment, he split off from headquarters one branch of the company in one county and rearranged the duties of everyone who worked there. Fulkerson created a new position, branch manager, and assigned to that one person a variety of functions—sales, purchasing, and dispatch, among others. Previously, these functions had been divided among people in several rigid categories at the central office and in the field. Another new position, office manager, likewise combined pieces of several functions. The change greatly reduced the isolation between Vortex's processes. The branch manager was responsible not just for quoting the customer a price for the repair of a door but also for getting the service trucks there at the agreed-upon time. Employees who actually repaired the doors were permanently attached to that branch and dealt only with customers in that county. Fulkerson comments: "Since there were only five service agents, they soon came to know and like each other and their customers."

Using the experimental branch as a model, he carved the company's entire territory into six independent branches and maintained a lightly staffed headquarters office. There are now ten branches in Southern California and one in Denver. Weekly communication meetings were instituted in every branch. The adjustment was hard at first, he says. Many employees "liked things just the way they were. It seemed like the people in the office didn't want new responsibilities or new challenges. The field guys didn't want to have to worry about quality or customer service. They just wanted to go out and fix the door."

Most of the employees couldn't adapt to the change. They were uncomfortable when left on their own, Fulkerson says. Turnover was 75% in the first year. The employees who remained—and the new ones who were hired—responded to the change quite differently. The redesign of jobs meant that employees had to master several sets of skills. Also, team leaders had to be technically adept, good at sales, and good managers. The employees didn't feel burdened by these multiple responsibilities, Fulkerson says, adding that "it turns out they enjoy doing all of these things."[10]

▼ Comparative Framework

Figure 16.1 shows five of the most common approaches to job design, contrasted in terms of impact and complexity. *Impact* refers to the extent to which a job design approach is likely to be linked to factors beyond the immediate job—such as reward systems, performance appraisal methods, leadership practices of managers, organization structure, physical working conditions, and team composition and norms—as well as its likely effects on changes in productivity and quality. *Complexity* means the extent to which a job design approach is likely to require (1) changes in many factors, (2) the involvement of individuals with diverse skills at various organizational levels; and (3) high levels of decision-making skills for successful implementation. In relation to Figure 16.1, the redesign of the housecleaning jobs at Maids International might be characterized in terms of both impact and complexity as somewhere between low and medium. In contrast, the redesign of the jobs at Vortex would be between medium and high in impact and complexity.

FIGURE 16.1

Comparison of Five Job Design
Approaches

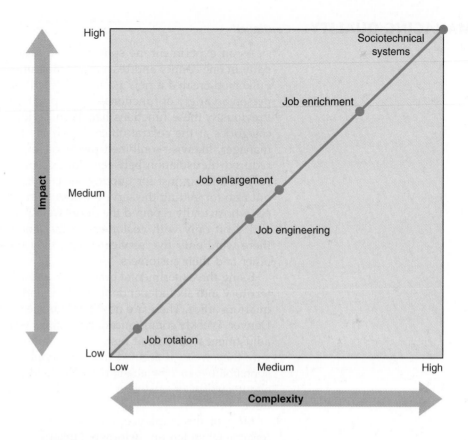

The five approaches shown in Figure 16.1 and summarized in the next section do not represent all the important job design approaches. For example, a job design perspective of renewed interest is the **human factor approach,** which focuses on minimizing the physical demands (costs) and biological risks at work and sometimes is referred to as *ergonomics*. The goal of the human factors approach is to ensure that the design of jobs doesn't exceed people's physical capabilities to perform them. This approach includes the design of aids (ranging from hand tools to computer software to instruments) used to perform jobs.[11]

▼ COMMON JOB DESIGN APPROACHES

This section provides an overview of the five common job design approaches shown in Figure 16.1: job rotation, job engineering, job enlargement, job enrichment, and sociotechnical systems. We expand on the job enrichment and sociotechnical systems approaches in later sections.

▼ Job Rotation

Job rotation involves moving employees from job to job, thereby giving them an opportunity to perform a greater variety of tasks. Job rotation is low in both impact and complexity because its primary purpose is to move employees among current jobs. Most often, job rotation focuses on adding variety to reduce employee boredom. Maids International used the job rotation approach with its four-person housecleaning teams by, for example, having a maid clean the kitchen in one house and the bedroom in another. However, if all the tasks are similar and routine, job rotation may not have the desired effect. For example, rotating automobile assembly-line workers from bolting bumpers on cars to bolting on tire rims isn't likely to reduce their boredom. Job rotation may be of benefit if it is part of a larger redesign effort and/or it is used as a training technique to improve the skills and flexibility of employees.

▼ Job Engineering

Late in the nineteenth century, Frederick W. Taylor established the foundation for modern industrial engineering. It is concerned with product design, process design, tool design, plant layout, work measurement, and operator methods. **Job engineering** focuses on the tasks to be performed, methods to be used, work flow between employees, layout of the workplace, performance standards, and interdependencies between people and machines. Analysts often examine these job design factors by means of time-and-motion studies, determining the time required to do each task and the movements needed to perform it efficiently.

Specialization of labor and efficiency are two of the cornerstones of job engineering. High levels of specialization are intended to (1) allow workers to learn a task rapidly, (2) permit short work cycles so performance can be almost automatic and involve little or no mental effort, (3) make hiring easier because low-skilled people can be easily trained and paid relatively low wages, and (4) reduce the need for supervision, owing to simplified jobs and standardization.

Many managers and industrial engineers now recognize that traditional job engineering also can create boring jobs. Yet it remains an important job design approach because its immediate cost savings can be measured easily. In addition, this approach is concerned with appropriate levels of automation—tending to look for ways to replace workers with machines to perform the most physically demanding and routine tasks.[12]

The following five questions further define the intent of the job engineering approach.

▲ *Job specialization*: Is the job highly specialized in terms of purpose and/or activity?

▲ *Task simplification*: Are the tasks simple and uncomplicated?

▲ *Job simplification*: Does the job require relatively little skill and training time?

▲ *Repetition*: Does the job require performing the same activity or activities repeatedly?

▲ *Automation*: Are many of the activities of this job automated or assisted by automation?[13]

The job engineering approach continues to be widely and often successfully used, especially when it is combined with a concern for the social context in which the jobs are performed. In Fremont, California, a GM–Toyota joint venture called New United Motor Manufacturing Inc. (NUMMI), has succeeded with an innovative form of Taylor's job engineering approach on the factory floor to (1) create world-class productivity and quality, and (2) increase worker motivation and satisfaction. The following Managing in Practice item reports on this unique program. NUMMI's approach is distinctive in two respects. First, it has a strong commitment to the social context in which work is performed. Second, it focuses intensively on creating standardized work through job engineering.

MANAGING IN PRACTICE

Job Engineering by Teams at NUMMI

In terms of social context, NUMMI tries to build an atmosphere of trust and common purpose. It employs various means to do so, but we present only a representative sample. The basic organizational unit at NUMMI is the production team, of which it has approximately 350. Each team consists of five to seven people and a leader. The idea is that small teams encourage participative decision making and bonding. Four teams comprise a group, led by a group leader who represents the first level of management. Beyond the production teams, the bigger team is everyone—all the workers, team leaders, managers, engineers, and staff in the plant and NUMMI's suppliers. The leadership of NUMMI wants workers to understand that the company isn't solely the property of management. In NUMMI's view, the primary purpose and responsibility of management is to support the production teams with problem-solving expertise. One expression of the big-team strategy is the no-layoff policy spelled out in NUMMI's collective-bargaining agreement with the union.

There are dramatic differences in job engineering at NUMMI and at most other organizations. For example, team members themselves hold the stopwatch. They learn the techniques of work analysis, description, and improvement. Team members begin by timing one another with stopwatches, looking for the safest and most efficient way to do each task at a sustainable pace. They pick the best performance, break it down into its fundamental parts, and explore ways of improving each element. The team then compares the resulting analyses with those of the other shift at the same work station and writes detailed specifications that become the standard work definition for everyone on both teams. Taking part in the analytical and descriptive work involves every team member in a commitment to perform each task identically. In one sense, therefore, standardized work is simply a means of reducing variability in task performance, which may seem to be a relatively trivial achievement. In fact, reduced variability leads to a whole series of interconnected improvements. For example, flexibility improves because all workers are now "industrial engineers" and can work in parallel to respond rapidly to changing demands. As a result, NUMMI can convert to a new line in four to six weeks, which might easily take four months in many automobile plants. Engineers in those plants often frantically recalculate thousands of tasks and try to force the new standards on workers.

Most of the production employees at NUMMI see automobile assembly as work that can never have much intrinsic value. One NUMMI worker stated: "What we have here is not some workers' utopia. Working on an assembly line in an automobile factory is still a lousy job. . . . We want to continue to minimize the negative parts of the job by utilizing the new system."[14]

Some of the concepts and tools of job engineering—such as carefully studying work flow between employees, methods to be used, and layout of the workplace—often are used in reengineering.[15]

▼ Job Enlargement

Job enlargement expands the number of different tasks performed by the employee. For example, one automobile assembly-line worker's job was enlarged from installing just one taillight to installing both taillights and the trunk. An auto mechanic switched from only changing oil to changing oil, greasing, and changing transmission fluid. Job enlargement attempts to add somewhat similar tasks to the job so that it will have more variety and be more interesting. As Figure 16.1 suggests, job enlargement is viewed as an extension of job engineering. However, it is more responsive to the higher level needs of employees by providing more variety in their jobs.

Although this approach often has positive effects, employees may resist it. Some employees view job enlargement as just adding more routine, boring tasks to their already boring job. Other employees may view it as eliminating the advantage of being able to perform their jobs almost automatically. These employees may value their opportunity to daydream about a big date that night or a vacation next month. Others may simply prefer to spend their time socializing with co-workers. If an enlarged job requires more careful attention and concentration, some employees may find it interesting, but others may view it negatively. Management should not underestimate the importance of individual differences in attempting to anticipate or understand the reactions of employees to redesigned jobs. Recall the Managing Quality feature on Vortex, where both the job enlargement and job enrichment approaches were used. Frank Fulkerson commented that many of the employees "liked things just as they were. It seemed like the people in the office didn't want new responsibilities or new challenges. The field guys didn't want to have to worry about quality or customer service. They just wanted to fix the door." After turnover of 75% in the first year after the changes, the remaining and new employees responded positively.

▼ Job Enrichment

Job enrichment adds tasks to employees' jobs by allowing them to assume more responsibility and accountability for planning, organizing, controlling, and evaluating their own work.[16] By giving teams added job engineering responsibilities, NUMMI enriched the individual jobs of production workers. The job enrichment approach originated in the 1940s at International Business Machines (IBM). In the 1950s, the number of companies interested in job enrichment grew slowly. Successful and widely publicized experiments at AT&T, Texas Instruments (TI), and Imperial Chemicals led to an increasing awareness of and interest in job enrichment in the 1960s.[17] The techniques used for enriching jobs often are specific to the job being redesigned. We discuss enrichment techniques when we present the job characteristics enrichment model.

▼ Sociotechnical Systems

The **sociotechnical systems model** considers every organization to be made up of people (the social system) using tools, techniques, and knowledge (the technical system) to produce goods or services valued by customers. The social and technical systems need to be designed with respect to one another and to the demands of groups in the external environment. To a large extent, this design determines how effective the organization will be. Although every organization is a sociotechnical system, it isn't necessarily based on the principles that are part of this approach.[18]

The fundamental goal of sociotechnical systems is to find the *best possible* match among the technology available, the people involved, and the organization's needs.[19] The sociotechnical systems approach recognizes the interdependence of tasks, which become the basis for forming natural work teams. After these work teams have been formed, the specific tasks to be performed by each member of a work team are considered. This approach has been applied most successfully—as has the job enrichment approach—to industrial organizations.

The sociotechnical systems approach emphasizes the diagnosis of demands by stakeholders (customers, suppliers, etc.) in the external environment and the internal adaptations needed to respond to those demands. From a job design perspective, passage of the Americans with Disabilities Act (ADA) in 1990 created one such demand for many U.S.-based organizations. The following Managing Diversity account suggests a few of the possible modifications that may be required of U.S. employers under the ADA.

MANAGING DIVERSITY

The Disabled and Job Design

Employers need to know who is a qualified person with a disability. The ADA defines this to be any individual who, with or without reasonable accommodation, can perform the essential functions of the job the individual has or wants. Essential functions are those that are necessary and fundamental to the job in question (as distinguished from incidental or marginal tasks) and those skills or abilities that are necessary to perform such tasks.

The definition of reasonable accommodation depends on the particular individual, the specific nature of his or her disability, and the specific job. Reasonable accommodation is the means provided by an employer to eliminate barriers to employment opportunities facing disabled persons and ensure that disabled persons can compete with non-disabled persons on a level playing field. There are two main types of barriers: (1) those relating to access to the job site or to common areas; and (2) those relating to performance of the job. The ADA says that reasonable accommodation may include: (1) modifying existing employment facilities to make them readily accessible to individuals with disabilities; and (2) making modifications such as job restructuring; part-time or modified work schedules; reassignment to vacant positions; acquiring, adjusting, or modifying equipment or devices; adjusting or modifying examinations; developing new training materials or policies; providing qualified readers or interpreters; and other similar accommodations.

Consider the reasonable accommodation by a firm for a computer operator who used a mouse for most of his work. He lost the ability to grip with his fingers and could no longer control the mouse. The accommodation in his

MANAGING DIVERSITY —*Continued*

case was to find an elastic hair band, glue velcro to the band, and glue some velcro to the mouse. The hair band then slipped over his fingers, and he had no problem using the mouse. The point of this incident is that establishing a list of disabilities for a given job, determining which disabilities can be accommodated, and specifying what the accommodations need to be is virtually impossible without reference to particular disabled individuals.[20]

▼ TECHNOLOGY AND JOB DESIGN

Technology refers to the application of science to invent techniques and machines to transform objects (material, information, and people) in support of desired goals.[21] Drawing from this definition, the **technical system** of an organization comprises the tools, techniques, methods, procedures, and knowledge used by employees to acquire inputs, transform inputs into outputs, and provide goods or services to clients and customers.[22] Our technology–job design discussion relates the concepts of work-flow uncertainty, task uncertainty, and task interdependence to job design. We also present some examples of how various information technologies are being used to implement these concepts. Of course, there are other approaches for relating technology to job design.[23] Earlier we outlined various ways that the work of individuals and teams is being changed by new information technologies, especially with groupware (see Chapters 9, 10, and 12). We defined *groupware* as specialized computer aids, communication tools, and designated physical facilities. We stated that groupware enables teams—and we now add individual employees—to work faster, share information, make decisions, and achieve their goals.

▼ Work-Flow and Task Uncertainty

Work-flow uncertainty is the degree of knowledge that an employee has about when inputs will be received and require processing. When there is little work-flow uncertainty, an employee may have little discretion (autonomy) to decide which, when, or where tasks will be performed. For the most part, the production workers at the NUMMI plant experience a low degree of work-flow uncertainty. In fact, the application of its job engineering approach through the use of work teams is intended to minimize work-flow uncertainty. **Task uncertainty** is the degree of knowledge that an employee has about how to perform the job and when it needs to be done. When there is little task uncertainty, an employee has a lot of knowledge about how to produce the desired results.[24] Through extensive training and the standardization of jobs, the NUMMI plant attempts to minimize task uncertainty. However, its production employees experience somewhat more task uncertainty when they meet as teams to study and refine work procedures. At NUMMI, all the teams are asked to participate in proposing continuous improvements, which is one of the elements in total quality management.

With high task uncertainty, there are few (if any) prespecified ways for dealing with some or many of the job's tasks. This condition means that experience, judgment, intuition, and problem-solving ability usually are required by the employee. Recall that Frank Fulkerson, president of Vortex, introduced higher levels of both task and work-flow uncertainty in formulating and implementing changes.

Figure 16.2 shows the possible combinations of work-flow uncertainty and task uncertainty. Each of the four cells contain examples of jobs that fall primarily into each category. Be careful not to stereotype particular jobs in thinking of them *only* in terms of a single position on the grid. Redesign often modifies jobs and changes their levels of task and work-flow uncertainty. Managerial jobs—including some top-management jobs—could range from the extreme upper right corner in cell 3 to closer to the center of the grid. Also, some jobs do not fit neatly into a single cell. For example, an auditor's job at an accounting firm might generally be plotted somewhere in the middle of the grid.

Job enrichment programs generally increase task uncertainty and/or work-flow uncertainty. However, the assembly-line job shown in cell 1 of Figure 16.2 could be enriched but still be generally classified as a cell-1 type of job— the situation at the NUMMI plant. Figure 16.2 also suggests how jobs could become too enriched. Some people who occupy cell-3 types of jobs could experience stress from too much work-flow and task uncertainty (see Chapter 8).

▼ Task Interdependence

Task interdependence is the degree to which decision making and cooperation between two or more employees is necessary for them to perform their jobs. At Austin Industries, erecting the structural steel framework of a high-rise building involves a high degree of task interdependence among the crane operator, ground crew, and assembly crew in moving and joining the steel girders. (Recall the discussion of independent, interdependent, and dependent task relations in Chapter 10.)

FIGURE 16.2

Technology Framework and Job Design

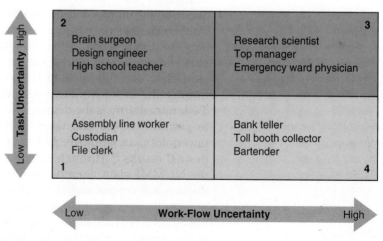

Source: Adapted from Slocum, J. W., Jr., and Sims, H. P., Jr. Typology for integrating technology, organization and job design. *Human Relations,* 1980, 33, 196; Susman, G. I. *Autonomy at Work—A Sociotechnical Analysis of Participative Management.* New York: Praeger, 1980, 132.

The three basic types of interdependent task relations are pooled, sequential, and reciprocal.[25] **Pooled interdependence** occurs when an employee is not required to communicate extensively with other individuals in the organization to complete their task(s). William Raveis Real Estate is primarily a residential brokerage firm based in Shelton, Connecticut. It has 40 offices and 1,200 sales associates, each of whom acts as an independent contractor. Each agent maintains a database of potential property buyers and sellers. Until a property is listed in the local multiple listing service (MLS), the sales associates control access to their data. The sales associates even purchase the laptop computers and printers they use in their work— and even pay for part of the software required. In the near future, the company plans to program actual contracts on the laptop so that the agents can negotiate deals and print out a final agreement in one meeting with buyer and seller. The firm also will be adding "pen capabilities" to the laptops so that agents can take notes during property "walk throughs."[26] Clearly, most of the time the jobs of the 1,200 associates within William Raveis Real Estate fit the concept of pooled interdependence.

Sequential interdependence occurs when one employee must complete certain tasks before other employees can perform their tasks. In other words, the outputs from some employees become the inputs for other employees. The sequence of interdependencies can be a long chain in some mass-production technologies. The automobile assembly line at the NUMMI plant is an example of sequential interdependence.

Reciprocal interdependence occurs when outputs from one individual (or group) become the inputs for others and vice versa. Reciprocal interdependencies are common in everyday life. Examples include (1) a family, (2) a basketball team, (3) a surgical team, (4) a decision-making team, and (5) a class project assigned to a small team of students. Reciprocal interdependence usually requires a high degree of collaboration, communication, and team decision making. The following Managing Quality feature on the Metz Baking Company demonstrates how groupware has improved the reciprocal interdependencies in producing, delivering, and maintaining quality baked goods at grocery stores. Metz is headquartered in Sioux City, Iowa, and covers 16 states.

MANAGING QUALITY

Metz Baking Company

Prior to the introduction of groupware aids, the company's 1,400 sales representatives manually estimated demand for baked goods on their daily routes. A route includes approximately 30 grocery stores, delis, and restaurants. "They'd make their best guess of what they needed for their entire route over the next week; we'd bake that amount of product, roughly divided by day; and they'd attempt to sell it on a daily basis," recalls Larry Hames, vice-president of MIS for Metz. These estimates weren't always on the mark. "If you ended up short by the end of your route, one of your accounts would have to do without. Or you might end up dumping all your excess product at the last stop," Hames says.

MANAGING QUALITY —*Continued*

The fact that shoppers often buy baked goods on impulse also meant that these weekly sales estimates—which were translated into nightly bake schedules—frequently were wrong. A sales rep would deliver too much product at the beginning of the week and run out by the weekend, according to Ken Franklin, senior vice-president of sales. "We have stringent 72-hour stale requirements. Our product has to be on the shelf the day the consumer is in the store, or we run the risk of not being able to sell it at all."

Metz invested more than $7.5 million in its sales automation efforts, which included 1,400 Norand Corporation palmtop computers. Now, all product data, price changes, and new-customer data are downloaded each evening from remote IBM AS/400 minicomputers into each sales rep's palmtop. At night, the palmtops are kept in a "docking station" at each of 250 Metz distribution centers scattered across 16 states. Just after dawn Metz sales reps pick up their handheld units and verify that the type and number of bakery products they ordered have been correctly recorded and loaded onto their trucks.

The sales representative is then ready to drive the route. At each store, the sales rep takes all stale Metz products off the shelves, enters the data into the palmtop and then fills the shelves with freshly baked goods. The palmtop automatically generates an invoice that takes into account how much stale product from the previous day wasn't sold and how much fresh product was delivered. The sales rep then enters the estimate of the next day's order. "This is the beauty of the new system," says Hames. Previously, a driver might jot down notes during the day of how product seemed to be moving at individual stores. "But more likely, they'd wait until the end of the day, look at the amount of stale product in the truck and estimate how much fresh product the entire route might need the next day," says Hames. "Now our drivers can track demand on a daily basis by account. No more ballpark figures."[27]

In designing new jobs or redesigning existing jobs, management often must consider and make changes in task uncertainty, work-flow uncertainty, and/or task interdependence. *Increasing* pooled interdependence *decreases* the amount of required coordination between jobs. That is, less coordination between jobs means less sequential and/or work-flow uncertainty for the individuals involved. Also, new information technologies may change task interdependence and reduce work-flow uncertainty. The introduction of groupware for use by the 1,200 sales associates at the William Raveis Real Estate firm appears to have enhanced the use of pooled interdependence and reduced some task uncertainty within the organization. The introduction of computer-based groupware for use by the 1,400 sales representatives at the Metz Baking Company enhanced the reciprocal interdependencies between the sales and baking functions. These aids also appeared to reduce both task and work-flow uncertainty for the sales representatives.

▼ JOB CHARACTERISTICS ENRICHMENT MODEL

Richard Hackman and Greg Oldham developed the job characteristics enrichment model.[28] It is one of the best known approaches to job enrichment. Before reading further, please complete the questionnaire in Table 16.1.

▼ Basic Framework

The **job characteristics enrichment model** focuses on increasing the amounts of skill variety, task identity, task significance, autonomy, and feedback in a job. The model suggests that the levels of these jobs characteristics affect three critical psychological states: (1) experienced meaningfulness of the tasks performed; (2) experienced personal responsibility for task outcomes; and (3) knowledge of the results of task performance. If all three psychological states are positive, a reenforcing cycle of strong work motivation based on self-generated rewards is activated. A job without meaningfulness, responsibility, and feedback is incomplete and presumably doesn't strongly motivate an employee. Because of our previous coverage of motivation (see Chapters 6 and 7), we focus here on the job characteristics and individual differences components of the model. Figure 16.3 shows an outline of the elements and their relationships in the job characteristics enrichment model.

▼ Job Characteristics

Five job characteristics are key to job enrichment efforts in this model. They are defined as follows.

- ▲ **Skill variety**—the degree to which a job requires a range of personal competencies and abilities to carry out the work.
- ▲ **Task identity**—the degree to which a job requires completion of a whole and identifiable piece of work, that is, doing a task from beginning to end with a visible outcome.
- ▲ **Task significance**—the degree to which the employee perceives the job as having a substantial impact on the lives of other people, whether those people are within or outside the organization.
- ▲ **Autonomy**—the degree to which the job provides freedom, independence, and discretion to the employee in scheduling tasks and in determining procedures to be used in carrying out the tasks.
- ▲ **Job feedback**—the degree to which carrying out the job-related tasks provides the individual with direct and clear information about the effectiveness of his or her performance.[29]

Skill variety, task identity, and task significance may be especially powerful in influencing the experienced meaningfulness of work. Autonomy usually fosters increased feelings and attitudes of personal responsibility for work outcomes. Job feedback directly gives the employee the knowledge of results from performing the job. This type of feedback comes from the work itself,

TABLE 16.1   Job Characteristics Inventory

Directions

The following list contains statements that could be used to describe a job. Please indicate the extent to which you agree or disagree with each statement as a description of a job you currently hold or have held, by writing the appropriate number next to the statement. Try to be as objective as you can in answering.

1	2	3	4	5
Strongly disagree	Disagree	Uncertain	Agree	Strongly agree

This job . . .

_____ 1. provides much variety.

_____ 2. permits me to be left on my own to do my work

_____ 3. is arranged so that I often have the opportunity to see jobs or projects through to completion.

_____ 4. provides feedback on how well I am doing as I am working.

_____ 5. is relatively significant in my organization.

_____ 6. gives me considerable opportunity for independence and freedom in how I do the work.

_____ 7. provides different responsibilities.

_____ 8. enables me to find out how well I am doing.

_____ 9. is important in the broader scheme of things.

_____10. provides an opportunity for independent thought and action.

_____11. provides me with considerable variety of work.

_____12. is arranged so that I have the opportunity to complete the work I start.

_____13. provides me with the feeling that I know whether I am performing well or poorly.

_____14. is arranged so that I have the chance to do a job from the beginning to the end (i.e., a chance to do the whole job).

_____15. is one where a lot of other people can be affected by how well the work gets done.

Scoring

For each of the five scales, compute a score by summing the answers to the designated questions.

Score

Skill variety: Sum the points for items 1, 7, and 11.   _____

Task identity: Sum the points for items 3, 12, and 14.   _____

Task significance: Sum the points for items 5, 9, and 15.   _____

Autonomy: Sum the points for items 2, 6, and 10.   _____

Job feedback: Sum the points for items 4, 8, and 13.   _____

    Total Score   _____

Summary Interpretation

A total score of 60–75 suggests that the core job characteristics contribute to an overall positive psychological state for you and, in turn, leads to desirable personal and work outcomes. A total score of 15–30 suggests the opposite. We present additional interpretative comments later in this section of the chapter.

Source: Adapted from Sims, H. P., Jr., Szilagyi, A. D., and Keller, R. T. The measurement of job characteristics. *Academy of Management Journal*, 1976, 19, 195–212.

FIGURE 16.3

Job Characteristics Enrichment
Model

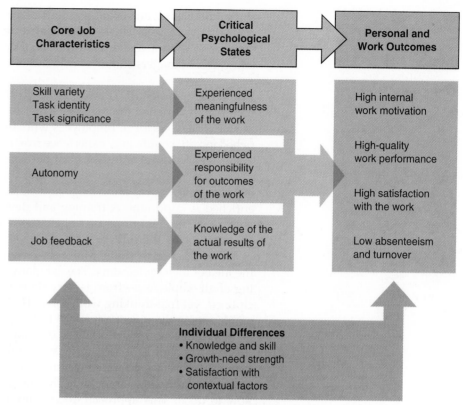

Source: Hackman, J. R., and Oldham, G. R. *Work Redesign.* Copyright © 1980. Addison-Wesley Publishing
Co., Inc., Reading, Massachusetts (adapted from Fig. 4.6 on p. 90). Reprinted with permission.

not from a superior's performance appraisal. Refer back to Table 16.1 and your
scores on each of the job characteristics. A score of 12–15 for a job characteristic is likely to contribute positively to one or more critical psychological
states. A score of 3–6 for a job characteristic, in contrast, is likely to contribute
negatively to one or more critical psychological states.

The job of surgeon can be used to further illustrate these points. This job
seems to rate high on all core job characteristics. It provides a constant opportunity for using highly varied skills, abilities, and talents in diagnosing
and treating illnesses. Task identity is high because the surgeon normally di-
agnoses a problem, performs the operation, and monitors the patient's recovery. Task significance also is high because the surgeon's work can mean life
or death to the patient. Autonomy is high because the surgeon often is the
final authority on the procedures and techniques used. However, the growing
prevalence and threat of malpractice suits may have lowered the surgeon's
sense of autonomy recently. Finally, the surgeon receives direct feedback from
the job, knowing in many cases almost immediately whether an operation is
successful.

▼ Individual Differences

Three major individual differences (see Figure 16.3) in this model are likely
to influence the way in which employees respond to enriched jobs. They in-

clude knowledge and skill, strength of growth needs, and satisfaction with contextual factors.[30] These individual differences can affect the relationship between job characteristics and personal or work outcomes in several important ways. Managers should consider them in designing or redesigning jobs.[31]

Knowledge and Skill   Employees with the knowledge and skill needed to perform an enriched job well are likely to experience positive feelings about the tasks they perform. Employees who are not competent to perform an enriched job effectively may experience frustration, stress, and job dissatisfaction. These feelings and attitudes may be especially intense for employees who desire to do a good job but realize that they are performing poorly. Accordingly, diagnosing the knowledge and skills of employees whose jobs are to be enriched is important. A training and development program may be needed with an enrichment program to help them learn the new skills needed for the job now and in the future.

To develop such skills, Motorola recently began a program built around the idea of lifelong learning. The company is dramatically increasing the training of all employees—from factory floor to executive suite. The goal is a disciplined, yet free-thinking work force. The intent of this initiative is to (1) train employees in the use of advanced techniques and procedures so they operate as a well-oiled machine, and (2) develop the knowledge and independence that the company will need to master rapidly changing technologies and markets. Motorola ties education to business goals. For example, it sets a goal to reduce product development cycle time and then creates a formal course on how to do it. This approach doesn't involve learning for its own sake. Employees are coached in specific tasks until they get them right, whether it's operating a tool or being more persuasive with customers.[32]

Growth-Need Strength   **Growth-need strength** is the degree to which an individual desires the opportunity for self-direction, learning, and personal accomplishment at work. This concept is essentially the same as Alderfer's growth needs and Maslow's esteem needs and self-actualization needs concepts (see Chapter 6). Most research suggests that individuals who have high growth needs tend to respond favorably to job enrichment programs. They derive greater satisfaction from work and are more highly motivated than people who have low growth needs. High growth-need individuals are absent less and produce better quality work when their jobs are enriched.[33] In contrast, one study recently suggested that the level of growth-need strength doesn't moderate the relationships between job characteristics and personal or work outcomes.[34] It reported that the sense of satisfaction with work and internal work motivation didn't appear to change after job enrichment. In general, research hasn't shown job enrichment to be negatively related to satisfaction or performance for individuals with low growth needs. Employee responses to enriched jobs usually range from indifferent to highly positive.[35]

Satisfaction with Contextual Factors   The degree to which employees are satisfied with contextual factors at work may affect their willingness or ability to respond positively to enriched jobs. Contextual factors include organizational policies and administration, technical supervision, salary and benefit programs, interpersonal relations, and work conditions (lighting, heat, safety hazards, etc.). Employees who are extremely dissatisfied with their superiors, salary level, and safety measures are less likely to respond favorably to enriched jobs than are employees who are satisfied with these conditions. Other contextual factors (e.g., employee satisfaction with the organization's culture, power and political processes, and team norms) also can affect employee responses to their jobs.[36]

A contextual factor of increasing concern is the growing use of electronic monitoring of work through the use of computers, video cameras, or telephones to "listen in" or "observe" employees as they perform their tasks. Such monitoring often occurs without employees being aware that it is taking place. Information technologies are being used to monitor attendance, lateness, speed of work (e.g., recording the number of computer keystrokes a worker performs per minute or hour), length and frequency of breaks, types of messages being transmitted on computer networks, nature and quality of conversations with customers or others, and so on. The intrusiveness of these technologies raises serious ethical concerns, which focus on the excessive invasion of privacy of employees while at work and a widespread concern that "Big Brother is watching."[37] The ethical concerns with the unbridled use of electronic monitoring have become so intense that Congress has introduced legislation to place some limits on it. Many European countries already have enacted antimonitoring laws.[38] The following Managing Ethics feature describes invasion of privacy and lack of fairness ethical concerns related to electronic monitoring.

MANAGING ETHICS

Electronic Monitoring of Work

Silent monitoring, where the employee doesn't know exactly when someone is listening, is spreading among U.S. companies that use service workers. The practice isn't new with telephone companies; AT&T was using it in the late nineteenth century. But it has now spread to airlines, banks, insurers, computer manufacturers, appliance makers, and others. These firms operate some 5,000 incoming telephone call centers around the country and most use monitoring of one kind or another.

Also, a PC may be personal, but it is far from private when part of a network. A password may keep out hackers but not necessarily the manager. The Norton–Lambert Company of Santa Barbara, California, which makes *Close Up* networking software, takes out trade journal ads to urge employers to "look in on Sue's computer screen. In fact, Sue doesn't even know you're there! Hot key again and off you go on your rounds of the company. Viewing one screen after another, helping some, watching others. All from the comfort of your chair." Another software supplier, Networking Dynamics Corporation of Glendale, California, sells programs called *Peek and Spy*. It boasts that dozens of *Fortune* 500 companies use them—most merely to peek, others to spy. *Peek* requires an employee's approval on each occasion for a supervisor to see the employee's PC screen. *Spy* allows access to the screen without the employee's knowledge or approval.

One major customer of electronic surveillance aids is American Airlines. It installed remote-screen surveillance software to supplement the ability to listen in on telephone calls at its reservation center at the Dallas–Fort Worth airport. American says the idea is to enable supervisors to help agents use the global Sabre reservation system more effectively. In addition to hearing what agents are telling customers on the phone, supervisors are able to see what agents are entering on their PC screens. In contrast, executives at GE's Answer Center elected not to buy programs of this sort. "It just goes against our philosophy of professionalism and trust. Unrequested assistance risks driving employees up the wall," says manager Bill Waers.[39]

▼ Job Diagnosis

Various methods may be used to diagnose jobs, determine whether job design problems exist, and estimate the potential for job enrichment success. We limit the discussion to two of these methods: structural clues and survey.

Structural Clues Method   The structural clues method involves checking for contextual factors often associated with deficiencies in job design.[40] The analysis of five specific structural factors usually reveals potential job design problems and possible employee acceptance of job enrichment.

▲ *Inspectors or checkers.* Autonomy usually is much lower when inspectors or checkers, rather than the employees themselves, examine work. Feedback is less direct because it doesn't come from the job itself.

▲ *Troubleshooters.* The existence of troubleshooters usually means that the exciting and challenging parts of a job have been taken away from the employees. Thus they have less sense of responsibility for work outcomes. Task identity, autonomy, and feedback usually are poor.

▲ *Communications and customer relations departments.* These departments usually cut the link between employees who do the job and customers or clients. These departments often dilute direct feedback and task identity for those creating the products or services.

▲ *Labor pools.* On the surface, pools of word processors, computer programmers, and other employees are appealing because they seem to increase efficiency and the ability to meet workload fluctuations. However, such pools may destroy workers' feelings of ownership and task identity.

▲ *Narrow span of control.* A manager with only a few subordinates (say, five to seven) is more likely to become involved in the details of their day-to-day tasks than a manager with a wider span of control. Centralization of decision making and overcontrol may result from too narrow a span of control and seriously reduce autonomy.

Survey Method   Several types of questionnaires make diagnosing jobs relatively easy and systematic.[41] One of these is the **job diagnostic survey** (JDS). Hackman and Oldham constructed it to measure the job characteristics in their model and the likely outcomes of job redesign.[42] The questionnaire in Table 16.1 measures these same job characteristics. You can develop your own job profile by using the totals on the scales in Table 16.1, each of which has a score from 3–15. You can calculate an overall measure of job enrichment, called the **motivating potential score** (MPS), as follows:

$$\text{MPS} = \frac{\dfrac{\text{Skill}}{\text{variety}} + \dfrac{\text{Task}}{\text{identity}} + \dfrac{\text{Task}}{\text{significance}}}{3} \times \text{Autonomy} \times \text{Feedback}$$

The MPS formula sums the scores for skill variety, task identity, and task significance and divides the total by 3. The combination of these three job characteristics has the same weight as autonomy and job feedback. The reason is that the job characteristics enrichment model (see Figure 16.3) requires that both experienced responsibility and knowledge of results be present for high internal job motivation. This outcome can be achieved only if reasonable degrees of autonomy and job feedback are present. The minimum MPS score, using Table 16.1, is 1. The maximum possible MPS score is 3,375, a clearly positive MPS score starts at 1,728, and a purely neutral MPS score is 729 (based on an average score of 9 per scale). What is your MPS score? Use your score results from the completed questionnaire to calculate it.

▼ Implementation Approaches

Five approaches may be used to implement a job enrichment program. All need not be used in every job enrichment effort, nor are they mutually exclusive. The two main approaches are vertical loading and the formation of natural work teams. The other three—establishment of customer relationships, employee ownership of the product, and employee receipt of direct feedback—often are used within one of the two principal approaches.

Vertical Loading **Vertical loading** refers to delegating to employees responsibilities that were formerly reserved for management or staff specialists. The elements of vertical loading include

- ▲ giving employees leeway in setting schedules, determining work methods, and deciding when and how to check on the quality of the work produced.
- ▲ allowing employees to make their own decisions about when to start and stop work, when to take breaks, and how to assign priorities; and
- ▲ encouraging employees to seek solutions to problems on their own, consulting with others only as necessary, rather than calling immediately for the manager when problems arise.

Many employees schedule their own work after vertical loading, although the manager may set deadlines or goals. Within these guidelines, employees are allowed some freedom in setting their own schedules and pace. **Flextime** allows employees, within certain limits, to vary their arrival and departure times to suit their individual needs and desires and helps in self-scheduling of work. With the new information technology capabilities (e.g., computer-based networks), an increasing number of jobs can be performed, at least part of the time, at the employee's residence, in hotels while traveling, and at customer locations.[43]

Natural Work Teams   The formation of natural work teams combines individual jobs into a formally recognized unit (e.g., a section, team, or department). The criteria for this grouping are logical and meaningful to the employee and include the following.

▲ *Geographic*: Salespersons might be given a particular section of the city, state, or country as their territory.

▲ *Types of business*: Insurance claims adjusters might be assigned to teams that serve specific business categories such as utilities, manufacturers, or retailers.

▲ *Organizational*: Word-processing operators might be given work that originates in a particular department.

▲ *Alphabetic or numeric*: File clerks could be made responsible for materials in specified alphabetical groups (A to D, E to H, etc.); library-shelf readers might check books in a certain range of the library's cataloging system.

▲ *Customer groups*: Employees of a public utility might be assigned to particular residential or commercial accounts.

Customer Relationships   One of the most important concepts of job enrichment is putting employees in touch with the users of their output. The establishment of customer relationships often is a logical outcome if natural work teams are formed. Employees too often end up working directly for their superiors rather than for customers or clients. For example, in word-processing centers, certain operators can be assigned to specific clients or to teams of, say, salespeople or engineers. When problems arise, operators can work directly with the client to resolve them.

Consider the approach used by Home Depot, a large retailer for residential fixer-uppers. It encourages employees to build long-term relationships with customers. Workers are trained in home-repair techniques and can spend as much time as is needed to help customers. There are no high-pressure sales tactics, and employees are on straight salary. In order to satisfy customers consistently, the leadership of Home Depot believes that employees must be committed. Every salesperson's bright-orange apron reads, "Hi. I'm _____, a Home Depot stockholder. Let me help you." Instead of receiving discounts on merchandise, employees get shares in the company. Salespeople are trained not to let customers overspend. "I love it when shoppers tell me they were prepared to spend $150 and our people have showed them how to do the job for four or five bucks," says Bernard Marcus, the chief executive of Home Depot. He further states: "Every customer has to be treated like your mother, your father, your sister, or your brother."[44]

Ownership of Product   Employees who assemble entire television sets or washing machines or type entire reports identify more with the finished products than do employees who perform only part of the same job. Allowing employees to build an entire product or complete an entire task cycle is likely to generate a sense of pride and achievement. The assignment of as much responsibility as possible for a certain geographic area also may create the feeling of ownership.

At Aetna Life and Casualty Company, changes in the way insurance policies are issued have improved customer service and given employees a sense of ownership in providing this service. Not long ago, Aetna had 22 business centers, with a staff of 3,000. About 15 days were required to get a basic policy out of the office, in part, because 60 different employees had to handle the application. Now, the entire operation is handled by 700 employees in 4 centers—and customers get their policies within 5 days. How? A single Aetna representative sitting at a PC tied to a network can now perform all the necessary steps. This representative may access an actuarial database, for example, to begin processing an application immediately. When all the relevant information is gathered, the policy is passed along the network to company headquarters in Hartford, Connecticut. It is printed and mailed within a day from Hartford. Computer-based technology also gave Aetna's salesforce more autonomy. Work teams of about 17 people have replaced the old hierarchy of managers and agents.[45]

Direct Feedback   The job-enrichment approach stresses feedback to the employee directly from performance of the task.[46] Reports or computer output may go directly to employees, instead of just to their supervisors. A common technique is to let people check their own work so that they can catch most of their own errors before others do. This technique also increases employee autonomy. Direct communication with customers or clients also may improve the timeliness and accuracy of feedback, thereby eliminating distortions and delays.

▼ Technology and Job Characteristics

We now merge our discussion of technology and job design—and the technology framework (see Figure 16.2)—with that of the job characteristics enrichment model (see Figure 16.3). To change one or more of the five job characteristics usually means making changes in one or more of the three technological dimensions. To avoid excessive complexity, we consider only a basic job redesign situation where management decides to use a combination of vertical loading and the formation of natural work teams.

Vertical loading increases the amount of task and work-flow uncertainty that employees must handle in redesigned jobs. Some of the changes caused by vertical loading tend to increase pooled interdependence and decrease sequential and reciprocal interdependence. For example, there is usually less need to obtain a quality control specialist's approval before proceeding with other tasks, which lessens sequential interdependence. The formation of natural work teams has the most direct impact on reducing task interdependence between departments or teams, with each team becoming a self-managed team. All the criteria for forming natural work teams tend to increase pooled interdependence and decrease sequential and reciprocal interdependence among departments, teams, and higher levels of the organization.

Figure 16.4 shows the technological changes that will probably accompany a job redesign program involving vertical loading and the formation of natural work teams. These changes, in turn, can be expected to lead to changes in job characteristics. In brief, technological dimensions and job characteristics are closely and intricately linked.[47]

FIGURE 16.4

Sample Job Characteristic and Technological Links

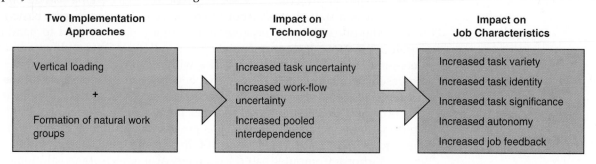

Two Implementation Approaches	Impact on Technology	Impact on Job Characteristics
Vertical loading + Formation of natural work groups	Increased task uncertainty Increased work-flow uncertainty Increased pooled interdependence	Increased task variety Increased task identity Increased task significance Increased autonomy Increased job feedback

The following Managing in Practice account presents a summary of a study on the long-term effects of work redesign for bank tellers. It demonstrates several linkages between the introduction of computer-based information technology and job enrichment.

MANAGING IN PRACTICE

Technology and Redesign of Tellers' Jobs

The research was conducted at the 38 member banks of a large Southwestern bank holding corporation over four years. The member banks were located in seven metropolitan areas. The respondents included 526 bank tellers, 85% of whom were women. Their average employment with the corporation was slightly less than four years.

The bank's management decided to implement an on-line computer network to speed up tasks the tellers had performed manually and to enrich the tellers' job. The purpose of the job redesign program was to make the job more professional and intrinsically rewarding. The automated information network was supposed to decrease errors and increase the speed of posting changes in customer accounts. Several changes targeted increased responsibility, authority, and accountability.

First, tellers were given a wider range of activities than before. Previously, they cashed checks and accepted deposits and loan payments. Commercial and traveler's check customers were referred to special tellers. Under the new system, each teller was trained in all functions and could provide all these services for a customer. Under the old system, tellers held documents on deposits and withdrawals in a tray until the documents were collected and taken to another workroom, where bookkeeping employees posted them. Under the new system, each teller had an on-line computer terminal. They posted deposits, payments, and withdrawals immediately, which bookkeeping later verified. Tellers also received more autonomy over routine decisions. Previously, they needed a supervisor's signature for immediate crediting of all deposits and for withdrawals of more than $100. After the job changes, tellers could post local checks immediately and perform withdrawals as long as the information system indicated adequate funds in a customer's account. Several other similar types of decisions were formally delegated to the tellers.

MANAGING IN PRACTICE —*Continued*

Feedback also was enhanced. Under the old system, errors weren't reported back to the tellers until the end of the day or, in some cases, the next morning. The new information technology allowed bookkeeping to transmit error messages as soon as errors were discovered. The system also recorded the total number of customers and transactions each teller handled each day. These figures were displayed on the teller's monitor when it was not being used to service a customer. Thus tellers could monitor their own work pace at all times. Finally, a closer link between tellers and customers was established. The receipt for each transaction was changed to include a special message at the bottom. It gave the name of the teller who had performed the transaction. The customer was invited to contact the teller first in the event of an error or question. The teller could then handle the question or inquiry or refer it to someone more appropriate if he or she could not do so.

An interesting pattern of results emerged. First, the job redesign program significantly increased employee perceptions of their core job characteristics (see Figure 16.3) in the predicted and desired directions. These changed perceptions remained at their new level for the duration of the study. Second, the satisfaction and commitment of tellers increased quickly but then diminished to their initial levels. Finally, although performance didn't increase initially, it did improve significantly over the study period.[48]

▼ Social Information Processing

The job characteristics enrichment model is based on the assumption that employees can respond reasonably, accurately, and objectively about the characteristics of their jobs. Their perceptions of job characteristics may be influenced by **social information,** which refers to comments, observations, and similar cues provided by people whose view of the job an employee values. Social information may be provided by people directly associated with the job, such as co-workers, managers, and customers, and by people not employed by the organization, such as family members and friends. Some aspects of a job aren't likely to be influenced by cues from others (a hot work environment will be hot despite what anyone tells a worker). However, most of an employee's perceptions of job characteristics are subject to the influence of others with whom the employee has contact.[49]

Based on this perspective, the **social information processing model** states that

▲ the individual's social environment may provide cues as to which dimensions might be used to characterize the work environment;

▲ the social environment may provide information concerning how the individual should weigh the various dimensions—whether autonomy is more or less important than skill variety or whether pay is more or less important than social usefulness or worth;

▲ the social context provides cues concerning how others have come to evaluate the work environment on each of the selected dimensions; and

▲ the social context may provide direct positive or negative evaluation of the work setting, leaving the individual to construct a rationale to make sense of the generally shared affective reactions.[50]

The potential impact of the social information processing model can be illustrated with a simple example. Two employees performing the same tasks with the same job characteristics under different managers might respond differently to the objective characteristics of their jobs on the job diagnostic survey (JDS). The differences in perceived social information cues might account for some of the variation in the employees' responses. For example, one manager may praise subordinates a great deal, whereas the other manager may criticize subordinates repeatedly. The social information processing model suggests that receiving praise or criticism could affect how employees respond to the JDS. An integrated perspective may be more accurate than one or the other points of view. The integrative perspective suggests that (1) job characteristics and social information (cues) combine to affect employees' reactions to their jobs and (2) introducing changes in the work environment can produce those reactions.[51] However, the intricate and varied ways that social information in the workplace can affect the perceptions of job characteristics is beyond the scope of this discussion.[52] To reduce possible distortions caused by social information influences, the employees' managers and possibly a trained job analyst should also rate the characteristics of jobs being considered for redesign.

▼ SOCIOTECHNICAL SYSTEMS MODEL

The importance of technology in job design and redesign always has been recognized in the sociotechnical systems model. Moreover, this model emphasizes grouping jobs by work team when the reciprocal and/or sequential interdependence among jobs cannot be reduced.[53] The use of pooled interdependence therefore tends to occur between work teams rather than between individual jobs. In addition, the model focuses on vertical job loading to a cluster of jobs within the team as a whole, rather than to each individual job. Many concepts and diagnostic tools in this model are being used by the advocates of reengineering. After accounting for the demands of the external environment, management can use the sociotechnical systems model to design work that integrates people with technology and to optimize the relationships between the technological and social systems.[54] When applied to manufacturing, the needed changes in technology sometimes are too difficult and costly to make in an existing plant. Thus the sociotechnical systems model more frequently works best in designing jobs for an entirely new plant. Numerous organizations in Western Europe and North America, including General Foods, GM, Weyerhauser, TRW, Rushton Mining, Volvo, and the Tennessee Valley Authority, have implemented sociotechnical systems projects.[55] Although many successes have been reported, so have some failures.[56]

Figure 16.5 presents the sociotechnical systems model. It consists of four major parts: environmental forces, social system, technological system, and moderators. We won't review the important environmental forces (e.g., customers, suppliers, and regulatory agencies) in this model because we have described them throughout the book.

FIGURE 16.5

Sociotechnical Systems Model

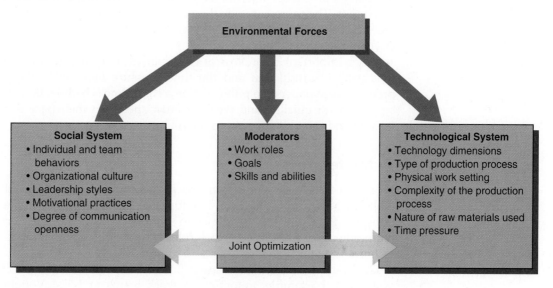

▼ Social System

The social system includes those aspects of the organization's ''human side'' that can influence how individuals and teams perform tasks and their attitudes toward work and the organization. We covered the social system factors listed in Figure 16.5 in previous chapters. (Chapters 9, 11, and 14, in particular, presented the main elements and processes of the work-related social system). For example, if employees characterize their organization as one marked by distrust, back-stabbing, and infighting, the creation of self-managed work teams is likely to be counterproductive until some degree of trust and cooperation is established.

▼ Technological System

Task uncertainty, work-flow uncertainty, and task interdependence need to be diagnosed. These three technological dimensions are likely to vary with the type of production process being used or planned. For example, the type of production process in a factory (assembly line or small unit) is an important technological characteristic, and different production processes require different approaches to job design. In a process-technology operation, such as an oil refinery, most work is automated. A relatively few workers spend much of their time monitoring dials and performing maintenance tasks. By contrast, small-unit technologies—plumbing, television repair, sales, and investment brokering—involve relatively large amounts of labor to achieve the required outputs.

Another technological characteristic is the physical work setting (amount of light, temperature, noise, pollution, geographical isolation, and orderliness). For example, if the workplace is too hot or noisy, employees may have difficulty performing tasks that require intense thought and concentration.

Complexity of the production process also is an important technological characteristic. A person might easily learn how to build an entire toaster, but one person probably could not learn how to build a major system of a complex jet aircraft. The more complex the production process, the greater are the degrees of task and work-flow uncertainty and the requirements for reciprocal task interdependence.

Other important technological characteristics are the nature of raw materials used in production and the time pressure inherent in the production process. Newspapers are published on a rigid time schedule. Bottlenecks must be dealt with quickly, and workers must speed up their pace if production falls behind schedule by even a few minutes.

▼ Moderators

Work roles act as moderators in the sociotechnical systems model. They establish a set of expected behaviors for each employee. They define the relationships between the people who perform tasks and the technological requirements of those tasks. Work roles provide the glue that binds the sociotechnical systems together.

Goals also moderate the relationship between the social and technological systems. For example, autonomous work teams at Loral Vought Systems' Camden, Arkansas, plant may have a goal of producing a certain number of subassemblies per day. So long as this goal is compatible with technical-system goals, the work team can perform somewhat autonomously. It can arrange the work any way it wants to, so long as it meets its output goal.

A final moderator includes the skills and abilities of the employees. The sociotechnical systems model is most likely to be effective in a plant with a highly skilled and educated work force. If the needed skills aren't available, changing the production process and simplifying jobs may be necessary.

▼ Key Principles

The degree to which an organization operates according to the principles of sociotechnical systems design can be assessed in terms of the following six principles.

▲ *Innovativeness*—organizational leaders and members maintain a futuristic versus historical orientation, including a propensity for risk taking and provision of rewards for innovation.

▲ *Human resource development*—the talents, knowledge, skills, and abilities of organizational members are developed and tapped through work design, supervisory roles, organizational structure, and the work-flow process.

▲ *Environmental agility*—the organization maintains awareness of the environment and responds appropriately to it by recognizing customer importance, proactivity versus reactivity, and structural, technical, and product or service flexibility.

▲ *Cooperation*—individuals and departments work together to accomplish common goals through teamwork, mutual support, shared values, and common rewards.

▲ *Commitment/energy*—employees are dedicated to accomplishing organizational goals and are prepared to expend energy in doing so.

▲ *Joint optimization*—the organization uses both its social and technical resources effectively, including the design of technology to support teamwork and flexibility.[57]

The following Managing Across Cultures item reveals some of the contrasting ways that Volvo's Uddevalla automobile plant and the NUMMI plant utilized design features of the sociotechnical systems model. The Uddevalla plant suffered from inadequate diagnosis of changing environmental forces and a lack of adequate attention to several crucial technological issues. Because Volvo was operating at low production levels, this relatively new plant had to be shut down in 1993. Its operation appeared to become "out-of-balance" by overemphasizing efforts to democratize and humanize the plant. The contrasts with the NUMMI plant (discussed earlier in the chapter) dramatize the core idea of the sociotechnical systems model, namely, the need to balance and integrate environmental forces, the technological system, the social system, and various moderators in the design of jobs, teams, and plants.

MANAGING ACROSS CULTURES

Volvo's Uddevalla Versus NUMMI

The Uddevalla plant evolved at a time when Volvo was experiencing production capacity bottlenecks in a relatively protected market. There were no efficient Japanese competitors for its niche at that time. In the mid 1980s, Volvo was selling everything it could make, and lack of production capacity was a key problem. The major constraint in breaking the capacity bottleneck was the tight Swedish labor market. The design of the Uddevalla plant was labor-market driven, not product-market driven. As one of the key managers involved in the plant design expressed it: "The problem we had was how could we make the plant attractive for Swedish workers to want to work in it."

In the newly designed plant, each of eight production teams took full responsibility for assembling the vehicle from the subsystems up—a work cycle of about two hours. The plant abolished the assembly line, and the eight teams worked in parallel. Because the work cycle was so long, Uddevalla teams paid much less attention than NUMMI teams to detailed, movement-by-movement standardization. Instead, the teams focused on the more general balance of tasks within the whole assembly cycle. The Uddevalla teams decided job rotation schedules, selected their own employees, and decided on their own overtime schedules. At NUMMI, union representatives and managers jointly select team leaders based on objective tests. At Uddevalla, teams selected their own leaders and often rotated the role. Both plants put great emphasis on worker training. NUMMI invested more time and effort than Uddevalla did in training workers in the principles and techniques of job engineering and its production system.

Uddevalla probably was the more desirable place to work than NUMMI. Uddevalla offered a much less regimented environment, more task variety, more autonomy, and more team self-management. However, NUMMI's pro-

MANAGING ACROSS CULTURES —*Continued*

duction system delivered the greatest efficiency and quality. One Volvo executive stated that Uddevalla would not have been built under today's circumstances. The context that produced Uddevalla changed: The labor bottleneck disappeared and efficient Japanese competitors hurt Volvo in its export markets.

Uddevalla workers had specific information on their work cycle performance. But this cycle was two hours long. They had no way to track task performance in more detail. This problem was compounded by the work culture that encouraged the employees to think that they should have considerable latitude in how they performed each cycle. Some proponents of the Uddevalla design principles argue that it offered a way around the line-balancing problems that limit the efficiency of traditional sequential assembly lines. NUMMI resolved those problems through a combination of modest doses of worker flexibility (far less extensive than Uddevalla's) and aggressive efforts to reduce setup times. The standardization of detailed work methods facilitated efforts to reduce setup times. Moreover, as the variety of models produced in a plant increases, workers have more difficulty recalling the correct procedure for each job. Shorter cycle times and well-defined methods help ensure quality at NUMMI. As a result, its assembly line can handle a relatively broad range of product types with minimal disruption.

No detailed documentation was available to Volvo workers describing how to perform each work task and specifying how long it should take. One of the Uddevalla workers argued, "You don't really need all that detail because you can feel it when the task isn't going right; you can feel the sticking points yourself." The workers at Uddevalla had no mechanisms for identifying, testing, or disseminating the improvements that individual workers might make to eliminate problems. Sustaining continuous improvements in the production of goods as standardized as automobiles without clear and detailed methods and standards is extremely difficult.[58]

This feature and the discussion of NUMMI earlier in the chapter suggests that its sociotechnical system may be the more appropriate type for relatively repetitive, labor-intensive activities such as auto assembly. However, in the long run, NUMMI's sociotechnical system could be undermined by the progressive automation of assembly tasks, changing employee expectations, and the continuing shift toward volatile markets, lower volumes, and greater product variety. If Uddevalla had survived, it probably would have had to evolve in dramatically new ways to be competitive. Whether Uddevalla could have done so quickly enough and whether it could have retained its distinctive sociotechnical system is unclear.

▼ Organizational Significance

The factors to be diagnosed in designing jobs under the sociotechnical systems model are complex. The basic issue is the management philosophy and values that define the organization's culture. Managers interested in improving both the social system and organizational effectiveness may find the job enrichment or sociotechnical models appropriate. Managers interested only in production and efficiency may concentrate on the job engineering, job enlargement, or job rotation approaches.

Technology is a primary variable in job design. Some jobs cannot be enriched without redesigning the whole operation. When changing a job is impossible, other techniques (such as flextime) may soften the effects of a boring job. Moreover, new information technologies, especially those involving robots in manufacturing, are being used increasingly to eliminate routine jobs and thus the need to redesign them. Perhaps the best approach is to understand fully the various job design approaches and to use the approach or combination of approaches that best fits the organization or department.[59]

Summary

Job design is a continuous task in organizations. Ideally, jobs will be both efficient and satisfying to employees. Five of the most common approaches to job design are job rotation, job engineering, job enlargement, job enrichment, and the sociotechnical systems model. These approaches vary significantly in terms of their relative impact on the organization and complexity of implementation. Job engineering includes traditional industrial engineering techniques that simplify a job in order to make it more efficient. Job enlargement and job rotation seek to make boring jobs more interesting by adding variety.

Job enrichment seeks to make jobs more meaningful and challenging. The job characteristics enrichment model focuses on modifying five job characteristics: task variety, task identity, task significance, autonomy, and job feedback. Technological dimensions that affect these job characteristics usually must be changed. Three important technological dimensions are task uncertainty, work-flow uncertainty, and task interdependence (pooled, sequential, and reciprocal). The approaches for implementing the job enrichment approach include vertical loading, formation of natural work teams, establishment of client relationships, employee ownership of the product, and employee receipt of direct feedback. Employees in properly designed jobs are more likely to be satisfied and perform better than employees in poorly designed jobs. Individual differences are important in redesigning jobs because some people may not want enriched jobs or may not want to work in teams. Also, some organizational or technological situations may not permit job enrichment.

When applied to job design, the sociotechnical systems model is a way to integrate the organization's technological and social systems after careful assessment of the environmental forces acting on the organization. Three moderators—work roles, goals, and skills and abilities—serve to influence optimization of the social and technological systems. Relative to the other approaches to job design, it is the most complex and offers the greatest potential impact on the organization as a whole. The principles of this model address six key factors: innovativeness, human resource development, environmental agility, cooperation, commitment and energy, and joint optimization.

Job design decisions, like other decisions, contain many contingencies that must be diagnosed. Perhaps the best way to understand and balance these contingencies is by having a thorough knowledge of the various job design approaches that can be applied.

Key Words and Concepts

Autonomy	Job feedback	Sociotechnical systems model
Flextime	Job rotation	Task identity
Growth-need strength	Motivating potential score	Task interdependence
Human factor approach	Pooled interdependence	Task significance
Job characteristics enrichment	Reciprocal interdependence	Task uncertainty
model	Reengineering	Technical system
Job design	Sequential interdependence	Technology
Job diagnostic survey	Skill variety	Vertical loading
Job engineering	Social information	Work-flow uncertainty
Job enlargement	Social information processing	
Job enrichment	model	

Discussion Questions

1. Why should job design be an important area of concern for organizations?

2. Why is job design important to reengineering?

3. What are the similarities and differences between job rotation and job enlargement?

4. How do the assumptions of job engineering differ from those of job enrichment?

5. Think about your role as a student as though it were a job. Analyze your student job in terms of task uncertainty, work-flow uncertainty, and task interdependence. Can this analysis vary by specific course and instructor? Explain.

6. Why does technology often need to be changed as a first step in changing job characteristics?

7. Does electronic monitoring of workers create any ethical dilemmas for you? Explain.

8. How would you compare each of the job characteristics in your instructor's job with those in your job as a student? Discuss their similarities and differences.

9. What clues might you look for in determining whether the manager's job of a local sports shoe store needs to be redesigned?

10. Why might some managers and employees welcome the sociotechnical systems approach to job design and others oppose it?

 # Developing Skills

Self-Diagnosis:
Redesign of the Data Entry Operator Job[60]

Job Objective

To get information from printed or written media that is used as input to a computer.

Current Situation

There are 15 Data Entry Operators in this unit reporting to one supervisor. They enter a wide variety of work which is supplied by various departments and teams. Some jobs are small, some much larger, and some are more sensitive or critical than others. Some work comes with a due date and

the remainder is pre-scheduled on a routine basis to meet the computer's requirements.

The work is supplied to the Data Entry Operators by an Assignment Clerk. The Assignment Clerk looks at the work before giving it to the Data Entry Operators to make sure that it is legible. If it is not, this person gives it to the supervisor who returns the work to the originating department. The Assignment Clerk attempts to see that each operator gets exactly one-fifteenth of the work even if this requires assigning parts of the same job to different operators. Because of the exactness of the work, each job is entered twice by different Operators and then verified through the computer to help keep errors to a minimum. However, some errors are not discovered until the finished job is turned out by the computer. Turnover is high and many due dates and schedules for the computers are not met.

Assignment

Some proposals are listed below that you could take that might result in improving work performance. Read over the list and decide whether you would or would not implement the proposal. Put an X in the appropriate space next to each of the items in the list. Next, rank order the action you would take first and number it 1. Then pick 2, etc., and continue to do the same for the changes that you think are necessary.

Possible Changes	Would	Would Not	Rank Order
1. Make sure the forms from which the Operators get their information are arranged in the best way.	___	___	___
2. Let some Data Entry Operators decide whether or not their work should be double entered and verified.	___	___	___
3. Do the work that has specific due dates first.	___	___	___
4. Train the Assignment Clerks on the PCs so they can help out when the workload is heavy.	___	___	___
5. Add another supervisor and split the group into two teams.	___	___	___
6. Have the Data Entry Operators inspect the media they receive for legibility.	___	___	___
7. When errors are discovered, feed back the details to the Data Entry Operator who made the error(s).	___	___	___
8. Have the Data Entry Operators verify their own work.	___	___	___
9. Assign responsibility for entering a whole job to an individual.	___	___	___
10. Arrange for departmental contacts for certain operators.	___	___	___
11. Let some Data Entry Operators schedule their own day.	___	___	___
12. Make sure that jobs for a particular team or account always go to the same Data Entry Operator.	___	___	___

Individual Analysis

For each of the changes that you would make, identify the concept in the job characteristics enrichment model that would be enhanced by the specific change. For each of the changes that you did not make, please justify each decision through the use of one or more concepts in the job characteristics enrichment model.

A Case in Point: McGuire Industry

In spite of a modern $30 million facility for overhauling engines, a Department of Defense industrial facility is having trouble meeting its production quotas. The morale of the civilian employees also seems to be low—absenteeism and tardiness are major problems. The plant is located in the southwestern United States. Approximately 80% of the 2,000 employees have a tenth grade through high school education. Other employees have one or more years of college. The engine facility is directed by a colonel who has had extensive management experience in military units. But he has never directed an industrial organization.

The engine facility was designed to utilize the latest technology in engine overhaul for military vehicles. Engines enter at one end of the half-mile-long plant where they are disassembled. Then, the parts are placed on conveyor lines to the areas that specialize in repairing, replacing, and cleaning particular components, such as turbine wheels and fuel controls. Work groups are highly specialized. They consist of 10–15 employees and a supervisor. Their workload is determined by the pace of incoming components. After a work group cleans and repairs a component, it is sent to a testing group. Then, the part is sent to the next group and combined with other components to produce a subassembly. When the subassemblies arrive at the other end of the building, they are combined to yield the final engine. It is sent to the testing department for an operational runup. Finally, the engines are packed for shipment to the appropriate military unit.

Employees are tightly controlled. They punch time clocks and take breaks only when a buzzer sounds. Their physical mobility is limited, and even the use of rest rooms is tightly controlled. Supervisors and white-collar workers have their own separate rest rooms.

Questions

1. Is the technical system compatible with the social system? Explain.
2. How might the skill variety, task identity, and task significance of the production employees be increased?
3. How might the autonomy and job feedback of the production employees be increased?
4. Should the production jobs be enriched? Explain.

References

1. Adapted from Denton, D. K. I hate this job! *Business Horizons*, January–February 1994, 46–52.
2. Ibid., 47.
3. Carlson, R., and Goldman, B. *Fast Forward: Where Technology, Demographics, and History Will Take America and the World in the Next Thirty Years*. New York: HarperCollins, 1994.
4. Griffin, R. W. *Task Design: An Integrative Approach*. Glenview, Ill.: Scott, Foresman, 1982.
5. The Juran Institute and Main, J. *The Road to Quality*. New York: Free Press, 1994.
6. Hammer, M., and Champy, J. *Reengineering the Corporation: A Manifesto for Business Revolution*. New York: Harper Business, 1993.
7. Hammer, M. Reengineering work: Don't automate, obliterate. *Harvard Business Review*, July–August 1990, 104–112.
8. Karlgaard, R. ASAP interview: Mike Hammer. *Forbes ASAP*, February 25, 1994, 69–75.
9. Omachonu, V. K., and Ross, J. E. *Principles of Total Quality*, Delray Beach, Fla.: St. Lucie Press, 1994, 297–308; Janson, R. How reengineering transforms organizations to satisfy customers. *National Productivity Review*, Winter 1992, 45–53.
10. Adapted from Barrier, M. Re-engineering your company. Adapted by permission, *Nation's Business*, February 1994. Copyright © 1994, U.S. Chamber of Commerce.
11. Howell, W. C. Human factors in the workplace. In M. D. Dunnette and L. M. Hough (eds.), *Handbook of Industrial & Organizational Psychology*, vol. 2, 2nd. ed. Palo Alto, Calif.: Consulting Psychologists Press, 1991, 209–269; Franchi, K., and Fleck, R.A., Jr. Ergonomic improvements in the office environment. *Business Horizons*, March–April 1994, 75–79.
12. Swanson, R. A. *Analysis for Improving Performance: Tools for Diagnosing Organizations & Documenting Workplace Expertise*. San Francisco: Berrett-Koehler, 1994.
13. Campion, M. A., and Thayer, P. W. Job design: Approaches, outcomes, and trade-offs. *Organizational Dynamics*. Winter 1987, 66–79.
14. Adapted from Adler, P. S. Time and motion regained. *Harvard Business*. January–February 1993, 97–108; Adler, P. S., and Cole, R. E. Designed for learning: A tale of two auto plants. *Sloan Management Review*, Spring 1993, 85–94.
15. Ehrbar, A. Reengineering gives firms new efficiency, workers the pink slip. *Wall Street Journal*, March 16, 1993, A1, A11.

16. Roberts, H. V., and Sergesketter, B. F. *Quality Is Personal: A Foundation for Total Management*. New York: Free Press, 1994.
17. Herzberg, F., Mausner, B., and Snyderman, B. *The Motivation to Work*. New York: John Wiley & Sons, 1959.
18. Trist, E., and Murray, H. (eds.), *The Social Engagement of Social Science: A Tavistock Anthology, Vol II: The Socio-Technical Perspective*. Philadelphia: University of Pennsylvania Press, 1993.
19. Susman, G. I. *Autonomy at Work: A Sociotechnical Analysis of Participative Management*. New York: Praeger, 1976.
20. Adapted from Wilhelm, P. G. Productive employment of the handicapped: Compliance strategies for the Americans with Disabilities Act. *SAM Advanced Management Journal*, Summer 1993, 9–15; Brannick, M. T., Brannick, J. P., and Levine, E. L. Job analysis, personnel selection, and the ADA. *Human Resource Management Review*, 1992, 2, 171–182.
21. Aichholzer, G., and Schienstock, G. (eds.), *Technology Policy: Toward an Integration of Social and Ecological Concerns*. New York: de Gruyter, 1994.
22. Quinn, J. B. *Intelligent Enterprise: A Knowledge and Service Based Paradigm for Industry*. New York: Free Press, 1992.
23. Wall, T. D., Jackson, P. R., and Davids, K. Operator work design and robotics system performance: A serendipitous field study. *Journal of Applied Psychology*, 1992, 77, 353–362.
24. Slocum, J.W., Jr., and Sims, H. P., Jr. A typology for integrating technology, organization, and job design. *Human Relations*, 1980, 33, 193–212; Wall, T. D., Corbett, J. M., Martin, R., Clegg, C. W., and Jackson, P. R. Advanced manufacturing technology, work design, and performance: A change study. *Journal of Applied Psychology*, 1990, 75, 691–697.
25. Thompson, J. D. *Organizations in Action*, New York: McGraw-Hill, 1967; Saavedra, R., Early, P. C.,and Van Dyne, L. Complex interdependence in task-performing groups. *Journal of Applied Psychology*, 1993, 78, 61–72.
26. La Plante, A. It's wired Willy Loman! *Forbes ASAP*, April 11, 1994, 46–55.
27. Ibid., 46–55 (adapted from).
28. Hackman, J. R., and Oldham, G. R. *Work Redesign*. Reading, Mass.: Addison-Wesley, 1980.
29. Ibid., 77–80. Also see Staw, B. M., and Boettger, R. D. Task revision: A neglected form of work performance. *Academy of Management Journal*, 1990, 33, 534–559.
30. Hackman, J. R., and Oldham, G. R. *Work Redesign*, Reading,

Mass.: Addison-Wesley, 1980, 82–88.

31. Johns, G., Xie, J. L., and Fang, Y. Mediating and moderating effects in job design. *Journal of Management*, 1992, 18, 657–676; Ackerman, P. L. Predicting individual differences in complex skill acquisition: Dynamics of ability determinants. *Journal of Applied Psychology*, 1992, 77, 598–614.

32. Kelly, K. Motorola: Training for the millennium. *Business Week*, March 28, 1994, 158–162.

33. Graen, G. B., Scandura, T. A., and Graen, M. R. A field experimental test of the moderating effect of growth-need strength on productivity. *Journal of Applied Psychology*, 1986, 71, 484–491.

34. Tiegs, R. B., Tetrick, L. E., and Fried, Y. Growth need strength and context satisfactions as moderators of the relations of the job characteristics model. *Journal of Management*, 1992, 18, 575–593.

35. Campion, M. A., and McClelland, C. L. Interdisciplinary examination of the costs and benefits of enlarged jobs: A job design quasi-experiment. *Journal of Applied Psychology*, 1991, 76, 186–198. Also see Wagner, J.A. III. Participation's effects on performance and satisfaction: A reconsideration of research evidence. *Academy of Management Review*, 1994, 19, 312–330.

36. Perlman, S. L. Employees redesign their jobs. *Personnel Journal*, November 1990, 37–40; Shostak, A. B. The nature of work in the twenty-first century: Certain uncertainties. *Business Horizons*, November–December 1993, 30–34.

37. Murphy, K. R. *Honesty in the Workplace*. Pacific Grove, Calif.: Brooks/Cole, 1993; Nebeker, D. M., and Tatum, B. C. The effects of computer monitoring, standards, and rewards on work performance, job satisfaction, and stress. *Journal of Applied Social Psychology*, 1993, 23, 508–536.

38. Griffith, T. L. Teaching Big Brother to be a team player: Computer monitoring and quality. *Academy of Management Executive*, February 1993, 73–80.

39. Adapted from Bylinsky, G. How companies spy on employees. *Forbes*, November 4, 1991, 131–140; Hays, L. Personal effect: Amid all the talk about the wonders of the networks, some nagging social questions arise. *Wall Street Journal*, November 15, 1993, R16; Sixel, L. M. Look who's watching. *Houston Chronicle*, April 24, 1994, 1E, 6E.

40. Whitsett, D. A. Where are your enriched jobs? *Harvard Business Review*, January–February 1975, 74–80.

41. Ilgen, D. R., and Hollenbeck, J. R. The structure of work: Job design and roles. In M. D. Dunnette and L. M. Hough (eds.), *Handbook of Industrial and Organizational Psychology*, vol. 2, 2nd ed. Palo Alto, Calif.: Consulting Psychologists Press, 1991, 165–207.

42. Hackman, J. R., and Oldham, G. R. Development of the job diagnostic survey. *Journal of Applied Psychology*, 1975, 60, 159–170; Idaszak, J. R. and Drasgow, F. A. Revision of the job diagnostic survey: Elimination of a measurement artifact. *Journal of Applied Psychology*, 1987, 72, 69–74.

43. Reid, A. *Teleworking*. Cambridge, Mass.: Blackwell, 1994.

44. Sellers, P. Companies that serve you best. *Fortune*, May 31, 1993, 74–88.

45. Gleckman, H. The technology payoff: A sweeping reorganization of work itself is boosting productivity. *Business Week*, June 14, 1993, 57–68.

46. Herold, D. M., and Parsons, C. K. Assessing the feedback environment in work organizations: Development of the job feedback survey. *Journal of Applied Psychology*, 1985, 70, 290–305.

47. Straus, S. G., and McGrath, J. E. Does the medium matter? The interaction of task type and technology on group performance and member reactions. *Journal of Applied Psychology*, 1994, 79, 87–97; Campion, M. A., Medsker, G. J., and Higgs, A. C. Relations between work group characteristics and effectiveness: Implications for designing effective work groups. *Personnel Psychology*, 1993, 46, 823–850.

48. Adapted from Griffin, R. W. Effects of work redesign on employee perceptions, attitudes and behaviors: A long-term investigation. *Academy of Management Journal*, 1991, 34, 425–435.

49. Thomas, J. G., and Griffin, R. W. The power of social information in the workplace. *Organizational Dynamics*, Winter 1989, 63–75.

50. Pfeiffer, J. Management as symbolic action: The creation and maintenance of organizational paradigms. In L. L. Cummings and B. M. Staw (eds.), *Research in Organizational Behavior*, vol. 3. Greenwich, Conn.: JAI Press, 1981, 1–32. Also see Sandelands, L. E. Perceptual organization in task performance. *Organizational Behavior and Human Decision Processes*, 1987, 40, 287–306.

51. Griffin, R. W., Bateman, T. S., Wayne, S. J., and Head, T. C. Objective and social factors as determinants of task perceptions and responses: An integrated perspective and empirical investigation. *Academy of Management Journal*, 1987, 30, 501–523; Ornstein, S. The hidden influences of office design. *Academy of Management Executive*, May 1989, 144–147; Head, T. C., Griffin, R. W., Bateman, T. S., Lohman, L., and Yates, V. L. The priming effect in task design research. *Journal of Management*, 1988, 14, 31–39.

52. Baldwin, M. W. Relational schemas and processing of social information. *Psychological Bulletin*, 1992, 112, 461–484.

53. Cherns, A. Principles of sociotechnical design revisited. *Human Relations*, 1987, 40, 153–162; Pava, C. Redesigning sociotechnical systems design: Concepts and methods for the 1990s. *Journal of Applied Behavioral Science*, 1986, 22, 201–221.

54. Trist, E., and Murray, H. (eds.), *The Social Engagement of Social Science: A Tavistock Anthology, Vol. II: The Socio-Technical Perspective*. Philadelphia: University of Pennsylvania Press, 1993.

55. Dumaine, B. Who needs a boss? *Fortune*, May 7, 1990, 52–60.

56. Wall, T. D., Kemp, N. J., Jackson, P. R., and Cleff, C. W. Outcomes of autonomous workgroups: A long-term field experiment. *Academy of Management Journal*, 1986, 29, 280–304.

57. Pasmore, W. A. *Designing Effective Organizations: The Sociotechnical Systems Perspective*. New York: John Wiley & Sons, 1988, 157–186; Argyris, C. Teaching smart people how to learn. *Harvard Business Review*, May–June, 1991, 99–109.

58. Adapted from Adler, P. S., and Cole, R. E. Designed for learning: A tale of two auto plants. *Sloan Management Review*, Spring 1993, 85–93; Adler, P.S. (ed.), *Technology and the Future of Work*. New York: Oxford University Press, 1992; Adler, P. S. Time and motion regained. *Harvard Business Review*, January–February 1993, 97–108.

59. Lawler, E. E. III. The new plant revolution revisited. *Organizational Dynamics*, Autumn 1990, 5–14.

60. *Source*: Halsey Jones, Professor of Management, Department of Management, University of Central Florida, 1994. Used with permission.

17 Organization Design

LEARNING OBJECTIVES

When you have finished studying this chapter, you should be able to:

▲ Explain the influence of environmental forces, strategic choices, and technological factors on the design of organizations.

▲ Indicate the relationship between reengineering and organization design.

▲ Point out the key differences and relationships in seven organization designs and the nature of mechanistic and organic systems.

▲ Describe functional, place, product, horizontal, and matrix designs and the conditions for their use.

▲ Discuss multidivisional, multinational, and network designs and conditions for their use.

OUTLINE

Preview Case: Xerox's New Design

Key Factors in Design

Environmental Forces

Strategic Choices

Technological Factors

Managing in Practice: Fannie Mae

Comparative Framework

Relation to Reengineering

Managing Quality: Ford Reengineers Accounts Payable

Mechanistic Versus Organic Systems

Hierarchy of Authority

Division of Labor

Managing in Practice: Gore's Organic System

Rules and Procedures

Impersonality

Managing Diversity: Sexual Harassment Complaint Procedures

Functional Design

Line and Staff Functions

Link to Task Environment

Chain of Command

Span of Control

Managing Ethics: Ethics Positions and Offices

Conditions for Use

Place Design

Link to Internationalization

Conditions for Use

Product Design

Typical Evolution

Multidivisional Design

Managing in Practice: Johnson & Johnson's Multidivisional Design

Conditions for Use

Integration of Units

Horizontal Design

Managing Quality: NCR's U.S. Group Quality Improvement Design

Matrix Design

Multinational Design

Basic Options

Conditions for Use

Managing Across Cultures: Ford's New Global Design

Network Design

Managing in Practice: Eastman Chemical's Network Design

Key Characteristics

Role of Information Technologies

External Networking

Managing Across Cultures: Procter & Gamble's New Network Design

DEVELOPING SKILLS

Self-Diagnosis: *Inventory of Effective Design*

A Case in Point: *Aquarius Advertising Agency*

563

PREVIEW CASE

Xerox's New Design

Xerox replaced its old "playbook" with a radically different organization design intended to change how employees think and act. The overhaul under CEO Paul Allaire reflects how a big company can adapt to rapidly changing technology and competition. The $18 billion company that unveiled the first plain-paper copier in 1959 has eliminated layers of management. Its old design made Xerox a classic American corporation in which the chairman and top executives made nearly all of the significant decisions.

"This is not an evolution, it's a revolution," said Colin O'Brien, who heads one of Xerox's nine new market-based divisions. "This company had been organized in a monolithic approach since 1959. It institutionalized the monolithic approach to management." About 12 years ago, Xerox was near collapse. It was bogged down by bureaucracy, slow to market its cutting-edge products, and lost sales to Japanese competitors such as Cannon and Sharp. Management and unions were bitter foes.

Under the old structure the chairman was at the top and factory workers at the bottom. Xerox operations were grouped into four gigantic units based on function: manufacturing, research and development, marketing, and finance. Today, Xerox's new divisions resemble independent businesses, with each performing nearly all functions. The company no longer has one all powerful president, but a six-person corporate office headed by Allaire. Three separate geographic units sell and service all Xerox products. The nine divisions—three each for the copier, printer, and software and services markets—have 23 business units, where most decisions are made about what machines to build, how to build them, and where to get materials.

Orders used to descend from the top of the pyramid and reports moved from the bottom up. Thick layers of management encouraged caution, slow decision making and inefficiency. To create diverse teams within the divisions, Xerox shifted scores of engineers into marketing, finance, and other areas. Decision-making authority has been increased among designers and engineers, led by the business unit managers.

A simple decision like the color of the buttons on a copier used to climb the hierarchy nearly to corporate headquarters. Now such decisions are made by the product divisions. Divisions are accountable for their own profits and loss, but they must share engineering designs across the company. On the manufacturing side, Xerox needs to ensure that divisions don't monopolize cost-effective practices. Also, salespeople remain accountable to all divisions because Xerox isn't breaking up its sales force. Thus, customers don't have to meet with a variety of representatives from different divisions.[1]

Organization design is the process of diagnosing and selecting the structure and formal system of communication, division of labor, coordination, control, authority, and responsibility necessary to achieve the organization's goals. The Preview Case demonstrated how slow and top-down decision making, increased competitive pressures, and changing technologies triggered a reevaluation of Xerox's organization design. Design decisions involve the diagnosis of complex and multiple factors.[2] Xerox discovered that its centralized decision-making process, numerous organizational levels, and primary division of labor based on function—manufacturing, research and development, marketing, and finance—could no longer cope with complex, diverse, and changing environmental factors.

Organization design both reflects and helps to shape the organization's culture, power and political behaviors, and job design. Organization design represents the outcomes from a decision-making process that encompasses environmental forces, technological factors, and strategic choices.[3] Specifically, organization design should

▲ ease the flow of information and decision making in meeting the demands of customers, suppliers, and regulatory agencies;

▲ clearly define the authority and responsibility for jobs, teams, departments, and divisions; and

▲ create the desired levels of integration (coordination) among jobs, teams, departments, and divisions.

One cornerstone of organization design is the design of individual jobs (see Chapter 16). A second cornerstone is the formation and use of teams—such as problem-solving teams, special-purpose teams, and self-managed teams (see Chapter 9). A third cornerstone is the design of interteam relations, including consideration of group goals, substitutability, types of task relations, and resource sharing (see Chapter 10). Recall that organization design mechanisms for managing interteam relations included organization hierarchy, linking roles, task forces, and integrating roles and teams. The fourth cornerstone includes both organizational culture and power and political behavior (see Chapters 14 and 15). Recall that organizational culture is a set of shared philosophies, values, assumptions, and norms that influence organizational decisions and actions. The organization's culture is likely to influence organization design decisions, such as changes in the delegation of authority or the use of teams. Power and political behavior usually come into play when major changes in organization design are being considered. Xerox changed from a design that concentrated power and influence in functional units to one that concentrated power and influence in business divisions that are closer to the customers. Paul Alliare, the chief executive officer, and other key people at Xerox had to deal with the potential loss of power and related political behavior in these functional units before they could implement these changes. In doing so, Alliare initiated a systematic 15-month design process that heavily involved more than 75 of Xerox's managers. After receiving their initial recommendations, he formed an Organizational Transition Board and charged it with refining the recommendations. This board consisted of 15 influential senior managers and 5 influential support staff.[4]

In this chapter, we first note how environmental forces, strategic choices, and technological factors can influence the design of an organization. We present a broad framework to suggest how particular patterns of these factors tend to fit different organization designs and briefly discuss how reengineering and organization design are related. Then, we introduce and compare mechanistic and organic systems and show how each type reflects a basic strategic choice by top managers and the organization culture. Next, we describe the functional, place, and product bases of design. Then, we explain how to use the horizontal and matrix designs to improve integration across units. Next, we present multinational design options as ways to respond to multiple demands, primarily owing to diversity in the customers, cultures, and geographic markets served. Finally, we describe the newest approach to organization design—the network organization—a method intended to overcome the limitations of the others in the face of complex, diverse, and changing environments, technologies, and strategic choices.

▼ KEY FACTORS IN DESIGN

Organization design decisions (e.g., greater decentralization and empowerment of employees) may solve one set of problems but create others. Because every organization design has some drawbacks, the key is to select an organ

-ization design that minimizes them. Table 17.1 identifies several variables for each of the three primary factors—environmental forces, strategic choices, and technological capabilities—that affect organization design decisions.

▼ Environmental Forces

The environmental forces that managers and other employees need to assess are (1) the *characteristics* of the present and possible future environments and (2) the *demands* of those environments on the need to process information, cope with uncertainties, and achieve desired levels of differentiation (division of labor) and integration (coordination).

Environmental Characteristics   The **task environment** includes the external stakeholders and forces that directly affect the organization.[5] Major stakeholders include customers, suppliers, regulatory agencies, shareholders, and creditors. After identifying the relevant stakeholders and forces in the task environment, management should assess their characteristics and relative importance to the organization.[6] Environmental characteristics basically vary in terms of complexity and dynamism.

Complexity refers to whether characteristics are few and similar (homogeneous) or many and different (heterogeneous). Employees involved in planning typically face a heterogeneous environment comprising numerous and diverse stakeholders. However, custodial employees face a homogeneous environment. Rating an environment as homogeneous or heterogeneous depends both on the number of factors and the number of subenvironments involved. Five factors in one subenvironment, such as the customer subenvironment, would not be as complex as five factors in three subenvironments, such as customers, suppliers, and competitors. As suggested by the formation of nine product divisions and three geographic units, Xerox recognized that the task environment had become too complex and dynamic for its functional design.

Dynamism relates to whether environmental characteristics remain basically the same (are stable) or change (are unstable). Xerox also saw the task environment as changing and decided to make its design more responsive to those changes. Dynamism also relates to the need for *speed* in responding to

TABLE 17.1   **Key Factors in Organization Design Decisions**

Factors	Sample Variables
Environmental forces	Degree of complexity Degree of dynamism
Strategic choices	Top management's philosophy Types of customers Geographic areas served Total quality values
Technological capabilities	Work-flow uncertainty Task uncertainty Task interdependence

customers' and other stakeholders' demands. Organizations increasingly must be able to respond quickly and flexibly, a need explicitly addressed by Xerox in its new design.

Types of Task Environments   Task environments are classified on the basis of complexity and dynamism in Figure 17.1. The four "pure" types of task environments are homogeneous–stable, heterogeneous–stable, homogeneous–unstable, and heterogeneous–unstable. You can locate the environment of an organization or its departments and divisions anywhere on this grid.

The *homogeneous–stable environment* (box 1) represents the easiest design situation. The task environment holds few surprises, and the manager's role is to be sure that employees consistently follow established routines and procedures. Managers and employees need relatively less skills, formal training, and job experience to operate successfully in this environment than in the others. Organizations that primarily operate in this environment include basic lawn care firms, local delivery service firms, car wash firms, mail service firms, and self-service storage firms. Of course, these firms do face uncertainties created by competitors' actions, customers changing preferences, and potential substitutes for their products and services.

FIGURE 17.1

Basic Types of Task Environments

	Homogeneous ← Degree of Complexity → Heterogeneous
Stable ↑	**Low Uncertainty** 1 — • Few environmental factors exist. • Factors are similar to each other. • Factors remain basically the same. *Example:* Salt manufacturers, Printing firms	**Moderate Uncertainty** 2 — • Many environmental factors exist. • Factors are not similar to each other. • Factors remain basically the same. *Example:* Registrar's offices in universities, Gasoline refining/distribution firms
Unstable ↓	**Moderately High Uncertainty** 3 — • Few environmental factors exist. • Factors are similar to each other. • Factors are continually changing. *Example:* Fast-food firms, Consumer products firms	**High Uncertainty** 4 — • Many environmental factors exist. • Factors are not similar to each other. • Factors are continually changing. *Example:* Telecommunications firms, Biotechnology firms

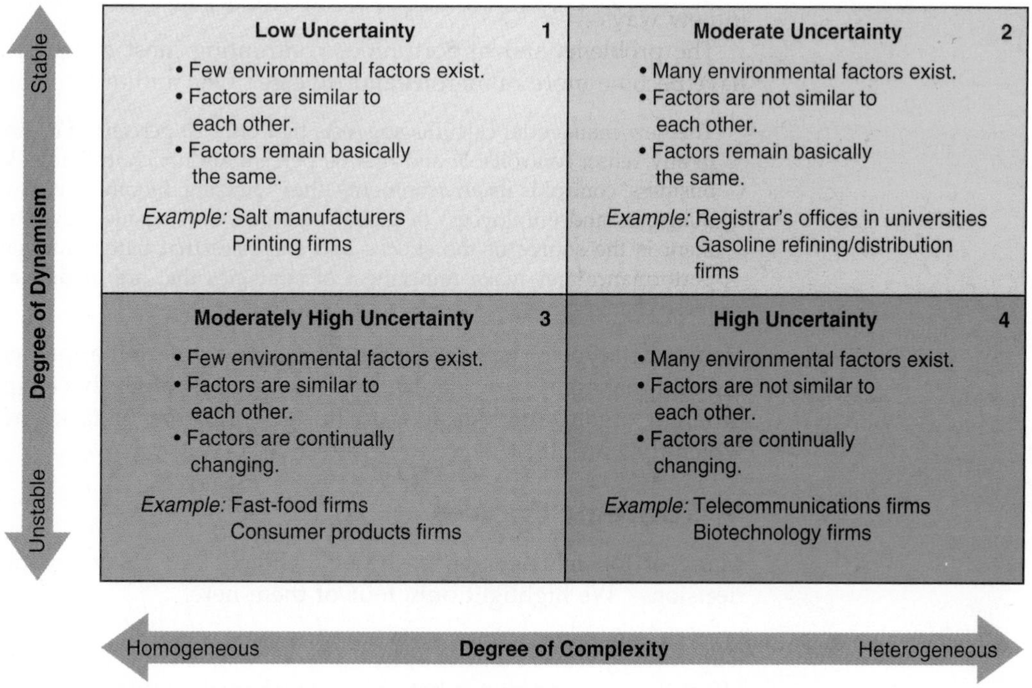

Source: Adapted from Rasheed, A., and Prescott, J. E. Dimensions of organizational task environments: Revisited. Paper presented at 1987 Academy of Management meeting, New Orleans, 1987; Duncan, R. What is the right organization structure? Decision tree analysis provides the answer. *Organizational Dynamics,* Winter 1979, 60–64.

The *heterogeneous–stable environment* (box 2) poses some risks for managers and employees, but the environment and the alternatives are fairly well understood. Managers can assign probabilities to the effects of various alternatives. The environment is relatively stable, but organization members may need considerable training and experience to understand and manage it. For example, the registrar's office of a college or university must communicate with academic departments, current and prospective students, the central administration, and government education agencies. The nature of these communications doesn't change frequently, and they usually are guided by extensive rules and procedures.

The *homogeneous–unstable environment* (box 3) requires managers, employees, and organization designs to be flexible. Frequent changes can be handled with reasonable levels of skill and motivation. Computer-based information systems often help keep track of the changes. McDonald's, for example, frequently offers new menu items, to attract and retain customers, but they all are relatively easy to make.

The *heterogeneous–unstable environment* (box 4) represents the most difficult organization situation because the environment contains numerous uncertainties. Of all task environments, this one requires the most managerial and employee sophistication, insight, and problem-solving abilities. Decision-making techniques can help, but they are no substitute for human judgment. Managers can't solve the problems confronting them merely by using standardized rules and procedures. Xerox operates in a heterogeneous–unstable environment. The company's organization design changes were intended to encourage employees at lower levels to take the initiative, innovate, and go after business in new ways.

The problems and opportunities confronting most complex organizations have become more numerous and diverse.[7] One authority commented:

> The new managerial calculus suggests that only 20 percent of business factors are, in any sense, controllable and that 80 percent are noncontrollable. What is beyond business' control is its environment—that "buzzing, blooming confusion" (to many managers and employees) of global, national, and business events. This environment is the source of the shocks and surprises that batter international business performance and make mincemeat of strategies that are inadequately attuned to these changes.[8]

Hence each type of task environment requires different approaches to designing and managing an organization. As we go through this chapter, we relate different organization designs to the general type of task environment for which they are most likely to be effective.

▼ Strategic Choices

Many of top management's strategic choices can affect organization design decisions.[9] We highlight only four of them here.

Top Management's Philosophy   Top management's values and philosophy affect the strategic choice between a mechanistic (centralized) and an organic (decentralized) design and control system. A mechanistic system usually requires more levels in the hierarchy with more resources devoted to monitoring and controlling employees than does an organic system. For example, quality control, human resources, and auditing functions may be given relatively large budgets and considerable authority in a mechanistic system.

Customers to be Served   Another important strategic choice involves top management's decisions about the types of customers it wants to serve. A firm that tries to sell to industrial, commercial, and residential customers often needs a different organization design than a firm that tries to sell only to industrial customers. Firms that sell multiple lines of goods or services, such as IBM, Xerox, and Procter & Gamble, often bring together the resources needed to manufacture and market each major product line.

Where to Market and Produce   Top management's strategic choice of where to produce and market goods and services is significant. For example, Allstate Insurance markets insurance only in North America. Ford Motor Company, KFC (formerly Kentucky Fried Chicken), and Sony have defined the world as their market. They need more complex designs than firms that only manufacture and market in a particular country or region of the world.

Strategy of Total Quality   An essential strategic choice is the degree to which top management and other organizational members pursue *total quality*. Total quality isn't merely a patch on the way management currently runs the organization. Rather, it is an organizational *strategy* that drives an ongoing, continuous process. It may require radical changes in organization design and day-to-day operations. The following core values and perspectives are generally recognized as characteristics of an organization that strives for total quality.

▲ Methods, processes, and procedures are designed to meet both internal and external customer expectations.

▲ Top management fully understands the quality process (often having been through the same training given to the others) and supports the strategy through both words and actions. Everyone in the organization receives quality training. Everyone has the perspective, goals, and the necessary tools and techniques for improving quality.

▲ Everyone makes a strong effort to reduce the cycle times of product and service outputs and support functions. They follow the maxim, "If it cannot be done any better, focus on doing it faster." Quality is designed into the products and services. Errors are prevented from occurring rather than being detected and then corrected.

▲ The organization constantly monitors customers, competitors, suppliers, and others to determine the level of quality or service that will have to be provided to customers over the next 12–36 months and how best to do so.

▲ The organization promotes cooperation with both suppliers and customers by developing a network system that helps drive up quality and hold down costs. Corporate citizenship and responsibility are fostered by sharing quality-related information with other organizations. The desire is to reduce negative impacts on the community by eliminating product waste generation and product defects and recalls.[10]

These examples of the importance of strategic choices to organization design illustrate a key point: Organization design often is created and modified as a result of strategic choices, as illustrated by Xerox in the Preview Case.

▼ Technological Factors

Recall that the technological factors of work-flow uncertainty, task uncertainty, and task interdependence affect job design. These same technological factors also influence organization design in terms of the creation of teams and departments, the delegation of authority and responsibility, and the need for formal integrating mechanisms.

Work-Flow and Task Uncertainty   In terms of organization design, *work-flow uncertainty* is the degree of knowledge in a department (or other unit) about when inputs will be received for processing. When work-flow uncertainty is low, a department has little discretion to decide which, when, or where tasks will be performed. *Task uncertainty* is the degree of knowledge in a department with respect to performing the tasks assigned to it.[11] When task uncertainty is low, employees generally know how to produce the desired outcomes. When task uncertainty is high, employees have few (if any) prespecified ways for dealing with the tasks assigned. In this case, key members of the department usually have to apply experience, judgment, and intuition—and jointly define and solve problems—in order to achieve the desired outcomes.

Parallel to the discussion of job design and technology in Chapter 16 (see, especially, Figure 16.3), we first consider the effects of work-flow uncertainty and task uncertainty on organization design and then discuss the effects of task interdependence on organization design.[12] Figure 17.2 shows possible linkages between work-flow uncertainty and task uncertainty. Both can range from low to high, again yielding four combinations.

FIGURE 17.2
───────────

Technology and Organization Design Framework

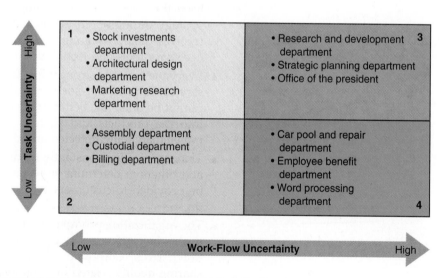

Source: Adapted from Slocum, J. W., Jr., and Sims, H. P., Jr. Typology for integrating technology, organization, and job design. *Human Relations*, 1980, 33, 196; Susman, G. I. *Autonomy at Work: A Sociotechnical Analysis of Participative Management.* New York: Praeger, 1980, 132.

Each cell shows departments that often are representative of that combination. An organizational unit may fit into more than one of these cells. Through organization redesign, most units can be modified and the task uncertainty and work-flow uncertainty changed. The office of the president and the strategic planning department generally are characterized by high task uncertainty and high work-flow uncertainty. However, some of the specific tasks that they perform could be classified anywhere on the matrix. Some departments do not fit neatly into a single cell. For example, the auditing department in an accounting firm might fit somewhere in the middle of Figure 17.2. One of the implications of the framework is to recognize similarities in technological characteristics by creating functional departments, such as those shown.

Task Interdependence   Recall that task interdependence may be pooled, sequential, or reciprocal. In terms of organization design, we can characterize them in the following manner.

▲ *Pooled interdependence* occurs when departments or teams are relatively autonomous and make an identifiable contribution to the organization. For example, the many sales and services offices of State Farm Insurance do not engage in day-to-day decision making, coordination, and communication with each other. The local offices are interdependent with regional offices that coordinate and set policies for the local sales and services offices. The performance of each local office is readily identifiable.

▲ *Sequential interdependence* occurs when one department or team must complete certain tasks before one or more other departments or teams can perform their tasks. For example, at Whirlpool's washing machine factory, the fabrication department provides its outputs to the assembly department, which, in turn, provides its outputs to the painting and finishing department, and so on.

▲ *Reciprocal interdependence* occurs when the outputs from one department or team become the inputs for another department or team and vice versa. For example, the planning, marketing, and research and development departments at AT&T are likely to be reciprocally interdependent in the development of new telecommunication services and the offering of these services to customers.

As Figure 17.3 shows, reciprocal interdependence is the most complex type, and pooled interdependence is the simplest type. Greater interdependence generally requires greater integration. Placing reciprocally interdependent departments or teams under a common superior often improves integration and minimizes information processing costs. For example, at Brooklyn Union Company, the marketing research, advertising, and sales departments report to the vice-president of marketing. Employees in these departments must communicate and coordinate more with each other than with employees in the maintenance department.

In previous chapters, we discussed how new information technologies are changing many jobs. These information technologies also affect the design of organizations and the flows of information through them.[13] The following

FIGURE 17.3

Types of Task Interdependence in
Organization Design

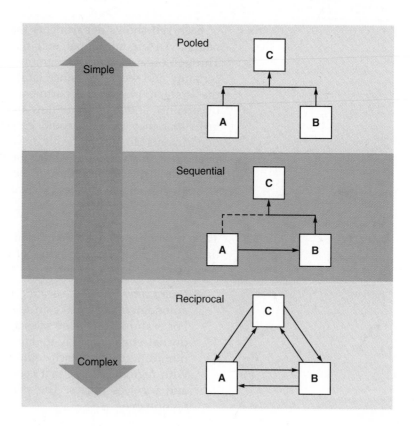

Managing in Practice feature reveals how "Fannie Mae" redesigned itself and
adopted new computer-based information technologies to improve its ability
to manage numerous task interdependencies. An increasingly unstable and
heterogeneous market prompted these changes.

MANAGING IN PRACTICE

Fannie Mae

The Federal National Mortgage Association (Fannie Mae) seemed the very
essence of a modern, high-tech organization. Fannie Mae, the nation's largest
buyer of home mortgages, was built on information stored in banks of mainframe computers. The computers processed huge quantities of loan information and permitted the company to pool millions of mortgages into easily sold
securities. By the early 1990s, those mainframes and a highly centralized management system had become barriers to Fannie Mae's future expansion.

Despite their enormous power, the Washington-based company's computers simply couldn't keep up with the growing volume of work. So Fannie Mae
began redesigning itself. It broke down the old centralized departments that
slowed things down and replaced them with work teams that linked financial,
marketing, and computer experts at the start of each loan. A network of more
than 2,000 personal computers now ties the new system together. New software makes the PCs accessible to employees with a minimum of training.

The $10 million investment in the new PCs and related equipment paid for
itself in less than a year. When interest rates plunged in 1992, home refinanc-

MANAGING IN PRACTICE —*Continued*

ing began to surge. Volume soared, but so did productivity: Fannie Mae handled $257 billion in new loans, nearly double its 1991 volume. But, it had to add only 100 more employees to a work force of nearly 3,000. "If we had not used this technology," says vice-chairman Franklin D. Raines, "our business would have collapsed." The Fannie Mae story is a small part of the information technology revolution that is sweeping America's offices and factories.[14]

▼ Comparative Framework

Figure 17.4 shows seven common organization design approaches. These approaches, and the conditions under which they are most likely to be effective, are contrasted in terms of the key factors in organization design. We combined the various environmental forces into a single continuum on the vertical axis. It ranges from a complex, dynamic environment to a simple, stable environment. We also combined the technological factors into a single continuum on the vertical axis. It ranges from complex and high uncertainty to simple and low uncertainty. We show strategic choices on the horizontal axis. At one end of the continuum is a cluster of choices that reflect diversity in customers, products, and geographic markets, represented by firms such as Ford Motor Company, IBM, and Procter & Gamble. At the other end of the continuum is a cluster of choices that reflect uniformity in customers, products, and geographic markets, represented by firms such as Avis Rent-a-Car, Allstate Insurance Company, and the Motel 6 chain.

The comparative framework shown broadly portrays how the design of an organization may differ and change as a result of various patterns of environmental forces, technological factors, and strategic choices. The simplest environment (lower left) implies that some version of the functional organization design is likely to be appropriate. The most complex environment (upper right) implies that some form of the network organization design is likely to be appropriate. In general, the designs become more complex from the functional design to the network design. The horizontal design options, shown on the diagonal line, change from simple and standard horizontal integrating mechanisms (such as a committee) to complex and varied options (such as the sophisticated computer-based network at Fannie Mae).

After considering the relationship between organization design and reengineering, we will review a key strategic choice that reflects both top management's philosophy, and the prevailing organizational culture, including power and political behavior. That choice determines whether the organization will tend to be mechanistic or organic. This strategic choice and other key factors in organization design decisions are shown as *foundation influences* in Figure 17.4.[15]

▼ Relation to Reengineering

In our discussion of the relationship of job design to reengineering (see Chapter 16), we defined *reengineering* as radically new ways of thinking about organizing and breaking away from outdated assumptions, rules, and proce-

FIGURE 17.4

Factors and Key Options in Organization Design

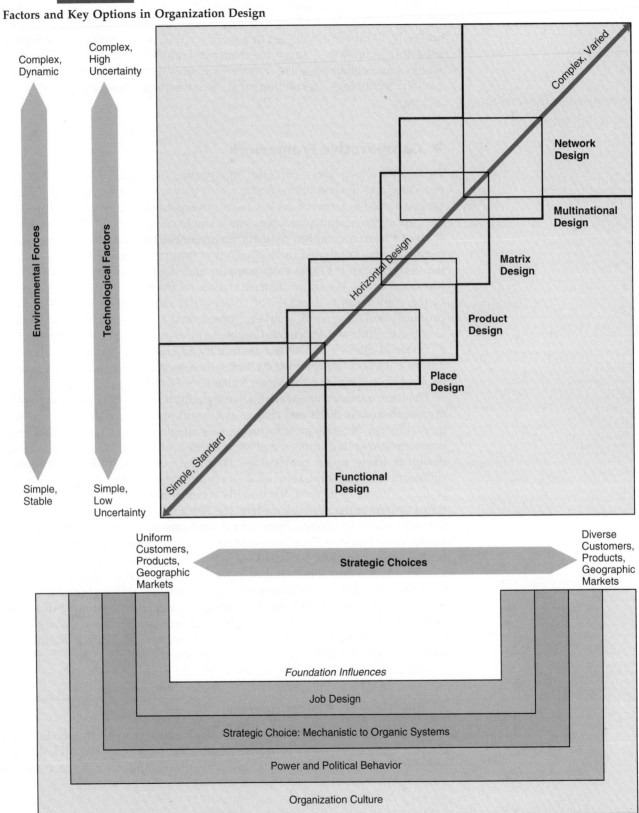

dures. The need to diagnose and address environmental forces, technological factors, and strategic choices in organization design is consistent with the reengineering approach. Therefore, we support the need to ask certain fundamental questions in undertaking a diagnosis to determine the appropriate organization design, two of which are: Why do we do what we do? Why do we do it the way we do?

But, unlike the reengineering approach, we do not suggest that "starting all over" or "starting from scratch" in changing the organization's design is always necessary or feasible. In some situations, an evolutionary approach to organization design may be more feasible and effective. As with reengineering, we provide guidance on the choice of organization design that is likely to deliver value to customers and other stakeholders.[16] A central tenet in reengineering is to make fundamental changes in business processes, which in turn affects organization design. The following Managing Quality feature reveals how Ford Motor Company reengineered its accounts payable process. Ford had compared its process against Mazda's, discovering that its process was slow, confusing, expensive, and error prone. Reengineering was the solution adopted.

MANAGING QUALITY

Ford Reengineers Accounts Payable

Under the old system, Ford's purchasing department would send a purchase order to a supplier with a copy going to the accounts payable department. When the goods arrived at Ford, a clerk at the receiving dock completed a form describing the goods and then sent it to accounts payable. Meanwhile, the supplier sent accounts payable an invoice. The system was ponderous. Many of the department's 500 clerks spent most of their time straightening out discrepancies in purchase order, receiving, and invoice documents. Sometimes resolution required weeks of time and enormous amounts of work to trace and correct documents.

Ford's new accounts payable process is radically different. Accounts payable clerks no longer match the purchase order and receiving document because the new process eliminated the invoice entirely. Now, when a buyer in the purchasing department issues a purchase order to a vendor, the buyer simultaneously enters the order into an on-line database. Suppliers, as before, send goods to the receiving dock. When they arrive, someone in receiving uses a computer terminal to see whether the received shipment corresponds to an outstanding purchase order in the database. Only two possibilities exist: It does, or it doesn't. If it does, the employee at the dock accepts the goods and pushes a button on the terminal keyboard to tell the database that the goods have arrived. The receipt of the goods is now recorded in the database. The computer will automatically issue and send a check to the supplier at the appropriate time. However, if the goods don't correspond to an outstanding purchase order in the database, the employee on the dock refuses the shipment and sends it back to the supplier.

The basic concept of the change at Ford is simple. Payment authorization, which used to be performed by accounts payable, is now accomplished at the receiving dock. The new process allowed Ford to reduce the number of people involved in supplier payment from 500 to 125.[17]

▼ MECHANISTIC VERSUS ORGANIC SYSTEMS

A **mechanistic system** is characterized by reliance on formal rules and regulations, centralization of decision making, narrowly defined job responsibilities, and a rigid hierarchy of authority. In contrast, an **organic system** is characterized by low-to-moderate use of formal rules and regulations, decentralized and shared decision making, broadly defined job responsibilities, and a flexible authority structure with fewer levels in the hierarchy.[18]

Top management typically makes strategic and philosophical choices that determine the extent to which an organization will operate as a mechanistic system or an organic system. Although mechanistic and organic systems are strategic choices, situational forces (such as a dynamic, complex environment versus a stable, simple environment) also are likely to influence the system choice. These alternative systems exist on a continuum from a pure mechanistic system to a pure organic system. The specific organization's version of the system reflects its own underlying organizational culture and power and political profile.

A mechanistic system is essentially a bureaucracy. Max Weber, a German sociologist and economist in the early 1900s, defined a **bureaucracy** as an organization having the following characteristics.

- ▲ The organization operates according to a body of rules, or laws, that are intended to tightly control the behavior of employees.
- ▲ All employees must carefully follow extensive impersonal rules and procedures in making decisions.
- ▲ Each employee's job involves a specified area of expertise, with strictly defined obligations, authority, and powers to compel obedience.
- ▲ The organization follows the principle of hierarchy; that is, each lower position is under the tight control and direction of a higher one.
- ▲ Candidates for jobs are selected on the basis of "technical" qualifications. They are appointed, not elected.
- ▲ The organization has a career ladder. Promotion is by seniority or achievement. Promotion depends on the judgment of superiors.[19]

The word *bureaucracy* often brings to mind rigidity, incompetence, red tape, inefficiency, and ridiculous rules. In principle, though, the basic characteristics of a mechanistic system may make it a feasible approach in some situations.[20] Thus any discussion of a mechanistic system must distinguish between the way it should ideally function and the way some large-scale organizations actually operate.[21]

The degrees to which an organization emphasizes a mechanistic or an organic system can vary substantially, as suggested in Figure 17.5. Organization B represents a relatively mechanistic system in terms of all the selected dimensions. Organization A has a more varied emphasis among the dimensions and represents an organic system. Organization A could be Xerox under its new design, whereas Organization B might approximate Xerox under its old design. Or, Organization A might approximate the system at Southwest Airlines, whereas Organization B might approximate the system at the U.S. or Canadian Postal Services.

The organic system emphasizes employee competence, rather than the employee's formal position in the hierarchy, as a basis for influence in decision

FIGURE 17.5

General Characteristics of Mechanistic and Organic Systems

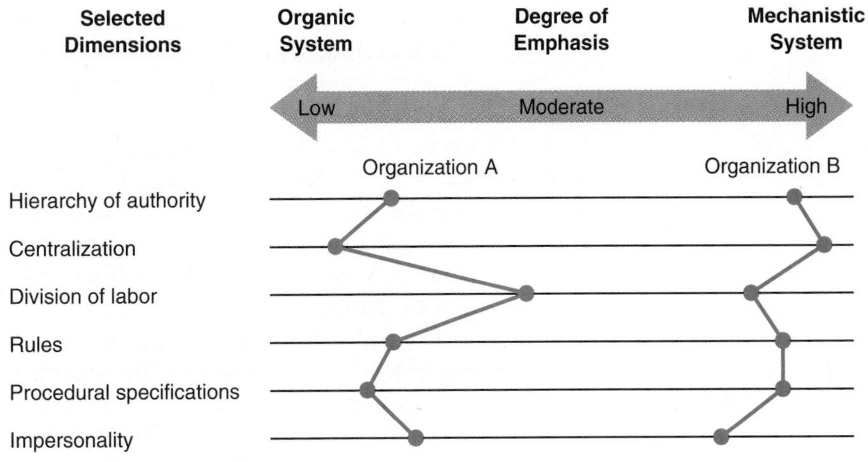

Selected Dimensions	Organic System	Degree of Emphasis	Mechanistic System

making. This system has a flexible hierarchy and empowers employees to deal with uncertainties in technology and the task environment.[22]

▼ Hierarchy of Authority

Hierarchy of authority represents the extent to which decision making processes are prescribed and formal power is allocated. In a mechanistic system higher level departments set or approve goals and detailed budgets for lower level departments and issue orders to them. The philosophy and strategy under the mechanistic system is to have as many levels in the hierarchy as necessary to achieve tight control, whereas the organic system has as few levels as necessary to achieve goals and foster innovation.

The hierarchy-of-authority dimension is related to centralization. **Centralization** means that all major, and oftentimes many minor, decisions are made only at the top levels of the organization.[23] Centralization is common in mechanistic systems, whereas decentralization and shared decision making between and across levels are common in an organic system.[24] At Xerox the chairman and other top executives used to make nearly all decisions of any consequence. In the old hierarchy, orders were sent down and reports were sent up the hierarchy.

▼ Division of Labor

Division of labor refers to the various ways of dividing up tasks and labor to achieve goals.[25] Adam Smith, the father of capitalism, recognized the importance of this concept in his book *An Inquiry into the Nature and Cause of the Wealth of Nations*, published in 1776. Smith suggested that, in general, the greater the division of labor in organizations, the greater would be the efficiency of the organizations and the amount of wealth created.[26]

The mechanistic system typically follows Smith's views. However, a continued increase in the division of labor may eventually become counterproductive. Employees who perform only very routine and simple jobs that require few skills may become bored and frustrated. The results may be low quality and productivity, high turnover, and high absenteeism. In addition, the managerial costs (many reports, more managers, and more controls to administer) of integrating highly specialized functions usually are high. In contrast, the organic system tends to reduce these costs by delegating decision making to lower levels of the organization. Delegation also encourages employees and teams to take on responsibility for achieving their tasks and linking them to those of the entire organization. The organic system takes advantage of the benefits from the division of labor, but it is sensitive to the adverse consequences of carrying division of labor too far. Xerox shifted its division of labor from huge functional units to nine product divisions and three separate geographic units.

The following Managing in Practice item about W. L. Gore & Associates presents a clear example of the organic system in action. Gore's philosophy is to (1) use hierarchy only as necessary, (2) empower and delegate to individuals and teams, and (3) assign employees to each product line. Headquartered in Newark, Delaware, the company manufactures Gore-Tex waterproof fabric for spacesuits and outdoor apparel, cable insulation, no-stick dental floss ("Glide"), industrial filters, and vascular grafting material for surgical repair. The firm has about 6,000 associates (never "employees"), 35 plants worldwide, and annual revenues of about $1 billion. Wilbert L. "Bill" Gore founded the firm in 1958, and it is privately held.

MANAGING IN PRACTICE

Gore's Organic System

Gore is built on what it calls *un-management* This company has no formal organizational chart. The only titles are those required for legal purposes, that is, president and secretary–treasurer, who happen to be Bill Gore's son and widow. Bill Gore died in 1986. Nobody gets hired until a company associate agrees to "sponsor" the person, which includes finding work for that person to do.

At Gore a "product specialist" takes responsibility for developing a product. As it progresses, that person recruits a team from within and outside the firm to work on it. Eventually, the team might become an entire plant. By then the team may have broken into multiple teams, or manufacturing cells. Team members are trained to perform most manufacturing tasks in their "cells." Each team has a leader, who evolves from within that team. The leader is not appointed, but achieves the position by assuming leadership. The leader must be approved in a consensus reached through discussion—not a vote. This approach reflects several of Bill Gore's leadership homilies: "Leadership is a verb, not a noun," "Leadership is defined by what you do, not who you are," and "Leaders are those whom others follow."

No plant has more than 200 associates because Bill Gore thought that people work best together when they know one another. Compensation is determined by a committee, which relies heavily on the evaluations of other associates. The company allows individuals the freedom to grow beyond what they are doing, and they are expected to use it.

MANAGING IN PRACTICE —*Continued*

Like any system, Gore's has its downside—decentralization causes some communications problems, trying to duplicate the Gore culture in some foreign locations has been difficult, and some employees don't like this organic system. "You have to take a lot of responsibility to work here, and not everybody is willing to do that," says Bert Chase, an associate. "This place is for people with bound wings who want to fly."[27]

▼ Rules and Procedures

Rules are formal, written statements specifying acceptable and unacceptable behaviors and decisions by organization members. One of the paradoxes of rules that attempt to reduce individual autonomy is that someone must still decide which rules apply to specific situations. Rules are an integral part of both mechanistic and organic systems. In a mechanistic system, the tendency is to create detailed uniform rules to handle tasks and decisions *whenever possible*. In an organic system, the tendency is to create rules *only when necessary* (such as safety rules to protect life and property). Managers and employees tend to question the need for new rules, as well as existing rules. In a mechanistic system, the tendency is to accept the need for extensive rules and to formulate new rules in response to new situations.

Procedures are the preset sequences of steps that managers and employees must follow in performing tasks and dealing with problems. Procedures often comprise rules that are to be used in a particular sequence. For example, in order to obtain reimbursement for travel expenses in most organizations, employees must follow specific procedures. Procedures have many of the same positive and negative features that characterize rules, and they often proliferate in a mechanistic system. Managers in organic systems usually know that rules and procedures can make the organization too rigid and thus lower employee motivation, innovation, and creativity. In a mechanistic system, rules and procedures tend to be developed at the top and issued through memorandums. Such memos may indicate the expectation of strict compliance and express the adverse consequences of not obeying the new rules or procedures. In an organic system, employee input is likely to be sought on changes in current rules and procedures or on proposed rules and procedures when they are absolutely necessary. In an organic system employees at all levels are expected to question, evaluate, and make suggestions, with an emphasis on collaboration and interdependencies.[28]

▼ Impersonality

Impersonality is the extent to which organizations treat their employees, as well as outsiders, according to objective, detached, and rigid characteristics. A highly mechanistic system is likely to emphasize matter-of-fact indicators (e.g., college degrees, certificates earned, test scores, training programs completed, and length of service) when making hiring, salary, and promotion decisions. Although these factors may be considered in an organic system, the emphasis is likely to be on actual achievements and the professional judgments of individuals rather than on rigid quantitative indicators. Merck is a leading pharmaceutical company and operates as an organic system. A college graduate applying for a job at Merck goes through an extensive interview process. This process may involve several managers, many (if not all) of the employees with whom the applicant would work, and even a casual and informal "interview" by a team of employees. The person responsible for filing the open position solicits opinions and reactions from these employees before making a decision. In some instances, the manager may even call a meeting of the employees and other managers who participated in the interview process to discuss a candidate.

In both mechanistic and organic systems, well-defined rules and procedures may have to be developed and applied through a relatively impersonal process in certain instances. For example, laws, court rulings, and regulatory agency decisions may even mandate impersonality, extensive rules, and rigid procedures.[29] Sexual harassment and safety appear to be two such areas. The following Managing Diversity account provides an example: It presents a few of the rules, procedures, and impersonal process for handling sexual harassment complaints at Texas A&M University. The approach presented is representative of that taken by many U.S. public and private organizations.

MANAGING DIVERSITY

Sexual Harassment Complaint Procedures

The first section of the Texas A&M University sexual harassment complaint rules and procedures sets out in detail the *informal procedures* that are available to the complainant. The second section states the precise *formal procedures* if the complainant elects to file a formal grievance. Step I, entitled Complaint Investigation, presents the rules and procedures to be followed.

If the complaint is against a faculty member, the following procedure applies. A formal complaint filed against a faculty member shall be directed to the dean of faculties, who, in turn, should notify the appropriate college dean and department head within three working days of receipt of the complaint. The college dean and department head should notify the faculty member concerned and investigate the case and determine within 12 working days whether further investigation or a recommendation for sanctions is warranted. Under appropriate circumstances, the dean of the college may decide to convene an ad hoc committee to review the facts surrounding the case and make recommendations of resolution of the complaint. Decisions regarding the complaint and any recommendations for sanctions by the college dean and department head shall be reported to the dean of faculties, who, in turn, shall advise the President through the Provost. The President shall notify the faculty member and the complainant of the decision.

Step II in section two details the optional procedure for the use of an ad hoc committee. Step III sets forth the procedures for appeal by a faculty member, staff member, or student if found guilty and sanctioned. The following statement appears for a faculty member found guilty. If a recommendation of

MANAGING DIVERSITY —*Continued*

sanctions is made against a tenured faculty member or a nontenured faculty member whose term of appointment has not expired, the faculty member may request a due process hearing by the Tenure Advisory Committee and, if necessary, by the Committee on Academic Freedom, Responsibility and Tenure, as provided in the *Texas A&M University Policy*, "Academic Freedom, Responsibility, and Tenure."[30]

▼ FUNCTIONAL DESIGN

Functional design creates positions and units on the basis of specialized activities. Departments of a typical manufacturing firm with a single product line often are grouped by function—engineering, human resources, manufacturing, shipping, purchasing, sales, and finance. Tasks also are usually divided functionally by the *process* used—receiving, stamping, plating, assembly, painting, and inspection (sequential interdependence). Figure 17.6 shows how the Callaway Golf Corporation uses both managerial functions and processes in its design. This firm is the largest golf club manufacturer in the United States. A common theme of functional design proponents was the desirability of standardizing and routinizing repetitive tasks whenever possible. Management could then concentrate on exceptions to eliminate any gaps or overlaps.

▼ Line and Staff Functions

Line functions are those jobs that directly affect the principal work flow in an organization. In a manufacturing firm, for instance, all production activities—engineering, stamping, plating, assembly, painting, inspection, and shipping—are considered to be line functions. **Staff functions** are support jobs

FIGURE 17.6

Callaway Golf's Design by Function and Process

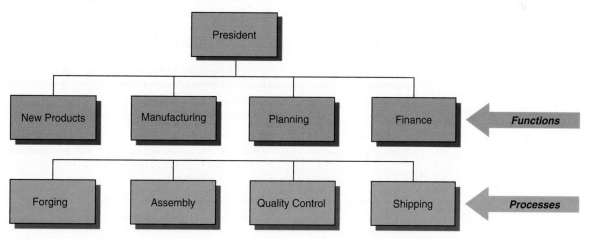

Source: Adapted from *Callaway Golf 1993 Annual Report*, Carlsbad, Calif., 1994.

FIGURE 17.7

Con Edison's Design for Line and Staff Functions

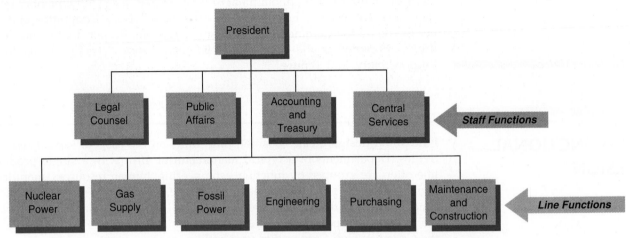

Source: Adapted from *Con Edison 1993 Annual Report*, New York, 1994.

that provide service and advice to line departments. They usually include the human resource, purchasing, legal, and finance departments. Figure 17.7 illustrates how Con Edison, a supplier of electricity to most parts of New York City, uses a line and staff design. For some activities, staff units may be given authority to ensure compliance with laws and regulations and to improve customer service. For example, the human resources department may have the authority to ensure proper hiring and training of employees.[31]

▼ Link to Task Environment

Table 17.2 illustrates a simple functional design in which separate departments specialize in dealing with each major stakeholder in the task environment. For example, the marketing department normally has more direct contact with customers than any of the other departments. At Callaway Golf the new products department has extensive direct contact with golf professionals. The executive team, especially the CEO, is likely to have direct decision-making

TABLE 17.2   Functional Form of Organization and the Task Environment

Department	Primary Links to External Stakeholders
Marketing	Customers, competitors
Manufacturing	Suppliers, customers, regulatory agencies
Purchasing	Suppliers
Human resources	Potential employees, unions, health and life insurance companies, regulatory agencies
Research and development	New scientific knowledge and technology
Legal services	Shareholders, regulatory agencies, courts
Finance and accounting	Creditors and debtors, regulatory agencies

FIGURE 17.8

Span of Control and Organization Shape

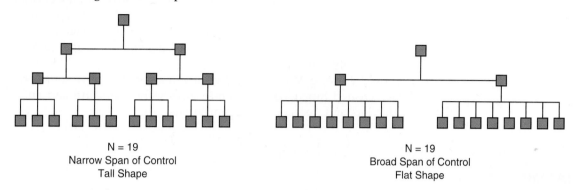

N = 19
Narrow Span of Control
Tall Shape

N = 19
Broad Span of Control
Flat Shape

involvement with many of the stakeholders. The reason is that the executive team, including the board of directors, is usually responsible for (1) setting the major strategies and policies to be followed by the departments in contacts with stakeholders; (2) approving the organization's strategic plan, which is to be followed by each functional department; (3) monitoring and evaluating the organization's effectiveness as a whole, as well as that of key departments; and (4) monitoring changes in the environment and making the key decisions based on their diagnosis, such as to approve major new plant construction, set dividend policy, approve acquisition of a supplier, and the like.[32]

▼ Chain of Command

In addition to distinguishing line from staff functions, early writers on organization design stressed two basic ideas about the chain of command. First, in a **scalar chain of command,** authority and responsibility are arranged hierarchically. They flow in a clear, unbroken vertical line from the highest executive to the lowest employee. Clarity is at the heart of the scalar chain. Second, these writers emphasized **unity of command,** which states that no subordinate should receive orders from more than one superior. Although modern organizations don't rigidly follow unity of command in their designs, overlapping lines of authority and responsibility can make both managing and working difficult. Without any unity of command, who may direct whom to do what may become cloudy and confusing. Of course, the issues of chain of command and span of control don't just apply to functional design. They must be addressed in all organization designs.

▼ Span of Control

Span of control refers to the number of employees supervised by a superior, which influences the organization's shape and structure. When the span of control is broad, relatively few levels exist between the top and bottom of the organization. Conversely, when the span of control is narrow, more levels are required for the same number of employees. As Figure 17.8 illustrates, an organization with 19 employees requires four levels with a narrow span and three levels with a broader span. The span of control varies with the nature of the tasks being performed and choice of design. For example, the use of self-managed teams allows a broader span of control and fewer organizational levels. Moreover, a manager of a relatively simple and repetitive operation, such as a McDonald's restaurant, might effectively manage 20–30 employees. At higher organizational levels, however, a general manager might effectively manage only 7–9 subordinates.

The following Managing Ethics feature suggests how some organizations have created functional roles and offices to help nurture and enforce ethical behaviors and decisions in organizations.

MANAGING ETHICS

Ethics Positions and Offices

Some companies have full-time ethics officers. Generally, they are at the corporate vice-president level and report directly to the chairman or an ethics committee of top officers. One of the most effective tools these ethics specialists employ is a hot line through which workers at all levels may register complaints or ask about questionable behavior.

At Raytheon Corporation, Paul Pullen receives about 100 calls a month. Some 80% of the calls involve minor issues that he can resolve on the spot or refer to the human resources department. Another 10% of callers simply are looking for a bit of advice. But about ten times a month, the callers report some serious ethical lapse that Pullen must address with senior management. Pullen states, "Most people have high standards, and they want to work in an atmosphere that is ethical. The complaints come from all levels, and they are typical of what you would find in any business: possible conflicts of interest, cheating on timecards, and cheating on expense reports."

Unfavorable publicity has motivated some companies to set up an ethics office. NYNEX Corporation—which owns New York Telephone, New England Telephone, and other divisions—took such action following a series of scandals. The scandals included revelations of lewd parties in Florida thrown for suppliers by a NYNEX executive. Fifty-six middle managers at NYNEX were disciplined or discharged for allegedly receiving kickbacks. Also, the Securities and Exchange Commission accused a former division president of insider trading. The company now emphasizes ethics. Graydon Wood, NYNEX's newly appointed ethics officer, says that the job requires a realistic view of human behavior: "You have to recognize that even with all the best programs, some employees do go wrong. Some marketing people didn't report properly, resulting in unjustified commissions. We fired them."

Dow Corning has a formal Business Conduct Committee, on which six managers serve three-year terms. Each member devotes as much as six weeks a year to the committee. Two members audit every business operation every three years, and the panel reviews up to 35 locations annually. Three-hour reviews are held with up to 35 employees at each location. Committee members use a code of ethics as the framework and encourage employees to raise ethical issues. Results of the audits are reported to a three-member Audit and Social Responsibility Committee of the board of directors.[33]

▼ Conditions for Use

A functional design has both advantages and disadvantages. On the positive side, it permits clear identification and assignment of responsibilities, and employees easily understand it. People doing similar tasks and facing similar problems work together, thus increasing the opportunities for interaction and mutual support. A disadvantage is that a functional design fosters a limited point of view that focuses on a narrow set of tasks. Employees may lose sight of the organization as a whole. Horizontal integration across functional departments often becomes difficult as the organization increases the number of geographic areas served and the range of goods or services provided. With the exception of marketing, most employees in a functional design have no direct contact with customers and may lose sight of the need to meet or exceed customer expectations.

A functional design may be effective when an organization has a narrow product line and doesn't have to respond to the pressures of serving different geographic areas or types of customers. The addition of specialized staff departments to a functional design may enable an organization to deal effectively with some degree of environmental complexity and dynamism. Staff departments may provide line departments with expert advice, such as dealing with certain technological factors. As shown in Figure 17.4, functional design is the most elementary type of organization design and often represents a cornerstone from which other types of designs evolve. The addition of horizontal design mechanisms, such as linking roles and task forces, also may facilitate the use of the basic functional design.

▼ PLACE DESIGN

Place design involves establishing an organization's primary units geographically while retaining significant aspects of functional design. Many of the tasks in a geographic territory are placed under one manager, rather than grouping functions under different managers or all tasks in one central office. Large companies such as American Airlines, Federal Express, and Allstate use place design in the form of regional and district offices. Similarly, many governmental agencies such as the Internal Revenue Service (IRS), the Federal Reserve Board, the federal courts, and the Postal Service use place design in providing their services.

▼ Link to Internationalization

Many international firms use place design to address cultural and legal differences in various countries and the lack of uniformity among customers in different geographic markets. For example, Kendall Healthcare Products Company established a German subsidiary to manufacture locally and market a broad line of products developed in the United States for German consumption. Localized manufacturing historically has made sense because health care product standards have varied considerably from country to country. Moreover, the German healthcare system has been a major consumer of Kendall's products.[34]

▼ Conditions for Use

Place design has several potential advantages. If each department or division is in direct contact with customers or other stakeholders, it can adapt more readily to their demands. For manufacturing, such contact might mean locating near raw materials or suppliers and/or in the primary market area for finished products. Potential gains may include lower costs for materials, freight rates, and (perhaps) labor costs. For marketing, locating near customers might mean lower costs or better service. Salespeople can spend more time selling and less time traveling. Being closer to the customer may help them pinpoint the marketing tactic most likely to succeed in that particular region.

Organizing by place clearly increases control and coordination problems. If regional units diverge in significant respects, top management may have difficulty achieving integration. Further, regional and district managers may want to control their own internal activities, such as purchasing and human resources. Employees may begin to emphasize their own geographically-based unit's goals and needs more than those of the organization as a whole. To help ensure uniformity and coordination, organizations such as the IRS, Southland (7-Eleven stores), Steak and Ale, Serle Optical, and Hilton Hotels make extensive use of rules that apply in all locations.

▼ PRODUCT DESIGN

Product design involves the establishment of self-contained units, each capable of developing, producing, and marketing its own goods or services. This type of organization design emphasizes pooled interdependence among self-contained product units. As Figure 17.9 shows, BancTec uses the product design (only part of BancTec's organization design is depicted here). This firm provides integrated systems, applications software, and maintenance and support services for the banking, utility, and insurance companies that must process large volumes of financial documents. The company targets its products to specific customers and manufacturers them in four geographically diverse plants to provide fast customer service. BancTec markets its services and products through its own sales force in the United States, United Kingdom, and Australia and uses distributors in Asia and South America. BancTec formed a joint venture with Thomson–CSF to market its products and services in Europe, Scandinavia, and North Africa.

▼ Typical Evolution

Organizations that produce multiple goods or services, such as Procter & Gamble, Heinz, PepsiCo, and American Brands, utilize some form of product design. It reduces the complexity that managers and others would face in a pure functional design. With pure functional design, a single vice-president of marketing at such a firm wouldn't be able to manage the diversity of products, customers, and geographic markets served. When the diversity of goods or services and types of customers reach a certain point, the creation of multiple marketing vice-president positions (one vice-president for each product line), to handle the resulting complexity can be more effective. This is the organization design used by American Brands, which offers more than 100

FIGURE 17.9

BancTec's Product Divisions

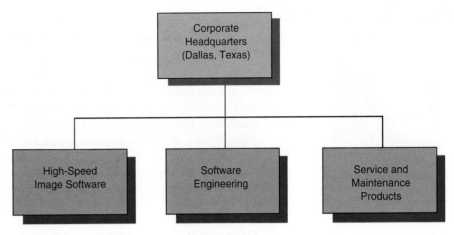

Source: Adapted from *BancTec 1993 Annual Report*, Dallas, 1994.

diverse products, including Master Locks, Titleist golfballs, and Foot Joy shoes. Moreover, a product design is an attractive alternative to a functional design when the task environment and/or technological factors for each product line are different. Organizations with a product design usually began with a functional design and then added some place design features as they began to serve new geographical markets. Greater environmental dynamism and complexity eventually create management problems that functional design or place design alone cannot effectively deal with. The addition of new product lines, diverse customers, and technological advances also may increase complexity and uncertainty (see Figure 17.4). When changing to a product design, however, companies usually do not discard functional or place designs altogether. Instead, the product design may incorporate features of functional and place designs into the organization of each product division.

▼ Multidivisional Design

A variation of the product design is the multidivisional design, sometimes referred to as the *M-Form*. **Multidivisional design** organizes tasks into divisions on the basis of the product or geographic markets in which their goods or services are sold. Divisional managers are primarily responsible for the day-to-day operating decisions within their units. Freed from day-to-day operating responsibilities, top corporate-level managers concentrate on strategic issues, such as allocating resources to the various divisions, assessing new businesses to acquire and divisions to sell off, and communicating with shareholders and others. These top managers often are supported by elaborate accounting and control systems and specialized staff.[35] As illustrated in the Preview Case on Xerox, they may delegate to product divisions the authority to develop their own strategic plans.

The following Managing in Practice account describes Johnson & Johnson (J&J) Corporation's multidivisional design. It also reveals some of J&J's efforts to overcome the limitations of this type of design by introducing horizontal design mechanisms. The company manufactures and markets a wide range of products, including anesthetics, Band-Aids, baby powder, and contact lenses.

MANAGING IN PRACTICE

Johnson & Johnson's Multidivisional Design

At Johnson & Johnson (J&J), the presidents of its 166 separately chartered companies are not just encouraged to act independently—they're expected to. They travel at will and decide who will work for them, what products they will produce, and which customers they'll sell to. They prepare budgets and marketing plans, and many oversee their own research and development. Although they are accountable ultimately to executives at corporate headquarters, some presidents see headquarters executives as rarely as four times a year. The J&J approach "provides a sense of ownership and responsibility for a business that you simply cannot get any other way," says chief executive Ralph S. Larsen.

However, decentralization caused problems with some large customers. Dozens of J&J representatives call on customers such as Wal-Mart Stores, Inc., or Kmart Corporation. But big retailers increasingly want to simplify their dealings with manufacturers by reducing the number of contacts with a supplier. Another concern for a decentralized company is overhead. Scores of units operating autonomously can lead to duplication of purchasing, billing, and distribution functions. Overhead at J&J was 41% of sales, compared with 30% for its more integrated rival, Merck & Company, and 28% for Bristol-Myers Squibb Company. To keep large retailers happy, J&J established "customer-support centers." These employee teams work on-site with retailers to ease distribution and ordering. Giant customers such as Kmart still get sales calls from dozens of different J&J units. But, the goods from most operating companies are now delivered to retailers' warehouses in single large shipments. "We're very excited about it," says James A. Glime, manager of business development at Kmart. "This makes sense, and it certainly supports our business."

The J&J organization design isn't static. Since taking over as CEO, Larsen has pushed the J&J companies to achieve more horizontal integration among such functions as payroll processing, computer services, purchasing, distribution, accounts payable, and benefits. This push is intended to share more services among units to cut down on duplication of efforts and improve relations with J&J's biggest customers. Larsen also launched an effort to unite customer service and credit functions. Code-named Pathfinder, it replaced four separate departments that used to do credit reviews, sometimes on the same customers. "If a customer has a question about a delivery, they don't have to call the baby company, then our consumer-products organization, and so on," says Larsen. "They make one phone call to one person who specializes in them, and no matter where the problem is, that person takes care of it."[36]

▼ Conditions for Use

A product (or multidivisional) design eases problems of integration by focusing expertise and knowledge on specific goods or services. For example, the sales efforts of a single marketing department at a firm like Johnson & Johnson would likely be ineffective in marketing products ranging from anesthetics to contact lenses to baby powder. Each product line is best handled by a department or division thoroughly familiar with it and its set of customers. Such a design clearly meets the needs of a company such as J&J, which provides diverse products to diverse customers (ranging from family-run pharmacies to global retailers to hospitals to government agencies) in diverse geographic locations throughout the world.

One disadvantage of the product (or multidivisional) design is that a firm must have a large number of managerial personnel to oversee all the product lines. Another disadvantage is the higher cost that results from the duplication of various functions. Johnson & Johnson addressed it by combining some processes and introducing horizontal mechanisms to link its independent units in dealing with common issues.

Adoption of a product (or multidivisional) design often reduces the environmental complexity facing any one team, department, or division. The employees in a product-based unit needs to focus only on the environment for one product line, rather than on those for multiple product lines. As with a functional design, an organization with a product or multidivisional design can further deal with complex, dynamic environments and common technological complexities and uncertainties by adding horizontal mechanisms, such as linking roles, task forces, and integrating roles and cross-functional teams. Johnson & Johnson did so with its payroll, computer services, purchasing, distribution, accounts payable, and benefits functions.

▼ INTEGRATION OF UNITS

Another essential part of organization design is to determine the desired horizontal integration among individuals, teams, departments, and divisions. **Horizontal design** refers to the processes and mechanisms for linking units that are in lateral relationships to each other, such as between marketing and manufacturing departments. Many of the dynamics between groups and teams (see Chapter 10) apply to horizontal relations. Horizontal design processes and mechanisms include dialogue, superordinate group goals and rewards, plans, linking roles, cross-functional teams, integrating roles and teams, and various groupware aids. They are affected primarily by three variables: (1) the degree of differentiation between units; (2) the degree of required integration between units; and (3) the degree of uncertainty (including task, work-flow, and environmental) confronting each unit. As Figure 17.10 shows, each variable has a range from low to high. The diagnosis of these variables and their impact on operations is a necessary step in designing an effective organization.

▼ Horizontal Design

Differentiation   **Differentiation** is the degree to which units differ in structure (low to high), members' orientation to a time horizon (short to long), managers' orientation to other people (permissive to authoritarian), and members' views of the task environment (certain to uncertain).[37] Production departments often have a high degree of formal structure with many rules and procedures, tight supervisory control, frequent and specific reviews of individual and departmental performance, and structured relationships between

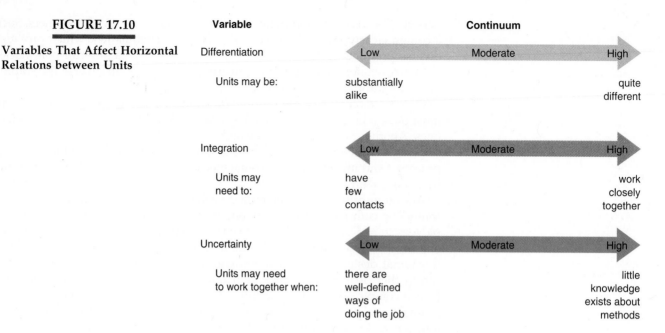

FIGURE 17.10

Variables That Affect Horizontal Relations between Units

co-workers (mechanistic system). Research departments and planning departments often are just the opposite with their personnel needing open and close working relationships (organic system). Production workers have short time horizons (minutes, hours and days) and think about immediate problems. Research and planning employees think in terms of months and even years into the future. In general, the greater the differences between departments, the greater is the challenge of getting them to work together (such as marketing with production).[38]

Integration   **Integration** is the degree of collaboration and mutual understanding required among units to achieve their goals, for which the division of labor and task interdependencies create the need. This need is greatest between units that are reciprocally interdependent and least when they are in a pooled interdependent relationship.

   Managers must be careful not to establish too much or too little horizontal integration. Too little integration probably will lead to lower quality decisions and the misuse of resources because each unit will "do its own thing." The costs associated with too much integration are likely to far exceed any possible benefits.[39] With excessive horizontal integration, units often get in the way of each other, rather than help each other perform their tasks and achieve their goals. This became a problem at Xerox in the efforts to achieve horizontal integration among its old functional units.

   In Chapter 10, we discussed seven approaches for fostering effective dynamics and outcomes between horizontal and interdependent teams and groups. These approaches also apply to achieving horizontal integration in organization design—for example, between functional units or between one or more functional units and others based on place design or product design. Recall that Xerox now has nine product divisions and three geographically based sales and service divisions. It achieves horizontal integration between them with a variety of horizontal mechanisms. Uncertainty is a key to determining how complex and varied such horizontal mechanisms need be.

Uncertainty   Uncertainty is the gap between what is known and what needs to be known to make effective decisions and perform tasks effectively. Factors that should be evaluated in determining the degree of uncertainty that a unit faces include

▲ the completeness of information and guidelines available to help employees perform their tasks;

▲ the frequency with which units can be expected to face problems that they have to solve jointly;

▲ the amount of actual thinking time required before units can try to implement solutions to mutual problems; and

▲ the probability that units can be reasonably certain of the results of their independent and mutual efforts.[40]

The following Managing Quality account explains the horizontal design created by NCR's U.S. Group to foster its total quality management (TQM) program. The company manufactures and services a wide range of computer-based products and systems. The "cash register" is one of its best known products. The U.S. Group comprises six regional divisions and employs about 15,000 people.

MANAGING QUALITY

NCR's U.S. Group Quality Improvement Design

The horizontal design mechanisms used to implement the TQM program at NCR's U.S. Group include the following.

U.S. Group Quality Council   This council consists of executives from each U.S. Group division. The quality council provides direction for the ongoing development of the entire group's quality system. Using employee effectiveness surveys and customer satisfaction measurements, the council acts as a "quality advocate" for the U.S. Group. The council meets monthly in conjunction with U.S. Group executive meetings and is accountable for the Group's quality efforts.

U.S. Process Advisory Council   The UPAC is the "hands-on" arm of the quality council. Under the council's direction, UPAC developed and maintains the U.S. Group's *Quality Policy and Quality Manual*. The advisory council also established an educational process to guide each division's quality efforts. This process involves not only the "how to do it" end of the system but the "how to measure it" side as well.

Division Quality Councils   The quality council and UPAC oversee the U.S. Group's overall quality approach, but the division quality councils often lead the efforts. These councils relate the information and policies provided by UPAC to each division's efforts to satisfy its customers. One person in each division is responsible for supporting its quality system.

MANAGING QUALITY —*Continued*

Assessing Quality   NCR employed a consulting firm to measure its quality gains and help assess the company's customer satisfaction levels. Indianapolis-based Customer Satisfaction Management (CSM) helps companies measure every aspect of customer satisfaction, from products to sales efforts to customer service. The consulting firm's research shows that one central goal exists for most businesses. "During a customer seminar with 40 company presidents," says Jeffrey W. Marr, CSM's vice-president of client services, "everyone present—40 out of 40—said that long-term customer satisfaction was 'priority number one.'"[41]

Conditions for Use   The combinations of the three variables—differentiation, required integration, and level of uncertainty—have several significant implications for horizontal organization design. The simplest situation involves low uncertainty, low differentiation, and low required integration between units, that is, when units are practically independent of each other. The produce and canned/boxed goods departments in a supermarket are an example.

An increase in the degree of uncertainty, differentiation, and integration is costly. It requires an increase in the expenditure of resources and the number of formal horizontal mechanisms (such as cross-functional teams) and the use of certain behavioral processes to obtain integration. For example, extensive collaboration among manufacturing, marketing, planning, design, and engineering at General Motors and the Oldsmobile Division was required to create the new Aurora automobile.

The most difficult interunit situation involves high uncertainty, high differentiation, and high required integration. Organizations must expend considerable resources and use a wide variety of formal horizontal mechanisms and behavioral processes to manage interunit relations under such conditions. For example, NCR's U.S. Group uses complex and varied horizontal mechanisms to implement its TQM program.

▼ Matrix Design

Matrix design is based on multiple support systems and authority relationships in which some employees report to two superiors rather than one.[42] As Figure 17.11 illustrates, matrix design usually involves a combination of functional and product designs through the use of dual authority, information, and reporting relationships and systems. Every matrix contains three unique sets of role relationships: (1) the top manager, who heads up and balances the dual chains of command; (2) the managers of functional and product departments, who share subordinates; and (3) the managers (or specialists) who report to both a functional manager and a product manager.[43] In an organization that has major operations throughout the world, matrix managers could be designated for each of the firm's major geographic areas, such as Europe, South America, North America, Pacific Rim, and the Middle East.[44]

Aerospace companies were the first to use the matrix design. Today, organizations in many industries (e.g., chemical, banking, insurance, packaged goods, electronics, and computer) and fields (e.g., hospitals, government agencies, and professional organizations) use various adaptations of the matrix design.

FIGURE 17.11

Partial Illustration of Basic Matrix
Design

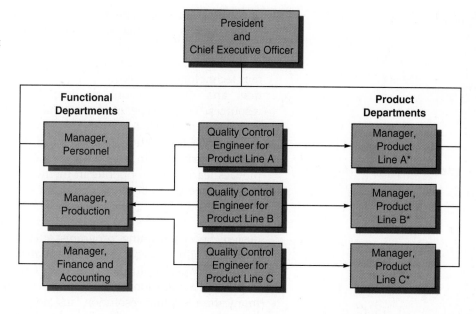

*These product managers also have full responsibility for the marketing activities associated with their own product lines.

Typical Evolution   The matrix design typically evolves in stages. The first stage may be the use of a temporary task force. Composed of representatives from different departments or divisions of the organization, the task force is created to study a problem and make recommendations. Task force members retain their usual departmental affiliations (an engineer continues to report to the head of engineering and a marketing representative to the head of marketing). But these temporary members also are accountable to the task force's leader.

The second stage usually involves the creation of a permanent team or committee to address a specified need or problem. Again, representatives from the various functional and product departments comprise the team or committee, each representing the view of the home department. The third stage may occur when a project manager is appointed and held accountable for integrating the team's activities and inputs for its final output. Project managers often must negotiate or "buy" the human resources necessary to carry out the tasks from the managers of functional departments. With the appointment of project managers, an organization is well on the way to a matrix design and faces all the difficulties and benefits of multiple-authority relationships.

These new multiple-authority relationships replace the simple, straightforward, single chain of command. These relationships are the distinguishing characteristic of the matrix design. While the traditional hierarchical design rests on formal reward or position power, the matrix design demands negotiations by peers with a high tolerance of ambiguous power relationships.[45] Managing these power relationships is one of the most challenging aspects of the matrix design.

Conditions for Use   The matrix design may be appropriate under the following conditions: (1) when managers and others must be highly responsive to both functional or product line (or place) concerns; (2) when organizations face complex, dynamic task environments coupled with complex and uncertain technologies that require employees to process lots of data and information; and (3) when organizations have multiple products and limited resources.[46] This type of design makes specialized, functional employees' knowledge available to all projects. Also, it uses people flexibly, as employees are assigned to functional and product departments simultaneously.

The matrix design demands substantial managerial resources while employees learn how to operate in the new organization. Learning may require two or three years because significant changes in attitude are required. Employees used to unity of command, a clear authority structure, and top-down orders may be uncomfortable with the flexibility required under a matrix design. Special training programs often are needed to implement the new design. In order to work properly, a matrix design must maintain a continuing tension between multiple orientations (such as functional specialty and product line). This tension, in turn, requires effective interpersonal skills in communication, conflict resolution, and negotiation.[47]

▼ MULTINATIONAL DESIGN

A **multinational design** attempts to maintain three-way organization perspectives and capabilities among products, functions, and geographic areas. Meeting the need for three-way consideration of issues is especially difficult because, in a multinational design, operating divisions are divided by distance and time and managers often are separated by culture and language.[48] A "perfect" balance, if such were ever possible, between these perspectives would require a three-way matrix design. Hence most multinational designs focus on the relative emphasis that should be given between place and product organization design.

▼ Basic Options

Figure 17.12 suggests the various combinations that might be selected and shows the likely effects of choosing a design based primarily on place or product line. For example, strong delegation of authority based upon *place* gives country or regional managers the ability to respond and adapt to local needs and forces. In contrast, product-line managers with worldwide authority may focus on achieving global efficiencies (integration) in production and universal (standard) products.

▼ Conditions for Use

The forces for more global integration in many industries include (1) the growing presence and importance of global competitors and customers, (2) the rise in market demand for products globally, (3) new information technologies,

FIGURE 17.12

Basic Options in Multinational Design

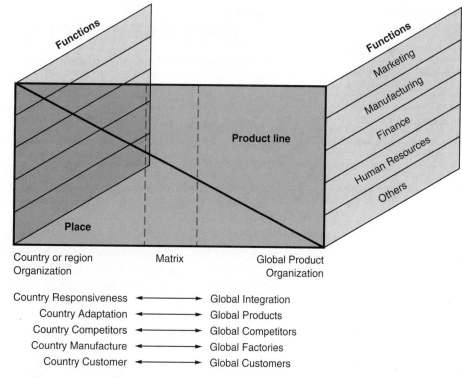

Country Responsiveness ⟷ Global Integration
Country Adaptation ⟷ Global Products
Country Competitors ⟷ Global Competitors
Country Manufacture ⟷ Global Factories
Country Customer ⟷ Global Customers

Source: Adapted from Galbraith, J. R., and Kazanjian, R. K. *Strategy Implementation: Structure Systems and Process*, 2nd ed. St. Paul, Minn.: West, 1986, 159.

and (4) efficient factories that can manufacture goods for customers throughout the world.[49] Thus worldwide product divisions in firms facing such forces are likely to dominate in decisions relative to the geographically based divisions. However, pressures from national governments and local markets also may be strong. Multinational corporations usually markets full product lines in all principal countries. However, such marketing opportunities may not be open to companies without negotiating with the host government. Thus an independent worldwide product-line division may not be as effective at opening up new territories as a geographically organized division. A division operating under a place design often can establish relations with host governments, invest in distribution channels, develop brand recognition, and build competencies that no single product-line division could afford. Thus valid reasons still exist for country or regional (Europe, North America, Latin America, Pacific Rim) organization.[50]

The following Managing Across Cultures item reports on the shift at the Ford Motor Company in 1994 from a multinational design that emphasized regional design to one that emphasizes global design. It reveals some of the tensions inherent in multinational design when top management tries to balance place, function, and product-line considerations.

MANAGING ACROSS CULTURES

Ford's New Global Design

Ford's reorganization puts each major function (e.g., product development, sales, and engine/transmissions) under an executive with authority to think and act globally—a radical departure from the previous design. With that design, Ford North America, Ford of Europe and, Ford Asia/Pacific operated as quasi-independent car companies. The autonomy of those geographic groups has been diminished in favor of global leaders with worldwide authority for their specific responsibilities.

The new design reflects the thinking of Alexander Trotman, chairman and chief executive officer, who took the helm at Ford Motor Company in November 1993. Trotman wanted a design that would let Ford avoid costly duplication of efforts in different parts of the world. To do so meant efficiently developing vehicles which, with minor modifications, can sell in most parts of the world. Ford spent more than $6 billion to develop a compact car, named the Mondeo in Europe and the Ford Contour/Mercury Mystique in the United States and Canada. That was more than four times the cost of Chrysler's new Dodge/Plymouth Neon. The high cost was partly due to the expensive and time-consuming coordination of efforts between Ford's engineering units in the United States, England, and Germany. Trotman stated, "We want to be a global company in primarily product development, manufacturing and purchasing to optimize the strength Ford has in various parts of the world. I don't think it was so in the past."

"It looks like Ford is at last dealing with its functional sclerosis," said James Womack, co-author of the influential book on the auto industry, *The Machine That Changed the World*. Womack said that Ford has long been plagued by a product-development organization that spent too much money and time in developing cars. Trotman identified the same weakness as head of Ford's North American operations in the early 1990s. In an effort to spark change, he created a team to study how Ford could develop a new Mustang coupe in three years, instead of the normal four to five years. This study lead to the formation of a single, cross-functional team housed in one location. The team produced the new Mustang in less than three years on a budget roughly 30% less than comparable programs in the past. Trotman is now overseeing the construction of a new "program team facility." All of Ford's future products will be developed by teams similar to the one that produced the Mustang.[51]

▼ NETWORK DESIGN

All the organization designs discussed so far have limitations that often hinder them in coping both effectively and efficiently with turbulent environments and technologies. The **network design** is intended to facilitate managing highly diverse, complex, and dynamic factors involving multiple units and many people, both within and external to the organization.[52] A primary concern in all of the other organization designs was how to allocate authority and control among positions, departments, and divisions. The network organization, while not ignoring these issues, focuses on sharing authority, responsibility, and control among people and units that must cooperate and communicate frequently to achieve common goals.[53] The various options available in network design are to be used as the tasks to be performed and the goals to be achieved change.[54]

The following Managing in Practice account presents the features of the network design recently adopted by Eastman Chemical Company. This company is a large division ($3.5 billion in annual sales) of the Eastman Kodak Company.

MANAGING IN PRACTICE

Eastman Chemical's Network Design

Figure 17.13 shows Eastman Chemical's schematic representation of its new network design. "Our organization chart is now called the pizza chart because it looks like a pizza with a lot of pepperoni sitting on it," says Ernest W. Deavenport, Jr., who as president is the "pepperoni" at the center of the pie. "We did it in circular form to show that everyone is equal in the organization. No one dominates the other. The space inside the circles is more important than the lines."

The large "pepperoni" typically represents the major cross-functional teams responsible for managing a key product line, a geographic area, a function, or a "core competence" in a specific technology or area such as innovation. The space around them is where the collaborative interaction is supposed to occur. The small pepperoni typically represent support teams (such as human resources) or special project teams that will be discontinued after their goals are accomplished.

Self-managed teams replaced several of the senior vice-presidents in charge of the key functions. Instead of having a head of manufacturing, for example, the company uses a team consisting of all its plant managers. "It was the most dramatic change in the company's 70-year history," maintains Deavenport. "It makes people take off their organization hats and put on their team hats. It gives people a much broader perspective and brings decision-making down at least another level."

FIGURE 17.13

Eastman Chemical's Network (Pizza) Design

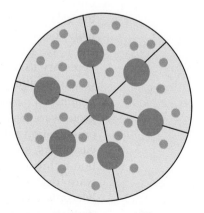

Source: Office of Public Affairs, Eastman Chemical Company, 1994.

MANAGING IN PRACTICE —*Continued*

In creating the new organization, the senior managers agreed that the primary role of the functions was to support Eastman's businesses in chemicals, plastics, fibers, and polymers. "A function does not and should not have a mission of its own," insists Deavenport. But over the years, the functional departments had grown strong and powerful, often at the expense of the company overall as they fought to protect and build their own turf. The company's managers now work on at least one cross-functional team, and most work on two or more. Tom O. Nethery, a group vice-president, leads an industrial-business group. He also serves on three teams that deal with such diverse issues as human resources, cellulose technology, and product-support services.[55]

▼ Key Characteristics

The network design is sometimes called a spiderweb or cluster organization. It resembles a mosaic of mutually interdependent mechanisms and managerial processes. This mosaic cannot be captured through the use of typical organization charts that show vertical authority and reporting relationships. This change is suggested by Eastman Chemical's "pizza" design. A network organization exists only when most of the following factors operate in support of one another.

▲ *Distinctive competence*—The organization maintains superiority through innovation and adaptation by combining resources in novel ways.

▲ *Responsibility*—People who must collaborate to perform their tasks share responsibility. The organization's design includes extensive use of cross-functional, special-purpose, and self-managed teams. At Eastman Chemical, each large "pepperoni" in Figure 17.12 typically represents a key cross-functional team responsible for managing a product line, a geographic area, a function, or a core competence in a specific technology (or area such as innovation).

▲ *Goal setting*—Common goals linked to satisfying the needs of one or more important external stakeholders, (e.g., customers/clients, suppliers, shareholders, lenders, and governments) are formulated.

▲ *Communication*—All-channel networks are used both internally (among the relevant employees, teams, departments and divisions) and externally (between the organization and key stakeholders). The primary focus is on lateral rather than vertical communication. The information necessary to make decisions is widely shared and distributed, and open communication is the norm.

▲ *Information technology*—Many information technologies (including groupware) assist employees in networking internally (with others in the organization who may even be at a great distance) or externally (with customers, suppliers, regulatory agencies, and so on). Typical information technologies and related groupware include E-mail, special PC software decision aids, voice-mail, mobile phones, fax, telecommuting, teleconferencing, local and wide-area computer networks, and the like.

▲ *Attitudinal sets*—Interdependent employees are primarily cooperative rather than competitive. They exhibit mutually reinforcing behaviors and attitudes of high trust, listening to each other, collaborating and compromising styles of conflict management, acceptance of mutual control, and flexibility in relationships.

▲ *Organizational culture*—The organization's culture focuses both on problems of external adaptation and on internal integration. This culture has a bias toward the organic system and as few organization levels as possible. Recall the comment of Deavenport at Eastman Chemical: "We did it (organization chart) in circular form to show that everyone is equal in the organization. No one dominates the other. The space inside the circles is more important than the lines."

▲ *Balanced view*—Individual teams, departments, and divisions do not view themselves as isolated islands having only their unique goals and ways of doing things. They view themselves in relation to other individuals and units with common superordinate goals and rewards. Network forms of exchange evolve over time, based on the history of earlier transactions. The basic assumption of network relationships is that each person or unit depends on resources controlled by others and that mutual gains are obtained by pooling resources and finding win-win solutions.[56]

▼ Role of Information Technologies

The principal developments in information technologies (including groupware) over the past ten years have both pushed and enabled organizations to move toward the network design. We discussed many of these specific technologies in previous chapters and explored them further in Chapter 19. Here we simply highlight four of the information technology advances that have enabled organizations to utilize internal and external networking.[57]

Open Systems   Portable software and compatible technology now exist. These capabilities extend to the external network of suppliers, consumers, regulatory agencies, and even competitors. The shift is away from departments or divisions with their own unique computing capability to a network of linked business processes. In addition, organizations can be in closer touch with their customers, suppliers, and others, enabling people to act not only in their own self-interest, but with a shared vision and commitment.

Distributed Computing   The shift is from centralized computing where all access was limited to a few people or departments to one network computing where "intelligence" becomes available to the primary user. Centralized and limited access computing systems are typical of a mechanistic system. In contrast, planning, information processing, and the application of knowledge to business problems are being distributed throughout organic organizations by empowering individuals and teams.

Real Time   The new information technologies now capture information online and update information banks in real time. This gives an instantaneous, accurate picture of many processes, such as sales, production, and cash flow. Information immediacy enables the real time network organization to continuously adjust to changing conditions. Just-in-time receipt of parts from suppliers and delivery of products to customers minimizes the need for warehousing and allows firms to shift from mass production to custom on-line production. Customer orders can arrive electronically and be processed instantly. Corresponding invoices may be sent electronically and databases automatically updated.

Global Networking   Information networks are the backbone of network organization design—the essential support system for transformation processes and operations. Global networking permits both real-time communication and access of electronically stored information at will from anywhere in the world. The network organization design redefines time and space for both employees and external stakeholders. In an open network design, any individual, team, or unit can quickly communicate and share information with any other individual, team, or unit. Work can be performed at a variety of locations, including employees' homes, with the office becoming part of a network rather than a place.

▼ External Networking

The network design is particularly effective in creating alliances with other organizations.[58] They could include customers, suppliers, and firms that would be defined as competitors under different circumstances. Corning, Inc., uses its 23 joint ventures with foreign partners such as Siemens (Germany), Samsung (South Korea), Asahi Chemical (Japan), and CIBA–GEIGY (Switzerland), to compete in a growing number of related high-technology markets.[59] The network design treats their alliances as forms of flexible partnerships.[60] For example, the flexibility with which Corning approaches its partnerships—letting the form be determined by the goals and letting the ventures evolve in form over time—is one reason for its success. But even more important is the time and effort expended by Corning executives to create the conditions for long-lasting, mutually beneficial relationships.

The network design is intended to create successful external relationships by having "six I's" in place: importance, investment, interdependence, integration, information, and institutionalization. The network relationship is important, and therefore it gets adequate resources, management attention, and sponsorship. Agreement for long-term investment tends to help equalize benefits over time. The network organizations are interdependent, which helps keep power balanced. The organizations are integrated in order to maintain essential points of contact and communication. Each partner is informed about the plans and directions of the other. Finally, the networking is institutionalized, that is, bolstered by a framework of supporting mechanisms from legal requirements to social ties to shared values. These mechanisms make trust possible.[61]

The following Managing Across Cultures feature reports on the new network design adopted at Procter & Gamble (P&G) to make it a speedier global marketer. It has required fundamental changes in P&G's organizational culture, and complete implementation is likely to take several more years. A large number of managers who couldn't change from the old mechanistic system have already left, retired early, or are seeking to leave.

MANAGING ACROSS CULTURES

Procter & Gamble's New Network Design

Procter & Gamble (P&G) has redesigned the way it develops, manufacturers, distributes, prices, markets, and sells products to deliver better value at every point in the supply chain. The new design has eliminated three management levels to make the company a swifter global marketer. As for P&G's product-line divisions, products will be tailored more swiftly to the wishes of consumers everywhere, such as South America, China, and Canada.

Achieving lower costs required fundamental changes in P&G's over-managed organization. Durk Jager, a protégé from Edwin Artzt's European days, pushed Artzt (the new CEO) relentlessly to break with the past. The *strengthening global effectiveness*, or SGE, effort emerged. A group of 11 teams collectively examined every part of the company. There were four rules: change the work, do more with less, eliminate rework, and reduce costs that can't be passed on to the consumer. Stephen David, a vice-president in charge of one of the teams stated, "The first thing we learned is that if you don't make the commitment to take some of your best people and pull them off line, you will not get the results." His project, originally scheduled for six to nine months with part-time participants, had to be converted to a full-time, year-long effort.

David's team, guided by consultants from Booz Allen, spent six months benchmarking the costs of the sales organization. The team analyzed 41 work processes that the company calls its customer management system. It found that P&G had the highest overhead in the industry and marketed 34 product categories, each with 17 basic pricing brackets and endless variations. The quarterly sales promotion plan for health and beauty products alone ran to more than 500 pages and was sent to every salesperson. Five P&G trucks used to pull up to a retailer's dock on any day, representing five separate contacts for order verification and delivery times. Richard E. Fredericksen, an executive at American Stores, a Salt Lake City–based multiregional food and drug retailer stated, "There were so many levels and so many parts; to get a purchase order correct was almost an act of God."

One goal of the overhaul is to make the distribution chain linking supplier, wholesaler, retailer, and consumer more like a continuous loop. This networking replaces the old piecemeal ordering system with continuous product replenishment (CPR). When a box of detergent is scanned at the checkout, the information is transferred directly to the manufacturer's computer. The computers are programmed to replenish the product automatically. This paperless exchange minimizes mistakes and bill-backs, reduces inventory, decreases out-of-stocks, and improves cash flow.

The company now requires that suppliers to the feminine products, diaper, hair care, and laundry detergent categories bid for global business. Artze also wants P&G to get improved products to market faster. It used to take 44 months to make a diaper change worldwide. Pampers Phases required only 20 months. Although P&G has long sought to make world products, the company has been slow in coordinating R&D, purchasing (suppliers), and marketing strategy. The company has modified its global management matrix. In this matrix, an executive might have operating responsibility for the U.S. diaper business and responsibility for a global diaper strategy. The company now stresses regional management over country management. In South America a regional matrix focused on customers has replaced a country-by-country design. Executives say that this matrix can handle twice the business with the same staff, facilitated by a computer-based global information network.[62]

Summary

Organization design is an intricate decision-making process. It is heavily influenced by the combination environmental forces, technological factors, and strategic choices. The task environment(s) confronting an organization as a whole and its various teams, departments, and divisions can vary greatly. This variability must be assessed in terms of the degrees of complexity, dynamism, diversity, and uncertainty.

Strategic choices—such as top-management's philosophy and decisions about the range of products or services to be provided, geographic markets to be served, and types of customers to be sought—have a direct impact on organization design. If top management and the prevailing organizational culture support tight, centralized control of day-to-day decisions, a mechanistic system is more likely than an organic system. The adoption of total quality values often requires a shift to a more organic system.

As in job design, technological considerations are important in organization design. The potential impact of three technological variables—work-flow uncertainty, task uncertainty, and task interdependence (pooled, sequential, and reciprocal)—on organization design can be considerable.

Different departments or divisions within the same organization may vary along the mechanistic to organic continuum. For example, in an organization with a functional design, a production department may operate as a mechanistic system, whereas the research and development department may operate as an organic system.

The four more traditional designs discussed were functional, product, place, and matrix. The conditions under which each may be appropriate were noted. An organization or its departments facing a somewhat simple, stable environment and simple technology generally can utilize a functional design effectively. The top managers may integrate the functional areas with the support of some horizontal mechanisms such as committees and cross-functional teams. Multidivisional design—a form of product design—is an option for firms providing a range of goods or services to geographically dispersed markets. The need for linking units also affects organization design. Horizontal and matrix designs support linking. The amount of horizontal integration needed is strongly influenced by three variables: differentiation, integration, and uncertainty. Diagnosis of these variables is an essential aspect of horizontal organization design. Horizontal mechanisms include superordinate group goals and rewards, task forces, formal planning activities, linking roles, cross-functional teams, and the like.

Multinational design attempts to maintain three-way organization perspectives and capabilities among products, functions, and geographic areas. Numerous options are available in multinational design. Network organization design represents a fundamental breakthrough in overcoming the disadvantages inherent in the other types of design. The network design heavily incorporates horizontal mechanisms and processes to manage complex sequential and reciprocal interdependencies among people, individuals, teams, and divisions—often located at great distances from each other. This design also draws on the revolution in information technologies (including groupware) that enable convenient and low-cost networks to form and change as needs and goals change. This design generally requires a management philosophy and organizational culture that supports an organic system.

Key Words and Concepts

Bureaucracy	Integration	Procedures
Centralization	Line functions	Product design
Complexity dimension	Matrix design	Rules
Differentiation	Mechanistic system	Scalar chain of command
Division of labor	Multidivisional design	Span of control
Dynamism dimension	Multinational design	Staff functions
Functional design	Network design	Task environment
Hierarchy of authority	Organic system	Uncertainty
Horizontal design	Organization design	Unity of command
Impersonality	Place design	

Discussion Questions

1. What are two similarities between functional and product organization design?

2. What are two differences between functional and product organization design?

3. Why do information technologies affect organization design?

4. Which organization design is used by the college in which you are enrolled?

5. Which other organization design could be used for the college in which you are enrolled? What might be the advantages and disadvantages of this alternative design?

6. Describe the mechanistic or organic characteristics of an organization of which you are a member. Are any changes needed? Explain.

7. Give three personal experiences with organizational rules that seemed to be either helpful or counterproductive in terms of organizational effectiveness.

8. How might top managers' philosophy and the organization's culture influence organization design decisions?

9. What difficulties are associated with the matrix design? Would you like to work in an organization that utilizes a matrix design? Why or why not?

10. What forces work for and against the establishment of a network design?

▲ Developing Skills

Self-Diagnosis:
Inventory of Effective Design[63]

Instructions

Listed are statements describing an effective organization design. Please indicate the extent to which you agree or disagree with each statement as a description of an organization you currently or have worked for. Write the appropriate number next to the statement.

```
1        2        3        4        5        6        7
|_____|_____|_____|_____|_____|_____|
Strongly  Disagree Somewhat  Uncertain Somewhat  Agree  Strongly
Disagree          Disagree            Agree             Agree
```

_____ 1. Employees who try to change things are usually recognized and supported.

_____ 2. The organization makes it easy to get the skills needed to progress.

_____ 3. Employees almost always know how their work turns out, whether it is good or bad.

_____ 4. Employees have flexibility over the pace of their work.

_____ 5. Managers facilitate discussion at meetings to encourage participation by subordinates.

_____ 6. Few policies, rules, and regulations restrict innovation in this organization.

_____ 7. Boundaries between teams, departments, and/or divisions rarely interfere with solving joint problems.

_____ 8. There are few hierarchical levels in this organization.

_____ 9. Everyone knows how their work will affect the work of the next person or team and the quality of the final product or service.

_____ 10. The organization is well informed about technological developments relevant to its processes, goods, or services.

_____ 11. The organization is constantly trying to determine what the customer wants and how to meet customer needs better.

_____ 12. The organization can adapt to most changes because its policies, organization design, and employees are flexible.

_____ 13. Different parts of the organization work together; when conflict arises, it often leads to constructive outcomes.

_____ 14. Everyone can state the values of the organization and how they are used to make decisions.

_____ 15. A great deal of information is shared openly, as appropriate.

Scoring and Interpretation

Sum the points given to statements 1–15. A score of 75–105 suggests an effective organization design. A score of 70–89 suggests a mediocre design that probably varies greatly in terms of how specific aspects of the organization work for or against effectiveness. A scores of 50–69 suggests a great deal of ambiguity about the organization and how it operates. A scores of 15–49 suggests that the design is contributing to serious problems.

A Case in Point:
Aquarius Advertising Agency

The Aquarius Advertising Agency is a middle-sized firm that offered two basic professional services to its clients: (1) customized plans for the content of an advertising campaign such as slogans and layouts; and (2) complete plans for media such as radio, TV, newspapers, billboards, magazines. Additional services included aid in marketing research to test advertising effectiveness.

Aquarius was organized in a traditional manner. The formal organization is shown in Figure 17.14. Each of the functions included similar tasks, and on top of that each client account was coordinated by an account executive who acted as a liaison between the client and the various specialists on the professional staff of the Operations and Marketing Division. The amount of direct communication and contact between clients and Aquarius specialists, client and account executives, and Aquarius specialists and account executives is indicated in Table 17.3. These sociometric data were gathered by a consultant who conducted a study of the patterns of formal and informal communication. Each intersecting cell of Aquarius personnel and the clients contains an index of the direct contacts between them.

An account executive was designated to be the liaison between the client and agency specialists and among various specialists within the agency. However, communication frequently occurred directly among the parties, bypassing the

FIGURE 17.14

Aquarius Advertising Agency Organization Chart

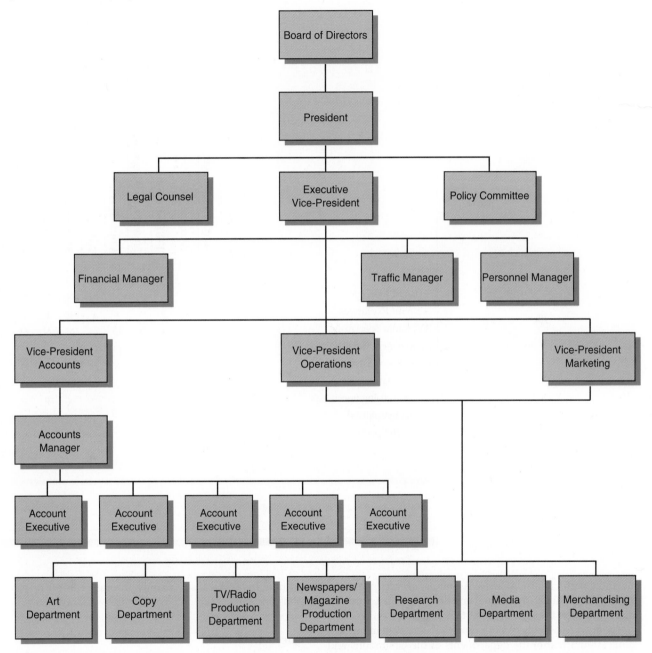

account executive. These direct contacts involved a wide range of interactions, including meetings, luncheons, telephone calls, and letters. A large number of direct communications occurred between agency specialists and their counterparts in the client organization. For example, an art

specialist working as one member of a team on a particular client account often would be contacted directly by the client's in-house art specialist. Also, agency research personnel communicated directly with research people at the client firm. Some of the unstructured contacts led to more formal

TABLE 17.3   Sociometric Index of Contacts of Aquarius Personnel and Clients

	Clients	Account Manager	Account Executives	TV/Radio Specialists	Newspaper/Magazine Specialists	Copy Specialists	Art Specialists	Merchandising Specialists	Media Specialists	Research Specialists	Traffic
Clients	X	F	F	N	N	O	O	O	O	O	N
Account Manager		X	F	N	N	N	N	N	N	N	N
Account Executives			X	F	F	F	F	F	F	F	F
TV/Radio Specialists				X	N	O	O	N	N	O	N
Newspaper/Magazine Specialists					X	O	O	N	O	O	N
Copy Specialists						X	N	O	O	O	N
Art Specialists							X	O	O	O	N
Merchandising Specialists								X	F	F	N
Media Specialists									X	F	N
Research Specialists										X	N
Traffic											X

F = Frequent—daily.
O = Occasional—once or twice per project.
N = None.

meetings with clients. At these meetings, agency personnel made presentations, interpreted and defended agency policy, and committed the agency to certain courses of action.

There were aspects of both a mechanistic system and organic system within the departments of the Operations and Marketing Divisions. Each department was organized hierarchically with a director, an assistant director, and several levels of authority. Professional communications were widespread and mainly concerned with sharing knowledge and techniques, technical evaluation of work, and development of professional interests. Control in each professional department was exercised mainly through control of promotions and supervision of work done by subordinates.[64]

Questions

1. How would you characterize the organization design that exists at the Aquarius Advertising Agency?
2. What are the advantages and disadvantages of the organization design at Aquarius?
3. Design an organization that could eliminate the disadvantages of the Aquarius organization design.

References

1. Adapted from Associated Press, Xerox streamlined to save itself from bureaucracy mire, *Bryan–College Station Eagle*, December 25, 1992, C8; Smart, T. Can Xerox duplicate its glory days? *Business Week*, October 4, 1993, 56–58; Bowen, J. S. and Walton, E. Reenacting the corporation: Organizational change and restructuring of Xerox. *Planning Review*, September/October 1993, 5–8.

2. Gallbraith, J. R., Lawler E. E. III, & Associates. *Organizing for the Future: The New Logic for Managing Complex Organizations*. San Francisco: Jossey-Bass, 1993.

3. Daft, R. L. *Organization Theory and Design*, 5th ed. St. Paul, Minn.: West, 1995.

4. Howard, R. The CEO as organizational architect: An interview with Xerox's Paul Allaire. *Harvard Business Review*, September–October 1992, 106–119.

5. Duncan, R. B. Characteristics of organizational environments and perceived environmental uncertainty. *Administrative Science Quarterly*, 1972, 17, 314.

6. Bluedorn, A. C. Pilgrim's progress: Trends and convergence in research on organizational size and environments. *Journal of Management*, 1993, 19, 163–192; Boyd, B. K., Dess, G. G., and Rasheed, A. M. Divergence between archival and perceptual measures of the environment: Causes and consequences. *Academy of Management Review*, 1993, 18, 204–226.

7. Hegarty, W. H. Organizational survival means embracing change. *Business Horizons*, November–December 1993, 1–4; Miller, D. Environmental fit versus internal fit. *Organization Sciences*, 1992, 3, 159–178.

8. Wilson, I. Evaluating the environment: Social and political factors. In W. D. Guth (ed.), *Handbook of Business Strategy*, Boston: Warren, Gorham and Lamont, 1985, 32.

9. Oster, S. M. *Modern Competitive Analysis*, 2nd ed. New York: Oxford University Press, 1994.

10. Adapted from Hodgetts, R. M., Luthans, F., and Lee, S. M. New paradigm organizations: From total quality to learning to world-class. *Organizational Dynamics*, Winter 1994, 5–19; Grant, R. M., Shani, R., and Krishnan, R. TQM's challenge to management theory and practice. *Sloan Management Review*, Winter 1994, 25–35.

11. Fry, L. W., and Slocum, J. W., Jr. Technology, structure and workgroup effectiveness: A test of a contingency model. *Academy of Management Journal*, 1984, 17, 221–246.

12. Miller, C. C., Glick, W. H., Wang, Y. D., and Huber, G. P. Understanding technology–structure relationships: Theory development and meta-analytic theory testing. *Academy of Management Journal*, 1991, 34, 370–399.

13. Pennings, J. M., and Harianto, F. Technological networking and innovation implementation. *Organization Science*, 1992, 3, 356–382; Hackel, S. H., and Nolan, R. L. Managing by wire. *Harvard Business Review*, September–October 1993, 122–132.

14. Adapted from Gleckman, H. The technology payoff: A sweeping reorganization of work itself is boosting productivity. *Business Week*, June 14, 1993, 57–68; Fannie and Freddi adapt to meet lending challenge. *Bank Management*, May 1993, 31; Freedman, D. H. Fannie Mae's fast footwork. *Forbes*, June 7, 1993, 31–34.

15. Miller, D. The architecture of simplicity. *Academy of Management Review*, 1993, 18, 116–138; Gresov, C., Haveman, H. A., and Oliva, T. A. Organizational design, inertia, and the dynamics of competitive response. *Organization Science*, 1993, 4, 181–208.

16. Hall, G., Rosenthal, J., and Wade, J. How to make reengineering really work. *Harvard Business Review*, November–December 1993, 119–131.

17. Adapted from Hammer, M., and Champy, J. *Reengineering the Corporation: A Manifesto for Business Revolution*. New York: Harper Business, 1993; Sherman, S. How to bolster the bottom line: Investments in information technology; Profiles of five companies. *Fortune*, Autumn 1993, 14–18, Special 1994 Information Technology Guide.

18. Burns, T., and Stalker, G. M. *The Management of Innovation*. London: Social Science Paperbacks, 1961, 96–125.

19. Adapted from Weber, M. *The Theory of Social and Economic Organization* (trans., T. Parsons). New York: Oxford University Press, 1947, 329, 334.

20. Goodsell, C. T. *The Case for Bureaucracy: A Public Administration Polemic*, 3rd ed. Chatham, N.J.: Chatham House, 1994; d'Lribarne, P. The honour principle in the bureaucratic phenomenon. *Organization Studies*, 1994, 15, 81–97.

21. Benveniste, G. *Professionalizing the Organization: Reducing Bureaucracy to Enhance Effectiveness*. San Francisco: Jossey-Bass, 1987.

22. Pinchot, G., and Pinchot, E. *The End of Bureaucracy and the Rise of the Intelligent Organization*. San Francisco: Berrett-Koehler, 1993.

23. Donaldson, G. *Corporate Restructuring: Managing the Change Process from Within*. Boston: Harvard Business School Press, 1994.

24. Nelson, R. B. *Empowering Employees Through Delegation*. Burr Ridge, Ill.: Irwin, 1994.

25. Jones, G. *Organizational Theory: Text and Cases*. Reading, Mass.: Addison-Wesley, 1995.

26. Smith, A. *An Inquiry into the Nature and Causes of the Wealth of Nations* (1776). New York: Modern Library, reprint, 1937, 48.

27. Adapted from Huey, J. The new post heroic leadership. *Fortune*, February 21, 1994, 42–50; Lester, T. The Gore's happy family. *Management Today*, February 1993, 66–68.

28. Kahn, W. A., and Kram, K. E. Authority at work: Internal models and organizational consequences. *Academy of Management Review*, 1994, 19, 17–50.

29. Sitkin, S. B., and Bies, R. J. (eds.), *The Legalistic Organization*. Thousand Oaks, Calif.: Sage, 1994.

30. Adapted from *University Regulations: Texas A&M University*. College Station: Texas A&M University, 1994, 38–39, 72–75.

31. Schneider, B., and Bowen, D. E. The service organization: Human resources management is crucial. *Organizational Dynamics*, Spring 1993, 39–52.

32. Shrivastava, P. *Strategy Formulation and Implementation: Conceptual and Practical Frontiers*. Cincinnati: South-Western, 1994.

33. Adapted from Labich, K. The new crisis in business ethics. *Fortune*, April 20, 1992, 167–176; Byrne, J. A. The best-laid ethics programs. *Business Week*, March 9, 1992, 67–69; Ferguson, W. C. Solving a crisis of confidence and trust: NYNEX Corporation's ethics training program. *Across the Board*, July/August 1993, 56–57; Cauley, L. NYNEX fines and reassigns executives who got draft of outside ethics report. *Wall Street Journal*, April 29, 1994, B4.

34. Morrison, A. J., Ricks, D. A., and Roth, K. Globalization versus regionalization: Which way for the multinational? *Organizational Dynamics*, Winter 1991, 17–29.

35. Hoskisson, R. E., Hill, C. W. L., and Kim, H. The multidivisional structure: Organizational fossil or source of value? *Journal of Management*, 1993, 19, 269–298; Palmer, D. A., Jennings, P. D., and Zhou, X. Late adoption of the multidivisional form by large U.S. Corporations: Institutional, political, and economic accounts. *Administrative Science Quarterly*, 1993, 38, 100–131.

36. Adapted from Weber, J. A big company that works. *Business Week*, May 4, 1992, 124–132; Tully, S. A dickens of a tale. *Fortune*, May 31, 1993, 167–169.

37. Lorsch, J. W., and Allen, S. A. III. *Managing Diversity and Interdependence: An Organizational Study of Multidivisional Firms*. Cambridge, Mass.: Harvard University Graduate School of Business Administration, 1973. Also see Lawrence, P. R., and Lorsch, J. W. *Organization and Environment: Managing Differentiation and Integration*. Homewood, Ill.: Irwin, 1969.

38. Crittenden, V. L. Closing the marketing/manufacturing gap. *Sloan Management Review*, Spring 1992, 41–52.

39. Boschken, H. L. Strategy and structure: Reconceiving the relationship. *Journal of Management*, 1990, 16, 135–150; Barker, J. R. Tightening the iron cage: Concertive control in self-managing teams. *Administrative Science Quarterly*, 1993, 38, 408–437.

40. Lawrence, P. R. Organization and environment perspective: The Harvard research program. In A. H. Van de Ven, and W. F. Joyce (eds.), *Perspectives on Organization Design and Behavior*. New York: John Wiley & Sons, 1981, 311–337.

41. Adapted from Poole, J., and Wise, J. The structure of quality. *NCR Alpha*, Spring 1992, 6–9.

42. Davis, S. M., and Lawrence, P. R. *Matrix*. Reading, Mass.: Addison-Wesley, 1977; Hanna, D. P. *Designing Organizations for High Performance*. Reading, Mass.: Addison-Wesley, 1988.

43. Ford, R. C., and Randolph, W. A. Cross-functional structures: A review and integration of matrix organization and project management. *Journal of Management*, 1992, 18, 267–294.

44. Hodgetts, R. M., and Luthans, F. *International Management*, 2nd ed. New York: McGraw-Hill, 1994.

45. Kolodny, H. F. Managing in a matrix. *Business Horizons*, March–April 1981, 17–35; Gresov, C. and Stephens, C. The context of interunit influence attempts. *Administrative Science Quarterly*, 1993, 38, 252–276.

46. Rosenweig, P. M., and Singh, J. V. Organizational environments and multinational enterprise. *Academy of Management Review*, 1991, 16, 340–361.

47. Joyce, W. F. Matrix organization: A social experiment. *Academy of Management Journal*, 1986, 29, 536–561.

48. Bartlett, C. A., and Ghoshal, S. *Transnational Management: Text, Case and Readings in Cross-Border Management*. Homewood, Ill.: Irwin, 1992.

49. Sundaram, A. K,. and Black, J. S. The environment and internal organization of multinational enterprises. *Academy of Management Review*, 1992, 17, 729–757.

50. Ghoshal, S., and Nohria, N. Horses for courses: Organizational forms for multinational corporations. *Sloan Management Review*, Winter 1993, 23–35.

51. Adapted from Ingassia, P., and Mitchell, J. Ford to realign with a system of global chiefs. *Wall Street Journal*, March 31, 1994, A3, A4; White, J. B. and Suris, O. How a "skunk works" kept the Mustang alive—on a tight budget. *Wall Street Journal*, November 21, 1993, A1, A12; Plumb, S. E. Trotman team eye's Ford future: Group has ambitious global and product plans for the '90s. *Wards Auto World*, November 1993, 25–28.

52. Snow, C. C., Miles, R. E., and Coleman, H. J. Managing 21st century network organizations. *Organizational Dynamics*, Winter 1992, 5–20; Nadler, D. A., Gerstein, M. C., and Shaw, R. B. *Organizational Architectures: Designs for Changing Organizations*. San Francisco: Jossey-Bass, 1992.

53. Powell, W. W. Neither market nor hierarchy: Network forms of organization. In B. M. Staw and L. L. Cummings (eds.), *Research in Organizational Behavior*, vol. 12. Greenwich, Conn.: JAI Press, 1990, 295–336; Fulk, J., and Boyd, B. Emerging theories of communication in organizations. *Journal of Management*, 1991, 17, 407–446.

54. Limerick, D. The shape of the new organization: Implications for human resource management. *Asia Pacific Journal of Human Resources*, 1992, 30, 38–52; Wells, C. and Grieco, M. Spinning a web? Networking the technical convergence of Europe. *Organization Studies*, 1993, 14, 621–637.

55. Adapted from Byrne, J. A. The horizontal organization: It's about managing across not up and down. *Business Week*, December 20, 1993, 76–81.

56. Mills, D. Q. *Rebirth of the Corporation*. New York: John Wiley & Sons, 1991; Parker, G. M. *Cross-Functional Teams: Working with Allies, Enemies, and Other Strangers*. San Francisco: Jossey-Bass, 1994; Banner, D. K., *Designing Effective Organizations: Traditional and Transformational Views*. Thousand Oak, Calif.: Sage, 1994; Davidow, W. H., and Malone, M. S. *The Virtual Corporation*. New York: HarperCollins, 1992.

57. Adapted from Tapscott, D., and Caston, A. *Paradigm Shift: The New Promise of Information Technology*. New York: McGraw-Hill, 1993. Information technology enters a second era. *Business Week*, October 25, 1993, Special advertising section, unpaginated; Stewart, T. A. The netplex: It's a new silicon valley, *Fortune*, March 7, 1994, 98–104; Verity, J. W. Truck lanes for the information highway. *Business Week*, April 18, 1994, 112–114.

58. Ghoshal, S., and Bartlett, C. A. The multinational corporation as an interorganizational network. *Academy of Management Review*, 1990, 15, 603–625.

59. Slocum, J.W., Jr., and Lei, D. Designing global strategic alliances: Integrating cultural and economic factors. In G. P. Huber and W. M. Glick (eds.), *Organizational Change for Improving Performance*. New York: Oxford University Press, 1993, 295–322.

60. Smith-Ring, P., and Van de Ven, A. H. Developmental processes of cooperative interorganizational relationships. *Academy of Management Review*, 1994, 19, 90–118.

61. Kanter, R. M. Becoming PALs: Pooling, allying, and linking across companies. *Academy of Management Executive*, August 1989, 183–193; Kupfer, A. The race to rewire America, *Fortune*, April 19, 1993, 42–61.

62. Adapted from Saporito, B. Behind the tumult at P&G. *Fortune*, March 7, 1994, 74–81; Laing, J. R. New and improved: Procter & Gamble fights to keep its place on the top shelf. *Barrons*, November 29, 1993, 8–11; Arzt, E. L. Customers want performance, price, and value; Procter & Gamble's revamped logistics system within a total quality management context. *Transportation & Distribution*, July 1993, 32–34.

63. Adapted from Pasmore, W. A. *Designing Effective Organizations: The Sociotechnical Systems Perspective*. New York: John Wiley & Sons, 1988, 157–186.

64. Veiga, J. F., and Vanouzas, J. N. *The Dynamics of Organization Theory*, 2nd ed. St. Paul, Minn.: West, 1984, 212–215. Used with permission.

18 Organizational Decision Making

LEARNING OBJECTIVES

After you have finished studying this chapter, you should be able to:

▲ Identify the core issues in ethical decision making.

▲ Explain three basic models of organizational decision making.

▲ Describe the phases of managerial decision making.

▲ Explain the common human biases in decision making.

▲ Describe two methods for stimulating creativity.

OUTLINE

Preview Case: Rules to Decide By

Ethical Decision Making

Ethical Intensity

Managing Diversity: Denny's Errors and Recovery

Decision Principles and Rules

Managing Ethics: Designing an Effective Code

Affected Individuals

Benefits and Costs

Determination of Rights

Decision-Making Models

Rational Model

Managing Quality: Providing Reliable Service

Bounded Rationality Model

Political Model

Phases of Managerial Decision Making

Problem Recognition

Managing in Practice: The Challenger Disaster

Problem Interpretation

Attention to Problems

Managing in Practice: Challenger Flashback

Courses of Action

Aftermath

Managing Across Cultures: Royal Dutch/Shell's Decision Making

Stimulating Creativity

Lateral Thinking Method

Devil's Advocate Method

DEVELOPING SKILLS

Self-Diagnosis: *Individual Ethics Profile*

A Case in Point: *Olson Medical Systems*

PREVIEW CASE

Rules to Decide By

Individuals and organizations often use rules to evaluate information and make decisions. Nine decision rules that managers and organizations actually use are presented in the following list. After you read the application cited for each rule, indicate next to it whether you think that the decision rule is *probably good* (PG) or *probably bad* (PB) for that specific situation.

_____ **1.** *Restaurant pricing*: Mark food up three times direct cost, beer four times, and liquor six times. Direct food cost should be no more than 35% of food sales.

_____ **2.** *Evaluating acquisitions*: Purchase firm only if the estimated after-tax earnings in year 3 after the acquisition exceed 12% of the purchase price.

_____ **3.** *Pricing seasonal clothing*: Mark up the wholesale price by 60% and discount the retail price every two weeks by 20% until the entire inventory is gone.

_____ **4.** *Washington hotel booking*: Seven days prior to date accept up to 50 rooms overbooking (on top of 724 rooms available); one day prior to date, accept up to 20 rooms being oversold (used by a well-known Washington, D.C., hotel).

_____ **5.** *Conducting legal research*: When an issue needs research, tell a law clerk to spend six hours in the library and then report back.

_____ **6.** *Evaluating bank teller performance*: Must process at least 200 transactions per day, have fewer than four clerical errors per day, and have fewer than five days per month when the cash balance and cash register contents do not match.

_____ **7.** *Bookstore ordering*: If author and title are not familiar and the book is not slated for a big review (such as in the *New York Times* Book Section), order ten copies. Never let inventory drop below two copies.

_____ **8.** *Banquet staffing*: Staff one server per 30 guests if catering a sit-down banquet function and one per 40 guests for a buffet.

_____ **9.** *Exporting products*: Ship the steel product as long as the profit margin is positive (used by a Japanese manufacturer serving both foreign and domestic markets).[1]

You are correct if you responded *probably bad* (PB) to all these decision rules. The danger inherent in each rule is as follows (the numbers used here correspond to those in the Preview Case): (1) ignores labor cost differences and local competitive conditions; (2) insensitive to exact income profile over time and inadequately considers long-term payoffs; (3) ignores competitors' prices and the special characteristics of each product class; (4) inappropriate with big convention in town when all hotels are overbooked; (5) results in overbilling and adverse reaction from clients with minor legal issues; (6) discourages high-quality service for elderly or handicapped persons and for new customers still learning how to bank; (7) ignores seasonality (holiday season) and local demand or interest in topic or author; (8) ignores that serving some items, such as lobster, is more labor intensive than serving chicken, and it also ignores that some conventions run on a much tighter time schedule and cannot afford delay; and (9) may ship product overseas when domestic demand, which has higher profit margins, is at capacity, thereby failing to receive the highest profit margin attainable.[2]

Rules are quick and easy ways to reach a decision without a detailed analysis. They can be explicitly stated and easily applied, as suggested by the Preview Case.[3]   A general type of rule used by organizations—as well as by individuals—is the **dictionary rule.** This rule ranks items the same way a dictionary does: one criterion (i.e., letter) at a time. The dictionary rule gives great importance to the first criterion. It is valid in decision making only if this first criterion is known to be of overriding importance.[4] The dictionary rule was incorrectly used in evaluating acquisitions (item 2) in the Preview Case.

In previous chapters, we presented recommendations for assessing and improving decision making. In Chapter 3, we discussed the powerful roles of perception and attribution in understanding behaviors in organizations and how they influence decisions. In Chapter 4, we presented four major problem-solving styles based on how individuals may gather and evaluate information differently. In Chapter 6, we described the process that should be followed in diagnosing problems of work motivation and the types of decisions that are likely to improve motivation and productivity. In Chapter 7, we discussed goal setting as a process for creating a sense of direction in day-to-day decision making and establishing priorities. Of course, goal setting is, itself, one type of organizational decision making. In Chapter 9, we reviewed the six phases of team decision making that should lead to more effective team decisions. As part of that discussion, we presented the nominal group technique as a specialized decision-making process for stimulating team creativity. In Chapter 11, we discussed the Vroom-Jago leadership decision model, which provides insight into leadership styles that typically result in high-quality decisions. In Chapter 13, much of the discussion of conflict and negotiation focused on coping with decision situations when there is disagreement over goals, over how to achieve goals, or over the decision process to be used to resolve a conflict (e.g., procedural conflicts). In Chapter 15, we saw that access to the decision-making process provides a source of power for individuals and teams.

In this chapter, we enrich and broaden those earlier discussions of organizational decision making. We start with five core questions related to ethical decision making.[5] Second, we briefly outline the features of three major decision-making models. Third, we use some of the features of those models in presenting the phases of managerial decision making. Finally, we review two approaches to stimulating creativity in decision making.

▼ ETHICAL DECISION MAKING

Organizational decisions reflect underlying ethical principles and rules. In all the preceding chapters, we illustrated this point by discussing one or more ethical issues relevant to the content of the chapter. **Ethics** deals with right or wrong in the actions and decisions of individuals and the organizations of which they are a part. Ethical issues in organizations are more common and complex than generally recognized. In fact, ethical issues influence the decisions that employees make daily.[6] Some ethical issues involve factors that make the choice of "right or wrong" muddy. Thus many employees experience ethical dilemmas.[7] The major areas of these ethical dilemmas are suggested in Table 18.1, which shows a ranking of 26 ethical issues according to their importance. This table is based on a survey of the 711 largest U.S. corporations. The managers in this study identified the 5 most important ethical issues as drug and alcohol abuse, employee theft, conflicts of interest, quality control, and discrimination.[8]

Ethical decision making is extremely complex.[9] Thus there are no simple rules, such as those cited in the Preview Case, for coping with decisions that

TABLE 18.1   Major Ethical Issues Facing U.S. Industries: In Rank Order of Importance

Rank	Issue	Rank	Issue
1.	Drug and alcohol abuse	15.	False or misleading advertising
2.	Employee theft	16.	Giving excessive gifts and entertainment
3.	Conflicts of interest		
4.	Quality control	17.	Kickbacks
5.	Discrimination	18.	Insider trading
6.	Misuse of proprietary information	19.	Relations with local communities
7.	Abuse of expense accounts	20.	Antitrust issues
8.	Plant closings and layoffs	21.	Bribery
9.	Misuse of company assets	22.	Political contributions and activities
10.	Environmental pollution		
11.	Misuse of other's information	23.	Improper relations with local government
12.	Methods of gathering competitor's information	24.	Improper relations with federal government
13.	Inaccuracy of books and records	25.	Inaccurate time charging to government
14.	Receiving excessive gifts and entertainment	26.	Improper relations with foreign governments and their representatives

Source: Ethics Resource Center and Behavior Research Center. *Ethics Policies and Programs in American Business: Report of a Landmark Survey of U.S. Corporations.* Washington, D.C.: Ethics Resource Center, 1990, 17. Used with permission.

have important ethical content. As with our earlier presentations of ethical issues, our intent here is to help you to learn ethical reasoning. Evaluation of alternatives can be improved by an examination of five core ethical issues.[10]

▼ Ethical Intensity

The ethical issues suggested in Table 18.1 are not of equal importance. **Ethical intensity** refers to the degree of importance given an issue-related moral imperative. Accordingly, ethical intensity will vary substantially from issue to issue for decision makers.[11] Ethical intensity is determined by the combined impact, as interpreted by the decision maker, of six components.

▲ The *magnitude of consequences* of the ethical issue is the total of the harm or benefits for individuals affected by the ethical act in question. A decision that causes a thousand people to suffer a particular injury has greater consequences than a decision that causes ten people to suffer the same injury. A decision that causes the death of a human being has a greater consequence than a decision that causes a minor personal injury.

▲ The *probability of effect* of the ethical decision is a joint result of the probability that the decision will be implemented and that the decision will cause the harm or benefit predicted. The production of an automobile that would be dangerous to occupants during routine driving has greater probability of harm than the production of a car that endangers occupants only when curves are taken at high speed. The sale of a gun to a known armed robber has a greater probability of harm than the sale of a gun to a law-abiding citizen.

▲ The *social consensus* of the ethical issue is the degree of public agreement that a proposed decision is evil or good. The evil involved in actively discriminating against minority job candidates has greater social consensus than the evil involved in not actively seeking out minority job candidates. The evil involved in bribing a customs official in Canada has greater social consensus than the evil involved in bribing a customs official in a country where such behavior is generally accepted as a way of doing business, such as the Philippines (both illegal under U.S. law). Employees will find it difficult to decide ethically if they do not know what good ethics prescribe in a situation; a high degree of social consensus reduces the likelihood of ambiguity.

▲ The *temporal immediacy* of the ethical issue is the length of time between the present and the start of consequences of the decision. A shorter length of time implies greater immediacy. The release of a drug that will cause 1% of the people who take it to have acute nervous reactions within one month after they take it has greater temporal immediacy than releasing a drug that will cause 1% of those who take it to develop nervous disorders after 30 years. The reduction in the retirement benefits of current retirees has greater temporal immediacy than the reduction in retirement benefits of employees who are currently between 20 and 30 years of age.

▲ The *proximity* of the ethical issue is the feeling of nearness (social, cultural, psychological, or physical) that the decision maker has for victims or beneficiaries of the decision. Layoffs in a person's department have greater ethical proximity (physical and psychological) than do layoffs in a remote plant. For North Americans, the sale of dangerous pesticides in North American markets has greater ethical proximity (social, cultural, and physical) than does the sale of such pesticides in Australia.

▲ The *concentration of effect* of the ethical decision is an inverse function of the number of people affected by a decision. A change in a warranty policy denying coverage to 10 people with claims of $10,000 each has a more concentrated effect than a change denying coverage to 10,000 people with claims of $10 each. Cheating an individual or small group of individuals out of $1,000 has a more concentrated effect than cheating an organization, such as General Motors or the Internal Revenue Service, out of the same sum.

These components of ethical intensity are all potential characteristics of the ethical issue itself. As a result, they are likely to have combined effects. Ethical intensity will increase with increases in one or more of its components. Likewise, it will decrease with decreases in one or more of its components, assuming that all other components remain constant. Of course, individuals may rate ethical intensity differently, simply because they place different values on the various principles of ethical decision making.

Ethical intensity often comes into play in coping with diversity issues such as racism. The following Managing Diversity feature clearly illustrates most of the components of ethical intensity, including magnitude of consequences, social consensus, temporal immediacy, and concentration of effect.

MANAGING DIVERSITY

Denny's Errors and Recovery

During 1993, little looked good for Denny's, which has about 1,500 restaurants. The U.S. Justice Department had sustained allegations of bias against African-American customers of the chain. A group of 32 African-American customers sued the company in federal court in San Jose, California. They alleged that African-Americans in California Denny's restaurants were required to prepay for meals and pay cover charges but that whites were not. Four additional discrimination suits—including one by a group of Secret Service agents, who said they were denied service in a Denny's—soon followed. The six African-American secret service agents were not served at a Denny's in Annapolis, Maryland, but their white colleagues were served.

Jerry Richardson, CEO of Flagstar Companies, which owns the Denny's chain, apologized to the customers. Richardson fired or transferred problem employees and initiated meetings with civil rights groups. He also created a cultural diversity team to sensitize employees about the nature of racism. Denny's entered into a consent decree with the Justice Department that requires spot testing of restaurants for discrimination.

The company agreed with the National Association for the Advancement of Colored People (NAACP) to invest $1 billion over seven years to double the number of Denny's franchises owned by minorities, add hundreds of African-American managers, and sharply increase purchasing from minority enterprises. "This is a company that started out trying to deal with their problem in a superficial way," says Guy T. Saperstein, an Oakland, California, lawyer who brought a class-action lawsuit against Denny's. But "now, they're dealing with it in a substantive, remedial way. It's good for everybody."[12]

▼ Decision Principles and Rules

There are no simple agreed-upon principles and rules for resolving all ethical issues.[13] Table 18.2 shows various principles and rules that have been advanced by people in business, philosophy, religion, and politics. We do not suggest that all are necessarily good and desirable. Rather, we present them in sequence ranging from those that justify self-serving decisions to those that require careful consideration of others' rights and costs.

Through laws, court rulings, and enforcement agencies, governments establish ethical principles and rules that organizations are expected to comply with in certain situations.[14] For example, Title VII of the 1964 U.S. Civil Rights Act forbids organizations from considering such personal characteristics as race, gender, religion, or national origin in decisions to recruit, hire, promote, or fire employees. This law is based on the ethical principle of distributive justice. As suggested in previous chapters, the **distributive justice principle**

TABLE 18.2 **Stated Principles of Behavior**

1. *Hedonist principle*—do whatever you find to be in your own self-interest.

2. *Might-equals-right-principle*—you are strong enough to take advantage without respect to ordinary social conventions and widespread practices or customs.

3. *Conventionalist principle*—bluff and take advantage of all legal opportunities and widespread practices or custom.

4. *Intuition principle*—go with your "gut feeling" or what you understand to be right in a given situation.

5. *Organization ethics principle*—ask whether actions are consistent with organization goals and do what is good for the organization.

6. *Means–end principle*—ask whether some overall good justifies any moral transgression.

7. *Utilitarian principle*—determine whether the harm in action is outweighed by the good.

8. *Professional ethics principle*—do only that which can be explained before a group of your peers.

9. *Disclosure principle*—ask how it would feel if the thinking and details of the decision were disclosed to a wide audience.

10. *Distributive justice principle*—an individual's treatment should not be based on arbitrarily defined characteristics.

11. *Categorical imperative principle*—act in a way you believe is right and just for any other person in a similar situation.

12. *Golden rule principle*—look at the problem from the position of another person affected by the decision and try to determine what response the other person would expect as most virtuous.

Source: Adapted from Lewis, P. V. Ethical decision-making guidelines: Executive/student perceptions. In L. H. Peters and K. A. Vaverek (eds.), *Proceedings of the Annual Meeting of the Southwest Division of the Academy of Management.* Denton, Texas. Southwest Division of the Academy of Management, 1988, 44, 48.

means that treating individuals differently should not be based on arbitrarily defined characteristics.[15] It states that (1) employees who are similar in *relevant* respects should be treated similarly and (2) employees who differ in *relevant* respects should be treated differently in proportion to the differences between them. On this basis, the U.S. Equal Pay Act of 1963 holds that it is illegal to pay women and men different wages when the jobs in the same organization require equal skill, effort, responsibility, and working conditions. Violations of the distributive justice principle in employment practices for many cultures—such as Russia, China, and Brazil—are not viewed with the same level of ethical intensity as in the United States and Canada.

There is no one method for ensuring that employees adhere to ethical principles and rules in their decision making. However, the following actions have been suggested for integrating ethical decision making into the day-to-day life of an organization.

▲ Develop a clear code of ethics and follow it.

▲ Establish a whistle-blowing and/or ethical concerns procedure and follow it.

▲ Involve employees in the identification of ethical problems to achieve a shared understanding and resolution of them.

▲ Monitor individual, team, and departmental performance regarding ethical issues.

▲ Include ethical decision making in the performance appraisal process.

▲ Publicize the organizational priorities and efforts related to ethical issues.[16]

The following Managing Ethics feature provides guidance on what a code of ethics should include and how it should be used. It presents five ways in which codes of ethics could do more to promote ethical behavior by asking and answering pertinent questions about such codes.

MANAGING ETHICS

Designing an Effective Code

Is the code a public document? Only about 50% of all codes are publicly distributed. If these statements are really "ethical" codes, they should state the organization's commitment to fair and ethical practice to all relevant stakeholders. The Johnson & Johnson (J&J) credo is an excellent example of a widely distributed corporate code. It has been translated into many languages and is conspicuously displayed by J&J employees throughout the world.

Does the code contain information specific to the organization's industry? If codes are to move beyond a checklist of general issues, they should include information relevant to the organization's specific industry. McDonald's detailed code for children's advertising, for instance, lists specific responsibilities of the company (including the fact that Ronald McDonald will never be a pitchman). This code not only covers the general philosophy in using cartoon characters but also the type of premium/offer advertising and conventional purchase premiums that are allowed for advertising aimed at children.

Does the code provide specific guidance? Over 80% of those who responded to one survey indicated that their code did provide specific guidance on gift giving and receiving. Some codes, however, use words such as *nominal, token,* or *modest value* when discussing gifts. This leaves the door open to widely varying interpretations. The Donnelly Corporation provides a creative approach: "If you can't eat it, drink it or use it up in one day, don't give it or anything else of greater value."

Is the Code Enforced? If a code is to have value, employees must know that they will suffer consequences if they violate it. Most codes include sanctions for violations, which range from a mild reprimand to termination. The Hercules Corporation outlines a procedure for dealing with both major and minor violations. The company also has an ethics committee that oversees the implementation and enforcement of the code.

Does the code include the organization's responsibility to the employee? Too many codes contain only a list of do's and don'ts for employees to follow. The rules seem to exist exclusively for the organization's protection. A statement of the organization's position is very helpful to employees who are asked to follow the "rules of the game" stated in the code. Xerox and United Technologies use representative written questions and answers to explain the principles set forth in the code.[17]

▼ Affected Individuals

Ethical decision making generally requires an assessment of who will experience benefits or costs as a result of a particular decision. For major decisions, this assessment may include a variety of stakeholders—shareholders, customers, lenders, suppliers, employees, and government agencies, among others. The more specific you can be about individuals and departments that may experience benefits or costs from a particular decision, the more likely it is that ethical decisions will be made. Remember, ethics is about the *effects* of decisions on identifiable individuals and organizations.

The ethical interpretation of the effects of decisions on identifiable individuals can change over time. Consider **employment at will,** a doctrine that holds that parties to an employment agreement have equal bargaining power and therefore that the right to fire is absolute and creates very little cost to either party. The employer presumably can easily find another employee, and the employee presumably can easily find another job.[18]

Based on the distributive justice principle, the categorical imperative principle, and the golden rule principle (principles 10, 11, and 12 in Table 18.2), the employment-at-will doctrine increasingly has been challenged successfully in wrongful termination cases in the courts. Before 1980, companies in the U.S. were free to fire most employees "at will." That is, they could be fired for any reason and without explanation. Employees rarely went to court to challenge a termination. The vast majority who did had their suits dismissed. The courts have been increasingly willing to rule for exceptions to at-will employment.[19] Two management errors underlie a significant number of the terminations that wind up in court.

▲ Managers are unclear about their actual reasons for terminating someone. Their lack of clarity makes it difficult to judge whether the grounds are justifiable. Likewise, managers fail to understand the categories within which a termination can be responsibly justified and the special requirements for fair play.

▲ Managers are so concerned with finding good justifications to cover themselves in court that they have difficulty understanding what fairness means from the vantage point of the about-to-be terminated employee. They fail to balance the employee's need to be treated fairly with the organization's needs for excellence and discipline.[20]

▼ Benefits and Costs

Judging the benefits and costs of a proposed decision requires a determination of the interests and values of those affected. When individuals value something, they want that situation to continue or to occur in the future. **Values** are the relatively permanent and deeply held desires of individuals. A sample of business managers were asked to rank a set of 18 values they considered most important in their lives. The top 5 were self-respect, family security, freedom, accomplishment, and happiness. The bottom 5 were pleasure, beauty, salvation, social recognition, and equality.[21] Managers need to guard against assuming that others share their priority of values. Conflicting values between stakeholders can lead to different interpretations of ethical responsibilities. Environmental groups, which probably have as one of their top values a world of beauty, often consider the managers of some organizations as both irresponsible and unethical in not showing more concern about air and water pollution, land use, and the like.

One common approach to the assessment of benefits and costs is utilitarianism. As noted in Table 18.2 (principle 7), **utilitarianism** emphasizes the provision of the greatest good for the greatest number in judging the ethics of decision making. An individual who is guided by utilitarianism considers the potential effect of alternative actions on those who will be affected and then selects the alternative benefiting the greatest number of people. The individual accepts the fact that this alternative may harm others. However, so long as potentially positive results outweigh potentially negative results, the individual considers the decision to be both good and ethical.[22] Some critics suggest that utilitarianism has been carried to extremes in North America. They suggest that there is too much short-run maximizing of personal advantage and too much discounting of the long-run costs of disregarding ethics, those living in poverty, and the environment. They believe that too many people are acquiring wealth for the purpose of personal consumption and that the means to get it are unimportant to such people.[23]

▼ Determination of Rights

The notion of rights also is complex and has changed over time. One aspect of rights focuses on who is entitled to benefits or to participation in the decision to change the allocation of benefits and costs.[24] Union–management negotiations frequently involve conflicts and dilemmas over management's rights to hire, promote, fire, and reassign union employees. Slavery, racism, gender and age discrimination, and invasion of privacy often have been attacked by appeals to values based on concepts of fundamental rights.

Employee responsibilities and rights issues are numerous and highly varied. A few examples include unfair and reverse discrimination, sexual harassment, employee rights to continued employment, employer rights to terminate employment "at will," employee and corporate free speech, due process, and acquired immune deficiency syndrome (AIDS). According to some experts, the attention to workplace rights is the most crucial internal issue facing organizations in the nineties.[25]

Privacy rights have become ethical dilemmas in terms of (1) distribution and use of employee data from computer-based human resource information systems;[26] (2) increasing use of paper-and-pencil honesty tests as a result of polygraph testing being declared illegal in most situations;[27] (3) procedures and bases for AIDS and drug testing; and (4) genetic testing.[28] The ethical dilemmas in each of these areas revolve around balancing the rights of the individual, the needs and rights of the employer, and the interests of the community at large.[29]

▼ DECISION-MAKING MODELS

The primary features of three decision-making models are presented briefly in this section. Our goal is to demonstrate the significant variations in how decision making is perceived and interpreted. These models are useful for identifying the complexity and variety of decision-making situations in an organization.[30]

▼ Rational Model

The **rational model** holds that decision making involves intentionally choosing among alternatives to maximize benefits to the organization. The rational perspective requires comprehensive problem definition, an exhaustive consideration of alternatives, and thorough data collection and analysis. Evaluation criteria are developed early in the process, and information exchange presumably is unbiased and accurate. Individual preferences and organizational choices are a function of the best alternative for the entire organization.[31] The rational model of decision making is based on the assumptions that (1) complete information concerning alternatives is available, (2) these alternatives can be ranked according to objective criteria, and (3) the alternative selected will provide the maximum gain possible for the organization (or decision makers). An implicit assumption is that ethical dilemmas do not exist in the decision-making process.

Xerox developed a companywide six-step process for virtually all decisions of any importance. A portion of this decision making process in presented in Table 18.3. Column 1 identifies each of the six steps. Column 2 presents the key question to be answered in each step. Column 3 indicates what's needed to proceed to the next step. Through this process, Xerox attempts to obtain rational decision making. Employees receive extensive training about various decision-making tools to work through these steps.[32]

Total quality management (TQM) introduces values, tools, and process aids that enable organizations to *rationally* meet or exceed customer expectations.[33]

TABLE 18.3   Portion of Xerox's Rational Decision-Making Process

Step	Question to Be Answered	What's Needed to Go to the Next Step
1. Identify and select problem	What do we want to change?	Identification of the gap; "desired state" described in observable terms
2. Analyze problem	What's preventing us from reaching the "desired state"?	Key cause(s) documented and ranked
3. Generate potential solutions	How *could* we make the change?	Solution list
4. Select and plan the solution	What's the *best* way to do it?	Plan for making and monitoring the change; measurement criteria to evaluate solution effectiveness
5. Implement the solution	Are we following the plan?	Solution in place
6. Evaluate the solution	How well did it work?	Verification that the problem is solved, or agreement to address continuing problems

Source: Adapted from Garvin, D. A. Building a learning organization. *Harvard Business Review*, July–August 1993, 78–91; Brown, J. S., and Walton, E. Reenacting the corporation: Organizational change and restructuring of Xerox. *Planning Review*, September/October 1993, 5–8.

The following Managing Quality account identifies some of the ways that service providers attempt to deliver reliable service *rationally.*

MANAGING QUALITY

Providing Reliable Service

Some managers believe that to try to eliminate mistakes isn't practical. This bias is problematic for it doesn't challenge managers to boldness and creativity in improving service to customers. A company with 100,000 weekly transactions, and with a 98% reliability rate, still undermines the confidence of 2,000 customers each week.

Hard Rock Cafe, a successful restaurant and retail chain with locations throughout the world, follows the service tenet of "double checking" to minimize errors. The tenet is: *Be careful and don't make a mistake in the first place. If a mistake does occur, correct it before it reaches the customer.* The Hard Rock Cafe in Orlando, Florida implements double checking through two "extra" people in the kitchen. One is stationed inside the kitchen and the other at the kitchen counter. The inside person reviews everything that is going on, looking for signs of undercooked or overcooked meals, wilting lettuce, and the like. The counter person, or "expediter," checks each prepared plate against the order ticket before the plate is delivered to the table. Although this system is an added expense, it has worked well for this restaurant. On a busy day, the Orlando outlet will serve 6,000 meals to customers who may have waited in line for a table for an hour or more.

Preston Trucking Company, a Maryland-based firm selected as one of America's ten best companies to work for, nurtures service reliability values in a different way. Preston has each employee sign a service excellence statement. Posted in each Preston facility, the statement reads in part: *Once I make a commitment to a customer or another associate, I promise to fulfill it on time. I will do what I say when I say I will do it ... I understand that one claim or one mistake is one error too many. I promise to do my job right the first time and to continually seek improvement.*

De Mar, a plumbing, heating, air conditioning and refrigeration company in Clovis, California, grew from just over $200,000 in annual revenue to $3.3 million in approximately six years. De Mar did so by identifying and then responding to customers' most important expectations. Customers wanted timely service in emergencies. De Mar responded by providing 24-hour-a-day, seven-day-a-week service. De Mar also guarantees same-day service for customers requiring it. Customers also wanted accurate cost estimates. De Mar answered by guaranteeing its estimates before doing the work.[34]

▼ Bounded Rationality Model

The **bounded rationality model** recognizes the limitations of the individual's rationality and reveals the day-to-day decision-making processes used by individuals. It partially explains why different individuals make different decisions when they have exactly the same information. As suggested in Figure 18.1, the bounded rationality model reflects the individual's tendencies to (1)

FIGURE 18.1
━━━━━━━━━━

Bounded Rationality Model

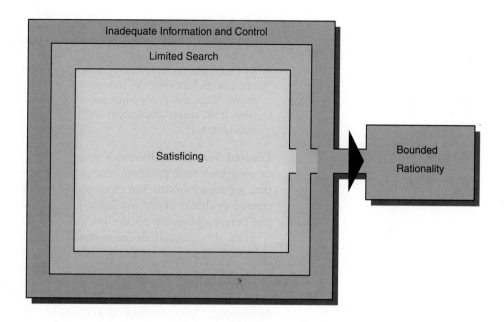

select less than the best goal or alternative solution (that is, to *satisfice*), (2) engage in a limited search for alternative solutions, and (3) have inadequate information and control of external and internal environmental forces influencing the outcomes of decisions.[35] This model also recognizes the reality that complete information—concerning available alternatives or the outcome of some course of action—may be impossible for an individual to obtain, regardless of how much time or resources are used.

Satisficing   The practice of selecting an acceptable goal or solution is called **satisficing.** In this case, *acceptable* might mean easier to identify and achieve, less controversial, or otherwise safer than the best available alternative. For example, profit goals often are quantified, such as a 12% rate of return on investment or a 6% increase in profits over the previous year. These goals may not be the maximum attainable. They may, in fact, represent little more than top management's view of reasonable goals, that is, challenging but not too difficult to achieve.[36]

In an interview almost 35 years after introducing the bounded rationality model, Herbert Simon described satisficing in these words for a management audience:

> Satisficing is intended to be used in contrast to the classical economist's idea that in making decisions in business or anywhere in real life, you somehow pick, or somebody gives you, a set of alternatives from which you select the best one—maximize. The satisficing idea is that first of all, you don't have the alternatives, you've got to go out and scratch for them—and that you might have shaky ways of evaluating them when you do find them. So you look for alternatives until you get one from which, in terms of your experience and in terms of what you have reason to expect, you will get a reasonable result.
> But satisficing doesn't necessarily mean that managers have to be satisfied with what alternative pops up first in their minds or in their computers and let it go at that. The level of satisficing can be raised—by personal determination, setting higher

individual or organizational standards, and by use of an increasing range of sophisticated management science and computer-based decision-making and
problem-solving techniques.

As time goes on, you obtain more information about what's feasible and what you
can aim at. Not only do you get more information, but in many, if not most, companies there are procedures for setting targets, including procedures for trying to
raise individuals' aspiration levels [goals]. This is a major responsibility of top
management.[37]

Limited Search   Individuals usually make a limited search for possible goals
or solutions to a problem, considering alternatives only until they find one
that seems adequate. For example, in choosing the best job, college graduates
cannot evaluate every available job in their field. They might hit retirement
age before obtaining all the information needed for a decision.

Even the rational decision-making model recognizes that identifying and
assessing alternatives cost time, energy, and money. In the bounded rationality
model, individuals stop searching for alternatives as soon as they discover an
acceptable goal or solution.

Inadequate Information and Control   Individuals frequently have inadequate information about problems and face environmental forces that they
cannot control. These conditions often influence the results of their decisions
in unanticipated ways. For example, management might decide to purchase
automatic stamping machines to make disc brakes for automobiles. By reducing labor costs, the machines could pay for themselves within two years. But
management might fail to anticipate either union resistance or declining automobile sales. In those cases, the machines could not be used effectively, and
their payout time could more than double.

In sum, the bounded rationality model provides insights into the limitations
of decision making in organizations. It implicitly recognizes the potential for
ethical dilemmas in decision-making situations, but provides no guidance on
how to resolve them.[38]

▼ Political Model

The **political model** suggests that organizational decisions reflect the desires
of individuals to satisfy their own interests. Preferences are established early,
usually on the basis of departmental goals, and seldom change as new information is acquired. Problem definitions, searches, data collection, and evaluation criteria are merely methods used to tilt the decision outcome in
someone's favor. Information exchange is biased toward the same end.

Decisions are a result of the distribution of power in the organization and
the effectiveness of the tactics used by the various participants in the process.[39]
The model doesn't allow for ethical dilemmas. However, it draws on the following behavioral principles presented in Table 18.2: (1) *hedonistic principle*—
do whatever you find to be in your own self-interest; (2) *might-
equals-right-principle*—you are strong enough to take advantage without respect to ordinary social conventions and widespread practices or customs; and
(3) *conventionalist principle*—bluff and take advantage of all legal opportunities
and widespread practices or customs.

▼ PHASES OF MANAGERIAL DECISION MAKING

Managerial decision making begins with a recognition or awareness of problems and concludes with an assessment of the results of actions taken to solve those problems. Figure 18.2 illustrates the phases of managerial decision making.[40] Although these phases appear to proceed in logical order, managerial decision making actually may be quite disorderly and complex as it unfolds. In fact, decisions often are made and problems solved in fits and starts. There seemingly is no beginning or end.[41] Managers usually deal with the unexpected crises and petty problems that require much more time than they're worth. The manager may well go from a budget meeting involving millions of dollars to a discussion of what to do about a broken decorative water fountain. Thus managerial work is hectic and fragmented and requires the ability to shift continually from person to person, from subject to subject, and from problem to problem.[42]

FIGURE 18.2

Phases of Managerial Decision Making

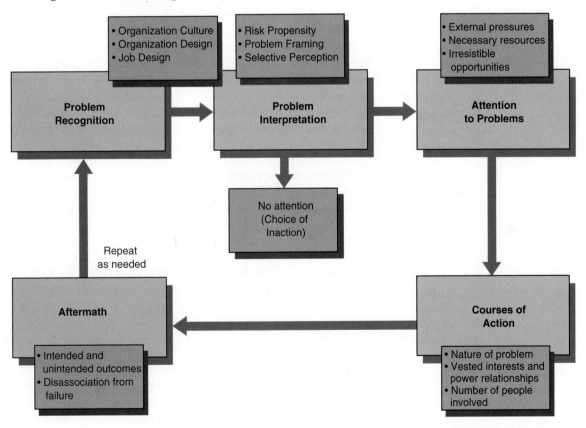

Source: Adapted from McCall, M. W., Jr., and Kaplan, R. E. *Whatever It Takes: The Realities of Managerial Decision Making,* 2nd ed. Englewood Cliffs, N.J.: Prentice-Hall, 1990.

▼ Problem Recognition

Managerial decision making rarely begins with a clean slate. Previous decisions and experiences and new information may determine whether a manager is aware or recognizes a problem. Moreover, the characteristic of individual managers play an important role in problem recognition[43] (see Chapter 4).

With **structured problems,** the problem recognition phase is straightforward. For example, a marketing manager promises the delivery of an order within 30 days. After 45 days, the customer calls and angrily states: "The order hasn't arrived. I need it pronto. What are you going to do?" The marketing manager is suddenly and forcefully made aware of a problem and the need to resolve it immediately.

With **unstructured problems,** the problem recognition phase, itself, often is a problem.[44] The "problem" of problem recognition can result from unclear or inadequate information about developments and trends in the environment. For example, Walt Disney, Hilton Hotels, and other organizations create marketing research departments to collect information about their customers to determine whether changing customer tastes and preferences are likely to create new problems. A challenge for successful organizations is to avoid the error of *perceptual defense* (see Chapter 3). People have a tendency to deny and protect themselves against threatening ideas or situations, especially when current success is threatened.[45] Mark Newton heads the department at Cincinnati Gas & Electric and is charged with helping the utility move into the future. He comments: "I look at denial as an unconscious coping mechanism to block out and not deal with major change that may have some pain associated with it."[46]

Let's return to the marketing manager who was called by an irate customer. This manager also has had a 200% turnover in sales representatives. When asked about this level of turnover, he replies: "That's the way it's always been, even before I became the marketing manager. I guess it's just part of the cost of doing business and the nomadic nature of sales reps." This response shows no awareness that a problem of high turnover might exist. Six months later, a new marketing manager is appointed. When reviewing the personnel files, she is astounded by the "major turnover problem, which must be corrected if we are ever to establish long-term and trusting relationships with our customers and eventually increase our sales to them."

The recognition of a problem usually triggers activities that may either lead to a quick solution or be part of a long, drawn-out process. The length of time required depends on the nature and complexity of the problem. For example, the new marketing manager may be confronted by a subordinate with an easily solved problem: "We are fifteen days late in the delivery of the West Publishing Company order. Should we ship it by our regular freight line, by air express, or what?" The marketing manager may immediately respond: "Send it air express." However, the 200% annual turnover in sales personnel represents a major problem. She may need several months to (1) determine the reasons for the turnover, (2) implement a program to reduce turnover, and (3) assess the results of the program.

Major disasters or accidents often have long incubation periods characterized by a number of events signaling danger. These events often go unrecognized or misinterpreted and accumulate over time.[47] Consider the following Managing in Practice account of the *Challenger* disaster.

MANAGING IN PRACTICE

The Challenger *Disaster*

A nagging question in the minds of most people following the *Challenger* space shuttle explosion on January 28, 1986, is how NASA management officials could have allowed the shuttle to take off. There appeared to be clear-cut warnings about problems with the shuttle's solid-fuel booster rocket joints. Whatever pressure the managers were facing to launch the shuttle, did they not know enough technically to realize that the lives of the crew were in serious danger? If, in fact, they did not know enough about the technical apparatus of the shuttle, as good managers, should they not have been in constant contact with their trained professionals regarding the spacecraft's safety?

The findings of the presidential commission investigating the loss of the *Challenger* revealed that NASA management officials *did* have sufficient information to cancel the flight. However, this information may not have reached all of the relevant managers. The information was made available to several key NASA managers by some engineering professionals as late as the evening before the flight. Allan J. McDonald, a senior engineer in charge of the solid-fuel booster rocket motor program at Morton Thiokol, Inc., NASA's principal contractor of booster rockets, argued strongly against the launch only hours before the *Challenger* was scheduled to lift off. In testimony before the presidential commission, McDonald and Roger Biosjoly, who had graphically demonstrated the erosion of the infamous O-rings in prior flights, testified about their objections. Their bosses had overruled them after presumably being pressured by NASA officials at the Marshall Space Flight Center. According to the testimony, McDonald stated that the engineers would not recommend a launch at temperatures below 53°F. The commission also learned that Rockwell International's engineers had also warned about the adverse effects of cold weather on the shuttle's tiles.

On the morning of the launch, temperatures ten degrees below the danger threshold were recorded by NASA technicians on the booster rocket's exterior. Jerry Mason, former senior vice-president at Thiokol, testified how the decision to launch was reached by polling appropriate managers. When asked if company officials polled the engineers, Mason replied, ''We only polled the management people.''[48]

A variety of conditions can increase the likelihood of incorrect problem recognition and formulation. The following are seven such conditions.

▲ *Someone gives you a problem.* When you are asked to help solve a problem that someone else has defined, you are likely to take that problem as a ''given'' and work within the constraints of the problem statement. The more authority or power that the person wields, the more likely you are to accept, without question, the statement of the problem.

▲ *A quick solution is desired*. If a decision is needed quickly, the amount of time spent in formulating or reformulating a problem is likely to be cut short. This was one of the conditions involved in the *Challenger* launch.

▲ *A low-quality solution is acceptable*. People attach a lower priority to some problems than others. When this is the case, less time is likely to be spent formulating and solving the problem than if a high-quality solution were essential.

▲ *The problem seems familiar*. A seemingly familiar problem is likely to get a ready-made solution rather than a tailor-made solution. Familiarity can lead to a quick solution or a fix.

▲ *Emotions are high*. Stressful or emotional situations often lead to an abbreviated search for a satisfactory statement of the problem. This was one of the conditions involved in the *Challenger* launch.

▲ *No prior experience in challenging problem definitions*. For most people, questioning a problem statement requires training and practice. The habit of questioning is hard to get into (and easy to fall out of). Those unaccustomed to challenging or reformulating a problem statement are unlikely to do so.

▲ *The problem is complex*. When a situation involves a lot of variables and the variables are hard to identify and/or measure, the problem is harder to formulate and solve.[49] This was another of the conditions involved in the *Challenger* launch.

▼ Problem Interpretation

The second phase in the decision-making process requires an interpretation of the problem. A high turnover rate for sales representatives might be the result of looking for applicants in the wrong places, poor selection procedures and training, lack of supervision, a poor compensation system, or some combination of these inadequacies. **Problem interpretation** refers to the process of giving meaning and definition to problems that have been recognized.[50] Problem recognition does not ensure sufficient, if any, problem attention. According to Figure 18.2, one option for managers simply is not to give a recognized problem any attention—the choice of inaction. This choice may be a consequence of (1) demands on the manager to deal with too many high-priority problems, (2) a belief that the problem will go away with time, or (3) the judgment that an attempt to do something about the problem will only worsen the situation.

Preconceptions, the filtering out of new information, and defensiveness contribute to ineffective problem interpretation.[51] As suggested in Figure 18.2, some of the key influences on problem interpretation include perceptions and attributions, organizational culture, and organization design. A common thread in these influences is the way information is processed and how it is used to interpret problems.[52] There is no simple one-to-one relationship between the availability of "objective" information and how it is processed in the problem-interpretation phase. Various biases can affect decision making, six of which we discuss next.

Risk Propensity   **Risk propensity** is the general tendency of the decision maker to take or avoid risks. A risk-averse decision maker is likely to focus on negative outcomes. The probability of loss is overestimated relative to the probability of gain. Therefore the decision maker requires a high probability of gain to tolerate exposure to failure. Conversely, a risk-seeking decision maker is likely to focus on potential positive outcomes. Probability of gain is overestimated relative to the probability of loss. Thus risk seekers may be willing to tolerate exposure to failure with a low probability of gain.[53] Many decisions can be understood in terms of a desire to avoid the unpleasant consequences of a decision that turns out poorly. Making a choice can be personally threatening because a poor outcome can undermine the decision maker's sense of competence, cause significant problems for the organization, and even get the decision maker fired. In general, most people have a low-risk propensity. They buy countless varieties of insurance to avoid the risk of large but improbable losses. They invest in savings accounts, CDs, and money market funds in order to avoid the risk of stock and bond volatility. Generally, they prefer certain outcomes to risky courses of action that have the same or higher expected outcomes.[54]

Problem Framing   **Problem framing** refers to whether a situation is presented or viewed in positive or negative terms. Individuals who are in favorable circumstances tend to be risk averse because they may feel they have more to lose. In contrast, those who believe that they are in an unfavorable situation may feel that they have little to lose and therefore may be risk seeking.[55] Stressing the potential losses implied by a decision heightens the importance of risk. In contrast, stressing potential gains lessens the perception that serious risks are involved. Specifically, positively framed situations foster risk taking by drawing managerial attention to opportunities rather than risks.[56] An example of positive versus negative framing is that of winning $3,000 for certain or winning $4,000 with an 80% probability. Most people prefer the certain gain to the uncertain chance of larger gain. Which would you choose? Although risk aversion commonly is assumed to hold for most decisions, many exceptions have been documented. People prefer to take risks when making a choice between a certain loss and a risky loss. For example, what happens when individuals are asked to choose between losing $3,000 for certain and losing $4,000 with an 80% probability? In this case, most people prefer the risky alternative.[57] Which would you choose?

Availability Bias   The **availability bias** refers to the tendency to recall specific instances of an event and therefore overestimate how often such an event occurs (and vice versa). For example, individuals who have been in a serious automobile accident often overestimate the frequency of such accidents. This type of bias may be expressed as what's out of sight often is out of mind. In other words, evident limited alternatives may exert more weight on likelihood judgments than they should. Bridge players provide a telling example. Experienced bidders take into account unusual events or hands. Less experienced players believe that they can make hands they often cannot, precisely because they fail to consider uncommon occurrences.[58]

Confirmation Bias   The **confirmation bias** refers to the natural tendency to seek support for an initial view of a situation rather than to look for disconfirming evidence. Unfortunately, the more complex and uncertain a situation, the easier one-sided support is to find. Realistic confidence requires seeking negative, as well as positive, evidence. People tend to overstate the strength of evidence (e.g., how well a candidate did in an interview) relative to the credibility of that type of evidence (the limited insight gained from any single interview). Whenever source credibility is low and the strength of the evidence is highly suggestive, overconfidence is likely to occur. Thus people may predict too readily that the interviewed candidate will win or lose, based on the fallible, limited evidence obtainable from a short interview.[59]

Selective Perception Bias   The **selective perception bias** refers to the tendency to see what the person expects to see. People seek information consistent with their own views and often downplay information that conflicts with their perceptions. An example might be parents who are unwilling to acknowledge that the reasons their child received a failing grade are poor performance and lack of effort, rather than poor instruction or instructor bias.

Law of Small Numbers Bias   The **law of small numbers bias** refers to the tendency of considering small samples as representative of the larger population (a few cases "proves the rule"), even when they are not.[60] Some Arab-Americans were the targets of hostile comments and actions by some non-Arabs after the invasion of Kuwait by Iraq. Apparently, these individuals incorrectly attributed the unsavory characteristics of Saddam Hussein (sample of 1) to Arabs and Arab-Americans in general.

Another potential bias is occupational specialization, which may lead to a form of *tunnel-vision*. Specialization fosters the channeling of information and problems to particular experts and departments, which can both aid and hinder problem recognition and interpretation. When the marketing manager and her staff have been assigned goals to ensure customer satisfaction—such as "98% of all orders are to reach customers on the promised date of delivery"—and to take corrective action when the goals are not achieved, specialization probably aids problem recognition and interpretation. Generally, however, unless accompanied by horizontal integrating mechanisms (such as cross-functional teams), specialization may well lead to ineffective efforts and conflicts between specialties and departments. Employees have been known to conceal and distort information as a means of advancing their individual and departmental goals. Someone also may fail to recognize the importance of new information if it doesn't clearly fall within an existing specialty or area of responsibility. Unfortunately, this tendency is most likely in a complex and uncertain environment, the very environment in which effective problem recognition and problem interpretation is crucial.[61] The likelihood of managers and employees learning to recognize and interpret problems effectively is strongly influenced by the organization's culture.[62]

▼ Attention to Problems

After problems have been recognized and interpreted, judgments need to be made as to which problems are to receive attention, how much, and in what order. Managers must be aware of the relative priorities they place on the problems they attend to, sometimes unconsciously. As Figure 18.2 suggests, the problems receiving the highest priority are likely to meet the following criteria.

▲ Attention to the problem is supported by strong *external pressure* (the executive vice-president insists on a report being completed within two weeks).

▲ Attention to the problem is supported by the *necessary resources* to take action (authorization given to approve overtime pay and hire temporary workers to complete the report within two weeks).

▲ Attention to the problem represents an *irresistible opportunity* (the report deals with assessing a proposed expansion in production capacity that could lead to a larger and more profitable firm, a promotion from production supervisor to production manager, or the potential of larger bonuses).

The number and variety of recognized problems needing attention almost always exceed the manager's capacity for addressing and solving all of them within the desired time frame. In addition, pressures from the external environment can change the most carefully planned priorities for attending to recognized problems.[63] Let's return to the *Challenger* disaster described in the preceding Managing in Practice account. We now review some of the apparent external pressures and the sense of irresistible opportunities that helped move the decision-making process to a launch decision.

MANAGING IN PRACTICE

Challenger *Flashback*

The *Challenger* tragedy was as much a failure of decision making as of technology. The normal procedures of NASA were circumvented. The objections of experts were either overruled or kept from key decision makers. The pressures on NASA were intense and varied. They included the desire to secure congressional funding by providing evidence of cost-effectiveness and productivity, the intense public interest in the heavily advertised "Teacher in Space" program, and the wish to demonstrate the capabilities of NASA technology. All of these factors created a powerful "pressure cooker" environment in which NASA decision makers adhered to a set of ideas and ignored negative information.

In the *Challenger* case, lift-off clearly was seen as more desirable than delay. With a "go" decision, the flight schedule could be kept, the public would not be disappointed, and the shuttle program would achieve another major goal. Any interpretation of possible system failure would have suggested the need to spend more money, a conclusion NASA found distasteful in light of its commitment to cost-effectiveness.

Because indecision and ambiguity often are stressful, any action may seem better than delay. This need for action often increases as a deadline draws near—exactly the condition that NASA officials faced with the *Challenger*. When the perceived costs of a bad decision or judgment seem high, a decision maker usually searches for alternatives and normally is sensitive to information about the flaws and pitfalls of a decision. With the *Challenger* mission, the fear seemed to be lost in a general atmosphere of enthusiasm. Top officials didn't want to be pressed to recognize the possibility of an accident being much more likely than normal because of cold weather.

MANAGING IN PRACTICE —*Continued*

The main motivations of people involved in the *Challenger* decision varied, depending on who they were. Top NASA managers were under great pressure to make a decision; their desire for action encouraged a decision to launch. Their concern for productivity and cost-effectiveness also made that decision more likely. By contrast, engineers at Morton Thiokol, the manufacturer of the solid-fuel rocket boosters, had less decision pressure, little concern about the decision's political and economic implications, and the greatest fear of disaster. They were the ones who objected to the launch. Top management at Thiokol had a different set of motivations. Highly dependent on NASA for a contract bringing in an estimated $400 million a year, Morton Thiokol's top managers could identify with NASA's concerns. Robert Lund, vice-president for engineering at Thiokol, testified how he initially opposed the launch. But he changed his position "after being told to take off his engineering hat and put on one representing management."[64]

▼ Courses of Action

The development and evaluation of courses of action (alternatives) and the implementation of the selected alternative can range from a *quick-action process* to a *convoluted-action process*. A quick-action process is appropriate when (1) the nature of the problem is well structured (two subordinates fail to show up for work, creating a problem in meeting a deadline for the next day); (2) a single manager (or at most, two managers) is clearly recognized as having the authority and responsibility to resolve the problem (the manager authorizes overtime for some of the other employees to meet the deadline); and (3) the search for information about the problem and alternatives is quite limited (the manager might call the customer to determine whether to schedule overtime, bring in help from a temporary employment service, or check with other managers to find out whether their departments are less busy and could loan some workers). This quick-action process may well take place within a matter of minutes or take as long as several days.

At the other extreme, the convoluted-action process is drawn-out and maze-like. The *Challenger* situation prior to launch should have triggered a convoluted-action process within NASA and Morton Thiokol because it met the following criteria.

▲ *The problem is unstructured.* NASA had never faced a launch situation at low temperatures. Research clearly indicated that the O-rings' effectiveness in directing the flow of gases was substantially reduced at low temperatures. Even at higher temperatures, there was evidence of problems with the O-rings.

▲ *A long period of time is required.* NASA and Morton Thiokol officials recognized how a redesign of the O-rings could delay the planned shuttle schedule by as much as two years. This worked against adopting the needed convoluted-action process.

▲ *Many vested interests and power relationships are involved.* We identified some of the vested interests and power relationships prior to launch in the *Challenger* Flashback account. After the disaster, even more vested interests and power relationships came into play: Congress, the Office of the President, the astronauts, the federal courts (in assigning liability), and the Justice Department, among others.

▲ *Many people are involved in an extensive search for solutions.* Prior to the *Challenger* disaster, only a few engineers at Morton Thiokol were deeply involved in an extensive search to solve the O-ring problem. After the disaster, many groups and individuals were involved in the search for solutions to that problem and the broader problem of the flawed decision-making process at NASA and Morton Thiokol.

In either the convoluted-action or quick-action processes, trade-offs, negotiations, conflict, and political processes usually are involved. The process leading up to the launch decision clearly suggests that they were present in the *Challenger* disaster. The worst trade-off was favoring the planned launch schedule over safety. Managers continuously face a variety of problems, many of which can be addressed by the quick-action process; far fewer require initiating the convoluted-action process. However, quick action may lead to poor decisions, when a deliberate approach would have been more appropriate.[65]

▼ Aftermath

During the **aftermath** of a decision, the results of the actions taken are evaluated. With structured problems, evaluation is usually rather simple. The costs and benefits associated with alternative actions can be easily calculated. Recall the example of the manager who scheduled overtime to meet a deadline when two workers failed to show up. If the overtime hours resulted in meeting the deadline, there is clear feedback that the decision led to the intended result.

The selection of a course of action and its implementation to deal with an unstructured problem may involve many individuals, teams, and subjective judgments, as in the *Challenger* situation. The assessment of the course of action taken may require months or even years before the outcomes are known and their consequences can be determined.[66] At least 18 months were required from the selection of the revised O-ring design to its use in a space shuttle launch. The long-term reliability of the redesign can only be determined under actual and repeated launch conditions. Unstructured problems usually require implementing a course of action in the face of risk and uncertainty.

Even the best managers and employees make mistakes. The challenge is to learn from these mistakes. Most employees and managers guard their reputations as capable people and may go to extremes not to acknowledge their mistakes. Moreover, individuals and teams tend to overestimate the effectiveness of their judgment decisions.[67] In the aftermath of the *Challenger* disaster, most of the officials involved at NASA and Morton Thiokol denied making mistakes. They engaged in self-delusions that the disaster was primarily a result of a naturally high-risk program.

Sometimes the negative aftermath of a decision will result in an escalating commitment. **Escalating commitment** is a process of continuing or increasing the commitment of resources to a course of action, even though a substantial amount of feedback indicates that the action is wrong.[68] Consider the following reflections on the Vietnam War and the anticipation of the escalating commitment process.

At an early state of the U.S. involvement in the Vietnam War, George Ball, then Undersecretary of State, wrote the following statement in a memo to Lyndon Johnson: "The decision you face now is crucial. Once large numbers of U.S. troops are committed to direct combat, they will begin to take heavy casualties in a war they are ill-equipped to fight in a noncooperative if not downright hostile country-side. Once we suffer large casualties, we will have started a well-nigh irreversible process. Our involvement will be so great that we cannot—without national humiliation—stop short of achieving our complete objectives. Of the two possibilities I think humiliation would be more likely than the achievement of our objectives—even after we have paid terrible costs." (Memo dated July 1, 1965, from Pentagon Papers, 1971).[69]

One of the explanations for escalating commitment is that individuals feel responsible for negative consequences, which motivates them to justify previous decisions. In addition, individuals may become committed to a course of action simply because they believe that consistency in action is a desirable form of behavior.[70] Our presentation in Chapter 3 on perception and attributions gives additional insights into the possible reasons for escalating commitment.

The following comments by two managers are instructive of the need to learn from the aftermath of a course of action, including those that turned out to be mistakes.

Everybody knows you make mistakes, so why not admit it. I make it a point to admit the blunders. Once I admit it, I feel better about it. It doesn't bother me. It's really a painful thing to keep trying not to admit some things. You have to carry that around as a burden until you get it off your chest.[71]

When one's decisions turn out all right, one should resist the temptation to spend very much time basking in the glory of those right decisions. They need to be reexamined on a continuous basis to be sure that the decision that was right yesterday continues to be right today.[72]

The following Managing Across Cultures piece reviews a variety of processes that Royal Dutch/Shell utilizes to evaluate risks, choose courses of action, assess the aftermath of decisions, and minimize errors such as escalating commitment.

MANAGING ACROSS CULTURES

Royal Dutch/Shell's Decision Making

With a century of experience, Royal Dutch/Shell (or "Shell") has developed a range of strategies for dealing with aspects of its business that seem unmanageable. The culture at Shell encourages individual initiative. Some 160 principal operating units have significant autonomy. They can make almost all of their own operating decisions, backed by other Shell companies that offer research and technical support. Such decentralization and autonomy help managers blend in with their local communities and to respond swiftly to new regulations, changing customer needs, and any crisis.

The committee of managing directors reviews the company's wide-ranging operations throughout the world. They do all the "big thinking" on a consensus basis. Key planning and personnel decisions must be unanimous, which puts real constraints on the chairman. The setup works. Shell avoided the

MANAGING ACROSS CULTURES —*Continued*

worst business fads of the 1980s. It didn't embark on a binge of buying other major oil companies, as did so many competitors, nor did it load up on debt. It also avoided costly detours into unfamiliar businesses, such as Mobil's acquisition of Montgomery Ward. The committee keeps the focus long term. Of all the risks an oil company faces, global instability—wars and revolution—may be the toughest to deal with. Shell uses three lines of defense: geographical diversification, sensible product diversification, and speed in adapting to change.

Shell is perhaps the most global of all energy companies. It explores for oil and gas in some 50 countries, refines in 34, and markets in more than 100. Political or economic turmoil in one place won't have much effect on the rest of the company. In countries where the political climate is especially delicate, Shell makes sure it gets high returns, usually by achieving a monopoly or near monopoly in the local market. If it can't earn good margins in risky countries, Shell pulls out.

The company limits product diversification to tightly linked and synergistic energy and chemical businesses, rarely straying far from what it knows best. This mix helps smooth out quarterly bumps. It strikes a good balance among upstream (exploration and production), downstream (refining and marketing), and related chemical (industrial, agricultural, and petrochemicals) activities and products. Speed in reacting is not only a defense for Shell but a competitive weapon. When Spain revoked the state oil company's monopoly on service stations, Shell rapidly established a presence and has developed a network of gas stations there. Just before the Iron Curtain parted, Shell invested in Interag, the state-owned company that had long distributed its products in Hungary. Shell has more than 1,000 such deals worldwide, many with local governments.

The development of alternative scenarios helps Shell prepare for the unexpected. Local operating companies simulate supply disruptions on a regular basis. Four times a year the crews of its 114-tanker fleet face surprise simulated accidents. When the real Gulf War erupted, Shell lost several hundred thousand barrels of oil per day from Kuwait and Iraq. But a scenario had been drafted for locating and bringing in alternative sources of crude oil.[73]

▼ STIMULATING CREATIVITY

Organizational creativity is the production of novel and useful ideas by an individual or team of individuals working together. This process may include the assistance of computer-based information technology (including groupware). Innovation builds on novel and useful ideas. Accordingly, **organizational innovation** is the implementation of creative and useful ideas through unplanned or planned organizational change.[74]

Creativity helps employees uncover problems, identify opportunities, and undertake novel courses of action to solve problems. We presented two approaches for stimulating creativity in organizations in Chapter 9, namely, the nominal group technique and electronic brainstorming. Moreover, we have repeatedly addressed issues and discussed processes for reducing barriers to creative and innovate thought and action. Some of these barriers include perceptual blocks, cultural blocks, and emotional blocks. *Perceptual blocks* include such factors as the failure to use all of the senses in observing, failure to investigate the obvious, difficulty in seeing remote relationships, and failure to distinguish between facets of cause-and-effect relationships. *Cultural blocks* include a desire to conform to established norms, overemphasis on competition or conflict avoidance and smoothing, the drive to be practical and narrowly economical above all things, and a belief that indulging in fantasy or other forms of open-ended exploration is a waste of time. Finally, *emotional blocks* include fear of making a mistake, fear and distrust of others, grabbing the first idea that comes along, and the like.[75]

NASA and Morton Thiokol officials did not exercise organizational creativity in confronting the O-ring problem. In fact, a seemingly endless series of memos reveal safety concerns from lower level employees of both NASA and Morton Thiokol. If NASA officials had listened and acted on the early warning signals, in all likelihood they could have prevented the disaster. One of the most striking memos from a Morton Thiokol engineer begins with the word, "Help!" The memo goes on to say that if the shuttle continues to fly with the O-rings as they are designed, NASA is almost guaranteed a disaster. The managers ignored the bad news. Instead of deliberately designing monitoring systems to pick up danger signals, NASA, in effect, designed a management system that would intentionally tune out danger signals and downgrade the seriousness of those that did get through.[76]

▼ Lateral Thinking Method

The **lateral thinking method** is a deliberate process for the generation of new ideas through a change in the individual's or team's typical logical pattern for processing and storing information. In contrast, the **vertical thinking method** is the logical step-by-step process of developing ideas by proceeding on a continuous path from one bit of information to the next. Table 18.4 presents the major differences between lateral thinking and vertical thinking. Edward de Bono, the British physician and psychologist who developed the lateral thinking method, stated that the two processes are complementary, not antagonistic:

> Lateral thinking is useful for generating ideas and approaches and vertical thinking is useful for developing them. Lateral thinking enhances the effectiveness of vertical thinking by offering it more to select from. Vertical thinking multiplies the effectiveness of lateral thinking by making good use of the ideas generated. Most of the time one might be using vertical thinking but when one needs to use lateral thinking, then no amount of excellence in vertical thinking will do instead.[77]

The lateral thinking method includes some special techniques for (1) developing an awareness of current ideas and practices, (2) generating alternative ways for looking at a problem, and (3) assisting in the development of new ideas. Here, we consider four lateral thinking techniques for assisting in the development of new ideas.[78]

Reversal   The reversal technique allows new ideas to be suggested by examining the current problem and turning it completely around, inside out, or upside down. Engineers at Conoco asked, "What's good about toxic waste?"

TABLE 18.4   **Characteristics of Lateral Versus Vertical Thinking**

Lateral Thinking	Vertical Thinking
1. Tries to find new ways for looking at things; is concerned with change and movement.	1. Tries to find absolutes for judging relationships; is concerned with stability.
2. Avoids looking for what is "right" or "wrong." Tries to find what is different.	2. Seeks a "yes" or "no" justification for each step. Tries to find what is "right."
3. Analyzes ideas to determine how they might be used to generate new ideas.	3. Analyzes ideas to determine why they do not work and need to be rejected.
4. Attempts to introduce discontinuity by making "illogical" (free association) jumps from one step to another.	4. Seeks continuity by logically proceeding from one step to another.
5. Welcomes chance intrusions of information to use in generating new ideas; considers the irrelevant.	5. Selectively chooses what to consider for generating ideas; rejects any information not considered to be relevant.
6. Progresses by avoiding the obvious.	6. Progresses using established patterns; considers the obvious.

Source: Based on de Bono, E. *Lateral Thinking: Creativity Step by Step.* New York: Harper & Row, 1970; de Bono, E., *Six Thinking Hats.* Boston: Little, Brown, 1985.

By so doing, they discovered a substance in waste that they now are turning into both a synthetic lubricant and—they hope—a promising new market. Ronald Barbaro, president of Prudential Insurance, considered the idea "You die before you die" and came up with "living benefit" life insurance. It pays people suffering from terminal illnesses death benefits before they die. Prudential has sold more than a million such policies.[79]

Cross-fertilization   The cross-fertilization technique involves asking experts from other fields to view the problem and suggest methods for solving it from their own areas. For the technique to be effective, these outsiders should be from fields entirely removed from the problem. An attempt can then be made to apply these methods to the problem. Hallmark Cards has its own variation of cross-fertilization. It has more than 600 artists, writers, and designers. Management brings in some 30 speakers a year to stimulate novel thinking. Writers and artists also are sent on what seem like vacations to soak up new atmospheres and obtain inspiration. Artist and manager Marita Wesely-Clough, just back from two weeks in Mexico, found "stimulus galore." It led her to suggest such new products as a line of cards whose colors mimic the shades of adobe walls.[80]

Analogies   An analogy is a statement about similarities between objects, persons, or situations. Some examples of analogies are: "This organization operates like a beehive" or "This organization operates like a fine Swiss watch." The method involves translating the problem into an analogy, refining and developing the analogy, and then retranslating to the problem to judge the suitability of the analogy. If an analogy is too similar to the problem, little will be gained. Concrete and specific analogies should be selected over more abstract ones. Analogies should describe a specific, well-known issue or process in the organization. For a mechanistic organization that is ignoring increased environmental change, an analogy might be: "We are like a flock of ostriches with our heads buried in the sand."

Random-Word Stimulation　A word is selected from a dictionary or specially prepared word list, and a link is sought between the word and the problem. One option is to select a word using a table of random numbers to choose a page in a dictionary and then a position on a page. For most problems, however, less-than-random procedure probably is adequate. One important point in using this method is to try to stay with a word once it is selected. A premature judgment about a word's relevance could result in many useful ideas being overlooked.

We presented only a few of the techniques and ideas for stimulating lateral thinking. Organizations such as Unilever, General Electric, Shell, and 3M Corporation have formally introduced this approach through their training programs. The lateral thinking method is consistent with a view of creative behavior as a complex person–situation interaction that is influenced by the past and current situation.[81]

▼ Devil's Advocate Method

The **devil's advocate method** calls for a person or small task force to develop a systematic critique of a recommended course of action. The devil's advocate attempts to point out weaknesses in the assumptions underlying the proposal, internal inconsistencies in it, and problems that could lead to failure if it were followed. The devil's advocate acts like a good trial lawyer by presenting arguments against the majority position as convincingly as possible.[82] Figure 18.3 illustrates the basic decision-making process when this method is utilized.

People assigned to the devil's advocate role should be rotated to avoid any one person or task force being identified as a critic on all issues. The devil's advocate role may be advantageous for a person and the organization. Steve Huse, chairperson and CEO of Huse Food Group, indicates that the devil's

FIGURE 18.3

Decision Making with a Devil's Advocate

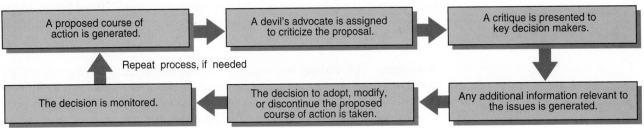

Source: Adapted from Cosier, R. A., and Schrivenk, C. R. Agreement and thinking alike: Ingredients for poor decisions. *Academy of Management*, February 1991, 71.

advocate role is an opportunity for employees to demonstrate their presentation and debating skills. How well someone understands and researches issues is apparent when that person presents a critique. The organization avoids costly mistakes by hearing viewpoints that identify potential pitfalls. In addition, the use of the devil's advocate approach may increase the probability of creative solutions to problems and reduce the probability of groupthink.[83] Recall that groupthink in decision making is caused by excessive consensus and similarity of views in groups—a sure killer of organizational creativity (see Chapter 9). The devil's advocacy method is effective in helping to bring to the surface and challenge assumptions in a proposed course of action—an essential element in stimulating creativity. Of course, the devil's advocate method should not be overused.[84] It is intended for especially important and complex issues.

Summary

Employees sometimes experience ethical dilemmas when making decisions. Five basic questions should be asked to check ethical decision making: What is the ethical intensity? What are the principles and rules? Who is affected? What are the benefits and costs? Who has rights?

Three approaches commonly used to describe decision making are the rational, bounded rationality, and political models. Each captures some of the decision-making situations and processes experienced by managers and employees. All three models are needed to cover the complexity and range of such situations and processes.

Managerial decision making is characterized as unending flows and cross-currents of decisions. The phases of managerial decision making include problem recognition, problem interpretation, attention to problems, courses of action, and aftermath. These phases do not unfold for real-world managers in a neat and orderly sequence.

Creativity is likely to be very important in addressing the most difficult type of situation. It is when there is ambiguity or disagreement over the goals to be sought and the best course of action to pursue. Organizational creativity and innovation are crucial to the production and implementation of novel and useful ideas. Two approaches for stimulating organizational creativity were noted: the lateral thinking method and the devil's advocate method.

Key Words and Concepts

Aftermath	Ethics	Risk propensity
Availability bias	Lateral thinking method	Satisficing
Bounded rationality model	Law of small numbers bias	Selective perception bias
Confirmation bias	Managerial decision making	Structured problems
Devil's advocate method	Organizational creativity	Unstructured problems
Dictionary rule	Organizational innovation	Utilitarianism
Distributive justice principle	Political model	Values
Employment at will	Problem framing	Vertical thinking method
Escalating commitment	Problem interpretation	
Ethical intensity	Rational model	

Discussion Questions

1. Think of an issue that created an ethical dilemma for you. How would you evaluate this dilemma in terms of each of the six components of ethical intensity?

2. Of the six ethical intensity components, which two are likely to be most important in the majority of situations? Explain.

3. What are the similarities and differences between the distributive justice principle and utilitarianism?

4. Rearrange the ethical principles in Table 18.2 in rank order from your most-preferred to least-preferred principle. What does this ranking tell you about how you are likely to interpret situations involving ethical dilemmas?

5. What are the three potential ethical dilemmas that managers may experience when conducting performance appraisals?

6. At which managerial level—first-line, middle, and top—is a manager most likely to use each of the decision-making models (rational model, bounded rationality model, and political model)?

7. How is the decision-making process for professionals likely to differ from that of nonprofessional employees?

8. What are the most common problems in achieving effective problem recognition?

9. How might creativity help employees who experience difficulties in problem identification and interpretation?

10. What are two differences between the lateral thinking method and the devil's advocate method?

▲ Developing Skills

Self-Diagnosis:
Individual Ethics Profile

The Individual Ethics Profile (IEP) is designed to help individuals identify the ethical preferences that guide their actions. The results can be useful for individuals who want to understand better the determinants of their own actions and gain new and broader ethics perspectives.

Instructions

Twelve pairs of statements or phrases follow. Read each pair and check the one that you most agree with. You may, of course, agree with neither statement. In that case, you should check the statement that you least disagree with.

You must select one statement in each pair; your IEP cannot be scored unless you do so.

_____ 1. The greatest good for the greatest number.

_____ 2. The individual's right to private property.

_____ 3. Adhering to rules designed to maximize benefits to all.

_____ 4. Individuals' rights to complete liberty in action, as long as others' rights are similarly respected.

_____ 5. The right of an individual to speak freely without fear of being fired.

_____ 6. Engaging in technically illegal behavior in order to attain substantial benefits for all.

_____ 7. Individuals' rights to personal privacy.

_____ 8. The obligation to gather personal information to ensure that individuals are treated equitably.

_____ 9. Helping those in danger when doing so would not unduly endanger oneself.

_____10. The right of employees to know about any dangers in the job setting.

_____11. Minimizing inequities among employees in the job setting.

_____12. Maintaining significant inequities among employees when the ultimate result is to benefit all.

_____13. Organizations must not require employees to take actions that would restrict the freedom of others or cause others harm.

_____14. Organizations must tell employees the full truth about work hazards.

_____15. What is good is what helps the organization attain ends that benefit everyone.

_____16. What is good is equitable treatment for all employees of the organization.

_____17. Organizations must stay out of employees' private lives.

_____18. Employees should act to achieve organizational goals that result in benefits to all.

_____19. Questionable means are acceptable if they achieve good ends.

_____20. Individuals must follow their consciences, even if it hurts the organization.

_____21. Safety of individual employees above all else.

_____22. Obligation to aid those in great need.

_____23. Employees should follow rules that preserve individuals' freedom of action while reducing inequities.

_____24. Employees must do their best to follow rules designed to enhance organizational goal attainment.

Instructions

Circle the numbers of the statements that you checked, indicating a preference for those statements over with their paired alternatives. When you have circled the numbers of all your choices, add the *number of circles* in each of the three columns. The total for any column can range from 0 to 8.

1	2	4
3	5	8
6	7	9
12	10	11
15	14	13
18	17	16
19	20	22
24	21	23

Total number circled   __   __   __

Divide the totals for each of the columns by 8. Enter the results on the following chart.

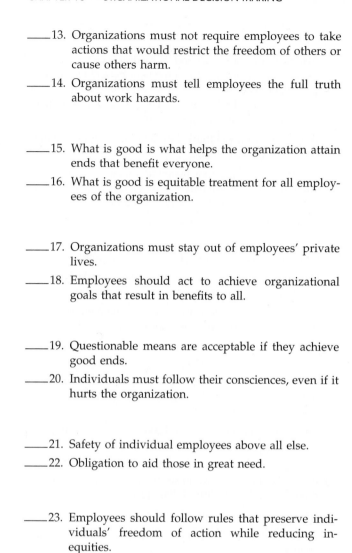

Utilitarian   Moral rights   Justice

Interpretation

The IEP measures a person's preferences among three major sets of ethical concepts. The first set is called *utilitarian* because it is based on the premise that actions must be judged good or bad in terms of their effects, especially the effect of producing the greatest good for the greatest number. Although this value set is consistent with the common organizational aims of efficiency and effectiveness, it may be limited in that affected parties who are not heard from can easily be ignored. The utilitarian concept is consistent with what many believe to be a dangerous premise, that is, that the ends can justify the means.

The second ethical concept is called *moral rights*. It is based on the idea that individuals' personal rights must not be violated. Such rights include the right to life and safety, the right to know information that directly affects them and their choice of actions, the right to privacy, the right to act in line with their beliefs or conscience without fear of reprisal, the right to speak freely (including the right to speak about illegal or unethical actions by their employer, without fear of reprisal), and the right to private property. Clearly in some cases the moral rights concept may conflict with the utilitarian concept.

The third ethical concept is called *justice*. It is based on the belief that benefits and burdens should be allocated fairly, that is, based on equity and impartiality. In other words, each person has a right to the greatest possible freedom consistent with similar freedom for all others. Further, justice demands that social and economic inequities be dealt with so that those who are the most disadvantaged receive the greatest benefits. The concept of affirmative action is one illustration of this value in action. At the same time, the justice concept set calls for all persons to be treated equitably and not arbitrarily. Thus one employee should not be paid more than another who has the same skills and is doing the same job because of gender or race.[85]

A Case in Point:
Olson Medical Systems

Olson Medical Systems (OMS) offers computer-based financial systems to hospitals and nursing homes throughout the United States. Founded ten years ago by T. G. Olson, a former health care administrator, OMS employs over 40 analysts and programmers.

Once a month, the executive team of OMS meets to discuss plans, problems, and opportunities of the company. T. G. Olson calls and chairs the meetings. The other members include Frank Telsor (marketing), Karen Smith (operations), Terry Heath (systems development), Damien O'Brien (finance/accounting), and Ali Hassan (systems analyst). At a recent meeting, "maintenance contract" appeared on the agenda, producing the following discussion.

Olson: Okay. Our last item is "maintenance contracts." O'Brien, this was your item.

O'Brien: Yes. I've been looking into the software maintenance contracts we have with some of our clients and I don't think we are getting a good return on investment. Based on my calculations, we would be better off selling enhanced versions of our Medicalc package every two years than offering maintenance contracts . . . unless, of course, we increase the price of the maintenance agreement.

Olson: How much would we have to increase the price?

O'Brien: Right now, we are breaking even.

Olson: So, what are you proposing?

O'Brien: I think we should increase the annual fee for Medicalc by at least two hundred dollars.

Telsor: If we do that, we're going to lose some business . . . maybe not the people who are with us already but some potential clients.

Olson: How many Medicalc users have maintenance contracts with us?

Telsor: I don't know.

O'Brien: I think it's about eighty percent.

Olson: What is the standard price, on a percentage basis, for maintenance packages?

Telsor: It varies slightly with the price of the software, but it is related to the frequency of changes.

Heath: Maybe we shouldn't be making so many changes. Last year, we made those changes to Schedule B and then Health and Social Services changed their minds. We could have been spending our time converting to the new IBM system.

Smith: It didn't help that we lost Stan Freedson. He knew Medicalc inside and out.

Olson: Yeah. Stan was good. Why don't we try to market the Medicalc maintenance agreement better? Does Health Data Systems or TMS make the kinds of changes we do and as frequently as we do? Let's let our clients know that our system is the most up-to-date in the market.

Telsor: Sometimes I think they'd rather buy the enhanced version every two years.

O'Brien: There are two hospitals in the Southwest that purchased the maintenance agreement, went off it for a year, and then renewed. Why, I wonder?

Telsor: One of them had a change of financial directors.

Olson: Ali, we haven't heard from you yet. Any thoughts on how to keep the cost of maintenance down?

Hassam: Not really. This sounds like a marketing problem to me . . . how to sell the service contracts.

Smith: I think we need more data. Maybe we should table this item until we know more about our clients' need and so forth.

O'Brien: What, specifically, do we need to know?

Olson: We need to know the projected changes in the schedules for the next couple of years and what it will cost to keep current.

Smith: Excuse me, I have to leave. I have a meeting with Joe Bergmann at eleven.

O'Brien: Why don't we just raise the price seventy-five dollars for new clients and see what happens? TMS raised theirs one hundred fifty dollars last year.

Olson: What do you think, Telsor?

Telsor: Well, we can try it. We may lose some potential clients.

Olson: Okay, let's try it.[86]

Questions

1. What problem statements were offered (explicitly or implicitly) during this meeting?
2. How are these statements related to each other (i.e., which statements are the means of solving others)?
3. What different purposes do problem statements serve (e.g., to keep people involved in the process, to avoid blame, etc.)? For what purposes were the statements offered in this case, in your opinion?
4. What other problem perspectives can you think of that might be useful to this team?
5. Which model of decision making (i.e., rational, bounded rationality, or political) best describes the decision-making process in this case? Explain and justify your answer.

References

1. Adapted from Schoemaker, P. J. H., and Russo, J. E. A pyramid of decision approaches. *California Management Review*, Fall 1993, 9–31.
2. Ibid.
3. Allan, L. G. Human contingency judgments: Rule based or associative. *Psychological Bulletin*, 1993, 114, 435–448.
4. Kleindorfer, P., Kunreuther, H., and Schoemaker, P. *Decision Sciences: An Integrative Perspective*. New York: Cambridge University Press, 1993.
5. Freeman, E. E. (ed.), *Business Ethics: The State of the Art*. New York: Oxford University Press, 1991.
6. Donaldson, T., and Dunfee, T. W. Toward a unified conception of business ethics: Integrative social contracts theory. *Academy of Management Review*, 1994, 19, 252–284.
7. De George, R. T. *Competing with Integrity in International Business*. New York: Oxford University Press, 1993.
8. Ethics Resource Center and Behavior Research Center. *Ethics Policies and Programs in American Business: Report of a Landmark Survey of U.S. Corporations*. Washington, D.C.: Ethics Resource Center, 1990.
9. Trevino, L. K., and Youngblood, S. A. Bad apples in bad barrels: A causal analysis of ethical decision-making behavior. *Journal of Applied Psychology*, 1990, 75, 378–385.
10. Freeman, R. E., and Gilbert D. R., Jr. *Corporate Strategy and the Search for Ethics*. Englewood Cliffs, N.J.: Prentice-Hall, 1988.
11. This section is based primarily on James, T. M. Ethical decision making by individuals in organizations: An issue-contingent model. *Academy of Management Review*, 1991, 16, 366–395. Also see Darley, J. M., and Shultz, T. R. Moral rules: Their content and acquisition. In M. R. Rosenzweig and L. W. Porter (eds.), *Annual Review of Psychology*, vol. 41. Palo Alto, Calif.: Annual Reviews, 1990, 525–556.
12. Adapted from DeLisser, E., and Holden, B. A. Denny's begins repairing its image—and its attitude. *Wall Street Journal*, March 11, 1994, B1, B6; Serwer, A. E. What to do when race charges fly. *Fortune*, July 12, 1993, 95–96; Hawkins, C. Denny's: The stain that isn't coming out. *Business Week*, June 28, 1993, 98–99.
13. Stark, A. What's the matter with business ethics? *Harvard Business Review*, May–June 1993, 38–48; Brady, F. N. *Ethical Managing: Rules and Results*. New York: Macmillan, 1990.
14. Paine, L. S. Managing for organizational integrity, *Harvard Business Review*, March–April 1994, 106–117.
15. Gilliand, S. W. The perceived fairness of selection systems: An organizational justice perspective. *Academy of Management Review*, 1993, 18, 694–734.
16. Harrington, S. J. What corporate America is teaching about ethics. *Academy of Management Executive*, February 1991, 21–30; Weiss, A. Seven reasons to examine workplace ethics. *HR Magazine*, March 1991, 69–74.
17. Adapted from Murphy, P. E. Improving your ethics code. *Business Ethics*, March–April 1994, 23.
18. Sheppard, B. H., Lewicki, R. J., and Minton, J. W. *Organizational Justice: The Search for Fairness in the Workplace*. New York: Lexington Books, 1992.
19. Hilgert, R. L. Employers protected by at-will statements. *HR Magazine*, March 1991, 57–60; Krueger, A. B. The evolution of unjust-dismissal legislation in the United States. *Industrial and Labor Relations Review*, 1991, 44, 644–660.
20. Trevino, L. K. The social effects of punishment in organizations:

21. A justice perspective. *Academy of Management Review*, 1992, 17, 647–676.
21. Wartzman, R. Nature or nurture? Study blames ethical lapses on corporate goals. *Wall Street Journal*, October 9, 1987, 21.
22. Hartley, R. E. *Business Ethics: Violations of the Public Trust*. New York: John Wiley & Sons, 1993.
23. Mitchell, T. R., and Scott, W. G. America's problems and needed reforms: Confronting the ethics of personal advantage. *Academy of Management Executive*, August 1990, 23–35.
24. Eide, A., and Hagtvet, B. *Human Rights in Perspective: A Global Assessment*. Cambridge, Mass.: Blackwell, 1992.
25. Osigweh, Y. C. Elements of an employee responsibilities and rights paradigm. *Journal of Management*, 1990, 16, 835–850.
26. Crossen, B. R. Managing employee unethical behavior without invading individual privacy. *Journal of Business Psychology*, 1993, 8, 227–243.
27. Bergmann, T. J., Mundt, D. H. Jr., and Illgen, E. J. The evolution of honesty tests and means for their evaluation. *Employee Responsibilities and Rights Journal*, 1990, 215–223.
28. Murphy, K. R. *Honesty in the Workplace*. Pacific Grove, Calif.: Brooks/Cole, 1993.
29. Weiss, J. W. *Business Ethics: A Managerial, Stockholder Approach*. Belmont, Calif.: Wadsworth, 1994.
30. Dean, J. W., Jr. *Decision Processes in the Adoption of Advanced Technology*. University Park, Pa.: Center for the Management of Technological and Organizational Change, Pennsylvania State University, May 1986.
31. Hogart, R. M., and Reder, M. W. (eds.), *Rational Choice: The Contrasts Between Economics and Psychology*. Chicago: University of Chicago Press, 1986.
32. Garvin, D. A. Building a learning organization. *Harvard Business Review*, July–August 1993, 78–91.
33. Juran, J. M. Made in the U.S.A.: A renaissance in quality. *Harvard Business Review*, July–August 1993, 42–50.
34. Adapted from Berry, L. L., Parasuraman, A., and Zeithaml, V. A. Improving service quality in America: Lessons learned. *Academy of Management Executive*, May 1994, 32–45.
35. March, J., and Simon, H. *Organizations*, 2nd ed. Cambridge, Mass.: Blackwell, 1993; Martin, J. E., Kleindorfer, G. B., and Brashers, W.R., Jr. The theory of bounded rationality and the problem of legitimation. *Journal for the Theory of Social Behavior*, 1987, 17, 63–82.
36. Silver, W. S., and Mitchell, T. R. The status quo tendency in decision making. *Organizational Dynamics*, Spring 1990, 34–46.
37. Roach, J. M. Simon says: Decision making is a "satisficing" experience. *Management Review*, January 1979, 8–9. Also see Simon, H. A. Bounded rationality and organizational learning. *Organization Science*, 1991, 2, 125–134.
38. Mumby, D. K., and Putman, L. L. The politics of emotion: A feminist reading of bounded rationality. *Academy of Management Review*, 1992, 17, 465–486.
39. Pfeffer, J. *Managing with Power: Politics and Influence in Organizations*. Boston: Harvard Business School, 1994.
40. The perspective of this discussion was developed from McCall, M. W., Jr., and Kaplan, R. E. *Whatever It Takes: The Realities of Managerial Decision Making*. 2nd ed. Englewood Cliffs, N.J.: Prentice-Hall, 1990.
41. McCall, M. W., Jr., and Kaplan, R. E. *Whatever It Takes: Decision Makers at Work*. Englewood Cliffs, N.J.: Prentice-Hall, 1985, xv.

42. Sayles, L. R. *The Working Leader*. New York: Free Press, 1993.

43. Thomas, J. B., Clark, S. M., and Goia, D. A Strategic sense making and organizational performance: Linkages among scanning, interpretation, action, and outcomes. *Academy of Management Journal*, 1993, 36, 239–270.

44. Dutton, J. E., and Ashford, S. J. Selling issues to top management. *Academy of Management Review*, 1993, 18, 397–428.

45. Cowan, D. A. Developing a process model of problem recognition. *Academy of Management Review*, 1986, 11, 763–776; Cowan, D. A. Developing a classification structure of organizational problems: An empirical investigation. *Academy of Management Journal*, 1990, 33, 366–390.

46. Kiechel, W., III. Facing up to denial. *Fortune*, October 18, 1993, 163.

47. Taylor, R. N. Strategic decision making. In M. D. Dunnette and L. H. Hough (eds.), *Handbook of Industrial and Organizational Psychology*, vol. 3, 2nd ed. Palo Alto, Calif.: Consulting Psychologists Press, 1992, 961–1007.

48. Adapted from Raelin, J.A . The professional as the executive's ethical aide-de-camp. *Academy of Management Executive*, August 1987, 1, 177–182; Maier, M. *Challenger*: The path to disaster (A), (B), and (C). *Case Research Journal*, Winter, 1994, 1–49; Vaughan, D. Autonomy, interdependence, and social control: NASA and the space shuttle *Challenger*. *Administrative Science Quarterly*, 1990, 35, 225–257.

49. Adapted from Volkema, R. J. Factors which promote "solving the wrong problem." Unpublished statement. Fairfax, Va.: Institute for Advanced Study in the Integrative Sciences, George Mason University, 1988.

50. Janis, I. L., and Mann, L. *Decision Making: A Psychological Analysis of Conflict, Choice, and Commitment*. New York: Free Press, 1977, 81–106; Gilber, D. T. How mental systems believe. *American Psychologist*, 1991, 46, 107–119.

51. Hrebiniak, L. G. *The We-Force in Management: How to Build and Sustain Cooperation*. New York: Lexington Books, 1994.

52. Gephart, R.P., Jr. The textual approach: Risk and blame in disaster sensemaking. *Academy of Management Journal*, 1993, 36, 1465–1514; Isabella, L. A. Evolving interpretations as a change unfolds: How managers construe key organizational events. *Academy of Management Journal*, 1990, 33, 7–41,

53. Sitkin, S. B., and Pablo, A. L. Reconceptualizing the determinants of risk behavior. *Academy of Management Review*, 1992, 17, 9–38.

54. Larrick, R. Motivational factors in decision theories: The role of self-protection. *Psychological Bulletin*, 1993, 113, 440–450.

55. Sitkin, S. B., and Pablo, A. L. Reconceptualizing the determinants of risk behavior. *Academy of Management Review*, 1992, 17, 9–38.

56. March, J. G., and Shapira, Z. Managerial perspectives on risk and risk taking. *Management Science*, 1987, 33, 1404–1418.

57. Kahneman, D., and Tversky, A. Prospect theory: An analysis of decision under risk. *Econometricka*, 1987, 47, 263–291.

58. Russo, J. E., and Schoemaker, P. J. H. Managing overconfidence. *Sloan Management Review*, Winter 1992, 7–17.

59. Klayman, J., and Ha, Y. W. Confirmation, disconfirmation, and information in hypothesis testing. *Psychological Review*, 1987, 94, 211–228.

60. Kahneman, D. Judgment and decision making: A personal view. *Psychological Science*, 1991, 2, 142–145; Smith, J. F., and Kida, T. Heuristics and biases: Expertise and task realism in auditing. *Psychological Bulletin*, 1991, 109, 472–489.

61. Starbuck, W. H., and Milliken, F. J. Executives' perceptual filters: What they notice and how they make sense. In D. C. Hambrick (ed.), *The Executive Effect: Concepts and Methods for Studying Top Managers*. Greenwich, Conn.: JAI Press, 1988, 35–66.

62. Kim, D. H. The link between individual and organizational learning. *Sloan Management Review*, Fall, 1993, 37–50; McGill, M., and Slocum, J.W., Jr. *The Smart Organization*, John Wiley & Sons, 1994.

63. Janis, I. L. *Crucial Decisions: Leadership in Policy Making and Crisis Management*. New York: Free Press, 1989.

64. Adapted from Kruglanski, A. W. Freeze-think and the *Challenger*. *Psychology Today*, August 1986, 48–49; Pearson, C. M., and Mitroff, I. I. From crisis prone to crisis prepared: A framework for crisis management. *Academy of Management Executive*, February 1993, 48–59; Boisjoly, R. M. Personal integrity and accountability: Case of *Challenger* launch decision. *Accounting Horizons*, March 1993, 59–69.

65. Beach, L. R. *Image Theory: Decision Making in Personal and Organizational Contexts*. Chichester, England: John Wiley & Sons, 1990; Bazerman, M. H. *Judgment in Managerial Decision Making*. New York: John Wiley & Sons, 1990.

66. Quinn, R. E. *Beyond Rational Management: Mastering the Paradoxes and Competing Demands of High Performance*, San Francisco: Jossey-Bass, 1988.

67. Neale, M. A., and Bazerman, M. H. *Cognition and Rationality in Negotiation*. New York: Free Press, 1991; Jagacinski, C. M. Personnel decision making: The impact of missing information. *Journal of Applied Psychology*, 1991, 76, 19–30.

68. Brockner, J. The escalation of commitment to a failing course of action: Toward theoretical progress. *Academy of Management Review*, 1992, 17. 39–61.

69. Staw, B. M. The escalation of commitment: A review and analysis. *Academy of Management Review*, 1981, 6, 577–587.

70. Bowen, M. G. The escalation phenomenon reconsidered: Decision dilemmas or decision errors? *Academy of Management Review*, 1987, 12, 52–66.

71. McCall, M. W., and Kaplan, R. E. *Consequences, Issues and Observations*. Greensboro, N.C.: Center for Creative Leadership, February 1985, 7.

72. Ibid., 8. Also see McCall, M. W., Jr., Lombardo, M. M., and Morrison, A. M. *The Lesson of Experience*, Lexington, Mass.: Lexington Books, 1988.

73. Adapted from Knowlton, C. Shell gets rich by beating risk. *Fortune*, August 26, 1991, 79–82; Norman, J. R. The opportunities are enormous. *Forbes*, November 9, 1992, 92–94; Schoemaker, P. J. H., and Van der Heijden, C. A. Integrating scenarios into strategic planning at Royal Dutch/Shell. *Planning Review*, May–June 1992, 41–46.

74. Woodman, R. W., Sawyer, J. E., and Griffin, R. W. Toward a theory of organizational creativity. *Academy of Management Review*, 1993, 18, 293–321.

75. Martin, L. P. Inventory of barriers to creative thought and innovative action. In J. W. Pfeffer (ed.), *The 1990 Annual: Developing Human Resources*. San Diego: University Associates, 1990, 131–141; Anderson, J. V. Wierder than fiction: The reality and myths of creativity. *Academy of Management Executive*, November 1992, 40–47.

76. Maier, M. *Challenger*: The path to the disaster (A), (B), and (C). *Case Research Journal*, Winter 1994, 1–49.

77. de Bono, E. *Lateral Thinking: Creativity Step by Step*. New York: Harper & Row, 1970, 50.

78. This discussion is based on Van Gundy, A. B. *Techniques of Structured Problem Solving*. New York: Van Nostrand, 1981, 234–244; de Bono, E. *Masterthinkers Handbook*. New York: International Center for Creative Thinking, 1985.

79. Farnham, A. How to nurture creative sparks. *Fortune*, January 10, 1994, 94–100.

80. Ibid.

81. Woodman, R. W., and Schoenfeldt, L. F. Individual differences in creativity: An interactionist perspective. In J. A. Glover, R. R. Ronning, and C. R. Reynolds (eds.), *Handbook of Creativity*. New York: Plenum Press, 1989, 77–91.

82. Schwenk, C. R. Devil's advocacy and the board: A modest proposal. *Business Horizons*, July–August 1990, 22–27.

83. Cosier, R. A., and Schwenk, C. R. Agreement and thinking alike: Ingredients for poor decisions. *Academy of Management Executive*, February 1990, 69–74.

84. Gundry, L. K., Prather, C. W., and Kickul, J. R. Building the creative organization. *Organizational Dynamics*, Spring 1994, 22–37.

85. Adapted from Sashkin, M., and Morris, W. C. *Experiencing Management*. Reading, Mass.: Addison-Wesley, 1987, 60–62.

86. Volkema, R. J. Problem Formulation at Olson Medical Systems. Used with permission. This case was developed under a grant from the National Institute for Dispute Resolution, 1988.

Part IV Change Processes

Chapter
19
Nature of Planned Organizational Change

Chapter
20
Approaches to Planned Organizational Change

Chapter
21
Career Planning and Development

647

19 Nature of Planned Organizational Change

When you have finished studying this chapter, you should be able to:

▲ Identify the goals of planned organizational change.

▲ Discuss the "revolutions" that are creating pressures on organizations to change.

▲ Describe individual and organizational resistance to change.

▲ Diagnose the pressures for and resistance to change in a work setting.

▲ Provide suggestions for overcoming resistance to change.

▲ Explain the importance of an accurate diagnosis of organizational functioning and problems.

▲ Describe some general models or approaches for organizational change.

OUTLINE

Preview Case: Managing in the Midst of Chaos

Goals of Planned Change

Improving Organizational Adaptability

Changing Individual Behaviors

Pressures for Change

Globalization

Managing Across Cultures: Arvin Industries

Information Technology and Computers

Changing Nature of Management

Managing Quality: The Non-manager Managers

Changing Nature of the Work Force

Managing Across Cultures: 12,000 World Managers View Change

Resistance to Change

Individual Resistance to Change

Managing Diversity: Ineffective Training Increases Resistance

Organizational Resistance to Change

Overcoming Resistance to Change

Managing Ethics: Overcoming Resistance to Integrity

Organizational Diagnosis

Managing in Practice: The Chairman's Rice Pudding

Readiness for Change

Principles of Change

Changing Organizations

A Systems Approach to Change

Innovation

Managing In Practice: The Nuts and Bolts of Innovation

Action Research

Organization Development

DEVELOPING SKILLS

Self-Diagnosis: *Rate Your Readiness for Change*

A Case in Point: *Planned Change at the Piedmont Corporation*

PREVIEW CASE

Managing in the Midst of Chaos

Whether it's called reengineering, restructuring, transformation, downsizing, or simply reorganization, it can spell chaos for managers and employees as they attempt to cope with their organization's move into the twenty-first century. The ability to manage in the midst of chaos is the newest skill required of organization leaders. Here are a few examples.

Willow Shire is a corporate vice-president of Digital Equipment Corporation At Digital, changing market forces have severely battered the world's number 3 computer maker. Its once admired corporate culture is considered an obsolete burden. Shire concedes that "morale is very low. When I first came here, I was surrounded by intelligent, aggressive people who were excited about what they were doing. Now people are tired, frustrated, and frightened." Shire argues that women at Digital are coping with the massive changes somewhat better than men. "We were never invested in the old boy club," she says. "So when it's time to tear down the old system, we have nothing to lose."

Duane Hartley is general manager of Hewlett-Packard's microwave instruments division. The company was hit hard by the upheaval in the computer business, but confronted its problems earlier than did IBM or Digital Equipment. Hartley says, "I don't think people really enjoy change, but if they can participate in it and understand it, it can become a positive for them." Reflecting on managers and companies that have fallen by the wayside during this era of changes, Hartley observed, "They didn't listen. They didn't listen to the customers, the market, or their own employees. They just flat got out of touch."

Rebecca McDonald is president of Tenneco's natural gas marketing subsidiary. Tenneco went through a period of heavy losses as the natural gas business moved from a regulated to a market-driven industry. Of Tenneco's troubles McDonald says, "Corporate arrogance was our culture. We assumed that we knew what our customers needed, but we never asked them. The hierarchy suppressed new ideas and made us very risk averse." She sees today's business as a "blank page—a chance to do everything over. How can that not be exciting?"[1]

A major challenge facing organizations is to manage change effectively.[2] In many sectors of the economy, organizations must have the capacity to adapt quickly in order to survive. Often the speed and complexity of change severely test the capabilities of managers and employees to adapt quickly and effectively. When organizations fail to change, the costs of that failure may be quite high. In 1985, 406,000 people worked for IBM worldwide and its profits were $6.6 billion. By 1994, one-third of the people and most of the profits were gone.

To a certain extent, all organizations exist in a changing environment and are themselves constantly changing. For example, the world of business is thought to be changing in the following ways.

▲ The average company will become smaller, employing fewer people.

▲ The traditional hierarchical organization will give way to a variety of organizational forms, such as networks of specialists.

▲ Technicians, ranging from computer repairers to radiation therapists, will replace manufacturing operatives as the worker elite.

▲ The vertical division of labor will be replaced by a horizontal division of labor.

▲ The emphasis of many businesses will shift from making a product to providing a service.

▲ Work itself will be redefined with more emphasis on constant learning and higher-order thinking.[3]

As you read this chapter and Chapter 20, you may well conclude that many of these changes already have taken place, at least in part.

Increasingly, organizations that emphasize bureaucratic or mechanistic systems are ineffective. Organizations with rigid hierarchies, high degrees of functional specialization, narrow and limited job descriptions, inflexible rules and procedures, and impersonal management can't respond adequately to demands for change. Organizations need designs that are flexible and adaptive. They also need systems that both require and allow greater commitment and use of talent on the part of employees and managers.

In this chapter, we examine the goals of planned organizational change, pressure for and resistance to change, the importance of accurate organizational diagnosis, and some models and processes for implementing organizational change. In Chapter 20, we present some specific approaches and techniques for making organizational and behavioral changes.

▼ GOALS OF PLANNED CHANGE

Distinguishing between change that inevitably happens to all organizations and change that is *planned* by members of an organization is important.[4] Our focus is primarily on intentional, goal-oriented organizational change. **Planned organizational change** represents the intentional attempt by managers and employees to improve the functioning of groups, teams, departments, divisions, or an entire organization in some important way.

Because managers and employees cannot control an organization's environment, they must continually introduce internal organizational changes that allow it to cope more effectively with new challenges. These challenges come from within the firm in terms of the demands and expectations of the work force and from sources outside the firm, such as increased competition, advances in technology, new government legislation and regulations, and pressing social demands. Organizations usually change in response to these pressures, and in some cases, organizations change in anticipation of them.

Planned change efforts always involve specific goals. These goals might include spurring productivity, developing new technology, increasing employee motivation, gaining greater customer satisfaction, or building market share. However, specific goals for improvement are based on two underlying objectives: (1) to improve the capacity or ability of the organization to adapt to changes in its environment; and (2) to change patterns of employee behaviors.

▼ Improving Organizational Adaptability

Organizations need effective approaches and techniques to adapt to changing markets, labor supplies, societal expectations, legal requirements, new ideas, and the like. Organizations typically create departments or specialized teams that plan for and implement needed changes. These adaptive departments or groups often have such names as product research, market research, long-range planning, strategic planning, research and development, public affairs, or organization development.

The departments that have traditionally been concerned with issues of organizational change may no longer provide sufficient adaptability. Thus the ability to manage organizational change effectively is no longer the exclusive concern of specialized departments: All parts of the organization must be challenged to become more adaptive. Table 19.1 lists several functions, such as manufacturing and marketing, and contrasts the "old" and "new" emphases. Because the entire organization must be concerned with change, organizational culture (see Chapter 14) plays an important role in the ability of organizations to adapt.

As Table 19.1 suggests, with product life cycles becoming shorter, organizations must shorten production lead times. Managers can increase the organization's capacity to adapt by using temporary or flexible designs and assembling teams to develop ideas, determine strategies, and analyze decisions. Adaptive, temporary structures also enable the organization to react quickly to new information, facilitate transitions to new operations, encourage broadly based and participative decision making, and develop future leaders.

▼ Changing Individual Behaviors

The second major objective of planned organizational change is to alter the behavior of individuals within the organization. An organization may not be able to change its strategy for adapting to its environment unless its members behave differently in their relationships with one another and their jobs. In

TABLE 19.1   **Changes in Basic Business Functions**

Function	Old Emphasis	New Emphasis
Manufacturing	Capital and automation more important than people; volume, low cost, and efficiency more important than quality and responsiveness	Short production runs; fast product changeover; people, quality, and responsiveness most important
Marketing	Mass markets; mass advertising; lengthy market tests	Fragmented markets; market creation; small-scale market testing; speed
Financial control	Centralized; specialized staff reviews proposals, sets policy	Decentralized; financial specialists members of business teams; high spending authority at local level
Management information systems	Centralized information control; information hoarded for sake of "consistency"	Decentralized data processing; personal computer proliferation; multiple databases permitted
Research and development	Centralized; emphasis on big projects; cleverness more important than reliability and serviceability; innovation limited to new products and services	All activities/functions hotbeds for innovation; not limited to new products and services; emphasis on "portfolio" of small projects; speed

Source: Adapted from Peters, T. A world turned upside down. *Academy of Management Executive*, 1987, 1, 231–241; Peters, T. Prometheus barely unbound. *Academy of Management Executive*, 1990, 4(4), 70–84.

the final analysis, organizations survive, grow, prosper, decline, or fail because of employee behaviors—the things that employees do or fail to do.

An example of the importance of changing employee behaviors occurred when the new CEO of an international bank announced a companywide change program. The bank's traditional hierarchical organization seemed ill-suited to respond to serious challenges stemming from deregulation in the United States and increased global competition. The only solution was a fundamental change in how the company operated. The CEO held a retreat with 15 top executives of the bank. They carefully examined the organization's culture and purpose and drew up a new mission statement. Following the retreat, the bank recruited a new vice-president for human resources from another organization well known for its excellent management. In a quick succession of moves, the bank adopted a new organization design, performance appraisal system and compensation plan, and training programs. The CEO implemented quarterly attitude surveys to track the progress of the change program. All these steps would seem to represent a textbook example of successful organizational change. Unfortunately, there was one principal problem. Two years after the CEO started the change program, virtually no changes in organizational behavior had occurred.[5] So, what went wrong?

The CEO and his top-management team correctly identified the need for change. But they incorrectly assumed that they alone knew how best to proceed. They believed that simply adopting a new mission statement, new programs, and a new organization design would achieve the change they desired. However, unless employee behaviors actually change, new programs and structures probably will have little, if any, impact on organizational effectiveness—as the bank's management learned to their chagrin.

Behavior should be a primary target of planned organizational change. Change programs must have an effect on employee roles, responsibilities, and working relationships. At some fundamental level, all organizational changes depend on changes in behavior.

▼ PRESSURES FOR CHANGE

Both advanced industrialized societies and developing countries are changing in important ways that have significant impacts on organizations.[6] The pressures on organizations for change are accelerating, so in a very real sense, organizations are undergoing several **business revolutions**—sudden, radical, and complete reorientations of the way business is done—around the world.[7] These business revolutions include (1) the globalization of markets, (2) the spread of information technology and computer networks, (3) the dismantling of organizational hierarchies, which fundamentally alters management's tasks, and (4) changes in the nature of the work force employed by organizations. These revolutions are the result of dramatic forces, or **pressures for change,** that profoundly affect all organizations and societies.

The current business revolutions may be comparable in scale to the Industrial Revolution of the nineteenth century. George Bennett, chairman of Symmetrix, a consulting firm, asks: "If 2% of the population can grow all the food we eat, what if another 2% can manufacture all the refrigerators and other things we need?"[8] Consider the following examples. The parking lot for General Electric's Louisville, Kentucky, appliance factory was built to hold 25,000 cars in 1953. Today, this parking lot needs to hold only 10,000 cars.

Volkswagen, the large German automaker, says that it really needs only two-thirds of its current workforce. Although sales are rising, Procter & Gamble is dismissing 12% of its employees. Not just manufacturing firms are downsizing. Cigna, the giant Philadelphia-based insurance firm, reduced its work force by 25% between 1990 and 1994.

We examine these business revolutions and explore the pressures for change that are affecting organizations. These are not the only pressures for change, but they certainly are among the more dramatic.

▼ Globalization

Organizations face global competition on an unprecedented scale. Increasingly, the main players in the world's economy are international or multinational corporations. The emergence of these global organizations creates pressures on domestic corporations to redesign and, in turn, internationalize their operations. There is a global market for most products, but in order to compete effectively in it, firms often must transform their cultures, structures, and operations.

The primary forces at work in **globalization** include

▲ the economic recoveries of Germany and Japan after their defeat in World War II;

▲ the emergence of "newly industrialized" countries, such as Korea, Taiwan, Singapore, and Spain;

▲ the dramatic shift from planned economies to market economies occurring in Eastern Europe, Russia and other republics of the former Soviet Union, and, to a lesser extent, China; and

▲ the emergence of new "power blocks" of international traders, such as the economic unification of Europe (which eventually will involve currency, some government operations, and lowered tariff barriers) and the "yen block" (Japan and its Pacific Rim trading partners).[9]

These powerful forces for globalization mean that organizations must recognize that the rest of the world does in fact exist. Although successful globalization strategies aren't easy to implement, many organizations have effectively moved outside their domestic markets. For example, Ford, Merck & Company, IBM, and Hewlett-Packard have strong, profitable operations in Europe. McDonald's, Walt Disney, du Pont, and Amway have successful Asian operations. Amway sells over $500 million worth of housewares door to door in Japan each year.[10] The following Managing Across Cultures feature describes Arvin Industries' successful globalization.

MANAGING ACROSS CULTURES

Arvin Industries

James K. Baker, chairman of Arvin Industries, can give you an authentic course in how to go global. In a little over ten years, Arvin transformed itself from a little-known automobile parts maker in Indiana into a global powerhouse with one-third of its sales overseas.

Arvin originally produced consumer electronics products, portable heaters, laminated panels, and auto parts. Historically, the auto parts accounted for

MANAGING ACROSS CULTURES —*Continued*

about 60% of sales, but almost all went to General Motors, Chrysler, and Ford. Arvin had no international revenues but could see the handwriting on the wall. Says Baker, "We realized that we had to change."

Arvin decided to concentrate on auto parts while acquiring complementary product lines and spreading geographically. The firm added Gabriel brand shock absorbers and MacPherson struts. It went in search of new customers and now sells to 17 automobile companies, including Toyota, Volvo, and Hyundai. Arvin now has factories in 16 countries and ships products to 130. Sales have tripled, and Arvin Industries has grown to No. 235 on the *Fortune* 500 list of the largest industrial firms.[11]

▼ Information Technology and Computers

Coping with international competition requires a flexibility that traditional organizations often do not possess. Fortunately, the revolution in information technology permits many organizations to develop the needed flexibility. A second revolution facing organizations stems from the proliferation of computer networks and the use of sophisticated information technology. **Information technology** (IT) comprises complex networks of computers, telecommunications systems, and remote-controlled devices. As discussed previously, information technology is having a profound impact on organizational operations, power relationships, and development and implementation of strategies.[12]

For example, information technology might affect a J.C. Penney store manager who sees an attractive sweater at Neiman-Marcus. She buys the sweater, photographs it, and faxes the photograph to Penney buyers around the world. Soon, a buyer in Bangkok locates a factory that can produce the sweater. Within two weeks, thousands of replicas are on their way to Penney stores. Information technology permits an IBM engineer to ask colleagues around the world for help when confronted with a difficult problem. General Electric recently spent hundreds of millions of dollars to create its own private global phone network. Employees now can communicate directly with each other from anywhere in the world using just seven digits. Information technology allows CRSS, the giant architectural firm, to exchange drawings with its client 3M almost instantly. In an event of great historic (and perhaps symbolic) significance, the London Stock Exchange recently replaced its trading floor with a computer–telecommunications network.[13]

Table 19.2 contains examples of information technologies that will be common in organizations of the future. Some, such as electronic data interchange and voice-mail, are in use in many advanced organizations today. In time, most (if not all) organizations will utilize these and even more advanced information technologies.

The latest frontier in information technology is a computer application known as virtual reality. **Virtual reality** is created by a display and control technology that surrounds the user with an artificial environment that mimics real life. The user of virtual reality does not passively view a computer screen but rather becomes a participant in a three-dimensional setting. Boeing is investigating potential applications of virtual reality to the design and testing of aircraft. Caterpillar has been testing virtual reality models of its earth-

TABLE 19.2   Information Technology of the Future

Individual Work Support	Group Work Support	Advanced Organizational Automation	Enhanced Communication
High bandwidth portable computer	Groupware	Electronic data interchange (EDI)	Language speech translator
Knowbot*	Cyberspace†	Virtual reality sales	E-mail and voice-mail
Advanced forms of multimedia	Virtual reality for teams	Automated customer response systems	Videophone and desktop videoconferencing
Virtual reality			Videoconferencing
			Telepresence‡

*A *knowbot* resides inside an individual's PC and is programmed to organize data and work for the user.
†The next step beyond virtual reality; incorporates the user's thoughts into computer processible form.
‡The transmission of holographic images from one office to another.

Source: Adapted from Thach, L., and Woodman, R. W. Organizational change and information technology: Managing on the edge of cyberspace. *Organizational Dynamics*, Summer 1994, 34.

movers to improve performance and driver visibility. Daniel Ling, leader of a research team on virtual reality at IBM, stated: "Virtual reality will eventually change the way people use computers. The applications are countless."[14]

Another new information technology, already in use at some companies, is **electronic data interchange** (EDI), which links an organization to its suppliers and customers electronically. An organization can link its manufacturing and inventory functions so that, as soon as the system runs low on a part, a central computer automatically executes an electronic purchase order signaling the supplier to ship new parts. This technology can save a company millions of dollars in reduced inventory costs and potential downtime from part shortages.[15] Consider, for example, how Motorola, Inc., makes and sells its Bravo pocket pagers. A salesman in Foster City, California, types an order into his Macintosh computer, specifies the unique code that will cause each pager to beep, and asks for delivery in two weeks. The order zips over phone lines to a mainframe computer in a new factory in Boynton Beach, Florida. The computer automatically schedules the pagers for production, orders the proper components, and informs the shipping docks to express mail them to Pacific Telesis Group in California.[16]

A version of EDI, known as **Computer-integrated manufacturing** (CIM), uses computer networks to link sales, production, and shipping. Figure 19.1 shows a CIM network. This technology is designed to break down barriers between departments, improve quality control, and reduce inventory costs by creating a just-in-time (JIT) manufacturing process. The employees involved can use their computers to "talk" to each other and watch the process unfold as the product moves through the system. The emphasis on using robots in manufacturing was to replace humans with machines and thus reduce labor costs. However, the major goal of CIM (and other versions of electronic data

FIGURE 19.1

Computer-Integrated
Manufacturing

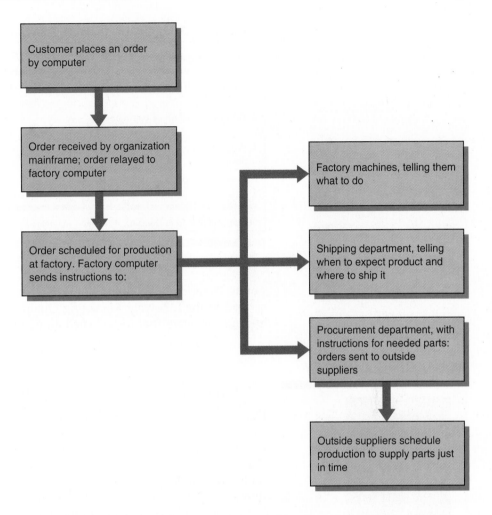

Source: Adapted from Yoder, S. K. Putting it all together. *Wall Street Journal Reports: Workplace of the Future*, June 4, 1990, 24.

interchange) is to improve competitiveness and adaptability by reducing the time needed to turn ideas and sales into products and get those products to the customer.

▼ Changing Nature of Management

A third business revolution concerns the changing nature of management. Both globalization and information technology have an impact on organizational management. In adaptive, flexible organizations the roles and practices of managers are being reconceptualized. Table 19.3 presents examples of these changing roles.

The old-style manager often told people what to do and how to do it. The new-style manager asks the right questions and helps employees do the job on their own. New-style managers may still be relatively rare. James Champy, CEO of a consulting firm that specializes in reengineering organizations, says, "We won't see them in great numbers for another five to ten years. But cor-

TABLE 19.3   Contast Between Old-Style and New-Style Managers

Old-Style Manager	New-Style Manager
▲ Thinks of self as boss	▲ Thinks of self as sponsor, team leader, or consultant
▲ Follows the chain of command	▲ Works with anyone necessary to get the job done
▲ Works within a rigid organization design	▲ Changes organization designs in response to market change
▲ Makes most decisions alone	▲ Shares decision making with others
▲ Hoards information	▲ Shares information

Source: Adapted from Dumaine, B. The new non-manager managers. *Fortune*, February 22, 1993, 81.

porate America is definitely going in that direction.''[17] Such people are described in the following Managing Quality account. An emphasis on quality and management that fosters such an emphasis clearly are connected.

MANAGING QUALITY

The Non-Manager Managers

Dee Zalneraitis is the information group manager of a division of R. R. Donnelley & Sons, America's largest printing company. Her division, located in Hudson, Massachusetts, converted to self-managed teams last year. Zalneraitis's new role is to teach, train, and nurture her 40 employees until they can confidently manage their own team, including hiring, firing, scheduling vacations, and the like. Once Zalneraitis believes that her people can handle their team, she hopes to move on. She states, ''I'd like to manage my way out of my current job in two years.''

Three years ago, Cindy Ransom of Clorox challenged her 100 employees to redesign completely their Fairfield, California, plant's operations. Teams of employees established training programs, set work rules and policies, and reorganized a traditional factory into five customer-focused business units. Ransom intervened only to answer an occasional question and help provide some overall vision for the new plant. The reorganization freed Ransom's time to focus on customers and suppliers.

New managers must learn to create new business swiftly in response to fast-changing markets. At Sony Medical, Anthony Lombardo uses an approach designed to create opportunities for rapid innovation. Sony Medical makes computer peripherals (such as color printers) used with ultrasound machines and other medical imaging equipment. Lombardo spends lots of time with customers (doctors and health maintenance organizations) to understand their needs. He constantly scans Sony for technologies that might meet those needs. When Lombardo identifies a need for a new product, he assembles a team of ten or so employees from different disciplines to tackle its development. The idea is to experiment constantly and, if an idea doesn't work, to move quickly to another one. Lombardo says the key is to constantly create, shift, and change teams of people as the market demands.[18]

▼ Changing Nature of the Work Force

In addition to coping with the revolutions stemming from globalization, information technology, and new management philosophies, organizations must attract employees from a changing work force (see Chapter 1). Throughout the book, we have explored the challenges of managing cultural diversity.

The work force continues to grow more diverse in terms of gender and race. Thus equal opportunity pressures on hiring practices and promotion decisions will persist for some time to come. Other trends add to the challenge for organizations. For example, the dual-career family rapidly is becoming the norm, rather than the exception, in many advanced societies. Further, the contingency work force continues to grow as a percentage of all workers. The **contingency work force** includes part-time employees, free-lancers, subcontractors, and independent professionals hired by companies to cope with unexpected or temporary challenges. By some accounts, almost 25% of U.S. workers now are in this category.[19] Experts expect this percentage to continue to grow as companies find efficiencies by operating with a small core of permanent employees surrounded by a changing cast of temporary help. Temporary-employment agencies, such as Manpower and Kelly Services, have grown by 240% in the last ten years and now employ some 1.6 million people. Manpower, the largest of these firms, has more employees than General Motors or IBM. Among the challenges facing organizations are those of motivating and rewarding part-time employees whose morale and loyalties may be quite different from those of permanent employees.

Increasingly, the work force is better educated, less unionized, and characterized by changing values and aspirations. Although changing values and expectations will not lessen the motivation to work, they are altering the rewards that people seek from work and the balance they seek between work and other aspects of life. The **quality of work life** represents the degree to which people are able to satisfy important personal needs through their work and is an important goal for many, if not most, working women and men. More than ever before, employees desire pleasant working conditions, more participation in decisions that affect their jobs, and support facilities, such as day care centers for their children. These and other employee expectations put additional pressures on organizations and affect their ability to compete effectively in the labor market.

Not only will the composition and values of the work force continue to change, but interorganizational and international mobility also will increase. Even permanent employees are likely to become less loyal to a particular organization and strengthen their ties to their profession or skill. Moreover, people may be forced to change occupations several times during their working lives to adjust to changing economic conditions. As a result, more and more individuals will work at diverse occupations during their lifetimes (see Chapter 21).

Although there are differences among countries and regions, global organizations face similar changes in the nature of their work forces worldwide.[20] All these business revolutions affect managers and organizations around the world, as the following Managing Across Cultures item indicates.

MANAGING ACROSS CULTURES

12,000 World Managers View Change

The *Harvard Business Review* collected data (by survey questionnaire) on a variety of organizational issues from almost 12,000 managers throughout the world. Twenty-five business publications in 25 countries on six continents assisted the journal in this effort. Each publication reproduced the survey questionnaire in its own language.

The questionnaire examined a number of issues, but one strong theme particularly stood out in the survey results. Change is occurring everywhere—regardless of country, culture, or organization—with managers reporting a rapidly changing business environment. Figure 19.2 contains data from six countries, showing the percentage of respondents' organizations that underwent a major redesign during a recent two-year period. For example, during that period, an incredible 71% of South Korean firms were restructured. Among the six countries shown in Figure 19.2, Hungary had the smallest amount of organizational redesign, at 36%. However, even that is a significant amount of reorganization for any two-year period.

Figure 19.3 summarizes results from the same six countries with regard to international expansion. Almost half of the German and Japanese respondents' firms expanded their international operations during the two-year reporting period. The United States trailed, with 26% of the managers reporting increased globalization.

These survey results reveal that globalizing markets, instantaneous communications, political realignments, changing demographics, technological

FIGURE 19.2

Percentage of Respondents Reporting Major Redesign of Their Organizations

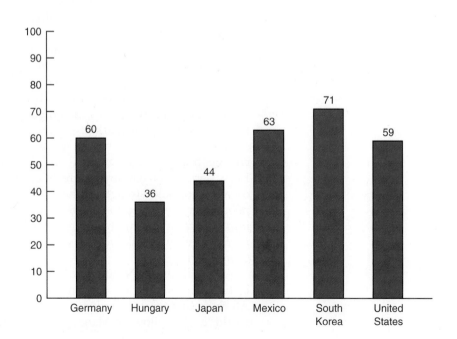

Source: Adapted from Kanter, R. M. Transcending business boundaries: 12,000 world managers view change. *Harvard Business Review*, May–June, 1991, 154.

MANAGING ACROSS CULTURES —*Continued*

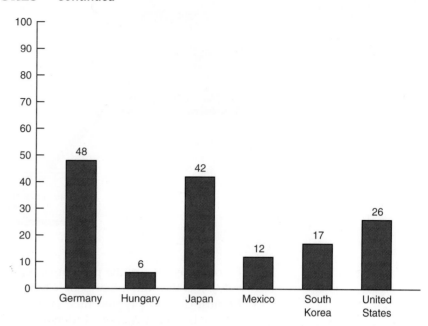

FIGURE 19.3

Percentage of Respondents Reporting International Expansion by Their Organizations

Source: Adapted from Kanter, R. M. Transcending business boundaries: 12,000 world managers view change. *Harvard Business Review,* May–June, 1991, 154.

transformations in both products and production, and new corporate alliances are changing the ways that organizations are designed and conduct their business.[21]

▼ RESISTANCE TO CHANGE

Inevitably, change will be resisted, at least to some extent, by both individuals and organizations. **Resistance to change** is baffling because it can take so many forms. Overt resistance may be manifested in strikes, reduced productivity, shoddy work, and even sabotage. Covert resistance may be expressed by increased tardiness and absenteeism, requests for transfers, resignations, loss of motivation, lower morale, and higher accident or error rates. One of the more damaging forms of resistance is lack of participation in and commitment to proposed changes by employees, even when they have opportunities to participate.[22]

As Figure 19.4 shows, resistance to change stems from a variety of sources. Some are traceable to individuals, but others involve the nature and structure of organizations. Managers and employees need to understand the reasons for and sources of resistance to change.[23]

▼ Individual Resistance to Change

Figure 19.4 shows six important sources of individual resistance to change. Of course, these are not the only reasons why individuals may resist change at work.

FIGURE 19.4

Sources of Resistance to Change

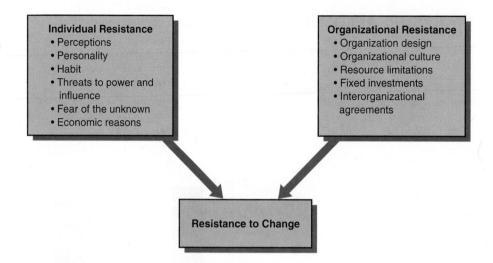

Perceptions   Recall the perceptual error called perceptual defense (see Chapter 3). It is the notion that people tend to perceive selectively those things that fit most comfortably into their current understanding of the world. Once individuals establish their understanding of reality, they resist changing it. Among other things, people may resist the possible impact of change on their lives by (1) reading or listening only to what they agree with, (2) conveniently forgetting any knowledge that could lead to other viewpoints, and (3) misunderstanding communication that, if correctly perceived, wouldn't fit their existing attitudes and values. For example, managers enrolled in management training programs are exposed to different managerial philosophies and techniques. They may ably discuss and answer questions about these philosophies while carefully segregating in their minds the approaches that they believe wouldn't work from those that they already practice.

Stereotypes (another type of perceptual error addressed in Chapter 3) also can serve as a perceptual resistance to change as the following Managing Diversity piece demonstrates.

MANAGING DIVERSITY

Ineffective Training Increases Resistance

"Caucasians are insensitive and aloof. African-Americans like watermelon. Women shouldn't manage because they're too emotional." These stereotypes were generated in a diversity workshop held in a government agency. They could have been used constructively to create awareness of how these perceptual biases might affect working relationships. Unfortunately, following the workshop, they were circulated throughout the agency by an inexperienced trainer without being accompanied by any explanation of where they came from or what they meant. Needless to say, this information created a tremendous amount of anger and hostility and made subsequent diversity training efforts more difficult.

In another case, a Midwestern manufacturer hired some diversity consultants to help deal with racial tensions in the workplace. The consultants split

MANAGING DIVERSITY —*Continued*

employees into two groups: minorities (identified as employees who felt op-
pressed) and Caucasians (identified as people who made others feel op-
pressed). Employees in the minority group shared their anger and resentment
toward the Caucasians. In the workshop, the Caucasians simply listened without responding.

These identities may have been useful if handled properly, but the exercise
outraged the Caucasian employees. Further, members of the minority group
left the workshop feeling vulnerable. Rather than bringing the groups closer
together, the manner in which this workshop was conducted drove a wedge
between employees and further worsened working relationships in the company. Frances Kendall, the diversity consultant brought in to repair the damage, stated, "The exercise didn't work for either group."

As demand for diversity training has grown, unfortunately so have incidents such as these. Many inexperienced and unqualified people have hung
out shingles as diversity trainers. Organizations need to be careful about
whom they employ to help with these important programs. Bad training experiences can seriously damage diversity efforts and increase resistance to
needed changes.[24]

Personality   Some aspects of their personalities (e.g., dogmatism and dependency) may predispose some individuals to resist change (see Chapter 2).
Recall that dogmatism is the rigidity of a person's beliefs. The highly dogmatic
individual is close-minded and more likely to resist change than a less dogmatic person. Another example is dependency.[25] If carried to extremes, dependency on others can lead to resistance to change. People who are highly
dependent on others often lack self-esteem. They may resist change until those
they depend on endorse the change and incorporate it into their behavior.
Employees who are highly dependent on their supervisors for performance
feedback probably will not accept any new techniques or methods unless the
supervisors personally endorse them and indicate to the employees how these
changes will improve performance.

A cautionary note: Don't overemphasize the role played by personality in
resistance to change. Recall the fundamental attribution error (see Chapter 3).
People tend to "blame" resistance to change in the workplace on individual
personalities. Although personality may be a factor, it seldom is the most
important dynamic in the situation.

Habit   Unless a situation changes dramatically, individuals may continue to
respond to stimuli in their accustomed ways. A habit may be a source of
satisfaction for individuals because it allows them to adjust to and cope with
their world. A habit also provides comfort and security. Whether a habit becomes a major source of resistance to change depends, to a certain extent, on
whether individuals perceive advantages from changing it. For example, if an
organization suddenly announced that all employees would immediately receive a 20% pay raise, few would object, even though the raise might permit
significant changes in their life-styles. However, if the organization announced
that all employees could receive a 20% pay raise only if they switched from

working from 9:00 A.M. to 5:00 P.M. to working during the evenings and nights, many would object. Employees would have to change many habits—when they sleep, eat, interact with their families, and so on.

Threats to Power and Influence   Some people in organizations may view change as a threat to their power or influence. Recall that the control of something needed by other people, such as information or resources, is a source of power in organizations (see Chapter 15). Once a power position has been established, individuals or groups often resist changes that they perceive as reducing their power and influence. For example, programs to improve the quality of work life (QWL programs) in organizations tend to focus on nonmanagerial employees and often are perceived as increasing their power. As a result, managers and supervisors may resist such programs. Novel ideas or a new use for resources also can disrupt the power relationships among individuals and departments in an organization and therefore often are resisted.

Fear of the Unknown   Confronting the unknown makes most people anxious. Each major change in a work situation carries with it an element of uncertainty. People starting a new job may be concerned about their ability to perform adequately. Women starting a second career after raising a family may be anxious about how they will fit in with other workers after a long absence from the workplace. An employee may wonder what might happen if he or she relocates to company headquarters in another state: "Would my family like it?" "Will I be able to find friends?" "What will top managers think of me if I refuse to relocate?" Uncertainty in such situations arises not just from the prospective change itself, but also from the potential consequences of the change. In order to avoid both making more demanding types of decisions and the fear of the unknown, some employees may refuse promotions that require relocating or that require major changes in job duties and responsibilities.

Economic Reasons   Money weighs heavily in people's considerations. They certainly can be expected to resist changes that could lower their income. In a very real sense, employees have invested in the status quo in their jobs. That is, they may have learned how to perform the work successfully, how to get good performance evaluations, and how to interact with others. Changes in established work routines or job duties may threaten their economic security. Employees may fear that after changes are made, they will not be able to perform up to their previous standards and subsequently will not be as valuable to the organization, their supervisor, or their co-workers.

▼ Organizational Resistance to Change

To a certain extent, the nature of organizations is to resist change. Organizations often are most efficient when doing routine things and tend to perform more poorly, at least initially, when doing anything for the first time. To ensure operational efficiency and effectiveness, organizations may create strong defenses against change. Moreover, change often opposes vested interests and violates certain territorial rights or decision-making prerogatives that groups, teams, and departments have established and accepted over time. Figure 19.4

shows several of the more significant sources of organizational resistance to change.

Organization Design   Organizations need stability and continuity in order to function effectively. Indeed, the term *organization* implies that individual, group, and team activities must have a certain structure. That is, individuals must have assigned roles, established procedures for getting the job done, consistent ways of getting needed information, and the like. However, this legitimate need for structure also may lead to resistance to change. Organizations may have narrowly defined jobs; clearly spelled-out lines of authority, responsibility, and accountability; and limited flows of information from the top to the bottom. The use of a rigid design and an emphasis on the hierarchy of authority usually causes employees to use only specific channels of communication and to focus narrowly on their own duties and responsibilities. Typically, the more mechanistic the organization, the more numerous are the levels of the organization through which an idea must travel. This organizational design, then, increases the probability that any new idea will be screened out because it threatens the status quo. More adaptive and flexible organizations, as discussed in this and the next chapter, are designed to reduce the resistance to change created by rigid organizational structures.

Organizational Culture   Organizational culture plays a key role in change. Recall that cultures are not easy to change and may become a principle source of resistance to needed changes (see Chapter 14). One aspect of an effective organizational culture is whether the culture has the flexibility to take advantage of opportunities to change. An ineffective organizational culture, from the perspective of our organizational change topic, is one that rigidly socializes employees into the old culture even in the face of evidence that it no longer works.

Resource Limitations   Some organizations want to maintain the status quo, but others would change if they had the resources to do so. Change requires capital, time, and skilled people. At any particular time, an organization's managers and employees may have identified changes that could or should be made, but they may have to defer or abandon some of the desired changes because of resource limitations.

Fixed Investments   Resource limitations aren't confined to organizations with insufficient assets. Wealthy organizations may be unable to change because of fixed capital investments in assets that they can't easily alter (e.g., equipment, buildings, and land). The plight of the central business districts in many cities illustrates this resistance to change. Most large cities developed before the automobile and can't begin to accommodate today's traffic volumes and parking demands. The fixed investments in buildings, streets, transit systems, and utilities are enormous and usually prevent rapid and substantial change. Therefore many older central areas are unable to meet the competition of suburban shopping centers.

Fixed investments aren't always limited to physical assets; they also may be expressed in terms of people. For example, consider employees who no longer are making a significant contribution to an organization but have enough seniority to maintain their jobs. Unless they can be motivated to higher task performance or retrained for other positions, their salaries and fringe benefits represent, from the organization's perspective, fixed investments that cannot easily be changed.

Interorganizational Agreements   Agreements between organizations usually impose obligations on people that can restrain their behaviors. Labor negotiations and contracts are the most pertinent example. Some ways of doing things that once were considered the prerogatives of management (the right to hire and fire, assign tasks, promote and demote, and so on) may become subject to negotiation and fixed in the negotiated contract. Other types of contracts also constrain organizations. For example, proponents of change may face delay because of arrangements with competitors, commitments to suppliers and other contractors, and pledges to public officials in return for licenses, permits, or financing.

▼ Overcoming Resistance to Change

Realistically, resistance to change will never cease completely. However, managers and employees can learn to identify and minimize it and become more effective change agents. The following Managing Ethics account describes how Martin Marietta overcame resistance to changing its ethical practices and culture.

MANAGING ETHICS

Overcoming Resistance to Integrity

During a period of time when the defense industry was under attack for fraud and mismanagement, Martin Marietta Corporation, a major U. S. aerospace and defense contractor, received more than its share of unfavorable scrutiny. The company had significant problems with improper travel billings and other lapses in ethical judgement, yet managers were resistant to change and skeptical that an ethics program could influence behavior. Current president Thomas Young recalls people asking, "Do you really need an ethical program to be ethical?" Many organizations' ethics programs could be described as a "compliance strategy," which emphasizes legal compliance. However, Martin Marietta quickly realized that meaningful ethical change required a change in culture. As a result, the company adopted an "integrity strategy" for changing behavior. Table 19.4 contrasts a compliance approach and an integrity approach.

Today the ethics program at Martin Marietta consists of a code of conduct, an ethics training program, and procedures for reporting and investigating ethics concerns. Ethics training focuses on ethical decision making, the challenge of identifying ethical dilemmas in balancing responsibilities, and developing knowledge concerning relevant laws and regulations. Importantly, the compensation system is tied to the ethics program, with executives and managers held responsible for promoting ethical conduct. A corporate ethics office manages the program and has representatives at all major company facilities. The firm's top management—the president, senior executives, and two rotat-

MANAGING ETHICS —*Continued*

TABLE 19.4   Approaches to Ethics Management

Characteristics of Compliance Strategy		Characteristics of Integrity Strategy	
Vision	Conformity to externally imposed standards	Vision	Self-governance according to chosen standards
Objective	Prevention of criminal misconduct	Objective	Enable responsible conduct
Leadership	Lawyer driven	Leadership	Management driven, with aid of lawyers and human resources staff
Methods	Education, reduced discretion, auditing and controls, and penalties	Methods	Education, leadership, accountability, organizational sytems and decision processes, auditing and controls, and penalties

Source: Adapted from Paine, L. W. Managing for organizational integrity. *Harvard Business Review,* March–April, 1994, 113.

ing members from field operations—oversee the ethics office. In turn, an ethics committee of the corporation's board of directors monitors top management.

Martin Marietta's attention to ethics has had a significant effect on the organizational culture and ultimately on the firm's reputation for integrity, quality, and reliability. Chief executive officer Norman Augustine says, "Ten years ago, many employees would have said that there were no ethical issues in our business. Today employees think their number-one objective is to be thought of as decent people doing quality work."[26]

Organizational members often have difficulty in clearly understanding situations that involve change. Analyzing a change problem may be quite complex when a large number of variables must be considered. Kurt Lewin, a pioneering social psychologist, developed a way of looking at change that has proved to be highly useful to action-oriented managers and employees.[27] Lewin viewed change not as an event but as a dynamic balance of forces working in opposite directions. His approach, called **force field analysis,** suggests that any situation can be considered to be in a state of equilibrium resulting from a balance of forces constantly pushing against each other. Certain forces in the situation—various resistances to change—tend to maintain the status quo. At the same time, various pressures for change are acting opposite to these forces and are pushing for change. The combined effect of these two sets of forces results in the situation depicted in Figure 19.5, which shows the sources of pressures for and resistance to change discussed in this chapter.

To initiate change, someone must act to modify the current equilibrium of forces by

▲ increasing the strength of pressure for change;

FIGURE 19.5

Force Field Analysis

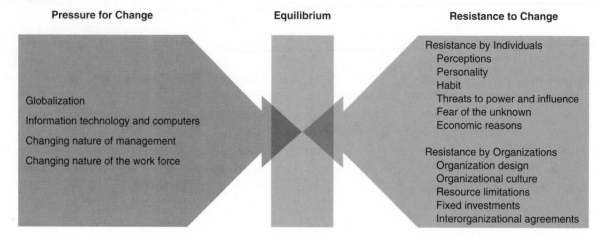

Using force field analysis to understand the processes of change has two primary benefits. First, managers and employees are required to analyze the current situation. By becoming skillful at diagnosing the forces pressing for and resisting change, individuals should be able to understand better the relevant aspects of any change situation. Second, a force field analysis highlights the factors that can be changed and those that cannot. People often waste a great deal of time considering actions related to forces over which they have little, if any, control. When individuals direct their attention to the forces over which they do have some control, they increase the likelihood of selecting effective options to change the situation.

However, careful analysis of a situation doesn't guarantee successful change. For example, people in control have a natural tendency to increase the pressure for change in any situation in order to produce the change they desire. Increasing such pressure may result in short-run changes, but it may have a high cost: Strong pressure on individuals and groups may create conflicts and disrupt the organization. Often the most effective way to make needed changes is to identify existing resistance to change and focus efforts on removing or reducing as much resistance as possible.

An important part of Lewin's approach to changing behaviors consists of carefully managing and guiding change through a three-step process.

▲ **Unfreezing.** This step usually involves reducing those forces maintaining the organization's behavior at its present level. Unfreezing is sometimes accomplished by introducing information to show discrepancies between behaviors desired by employees and behaviors they currently exhibit.

▲ **Moving.** This step shifts the behavior of the organization or department to a new level. It involves developing new behaviors, values, and attitudes through changes in organizational structures and processes.

▲ **Refreezing.** This step stabilizes the organization at a new state of equilibrium. It is frequently accomplished through the use of supporting mechanisms that reinforce the new organizational state, such as organizational culture, norms, policies, and structures.[28]

Successful methods for dealing with resistance to change often include the following components.

▲ *Empathy and support.* Understanding how employees are experiencing change is useful. It helps identify those who are troubled by the change and understand the nature of their concerns. When employees feel that those managing change are open to their concerns, they are more willing to provide information. This openness, in turn, helps establish collaborative problem solving, which may overcome barriers to change.

▲ *Communication.* People are more likely to resist change when they are uncertain about its consequences. Effective communication can reduce gossip and unfounded fears. Adequate information helps employees prepare for change.

▲ *Participation and involvement.* Perhaps the single most effective strategy for overcoming resistance to change is to involve employees directly in planning and implementing change. Involvement in planning change increases the probability that employee interests will be accounted for and thus lowers resistance to change. Involved employees are more committed to implementing the planned changes and more likely to ensure that they work.[29]

▼ ORGANIZATIONAL DIAGNOSIS

An accurate diagnosis of organizational problems is absolutely essential as a starting point for planned organizational change.[30] In a humorous way, the following Managing in Practice feature suggests the importance of organizational diagnosis.

MANAGING IN PRACTICE

The Chairman's Rice Pudding

A senior manager was given the responsibility of examining all operations and procedures at corporate headquarters. She formed a task force to help with this review. The top executives of the organization had their own private kitchen and dining room. Although this perk wasn't high on its list of priorities, the task force eventually got around to taking a look at this kitchen's operation.

The task force discovered that two rice puddings were made every day at 12:15 P.M. and thrown away at 2:45 P.M. Mysteriously, the rice puddings were not listed on the dining room's menu. The kitchen's chef was questioned about this practice. He admitted that, to the best of his knowledge, no one had ever eaten one of these puddings. Nor did he know why they were being made. He had been the chef for eight years. The practice was in place when he joined the organization, and he had simply continued it.

MANAGING IN PRACTICE —*Continued*

Intrigued, the task force decided to investigate the origin of this odd ritual. The explanation found was as follows. Seventeen years before, the then-chairman of the organization had strolled through the kitchen one day. In a conversation with the chef at the time, he had mentioned how much he liked rice pudding. The chef then instructed his kitchen staff to prepare two rice puddings each day but not to include them on the menu. When the chairman came to lunch, his waiter could then offer him a rice pudding. The second rice pudding was made in case anyone else in the chairman's lunch party also should request one.

The chairman who apparently had a rice pudding occasionally retired four years later. Thirteen years after his retirement, the kitchen staff was still making rice puddings. By now, however, none of them knew why they were doing so, nor did any of the patrons of the dining room know that the pudding was available.[31]

All organizations have "rice puddings"—patterns of behavior and procedures that, at one time and place, made perfect sense but no longer do. Diagnosing needed change, in part, means uncovering the organization's "rice puddings." Four basic steps should be undertaken in **organizational diagnosis:**

▲ recognizing and interpreting the problem and assessing the need for change;

▲ determining the organization's readiness and capability for change;

▲ identifying managerial and work-force resources and motivations for change; and

▲ determining a change strategy and goals.[32]

Information needed to diagnose organizational problems may be gathered by questionnaires, interviews, observation, or from the firm's records. Typically, some combination of these data-gathering methods is used.[33] An advantage of the information-collecting process is that it increases awareness of the need for change. Even when widespread agreement exists concerning the need for change, people may have different ideas about the approach to be used and when, where, and how it should be implemented. Thus some systematic attempt should be made to determine the initial focus of a change effort.

▼ Readiness for Change

Any planned change program requires a careful assessment of individual and organizational capacity for change. Two important aspects of individual readiness for change are the degree of employee satisfaction with the status quo and the perceived personal risk from possible changes. Figure 19.6 shows the possible combinations of these considerations. When employees are dissatisfied with the current situation and perceive little personal risk from a change, their readiness for change probably would be high. In contrast, when em-

FIGURE 19.6
_____

Employee Readiness for Change

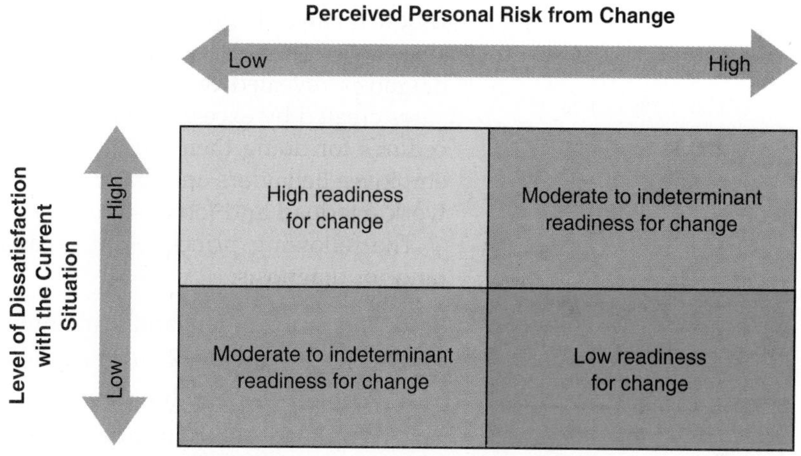

Perceived Personal Risk from Change

Low   High

Level of Dissatisfaction with the Current Situation

High

| High readiness for change | Moderate to indeterminant readiness for change |

Low

| Moderate to indeterminant readiness for change | Low readiness for change |

Source: Adapted from Zeira, Y., and Avedisian, J. Organizational planned change: Assessing the chances for success. _Organizational Dynamics_, Spring 1989, 37.

ployees are satisfied with the status quo and perceive high personal risk in change, their readiness for change probably would be low.[34]

With regard to individual readiness for change, another crucial variable is employee expectations regarding the change effort.[35] Expectations play an essential role in behavior. If people expect that nothing of significance will change, regardless of the amount of time and effort they devote, this belief can become a self-fulfilling prophecy. And when employee expectations for improvement are unrealistically high, unfulfilled expectations can make matters worse. Ideally, expectations regarding change should be positive yet realistic.

The various types of resistance to change described earlier represent another important aspect of readiness for change. Both individual and organizational resistance to change must be diagnosed. In addition, the organization's capacity to change must be accurately assessed. Approaches that require a massive commitment of personal energy and organizational resources probably will fail if the organization has few resources and its members do not have the time or opportunity to implement the needed changes. Under such circumstances, the organization may benefit most from starting with a modest approach. Then, as the organization develops the necessary resources and employee commitment, it can increase the depth and breadth of the change.

▼ Principles of Change

When managers and employees conduct an organizational diagnosis, they should recognize two crucial factors. First, organizational behavior is the product of many interacting forces. Therefore what is observed or diagnosed— employee behaviors, problems, and the current state of the organization—has multiple causes. Trying to isolate single causes for complex problems can lead to simplistic and ineffective change strategies. Second, much of the information gathered about an organization during a diagnosis will represent symptoms rather than causes of problems.[36] Obviously, focusing change strategies on symptoms won't solve underlying problems. For example, in one organization, an awards program that recognized perfect attendance failed to reduce absenteeism because it didn't deal with the causes of the problem. Careful diagnosis revealed that employees were absent from work because of pressures created by excessive workloads and an inefficient, frustrating set of procedures for doing their jobs. The awards offered weren't sufficient to change employee behaviors and, more important, didn't address the real problems of work overload and job design.

The following principles of organizational change emphasize the importance of diagnosis.

▲ You must understand something thoroughly before you try to change it.

▲ You cannot change just one element of a system.

▲ People resist anything they feel is punishment.

▲ People are reluctant to endure discomfort, even for the sake of possible gains.

▲ Change always generates stress.

▲ Participation in setting goals and devising strategies reduces resistance to change and increases commitment.

▲ Behavioral change comes in small steps.[37]

▼ CHANGING ORGANIZATIONS

Many approaches can be used to diagnose and initiate organizational change. We consider four of the most important and widely used approaches: a systems approach, the process of innovation, the process of action research, and the applied behavioral science called organization development.

▼ A Systems Approach to Change

The **systems model of change** describes the organization as six interacting variables that could serve as the focus of planned change: people, culture, task, technology, design, and strategy. The **people variable** applies to the individuals working for the organization, including their individual differences—personalities, attitudes, perceptions, attributions, problem-solving styles, needs, and motives. The **culture variable** reflects the shared beliefs, values, expectations, and norms of organizational members (see Chapter 14).

The **task variable** involves the nature of the work itself—whether the job is simple or complex, novel or repetitive, standardized or unique. The **technology variable** encompasses the problem-solving methods and techniques used and the application of knowledge to various organizational processes. It includes such things as the use of information technology, robot and other automation, manufacturing processes, tools, and techniques (e.g., computer-integrated manufacturing).

The **design variable** is the formal organizational structure and its systems of communication, control, authority, and responsibility (see Chapter 17). Finally, the **strategy variable** comprises the organization's planning process. It typically consists of activities undertaken to identify appropriate organizational goals and prepare specific plans to acquire, allocate, and use resources in order to accomplish those goals.

As Figure 19.7 indicates, these six variables are highly interdependent. A change in any one variable usually results in a change in one or more of the others. For example, a change in the organization's strategic plan might dictate a change in organization design to an adaptive or network form. This change, in turn, could result in the reassignment of people. At the same time, the redesign may also lead to a change in the technology used, which would affect the attitudes and behaviors of the employees involved, and so on. Any of these changes occur within a particular culture, which might either support or resist them. Moreover, change itself may either modify or reinforce the existing culture. An advantage of a systems approach to organizational change is that it helps managers and employees think through such interrelationships. The systems approach reminds us that we cannot change a part of the organization without, in some sense, changing the whole.

Organizational change can be introduced by altering these variables singly or in combination, but all six usually are present in an organizationwide change process. However the systems approach to change emphasizes the importance of understanding all six variables before making changes in any one of them. The systems model shown in Figure 19.7 provides the framework for examining specific approaches and techniques of organizational change in Chapter 20.

▼ Innovation

Innovation is the initiation or adoption of new products, services, processes, procedures, or ideas by an organization. The capacity to innovate is central to the ability of an organization to adapt to changes in its environment.[38]

FIGURE 19.7

A Systems Model of Change

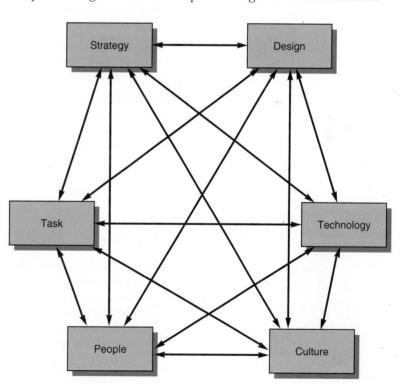

Many critics of U.S. industry argue that its most serious shortcoming in the face of increased global competition is a lack of innovation. The reasons given for an inability to generate sufficient innovation include (1) an overemphasis on short-term profits, (2) an unwillingness to invest owing to the high cost of capital, (3) government regulation, (4) resistance to change (including many of the issues discussed in this chapter), (5) rigid organization design and procedures that stifle new ideas, and (6) reward structures that punish creativity and risk taking. Other critics, however, suggest that the central issues involve management philosophy, practices, and culture.

The conclusions stemming from studies of innovation at the Xerox Palo Alto Research Center (PARC) support the latter view. Investigations of organizational innovation spanning the last 20 years at PARC suggest that effective innovation will occur only by creating "continuously innovating companies." Such an organization continuously "reinvents" itself and its products or services.

The studies at PARC also reached the following conclusions regarding innovation.

▲ Innovation in work practices is as important as innovation in new-product development and manufacture.

▲ Innovation is everywhere in the organization, not just in research and development labs and research centers.

▲ Organizations need to learn how to identify these many innovations and share them throughout the system.

▲ Specialized research centers in the organization cannot just produce innovation, which must be "coproduced." Large numbers of employees must share a vision of the importance of innovation in order for change to occur and be disseminated throughout the organization.

▲ The organization's ultimate innovation partner is the customer. Innovation, like everything else the organization does, must allow the organization to meet customer needs better.[39]

The following Managing in Practice account describes the philosophy and culture for innovation at Illinois Tool Works (ITW). Some of the points just mentioned—a focus on work practices and linking innovations to customer needs—are reflected in the operations of ITW.

MANAGING IN PRACTICE

The Nuts and Bolts of Innovation

Illinois Tool Works is relatively unknown to the general public despite being a huge corporation with sales in excess of $2 billion per year. This obscurity stems from the products it produces, most of which are attached to or become part of somebody else's products. The company manufactures nails, screws, bolts, strapping, wrapping, valves, capacitors, filters, and adhesives. It also manufactures tools and machines to assemble products containing these components. (One product that many people would recognize is the plastic loops that hold six-packs together—ITW invented them.) It has a reputation for be-

MANAGING IN PRACTICE *—Continued*

ing extraordinarily innovative in many relatively mundane areas. For some time, ITW has placed first in its industry in *Fortune* magazine's list of most admired companies. (In 1994, the company slipped to second behind Gillette in the "metal products" industry—an industry that contains dozens of firms.) How has it been so successful in innovation?

The Illinois Tool Works factory in Elgin, Illinois—noisy, grimy and hot— hardly looks like a cutting-edge innovative operation. Yet, something little short of miraculous has taken place there. Productivity tripled in just eight years, and the factory regained market share previously lost to low-cost competitors. Across the entire company, ITW has lowered costs and prices, increased market share, and become dramatically more inventive. In addition, the firm expanded internationally and now operates in more than 30 countries.

The company's version of the adaptive organization might be described as an amoeba. When engineers and marketers develop a new product, the organization typically sets up a new entity. It has 90 product divisions, loosely arranged in nine groups. These divisions usually are small (less than $30 million in annual revenue) and autonomous. The company is highly decentralized, with divisions controlling their own manufacturing, marketing, and research and development. Employees work hard at staying in close touch with their customers and attribute much of the impetus for innovation to this effort. Employees spend as much time seeking innovative ways to organize their methods of production as they do focusing on product development.

The company determined that, in most of its factories, 80% of the business comes from 20% of the customers. These large customers order only a handful of products but do so in large quantities. The other 80% of the customers (the "small-batch guys") can dramatically reduce the productivity of the entire plant if all products are treated the same. The solution is segregation. The most sophisticated, high-speed, low-inventory (such as just-in-time materials handling) manufacturing and assembly operations are used with the high-volume products. Other products are segregated into separate enclaves, and the procedures used are most appropriate for the product, volume, and so on. Another work system innovation at ITW is known as the "focused factory." Here, high-volume specialty products are spun off into separate small operations usually employing less than 25 people.[40]

▼ Action Research

Action research is a data-based, problem-solving process of organizational change that closely follows the steps involved in the scientific method.[41] It represents a powerful approach to organizational change and consists of three essential steps:

- ▲ gathering information about problems, concerns, and needed changes from the members of an organization;
- ▲ organizing this information in some meaningful way and sharing it with the employees involved in the change effort; and
- ▲ planning and carrying out specific actions to correct identified problems.

The action-research sequence often includes an evaluation of the implemented actions. An organizational change program may go through repeated cycles of data gathering, information sharing, and action planning before its conclusion.

The strength of the action-research approach to change lies in (1) its careful diagnosis of the current situation in the organization and (2) its involvement of employees in the change process. Managers can effectively change an organization or group only if they understand the current situation, including what tasks are done well and what tasks need to be improved. In addition, employee involvement can spur change for at least two reasons. First, people are more likely to implement and support a change that they have helped create. Second, once managers and employees have identified the need for change and have widely shared this information, the need becomes difficult for people to ignore. The pressure for change thus comes from within the group, department, or organization, rather than from outside. This internal pressure is a particularly powerful force for change.[42]

▼ Organization Development

Organization development (OD) is a planned, systematic process of organizational change based on behavioral science research and theory.[43] The goal of OD is to create adaptive organizations capable of repeatedly transforming and reinventing themselves as needed to remain effective.[44] As a field of behavioral science, OD draws heavily from psychology, sociology, and anthropology. Organization development relies on information from motivation theory, personality theory, and learning theory (see Chapters 6, 2, and 5, respectively), and on research on group dynamics, leadership, power, and organization design (see Chapters 9, 10, 11, 15, and 17, respectively). It is based on many well-established principles regarding the behaviors of individuals and groups in organizations. In short, OD rests on many of the facets of organizational behavior presented in this book.

Organization development isn't a single technique but a collection of techniques that have a certain philosophy and body of knowledge in common. The basic tenets that set OD approaches apart from other organizational change approaches include the following.

- ▲ OD seeks to create self-directed change to which people are committed. The problems and issues to be solved are those identified by the organization members directly concerned.
- ▲ OD is a systemwide change effort. Making lasting changes that create a more effective organization requires an understanding of the entire organization. It isn't possible to change part of the organization without changing the whole organization in some sense.
- ▲ OD typically places equal emphasis on solving immediate problems and the long-term development of an adaptive organization. The most effective change program isn't one that just solves present problems but one that also prepares employees to solve future problems.
- ▲ OD places more emphasis than do other approaches on a collaborative process of data collection, diagnosis, and action for arriving at solutions to problems. Action research (discussed in the preceding section) is a primary change process used in most OD programs.

▲ OD has a dual emphasis on organizational effectiveness and human fulfillment through the work experience.[45]

A recent survey of 110 of the *Fortune* 500 industrial corporations revealed that all but 3 of these organizations had viable OD change activities underway. Some 82% of these organizations considered their OD change programs to be effective.[46] Many of the techniques and methods for changing organizations described in Chapter 20 often make up part of an OD program.

Summary

A rapidly changing environment places many demands on managers and employees, including the need to plan for and manage organizational change effectively. Planned organizational change attempts to alter the design and processes of an organization to make it more effective and efficient. Organizational change requires adaptation by the organization as a whole and by its individual members, who must alter their patterns of behavior.

Pressures for change stem from globalization, increasingly heavy use of computers and information technology, the changing roles and practices of management, and the changing nature of the work force. Individuals may resist change because of their perceptions or personalities. In addition, habitual behaviors, a fear of the unknown, economic insecurities, and threats to established power and influence may generate further resistance to change. Organizational resistance to change may be caused by organizational structure and culture, resource limitations, fixed investments not easily altered, and interorganizational agreements.

Force field analysis can help managers and employees diagnose and overcome resistance to change. The change process passes through three stages: unfreezing, moving, and refreezing. To foster change, managers must encourage pressures for change and discourage resistance to change. Resistance to change can be reduced through good communications and high levels of employee involvement in the change process.

An accurate, valid diagnosis of current organizational functioning, activities, and problems is an essential foundation for effective organizational change. The readiness for change, availability of resources for change, and possible resistances to change are among the factors that should be diagnosed.

The primary variables in the systems model of change are people, culture, task, technology, design, and strategy. A systems approach to change recognizes the interdependent nature of these variables. Innovation processes are a crucial part of an organization's ability to adapt to changes in its environment. Successful change programs often utilize an action-research sequence of information gathering, feedback, and action planning. Organization development (OD) is a field of applied behavioral science that focuses on understanding and managing organizational change.

Key Words and Concepts

Action research	Contingency work force	Force field analysis
Business revolutions	Culture variable	Globalization
Computer-integrated manufacturing	Design variable	Information technology
	Electronic data interchange	Innovation

Moving
Organization development
Organizational diagnosis
People variable
Planned organizational change

Pressures for change
Quality of work life
Refreezing
Resistance to change
Strategy variable

Systems model of change
Task variable
Technology variable
Unfreezing
Virtual reality

Discussion Questions

1. What are the basic objectives of planned organizational change? Which one seems most fundamental to you? Defend your answer.

2. What are some of the external and internal pressures for change at your college or university? Explain. (You might consider funding, student life, curriculum development, or similar types of pressures.)

3. Identify the primary sources of individual resistance to change. Which have you had the most experience with? Describe a personal experience with individual resistance to change.

4. Identify the major sources of organizational resistance to change. Which have you had the most experience with? Describe a personal experience with organizational resistance to change.

5. Based on your own work experience, use force field analysis to analyze a situation that needed changing. Start

by describing the setting and situation. What were the main pressures and resistances to change operating in the situation?

6. Use the three-step process of unfreezing, moving, and refreezing to describe some major behavioral change from your own experience.

7. Based on your own work experience, analyze a change situation in terms of the readiness for change on the part of individuals involved.

8. What are six major systems variables that affect an organization's ability to change? Describe them and give an example to show how they are interrelated.

9. Why might innovation be low in an organization? Explain why innovation is crucial in effective organizations.

10. What does the process of action research involve? Suggest a situation in which it might be used effectively.

▲ Developing Skills

Self-Diagnosis:
Rate Your Readiness for Change

Instructions

Think of an organization where you currently work or used to work and assign values to the following. Give three points for a high ranking (We're good at this.); two for a medium ranking (We could use some improvement on this.); and one point for a low score (We have a problem with this.).

Readiness Scores: High = 3; Medium = 2; Low = 1.

1. _____   *Leadership*: Who are the leaders involved in the change? Successful change is more likely if high-level leadership is involved and has a stake in the change effort. Leadership that is primarily from lower levels of the hierarchy, is not well connected, or comes only from staff positions should be scored low.

2. _____   *Motivation*: Give high points for a strong sense of urgency from the top of the organization or for a cul-

ture that emphasizes continuous improvement. Give low points for large numbers of employees who have been in their jobs for many years or for a conservative culture that discourages risk taking.

3. _____   *Direction*: How clear are managers' and employees' visions of the future? Can employees be mobilized for action? Positive answers rate a 3. If managers and employees believe that only minor changes are needed and little change is likely, give it a 1.

4. _____   *Customer focus*: If employees know who their customers are, know their needs, and have direct contact with them, the ranking should be high. If only a few employees are customer-oriented, the ranking should be low.

5. _____   *Rewards*: Change is easiest when managers and employees are rewarded for being innovative and taking risks. Team-based rewards are better than individual rewards. Rewarding continuity rather than change and making heroes out of people just for staying within a budget deserve low ratings.

6. _____ *Organizational structure*: Flexible structures with little need for constant reorganizations earn the most points. Rigid structures and frequent reorganizations with little success earn fewer points.

7. _____ *Communication*: Change is easier when employees understand and use many channels of communication (rate high). Change is more difficult if few communication channels exist or if information flows only one-way, i.e., top-down (rate low).

8. _____ *Prior change experience*: Score 3 if your organization has handled a major change successfully in its history. Score 1 if it has had no prior experience with attempting major changes or if failed change efforts have left bitterness and anger.

9. _____ *Morale*: If employees enjoy working for your company and readily accept individual responsibility, change will be easier (score high). Poor morale or team spirit or low levels of trust between managers, employees, or departments make change more difficult (score low).

10. _____ *Decision making*: Rate high if decisions are made quickly and include suggestions from a wide variety of individuals and departments. Rate lower for slow decision-making processes, high levels of conflict, and confusion and resentment after decisions are made.

Scoring

If your score is

24–30, implementing change is likely to be successful. Focus resources on lagging factors (1's and 2's) to improve the odds even further.

17–23, change is possible, but may be difficult. Factors receiving the lowest scores need improvement before major changes are attempted.

10–16, implementing meaningful change is unlikely. Improve change readiness in areas indicated by 1's before starting change efforts. Pilot programs, in selected parts of the organization probably will be needed.[47]

A Case in Point: Planned Change at the Piedmont Corporation

The Piedmont Corporation produces and markets a variety of computer products for the global market. In order to compete in this industry, firms need to introduce new products rapidly to meet changing customer demand. This requires close coordination among different functional departments, including research and development, marketing, production, and sales. For major new products, Piedmont creates special task forces responsible for coordinating the different contributions needed to develop, produce, and sell the product. Each task force is headed by a product manager and includes representatives from the different functional departments.

Stan Ledford headed the Omega task force, which was in the early stages of developing a plan for introducing the new Omega word processor. The task force was just starting its activities and had held four half-day meetings since its inception about a month earlier. Stan felt frustrated by the progress of these meetings and attributed these feelings to members' inability to work well together. They frequently interrupted each other and strayed from the agenda that Stan gave out at the start of each meeting. They also had forceful yet divergent opinions on how the Omega should be rolled out, and they had difficulty making even minor decisions. In talking these problems over with a close friend and fellow product manager, Stan was advised that members of his division's human resources department might be able to help. He was quickly put in touch with Sue Srebla, an internal consultant for Piedmont who specialized in organization development. Sue suggested that the two of them meet and explore Stan's problems and determine whether Sue (or someone else) might help to resolve them.

At the meeting, Stan shared his ideas about the task force's problems. Sue listened attentively, periodically asking questions to clarify what Stan was saying. She then talked about her experience helping groups to solve such problems and tentatively outlined a team-building strategy for Stan's consideration. The strategy would be aimed at helping team members to examine their meetings and task interactions and to devise ways of improving them. Sue would facilitate this process by interviewing team members about their perceptions of the problems and feeding the data back to members at a special meeting. Sue would help members analyze the interview data and devise appropriate solutions. Sue suggested that Stan should take an active leadership role in the team building and that team members should be involved in deciding whether to proceed with the team building and whether to use Sue as their consultant. Stan agreed to put this issue on the agenda for the team's next meeting and asked Sue to attend to answer questions and to establish relations with members.

At the team's next meeting, Stan explained his frustration with the group's progress and his desire to do something constructive about it. He described his meeting with Sue and outlined the team-building proposal as well as Sue's expertise in this area. Members were encouraged to ask questions and to share their reactions. This led to a spirited discussion about the need for good task interactions among group members. It also led to sharing their expectations about Sue's role in the team building as well as her expectations of members' roles. All members agreed to try the team building, and they set a date for the interviews and the subsequent feedback and problem-solving meeting.

Over the next week, Sue conducted a one-hour interview with each member of the Omega task force. Although she asked several questions, they were aimed at three major areas: things the team did well, things that impeded task performance, and suggestions for improvement. Sue summarized the interview data under those three headings and placed them on large sheets of newsprint that could be affixed to the walls of the meeting room. Only general themes appeared on the newsprint in order to preserve the anonymity of members' responses. Members could choose to be as open as they wanted at the feedback meeting. On the evening before the meeting, Sue shared the summarized data with Stan so that he would be prepared to lead the meeting and to help the group address important issues.

The feedback session started with members setting expectations for the meeting and agreeing to share perceptions openly with a spirit of constructive problem solving. Sue briefly reviewed the major themes on the newsprint and encouraged members to elaborate on their responses and to share opinions about the underlying causes of the problems. Several strengths of the team were identified, including member's expertise, willingness to work hard, and fierce loyalty to the product. Among the impediments to team performance were members' lack of input into the agenda for meetings, Stan's laissez-faire leadership style, and one or two members' domination of the meetings.

Members engaged in an open discussion of the feedback and ended the meeting with concrete suggestions for improvement. These included setting clearer parameters for group decision making, allowing members to gain greater involvement in setting the agenda, and paying more attention to members' interactions and to how the group is functioning. Sue provided conceptual input about the role of group norms in determining members' behaviors, and the group decided to list norms that it would like to operate under. Members also agreed to set aside some time at the end of each meeting to review how well their behaviors matched those norms. This would enable the group to detect ongoing problems and to solve them. At the end of the feedback session, the group thanked Sue for the help and asked whether she would be willing to provide further assistance if new problems emerged that the group could not handle. Sue assented to this request and ended this cycle of consulting with the Omega task force.

Over the next few months, Stan and his team implemented most of the suggestions from the feedback session. Although they had some problems taking time to assess their norms at each meeting, members gradually saw the benefits of doing this and made it a regular part of meetings. Periodically, the team encountered new problems that were difficult to deal with, such as bringing new members on board, and asked Sue for help. Her inputs helped team members solve their own problems, and with time, the team called on her less and less. Although far from perfect, the Omega team was judged by Piedmont executives to be one of its most effective new-product task forces.[48]

Questions

1. Using the force field analysis techniques discussed in the chapter, analyze this case. Be specific about the pressures for change and the resistance to change that seem to be operating in this situation. Identify which types of pressure and resistance are likely to be the strongest.
2. Use the systems model of change to identify key variables that might be changed in order to increase the overall effectiveness of Piedmont Corporation.
3. Describe the readiness for change that seems to be exhibited by individuals in this case.
4. Would you describe the change approach in use as action research? Why or why not?

References

1. Adapted from Huey, J. Managing in the midst of chaos. *Fortune*, April 5, 1993, 38–48.
2. Hammer, M., and Champy, J. *Reengineering the Corporation.* New York: Harper Business, 1993; Kanter, R. M., Stein, B. A., and Jick, T. D. *The Challenge of Organizational Change.* New York: Free Press, 1992; Woodman, R. W., and Pasmore, W. A. (eds.), *Research in Organizational Change and Development*, vol. 7. Greenwich, Conn.: JAI Press, 1993.
3. Kiechel, W. How we will work in the year 2000. *Fortune*, May 17, 1993, 39.
4. See, for example, Cummings, T. G., and Worley, C. G. *Organization Development and Change*, 5th ed. St. Paul, Minn.: West, 1993, 52–71.
5. Beer, M., Eisenstat, R. A., and Spector, B. Why change programs don't produce change. *Harvard Business Review*, November–December 1990, 158.
6. Doyle, F. P. People-power: The global human resource challenge for the '90s. *Columbia Journal of World Business*, Spring/Summer 1990, 36–45; Offermann, L. R., and Gowing, M. K. Organizations of the future. *American Psychologist*, 1990, 45, 95–108.

7. Stewart, T. A. Welcome to the revolution. *Fortune*, December 13, 1993, 66–80.

8. Ibid., 66.

9. Peters, T. Prometheus barely unbound. *Academy of Management Executive*, 1990, 4(4), 70–84.

10. Wysocki, B. Going global in the new world. *Wall Street Journal Reports: World Business*, September 21, 1990, 3.

11. Adapted from Nulty, P. A quick course in going global. *Fortune*, January 13, 1992, 64.

12. Barry, B. Information technology and organizational development. In R. W. Woodman and W. A. Pasmore (eds.), *Research in Organizational Change and Development*, vol. 3. Greenwich, Conn.: JAI Press, 1989, 213–231; Gerstein, M. S. *The Technology Connection: Strategy and Change in the Information Age*. Reading, Mass.: Addison-Wesley, 1987; Gleckman, H. The technology payoff. *Business Week*, June 14, 1993, 56–68; Lederer, A. L., and Nath, R. Making strategic information systems happen. *Academy of Management Executive*, 1990, 4(3), 76–83.

13. These examples are drawn from Peters, Prometheus barely unbound, *Academy of Management Executive*, 1990, 4(4), 72–73.

14. Bylinsky, G. The marvels of "virtual reality." *Fortune*, June 3, 1991, 138–142.

15. Thach, L., and Woodman, R. W. Organizational change and information technology: Managing on the edge of cyberspace. *Organizational Dynamics*, Summer 1994, 30–46.

16. Yoder, S. K. Putting it all together. *Wall Street Journal Reports: Workplace of the Future*, June 4, 1990, 24.

17. Dumaine, B. The new non-manager managers. *Fortune*, February 22, 1993, 81.

18. Ibid., 80–84 (adapted from).

19. Fierman, J. The contingency work force. *Fortune*, January 24, 1994, 30–36.

20. Johnston, W. B. Global work force 2000: The new world labor market. *Harvard Business Review*, March–April 1991, 115–127; O'Reilly, B. Your new global work force. *Fortune*, December 14, 1992, 52–66.

21. Adapted from Kanter, R. M. Transcending business boundaries: 12,000 world managers view change. *Harvard Business Review*, May–June 1991, 151–164.

22. Neumann, J. E. Why people don't participate in organizational change. In R. W. Woodman and W. A. Pasmore (eds.), *Research in Organizational Change and Development*, vol. 3. Greenwich, Conn.: JAI Press, 1989, 181–212; Pasmore, W. A., and Fagans, M. A. Participation, individual development, and organizational change: A review and synthesis. *Journal of Management*, 1992, 18, 375–397.

23. For additional perspectives on resistance to change, see Argyris, C. *Overcoming Organizational Defenses*. Boston: Allyn & Bacon, 1990; Argyris, C. Reasoning, action strategies, and defensive routines: The case of OD practitioners. In R. W. Woodman and W. A. Pasmore (eds.), *Research in Organizational Change and Development*, vol. 1. Greenwich, Conn.: JAI Press, 1987, 89–128; Bartunek, J. M. Rummaging behind the scenes of organizational change—and finding role transitions, illness, and physical space. In R. W. Woodman and W. A. Pasmore (eds.), *Research in Organizational Change and Development*, vol. 7. Greenwich, Conn.: JAI Press, 1993, 41–76.

24. Adapted from Caudron, S. Training can damage diversity efforts. *Personnel Journal*, April 1993, 51.

25. Bornstein, R. F. The dependent personality: Developmental, social and clinical perspectives. *Psychological Bulletin*, 1992, 112, 3–23.

26. Adapted from Paine, L.S. Managing for organizational integrity. *Harvard Business Review*, March–April, 1994, 112–115.

27. Lewin, K. *Field Theory in Social Science*. New York: Harper & Row, 1951; Lewin, K. Frontiers in group dynamics. *Human Relations*, 1947, 1, 5–41.

28. Cummings, T. G., and Worley, C. G. *Organization Development and Change*, 5th ed. St. Paul, Minn.: West, 1993, 53.

29. Ibid., 148–149.

30. Ibid., 84–109; Burke, W. W. *Organization Development: A Process of Learning and Changing*, 2nd ed. Reading, Mass.: Addison-Wesley, 1994, 96–124; Jackson, C. N., and Manning, M. R. (eds.), *Organization Development Annual Volume III: Diagnosing Client Organizations*. Alexandria, Va.: American Society for Training and Development, 1990; Weisbord, M. R. Towards a new practice theory of OD: Notes on snapshooting and moviemaking. In W. A. Pasmore and R. W. Woodman (eds.), *Research in Organizational Change and Development*, vol. 2. Greenwich, Conn.: JAI Press, 1988, 59–96.

31. Adapted from Carnall, C. A. *Managing Change in Organizations*. London: Prentice-Hall, 1990, 68–69.

32. Beckhard, R. Strategies for large system change. *Sloan Management Review*, 1975, 16, 43–55; Beckhard, R., and Harris, R. T. *Organizational Transitions: Managing Complex Change*. Reading, Mass.: Addison-Wesley, 1987, 29–44; Spector, B. A. From bogged down to fired up: Inspiring organizational change. *Sloan Management Review*, Summer 1989, 29–34.

33. Woodman, R. W. Issues and concerns in organizational diagnosis. In C. N. Jackson and M. R. Manning (eds.), *Organization Development Annual Volume III: Diagnosing Client Organizations*. Alexandria, Va.: American Society for Training and Development, 1990, 5–10.

34. Zeira, Y., and Avedisian, J. Organizational planned change: Assessing the chances for success. *Organizational Dynamics*, Spring 1989, 31–45.

35. Eden, D. Creating expectation effects in OD: Applying self-fulfilling prophecy. In W. A. Pasmore and R. W. Woodman (eds.), *Research in Organizational Change and Development*, vol. 2. Greenwich, Conn.: JAI Press, 1988, 235–267; Woodman, R. W., Organizational change and development: New arenas for inquiry and action. *Journal of Management*, 1989, 15, 209–210; Woodman, R. W., and Tolchinsky, P. D. Expectation effects: Implications for organization development interventions. In D. D. Warrick (ed.), *Contemporary Organization Development: Current Thinking and Applications*. Glenview, Ill.: Scott, Foresman, 1985, 477–487.

36. Woodman, R. W. Issues and concerns in organizational diagnosis. In C. N. Jackson and M. R. Manning (eds.), *Organization Development Annual Volume III: Diagnosing Client Organizations*. Alexandria, Va.: American Society for Training and Development, 1990, 7.

37. Sikes, W. Basic principles of change. In W. Sikes, A. B. Drexler, and J. Gant (eds.), *The Emerging Practice of Organization Development*. Alexandria, Va.: NTL Institute for Applied Behavioral Science, 1989, 179.

38. Henderson, R. Managing innovation in the information age. *Harvard Business Review*, January–February, 1994, 100–105.

39. Brown, J. S. Research that reinvents the corporation. *Harvard Business Review*, January–February, 1991, 102–111.

40. Based on Henkoff, R. The ultimate nuts and bolts company. *Fortune*, July 16, 1990, 70–73; Welsh, T. Best and worst corporate reputations. *Fortune*, February 7, 1994, 86.

41. For a description of action research, see French, W. L., and Bell, C. H. *Organization Development: Behavioral Science Interventions for Organization Improvement*, 4th ed. Englewood Cliffs, N.J.: Prentice-Hall, 1990, 98–111; see also Agunis, H. Action research and scientific method: Presumed discrepancies and actual similarities. *Journal of Applied Behavioral Science*, 1993, 29, 416–431.

42. See, for example, the classic statement by Cartwright, D. Achieving change in people: Some applications of group dynamics theory. *Human Relations*, 1951, 4, 381–392.

43. Porras, J. I., and Robertson, P. J. Organizational development: Theory, practice, and research. In M. D. Dunnette and L. M. Hough, (eds.), *Handbook of Industrial and Organizational Psychology*, vol. 3, 2nd ed. Palo Alto, Calif.: Consulting Psychologists Press, 1992, 719–822; Woodman, R. W. Organization develop-

ment. In N. Nicholson (ed.), *The Blackwell Dictionary of Organizational Behavior*. Oxford: Blackwell, 1994 (in press).

44. Woodman, R. W. Observations on the field of organizational change and development from the lunatic fringe. *Organization Development Journal*, 1993, 11, 71–74.

45. Beer, M. *Organization Change and Development: A Systems View*. Santa Monica, Calif.: Goodyear, 1980, 10; Woodman, R. W. Organization development. In N. Nicholson (ed.), *The Blackwell Dictionary of Organizational Behavior*. Oxford: Blackwell, 1994.

46. McMahan, G. C., and Woodman, R. W. The current practice of organization development within the firm: A survey of large industrial corporations. *Group & Organization Management*, 1992, 17, 117–134.

47. Adapted from Stewart, T. A. Rate your readiness to change. *Fortune*, February 7, 1994, 107–108.

48. Reprinted by permission from pages 61–63 of *Organization Development and Change*, 5th ed. by T. G. Cummings and C. G. Worley; Copyright © 1993 by West Publishing Company. All rights reserved.

20 Approaches to Planned Organizational Change

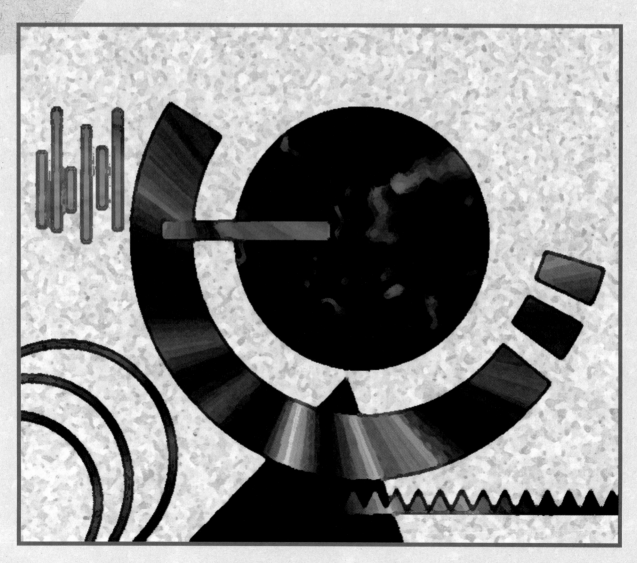

LEARNING OBJECTIVES

When you have finished studying this chapter, you should be able to:

▲ Identify and describe five people- and culture-focused approaches to organizational change.

▲ Explain some key issues in changing organizational culture.

▲ List and explain the approaches to organizational change that focus on task and technology.

▲ Describe design and strategy-focused approaches to organizational change.

▲ Discuss ethical issues in organizational change.

OUTLINE

Preview Case: A Grim Fairy Tale

The Challenge of Change

Organizationwide Change

Contingency Perspective

People- and Culture-Focused Approaches

Survey Feedback

Team Building

Process Consultation

Quality-of-Work-Life Programs

Managing Diversity: Workplace Flexibility at Corning

Changing Cultures

Managing in Practice: Changing Big Blue's Culture

High Performance–High Commitment Work Systems

Task- and Technology-Focused Approaches

Job Design

Sociotechnical Systems

Quality Circles

Managing Across Cultures: Quality Circles in Japan

Reengineering

Total Quality Management

Managing Quality: Quality at AT&T Universal Card Services

Design- and Strategy-Focused Approaches

Adaptive Organization Designs

Managing in Practice: The Adaptive Organization

Strategic Change

Ethical Issues in Organizational Change

Managing Ethics: The Tyranny of Change

DEVELOPING SKILLS

Self-Diagnosis: *Attitudes Toward Change*

A Case in Point: *Understanding Quality Systems—The Westinghouse Corporation*

PREVIEW CASE

A Grim Fairy Tale

Once upon a time, an American automobile company and a Japanese automobile company decided to have a boat race on the Mississippi River. Teams from both companies practiced long and hard to reach their peak rowing performance. On the big day, the teams were as ready as they could possibly be.

The Japanese team won by a mile. After the race, the American team became discouraged by the loss and their morale sagged. Corporate management decided that the reason for the crushing defeat had to be found. A task force of executives was created to diagnose the problem and to recommend appropriate corrective action.

After much study, the task force concluded that the problem seemed to center around the fact that the Japanese team had 8 people rowing and 1 person steering. The American team, in contrast, had 1 person rowing and 8 people steering. Not wanting to rush to judgement, the task force recommended that a consulting firm be employed to further study the problem. After some time and the accumulation of considerable consulting fees, the consulting firm also concluded that: "too many people were steering and not enough rowing."

To prevent further losses to the Japanese team, it was decided the management structure of the rowing enterprise needed to be redesigned. The new management team consisted of 4 steering managers, 3 area steering managers, and 1 staff steering manager. In addition, a new incentive system was developed for the person rowing the boat in order to provide motivation to work harder.

A new race was agreed upon and this time the Japanese team won by two miles. The American company then decided to downsize. The rower was laid off for poor performance. The company sold off the boat and paddles, cancelled capital investments planned for a new boat, granted a high performance award to the consulting firm, and distributed the money budgeted for next year's race as bonuses for senior executives.[1]

T he Preview Case contains a tongue-in-check parable that appeared on an organization's computer bulletin board. Like much satire, it contains a kernel of wisdom and truth. As we pointed out in Chapter 19, the world facing organizations is changing, and "business as usual" for many firms is a sure prescription for disaster. We can easily imagine the story in the Preview Case being composed by a disgruntled employee irritated by his or her company's unimaginative approach to needed organizational changes.

Managing organizational change presents complex challenges.[2] Planned changes may not work, or they may have consequences different from those intended. When trying to improve organizational adaptability and employee behaviors, managers and employees must understand the nature of the changes needed and the likely effects of alternative approaches to bring about that change. In this chapter, we discuss specific approaches and techniques for changing organizations and employee behaviors. Each approach may be valuable under certain conditions.

▼ THE CHALLENGE OF CHANGE

Organizational change can be difficult and costly. Despite the challenges, many organizations successfully make needed changes. Adaptive, flexible organizations have a competitive advantage over rigid, static ones.[3] Thus managing change has become a central focus of effective organizations worldwide. This focus is creating its own vocabulary. For example, Table 20.1 contains

TABLE 20.1   The Language of Organizational Change

Concept	Explanation
The learning organization	The notion that learning is central to success and effectiveness. Management must learn to see the "big picture" and understand subtle relationships among parts of the system.
Reengineering	A fundamental rethinking and redesign of systems and processes. Work should be organized around outcomes not tasks or functions.
Core competencies	The notion that companies need to identify and organize around what they do best. Strategy should be based on these core competencies rather than products or markets.
Organizational architecture	The idea that managers need to think broadly about the organization in terms of how work, people, and designs fit together.
Time-based competition	The notion that time is money. Time is manageable and can be a source of competitive advantage affecting productivity, quality, and innovation.

Source: Adapted from Byrne, J. A. Management's new gurus. *Business Week*, August 31, 1992, 45.

some of the current concepts made popular by the increasing emphasis on effective organizational change. These ideas have appeared in various forms throughout the book. In many respects, managing change effectively means understanding and using many of the important principles and concepts of organizational behavior that we have explored in this book.

▼ Organizationwide Change

Meeting the challenge posed by organizational change often means not doing things piecemeal. To be successful, change usually must be organizationwide. A good example of the comprehensive nature of successful change programs is provided by cutting-edge manufacturing organizations in the United States, Canada, Japan, and elsewhere. For about 25 years, a quiet revolution has been underway in the design and management of manufacturing facilities. These "revolutionary" plants go by a variety of names: high-involvement plants, new-design plants, high-performance–high-commitment work systems, quality-of-work-life organizations, productive workplaces, and the like. Procter & Gamble may have been the first company to design and build such a plant in the late 1960s. It was quickly followed by Sherwin-Williams, TRW, Mead Corporation, Cummins Engine, General Foods, Chaparral Steel, and Westinghouse, among others. In the 1980s, the pace accelerated, and by the 1990s, there were more than 500 such facilities in operation in North America and many more around the world, most notably in the Scandinavian countries and Japan. These new plants differ from more traditionally organized and managed facilities in several important ways.

Selection   Emphasis is placed on providing job applicants with a great deal of information concerning the jobs they are applying for. This approach allows for a high degree of self-selection out of a culture and work environment that might not be a good fit for an individual. Typically, production employees, rather than a human resources staff only, handle major portions of the selection process.

Pay System   The most common approach in new-design plants is skill-based pay (see Chapter 7). Under this pay system, individuals are paid according to how many skills they can learn and perform. This approach tends to create a flexible, highly trained work force and promotes the development of effective work teams capable of handling a variety of challenges, including production scheduling, quality control, and customer service.

Plant Physical Layout   High-involvement plants are characterized by few barriers or status differences between managerial and nonmanagerial employees. For example, managers and employees park in the same lots, eat in the same cafeteria, and so on.

Job Design   Employees typically have challenging work that involves doing a whole, identifiable task and having responsibility for controlling how it is done. The use of autonomous or self-managed work teams and other participative group structures is common.

Organization Design   High-involvement plants are characterized by flat structures and wide spans of control. A plant may have only two layers of management, with work teams having considerable autonomy to manage themselves. Such plants also have relatively small central office staffs because many activities—such as quality control, selection of new employees, inventory control, and production scheduling—are handled directly by the work teams.

Plant Culture   New-design plants are characterized by high degrees of participative management with decision-making responsibility pushed as low in the organization as possible. The competitive advantage of high-involvement plants stems from having employees who can solve problems, coordinate their work with the efforts of others, and manage the production process effectively.[4]

How does an organization turn a traditional manufacturing or service operation into an adaptive, high-involvement facility? Answering that question is where the various approaches to change come into play.

▼ Contingency Perspective

Disagreement exists about the best approaches to organizational change.[5] Many different approaches have been used successfully in organizational change efforts, but a successful approach in one organization may not necessarily work in another. Thus we emphasize a contingency perspective, which recognizes no single best approach to change and holds that no approach is likely to be effective under all circumstances.

Recall our systems model of change, which comprises six variables: people, culture, task, technology, design, and strategy (see Chapter 19). We use this systems model to organize approaches to change into three major categories: people- and culture-focused approaches, task- and technology-focused approaches, and design- and strategy-focused approaches. We explore various specific change strategies and techniques within each of these general categories. Although the chapter is organized as if each approach to organizational change were independent, that isn't the case in practice. A well-managed and carefully coordinated combination of approaches often is needed for effective change.[6] Successful organizational change programs typically use a combination of approaches at the same time.

▼ PEOPLE- AND CULTURE-FOCUSED APPROACHES

People- and culture-focused approaches to change rely on active involvement and participation by many employees. If successful, people-focused approaches improve individual and group processes in decision making, problem identification, problem solving, communication, working relationships, and the like. Changes focused on organizational culture can have an impact on the shared values, expectations, attitudes, and behaviors of organizational members. As we have pointed out previously, comprehensive programs of organizational change must, at least to some degree, deal with changes in organizational culture.

We examine four approaches to organizational change that initially focus on people: survey feedback, team building, process consultation, and quality-of-work-life (QWL) programs. In addition, we briefly review cultural change and explore a potentially effective work culture, the development of which is often the goal of organizational change efforts.

Table 20.2 summarizes the change approaches discussed in this section, the primary focus of each approach, and the relative direct impact of each on the six major system variables. Each approach usually has a high, moderate, or

TABLE 20.2   Comparison of Relative Direct Impact of People- and Culture-Focused Approaches on System Variables

Change Approach	Relative Direct Impact on System Variables					
	People	*Culture*	*Task*	*Technology*	*Design*	*Strategy*
Survey feedback	High	Low to moderate	Low to moderate	Low	Low to moderate	Low
Team building	High	Low to moderate	Low to high	Low	Low to moderate	Low
Process consultation	High	Low	Low to moderate	Low	Low	Low
Quality of work life	High	High	Low to moderate	Low to moderate	Low to moderate	Low to moderate
High-performance– high-commitment work systems	High	High	Moderate to high	High	Low to high	Low to moderate

low direct impact on each variable. Those approaches that could have different degrees of direct impact are given a range. For example, the direct impact of team building on the task variable can vary from low to high, depending on the focus and goals of the team-building activities.

The direct impacts shown in Table 20.2 represent the initial focus, or target, of the change effort. However, keep in mind that the systems perspective means that to change part of an organization is to change the whole in the long run. Thus each change approach, if successful, ultimately will affect all six major system variables.

▼ Survey Feedback

Survey feedback consists of (1) collecting information (usually by questionnaire) from members of an organization or work group, (2) organizing the data into an understandable and useful form, and (3) feeding it back to the employees who generated the data.[7] Some or all of the employees then use this information as a basis for planning actions to deal with specific issues and problems. Survey feedback follows the action-research process (see Chapter 19). The primary objective of survey feedback is to improve the relationships among the members of groups or teams or between departments through the discussion of common problems, rather than to introduce a specific change, such as a new computer system. Survey feedback also is frequently used as a diagnostic tool to identify team, department, and organizational problems. Because of its value in organizational diagnosis, survey feedback often is utilized as part of large-scale, long-term change programs in combination with other approaches and techniques.

Survey feedback usually begins with the commitment and endorsement of top management. Top managers or other employees may collaborate with outside consultants and human resource professionals in designing the questionnaire to be used. Employees in the survey feedback program then complete a standardized questionnaire. Generally, surveying members of the entire organization (or at least everyone in a department, team, or work group) yields the best results. The questionnaire, which people often answer anonymously, may ask for employees' perceptions and attitudes about a wide range of issues, including communication processes, motivational incentives, decision-making practices, coordination among departments and individuals, job satisfaction, and so on. The Developing Skills section at the end of this chapter contains a questionnaire that can be used to assess attitudes toward change during a survey feedback program.

Typically, all employees receive a summary of the responses from the entire organization, department, or team, as well as their own individual responses. Group discussion and problem-solving meetings are then held to discuss the data fed back. The teams involved need to have the discretion to consider and take action based on the survey findings and analysis. Employees can receive feedback of the data in one of three ways: (1) almost simultaneously; (2) in a "waterfall" pattern, with team meetings held at the highest organizational levels first, followed by team meetings at each succeeding lower level; or (3) in a "bottom-up" fashion, with team meetings held first at the lowest participating levels of the organization.

A major strength of survey feedback is that it deals with managers and employees in the context of their own jobs, problems, and work relationships. Thus employees often perceive that the data generated and the process employed are highly relevant to their goals and concerns. Survey feedback can effectively meet both organizational goals and individual and group needs. It doesn't usually bring about fundamental changes in organization design, task design, technology, or strategy. Nor would survey feedback, used in isolation, be likely to result in cultural change. However, survey feedback helps bring problems to the surface and clarifies issues, which in turn may indicate the need for changes in culture, tasks, technology, design, or strategy.

▼ Team Building

Team building is a process by which members of a work group or team diagnose how they work together and plan changes to improve their effectiveness. Many different work groups comprise an organization, and much of its success depends on how effectively people can work together as a team.[8]

Some interdependence among its members should exist before a group attempts team building. That is, the work of team members requires group effort, and effective performance by one member depends on that of the others. When such task interdependence doesn't exist, team building is inappropriate, and managers should use other types of change programs.

Team building attempts to improve the effectiveness of work groups by having members focus on

▲ setting goals or priorities for the team,

▲ analyzing or allocating the way work is performed,

▲ examining the way the team is working, and/or

▲ examining relationships among the people doing the work.[9]

Team building begins when members recognize a problem in group functioning for which this approach seems appropriate. During team building, members of the work group contribute information concerning their perceptions of issues, problems, and working relationships. They may gather data informally during group meetings or prior to meetings, using interviews or questionnaires. They then analyze these data and diagnose work problems. Using problem diagnosis as the starting point, members of the team plan specific actions and assign individuals to implement them. At some later stage, team members evaluate their plans and progress and determine whether their actions solved the problems. Effective team building often involves use of the action-research process.

Of course, every organization has groups of people who work together. However, not every organization has effective teams that are capable of self-management. Table 20.3 contrasts traditional work groups and new teams, which provide the leadership and direction needed in adaptive, high-performance organizations. Although no sure prescription exists for building the types of teams described, the following suggestions are useful.

▲ Establish urgency and direction. Team members need to develop an understanding of the importance of what they are doing and a shared vision of where they are going.

TABLE 20.3 Contrasts Between Traditional Work Groups and New Teams

Traditional Work Group	New Team
Strong leader (single individual)	Shared leadership roles
Individual accountability	Both individual and mutual accountability
Individual work products	Collective work products
Runs efficient meetings	Uses problem-solving meetings with open-ended discussion
Often measures its effectiveness indirectly	Measures performance directly by assessing collective work products

Source: Adapted from Katzenbach, J. R., and Smith, D. K. The discipline of teams. *Harvard Business Review*, March–April, 1993, 113.

▲ Select team members based on skills and potential rather than personality.

▲ Pay particular attention to first meetings and actions.

▲ Set some performance goals that are attainable immediately to build success and confidence.

▲ Bring new challenges and information to the team regularly to maintain momentum and enthusiasm.

▲ Use positive feedback, recognition, and rewards.[10]

Team building addresses immediate group problems and helps team members learn how to deal with new problems continually. An effective team can recognize barriers to its own effectiveness and design and take action to remove them. Team building has resulted in many positive outcomes for organizations. They include positive changes in employee participation, involvement, job satisfaction, and other work attitudes; organizational climate; group decision-making and problem-solving skills; and other aspects of team behavior.[11] These positive changes result in high-performance work teams. As team effectiveness grows, the potential impact on organizational performance increases. Another good way to define team building is that it consists of the activities designed to move the team up the performance curve shown in Figure 20.1

About 20% of U.S corporations are operating with self-managed teams, considered by many to be the best example of high-performing teams. These teams comprise perhaps 7–9% of all employees. Estimates are that 40–50% of all employees will work in such teams by the year 2000. At Chrysler Corporation, high-performance teams saved the firm's oldest plant in New Castle, Indiana, from almost certain closure. Chrysler's teams assign tasks, talk to customers, order repairs, and schedule their own work hours. Absenteeism and grievances have plummeted. Defects per million parts made have dropped from 300 to 20. Production costs also have shrunk.[12] At Ford Motor Company, a group known as "Team Mustang" saved the mustang automobile from extinction by developing a new version of the popular car in 25% less time and using 30% less money than required to introduce any other comparable new car in the automaker's history.[13]

FIGURE 20.1

The Team Performance Curve

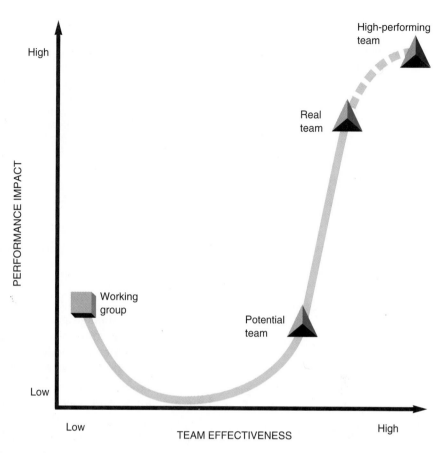

Source: Adapted from Katzenbach, J. R., and Smith, D. K. *The Wisdom of Teams.* Boston: Harvard Business School Press, 1993, 84.

Team building frequently is an important part of an organization development (OD) program. Organization development practitioners place great value on collaborative behaviors in achieving organizational change. Many OD programs are based on the assumption that widespread participation by employees is necessary to effect and sustain meaningful change. Increased involvement and participation are among the strongest expected outcomes of team building.[14] In addition to its other potential benefits, team building can provide a useful way to involve employees in an organizational change program and to increase collaborative efforts.

▼ Process Consultation

Process consultation is guidance provided by a consultant to help members of an organization perceive, understand, and act on process events that occur in the work environment.[15] *Process events* are the ways in which employees do their work, including the behavior of people at meetings; formal and informal encounters among employees at work; and, in general, any of the behaviors involved in performing a task. Figure 20.2 indicates some of the differences between process and content when tasks and interpersonal relationships are changed.

FIGURE 20.2

Some Examples of Differences
Between Content and Process

Focus of Change

	Task	**Interpersonal**
Content	Task goals	Who is involved
Process	How the task is done, decision making and problem solving	Communications, leadership, personal relationships

Source: Adapted from Schein, E. H. *Process Consultation, Vol. II*, Reading, Mass: Addison-Wesley, 1987, 40.

Process consultation involves the use of a skilled third party, or facilitator, who may be an outsider to the organization (e.g., an external behavioral science consultant) or a member of the organization (e.g., a human resource professional or a manager skilled in process activities). Process consultation typically addresses one or more of the following areas of concern.

▲ *Communication.* Managers and employees must understand the nature and style of the communication process in the organization and make this process as open and valid as possible. In particular, communication patterns in meetings can contribute to or reduce group effectiveness.

▲ *Leadership.* A work group or team must understand leadership styles and how individuals can adjust their styles to fit different situations better. In addition, by understanding influence processes, team members can learn to rotate leadership according to individual expertise, an important group skill.

▲ *Decision making and problem solving.* Efficient decision-making and problem-solving processes are crucial for individual and group effectiveness in organizations. Managers and employees must understand how decisions are made in their organizations and learn effective problem-solving behaviors.

▲ *Norms and roles.* Managers and employees should be aware of the processes by which individuals take on certain roles. In addition, teams need to examine the appropriateness of norms that influence behavior and learn how to change norms by a conscious process.

▲ *Conflict resolution.* How organizations resolve conflicts between individuals, teams, and departments is another important process. Process consultation may provide an effective approach to diagnosing, understanding, and resolving organizational conflict.[16]

Process consultation often is effective in changing attitudes and norms, improving interpersonal and decision-making skills, and increasing group cohesiveness and teamwork. There is little evidence that process consultation *directly* affects outcomes, such as task performance. However, the use of process consultation could contribute to a reduction in conflict in labor–management relations, leading to improved organizational performance in the long run.[17] Process consultation is seldom the sole component of an organizational change program; rather, it usually is used in combination with other approaches.

▼ Quality-of-Work-Life Programs

Quality-of-work-life (QWL) programs are activities undertaken by an organization to improve conditions that affect an employee's experience with an organization. Many QWL programs focus on security, safety and health, participation in decisions, opportunities to use and develop talents and skills, meaningful work, control over work time or place, protection from arbitrary or unfair treatment, and opportunities to satisfy social needs.[18]

Quality-of-work-life programs became popular in response to demands from employees for improvements in working conditions. In addition, QWL programs have been undertaken to increase productivity and quality of output through greater involvement and participation by employees in decisions that affect their jobs. Typically, such programs are broad-based and, to a certain extent, lack the precise definition and focus of survey feedback and team building.

Organizations with active QWL programs include GM, Ford, Chrysler, Motorola, Honeywell, Westinghouse, Digital Equipment, Hewlett-Packard, AT&T, Bethlehem Steel, Polaroid, and GE. Such programs may involve the use of a wide variety of specific techniques to improve employees' work experiences, such as team building, job redesign, participative management, quality circles, work-environment improvements, and flextime or other alternative work schedule programs. **Flextime** programs give employees some control over their own work schedules. For example, employees might be allowed to begin work anytime between 7 and 9 A.M. and to stop work between 4 and 6 P.M., depending on their starting times. Or employees might have the option of working a compressed work schedule of four ten-hour days, instead of five eight-hour days.

In addition to flextime, **alternative work schedule** programs might include the use of part-time employment, job sharing (where two individuals share the same job, each working part of the day or week), or work at home. A survey of companies affiliated with the Conference Board found that 92% used flextime, 69% allowed compressed work schedules, 95% utilized part-time employees, 67% had some job sharing, and 76% had some employees who were allowed to do at least part of their jobs at home (called telecommuting).[19]

Aetna Life and Casualty Company is using nearly all these alternative work schedule options with good results. Although they have meant many adjustments, particularly by managers whose subordinates use them, on balance managers and employees are pleased. Making alternative work schedules available allowed Aetna to retain some highly valued employees who otherwise would have quit. One Aetna manager said, "We're not doing flexible work scheduling to be nice, but because it makes business sense."[20] Xerox shares that conclusion. Tough productivity goals led one of its divisions to experiment with, in their words, "radical measures" to improve working conditions and output. After Xerox adopted flexible work schedules (employees have total freedom to set their own work hours), absenteeism fell by one-third, teamwork increased, and morale improved. Xerox particularly feels that productivity among dual-career couples with child care problems has risen and that these employees also now report less job stress.[21] In addition to these positive outcomes, firms also are discovering that alternative work schedules and other forms of workplace flexibility can help to manage diversity, as the following Managing Diversity account indicates.

MANAGING DIVERSITY

Workplace Flexibility at Corning

Corning, Inc., became concerned about retaining and developing talented women and African-Americans. Management formed a task force to ensure that employees had the opportunity to "participate fully, to grow professionally, and to develop their potential." To meet these goals, the task force concluded that Corning needed greater workplace flexibility, not only in terms of work schedules but also in terms of expectations about conformity in dress, behavior, and social activities. To develop greater workplace flexibility, the company adopted several programs and changes:

▲ race and gender awareness training, which focuses on aspects of organizational culture that inhibited flexibility;

▲ child care services and expanded family care leaves;

▲ career planning that recognizes the diversity in needs and goals of employees; and

▲ management performance ratings that hold managers accountable for workplace flexibility goals.

Corning sought to change its culture to one that values diversity as a strength and that helps the company relate to the diversity of its customers. These changes seem to be working. Corning reports that recruitment, retention, and advancement of women and African-American employees all have improved.[22]

Quality-of-work-life programs usually have two major objectives: (1) improving the quality of work life for employees; and (2) improving group, team, and/or organizational productivity. Such programs encompass so many activities that documenting their precise effects is difficult. However, considerable success has been reported in increasing levels of employee involvement, improving working conditions, and changing organizational culture. Improvements in work attitudes, such as organizational commitment, also may occur.[23] Improvements in productivity have been reported, although the relationship between QWL programs and productivity changes is complex, often indirect, and not easily measured. For example, Figure 20.3 suggests that QWL programs have the potential for improving communication, coordination, motivation, and performance capabilities. These improvements, in turn, may translate into increased productivity.

Quality-of-work-life programs can have negative outcomes. For example, middle managers and first-line supervisors sometimes resist QWL programs, perceiving them as increasing employee participation at the expense of their power and right to make decisions. Unless such resistance is overcome, a QWL program may fail or be achieved at a high cost in terms of managerial or supervisory turnover.

▼ Changing Cultures

Earlier, we explored changing organizational cultures and pointed out just how difficult such changes can be (see Chapter 14). To begin with, there are

FIGURE 20.3

Potential Effects of QWL
Programs on Productivity

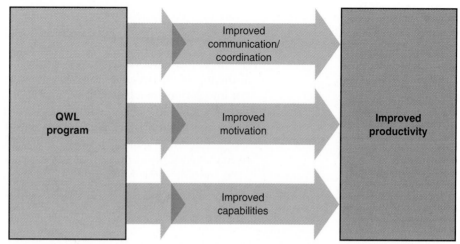

Source: Lawler, E. E., and Ledford, G. E. Productivity and the quality of work life. *National Productivity Review*, Winter 1981–1982, 29. Reprinted with permission of the publisher. National Productivity Review, 33 West 60th St., New York, NY 10023.

problems just in assessing the culture accurately before any plans for changes can be developed. In addition, some aspects of culture (such as the deepest core values shared by employees) may be almost impossible to change. Despite these challenges, some organizations have successfully changed their cultures. How did they do it?

A detailed examination of cultural change, conducted by Harrison Trice and Janice Beyer, suggests that the odds for success can be increased by attention to seven main issues.[24] First, *capitalize on dramatic opportunities*. The organization needs to take advantage of the moment when obvious problems or challenges that are not being met "open the door" to needed change. When Ford acquired Jaguar, obvious quality problems with the Jaguar automobile made justifying needed changes easier.

Second, *combine caution with optimism*. Managers and employees need to be optimistic with regard to the advantages of cultural change; otherwise they will be unwilling to make the attempt. Yet, as cultural change can have negative impacts, the organization needs to proceed with caution. Expectations for improvement must be positive yet realistic.

Third, *understand resistance to cultural change*. Resistance to change needs to be diagnosed. Identifying and reducing sources of resistance is valuable in cultural change as well as in other change programs.

Fourth, *change many elements, but maintain some continuity*. "Don't throw the baby out with the bathwater" is a common saying that sums up the importance of recognizing what is of value and retaining it. Hewlett-Packard successfully changed its culture as it grew and prospered, yet managed to retain a core of cultural ideas and beliefs that have served it well.

Fifth, *recognize the importance of implementation*. One survey indicated that over 90% of planned changes in strategy and culture were never fully implemented. A large percentage of failed change programs are really failures of implementation rather than failures of ideas. Organizations need to recognize that having a vision and a plan, although important, are only part of the battle. Planned changes must be carried through.

Sixth, *modify socialization tactics.* Socialization is the primary way that people learn their cultures. Thus changing socialization processes can be an effective approach to cultural change.

Finally, *find and cultivate innovative leadership.* Cultural change must begin at the top of the organization, and good leadership is crucial. When Lockheed got into serious trouble with its L-1011 jet airliner, an ineffective culture at its primary manufacturing facility was identified as a major part of the problem. The turnaround at Lockheed began with the appointment of Dale Daniels as vice-president of manufacturing at the L-1011 plant. Daniels brought a change in managerial philosophy that effectively changed the culture of the firm.

In the following Managing in Practice account, we explore the challenges facing IBM as it attempts to change its organizational culture.

MANAGING IN PRACTICE

Changing Big Blue's Culture

IBM faces practically every challenge known to organizations and is being forced to make dramatic, painful changes. Its culture and organizational design grew out of an era when the firm had no serious competitors. IBM's mistakes have become legendary in the computer business. The company was slow to recognize that the market had moved away from large, mainframe computers to desktop PCs linked into networks. IBM lost touch with its customers and was described as having a *Field of Dreams* mentality: "If you build it, they will come." The organization tried to hang on to its proprietary hardware and software long after customers had begun demanding systems that are compatible with other manufacturers' products. It continued to emphasize hardware in a business where software and customer service have become crucial. Perhaps most damaging was IBM's slowness in bringing new products to a marketplace characterized by rapid and constant introduction of new machines and new technologies.

Formidable as these problems are, some management experts think that IBM's greatest challenge will be to change its culture. Traditionally, IBM has been a bureaucratic company with highly centralized decision making. Managers are used to having large support staffs and using a deliberative, hierarchical decision-making process. Detailed procedures exist for almost every aspect of the business. When a group of IBM executives left IBM and started their own company, one of their first acts reportedly was to install Big Blue's bulky procedures manual in the middle of the plant floor, encased in plastic, to signify that they were doing things differently.

The IBM culture has been described as "addicted to perks, parties, and bureaucracy." The firm's sheer size makes it difficult to change the culture quickly. Despite its downsizing (IBM has eliminated 180,000 jobs in the past eight years, with 125,000 of them in just the past four years), Big Blue is still more than four times larger than the second largest computer maker (Digital) and ten times larger than Apple. IBM wants to decentralize, giving more autonomy to leaner, more flexible business units. IBM seeks to create a culture that focuses on service and customer satisfaction.

MANAGING IN PRACTICE —*Continued*

Whether IBM will successfully change its culture remains to be seen. No one doubts the sincerity and dedication of many managers and employees to try. However, it will be difficult. An internal survey of 1,200 top IBM managers indicated that almost 40% of them apparently still don't understand or won't accept "the need for change." Kim Clark, of Harvard University, sees great similarities between IBM and General Motors. "What you have here are two companies that at one point dominated their industries by producing very large products—mainframe computers and big American cars. And they created organizations that were very good at doing that. Then the world changed."[25]

▼ High-Performance–High-Commitment Work Systems

At the beginning of this chapter, we described the new plant revolution in many manufacturing facilities in the United States and around the world. The goal of many cultural change efforts is to produce a "high-involvement" type of work culture. One example of this type of culture is known as a **high-performance–high-commitment (HP–HC) work system.**[26] These systems blend technology and teamwork to create a sense of ownership among employees while utilizing the most sophisticated work practices and technologies.

High-performance–high-commitment work systems have the following characteristics.

▲ *Delegation.* People who have the most relevant and timely information or the most appropriate skills for a task are given responsibility for decisions and actions.

▲ *Teamwork across boundaries.* All employees in the organization are focused on servicing the product and the customer for the product, rather than their function or department.

▲ *Empowerment.* Everyone is expected to accept and exercise the responsibility necessary to do their jobs and help others accomplish theirs. Providing opportunities to be responsible empowers people—the opposite of limiting roles and contributions. No one feels free to say, "It's not my job."

▲ *Integration of people and technology.* People are in charge of the technology, instead of the technology being in charge of the people.

▲ *A shared sense of purpose.* People in the work culture share a vision of the organization's purpose and the methods for accomplishing this purpose.[27]

An assumption underlying the HP–HC work system is that superior technology, efficient task design, matching organizational designs and processes, good planning, and the like are necessary—but not sufficient—for high performance. Individuals and teams must be *committed* to make the technology, task design, structure, and strategy work. The HP–HC work system is designed to manage human, technological, and financial resources efficiently and to more fully engage the talents and capacities of employees.

▼ TASK- AND TECHNOLOGY-FOCUSED APPROACHES

The task-focused approach to change emphasizes making changes in the work of employees, groups, and teams. The technology-focused approach concentrates on the technological processes and tools used to perform the work. We examine five approaches to organizational change that focus (at least initially) on task and technology: job design, sociotechnical systems, quality circles, reengineering, and total quality management. Two of these—job design and sociotechnical systems—have been explored in Chapter 16. We note them again here, because they also represent major approaches to changing organizations.

Table 20.4 shows the primary focus of the change approaches discussed in this section along with the relative impact of each on the six major system variables. As you might expect, the five approaches have a relatively high impact on the task and technology variables.

▼ Job Design

As a change approach, **job design** represents a deliberate, planned restructuring of the way work is performed in order to increase employee motivation, involvement, and efficiency—and ultimately to improve performance. Recall that job design encompasses a group of specific organizational change techniques, including job engineering, job rotation, job enlargement, job enrichment, and the redesign of core task characteristics (see Chapter 16).

Each technique is an effective approach to organizational change under certain conditions. All can positively affect task performance, absenteeism, turnover, and job satisfaction. However, managers sometimes use specific job design approaches inappropriately. For example, job enrichment programs may fail if managers wrongly assume that all employees want enriched work and do not allow for differences in employee needs and values. Job design techniques perhaps are most successful in the context of a comprehensive organizational change program that examines the complex fit among the tasks

TABLE 20.4   Comparison of Relative Direct Impact of Task- and Technology-Focused Approaches on System Variables

Change Approach	Relative Direct Impact on System Variables					
	People	*Culture*	*Task*	*Technology*	*Design*	*Strategy*
Job design	Low to high	Low to moderate	High	Low to high	Low	Low
Sociotechnical systems	High	High	Moderate to high	High	Low to moderate	Low to moderate
Quality circles	Low to moderate	Low	Moderate to high	Low to high	Low	Low
Reengineering	Moderate to high	Moderate to high	High	High	Low to high	Low to high
Total quality management	Moderate to high	Moderate to high	High	High	Low to high	Low to high

to be performed, the types of technology used, the design and culture of the organization or team, and the nature and characteristics of the people doing the work.[28] Studies have shown improvements in the quality of work life and performance and reduced turnover and conflict in organizations that have involved employees in redesigning their own jobs.[29]

▼ Sociotechnical Systems

The **sociotechnical systems** (STS) approach simultaneously focuses on changing both the technical and social aspects of the organization to optimize their relationship and thus increase organizational effectiveness.[30] The STS approach regards the organization as more than just a technical system for making products and providing services. Ultimately, the organization is a collection of human beings—a social system. Changes made in the technical system affect the social fabric of the organization. Thus managing organizational change effectively means dealing with both the social and technical aspects of that change.

Sociotechnical approaches to organizational change usually incorporate a major redesign of the way work is done (the task variable), in addition to emphasizing technological and social issues (the technology and people variables). We described the sociotechnical systems approach to job design in detail in Chapter 16.

We have discussed self-managed teams throughout the book. From the perspective of organizational change, the idea of autonomous, or self-managed, work groups is a major contribution of sociotechnical systems theory. **Autonomous groups** or **self-managed teams** are work groups that plan their work, control its pace and quality, and make many of the decisions traditionally reserved to management.[31] A self-managed team may determine its own job assignments, work schedules, and even the quantity and quality of its output. The STS approach involves redesigning work groups to give them as much control as possible over virtually all the resources and skills needed to manufacture a specific product or deliver a specific service to a customer. The role of management in STS is to ensure that teams have sufficient resources to accomplish their tasks.

Sociotechnical approaches have been used extensively to design, build, and manage new plants. The high-involvement plants described earlier in the chapter, as well as high-performance–high-commitment work systems, typically incorporate many aspects of the STS approach to change.

▼ Quality Circles

Quality circles are work groups, generally containing less than a dozen volunteers from the same work area, who meet regularly to monitor and solve job-related quality and/or production problems. Quality circles also may be utilized to improve working conditions, increase the level of employee involvement and commitment, and encourage employee self-development. In these instances, they frequently are an important component of QWL programs. Adapted initially from Japanese quality-control practices, their use spread rapidly in the United States. The activities and focus of quality circles has been described as follows:

The [quality circle] members receive training in problem solving, statistical quality control, and group process. Quality circles generally recommend solutions for quality and productivity problems which management then may implement. A facilitator, usually a specially trained member of management, helps train circle members and ensures that things run smoothly. Typical objectives of QC programs include quality improvement, productivity enhancement, and employee involvement. Circles generally meet four hours a month on company time. Members may get recognition but rarely receive financial rewards.[32]

Table 20.5 contains examples of the problem-solving tools typically used by quality circles.

Quality circles typically have a narrower focus than many of the other change techniques described. They also differ from other approaches in that management retains more control over the activities of the employees than is possible, or desirable, in most of the other approaches. Although the effects of quality circles often are not carefully evaluated, some comparisons of expected to actual outcomes have been made.[33] So far, the results seem to be mixed.

Productivity and quality gains—sometimes substantial—have been reported. For example, at Stanley Works, a New England manufacturer of tools and hardware, quality circles contributed to reducing the scrap rate from 15% to 3%.[34] As integral parts of comprehensive QWL programs, quality circles have fostered greater employee involvement in decision making and other aspects of work.[35]

However, a number of failures also have been reported. Although quality circles may make a contribution relatively quickly, sustaining an initial success over a period of time requires considerable energy and creating new challenges to maintain employee interest. Quality circles may not fit well into an organization's culture and are not likely to move the organization toward a highly participative culture if other changes are not made at the same time. Quality circles appear to cope successfully with only a limited range of problems; accurate diagnosis is essential to ensure that the problems facing the organization can be best addressed by this approach. Although quality circles

TABLE 20.5   Quality Circle Problem-Solving Tools

Tool	Description
Histograms	Presentation of quality data (e.g., defect rates) in histogram form
Graphs	Pie charts, line graphs, and the like
Check sheets	Basic data recording sheets for classifying events
Cause-and-effect diagrams	"Fishbone" diagrams that show how problems are related to four causal agencies: methods, manpower, machines, and materials
Control charts	Displays the variation in a process over time

Source: Adapted from Steel, R. P., and Jennings, K. R. Quality improvement technologies for the 90s: New directions for research and theory. In W. A. Pasmore and R. W. Woodman (eds.), *Research in Organizational Change and Development*, vol. 6. Greenwich, Conn.: JAI Press, 1992, 5.

have both succeeded and failed in North America, they have continued to thrive in Japan, as the following Managing Across Cultures feature describes.

MANAGING ACROSS CULTURES

Quality Circles in Japan

Quality circles were among the first Japanese management practices used in the U.S. When visiting Japan in the 1970s, American managers noticed groups of workers meeting to address quality problems. The managers recognized this as a practice that could easily be copied and they returned home to institute it in their own companies. Quality circles took off in the U.S. as the Japanese management mania peaked, and firms like Lockheed and Westinghouse reported early successes. The quality circle movement really boomed in the early 1980s, as most large American companies introduced the practice.

The bloom was soon off the rose, however, as firms found themselves devoting a lot of time and attention to quality circles and receiving relatively little in return. There were a number of reasons for the lack of results. Employees were only encouraged to work on quality problems during their meetings (usually about an hour a week) and spent the rest of their week just "doing their jobs." Supervisors were often not involved in the program and were indifferent, if not downright hostile, to it. Perhaps the biggest problem was that quality circles were "just a program," cut off from and often opposed to the way the organization usually worked.

Not surprisingly, companies started to disband their quality circle programs, which were soon dismissed as just another passing fad. In the context of the current interest in total quality management, many managers look back on quality circles as essentially a false start on the road to quality. It is interesting in this light to note that many Japanese companies still operate quality circles and that they are seen as a critical part of the total quality effort in these companies. According to the Japanese Union of Scientists and Engineers, 5.5 million workers take part in 750,000 quality circles. Managers as well as employees are involved, and the circles are considered a normal part of working life, rather than a "program."[36]

▼ Reengineering

Reengineering is another term that has appeared frequently throughout the book. We revisit this concept in the context of organizational change because it represents a major change approach currently popular with organizations. **Reengineering,** sometimes called process redesign, is a fundamental rethinking and radical redesign of business processes to reduce costs and improve quality, service, and speed.[37] Reengineering represents a more radical approach to change than do most of the other methods discussed. During reengineering, the most fundamental ideas and assumptions of the organization are challenged. Recall that reengineering begins with no assumptions and asks fundamental questions such as: Why does the organization do what it does? Why does it do it the way that it does?

Reengineering is compatible with organizational diagnosis (see Chapter 19). There, we suggested that every organization has "rice puddings"—procedures and practices that made sense at one time but no longer are effective. As with a valid diagnosis, reengineering aims to ferret out the "rice puddings" and do away with them. At GE, chairman Jack Welch compared his company to a 100-year-old attic that collected a lot of useless junk over the years. Welch views reengineering as the process of cleaning all the junk out of the attic. GE calls its reengineering, or process redesign, activities "workout."[38]

When an organization reengineers its business processes, the following changes typically occur.

▲ Work units change from functional departments to process teams.

▲ Individual jobs change from simple to multidimensional tasks.

▲ People's roles change from being controlled to being empowered to make decisions.

▲ Performance appraisal changes from measuring activities (attending meetings, arriving at work on time) to measuring results (customer satisfaction, costs, performance).

▲ Managers change from supervisors to coaches.

▲ Organization designs change from tall to flat hierarchies.[39]

Reengineering thus shares many of the objectives of other change approaches. Despite these similarities, reengineering programs (if they truly are reengineering) represent a dramatic and revolutionary, rather than evolutionary or gradually transformational, approach to organizational change.

▼ Total Quality Management

Total quality management (TQM) focuses on meeting or exceeding customer expectations. Quality ultimately is defined by the customer. When an organization achieves "total quality," all activities and processes are designed and carried out to meet all customer requirements while reducing both the time and cost required to provide them.[40] Table 20.6 shows the important elements of TQM.

Note that TQM is partly technical. Just-in-time (JIT) inventory systems, for example, frequently are utilized by TQM organizations. TQM is partly cultural—the shared values must emphasize quality, and employees must be empowered to carry out needed changes. The concept of **continuous improvement** is central to TQM. One-time programs or "quick-fix" solutions for productivity or quality problems are unacceptable.

A focus on quality and continuous improvement is crucial to competing effectively in the global economy. The U.S. government created the Malcolm Baldrige National Quality Award to honor organizations that attain "world-class" quality in their products, services, and operations. (The award is named after a Reagan administration secretary of commerce who was killed in a 1987 accident.)

The examiners and judges look for accomplishments in eight principal areas by organizations competing for the Baldrige award. These areas also provide insight into the key components of TQM.

▲ A plan to keep improving all operations continuously.

TABLE 20.6   Elements of Total Quality Management

Element	Definition
Changing the corporate culture	All employees assume responsibility for quality
Top management commitment	Active quality leadership by top management
Training	Employee training in quality analysis tools
Continuous process improvement	Expand understanding of business processes and focus on their continuous improvement
Employee empowerment	Empowerment of employees to take action when quality problems are detected
Supplier relationship management	Proactive supplier relations and prequalifying sources of supply
Cross functional problem solving	Cross-functional teams analyzing and solving cross-functional quality problems
Customer relationship management	Continuing focus on internal and external customer preferences

Source: Adapted from Steel, R. P., and Jennings, K. R. Quality improvement technologies for the 90s: New directions for research and theory. In W. A. Pasmore and R. W. Woodman (eds.), *Research in Organizational Change and Development*, vol. 6. Greenwich, Conn.: JAI Press, 1992, 19.

▲ A system for measuring these improvements accurately.

▲ A strategic plan based on benchmarks that compare the company's performance with the world's best.

▲ A close partnership with suppliers and customers that feeds improvements back into the operation.

▲ A deep understanding of the customers so that their wants can be translated into products or services.

▲ A long-lasting relationship with customers, going beyond the delivery of the product to include sales, service, and ease of maintenance.

▲ A focus on preventing mistakes, rather than merely correcting them.

▲ A commitment to improving quality that runs from the top of the organization to the bottom.[41]

Recent winners of the Baldrige Award include Motorola, Westinghouse, Xerox, the Cadillac Division of General Motors, Texas Instruments, Federal Express, The Ritz-Carlton Hotel Company, and AT&T Universal Card Services.[42] Motorola provides a good example of the payoff from emphasizing quality. The company is the market leader in cellular phones, pagers, two-way radios and some types of microprocessors. It is beating Japanese rivals by manufacturing consumer electronics with better quality at lower prices. Part of its strategy is a TQM program that produced a Baldrige award and, more important, has reduced its defect rate in manufacturing by an astounding 99%. This reduction in defects, in turn, generated savings currently running about $900 million a year.[43] The following Managing Quality feature examines AT&T Universal Card Services, another Baldrige winner.

MANAGING QUALITY

Quality at AT&T Universal Card Services

AT&T Universal Card Services (UCS), a 1992 winner of the Malcolm Baldrige National Quality Award, has had the luxury of building an organization based on quality and empowerment from the ground up. Launched in March 1990, the Universal Card is the second-biggest credit card in the industry and is still growing.

More than 100 quality measurements are taken daily from various portions of the business. These measurements are displayed on TV monitors and walls all over the company. They are also followed closely by UCS employees, who get a bonus equal to 12 percent of their daily salary for every day UCS meets its quality targets. On average, employees earn about $2,200 a year from these bonuses.

UCS employees can take advantage of numerous training opportunities, ranging from traditional classes to computer-based instruction. Hourly employees undergo about 84 hours of training per year beyond the 8-week orientation for new customer-service employees.

With this level of training and motivation for quality as a backdrop, UCS phone associates are empowered to do whatever is necessary when cardmembers call for help, regardless of company rules. One time an associate received a collect call from a tourist in Paris who had become stranded when his card had been "eaten by the automatic teller machine" on a Saturday afternoon. The cardmember was desperate, as he was scheduled to leave the next day and was broke. While the cardmember stayed on the line, the associate contacted the American embassy in Paris and arranged for a limo to take the traveler to the only bank still open in the city, where the associate had authorized an emergency cash advance. It is in situations such as these that motivation, training, and empowerment come together to produce customer satisfaction, if not outright "delight."[44]

▼ DESIGN- AND STRATEGY-FOCUSED APPROACHES

Organizationwide change programs frequently are aimed at changing organization design and strategy, as well as culture. Design-focused approaches to change involve redefining positions or roles and relationships among positions and redesigning department, division, and/or organization structure. Strategy-focused approaches involve a reexamination of the organization's basic mission or goals and the specific plans or strategies for attaining those goals. Table 20.7 compares the relative impacts of organizational change approaches focusing on adaptive organization designs and strategic change.

▼ Adaptive Organization Designs

As organizations grow increasingly complex, and face the challenge of managing constant change, they often need new ways of organizing their activities. They particularly need more flexibility and adaptive capabilities than the traditional mechanistic system, with its rigid hierarchy and standardized procedures, allows. Here, we explore three forms of organizational design that characterize flexible, adaptive organizations: collateral organization, matrix or-

TABLE 20.7   Comparison of Relative Direct Impact of Design- and Strategy-Focused Approaches on System Variables

Change Approach	Relative Direct Impact on System Variables					
	People	*Culture*	*Task*	*Technology*	*Design*	*Strategy*
Adaptive designs	High	Moderate to high	Low to moderate	Low to moderate	High	Low to high
Strategic change	Low to high	Low to high	Low to high	Low to high	High	High

ganization, and network organization. First, let's explore the general concept of **adaptive organizations** as presented in the following Managing in Practice piece.

MANAGING IN PRACTICE

The Adaptive Organization

The adaptive organization is still more dream than reality, but organizations such as Apple Computer, Cypress Semiconductor, Levi Strauss, and Xerox are experimenting with new organizational arrangements designed to unleash employee creativity and make their organizations more competitive. Paul Allaire, CEO of Xerox, states: "We're never going to out-discipline the Japanese on quality. To win, we need to find ways to capture the creative and innovative spirit of the American worker. That's the real organizational challenge."

One objective of the new, adaptive organization is to eliminate the traditional, bureaucratic organization chart in favor of ever-changing networks of teams, projects, alliances, and coalitions. In the adaptive organization, employees will rely less on guidance from their manager. Individuals will continuously examine the work process and be charged with the responsibility to improve it, even if this means going outside the boundaries of their regular job. For example, at Xerox, a team of employees from accounting, administration, distribution, and sales developed a system that saves the company $200 million a year in inventory costs.

Much of the "structure" of the adaptive organization will be temporary, flexible, and determined more by what needs to be done than by traditional boundaries between functions, products, and levels of the hierarchy. Raymond Gilmartin, CEO of Becton Dickinson, a producer of high-technology medical equipment, says: "Forget structures invented by guys at the top. You've got to let the task form the organization."

All the designs for an adaptive organization have one thing in common—flexibility. A scientist or marketing expert who has the knowledge and experience to be the leader on one project may turn around and be a follower on the next project. The adaptive organization will work like global construction firms (such as Bechtel or Brown & Root). These firms carefully gather selected groups of employees and outside contractors with the right skills for each new airport, dam, or refinery.[45]

A related concept is that of the **virtual corporation,** defined as a temporary network of independent companies linked by information technology to share skills, costs, and access to customers. Companies unite temporarily to exploit some specific opportunity. Both adaptive organizations and virtual corporations—networks of adaptive organizations—demand new managerial skills. Managers will have to build relationships, negotiate win–win deals, be able to find competent venture partners, and provide the temporary organization with a balance of freedom and control.[46]

Collateral Organization   A **collateral organization** is a parallel, coexisting organization that can be used to supplement an existing formal organization.[47] The collateral, or parallel, organization utilizes groups of people outside normal communication and authority channels to identify and solve difficult problems that the formal organization may be unwilling or unable to solve. A collateral organization has norms—ways of working together, making decisions, and solving problems—that are different from those of the rest of the organization. However, the collateral organization requires no new people, is carefully linked to the formal organization, and coexists with it. Collateral organizations have the following characteristics.

▲ All communication channels are open and connected. Managers and employees freely communicate without being restricted to the formal channels of the organizational hierarchy.

▲ There is a rapid and complete exchange of relevant information on problems and issues. The outputs of the collateral structure are ideas, solutions to problems, and innovation.

▲ The norms in use encourage careful questioning and analysis of goals, assumptions, methods, alternatives, and criteria for evaluation.

▲ Managers can approach and enlist others in the organization to help solve a problem; they are not restricted to their formal subordinates.

▲ Mechanisms are developed to link the collateral and formal organization.[48]

Collateral organization designs have been used successfully by automobile manufacturers, banks, high-tech firms, hospitals, research and development laboratories, universities, and other organizations. The fire department of Bryan, Texas, is using a collateral structure successfully to provide effective communication and coordination across shifts. The fire department also provides emergency medical services to the community and found that an adaptive organization design was needed to identify and solve problems that were interfering with the provision of efficient fire and emergency services 24 hours a day.

Collateral organizations seem appealing, but benefits from this approach are not yet well documented. Perhaps a major advantage of the collateral form of organization is that it gives managers a way to match problems with organizational structures best suited to solve them. For example, the formal organization may best deal with routine production problems, whereas poorly structured or defined problems may best be handled by problem-solving groups operating outside the formal structure.

Some results suggest that the real advantages of collateral organizations may be other than in problem solving. Collateral organizations create more complex roles for employees. Employees interact with different people than they would in a group restricted to the formal hierarchy, and they interact with them in different ways—that is, the norms have been changed. These complex roles may provide opportunities for individuals to be involved, engage in meaningful work, have control over their jobs, and gain satisfaction from their work. In addition, collateral organizations may be particularly good at developing managerial skills, coping with crises requiring decentralized decision making, and fostering organizational innovation.[49]

Matrix Organization Many organizations have turned to a matrix design to address the limitations of mechanistic or bureaucratic structures. Recall that a **matrix organization** represents a balance between organizing resources according to products or functions.

A mutually beneficial relationship often exists between the matrix form of organization and the capacity to change. For example, many features of OD programs, such as an emphasis on collaborative behavior and the effective use of teams, also are important for implementing a matrix structure with its decentralized decision making and extensive use of temporary task forces and teams. In general, the matrix form helps to create a culture receptive to organizational improvement efforts.

Changing an organization to a matrix form is never easy. Often, managers need a people-focused change strategy to facilitate the transition. For example, team building has helped organizations introduce matrix designs successfully. One senior executive put it this way: "The challenge is not so much to build a matrix structure as it is to create a matrix in the minds of our managers."[50]

The matrix design is appealing because of its flexibility and adaptability. It may be superior to other organizational forms when an organization uses complex technology, faces rapidly changing market conditions, and needs a high degree of cooperation among projects and functions. However, a matrix design is costly to implement and maintain and can be extremely difficult to manage effectively.

Network Organization The **network organization** as described in Chapter 17, is a complex mosaic of lateral communication, decision-making, and control processes. Although a network organization might have an organization chart showing the typical hierarchical authority and communication relationships, this chart cannot begin to describe the reality of this complex organizational form. Figure 20.4 shows three basic types of network organizations.

The components business of General Motors represents an internal network. Corporate headquarters serves a "brokerage function" that coordinates eight components divisions' activities. The separate divisions each sell some of their products on the open market. The Bavarian Motor Works is a stable network. Every part of the BMW automobile is a candidate for outsourcing and somewhere between 55% and 75% of the total cost of the car is in outside parts. Lewis Galoob Toys operates as a dynamic network. It has only about 100 permanent employees to run the core business. Most of its products are invented, designed, and engineered outside the firm. Galoob also contracts for manufacturing and packaging with other organizations. Galoob operates as a "broker," coordinating the activities of independent specialty firms.[51]

Network organizations share some features with both matrix and collateral organizations, yet place more emphasis on sophisticated information technol-

FIGURE 20.4

Examples of Network Designs

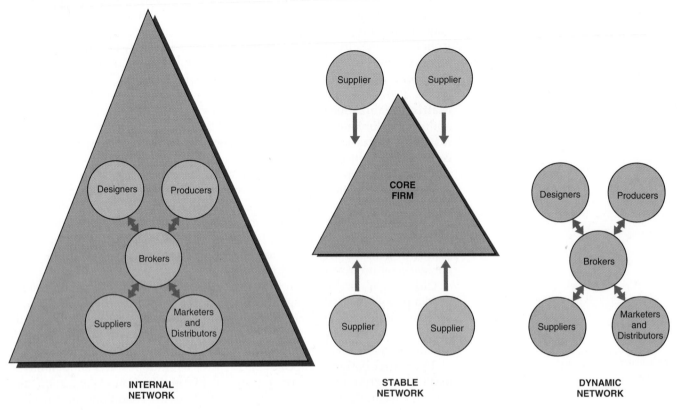

ogies to coordinate activities and perform work. Managers in a network organization function much like switchboard operators in terms of coordination and control. They can pull together temporary teams of employees to bring expertise to bear on projects and concerns as needed. The collaborative behaviors and attitudes characterizing the network organization are similar to those typical of the high-performance–high-commitment work system described earlier. Many adaptive organizations are using some version of network designs, especially global organizations that need this flexibility to function effectively in the international arena.

▼ Strategic Change

Issues of strategic change need to be addressed in comprehensive organizational change programs. At its most basic level, a strategy is a *plan*—an intended course of action to attain organizational goals. **Strategic change** is planned organizational change designed to alter the organization's intended courses of action to attain its goals. Strategic change may include assessment and redefinition of the goals themselves.

A good example of a strategic change program is provided by the process of open systems planning. **Open systems planning** is designed to help an organization systematically assess its environment and develop a strategic response to it. It consists of the following steps.

▲ Assess the external environment in terms of its expectations and demands on the organization's behavior.

▲ Assess the organization's current response to these environmental demands.

▲ Identify the organization's core mission.

▲ Create a realistic scenario of future environmental demands and organizational responses.

▲ Create an ideal scenario of future environmental demands and organizational responses.

▲ Compare the present with the ideal future and prepare an action plan for reducing the discrepancy.[52]

Central to many approaches to strategic change, including open systems planning, is the concept of visioning. In general, **visioning** refers to choosing a desired future state or condition for the organization. Visioning includes identifying and articulating for organizational members the central or core mission and goals of the system and specifying, at least broadly, how the goals or future state is to be attained. In Chapter 11, we discussed visioning as a crucial component of leadership; it also is a crucial aspect of most approaches to strategic organizational change. BankAmerica Corporation made one of the most dramatic turnarounds in U.S. banking history, after sustaining almost $2 billion in losses, in large part by adopting a new strategic vision when the old one no longer worked. Had BankAmerica attempted minor, piecemeal changes, rather than a comprehensive organizationwide change in strategy, culture, and design, the firm probably would not have survived as an independent organization.[53]

▼ ETHICAL ISSUES IN ORGANIZATIONAL CHANGE

Serious ethical issues may arise in any organizational change program, no matter how carefully thought out and managed it might be. Managers and employees need to be aware of potential ethical issues in four main areas: change approach selection, change target selection, managerial responsibilities, and manipulation.[54] The following Managing Ethics feature describes the experience of one consultant who came to realize the ethical implications of organizational change. Changes affect people and their jobs, and change agents need to be acutely aware of this fact.

MANAGING ETHICS

The Tyranny of Change

Some time ago I had occasion to visit a large and successful organization for which I had recently completed some consulting work. I entered the building at three o'clock on a rainy Friday afternoon. As I walked through the marketing department, I was struck by the sense of emptiness and quiet which pervaded the place. Lights were turned off, chairs were unoccupied, corridors were empty, and desk-tops were conspicuously neat. I looked into five offices and found them all vacant. Finally, I encountered one of the upper middle managers. I asked her where everyone was and she replied that they were all

MANAGING ETHICS —*Continued*

out playing football. Football? In a company which has no team and does not actively promote outside group activities? On a rainy day? During a busy time? My blank look prompted a further explanation:

"Things got so bad around here that people thought a game might help dispel some of the gloom. So Marketing is out playing Finance. . . . We are being reorganized. . . . We are expecting some kind of big announcement about all the changes the middle of next week. Everyone is worried or scared. You know, initially this big change thing, this organization development effort, seemed kind of exciting. But now it's real old. And I'm so tired of it."[55]

When choosing the change approach or combination of approaches deemed best for the situation, managers and employees should recognize the ethical issues involved in selecting the criteria to be used. Does the manager or change agent have a vested interest in using a particular technique so that other alternatives might not receive a fair hearing? Do individuals involved in the organizational diagnosis have biases that might predetermine the problems identified and thus influence the change approach chosen?

Selection of the change target raises ethical concerns about participation in the change program. What is to be the target of change? Which individuals, teams, or departments of the organization will the change effort focus on? Which members of the organization participate in diagnosing, planning, and implementing the change and to what degree? Who will make this determination? Issues of power and political behavior raise serious ethical concerns when managers attempt to make inappropriate changes or choices concerning what is to be changed that overstep the boundaries of their legitimate roles. To what extent can managers make choices about changing the behaviors of employees, and where should the line be drawn in this regard?

A major ethical concern in the area of managerial responsibility involves whose goals and values are to guide the change effort. Organizational change is never value neutral. The value systems of managers and employees always underlie assumptions about what the organization should be doing. Ethical concerns arise if managers involved in the change process fail to recognize the potential problems associated with incompatible goals and values held by organizational members. Whose vision guides the change? Whose values influence the adoption of goals and methods chosen to accomplish them?

Finally, manipulation also raises the question of power in the change process. Making changes in organizations without some employees feeling manipulated in some way is difficult. Often the organization needs to make changes that do, in fact, result in some individuals or groups being worse off after the change than they were before. Ethical issues concern the degree of openness surrounding planned changes. To what extent should the organization disclose all aspects of the change in advance? To what degree do employees have the right to participate in, or at least be aware of, changes that affect them, even indirectly?

These questions are not easily addressed. Hence managers and employees need some basis for recognizing the potential ethical concerns involved in organizational change, so that fair and informed choices can be made. As a starting point, organizations need to be sensitive to the probability that ethical problems will emerge during planned change programs.

Summary

Managers and employees must understand the likely effects of various change approaches and carefully match change programs with the problems they are intended to solve.

When the initial focus of the change effort is on people, managers might choose to use survey feedback, team building, process consultation, or quality-of-work-life programs. Comprehensive change often means that the culture of the organization must be considered. Although cultural change is difficult, the probability of success can be increased by careful attention to some key issues. Creating a high-performance–high-commitment work system often is the goal of cultural change efforts.

When the initial focus is on task or technology, managers typically utilize job design, sociotechnical systems, quality circles, reengineering, or total quality management. The last two may involve significant changes in organizational culture. Design-focused approaches to change might include creating more adaptive organizational structures, such as collateral, matrix, or network designs. Strategic change often is the focus of organizationwide change efforts. Open systems planning is one method of strategic change.

No approach to organizational change is likely to be successful unless it addresses several, if not all, of the people, culture, task, technology, design, and strategy variables. Comprehensive organizational change programs, regardless of their initial focus, often make simultaneous changes in several aspects of the organization. In practice, the approaches presented in this chapter are commonly used in combination to manage organizational change.

Managers and employees need to be aware of and knowledgeable about potential ethical issues that can arise during organizational change. Ethical issues may emerge during selection of the change approach, selection of the change targets, managerial responsibilities for the goals selected, and potential manipulation of employees.

Key Words and Concepts

Adaptive organizations
Alternative work schedule
Autonomous groups
Collateral organization
Continuous improvement
Flextime
High-performance–high-
    commitment (HP–HC)
    work system

Job design
Matrix organization
Network organization
Open systems planning
Process consultation
Quality circles
Quality-of-work-life (QWL)
    programs
Reengineering

Self-managed teams
Sociotechnical systems
Strategic change
Survey feedback
Team building
Total quality management
Virtual corporation
Visioning

Discussion Questions

1. Describe an ideal "adaptive organization" and then describe an organization with which you are familiar. Compare the two descriptions and suggest how the real organization could become more like your ideal of an adaptive organization.

2. Can employees always have a high level of participation in organizational change programs? Why or why not?

3. Write a brief summary description of each of the five people- and culture-focused change approaches presented in this chapter.

4. Write a brief summary description of each of the five task- and technology-focused change approaches presented in this chapter.

5. What are the similarities and differences between survey feedback and team building?

6. Compare and contrast quality-of-work-life programs and high-performance–high-commitment work systems.

7. Explain why both HP-HC work systems and total quality management may require significant changes in organizational culture to be effective.

8. Compare and contrast reengineering and TQM.

9. Based on your own experiences, describe an organization, group, or team that needed change. Which of the change approaches presented would you use? Why?

 ## Developing Skills

Self-Diagnosis: Attitudes Toward Change

Instructions

Use this questionnaire to assess your own attitudes toward change. As you answer the questions, think of your current job or a job you used to have. Respond to the questions using the following scale.

Strongly Disagree	Disagree	Slightly Disagree	Neither Agree nor Disagree	Somewhat Agree	Agree	Strongly Agree
1	2	3	4	5	6	7

_____ 1. I look forward to changes at work.

_____ 2. I usually resist new ideas.

_____ 3. Most employees benefit from change.

_____ 4. I dislike change because management usually fails to support it.

_____ 5. Change usually benefits the organization.

_____ 6. Most changes are bad ideas.

_____ 7. Change is necessary.

_____ 8. I tend to use my power to resist change.

_____ 9. I often suggest new approaches to things.

_____ 10. I often feel less secure after changes in my job.

_____ 11. Change usually helps improve unsatisfactory situations at work.

_____ 12. I will go along with a change only when everyone else does.

_____ 13. I try to stay aware of new ideas in areas related to my job.

_____ 14. Change usually reduces my ability to control what goes on at work.

Scoring

Add the responses to questions 1 ____, 3 ____, 5 ____, 7 ____, 9 ____, 11 ____, 13 ____ Total ____

Reverse the scores on questions 2, 4, 6, 8, 10, 12, and 14 (1 = 7, 2 = 6, 3 = 5, 4 = 4, 5 = 3, 6 = 2, 7 = 1). Now add these together: 2 ____, 4 ____, 6 ____, 8 ____, 10 ____, 12 ____, 14 ____ Total ____

Now add the two totals. TOTAL SCORE ____

Interpretation

Scores can range from 14 to 98. Scores from 70 to 98 indicate very positive attitudes toward change at work. Scores of 42 or below suggest relatively negative attitudes toward change. Scores from 43 to 69 suggest that you are somewhat ambivalent toward change.[56]

A Case In Point: Understanding Quality Systems—The Westinghouse Corporation

During the 1970s, the Westinghouse Defense and Electronics Group anticipated significant growth in its electronic defense business. To satisfy this growth requirement, a new satellite facility was built in College Station, Texas. The facility was named Westinghouse Electronic Assembly Plant (EAP) and was developed in response to a growing market in high-technology wiring assemblies. In addition, the plant was designed to provide a competitive advantage for Westinghouse Corporation by having a "factory of the future" in its assembly-plant system. The plant design team created a state-of-the-art assembly system that included modern management practices, advanced information systems, and the latest in engineering technologies. Due to the anticipated growth and competition in the electronics defense business, EAP would be required to handle a broad range of product lines, small lot sizes, a high rate of change in product design, and ever-increasing quality requirements.

In 1983, the 186,000-square-foot Westinghouse Electronic Assembly Plant opened its doors and began producing printed wiring assemblies. These "circuit board" assemblies are part of a larger component that the parent plant, Westinghouse-Baltimore, supplies to external customers for use in land-based and airborne radar systems. EAP employs more than five hundred people—approximately four hundred technicians, sixty professionals, and forty managers.

By industry standards, the plant's start up was relatively smooth. The investments in the latest equipment and team-concept management technologies seemed to be paying off as the learning curve and adjustment period leveled off. It was not too long before the plant seemed to operate in a rather efficient and productive manner.

As with any organization, change was inevitable. In the latter part of 1984, the U.S. government clamped down on all defense contractors. New compliance procedures were established for all military suppliers. A major competitor of the Westinghouse Defense and Electronic Group was shut down after the government completed its internal audit of its facilities and found major problems with the product- and process-quality systems of its suppliers. An inability to change internal quality systems was threatening the very survival of defense contractors.

Although EAP was producing "good" quality (roughly 90 percent meeting standards on the first time through), the new compliance procedures required substantial changes and improvements in work processes and procedures. In March 1985, the EAP management team asked each member to answer the question, "If you owned this business, how would you fix it?" Using the ideas of the management team, a committee was formed under the direction of Keith Hudspeth, then product line manager, to develop a plan of action for solving the quality problem at EAP.

Hudspeth and his team started their investigation by reevaluating the production process in the plant. A few key questions were formulated to guide this evaluation: (1) How do we change our system to comply with our new customer requirements? (2) What information are our work teams currently using to manage their processes? and (3) Are we, management, managing the proper business processes?

After some lengthy discussions with nonexempt technicians, first-line supervisors, and other management team members, some answers were developed to these questions. First, in order to change the system to comply with the new customer requirements, technicians must know what the new requirements are and how important they are to survival. Management must create an awareness of the problem with all employees. Second, the supervisors keep track of a variety of information concerning work team performance. Supervisors need to have the technicians involved and measuring the critical information of the business. The plant must get "back to the basics" in measuring performance. Finally, because the plant was so new, there was a tendency to continue with the same "close supervision" management style used for a start-up operation. Management has to realize that the plant is in full operation and to let the employees begin to manage the daily operations of the business.

With these issues on the table, Hudspeth's committee established three task teams consisting of a cross-section of managers, engineers, and technicians who were given the responsibility to propose a plan of attack for EAP. From all the information that Hudspeth and his team had previously gathered in their production system analysis, the issues for the new task teams were formalized:

1. A need existed for a system to allow EAP to relay the vision and goals of the customer requirements to all employees.

2. A need existed for a system to change the current internal measures and allow EAP employees to measure the important aspects of the business from the customer's viewpoint.

3. The plant needed a system that would allow employees to assume responsibility for their own destiny, and EAP must reward and recognize employee efforts in this direction.

Each task team was given an issue and was asked to report back to the committee with their ideas. This input would be incorporated into a total plan to resolve EAP's pressing concerns.[57]

Questions

1. List the ideas and concepts from this chapter that appear, in one form or another, in this case.

2. Assume that you are part of the Westinghouse team responsible for developing a comprehensive plan to resolve these issues. Ask yourself, "If I owned this business, how would I fix it?" Explain and defend your plan.

References

1. Adapted from a story posted on a computer bulletin board and reprinted on Internet. Author unknown.

2. Huber, G. P., and Glick, W. H. (eds.), *Organizational Change and Redesign*. New York: Oxford University Press, 1993; Kochan, T.

A., and Useem, M. (eds.), *Transforming Organizations*. New York: Oxford University Press, 1992; Kanter, R. M., Stein, B. A., and Jick, T. D. *The Challenge of Organizational Change*. New York: Free Press, 1992.

3. *High Performance Work Practices and Firm Performance*. Washington, D.C.: U.S. Department of Labor, 1993.

4. These descriptions were drawn primarily from Lawler, E. E. The new plant revolution revisited. *Organizational Dynamics*, Autumn 1990, 5–14; Also see Lawler, E. E. *High-Involvement Management*. San Francisco: Jossey-Bass, 1986; Weisbord, M. R. *Productive Workplaces: Organizing and Managing for Dignity, Meaning, and Community*. San Francisco: Jossey-Bass, 1987; Woodman, R. W. Organizational change and development: New arenas for inquiry and action. *Journal of Management*, 1989, 15, 205–228.

5. Woodman, R. W. Change methods. In N. Nicholson (ed.), *The Blackwell Dictionary of Organizational Behavior*. Oxford: Blackwell (in press).

6. Macy, B. A., and Izumi, H. Organizational change, design, and work innovation: A meta-analysis of 131 North American field studies—1961–1991. In R. W. Woodman and W. A. Pasmore (eds.), *Research in Organizational Change and Development*, vol. 7. Greenwich, Conn.: JAI Press, 1993, 235–313; Robertson, P. J., Roberts, D. R., and Porras, J. I. An evaluation of a model of planned organizational change: Evidence from a meta-analysis. In R. W. Woodman and W. A. Pasmore (eds.), *Research in Organizational Change and Development*, vol. 7. Greenwich, Conn.: JAI Press, 1993, 1–39; Robertson, P. J., Roberts, D. R., and Porras, J. I. Dynamics of planned organizational change: Assessing empirical support for a theoretical model. *Academy of Management Journal*, 1993, 36, 619–634.

7. For descriptions of survey feedback and its effects, see Cummings, T. G., and Worley, C. G. *Organization Development and Change*, 5th ed. St. Paul, Minn.: West, 1993, 136–142; French, W. L., and Bell, C. H. *Organization Development: Behavioral Science Interventions for Organization Improvement*, 4th ed. Englewood Cliffs, N.J.: Prentice-Hall, 1990, 169–172.

8. Hirschhorn, L. *Managing in the New Team Environment*. Reading, Mass.: Addison-Wesley, 1991; Johansen, R., Sibbet, D., Benson, S., Martin, A., Mittman, R., and Saffo, P. *Leading Business Teams*. Reading, Mass.: Addison-Wesley, 1991; Katzenbach, J. R., and Smith, D. K. *The Wisdom of Teams: Creating the High-Performance Organization*. Boston, Mass.: Harvard Business School Press, 1993.

9. Beckhard, R. Optimizing team building efforts. *Journal of Contemporary Business*, 1972, 1(3), 23–32; Dyer, W. G. *Team Building: Issues and Alternatives*, 2nd ed. Reading, Mass.: Addison-Wesley, 1987, 22–23.

10. Katzenbach, J. R., and Smith, D. K. *The Wisdom of Teams: Creating the High-Performance Organization*. Boston: Harvard Business School Press, 1993, 119–126.

11. Sundstrom, E., DeMeuse, K. P., and Futrell, D. Work teams: Applications and effectiveness. *American Psychologist*, 1990, 45, 120–133; Woodman, R. W., and Sherwood, J. J. The role of team development in organizational effectiveness: A critical review. *Psychological Bulletin*, 1980, 88, 166–186.

12. Lublin, J. S. Trying to increase worker productivity, more employers alter management style. *Wall Street Journal*, February 13, 1992, B3.

13. White, J. B., and Suris, O. How a "skunk works" kept the mus-

tang alive—on a tight budget. *Wall Street Journal*, September 21, 1993, A1, A12.

14. Woodman, R. W., and Sherwood, J. J. Effects of team development intervention: A field experiment. *Journal of Applied Behavioral Science*, 1980, 16, 211–227.

15. Schein, E. H. *Process Consultation, Vol. I: Its Role in Organization Development*, 2nd ed. Reading, Mass.: Addison-Wesley, 1988, 11.

16. Burke, W. W. *Organization Development: Principles and Practices*. Boston: Little, Brown, 1982, 282–286; Cummings, T. G., and Worley, C. G. *Organization Development and Change*, 5th ed., St. Paul, Minn.: West, 1993, 201–211.

17. Cutcher-Gershenfeld, J. The impact on economic performance of a transformation in workplace relations. *Industrial and Labor Relations Review*, 1991, 44, 241–260.

18. Pasmore, W. A. A comprehensive approach to planning an OD/QWL strategy. In D. D. Warwick (ed.), *Contemporary Organization Development: Current Thinking and Applications*. Glenview, Ill.: Scott, Foresman, 1985, 205.

19. Trost, C. To cut costs and keep the best people, more concerns offer flexible work plans. *Wall Street Journal*, February 18, 1992, B1.

20. Hymowitz, C. As Aetna adds flextime, bosses learn to cope. *Wall Street Journal*, June 18, 1990, B1, B5.

21. Shellenbarger, S. More companies experiment with workers' schedules. *Wall Street Journal*, January 13, 1994, B1.

22. Adapted from Hall, D. T., and Parker, V. A. The role of workplace flexibility in managing diversity. *Organizational Dynamics*, Summer 1993, 8.

23. Fields, M. W., and Thacker, J. W. Influence of quality of work life on company and union commitment. *Academy of Management Journal*, 1992, 35, 439–450.

24. Trice, H. M., and Beyer, J. M. *The Cultures of Work Organizations*. Englewood Cliffs, N.J.: Prentice-Hall, 1993, 393–428.

25. Hays, L. Gerstner is struggling as he tries to change ingrained IBM culture. *Wall Street Journal*, May 13, 1994, A1, A5; Huey, J. Managing in the midst of chaos. *Fortune*, April 5, 1993, 44; Kirkpatrick, D. Breaking up IBM. *Fortune*, July 27, 1992, 44–58; Miller, M. W. As IBM losses mount, so do the complaints about company perks. *Wall Street Journal*, October 27, 1993, A1, A14.

26. Mohrman, S. A., and Cummings, T. G. *Self-Designing Organizations: Learning How to Create High Performance*. Reading, Mass.: Addison-Wesley, 1989; Woodman, R. W. Organizational change and development: New arenas for inquiry and action. *Journal of Management*, 1989, 15, 218–219.

27. Sherwood, J. J. Creating work cultures with competitive advantage. *Organizational Dynamics*, Winter 1988, 5–26.

28. Griffin, R. W., and Woodman, R. W. Utilizing task redesign strategies within organization development programs. In D. D. Warwick (ed.), *Contemporary Organization Development: Current Thinking and Applications*. Glenview, Ill.: Scott, Foresman, 1985, 308–319.

29. Perlman, S. L. Employees redesign their jobs. *Personnel Journal*, November 1990, 37–40.

30. Pasmore, W. A. *Designing Effective Organizations: The Sociotechnical Systems Perspective*. New York: John Wiley & Sons, 1988.

31. Manz, C. Beyond self-managing work teams: Toward self-leading teams in the workplace. In W. A. Pasmore and R. W. Woodman (eds.), *Research in Organizational Change and Development*, vol. 4. Greenwich, Conn.: JAI Press, 1990, 273–299.

32. Lawler, E. E., and Mohrman, S. A. Quality circles after the fad. *Harvard Business Review*, January–February 1985, 66.

33. Adam, E. E. Quality circle performance. *Journal of Management*, 1991, 17, 25–39; Steel, R. P., and Jennings, K. R. Quality improvement technologies for the 90s: New directions for research and theory. In W. A. Pasmore and R. W. Woodman (eds.), *Research in Organizational Change and Development*, vol. 6. Greenwich, Conn.: JAI Press, 1992, 1–36.

34. Calonius, E. Smart moves by quality champs. *Fortune*, Spring/Summer 1991, 24.

35. Bruning, N. S., and Liverpool, P. R. Membership in quality circles and participation in decision making. *Journal of Applied Behavioral Science*, 1993, 29, 76–95.

36. Reprinted by permission from page 178 of *Total Quality: Management, Organization, and Strategy* by J. W. Dean and J. R. Evans; Copyright © 1994 by West Publishing Company. All rights reserved.

37. Hammer, M., and Champy, J. *Reengineering the Corporation*. New York: HarperCollins, 1993, 32.

38. Dean, J. W., and Evans, J. R. *Total Quality: Management, Organization, and Strategy*. St. Paul, Minn.: West, 1994, 159; Also see Ashkenas, R. N., and Jick, T. D. From dialogue to action in GE work-out. In W. A. Pasmore and R. W. Woodman (eds.), *Research in Organizational Change and Development*, vol. 6. Greenwich, Conn.: JAI Press, 1992, 267–287.

39. Hammer, M., and Champy, J. *Reengineering the Corporation*. New York: HarperCollins, 1993, 65–82.

40. Ciampa, D. *Total Quality*. Reading, Mass.: Addison-Wesley, 1992, 41. Also see Hodgetts, R. M., Luthans, F., and Lee, S. M. New paradigm organizations: From total quality to learning to world class. *Organizational Dynamics*, Winter 1994, 5–19; Lawler, E. E. Total quality management and employee involvement. *Academy of Management Executive*, February 1994, 68–76.

41. Yoder, S. K., Fuchsberg, G., and Stertz, B. A. All that's lacking is Bert Parks singing "Cadillac, Cadillac." *Wall Street Journal*, December 13, 1990, A1, A4.

42. Caudron, S. Keys to starting a TQM program. *Personnel Journal*, February 1993, 33.

43. Hill, G. C., and Yamada, K. Motorola illustrates how an aged giant can remain vibrant. *Wall Street Journal*, December 9, 1992, A1.

44. Reprinted by permission from page 205 of *Total Quality: Management, Organization, and Strategy* by J. W. Dean and J. R. Evans; Copyright © 1994 by West Publishing Company. All rights reserved.

45. Dumaine, B. The bureaucracy busters. *Fortune*, June 17, 1991, 36–50; Mitroff, I. I., Mason, R. O., and Pearson, C. M. Radical surgery: What will tomorrow's organizations look like? *Academy of Management Executive*, May 1994, 11–21.

46. Bryne, J. A., Brandt, R., and Port, O. The virtual corporation. *Business Week*, February 8, 1993.

47. Bushe, G. R., and Shani, A. B. *Parallel Learning Structures: Increasing Innovation in Bureaucracies*. Reading, Mass.: Addison-Wesley, 1991; Woodman, R. W. Collateral organization. In N. Nicholson (ed.), *The Blackwell Dictionary of Organizational Behavior*. Oxford: Blackwell, 1994 (in press).

48. Bushe, G. R., and Shani, A. B. Parallel learning structure interventions in bureaucratic organizations. In W. A. Pasmore and R. W. Woodman (eds.), *Research in Organizational Change and Development*, vol. 4. Greenwich, Conn.: JAI Press, 1990, 167–194; Zand, D. E. Collateral organization: A new change strategy. *Journal of Applied Behavioral Science*, 1974, 10, 63–89.

49. Rubinstein, D., and Woodman, R. W. Spiderman and the Burma raiders: Collateral organization theory in action. *Journal of Applied Behavioral Science*, 1984, 20, 1–21.

50. Bartlett, C. A., and Ghoshal, S. Matrix management: Not a structure, a frame of mind. *Harvard Business Review*, July–August 1990, 145.

51. Snow, C. C., Miles, R. E., and Coleman, H. J. Managing 21st century network organizations. *Organizational Dynamics*, Winter 1992, 5–20. Reprinted, by permission of publisher, from *Organizational Dynamics*, Winter/1992 © 1992. American Management Association, New York. All rights reserved; Slocum, J. W., Jr., McGill, M., and Lei, D. The new learning strategy: Anytime, anything, anywhere. *Organizational Dynamics*, Autumn 1994 (in press).

52. Cummings, T. G., and Worley, C. G. *Organization Development and Change*, 5th ed. St. Paul, Minn.: West, 1993, 505–506.

53. Clausen, A. W. Strategic issues in managing change: The turnaround at BankAmerica Corporation. *California Management Review*, Winter 1990, 98–105.

54. Boccialetti, G. Organization development ethics and effectiveness. In W. Sikes, A. B. Drexler, and J. Gants (eds.), *The Emerging Practice of Organization Development*. Alexandria, Va.: NTL Institute for Applied Behavioral Sciences, 1989, 83–92; Connor, P. E., and Lake, L. K. *Managing Organizational Change*. New York: Praeger, 1988, 171–175.

55. McKendall, M. The tyranny of change: Organizational development revisited. *Journal of Business Ethics*, 1993, 12, 93. Reprinted by permission of Kluwer Academic Publishers.

56. Adapted from Dunham, R. B., Grube, J. A., Gardner, D. G., Cummings, L. L., and Pierce, J. L. The development of an attitude toward change instrument. Paper presented at the annual meeting of the Academy of Management, Washington, D.C., August 1989.

57. Case prepared by Gary C. McMahan during his tenure as Westinghouse Manufacturing Fellow, Department of Management, Texas A&M University, January 1990. Reprinted with permission.

21 Career Planning and Development

When you have finished studying this chapter, you should be able to:

▲ Describe the socialization process.

▲ Define career and describe its components.

▲ Explain the factors that influence a person's choices of career and occupation.

▲ Describe the four career stages that most people pass through.

▲ Identify the central activities and career concerns associated with each career stage.

▲ Discuss the factors that affect career planning.

▲ List the problems facing dual-career couples, women managers, and employees who have been outplaced.

OUTLINE

Preview Case: Winning the Career Game

Organizational Socialization: The Process of Joining Up

Anticipatory Socialization Stage

Managing Quality: Realistic Job Previews at Nissan

Encounter Stage

Managing Diversity: Pepsi-Cola's Designate Program

Change and Acquisition Stage

Career Changes

Managing Across Cultures: Speed Bumps on a Career Path

Matching Organizational and Individual Needs

Career Choice

Managing in Practice: Cross Colours

Occupational Choice

Organizational Choice

Career Stages

Career Movement Within an Organization

Working-Life Career Stages

Career Planning Issues

Effects of Career Planning

Dual-Career Couples

Managing Across Cultures: 3M

Child Care

Women in Management

Outplacement

Managing in Practice: Coping with Job Loss

DEVELOPING SKILLS

    Self-Diagnosis: *Life Success Scale*

    A Case in Point: *Tradeoffs*

PREVIEW CASE

Winning the Career Game

To say that the future is rosy and splendid careers await you requires a very optimistic outlook. The new global economy is causing organizations to rethink how they hire and promote people. In response, people have to rethink their jobs and careers. Jobs with regular pay, hours, and a fixed place in an organization's chart have started to fade away. IBM has pared down to about 256,000 employees worldwide from a high of 406,000. General Motors, Procter & Gamble, and Microsoft, among others, have reduced employment in an attempt to maintain their competitive edge in the marketplace.

To prosper in this new world of work, you must be prepared to "reinvent" yourself over your career. Terri Stynes, a manager at Bank of America's credit card operation in San Francisco, had 75 employees reporting to her. The bank decided to relocate the operation to Phoenix. After discussing her job options with her husband, Stynes decided not to move to Phoenix and resigned. Leafing through 100-page Career Opportunity Bulletins at the Bank of America, she eventually found a job in counseling and working with substance abusers. Most employees know that organizational loyalty isn't rewarded and that jobs disappear daily. The challenge for you is to be creative in thinking about your career and jobs that you will have during it.[1]

If you were in Terri Stynes's situation, would you make the same decision? During the past two decades, a new breed of employee has come into the work force. Their attitude toward life and work is vastly different from that of their parents. They aren't as motivated by traditional lures of money, titles, security, and ladder climbing. They insist on getting satisfaction from their jobs and are reluctant to make personal sacrifices for the sake of the organization. They believe that other interests—leisure, family, life-style, the pursuit of learning—are just as important as work.

In Chapter 1, we highlighted the composition, needs, and values of the new work force. They will influence your career is five specific ways.[2] First, the new global economy requires that you be able to operate comfortably in various settings, including different cultures. Throughout this book, we have identified the skills that you will need to learn and maintain as a professional in a global economy. We also have illustrated the challenges facing managers who now must direct the work of employees whose values, ethics, and culture are different than theirs.

Second, you will likely perform more and more work as a team member on projects that have a beginning and an end. Organizations increasingly will bring together a team of highly skilled people to develop and complete a project and then disband. Managers must learn how to share power with people they once regarded as subordinates. Ralph Stayer, CEO of Johnsonville Foods, comments that effective teams will not be like a pack of sled dogs but more like a flight of wild geese. The leader always changes, but the geese fly in formation. Flying as a flock enables geese to travel 173% farther than if each goose flew solo. Globalization and the explosion of information technology together increase the likelihood of people working in teams across great distances.

Third, you will have to compete harder for fewer middle management jobs, which means less and slower movement up the organizational hierarchy. Under Jack Welch's leadership at GE, the number of general management jobs has declined by 66%. In the services industry, NationsBank, American Airlines, and Banc One, among others, are scrambling to streamline their operations. Freed from performing routine tasks, such as processing mortgage applications at Banc One, employees can become available to develop new services for customers.

Fourth, you can count on not spending 30 years with the same employer. Dick Ferrington lives with his wife, two teenaged children, several pets, and a house, but has no permanent organizational address. Last year, he served as an interim vice-president for human resources in one company, a compensation specialist for another, and now has an office at home (equipped with a PC, fax board, printer). He knows how to put together a team of specialists to solve problems for an organization but probably will not work for any one organization again.

Finally, you will have to be self-reliant and assume the responsibility for managing your own career. To develop your sense of self-reliance, Vicky Farrow, director of work-force development at Sun Microsystems, offers the following advice to help employees assume control over their own careers.

▲ Think of yourself as a business. What is your area of expertise? To whom are you going to sell this?

▲ Know your profession and what's going on there. Is your profession becoming obsolete?

▲ Be willing to change careers. Few people will have a chance to stay in one career for their whole lives.

▲ Be a team player. Develop a network of contacts that can help you solve problems.[3]

With these realities as a background, in this chapter we introduce you to ways of managing a career. First, we discuss the socialization processes that organizations use to attract and orient employees to their culture and organization. Second, we discuss the three career stages that most people pass through, perhaps changing jobs and careers more than once during their lifetimes, that pose managerial and psychological challenges for them. How people cope with these challenges affects their family and work life. Finally, we focus on challenges facing dual-career couples, executive women, and employees who have been outplaced by their own organization.

▼ ORGANIZATIONAL SOCIALIZATION: THE PROCESS OF JOINING UP

Recall the jobs that you have held. What were your feelings during your first few weeks on each job? That time may have been filled with frustration. As a newcomer, you faced a new environment, one different in many respects from others you had previously faced. The people working with you were new and unfamiliar. At the same time, you may have had to establish a new residence in an unfamiliar town, which required finding a place to live, getting the phone and utilities turned on, establishing a new checking account, getting a driver's license, and so on. Unless you had found a job and city that were similar to those you worked and lived in before, you had to learn new behaviors, skills, and ways of relating to people. Getting settled personally minimizes frustration in beginning a new job and will let you become productive more quickly.

Because of the complexity of most jobs, a new employee needs to "learn the ropes" fast. The ease and speed with which an individual learns a job is important from both the individual's and the organization's point of view. The process by which employees learn about their new job and work environment is called *organizational socialization.*[4] In Chapter 14, we defined organizational socialization as the process by which organizations bring new employees into their culture. At Arthur Andersen, a major accounting and consulting firm, the formal socialization process lasts ten weeks. All new employees are required to attend Andersen's school in Lake Charles, Illinois, to learn about the Andersen way of doing business. At Hoechst Celanese Corporation, newcomer socialization lasts several weeks. In many fast-food restaurants, such as Wendy's and McDonald's, newcomer socialization lasts only several hours. Employee turnover in many fast-food restaurants is well over 100% a year. Thus some individuals claim that spending time socializing and training people is a waste of money and time. Most employees do not stay long enough for the organization to realize any gains from such time-consuming socialization programs. However, effective socialization programs often reduce the rate of turnover.

In one sense, socialization never ends. It begins well before the individual actually arrives at work and continues for long after entry. Hence we need to discuss the socialization process in three distinct—but related—stages: anticipatory socialization, encounter, and change and acquisition. Figure 21.1 depicts these stages.

FIGURE 21.1

Stages in Employee Socialization

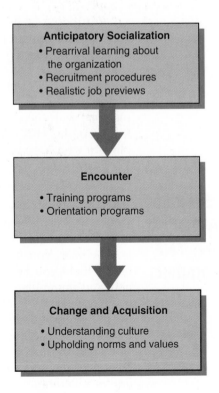

Anticipatory Socialization
- Prearrival learning about the organization
- Recruitment procedures
- Realistic job previews

Encounter
- Training programs
- Orientation programs

Change and Acquisition
- Understanding culture
- Upholding norms and values

▼ Anticipatory Socialization Stage

Before individuals actually join an organization, they may know quite a bit about it. Friends, relatives, or people already working for the organization often provide information to prospective employees. Other valuable sources of information are newspaper articles, the organization's annual reports, and news items in trade and professional journals about the organization. In essence, people begin to socialize themselves before joining an organization to help them get a job that they want. **Anticipatory socialization** is the process of accepting the beliefs and values of an organization before an individual actually joins it. Anticipatory socialization is especially prevalent among students enrolled in professional schools (e.g., business, engineering, law, and medicine) as they learn and practice the traditional behaviors and values of the profession. However, such efforts may have biased the newcomer's perceptions of an organization.

PepsiCo has a fast-track development program for its college-level newcomers. It is a make-or-break experience: The company demands a lot, and the pressure is intense to reach sales and cost goals. Working 70 or more hours per week and moving to various cities are common requirements. This information is widely known, and individuals considering going to work for PepsiCo often are well informed about the required behaviors and values before responding to a job offer.[5]

To avoid the negative reactions of newcomers who discover that the organization isn't what they were led to believe, many organizations conduct realistic job previews. A **realistic job preview** provides applicants with an accurate description of the job they will perform and the department they will work in.[6] Employees exposed to such previews usually report higher job satisfaction and have lower turnover than those who receive the standard, glowing—and often misleading—information about the job. The following Managing Quality feature highlights how Nissan uses realistic job previews at its Smyrna, Tennessee, plant to reduce absenteeism, turnover and to improve quality.

MANAGING QUALITY

Realistic Job Previews at Nissan

Phyllis Baines has two minutes to grab 55 nuts, bolts, and washers, assemble them in groups of 5, and attach them in order of size to a metal rack. But she fumbled nervously with several pieces and finished the task seconds after her allotted time. "I've got to get a little better at this, don't I?" She frowned as she pulled the last of the fasteners out of a grimy plastic tray. Her tester, Harold Hicks, encouraged her: "You're close. For the first night, you're probably doing a little better than normal."

You may suspect that Baines (not her real name) is going through first-night jitters at an adult education class in home repair. However, she is trying to land a job at the Nissan Motor Manufacturing Corporation plant in Smyrna, Tennessee. The 31-year-old department store employee will be devoting 70 hours worth of her nights and weekends during the next few months doing similar exercises.

MANAGING QUALITY —*Continued*

Baines and about 270 other job seekers are participating in Nissan's pre-employment program. In exchange for a shot at highly paid assembly-line and other hourly jobs and Nissan's promise not to inform their employers, the moonlighters work as many as 360 hours without being paid. They are tested and instructed in employment fundamentals by the Japanese automaker. "We hope the process makes it plain to people what the job is," says Thomas P. Groom, Nissan's manager of employment. "It's an indoctrination process," he says, as well as a screening tool.

Not all participants are fully satisfied with the program. A candidate who works as a machine adjuster at an envelope factory says that the lack of a job guarantee by Nissan "worries you, because you get your hopes up." And some candidates bemoan the lack of pay for their time. But many participants feel that the training and experience they receive outweigh any additional obstacles to getting hired. For one thing, they get a shot at some of the best-paying jobs in the state. If they are not hired, they can take the skills they have learned elsewhere. Judy McFarland, a press operator who went through the program, said: "It gave me a chance to see what Nissan expected of me without their having to make a commitment to me or me to them."[7]

▼ Encounter Stage

The second stage in organizational socialization begins when individuals actually start their new jobs. During this stage, they learn the skills and roles—information, interpersonal, and decisional—required by their new job and become oriented to the practices, procedures, and culture of the organization. Orientation may be informal or a formal program that introduces new employees to their job responsibilities, their co-workers, and the company's policies. Effective orientation programs serve two purposes: (1) they inform new employees about benefits, company policies, and procedures; (2) they fine-tune employee job-related and cultural expectations. Formal orientation programs reduce the time and effort required by managers to train new employees. In addition, if busy managers assign orientation to an assistant or a secretary, certain key points may be covered too lightly or skipped over.

PepsiCo has an effective orientation program that lasts several days. Chief executive officer Wayne Calloway believes that if sales are to continue to grow at 17% annually, the company needs to recruit employees and give them the self-confidence to take risks. The orientation program tells newcomers that it's okay to take risks and to think outside their own jobs. Calloway likes to identify high-performing employees early in their careers and send them to posts around the world for an education in the school of hard knocks. Therefore, to prepare them for life at PepsiCo, new employees learn that most successful employees have

▲ the ability to handle business complexities;
▲ the ability to lead and manage people; and
▲ the drive to achieve outstanding results.

Perhaps the biggest challenge any global organization faces is to ensure the continuity of common values. For members of the human resources department at Pepsi-Cola International, a division of PepsiCo, the challenge was to create practices that had universal appeal. To achieve this objective and focus on issues of cultural diversity, Pepsi-Cola International created the Designate Program. This program helps it manage cultural diversity by bringing non-U.S. employees to the United States for a period of specialized training in the domestic U.S. Pepsi system, as described in the following Managing Diversity account.

MANAGING DIVERSITY

Pepsi-Cola's Designate Program

Individuals are selected for the program by their division managers because of their significant potentials for growth. Furthermore, all employees must agree before starting the program to return to their home countries. The key outcome of the program is the ability to transfer the skills learned in the program to their overseas market.

What values are stressed? First, employees should listen carefully to what others have to say, giving recognition to or sharing recognition with others. Teamwork is important. Second, employees should focus on business issues rather than personal issues when giving subordinates feedback on their performance. Although cultural differences are important, sticking to business issues is more important. The objective is to learn the business values of Pepsi-Cola that transcend cultural beliefs. These values include openly confronting problems and different points of view, staying focused under pressure, figuring out what needs to be done and charting a course of action, acting with maturity and good judgment, and jointly setting goals with people so that they can judge their own accomplishments. Third, employees should overcommunicate at every opportunity and never take communication for granted. Although "handling business complexity" might be translated differently in China and France, the outcome should be the same: to generate additional sales in the region.[8]

▼ Change and Acquisition Stage

Sometime after joining an organization, individuals attain full member status by learning and practicing the new attitudes and behaviors. In the change and acquisition stage, individuals develop self-images and behaviors that are consistent with the organization's culture. Often a ceremony, such as a dinner, lunch, or reception, formally recognizes new employees as full members. Their titles change from trainee or apprentice to assistant manager or supervisor. At Brooklyn Union Company, this ceremony occurs at a luncheon hosted by the president, during which employees receive their permanent identification numbers and are assigned parking spaces in a covered garage. In contrast, at the Fort Worth Museum of Science and History, there is no ceremony. Don Otto, the museum director, sends a memo to all employees indicating that a change has taken place in a person's status. Otto and the person then go out to lunch.

Whatever form it takes, the settling-in phase of the socialization process marks important shifts for both individuals and organizations. Employees make permanent adjustments in their personal lives and to their jobs. They juggle child and/or elder care and job responsibilities. They have people reporting to them and now must manage people instead of tasks. The hardness adjustments for first-time managers are switching from relying on formal authority to establishing credibility to get the job done, from striving for control to building subordinate commitment, and from managing oneself to leading a team.[9]

CAREER CHANGES

A **career** is a sequence of work-related positions occupied by a person during a lifetime.[10] The popular view of a career usually is restricted to the idea of moving up the organizational ladder. As we have noted, this opportunity no longer is available to most people. Actually, a career consists of attitudes and behaviors that are part of ongoing work-related activities and experiences. A person may remain at the same level, acquiring and developing new skills, and have a successful career without ever being promoted. Or people can build a career by moving among various jobs in different fields and organizations. Thus a career encompasses not only traditional work experiences but also the diversity of career alternatives, individual choices, and individual experiences. Let's consider five aspects of career to clarify the concept.

▲ The nature of a career in itself doesn't imply success or failure or fast or slow advancement. Career success or failure is best determined by the individual, rather than by others.

▲ No absolute standards exist for evaluating a career. Career success or failure is related to the concept of self-actualization in the needs hierarchy (see Chapter 6). Individuals should evaluate their own career goals and progress in terms of what is personally meaningful and satisfying.

▲ An individual should examine a career both subjectively and objectively. Subjective elements of a career include values, attitudes, personality, and motivations, which may change over time. Objective elements of a career include job choices, positions held, and specific skills.

▲ **Career development** involves making decisions about occupation and engaging in activities to attain career goals. The central idea in the career development process is time. The shape and direction of a person's career over time are influenced by many factors (e.g., the economy, availability of jobs, skill acquisition, personal characteristics, family status, and job history.

▲ Cultural factors play a role in careers. Cultural norms in countries such as Japan, the Philippines, and Mexico also influence the direction of a person's career. For example, women are discriminated against as managers in most cultures. In other cultures, social status and educational background largely determine career paths.

The following Managing Across Cultures item illustrates some of the problems facing women employees in Mexico.

MANAGING ACROSS CULTURES

Speed Bumps on a Career Path

Mercedes Trulillo de Casanova angrily recalls the day she told her supervisors that she was getting married. One of them pulled out a form that she had signed when joining the company. It stated that if she got married, she would leave. She would have liked to keep working because she and her husband wanted to save enough money to buy a home. After receiving a month's severance pay from Hylsa, S.A., she found another job at Focos, S.A. Four years later, when she found out that she was pregnant, her supervisor told her that she couldn't return after giving birth. The company didn't employ women with young children. According to the company, it had adopted the policy to protect the integrity of the family. Discrimination? Not in Mexico. Although gender discrimination is prohibited in government work, a private organization can dismiss an employee without any repercussions. The Mexican Bar Association has been trying for years to reverse this ruling, but to no avail.

The difficulties that women face are rooted in the cultural machismo that has prevailed for generations. It starts in the home where Mexican men don't want to help their wives with housework. Women are socialized early that their role is taking care of the home and family; the husband's place is making a living. Once women are hired, they are not likely to be promoted to management positions because those jobs usually are reserved for men. Even with a college degree, most women are not promoted beyond the position of executive secretary. The huge pay differentials between Mexican men and women approach 75% in many instances. Older women (past 35) are routinely passed over in favor of younger women. With a large pool of women under 19, organizations have little trouble hiring.[11]

▼ Matching Organizational and Individual Needs

Effective career development requires a fit between the individual and organization.[12] An individual's career is a process, or sequence, of work-related experiences. The organization has an important stake in this process and often attempts to match its needs with the employee's needs and career goals. To the extent that the matching process is done well, both organization and employee benefit. The organization is more effective and productive, and the individual is more satisfied, happy, and successful.

Figure 21.2 highlights the organizational and individual issues inherent in career planning and development. It also shows some of the continuing matching processes needed to integrate organizational needs with individual needs and career goals.

Organizational Issues   A society's technology, cultural values, laws, and institutions determine the labor market and strongly influence the structure of occupations. The culture in which an organization operates broadens or constrains the career opportunities for employees. An important organizational activity is identifying human resource needs and making plans for meeting them. How many people will be needed? When will they be needed? Where

FIGURE 21.2

Matching Organizational and Individual Issues in Career Planning and Development

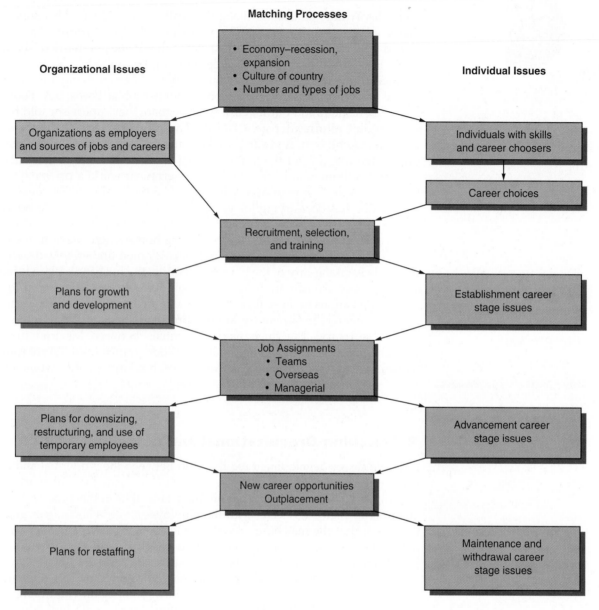

will they come from? What skills will they need? Organizations must continuously recruit, develop, transfer, and promote people to perform its functions. These planning and managing activities never stop unless the organization goes out of existence.

Individual Issues   The individual must develop a career plan in order to be successful. Ralph Waldo Emerson's classic 153-year-old essay, "Self-reliance" offers the best advice for people seeking a career: "Trust thyself." To be successful in the future, people will need to commit themselves to a lifetime of learning, including the development of a career plan. A **career plan** is the individual's choice of occupation, organization, and career path. (We discuss the career planning process in more detail later in this chapter.) If opportunities provided by the organization are not attractive career alternatives for individuals, the organization will be plagued by personnel problems, including those of recruiting and retaining qualified employees.

The Matching Process   The central portion of Figure 21.2 shows ways that an organization can attempt to match its human resource needs with its employees' career stages. The careers of most people seem to progress through similar stages: establishment, advancement, maintenance, and withdrawal. People's needs, values, and goals change as they go through these stages. The staffing needs of the organization also change over time. For example, reengineering changes both individual and organizational needs. Reengineering pushes decision-making authority as far down the organization as possible—often to self-managed teams—but, in many cases, causes layoffs. That is, organizations require fewer employees but those that they do need have to possess greater interpersonal and technical skills to solve complex problems. Thus many organizations strive to translate their needs into opportunities that employees will consider attractive in terms of their own needs and career goals. The success of this matching process determines, in part, organizational effectiveness.

▼ Career Choice

During the 1990s, an estimated 25 million people will join the work force.[13] Nearly 85% of these new workers will be women, blacks, and people with disabilities. The most successful organizations will be those that recognize the challenge and opportunity of these changes. Organizations that promote the value of a diverse work force of different races, ethnic backgrounds, ages, and abilities will have a competitive advantage. Successful organizations will give people career choices knowing that more and more people will make multiple career choices during their working lives. The following Managing in Practice feature highlights how Carl Jones, CEO of Cross Colours, made some career choices.

MANAGING IN PRACTICE

Cross Colours

Born in Memphis and raised in South Central Los Angeles, Carl Jones was anxious to do his own thing. He dropped out of school in 1982 and borrowed $20,000 to start his own silk-screen printing firm. He learned the fine points of the garment business and snared some big clients, including Guess and Sassoon. In 1985, he started another company, Surf Fetish, that became known for its multiprinted active wear by taking beachwear to the streets. By 1988, Jones was tired of this business. Friends, bankers, and others thought that Jones had lost his head. Surf Fetish was doing $20 million a year. But following

MANAGING IN PRACTICE —*Continued*

his instincts, he mortgaged his Beverly Hills home, sold some of his 17 Harley Davidson motorcycles, and raised $1 million to start another career. Jones thought that the Afrocentric movement was just beginning in the United States. By 1990, he had convinced Thomas Walker that the time was right to harness a new craze in clothing for men. Together they founded Cross Colours. Targeting African-Americans, they have rung up sales of more than $100 million and were recently named the Black Enterprise of the year.

Cross Colours now employs more than 250 people. The average age of its employees is 25. In its headquarters, swatches of material are everywhere—and so is energy. Jones's management style is loose and democratic, yet demanding and team-oriented. Managers shun suits for baggy jeans and sneakers. Jones forbids titles on business cards and Colours has no career ladders.

Both Jones and Walker are training teenagers to enter the apparel business. Cross Colours joined forces with L.A.'s Common Ground to create entry-level jobs for kids from South Central Los Angeles. They started mentoring programs for youth and hope that these programs will inspire young people to stay in high school and learn skills to compete in tomorrow's job market. They also want to open a sewing factory in South Central that will offer jobs and train people.[14]

During the course of your career, you may make several career choices because such decisions are seldom irreversible these days. People such as Carl Jones and Thomas Walker do not feel locked into their choices for life; instead, they create or find other career opportunities. Studies of college graduates indicate that, five years after graduation, at least 50% have changed organizations at least once and 20% have changed occupations.

▼ Occupational Choice

Researchers and managers have long been fascinated by the possibility that individuals attracted to a specific occupation might have certain common characteristics or attributes. They also have tried to determine whether certain sets of characteristics might be used to predict specific career choices and effective performance in those careers. Although finer distinctions might be made, at least two general categories of personal characteristics seem to be related to career choices: personality and social background.

Personality: Vocational Behavior   John Holland advanced the most detailed theory relating personality to vocational behavior.[15] He identified six basic personality types, each of which best matches (is congruent with) the demands and expectations of a particular career. Holland claims that these six classifications of personality types are good predictors of career aspiration and choice. For example, Carl Jones of Cross Colours has an enterprising personality type that matches his career choice. Research supports the existence of a relationship between personality orientation and career choice. Evidence also points to the likelihood of people remaining in a chosen occupation if it matches their personality orientation. In incongruent environments, people

TABLE 21.1 Holland's Personality Type Descriptions

Personality Type	Corresponding Problem-Solving Style	Personality Traits	Representative Occupations
Realistic	Sensation thinker (ST)	Stable, materialistic, persistent, practical	Architecture, trades (plumber, electrician), machinist, forest ranger
Investigative	Intuitive thinker (NT)	Analytical, critical, curious, intellectual, rational	Physicist, anthropologist, chemist, mathematician, biologist
Artistic	Intuitive feeler (NF)	Emotional, idealistic, imaginative, impulsive	Poet, novelist, musician, sculptor, playwright, composer, stage director
Social	Sensation feeler (SF)	Cooperative, friendly, sociable, understanding	Professor, psychologist, counselor, missionary, teacher
Enterprising	Sensation thinker (ST) Intuitive thinker (NT)	Adventurous, ambitious, energetic, optimistic, self-confident, talkative	Manager, salesperson, politician, lawyer, buyer
Conventional	Sensation thinker (ST)	Conscientious, obedient, orderly, self-controlled	Certified public accountant, statistician, bookkeeper, administrative assistant, postal clerk

Source: Adapted from Holland, J. V. *Making Vocational Choices: A Theory of Careers.* Englewood Cliffs, N.J.: Prentice-Hall, 1973, 111–117; Spokane, A. A. Review of research on person–environment congruence in Holland's theory of careers. *Journal of Vocational Behavior,* 1985, 26, 306–343; Moore, T. Personality tests are back. *Fortune,* March 30, 1987, 74–82.

will be less satisfied with the job, their job performance will be lower, and they will be more likely to change careers.

Table 21.1 lists the six basic personality types in Holland's theory, along with some of their corresponding personality traits, interests, and representative occupations. The second column shows the problem-solving style (see Chapter 4) that seems to fit best each personality type. Note that no single problem-solving style appears to be typical of the enterprising personality type.

Occupational Interests The right-hand column of Table 21.1 lists some of the occupational interests of the six personality types. Because an occupation involves specific activities, people having the same occupation may share certain interests to a greater extent than do people in general. Thus a person's interests can be compared to the profile of interests for samples of individuals in various occupations. This information can help an individual choose a vocation. People often pursue careers that match their interests, and such interests may play a part in career success or, at least, in their remaining in a chosen occupation.

Personality: Self-Esteem   Another personality dimension related to occupational choice is a person's self-esteem (see Chapter 2). Recall that self-esteem is an individual's evaluation of himself or herself. A person's self-esteem may strongly influence initial vocational choice. However, this choice may change over time as the value placed on an occupation and a career by others changes and as the person gains experience.

Social Background   The social background of the individual also influences career choice. Social background refers to early childhood experiences, the socioeconomic status of the family, the educational level and occupations of parents, and so on. All these factors affect an individual's occupational goals and career choices by providing socialization experiences and setting practical constraints. For example, people may be more likely to consider a white-collar or professional career if one or both parents have such a career. The practical constraint of being unable to afford a college education may limit later occupational choices. Other, more subtle constraints include the socialization of girls to expect adult roles different from those of boys (e.g., the roles of wife and mother versus the role of breadwinner). This early socialization may later influence the vocational choices made by many women.

▼ Organizational Choice

Choosing an organization is the second major career decision that most people make. A primary factor in choosing a specific organization is the availability of opportunities for individuals at any given time. Individuals also use infor-

TABLE 21.2   Questions That You Should Ask When Assessing an Organization

1. How large is the organization's industry and what are its prospects for growth?
2. What major changes are foreseen in the industry? How is the organization ready to respond?
3. What goods and services does it produce?
4. What are the organization's most important product developments?
5. Who are the organization's main competitors? How do they compete?
6. Where does the organization have other plants or divisions?
7. What jobs have its top managers held during their careers?
8. What do employees find most satisfying about working for the organization?

Source: For the rest of an extensive list of such questions, see Dlabay, L., and Slocum, J. W., Jr. *How to Pack Your Career Parachute*. Reading, Mass.: Addison-Wesley, 1989.

mation about an organization to form opinions about working there. Anticipatory socialization often is a key in making an organizational choice. Table 21.2 on p. 732 presents some typical questions that individuals have about an organization. Individuals tend to judge an organization by how well it fits their career goals and plans. They tend to base their choice on perceptions of a fit between known organizational characteristics and their personal characteristics, values, and goals.

▼ CAREER STAGES

A **career stage** in a person's life is a period of time characterized by distinctive and fairly predictable developmental tasks, concerns, needs, values, and activities.[16] We examine career stages from two perspectives: (1) an individual's career movement within a specific organization; and (2) an individual's passage through career stages spanning an entire working life.

▼ Career Movement Within an Organization

People most often think of career movement as advancing up some management or technical hierarchy with ever-increasing salary, status, and responsibilities. At J.C. Penney, Kmart, and Nordstrom's—all retail department stores—new college graduates with business degrees begin their employment as management trainees. They advance to assistant buyer or assistant merchandiser, buyer, assistant manager of a department (e.g., women's or men's apparel, jewelry, or housewares), department manager, and finally store manager.

Career moves in an organization usually are more complex than that. Individuals actually move in three directions in an organization: vertically, horizontally, and (more subtly) inclusively, as Figure 21.3 shows.[17] Vertical movement is represented by a change up or down the cone. Horizontal movement is represented by a change around the circumference of the cone from one functional or technical area to another. The inclusion movement is a change from the outer surface of the cone toward the center. An understanding of the types of career moves in an organization can be extremely valuable in an individual's career planning and development.

Vertical Movement   A change up or down formal organizational levels is a **vertical career movement.** During a career in a particular organization, most people move vertically upward, typically receiving a series of raises and promotions. As organizations continue to downsize their work forces and outsource many functions, relatively fewer senior individuals are needed to manage the organization. Thus some individuals reach their final hierarchical level early in their careers. Organizations differ dramatically in the number of hierarchical opportunities available: Some may be quite flat, with few steps to the top, and others may have many levels, or ranks.

Horizontal Movement   A lateral change to another functional or technical area is a **horizontal career movement.** This type of movement is becoming more common as the possibility of vertical movement diminishes. Individuals at Hoechst Celanese, Arco, and IBM, among others, move horizontally to im-

FIGURE 21.3

A Model of Career Movement in
Organizations

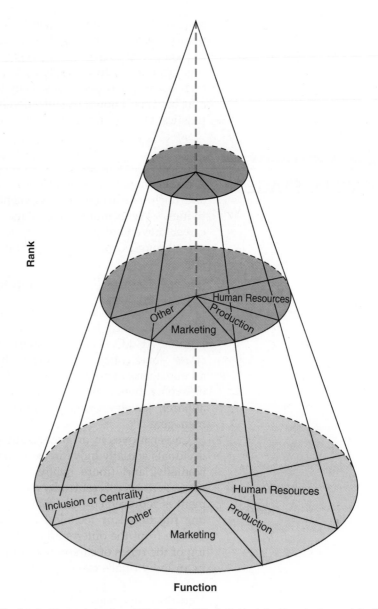

Source: Reprinted with permission from NTL Institute. "The Individual, the Organization, and the Career: A Conceptual Scheme" by Edgar H. Schein, p. 404, *The Journal of Applied Behavioral Science*, vol. 7, no. 4, copyright 1971.

prove their knowledge of different functional areas of the organization. By making a horizontal move, employees broaden their perspectives, learn new skills, and gain visibility to managers in other departments. The management trainee who is rotated among positions in production, marketing, and human resources at the same organizational level provides an example of horizontal movement. Some organizations deliberately use rotation to groom people for eventual promotion to the ranks of general management, where managers need the ability to see and understand overall operations.

Matt Bohn at Hoechst Celanese believes that horizontal moves were essential to his moving up and gaining a wider understanding of all the company's businesses—pharmaceuticals, cosmetics, chemicals, fibers, and films. When he joined the company after graduation from college, he took a sales job and served customers in the Northeast. After seven years, he received a promotion and transferred to Dallas. Five years ago, after a career spent mostly in information management systems and marketing in Dallas, he left that job to take a marketing position in the organization's chemical products line at corporate headquarters in Bridgewater, New Jersey. After spending two and a half years at headquarters, he realized that to be considered for a future promotions, he needed operating experience at one of the company's plants. He took a job as manager of quality control at a plant in North Carolina. Spending four years in the plant broadened his manufacturing, purchasing, and quality control knowledge. Recently, Bohn transferred back to Dallas to take a position responsible for marketing products for several plants in the chemical group of Hoechst Celanese.[18]

Inclusion: Movement Toward the Center   Movement toward the inner circle, or core, of an organization is an **inclusion career movement.** It occurs when a manager earns trust, develops greater understanding of the organization, takes on greater responsibility, and is consulted on important matters more frequently. A relationship often exists between vertical and inclusion movement; yet a person often can make one move without the other. Someone can become more "central" to the organization without being promoted to a higher rank by acquiring experience and the trust and confidence of a top manager and co-workers. Similarly, a person can move up in the hierarchy and still not be included in important core activities and decisions, as illustrated by the phrase "being kicked upstairs." Inclusion is the most subtle and confusing aspect of career moves within an organization. People may go through their entire careers completely unaware of their positions in terms of inclusion or, perhaps, even be oblivious to the existence of inclusion.

▼ Working-Life Career Stages

Individuals typically move through four distinct career stages during their working lives: establishment, advancement, maintenance, and withdrawal.[19] Figure 21.4 summarizes these stages and indicates the expected relative levels

FIGURE 21.4

Working-Life Career Stages

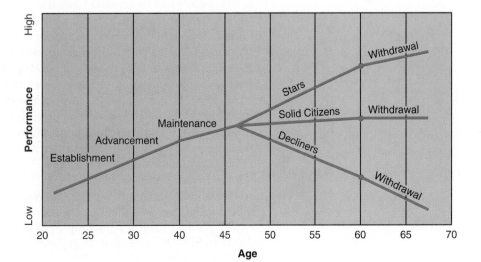

of performance as employees move through their careers. However, not all careers will be like those shown. For example, some people may take longer than others in choosing careers; similarly, some may choose a different occupation later in life and thus have to learn new skills, which others learned earlier in their careers. Carl Jones didn't start Cross Colours until he was 35; Anita Roddick, CEO of the Body Shop didn't form her firm until she was 38; and Mary Kay Ash, founder and CEO of Mary Kay Cosmetics, didn't start her company until she had had a successful 25-year career in sales.

Establishment Career Stage   When first joining an organization, a person immediately faces several challenges.[20] First, the new employee must learn to perform at least some tasks competently and to decide which tasks are essential and which require less attention. At the same time, the newcomer must also be socialized to learn how tasks get done, using both formal and informal channels of communication. Finally, the new employee must perform these tasks while being closely watched by one or more managers for competency and indications of future potential.

Much of a new employee's work in the **establishment career stage** involves fairly routine tasks. A person shouldn't become bogged down in detail work but show initiative and be innovative in finding solutions to problems. New employees typically are assigned parts of larger projects being directed by more senior employees or managers. Young people often find this situation frustrating. Such a reaction is understandable, but those who try to escape subordinate positions too quickly miss an important aspect of career development: They fail to learn what others have gained by experience. More important, if they undertake tasks for which they aren't prepared, newcomers may be tagged as mediocre performers, a reputation that is hard to overcome. Effectively handling the subordinate–superior relationship and assigned tasks can be crucial in building an effective career.

Ideally, a newcomer will be assigned to a mentor who knows the organization, is successful, and has been trained to work with newly hired employees.[21] A **mentor** typically is an older and more experienced employee who will sponsor and speak to others about the newcomer's accomplishments. The mentor identifies tasks and committees that are crucial to the organization's success, points out those who have the power or "clout" to make things happen in the organization, and offers advice about organizational life not found in organizational charts and orientation brochures.

Mentors tend to be people with power and status in the organization. As a result, they are able to assist young employees without threat to their own careers when younger employees make mistakes. By observing the mentors, employees also get a realistic impression of the organization's performance expectations. As new employees come to understand the politics of the organization, they confront their conceptions about managerial work and gain some appreciation for the ambiguities and complexities of the job.

How do mentors pick an employee? First, a mentor usually is impressed with the person's performance. The mentor may find out about that performance informally from others. Mentors normally have access to the managerial grapevine, so they know about the successes and failures of many employees. Second, the mentor finds the employee easy and pleasant to be around. They may share similar attitudes, backgrounds, or leisure time activities, such as tennis or golf. Third, in some organizations (e.g., British Petroleum, Heineken, and Honeywell) new employees are encouraged to approach would-be mentors and actively ask for help or attempt to initiate a working relationship in other ways. Another tool for helping mentoring programs work is to integrate the results of such programs into a manager's performance appraisal.[22] Amtrak, Coca-Cola, Merck, and Baxter Health Care, among others, all tie compensation to a manager's performance on mentoring. At Amtrak, manager promotion and compensation are tied to a review of career development and mentoring plans for at least ten female and minority employees. McDonald's ''Black Career Development Program'' provides mentoring opportunities for fast-track African-American managerial employees. Senior managers at McDonald's must advise employees on plans that they have for improving the company's response to increased work-force diversity.

What do mentors want in return for helping a protégé? First, they expect the individual to work hard and complete assigned tasks satisfactorily. Second, they expect the individual to be a loyal supporter within the organization and work the office politics to help ensure that certain projects sponsored by the mentor progress smoothly. Third, mentors expect recognition from others for helping bring along young talent and enhancement of their own standing by the younger employee's success. Yi Li, a quality assurance specialist for Electronic Data Systems, believes that a protégé's performance can enhance or limit a manager's performance. Having outstanding protégés shows that the mentor can pick and develop good people. Being chosen by few people for mentoring might signal others that this person cannot attract good people to work with.[23] Finally, the mentor may receive need satisfaction (especially self-esteem and self-actualization) by helping younger employees learn the ropes.

How important is it for you to have a mentor? Most successful managers have had one or more mentors during their careers. For women, having a mentor is much more important than it is for men. Many women are unable to climb the organization's ladder themselves because of the corporate culture. That is, they cannot break through the glass ceiling.[24] The **glass ceiling** refers to artificial, invisible barriers based on attitudes and organization folklore that women and members of minorities face that prevent them from rising above a certain level in an organization. The glass ceiling isn't a barrier based on an individual's inability to handle a higher level job; rather it is a barrier that keeps people from advancing because of who they are.

To overcome some mentoring obstacles for women and minority employees, Honeywell, Corning, Du Pont, and other organizations formally team young women and minorities with more experienced executives.[25] At Honeywell, senior managers encourage and expect more informal contacts, such as picnics and bicycle rides instead of golf matches and poker games, between senior and junior managers. Tennis and swimming activities are part of organizational retreat activities. Coed managerial groups can be seen at Corning's favorite lunch spots and informal get-togethers after work. It isn't that lunch, tennis, or swimming events in themselves are important but that women and minorities who are excluded from them miss out on important contacts, essential information, and useful gossip. Inclusion could bring news of someone being transferred or plans for a new product. Such news often is at the heart of one elusive element of success: being in the right place at the right time.

The potential gains from having a mentor are offset by some risks. Employees who stake their careers on mentors with little power or who have fallen from power may find that their own career suffer. Indeed, they might find themselves without a job if a layoff occurs following the defeat of the mentor in a political power struggle. In addition, mentors are only human, so not all their advice will be helpful or even useful. Finally, young employees may become so dependent on their mentors that the development of their own careers is slowed. They might be portrayed as not having self-reliance or independent judgment and may even become resistant to change because of that dependency (see Chapter 19).

Table 21.3 summarizes the concerns of employees at this career stage. It requires time for adjustment to the reality of the job, orientation to the organization, and establishment of an effective working relationship with a supervisor. Completing routine jobs successfully can quickly lead to more challenging assignments. If new employees can pass through this stage successfully, they usually can achieve their career goals.

TABLE 21.3   Concerns of Employees at the Establishment Stage—Ages 20–25

▲ Central Activities: Helping, learning, and following directions
▲ Primary Relationships: Being a subordinate and finding a mentor
▲ Needed from a Superior: Coaching, feedback, and visibility to senior management

Table 21.4 shows the characteristics of successful employees at this career stage. Successful people want challenging work, describe themselves as effective, have established a mentoring relationship with a senior manager, are willing to job hop (if necessary) to gain personal goals, and understand the organization's reward system.

TABLE 21.4   Characteristics of Successful Employees at the Establishment Stage

▲ Want to be promoted soon.
▲ Describe themselves as successful.
▲ Indicate that the job is not challenging.
▲ Have been tapped by a senior manager who is mentoring them.
▲ Have a considerate and supportive manager.
▲ Are eager and willing to move between organizations if this leads to greater job challenge, experience, and visibility to upper management.
▲ Understand how rewards (salaries, raises, promotions) are obtained in the organization.

Advancement Career Stage   The **advancement career stage** often involves new experiences: special assignments, transfers, promotions, offers from other organizations, and doing tasks that will increase the employee's visibility to higher management.[26]In accepting a promotion or new job assignment involving supervisory managerial duties, employees now have to manage people, not just tasks. To use the analogy of an orchestra, a newly appointed manager moves from being violinist who concentrates on playing one instrument to being the conductor, who coordinates the efforts of many musicians and must know something about the role of each instrument in playing various compositions.

At this stage in a career, the individual must adjust to the daily reality of managerial life, which often is pressure packed, hectic, and time-consuming. New managers must learn to respond to the seemingly unending and sometimes conflicting demands made on their time by subordinates, bosses, and peers. Their success now depends as much on the success of their subordinates as on their own abilities. They must also learn how to hold subordinates accountable, yet tolerate mistakes and deficiencies, while also providing leadership to generate high performance. Performance feedback becomes essential to feelings of success or failure.

An important individual decision to be made at this stage concerns specialization. Specializing (as in sales, accounting, or human resources) allows a person to become an expert in one area. The potential danger, though, is that of being pigeonholed. An alternative is to develop a set of specialized skills and apply them in a variety of areas. For example, a computer specialist (programmer or systems analyst) can apply those skills in marketing, accounting, human resources, manufacturing, and finance. The risk then is that of becoming a jack of all trades and a master of none. Thus the individual must balance the potential career rewards and potential career risks of these options.

As they approach the age of 40, many employees have developed skills that make them attractive to other organizations. Top managers recognize this situation and use golden handcuffs to retain valued employees. **Golden handcuffs** are the salary, perks (e.g., country club memberships, plush office, and company car), and fringe benefits (e.g., deferred compensation plans and stock options) that organizations use to tie employees to them. The independence once sought by the college graduate has now been replaced by a growing commitment to and dependence on the organization.

Peer relationships are especially important at this stage. The individual relies less and less on a mentor for direction and advice and, instead, turns to peers. They provide an outlet for discussing inequalities, such as who did and didn't get promoted and why, the size of pay increases and bonuses, and the like. The transition from relating to a mentor to relating to peers is not easy. Peers may exploit flaws in others when the opportunity arises. For example, if someone fails to receive an expected promotion, the individual will likely turn to peers for emotional support. The individual hopes that they will agree that the wrong person was promoted and offer advice and comfort. However, some of them may secretly be glad that the person was not promoted because this opens opportunities for them to get promoted faster. Once someone has been passed over, the chances for being considered again decrease.

During the advancement stage, a person's struggles with decisions at work often are compounded by struggles with personal decisions. Work and personal decisions often are interrelated. Whether to take a promotion or a horizontal move with its corresponding relocation, longer hours, more travel, and increased stress requires consideration of its effects on an individual's personal and family life. Whether to stay with an organization and become increasingly tied to it by golden handcuffs is yet another consideration. College graduates will change jobs an average of four times during their careers; those job changes will occur primarily during the advancement stage.

Table 21.5 summarizes the concerns of employees at this career stage. As the potential for advancement is either realized or not, self-esteem and the probability of future advancement are determined.

TABLE 21.5   Concerns of Employees at the Advancement Stage—Ages 26–39

▲ Central activities: specialization, independent contributor, professional standing

▲ Primary relationship: peers

▲ Needed from superior: exposure, challenging work, sponsorship

Table 21.6 illustrates some of the characteristics of successful employees at this stage of their careers. Note that four characteristics of the establishment stage remain valid for successful employees at the advancement stage: They feel successful, believe that the job is not challenging, have an open and supportive manager, and want to be promoted soon. The newly acquired characteristics of successful managers at this stage are that they now have a different mentor and make few interorganizational moves. Because the manager and the former mentor might now be at similar organizational levels, a different mentor often is needed to maintain the manager's visibility to senior management, secure challenging job assignments, and the like.

TABLE 21.6   Characteristics of Successful Employees at the Advancement Stage

▲ Feel successful.

▲ Believe that their current job is not challenging.

▲ Have an open and supportive manager.

▲ Want to be promoted again, soon.

▲ Have another mentor.

▲ Make fewer interorganizational moves but more intraorganizational moves.

Maintenance Career Stage   Moving into the **maintenance career stage** is often associated with various personal changes.[27]Changes in physical appearance and stamina occur more rapidly after the age of 40: Hair begins to turn gray, skin begins to wrinkle, and muscles begin to complain during tennis and racquetball games. In addition to these types of changes, some 35% of today's managers probably will experience a mid-life crisis. A **mid-life crisis** results in radical changes in a person's behavior and usually occurs between the ages of 39 and 44.[28]A career that hasn't matched a person's dreams and expectations can lead to feelings of resentment, sadness, frustration, and severe personal problems. Someone experiencing such a crisis may quit a stable job and take a less secure one, become a middle-aged dropout, be unable to cope with family problems, or get divorced.

During this stage, a person may take one of three typical career paths: star, solid citizen, or decliner. The path selected will depend largely on the direction a career has taken during the first two stages. Those who have been picked by top managers as **stars** will continue to receive promotions, new job assign-ments, greater responsibility, and higher status. These people believe that they have almost made it. Special assignments and expanded mentoring roles are important to stars. Assignments may entail dealing with others outside the organization, such as governmental agencies and influential customers.

Many employees become **solid citizens.** They are reliable and do good work but, for one reason or another, have little chance of promotion. They may lack the technical skills needed to move to a higher level position, the desire for further promotion, or the interpersonal skills needed to play the organization's political game—or they may be too valuable in their present positions for the organization to move them to other jobs. Managers having these characteristics constitute the largest managerial group in any organiza-tion and accomplish most of its managerial work.

Regardless of the reason, some of the solid citizens have reached a **career plateau,** a level at which the likelihood of future promotions is very low.[29] Plateauing does not ordinarily lead to a decline in performance, nor does it necessarily reflect poor performance in the past. Rather, a plateau is reached in most cases simply because far more qualified people are available for higher level positions than there are positions. As organizations downsize, the op-portunities for promotion decline even more. Organizations need fewer em-ployees and hence fewer managers. Solid citizens face doing the same job for many years. They need to be patient, trying not to overreact to mistakes and helping newcomers learn from their mistakes. Many develop nonwork inter-ests and become deeply involved in community and family activities.

Decliners have little chance for promotion. They often are given staff jobs that top managers have labeled dead-end positions. The performance of these employees is likely to decline to a point where it becomes marginal. They simply try not to make mistakes that will result in their getting fired. Decliners tend to have few relationships at work. Because they lack influence in the organization, their attempts at mentoring fail. They do not receive challenging assignments, and salary increases are minimal. By accepting positions out of the mainstream of decision making, they hope to hang on until retirement.

Table 21.7 compares the results for employees who have taken the "star" and "decliner" paths at this stage of their careers. These results are grouped into three categories: the organization, the job, and the manager.[30] The *organ-ization* refers to characteristics of the organization's structure that influence careers. Stars gravitate to organizations such as PepsiCo, Promus, Johnson & Johnson that reward risk taking and let employees exercise judgment in mak-ing decisions about products, markets, and manufacturing processes. They are bound by few rules and regulations. Employees are encouraged and rewarded to take the initiative. Decliners find themselves in organizations that stifle initiative with numerous rules and regulations. The reward system encourages the status quo by sending people who take a risk and fail off to "corporate Siberia."

The *jobs* that stars take eventually involve managing people on important projects for the organization, gaining them access and visibility to senior man-agement. Working 60–70 hours a week to meet tight time and financial dead-lines without burning out is crucial to their success. The hectic pace of the job requires that they delegate details to others and focus on policy decisions that have broad implications for the firm. They are self-directed learners. Decliners

TABLE 21.7   Career Path Characteristics for Stars and Decliners

	Stars	Decliners
The Organization	▲ Culture supports experimentation	▲ Culture supports maintenance
	▲ Few rules and regulations to follow	▲ Many rules and procedures to follow
	▲ Frequent changes in products and processes	▲ Stable environment
	▲ Employees held accountable for results	▲ Little support for risk taking
	▲ Rewards are greater influence, involvement, and status	▲ Rewards are personal freedom and job satisfaction
The Job	▲ High "people" involvement	▲ Low "people" involvement
	▲ Develops policy	▲ Administers policy
	▲ High stress and variety of work	▲ Medium–low stress and work on routine problems
	▲ People problems	▲ Impersonal feedback
	▲ Jobs that promote visibility and increase learning leadership skills	▲ Little upward visibility
The Manager	▲ High people orientation	▲ Low people orientation
	▲ Open mind to solving problems differently	▲ Limiting framework
	▲ Able to articulate their own learning processes	▲ Inarticulate regarding their own learning processes
	▲ Frequently moved into key jobs	▲ Little movement from current job

tend to be good in technical jobs that are not strategically important to the organization and do not involve managing others. Therefore their jobs give them little visibility to senior managers.

Finally, the *manager* of a star has moved frequently and mentored other stars. These managers are able to transfer what they have learned to others with an open mind. Stars find these managers to be approachable, have access to resources that help them reach their objectives, and are part of the organization's political network. Managers of decliners have not moved frequently, have limited access to top managers, and have dead-end jobs themselves. They might even feel threatened by others and therefore tend to seek simple as opposed to complex jobs.

In summary, the maintenance stage is the time when most employees review their careers. Table 21.8 shows their concerns. Stars continue to receive promotions and are assigned increasingly challenging and important tasks. Solid citizens are satisfied with their careers, demonstrate loyalty to the organization, and can serve as mentors. Decliners are assigned duties that are out of the mainstream of the organization.

TABLE 21.8   Concerns of Employees at the Maintenance Stage—Ages 40–60

▲ Central activities: training and directing others

▲ Primary relationship: mentoring

▲ Needed from superiors: autonomy, opportunity to develop others

Withdrawal Career Stage   The **withdrawal career stage** occurs for most people when they reach about 60 years of age. Even though they are still energetic, they are being passed over or given the opportunity for early retirement. In general, employees at this career stage can afford to cope with reduced career prospects. Most will hang on to their jobs as long as they can. As the work force becomes more competitive, high-performing employees at this career stage can bring together the resources and people to push new ideas to a successful conclusion, playing the role of maverick or internal entrepreneur. These roles are legitimate so long as they are performed successfully. A person's identity as a maverick or entrepreneur often is based on a solid reputation in the company.

At this stage, senior employees often seek to establish mentoring relationships with younger employees. Many will spend considerable time and energy on developing their replacements. They learn to think about the needs of the organization beyond the time of their involvement in it. Others devote time to establishing relationships outside their organizations and representing their organizations in business, professional, and community affairs.[31]

▼ CAREER PLANNING ISSUES

Career planning entails evaluating abilities and interests and considering alternative career development activities.[32] The process results in decisions to enter a certain occupation, join a particular organization, accept or decline new job opportunities (relocations, promotions, or transfers), and ultimately leave an organization for another job or retirement.

▼ Effects of Career Planning

A career planning program can help an organization meet its continuing staff requirements.[33] In large organizations, a typical career planning program might include

▲ career counseling by members of the human resources department;

▲ workshops to help employees evaluate their skills, abilities, and interests and to formulate career development plans;

▲ self-directed programs aimed at helping employees guide their own careers through self-assessment; and/or

▲ communication of job opportunities through job postings, videotapes, and publications.

Career planning has both positive and negative effects. Career planning may increase managers' work loads by requiring them to provide counseling and on-the-job development assistance. Career planning may lead to greater employee demand for career development resources, such as training, education assistance (tuition reimbursement), and staff counseling. Employees may request more information on job vacancies, pay practices, and career opportunities, and raise fundamental questions regarding individual strengths, weaknesses, and goals for the first time. Greater expectations may increase employee anxiety, and unfulfilled expectations may lead to disappointment and reduce commitment. As a result, some employees may become less motivated to perform well, and others may seek work elsewhere.

Despite these negative effects, American Airlines, Gulf Oil, IBM, GE, Xerox, the IRS and others have developed career planning programs to reduce turnover, enhance the quality of working life, and improve job performance.[34] These organizations recognize that stimulating realistic career aspirations is in their best interests and those of their employees. Moreover, these organizations have tried to dispel the "up-or-out" notion of career because many employees ultimately will be plateaued. Therefore horizontal career moves within specialized job areas can be attractive to many employees if career information focuses on personal development, work content, and job importance, rather than solely on promotability.

Career planning also may provide employees with information to enable them to make better career decisions. Rather than raising expectations with promises that probably will not be fulfilled, many companies candidly describe what their programs can and cannot do, along with identifying anticipated job opportunities. Let's now turn to three key career issues facing employees: dual-career couples, women in management, and outplacement.

▼ Dual-Career Couples

The traditional family with the husband as the breadwinner and wife as a homemaker and child care-taker is fast becoming obsolete. Although wives still bear a disproportionate share of the housework, the U.S. Department of Labor reports that 81% of all marriages involve dual careers.[35] **Dual careers** refers to both partners working outside the home. When both hold down full-time jobs, they typically earn more than $50,000, but experience severe stress.[36]

Stressors   *Family stressors* are especially important when there are children under age 6, who generally need more attention than older children. The amount and quality of each parent's time with the children must be balanced against the demands of each person's job. Research indicates that women managers are more likely than male managers to experience job burnout from family, as opposed to work schedule stress.

Work *schedule* stressors increase as individuals rise in the organization; job demands increase, with long hours, travel, and little time for vacations. Job demands often conflict with family demands and trade-offs are made—many times unsuccessfully. For example, a meeting in Chicago lasts longer than expected, which means that a flight connection is missed, which causes a parent to miss a child's school play or sporting event after promising to attend, which the parent attempts to make up for with a present from the airport gift store.

Work role stressors involve role ambiguity, conflict, and overload (see Chapter 8). *Organizational stressors* relate to organizational politics and lack of career progress. Men are much more likely than women to exhibit this type of stress. Women do not show the effects of organizational stress in family matters as much as men do. Men seldom separate work and home problems.

Relocation   The increase in the number of dual-career couples poses problems for many companies when they try to relocate employees. In 1977, Merrill Lynch conducted a relocation survey and asked companies whether employees were resisting transfers because of working spouses. At that time, less than 20% indicated a concern. By 1981, that figure had increased to 26%, and Merrill Lynch estimates that it now is more than 35%.

Seventy percent of the companies surveyed believed that the spouse's job will play a larger role in future relocation decisions.[37] One of the principal challenges for multinational employers (e.g., Mobil, Intel, and 3M) always has been to select stars for overseas assignments who will succeed abroad and successfully reintegrate in their home country. Taking a job with a foreign corporation and relocating to a different country present special difficulties for the dual-career couple. In many countries, spouses of the transferred employee can't continue their careers because they have no job prospects. The loss of spousal income is an obvious concern. As a result, couples have no choice but to come up with creative solutions. For example, some dual career couples are working in two different foreign countries that are close to one another.

In an attempt to satisfy the needs of both partners, some multinational organizations are establishing policies to eliminate as many barriers as possible to an international assignment for dual-career couples. How 3M tackled this challenge is the focus of the following Managing Across Cultures account.

MANAGING ACROSS CULTURES

3M

Presently 60 to 70 families are participating in 3M's program that attempts to attract high-potential employees to international assignments. What are some of the unique features of this program? First, when a spouse is employed by another company or self-employed, the non–3M person receives a dislocation allowance of up to $5,000. Second, another payment is made when the trailing spouse accompanies the 3M employee on the premove relocation visit. Third, the spouse may be reimbursed for language training and other skill training in the new location. Finally, when the employee's foreign assignment ends and they return to their host country, 3M works with the spouse to find another job. Every effort is made by 3M to place the person in a job that is the same as or comparable to the person's former position.[38]

▼ Child Care

Child care always has been a problem for the working poor. Traditionally, they have relied on neighbors or extended families and, in the worst cases, have left their children alone at home or to roam the streets. However, three major events have transformed this problem into one for the vast majority of working women, including female managers.[39]First, the feminist movement of the 1960s encouraged homemakers to seek fulfillment in a career. Women now make up over 55% of the labor force, and they are expected to fill about 60% of the jobs created between 1994 and 2000. Second, economic recessions and inflation hit the family pocketbook hard. Between 1973 and 1991, the median income for families—adjusted for inflation—fell by more than 13%. Suddenly, the middle-class dream of a house, car, and a college education for the children carried a dual-income price tag. So for most families, two paychecks are a necessity. Third, the number of single-parent heads of household has skyrocketed. Since more than 50% of all marriages end in a divorce, single parents are faced with the challenge of raising children from a dissolved marriage alone. The financial burden of this arrangement is difficult for the single parent.

More than 14 million preschoolers in the United States spend their days with someone other than their mothers.[40] As U.S. women continue to enter the work force, the number will increase. By 2000, an estimated 80% of the women aged 25–44 will be working outside the home. Of those 80%, 90% will be mothers. This percentage represents a dramatic increase since the 1970s, when only 29% of working women were mothers.

Employers are aware that day care worries can weigh heavily on mothers and fathers alike and can hurt productivity.[41] As the competition for good workers increases, many organizations will be forced to grapple with the problems that working parents face or risk losing desirable employees. Among others, IBM offers employees a free child care referral service and plans to spend more than $22 million during the next few years to improve the availability and quality of day care in the towns and cities where most of its employees live. Johnson & Johnson has an on-site day care center at its headquarters in New Brunswick, New Jersey. Johnson & Johnson subsidizes part of its cost, but employees using the center still pay $110 to $130 a week, depending on the age of the child. American Bankers Insurance Group of Miami, like other smaller organizations, maintains a day care center for employees' children between the ages of 6 weeks and 5 years. After that, the child can attend a company-run private school for an additional three years. The school provides care for the children from 8:00 A.M. to 6:15 P.M. and remains open during public school holidays and summer vacations. These companies believe that the centers have resulted in a 53% decline in absenteeism and tardiness and a 65% decrease in female executive turnover.

▼ Women in Management

Women rarely occupy the top positions at the largest U.S. corporations. The proportion of women who hold senior management positions has increased slightly from less than 3% in 1979 to about 5% in 1994.[42] Although the percentage of all management positions filled by women has increased from 18.5% in 1970 to approximately 40% in 1994, women still are underrepresented in powerful management positions in most organizations. In some corporations (e.g., Allstate Insurance Company, CBS, Dayton-Hudson, AT&T, and Corning) women are making some progress in entering executive suites. These corporations are cutting back on the travel, relocation, and long hours that exclude many women with families. These firms also offer benefits, such as extended leaves, flex-time, and elder care assistance, that help women balance family requirements, which still fall most heavily on their shoulders, and job demands.

Traditionally the top management jobs have been held by men, which is a principal reason for the glass ceiling that slows and in some instances prevents women from moving into higher level managerial jobs. Assigning mentors to women is one way to dismantle the glass ceiling. Organizations also are tackling this problem by revising procedures affecting promotion and holding decision makers accountable for eliminating gender bias in the promotion process.

Women in management positions face three types of pressures.[43] First, there is the pressure of the job itself. The demands to satisfy irate customers, return numerous phone calls, and handle disgruntled subordinates seem endless. They must continuously address problems that seemingly have no answers but are only symptomatic of larger problems. They must gather information from peers, superiors, and subordinates. Many things must be done quickly, and information is often limited. The glass ceiling often prevents women from forming these close work associations that cut across departments and divisions. Therefore they often don't have the same networks to rely on when making decisions that male managers have, yet face the same job demands.

Second, a woman going into a high-level meeting often sees few other women. Thus the pressure of being in the minority and representing women as a group is great. Deborah Hueppler, CEO at Just Brakes Corporation, remembers her first day at a Dartmouth College engineering class. She was the only woman and found herself sitting next to empty desks in a classroom of 150 seats.[44] In addition to being watched closely by other managers, women must overcome the "good ole boy" feeling that still exists in senior management. It protects men when they make managerial mistakes because they are part of the closed circle sometimes referred to as the "men's hut."

Third, women are still expected to take major responsibility for maintaining a household, raising a family, and providing a caring and comforting environment at home. The role reversal—being tough, no-nonsense, and efficient in the office but being tender, playful, and caring at home—can be stressful.

Major Success Factors   Table 21.9 compares the success factors for female and male managers.[45] For women, six factors are more important than for men. For women, getting help from a mentor is extremely important in breaking through the glass ceiling. The mentor provides all types of advice and general encouragement. The lack of female manager role models means that a mentor must spend moretime grooming female than male managers. Mentors can help them become visible and get middle-management jobs with profit-and-loss responsibility. Having an outstanding track record, along with a mentor who helps promote her success, is more important for a woman than it is for a man.

Successful female managers often stand out in terms of completing assignments, being technically competent, having the ability to head off potential problems, and being highly professional. Successful women also demonstrate an ability to handle the three pressures discussed earlier. These women were "willing to pay the price" and generally make family life secondary to career until they become established. Being mobile, never questioning a relocation,

TABLE 21.9   Success Factors for Female and Male Managers

Factor	Percentage of Managers Who Agree on Importance of Factor	
	Successful Women	Successful Men
▲ Help from above (mentor)	100%	55%
▲ Track record	89	75
▲ Desire to succeed	84	45
▲ Ability to manage subordinates	74	50
▲ Willingness to take career risks	74	15
▲ Ability to be tough, demanding, and decisive	68	20

Source: Adapted from Morrison, A. M., White, R. P., Van Velsor, E., and the Center for Creative Leadership. *Breaking the Glass Ceiling: Can Women Reach the Top of America's Largest Corporations?* Reading, Mass.: Addison-Wesley, 1987, 190; Hellwig, B. The breakthrough generation: 73 women ready to run corporate America. *Working Women*, April 1985, 99–148; Morrison, A. M., and Von Glinow, M. A. Women and minorities in management. *American Psychologist*, 1990, 45, 200–208.

and being dedicated to the organization are more important for female than for men executives. The ability to manage subordinates, especially men, is crucial. This ability includes hiring the right people and pulling in key people from other departments to get the job done.

Female managers also must take more career risks than men. Such risks include moving into an unfamiliar department, relocating to a foreign country, taking a promotion before being ready, or transferring to a lower level job if that job gives a better shot at the top eventually. Subordinates often describe female executives as being tough, decisive, aggressive, strong-willed, and not afraid to speak their minds.

Conditions in Other Cultures   Almost no Japanese women occupy managerial positions higher than clerical supervisors, especially in large, multinational corporations. As a society, Japan expects women to work until marriage, quit to raise children, and return, as needed, to low-level and part-time positions after the age of 40. Although some cracks are appearing in these traditional patterns for Japanese women, they have fewer opportunities than women in the United States. Women from wealthy families in the Philippines can hold influential managerial positions because of family connections. However, less than 3% of the working women hold administrative or managerial positions. In Mexico, women hold only 1.6% of all managerial jobs, compared with about 15% in the United States.

▼ Outplacement

Called the dismantling of the Fortune 500 by many, between 1980 and 1994, millions of managers lost their jobs. More and more companies are being forced to cut costs to stay competitive. A result, the number of attractive management positions has shrunk dramatically. Fierce global competition and heavy corporate debt loads have forced organizations to cut back on the number of managers more than ever before. A *Fortune* survey reported that 86% of the top 1,000 organizations significantly downsized during the past five years. By 1997, the managerial ranks of these corporations are expected to shrink even further.[46]

The managers most vulnerable to layoff are middle managers who are in the maintenance or decline stage of their careers and whose contributions to the organization are difficult to measure. To handle this steady flow of managerial departures, organizations increasingly are using outplacement agencies. These firms have grown from small businesses 20 years ago to an industry with more than $1 billion in annual revenues. **Outplacement firms** are organizations that assist laid-off managers in career planning and job hunting. Such assistance includes testing to pinpoint job preferences, extensive counseling, and the use of an office and support services. If nothing else, outplacement firms give these managers a place to go regularly to maintain some structure in their lives and some sense of involvement with others. Drake Beam Morin, the nation's largest outplacement firm, indicates that, on average, more than eight months are required for a manager to find a new position, or two months longer than in 1989. Many managers go through stages of mourning, similar to that following other tragic events in life.[47]

Outplacement counselors say that people who bounce back the quickest are those who can express their anger and who immediately move on to the next phase of their lives.[48] Outplacement firms help by having people take a realistic look at themselves and their financial situations and assess their options. Large corporations typically give laid-off managers a severance check, but they also may pick up the expenses of the outplacement firm, which range between 10% and 20% of the manager's former salary. Nothing an outplacement firm can do compares to what displaced managers can do for themselves, as the following Managing in Practice item illustrates.

MANAGING IN PRACTICE

Coping with Job Loss

Robert Humes, a manager with Squibb, has coped well with his outplacement because he never relied solely on his job to provide him with a sense of self-esteem. He realized that, when Bristol-Myers acquired Squibb in 1989, a Bristol-Myers manager would take over his responsibility. He knew that he would be replaced as soon as the merger was completed. But after 18 years of working for Squibb, he still found the layoff hard to take. His typical day begins with a visit to the office of an outplacement firm in Princeton, New Jersey. He makes a few calls and dictates a letter or two to a staff secretary. He has inquired about 50 jobs and pursued about 6. He received an offer from one corporation in Texas, but he didn't want to move that far. Humes insists that he is flexible and open to jobs in organizations much smaller than Squibb and to jobs that probably cannot match his former six-figure salary. He maintains his active involvement in the Princeton chapter of the Red Cross because it enables him to keep up with business contacts and gives him a feeling of self-worth.[49]

Losing your job is an emotional blow, but it doesn't have to be a career disaster. Jim Tarter, senior principal at King, Chapman, Broussard & Gallagher, a major human resources consulting firm, indicates that you can take several steps to make the period of unemployment shorter.

▲ Stay calm. The worst mistake that you can make is to reach out frantically for the first job you can find. Get into the market with a plan, not emotions.

▲ Save your network of contacts and friends until you are ready to move. More than 70% of new managerial jobs come from networking.

▲ Be flexible. The more broadly that you define your skills, the greater are your options.

▲ Try to avoid emotional highs and lows. Searching for a new job is a roller coaster. You can ride it better if you keep your expectations for each new job prospect low and avoid disappointment after failed interviews.

▲ Don't pretend that you weren't fired. It doesn't carry the same stigma as it did five years ago, and interviewers probably will learn the truth anyway.

▲ Maintain a daily routine. Visit the outplacement firm regularly, eat well, exercise, and take time to relax.[50]

Summary

In this chapter we focused on how individuals make career path decisions. As organizations downsize and outsource work, the need for huge permanent work forces is declining. As a result, most individuals will make several job, organization, and career moves during their working lives. The first step in embarking on a career path is to join an organization. Organizations try to socialize newcomers through a sequence of activities: getting in, breaking in, and settling in. Individual and organizational factors affect the choice of a career, including the probability that a person will choose one in which he or she is likely to be successful. Individual factors that affect occupational choice include personality, vocational interests, self-esteem, and social background. Organizational factors include the type of industry, the nature of the organization, organizational culture, and the characteristics of the job. When there is a good match between the person and the organization, the employee is likely to be satisfied with the job, be a high performer, and develop a solid commitment to the organization.

There are three distinct types of career movements within an organization: vertical, horizontal, and inclusion. Each presents a new series of challenges and career issues. A person's working life can be divided into four career stages, each of which presents certain problems that have to be resolved. In the establishment stage, the newcomer is a subordinate and will be expected to follow directives and perform routine tasks well. During this stage, the newcomer should find a mentor in the organization.

After passing through the establishment stage, the individual moves into the advancement stage. The central activity at this stage involves specialization and making an independent contribution. Instead of relying solely on a mentor for sponsorship, individuals will likely turn to peers for encouragement and support.

As employees pass age 40, they probably will enter the maintenance career stage. One of three paths can be followed during this stage: (1) those who are selected as stars will continue to receive assignments that involve greater levels of challenge, authority, and responsibility; (2) others become known as solid citizens who have little chance for further promotion because they have reached a career plateau but will continue to perform well; and (3) others become decliners because they let their performance slip, become indifferent, and will be bypassed and cut off from the mainstream of decision making.

In the withdrawal stage, the individual begins to think about retiring. Some play the maverick role and others the internal entrepreneurial role; still others spend time establishing relationships outside the organization. As managers proceed through the withdrawal stage, they begin to feel the loss of power and have to learn not to second-guess the decisions of subordinates.

Three important issues in career planning are (1) the impact of career choices on dual-career couples regarding relocation and child-care; (2) problems facing working women, especially the glass ceiling, in their efforts to move up in organizations, and (3) facing the loss of a job and going through outplacement.

Key Words and Concepts

Advancement career stage	Dual careers	Mid-life crisis
Anticipatory socialization	Establishment career stage	Outplacement firms
Career	Glass ceiling	Realistic job preview
Career development	Golden handcuffs	Solid citizens
Career plan	Horizontal career movement	Stars
Career plateau	Inclusion career movement	Vertical career movement
Career stage	Maintenance career stage	Withdrawal career stage
Decliners	Mentor	

Discussion Questions

1. Why should people be concerned about managing their careers? What can happen if people do not actively plan and manage their careers?

2. How important will the amount and type of work be in your career? What makes you feel that way?

3. Do you plan to choose an occupation that matches your talents, values, and personality? What are some obstacles to finding such a match?

4. Have your educational experiences in college given you a realistic picture of what being a new employee in an organization is like? Why or why not?

5. What are the advantages to organizations of utilizing realistic job previews? To perspective employees?

6. Why are mentors important to people in the establishment career stage? How can mentors contribute to the development of protégés early in their careers?

7. What are some of the problems that female managers face as they attempt to get promoted?

8. Describe the pressures facing dual-career couples?

9. What are some career issues facing employees during the maintainence stage of their careers?

10. What are some functions that outplacement firms perform for managers who have lost their jobs?

11. Employees often say that success in a career, at least as measured by society's yardsticks of money and status,

doesn't guarantee personal happiness. Do you agree? Why or why not?

12. Discuss the special problems that employees face when they relocate to a foreign country. Why might such an assignment be career ending?

▲ Developing Skills

Self-Diagnosis: Life Success Scale[51]

Instructions

People have different ideas about what it means to be successful. Please rate each of the following ideas on life success by circling the number that best represents its importance to you.

	Always Important	Very Often Important	Fairly Often Important	Occasionally Important	Never Important
1. Getting others to do what I want	5	4	3	2	1
2. Having inner peace and contentment	5	4	3	2	1
3. Having a happy marriage	5	4	3	2	1
4. Having economic security	5	4	3	2	1
5. Being committed to my organization	5	4	3	2	1
6. Being able to give help, assistance, advice, and support to others	5	4	3	2	1
7. Having a job that pays more than peers earn	5	4	3	2	1
8. Being a good parent	5	4	3	2	1
9. Having good job benefits	5	4	3	2	1
10. Having a rewarding family life	5	4	3	2	1
11. Raising children to be independent adults	5	4	3	2	1
12. Having people work for me	5	4	3	2	1
13. Being accepted at work	5	4	3	2	1
14. Enjoying my nonwork activities	5	4	3	2	1
15. Making or doing things that are useful to society	5	4	3	2	1
16. Having high income and the resulting benefits	5	4	3	2	1
17. Having a sense of personal worth	5	4	3	2	1
18. Contributing to society	5	4	3	2	1
19. Having long-term job security	5	4	3	2	1
20. Having children	5	4	3	2	1
21. Getting good performance evaluations	5	4	3	2	1
22. Having opportunities for personal creativity	5	4	3	2	1
23. Being competent	5	4	3	2	1
24. Having public recognition	5	4	3	2	1

25. Having children who are successful emotionally and professionally	5	4	3	2	1
26. Having influence over others	5	4	3	2	1
27. Being happy with my private life	5	4	3	2	1
28. Earning regular salary increases	5	4	3	2	1
29. Having personal satisfaction	5	4	3	2	1
30. Improving the well-being of the work force	5	4	3	2	1
31. Having a stable marriage	5	4	3	2	1
32. Having the confidence of my bosses	5	4	3	2	1
33. Having the resources to help others	5	4	3	2	1
34. Being in a high-status occupation	5	4	3	2	1
35. Being able to make a difference in something	5	4	3	2	1
36. Having money to buy or do anything	5	4	3	2	1
37. Being satisfied with my job	5	4	3	2	1
38. Having self-respect	5	4	3	2	1
39. Helping others to achieve	5	4	3	2	1
40. Having personal happiness	5	4	3	2	1
41. Being able to provide quality education for my children	5	4	3	2	1
42. Making a contribution to society	5	4	3	2	1

Scoring

The STATUS/WEALTH SCORE is found by adding responses to items:

____	____	____	____	____	____	____	____	____/8 = ____
1	7	12	16	24	26	34	36	Total

The CONTRIBUTION TO SOCIETY SCORE is found by adding responses to items:

____	____	____	____	____	____	____	____	____/8 = ____
6	15	18	22	33	35	39	42	Total

The FAMILY RELATIONSHIPS SCORE is found by adding responses to items:

____	____	____	____	____	____	____	____	____/8 = ____
3	8	10	11	20	25	31	41	Total

THE PERSONAL FULFILLMENT SCORE is found by adding responses to items:

____	____	____	____	____	____	____	____	____/8 = ____
2	14	17	23	27	29	38	40	Total

The PROFESSIONAL FULFILLMENT SCORE is found by adding responses to items:

____	____	____	____	____	____/5 = ____
5	13	21	32	37	Total

The SECURITY SCORE is found by adding responses to items:

____	____	____	____	____	____/5 = ____
4	9	19	28	30	Total

To compare your scores with those of managerial men and women, please use the following norms.

Norms

	Women (n = 439)	Men (n = 317)
Status/wealth	3.48	3.65
Social contribution	4.04	4.07
Family relationships	4.44	4.28
Personal fulfillment	4.60	4.43
Professional fulfillment	4.21	4.15
Security	4.30	4.21

In what areas do your scores differ from those of managers? Why?

A Case in Point: Tradeoffs

What a great beginning. Two weeks after graduating, Martha Wilson started her first day with Comtec, a small software manufacturer in Richardson, Texas. The company gave her time off to find an apartment, get a Texas driver's license, and straighten out some personal matters.

Wilson had been hired as a management trainee and promised supervisory assignment within a year. However, because of a management reorganization, she was placed in charge of an five-person customer service group only five months after starting work. The group's job was to handle customer problems as quickly as possible, with manufacturing if necessary. The reorganization streamlined work, upgraded some clerical jobs, and made greater use of the computer to provide customer service. It was a drastic departure from the old way of doing things and created a great deal of anxiety among Wilson's five-person group.

Management realized that the supervisors needed leeway to redesign their own departments, so management gave them a free hand to run their units as they saw fit. Wilson used this latitude to implement team meetings and a training class. She also promised all her people that they would get raises if they worked hard to learn their new jobs. By working long hours, participating in training class, and with her leadership style, she was able to increase productivity, reduce customer complaints, and cut turnover and absenteeism in her unit. Top management quickly noticed these results, and Wilson earned a reputation in the company was a "superstar" despite being viewed by other managers as free spirited and unorthodox. Top management tolerated her style because of her excellent results.

After three years, Wilson received an offer from BanTec to manage a marketing department. Taking the job would involve moving to Phoenix, finding a place to live, establishing new friends, and so on. The pay was excellent, and it offered her an opportunity to turn around a department whose results had been poor. She felt that her work at Comtec was finished and didn't see any immediate opportunity for advancement. Most of her mentors at Comtec had left the organization. She decided to take the job. Comtec threw a huge party for her and top management indicated that if she ever wanted to return, all she needed to do was just pick up the phone.

The new job was exciting. BanTec had clients in Mexico and Canada and was preparing to open a manufacturing plant in Leeds, England. Her boss, Larry Wilson, also encouraged her to think about getting an MBA at a local university to broaden her business horizons. Within nine months, she started graduate school and developed a relationship with Art Cunningham. Art worked for Baxter International and had been transferred recently from Chicago to Phoenix. Martha's job was exciting and required lots of travel. Being out of the office a lot, she learned to delegate decisions to subordinates. She encouraged them to participate in training sessions and juggle their competing needs and expectations. She got in the habit of taking ten minutes every Friday to note "big mistakes made and lessons learned." These notes helped her set benchmarks for the next week. The performance of her department increased dramatically because she trusted subordinates to make decisions and spent less time on details.

After three years, she had completed her MBA degree, had traveled overseas extensively, and had become engaged to Art. The president of BanTec asked her to come by for a chat about her career. He asked her to consider an assignment as vice-president for operations at BanTec's plant in Monterrey, Mexico. He indicated that her management style and experience would be valuable in improving productivity and morale at that plant. She knew that eventually she would need some manufacturing experience if she ever wanted to become a top manager at BanTec; all its top managers had manufacturing or engineering experience. She would be reporting to Enrique Rangel, the plant manager. She knew Rangel from her frequent visits to the plant but didn't know whether she would be able to adapt to his strict, task-oriented style. Furthermore, there were no women in management positions in the plant. Employees in the plant joked that Rangel's idea of MBO was "Management by Oppression." Martha told the president that she would need some time to think over the offer.

Questions

1. What career stage is Martha in? What personal concerns is she facing?

2. Describe stressors that she will face if she and Larry become a dual-career couple?

3. What decision would you make if you were Martha? What did you consider in making that decision?

References

1. Adapted from Henkoff, R. Winning the new career game. *Fortune*, July 12, 1993, 46–49; Sherman, S. A brave new Darwinian workplace. *Fortune*, January 25, 1993, 50–56.

2. Kiechel, W. III. A manager's career in the new economy. *Fortune*, April 4, 1994, 68–72.

3. *Ibid*, 71

4. Allen, N. J., and Meyer, J. P. Organizational socialization tactics: A longitudinal analysis of links to newcomers' commitment and role orientation. *Academy of Management Journal*, 1990, 33, 847–858; Ostroff, C., and Kozlowski, S. W. J. Organizational socialization as a learning process: The role of information acquisition. *Personnel Psychology*, 1992, 849–874.

5. Calloway, W. Building a culture of growth. *Fortune*, March 7, 1994, 70–72.

6. Wanous, J. P. *Organizational Entry*. Reading, Mass.: Addison-Wesley, 1981; Meglino, B. M., DeNisi, A. S., Youngblood, S. A., and Williams, K. K. Effects of realistic job previews: A comparison using an enhancement and a reduction preview. *Journal of Applied Psychology*, 1988, 73, 259–266; Vandenberg, J., and Scarpello, V. The matching method: An examination of the processes underlying realistic job previews. *Journal of Applied Psychology*, 1990, 75, 60–67.

7. Adapted from Buss, D. Job tryouts without pay get more testing in U.S. auto plants. *Wall Street Journal*, January 10, 1985, Section 2, 29.

8. Adapted from Fulkerson, J. R., and Schuler, D. S. Managing worldwide diversity at Pepsi-Cola International. In S. E. Jackson and Associates (eds.), *Diversity in the Workplace*. New York: Guilford Press, 1992, 248–278.

9. Ostroff, C., and Kozlowski, S. W. J. The role of mentoring in the information gathering process of newcomers during early organizational socialization. *Journal of Vocational Behavior*, 1993, 42, 170–183.

10. Feldman, D. C. *Managing Careers in Organizations*. Glenview, Ill.: Scott, Foresman, 1988.

11. Adapted from Rangel, E. Speed bumps on a career path. *Dallas Morning News*, March 1, 1994, D1, D4; Rangel, E. Women battle job bias in Mexico's corporations. *Dallas Morning News*, March 1, 1994, A1, A10.

12. Bretz, R. D., Jr., and Judge, T. A. Person–organization fit and the theory of work adjustment: Implications for satisfaction, tenure and career success. *Journal of Vocational Behavior*, 1994, 44, 32–54.

13. Keeney, P. Diversity at work. *Equal Opportunity*, Winter 1993, 33–35.

14. Adapted from Adelson, A. Black enterprise names Cross Colours as no. 1. *New York Times*, May 15, 1993, 19; Branch, S. How hip-hop fashion won over mainstream America. *Black Enterprise*, February 1993, 112–120.

15. Holland, J. V. *Making Vocational Choices*. Englewood Cliffs, N.J.: Prentice-Hall, 1973; Hyland, A. M., and Muchinsky, P. M. Assessment of the structural validity of Holland's Model with job analysis. *Journal of Applied Psychology*, 1991, 76, 75–80.

16. London, M. Relationship between career motivation, empowerment and support career development. *Journal of Occupational and Organizational Psychology*, 1993, 66, 55–69.

17. Schein, E. H. The individual, the organization, and the career: A conceptual scheme. *Journal of Applied Behavioral Science*, 1971, 7, 401–426.

18. Interview with John Slocum, Dallas, Texas, April 26, 1994.

19. This section is based primarily on the work of Don Super and his associates. For an overview, see Super, D. E. A life-span, life-space approach to career development. *Journal of Vocational Behavior*, 1980, 16, 282–298; Ornstein, S., and Isabella, L. A. Making sense of careers: A review of 1989–1992. *Journal of Management*, 1993, 19, 243–267.

20. Slocum, J. W., Jr., and Cron, W. L. Job attitudes and performance during three career stages. *Journal of Vocational Behavior*, 1985, 26, 126–145; Aryee, S., Chay, Y. W., and Chew, T. An investigation of the predictors and outcomes of career commitment in three stages. *Journal of Vocational Behavior*, 1994, 44, 1–16.

21. Kram, K. E. *Mentoring at Work: Developmental Relationships in Organizational Life*. Glenview, Ill.: Scott, Foresman, 1985; Whitely, W. T., and Coetsier, P. The relationship of career mentoring to early career outcomes. *Organization Studies*, 1993, 14, 419–441; Ohlott, P. J., Ruderman, M. N., and McCauley, C. D. Gender differences in managers' developmental job experiences. *Academy of Management Journal*, 1994, 37, 46–67.

22. Whitely, W., Dougherty, T. W., and Dreher, G. G. Relationship of career mentoring and socioeconomic origin to mangers' and professionals' early career progress. *Academy of Management Journal*, 1991, 34, 331–351; Olian, J. D., Carroll, S. J., and Giannantonio, C. M. Mentor reactions to protégés: An experiment with managers. *Journal of Vocational Behavior*, 1993, 43, 266–278; Ragins, B. R., and Cotton, J. L. Gender and willingness to mentor in organizations. *Journal of Management*, 1993, 19, 97–111; Turban, D. B., and Dougherty, T. W. Role of protégé personality in receipt of mentoring and career success. *Academy of Management Journal*, 1994, 37, 688–702.

23. Personal interview with John Slocum, Dallas, Texas, April 28, 1994.

24. Powell, G. N., and Butterfield, D. A. Investigating the "glass ceiling" phenomenon: An empirical study of actual promotions to top management. *Academy of Management Journal*, 1994, 37, 68–86; Greenhaus, J. H., and Parasuraman, S. Job performance attributions and career advancement prospects: An examination of race and gender effects. *Organizational Behavior and Human Decision Processes*, 1993, 55, 273–297.

25. Gattiker, U. E., and Larwood, L. Predictors for career achievement in the corporate hierarchy. *Human Relations*, 1990, 43, 707–726.

26. Sheridan, J. E., Slocum, J. W., Jr., Buda, R., and Thompson, R. Effects of corporate sponsorship and departmental power on career tournaments: A study of intra-organizational mobility. *Academy of Management Journal*, 1990, 33, 578–602; Kelly, R., and Caplan, J. How Bell Labs creates star performers. *Harvard Business Review*, July—August 1993, 128–139.

27. Stout, S. K., Slocum, J. W., Jr., and Cron, W. L. Career transitions of superiors and subordinates. *Journal of Vocational Behavior*, 1987, 30, 124–137.

28. McGill, M. E. *The 40-to-60 Year Old Male*. New York: Simon and Schuster, 1980; Paul, R., and Townsend, J. Managing the older worker: Don't just rinse away the gray. *Academy of Management Executive*, 1993, 7, 67–74; Fierman, J. Beating the midlife career crisis. *Fortune*, September 6, 1993, 58–60.

29. Slocum, J. W., Jr., Cron, W. L., Hansen, R., and Rawlings, S. Business strategy and the management of the plateaued performer. *Academy of Management Journal*, 1985, 28, 133–154; Feldman, D. C., and Weitz, B. A. Career plateaus reconsidered. *Journal of Management*, 1988, 14, 69–80; Chao, G. T. Exploration of the conceptualization and measurement of career plateau: A comparative analysis. *Journal of Management*, 1990, 16, 181–193.

30. Cron. W. E., Jackofsky, E. F., and Slocum, J. W., Jr. Job performance and attitudes of disengagement stage salespeople who are about to retire. *Journal of Personal Selling and Sales Management*, 1993, 13, 1–14; Feldman, D. C. The decision to retire early: A review and conceptualization. *Academy of Management Review*, 1994, 19, 285–311.

31. Heppner, M. J., Multon, K. D., and Johnston, J. A. Assessing psychological resources during career change: Development of the careers transitions inventory. *Journal of Vocational Behavior*, 1994, 44, 55–74.

32. Adler, N., and Izraeli's, D. N. *Women Managers in a Global Economy*. Cambridge, Mass.: Oxford, 1993; Ayree, S., and Debrah, Y. A. A cross-cultural application of a career planning model. *Journal of Organizational Behavior*, 1993, 14, 119–127.

33. Blau, G., Linnenham, F., Brooks, A., and Hoover, D. K. Vocational behavior 1990–1992: Personnel practices, organizational behavior, workplace justice, and industrial/organizational measurement issues. *Journal of Vocational Behavior*, 1993, 43, 133–197.

34. Richman, L. S. How to get ahead in America. *Fortune*, May 16, 1994, 46–54.

35. Karanbayya, R., and Reilly, A. H. Dual earner couples: Attitudes and actions in restructuring work for family. *Journal of Organizational Behavior*, 1992, 13, 585–603; Schneer, J. A., and Reitman, F. Effects of alternate family structures on managerial careers. *Academy of Management Journal*, 1993, 36, 830–843.

36. Jones, F., and Fletcher, B. C. An empirical study of occupational stress transmission in working couples. *Human Relations*, 1993, 46, 881–904; Ayree, S. Dual-earner couples in Singapore: An examination of work and nonwork sources of experienced burnout. *Human Relations*, 1993, 46, 1441–1469; Wiersma, U. J. A taxonomy of behavioral strategies for coping with work–home role conflict. *Human Relations*, 1994, 47, 211–222.

37. Noe, R. A., and Barber, A. E. Willingness to accept mobility opportunities: Destination makes a difference. *Journal of Organizational Behavior*, 1993, 14, 159–175; Landau, J. C., Shamir, B., and Arthur, M. B. Predictors of willingness to relocate for managerial and professional employees. *Journal of Organizational Behavior*,

1992, 13, 667–680; Harvey, M. Inpatriation training: The next challenge for international human resource management. *Journal of International Business Studies*, 1994, in press.

38. Reynolds, C., and Bennett, R. The career couple challenge. *Personnel Journal*, March 1991, 46–50; Greenhaus, J. H. *Career Management*. Chicago: Dryden, 1987.

39. Wharton, A. S., and Erickson, R. J. Managing emotions of the job and at home: Understanding the consequences of multiple emotional roles. *Academy of Management Review*, 1993, 18, 457–486.

40. Shellenbarger, S. Work and family. *Wall Street Journal*, October 3, 1993, B1.

41. Goff, S. J., Mount, M. K., and Jamison, R. L. Employer-supported child care, work/family conflict, and absenteeism: A field study. *Personnel Psychology*, 1990, 43, 739–810; Kossek, E. E. Diversity in child care assistance needs: Employee problems, preferences, and work-related outcomes. *Personnel Psychology*, 1990, 43, 769–791.

42. Powell, G. N., and Butterfield, D. A. Investigating the "glass ceiling" phenomenon: An empirical study of actual promotions to top management. *Academy of Management Journal*, 1994, 37, 68–87; Blum, T., Fields, D. L., and Goodman, J. S. Organization-level determinants of women in management. *Academy of Management Journal*, 1994, 37, 241–268; Dalton, D. B., and Kesner, I. F. Cracks in the glass ceiling: The silent competence of women. *Business Horizons*, March–April 1993, 6–12; Scandura, T. A., and Ragins, B. R. The effects of sex and gender role orientation on mentorship in male-dominated occupations. *Journal of Vocational Behavior*, 1993, 43, 251–265.

43. Kunde, D. Doing it by the numbers. *Dallas Morning News*, May 16, 1993, H1–H2; Hood, J. N., and Koberg, C. S. Patterns of differential assimilation and acculturation for women in business organizations. *Human Relations*, 1994, 47, 159–182.

44. Hall, C. Just Brakes exec unstopable in her career. *Dallas Morning News*, February 6, 1994, H1, H6, H7.

45. These characteristics were taken from Hill, L. A. *Becoming a Manager: Mastery of a New Identity*. Cambridge, Mass.: Harvard Business School Press, 1994; Freeman, S. J. M. *Managing Lives: Corporate Women and Social Change*. Amherst, Mass.: University of Massachusetts Press, 1990; Powell, G. N. *Women and Men in Management*, 2nd ed. Newbury Park, Calif.: Sage, 1993.

46. Henkoff, R. Winning the new career game. *Fortune*, July 12, 1993, 46–49.

47. Schellhardt, T. D. Managing your career. *Wall Street Journal*, February 23, 1994, B1.

48. Jackofsky, E. F., Ornstein, S., and Rogers, R. J. Seeking reemployment: Industrial and labor market impact on search behaviors of managers. Unpublished manuscript, Cox School of Business, Southern Methodist University, Dallas, Texas, 1994; Leana, C. R., and Feldman, D. C. *Coping with Job Loss*. New York: Lexington Books, 1992.

49. Adapted from Kirkpatrick, D. The new unemployed executive. *Fortune*, April 8, 1991, 36–39, 42, 46–48.

50. Personal interview with Dr. James Tarter, senior principal, King, Chapman, Broussard & Gallagher, Dallas, Texas, April 29, 1994.

51. Parker, B., and Chusmir, L. H. *Development and Validation of the Life Success Measures Scale*. Miami Florida International University, 1994. Used with permission.

Appendix

Tools and Techniques for Studying Organizational Behavior

This appendix introduces you to the tools and techniques used to assess problems in organizational behavior. We suggest ways to think about issues and apply sound research methods to solve them. Through examples we show how several organizations used research to answer specific questions that puzzled their managers.

▼ THE SCIENTIFIC APPROACH

Good management involves the ability to understand job-related problems and to make valid predictions about employee behavior. The key is understanding the *scientific approach*, a method for systematically collecting and analyzing information in an unbiased manner. Figure A.1 illustrates the three basic steps of the scientific approach: observation, measurement, and prediction. These steps are so basic that, without even realizing it, most people use them every day.

The Marriott Corporation used the scientific approach to understand how family issues affected productivity.[1] Marriott is one of the country's largest employers. Of its 206,000 employees, more than half are women, a large percentage are part time, and one-third have children younger than twelve years old. Most Marriott employees live in major metropolitan areas, where the company has intense labor competition. Marriott managers had some anecdotal information that employees were having difficulty satisfying both their work and home requirements. According to Donna Klein, Director of Work and Family Life, many Marriott employees quit at the beginning of summer because they didn't have anyone to take care of their children.

To assess the size of the problem, Marriott undertook a large sample survey nationwide, using questionnaires, interviews, and observation, to document its employees' problems. Klein's team collected data from more than 1,600 employees in five metropolitan areas: Atlanta, Boston, Chicago, Los Angeles, and Washington, D.C. The results indicated that family issues strongly affected Marriott's work force. The company also obtained data that hadn't been collected before: the average number of children (2.2); the percentage of employees who have dependents under age 12 (35%); and the percentage who have children under age 5 (15%). The survey also discovered the amount of work time employees missed because of child care problems and the kind of child care they needed. The company discovered that, on average, employees with children younger than 12 were absent four days a year and were late five days a year because of child care problems. Each year, nearly 33% of

757

FIGURE A.1

Scientific Approach

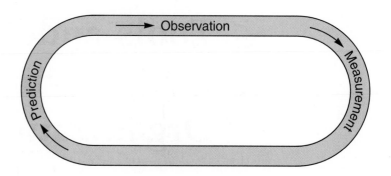

employees took two days off because they couldn't find a replacement when their day care arrangements broke down. Moreover, 20% of all Marriott employees had left a previous employer because of work–family conflicts. The survey also indicated that male and female employees reported an equal number of problems, that elder care issues were growing in importance, and that problems with child care arrangements limited an employee's ability to work certain schedules and overtime. Marriott managers predicted that, unless the organization took some action to remedy these problems, turnover, absenteeism, and tardiness would continue at their present levels or even increase.

In response to the identified needs, Marriott made the following core of programs available nationwide to its employees.

▲ The Child Care Choices referral program provides employees with professional help in locating affordable child care.

▲ The Child Care Discount program gives employees a 10% discount or waives registration fees for Marriott employees.

▲ The Family Care Spending Account enables employees to use a payroll deduction plan to pay for child care tax free.

▲ The Elder Care Program provides information and seminars about services available to older employees and their relatives.

Marriott based these and other programs on its scientific approach to studying the problem.

The scientific approach also requires a systematic test of assumptions. Such testing may reveal that a problem doesn't exist or is less or more serious than initially assumed. The scientific approach guards against preconceptions or personal bias by requiring as complete an assessment of the problem or issue as resources permit.

▼ PREPARATION OF RESEARCH DESIGNS

A *research design* is a plan, structure, and strategy of investigation intended to obtain answers to one or more questions.[2] The *plan* is the researcher's overall program for the research. It includes a list of everything the researcher will do during the project from its beginning through analysis of the data to submission of the final report. The plan should identify the types of data to be collected, sample populations, research instruments, methods of analysis, tentative target completion dates, and the like. The *structure* is an outline of the specific variables to be measured. Diagrams can be used to show how the variables—and their assumed relationships—are to be examined. The *strategy* presents the methods to be used to validate the data, to achieve research objectives, and to resolve problems encountered during the research.

▼ Purposes of Research Designs

A research design has two major purposes: to provide answers to questions and to provide control for nonrelevant effects that could influence the results of the study.[3] Investigators devise research designs to obtain answers to questions as objectively, accurately, and economically as possible. The design determines what observations to make, how to make them, and how to analyze them. A *nonrelevant* effect is anything the investigator has little control over but that could affect study results. In the Marriott Corporation example, nonrelevant effects might include a national health care program that could reduce employees' problems and weather-related problems that could affect employees' ability to get to work.

▼ Fundamentals of Research Designs

Rarely does a research design satisfy all the criteria associated with the scientific approach, but investigators should try to satisfy as many as possible in choosing a design. The ultimate findings of a poorly conceived research design may be invalid or have limited applicability. The ultimate product of a well-conceived design is more likely to be valid and receive serious attention.

▼ Hypothesis

The design of a research project typically involves stating a hypothesis so that inferences of a causal relationship between an independent (causal) variable and a dependent (effect) variable can legitimately be drawn or discarded. A *hypothesis* is a statement about the relationship between two or more variables. It asserts that a particular characteristic or occurrence of one of the factors (the *independent* variable determines the characteristic or occurrence of another factor (the *dependent* variable). A manager might state the following hypotheses with regard to drug testing.

- ▲ Employees who use illegal drugs are more likely to steal from customers and do shoddy work than employees who do not use illegal drugs.
- ▲ Spending $12,000 a year testing for the presence of illegal drugs will be less costly than not testing for these drugs.
- ▲ Customers will use the services of organizations whose employees are drug-free more often than organizations whose employees aren't drug-free.

After researchers state a hypothesis, they collect facts and analyze it (usually statistically) to determine whether the facts support or don't support it. A cause-and-effect relationship often isn't easy to establish. With all this in mind, let's examine the basic parts of an experimental design.

▼ Experimental Design

Some types of research designs provide more valid grounds for drawing causal inferences than do others. The concept of causality in relation to experimental designs is complex,[4] and a thorough analysis is beyond the scope of this appendix. Here we limit the discussion to points that are essential to understanding adequate research design requirements. We use the example of physical fitness and wellness programs in organizations to introduce these points.

In the past fifteen years, U.S. and Canadian businesses have become increasingly aware of the importance of physical fitness and wellness in the workplace.[5] The estimated cost of medical treatment for workers and lost productivity is more than $175 billion per year. The tremendous growth of workplace health programs has resulted partially from the belief that an organization should take some of the responsibility for the welfare of its most valuable asset, its employees. Organizations sponsoring fitness and wellness programs include *Fortune* 500 companies, municipal public safety agencies (such as fire and police departments), insurance providers, federal and state agencies, manufacturing organizations, and universities.

Many organizations have adopted one of three levels of fitness and wellness programs to control costs and maintain a healthier work force. Level I programs comprise efforts aimed at making individuals aware of specific consequences of unhealthful habits. These programs may include newspaper articles, health fairs, screening sessions, posters, flyers, and classes. Level II programs involve jogging, help for employees to stop smoking, and various aerobic exercises and strength training that last some eight to twelve weeks. Level III programs help individuals maintain healthy life-styles and behaviors. A Level III program typically fosters ongoing participation in a healthy life-style by providing an on-site fitness center (including equipment, space, and locker facilities) making healthy food (such as low-fat, low-cholesterol items) available in lounges and cafeterias, and removing unhealthy temptations (for example candy and cigarettes) from the workplace.

Johnson & Johnson wanted to test the hypothesis that employees who participated in Level III fitness and wellness programs would have lower health costs than employees who participated in Level I or II programs.[6] The company believed that the Level III approach, with its constant reinforcing messages, would change the health-related behaviors of employees more permanently than Level I or II programs. The company also believed that participation in Level III programs would change the work environment, providing additional positive reinforcement for changes in employee behaviors. More than 11,000 employees were divided into two groups. All agreed to participate in either a Level I and II or Level III program for thirty months. Initial analysis of the groups indicated that medical costs and other factors, such as age, gender, and marital status, prior to the experiment were about the same. After thirty months, the company concluded that employees participating in Level III programs had fewer admissions to hospitals, visited doctors less, and were absent from work less than employees who had participated in Level I and II programs.

Two groups are always used in an experiment: experimental and control. Members of the *experimental group*—in the Johnson & Johnson case, employees who participated in Level III fitness programs—are exposed to the treatment, or the independent variable. Members of the *control group*—employees in the Johnson & Johnson Level I and II fitness programs—are not exposed to the treatment. After a thirty-month period, the company compared the medical and performance data on employees in the two groups. The results showed that Level III participants had fewer medical expenses and performed better than those not in the Level III programs.

Johnson & Johnson randomly chose employees to participate in this experiment. In this *random selection*, each person had an equal chance of being selected. The company then randomly selected members of the control and experimental groups from the participants. One way to obtain a random selection involves assigning each person a number and then consulting a table of random numbers. Another way is to flip a coin for each person; heads are participants (or members of the control group); tails are nonparticipants (or members of the experimental group). Random selection ensures that an experimenter's preconceptions or biases do not influence the choice of participants or assignment to either the control group or the experimental group.

Another way of selecting people to participate is *matching*. In matching, participants must be alike in all aspects relevant to the experiment. For example, in the Johnson & Johnson example, employees could be matched by length of employment, job level, prior medical costs, marital status, age, educational level, and so on. Employees who fit the same profile would then be divided into experimental and control groups (probably by random selection).

The use of a control group permits investigators to rule out other causes for improvement in job performance, which include the following significant possibilities.

▲ *Natural maturing or development.* Whether or not employees participated in the program, day-to-day experiences that had nothing to do with that training could have affected their performance. Moreover, employees could reduce their medical expenses during the experimental period (thirty months) whether or not they attended a Level III fitness program. However, if the maturing process could be assumed to be the same for members of both the experimental and control groups—and it if could be assumed further that the effect of the fitness program wasn't caused by any extraordinary circumstances—the effects of maturation could be ruled out when comparing the two groups.

▲ *Influence of the measurement process itself.* If employees felt that they were being studied, they might respond differently than if they felt that they were not being studied. If the employees felt like guinea pigs in the experiment or if they felt that they were being tested and had to make a good impression, the measurements obtained could distort the experimental results. Variations in experimental designs can be used to account for the effects of the measuring process but are complex.[7]

▲ *Contemporaneous events other than the exposure of the employees to the program.* Events that occurred during the training that the researcher couldn't control might affect employee performance and the outcome of the experiment. For example, while employees were participating in the fitness programs, a feature story in the *Wall Street Journal* indicated that the Surgeon General of the United States believed that all people should engage in regular, vigorous exercise. The article also said that before exercising people should be screened medically and then be encouraged to maintain a regular exercise program. The story indicated that people who exercised regularly had lower medical expenses and were more productive than those who didn't. If most of the Johnson & Johnson employees in either fitness program read the story, they might start exercising regardless of the fitness program they were enrolled in. Like maturational effects, however, if such an event affected members of the experimental and control groups the same way, it wouldn't result in differences between the two groups.

TYPES OF RESEARCH DESIGN

Many different types of research design exist, and numerous textbooks have been written on the subject.[8] There is growing recognition that managers and others need a basic knowledge of certain research methods in order to understand the contributions and limitations of research in organizational behavior. A discussion of these methods should rein in the tendency to rush into cause-and-effect analyses and solutions to problems.

Managers should familiarize themselves with several research designs so that they can select the best design for the problem at hand. They should select the design that will do the most complete job, which depends on

▲ the types of information the design provides;

▲ the validity of the data, that is, how confident the investigator can be about inferences based on the findings; and

▲ the amounts of time, money, and other resources required and available to perform the research.

Instead of properly evaluating these and other considerations, managers often approve a research design, become comfortable with it, and then apply it inappropriately to situations. Unfortunately, prior habits, experiences, and biases often determine the choice of a research design. Instead of becoming solely interested in, say, laboratory experiments or field surveys, managers should understand and appreciate the usefulness and limitations of various types of research design.

The four most common types of research design are the case study, the field survey, the laboratory experiment, and the field experiment. They may be interrelated in many ways, and Figure A.2 suggests one type of relationship.

▼ Case Study

In a *case study* a researcher seeks detailed information about an individual or a group through records, interviews, questionnaires, and observations. The case study is particularly useful for stimulating insights into problems in relatively new areas where there is little experience to guide the researcher.

Three distinctive features of the case study make it an important tool for stimulating new insights. First, the researcher can adopt an attitude of alert

FIGURE A.2

One Type of Relationship Among
Research Designs

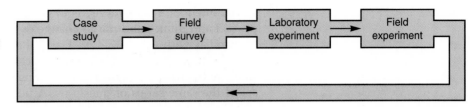

Note: A logical sequence of research might follow the above diagram.

receptivity, of seeking rather than testing. The factors being studied guide the investigator, who is not limited to testing existing hypotheses. Second, the case study is intense. The researcher attempts to obtain sufficient information to characterize and explain the unique aspects of the case being studied and other cases having common factors. Third, the case study tests the researcher's ability to assemble many diverse bits of information and base a unified interpretation on them.

If the investigator is comfortable with these three key features, the case study can be an effective way to analyze organizational behavior. It is highly adaptable to many problems found in organizations, such as in obtaining the reactions of a newcomer to an established work group. A newcomer to a group tends to be sensitive to social customs and practices that members probably take for granted. For example, a six-person work group loses one member because of retirement, and a newcomer to the plant fills this vacancy. The social practices of the group (for example, lunch breaks, kidding each other while working, and the bowling team) and its production standard (no more than 100 axles per day) must be communicated to this newcomer. In an analysis of the newcomer's reactions, the depth of understanding that can be attained through the case study is its major advantage.

The investigator must also consider the limitations of the case study. The method's main disadvantage is that generalizing the results of one case study to other cases usually isn't practical or logical. That is, only rarely can two cases be compared meaningfully in terms of their essential characteristics (for example, growth potential, number of employees, location, number of products made, levels of hierarchy, and the technology used to manufacture goods). Therefore case studies can rarely be repeated exactly or their findings applied validly to other settings.

A further disadvantage is that a case study usually doesn't lend itself to a systematic investigation of cause-and-effect relationships. Although a case study extending over time can offer the opportunity to determine changes, the range of variations observed in the case study may be too limited for practical cause-and-effect analysis. Case studies therefore may not allow the researcher to accept or reject a hypothesis; however, they frequently provide many clues and insights for further investigation.

▼ Field Survey

In a *field survey* data are collected through interviews or a questionnaire from a sample of people selected to represent the group being studied. Using a sample avoids an expensive and time-consuming census, or contacting every person in the group being studied.

The intent of a field survey is to gather information—to discover how people feel and think—and not to change or influence the respondents. You may be familiar with the ABC–Lou Harris Poll. This field survey asks people to express their opinions about topics such as the economy, presidential decisions, and proposed legislation in Congress. Each person in the sample is asked the same series of questions. A field survey generally requires a large sample in order to draw valid conclusions. Of those initially selected, many fail to respond: Typically, only about 20 to 30% of the people who receive a questionnaire fill it out and return it. Researchers tabulate the responses, analyze them, draw conclusions, and state the results.

The field survey isn't the best research design for obtaining some types of data; its use is limited to data about things of which the respondents are consciously aware. If people's unconscious motivations are important, an in-depth personal interview would be more productive and valid.

Problems with inferring cause-and-effect relationships also arise in the field study. Consider an analysis of the relationships between job satisfaction, leadership styles, and performance. Does job satisfaction lead to higher performance, causing leaders to change their personal styles? Or is leadership related to job satisfaction, causing high performance? Because of the large number of unmeasured variables usually involved in a field survey, such questions concerning causal relationships among the variables can't be answered.

▼ Laboratory Experiment

Compared with the case study and the field survey, the *laboratory experiment* increases the investigator's ability to establish cause-and-effect relationships among the variables. By conducting an experiment in an artificial setting, the investigator can create and control the exact conditions desired.

The essence of the laboratory experiment is to manipulate one or more independent variables and observe the effect on one or more dependent variables. For example, an autocratic leader tells one group of three blindfolded subjects to build a tower as high as possible with Tinker Toys. A democratic leader asks another group of blindfolded subjects to perform the same task. The dependent variable is the height of the tower; the independent variable is leadership style.

The laboratory setting permits the investigator to control the conditions under which the experiment is carried out. Laboratory experiments are most useful when the conditions required to test a hypothesis are not practically or readily obtainable in natural situations and when the situations can be replicated under laboratory conditions. For example, Chili's restaurants has built a challenge course to demonstrate how teamwork can improve managerial effectiveness. The challenge course comprises fifteen vertically low events, such as having members of a group exchange places while standing on a horizontal telephone pole suspended six inches off the ground, and eight vertically high events, such as a sixty-foot-high climbing and rappelling tower. By manipulating the types of challenges facing the group, Wade Bibbee, the course's director, can observe the changes in team effectiveness, cooperation, and commitment and draw some conclusions about ways to increase teamwork.

Using the laboratory research design has several disadvantages. For practical reasons, college students are the most common source of subjects in studies of organizational behavior. However, justifying their representation of managers actually involved in making decisions is difficult. Many students are young, transient, haven't yet occupied positions of responsibility, and don't depend on successful completion of a task under laboratory conditions for their livelihoods. To what populations and treatment variables then can the laboratory results of experiments involving students be generalized?

In addition, simulating many of the properties of organizational structure and process in the laboratory can be extremely difficult. Much of the work undertaken in the laboratory deals with things that can't be reproduced in or applied to real-life situations. For example, a firm couldn't readily redesign its organizational hierarchy to fit an ideal model. Even if it could find and hire "perfect" personnel, the changeover likely would result in serious morale and productivity problems. Conversely, many behavioral problems in organizations can't be isolated to permit their examination under laboratory conditions. Investigators thus tend to focus narrowly on problems that can be addressed in the laboratory. Ideally, laboratory experiments should be derived from studies of real-life situations, and results should be continually checked against them.

▼ Field Experiment

A *field experiment* is an attempt to apply the laboratory method to ongoing real-life situations. The field experiment permits the manipulation of one or more independent variables in an organization. The researcher can study the changes in the dependent variables and can infer the direction of causality with some degree of confidence.

The subjects in a field experiment ordinarily know that they are being observed, so the researcher must use procedures that minimize the possibility of subjects changing their behavior simply because they are being observed. Compared to the laboratory experiment, the field experiment provides the investigator with fewer controls. Let's consider how the Prudential Insurance Company used a field experiment to determine the success of its general fitness program.

The company developed a general fitness program and for five years studied its effects on 190 white-collar workers who held sedentary jobs.[9] The program was designed to provide participants with a healthy work environment. The company provided smoke-free offices, an on-site fitness center with an instructor, and low-cholesterol food in the cafeteria and removed candy and cigarette machines from the premises, among other things. The study included employees who worked for the company at least a year before and a year after their participation. Doctors measured the participants' level of cardiorespiratory fitness (aerobic capacity) with a treadmill exercise test prior to the field experiment. Each individual was placed in one of five fitness categories (low to high) as defined by the American Heart Association in relation to that person's age, gender, and aerobic activity. The results of the study showed that the percentage of individuals in the experimental group who were in the low and fair fitness categories declined from 57 to 33%. These individuals moved into the average, good, and high fitness categories. The proportion of the participants in the high and good categories increased from 16 to 39%. Participants in the control group all remained in their original categories, with neither improvement nor regression.

One striking result of the marked improvement in employee fitness levels in the experimental group was that their average sick days dropped 20% compared to the year before the program began. When these days were converted to dollars, the experimental group racked up a 32% reduction in costs for the program's first year. Similarly, their major medical costs dropped by 46% during a period when national health care costs increased by 13.9%. In contrast, over the five years of the study, the medical costs for those in the control group rose by 29%. The savings in annual disability and major medical costs per participant in the experimental group were $353.88, compared to the fitness program's cost of $120.60 per participant.

▼ Comparison of Research Designs

Each of the four types of research design has both strong and weak points. By selecting one, the researcher must often forgo some of the advantages of the others but, at the same time, avoids their disadvantages.

▼ Realism

A primary advantage of doing research in a natural setting, such as a field experiment within an organization, is the ability to increase the level of realism. The researcher can be confident that the employees are generally behaving under natural and ongoing conditions. They offer an advantage over the laboratory setting, which typically involves artificial conditions. However, the investigator in the field loses the ability to manipulate the independent variable or variables as freely as in the laboratory.

▼ Scope

Case studies and field surveys usually have a broad scope and incorporate many variables of interest not the investigator. Laboratory experiments, by their nature, are the most limited in scope, and a field experiment often is simply an expansion of a laboratory experiment.

▼ Precision

Laboratory research usually is more precise than field research. In the laboratory, the use of multiple measures of the same variable or variables under controlled conditions allows the researcher to obtain more accurate information about the variables than do other strategies. The use of videotape, for example, permits the investigator to record an entire experiment and then study it at a later time, examining such things as behavior, expressions, and gestures.

▼ Control

Investigators try to control an experiment so that the events being observed will be related to hypothesized causes, not to some unknown, unrelated events. The laboratory experiment allows researchers to reproduce a situation repeatedly so that they do not have to rely on a single observation for their conclusions. By replicating a study, predictions about cause-and-effect relationships can be refined from "sometimes" to, say, "ninety-five times in one hundred." The laboratory experiment also avoids many factors present in the field over which the investigator has little control (personnel changes or employees forgetting to fill out questionnaires, for example). However, the results obtained from ideal circumstances may not fit the real situation.

▼ Cost

Research designs differ in terms of relative costs and resources required. Designs vary in initial setup costs, that is, in the time and resources needed to plan and initiate them. They also vary in the cost per additional sample. For example, a laboratory experiment has relatively low setup costs, requires relatively few other resources, and costs relatively little for additional subjects—and the resources required can be found in most colleges. Because of high costs, field experiments and surveys tend to be carried out by large research organizations rather than by a researcher and a few assistants. These designs require a large number of subjects and computer facilities to analyze the data.

▼ Summary

All research designs have both strengths and weaknesses. Too much has been written about the reasons that one strategy is weak or one strategy is better than others: No one strategy is best in every case. Far more important is determining how each type of research design differs from and is complementary to the others. Rather than search for the ideal, effective investigators select the research design that is best for their purposes and circumstances at the time, use all the strengths of that design, and limit or offset its weaknesses whenever possible.

▼ DATA COLLECTION METHODS

Managers observe events and gather data all day, every day. Some data they reject, some they store away, and some they act on. The problem with this ordinary method of data gathering, as opposed to scientific data gathering, is that day-to-day observations of behavior frequently are unreliable or biased by personal attitudes or values. Also, the sample of behaviors observed often is limited and doesn't truly represent typical behavior; hence it isn't a good basis for generalizations. Hence erroneous conclusions frequently are drawn from observations of human behavior.

The quality of research depends not only on the adequacy of the research design but also on the adequacy of the data-collection methods used. The investigator can collect data in various ways: by interviews, questionnaires, observation, on reactive measures, or qualitative methods.[10] The rules for using these data-collection methods to make statements about the relevant subject matter may be built into the data-collecting technique, or they may be developed during the investigator's study. The Marriott Corporation used interviews, observations, and questionnaires to study the relationship of employee productivity to family needs.

▼ Interviews

The interview is one of the oldest and most often used methods for obtaining information. It relies on the willingness of people to communicate. Asking someone a direct question can save considerable time and money if the respondent is willing to talk and the answer is honest.

An interview's quality depends heavily on the mutual trust and goodwill established between interviewer and respondent. A trained interviewer builds these relationships early in the interview so that more of the responses will be useful. One way to build trust is to assure the respondent that all answers will be confidential. In addition, an interviewer must be a good listener in order to draw information from the respondent.

However, the interview method has several major shortcomings. First, people may be unwilling to provide certain types of information readily to an interviewer face-to-face. Employees, for example, may be unwilling to express negative attitudes about a superior when the interviewer is from the organization's human resources department. Getting employees to talk openly—even to a skilled outsider—and answer questions about their jobs, other individuals, and the organization is a difficult task because trust is necessary for that to happen. Thus the importance of establishing trust cannot be overstated. The second shortcoming of this method is that interviews take time, which costs money. Third, to achieve reliability, interviewers must be well-trained, present questions in a way that ensures validity, and eliminate personal biases. Their questions must be tested in advance of the actual interviews for hidden biases. Fourth, the questions asked by the interviewer limit the answers that respondents may freely give.

▼ Questionnaires

Questionnaires are sets of written items to which the subject is asked to respond. They probably are the most frequently used data-gathering device. Questionnaires are used to measure the respondent's attitudes, opinions, or demographic characteristics covering a wide variety of variables. Numerous types of questionnaires are used to measure variables such as job satisfaction, need fulfillment, company satisfaction, job stress, leadership style, values, vocational interest, and the like.

Developing a questionnaire is more of an art than a science. Factors such as the research budget, the purpose of the study, and the nature of the population to be sampled must be addressed before a sound decision can be made about the use of a questionnaire. After carefully thinking through the reasons for using a questionnaire and deciding to use this method, an investigator must construct the specific questionnaire that fits their intended purpose. To illustrate how the structure of questionnaire items can vary, consider the measurement of job satisfaction. At one end of the continuum, an investigator could measure satisfaction by asking, "Are you satisfied with your job?" A person would respond by checking either (a) yes or (b) no, the only two alternatives provided for a highly structured question. A somewhat less structured question is one that asks the person to indicate agreement with the statement, "I find my job quite satisfying," using the response categories (a) strongly agree, (b) agree, (c) neither agree nor disagree, (d) disagree, and (e) strongly disagree.

An example of a totally unstructured question is one that asks, "What do you like or dislike about your job?" for which the response is open-ended.

Using questionnaires to collect data has both advantages and disadvantages. Among the advantages of questionnaires are the following.

▲ They provide a relatively inexpensive way to collect data.

▲ They can be administered by relatively unskilled people.

▲ They can be mailed to people individually or given to people in groups.

▲ They provide the same stimulus to everyone surveyed.

▲ They often can be answered anonymously, which may lead to more open and truthful responses than might be obtained, for example, during an interview.

Questionnaires may have one or more of the following disadvantages.

▲ Missing data may be a problem if people do not answer all the questions.

▲ A low response rate may invalidate the results.

▲ This method cannot be used with individuals who have severe reading problems. When employees cannot read English, translations are needed. Unfortunately, translations aren't always precise.

▲ The respondent has no flexibility in answering, which limits the amount of information that can be obtained.

Suppose that you wanted to study sexual harassment at work. How might you undertake such a study? Probably the best way to do so is to ask employees to answer a questionnaire. That gives them privacy in describing sexual harassment practices encountered or observed in the organization that an interview wouldn't. Also, not requiring them to sign the questionnaire assures them of anonymity.

Why would you want to study such practices? One reason is the magnitude of the problem. More than half of all employees report some type of sexual harassment from a co-worker. A broad definition of sexual harassment is sexually related behaviors, such as telling sexual jokes to groups, flirting, displaying sexual cartoons, giving wolf whistles, and making sexual comments that are annoying and unwelcome. About 10% of all women employees have quit their jobs because of sexual harassment.[11]

The questionnaire in Table A.1 has been used to measure the degree of sexual harassment in offices. Before designing this questionnaire, the investigators actually observed the eight behaviors measured. They also asked managers whether they considered these behaviors to be sexual harassment. The investigators then selected a scale to measure the extent to which these behaviors actually occurred. They chose structured scales to indicate the extent to which individuals believe that sexual harassment exists on the job. Complete the questionnaire yourself to measure how much sexual harassment you have observed in your college, university, or job.

▼ Observation

Managers observe the actions of others and, based on these observations, infer others' motivations, feelings, and intentions. A principal advantage of the observation method is that the observer actually can see the behavior of indi-

TABLE A.1   Sexual Harassment in the Workplace

We would like you to describe the environment in which you work. By environment, we mean daily routines that shape employees' behaviors. Make your descriptions as objectively and factually accurate as possible without regard to whether you like or dislike your job. Please use the following scales and circle the one that best describes the practices that occur in your place of work (or where you have worked).

1. How often does joking or talking about sexual matters happen at your workplace?
   1. Frequently
   2. Occasionally
   3. Sometimes
   4. Never

2. Where you work, how much social pressure is there for women to flirt with men?
   1. A lot
   2. Some
   3. None

3. Where you work, how much social pressure is there for men to flirt with women?
   1. A lot
   2. Some
   3. None

4. How much of a problem at your place of work do you consider sexual harassment to be?
   1. A major problem
   2. A problem
   3. Can't say
   4. A minor problem
   5. No problem

5. How many women dress to appear sexually attractive to men at work?
   1. Most
   2. Many
   3. Some
   4. Hardly any
   4. None

6. How many men dress to appear sexually attractive to women at work?
   1. Most
   2. Many
   3. Some
   4. Hardly any
   4. None

7. How many women present themselves in sexually seductive ways to men at work?
   1. Most
   2. Many
   3. Some
   4. Hardly any
   5. None

8. How many men present themselves in sexually seductive ways to women at work?
   1. Most
   2. Many
   3. Some
   4. Hardly any
   5. None

Scoring

Add your points to get a total. The lower the score, the more likely are sexual harassment practices occurring in your place of work.

Source: Adapted from Gutek, B. A., Konrad, A. M., and Cohen, A. G. Predicting social-sexual behavior at work: A contact hypothesis. *Academy of Management Journal*, 1990, 33, 560–577.

viduals rather than relying on verbal or written descriptions of it, which may be inaccurate or biased.

One problem with the observation method is inherent in the observers. They must digest the information noted and then draw inferences from what they have observed. However, these inferences often are incorrect. Suppose, for example, that a person intensely dislikes college football because of its violence, corruption in recruiting of athletes, and emphasis on winning. These previously formed personal opinions may well invalidate any observations and inferences that person might make after watching a game.

▼ Nonreactive Measures

A manager who wants to know something about someone might turn to nonreactive sources of information instead of asking or observing that person directly. *Nonreactive measures* don't require the cooperation of the person. Company records provide investigators with valuable data on absenteeism, turnover, grievances, performance ratings, and demographics. In some cases, these sources may yield more accurate data than that obtained by directly questioning the employee. Nonreactive measures have the advantage of being inconspicuous because they are generated without the person's knowledge of their use. For example, radio dial settings can be used to determine the listener appeal of different radio stations. A Dallas automobile dealer estimates the popularity of different radio stations by having mechanics record the radio dial position on all cars brought in for service. The dealer then uses this information to select radio stations to carry its advertising. The wear on library books, particularly on the corners where the pages are turned, offers another example of a nonreactive measure librarians can use to learn the popularity of a book.

▼ Qualitative Methods

Investigators also use *qualitative methods* to describe and clarify the meaning of naturally occurring events in organizations. These methods are open-ended and interpretative because qualitative data are rarely quantifiable. Hence the researcher's interpretation and description are highly significant.

Qualitative methods rely on the experience and intuition of the investigator to describe the organizational processes and structures that are being studied. The type of data collected requires the qualitative researcher to become closely involved in the situation or problem being studied. For example, a qualitative method used for years by anthropologists is enthnography. As applied to organizational behavior, *ethnography* requires the investigator to study the organization for long periods of time as a participant observer. That is, the investigator takes part in the situation being studied in order to understand what it is like for those involved in it. One researcher studying a big-city police department accompanied police officers on their daily duties. This person informally interviewed police officers, read important police documents, used nonreactive methods to gather other data, and, as a result, provided vivid descriptions of what police work was really like.

▼ Criteria for Data Collection

Any data-collection method used to measure attitudes or behaviors must meet three important requirements: reliability, validity, and practicality.[12]

Reliability   The accuracy of measurement and the consistency of results determine *reliability*, which is one of the most important characteristics of any good data-collection method. A bathroom scale would be worthless if you stepped on it three times in sixty seconds and got a different reading each time. Similarly, a questionnaire would be useless if the scores obtained on successive administrations were inconsistent. Different scores obtained for the same individual at different times reflects low reliability, unless something happened (experimental change) between each measurement to warrant the change.

Control normally is the only prerequisite for reliability. So long as the directions for a data-collection method are clear, the environment is comfortable, and ample time is given for the subject to respond, the method should give reliable results. Furthermore, all data-collection methods, except those utilizing nonreactive sources, are affected to some degree by random changes in the subject (e.g., fatigue, distraction, or emotional strain). These conditions also can affect the researcher's reliability, especially in the observation method. Finally, changes in the setting, such as unexpected noises or sudden changes in weather, also can affect data reliability.

Validity   Even a reliable data-collection method isn't necessarily valid. *Validity* is the degree to which a method actually measures what it claims to measure. Validity is an evaluation, not a fact and usually is expressed in broad terms, such as high, moderate, or low, instead of precise quantities. A method can reliably measure the wrong variables. For example, a low score on a math test denies a job to a potential machine repairer. The test may have reliably measured the applicant's abstract math ability. It may not, however, be a valid measure of the applicant's actual skill at repairing machines.

The validity of many psychological tests used by organizations in employee selection is being questioned. The U.S. Equal Employment Opportunity Commission insists that the use of tests that cannot be validated be discontinued. Tests that are not valid are worse than useless: They are misleading and dangerous. At times, such tests have been used—either consciously or unwittingly—to discriminate against certain minority or ethnic groups. Those who challenge the use of vocabulary testing in the hiring process question not their reliability but the validity.

Practicality   Do not underestimate the importance of *practicality*, the final requirement of a good data-collection method. Questionnaires, interviews, and other methods should be acceptable to both management and the employees who are asked to participate in a study. Unions and various civil rights groups have raised questions about what management has the right to know. In the case of testing for drugs, the question of who has the right to know the results of the tests is crucial. Most organizations maintain confidentiality by recording positive tests only on the doctor's records.

Some organizations, such as IBM and Kodak, have adopted the following practical plan to test for the presence of illegal drugs in their new hires.[13] First, all applicants are notified of the screening test and procedures on the physical examination form. It identifies the types of tests, such as hair analysis or urinalysis, that will be used. Second, the applicant is not permitted to change a test date after appearing at the doctor's office and realizes that drug testing is part of the physical examination. Third, in the event of a positive test, the test is repeated using the same sample in order to ensure validity. Samples are kept in the doctor's office for 180 days in case of a lawsuit. Fourth, all records are confidential. Only the applicant knows the results of these tests.

Where employees are unionized, the union must approve the data-collection method. The use of a planning committee composed of representatives from each management level and the unions can increase widespread acceptance. The investigator can consider their viewpoints in deciding which data-collection method to use. The method chosen also should ensure easy accessibility to participants and test administrators to save time and money and to minimize disruption of normal operations.

▼ ETHICS IN RESEARCH

Investigators who obtain data from the general public, students, or employees must recognize the ethical and legal obligations they have to their subjects. Generally, managers and researchers face three types of ethical issues:

▲ misrepresentation and misuse of data;

▲ manipulation of the participant; and

▲ value and goal conflict.

▼ Misrepresentation and Misuse of Data

Misrepresentation and misuse of data are widespread problems. The issue for the investigator is to decide between fully disclosing all the information obtained or sharing just some of it. For example, a manager may easily gather data about a department's performance under the guise of asking about a competitor's. People might talk freely and give the manager essential information about the department. What happens, however, if a higher level manager asks for that information? The dilemma for the manager is that he or she gathered the data in a confidential manner and is now asked to reveal its contents.

Many organizations use computer monitoring to measure a person's performance.[14] *Computer monitoring* refers to the collection of detailed, minute-by-minute information on employee performance through computers for management's use. Often computer monitoring is sold to employees as a way to help them improve their performance and gain valuable rewards, such as prizes and/or bonus checks. An estimated seven million workers currently are being monitored electronically, often without their knowledge. They include employees who work at computer terminals in data-processing service bureaus, insurance, airlines, telemarketing, and telephone service. Many managers in these organizations, however, collect these data to discipline employees who talk too long on the phone with customers, make personal calls, and the like.

In laboratory experiments, investigators sometimes present false statements or attribute true statements to false sources. The code of ethics of the American

Psychological Association states that "Only when a problem is significant and can be investigated in no other way is the psychologist justified in giving misinformation to research subjects."[15] Many researchers feel an ethical obligation to inform the subjects of any false information presented as soon as possible after terminating the research.

The U.S. Department of Health, Education, and Welfare issued an extensive report recommending research requirements to protect human subjects. One recommendation was that a committee conduct objective and independent reviews of research projects and activities involving the use of human subjects when federal funds are involved. Most universities, for example, have an independent review committee composed of various directors of research from the colleges within the university. Each member arrives at a decision based on professional judgment as to whether the research will place the participants at risk. If a majority of the review committee members believe that the procedure employed will not put the subjects at risk, the committee will approve the proposal. After this approval, each subject must sign an agreement of informed consent. The basic elements of informed consent include

▲ a fair explanation of the procedures to be followed, including those that are experimental;

▲ a description of the study;

▲ an offer to answer any inquiries concerning the procedures;

▲ an announcement that the subject is free to withdraw consent and to discontinue participation in the activity at any time; and

▲ upon completion of the research, an offer to make available an abstract of the report to all participants.

▼ Manipulation

Manipulation involves tampering with a person's exercise of free will. Basically, manipulation occurs when the investigator requires employees to do something opposed to their personal values. Many college students participating in laboratory experiments are asked to lie to others about the results of the experiment. Such practices are illegal unless the experimenter, immediately after the experiment, tells all subjects the reasons for such manipulation.

▼ Value and Goal Conflicts

The third major issue is that of value and goal conflict. The American Civil Liberties Union and other organizations protest the use of employee alcohol and drug testing unless the organization can show probable cause. Some experts estimate that one fourth of the U.S. work force may be substance abusers, which cost businesses more than $300 billion in 1993.[16] Although no single symptom is indicative of substance abuse, behavioral changes, such as increased absenteeism, disappearance from the work area, failure to complete tasks, accidents, and changes in work quality may suggest substance abuse. General Motors and Pennzoil, among others, have set up sting operations to uncover substance abusers in their organizations. Such operations are extremely controversial because they entail surveillance, search, and detection to identify employees involved in the sale and abuse of illegal drugs. Drug testing, commonly through urinalysis, is used by 96% of U.S. corporations to detect substance abuse. Organizations must be careful not to violate federal, state, and local laws, especially a constitutionally protected right to privacy. Some courts have decided that random drug testing violates this right.[17]

References

1. Solomon, C. M. Marriott's family matters. *Personnel Journal*, 1991, 70(10), 40–42.

2. McCall, M. W., Jr., and Bobko, P. Research methods in the service of discovery. In M. D. Dunnette and L. M. Hough (eds.), *Handbook of Industrial and Organizational Psychology*. Palo Alto, Calif.: Consulting Psychologist Press, 1990, 381–418.

3. Cook, T. D., Campbell, D. T., and Peracchio, L. 1990. Quasi-experimentation. In M. D. Dunnette and L. M. Hough (eds.), *Handbook of Industrial and Organizational Psychology*. Palo Alto, Calif.: Consulting Psychologist Press, 1990, 39–74.

4. Campbell, J. P. The role of theory in industrial and organizational psychology. In M. D. Dunnette and L. M. Hough (eds.), *Handbook of Industrial and Organizational Psychology*. Palo Alto, Calif.: Consulting Psychologist Press, 1990, 39–74.

5. Erfurt, J.C., Foote, A., and Heirich, M. A. The cost effectiveness of worksite wellness programs for hypertension control, weight loss, smoking cessation, and exercise. *Personnel Psychology*, 1992, 45(1), 5–29. Also see Sell, A. R., and Newman, R. G. Alcohol abuse in the workplace—A managerial dilemma. *Business Horizons*, 1992, 35(6), 64–71; Santora, J. E. Sony promotes wellness to stabilize health care costs. *Personnel Journal*, 1992, 71(9), 40–44.

6. Bly, J. L., Jones, R. C., and Richardson, J. E. Impact of worksite health promotion on health care costs and utilization: Evaluation of Johnson & Johnson's Live for Life program. *JAMA*, 1986, 256(23), 3235–3240. Also see Santora, J. E. Sony promotes wellness to stabilize health care costs. *Personnel Journal*, 1992, 71(9), 40–44.

7. Schmidt, N. W., and Klimoski, R. J. *Research Methods in Human Resource Mangement*. Cincinnati: Southwestern, 1991.

8. Gilbert, N. (ed.). *Researching Social Life*. Newbury Park, Calif.: Sage, 1993.

9. Bowne, D. W., Russell, M. L., Morgan, S. A., Optenberg, S., and Clarke, A. Reduced disability and health care costs in an industrial fitness program. *Journal of Occupational Medicine*, 1984, 26, 809–816; Davis, D., and Cosenza, R. M. *Business Research for Decision Making*, 3rd ed. Belmont, Calif.: Wadsworth, 1993.

10. Lawler, E. E., III, Mohrman, S. A., Ledford, G. E., Jr., and Cummings, T. G. *Doing Research That Is Useful for Theory and Practice*. San Francisco: Jossey-Bass, 1985; Rosenfeld, P., Edwards, J. E., and Thomas, M. D. *Improving Organizational Surveys*. Thousand Oaks, Calif.: Sage, 1993.

11. Gutek, B. A., Konrad, A. M., and Cohnen, A. G. Predicting social-sexual behavior at work: A contact hypothesis. *Academy of Management Journal*, 1990, 33, 560–577. Also see Wells, C. L., and Kracher, B. J. Justice, sexual harassment, and the reasonable victim standard. *Journal of Business Ethics*, 1993, 12, 423–432.

12. McCall, M. W., Jr., and Bobko, P. Research methods in the service of discovery. In M. D. Dunnette and L. M. Hough (eds.), *Handbook of Industrial and Organizational Psychology*. Palo Alto, Calif.: Consulting Psychologist Press, 1990, 381–418; Schwartzman, H. B. *Ethnography in Organizations*. Thousand Oaks, Calif.: Sage, 1992.

13. Drug testing in workplace rising rapidly. *Dallas Morning News*, April 2, 1993, D-1; Crow, S. M., and Hartman, S. J. Drugs in the workplace: Overstating the problems and the cures. *Journal of Drug Issues*, 1992, 22, 923–938.

14. Smith, M. J., Carayon, P., Sanders, K. J., Lim, S-Y., and LeGrande, D. Employee stress and health complaints in jobs with and without electronic performance monitoring. *Applied Ergonomics*, 1992, 12(1), 17–28; Griffith, T. Teaching big brother to be a team player: Computing monitoring and quality. *Academy of Management Executive*, 1993, 7(1), 73–80; Grant, R. A., and Higgins, C. A. The impact of computerized performance monitoring on service work: Testing a causal model. *Information Systems Research*, 1992, 116–142.

15. American Psychological Association. Ethical principles of psychologists and code of conduct. *American Psychologist*, 1992, 47, 1598–1611.

16. Mason, D. Substance abuse tab: Pay now or later. *Business First—Columbus*, 1993, 9(29), 38(A)–40(A).

17. Fellows, H. D., Jr. Legal aspects of drug and alcohol testing in the workplace. *Risk Management*, 1993, 40, 21–27.

Integrating Cases

▼ A DAY IN THE LIFE OF YOLANDA VALDEZ

Yolanda Valdez, senior vice-president for marketing of ClearVision Optical Group, arrived at her office at 7:25 A.M. Settling in at her desk, she began to think about the problems she should handle in the course of the day.

ClearVision Optical Group is a specialty retailer operating under the name of ClearVue with annual sales of over $20 million. The optical group owns 750 stores in forty states, Canada, Mexico, Puerto Rico, The Netherlands, and England. It is the United States' largest provider of eye care products and services, and it seeks to expand its market share in other free world countries. ClearVision is one group of S. G. Davis, an Illinois-based company that also has pharmaceutical and medical product groups. The optical group is planning to expand into other broadly based health care markets, and in 1980 it began experimenting with small shops that sell only sunglasses. ClearVision is a marketing-oriented company that bases its strategy on understanding customer needs and developing and delivering distinctive characteristics that appeal to customers. An example of this is ClearVue's in-store labs that cut lenses for eyeglass frames on a "while-you-wait" basis, often getting the customer's prescription filled within an hour. This service differentiates ClearVue from its competitors, who typically do not offer such speedy service.

Valdez' duties as senior vice-president for marketing broadly include determination and evaluation of the strategic and operational directions for the company. Her specific responsibilities include marketing research, advertising programs, the eyeglass frame line, contact lenses, and in-store merchandising-display programs.

A high-priority item on Valdez' list of things to accomplish today was to construct a questionnaire to survey customer attitudes about the firm's line of frames. This was to be circulated to each of ClearVue's retail store managers to determine whether the current frame styles were preferred by customers and if the selection of frames was adequate at each price level. Valdez realized that she would have a greater likelihood of uninterrupted work before most of the other employees came at 8:30, so she began working on the questionnaire at 7:45. She had scarcely begun clarifying her definition of the problem and stating her objectives when her secretary, Linda Brown, came in with a list of activities planned for the day.

A meeting with the research analysis group working on contact lenses was scheduled for 9:15. There was another meeting set for 10:15 with the group working on fall displays for use in the stores. Valdez was scheduled to lunch with a representative of a prospective advertising agency at 12:00, and she had an appointment with the president at 3:00 to discuss progress on an evaluation of the firm's frame suppliers. She told her secretary she needed some letters typed and put in the mail before the afternoon and a summary of the supplier evaluation typed before her meeting with the president. Her secretary reminded Valdez that the vice-president for finance wanted to see her that day to discuss the details of financing for the new sunglass stores.

When Linda left, Valdez settled back to work on the questionnaire. She outlined what she hoped to accomplish and wrote down a list of specific pieces of information she wanted to get from the store managers. At 8:20 the senior vice-president for operations in the western division called and asked Valdez if she could get a cup of coffee with him and discuss some new ideas he had for marketing children's eyewear. Yolanda agreed to meet him in five minutes. They discussed the plans she was currently considering and how the new suggestions would modify those plans. As she was walking back to her office at 8:45, a woman who worked in the optical lab on the premises asked her if she could give her some advice. Yolanda said she could spare a moment. The woman questioned her on career opportunities in marketing, both in the company and in the entire field. She confessed that she had wanted to get more training and go into marketing, but had never taken the opportunity. Yolanda told her about her experiences in the field and advised her about the best route to take to get into the company's marketing department. After she left, Valdez called the president and asked for his opinion of a major new advertising and display campaign for children's eyewear based on the suggestions she had received. They discussed various ways in which the advertising budget could be reallocated to finance such a campaign. They decided that some funds could be taken from fashion eyewear programs, and some additional money could be trimmed form other elements of the budget and allocated to this campaign. The president mentioned that he would like to see the ideas Valdez had for this campaign before they were sent to an advertising agency.

As Valdez hung up, she realized it was time for the meeting with the contact lens group. She walked into the conference room and sat down at the head of the table. She chatted informally with a few of the people in the group before they got down to business. Valdez listened to their presentation, and after they were finished, she stated some new ideas on the situation and thanked them for the results. She set some goals for the contact lens group that she wanted accomplished before the next meeting. This meeting was over at 10:15, and the group working on fall store displays came in for their meeting. Valdez told them about the children's eyewear. The meeting ended at 11:20.

As Valdez walked out of the conference room, she was stopped by a man from the display group. He talked to Valdez for a few moments about some ideas he had for different types of displays for the sunglass stores. Then he hesitated for a moment and asked Valdez if he could speak to her about a situation that had been troubling him. Valdez said she would like to help with the problem if possible. The man told her that he had been experiencing conflict with his team leader in the display group: he felt she had not been allowing free expression of ideas, and "had it in" for him. The man admitted that he did not know how to cope with the situation and had been considering looking for another job. Valdez promised to look into the matter further.

When she returned to her office and found a stack of phone messages waiting for her, she first returned the call of the vice-president for finance and arranged to meet with him at 1:30. She also returned the call of the vice-president for manufacturing. He needed to talk to her about manufacturing problems with one of the new specialty lenses, so they set up a time to discuss the problem at 2:00. Leaving the rest of the messages on her desk, Valdez left for her lunch appointment with the ad agency representative. At lunch, she discussed plans for network TV advertising and asked for ideas and strategies for effective new messages and the most effective timing for ads. All the time, she was attempting to evaluate whether or not ClearVision should hire this new agency for its next campaign. Since this would be Clear-Vision's first use of network TV advertising, it was a particularly important decision. After lunch, they drove to the agency's offices and discussed in detail the creative and media scheduling aspects of the campaign.

Valdez was back in her office at 1:15. She made some routine calls to subordinates to check on their progress on certain projects until 1:30. Then the vice-president for finance came in to discuss the acquisition of an existing chain of sunglass stores. They talked about integrating these stores into ClearVision Optical Group's strategic plan until Keisha Jackson, the vice-president for personnel, knocked on the door. The vice-president for finance stayed to hear what Jackson had to say, and the three discussed possible solutions to the new company employee benefits program.

They left at 2:30. Valdez collected her phone messages and began returning calls. She had just finished talking with a frame supplier representative in New York and an ad agency reporting the completion of a print ad campaign for the next quarter when she had to leave for her meeting with the president. Valdez talked with him for half an hour about expansion strategy and another half-hour about her evaluation of the frame suppliers the firm was currently using.

At 4:00 Valdez went back to her office and found a report on her desk about an inventory control model that gave appropriate purchase quantities and intervals for the current frame line. One of her subordinates in the frame management group had researched the matter and felt that frame purchasing could be more efficient. Valdez recalled that she had told the man to come up with a better method if he could, and this report gave his findings on the matter. Valdez read the report carefully and thought about its implications. She called the man in and asked him to explain some aspects of the model more clearly. They discussed how the model would work in practice and the dollar savings that would result form it. The man left Valdez' office at 4:45, and Valdez began working on the frame line questionnaire again. Five minutes later, Linda Brown came in with some letters for her to sign and some personnel evaluations the head of personnel had sent over to be filled out. She decided to forget about the questionnaire and work on it at home, where she was less likely to be interrupted. She worked on the performance evaluations until 5:45, when she packed her papers in her briefcase and headed for home.

QUESTIONS

1. What characteristics of managerial work did Valdez' day illustrate?

2. What roles did Valdez play?

3. How did she spend her day? Explain.

4. What fundamental concepts of the contingency approach are illustrated in this case?

▼ BOB KNOWLTON

Bob Knowlton was sitting alone in the conference room of the laboratory. The rest of the group had gone. One of the secretaries had stopped and talked for a while about her husband's coming induction into the Army, and had finally left. Bob, alone in the laboratory, slid a little further down in his chair looking with satisfaction at the results of the first test run of the new photon unit.

He liked to stay after the others had gone. His appointment as project head was still new enough to give him a deep sense of pleasure. His eyes were on the graphs before him but in his mind he could hear Dr. Jerrold, the head of the laboratory, saying again, "There's one thing about this place that you can bank on. The sky is the limit for a person who can produce." Knowlton felt again the tingle of happiness and embarrassment. Well, dammit, he said to himself, he had produced. He wasn't kidding anybody. He had come to the Simmons Laboratories two years ago. During a routine testing of some rejected Clanson components he had stumbled on the idea of the photon correlator, and the rest just happened. Jerrold had been enthusiastic; a separate project had been set up for further research and development of the device, and he had gotten the job of running it. The whole sequence of events still seemed a little miraculous to Knowlton.

He shrugged out of the reverie and bent determinedly over the sheets when he heard someone come into the room behind him. He looked up expectantly. Jerrold often stayed late himself, and now and then dropped in for a chat. This always made the day's end especially pleasant for Bob. It wasn't Jerrold. The man who had come in was a stranger. He was tall, thin, and rather dark. He wore steel rimmed glasses and had on a very wide leather belt with a large brass buckle. Lucy remarked later that it was the kind of belt the Pilgrims must have worn. The stranger smiled and introduced himself. "I'm Simon Fester. Are you Bob Knowlton?" Bob said yes and they shook hands. "Doctor Jerrold said I might find you in. We were talking about your work, and I'm very much interested in what you are doing." Bob waved to a chair. Fester didn't seem to belong in any of the standard categories of visitors: customers, visiting fireman, stockholder. Bob pointed to the sheets on the table. "These are the preliminary results of a test we're running. We've got a new gadget by the tail and we're trying to understand it. It's not finished, but I can show you the section that we're testing." He stood up, but Fester was deep in the graphs. After a moment he looked up with an odd grin. "These look like plots of a Jennings surface. I've been playing around with some autocorrelation functions of surfaces—you know that stuff." Bob, who had no idea what he was referring to, grinned back and nodded, and immediately felt uncomfortable. "Let me show you the monster," he said, and led the way to the workroom.

After Fester left, Knowlton slowly put the graphs away, feeling vaguely annoyed. Then, as if he had made a decision, he quickly locked up and took the long way out so that he would pass Jerrold's office. But the office was locked. Knowlton wondered whether Jerrold and Fester had left together.

The next morning Knowlton dropped into Jerrold's office, mentioned that he had talked with Fester, and asked who he was.

"Sit down for a minute," Jerrold said. "I want to talk to you about him. What do you think of him?" Knowlton replied truthfully that he thought Fester was very bright and probably very competent. Jerrold looked pleased.

"We're taking him on," he said. "He's had a very good background in a number of laboratories, and he seems to have ideas about the problems we're tackling here." Knowlton nodded in agreement, instantly wishing that Fester would not be placed with him.

"I don't know yet where he will finally land," Jerrold continued, "but he seems interested in what you are doing. I thought he might spent a little time with you by way of

getting started." Knowlton nodded thoughtfully. "If his interest in your work continues, you can add him to your group."

"Well, he seemed to have some good ideas even without knowing exactly what we are doing," Knowlton answered. "I hope he stays; we'd be glad to have him."

Knowlton walked back to the lab with mixed feelings. He told himself that Fester would be good for the group. He was no dunce, he'd produce. Knowlton thought again of Jerrold's promise when he had promoted him—"the person who produces gets ahead in this outfit." The words now seemed to him to carry the overtones of a threat.

The next day, Fester didn't appear until midafternoon. He explained that he had had a long lunch with Jerrold, discussing his place in the lab. "Yes," said Knowlton, "I talked with Jerry this morning about it, and we both thought you might work with us for a while."

Fester smiled in the same knowing way that he had smiled when he mentioned the Jennings surfaces. "I'd like to," he said.

Knowlton introduced Fester to the other members of the lab. Fester and Link, the mathematician of the group, hit it off well together, and spent the rest of the afternoon discussing a method of analysis of patterns that Link had been worrying over for the last month.

It was six-thirty when Knowlton finally left the lab that night. He had waited almost eagerly for the end of the day to come—when all lab personnel would all be gone and he could sit in the quiet room, relax, and think it over. "Think what over?" he asked himself. He didn't know. Shortly after five they had all gone except Fester, and what followed was almost a duel. Knowlton was annoyed that he was being cheated out of his quiet period, and finally resentful, determined that Fester should leave first.

Fester was sitting at the conference table reading, and Knowlton was sitting at his desk in the little glass enclosed office that he used during the day when he needed to be undisturbed. Fester had gotten the last year's progress reports out and was studying them carefully. The time dragged. Knowlton doodled on a pad, the tension growing inside him. What the hell did Fester think he was going to find in the reports?

Knowlton finally gave up and they left the lab together. Fester took several of the reports with him to study in the evening. Knowlton asked him if he thought the reports gave a clear picture of the lab's activities.

"They're excellent," Fester answered with obvious sincerity: "They're not only good reports; what they report is damn good, too!" Knowlton was surprised at the relief he felt, and grew almost jovial as he said goodnight.

Driving home, Knowlton felt more optimistic about Fester's presence in the lab. He had never fully understood the analysis that Link was attempting. If there was anything wrong with Link's approach Fester would probably spot it.

"And if I'm any judge," he murmured, "he won't be especially diplomatic about it."

He described Fester to his wife who was amused by the broad leather belt and the brass buckle.

"It's the kind of belt the Pilgrims must have worn," she laughed.

"I'm not worried about how he holds his pants up," he laughed with her. "I'm afraid that he's the kind that just has to make like a genius twice each day. And that can be pretty rough on the group."

Knowlton had been asleep for several hours when he was jerked awake by the telephone. He realized it had rung several times. He swung off the bed muttering about damn fools and telephones. It was Fester. Without any excuses, apparently oblivious of the time, he plunged into an excited recital of how Link's patterning problem could be solved.

Knowlton covered the mouthpiece to answer his wife's stage whisper, "Who is it?"

"It's the genius."

Fester, completely ignoring the fact that it was two in the morning, proceeded in a very excited way to state in the middle of an explanation of a completely new approach to certain of the photon lab problems that he had stumbled on while making analyses of some past experiments. Knowlton managed to put some enthusiasm in his own voice and stood there, still half-dazed and very uncomfortable, listening to Fester talk endlessly it seemed to him, about what he had discovered. That was not only probably a new approach but also an analysis which showed how inherently weak the previous experiment had been and how further experimentation along that line would certainly have been inconclusive. The following morning Knowlton spent the entire morning with Fester and Link, the mathematician, the morning meetings having been called off so that Fester's work of the previous night could be gone over intensively. Fester was very anxious that this be done and Knowlton was not too unhappy to call the meeting off for reasons of his own.

For the next several days Fester sat in the back office that had been turned over to him and did nothing but read the progress reports of the work that had been done in the last six months. Knowlton caught himself feeling apprehensive about the reaction that Fester might have to some of his work. He was a little surprised at his own feelings. He had always been proud—although he had put on a convincingly modest face—of the way in which his team had broken new ground in the study of photon measuring devices. Now he wasn't sure. It seemed to him that Fester might easily show that the line of research they had been following was unsound or even unimaginative.

The next morning, as was the custom in Bob's group, the members of the lab, including the secretaries, sat around the table in the conference room for a group meeting. Bob always prided himself on the fact that the work of the lab was guided and evaluated by the team as a whole. He was fond of repeating that it was not a waste of time to include secretaries in such meetings because often what started out as a boring recital of fundamental assumptions to a naive listener uncovered new ways of regarding these assumptions that would not have occurred to the lab member who had long ago accepted them as a necessary basis for the research he was doing. These group meetings also served Bob in another sense. He admitted to himself that he would have felt far less secure if he had had to direct the work out of his own mind, so to speak. With the team meeting as the principle of leadership, it was always possible to justify the exploration of blind alleys as valuable because of the general educative effect of the team. Fester was there, Lucy and Martha were there, Link was sitting next to Fester, their conversation concerning Link's mathematical study apparently continuing from yesterday. The other members, Bob Davenport, George Thurlow and Arthur Oliver, were there and waiting quietly.

Knowlton, for reasons that he didn't quite understand, proposed for discussion this morning a problem that all of them had previously spent a great deal of time discussing. The team had come to an implicit conclusion that a solution was impossible and that there was no feasible way of treating it in an experimental fashion. When Knowlton proposed the problem, Davenport remarked that there was hardly any use of going over it again. He was satisfied that there was no way of approaching the problem with the equipment and the physical capacities of the lab.

This statement had the effect of a shot of adrenalin on Fester. He said he would like to know what the problem was in detail, and walking to the blackboard, began setting down "the factors" as various members of the group began both discussing the problem and simultaneously listing the reasons why it had been abandoned. Very early in the description of the problem it was evident that Fester was going to disagree about the impossibility of solving it. The group realized this and finally the descriptive materials and their recounting of the reasoning that had led to its abandonment dwindled away. Fester began his analysis, which as it proceeded might have well been prepared the previous night although Knowlton knew this was impossible. He couldn't help being impressed with the organized and logical way that Fester was presenting ideas that must have occurred to him only a few minutes before.

Fester had some things to say, however, which left Knowlton with a mixture of annoyance, irritation and, at the same time, a rather smug feeling of superiority over Fester in at least one area. Fester was of the opinion that the way that the problem had been analyzed was really typical of what happened when such thinking was attempted by a team, and with an air of sophistication which made it difficult for a listener to dissent, he proceeded to make general comments on the American emphasis on team ideas, satirically describing the ways in which they led to a "high level of mediocrity."

During this time Knowlton observed that Link stared studiously at the floor and he was very conscious of George Thurlow's and Bob Davenport's glances towards him at several points of Fester's little speech. Inwardly, Knowlton couldn't help feeling that this was one point at least in which Fester was off on the wrong foot. The whole lab, following Jerry's lead, talked if not practiced, the theory of small research teams as the basic organization for effective research. Fester insisted that the problem could be approached and that he would like to study it for a while himself.

Knowlton ended the morning session by remarking that the meetings would continue and that the very fact that a supposedly insoluble experimental problem was now going to get another chance was another indication of the value of such meetings. Fester immediately remarked that he was not at all averse to meetings for the purpose of informing the group of the progress of its members—that the point he wanted to make was that creative advances were seldom accomplished in such meetings, that they were made by the individual "living with" the problem closely and continuously, a sort of personal relationship to it. Knowlton went on to say to Fester that he was very glad that Fester had raised these points and that he was sure the team would profit by re-examining the basis on which they had been operating. Knowlton agreed that individual effort was probably the basis for making the major advances, but that he considered the group meetings useful primarily because of the effect they had on keeping the team together and on helping the weaker members of the team keep up with the advances of the ones who were able to advance more easily and quickly along the analysis of problems.

It was clear as days went by and meetings continued as they did, that Fester came to enjoy them because of the pattern which the meetings assumed. It became almost typical for Fester to hold forth and it was also clear that he was, without question, more brilliant, better prepared on the various subjects which were germane to the problems being studied. He was probably more capable of going ahead than anyone there, and Knowlton grew increasingly disturbed as he realized that his leadership of the team had been, in fact, taken over. In Knowlton's occasional meetings with Dr. Jerrold, whenever the subject of Fester was mentioned, he would comment only on the ability and obvious capacity for work that Fester had, somehow never feeling that he could mention his own discomforts, not only because they revealed a weakness on his own part but also because it was quite clear that Jerrold himself was considerably impressed with Fester's work and with the contacts he had with him outside the Photon Laboratory.

Knowlton at this time began to feel that the intellectual advantages that Fester had brought to the team perhaps did not quite compensate for what he felt were evidences of breakdown of the cooperative group spirit which he had seen in the group before Fester's coming. More and more of the morning meetings were skipped. Fester's opinion concerning the abilities of others of the team, with the exception of Link, was obviously low. At times during morning meetings or in smaller discussions he had been rude, refusing at certain times to pursue an argument when he claimed it was based on the other person's ignorance of the facts involved. His impatience of the others also led him to make remarks of this kind to Dr. Jerrold. This Knowlton inferred from a conversation he had had with Jerrold in which Jerrold had been asking whether Davenport and Oliver were going to be continued on; and his not mentioning Link, the mathematician, led Knowlton to feel that this was the result of conversations that Fester had had privately with Jerrold himself.

It was not difficult for Knowlton to make a quite convincing case on the question of whether the brilliance of Fester was actually a sufficient recompense for the beginning of this breaking up of the team. He took the opportunity to speak privately with Davenport and with Oliver and it was quite clear that both of them were uncomfortable with the relationship with Fester. Knowlton didn't press the discussion beyond the point of hearing them in one way or another say that they did sometimes feel awkward and that it was sometimes difficult for them to understand the arguments he advanced. They often felt too embarrassed to ask Fester to fill in the background on which he felt such arguments were valid. Knowlton did not interview Link in this manner.

About six months after Fester's coming into the Photon lab, a meeting was scheduled in which the sponsors of much of the research going on were coming to get some idea of the work and its progress. It was customary at these meetings for project heads to present the research being conducted in their own group. The members of the laboratory team were invited to other meetings which were held later in the day and open to all, but the special meetings were usually made up only of the project heads, the head of the laboratory and the sponsors. As the time for the special meeting approached, it seemed to Knowlton that he must avoid the presentation at all costs. His reasons for this were that he could not trust himself to present the ideas that Fester had advanced and on which work had been done, because of his apprehension as to whether he could present them in sufficient detail and answer questions about them. On the other hand he did not feel he could ignore these newer lines of work and present only the material which had been done or had been started before Fester's arrival which he was perfectly competent to do. He felt also that it would not be beyond Fester, in his blunt and undiplomatic way, if he were present at the meeting, to make comments on his own presentation and reveal the inadequacy which Knowlton felt he had. It seemed quite clear also, that it would not be easy to keep Fester from attending the meeting in spite of the fact that he was not on the administrative level which was invited.

Knowlton found an opportunity to speak to Jerrold and raised the question. He remarked to Jerrold that, of course, with the meetings coming up and with the interest in the work and with the contributions that Fester had been making he would probably like to come to these meetings but there was a question of the feelings of the others in the group if Fester were invited. Jerrold passed this over very lightly by saying that he didn't think the group would fail to understand Fester's rather different position. He thought that Fester by all means should be invited. Knowlton then immediately said that he had thought so too and that he felt that Fester should present the work because much of it was work that he had done; and that, as Knowlton put it, this would be a nice way to recognize Fester's contributions and to reward him since he was eager to be recognized as a productive member of the lab. Jerrold agreed and so the matter was decided.

Fester's presentation was very successful and in some ways dominated the meeting. He attracted the interest and attention of many of those who had come and following his presentation the questions persisted for a long period. Later that evening at the banquet, to which the entire laboratory was invited, a little circle of people formed about Fester during the cocktail period before the dinner. Jerrold was among the circle and discussion concerning the application of the theory Fester was proposing. All of this disturbed Knowlton and his reaction and behavior was characteristic. He joined the circle, praised Fester to Jerrold and to others, and remarked how able and how brilliant some of his work was.

Knowlton, without consulting anyone, began at this time to take some interest in the possibility of a job elsewhere. After a few weeks he found that a new laboratory of considerable size was being organized in a nearby city. His training and experience would enable him to get a project head job equivalent to the one he had at the lab, with slightly more money.

He immediately accepted it and notified Jerrold by a letter which he mailed on a Friday night to Jerrold's home. The letter was quite brief and Jerrold was stunned. The letter merely said that he had found a better position; that there were personal reasons why he didn't want to appear at the lab any more; that he would be glad to come back at a later time from where he would be, some forty miles away, to assist if there was any mixup at all in the past work; that he felt sure that Fester could, however, supply any leadership that was required for the group; that his decision to leave so suddenly was based on some personal problems; and he hinted at problems of health in his family, his mother and father. All of this was fictitious. Of course, Jerrold took it at face value but still felt that this was very strange behavior and quite unaccountable since he had always felt his relationship with Knowlton had been warm and that Knowlton was satisfied and, as a matter of fact, quite happy and productive.

Jerrold was considerably disturbed because he had already decided to place Fester in charge of another project that was going to be set up very soon and had been wondering how to explain this to Knowlton in view of the obvious help and assistance and value Knowlton was getting from Fester and the high regard in which he held him. He had, as a matter of fact, considered the possibility that Knowlton could add to his staff another person with the kind of background and training that had been unique in Fester and had proved so valuable.

Jerrold did not make any attempt to meet Knowlton. In a way he felt aggrieved about the whole thing. Fester, too, was surprised at the suddenness of Knowlton's departure and when Jerrold, in talking to him, asked him whether he preferred to stay with the photon group instead of the Air Force project which was being organized, he chose the Air Force project and went on to that job the following week. The photon lab was hard hit. The leadership of the lab was given to Link with the understanding that this would be temporary until someone could come in to take over.

QUESTIONS

1. What attributions did Bob Knowlton make?
2. What team norms seemed to be operating in Bob Knowlton's team?
3. How do you characterize the decision-making styles of Dr. Jerrold, Bob Knowlton, and Simon Fester?
4. What leadership style did Bob *need* from Dr. Jerrold after Simon arrived? Explain.
5. What leadership style did Bob seem to get from Dr. Jerrold *before* and *after* Simon arrived?
6. What leadership style did Bob use with his subordinates? Was it effective? Explain.
7. What leadership style did Bob use with Simon? Was it effective? Explain.
8. What would you have done with Simon if you were Bob?
9. What would you have done to influence Dr. Jerrold if you were Bob?

SOURCE: Case developed by Dr. Alex Bavelas. Used with permission.

▼ CONSCIENCE OR THE COMPETITIVE EDGE?

The plane touched down at Bombay airport precisely on time. Olivia Jones made her way through the usual immigration bureaucracy without incident and was finally ushered into a waiting limousine, complete with uniformed chauffeur and soft black leather seats. Her already considerable excitement at being in India for the first time was mounting. As she cruised the dark city streets, she asked her chauffeur why so few cars had their headlights on at night.

The driver responded that most drivers believed that headlights use too much petrol! Finally, she arrived at her hotel, a black marble monolith, grandiose and decadent in its splendour, towering above the bay.

The goal of her 4-day trip was to sample and select swatches of woven cotton from the mills in and around Bombay, to be used in the following season's youthwear collection of shirts, trousers, and underwear. She was treated with the utmost deference by her hosts, who were invariably Indian factory owners, or British agents for Indian mills. For 3 days she was ferried from one air-conditioned office to another, sipping iced tea or chilled lemonade, poring over leather-bound swatch catalogues, which featured every type of stripe and design possible. On the fourth day, Jones made a request which she knew would cause some anxiety in the camp. "I want to see a factory," she declared.

After much consultation and several attempts at dissuasion, she was once again ushered into a limousine and driven through a part of the city she had not previously seen. Gradually, the hotel and the western shops dissolved into the background and Jones entered downtown Bombay. All around was a sprawling shantytown, constructed from sheets of corrugated iron and panels of cardboard boxes. Dust flew in spirals everywhere among the dirt roads and open drains. The car crawled along the unsealed roads behind carts hauled by man and beast alike, laden to overflowing with straw or city refuse—the treasure of the ghetto. More than once the limousine had to halt and wait while a lumbering white bull crossed the road.

Finally, in the very heart of the ghetto, the car came to a stop. "Are you sure you want to do this?" asked her host. Determined not to be fainthearted, Jones got out of the car.

White-skinned, blue-eyed, and blond, clad in a city suit and stiletto-heeled shoes, and carrying a briefcase, Jones was indeed conspicuous. It was hardly surprising that the inhabitants of the area found her an interesting and musing subject, as she teetered along the dusty street and stepped gingerly over the open sewers.

Her host led her down an alley, between the shacks and open doors and inky black interiors. Some shelters, Jones was told, were restaurants, where at lunchtime people would gather on the rush mat floors and eat rice together. In the doorway of one shack there was a table which served as a counter, laden with ancient cans of baked beans, sardines, and rusted tins of a fluorescent green substance that might have been peas. The eyes of the young man behind the counter were smiling and proud as he beckoned her forward to view his wares.

As Jones turned another corner, she saw an old man in the middle of the street, clad in a waist cloth, sitting in a large tin bucket. He had a tin can in his hand with which he poured water from the bucket over his head and shoulders. Beside him two little girls played in brilliant white nylon dresses, bedecked with ribbons and lace. They posed for her with smiling faces, delighted at having their photograph taken in their best frocks. The men and women moved around her with great dignity and grace, Jones thought.

Finally, her host led her up a precarious wooden ladder to a floor above the street. At the top Jones was warned not to stand straight as the ceiling was just 5 feet high. There, in a room not 20 feet by 40 feet, twenty men were sitting at treadle sewing machines, bent over yards of white cloth. Between them on the floor were rush mats, some occupied by sleeping workers awaiting their next shift. Jones learned that these men were on a 24-hour rotation, 12 hours on and 12 hours off, every day for 6 months of the year. For the remaining 6 months they returned to their families in the countryside to work the land, planting and building with the money they had earned in the city. The shirts they were working on were for an order she had placed 4 weeks earlier in London, an order of which she had been particularly proud because of the low price she had succeeded in negotiating. Jones reflected that this sight was the most humbling experience of her life. When she questioned her host about these conditions, she was told that they were typical for her industry—and for most of the third world, as well.

Eventually, she left the heat, dust, and din of the little shirt factory and returned to the protected, air-conditioned world of the limousine.

"What I've experienced today and the role I've played in creating that living hell will stay with me forever," she thought. Later in the day, she asked herself whether what she had seen was an inevitable consequence of pricing policies that enabled the British customer to purchase shirts at £12.99 instead of £13.99 and at the same time allowed the company to make its mandatory 56 percent profit margin? Were her negotiating skills—the result of many years of training—an indirect cause of the terrible conditions she had seen?

Once Jones returned to the U.K., she considered her position and the options open to her as a buyer for a large, publicly traded, retail chain operating in a highly competitive environment. Her dilemma was twofold: Can an ambitious employee afford to exercise a social conscience in his or her career? And can career-minded individuals truly make a difference without jeopardizing their future?

QUESTIONS

1. What should Jones do?

2. What would you do if you were in her shoes?

SOURCE: This case was prepared by Kate Button, journalist, and Dr. Christopher K. Bart, McMaster University, Canada. This case was written solely for the purpose of stimulating student discussion. All events and individuals are real, but names have been disguised at the request of the principals involved. Copyright © 1993 by the *Case Research Journal* and Kate Button and Christopher K. Bart. This case appeared in the *Case Research Journal*, Winter 1994, 68–72. Used with permission.

THE SHIFTLESS WORKER?

Charlie McManus, with a troubled look on his face, sat back in his chair and gazed out the window of his office past the plant to the surrounding mountains. It was a beautiful, sunny day, and he had hoped to be able to duck out by mid-afternoon and be somewhere far up Foster's Creek by 4:30 or so. He would rather be worrying some brook trout instead of worrying about the implications of a situation developing out in area 7.

He could not quite put his finger on it, but there seemed to be something going on out there. Reports of the failure of operators to complete all the necessary checks on their shifts and some indications of minor grumblings among the work force had him wondering if everything was all right in the area. As the manager of department B, he was thinking about whether or not he should try to get better information about what, if anything, was going on and intervene in some way or just let things ride unless something more definite came up. He continued to review in his mind the company and the situation with which he was dealing.

The Company

Lost River Processing, Inc., a wholly owned subsidiary plant of a large conglomerate, processes ore mined in the nearby mountains into an intermediate product serving as input material for a broad range of industrial processes. The plant's production output is sold to other plants owned by the parent conglomerate, as well as to outside purchasers.

The particular mineral business in which the company engages is highly competitive, with a number of strong competitors located around the country. Since the end product produced by all these plants has the basic characteristics of a commodity, it is important to strive to be a low-cost producer, especially under the current industry condition of overcapacity of production facilities. It is also important to maintain high quality standards because quality is a major factor in securing and maintaining highly sought sole-supplier relationships with customers, which are becoming more common in the industry.

The plant, located in Ashley Springs, Wyoming (population, forty-five hundred), has been an institution in the community for over forty years, employing approximately five hundred workers in operations that continue around the clock. Most employees are from the surrounding rural, largely agricultural region. Many have grown up on farms and ranches in the area and still farm during their off time and on weekends. They tend to be a hard-working, independent, self-motivated work force in general, although there are some exceptions.

The plant has been nonunion for many years, and remaining so is an important objective of management. The chief advantage of the nonunion status as viewed by management is their flexibility to make changes as needed and

as technological developments demand, without protracted negotiations or costly concessions to a union.

In seeking to continue its nonunion status, the company attempts to follow enlightened human resource practices and strives to maintain benefits and grant annual wage and salary increases comparable to those achieved by unions in directly competing firms in the area.

The plant manager for the last several years has been a very capable, yet friendly, unassuming, down-to-earth individual who relates very well with and has the respect of the work force.

For the past two or three years, the company has been cautiously restructuring its work force and adopting some new management practices in line with a decision to eliminate some layers of supervision and push decision making farther down in the organization. These moves are one response to the need for continually reducing costs in order to remain competitive.

Over the longer range, the plant is planning to move progressively toward an operation run on the concept of self-managed groups. Because the work force tends to have low turnover and be well trained and responsible, management feels this move is well founded and offers the potential for real savings.

The plant organization is structured (as shown in Figure 1) with operators in each area responsible to shift supervisors, who in turn report to department managers. The various department managers report to the superintendent in their functional area, who reports to the plant manager, the highest position at the plant site.

Area 7

Area 7 is one of the processing areas falling under the supervision of the manager of department B, Charlie McManus. The area is worked by several crews assigned to assure coverage on an around-the-clock basis. The crews on each shift report to a shift supervisor, and the crews and supervisors rotate shifts monthly.

The supervisors are senior workers who have moved up to the position. Most have had eight or more years of experience in the plant before moving into their supervisory positions. As a result they are very knowledgeable about plant operations in their areas and also know all their fellow workers quite well.

There were, however, a few exceptions to this internal progression from experienced worker to supervisor within the plant. The parent corporation had operated a similar plant in South Carolina for many years. Increasing pressures to lower costs, combined with overcapacity in the industry, made continued operation of the old plant uneconomic, and it was eventually closed a little over a year ago.

When the plant was closed, some supervisors who were not able to take early retirement or move to other nearby plants were offered transfers to the Wyoming plant. Four

FIGURE 1

Organization Chart for Lost River Processing, Inc.

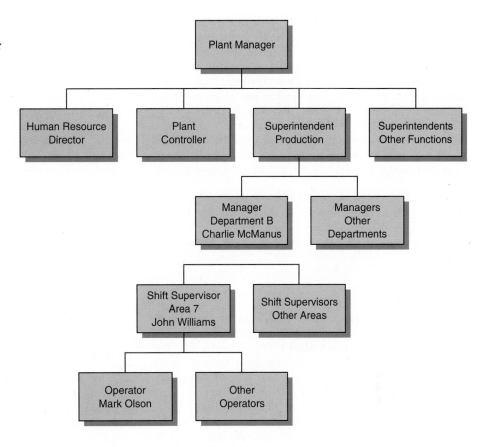

eventually elected to transfer and had arrived at the plant about one year ago. They were then placed in supervisory positions roughly equivalent to the positions they had held in South Carolina. Three of them were assigned to department B under Charlie McManus.

These new supervisors from the East had worked in an environment quite different from the Ashley Springs plant, with a quite different work force. The South Carolina plant had employed a racially diverse work force of relatively uneducated, predominantly rural people and had a turnover rate that was moderate to high by Ashley Springs standards. These workers were not highly trained and their supervisors tended to manage them quite closely. As a result, these supervisors had learned to be quite directive and spent a fair amount of their time making sure that their workers did what they had been assigned. These supervisors had subsequently brought these supervisory tendencies and practices with them to the West.

John Williams, Supervisor

John Williams, who was among the transferred supervisors, is one of the shift supervisors in area 7, responsible for several crews of operators involved in production work in that part of the plant. Among other duties, one of his crews is responsible for making sure that certain pumps are functioning properly, that several bins collecting by-products produced during the process are emptied on schedule, and that the work area is kept clean.

John has been complaining to his manager Charlie, even asking for help on one occasion, that one of the operators on one of his crews, Mark Olson, has not been performing the job as well as John would like. Over the past several months, according to John, this worker has on occasion either simply failed to perform or performed very poorly several of job responsibilities.

For example, the settling pond pumps are supposed to be checked every four hours, and certain readings written down. John mentioned that when assigned to this task, Mark does not check them this often and often fails to record the readings as required.

On the third shift, an operator is responsible for emptying the bins of coke and silica, which are produced as by-products, by performing a procedure called vactoring. On the second shift, the dryer bins are serviced in the same way. When assigned as the operator on these shift, Mark reportedly often fails to place the appropriate bins as they should be.

Part of each operator's assigned responsibility is a clean-up area. As the supervisor, John usually has to call Mark's attention to his clean-up area before the monthly inspection.

John reported he has tried talking with Mark about his performance several times, but it hasn't seemed to make any difference. He recognizes that Mark is one of the more intelligent employees among his crew of operators. As such, John is certain Mark is capable of performing well, if he chooses to do the job right. John expressed his concern to Charlie that Mark "always seems to find new ways to screw up—or just seems to forget to do certain aspects of his job assignments."

John indicated that Mark had also told him during one of the talks they have had that he doesn't really like his job very much and has been looking around for either a transfer within the plant or for some other opportunity outside the company.

Mark Olson

As he tried to keep track of all employees in his department, Charlie had been following Mark Olson's progress with the company since he was hired. Mark had been working for the company for several years, and by most indications, it seemed to Charlie, it had generally been a good experience for him. In the course of their infrequent, informal chats, Mark had never given Charlie any indication that he was dissatisfied with his job, and until recently, his performance had always been rated quite highly. The job has no doubt become somewhat routine for Mark now that he has learned all the tasks performed by the crew, and shift work is not particularly enjoyable. These are conditions however, that everybody comes to terms with eventually. At the same time, the pay, the working conditions, and the company are pretty good.

One thing that has been bothering Mark—and some others, according to scuttlebutt Charlie has picked up in the department—has been the attitude of the new supervisors the company transferred in from back East. The crews' attitude is that these new people seem to have taken over the department, and all the day-to-day operations are being run by these "out of towners." "They treat us like a bunch of slaves, don't let us make decisions, and treat us like we're stupid" was one comment overheard in the shower room a few weeks ago.

Mark appeared to Charlie to be one example of an operator who has not been performing the job as well as he is capable of doing, perhaps partly in response to the attitude of these supervisors. Over the past several months, according to his supervisor, Mark has on occasion simply failed to perform, or performed poorly, several of his job responsibilities. Mark admitted to a friend, who mentioned it to Charlie, that he purposely chose random tasks to "forget" to do. "I'm acting like this to drive them crazy, and just waiting for a job bid," Mark told his friend in the human resource department.

Charlie ended his reverie and arose from the chair. He was still not sure if he was dealing with any real issue or just the usual griping and interpersonal problems heard among the crews. Still, these problems and comments seemed to be arising more frequently than before in department B. He was concerned about young Mark Olson, for whom he had great hopes in the company.

Charlie wondered what should be done about the situation. In line with the downward delegation of authority in the plant, he generally did not intervene in cases of problem employees, but rather left resolution of such situations up to his supervisors. But in this case, he wondered if the supervisor might be part of the problem. He wasn't sure of just what he was dealing with here and didn't know if he should intervene in some way or not.

It was now 4:00, and Charlie headed out the door for the parking lot and his waiting pickup, gassed up and ready to go with his fly rod and some new Montana nymphs he was itching to try. He had decided to put in some good thinking time before tomorrow, when he would return with his decision.

QUESTIONS

1. What is your analysis of the situation faced by Charlie McManus? What are the key issues facing him?

2. How do you explain the behavior of the operator in this situation? Why do you think he is performing the way he is?

3. What do you think Charlie McManus should do? Explain in detail how you think he should proceed?

4. What do you think the supervisor John should do? How do you think the operator Mark will react to what you propose?

5. What are the implications of the short-term, operational decisions in this situation for the long-range strategic goals of the plant?

6. In this specific situation, the issue was an inappropriate supervisory style and its impact on worker behavior. What other issues are likely to arise in the transition from a traditional hierarchically structured unit to a group-oriented, self-managed organization? What managerial practices might be considered in dealing with them?

SOURCE: This case was prepared by William E. Stratton of Idaho State University and is intended to be used as a basis for class discussion, rather than to illustrate either effective or ineffective handling of the situation. The names of the firm, individuals, and locations have been disguised to preserve the firm's anonymity. Presented and accepted by the refereed Midwest Society for Case Research. All rights reserved to the author. Copyright © 1990 by William E. Stratton. See R. A. Cook (ed.), *Annual Advances in Business Cases 1990* South Bend, Ind.: Midwest Society for Case Research, 1990. 610–615. Used with permission.

THE ROAD TO HELL

John Baker, chief engineer of the Caribbean Bauxite Company Limited of Barracania in the West Indies, was making his final preparations to leave the island. His promotion to production manager of Keso Mining Corporation near Winnipeg—one of Continental Ore's fast-expanding Canadian enterprises—had been announced a month before, and now everything had been attended to except the last vital interview with his successor, the able young Barracanian Matthew Rennalls. It was vital that his interview be a success and that Rennalls leave Baker's office uplifted and encouraged to face the challenge of his new job. A touch on the bell would have brought Rennalls walking into the room, but Baker delayed the moment and gazed thoughtfully through the window, considering just exactly what he was going to say and, more particularly, how he was going to say it.

Baker, an English expatriate, was forty-five years old and had served his twenty-three years with Continental Ore in many different places: the Far East, several countries of Africa; Europe; and for the last two years, the West Indies. He had not cared much for his previous assignment in Hamburg and was delighted when the West Indian appointment came through. Climate was not the only attraction. Baker had always preferred working overseas in what were called the "developing countries" because he felt he had an innate knack—more than most other expatriates working for Continental Ore—of knowing just how to get on with regional staff. After only twenty-four hours in Barracania, however, he realized that he would need all of his innate knack if he were to deal effectively with the problems in this field that now awaited him.

At his first interview with Glenda Hutchins, the production manager, the whole problem of Rennalls and his future was discussed. Then and there, it was made quite clear to Baker that one of his important tasks would be the grooming of Rennalls as his successor. Hutchins had pointed out that not only was Rennalls one of the brightest Barracanian prospects on the staff of Caribbean Bauxite—at London University, he had taken first-class honors in the B.Sc. engineering degree—but, being the son of the minister of finance and economic planning, he also had no small political pull.

Caribbean bauxite had been particularly pleased when Rennalls decided to work for it, rather than for the government in which his father had such a prominent post. The company ascribed his action to the effect of its vigorous and liberal regionalization program that, since World War II, had produced eighteen Barracanians at the middle management level and had given Caribbean bauxite a good lead in this respect over all other international concerns operating in Barracania. The success of this timely regionalization policy had led to excellent relations with the government—a relationship that gained added importance when Barracania, three years later, became independent, an occasion that encouraged a critical and challenging attitude toward the role foreign interests would play in the new Barracania. Hutchins, therefore, had little difficulty convincing Baker that the successful career development of Rennalls was of prime importance.

The interview with Hutchins was now two years in the past, and Baker, leaning back in his office chair, reviewed just how successful he had been in the grooming of Rennalls. What aspects of the latter's character had helped, and what had hindered? What about his own personality? How had that helped or hindered? The first item to go on the credit side, without question, would be the ability of Rennalls to master the technical aspects of his job. From the start, he had shown keenness and enthusiasm, and he had often impressed Baker with his ability in tackling new assignments and the constructive comments he invariably made in departmental discussions. He was popular with all ranks of Barracanian staff and had an ease of manner that stood him in good stead when dealing with his expatriate seniors.

Those were all assets, but what about the debit side? First and foremost was his racial consciousness. His four years at London University had accentuated this feeling and made him sensitive to any sign of condescension on the part of expatriates. Perhaps to give expression to this sentiment, as soon as he returned home from London, he threw himself into politics on behalf of the United Action Party, which was later to win the preindependence elections and provide the country with its first prime minister.

The ambitions of Rennalls—and he certainly was ambitious—did not, however, lie in politics. Staunch nationalist that he was, he saw that he could serve himself and his country best—was not bauxite responsible for nearly half the value of Barracania's export trade?—by putting his engineering talent to the best use possible. On this account, Hutchins found that she had an unexpectedly easy task in persuading Rennalls to give up his political work before entering the production department as an assistant engineer.

It was, Baker knew, Rennall's well-repressed sense of racial consciousness that had prevented their relationship from being as close as it should have been. On the surface, they could not have seemed more agreeable. Formality between the two was minimal. Baker was delighted to find that his assistant shared his own peculiar "shaggy dog" sense of humor, so jokes were continually being exchanged. They entertained one another at their houses and often played tennis together—and yet the barrier remained invisible, indefinable, but ever present. The existence of this screen between them was a constant source of frustration to Baker, since it indicated a weakness that he was loath to accept. If successful with people of all other nationalities, why not with Rennalls?

At least he had managed to break through to Rennalls more successfully than had any other expatriate. In fact, it was the young Barracanian's attitude—sometimes overbearing, sometimes cynical—toward other company expatriates that had been one of the subjects Baker raised last year when he discussed Rennall's staff report with him. Baker knew, too, that he would have to raise the same subject again in the forthcoming interview, because Martha Jackson, the senior person in charge of drafting, had complained only yesterday about the rudeness of Rennalls. With this thought in mind, Baker leaned forward and spoke into the intercom: "Would you come in, Matt, please? I'd like a word with you." Rennalls came in, and Baker held out a box and said, "Do sit down. Have a cigarette."

He paused while he held out his lighter and then went on. "As you know, Matt, I'll be off to Canada in a few days' time, and before I go, I thought it would be useful if we could have a final chat together. It is indeed with some deference that I suggest I can be of help. You will shortly be sitting in this chair doing the job I am now doing, but I, on the other hand, am ten years older, so perhaps you can accept the idea that I may be able to give you the benefit of my longer experience."

Baker saw Rennalls stiffen slightly in his chair as he made this point, so he added in explanation, "You and I have attended enough company courses to remember those repeated requests by the human resources manager to tell people how they are getting on as often as the convenient moment arises, and not just the automatic once a year when, by regulation, staff reports have to be discussed."

Rennalls nodded his agreement, so Baker went on, "I shall always remember the last job performance discussion I had with my previous boss back in Germany. She used what she called the 'plus and minus technique.' She firmly believed that when managers seek to improve the work performance of their staff by discussion, their prime objective should be to make sure the latter leave the interview encouraged and inspired to improve. Any criticism, therefore, must be constructive and helpful. She said that one very good way to encourage a person—and I fully agree with her—is to discuss good points, the plus factors, as well as weak ones, the minus factors. So I though, Matt, it would be a good idea to run our discussion along these lines."

Rennalls offered no comment, so Baker continued, "Let me say, therefore, right away, that as far as your own work performance is concerned, the pluses far outweigh the minuses. I have, for instance, been most impressed with the way you have adapted your considerable theoretical knowledge to master the practical techniques of your job—that ingenious method you used to get air down to the fifth shaft level is a sufficient case in point. At departmental meetings, I have invariably found your comments well taken and helpful. In fact, you will be interested to know that only last week I reported to Ms. Hutchins that, from the technical point of view, she could not wish for a more able person to succeed to the position of chief engineer."

"That's very good indeed of you, John," cut in Rennalls with a smile of thanks. "My only worry now is how to live up to such a high recommendation."

"Of that I am quite sure," returned Baker, "especially if you can overcome the minus factor which I would like now to discuss with you. It is one that I have talked about before, so I'll come straight to the point. I have noticed that you are more friendly and get on better with your fellow Barracanians than you do with Europeans. In point of fact, I had a complaint only yesterday from Ms. Jackson, who said you had been rude to her—and not for the first time, either.

"There is, Matt, I am sure, no need for me to tell you how necessary it will be for you to get on well with expatriates, because until the company has trained sufficient personnel of your caliber, Europeans are bound to occupy senior positions here in Barracania. All this is vital to your future interests, so can I help you in any way?"

While Baker was speaking on this theme, Rennalls sat tensed in his chair, and it was some seconds before he replied. "It is quite extraordinary; isn't it, how one can convey an impression to others so at variance with what one intends? I can only assure you once again that my disputes with Jackson—and you may remember also Godson—have had nothing at all to do with the color of their skins. I promise you that if a Barracanian had behaved in an equally peremptory manner, I would have reacted in precisely the same way. And again, if I may say it within these four walls, I am sure I am not the only one who has found Jackson and Godson difficult. I could mention the names of several expatriates who have felt the same. However, I am really sorry to have created this impression of not being able to get on with Europeans—it is an entirely false one—and I quite realize that I must do all I can to correct it as quickly as possible. On your last point, regarding Europeans holding senior positions in the company for some time to come, I quite accept the situation. I know that Caribbean bauxite—as it has been doing for many years now—will promote Barracanians as soon as their experience warrants it. And, finally, I would like to assure you, John—and my father thinks the same, too—that I am very happy in my work here and hope to stay with the company for many years to come."

Rennalls had spoken earnestly, and Baker, although not convinced by what he had heard, did not think he could pursue the matter further except to say, "All right, Matt, my impression may be wrong, but I would like to remind you about the truth of that old saying 'What is important is not what is true, but what is believed.' Let it rest at that."

But suddenly Baker knew that he did not want to "let it rest at that." He was disappointed once again at not being able to break through to Rennalls and at having again had to listen to his bland denial that there was any racial prejudice in his makeup.

Baker, who had intended to end the interview at this point, decided to try another tack. "To return for a moment to the plus and minus technique I was telling you about just now, there is another plus factor I forgot to mention. I would like to congratulate you not only on the caliber of your work but also on the ability you have shown in overcoming a challenge that I, as a European, have never had to meet.

"Continental Ore is, as you know, a typical commercial enterprise—admittedly a big one—that is a product of the economic and social environment of the United States and Western Europe. My ancestors have all been brought up in this environment for the past two or three hundred years, and I have, therefore, been able to live in a world in which commerce (as we know it today) has been part and parcel of my being. It has not been something revolutionary and new that has suddenly entered my life. In your case," went on Baker, "the situation is different, because you and your forebears have only had some fifty and not two or three hundred years. Again, Matt, let me congratulate you—and people like you—on having so successfully overcome this particular hurdle. It is for this very reason that I think the outlook for Barracania—and particularly Caribbean Bauxite—is so bright."

Rennalls had listened intently, and when Baker finished, he replied, "Well, once again, John, I have to thank you for what you have said, and, for my part, I can only say that it is gratifying to know that my own personal effort has been so much appreciated. I hope that more people will soon come to think as you do."

There was a pause, and, for a moment, Baker thought hopefully that he was about to achieve his long-awaited breakthrough. But Rennalls merely smiled back. The barrier remained unbreached. There were some five minutes' cheerful conversation about the contrast between the Caribbean and Canadian climates and whether the West Indies had any hope of beating England in a soccer game before Baker drew the interview to a close. Although he was as far as ever from knowing the real Rennalls, he was nevertheless glad that the interview had run along in this friendly manner and, particularly, that it had ended on such a cheerful note.

This feeling, however, lasted only until the following morning. Baker had some farewells to make, so he arrived at the office considerably later than usual. He had no sooner sat down at his desk than his secretary walked into the room with a worried frown on her face. Her words came fast. "When I arrived this morning, I found Mr. Rennalls already waiting at my door. He seemed very angry and told me that he had a vital letter to dictate that must be sent off without any delay. He was so worked up that he couldn't keep still and kept pacing about the room, which is most unlike him. He wouldn't even wait to read what he had dictated. Just signed the page where he thought the letter would end. It has been distributed, and your copy is in your tray."

Puzzled and feeling vaguely uneasy, Baker opened the envelope marked "confidential" and read the following letter:

14 August 1990

FROM: Assistant Engineer

TO: Chief Engineer Caribbean Bauxite Limited

SUBJECT: Assessment of Interview between Messrs. Baker and Rennalls

It has always been my practice to respect the advice given to me by seniors, so after our interview, I decided to give careful thought once again to its main points and to make sure that I had understood all that had been said. As I promised you at the time, I had every intention of putting your advice to the best effect.

It was not, therefore, until I had sat down quietly in my home yesterday evening to consider the interview objectively that its main purpose became clear. Only then did the full enormity of what you said dawn on me. The more I thought about it, the more convinced I was that I had hit upon the real truth—and the more furious I became. With a facility in the English language which I—a poor Barracanian—cannot hope to match, you had the audacity to insult me (and through me every Barracanian worth his salt) by claiming that our knowledge of modern living is only a paltry fifty years old, while yours goes back two hundred to three hundred years. As if your materialistic commercial environment could possibly be compared with the spiritual values of our culture! I'll have you know that if much of what I saw in London is representative of your most boasted culture, I hope fervently that it will never come to Barracania. By what right do you have the effrontery to condescend to us? After all, you Europeans think us barbarians, or, as you say amongst yourselves, we are "just down from the trees."

Far into the night I discussed this matter with my father, and he is as disgusted as I. He agrees with me that any company whose senior staff think as you do is no place for any Barracanian proud of his culture and race. So much for all the company claptrap and specious propaganda about regionalization and Barracania for the Barracanians.

I feel ashamed and betrayed. Please accept this letter as my resignation, which I wish to become effective immediately.

cc: Production Manager
Managing Director

QUESTIONS

1. What were Baker's intentions in the conversation with Rennalls? Were they fulfilled or not, and why?

2. Was Baker alert to nonverbal signals? What did both Baker and Rennalls communicate to one another by nonverbal means?

3. How did Baker's view of himself affect the impression he formed of Rennalls?

4. What kind of interpersonal relationship had existed between Baker and Rennalls prior to the conversation described in the case? Was the conversation consistent or inconsistent with that relationship?

5. What, if anything, could Baker or Rennalls have done before, during, or after the conversation to improve the situation?

6. How would you characterize the personality attributes of Baker and Rennalls?

7. What perceptual errors and attributions are evident?

SOURCE: Prepared and adapted with permission from G. Evans, late of Shell International Petroleum Co. Ltd., London, for Shell-BP Petroleum Development Company of Nigeria, Limited.

▼ RESISTANCE TO CHANGE?

Forest Park Hotels had been started as an outgrowth of a strategic planning process initiated by the board of directors of Golden Horizons, Inc. A desire to diversify out of a singular focus on "intermediate care" nursing home facilities resulted in an initial decision to explore the opportunities in hotel operations. Based on extensive research, the development of a small chain of high-quality hotels appeared to provide a natural strategy for continued growth through diversification.

In just five years from the purchase of the first hotel, the chain had grown to six and was meeting both sales and profitability goals. The initial strategic plan adopted by the board had targeted the acquisition or construction of one hotel every twelve to eighteen months. According to Paul Halsey, CEO of Golden Horizons, "The growth of the Forest Park Hotel Division had happened at a faster rate than any of us had anticipated. Our positive cash flow allowed us to take advantage of some unique opportunities, both for construction and acquisition. If current operations continue at the present pace and attractive acquisitions become available, I would anticipate the continued rapid expansion of this division."

Centralization

Rapid growth of the hotel division with properties located in Atlanta, Dallas, Orlando, Minneapolis, New Orleans, and St. Louis brought with it the need for many changes. A corporate office was formed for the hotel division, and professionals were hired form outside the organization to fill several key positions, providing the experience necessary to continue with the present plans for expansion. As the operating plans for the new division were established, the division vice-president, with the input and consensus of the hotel general managers, decided to centralize the accounting, marketing, and purchasing functions. These decisions were well-received, and immediate cost savings and operational improvements were noted.

However, a later decision implementing a centralized human resources program to achieve equity in the hiring, training, development, and compensation of the managerial and professional (exempt) employees had been difficult. Although the general managers had enjoyed the autonomy of making their own human resources decisions, they grudgingly realized, for both legal reasons and for the planned growth of the division to be successful, change was necessary. The unanticipated rapid growth of the hotel division had created the need to prepare employees for promotions and transfers to meet future human resource needs.

Centralized Human Resource Program Implemented

Under the recently accepted human resource program, minimum qualifications for each position classified as being exempt from wage and hour regulations (including overtime provisions) were established through standardized job specifications. Training and development programs had also been outlined to prepare employees for promotions and transfers. A list of promotable employees was developed at each hotel and then forwarded to the division office to be compiled and shared with all of the general managers. In addition, minimum and maximum salary levels had been established for all exempt positions based on competitive salary and benefit surveys.

All of these guidelines had been developed by Cara Reynolds, division vice-president of human resources, and then sent to all general managers for possible changes before being officially adopted. When the proposed guidelines were sent to the hotels, the general managers had been instructed to work with the local human resource directors and other key members of their management teams in identifying any potential problems the guidelines could pose. After both formal and informal discussions between the vice-president of human resources, general managers, and local personnel directors, several modifications were made to the guidelines and the division vice-president endorsed the implementation of the following policy and procedures:

To provide for the future human resource needs of the hotel division while ensuring equity in the hiring, transferring, promoting, and compensating of all exempt employees, the following procedures will be followed to maintain our status as an equal opportunity employer:

1. The corporate human resource office will assist the human resources manager and management staff in each hotel in maintaining the proper levels of staffing.

2. Initial exempt employee staffing requirements and subsequent changes can only be made with the prior

approval of the division vice-president, the vice-president of human resources, and the general manager of the hotel making the request.

3. All job candidates must meet the minimum specifications set forth in the job description for each exempt position.

4. When qualified local candidates are not available, the costs of reasonable interviewing expenses including transportation will be reimbursed through the corporate human resource office.

5. Final approval must be obtained from the vice-president of human resources before any job offers are extended, and all personnel records including payroll or exempt employees will be maintained in the corporate office.

Everyone appeared to understand and accept the new procedures as they were implemented. Some minor problems were encountered, but these had been quickly resolved to everyone's satisfaction. However, the first serious challenge to the new program came just six months after the program had been implemented.

Request for an Exception

The challenge came from the management team of the Atlanta hotel that had been acquired first and formed the foundation for the present chain. Not only was it the first hotel, but it was also managed by Jim Evans, the general manager with the longest tenure. Jim had earned an enviable record of success by managing the most profitable operation in the division. Jim knew he was facing a problem and had made several calls to Cara seeking an exception to the newly adopted guidelines.

The problem was in the culinary department, which was under the supervision of the hotel's food and beverage director, Joseph Langemier. Jim's personnel staff had been unable to fill a key position, evening sous chef, in the hotel's gourmet dining room.

As Cara read the following memo from Joseph, he sensed the frustration of the local hotel's management staff.

TO: Cara Reynolds

FROM: Joseph Langemier

RE: Human Resource Policies and Procedures

This is to follow up our conversation in which it seems we have differences of understanding as to the needs in the culinary department. After the resignation of George Deal, evening sous chef, the executive chef (Aaron Murphy) and I agreed to readjust our organizational structure with regard to the outstanding requisition to fill the sous chef position. We agreed to have the evening sous chef position currently held by George to be filled with a sous chef of perhaps not the same caliber in terms of years of experience, but rather by an individual with an excellent culinary background.

Because of my association with very good professionals in the past, I am in the position of recommending candidates from time to time. This has been the case with Walter Steiner. He may not have the years of supervisory experience you seem to feel necessary, but he definitely has the culinary background to qualify for the position of sous chef. With this in mind, I have asked Executive Chef Murphy to talk to Walter and determine his interest in being considered for the sous chef position. It was only after the executive chef talked to Walter that we recommended that he be flown from Baltimore to Atlanta to see the hotel and dining room and interview for the position.

He has indicated that he will not take less than the maximum amount specified in the salary range for the position since he is currently making just four thousand dollars less than this amount between wages and overtime. In addition, he has chosen not to be promoted in the past because he wanted to gain the experience of working for a first-class operation similar to the one he has been working for during the last two years.

By adhering to your human resource policies, we are punishing Walter by insisting on hiring a person with supervisory experience. Would he have been considered to be qualified for the current position if he had been a supervisor in a steak and potatoes-type restaurant? That would qualify him to meet your supervisory qualifications but not our culinary requirements. Your refusal to consider Walter for the job indicates that you do not understand the differences between a culinarian and a supervisor.

Cara realized the anger coming through in the memo because Joseph was aware that Cara had been a hotel food and beverage manager before moving into the human resource function and, as such, was very knowledgeable of culinary duties. After reading the memo, Cara decided to review the job description and gather more information before making any decisions.

Job Title: Sous Chef
  General Description:
Assume full responsibility for the preparation, production, and presentation of quality food products for the dining room.
Duties and Responsibilities:
Supervise and coordinate all personnel under direct supervision.
  Observe and train all food preparation workers in the preparation, portion control, and presentation of food items based on prescribed standards.
  Requisition and maintain necessary supplies.
  Consult with executive chef on menu changes, work schedules, payroll, and personnel matters.

Assure adequate sanitation standards.

Other duties are assigned by the executive chef or executive sous chef.

Job Relationships:

Work under the direction of the executive chef and the executive sous chef. Supervise all preparation personnel in assigned location.

Job Specifications:

High school education: advanced training in food preparation, kitchen supervision, and sanitation preferred.

Minimum of two years' supervisory experience of food preparation in a full-service restaurant.

Must be knowledgeable of all basic cooking techniques, meats, and sauces.

Must be able to maintain rapport with superiors and subordinates.

Cara realized that Atlanta was experiencing a boom in new hotel construction for the 1996 Olympics that was resulting in an abnormally high turnover of skilled employees and upward pressure on salaries. In addition, the individual who had previously held the now-vacant position had been "lured" away by a new hotel as the executive sous chef (both a promotion in responsibility and title with a significant increase in pay). However, surveys completed by the Atlanta human resource staff within the last three months indicated the hotel had remained competitive in the salaries and benefits paid to comparable sous chefs. In fact, the salary guidelines established for the sous chef position in question were slightly above average for comparable hotels.

A review of the personnel files showed that the three sous chefs currently on staff met all minimum criteria set forth in the new human resource guidelines, and the open personnel requisition was for a person who would be in a comparable position. The fact that the position in question had now been vacant for one month and the hotel was entering its busiest season was puzzling since discussions with the local personnel manager indicated that two individuals meeting the guidelines had been screened and referred for interviews, but no interview comment forms had been returned. The personnel manager had also mentioned that Joseph and Walter had previously worked together and, based on some of Joseph's comments, they may have been "drinking buddies."

QUESTIONS

1. Describe the change process, problems encountered with implementing the planned change, and techniques used to promote change.

2. If one of the most experienced managers with a consistently profitable operation is requesting an exception to the guidelines, are there other underlying problems, or is he simply not accepting the new centralized human resource system?

3. How should Cara Reynolds respond to Joseph and the local management team?

4. What should Cara Reynolds do to prevent situations similar to this from happening again?

SOURCE: The names of the parties, as well as all place names, in the case have been disguised. This case was prepared by Roy A. Cook of Fort Lewis College and Jeryl L. Nelson of Wayne State College as a basis for class discussion rather than to illustrate either effective or ineffective handling of an administrative situation. Presented to the Midwest Society for Case Research Workshop, 1989. All rights reserved to the authors. Copyright © 1989, Roy A. Cook and Jeryl L. Nelson. See L. L. Goulet (ed.), *Annual Advances in Business Cases, 1989* South Bend, Ind.: Midwest Society for Case Research, 1989, 539–544.

AUTHOR INDEX

Abelson, M.A., 488
Abramson, N.R., 113–114
Ackerman, P.L., 544
Adam, E.E., 702
Adams, J.S., 193
Adelman, M.B., 412
Adelson, A., 730
Ader, R., 247
Adler, N.J., 17, 185, 743
Adler, P.S., 534, 556
Adler, S., 40
Affleck, G., 95
Agunis, H., 675
Aichholzer, G., 537
Ajzen, I., 53, 54
Akin, G., 139
Albanese, R., 270
Albano, C., 388
Albrecht, T.L., 412
Alderfer, C.P., 176
Alexander, K.L., 505
Allan, L.G., 612
Allen, D.S., 248
Allen, M., 412
Allen, N.J., 488, 722
Allen, R.L., 225
Allen, R.W., 509, 514, 517
Allen, S.A. III, 589
Alvarez, E.B., 7
Ancona, D.G., 330
Anderson, J.V., 636
Anderson, T., 448, 450
Andrews, S.B., 507
Angle, L.L., 509, 517
Angrist, S.W., 129
Anonyus, C., 94
Arbose, J., 240
Argyris, C., 555, 661
Arliss, L.P., 418
Armitage, M.A., 252
Arthur, E., 226
Arthur, M.B., 374, 745
Artz, E.L., 602
Aryee, S., 736, 743, 744
Ashford, S.J., 257, 626
Ashforth, B.E., 250
Ashkenas, R.N., 704
Athos, A., 192
Austin, N., 477
Avedisian, J., 671

Avolio, B.J., 375, 377
Axtell, R.E., 416
Ayman, R., 356

Babladelis, G., 95
Bacharach, S.B., 500
Baker, M.S., 170
Baker, S., 505
Bakor, F., 11
Baldwin, M.W., 552
Bales, R.F., 284
Balkin, D.B., 225
Ball, G.A., 152
Bamford, J., 377
Bandura, A., 141, 142, 152
Banks, W.P., 71
Banner, D.K., 599
Banning, K., 184
Barber, A.E., 199, 745
Barber, P., 75
Barker, J.R., 590
Barnard, C.I., 500
Barnes, F.C., 304
Barnum, C.F., 393
Baron, R.A., 90, 93, 245, 255, 430, 441
Baron, R.M., 52, 83, 89, 237, 246
Barrett, A., 162
Barrick, M.R., 48
Barrier, M., 530
Barry, B., 655
Bartholomew, S., 17
Bartlett, C.A., 14, 122, 594, 600, 709
Bartunek, J.M., 297, 429, 661
Baskerville, P.M., 455
Bass, B.M., 349, 377
Bastianutti, L.M., 299
Batemen, T.S., 552
Bates, M., 108
Baum, A.S., 237, 255
Baum, H.S., 514
Bautista, J., 77
Bawne, D.W., 765
Bazerman, M.H., 450, 633
Beach, L.R., 633
Beck, C.E., 405
Beck, E.A., 405
Becker, W.S., 178
Beckhard, R., 670, 691

Beckmann, J., 54
Beehr, T.A., 236
Beeman, D.R., 515
Beer, M. 653, 677
Belasco, J.A., 348
Bell, C.H., 675, 690
Bellafente, G., 106
Belohlav, J.A., 12
Bennett, R., 745
Bennis, W., 344
Benson, S., 277, 691
Benveniste, G., 576
Berelson, B., 281
Berenbeim, R.E., 374
Bergmann, T.J., 620
Berner, J., 407
Berry, L.L., 211, 622
Beswick, R.W., 406
Bettenhausen, K.L., 285
Betz, E.L., 176
Beyer, J.M., 375, 466, 473, 474, 487, 697
Bhagat, R.S., 250
Bies, R.J., 580
Biggart, N.W., 498
Bird, A., 501, 502
Bittman, M., 106
Bizup, A., 268
Black, J.S., 49, 452, 595
Blackburn, R., 312, 322, 437, 509
Blake, R., 71, 79, 80, 317, 444, 453
Blake, S., 482
Blanchard, K.H., 357, 360, 399
Blass, T., 48
Blau, G., 743
Blaylock, R., 368
Bluedorn, A.C., 566
Blum, T.C., 405, 746
Bly, J.L., 760
Bobko, P., 257, 758, 772
Boccialetti, G., 711
Boeker, W., 315
Boettger, R.D., 150, 186, 541
Boisjoly, R.M., 632
Boje, D.M., 474
Bolman, L.G., 276
Bond, M.H., 83
Bonnett, D.G., 218
Booth-Kewley, S., 253
Bornstein, R.F., 663
Boschken, H.L., 590

Boss, R.W., 48
Bouchard, T.J., 42
Boulding, K.E., 313
Bowen, D.E., 12, 582
Bowen, J.S., 564
Bowen, M.G., 634
Bowie-McCoy, S.W., 224
Bowman, E.D., 162
Boyatzis, R.E., 180, 518
Boyd, B.K., 566, 597
Boyle, D.C., 158
Boynton, A.C., 17, 312, 437
Bradac, J.J., 398
Bradford, D.L., 511
Brady, F.N., 616
Branch, S., 730
Brandt, R., 708
Brannick, J.P., 537
Brannick, M.T., 537
Brashers, W.R., Jr., 623
Brass, D.J., 214, 503
Breckler, S.J., 52
Brenner, S.N., 15
Brett, J.F., 215
Brett, J.M., 412
Bretz, R.D., 511, 727
Briznitz, S., 237
Brief, A.P., 48, 238
Brock, P., 14, 122
Brockner, J., 633
Brody, N., 42
Brokaw, L., 4, 173, 208, 212
Brook, C., 102
Brookes, A., 743
Brown, J.S., 621, 674
Brown, W.B., 330
Brownell, J., 413
Bruning, N.S., 702
Buda, R., 738
Burack, C., 214
Burke, M.J., 238
Burke, W.W., 669, 694
Burkhardt, M.E., 503
Burnham, D., 180
Burns, T., 576
Burrell, N.A., 431
Burton, G.E., 297
Bushe, G.R., 127, 708
Buss, D.M., 43, 724
Butcher, L., 122
Butterfield, D.A., 320, 737, 746
Buzzanell, P.M., 431
Bylinsky, G., 546, 656
Byosiere, P., 236, 252
Byrne, D., 90, 93, 245, 246, 255
Byrne, J.A., 481, 584, 598, 687, 708
Byrum-Robinson, B., 255, 256

Caggiano, C., 201
Cairns, A.B. III, 416

Caldwell, D., 330, 488
Calloway, W., 723
Calonius, E., 702
Calta, M., 106
Cameron, K.S., 478, 504
Campbell, D.T., 759
Campbell, J.P., 760
Campion, M.A., 292, 533, 544, 549
Capen, M.M.A., 125
Caplan, J., 738
Carayou, P., 373
Carlson, R., 528
Carnall, C.A., 670
Carr-Ruffino, N., 388
Carr-Ruffins, R., 417
Carroll, A.B., 61, 479
Carroll, G.R., 485
Carroll, S.J., 737
Carson, R.C., 51
Cartwright, D., 346, 499, 676
Cartwright, S., 476
Cascio, W.F., 11, 242
Case, T.L., 391, 497
Casse, P., 452
Caston, A., 599
Castro, M.A.D., 250
Catlin, L., 382
Caudron, S., 483, 663, 705
Cauley, L., 477, 584
Chah, D., 433
Chaiken, S., 52
Chang, G., 354
Champy, J., 55, 529, 575, 650, 703, 704
Chao, C.T., 11, 741
Chapman, N.J., 226
Chartier, M.R., 413
Chatman, J., 488
Chaw, S.W., 471
Chemers, M.M., 356
Cherns, A., 552
Chew, T., 736
Chope, R., 224
Chowdhury, J., 216
Christie, R., 518
Church, G.J., 170
Chusmir, L.H., 752
Ciampa, D., 704
Citera, M., 371
Clark, L.W., 88
Clark, S.M., 626
Clarke, A., 765
Clausen, A.W., 711
Clay, T.W., 736
Cleff, P.W., 552
Clegg, C.W., 537
Coates, J.F., 11
Cobb, A.T., 317
Coe, C.K., 127
Coetsier, P., 736
Cohen, A., 59
Cohen, A.R., 511

Cohen, N., 247
Cohen, S., 247
Cohnen, A.G., 769
Cole, R.E., 534, 556
Coleman, H.J., 596, 709, 710
Coleman, H.L.K., 398
Collings, V.B., 77
Collins, W.A., 41
Colvin, C., 253
Conger, J.A., 343, 377
Conlon, D.E., 453
Connor, P.E., 711
Contrada, R., 237, 255
Cooper, C.L., 240, 476
Cook, K.S., 403
Cook, M., 86
Cook, R.A., 457
Cook, T.D., 759
Cooper, J.N., 11
Cooper, M.L., 244, 245
Cooper, W.H., 299, 300
Copeland, L., 24
Corbett, J.M., 537
Cordes, C.L., 250, 251
Cosenza, R.M., 765
Cosier, R.A., 107, 288, 430, 638, 639
Cotton, J.L., 10, 273, 737
Cowan, P.A., 626
Cowherd, D.M., 193
Cox, T.H., 482
Crittenden, V.L., 590
Cron, W. L., 155, 167, 215, 736, 740, 741
Cronin, M.P., 179
Cropanzano, R., 371
Crossen, B.R., 620
Crossen, C., 412
Crow, S.M., 772
Crown, D.F., 48
Crump, C.E., 258, 259
Cummings, L.G., 327
Cummings, L.L., 40, 48, 52, 178, 198, 317, 371, 377, 481, 496, 509, 517, 522, 552, 597, 651, 669, 680, 690, 694, 699, 711, 714, 767
Cummins, R.C., 238
Cunningham, R., 133
Cunnington, B., 324
Cullen, J.B., 490
Curphy, G.J., 349
Cutcher-Gershenfeld, J., 694
Czander, W.H., 433

d'Lribarne, P., 576
Daft, R.L., 391, 564
Daily, B., 396
Dalrymple, D.J., 155, 166
Dalton, D.R., 152, 430, 746
Daly, J.A., 392
Darley, J.M., 614
Davenport, T.H., 28, 396

Davey, A.J., 110
Davidow, W.H., 599
Davids, K., 537
Davis, D., 765
Davis, S.M., 592
deBono, E., 636, 637
deForest, M.E., 416, 451
DeGeorge, R.T., 613
DeLisser, E., 616
DeLuca, J.M., 8, 143
DeMeuse, K.P., 692
DeNisi, A.S., 723
DePaulo, B.M., 86, 398, 417
DeWine, S., 442
Deal, T.E., 276, 477
Dean, J.W., Jr., 272, 479, 620, 703, 704, 706
Dearborn, D., 75
Debrah, Y.A., 743
Defares, P.B., 247
Delbecq, A.L., 297
Deming, W.E., 12
Dempsey, B.L., 296
Denison, D.R., 491
Dennis, A.R., 299
Denton, D.K., 11, 410, 528
Derlega, V.J., 412
Dess, G.G., 566
Desselles, M.L., 162
Deutsch, C.H., 225
Diamond, M.A., 285
Dibble, J.A., 393
Dickinson, A.M., 281
Dickson, W.J., 285
Diehel, M., 298
Digman, J.M., 45
Dindra, K., 412
Doel, S, 452
Doktor, R.H., 468
Donlan, T.G., 134
Donaldson, G., 577
Donaldson, T., 613
Dorfman, P.W., 77
Dougherty, T.W., 250, 251, 737
Downs, T.M., 412
Doyle, F.P., 653
Drake, B.H., 482
Drake, E., 482
Drasgow, F.A., 546
Dreher, G.G., 737
Drexler, A.B., 672, 711
Driskill, J.E., 282
Drucker, P.F., 8, 218, 475
Dubinsky, A.J., 127
Dunbar, R.L., 107
Duncan, R.B., 566, 567
Dunfee, T.W., 613
Dunham, R.B., 48, 199, 714
Dumaine, B., 47, 120, 331, 342, 474, 476, 552, 658, 707
Dunnette, M.D., 45, 46, 54, 76, 107, 174, 236, 269, 284, 287, 319, 320, 342, 360,

428, 437, 439, 441, 468, 532, 546, 627, 676, 758, 759, 760, 772
Dutton, J.E., 626
Duxbury, L.E., 437
Dwyer, D.J., 257, 259
Dyer, W.G., 691

Eagly, A.H., 52
Earley, P.C., 209, 214, 216, 539
Easton, G.S., 13
Economy, P., 449
Eden, D., 671
Edwards, J.E., 767
Egri, C.P., 522
Ehrbar, A., 535
Ehrenfeld, T., 224
Ehrlich, S.B., 371
Eichenwald, K., 219
Eide, A., 620
Eisenberg, E.M., 401, 405
Eisenstat, R.A., 653
Elderkin, K., 14, 122
Elizur, D., 176
Ellis, C., 221, 440
Ellis, R.A., 48
Ellison, K., 240
Elmer-DeWitt, P., 122
Engler, B., 41, 48, 50
Erez, M., 269, 433
Erfurt, J.C., 760
Ergi, C.P., 496
Erickson, R.J., 437, 746
Esterhuysen, P.W., 331
Everly, G.S., 254
Evans, J.R., 272, 479, 703, 704, 706
Evans, P.A., 468
Eysenck, H.J., 40, 50

Fagans, M.A., 661
Fagenson, E.A., 252, 439
Falbe, C.M., 347, 499, 510
Fang, Y., 544
Farnham, A., 473, 637
Farnsworth, S.R., 216
Feldman, D.C., 287, 412, 453, 726, 741, 749
Fellows, H.D., Jr., 775
Ferris, G.R., 198, 488, 513, 514, 515
Ferguson, W.C., 584
Festinger, L., 433
Fiedler, F.E., 270, 353, 356
Field, R.H.G., 369
Fields, D.L., 405, 746
Fields, M.W., 696
Fierman, J., 659, 740
Fillingham, R.B., 255
Finch, M., 396
Finegan, J., 28, 117

Finkelstein, S., 497
Finley, D., 199
Fishbein, M., 53, 54
Fisher, A.B., 10, 242
Fisher, B., 224
Fisher, C.D., 87
Fisher, R., 448
Fisher, R.J., 311
Fiske, S.T., 82
Fleck, R.A., Jr., 532
Fleming, J.E., 137
Fletcher, B.C., 744
Foote, A., 760
Ford, R.C., 592
Formisano, R.A., 199
Fortin, S.P., 441
Fox, M.L., 238, 257, 259
Frame, P., 280
Franchi, K., 532
Freedman, D.H., 573
Freedman, S.M., 256
Freeman, E.E., 613
Freeman, R.E., 614
Freeman, S.J., 478, 747
Frei, R.L., 441
French, J.R.P., 346, 499
French, W., 227
French, W.L., 675, 690
Fried, Y., 544
Friedman, H.S., 253
Friedman, M., 253
Friend, R., 237, 255
Frone, M.R., 244, 245
Frost, P.J., 496, 522
Fry, L.W., 570
Fulk, J., 391, 597
Fulkerson, J.R., 725
Fuchsberg, G., 480, 705
Funhouser, G.R., 286
Fusilier, M.R., 238
Futrell, D., 692

Gabriel, G., 117
Galbraith, J.R., 564, 595
Galem, S., 288
Galen, M., 437
Gales, L.M., 312, 437
Gallupe, R.B., 299, 300
Galvin, R.W., 432
Ganster, D.C., 238, 246, 253, 257, 259
Gant, J., 672, 711
Gantt, G., 457
Garcia, J.E., 270
Gardenswartz, L., 484
Gardner, D.G., 48, 714
Gardner, P.D., 11, 197
Gardner, W.L., 107, 398
Gargivlo, M., 404
Garko, M.G., 395

Garvin, D.A., 621
Gatewood, R.D., 479
Gattiker, U.E., 737
Gebhardt, D.L., 258, 259
Geis, F.L., 518
Gelfand, M.J., 284, 320, 321, 439
George, J.M., 40, 216, 238
George, K., 243
Gephart, R.P., Jr., 628
Gershenfeld, M.K., 274
Gersick, C.J., 274, 276
Gerstein, M.C., 596
Gerstein, M.S., 277, 655
Gerton, J., 398
Ghoshal, S., 594, 600, 709
Giacalone, R.A., 82
Giannantonio, C.A., 163, 737
Gibbs, B.W., 127
Gilber, D.T., 628
Gilbert, D.R., Jr., 614
Gilbert, N., 762
Gilbertson, D., 518
Gilliand, S.W., 617
Gilmore, M.R., 403
Ginnette, R.C., 349
Gioia, D.A., 413, 517
Gist, M.E., 141
Glass, D., 237, 255
Gleckman, H., 549, 573, 655
Glenn, J.R., Jr., 197
Glick, W.H., 686, 570, 600
Glover, J.A., 52, 638
Goddard, R.W., 61
Goff, S.J., 746
Goia, D., 626
Goldberger, L., 237
Goldhar, J.D., 17
Goldman, B., 528
Goldstein, J., 483, 484
Gomez-Majra, L.R., 11, 225
Goodman, J.S., 405, 746
Goodsell, C.T., 576
Goodson, J., 248
Goddstein, L.D., 98, 274
Gordon, R.D., 410
Goss, T., 192
Gowing, M.K., 653
Graen, G.B., 544
Graen, M.R., 544
Grant, L., 11
Graham, G.H., 417
Graham, J.L., 185
Graham, J.W., 481
Grant, R.A., 773
Grant, R.M., 569
Graziano, W.G., 52, 83, 89, 237
Greco, S., 182, 222
Green, G.M., 11
Greene, C.N., 502
Greenberg, J., 197, 198

Greenberger, D.B., 52, 94
Greenhaus, J.H., 737, 745
Greenwald, J., 315
Greenwood, R.G., 218
Greer, C.R., 150, 186, 250
Gregory, A.M., 261
Gresov, C., 573, 593
Grieco, P., 597
Griffin, R.W., 529, 551, 552, 635, 701
Griffith, T.L., 545, 773
Griggs, L., 24
Grise, M.L., 299
Grube, J.A., 714
Gudykunst, W.B., 326, 401
Gundry, L.K., 639
Gunn, E., 446
Gunnar, M.R., 41
Gupta, U., 438
Gustafon, D.H., 297
Gutek, B.A., 769
Guth, W.D., 568
Gutierrez, N.C., 221
Gutknecht, J.E., 198
Guzzo, R.A., 319

Ha, Y.W., 630
Hackel, S.H., 571
Hackman, J.R., 287, 541, 543, 544, 546
Hage, D., 11
Hagerty, L., 27
Hagtvet, B., 620
Hair, J.F., Jr., 217
Haley, U., 107
Halhed, B.R., 279
Hall, C.S., 10, 41, 747
Hall, D.T., 8, 11, 696
Hall, E., 399
Hall, G., 575
Hall, L., 448
Halverson, C.B., 399
Hambrick, D.C., 630
Hamilton, G.G., 498
Hamlin, S., 413
Hammer, E., 155
Hammer, M., 55, 529, 575, 650, 703, 704
Hammer, W.C., 155
Hanisch, K.A., 57
Hanna, D.P., 592
Hansen, R., 741
Hanson, J.R., 268, 401, 508
Harari, O., 170
Harder, J.W., 193
Hare, A.P., 281
Harianto, F., 571
Harpaz, I., 217
Harper, R.G., 415
Harrell, A., 190
Harrington, S.J., 217, 618

Harris, R.T., 670
Harris, T.J., 258, 260
Harrison, J.R., 485
Harrison, R.P., 414
Harsman, C.L., 271
Hartke, D.D., 356
Hartley, R.E., 620
Hartman, R.I., 272
Hartman, S.J., 772
Harvey, J.H., 90
Harvey, M., 745
Hatch, M.J., 466
Hauver, L.A., 441
Haveman, H.A., 573
Hawkins, C., 138, 616
Hays, L., 546, 699
Head, T.C., 552
Healey, J.R., 272
Heck, R.H., 477
Hegarty, W.H., 568
Heirich, M.A., 760
Heintzman, M., 416
Heller, F.A., 507
Hellriegel, D., 14, 115, 422
Hellweg, S.A., 451
Henderson, R., 673
Hendrick, C., 282
Heneman, R.L., 94
Henkoff, R., 13, 212, 432, 506, 675, 720, 749
Henley, N., 417
Henry, W.A. III, 280
Heppner, M.J., 743
Herbert, T.T., 98
Herman, S.M., 280
Herold, D.M., 549
Hersey, P., 357
Herzberg, F.I., 183, 184, 185, 535
Heskett, J.L., 467, 469, 477, 478
Hettma, P.J., 43
Hibino, S., 77
Hickson, D.J., 325
Higgins, C.A., 437, 773
Higgs, A.C., 292, 549
Hightower, S., 316
Hilgert, R.L., 619
Hill, C.W., 209, 587
Hill, G.C., 705
Hill, L.A., 747
Hill, R.C., 13
Hill-Storks, H., 34
Hinkin, T.R., 346, 347, 499
Hinnings, C.R., 325
Hinton, P.R., 85, 90
Hirokawa, R.Y., 297
Hirsch, S.H., 115, 127
Hirschhorn, L., 691
Hiser, T., 184
Hitt, M.A., 478
Hodgetts, R.M., 471, 569, 592, 704
Hoffman, L.R., 282

Hofheinz, P., 352
Hofstede, G., 26, 269, 467, 468, 477
Hogan, R.T., 45, 46, 76, 282
Hogart, R.M., 621
Holden, B.A., 616
Holden, C., 42
Holland, J.V., 730
Hollander, E.P., 497
Hollenbeck, J.R., 48, 215, 437, 546
Hollis, D., 248
Holmes, T.H., 245
Holton, B., 455
Holton, C., 455
Homans, G.C., 269
Hood, J.N., 747
Hooper, L., 120
Hoover, C.W., 86
Hoover, D.K., 743
Hori, S., 192
Hoskisson, R.E., 587
Hough, L.H., 627
Hough, L.M., 45, 46, 54, 76, 107, 174, 236,
        269, 284, 287, 319, 320, 342, 360, 428,
        437, 439, 468, 532, 546, 676, 758, 759,
        760, 772
House, R.J., 180, 360, 369, 374, 517, 518
Howard, L.W., 197
Howard, R., 120, 565
Howell, J.M., 374, 375
Howell, J.P., 77
Howell, W.C., 532
Hoy, F., 110, 444
Hrebiniak, L.G., 628
Huber, G.P., 570, 600, 686
Huey, J., 475, 579, 650, 699
Hughes, R.L., 349
Huk Ng, S., 398
Hulin, C., 54, 57, 59
Hyland, A.M., 730
Hymowitz, C., 695

Iaffaldano, M.T., 58
Ibarra, H., 10, 405, 507
Idaszak, J.R., 546
Ilgen, D.R., 188, 437, 546
Illgen, E.J., 620
Impoco, J., 11
Ingassia, P., 596
Ingersol, D., 226
Ingram, T.N., 127
Ireland, R.D., 478
Isaacs, W.N., 326, 407
Isabella, L.A., 243, 628, 735
Ivancevich, J.M., 237, 256, 257
Izraeli's, D.N., 743, 756
Izumi, H., 689

Jackofsky, E.F., 24, 470, 471, 741, 749
Jackson, C.N., 669, 670, 671

Jackson, D.N., 48, 110
Jackson, L.A., 197
Jackson, P.R., 537, 552
Jackson, S.E., 7, 8, 143, 221, 321, 405, 437
Jagacinski, C.M., 633
Jago, A.G., 364
Jakubowski, P., 388
James, K., 371
James, L.R., 52
James, T.M., 614
Jamieson, D., 7
Jamison, R.L., 746
Janis, I.L., 289, 628, 631
Janson, R., 530
Jarratt, J., 11
Jax, S.M., 236
Jennings, K.R., 702, 705
Jennings, P.D., 417, 587
Jensen, M.A.C., 274, 275
Jick, T.D., 650, 686, 704
Johansen, R., 277, 691
Johns, G., 544
Johnson, A.E., 48
Johnson, C., 298
Johnson, G., 457
Johnson, J.L., 446
Johnson, S., 399
Johnston, J.A., 743
Johnston, W.B., 11, 659
Jones, F.R., 227, 744
Jones, G.R., 209, 488, 577
Jones, H, 558
Jones, J.E., 413
Jones, R.C., 760
Jourard, S.M., 412
Joyce, J., 225
Joyce, W.F., 591, 594
Judge, T.A., 511, 727
Jung, C.G., 108
Juran, J.M., 621

Kabanoff, B., 444
Kacmar, K.M., 198, 514, 515
Kaeter, M., 428
Kahn, A., 438
Kahn, R.L., 236, 252, 313, 435, 436
Kahn, W.A., 323, 579
Kahneman, D., 629, 630
Kakuyama, T., 215
Kameda, N., 395, 396
Kanfer, R., 174
Kansas, D., 73
Kanter, R.M., 507, 600, 650, 660, 661, 686
Kaplan, D., 313
Kaplan, R.E., 625, 634
Karanbayya, R., 744
Karlgaard, R., 530
Karp, K., 412
Katzenbach, J.R., 272, 691, 692, 693

Kazanjian, R.K., 595
Keck, S.L., 321
Keebler, J., 310
Keeney, P., 729
Keleman, R.S., 287
Keller, R.T., 375, 542, 738
Kelley, H.H., 93
Kelly, E.P., 88
Kelly, K., 544
Kemp, N.J., 552
Kendall, L.M., 57
Kennedy, A.A., 477
Kenny, D.A., 86, 398
Kerr, J., 473
Kerr, S., 351
Kerwin, K., 315, 327
Kesner, I.F., 746
Kets de Vries, M.F.R., 433
Keys, B., 198, 497
Keys, J.B., 391
Kickul, J.R., 639
Kida, T., 630
Kiechel, W., 8, 412, 626, 720, 721
Kiersay, D., 108
Kilmann, R.H., 455, 464, 467, 473
Kilpatrick, J., 457
Kim, D.H., 630
Kim, H., 587
Kim, J.A., 147
Kim, W.C., 198
Kim, Y.Y., 95
Kinchla, R.A., 74
Kindel, S., 290
King, J., 129
King, W.C., 441
Kinlaw, D.C., 292
Kipnis, D., 510, 511
Kirkbride, P.S., 471
Kirkpatrick, D., 333, 699, 749
Klaas, B.S., 453
Klayman, J., 630
Klein, H.J., 215
Kleindorfer, G.B., 623
Kleindorfer, P., 613
Klimoski, R.J., 761
Kneale, D., 477
Knight, P.A., 58
Knowlton, B., 80
Knowlton, C., 635
Koberg, C.S., 747
Kochan, T.A., 686
Kofodimas, J., 433
Kogod, S.K., 401
Kohn, A., 431
Kolb, D.M., 429, 431
Kolesar, P.J., 328, 329
Kolodny, H.F., 593
Komaki, J.L., 162
Konrad, A.M., 769
Kormanski, C., 274

Kossek, E.E., 10, 746
Kotter, J.P., 343, 467, 469, 477, 478, 512
Kottler, J., 429
Kowalski, R.M., 85
Kozlowski, S.W.J., 141, 722, 726
Kracher, B.J., 769
Krackhardt, D., 268, 401, 503, 508
Krajicek, D., 71
Kram, K.E., 323, 579, 736
Kramer, R.M., 327
Kreitner, R., 147
Krishnan, R., 569
Kroeger, O., 115
Krueger, A.B., 619
Kruglanski, A.W., 86, 632
Kuhl, J., 4
Kumar, K., 8, 482
Kunde, D., 11, 747
Kunreuther, H., 613
Kupfer, A., 279, 600
Kurowski, L.L., 284, 320, 321, 439
Kurtz, T., 413

La Farge, V., 198
La Fromboise, T., 398
La Plante, A., 278, 407, 539, 540
Labich, K., 138, 584
Lachman, R., 324, 347, 503
Laden, M., 320
Lafasto, F.M.J., 291
Laing, J.R., 602
Lake, L.K., 711
Lamb, C.W., Jr., 217
Lambert, R.A., 182
Landau, J.C., 745
Landy, F.J., 57, 177, 253
Lane, H.W., 113–114
Lang, S., 346
Lange, A., 388
Langford, B.Y., 393
Larcker, D.F., 182
Larrick, R., 629
Larson, C.E., 291
Larson, U.R., 191
Larwood, L., 737
Latham, G.P., 173, 209, 212, 222, 223, 230, 314
Lawler, E.E. III, 223, 557, 564, 688, 697, 702, 704, 767
Lawler, E.J., 500
Lawrence, P.R., 589, 591, 592
Lazarus, R.S., 238
Le Grande, D., 773
Leana, C.R., 749
Leary, M.R., 85
Leathers, D.G., 416
Lederer, A.L., 655
Ledford, G.E., Jr, 345, 697, 767
Lee, Chang-Won, 443
Lee, C., 216, 257

Lee, C.A., 325
Lee, R.T., 250
Lee S.M., 704
Lee, T., 465
Lefcourt, H.M., 48, 49
Lei, D., 15, 600, 709
Leigh, J.H., 243
Lengel, R.H., 391, 392
Leopold, M., 483, 484
Lesly, E., 406, 509
Lester, T., 579
Leuser, D.M., 202, 203
Levine, D.I., 193
Levine, E.L., 537
Levine, R.V., 78, 79
Levy, P.E., 95
Lewicki, R.J., 446, 450
Lewin, K., 667
Lewis, P.V., 617
Liebert, R.M., 41, 48
Lievowitz, J., 275
Likert, J., 317
Likert, R., 317
Lim, S.Y., 773
Limerick, D., 324, 597
Lincoln, J.R., 56
Lindsay, C.P., 296
Lindsley, D.H., 214
Lindzey, G., 41
Linnenham, F., 743
Linowes, R.G., 84, 192, 468
Liska, L.Z., 363
Litterer, J.A., 446
Lituchy, T.R., 216
Liverpool, P.R., 702
Lobel, S.A., 482
Locke, E.A., 162, 173, 209, 212, 222, 230, 314, 433
Loden, M., 171
Lohman, L., 552
Lombardo, M.M., 634
London, M., 733
Long, P., 162
Longenecker, C.O., 413, 517
Lopez, J.A., 477
Lorenzi, P., 143, 375
Lorsch, J.W., 589
Low, B.S., 43
Lublin, J.S., 17, 250, 477, 692
Lucas, G.H., 243
Lucia, A., 153
Lustig, M.W., 284
Luthans, F., 147, 158, 569, 592, 704
Lykken, D.T., 42
Lyness, S.A., 253

Machan, D., 513
Mackey, J., 133
Macy, B.A., 689
Macy, H., 8

Maddi, S.R., 41
Madison, D.L., 514
Maes, S., 247
Magnet, M., 447, 448
Mahaffie, J.B., 11
Maier, M., 627, 636
Main, J., 529
Mallory, M., 439, 509
Malone, M.S., 406, 599
Mann, L., 628
Manning, M.R., 250, 669, 670, 671
Manz, C.C., 143, 291, 701
March, J., 623
March, J.G., 629
March, S., 439
Marcial, G.G., 375
Marcoulides, G.A., 477
Margulis, S.T., 412
Markus, H., 412
Marlow, E., 407
Martin, A., 277, 691
Martin, J.E., 623
Martin, L.P., 636
Martin, R., 537
Martineau, J.W., 142, 214
Martinko, M.J., 107
Maslow, A.H., 174
Mason, D., 774
Mason, R.O., 107, 707
Matarzzo, J.D., 415
Mathieu, J.E., 58, 142, 214
Matsui, T., 215
Matteson, M.T., 237, 256, 257
Mauborgne, R.A., 198
Mausner, B., 183, 535
Maxon, T., 124
Mayes, B.T., 77, 238, 253, 514
McBurney, D.H., 77
McCall, Jr., M.W., 625, 634, 758, 772
McCauley, C.D., 736
McCaulley, M.H., 111
McClelland, C.L., 544
McClelland, D.C., 179, 180, 518
McClure, L., 127
McCume, W.B., 332
McDaniel, C., 217
McDowell, R.N., 143
McGill, M.E., 193, 464, 630, 709, 740
McGrath, J.E., 549
McGue, M., 42
McIntyre, R.P., 125
McKee, B., 273
McKendall, M., 712
McKersie, R.B., 446
McLeod, P.A., 482
McMahan, G.C., 216, 230, 677, 715
McMillan, J.J., 431
McPherson, G., 227
McQuade, K., 14, 122
McQuaid, S.J., 24, 470, 471
Madsker, G.J., 292, 549

Mechanic, D., 509
Meglino, B.M., 723
Meindl, J.R., 371, 377
Mendenhall, M., 452
Metts, S., 412
Meyer, J.P., 218, 488, 722
Miceli, M.P., 481
Michaelsen, L.K., 8, 482
Milbank, D., 252
Miles, E.W., 441
Miles, R.E., 596, 709, 710
Miller, C.C., 570
Miller, D., 433, 568, 573
Miller, D.P., 398
Miller, J.G., 94
Miller, J., 269
Miller, J.L., 197, 269
Miller, K.I., 95
Miller, M.W., 185, 699
Milliken, F.J., 311, 630
Mills, D.Q., 599
Miner, J.B., 50, 58, 59, 65, 243, 252
Mink, B.P., 331
Mink, O.G., 331
Mintiz, B., 447
Minton, D., 154
Minton, J.W., 446, 619
Mintzberg, H., 19, 329
Mishra, A.K., 491
Mitchell, J., 596
Mitchell, T.R., 52, 141, 269, 360, 620, 623
Mitroff, I.I., 632, 707
Mittman, R., 277, 691
Mohrman, S.A., 345, 699, 702, 767
Mollander, E.A., 15
Monge, P.R., 401
Moore, S.F., 170
Moorman, R.H., 197
Morgan, G., 431
Morgan, R.B., 86, 481
Morgan, S.A., 765
Morris, W.C., 292, 335, 641
Morrison, A.J., 585
Morrison, A.M., 10, 634
Morrison, E.W., 485
Morrison, K., 111
Morton, J.S., 317
Moscovici, S., 288
Moshavi, S., 438
Motowidlo, S.J., 250
Mount, M.K., 48, 746
Mouton, J.S., 444, 453
Mowday, R.T., 58
Muchinsky, P.M., 58, 70, 262, 730
Mullen, B., 298
Multon, K.D., 743
Mumby, D.K., 624
Mundy, D.H., 620
Munter, M., 396, 399, 401
Murnighan, J.K., 285, 297
Murphy, C., 351

Murphy, K.R., 398, 545, 620
Murphy, P.E., 618
Murray, H., 238, 276, 295, 536, 552
Musen, G., 80
Myers, D.G., 52, 90, 93, 94, 95

Nadler, D.A., 596
Nagai, H., 113, 114
Nanus, B., 344
Napier, R.W., 274
Nath, R., 655
Navran, F.J., 434
Near, J.P., 481
Neale, M.A., 226, 633
Nebeker, D.M., 188, 545
Nelson, D.L., 256
Nelson, G., 518
Nelson, R.B., 360, 577
Neuijen, B., 269, 467, 477
Neumann, J.E., 661
Newman, R.G., 760
Nichol, V., 10
Nicholson, N., 676, 677, 688, 708
Niehoff, B.P., 197
Niehouse, O.I., 251
Nielsen, R.P., 481
Nicotera, A.M., 440, 442
Nobu, T., 395, 396
Noe, R.A., 745
Nohria, N., 595
Nolan, R.L., 571
Nolle, T., 278
Norman, J.R., 120, 635
Northcraft, G.B., 216
Nulty, P., 438, 655
Nunamaker, J.F., Jr., 299
Nurick, A.J., 198
Nurius, P., 412
Nutt, P.C., 110, 112
Nykodym, N., 243

O'Boyle, T.F., 240
O'Brian, B., 447
O'Mara, J., 7
O'Reilly, B., 659
O'Reilly, C.R., 55, 472, 488
Obert, S.L., 274
Offerman, L.R., 252, 497, 653
Ohayv, D.D., 269, 467, 477
Ohlott, P.J., 736
Olaniran, B.A., 299
Oldham, G.R., 541, 543, 544, 546
Olian, J.D., 737
Oliva, T.A., 573
Olson, J.M., 52, 54
Omachonv, U.K., 530
Oneal, M., 437

Onglatco, L.U., 215
Optenberg, S., 765
Organ, D.W., 163
Orlikowski, W.J., 391
Ornstein, S., 82, 552, 735, 749
Orton, J.D., 322
Osborn, A.F., 298
Osigweh, Y.C., 620
Oster, S.M., 568
Ostroff, C., 58, 141, 722, 726
Overman, S., 483
Owen, K.Q., 331

Pablo, A.L., 519, 629
Pacanowsky, M.E., 389
Packard, J.S., 250
Paige, R., 360
Paine, L.S., 290, 480, 616, 667
Palmer, D.A., 587
Parasuraman, A., 211, 622, 737
Pare, T.P., 414, 438
Parker, B., 752
Parker, G.M., 599
Parker, V.A., 8, 696
Parrott, C.S., 11
Parrott, R.L., 416
Parry, D., 442
Parsons, C.K., 549
Pascale, R., 192, 486
Pasewark, R.J., 369
Pasmore, W.A., 62, 377, 468, 478, 480, 555,
     604, 650, 655, 661, 669, 671, 689, 695,
     701, 702, 704, 705, 708
Patterson, L., 397
Pattison, P., 11
Paul, R., 740
Paunonen, S.B., 48
Pava, C., 552
Pearce, J.L., 170, 274
Pearson, C.M., 632, 707
Pennings, J.M., 325, 571
Penrod, S., 53
Peracchio, L., 759
Pereek, U., 64
Perlman, S.L., 545, 701
Perry, N.J., 324
Pervin, L.A., 42, 44, 51, 239
Peters, L.H., 356, 617
Peters, T.J., 477, 652, 654, 655
Peterson, R.B., 453
Petrick, J.A., 314
Petronio, S., 412
Pettigrew, T.F., 316
Pfeffer, J., 323, 497, 498, 503, 516, 624
Pfeiffer, J.W., 64, 98, 255, 261, 274, 302,
     399, 401, 412, 413, 521, 552, 636
Phillips, J.S., 256, 257
Phillips, S.L., 271
Pierce, J.L., 48, 714

Pinchot, E., 577
Pinchot, G., 577
Pincus, A.L., 45
Plumb, S.E., 310, 596
Podsakoff, P.M., 36, 499, 502
Pohlmann, J.T., 356
Poindexter, J.T., 170
Pondy, L.R., 438
Poole, J., 592
Poppo, L., 322
Porras, J.I., 676, 689
Port, O., 708
Porter, L.W., 58, 274, 509, 514, 517, 614
Porter, R.E., 398
Post, J.E., 411
Powell, G.N., 320, 737, 746, 747
Powell, W.W., 597
Prather, C.W., 639
Pratt, M.G., 416
Prescott, J.E., 567
Pritchard, R.D., 188
Proter, R.E., 451
Putnam, L.L., 624

Quenk, N.L., 108, 110, 112
Quick, J.C., 124, 247, 256, 487
Quick, J.D., 247, 256
Quinn, J.B., 537
Quinn, J.F., 314
Quinn, R.E., 633
Quinn, R.P., 436

Raelin, J.A., 627
Rafaeli, A., 23, 416
Ragins, B.R., 10, 508, 517, 518, 737, 746
Rahe, R.H., 245
Rahim, M.A., 446, 455
Randolph, W.A., 592
Rangel, E., 727
Rasheed, A.M., 566, 567
Rastegary, H., 253
Ratan, S., 44
Raven, B.H., 346, 499
Rawlings, S., 741
Ray, G., 286
Reder, M.W., 621
Reddy, W.B., 521
Reed, J., 133
Reid, A., 547
Reilly, A.H., 744
Reinsch, N.L., Jr., 406
Reitman, F., 744
Renwick, P.A., 514
Rescorla, R.A., 139
Reynolds, C.R., 52, 638, 745
Richardson, D.R., 430
Richardson, J.E., 760

Richman, L.S., 744
Richter, J., 11
Ricks, D.A., 585
Riecher, A., 236, 240, 252
Rigdon, J.E., 435
Ripley, D.E., 17
Ritti, R.P., 286
Roach, B., 109
Roach, J.M., 624
Roberson, L., 221
Roberts, C.K., 236
Roberts, D.R., 419, 689
Roberts, H.V., 535
Roberts, J.L., 477
Roberts, M., 258, 260
Robertson, P.J., 676, 689
Robichaux, M., 438
Roethlisberger, F.J., 285
Rogers, R.J., 749
Roitblat, H.L., 80
Ronning, R.R., 52, 638
Rosen, B., 13
Rosener, J.B., 171, 320
Rosenfeld, P., 767
Rosenfeld, T., 82
Rosenman, R., 253
Rosenthal, J., 575
Rosenthal, R.A., 436
Rosenzweig, M.R., 614
Rosenzweig, P.M., 170, 594
Ross, J.E., 328, 530
Ross, U.H., 453
Rosse, J.G., 48
Rost, K.M., 297
Rotemberg, J.J., 313
Roth, D.L, 255
Roth, K., 585
Rothman, H., 27
Rothstein, L.R., 43, 433
Rothstein, M., 110
Rowe, A.J., 107, 484
Ruble, T.L., 107
Ruderman, M.N., 736
Rusk, T., 398
Russ, G.S., 391
Russell, M.L., 244, 245, 765
Russo, J.E., 612, 629

Saal, F.E., 58
Saavedra, R., 214, 539
Sackman, S.A., 466, 476
Saffo, P., 277, 691
Salancik, G.R., 323
Salas, E., 282, 298
Samovar, L.A., 398, 451
Sadelands, L.E., 552
Sanders, G., 269, 467, 477
Sanders, K.J., 773
Santora, J.E., 760

Saporito, B., 602
Sarason, I.G., 247
Sashkin, M., 292, 335, 641
Saunders, D., 446
Sawyer, J.E., 635
Saxton, M.I., 467, 473
Sayles, L.R., 625
Sayles, R.L., 343
Scandura, T.A., 544, 746
Scarpello, V., 723
Scott, D.L., 279
Scott, J., 285
Scott, W.G., 269, 620
Schaeffer, A., 433
Schaubroeck, J., 238, 246, 253
Schein, E.H., 275, 315, 326, 407, 466, 467,
    471, 693, 694, 733
Schellhardt, T.D., 749
Schienstock, G., 537
Schifrin, M., 438
Schlenker, B.R., 85
Schmidt, K.D., 451
Schmidt, N.W., 761
Schmidt, S.M., 510, 511
Schneider, B., 12, 582
Schneer, J.A., 744
Schnake, M.E., 270
Schneck, R.E., 325
Schoemaker, P.J.H., 612, 613, 629, 635
Schoenfeldt, L.F., 52, 87, 638
Schriesheim, C.A., 346, 347, 351, 380, 499
Schrivenk, C.R., 638
Schuler, R.S., 8, 224, 437, 725
Schultz, D., 41, 48
Schulz, J.D., 436
Schwab, R.C., 330
Schwartzman, H.B., 772
Schwarz, R.M., 452
Schweizer, J., 158
Schwenk, C.R., 288, 638, 639
Sekuler, R., 71, 79, 80
Sell, A.R., 760
Sellers, P., 548
Selye, H., 237
Sergesketter, B.F., 535
Serpa, R., 467, 473
Serwer, A.E., 197, 616
Sessa, V.I, 405, 406
Sethia, N.K., 473
Shack, M.L., 441
Shaffer, D.R., 52
Shalley, C.E., 209
Shamir, B., 374, 745
Shani, A.B., 708
Shani, R., 569
Shapira, Z., 629
Sharkey, T., 514
Sharkey, T.W., 515
Shaw, J.B., 87
Shaw, R.B., 596
Shay, K.A., 255

Shea, G.P., 319
Shell, B.H., 111
Shellenbarger, S., 244, 320, 407, 695, 746
Shepard, H.A., 453
Sheppard, B.H., 450, 619
Sheridan, J.E., 738
Sherif, C., 317
Sherif, M., 317, 327
Sherman, M., 153
Sherman, S., 575, 720
Sherwood, J.J., 69, 693, 699
Shipper, F., 291
Shostak, A.B., 243, 545
Shrivastava, P., 583
Shultz, T.R., 614
Sibbet, D., 277, 691
Siconolfi, M., 219
Sikes, W., 672, 711
Silbey, S.S., 431
Silver, W.S., 623

Simon, B., 316
Simon, H.A., 75, 439, 623, 624
Simpson, J.A., 268
Sims, C., 438
Sims, Jr., H.P., 143, 375, 517, 537, 538, 542,
    570
Sims, R.R., 289
Singh, J.V., 518, 594
Sitkin, S.B., 519, 580, 629
Sixel, L.M., 546
Skinner, B.F., 140
Skow, L., 451
Slocum, Jr., J.W., 14, 15, 24, 115, 193, 215,
    422, 464, 470, 471, 473, 537, 538, 570,
    600, 630, 709, 735, 736, 737, 738, 740,
    741
Slutsker, G., 432
Smart, T., 564
Smith, A., 577
Smith, D.K., 272, 691, 692, 693
Smith, G., 217
Smith, J.F., 630
Smith, K.G., 433
Smith, K.K., 317
Smith, M.J., 773
Smith, P.C., 57
Smith, T., 302
Smith-Ring, P., 600
Snoek, J.D., 436
Snow, C.C., 596, 709, 710
Snyderman, B.B., 183, 535
Snyman, J.H., 77
Soft, R.L., 392
Solomon, C.M., 346, 468, 757
Sonnenfeld, J.A., 221, 440
Spangler, W.D., 180, 374
Spector, B.A., 653, 670
Spich, R.S., 287

Spiegler, M.D., 41, 48
Spielberger, C.D., 247
Squire, L.R., 80
Stahl, M.J., 190
Stalker, G.M., 576
Stangor, C., 52, 83, 89, 237
Starbuck, W.H., 630
Stark, A., 616
Staw, B.M., 40, 52, 178, 198, 317, 327, 371,
    377, 481, 496, 509, 517, 522, 541, 552,
    597, 634
Stayer, R.C., 348
Steel, R.P., 702, 705
Steers, R.M., 58
Stein, B.A., 650, 686
Steiner, G.A., 281
Steinmetz, G., 219
Stephens, C., 490, 593
Stertz, B.A., 705
Stevenson, W.B., 274
Stewart, R., 19
Stewart, T.A., 55, 120, 240, 498, 505, 599,
    653, 679
Stiles, W.B., 391
Stogdill, R.M., 350, 351
Stoneman, K.G., 281
Stoner, C.R., 272
Stout, S.K., 740
Strasser, S., 52
Strati, A., 416
Straus, S.G., 549
Strobe, W., 298
Stumpf, S.A., 107
Sullivan, J., 395, 396
Sullivan, L.A., 197
Sullivan, R.E., 436
Sullivan, S.E., 250
Sundaram, A.K., 595
Sundstrom, E., 508, 517, 518, 692
Super, D.E., 735
Suris, O., 596, 692
Surtees, L., 360
Susman, G.I., 536, 538, 570
Sussman, L., 408, 409, 410
Sutton, R.I., 243
Swaffin-Smith, C., 510
Swanson, R.A., 533
Swort, E.B., 184
Szilagyi, A.D., 542

Takagi, H.A., 113–114
Tannenbaum, S.I., 142, 214
Tapscott, D., 599
Tarter, J., 751
Tatum, B.C., 545
Taylor, M.S., 48
Taylor, R.N., 107, 627
Taylor, S.M., 163
Teitelbaum, R.S., 487

Tellegen, A., 42
Tennen, H., 95
Tesser, A., 52
Tetrick, L.E., 544
Tett, R.P., 110, 218
Tetzeli, R., 406
Thach, L., 656
Thacker, J.W., 696
Thayer, J., 253
Thayer, P.W., 533
Theroux, J., 106
Theus, K.T., 330
Thomas, D.A., 11
Thomas, J.B., 214, 626
Thomas, J.G., 336, 551
Thomas, K.W., 428, 440, 441, 455
Thomas, M.D., 767
Thomas, R.R., Jr., 7, 482
Thompson, G., 465
Thompson, J.D., 312, 539
Thompson, M.P., 408
Thompson, R., 738
Thornberry, N., 102
Thornburg, L., 321, 327
Tjosvold, D.W., 273, 315, 430
Tjosvold, M.M., 273
Todor, W.D., 152
Tolchinsky, P.D., 671
Toor, M., 170
Toshio, Y., 403
Townley, B., 497
Townsend, J., 740
Tracey, J.B., 510
Trevino, L.K., 59, 62, 152, 480, 613, 619
Triandis, H.C., 269, 284, 320, 321, 439, 468
Trice, H.M., 375, 466, 473, 474, 487, 697
Trist, E., 276, 295, 536, 552
Trost, C., 240, 256, 695
Tuckman, B.W., 274, 275
Tully, S., 208, 354, 588
Turban, D.B., 737
Tushman, M.L., 321
Tversky, A., 629
Tyler, L.S., 224

Uchitelle, H., 8
Ungson, G.R., 330
Unruh, J., 417
Ury, W., 448
Useem, M., 686

Van de Ven, A.H., 297, 591, 600
Vander Heijden, C.A., 635
Van Dyne, L., 214, 539
Van Fleet, D.D., 27, 342, 360
Van Gundy, A.B., 636

Van Loo, M.F., 197
Van Velsor, E., 10
Valacich, J.S., 299
Vandenberg, J, 723
Varca, P.E., 11
Vaughan, D., 627
Vaught, B.C., 110
Vaverek, K.A., 617
Veiga, J.F., 606
Verity, J.W., 599
Victor, B., 490
Virgile, L., 184
Vogel, D., 15
Vogel, T., 138
Volkema, R.J., 628, 642
Von Fersen, L., 80
Von Glinow, M.A., 473
Vroom , V.H., 187, 364

Wade, J., 575
Wagner, J.A., III, 544
Wagner, M., 216
Wahn, J., 197
Walker, G., 323
Walker, H.A., 500
Wall, T.D., 537, 552
Walsh, J.P., 76
Walton, E., 564, 621
Walton, R.E., 446
Walz, P.M., 11
Wang, Y.D., 570
Wang, Z., 507
Wanous, J.P., 723
Warrick, D.D., 671
Wartzman, R., 619
Warwick, D.D., 695, 701
Waterman, R.H., 477
Watson, W.E., 8, 482
Wayne, S.J., 518, 552
Weber, J., 364, 588
Weber, M., 576
Week, D., 443
Weick, K.E., 322

Weigelt, K., 182
Weigold, M.F., 85
Weihrich, H., 221
Weingart, L.R., 412
Weintraub, J., 102
Weintraub, R., 439
Weisbord, M.R., 669, 688
Weiss, A., 397, 618
Weiss, H.M., 40
Weiss, J.W., 620
Weiss, S.E., 452
Weitz, B.A., 741
Welles, E.Q., 124
Wells, C.L., 597, 769
Wells, G., 90
Welsh, T., 505, 675
Wendt, A.C., 224
Werther, W.B., Jr., 127
Wharton, A.S., 437, 746
Whetten, D.A., 504
White, J.B., 596, 692
White, R.P., 10
White, T., 382
Whitely, W.T., 736, 737
Whitsett, D.A., 546
Whyte, G., 289
Wiebe, D.J., 255
Wieman, J.M., 392, 414
Wiens, A.N., 415
Wiesma, U.J., 744
Wiggins, J.S., 45
Wilhelm, P.G., 197, 537
Wilke, J.R., 333, 505
Wilkinson, I., 510
Willey, S.L., 336
Williams, C.R., 215
Williams, G., 521
Williams, K.K., 723
Williamson, G.M., 247
Wilson, I., 568
Winer, B., 178
Winter, D.G., 183
Wintermantel, D., 184
Wise, J., 592
Witten, M.G., 405

Wofford, J.C., 363
Wolfe, D.M., 436
Wolff, E., 79
Wood, R., 141
Wood, W., 268
Woodburg, R., 124
Woodman, R.W., 52, 62, 243, 297, 377, 468, 478, 480, 518, 635, 638, 650, 655, 656, 661, 669, 670, 671, 676, 677, 688, 689, 692, 693, 699, 701, 702, 704, 705, 708, 709
Worchel, S., 268
Worley, C.G., 651, 669, 680, 690, 694, 711
Woycke, J., 180, 374
Wright, P.M., 216, 429
Wright, T.A., 218
Wysocki, B., 654

Xie, J.L., 544

Yukl, G.A., 342, 346, 499, 510
Yamada, K., 705
Yancy, E.J.,
Yanouzas, J.N., 606

Zajac, D.M., 58
Zaleznik, A., 434
Zand, D.E., 708
Zander, A., 270, 346
Zanna, M.P., 52, 54
Zartman, I.W., 450
Zebrowitz-McArthur, L., 83
Zeira, Y, 671
Zeithaml, V.A., 211, 622
Zelditch, M., 500
Zhou, X., 587
Zigarmi, D., 360
Zimmerman, M., 219

SUBJECT AND ORGANIZATION INDEX

ABB, 352
Academy culture, 465
Accommodating style, 442
Acculturation, 482
Achievement motivation theory
  achievement motive, 179
  affiliation motive, 179
  defined, 179
  measured, 179
  power motive, 179
  presidents' motives, 180
Achievement motive, 179
Achievement-oriented leadership, 361
Action research, 675
Adaptive organizations, 706
Advancement career stage, 738
Aetna Life and Casualty, 549, 695
Affective conflict, 429
Affiliation motive, 179
Affiliation needs, 175
Affirmative action, 221
African-Americans, 397, 483, 616
  networking, 508
  networks, 405
  training, 662
  see Diversity
Aftermath, 633
Aggressive communication, 389
Alternative work schedule, 695
American Airlines, 123, 396, 448
American Bankers Insurance, 746
American Brands, 586
American Civil Liberties Union, 774
American Heart Association, 765
Americans with Disabilities Act, 536
Amoco, 242
Amoral management, 60
Amtrak, 737
Amway, 654
Analogies, 637
Andersen Consulting, 528
Antecedent, 144
Anticipatory socialization, 723
Apple Computer, 71, 73, 279, 466, 698, 707
Approach-approach conflict, 433
Approach-avoidance conflict, 433
Arabs, 24
Arthur Anderson, 473, 722
Arvin Industries, 654

Asian-Americans, 397
Assertive communication, 388
AT&T, 153, 242, 258, 485, 535, 695
Attitudes
  affective component, 52
  attitudinal sets, 316
  attitudinal structuring, 447
  behavioral component, 52
  behavioral intentions model, 53
  cognitive component, 52
  defined, 52
  job satisfaction, 55
  organizational commitment, 58
  toward change, 714
  work attitudes, 55
Attitudinal sets, 316, 598
Attitudinal structuring, 447
Attribution model, 371
Attribution process
  casual attributions, 95
  defined, 90
  factors, 93
  fundamental attribution error, 94
  internal vs. external causes, 92
  success vs. failure, 94
Attributions, 371
AT&T Universal Card Services (UCS), 705
Audio King, 438
Authoritarian personality, 51
Authority, 498
  leadership, 344
  legitimate power, 347, 500
  position power, 354
  power, 498
Austria, 470
Automation, 533
Autonomous groups, 701
Autonomy, 541
Availability bias, 629
Aversive events, 145
Avoidance-avoidance conflict, 433
Avoidance learning, 149
Avoiding style, 441

Baby boom generation, 43
Baby busters generation, 43
Baldrige National Quality Award, 704

BancTec, 586
Bank of America, 464, 466, 711, 719
Baseball team culture, 465
Bavarian Motor Works (BMW), 709
Baylor Hospital, 140
Beech-Nut, 290
Bechtel, 707
Becton Dickinson, 707
Behavioral effects of stress, 247
Behavioral intentions model, 53
Behavioral modification
  charting behavior, 158
  ethics, 163
  identifying behaviors, 158
  limitations, 162
  model, 159
Bell Atlantic, 476
Ben & Jerry's Homemade Ice Cream, 106
Bethlehem Steel, 695
"Big five" personality factors, 45
Black Enterprise Magazine, 508
Black Entertainment Television, 509
Bloomingdale, 213
Body language, 400
Body Shop, 14, 22, 121, 347, 502
Boeing, 655
Bonne Bell, 259
Booz, Allen, & Hamilton, 513
Bounded rationality model, 622
Boundary-spanning roles, 330
Brainstorming, 298
Brazil, 240, 470
Brooklyn Union, 571
Brown & Root, 707
Buddhist culture, 400
Bureaucracy
  defined, 576
  division of labor
  hierarchy of authority, 577
  impersonality, 579
  mechanistic system, 576
  procedures, 579
  rules, 579
Burger King, 428
Business revolutions, 653
Bypassing, 395

Cafeteria-style benefit plans, 199

California Edison, 506
Callaway Golf, 581, 582
Campgrounds of America (KOA), 243
Canada, 240, 687
    culture, 23
    problem-solving styles, 113
    Shell Canada, 227
Career changes
    choices, 729
    culture, 726
    individual issues, 728
    Mexico, 727
    model, 728
    occupational choice, 730
    organizational issues, 727
Career development, 726
Career planning
    child care, 745
    dual-career couples, 744
    outplacement, 748
    women in management, 746
Career plateau, 741
Career stages
    advancement, 738
    establishment, 736
    horizontal movement, 733
    inclusion movement, 735
    maintenance, 740
    model, 735
    vertical movement, 733
    withdrawal, 743
Careers, 726
    advancement career stage, 738
    career planning, 743
    career plateau, 741
    changes, 726
    child care, 745
    Cross Colours, 729
    diagnosis, 752
    decliners, 741
    diversity, 725
    glass ceiling, 737
    golden handcuffs, 739
    Hoechst Celanese, 734
    influences on, 719
    job loss, 749
    life success scale, 752
    maintenance career stage, 740
    mentor, 736
    mid-life crisis, 740
    Nissan, 723
    organizational choice, 732
    organizational socialization, 721
    outplacement, 748
    Pepsi-Cola, 725
    personality, 730
    promotion, 12
    self-esteem, 732
    social background, 732
    solid citizens, 741
    stages, 733

stars, 741
stress, 243
3M, 745
    women in management, 746
    working-life stages, 735
Caterpillar, 212
Celestial Seasonings, 27
Centralization, 577
Challenger disaster, 627, 631
Change
    career, 726
    environmental forces, 28
    organizational culture, 475
    politics, 496
    reengineering, 128
    sociotechnical systems, 535, 552
    strategies, 32
    technology, 549
    work force, 659
    see Organizational change
Channels, 393
Chaparral Steel, 352, 687
Charisma, 347
Charismatic leaders, 374
Chevron, 244, 256
Child care, 226, 745
Chili's challenge course, 764
China, 269, 295, 400, 479, 506, 654
Chrysler, 655, 692, 695
CIGNA, 326, 654
Citicorp, 61, 242
Classical conditioning, 139
Clorox, 658
Closure, 80
Club culture, 465
CMB Packaging, 354
Coacting group, 270
Coalition, 311
Coalitions, 274
Coca-Cola, 465
Coercive power, 347, 499
Cognitive conflict, 429
Cognitive dissonance, 433
Cognitive moral development, 59
Cohesiveness, 288
Colgate-Palmolive, 175, 498
Collaboration, 443
Collaborating style, 443
Collateral organization, 708
Collectivism, 269
Commonwealth Electric, 481
Communication
    African-Americans, 405
    aggressive communication, 389
    American Airlines, 396
    Asian-Americans, 397
    assertive communication, 388
    biases, 397
    body language, 400
    bypassing, 395
    collaborating style, 443

centralization, 403
channels, 393
communication skills, 18
compromising style, 444
cultural barriers, 398
cultural context, 399
data, 391
decoding, 393
dialogue, 325, 407
Digital Equipment, 396
direct feedback, 549
distortion, 398
diversity, 397
electronic mail (E-mail), 406
encoding, 393
errors, 394
ethnocentrism,
external networks, 401
face-saving, 398
Federal Express, 410
feedback, 394, 411
Flying Tiger Line, 410
gender differences, 417
groupware, 406
high context culture, 399
Honda, 414
impression management, 85, 375, 398
information roles, 21
ingratiation, 398
integrative negotiations, 447
intercultural communication, 398
interpersonal barriers, 394
interpersonal communication, 389
Japanese, 393
language routines, 396
lateral networks, 401
listening, 413
low-context culture, 399
lying, 398
nonassertive communication, 389
meanings, 393
media richness, 391
messages, 392
meta-communication, 408
Mexico, 450
network design, 596
network types, 402
networks, 401
neurotic tendencies, 433
noise, 395
nonverbal communication, 414
openness, 408
person-role conflict, 436
personal space, 400
personality, 394
Pillsbury Corporation, 428
positive, 430
problem framing, 629
receiver, 390
receptors, 391
resource sharing, 323

role ambiguity, 437
role conflict, 435
role set, 435
self-disclosure, 412
self-promotion
voice quality, 83
Communication skills, 18
Competition, 315
Complexity, 566
Compliance conformity, 287
Compromising style, 444
Computer-integrated manufacturing, 656
Computer monitoring, 773
Conceptual skills, 18
Conference Board, 695
Confirmation bias, 629
Conflict
    accommodating style, 442
    affective conflict, 429
    aggressive communication, 389
    approach-approach conflict, 433
    approach-avoidance conflict, 433
    avoidance-avoidance conflict, 433
    avoiding style, 441
    Audio King, 438
    balanced, 431
    cooperation, 317
    Challenger disaster, 627, 631
    cognitive dissonance, 433
    collaboration, 443
    collaborating style, 443
    compromising style, 444
    defined, 428
    dialogue, 325
    distributive negotiations, 446
    distributive process, 448
    disturbance handler role, 22
    diversity, 439
    family conflict, 437
    forcing style, 442
    General Computer, 440
    goals, 315
    goal conflict, 429
    groupthink, 430
    horizontal conflict, 439
    integrating roles, 331
    integrative process, 448
    intergroup conflict, 438
    interpersonal conflict, 435
    interrole conflict
    intersender role conflict, 435
    intragroup conflict, 437
    intraorganizational negotiations, 448
    intrapersonal conflict, 432
    intrasender role conflict, 435
    line-staff conflict, 439
    negative, 430
    network analysis, 508
    semantics, 396
    sender, 389
    status, 416

stress, 243
stressors, 744
superordinate group rewards, 327
superordinate group goals, 327
telecommuting, 406
transmitters, 391
U-Haul, 437
Union Pacific Railroad, 396
USA Truck, 436
USAir, 439
vertical conflict, 438
voice mail, 406
vertical networks, 401
Wal-Mart, 445
women, 397
work-family, 245
Xerox, 405
Conflict management (see Conflict)
Conformity, 287
Consequence, 144
Consideration, 350, 380
Consolidated Edison, 173
Content theories of motivation, 174
Context, 276
Continental Airlines, 447
Contingencies of reinforcement, 144
Contingency leadership model, 352
Contingency work force, 659
Continuity, 80
Continuous improvement, 704
Continuous reinforcement, 155
Control
    electronic monitoring, 545
    job design, 530
    networks, 404
    coercive power, 347
    neurotic tendencies, 433
    norms, 287
    span of control, 583
Cooperation, 317
Coopers & Lybrand, 143
Core competencies, 687
Corning Glass, 346, 483, 696, 737
Counteracting group, 270
Creativity
    brainstorming, 298
    cross-fertilization technique, 637
    cultural blocks, 636
    devils' advocate method, 638
    electronic brainstorming, 299
    emotional blocks, 636
    entrepreneurial role, 22
    Hallmark Cards, 637
    Huse Food Group, 638
    intuition, 109
    intuitive-type, 110
    lateral thinking method, 636
    nominal group technique, 296
    North American Life & Casualty, 299
    organizational creativity, 635
    organizational innovation, 635

Peak Electronics, 148
perceptual blocks, 636
random-word stimulation, 638
reversal techniques, 636
teams, 296
Thermos, 342
vertical thinking method, 636
workout, 22
Cross Colours, 729
Cross-fertilization technique, 637
Cross-functional teams, 272, 322, 331, 597
    Thermos, 331
CRSS, 655
Cultural context, 399
Cultural diversity, 482
Cultural heroes, 467
Cultural symbols, 467
Cultural values, 467
Culture
    acculturation, 482
    achievement motivation, 179
    American managers, 84
    Arabs, 24
    Austria, 470
    body language, 400
    Brazil, 470
    British, 121, 401, 506
    Buddhist, 400
    Canada, 11, 23, 240
    careers, 727
    China, 295, 400, 506
    communication barriers, 398
    cultural context, 399
    Denmark, 471
    ethics, 615
    ethnic culture, 482
    ethnocentrism, 401
    Europeans, 351
    face-saving, 398
    France, 25, 351, 471
    Germany, 24
    global skills, 16
    globalization, 654
    Greeks, 400
    high context culture, 399
    Hondurans, 400
    Hong Kong, 470
    Hungary, 186
    intercultural communication, 398
    Japan, 25, 56, 84, 146, 188, 191, 247, 393,
        501, 748
    Japanese women, 748
    Latin America, 24
    learning, 77
    low-context culture
    machismo, 23
    Medtronics, 318
    Mexico, 184, 217, 239, 415, 450, 727
    motivation, 179, 184
    Muslim, 400
    national cultures, 469

negotiations, 450
Netherlands, 26
personal space, 400
personality, 43
positive multiculturalism, 321
power distance, 470
prejudices, 284
stress, 239
stress death, 247
Sweden, 352
time perception, 78
uncertainty avoidance, 470
United States, 56
values, 555
Venezuela, 400
views of change, 660
Volvo, 555
women, 727
work attitudes, 56
Culture variable, 672
Cummins Engine, 687
Cunningham Communications, 4
Customers, 548
    goals, 210
    see Total Quality Management
Cypress Semiconductor, 47, 707

Dart Group, 47
Data, 391
Datatec, 178
Day care centers, 10
De Mar, 622
Decentralization, 578, 588
Decision effectiveness, 364
Decision making
    aftermath, 633
    analogies, 637
    attitudes, 52
    availability bias, 629
    bounded rationality model, 622
    Challenger disaster, 627, 631
    cognitive conflict, 429
    cognitive dissonance, 433
    confirmation bias, 629
    control, 624
    convoluted-action, 632
    decentralization, 588
    decision roles, 22
    decision rules, 612
    decision tree, 366
    dictionary rule, 612
    effect uncertainty, 312
    environments, 568
    escalating commitment, 633
    ethical intensity, 614
    ethical issues, 614
    ethics, 613
    framing, 375
    goal conflict, 429

groupthink, 288
information, 624
law of small numbers bias, 630
managerial decision making, 625
Morton Thiokol, 627, 632
NASA, 627, 631
networks, 404
organization design, 564
organizational creativity, 635
organizational innovation, 635
perceptual defense, 626
political model, 624
power, 506
problem definition, 292
problem framing, 629
problem interpretation, 628
problem recognition, 626
problem-solving, 107
quick-action, 632
rational model, 621
response uncertainty, 312
risk propensity, 628
role ambiguity, 437
Royal Dutch/Shell, 634
satisficing, 623
search, 624
selective perception bias, 630
strategic choices, 568
structural problems, 626
task uncertainty, 537
team, 291
time pressures, 632
total quality management, 622
uncertainty, 311
uncertainty absorption, 312
unstructured problems, 626
Vietnam War, 634
work-flow uncertainty, 537
Xerox, 621
Decision roles
    defined, 22
    disturbance handler, 22
    entrepreneurial, 22
    negotiator, 22
    resource allocator, 22
Decoding, 393
Delegating style, 359
Delta Airlines, 465, 485
Denmark, 470
Denny's, 616
Dependent task relations, 323
Depersonalization, 250
Design variable, 672
Devil's advocate method, 638
Diagnosis
    goal-setting, 229
    groups, 268
    life success, 752
Dialogue, 325, 407
    collaborating style, 443
    compromising style, 444

Diet Centers, 161
Differentiation, 589
Digital Equipment, 242, 396, 483, 650, 695,
    698
Directive leadership, 361
Disabled, 536
Discipline, 154
Distortion, 398
Distributive justice, 193
Distributive justice principle, 616
Distributive negotiations, 446
Diversity
    affirmative action, 221
    African-Americans, 397, 405, 508, 616,
        662
    age, 11
    Americans with Disabilities Act, 536
    Asian-Americans, 397
    biases, 397
    Body Shop, 121
    Canada, 11
    career choice, 729
    career issues, 727
    child care, 226, 745
    CIGNA, 326
    conflict, 439
    contingency work force, 659
    Coopers & Lybrand, 143
    Corning Glass, 346, 696
    Cross Colours, 729
    cultural training, 725
    Datatec, 178
    defined, 7
    diagnosis, 34
    dialogue, 325, 407
    disabled, 536
    diversity questionnaire, 484
    Dow Chemical, 226
    dual-career couples, 744
    empowerment, 8
    ethnic culture, 482
    ethnicity, 10
    family care, 10
    female voice, 83
    first-impression errors, 87
    gender, 10, 440, 445
    gender-role stereotypes, 97
    generational tension, 43
    General Computer, 440
    glass ceiling, 10, 737
    group identification, 319
    GTE, 128
    Hewlett-Packard, 7
    Hispanic managers, 11
    Hispanics, 178
    Hoechst Celanese, 9
    human resource practices, 143
    job burnout, 251
    job design, 536
    language, 8
    language barriers, 178

leadership, 346
leadership development, 346
male voice, 83
mentoring, 736
mentors, 737
Mexico, 184, 217, 727
motivation, 171, 184
nonverbal cues, 417
organization culture, 725
organization design, 580
Pacific Bell, 221
PepsiCo, 725
perception errors, 87
positive multiculturalism, 321
prejudices, 284
Prudential Insurance, 483
questionnaire, 34
race, 10, 320, 440
race & ethnicity, 10
recruiting practices, 221
religion, 445
sex stereotyping, 88
sexual harassment, 580, 769
similarity errors, 86
stereotyping, 87
Tabra, 284
teams, 284
Tom's of Maine, 377
training, 662
Unity Forest Products, 117
vision, 346
Wal-Mart, 445
women, 397, 727, 746
women managers, 97, 320, 746
work, 7
work-family conflict, 245
work force, 7, 659
working mothers, 244
workplace flexibility, 696
Division of labor, 577
Dogmatism, 50
Donnelly, 618, 658
Dow Brazil, 313
Dow Chemical, 225
Dow Corning, 584
Downsizing, 11, 40, 249
Diamond International, 157
Dual-career couples
defined, 744
relocation, 744
stressors, 744
DuPont, 654
Dynamism, 566

Eastman Chemical, 597
Eastman Kodak, 242
Effect uncertainty, 312
Effectiveness, 365
decision effectiveness, 364
overall, 365

Electronic brainstorming, 299
Egypt, 240
Electronic data interchange, 656
Electronic Data Systems, 737
Electronic mail (E-mail), 406
Electronic monitoring, 545
Electronic Systems Personnel, 222
Elyria Foundry, 208
Emotional effects of stress, 246
Employee assistance program, 373
Employment-at-will, 619
Empowerment, 345
Encoding, 393
England, 78
Entrepreneurship
Cross Colours, 729
SEI, 8
Environment
complexity, 566
dynamism, 566
functional design, 582
influence, 28
organization design, 566
sociotechnical systems model, 552
task environment, 566
types, 567
uncertainty, 568
Equity theory
distributive justice, 193
inequity, 194
inputs, 194
model, 194
outcomes, 194
procedural justice, 198
significance, 197
ERG Theory, 176
Escalating commitment, 633
Escape learning, 149
Establishment career stage, 736
Esteem needs, 176
Ethical behavior, 86, 479, 711
Ethical dilemma, 14
Ethics
American Civil Liberties Union, 774
amoral management, 60
Beech-Nut, 290
behavioral, 59
behavioral modification, 163
Body Shop, 14, 121
categorial imperative principle, 617
Challenger disaster, 627
code of ethics, 618
cognitive moral development, 59
communication, 394
compromising, 445
computer monitoring, 773
concentration of effect, 615
consequences, 614
conventionalist principle, 617
decision making, 613
decision principles, 616

decisions, 15
defined, 14
Denny's, 161
diet centers, 161
dilemmas, 620
distributive justice, 617
distributive justice principle, 616
Donnelly, 618
Dow Brazil, 313
Dow Corning, 584
drug testing, 772
electronic monitoring, 545
employee assistance program, 373
employee theft, 196
employment-at-will, 619
ethical culture, 490
ethical intensity, 614
ethics positions, 584
ethics profile, 640
expense accounts, 15
foreign payments, 15
goal conflict, 429
goals, 280
golden rule principle, 617
groupthink, 289
hedonist principle, 617
immoral management, 60
individual differences, 59
inequity, 194
interviews, 768
intuition principle, 617
issues, 614
Johnson & Johnson, 618
lawsuits, 149
leadership, 86, 373
Machiavellianism, 518
McDonald's, 618
means-end principle, 617
medical practices, 149
Medtronics, 318
Mexico, 727
might-equals-rights principle, 617
moral management, 60
NBC News, 280
NYNEX, 584
organization ethics principle, 617
organizational change, 711
organizational culture, 479
out placement, 748
perceptions, 86
performance appraisal, 516
Pillsbury, 428
political model, 624
power, 313
privacy, 545
privacy rights, 620
probability of effect, 614
problem-solving styles, 121, 126
procedural justice, 198
proximity, 615
Prudential Bache Securities, 219

questionnaire, 15
Raytheon, 584
research, 773
rights, 620
role overload, 241
Sears, 480
social consensus, 615
stakeholders, 619
Synerdyne, 165
temporal immediacy, 615
theft, 196
Tom's of Maine, 376
utilitarian principle, 617
utilitarianism, 620
values, 619, 712
Wal-Mart, 445
whistle-blowing, 481
women in management, 746
Ethical intensity, 614
Ethnocentrism, 401
Ethnography, 771
Exchange process, 511
Expectancy effects, 89
Expectancy theory
defined, 187
first and second level outcomes, 188
instrumentality, 189
research findings, 190–191
valence, 189
Expert power, 347, 500
External adaptation and survival, 468
External locus of control, 49
Extraversion, 49
Extrinsic factors, 183
Exxon, 242

Face-saving, 398
Family conflict, 437
Federal Aviation Administration (FAA), 522
Federal Communications Commission, 477
Federal Express, 410, 705
Federal National Mortgage Association, 572
Feedback
constructive, 411
defined, 394
goal setting, 216
job design, 549
job feedback, 541
performance appraisal, 222
survey feedback, 690
Feeling, 109
Feeling-type person, 111
Female managers, 320
Females
leadership, 346
Field dependence/independence, 76

Fielder's contingency model
group atmosphere, 353
how well does it work, 355
implications, 356
leadership style, 354
power position, 354
task structure, 353
Fight-or-flight response, 237
Figurehead role, 20
Fixed interval schedule, 155
First-level outcomes, 188
Fixed ratio schedule, 156
Flexible benefit plans, 225
Flextime, 547, 695
Fluor, 323
Flying Tiger Line, 410
Follower readiness, 357
Force field analysis, 667
Forcing style, 442
Ford Motor, 256, 468, 596, 654, 692, 695, 697
Fort Worth Museum of Science and History, 506
Fortress culture, 465
Fortune Magazine, 46, 505, 655, 675, 677
Framing, 375
France, 25, 351, 471
Franco-British CMB Packaging, 354
Free Rider, 270
Friendship group, 270
Frigitemp Corporation, 60
Functional design, 581
Fundamental attribution error, 94

Gain-sharing plans, 224
Gardner Motor Homes, 243
Gates, B., 170
General Computer, 440
General Electric, 198, 212, 468, 653, 655, 695, 704
General Foods, 687
General Motors, 242, 280, 310, 655, 659, 695, 699, 705, 709
General theory of behavior, 41
Germany, 24, 240, 654, 660
Gillette, 478, 479, 675
Glass ceiling, 10, 737
Global challenge, 15
Global economy, 16
Global networking, 600
Globalization, 654
Goals
bankers, 210
competition, 315
customers, 210
defined, 173, 208
employees, 210
goal conflict, 315, 429

groups, 280, 314
groups, 314
high achievers, 180
individual, 269
job design, 554
motivation, 173
network design, 598
norms, 285
satisficing, 623
stockholders, 210
superordinate group goals, 327
suppliers, 210
team, 269
Goal commitment, 215
Goal conflict, 315, 429
Goal setting
challenge, 213
customer service, 210
diagnosis, 229
defined, 208
Elyria Foundary, 208
essentials, 208
ethics, 219
goal commitment, 215
impact on performance, 214
ISO 9000, 211
management by objectives, 218
mediators, 216
Mexico, 217
model, 213
moderators, 215
performance, 212, 216
purposes, 209
questionnaire, 229
reward systems, 223
satisfaction, 217
self-efficacy, 214
stakeholders, 209
Westinghouse Electric, 230
Goal-Setting Model
challenge, 213
mediators, 216
moderators, 215
performance, 216
rewards, 217
significance, 218
Golden handcuffs, 739
Goodyear, 242
Great Britain, 471, 506
Greece, 40, 73, 471
Greeks, 400
Group atmosphere, 353
Group identification, 319
Groups
adjourning stage, 276
Apple Computer, 279
attitudinal sets, 316
autonomy, 271
Beech-Nut, 290
brainstorming, 298

China, 295
coacting group, 270
coalitions, 274, 311
cohesiveness, 288
collectivism, 269
compliance conformity, 287
context, 276
counteracting group, 270
cross-functional teams, 272, 331
decision making, 291
defined, 269
dependent task relations, 323
development, 274
diagnosis, 268
dialogue, 325
diversity, 284
effect uncertainty, 312
electronic brainstorming, 299
forming stage, 274
free rider, 270
friendship group, 270
goals, 269, 280, 314
group atmosphere, 353
groupthink, 288
groupware, 277, 406
individual, 269
individual power, 520
individualism, 269
information technology, 277
interacting group, 271
leadership, 291, 353, 357
Maryland Plastics, 268
networks, 401
nominal group technique, 296
norming stage, 275
norms, 162, 285, 434
Oldsmobile Division, 310
performing stage, 276
personal acceptance conformity, 287
personality, 45
power, 313
prejudices, 284
problem-solving styles, 281
problem-solving teams, 272
relations-oriented role, 282
resource sharing, 323
response uncertainty, 312
see Teams
self-managed teams, 273
self-oriented role, 283
size, 281
state uncertainty, 311
storming stage, 274
stress, 243
Tabra Inc., 284
task group, 270
task-oriented role, 282
types, 270
uncertainty absorption, 312
videoconferencing, 278

Groupthink, 288, 430
Groupware, 277, 333, 391, 406, 537
GTE, 128, 365
Growth-need strength, 544

Hallmark Cards, 637
Halo effect, 88
Hard Rock Cafe, 622
Hardiness, 255
Hardy personality, 253, 255
Harvard Business Review, 660
Harvard University, 239
Heredity, 42
Hersey and Blanchard's situational model
 leadership styles, 359
 model, 358
 Northern Telecom, 359
Hewlett-Packard, 15, 218, 470, 472, 522,
 650, 654, 695, 697
Hierarchy, 330
Hierarchy of authority, 577
High context culture, 399
High performance-high commitment work
 culture, 478, 699
Hill Holliday, 47
Hispanics, 178
 see Diversity
Hoechst Celanese, 734
Home Depot, 548
Honda, 192, 414
Hondurans, 400
Honeywell, 695, 737
Hong Kong, 470
Hope Creek, 332
Horizontal career movement, 733
Horizontal conflict, 439
Horizontal design, 589
House's path–goal model
 contingency variables, 361
 leader behaviors, 360
 leader effects, 361
 model, 361
Human capital, 365
Hungary, 186, 660
Huse Food Group, 638
Hygiene factors, 183
Hyundai, 655

IBM, 71, 185, 242, 356, 465, 468, 485, 650,
 654, 659, 698, 772
Illinois Tool Works (ITW), 674
Illegal drugs, 772
Immoral management, 60
Impersonality, 579
Implicit personality theories, 83
Impression construction, 85

Impression management, 85, 375, 398
Impression motivation, 85
Inclusion career movement, 735
Independent task relations, 322
India, 470, 479
Individuals
 behaviors, 28
 change, 652
 conflict, 429
 conformity, 287
 feedback, 411
 goals, 269
 group, 269
 groupthink, 288
 impression management, 398
 individualism, 269
 job design, 543
 power, 520
 relations-oriented role, 282
 self-oriented role, 283
 task-oriented role, 282
Individual differences, 40, 59
Individual problem-solving styles (see
 Problem-solving styles)
Individualism, 269
Indonesia, 78
Influence strategies, 510–511
Information roles,
 defined, 21
 disseminator, 21
 monitor, 21
 spokesperson, 21
Information technology
 computer-integrated manufacturing, 656
 defined, 277, 655
 distributed computing, 599
 electronic brainstorming, 299
 electronic data exchange, 656
 electronic mail (E-mail), 406
 electronic offices, 17
 Federal National Mortgage Association,
  572
 global networking, 600
 groupware, 277, 333, 391, 406
 job design, 550
 network design, 598
 open systems, 599
 organizational change, 655
 power, 504
 real time, 599
 telecommuting, 406
 videoconferencing, 279
 virtual corporation, 708
 virtual reality, 655
 voice mail, 406
 Westinghouse, 278
Initiating structure, 350, 380
Innovation, 673
Innovative Office Systems, 219
Instrumentality, 189

Integration, 590
Integrating roles, 331
Integrative negotiations, 447
Intellectual capital, 505
Interacting group, 271
Interactionist perspective, 51
Intercultural communication, 398
Interdependent task relations, 322
Intergroup conflict, 438
Intergroup dynamics
    attitudinal sets, 316
    boundary-spanning roles, 330
    competition, 315, 317
    cooperation, 317
    cross-functional teams, 322, 331
    dependent task relations, 323
    dialogue, 325, 407
    diversity, 319, 439
    effect uncertainty, 312
    female managers, 320
    Fluor, 323
    goal conflict, 315
    goals, 314
    group identification, 319
    hierarchy, 330
    Hope Creek, 332
    independent task relations, 322
    integrating roles, 331
    interdependent task relations, 322
    linking roles, 330
    Medtronics, 318
    Oldsmobile Division, 310
    planning, 329
    positive multiculturalism, 321
    power, 313
    questionnaire, 335
    resource sharing, 323
    response uncertainty, 312
    state uncertainty, 311
    substitutability, 324
    superordinate group goals, 327
    superordinate group rewards, 327
    total quality management, 328
    uncertainty, 311
    uncertainty absorption, 312
Internal integration, 468
Internal locus of control, 49
International (see Multinational design,
    594)
Interpersonal communication
    defined, 389
    network, 401
    see Communication
Interpersonal conflict, 432, 435
Interpersonal roles
    defined, 20
    figurehead, 20
    leadership, 20
    liaison, 21
Interpersonal skills, 18

Interrole conflict, 436
Interval schedule, 155
Intragroup conflict, 437
Intraorganizational negotiations, 448
Intrasender role conflict, 435
Introversion, 49
Intuition, 109
Intuitive-feelers
    defined, 122
    limitations, 123
    professions, 123
    relating to others, 123
Intuitive-thinkers
    defined, 117
    limitations, 118
    professions, 118
    relating to others, 118
Intuitive-type person, 110
ISO 9000, 211
Israel, 470
Italy, 78

Jaguar, 697
Japan, 43, 56, 77, 84, 240, 247, 269, 471,
    501, 654, 660, 686, 701, 703
    culture, 25, 188, 393
    Japanese CEO, 501
    problem-solving styles, 113
    productivity, 191
    quality circles, 703
    recruiting practices, 146
    stress death, 247
    work attitudes, 56
J.C. Penney, 655
Job burnout, 250
Job characteristics enrichment model, 541
    see Job design
Job characteristic inventory, 542
Job descriptive index, 57
Job design
    achievement motivation, 179
    Aetna Life & Casualty, 549
    Anderson Consulting, 528
    AT&T, 535
    automation, 533
    autonomy, 541
    complexity, 531
    customers, 548
    defined, 540
    disabled, 536
    electronic monitoring, 545
    flextime, 547
    groupware, 537
    growth-need strength, 544
    growth needs, 176
    Home Depot, 548
    impact, 531
    independent task relations, 322

    individual differences, 543
    interdependent task relations, 322
    job characteristics, 541, 549
    job characteristics inventory, 542
    job diagnosis, 546
    job diagnosis survey, 546
    job engineering, 533
    job enlargement, 535
    job enrichment, 535
    job feedback, 541
    job rotation, 532
    job simplification, 533
    job specialization, 533
    Loral Vought Systems, 554
    Maids International, 528
    Metz Baking Company, 539
    motivating potential score, 547
    Motorola, 544
    NUMMI, 534, 538, 555
    organization design, 565
    organizational change, 700
    pooled interdependence, 539
    reciprocal interdependence, 539
    reengineering, 529
    repetition, 533
    role, 435
    role conflict, 435
    satisfaction, 544
    self-actualization needs, 176
    sequential interdependence, 539
    skill, 544
    skill variety, 541
    social information processing model, 551
    social system, 553
    sociotechnical systems model, 535, 552
    structural clues method, 546
    task identity, 541
    task interdependence, 538
    task significance, 541
    task simplification, 533
    task uncertainty, 537
    teams, 548
    technology, 549
    technological system, 553
    technology, 537
    telecommuting, 406
    tellers jobs, 550
    Texas Instruments, 535
    vertical loading, 547
    Volvo, 555
    Vortex, 530
    William Raveis Real Estate, 539
    work-flow uncertainty, 537
Job diagnosis, 546
Job diagnostic survey, 546
Job engineering, 533
Job enlargement, 535
Job enrichment, 535
Job feedback, 541
Job loss, 749

Job rotation, 532
Job satisfaction
    behavior, 58
    defined, 55
    sources, 57
Johnson & Higgins, 505
Johnson & Johnson, 227, 259, 363, 588, 618,
    746, 760, 762
Johnsonville Foods, 348, 719
Jostens Learning, 249
Just Brakes, 747
Justice Department, 481
Just-in-time inventory systems, 704

Kelly Services, 659
Kendall Healthcare Products, 585
King, Chapman, Broussard & Gallagher,
    750
Knowledge as power, 503
Kodak, 772
Korea, 654

Language routines, 396
Lateral thinking method, 636
Latin America, 24
Law of small numbers bias, 630
Leader, 343
Leader behaviors, 350
Leadership
    attribution model, 371
    behavioral models, 350
    behaviors, 343
    consideration, 350
    contingency models, 352
    contingency variables, 370
    Corning Glass, 346
    cultural heroes, 467
    Cunningham Communications, 6
    defined, 342
    diversity, 346
    emerging models, 371
    empowerment, 345
    ethics, 86, 373
    European, 351
    Fiedler's model, 353
    framing, 375
    groups, 291
    Hersey & Blanchard's model, 357
    House's path–goal model, 360
    initiating structure, 350
    leader, 343
    leadership difference, 369
    leadership role, 20
    leader-subordinate relationships, 344
    least-preferred co-workers, 354
    networks, 403

Ohio State studies, 350
    psychological oppression, 46
    quality, 363, 367
    skills, 344
    sources of power, 346
    subordinates, 344
    Thermos, 342
    traditional model, 348
    transformational model, 374
    Vroom–Jago model, 364
    W.L. Gore & Associates, 578
Leadership role, 20
Learning
    classical conditioning, 139
    defined, 139
    diversity, 143
    operant conditioning, 140
    organizational culture, 472
    perception, 77
    reflex, 139
    social learning, 141
Learning organization, 687
Learning & reinforcement
    behavioral modification, 158
    contingencies of reinforcement, 144
    organizational rewards, 147
    schedules of reinforcement, 155
    types of learning, 139
Learning theory, 138
Least preferred co-worker (LPC), 354
Legitimate power, 347, 500
Levi Strauss, 707
Lewis Galoob Toys, 709
Liaison role, 21
Life stressors, 245
Line functions, 581
Line-staff conflict, 439
Linking role, 330
Listening, 413
Liz Claiborne, 347
L.L. Bean, 259
Lockheed, 698
Locus of control
    defined, 49
    diagnosis, 63
    measure, 63–64
    political behavior, 518
Loew's Anatole Hotel, 372
Long John Silver's Seafood, 224
London Stock Exchange, 655
Loral Vought Systems, 137, 140, 176, 500,
    554
Lotus, 465
Low-context culture, 399
Lying, 398

Machiavellianism, 518
Maids International, 528

Malcolm Baldrige Award, 13
Maintenance career stage, 740
Management by objectives
    criticisms, 223
    defined, 218
    diversity, 221
    ethics, 219
    goal setting, 219
    implementation, 222
    organizational culture, 472
    participation, 222
    performance appraisal, 222
    significance, 223
Managers
    behaviors, 343
    changing roles, 657
    defined, 342
    female, 320
    Hispanic, 11
Managerial decision making, 625
Managerial roles, 20, 23
    see Roles
Manpower, 659
Marriott, 757
Martin Marietta, 666
Mary Kay Cosmetics, 375, 473
Mary T., 273
Maryland Plastics, 268
Matrix design, 592
Matrix organization, 709
MCA, 508, 509
McCulloch, 60
McDonald's, 267, 618, 654, 737
MCI Communications, 343
McKinsey & Co., 474, 513
Mead, 687
Meanings, 393
Mechanistic system, 576
Media richness, 391
Medtronics, 318
Men
    nonverbal cues, 417
Mentor, 736
Merck, 505, 654
Merrill Lynch, 155
Messages, 392
Meta-communication, 408
Metz Baking, 539
Mexico, 77, 184, 217, 239, 470, 660–661
    careers, 727
    goal setting, 217
    machismo, 23
    negotiations, 450
    nonverbal communication, 415
    women, 727
Microsoft, 71, 170, 465
Mid-life crisis, 740
Mirage Resorts, 198
Miramax Films, 47
Monetary incentives, 182

Moral management, 60
Morton Thiokol, 627, 632
Motown Records, 508, 509
Motivating potential score, 547
Motivation
  achievement motivation theory, 179
  cafeteria-style benefits, 199
  challenges, 173
  content theories, 174
  defined, 170
  diversity, 171, 178
  equity, 193
  ERG Theory, 176
  ethics, 196
  expectancy theory, 187
  goal, 173
  growth-need strength, 544
  intrinsic, 183
  Japan, 191
  job characteristics enrichment model,
      541
  leadership, 349
  matching content theories, 186
  matching process theories, 198
  Mexico, 184
  motivating potential score, 547
  motivators-hygiene theory, 183
  need for power, 517
  needs hierarchy theory, 174
  perception, 79
  process theories, 187
  superordinate group goals, 327
  superordinate group rewards, 327
Motivation-hygiene theory
  hygiene factors, 183
  motivators, 183
  significance, 185
Motivators factors, 183
Motorola, 184, 431, 447, 544, 656, 695, 705
Moving, 668
Multidivisional design, 587
  see Organization design
Muslim culture, 400

National Aeronautic and Space
    Administration (NASA), 481, 522, 627,
    631
Nations Bank, 227
Nature-nurture controversy, 42
Need for power, 517
Needs, 172
Needs hierarchy theory
  affiliation, 175
  defined, 174
  esteem, 176
  physiological, 174
  security, 175
  self-actualization, 176
  significance, 176

Negative reinforcement, 149
Negotiations
  American Airlines, 448
  attitudinal structuring, 447
  collaborating style, 443
  compromising style, 444
  Continental Airlines, 447
  distributive negotiations, 446
  distributive process, 448
  ethics, 620
  exchange process, 511
  influence strategies, 510
  integrative negotiations, 447
  integrative process, 448
  intergroup conflict, 438
  intraorganizational negotiations, 448
  job design, 534
  matrix, 449
  Mexico, 450
  negotiator role, 22
  outcomes, 449
  procedural conflict, 430
  win-lose, 448
Neiman-Marcus, 655
Netherlands, 26
Network analysis, 508
Network design, 596
Network organization, 709
Networks, 507
Neurotic tendencies, 433
New Balance Shoes, 28
Next Computer, 47
Nigeria, 240
Nike, 28
Noise, 395
Nominal group technique, 296
Nonassertive communication, 389
Nonverbal communication
  body language, 415
  defined, 400, 414
  men, 417
  Mexico, 415
  paralanguage, 415
  physical environment, 415
  status, 416
  time, 415
  types, 414
  women, 417
Nordstrom's, 192
Norms
  behavioral modification, 162
  cohesiveness, 288
  conformity, 287
  defined, 285
  enforcement, 287
  goals, 285
  group development, 275, 434
  relationship to attitudes, 53
North American Free Trade Agreement,
    184, 189, 240

North American Life and Casualty, 299
Northern Telecom, 359
Northwestern National Life Insurance, 240,
    252
NUMMI, 534, 538, 555
NYNEX, 584

Occupational choice
  interests, 731
  personality, 730
  self-esteem, 732
  social background, 732
Omission, 150
Open systems planning, 710
Operant conditioning 140
Organic system, 576
Organization decision making (see
    Decision making)
Organization design
  adaptive organization, 707
  American Brands, 586
  Banc Tec, 586
  boundary-spanning roles, 330
  Brooklyn Union Co., 571
  Calloway Golf, 581, 582
  centralization, 577
  change, 665
  changing, 660
  collateral organization, 708
  comparative framework, 573
  cross-functional teams, 331
  customers, 569
  decentralization, 354, 578
  defined, 26
  differentiation, 589
  division of labor, 577
  Eastman Chemical, 597
  environments, 566
  ethics positions, 584
  external networking, 600
  Federal National Mortgage Association,
      572, 573
  Ford Motor, 596
  functional design, 581
  hierarchy, 330
  hierarchy of authority, 577
  horizontal conflict, 439
  horizontal design, 589
  impersonality, 579
  information technologies, 599
  integrating roles, 331
  integration, 590
  internationalization, 585
  job design, 565
  Johnson & Johnson, 588
  Kendall Healthcare Products, 585
  line functions, 587
  line-staff conflict, 439

linking roles, 330
M-form, 587
management philosophy, 568
managers, 343
matrix design, 592
matrix organization, 709
mechanistic system, 576
multidivisional design, 587, 594
NCR's U.S. Group, 591
network design, 596
network organization, 709
networks, 404
Northern Telecom, 359
organic system, 576
place design, 585
pooled interdependence, 571
power, 503
procedures, 579
process, 27
Procter & Gamble, 26, 601
product design, 586
profit centers, 352
Raytheon, 584
reciprocal interdependence, 571
reengineering, 573
resistance to change, 665
Royal Dutch/Shell, 634
rules, 579
scalar chain of command, 583
sequential interdependence, 571
sexual harassment, 580
span of control, 583
staff functions, 581
strategic choices, 568
status, 416
task environment, 566, 582
task force, 593
task interdependence, 571
task uncertainty, 570
technology, 570
teams, 593
total quality management, 569, 591
uncertainty, 591
unity of command, 583
vertical conflict, 438
Vortex, 531
W.L. Gore & Associates, 578
work-flow uncertainty, 570
Xerox, 564
Organization development, 676
Organizational architecture, 687
Organizational behavior, 25
Organizational change
    academy culture, 465
    action research, 675
    adaptability, 651
    adaptive organization, 707
    attitudes, 714
    business revolutions, 653
    chaos, 650

collateral organization, 708
contingency perspective, 688
cultural change, 696
ethics, 666, 711
fear, 664
force field analysis, 668
globalization, 654
habits, 663
high-performance-high commitment
    work system, 699
individual behaviors, 652
individual resistance, 661
information technologies, 655
innovation, 673
interorganizational agreements, 666
job design, 700
learning organizations, 687
managerial, 657
network organization, 709
organization development, 676
organizational resistance, 664
organizationwide, 687
overcoming resistance, 666
pressures for change, 653
principles, 671
process consultation, 693
quality circles, 701
quality-of-work-life programs, 695
readiness, 670
readiness for, 678
reengineering, 703
refreezing, 669
resistance to, 661
resource limitations, 665
self-managed teams, 701
sociotechnical systems, 701
strategic change, 710
survey feedback, 690
systems approach, 672
team building, 691
time-based competition, 687
total quality management, 705
trends, 650
unfreezing, 668
virtual corporation, 708
virtual reality, 655
workforce, 659
Organizational commitment, 58
Organizational creativity, 635
Organizational culture
    Bank of America, 464
    baseball team culture, 465
    Body Shop, 121
    Celestial Seasonings, 27
    change, 665, 689, 696
    changing, 475
    club culture, 465
    components, 466
    cultural diversity, 482
    cultural heroes, 467

    cultural symbols, 467
    cultural values, 467
    defined, 466
    developing, 467
    ethical behavior, 479
    ethical culture, 490
    external adaptation, 468
    fortress culture, 465
    high performance-high commitment
        work culture, 478
    high performance-high work system, 699
    IBM, 698
    impact, 31
    internal integration, 468
    legends, 474
    levels, 466
    maintaining, 471
    national culture, 468
    network design, 599
    Nissan, 723
    organizational rites & ceremonies, 473
    organizational socialization, 485
    participative management, 478
    performance, 477
    Procter & Gamble, 490
    resistance to change, 665
    reward systems, 473
    role modeling, 472
    socialization, 721
    status, 473
    survival, 468
    total quality culture, 478
    types, 465
    whistle-blowing, 481
    Xerox, 405
Organizational diagnosis, 669
Organizational iceberg, 6
Organizational innovation, 635
Organizational politics, 513
Organizational rewards, 147
Organizational rites and ceremonies, 473
Organizational socialization
    defined, 485
    outcomes, 488
    process, 485
    see Socialization
Outplacement firms, 749
Outsourcing, 16

Pacific Bell, 221
Pacific Telesis Group, 656
Parallel organization, 708
Participating style, 359
Participative leadership, 361
Participative management, 478
Peak Electronics, 148
People variable, 672
PepsiCo, 118, 724

Perception
    accuracy, 86
    attribution process, 90
    availability bias, 629
    change, 662
    closure, 80
    confirmation bias, 629
    conflict, 429
    continuity, 80
    culture, 84
    defined, 71
    decision making, 626
    errors, 86, 394
    expectancy effects, 89
    external factors, 74
    groupthink, 288
    halo effect, 88
    icons, 71
    impression management, 85
    internal factors, 75
    interpretation, 73
    law of small numbers bias, 630
    learning, 77
    motivation, 79
    office design, 81
    organization, 71
    perceptual defense, 87
    perceptual grouping, 80
    perceptual organization, 79
    perceptual selection, 74
    person perception, 82
    personality, 76
    pollyanna principle, 79
    primacy effect, 82
    problem framing, 629
    problem interpretation, 628
    process of, 71
    projection, 88
    proximity, 80
    resistance to change, 662
    selection, 71
    selection decisions, 70
    selective perception, 75
    selective perception bias, 630
    sex stereotyping, 88
    similarity, 80
    social information processing model, 551
    stereotyping, 87
    stimuli, 71
    stress, 237
    time perception, 78
    voice quality, 83
    women managers, 97
Perceptual defense, 87
Perceptual grouping, 80
Perceptual organization, 79
Perceptual selection
    defined, 74
    external factors, 74
    internal factors, 75

Perceptual set, 77
Performance
    feedback, 411
    goal setting, 212, 216
    groups, 276
    motivation, 172, 190
    norms, 285
    organizational culture, 477
    reward systems, 223
    stress, 248
Performance appraisal
    Electronic Systems Personnel, 222
    feedback, 222
    political behavior, 515
Person perception, 82
Person-role conflict, 436
Personal acceptance conformity, 287
Personal space, 400
Personality
    accommodating style, 442
    artistic, 731
    authoritarianism, 51
    avoiding style, 441
    behavior, 48
    careers, 730
    collaborating style, 443
    communication, 394
    conventional, 731
    defined, 41
    dogmatism, 50
    enterprising, 731
    environment, 42
    extraversion, 49
    family, 44
    field dependence-independence, 76
    forcing style, 442
    group membership, 45
    hardiness, 255
    healthy, 412
    heredity, 42
    interactionist perspective, 51
    intrapersonal conflict, 432
    introversion, 49
    investigative, 731
    leadership, 347
    life experiences, 45
    locus of control, 49, 518
    Machiavellianism, 519
    neurotic tendencies, 433
    perception, 76
    person-role conflict, 436
    political behavior, 517
    problem-solving styles, 731
    psychological appression, 46
    realistic, 731
    resistance to change, 663
    self-disclosure, 412
    self-esteem, 48
    social, 731
    sources, 41

    stress, 238, 252
    structure, 45
    traits, 349, 731
    Type A personality, 253
    Type B personality, 253
Personality trait, 45
Peru, 471
Physiological effects of stress, 246
Physiological needs, 174
Philippines, 470
Phillips Petroleum, 256
Physiological effects of stress, 246
Pillsbury, 428
Place design, 585
Planned organizational change
    changing individual behaviors, 652
    defined, 651
    improving organizational adaptability,
        651–652
    see Organizational change
Planning, 292, 329
Playcare Development Center, 226
Polaroid, 695
Political behavior
    abuse of, 515
    avoidance of, 516
    creation of, 514
    defined, 512
    innovation, 496
    locus of control, 518
    Machiavellianism, 518
    need for power, 517
    organizational politics, 513
    performance appraisal, 516
    personality, 517
    risk-seeking propensity, 519
    succession, 513
    use of, 515
Political model, 624
Pollyanna principle, 79
Pooled interdependence, 539, 571
Portugal, 471
Position power, 354, 357
Positive discipline, 153
Positive events, 145
Positive multiculturalism, 321
Power
    aggressive communication, 389
    authority, 498
    change, 664
    chief executive officers, 497
    coercive power, 499
    compromising style, 444
    decision making as power, 506
    defined, 497
    dependent task relations, 323
    diagnosis, 520
    distributive process, 448
    effective use, 510
    empowerment, 345

exchange process, 511
expert power, 313, 500
forcing style, 442
golden handcuffs, 739
groups, 313
influence, 521
influence strategies, 509
integrative process, 448
interpersonal sources, 498
knowledge as power, 503
legitimate power, 500
lower level employee, 509
measure, 520
mentors, 736
networks, 404
networks as power, 507
norms, 162
political model, 624
position power, 354
power motive, 179
referent power, 502
resources as power, 505
reward power, 499
status, 473
structural sources, 503
substitutability, 324
uses, 347
vested interests, 632
visibility, 521
Power motive, 179
PPG Industries, 275, 498
Pressures for change, 653
Preston Trucking, 622
Price Waterhouse, 88, 505
Primacare, 367
Primacy effect, 82, 87
Primary reinforcer, 146
Principle of contingent reinforcement, 147
Principle of immediate reinforcement, 147
Principle of reinforcement deprivation, 147
Principle of reinforcement size, 147
Principled organizational dissent, 481
Pro Fasteners, 182
Problem framing, 629
Problem interpretation, 628
Problem recognition, 626
Problem-solving, 107
Problem-solving styles
    Canadian students, 113
    defined, 109
    diagnosis, 131
    diversity, 128
    ethics, 126
    feeling, 109
    feeling-type, 111
    groups, 281
    intuition, 109
    intuitive-feelers, 122
    intuitive-thinkers, 117
    intuitive-type, 110

Japanese students, 113
    model, 107
    personality, 731
    processes, 106
    sensation-thinkers, 115, 120
    sensation-type, 109
    sensing, 108
    thinking, 109
    thinking-type, 113
Problem-solving teams, 272
Procedural conflict, 430
Procedural justice, 198
Procedures, 579
Process, 27
Process consultation, 693
Process theories of motivation
    equity, 193
    expectancy, 187
Procter & Gamble, 26, 465, 485, 490, 601,
    654, 687
Product design, 586
Productivity, 188, 191, 223
Profit centers, 352
Profit-sharing plans, 224
Projection, 88
Proximity, 80
Prudential Bache Securities, 219
Prudential Insurance, 483, 765
Psychological functions
    feeling, 111
    intuition, 110
    sensation, 109
    thinking, 113
Punishment
    defined, 150
    effective use, 153
    effects, 152
    interpersonal, 151
    negative effects, 151
    positive discipline, 153

Quality
    defined, 12
    quality improvement teams, 268
    see Total Quality Management
Quality circles, 701
Quality of work life, 659, 695

Random-word stimulation, 638
Ratio schedule, 156
Rational model, 621
Raytheon, 584
Readiness for change, 670
    measure, 678
Realistic job preview, 723
Receptors, 391

Reciprocal interdependence, 539, 571
Reebok, 28
Reengineering, 54
    attitudes, 54
    defined, 54, 128, 529
    Ford Motor, 575
    GTE, 128
    job design, 529
    organization design, 573
    organizational change, 703
    rethink, 530
    retool, 530
    sociotechnical systems model, 552
Referent power, 347, 502
Reflex, 139
Refreezing, 669
Reinforcement
    comparisons, 156
    contingent reinforcement, 147
    continuous, 155
    defined, 145
    deprivation, 147
    fixed interval, 155
    fixed ratio, 156
    guidelines, 154
    immediate reinforcement, 147
    intermittent, 155
    negative reinforcement, 149
    omission, 150
    positive reinforcement, 145, 147
    principle of positive reinforcement, 147
    punishment, 150
    rewards, 145
    secondary reinforcer, 146
    size, 147
    variable interval, 156
    variable ratio, 156
Relations-oriented role, 282
Relationship behavior, 357
Research designs
    case study, 762
    comparisons, 766
    control, 761
    data collection methods, 767
    ethics, 773
    experimental, 760
    experimental group, 760
    field experiment, 765
    field survey, 763
    hypothesis, 759
    interviews, 768
    laboratory experiment, 764
    matching, 761
    nonreactive measures, 771
    observation, 769, 771
    purposes, 759
    qualitative methods, 771
    questionnaires, 768
    random selection, 761
    reliability, 772

validity, 772
Resistance to change
  individual, 661
  organizational, 664
  overcoming, 666
Resource sharing, 323
Resources as power, 505
Response uncertainty, 312
Reward power, 347, 499
Reward systems
  banking time off, 226
  flexible benefit plans, 225
  gain-sharing, 224
  monetary incentives, 182
  organizational culture, 473
  organizational rewards, 147
  performance, 223
  profit-sharing plans, 224
  Scanlon plan, 224
  skill-based pay, 227
  Westinghouse, 230
Rewards, 145
  defined, 145
  fixed interval, 157
  fixed ratio, 157
  goal setting, 217
  hygiene factors, 183
  material rewards, 148
  Mexico, 184
  monetary incentives, 182
  motivator factors, 183
  reinforcement, 156
  reward power, 347
  self-administered, 148
  size, 192
  social, 148
  status symbols, 148
  supplemental benefits, 148
  task, 148
  variable interval, 157
  variable ratio, 157
Risk propensity, 628
Risk-seeking propensity, 519
Ritz-Carlton Hotel, 705
Rohr Industries, 498
Role, 19, 435
Role ambiguity, 243, 437
Role conflict, 243, 435, 747
Role overload, 241
Role set, 435
Roles
  disseminator role, 21
  disturbance handler role, 22
  entrepreneurial role, 22
  figurehead role, 20
  leadership role, 20, 21
  liaison role, 21
  monitor role, 21
  resource allocator role, 22
  role modeling, 472
  spokesperson role, 21

Royal Dutch/Shell, 634
Rules, 285, 579
  decision rules, 612
  dictionary rule, 612
Russia, 479, 654

Safeway, 259
Saint Louis Bread, 173
Solomon Brothers, 173
Sanyo Electric, 191
Sara Lee, 259
Satisfaction
  equity theory, 193
  goal setting, 217
  hygiene factors, 183
  job design, 544
  motivation factors, 183
Satisficing, 623
Scalar chain of command, 583
Scanlon plan, 224
Scientific approach, 757
Sears, 480, 482
Second-level outcomes, 188
Secondary reinforcer, 146
Security needs, 175
SEI, 8
Selective perception bias, 630
Self-actualization needs, 176
Self-disclosure, 412
Self-efficacy
  goal setting, 214
  social learning, 141
Self-esteem, 48
  careers, 732
Self-fulfilling prophecy, 89
Self-managed teams, 273, 322, 597, 692, 701
Self-oriented role, 283
Self-serving bias, 95
Selling style, 359
Semantics, 396
Sensation-feelers
  defined, 120
  limitations, 121
  professions, 121
  relating to others, 120
Sensation-thinkers
  defined, 115
  limitations, 116
  professions, 116
  relating to others, 115
Sensation-type person, 109
Sensing, 108
Sequential interdependence, 539, 571
Service organizations, 12
Sexual harassment, 580
  defined, 769
  questionnaire, 770
Shell Canada, 227
Sherwin-Williams, 687

Similarity, 80
Singapore, 240, 654
Sir Speedy, 243
Skill variety, 541
Skills
  communications, 18
  conceptual, 18
  defined, 17
  global, 16
  interpersonal, 18
  leadership, 344
  skill-based pay, 227
  technical, 17
Social information processing model, 551
Social learning, 141
Social systems, 27
Socialization
  anticipatory stages, 723
  change & acquisition, 725
  dilemmas, 488
  encounter stage, 724
  Nissan, 723
  organizational, 722
  PepsiCo, 724
  process, 721
  realistic job preview, 723
  stages, 722
  successful, 488
  unsuccessful, 488
Sociotechnical systems, 535, 701
Sociotechnical systems model, 552
Solid citizens, 741
Sony Medical, 658
South Africa, 240
South Korea, 660
Southwest Airlines, 123, 486, 502
Spain, 654
Span of control, 583
Square D, 498
Squibb, 749
Staff functions, 581
Stakeholders, 209, 272, 619
Stanley Works, 702
State uncertainty, 311
Status, 416
Stereotyping, 87, 320
Stockholders, 210
Stonebriar Country Club, 165
Strategic change, 710
Strategic choices, 568
Strategies
  change, 32
  new balance, 28
  outsourcing, 16
Strategy variable, 672
Stress
  behavioral effects, 247
  career development, 243
  conflict, 243
  defined, 236
  depersonalization, 250

downsizing, 249
dual-career couples, 744
emotional effects, 246
family, 244
fight-or-flight response, 237
generational tension, 43
hardiness, 255
health, 247–248
individual coping, 255
interpersonal relations, 243
job burnout, 250
job conditions, 242
job loss, 749
karoushi, 247
life stressors, 245
management of, 255
organizational coping, 256
overtasking, 242
past experience, 238
perception, 237
personality, 238, 252
physiological effects, 246
role ambiguity, 243
role conflict, 243
role overload, 241
social support, 238
sources, 239
stressors, 236
Type A personality, 253
Type B personality, 253
wellness programs, 258
work-family conflict, 245
work stressors, 240
Stress management
    defined, 255
    individual methods, 255
    organizational methods, 256
    see Stress
Stressors
    defined, 236
    life, 244
    work, 240
    see Stress
Strong culture, 477
Structural problem, 626
Subcultures, 476
Subordinates, 344
Substitutability, 324
Superordinate group goals, 327
Superordinate group rewards, 327
Supportive leadership, 360
Survey feedback, 690
Symmetrix, 653
Systems model of change, 672
Sweden, 240, 470–471
Synerdyne, 165

Taiwan, 77, 78, 654
Tampa Electric, 154

Tandem Computers, 226
Task behavior, 357
Task environment, 566
Task group, 270
Task identity, 541
Task interdependence, 538, 571
Task-oriented role, 282
Task significance, 541
Task structure, 353, 357
Task uncertainty, 537
Task variable, 672
Team building, 691
Team goals, 280
Teams
    action, 293
    action planning, 294
    autonomy, 271
    brainstorming, 298
    Chaparral Steel, 352
    context, 276
    creativity, 296
    cross-functional teams, 322, 331
    Cunningham Communications, 5
    decision making, 292
    defined, 272
    diversity, 284
    Eastman Chemical, 597
    evaluation planning, 294
    France, 351
    free rider, 270
    goal setting, 220
    goals, 269, 280, 554
    Hope Creek, 332
    individual behaviors, 283
    integrating roles, 331
    job design, 534, 548
    leadership, 291
    Mary T., 273
    Maryland Plastics, 268
    networks, 404
    NUMMI, 534
    observers, 282
    Oldsmobile Division, 310
    organization design, 593
    organizational culture, 471
    PPG Industries, 275
    problem definition, 292
    problem-solving teams, 272
    processes, 30
    Procter & Gamble, 601
    questionnaire, 335
    reciprocal interdependence, 539
    self-managed teams, 692, 701
    solution generation, 291
    team building, 691
    Thermos, 342
    Westinghouse, 278
    see Groups
Technical skills, 17
Technology
    automation, 533

    defined, 537
    interdependence, 539
    job characteristics, 549
    Johnson & Johnson, 363
    Metz Baking, 539
    NUMMI, 534, 535, 555
    organization, design, 570
    sociotechnical systems model, 552
    task uncertainty, 537, 570
    technological system 553
    tellers' jobs, 550
    Volvo, 550
    work-flow uncertainty, 570
Technology variable, 672
Tele-Communications, 476
Telecommuting, 406
Telling style, 359
Tenneco, 650
Texas Instruments, 535, 705
Theft, 196
Thematic Apperception Test, 179
Theophrastus, 40
Thermos, 331, 342, 345
Thinking, 109
Thinking-type person, 113
3M, 655, 745
Time-based competition, 687
Tom's of Maine, 377
Total quality culture, 478
Total quality management
    Alcoa, 328
    assurance, 211
    AT&T Universal Card Services, 706
    challenge course, 764
    customer service, 211
    customers, 548
    De Mar, 622
    decision quality, 364
    defined, 12
    Deming, 12
    Diamond International, 157
    Ford Motor, 575
    Gillette, 479
    Hard Rock Cafe, 622
    Home Depot, 193
    Honda, 191, 414
    horizontal design, 591
    integrative negotiations, 447
    ISO 9000, 211
    job design, 548
    leadership styles, 363
    listening, 414
    Malcolm Baldrige Award, 13
    managerial role, 658
    Marriott, 757
    Mary T., 273
    motivation, 192–193, 217
    Motorola, 431, 447
    NCR's U.S. Group, 591
    North American Free Trade Act, 217
    organization design, 569

organizational change, 704
Peak Electronics, 148
Preston Trucking, 622
Primacare, 167
Pro Fasteners, 182
rational model, 621
realistic-job preview, 723
reengineering, 575
reinforcement, 148, 157
reliability, 211
responsiveness, 211
service quality, 211
Southwest Airlines, 487
superordinate group goals, 328
superordinate group rewards, 328
tangibles, 211
teams, 268, 272
total quality culture, 478
USAA, 13
values, 329, 569
vision, 329
wellness, 760
Westinghouse Electric, 230
Whole Foods Market, 133

Toyota, 655
Toys 'R' Us, 198
TRW, 242, 687
Traits model, 349
Transformational leadership
    charismatic leaders, 374
    framing, 375
    implications, 377
    impression management, 375
Transmitters, 391
Type A personality, 253
Type B personality, 253

U-Haul, 437
Uncertainty, 311, 591
Uncertainty absorption, 312

Unfreezing, 668
Union Pacific Railroad, 396
United Kingdom, 240, 507
United Parcel Service, 138, 465
United States, 23, 269
Unity of command, 583
Unity Forest Products, 116
University of Virginia, 467
Unstructured problems 626
USAA, 13
USA Truck, 436
USAir, 439
U.S. Bank of Washington, 241
U.S. Peace Corps, 78
U.S. Navy, 239, 496
Utilitarianism, 620

Valence, 189
Valeo, 351
Values
    Bank of America, 464
    cultural values, 467
    diversity, 725
    ethics, 619
    organizational change, 712
    total quality management, 329, 569
Variable interval schedule, 156
Variable ratio schedule, 156
Venezuela, 400
Vertical career movement, 733
Vertical conflict, 438, 439
Vertical loading, 547
Vertical thinking method, 636
Videoconferencing, 278
Virtual corporation, 708
Virtual reality, 655
Vision
    diversity, 346
    framing, 375
    leadership, 344
    MCI Communications, 343
    Thermos, 345
    transformational leaders, 377

Visioning, 711
Voice mail, 406
Volkswagen, 654
Volvo, 655
Vortex, 530, 535
Vroom–Jago leadership model
    decision effectiveness, 364
    decision tree, 365
    defined, 364
    implications, 369
    overall effectiveness, 365
    Primacare, 367

Wal-Mart, 445
Walt Disney, 654
Warnaco, 47
Washington Mutual Savings, 497
Weirton Steel, 505
Wellness, 760
Wellness programs, 258
Westinghouse, 230, 278, 687, 695, 705, 714
Whistle-blowing, 481
William Raveis Real Estate, 539
Wisconsin Energy, 244
W.L. Gore & Associates, 578
Work-flow uncertainty, 537
Working Mother Magazine, 244
Women in management (see Diversity)
Women managers, 320, 397, 417, 746
Wright-Patterson Air Force Base, 505

X generation, 43
Xerox, 71, 119, 242, 405, 564, 590, 695, 705, 707
    decision making, 621
Xerox Palo Alto Research Center (PARC), 674

Zone of indifference, 500